Automatic Speech & Speaker Recognition

OTHER IEEE PRESS BOOKS

Speech Analysis, *Edited by R. W. Schafer and J. D. Markel*
The Engineer in Transition to Management, *I. Gray*
Multidimensional Systems: Theory & Applications, *Edited by N. K. Bose*
Analog Integrated Circuits, *Edited by A. B. Grebene*
Integrated-Circuit Operational Amplifiers, *Edited by R. G. Meyer*
Modern Spectrum Analysis, *Edited by D. G. Childers*
Digital Image Processing for Remote Sensing, *Edited by R. Bernstein*
Reflector Antennas, *Edited by A. W. Love*
Phase-Locked Loops & Their Application, *Edited by W. C. Lindsey and M. K. Simon*
Digital Signal Computers and Processors, *Edited by A. C. Salazar*
Systems Engineering: Methodology and Applications, *Edited by A. P. Sage*
Modern Crystal and Mechanical Filters, *Edited by D. F. Sheahan and R. A. Johnson*
Electrical Noise: Fundamentals and Sources, *Edited by M. S. Gupta*
Computer Methods in Image Analysis, *Edited by J. K. Aggarwal, R. O. Duda, and A. Rosenfeld*
Microprocessors: Fundamentals and Applications, *Edited by W. C. Lin*
Machine Recognition of Patterns, *Edited by A. K. Agrawala*
Turning Points in American Electrical History, *Edited by J. E. Brittain*
Charge-Coupled Devices: Technology and Applications, *Edited by R. Melen and D. Buss*
Spread Spectrum Techniques, *Edited by R. C. Dixon*
Electronic Switching: Central Office Systems of the World, *Edited by A. E. Joel, Jr.*
Electromagnetic Horn Antennas, *Edited by A. W. Love*
Waveform Quantization and Coding, *Edited by N. S. Jayant*
Communication Satellite Systems: An Overview of the Technology, *Edited by R. G. Gould and Y. F. Lum*
Literature Survey of Communication Satellite Systems and Technology, *Edited by J. H. W. Unger*
Solar Cells, *Edited by C. E. Backus*
Computer Networking, *Edited by R. P. Blanc and I. W. Cotton*
Communications Channels: Characterization and Behavior, *Edited by B. Goldberg*
Large-Scale Networks: Theory and Design, *Edited by F. T. Boesch*
Optical Fiber Technology, *Edited by D. Gloge*
Selected Papers in Digital Signal Processing, II, *Edited by the Digital Signal Processing Committee*
A Guide for Better Technical Presentations, *Edited by R. M. Woelfle*
Career Management: A Guide to Combating Obsolescence, *Edited by H. G. Kaufman*
Energy and Man: Technical and Social Aspects of Energy, *Edited by M. G. Morgan*
Magnetic Bubble Technology: Integrated-Circuit Magnetics for Digital Storage and Processing, *Edited by H. Chang*
Frequency Synthesis: Techniques and Applications, *Edited by J. Gorski-Popiel*
Literature in Digital Processing: Author and Permuted Title Index (Revised and Expanded Edition), *Edited by H. D. Helms, J. F. Kaiser, and L. R. Rabiner*
Data Communications via Fading Channels, *Edited by K. Brayer*
Nonlinear Networks: Theory and Analysis, *Edited by A. N. Willson, Jr.*
Computer Communications, *Edited by P. E. Green, Jr. and R. W. Lucky*
Stability of Large Electric Power Systems, *Edited by R. T. Byerly and E. W. Kimbark*
Automatic Test Equipment: Hardware, Software, and Management, *Edited by F. Liguori*
Key Papers in the Development of Coding Theory, *Edited by E. R. Berkekamp*
Technology and Social Institutions, *Edited by K. Chen*
Key Papers in the Development of Information Theory, *Edited by D. Slepian*
Computer-Aided Filter Design, *Edited by G. Szentirmai*
Laser Devices and Applications, *Edited by I. P. Kaminow and A. E. Siegman*
Integrated Optics, *Edited by D. Marcuse*
Laser Theory, *Edited by F. S. Barnes*
Digital Signal Processing, *Edited by L. R. Rabiner and C. M. Rader*
Minicomputers: Hardware, Software, and Applications, *Edited by J. D. Schoeffler and R. H. Temple*
Semiconductor Memories, *Edited by D. A. Hodges*
Power Semiconductor Applications, Volume II: Equipment and Systems, *Edited by J. D. Harnden, Jr. and F. B. Golden*
Power Semiconductor Applications, Volume I: General Considerations, *Edited by J. D. Harnden, Jr. and F. B. Golden*
A Practical Guide to Minicomputer Applications, *Edited by F. F. Coury*
Active Inductorless Filters, *Edited by S. K. Mitra*
Clearing the Air: The Impact of the Clean Air Act on Technology, *Edited by J. C. Redmond, J. C. Cook, and A. A. J. Hoffman*

Automatic Speech & Speaker Recognition

Edited by

N. Rex Dixon
IBM Thomas J. Watson
Research Center

Thomas B. Martin
President
Threshold Technology, Inc.

A volume in the IEEE PRESS Selected Reprint Series, prepared under the sponsorship of the IEEE Acoustics, Speech, and Signal Processing Society.

IEEE PRESS

The Institute of Electrical and Electronics Engineers, Inc. New York

PRINTED IN THE UNITED STATES OF AMERICA

IEEE International Standard Book Numbers: Clothbound: 0-87942-117-7
Paperbound: 0-87942-118-5

Library of Congress Catalog Card Number 78-65703

Sole Worldwide Distributor (Exclusive of the IEEE):

JOHN WILEY & SONS, INC.
605 Third Ave.
New York, NY 10016

Wiley Order Numbers: Clothbound: 0-471-05833-5
Paperbound: 0-471-05834-3

CONTENTS

Part I
Introduction

INTRODUCTORY COMMENTS

In the relatively recent past, workers from a number of disciplines have merged into a field called speech processing. These disciplines include mathematics, physics, psychology, linguistics, engineering, artificial intelligence, computer sciences, and the speech and hearing sciences.

Using speech as input to some device, we would like to be able to automatically (1) confirm (verify) or reject a talker's purported identity, (2) recognize (identify) an unknown talker, (3) convert what the talker says into a standard-orthographical representation, (4) have the device respond to the" meaning" of what is said without auxilliary input, and/or (5) determine whether some specific subject(s) were mentioned or word(s) uttered. These tasks are referred to as (1) speaker verification, (2) speaker recognition, (3) speech recognition, (4) speech understanding, and (5) word spotting, respectively.

From an historical point of view, automatic speech and speaker recognition have attracted and repelled segments of the scientific and technical community in cyclic fashion since before the emergence of modern electronics. The periodicity of the onsets of interest has been somewhat linked to palpable innovations in the primary disciplines of the workers involved and surges in the availability of financial support.

In contrasting speaker verification and speaker recognition, it can be easily shown that recognition is by far the more difficult of the two tasks. Even on an *a priori* probability of correct decision basis, verification is 0.50 whereas recognition is one over *N*, where *N* can be very large. Also, it can be assumed that in speaker verification the speaker is completely cooperative, but not necessarily in speaker recognition, thereby making the recognition task more difficult.

A number of techniques have been developed for automatic recognition of isolated, single-word-length utterances. In fact, the vast majority of recognition work prior to 1972 was at the presegmented level. Since that time, there has been widespread interest in the continuous-speech problem. Operationally defined, discrete utterance recognition (DUR) is the process of recognizing (or 'understanding') any utterance in which the following assumptions are made:

- The whole utterance exists as a predefined, known pattern of whatever constituency.
- It is not generally necessary to make internal decisions relative to within-pattern syntactic boundaries or prosodics.
- It is not necessary to account for variation among occurrences of a "pattern" other than those of duration and/or over-all energy.
- There is a known, finite number of patterns to be recognized, each having been used to "train" the recognizer, i.e., each is a unique unit in the experiential vocabulary of the system.

On the other hand, true continuous-speech recognition permits very few assumptions concerning input, other than those the average listener might make in the natural process. In practice, most continuous-speech recognition work involves, as a necessary convenience, a set of constraints on input data. These usually relate to:

- the "normalcy", age, sex, and/or identity of the talker,
- the environmental conditions—ambient environment—in which the user is speaking,
- the syntax and lexicon of "admissible" utterances, and/or
- the number of different lexical entities.

It must be pointed out that, *ceteris paribus*, continuous-speech recognition is much more difficult than "understanding". In recognition, tolerance for error is minimal; a printout of "Eye want shoe two stop sending bills." would not be acceptable to a reader, but if the system correctly decoded four key words, it could interpret ("understand") the command perfectly. Thus, in understanding, the only errors made by the system are those which result in the wrong action being taken. For recognition purposes, there are three word-level errors in the above utterance, so accuracy would be zero at the sentence level and only 77.5% at the word level. For understanding, accuracy would be 100%, if all the system needed was "...want...stop sending bills." Obviously, the understanding process would be very sensitive to small word-level errors where a minimal phonetic difference shifts "meaning." Such a case might be "Move the eight blocks sideways." versus "Move the eighth block sideways." It is, at present, always necessary to construct a "command language" to be used by such a system so that minimally different commands do not coexist at the same level.

Another form of speech recognition—usually referred to as "word spotting"—can be employed to advantage in the recognition process. In this, a passage of continuous speech is scanned in an attempt to detect a particular pattern sequence corresponding to a fairly stable "content" word. Generally, such methods use long and/or stressed words, so as to minimize error. Usually, some technique is employed to "normalize" the utterance to be spotted with regard to duration and/or overall energy. These techniques yield good results, so long as care is taken to minimize the occurrence of similar image sequences across word boundaries; for example, find "recognize speech" in "That machine can really wreck a nice beach." One of the most debilitating aspects of continuous speech for word spotting, and recognition, for that matter, is the phenomenon of homophony—or "sound alikes." In DUR, one must only avoid sets of words like two-too-to, pare-pair-pear, ate-eight, etc., but in continuous speech, homophony becomes very complex, involving word sequences as well as single words.

Evaluating a particular system's performance, in terms of its predefined goals, presents no difficulty at all. One simply measures, at the processing level of interest, the degree to which the system does what it was designed to do. Ultimately, of course, performance must be measured at the level where the system provides a service to the user. If the aim is a speech-driven typewriter, the system can be evaluated at the word and sentence levels (and perhaps as a punctuator). However, many problems arise when an attempt is made to compare one system with another in ways which are mutually agreeable to the respective owners. While a number of attempts have been made to provide bases upon which systems can be evaluated, no real success has been achieved here. The main problem involves the determination of the relative difficulty of the tasks for which different systems have been designed. Unfortunately, extant systems are so extremely difficult to adapt to new, perhaps completely different tasks, that running comparative studies on the same task has not been done. In the absence of a common task, little agreed-upon success has been achieved in attempts to establish measures which relate different tasks in terms of difficulty.

In editing an IEEE Reprint Series book, it is necessary to make a number of decisions in the process of attempting to ensure success in achieving its purpose; that is, it should provide a ready reference for active workers in the field concerning their own and others' work, as well as a representative set of papers for familiarization of technically oriented individuals who are merely interested in the current state of the art.

The first decisions had to do with the rationale to be used in selecting papers to be included. It was decided that since the current state of the art was of primary interest, and since space was at a premium, only those postdating 1970 would be included. Also, it was decided that only papers which either constituted categorical reviews, system descriptions and/or presentations of experimental results would be included. We assumed these papers would contain lists of references on antecedent and/or ancillary work, if a reader needed them.

The final group of papers for inclusion was selected out of a much larger set by surveying the opinions of a number of respondent colleagues in speech processing. As is the case with any dynamic technical field, good descriptions of some of the work in speech and/or speaker recognition have not been published in the open literature and are not, therefore, available for reprinting here.

Computers that Talk and Listen: Man–Machine Communication by Voice

JAMES L. FLANAGAN, FELLOW, IEEE

Abstract—Computer techniques now emerging in the laboratory promise new capabilities for voice communication between man and machine. Three modes of interaction are of special interest: computer voice readout of stored information, automatic verification of a caller's identity by means of his voice signal, and automatic recognition of spoken commands. Applications extend to: voice-directed installation of telephone equipment, authentication by voice of a credit customer or of an individual requesting readout of privileged information, and voice-controlled services such as repertory dialing or automatic booking of travel reservations.

I. About the Paper

THIS PAPER has a checkered history. Over a year ago, in July 1974, the PROCEEDINGS Editor wrote and asked me to contribute a paper. I replied I would, and would send him a manuscript around the end of the year entitled "Man–Machine Communication by Voice." Exigencies of current work proceeded to modify this outlook, and the promised preparation receded almost with real time. In the interim, research on man–machine communications continued to progress, and a topic which earlier might have been served by one paper has become, most appropriately, the thrust of a complete issue. And so, my earlier promise is consummated, in the gratifying commitment of introducing this issue.

II. New Services for Communication

Research coming to fruition over the past several years has made clear that the techniques of man–machine communication by voice constitute a whole new range of communication services—services that can extend man's capabilities, serve his social needs, and increase his productivity. To insist that machines communicate with man on a level he finds effective, namely, by natural voice, seems a fitting requirement for machines—as the servants of man. The ability to speak makes the immense sophistication of modern computers immediately available over the ubiquitous voice channel, and from a terminal no more complicated than an ordinary telephone set.

Toward assessing the outlook for this new era, I would like to comment about where we have been, where we have gotten to, and where we are going. To facilitate discussion, I will choose examples mainly from work I know most about and am close to. I trust the reader will not find this stance parochial, but will make his interpretations in terms of the whole field.

III. Payoffs from Past Speech Research

Around 5 years ago, many of us in speech communications research were observing (probably along with our managements) that the cost of bandwidth was decreasing at a rate faster than we were learning to conserve it by shrewd coding. All our stellar efforts at efficient narrow-band coding and analysis/synthesis telephony were going for naught—thwarted by coaxial carrier, millimeter waveguide, and the promise of fiber optics. Was "vocoderism"[1] to blossom and fade, completely unsullied by crass commercialism? What to do with our accumulated understanding about the acoustics of the speech signal and how it can be represented parametrically?

Those of us more scientifically opportunistic, and perhaps with a more heightened instinct for survival, started to eye all the nice computers we had been using to simulate complex digital transmission systems, and to ask "If you're so smart, how come you can't talk?" Unlike Br'er Rabbit, who took the wrong tack and smacked his silent antagonist on the nose, we (along with many of our contemporaries) decided that with a little help from acoustics and speech technology, computers could talk! To convince ourselves of this, we pulled together some of our current work and wrote [1]. Computer voice response, at least for us, began to take a positive form. Numerous others progressed similarly.

About the same time, our interests were directed to an issue which also was to benefit from accumulated understanding in analysis/synthesis and in parametric representation of speech. Our industry and many others were beginning to lose substantial sums through unauthorized use of credit media—in our case, telephone credit cards. Furthermore, the business community was casting about for such things as new ways to apply the convenience of a telephone call to banking transactions, credit purchases, and to the accessing of privileged information. Authentication of a caller's claimed identity by means of measurements on his voice signal took on a strong interest. As a result, overt efforts were begun toward researching techniques for automatic verification of speakers. (See, for example, [26], [28].)

Also at about the same point, research in automatic recognition of speech received a notable impetus through an infusion of contract support from the Advanced Research Projects Agency (ARPA). Despite efforts to attenuate it, this support survived and evolved some new directions of work, particularly in the study of linguistic constraints and automatic analysis of syntax and semantics. While we did not participate initially in this rejuvenation, the climate eventually shifted, and the old challenge of automatic speech recognition again took on respectability. We scurried to catch up.

In the recognition area, too, accumulated knowledge from analysis/synthesis studies provided main points of departure, and provided main underpinnings for initial designs of auto-

Manuscript received July 16, 1975; revised September 16, 1975.

The author is with the Acoustics Research Department, Bell Laboratories, Murray Hill, NJ 07974.

[1] The term *vocoder*—formed from the words *voice coder*—has become largely a generic term, applied to a class of transmission systems based on analysis and synthesis of the speech signal.

Reprinted from *Proc. IEEE,* vol. 64, pp. 405–415, Apr. 1976.

matic speech recognizers. This technology, which has been immediately pressed into application, essentially reflects the current capabilities of automatic recognition. The capabilities are that for systems with designated speakers, vocabularies of several hundred individual words are tractable; whereas for speaker-independent systems, smaller vocabularies, such as spoken digits, are quite realistic.

These prospects for making computers talk and listen—although limited in many aspects—now take the form of a genuine target of opportunity. These "3-modes" of interaction by voice—namely, voice response, speaker verification, and speech recognition—can serve some of man's real-world communication needs right now. Confident enough are we of these techniques that we are committed within the coming year to demonstrate an experimental airlines information and reservation system based upon them. I will return to some additional description of this system later in the discussion. Looking toward this objective, I would like to comment about the engineering feasibility and practicability for these 3-modes of man-machine communication.

IV. Computer Voice Response

Interest in talking machines stems from as far back as the ancient Greek and Roman civilizations (Fig. 1). Only with the advent of electronics did speech synthesis pass from a curiosity to a potentially useful communication technique. Computers in partnership with the theory of sampled-data systems expanded the sophistication of speech synthesis, and established a new application; namely, voice readout of computer-stored data [1]-[9].

The ingredients of a computer voice response system are shown in Fig. 2. The machine is required to speak some message, typically specified in ordinary English text. A synthesis program must access from a stored vocabulary a description of the required sequence of words. It must put them together, head-to-tail, with the proper duration, intensity, and inflection for the prescribed context. This description of the connected utterance is then given to a synthesizer device which generates a signal for transmission over a voice circuit.

While many different approaches to speech synthesis exist [9], the techniques are distinguished largely by the storage capacity needed for the vocabulary and by the complexity of the control rules for generating the speech. Three different techniques serve to illustrate the range of complexity. They are, respectively, adaptive differential pulse-code modulation (ADPCM), formant synthesis, and text synthesis. Their typical bit rates for vocabulary storage are compared in Fig. 3.

The first and simplest technique utilizes a vocabulary composed of human-spoken words whose waveforms are digitally coded. The coding method is chosen to effect an advantageous compromise among signal quality, the storage capacity required for the word vocabulary, and the simplicity of the program for assembling the output messages. This coding is exemplified by ADPCM, typically at 24 kbits/s [10].

Adaptive quantization applied in differential coding provides dynamic adjustment of quantizer step size according to signal characteristics, and it achieves a quality improvement equivalent to around 2 bits of quantization. As shown in Fig. 4(a), the coder and decoder have the conventional DPCM arrangement, with the exception of a logic L. This logic observes the bit stream produced by the coder and adjusts the quantizer step size to minimize slope overload and granular distortion [10]. Algorithms for adaptation can involve memory for

Fig. 1. Interest in talking machines is not new!

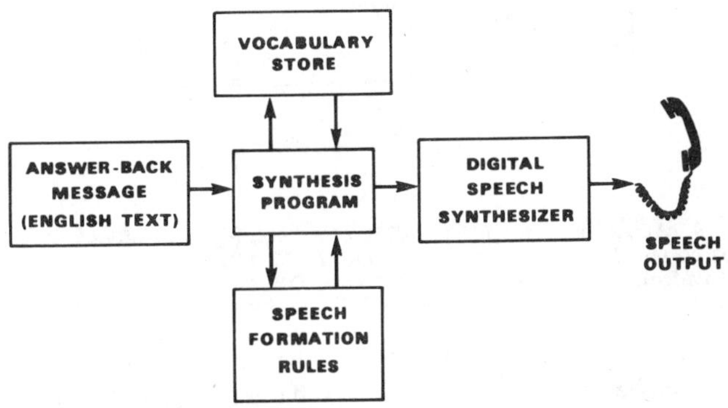

Fig. 2. Block diagram of a computer voice response system [5].

CODING	DATA RATE	DURATION OF SPEECH IN 10^6 BITS OF STORAGE
ADPCM	20K BITS/s	1 min
FORMANT SYNTHESIS	500 BITS/s	30 min
TEXT SYNTHESIS	75 BITS/s	240 min

Fig. 3. Comparison of data rates for storage of speech vocabularies.

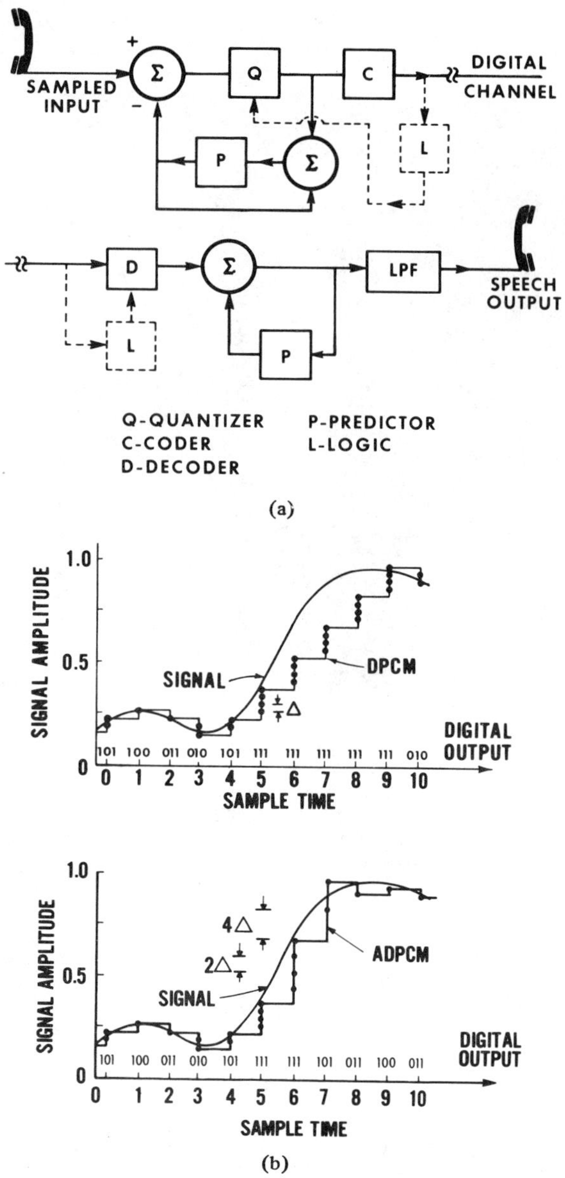

Fig. 4. Adaptive differential coding of speech [10]. (a) Block diagram of coder (adapted from U.S. Patent 3 772 682). (b) Comparison of waveforms coded by 3-bit DPCM and ADPCM.

one or more past code words,and the rate of adjustment can vary between instantaneous and syllabic. Signal coding at 3 bits/sample, by an exponential logic that has one code word of memory, is illustrated in Fig. 4(b). The ADPCM is seen to provide a better estimate of the signal than does the conventional DPCM.[2]

For message assembly, the synthesis program merely pulls the digitally coded words from disc store in the required sequence, and supplies them to an ADPCM decoder which produces the analog output signal. In this case, then, the digital synthesis device of Fig. 2 is nothing more than the simple ADPCM decoder. In this instance the only control of prosody that can be effected in assembling the message is the adjustment of time intervals between successive words, and, if necessary, their relative intensities. No control of voice pitch or merging of vocal resonances at word boundaries is possible. This technique is most appropriate, therefore, for messages requiring modest vocabulary size and having very lax semantic constraints. Typical messages are voice readout of numerals such as telephone numbers, instructions for sequential operations such as equipment assembly or wiring, stock price quotations, and inventory reporting.

This answer-back technique is presently being used experimentally for automated directory assistance [11], for voice-directed wiring [12], and for travel information [13]. Because the instructions for tasks such as point-to-point wiring in the assembly of electronic equipment are not highly contextual, and since the wiring list is often designed by a computer and supplied as a card deck or magnetic tape, a convenient means for converting the wiring list directly into spoken form is shown in Fig. 5. In this case, the computer voice output is recorded automatically on a cassette tape and taken to the work location. This system has been used experimentally for production-line assembly of telephone switch gear and for field installation of cabling [14]. Fig. 6 shows a central-office installer custom wiring the main distributing frame of an electronic switching system—some 13 000 point-to-point connections (read automatically from as many punched cards, representing the computer-designed wire list), and corresponding to a total of some 30 hours of talk!

Field studies suggest that this voice-directed technique reduces the time required to complete the job by about 20 percent and, perhaps more importantly, reduces the errors in wiring by about 50 percent over the old method of visually locating and reading each instruction from a bundle of computer printout (shown in the back corner of Fig. 6). For other types of installations, say climbing a pole to splice a cable (perhaps in a high wind), there are distinct advantages to eliminating the bundle of printout and to using a hand set to dial the computer for spoken instructions.

The second voice response technique of Fig. 3 is called formant synthesis. It utilizes a synthesis method in which a word library (again spoken initially by a human) is analyzed and parametrically stored as the time variations of vocal-tract resonances, or formants. Speech formants are represented by the dark bars on the sound spectrogram in the bottom panel of Fig. 7. These frequency variations as well as the fundamental frequency, or voice pitch, can be computer analyzed, as shown in the upper two panels of Fig. 7. These data can be represented by bit rates as low as 500 bits/s, as indicated in Fig. 3 [15]. Alternatively, equivalent data can be obtained in terms of the linear-prediction coefficients for the signal [16]-[18].

In formant synthesis the synthesizer device is a digital filter, as shown in Fig. 8. The filter's transmission resonances and antiresonances (poles and zeroes) are controlled by the computer, and its input excitation is derived by programmed rules for voice pitch (P) and for the amplitudes of voiced sounds (A_v) and noise-like unvoiced sounds (A_n) [1]-[9]. Because of the parametric description of the speech information, this synthesis method can control and modify the prosodic characteristics (pitch, duration, intensity) of the synthetic speech, and it can produce smooth formant transitions at successive word boundaries. Like the ADPCM method, this technique has also been used experimentally for generating automatic-intercept messages (telephone numbers) and for producing wiring instructions by voice [20].

[2] In this illustration, the ADPCM logic is seen to be an exponential algorithm that doubles the quantizer step size whenever slope overload is indicated by a single code word. Similarly, the step size contracts by $\frac{1}{2}$ whenever low-level hunting is indicated.

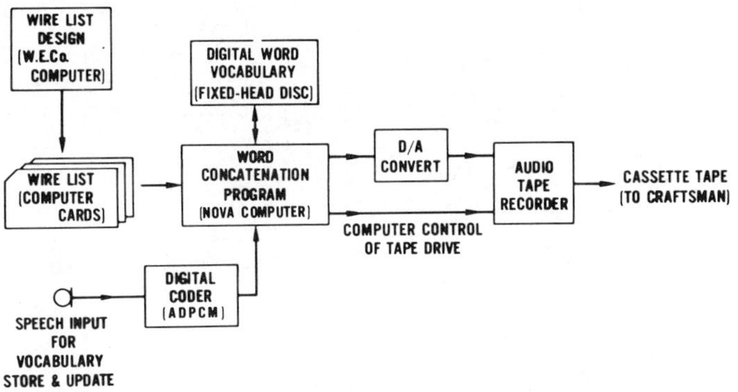

Fig. 5. Diagram of a computer system for automatically converting a wire list for telephone equipment into spoken instructions [12], [14], [20].

Fig. 6. Telephone installer wiring a central-office distributing frame from computer-generated spoken instructions [12], [14], [20].

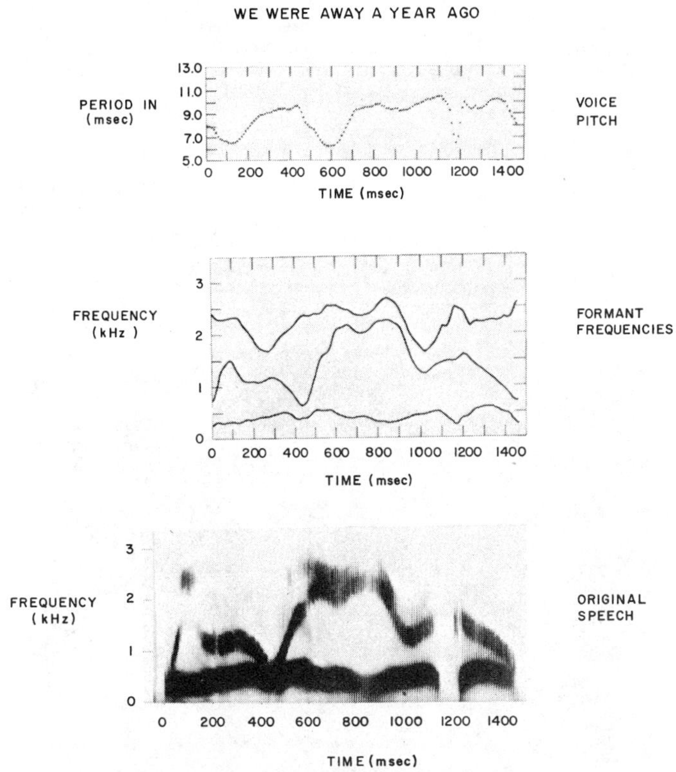

Fig. 7. Analysis of the sentence "We were away a year ago." The sound spectrogram in the bottom panel shows the time variation of vocal-tract resonances, or formants (dark bars). Computer-derived estimates of the formant frequencies and the voice pitch period are shown in the top two panels [15].

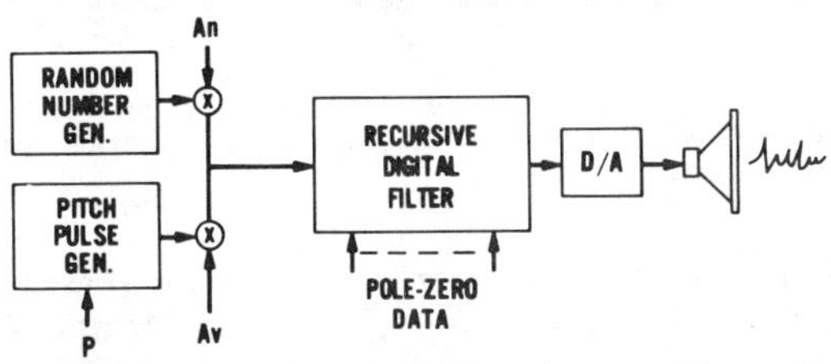

Fig. 8. Block diagram of a digital formant synthesizer [19].

The third, and most forward-looking voice response technique mentioned in Fig. 3 is called text synthesis [21], [22]. It strikes at the problem of storing and voice-accessing voluminous amounts of information, or of converting any printed message into spoken form. It generates speech from an information input corresponding to a typewriter rate, about 75 bits/s. In one design [21], the vocabulary is literally a stored pronouncing dictionary—each entry of which (just as in an ordinary desk dictionary) has the English word, a phonetic transcription of the word, word stress marks, and some rudimentary syntax information. The synthesis program includes a syntax analyzer which examines the English message to be generated and determines the role of each word in the sentence. Using the results of parsing by the syntax analyzer, the stored rules for prosody then calculate the sound intensity, sound duration, and voice pitch appropriate for each phoneme in the particular context, as illustrated in Fig. 9(a).

At the heart of the synthesis program is a dynamic articulatory model of the human vocal tract, depicted on the scope of Fig. 9(b) [23]. The calculated controls cause the vocal-tract model to execute a sequence of "motions." These motions are described in terms of changes in the coefficients of a wave equation for sound propagation in a nonuniform tube. From the time-varying wave equation, the eigenfrequencies (or formants) of the deforming tract are computed iteratively, 100 times/s. These resonant frequencies, along with the calculated pitch and intensity information, are given to the same digital formant synthesizer shown in Fig. 8. This system therefore generates its synthetic speech completely from stored rules and without resorting to any vestige of human-produced speech. English text can be typed directly into the system, as shown in Fig. 9(b), and the message synthesized on line.

Experiments in progress are examining the possibility for increasing the sophistication of the speech synthesizing device of this system. Since the system, through its model of

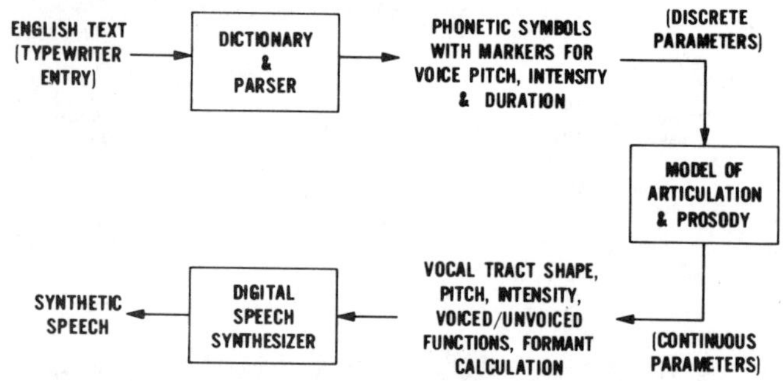

(a)

(b)

Fig. 9. System for synthesizing speech directly from printed text [21]. (a) Functional diagram of system. (b) Computer console display for text-synthesis system.

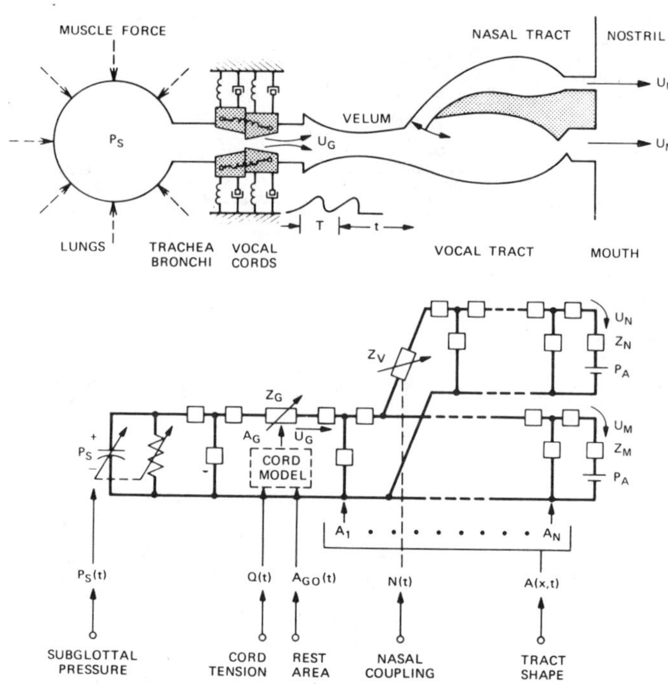

Fig. 10. Speech synthesizer based upon computer models for vocal-cord vibration, sound propagation in a yielding-wall tube, and turbulent flow generation at places of constriction [24]. The control inputs are analogous to the human physiology and represent: subglottal air pressure in the lungs (P_S), vocal-cord tension (Q), and area of opening at rest (A_{g_0}), the cross-sectional shape of the vocal tract ($A(x)$) and the area of coupling to the nasal tract (N).

articulation, already calculates physiologically based parameters in deriving controls for the formant synthesizer, the possibility exists for controlling a synthesis device which is more directly based upon the human speech mechanism [24]. One such synthesis device is shown in Fig. 10. This synthesizer approximates the human vocal system (schematized at the top of Fig. 10) by the bilateral transmission line (shown at the bottom of Fig. 10). Included in the transmission-line formulation is an aerodynamic oscillator which models the behavior of the human vocal cords. As input controls, the synthesizer requires physiologically based parameters corresponding to: subglottal lung pressure, vocal-cord tension and rest area of opening, the cross-sectional shape of the vocal tract, and the area of coupling to the nasal tract. Initial experiments have demonstrated the feasibility of synthesizing connected speech from this formulation.

V. Speaker Verification

Research over the past several years has now led to systems for authenticating the claimed identity of a caller by means of measurements on his voice signal [25]–[30]. When the possibilities for computer voice response began to take solid form about five years ago, it also became apparent that issues would arise about accessing privileged information—for example, personal information provided by insurance clients, inventory status of manufactured products, or bank-account data to be used by designated agents. Similarly, the strong desires to reduce the amount of written material and paper exchanged in our business community gave notable impetus to the notion of a "checkless society," and to the possibilities for accomplishing banking and credit transactions by voice [27]. Furthermore, various needs existed to streamline security procedures by means of "voice-locks" that, through on-the-spot analysis, could determine authorized access to restricted areas [29].

In their legitimate applications, all these situations are characterized by a cooperative individual who desires the machine to perform a useful service for him. The individual is willing to indicate his claimed identity and to have the machine judge whether the claim is correct. This is quite distinct from the problem of absolute identification of an unknown individual, or the "catch the criminal by his voice pattern" approach [31]. Not only is the verification task more tractable technically, it is also of much more importance and utility in the business sphere.

The tasks of verification versus identification can be distinguished as in Fig. 11. In verification the customer enters his identity claim and speaks his prearranged verification phrase. The machine makes measurements on the offered voice sample and compares the results to stored reference data it has on file for the claimed identity. It must then decide whether the claim is valid. In other words, it must generate one bit of information. Its judgment of closeness is conditioned upon its knowledge of the universe of possible users, and upon its information about the average closeness of the patterns of other users. That is, given the voice sample x and the claimed identity i, the machine will accept the claim if x is likely enough to have originated from i. In a simple form, "likely enough" means: $p_i(x) > c_i \langle p_n(x) \rangle_n$,

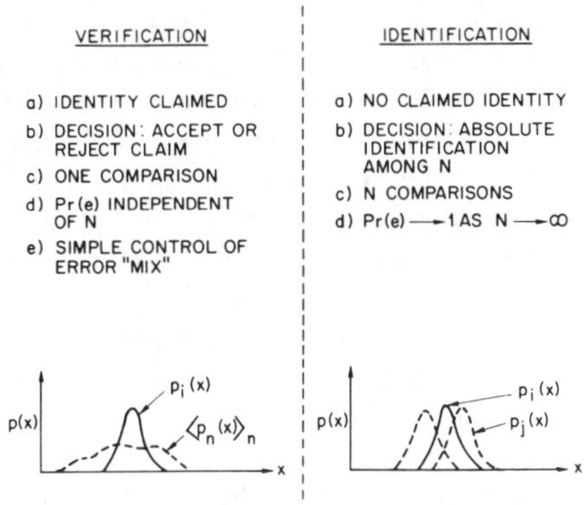

Fig. 11. Features that distinguish speaker verification and speaker identification.

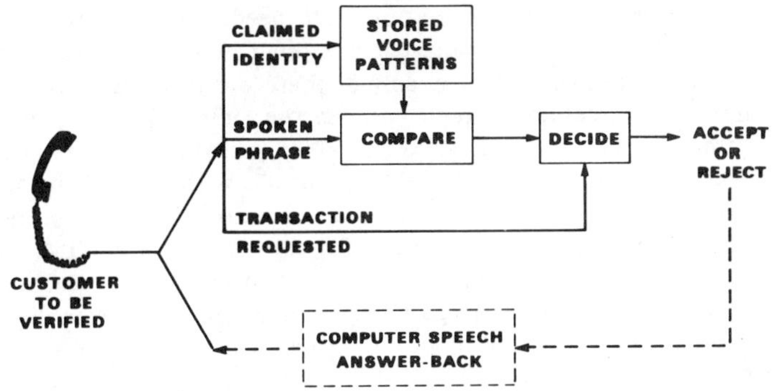

Fig. 12. Diagram of speaker verification system under test in a telephone system [14], [33].

	REJECT CUSTOMER	ACCEPT IMPOSTOR	ACCEPT MIMIC
COMPUTER	1	1	4
HUMAN	4	4	22

Fig. 13. Error rates in laboratory measurements on a speaker verification system [30].

where c_i is a constant and

$$\langle p_n(x)\rangle_n = \sum_{n=1}^{N} p_n(x)P_r(n)$$

and where N is the population of possible users of the system, and $P_r(n)$ is the probability that the nth user accesses the system. Generally $\langle p_n(x)\rangle_n$ approaches some limiting density as N becomes large, so the tendency is for the system performance to be independent of N. The machine therefore trades on the reasonableness of the probability that a close voice will attempt to be an impostor. Obviously the machine can do nothing about the impostor who, having learned his closeness to a given legitimate customer, can thwart the system at will. Additionally, however, the machine's decision can be made with an error "mix" (i.e., misses versus false alarms) that is tailored to the gravity of the requested transaction.

By contrast, the task of identification involves no claimed identity from the caller, but essentially the question "Who am I?" The machine must examine its library of stored patterns and, in the absence of a more sophisticated strategy, make N comparisons and indicate the closest match. That is, given only the voice sample x, the machine must pick the speaker from whom x is most likely to have originated–i.e., for all n choose the i for which $p_i(x) > p_n(x)$. As the user population N becomes large, the density of $p_n(x)$'s increases, and the probability of error increases.

The verification problem, therefore, is judged not only more tractable, but also of more practical interest. It consequently has received more emphasis in terms of a system design. At least one system has been implemented to accomplish the functions illustrated in Fig. 12. The system uses a sentence length utterance for verification, and it has the capability for measuring the temporal patterns of voice pitch, intensity, and spectral distribution (as reflected by the speech formants, or linear-prediction coefficients) [30]. The decision threshold and error mix can be dictated by the importance of the transaction. In the clinical environment of the laboratory, and with low-noise high-quality speech input, the system functions with an accuracy of 99 percent, or with a 1-percent error, when evaluated with all customers using the same verification phrase ($N = 77$) [30]. Data for the computer when using an equal-error criterion (equal rate of false alarms and misses) is shown in Fig. 13. Of those instances (one-half of the total) where the caller was a legitimate customer, it rejected him (false alarmed) 1 percent of the time. Of those instances (also one half of the total) where the caller was claiming an incorrect identity, it accepted the impostor (missed) 1 percent of the time.

An obvious related issue is how good is the human ear at making the same judgment? Using exactly the same speech data as given to the computer, a parallel experiment [28] asked human listeners to judge whether an unknown voice was the same as or different from stored reference samples. (At least one bank has used human listening for customer verification in voice banking.) The corresponding data for humans are shown also in Fig. 13. The human listeners are seen to perform less accurately than the computer.

Finally, a further related issue is how successful might skilled mimics be at violating the system? In a third series of experiments [32], professional voice mimics were selected from the radio and TV broadcasting industry and asked to train on the system, practicing over and over, to imitate customer voices. Under these most favorable circumstances, and with all subjects using the same phrase, the skilled mimics could increase the error scores somewhat on the computer system, to 4 percent, and by a sizable factor in the human listener experiment, to 22 percent.

Encouraged by these tests, this verification system has now been moved, in a simplified form, into the environment of the real telephone plant [33]. It presently operates over dialed up connections and with conventional telephone sets having carbon microphones. Using only the measures of voice pitch and intensity, it achieves a verification accuracy of 91 percent on a customer set of 100 persons and with several thousand potential impostors.[3] This level of performance seems acceptably high for a broad range of business transactions, such as reading out customer bank balances and making credit transactions that fall within prescribed limits.

[3] Indications are that it might prove robust enough for verification over long-distance connections. The system was demonstrated at a recent meeting of the Acoustical Society of America, where verifications were effected over telephone toll lines between Austin, TX, and Murray Hill, NJ.

The amount of information that needs to be stored for reference data seems manageable enough by present standards of disc capacities. For example, there are about six million holders of telephone credit cards in the United States. Something on the order of 4000 bits of information appears adequate to represent a customer reference.[4] With state-of-the-art disc stores, therefore, only about 20 disc spindles are required to store the references for all telephone credit-card customers in the country. This much disc capacity is commonly found in most large banks or data-processing establishments. Therefore, duplication of all customer patterns in several regions over the country seems feasible and economically attractive. This duplication would make customer patterns always accessible by a relatively short-distance call.

A continuing point of research interest is the possibility of voice classification, as opposed to storage of individual reference patterns. In this instance a customer speaks or keys a code that identifies him and describes certain distinctive attributes of his voice. He then speaks a prescribed sample, and the machine makes measurements to determine whether the indicated attributes are in fact present. This approach, if proven successful, eliminates the need for any reference storage.

Another direction of research interest relates to the dependence of the verification procedure upon speaking a prescribed text [34]. A prescribed text must, of course, be prearranged and remembered, but it gives added security (first through knowledge of the specific utterance and additionally, through custom-tailoring to the customer voice). It also enables the machine to measure characteristic prosody that a speaker uses in his dialect, as well as to make physical measures on text-independent features such as the characteristic spectral shape of the particular voice.

Still a further issue speaks to the question of achieving security in depth and using extemporaneous procedures to to guard adequately against accepting voice samples that might have been recorded at some earlier time. All these issues represent refinements that broaden the applications of voice verification.

VI. Speech Recognition

Every field has its Holy Grail, and automatic speech recognition (ASR) is ours. Its early manifestations took the form of the speech typewriter [35], [36]. The advent of computers has shifted this interest more toward the possibilities for commanding machines by voice to perform services such as computation, accounting, switching, logical functions, and voice readout of requested information. As one who, along with his immediate associates, has followed this field mostly from a distance, and who only recently has come into direct contact with it, I prefer to leave comment in depth to those who have dedicated their major efforts to it, and who have pioneered it in the computer age. No more outstanding can I suggest than Martin, Reddy, and Jelinek (all in this issue). Nevertheless, unencumbered by their wisdom, I will, from my narrow view and narrower experience, comment about several aspects.

A formula for success in ASR seems not unlike that for speech synthesis. To wit, be prudent enough to make something immediately useful, while at the same time chewing away on the farther-out problems. (My recent admonitions about this drew mixed reactions, but no tomatoes, in Stockholm, Sweden [37]). Present technology and understanding clearly support highly useful and well circumscribed applications of automatic speech recognition. These applications invariably relate either to relatively small word vocabularies (such as digits) spoken by a sizable population of users, or to rather large word vocabularies (several hundred) for speakers who allow the machine to calibrate their voices [38]–[50]. Already being demonstrated in the market place are systems for baggage and parcel sorting, for quality control and accounting on production lines, and for voice direction of machine tools (Martin, this issue).

More ambitious projects look toward speech understanding systems that will accept and understand unrestricted connected discourse from all speakers. I am not optimistic about the latter, at least not in my lifetime, nor yours. Again my preference is to achieve by pulling back from the broader issue, and taking a smaller bite—to look toward automatic recognition of connected discourse only in a rigorously limited frame—namely, for a designated speaker (on whom the machine has trained), for a highly stylized format (say, simple declarative sentences produced from a prescribed, but sizable, vocabulary), and for a highly delimited topic area [46]. Within this context, I believe it is possible to make admirable progress over the next decade, even to the extent of getting automatically-typed letters of first-draft quality, in stylized form, about a delimited topic, and from a machine which is calibrated to a given voice. Very likely, the fundamental understanding of syntax analysis and speech constraints now being accumulated in text synthesis will advance progress toward this recognition goal.[5]

Representative of the here and now is digit recognition with relatively high precision across speakers [39], [47]. A fundamental concept is the measurement of several signal features, any one of which is relatively unreliable, but when taken in combination lead to reliable recognition decisions. One such scheme is illustrated in Fig. 14 [47], where the relatively gross measures of zero-crossing rate, signal energy, and spectral compactness and slope are used as features for digit classification. The digit recognition scores it produces are shown in Fig. 15. [Again, alas, the male bias of this paper shows through—apologies to my female engineer and programmer colleagues for these disparate scores!]

In the direction of larger word vocabularies for designated speakers, the recognition system shown in Fig. 16 is representative [48]. The top part of Fig. 16 shows the flow chart for the system which is based on correlation coefficients and which utilizes a dynamic programming algorithm for time warping the measured utterance onto the reference library of the designated speaker. The lower part of Fig. 16 shows its connection in a telephone system for word recognition and reply to the customer. The system performs at a level of 96 percent correct on a 200-word library over conventional telephone connections. A typical display of its analysis is shown in Fig. 17. The top panel shows energy and illustrates automatic location of the beginning and ending of a word. The lower panel shows error measures as the vocabulary is searched, and the correct recognition of the telephone utterance of "Washington."[6] Using conventional telephone equipment and

[4] For convenience, (rather than economy), the present experimental system uses more than 4000 bits of storage per reference.

[5] It seems notable that the type of linguistics research proving valuable in synthesis and recognition work stands in strong contrast to the classical linguistic penchants for armchair theorizing. The speech synthesizer—now emerging as a quantitative test bed for linguistic theories—is an unrelenting caller of bluffs.

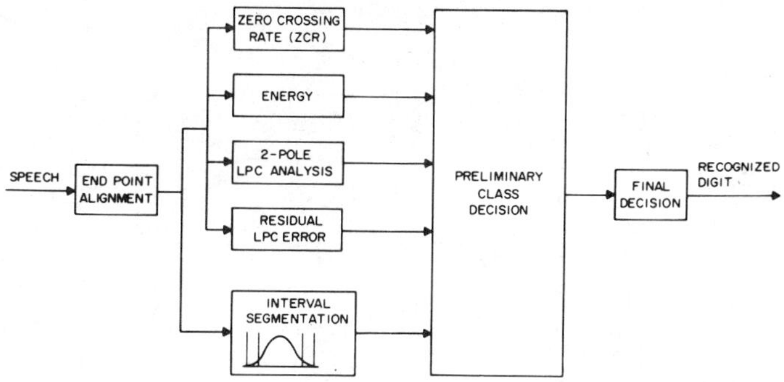

Fig. 14. System for recognition of spoken digits by feature analysis [47].

	NUMBER OF SPEAKERS	PERCENT CORRECT
MEN:	25	96.8
WOMEN:	30	92.3
TOTALS :	55	94.4

Fig. 15. Performance data for digit recognition [47].

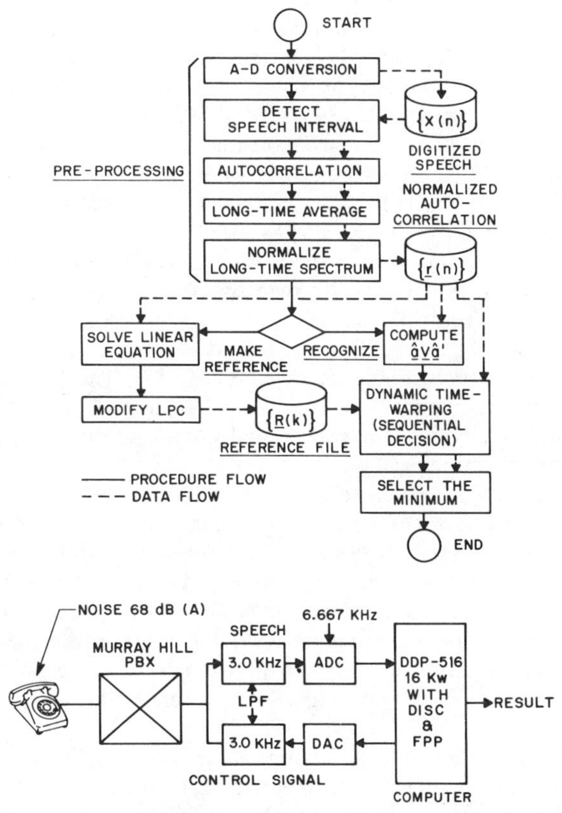

Fig. 16. Word recognition system for designated speakers [48].

dialed-up connections, this system is being combined with the verification and answer-back systems mentioned earlier to implement a complete "3-mode" experimental system for man-machine communication.

[6] The multiple, upward-pointing paths in the lower panel represent candidates which exceeded an adaptive threshold and were rejected.

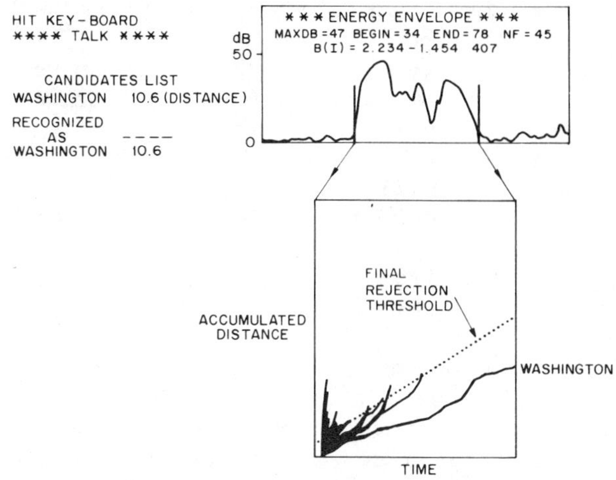

Fig. 17. Display of the dynamic-programming library search in the word recognition procedure [48].

VII. 3-Mode System for Man-Machine Communication

Toward harnessing the speech technology we have in hand (and with the parallel intent of gaining support for frontier-type activity), we have committed effort to an experimental vehicle that is an airlines information and ticketing service. This is a real-world application which at least one major airline has been considering for some time. The system being assembled in the laboratory combines 3-modes: voice answer-back based upon a digital word vocabulary coded with 24 kbits/s ADPCM [10], speaker verification as described earlier [33], and automatic recognition of a 100-word vocabulary for speakers who have trained the system [48]. One experimental scenario is as follows:

A frequent credit customer of the airlines dials the computer. The voice response answers with:

Computer: This is ABC Airlines information and ticketing service. Please key-in your account number.
(Customer does, computer looks it up, and comes back with):

Computer: Good morning, Mr. XYZ. Please speak your verification phrase for credit charging.
(Customer does, computer churns it and, if result favorable, comes back with):

Computer: Thank you, Mr. XYZ, I confirm your charge account. Where would you like to fly to?

Customer: Washington.

Computer: From what airport would you like to fly to Washington?[7]

Customer: Newark.

Computer: On what date would you like to fly from Newark?

Customer: (gives data; or may say no date).

Computer: At what time [on date, or of day] do you wish to depart?

Customer: (gives time).

[7] Note two things. 1) At each stage the answerback message has a woven-in confirmation of the last recognition. If the last recognition is incorrect, the customer can push a dial button and have the previous question repeated. 2) At each stage the recognition vocabulary is contracted in size to the answer ensemble appropriate to the question. This vocabulary contraction is an important contribution towards robustness of the system.

Computer: Just a moment, please, I will give you the flights available within two hours of [time].
(Computer goes to the current airlines timetable stored in disc file, looks up flights available, reads them out, and asks):
Computer: Which flight do you wish to book?
Customer: Flight 123.
Computer: Do you wish First Class or Economy on Flight 123?
Customer: First Class.
Computer: How many First Class seats do you wish?
Customer: One.
Computer: A moment, please, while I check availability of one seat.
Computer: I am pleased to confirm [reads it all back].
Your ticket will appear on your teletypewriter within the hour. Your bill will be sent at the end of the month.
Computer: Do you wish to book further?
Customer: No.
Computer: Thank you for calling ABC Airlines.
(Hangs up.)

At this writing a variant of this system is working in the laboratory over dialed-up connections and from conventional telephone sets in the local exchange. Continued tests will examine the robustness of the system, the traffic habits of the users, and the options needed.[8] The point is that this capability exists and our present technology, properly delimited, supports it. It is a gratifying payoff from many things learned in the interest of vocoder technology and band conservation which did not have as notable potential.

One further point remains before concluding this commentary. A lot of the foregoing discussion has assumed an analog voice channel connecting man to computer. While, at the present time, analog-voice is far and away the most ubiquitous facility, it may not always be so. Digital voice systems and data systems will continue to the fore, and it is not too early to consider the impact of switched digital networks upon opportunities for man–machine communication.

VIII. Digital Interfaces for Man-Machine Communication

The preceding discussion has not considered much about the communication carrier between man and machine. In many instances the carrier may have to serve computer-to-computer communications and man-to-man communications as well. Conventional analog dialed-up connections may not always be the medium, at least in end-to-end form, but may serve to get signals only part way in the path.

The concept of block-addressed packet-switched communication has been examined for several years [51]. Communication is by discrete digital packets which are "mailed" and routed through a delivery network, the transmission path varying according to demands on the system. This notion is distinct from that of a dialed-up hard-wire connection which is established and held for the duration of the information exchange. Ideally, when a user is being properly served in both systems he should not be able to distinguish between the carriers.

[8] Including options to branch to a human operator, if necessary.

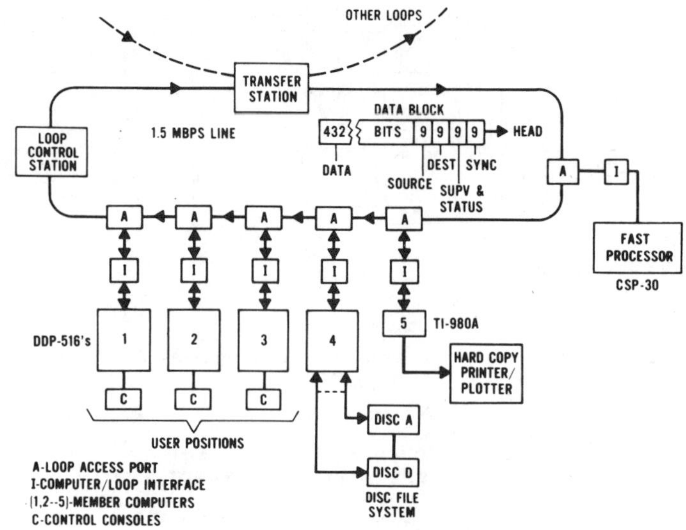

Fig. 18. Block diagram of a packet-switched data transmission system used for communication between laboratory computers [53].

The exact place of packet switching in the hierarchy of switched digital networks has yet to become clear. Experimentally at least the concept has promising features for allowing computers to share expensive peripherals, to join together in a common computational cause, and to remotely access processing power. A number of experimental systems are examining these potentials (for example, [51]–[55]).

One of the simplest of these experimental systems is illustrated in Fig. 18. It links several laboratory computers for projects in communications acoustics, including those already mentioned in the foregoing discussion. Data-packet transmission is at 1.5 Mbits/s over a coaxial line. Three independent user machines can access a large disc file, a hard copy printer/ plotter, and a fast processor (125 ns, 32K) when requested. Each user machine has its own assortment of input–output equipment (multiplexed A/D, D/A, card reader, magnetic tape, fixed-head discs, scope and light pen), but each is modest in processor power and storage [1], [14]. The loop system permits user machines to receive and to mail digital "letters" containing requests for service and computational parameters to other machines.

One is easily convinced of the viability of the letter-mailing concept for data communication. Less clear is how the same carrier might serve two-way voice communication. Two-way speech communication tends to be "bursty" in information rate, and this property is a nice fit to the packet-switched concept. Some experiments with the large ARPA network, using data-reduced digital speech, seem to indicate useful possibilities, provided round-trip delays can be kept within acceptable limits.

Still more generally, the digital domain has a number of advantages for speech transmission that do not accrue in analog transmission. A favorable digital format can be chosen to represent the signal according to characteristics of the transmission system—such as the bit rate the system will support at a given error rate, and whether the distribution of transmit errors is random or bursty (as it tends to be in mobile-radio channels).

Direct digital conversion between code formats is also attractive. Relatively straightforward digital circuitry can in many instances convert the format of one bit stream (say, adaptive delta modulation) to another (say DPCM) [56]. This direct conversion eliminates the need to revert to analog baseband, with the attendant accumulation of decoding and recoding noise.

Another attractive system possibility is allowing the quality of transmission to vary continuously and gracefully as transmission demands upon the system fluctuate. A prime possibility is a digital version of time-assignment speech interpolation (TASI) [57], in which a number of analog transmission channels are used to serve a larger number of conversations. This can be done because in normal conversations all partners are not talking simultaneously. The system depends upon being able to find an idle channel whenever a speech burst develops in a given conversation. In the analog implementation, overload or "freeze-out" tends to be catastrophic, with signal portions being clipped off and irretrievably lost. To guard against this, the safety factor is kept high and the full potential in bandwidth saving is not always realized.

In contrast, a digital implementation of time-assigned channels has the attractive possibility that signals can be gracefully varied in quality, or in the bit-rate allocated per channel, as the demand for transmission service fluctuates. Digital storage and buffering on a per-channel basis is also possible. These features, in combination, can effectively minimize catastrophic freeze-out, while maintaining the transmission channel efficiently loaded at all times. The range of acceptable quality that accomodates surges in demand on the system can be selected through prudent design. At least one variable-quality digital system has already been implemented [58].

IX. A Face to the Future

What can we comfortably look toward as feasible technology within the coming five years or so?

Computer voice response is already with us, at least in rudimentary forms such as the digital word store described earlier. More sophisticated storage and readout of voluminous amounts of contextual material is also presently possible, provided one is willing to commit substantial (and expensive) computer muscle to the task, and provided one is willing to accept a great amount of automaton-quality in the signal. Knowledge about synthesis-by-rule has not yet progressed to the point of producing human-sounding speech, that is, speech which sounds like any human, much less to a quantitative description of the subtleties of individual dialect. The next several years' work should see the former better resolved, but probably not the latter.

The capabilities of automatic speaker verification now seem relatively well established. The practical precision that is possible seems applicable to a middle-spectrum of business transactions. Present performance of first-generation designs achieves the 90% correct level, and does it over conventional dialed-up telephone circuits. Through more sophistication in the verification procedure, and through security "in-depth" (for example, by using sequences of custom-selected speech material keyed to temporal factors), this performance probably can be pushed up by perhaps another 5 percent. Automatic verification therefore seems most attractive not for highest gravity transactions, nor for lowest (which do not justify any added expense), but for a gamut of transactions such as department store credit purchases, voice-lock access to restricted areas, telephone credit calls, routine checking-account transactions, and accessing privileged information to authorized personnel. As microprocessor capabilities proliferate in communications equipment, verification by voice should be even further facilitated.

The prospects of speaker classification seem attractive, and research effort should be worthwhile here. This problem is a good example of where modest incremental investment might have significant and immediate return—just the type of problem we usually look to include in a research "mix."

Speech recognition at its present stage is a relatively untapped resource. The next few years should see a rapid growth in the use of word- and phrase-vocabularies for the designated-speaker type of system mentioned earlier. Most especially this includes systems which can be operated over voice-grade dialed-up connections. This disciplined and highly delimited form of speech recognition should find many real-world applications. Perhaps a good current possibility is a voice repertory dialer for mobile-radio telephone. The auto-driving telephone user would no doubt find it convenient to simply speak the name of the person he wished to talk to (selected from, perhaps, a couple of hundred names stored by the microprocessor in the glove compartment of his automobile) and immediately be connected.

The speech typewriter or automated secretary, on the other hand, in its full-fledged form, i.e., accepting unrestricted connected text by any speaker, may not happen this century, if ever. A more circumscribed version of the voice typewriter—for example, a machine that produces first-draft quality for a highly specific topic area and for a speaker who has trained the machine—may be possible in this decade.

As communication system designs move more toward digital coding and transmission of speech, considerable opportunities open up for services such as variable-quality signalling, privacy or encryption, error protection in fading channels, and efficiently combining signal processing, computational functions and switching functions with the communication process—in fact, it may ultimately become difficult to distinguish these functions in a given system.

What are our limitations in seeing these technologies emerge? The established and proven ideas need only good engineering exploitation and economic stimulus. The more speculative outlooks depend for their evolution upon the originality, creativeness and innovativeness of the engineers who identify and prosecute the critical problems. As always, there are fewer people who know what to do, rather than how to do it. But this, perhaps, is as it must be and should be. Our horizons are limited only by our abilities to conceive bold and innovative techniques for communication.

Acknowledgment

Several associates provided valuable comments on this manuscript—in addition to doing large amounts of the work discussed herein. I thank especially L. R. Rabiner, A. E. Rosenberg, J. L. Hall, C. H. Coker, N. S. Jayant, R. W. Schafer, F. Itakura, R. E. Crochiere, N. Umeda, and M. O. Harris.

References

[1] J. L. Flanagan, C. H. Coker, L. R. Rabiner, R. W. Schafer, and N. Umeda, "Synthetic voices for computers," *IEEE Spectrum*, vol. 7, pp. 22–45, Jan. 1970.

[2] R. D. Trupp, "Computer-controlled message synthesis," *Bell Labs Rec.*, pp. 175–180, June/July 1970.

[3] N. R. Dixon and H. D. Maxey, "Terminal analog synthesis of continuous speech using the diphone method of segment assembly," *IEEE Trans. Audio Electroacoust.*, vol. AU-16, pp. 40–50, Jan. 1968.

[4] W. D. Chapman, "Techniques for computer voice response," in *IEEE Int. Conv. Rec.*, Paper 2F.2, pp. 98–99, 1971.

[5] J. L. Flanagan, "Voices of men and machines," *J. Acoust. Soc. Amer.*, vol. 51, pp. 1375–1378, 1972.
[6] Y. Kato, K. Ochiai, and T. Araseki, "A terminal analog speech synthesizer in a small computer," in *IEEE Int. Conv. Rec.*, Paper 2F.4, pp. 102–103, 1971.
[7] V. G. Velichko and V. I. Kulya, "A method of reading out information from a computer in the form of speech," *Soviet Automat. Contr.*, vol. 4, pp. 41–44, 1971.
[8] K. Nakata and T. Miura, "A method of speech synthesis for multiplexed audio response," *Electron. Commun., Japan*, vol. 52-C, pp. 126–134, 1969.
[9] J. L. Flanagan and L. R. Rabiner, Eds., *Speech Synthesis*. Stroudsburg, PA: Dowden, Hutchinson and Ross, 1973.
[10] P. Cummiskey, N. S. Jayant, and J. L. Flanagan, "Adaptive quantization in differential-PCM coding of speech," *Bell Syst. Tech. J.*, vol. 52, pp. 1105–1118, 1973.
[11] M. Lesk, "User-activated BTL directory assistance," internal rep., Bell Lab., 1972.
[12] L. H. Rosenthal, L. R. Rabiner, R. W. Schafer, P. Cummiskey, and J. L. Flanagan, "A multiline computer voice response system utilizing ADPCM coded speech," *IEEE Trans. Acoustics, Speech and Signal Processing*, vol. ASSP-22, pp. 339–352, 1974.
[13] C. E. Schmidt and A. E. Rosenberg, "Bell Labs flight information system—An application of the voice response system on the Nova 800," internal rep. Bell Lab., 1975.
[14] J. L. Flanagan, "Digital techniques in communications acoustics," 1973 *IEEE NEREM Rec.*, vol. 15, pt. 2, *Signal Processing*, IEEE Cat. No. 73CHO 840-9, NEREM, Boston, November 1973.
[15] L. R. Rabiner, R. W. Schafer, and J. L. Flanagan, "Computer synthesis of speech by concatenation of formant coded words," *Bell Syst. Tech. J.*, vol. 50, pp. 1541–1558, 1971.
[16] B. S. Atal and S. L. Hanauer, "Speech analysis and synthesis by linear prediction of the speech wave," *J. Acoust. Soc. Amer.*, vol. 50, pp. 637–655, 1971.
[17] F. Itakura and S. Saito, "An Analysis-Synthesis Telephony Based on Maximum Likelihood Method," in *Proc. Int. Congr. Acoust.* (Tokyo, Japan), C-5-5, August 1968.
[18] J. P. Olive, "Fundamental frequency rules for the synthesis of simple declarative English sentences," *J. Acoust. Soc. Amer.*, vol. 57, pp. 476–482, 1975.
[19] L. R. Rabiner, L. B. Jackson, R. W. Schafer, and C. H. Coker, "A hardware realization of a digital formant speech synthesizer," *IEEE Trans. Commun. Technol.*, vol. COM-19, pp. 1016–1020, 1971.
[20] J. L. Flanagan, L. R. Rabiner, R. W. Schafer, and J. Denman, "Wiring telephone apparatus from computer-generated speech," *Bell Syst. Tech. J.*, vol. 51, pp. 391–397, 1972.
[21] C. H. Coker, N. Umeda, and C. P. Browman, "Automatic synthesis from ordinary English text," *IEEE Trans. Audio Electroacoust.*, vol. AU-21, pp. 293–298, 1973.
[22] J. Allen, "Speech synthesis from unrestricted text," in *Speech Synthesis*, J. L. Flanagan and L. R. Rabiner, Eds. Stroudsburg, PA., Dowden, Hutchinson and Ross, ch. 38, pp. 416–427, 1973.
[23] C. H. Coker, "Speech synthesis with a parametric articulatory model," in *Proc. Kyoto Speech Symp.* (Kyoto, Japan), A-4-1, (1968).
[24] J. L. Flanagan, K. Ishizaka, and K. Shipley, "Synthesis of speech from a dynamic model of the vocal cords and vocal tract," *Bell Syst. Tech. J.*, vol. 54, pp. 485–506, Mar. 1975.
[25] S. K. Das and W. S. Mohn, "Pattern recognition in speaker verification," in *Proc. FJCC*, vol. 35 (Las Vegas, NE), 1969.
[26] G. Doddington, J. L. Flanagan, and R. C. Lummis, "Automatic speaker verification by non-linear time alignment of acoustic parameters," U.S. Patent 3 700 815, issued Oct. 24, 1972.
[27] R. C. Lummis, "Speaker verification: A step toward the "checkless" Society," *Bell Lab. Rec.*, vol. 50, pp. 254–259, Sept. 1972.
[28] A. E. Rosenberg, "Listener performance in speaker verification tasks," *IEEE Trans. Audio Electroacoust.*, vol. AU-21, pp. 221–225, 1973.
[29] G. Doddington, "Speaker verification," Rome Air Development Center, Griffiss AFB, NY, Tech. Rep. RADC-TR-Ul-963700-F, Apr. 1974.
[30] A. E. Rosenberg and M. R. Sambur, "New techniques for automatic speaker verification," *IEEE Trans. Acoust. Speech Signal Processing*, vol. ASSP-23, 169–176, 1975.
[31] Nat. Acad. Sci.—Nat. Res. Council, Committee on Hearing, Bioacoustics, and Biomechanics, Rep. Working Group 53, "Research on Speaker Verification," Mar. 1971.
[32] R. C. Lummis, "Speaker verification by computer using speech intensity for temporal registration," *IEEE Trans. Audio Electroacoust.*, vol. AU-21, pp. 80–89, 1973.
[33] A. E. Rosenberg, "Evaluation of an automatic speaker verification system over telephone lines," *J. Acoust. Soc. Amer.*, 1975.
[34] B. S. Atal, "Effectiveness of linear prediction characteristics of the speech wave for automatic speaker identification and verification," *J. Acoust. Soc. Amer.*, vol. 55, pp. 1304–1312, 1974.
[35] J. Dreyfus-Graf, "Phonetograph und Schallwellen-Quantelung," in *Proc. Stockholm Speech Commun. Seminar* (Stockholm, Sweden), Sept. 1962: also, J. Dreyfus-Graf, "Phonétographe: Présent et futur," *Bull. Tech. PTT (Berne)*, May 1961.
[36] D. B. Fry and P. Denes, "The solution of some fundamental problems in mechanical speech recognition," *Language and Speech*, vol. 1, pp. 35–58, 1958.
[37] J. L. Flanagan, "Introductory comments of chairman, session II," in *Proc. Stockholm Speech Commun. Seminar* (Stockholm, Sweden), Aug. 1–3, 1974.
[38] V. M. Velichko and N. G. Zagoruyko, "Automatic recognition of 200 words," *Int. J. Man-Machine Studies*, vol. 2, pp. 223–234, (1970).
[39] G. I. Tsemel, *Recognition of Spoken Signals*. Moscow, USSR; English translation, Springfield, VA.: Joint Publications Research Service, National Tech. Inform. Service, 1972.
[40] L. V. Bondarko, N. G. Zagoruyko, V. A. Kozhevnikov, A. P. Molchanov, and L. A. Chistovich, *Model' vospriyatiya rechi chelovekom* (Model of the Perception of Speech by Man), Novosibirsk, USSR: "Nauka," 1968.
[41] K. H. Davis, R. Biddulph, and S. Balashek, "Automatic recognition of spoken digits," *J. Acoust. Soc. Amer.*, vol. 24, pp. 637–642, 1952.
[42] D. R. Reddy, L. D. Erman, and R. B. Neely, "A model and a system for machine recognition of speech," *IEEE Trans. Audio Electroacoust.*, vol. AU-21, pp. 229–238, 1973.
[43] D. R. Reddy, L. D. Erman, R. D. Fennell, and R. B. Neely, "The HEARSAY speech understanding system: An example of the recognition process," presented 3rd Int. Joint Conf. Artificial Intelligence, Stanford, CA, Aug. 1973.
[44] W. A. Woods, *et al.*, "Natural communication with computers: Speech Understanding Research at BBN," Rep. 2976, Vol I, Bolt, Beranek and Newman, Inc., Cambridge, MA, under ARPA DAHC15-71-C-0088, Dec. 1974.
[45] T. Martin, "Acoustic recognition of a limited vocabulary in continuous speech," Ph.D. dissertation, School of Arts and Sciences, Univ. Pennsylvania, Philadelphia, 1970.
[46] S. E. Levinson, "An artificial intelligence approach to automatic speech recognition," Ph.D. dissertation, Dep. Elec. Eng., Univ. Rhode Island, Kingston, 1974.
[47] M. R. Sambur, and L. R. Rabiner, "A speaker-independent digit-recognition system," *Bell Syst. Tech. J.*, vol. 54, pp. 81–102, 1975.
[48] F. Itakura, "Minimum prediction residual principle applied to speech recognition," *IEEE Trans. Acoust., Speech Signal Processing*, vol. ASSP-23, pp. 67–72, 1975.
[49] J. H. King, Jr., and C. J. Tunis, "Some experiments in spoken word recognition," *IBM J.*, vol. 10, pp. 65–79, 1966.
[50] D. E. Walker, "Speech understanding research," Stanford Res. Inst. Annu. Tech. Rep., AD-757049, Oct. 4, 1971–Oct. 2, 1972, DAHC-04-72-C-0009, 1973.
[51] L. G. Roberts and B. D. Wessler, "Computer network development to achieve resource sharing," in *AFIPS Proc., SJCC*, vol. 36 (Atlantic City, NJ), pp. 543–549, 1970.
[52] A. G. Fraser, "Spider—A data communications experiment," Bell Lab. Comput. Sci. Tech. Rep. 23, 1974.
[53] C. H. Coker, "An experimental interconnection of computers through a loop transmission system," *Bell Syst. Tech. J.*, vol. 51, pp. 1167–1175, 1972.
[54] R. E. Kahn, "Resource-sharing computer communications networks," *Proc. IEEE*, vol. 60, pp. 1397–1407, Nov. 1972.
[55] —, "The organization of computer resources into a pocket radio network," in *AFIPS Proc.*, vol. 44, pp. 177–186, 1975.
[56] D. J. Goodman and J. L. Flanagan, "Direct digital conversion between linear and adaptive delta modulation formats," in *Proc. IEEE Int. Commun. Conf.* (Montreal, Canada), June 1971.
[57] E. F. O'Neil, "TASI," *Bell Labs Rec.*, vol. 37, pp. 83–87, 1959.
[58] F. S. Boxall, "A digital carrier-concentration system with elastic traffic capacity," *IEEE Trans. Commun. Technol.*, vol. COM-22, pp. 1636–1642, 1974.

Part II
Reviews of Speech Recognition

Automatic Speech Recognition: A Critical Survey and Discussion of the Literature

S. R. HYDE

Introduction

This chapter* covers the literature now available on the subject of automatic speech recognition and presents some specific conclusions which were drawn as a result of this study. The literature refers to about 30 quite separate studies. It shows that there is much overlap in the work and a similarity in the degree of achievement.

In the literature available in 1970 it is possible to identify about 60 different studies. A few of these are claiming recognition scores of about 98 percent for about 30 isolated words spoken by about 30 speakers. In general these figures represent improved performance using earlier techniques and not the implementation of fundamentally new ideas on the subject. There are still no devices which can perform even moderately well on normal (conversational) speech in normal (noisy) environments by a normal range of talkers. Although this chap-

* Originally written as a British Post Office research report in 1968.

Reprinted with permission from *Human Communication: A Unified View*, E.E. David, Jr. and P. B. Denes, Eds., pp. 399–438. Copyright 1972 by McGraw Hill, New York.

ter itself may not therefore adequately represent the current position, the conclusions are still valid.

The chapter is divided into three major parts. In the first part we give a summary of the nature of the speech process and outline some of the lines of general speech research which have influenced speech recognition studies. If further reading is required Flanagan's book [1] provides a good coverage of the field of speech research and contains many valuable references.

In the second part we examine the automatic speech recognition literature. If a more comprehensive description of the earlier studies is required the reader is referred to the literature reviews of Lindgren [2] and Marill [3], to secs. 11.2, 11.4, and 12.2 of Saposhkov [4], and to sec. 5.5 of Flanagan [1].

In the third part we present certain conclusions drawn from the study regarding the important conditions to be met in a general-purpose recognition device. These conclusions cover several aspects of the recognition problem and each conclusion is briefly discussed as it is introduced.

The Nature of Speech

Speech is a form of communication between human beings which involves the generation and reception of a complex acoustic signal. The process by which thoughts in the mind of the talker are communicated, and so form reciprocal thoughts in the mind of the listener, may be thought of as a coding operation which takes place over a hierarchy of processing levels. At the highest level we have the thoughts, or possibly the fundamental concepts which give rise to these thoughts. The thoughts are encoded on a lower level, which we shall refer to as the *linguistic level,* in the form of words. The words are encoded on successively lower levels, involving neural processing and articulatory movements, until the lowest level is reached with the acoustic signal.

At each level redundancy is used to overcome the inherent ambiguities at that level. One form of redundancy is seen in the multiplicity of perceptual "cues" used to distinguish between different speech elements. Thus the sound /s/ is distinguished from other speech sounds by the presence of fricative noise, by the initial rate of rise in energy, by the concentration of energy in certain regions of the frequency spectrum, by its relative intensity, etc. Another form of redundancy involves feedback between levels. Thus an error made in identifying a speech sound from its acoustic pattern may be corrected by reference to rules governing the production of such sounds (physical, linguistic, etc.), knowledge about the vocal characteristics of the talker, and even whether the total message "makes sense."

Naturally, the redundancy added at each processing level results in an increase in the channel capacity necessary to transmit the information. The acoustic waveform covers a frequency range of about 10 kHz, although almost no intelligibility is lost if the range is limited to the region 200 Hz to 4 kHz. It has been estimated that, if the basic message could be extracted from the speech signal (by automatic recognition) and transmitted in the form of phonemic elements (see reference to the phoneme later), a saving of the order of 1,000:1 would be possible in the required channel capacity compared with that needed to transmit the acoustic waveform.

The acoustic signal is the result of the interaction of two separate functions of the human vocal system. We shall refer to these functions as the *spectral-envelope function* and the *excitation function.* To a first order these functions are independent of each other.

The spectral-envelope function is due to multiple acoustic resonance in the vocal tract. It is varied by means of the articulators: the tongue, lips, jaw, and velum. An adequate description of the envelope function is possible in terms of the frequency positions and relative amplitudes of the first three or four spectral peaks. These peaks are termed *formants* in voiced sounds, and it is convenient to consider them as separate measurable entities. Much of the message information in speech is conveyed by the envelope function and, in theory, it should be possible to extract this information if formant measures and the variation in overall energy level are known.

The excitation function, on whose spectrum the pattern of the vocal-tract resonances is impressed, is produced by two basically different processes.

One of these processes is due to the action of the vibrating vocal cords, which give a pulse-like air-flow waveform whose spectrum is very rich in harmonic components. The spectrum is seen as a series of harmonically related spectral lines, of which the first 50 to 100 have significant energy. The sensation of vocal pitch depends on the frequency with which the individual pulses occur.

The second excitation process is due to air turbulence generated by forcing a strong current of air through a narrow constriction in the vocal tract, for example between the tongue and the alveolar ridge. The hissing sound produced is random in nature and is referred to as *fricative noise.* The spectrum is continuous and covers a wide frequency range, but is modified by the vocal-tract resonances, particularly those associated with that part of the tract in front of the point of generation.

Although an electrical analog of the speech waveform may be viewed by means of an oscilloscope, a much more informative display is obtained from a running description of the short-time energy spectrum. This can be obtained by means of the sound spectrograph [1, p. 126], which analyzes a recorded section of speech and displays the result as a three-dimensional graph called a *spectrogram*. In this the two spatial dimensions represent frequency (vertical displacement) and time (horizontal displacement), and intensity is represented by the intensity (blackness) of the trace.

Spoken words are perceived as consisting of successions of elemental sound units. These perceptual units are referred to by the phonetician as *phonemes*. They function in the spoken language much as do letters in the written language. The various sounds which are perceived by the listener as being appropriate to the same phoneme are seen to result in spectrogram patterns with certain common characteristics. In fact, with suitable training it is often possible to "read" the spectrogram and repeat what was said. However, the patterns associated with a particular phoneme vary considerably with the talker, speed of utterance, presence of nearby phonemes, etc.; and quite different sounds, for example due to dialectal differences, may be correctly described by the listener as being due to the same phoneme.

Since the set of phonemes in a given language is quite small (there are about 40 different phonemes in English) compared with the set of all possible words, it is the phoneme which is often chosen as the unit of recognition in automatic speech recognition. Such a choice may be adequate for the case of a single cooperative talker and a small vocabulary of isolated words but is insufficient for the recognition of normal conversational speech.

Outline of General Speech Research

Speech research in general owes much to earlier workers in experimental phonetics such as Jones [5]. This work was able to quantify the relation between perceived phonemic quality and the occurrence of articulatory events related to tongue position and movement, lip shape, etc. It also revealed the independent nature of the sound-source and vocal-tract functions.

The fact that recognizable vowel sounds could be generated by combinations of acoustic resonators was known to Helmholtz and Rayleigh [6, p. 477], but the true nature of the dependence of the spectrum on the vocal-tract-area function was to await the development of cineradiographic techniques (e.g., the study by Russell, Ref. 7) and experiments with electrical vocal-tract analogs by Dunn [8] and Fant [9].

The mechanism of the operation of the human larynx (vocal cords, supporting cartilages, and operating muscles) was established by the work on cadaver larynxes by Van den Berg [10, 11], and the relation between intonation, intensity, etc., and prosodic information (grammatical stress, talker's emotional state and sex, etc.) has been investigated by workers such as Lieberman [12].

Important relationships between articulatory events and neural motor-function control have been revealed by electromyographic studies (e.g., Ref. 13). These suggest that, at the neural level, the physical correlates of phonemic elements are less dependent on phonemic environment than at the acoustic level.

An idea of the tolerance of the ear to certain forms of severe waveform distortion can be obtained from the paper by Licklider and Pollack [14]. They found that even limiting the waveform to two amplitude levels (infinite clipping), so preserving only information about the times at which the signal crosses the zero axis ("zero crossings"), still permits a high degree of intelligibility.

A great deal of useful research has been concerned with relations between the perceptual and acoustic aspects of speech communication. A comprehensive study of speech sounds analyzed by an early Bell Laboratories spectrograph led to the book by Potter, Kopp, and Kopp [15]. After twenty years this book is still considered to comprise a most valuable collection of data.

A considerable body of data concerning the acoustic correlates of phonemic quality (e.g., the acoustic patterns of vowels, semivowels, etc.) has resulted from the work directed by Peterson at the Communication Sciences Laboratory, University of Michigan, in which Lehiste has been most prominent (e.g., Refs. 16 and 17).

In a classic study, Peterson and Barney [18] obtained the perceptual responses of a large number of listeners to vowel sounds in speech by a large number of talkers, and plotted these as a function of the measured frequencies of the first two formants (F1 and F2). This showed a high degree of overlap between the different vowel judgments. For instance, the formant measurements for a particular vowel sound by one talker might be identical with those for a different vowel sound by another talker. This is particularly so when the range of speakers is not restricted in sex or age.

Clearly, specifying the first two formant frequencies alone does not provide sufficient information to uniquely identify a given vowel sound. It might be suggested that additional measures are required, perhaps related to higher formants. It is more likely that the judgment is related to perceived talker characteristics, so that the listener must become familiar with the talker's voice before reliable judgments can be made.

This notion is supported by an experiment reported by Ladefoged and Broadbent [19]. Using synthetic speech they generated utterances which sounded like the words "bit," "bet," and "bat." These utterances differed only in the formant frequencies used for the vowel sounds. In fact, F2 was the same in each case but F1 was higher for "a" than for "e" and higher for "e" than for "i." Each word was introduced by a short sentence, also in synthetic speech, and a panel of listeners was asked to decide which of the three words had been presented.

It was found that the listener's responses to the vowel sound could be controlled by varying the average value of F1 used in the introductory sentence. Thus, if a higher than average F1 was used throughout the preamble, a word which was earlier judged to be "bet" was now judged by the same panel to be "bit."

The great advantage in using synthetic speech for this type of experiment is in the precise way in which selected parameters may be varied while keeping others fixed. This is an advantage in many branches of speech research where the subject of study must be related to perceptual standards, as in automatic recognition. The value of synthetic speech in speech research was recognized and exploited in work performed at Haskins Laboratories on the isolation of the more important "cues" by which speech sounds are identified. A summary of the work performed in the early and middle 1950s is given by Delattre [20].

We conclude this introduction with a brief look at a group of papers of particular relevance to work on automatic recognition. These are concerned with theories on the way in which the human listener perceives speech when presented with the acoustic speech signal.

One such theory, known as *analysis by synthesis,* was proposed by Halle and Stevens of MIT [21, 22]. This postulates that in order to relate the speech signal to permissible strings of speech elements, the listener generates an internal speech signal under the known generative rules and matches these signals to signals derived from the incoming speech. A similar theory, called the *motor theory of speech perception,* has been suggested by Liberman of Haskins Laboratories [23]. This also suggests that the listener makes use of the mechanism for generating speech in order to turn the continuous acoustic signal into the discrete units in which speech is perceived.

The main difference between these two theories seems to be in the purpose for which the ideas are introduced. The MIT model is proposed in an explicit form, without regard for the detailed accuracy of the proposal, in order to stimulate research into specific attempts at speech recognition. The Haskins theory is used as a starting point from which research can proceed into the perceptual effects themselves.

Fant has criticized the details of these suggested active perceptual systems and has suggested a further model of the operations involved [24].

Fant is also co-author of a theory of speech production which has been fruitful in stimulating work on automatic recognition. This is the *distinctive-features* theory [25], which views the various phonemes of speech in terms of a smaller set of binary oppositions related to the manner of production. These oppositions are referred to by such terms as vocalic/nonvocalic, nasal/oral, tense/lax, etc. Some of these quantities can be directly related to measurable acoustic phenomena, such as the overall energy level and the presence of concentrations of energy in certain regions of the frequency domain; but the acoustic correlates of others have proved very elusive, and Fant himself has, more recently, been critical of some of the quantities chosen for the original set [24].

Survey of the Literature on Automatic Speech Recognition

The aim of this survey is not to give a detailed explanation of each system or to criticize the methods used, but to reveal the main theme on which each approach is based and to give an idea of the degree of success attained. This latter quantity, where given, usually takes the form of a percent-correct recognition score as reported by the experimenter. This measure should be used with great caution when comparing different systems, as it depends so much on the input material chosen and on the criteria used to determine it.

Earlier Studies

The first truly successful recognizer was reported in 1952 by Davis, Biddulph, and Balashek of Bell Laboratories [26]. This device could recognize the ten digits, spoken over the telephone by a single talker, with an accuracy approaching 100 percent. On the speech of a different talker, however, the accuracy could be as low as 50 percent. The talker was expected to speak clearly and to pause between digits. The recognition method used was to assign the spoken word to the most probable digit category on the basis of approximate F1/F2 measurements during vowel sounds.

The choice of the spoken digits as recognition material is a natural one due to the modest size of the vocabulary and its application in machine control, automatic dialing, etc. It does, however, contain word pairs which are easily confused even by humans, such as "five" and "nine."

In the following years the 1952 machine was considerably refined so that the device reported in 1958 [27] gave virtually perfect recognition for a single talker and could be used by other talkers if they learned to modify their voices, but it was not possible to significantly enlarge the vocabulary or increase the number of users without a considerable retraining period.

In 1956 Wiren and Stubbs [28] at Northeastern University produced a device which partially implemented the distinctive-feature binary oppositions. Phoneme classification was based on voiced/unvoiced, turbulent/nonturbulent, stop/fricative, and acute/grave determinations. This gave 94 percent correct recognition of the vowels in short words by 21 talkers. Also in 1956, Olson and Belar of RCA [29] reported a machine with a vocabulary of ten monosyllabic words with which a syllable recognition accuracy of 98 percent could be obtained in complete sentences by a single talker. "Careful" pronunciation was required with a pause between each syllable. Eight frequency bands and five time intervals per syllable were used to define an eight-cell by five-cell matrix. In each cell a "1" or a "0" was stored depending on whether the signal energy appropriate to that cell was above or below a threshold level. The decoded matrix pattern was used to operate a typewriter key and so a typed transcript of the sentence was obtained.

A later version of the Olson and Belar syllable recognizer was reported in 1961 [30]. Again this made use of eight frequency bands and five time samples, but these time samples were only taken when a significant change occurred in the spectral power distribution. The machine's vocabulary was increased from 10 to 100 syllables, but no recognition performance figures were given.

Following suggestions by Fry, Denes produced a speech recognizer at University College, London, in 1959 [31]. This consisted of a spectrum analyzer, a spectral pattern-matching system, and stored probabilistic information concerning the probability of any phoneme recognized by the machine following another in spoken English. The phoneme-recognition set comprised four vowels and nine consonants. The overall performance was not particularly good, but use of the linguistic data (phoneme pair probabilities) improved the word recognition accuracy from 24 to 44 percent.

We conclude this look at the earlier literature with the pioneering study by Forgie and Forgie at Lincoln Laboratories, reported in 1959 [32]. This used a 35-channel filter bank whose outputs were envelope-detected, sampled, and fed to a computer. The computer program made use mainly of the frequency positions of F1 and F2 and of fundamental voice-frequency measurements. It could recognize ten English vowels in isolated words of the form /b/-vowel-/t. For 21 male and female talkers, with no adjustment for the talker, the vowel recognition accuracy was 93 percent.

This work demonstrated the value of the digital computer in recognition studies; and the combination of computer and vocoder-type hardware analyzer was to appear in many future investigations, as we shall see in the following section.

Reports Since 1960

The availability of powerful, high-speed computers in recent years has brought about a significant change in research in this field.

One common use for a computer has been in place of the hardware concerned with classifying the utterance on the basis of output signals from a hardware spectrum analyzer. The spectrum analyzer is typically of the vocoder type, having a bank of filters followed by rectifying and smoothing circuits. Spectral analysis of speech in this manner is well established, and many such analyzers exist in speech-research centers. The computer time involved in simulating a conventional vocoder-type analyzer is therefore hardly justified. However, the recognition strategy, which determines the processing necessary in the later stages, is often subject to considerable modification as the study progresses. The flexibility which the computer offers is therefore very valuable in these stages.

Where the spectral analysis section is also subject to investigation there are considerable advantages in simulating the whole system by computer. However, where real-time operation is required, or where large amounts of speech material are to be processed, it has been common to fix the design during an initial period of complete simulation and then to build hardware units for those sections requiring long computer time. Now even this restriction has been greatly relaxed with the development of the "fast Fourier transform" algorithm of Cooley and Tukey [33]. Thus in many present-day laboratory investigations valuable research can be conducted with no further equipment than a tape recorder, an analog-to-digital converter, and a general-purpose computer.

The most interesting use to which computers have been put in some recently reported investigations has been in on-line computer studies using man-machine communication peripherals such as the light pen and RAND tablet. These highly flexible systems allow for rapid manipulation of the speech signal in intensive experimental sessions, which permit progress at a speed undreamed of in the special hardware days.

Hardware Studies

We begin this section with a look at three hardware devices reported from Japan in the early 1960s. A number of practical recognizers were demonstrated in that country at about this time and rather high recognition scores were claimed, although it has been suggested that this is partly due to the phonetic simplicity of the Japanese language.

A study of vowel recognition by Suzuki and Nakata of the Radio Research Laboratory, Tokyo, was reported in 1961 [34]. A 26-channel spectrum analyzer and separate wideband, formant-related channels were used. The channel outputs were separately grouped and connected to individual vowel-decision circuits. The speech was segmented into voiced and unvoiced segments, and envelope-intensity and fundamental voice-frequency measurements were also used. To reduce the errors due to formant movement during vowel sounds, separate recognition decisions were made at intervals throughout voiced segments. The final classification was then made by observing the phoneme most frequently recognized. If one phoneme was not clearly in the majority, the two most frequent were indicated.

Sakai and Doshita of Kyoto University reported a more comprehensive recognizer in 1962 [35]. This used separate circuits for segmenting the speech into vowels and consonants and for classifying the segmented phonemes. Zero-crossing analysis was combined with measurements of the variations of energy in various frequency regions. The segmentation operation made use of measures of the "stability" of, and the "distance" between, the digital patterns generated. Details of the recognition experiments were not given but it was claimed that 90 percent correct recognition was obtained on vowels and 70 percent on consonants, although it was pointed out that some phonemes were not allowed as input.

A device for recognizing Japanese digits spoken in isolation was reported by Nagata et al. of the Nippon Electric Co. in 1963 [36]. Recognition decisions were based on the number of voiced intervals in each utterance, the presence of an unvoiced consonant, and formant frequencies and frequency slopes at three time points in each voiced interval. Eight such features were detected, and the state of each was indicated by energizing one of a number of output lines. There were 56 lines in all, of which eight were energized at the end of each utterance. The output lines were connected to the columns of a resistor matrix. The rows of the matrix represented the 10 digits. The resistors were chosen such that the row appropriate to a particular digit had the highest voltage when the sequence of detected features made that digit the most likely. An indication of the fundamental voice frequency was derived and used to change the decision matrix for female talkers.

The matrix resistors were adjusted to suit a single male talker based on an analysis of 500 utterances of the digits. One thousand utterances by the same talker resulted in an error rate of 0.3 percent. The matrix was then adjusted on the basis of 600 utterances by 20 male talkers. One thousand utterances by the same talkers then gave a 2.1 percent error rate. After further adjustments, 500 utterances by 10 female talkers gave a 7 percent error rate.

A hardware study of massive proportions has been the subject of periodic reports by Martin et al. of RCA [37]. This system makes use of analog threshold logic (ATL) elements which are based on a model of the biological neuron. The ATL element is a transistor circuit having excitory and inhibitory inputs which provides an output only when the linear sum of input currents (inhibitory inputs are subtracted) exceeds a preset threshold. This output is then proportional to the sum of the inputs until saturation is reached. When reported in 1964 the system contained well over 500 of these circuits. The recognizer employed a 19-channel spectrum analyzer (which could handle a 60-dB dynamic range), ATL elements, AND gates, and monostable multivibrators. Various features of the speech signal were used for the recognition of individual phoneme patterns, such as steady-state and transitory spectral-energy patterns and intensity ratios. An interesting feature of the system was that no formant peaks or troughs were measured; it was found that a more invariant measurement was obtained from the "spectral regions of increasing and decreasing energy," i.e., the formant skirt slopes. The channel filters had Q factors ranging between 1 and 2.

In an article by Falter in 1965 [38] the machine's performance on CVC utterances by six male talkers was given. Recognition accuracies ranging from 82 to 99 percent were obtained for 22 different phonemes including vowels, stops, and vowel-like consonants. Work in hand at that time was expected to lead to improved performance on these phonemes and others not discussed, and it was claimed that the principle of operation could permit the recognition of connected speech. A great advantage of the approach adopted in this study is that it is possible to distinguish between patterns which differ only slightly in their physical characteristics. These differences can be detected and given greater weight then they would have in an overall view of the patterns.

A study made at the University of Illinois was described by Gazdag in 1966 [39]. In fact the recognition process was not completely implemented, so requiring human effort in the final stages, and the system was not fully tested at the time of reporting, but the report was mainly concerned with a mathematical investigation of the fundamental ideas involved. A 12-channel spectrum analyzer was used (highest frequency 3 kHz), and the measurement space defined by its outputs was partitioned by six hyperplanes, implemented by summing amplifiers and trigger circuits, each trigger circuit changing state as its amplifier's output passed through zero. The output pattern was thus in the form of six binary quantities whose time variation was characteristic of the spoken word. The outputs were recorded on a multichannel pen recorder and transcribed by human operators in sequences of six-digit binary numbers.

The machine was tested on 10 digits spoken by four talkers. Detailed results were not given but the performance was described as "promising." It was also claimed that the system was invariant to time variations but no proof of this was given.

A system for recognizing Italian numerals was described in 1967 by Gilli and Meo [40]. This used a 17-channel spectrum analyzer followed by threshold detectors which reduced the range of outputs from each channel to binary statements. These signals were sampled and connected to separate circuits for the recognition of each digit. The decisions were mainly based on the sequential occurrence of vowel and consonant patterns and patterns due to certain transitions.

For the 10 numerals spoken by 10 talkers, which were used to provide data on which the machine was designed, no errors occurred. For new utterances by the same talkers, correct recognition was obtained for 90 percent of the utterances. The authors claimed that the results proved that the crude patterns obtained were sufficient for recognition of the digits by a simple machine and that a redesign could have eliminated most of the errors.

Bezdel [41] of Standard Telecommunication Laboratories (STL) has described a system for discriminating sound class on the basis of zero-crossing analysis. This depends on the rate, and the differential rate, at which zero-crossing frequencies fall in previously defined bands. Some of the classes separated include long and short voiced and unvoiced sounds, two vowel classes, two fricative classes, and long and short periods of silence. It was claimed that an advantage of the system is that separate segmentation is not necessary, as this is inherent in the processing involved.

A word recognizer reported by Ross of RCA [42] was an extension of work by Olson and Belar. It used a four-channel spectrum analyzer and a digital disk storage system. A 20-bit binary pattern was generated for each word by sampling five two-state signals derived from the four frequency channels. Four of these signals were obtained by calculating the ratio of the mean energy level in each frequency channel to the mean energy in the overall signal. The fifth signal resulted from a comparison of the energy in the highest frequency channel with that in the two lowest. Each of these signals was compared with a threshold level to produce five binary outputs. The resulting patterns were classified by means of a "nearest neighbor" comparison with patterns stored in the machine. The permissible "distance" between patterns giving the same output response was under the control of the experimenter. The training procedure was to present a number of utterances representing a single word in sequence. If the incoming pattern was not sufficiently close to any of the patterns already stored, the new pattern was added to the stored patterns. Thus a set of different patterns were retained for each word in the machine's vocabulary.

After training, a new input pattern was given the same label as that of the nearest stored pattern if it was within the specified distance of one of these. Otherwise it was rejected. The machine was tested on spoken digits. When the permitted distance was set to one bit (i.e., two patterns were considered the same if they differed by only one bit out of the 20 pattern bits) 86 stored patterns were required to correctly identify the members of the training set. For ten new samples of each spoken digit, 56 gave the correct response, 8 gave incorrect responses, and 36 gave no response. When the permitted distance was zero (requiring an exact match), with 218 patterns stored, 46 out of 100 new digits gave the correct response, 2 gave incorrect responses, and 52 gave no response.

Computer Studies

Denes and Mathews [43] in 1960 reported a system for recognizing the 10 digits from complete word patterns. This used a 17-channel spectrum analyzer, the outputs of which were sampled and recorded on magnetic tape. This signal then formed the input to a computer. Time-frequency patterns for a number of utterances of each word were averaged and stored as reference patterns. Patterns from unknown utterances to be classified were compared, by a cross-correlation process, with each stored pattern in turn. The classification of the reference pattern giving the best match was chosen as that of the unknown utterance. A comparison was made of the results with and without time normalization of the patterns.

One female and six male talkers were used and the only restriction imposed on their pronunciation of the digits was that they should pause between each. The error rate averaged over all talkers was 6 percent with time normalization and 12 percent without. The authors concluded that forming the reference patterns by averaging over several talkers and the use of time normalization were both valuable techniques. They also suggested that, in time normalization, the consonant and vowel parts of the pattern should be treated separately rather than the whole pattern being simply stretched or compressed.

Another digit recognizer was briefly described in an abstract published in 1960 by Sebestyen of Litton Industries [44]. This combined an 18-channel vocoder analyzer and computer. The computer implemented linear transformations of the analyzer output signals to obtain maximal clustering of the data in the 361-dimensional space formed by time-sampling the channel outputs. Time normalization was used, and the normalization factor was included as one of the space dimensions.

Four hundred utterances of the 10 numerals by 10 talkers were used. It was claimed that, if at least seven examples of each numeral were used to optimize the clustering transformations, no recognition errors were made even when the talkers used in testing the recognizer were different from those used in training it.

The phoneme-recognition study by Meeker et al. of RCA [45] also used an 18-channel vocoder-type analyzer and a computer. Boundaries between phoneme-like segments were detected from changes in the channel energy levels. Long voiced segments in CVC words were considered to be vowels. For these the frequencies of the first two formants were determined at the center of the segment. The vowels were classified by comparison with the published data of Peterson and Barney [18]. Three types of consonant segment were recognized: stop, fricative, and nasal/liquid.

A total of 7,200 vowel sounds from words spoken by 10 male talkers were classified with an accuracy of about 40 percent. After an analysis of the results it was concluded that if the decision rules had been based on the speech of each talker separately, and if use had been made of vowel duration, the vowel recognition score would have been 97 percent. Ten consonants in 6,000 words were recognized with an accuracy of 60 percent.

A word-recognition system was reported in 1966 by Gold of MIT [46]. This used a 16-channel spectrum analyzer (maximum frequency 3 kHz), a pitch extractor, and a voicing detector. The computer program segmented the words into approximate phonemic units on the basis of voicing, magnitude, and spectral information. A further 15 spectral, durational, and intensity measurements were then made on a group of five segments centered on one segment which was defined as stressed. A scoring method based on the similarity with previous measurements on known words was used to classify the word. For 50 isolated words by 10 talkers, 86 percent were correctly identified and 96 percent received either the highest or the second-highest score.

An example of a system produced entirely by computer simulation is that of Sholtz and Bakis of IBM [47]. In this the spectral analyzer was assumed to have 40 filters, and the power output of each channel was obtained by convolving the time-sampled input signal with the impulse response of the appropriate filter. The input was in the form of isolated words. These were segmented into consonants and vowels (including vowel-like consonants) and compared with a library of stored word patterns. If a suitable match was obtained, the appropriate word was considered to be recognized; otherwise the utterance was rejected.

Eleven vowel and three consonant categories were used. Segment classification was on the basis of the following measurements:

1. Silence (power level 20 dB below average).

2. Total power slope (approximation to the time derivative of the total power).

3. A number of measurements obtained from the ratio of power contained in various bands; for example, the vowel/consonant decision was based on the ratio of the power in the band 0–800 Hz to that in the band 7–8 kHz. If greater than a given threshold value, vowel; otherwise consonant.

For each vowel applied to the classification process a set of 24 numbers was obtained relating to its power spectrum and time variation. The numbers were considered to specify a point in 24-dimensional space. This space was divided into 11 regions (ten vowel classes and one reject class) by hyperplanes implementing a Bayes decision, assuming equal a priori probabilities. The three consonant categories were stop (based on a rapid increase in power level following silence) and two types of fricative. In some cases a segment which did not fit into any of these three categories was rejected.

Utterances by 10 talkers were used to develop the recognition procedure. The system was then applied to words spoken by 40 new talkers in order to optimize the dictionary categories. If one word caused a particular sequence of phoneme categories, that word was assigned as the dictionary meaning of that sequence. If several words gave the same sequence, the most frequently occurring word was assigned as the dictionary meaning. When the recognition procedure was applied to the whole set of utterances (total of 493 words by 25 male and 25 female talkers), 97 percent of the words gave the correct response. It was claimed that the results were independent of the sex of the talker and that the process was more tolerant of intertalker differences than previously reported systems.

A word recognizer using a low-data-rate spectral-matching process has been developed by Shearme and Leach of J.S.R.U. [48]. The output of a 20-channel vocoder analyzer is sampled and fed to a computer. Each time sample is considered to define a point in 20-dimensional space. The variation of this point traces out a path in the space which is characteristic of the word and of the talker. Twenty different "prototype spectra" are chosen which represent certain fixed points in the space. The path taken by the signal during an utterance is specified by noting the nearest prototype point at each sampling instant. The result is a series of numbers in the range 1 to 20. It is this sequence which forms the pattern to be recognized in the matching process. Separate number sequences due to the utterance of words of known classification are first stored in the computer as "template" patterns. Unknown-word patterns are then compared with each prototype pattern and the classification of that giving the highest score is chosen.

For 32 isolated words by 10 talkers and using nine template patterns for each vocabulary word, an accuracy of 90 percent correct identification was obtained. No example of the input word by the talker under test was included in the set of prototype patterns. The scoring method provides two confidence measures, one relating to the probability of correct recognition and the other the probability that the word giving the highest score was, in fact, outside the vocabulary of the machine. One advantage of this type of system is the ease with which the template patterns may be changed to suit a different talker, dialect, or language. Another is the fact that the unit of recognition can be easily extended to a longer utterance than the word.

Purton [49] has produced a system which makes use of an autocorrelation technique. The signal is first split into two bands approximating the ranges of F1 and F2. The two waveforms are then infinitely clipped to produce zero-crossing signals. These signals are separately autocorrelated and time-sampled to produce a 36×30 matrix for each utterance. This pattern is compared with master patterns and the best match determined by a scoring method. The master patterns are formed from several utterances of known classification by one or by several talkers.

In single-talker experiments using a machine vocabulary of 10 words, 696 utterances gave individual accuracies ranging from 78 to 99 percent. The average accuracy was 89 percent. By using an "updating" procedure, where incoming patterns giving high scores are used to improve the master patterns, an average accuracy of 93 percent was obtained with 385 utterances by six talkers. As with the previous system, this system has the advantage that the stored patterns can be easily changed to suit the machine's use. Admitted disadvantages are the large storage requirements and the long processing time (about 3 s per utterance). It was claimed that these can be improved without loss of performance.

Lavington and Rosenthal [50] have been working on the recognition of verbal commands at Manchester University (Department of Computer Science). Their recognition system makes use of simple measurements of zero-crossing intervals, turn-arounds (points of zero time derivative), and amplitude-envelope information.

A total of 70 words from a vocabulary of 16 CVC monosyllables by 19 talkers with various accents were recognized with only one misclassification error and three "minor" errors. In each word the first consonant was /s/, /f/, /t/, or /n/, the final consonant was /s/ or /n/, and the vowel was /i/ or "or" (it is not clear whether this was /ɔ/ or /ɔr/, but in view of the range of dialects it is probable that both were included). The program was enlarged to accept all the initial consonants occurring in the 10 digits. There were 101 examples of these consonants pronounced by the same talkers and recognized without error, provided that no distinction was made between /θ/ and /f/.

Distinctive Features

In 1961 Hughes of MIT published a report on a limited recognition system based on a distinctive-features approach to phoneme classification [51]. The aim of the study was limited, being concerned with demonstrating that the distinctive-features approach was a valid one in speech recognition. The input to a computer program was in the form of purely spectral information from a 35-channel spectrum analyzer. Five acoustic features were detected: the frequencies of the first two formants, the presence of fricative noise, the approximate shape of the fricative spectrum, the occurrence of discontinuous changes in energy level and in formant frequencies, and the presence of silence. Six vowel and five consonant phoneme classifications were used, and no attempt was made to distinguish between consonants with similar spectral characteristics or between liquids, nasals, and glides.

For seven talkers pronouncing one- or two-syllable isolated words it was found that fairly good results were obtained for words containing a single stressed vowel but otherwise the results were poor.

Hughes was concerned with another distinctive-features scheme published in 1965 [52]. Again the input to the computer was in the form of spectral samples. Although the acoustic correlates of vowels and consonants were tested, detailed results were given only for vowels. A single-speaker approach was adopted and the results of machine recognition were compared with the performance of a panel of listeners as well as with the intentions of the talker.

In this study the vowel decisions were associated with measurements on the F1-F2 plane. The acute/grave, diffuse/compact, and flat/plain oppositions were implemented by means of linear decision boundaries (straight lines); the tense/lax decision was based on the relative distance from the neutral vowel and on the time duration. Consonant classification was based on the frequency of energy concentration and intensity for fricatives and various spectral and temporal measurements for stops and affricates. The decisions based on these measurements were given empirically derived weights in the classification process. The use of simple linguistic constraints concerned with vowel duration was also found to be useful in resolving some ambiguities. It was pointed out by the authors that it is necessary to distinguish between formant variations due to diphthong shifts and those due to the influence of adjacent phonemes.

The test material consisted of two-syllable nonsense utterances, a number of monosyllabic English words, and two English sentences. The overall vowel phoneme recognition accuracy was 92 percent, although it was believed that this could have been improved by a simple decision-boundary shift. The machine performance was similar to that of the human judges on excised vowels, and in some cases machine and listeners agreed on classifications that were different from those intended.

Adaptive (Learning) Recognizers

A report by Talbert et al. [53] demonstrates the application of "Adaline" networks (adaptive-threshold elements) to a speech-recognition task. For a description of the Adaline network, various adaptive systems using these networks and a discussion of important training theorems, see the book by Nilsson [54]. The reported system could recognize a small number of words by means of an eight-channel spectrum analyzer, four-level amplitude quantization and 10 time samples per word to generate a 240-spot binary pattern. This pattern was connected to a combination of Adaline networks simulated by computer. In a training operation several examples of each spoken word were presented to the system, which assigned a separate output signal to each word group. The training set was presented sequentially until each utterance was correctly categorized. New utterances were then presented for the system to identify.

It was found that, for the chosen set of "phonetically balanced" words, when the same talker was used for training and testing, 100 test utterances were recognized without error. For the 10 digits by a single talker, a 2 percent error rate was obtained. It was also found that when recognizing the utterances by five different talkers, better results were obtained if only one talker was used for training than when all five talkers were used to speak the training set. In an experiment in which new words were progressively added to the system's vocabulary, low error rates were obtained up to a vocabulary size of 16 words, but above this the error rate increased rapidly. This gave a measure of the "capacity" of the device.

A more detailed study of the application of adaptive-threshold elements to speech recognition was reported in 1965 by Dammann of IBM [55]. This phoneme-recognition system used a 15-channel spectrum analyzer and 13-level amplitude quantization, and the output, sampled every 10 ms, was fed to 10 adaptive threshold elements simulated by computer. Various phoneme categories were tried, but the best results were obtained with 20 classes, making no distinction between different stop consonants, between certain fricatives, or between a number of voiced continuants.

After training the system on the speech of a single talker, requiring 100 repetitions of the training set, 278 new isolated words by the same talker gave a phoneme-class recognition accuracy of 91.7 percent. For 343 words by a second talker the accuracy was 80 percent.

The adaptive word-recognition system of King and Tunis reported in 1966 [56] was rather more successful. This used a 15-channel spectrum analyzer and a computer. The computer program made use of a "peak picking" routine to find the frequency positions of the formants and based the recognition on a frequency-time matrix whose entries were 1 (peak) or 0 (no peak). The computer then implemented various transformations on this pattern in a series of experiments and classified the word by means of adaptive linear decision functions which had been trained on previous input data.

Two different vocabularies of 15 words each were recorded a number of times by a range of talkers. The recordings were used in various ways to test the system; for instance, the performance was observed when the same talker was used for the training and testing material, when different talkers were used, and when the material was formed from the combined utterances of several talkers. Different vocabulary sizes were also tried. The best result, obtained by using the same talker for training and recognition, gave only a 0.2 percent error rate. The worst result in the single-talker experiments (which was using a female talker) gave a 2.5 percent error rate. The training set consisted of 15 words repeated 35 to 50 times each. The recognition set consisted of different utterances of the same words repeated 90 to 115 times each. The worst result was obtained when the system was trained by one talker and then tried to recognize utterances by another talker. In that case the error rate was 46 percent, but when examples of both talkers were included in the training set, the error rate was 0.8 percent.

The above experiments made use of all the information contained in the matrix resulting from the utterance of each word. In a further set of experiments this matrix was transformed in various ways before the classification operation. In the first transformation a layer of feature detectors was used to detect the presence of steady formant patterns and of formant glides; in the second transformation detectors were applied to each column to detect particular sounds, e.g., particular formant distributions; in the third transformation the number of columns was reduced to three, so permitting only three time regions per word: early, middle, and late. None of these transformations resulted in better performance than was obtained without them, but the second and third transformations in series gave comparable results (0.6 to 1.9 percent errors) with significantly less information.

A word recognizer described by Fraipont in 1966 [57] divided the frequency range 300 Hz–3 kHz into ten channels, each of which was envelope-detected. Two more signals were formed from the energy above 3 kHz and the overall spectrum. These 12 signals were sampled for ½ second after the onset of a word, and the resulting 192 samples were punched on to paper tape which was subsequently fed into a computer. Word recognition was by means of linear decision hyperplanes which were adjusted to give optimum performance during a training session. The machine vocabulary comprised the 10 digits and five other words.

The training data were formed by 26 talkers each speaking the vocabulary words once. After training the machine for four hours the training set gave a correct-recognition score of 99 percent. Ten new talkers then spoke each of the words twice. This set resulted in 87 percent correct recognition, 6 percent errors, and 7 percent rejected.

Unusual Forms of Analysis

The successful transmission of speech over vocoder systems suggests that the smallest set of data containing sufficient information to specify the acoustic signal comprises eight measurements: the frequencies and amplitudes of the first three formants, the pitch of the voice in voiced sounds, and a binary indication concerning whether the sound is voiced or unvoiced. Of course, to these eight measurements must be added the human ability to resolve ambiguities by the use of linguistic and other constraints.

A recognition system proposed and tested by Teacher and Piotrowski [58] makes use of the single-equivalent-formant theory (SEF) devised by L. Focht of Philco Corporation. This theory is based on the experimentally established fact that a single resonance operating on a typical larynx-tone signal can elicit a sensation of vowel quality in the listener. It is argued that, if it were possible to obtain an estimate of the necessary resonance frequency from the acoustic waveform of natural speech, then the number of measurements required to classify these sounds would be reduced to four, i.e., only half that for a vocoder, with a consequent reduction in processing complexity. It has been shown that the SEF is closely related to the "dominant" formant in voiced sounds; this is usually defined as the formant having the highest amplitude when the speech signal is passed through a weighting network having a spectral "tilt" of +9 dB/oct.

In preliminary experiments with a simple word recognizer based on the SEF principle it was found that a small vocabulary of randomly chosen words could be recognized with an accuracy of 98 percent; however, it was expected that some confusion would occur between phonetically similar words with the system as it was at that time (1965).

In 1967 a complete, portable digit recognizer based on this earlier work was exhibited [59]. It contained a "pitch extractor" to give an indication of the beginning of each glottal cycle. The spectrum was modified by 9 dB/oct preemphasis. The SEF parameters were estimated from the period between the onset of the glottal cycle and the first zero crossing, and the maximum amplitude reached during this period. Logic circuits detected the occurrence of sequences of sound segments and identified the digit spoken.

The design was based on utterances by 10 male talkers. Further digits spoken by these talkers gave 90 percent correct recognition. When the system was tested on 34 new talkers, 25 percent of these were found to give good results.

A word-recognition system was reported by Weiss of the Federal Scientific Corporation (FSC) in 1966 [60]. This reduces the amount of data to be processed by sampling the spectrum at only three time positions in each phoneme pattern: at the initial and final boundaries and at the point of maximum power. The spectrum analyzer used was a commercial device manufactured by FSC called the Simoramic analyzer. This uses delay line feedback in a correlation technique simulating a continuum of filters of uniform bandwidth. The spectral resolution depends on the number of recirculations, and the amplitude-frequency information (spectral cross section) is translated into a short, repetitive, amplitude-time signal, where frequency is measured along the time axis for each "sweep." This signal was sampled at the equivalent of 30-Hz intervals in frequency and stored for computer analysis. The computer program determined the frequencies of F1, F2, and F3 at each of the three "critical instants" for each vowel, and in the most successful experiment, use was made of a simple fricative/vowel phoneme classification and of a voiced/unvoiced indication.

For 30 isolated words (including 16 minimal phoneme pairs) each spoken twice by 19 talkers, using the first set of utterances to "train" the system and the second set as input material in the recognition experiment, 92.4 percent correct word recognition was obtained when basing the measurements on the single vowel segment in each word. It was also found that ignoring the data obtained at the point of maximum power, i.e., the point at which the vowel pattern was least influenced by adjacent phonemes, a drop of only 3 percent was found in the recognition performance. In the experiment no more than 15 data values per word were used. The recognition strategy assumed a normal distribution for the measured data about mean values, and a likelihood classification procedure was employed which minimized the expected probability of error.

A vowel-recognition system described by Cannon of the Aerospace

Medical Research Laboratory [61] performs the spectral analysis by means of an "analog ear." This simulates the operation of the cochlea by means of a 24-section low-Q ladder network, where the cutoff frequencies of the sections decrease logarithmically with distance from the input end. Outputs were taken at four points equally spaced over the region of maximum activity. The outputs were sampled at a high rate in 4-ms bursts synchronized with the onset of each glottal cycle. Analysis was performed by a computer by means of correlation operations. The 4-ms samples were first autocorrelated. The autocorrelation functions obtained were then cross-correlated with each of a set of seven stored prototype patterns of similar form. This produced a set of 28 cross-correlation coefficients (four signals per sound and seven prototype patterns). The coefficients obtained were considered to specify a point in 28-dimensional space. This space was partitioned into vowel regions by a simple linear adaptive network, giving seven vowel-recognition classes.

After using 250 utterances by 10 talkers in the training operation, 71 sounds by five talkers were classified with an accuracy of 97 percent. The utterances were apparently isolated vowels, and the talkers had various regional accents. The prototype patterns were obtained by averaging the autocorrelation coefficients over several utterances by each talker and then over all talkers so that only information common to all talkers was retained.

A report by Reddy on work for a Ph.D. thesis conducted at Stanford University [62] is of particular interest not for the success achieved but for the way in which the computer installation was employed. The recognition strategy involved ad hoc measurements on the speech waveform which were developed during on-line computer sessions. The microphone signal was input directly to the computer's disk store via an analog-to-digital converter. The stored waveform (up to 2 s long) was presented on a cathode-ray tube, and the signal could be monitored repeatedly by loudspeaker. A light pen was used to select portions of the displayed waveform for analysis, and, if required, segments of stored speech could be selected and joined together and then heard on the loudspeaker.

In many speech-analysis systems spectral analysis accounts for a significant amount of the computer time involved. In Reddy's work spectral analysis had a relatively minor role and formed one of the final stages of analysis before classification. A 2-s utterance was first divided into sustained and transitional segments on the basis of intensity and zero-crossing measurements; for each voiced segment a typical pitch period was then identified near the center of the segment, and a Fourier expansion of this period gave the amplitudes of the first 100 harmonics of the fundamental frequency. Approximate spectral energy distributions for unvoiced segments were obtained by the Fourier expansion of a 10-ms sample near the center. These computer routines resulted in a list of 21 parameter values related to duration, intensity, and frequency measurements. The segments were then classified, on the basis of these values, as vowel-like, fricative-like, etc., and tests were made to reject those segments which were due to transitions between speech elements. The remaining segments were then associated with English phonemes.

For a single talker pronouncing 1- to 2-s connected utterances, both nonsense and meaningful, 81 percent of 287 phoneme patterns were correctly recognized. For the reported study the time necessary to analyze each utterance was about 40 times real time. It was claimed that this is significantly less than that for many other comparable studies. It was also claimed that some of the measurements found useful could not have been easily derived from the output of a filter bank.

General Comments on the Literature

Many of the reported systems have been designed to recognize short isolated utterances, and some of these are seen to provide rather good recognition scores. While several of the better systems could probably be expanded to permit the recognition of larger vocabularies or to accept a wider range of talkers, it is most unlikely that any of them could be modified to cope with normal connected speech. In general they perform the recognition by means of ad hoc rules based on knowledge of the acoustic waveform alone, whereas human recognition requires instinctive and acquired knowledge from a number of sources.

Those systems which use adaptive techniques work rather well within the limitations of their input material, but again these are ad hoc schemes which could not cope with the highly ambiguous acoustic patterns found in normal speech.

Although in theory a successful phoneme-pattern recognizer would have wider application than a word recognizer with similar limitations on the size of the recognition set, most of the phoneme recognizers covered by this survey, like the word recognizers, depend too much on the measurable acoustic patterns. The feature-abstraction scheme by Martin et al. [37] looks more promising than many others, but this still seems to require a separable pattern for each phoneme, and this is just not found in normal connected speech. The arguments in favor of using feature recognition and against the existence of a unique phoneme–acoustic-correlate relationship are developed in the next section.

The reported distinctive-feature schemes, though based on a theory of human perception, do not exhibit a marked degree of talker invariability or processing simplicity.

Some of the reported investigations have achieved results which appear contradictory; thus, Denes and Mathews [43] and King and Tunis [56] found it better to form the stored patterns used in the recognition process from utterances by several different talkers; whereas Talbert et al. [53] and Shearme and Leach [48] found it better to store and use the patterns due to different talkers separately. These effects obviously depend on the type of pattern stored, the way in which different patterns are combined, and the degree of variability between similar utterances by the different talkers used in each study.

The processes by which the large amount of data contained in the acoustic waveform can be reduced, while retaining sufficient data on which to base the recognition procedure, are of considerable interest. Some designers have taken conventional vocoder analysis techniques and simply reduced the number of measurements in the frequency, time, and amplitude directions. Others have based their data reduction on the results of earlier studies. Weiss [60] found that the most valuable data were preserved if he took spectral samples near the junctions between phonemic elements; Reddy [62] segmented the speech into phoneme-sized elements on the basis of simple measurements and then performed a detailed spectral analysis on a single glottal period near the center of each; Gold [46] gave greatest attention to stressed segments; and Shearme and Leach [48] divided their measurement space up into cells which were most closely spaced in the more populated regions.

It must be accepted that an arbitrary reduction in the data preserved for recognition will be reflected in the restrictions necessary on the input material and in the reliability of the recognition results. For a high-performance recognizer requiring minimal restrictions on the input speech it is unlikely that a significant degree of data reduction will be possible; in fact it will be necessary to add a certain amount of a priori information before the recognition process can be completed.

In summary, the reported studies suggest that the aims of reliable machine control, requiring the recognition of a small vocabulary of isolated utterances by a limited range of cooperative talkers, could be achieved in the near future; but the recognition of less restricted connected speech requires knowledge of the speech process which is not yet available.

It is unlikely that a recognition system which could match the full range of human ability will ever be economically feasible, but it is quite possible that future recognizers will be able to perform valuable recognition on input speech having no severe restrictions. The next step toward this aim will probably be a device which can accept normal connected speech as input and will scan this for the occurrence of any of a small number of preselected words or phrases. This would have the advantage that the available storage and computing effort would be concentrated on the detection of these few utterances, and the system could provide a valuable test bed for the development of more advanced recognition strategies.

The following section of this report, based on a wider study than that covered by this recognition-literature review, is concerned with some of the requirements which it is believed must be met to make possible a recognizer of this type.

Discussion

In this section we discuss certain conclusions reached by the writer as a result of the literature study. These conclusions are concerned with the important conditions which it is believed must be met if a general speech-recognition device is to have a reasonable chance of success. They are of three main types: (1) those which have already been explicitly stated in the literature and are now generally accepted by workers in this field, (2) those which are clearly implied by certain reported experiments but which have not been explicitly stated or which are apparently not widely known, and (3) personal opinions formed by the writer from his study of the literature on general speech research. The class into which a particular conclusion falls is not generally indicated but references to supporting works are given in a few cases.

1. *The mechanical recognition operation must be closely related to the way in which a human recognizes speech.* It is unlikely that there exist in the speech waveform invariant features which can be used for general speech recognition that are not already exploited by the human listener. The human-speech communication process is remarkably resistant to very severe corrupting influences. There is evidence that the listener can make use of information from a great many sources, employing both instinctive and acquired knowledge, and different forms of information in the speech wave itself. It is most unlikely that, in developing the speech facility, the evolutionary process has omitted valuable information which can be derived by mechanical processing.

2. *The most efficient way to isolate important perceptual features in speech is by the use of speech synthesis and human judgment.* Of course, the analysis of natural utterances must form the first step in detecting the important features for recognition; but in determining the

relative weight to be given to the observed features, speech-synthesis techniques provide essential stability and precision which can be obtained by no other method.

3. *Feature extraction is better than pattern matching in recognition at the acoustic level.* It is possible to separate many of the reported recognition systems into two groups related to the fundamental nature of the recognition process employed. We shall refer to these two processes as the pattern-matching process and the feature-extraction process These processes have inherent advantages and limitations which should be considered before a particular method is selected; of course, some systems make use of both processes, but even then one process may be dominant and so have a general influence on the utility of the machine.

The pattern-matching process usually compares the patterns produced by the incoming speech with patterns stored in the machine, and then decides on the classification by detecting the stored pattern which gives the best match. The patterns are usually produced by a particular transformation of the speech wave, for instance by means of spectral or correlation analysis. The stored patterns are chosen to be typical of the utterances within the vocabulary of the machine.

The feature-extraction process generally employs a number of specialized circuits or processing routines designed to detect the presence of various features known to be characteristic of the speech sound elements. These features might be related to the simultaneous presence of formants in defined regions of the frequency domain, to the rate of change of formant frequency, to the overall energy level, to the presence of voicing, etc. Recognition of an utterance is then based on the sequential occurrence of certain features, and the output may be in the form of a simple indication that a particular sound element has been detected.

The advantages of the pattern-recognition system include the ease with which the stored patterns may be changed to suit changes in language, talker, or the size of the unit of recognition, the comparative simplicity of the overall system, and the ease with which the system can be made self-adaptive. The main disadvantage is that, since the matching process must cover the whole range in which a pattern can occur (e.g., the whole range of important speech frequencies), it is difficult to discriminate against prominent but irrelevant data. The advantages and disadvantages of the feature-extraction system are largely the reverse of these. It is frequently more complicated, requires a period of intensive study to cope with changes of language, etc., and is difficult to make self-adaptive; however, as each section is designed for the optimum detection of a particular feature, it is easier to specifically exclude irrelevant data and to distinguish between very similar though distinctly different sounds.

It is most likely that a combination of these two systems should be used for optimum results, that is, feature extraction should form the basis of recognition at the lowest level, the level of sound elements, but that patterns formed by sequences of sound elements should be recognized by a pattern-matching process.

4. *The question of whether to base the recognition on phonemes or syllables has yet to be resolved.* There is some evidence to support the view that the syllable is the basic unit of speech articulation (see, for example, Kozhevnikov and Chistovich, Ref. 63). It is not clear, however, that it is also the basis of perception. The significance of rhythm and other aspects of syllabic stress show that the syllable has an important function in speech perception, but the ease and consistency with which the phonetician can describe an utterance in terms of phonemic units argues for a subsyllabic unit of perception. This fact and the implicit signal-processing economy have convinced many workers that phoneme-level recognition is a sensible approach to mechanical processing.

The view expressed by Kozhevnikov and Chistovich is that making recognition decisions in terms of phoneme units is probably valid as long as the decisions are taken with regard to information distributed over the whole syllable. Although this view was reached on the basis of experimental evidence, the question has not been finally resolved and some work remains to be done on the subject.

5. *The speech signal cannot be directly segmented into phoneme units.* The term *phoneme* is often used in the literature in a way which might confuse the reader. Thus the use of a "phoneme recognizer" suggests that speech is composed of phonemes and that these phonemes can be physically isolated and identified. In fact, the term phoneme refers to a conceptual grouping of speech sounds and allows the listener to describe a speech utterance in terms of an alphabet of phonemic symbols. The phoneme is the smallest meaningful sound unit of speech which the listener can perceive. The acoustic correlates of a given phoneme depend on the language, the dialect, and the individual talker. There is no one-to-one relationship between sound elements measurable in the speech waveform and the listener's description in terms of a sequence of phonemes. The term "phoneme unit" might reasonably apply to a speech sound having phonemic proportions, but the notion that the speech wave can be segmented into units which can be equated one-for-one with the phonemic description is wrong.

It is true that speech sounds made in isolation can be related to phonemic elements and that modified forms of these sounds can often be detected in connected speech, but it is equally true that quite different sound elements may be correctly given the same phoneme label, that a signal which seems, acoustically, to be a single sound may be described by a sequence of phonemes, and that a phoneme can even be ascribed to an element whose acoustic correlate may be totally absent. Thus, in the Cockney pronunciation of the word "bottle," the /t/ may be replaced by a glottal stop and the /l/ by a sound related to /w/; whereas the standard English pronunciation results in a laterally released /t/ followed by /l/. If there is no intention to distinguish between the two dialects it is quite legitimate to transcribe both as /bɒtl/.

It is evident that a recognizer designed to recognize phoneme units without reference to knowledge about the talker or to linguistic information would have only limited application in the recognition of normal conversational speech. In the case of a small vocabulary of words and a few talkers such a system might be quite adequate. The argument against trying to use phoneme recognition alone in speech recognition was clearly put by Denes in 1963 [64].

6. *Crudely quantized measurements of spectral and temporal quantities are inadequate.* Quite small changes in formant frequencies can result in significant changes in the perceived speech sound. Certain brief sounds may persist for very short periods only. Many of the reported recognition schemes employ measurement processes whose resolutions in time and frequency are quite inadequate to preserve such information. The precision required in the measurement of normal speech has never been properly determined.

Formant frequency measurement by zero-crossing analysis has been popular for some years due to the simplicity of the method, but this technique can lead to serious error unless the formant being measured is much larger than other spectral peaks. This was demonstrated in the paper published by E. Peterson in 1951 [65].

7. *A simple single measurement of the spectrum cross section in high-pitched voiced sounds may not be sufficient to accurately determine the formant frequencies.* When the fundamental frequency of larynx vibration is higher than the formant bandwidths (of the order of 150 Hz), as it often is in female and child speech, it is quite possible that a particular formant does not occur sufficiently close to a voice harmonic to be adequately specified by a simple spectrum measurement. It might be necessary to track a formant as it crosses the various harmonics prior to the point of measurement, to measure nearby voice harmonics and decide on the position of the peak by interpolation, or to employ a form of "pitch synchronous" analysis to examine the waveform at particular points in the glottal cycle.

8. *The human listener can recognize extremely brief sounds.* It is probable that the excitation of the vocal-tract resonances by a single glottal pulse is sufficient for the human listener to identify a given vowel sound. It also appears that the listener can make use of extremely rapid formant shifts involving large formant-frequency changes between successive glottal pulses (which are typically spaced about 10 ms apart). Narrowband spectrum analyzers and spectrum-sampling rates of the order of 100 s^{-1} are probably inadequate to preserve this information. Martin et al. [37] restricted channel-filter Q factors to less than two for this reason, and Reddy [62] claimed that his system made use of data which could not be easily obtained from the output of a normal spectrum analyzer. The ability to converse intelligibly over vocoder systems shows that conventional hardware spectrum analyzers preserve sufficient information for such purposes, but some loss in intelligibility must be admitted, and a moderate amount of degradation can be compensated for by the use of grammatical context. In demonstrating speech recognition techniques it might be necessary to supplement conventional channel-type spectrum analyzers with special circuits or computer routines operating on the unprocessed input signal in order to preserve very brief features.

9. *Time normalization, by simply stretching or compressing one pattern to compare with another, is of very limited value.* Except where the necessary changes are very slight, this type of time normalization is of little value even when the patterns due to different types of speech sound are treated separately. The reason is apparent if spectrograms are examined of different utterances of a sound like /bɪb/. Considering F2 alone, in the vowel /ɪ/ spoken in isolation it normally takes a high position, near 2 kHz typically; at the point of release of the initial stop and the point of closure of the final stop it takes a low position, typically below 500 Hz. The variation of F2 throughout the sound depends on the speed at which the lips open and close. If the sound is long the central part may show F2 in its normal /ɪ/ position for a considerable time. If the sound is very short, F2 may rise and fall very rapidly without actually attaining its "target" position in the vowel. To stretch this short vowel pattern consisting entirely of formant transition and compare it with the longer example, where the transition regions occupy a very small fraction of the time, would result in a high error measurement. If, however, a measure of the formant's time derivative were available, it might be possible to predict its target position and so to estimate which vowel was intended. This is equivalent to taking account of articulator inertia and thus is related to analysis-by-synthesis. The fact that the listener does take account of phonemic environment in identifying a vowel sound has been demonstrated by Lindblom and

Studdert-Kennedy [66]. This work shows that the intended vowel is actually heard even though the formants do not reach their target positions.

10. *Some consonant judgments are discrete while vowel quality judgments are continuous.* The human recognition of continuous vowels and consonants on one hand and rapid vowel transients and stops on the other seem to be based on different processing mechanisms. Thus varying vowel formant frequencies and amplitudes continuously causes a continuous change in perceived vowel quality, whereas a continuous change in formant frequency and amplitude transitions causes discrete jumps in consonant perception. For instance, if the vowel /æ/ is synthesized with an initial transition in F2 which begins at some given point in frequency and this starting frequency is gradually varied from a low frequency to a high frequency, at first the syllable /bæ/ is heard; at some starting frequency near 1.0 kHz the sound suddenly changes to /dæ/; at a little higher frequency the sound becomes /gæ/, and this persists for all higher frequencies. This effect was demonstrated by work at Haskins Laboratories [20] in early experiments with synthetic speech.

It is known that in visual perception some parts of the human recognition mechanism specialize in the detection of particular visual features, say curves having a particular curvature lying at a particular angle in the field of vision. It seems reasonable to suggest that some parts of the hearing mechanism are similarly specialized, say to detect positive or negative transitions in spectral peaks having time derivatives lying within specific values.

11. *Nondistinctive articulatory states (e.g., nasalization) can cause severe modification of spectral patterns without changing listener phoneme judgments.* This is one of the arguments against the use of simple spectral pattern matching for phoneme-level identification. Nasalization of a vowel sound introduces additional resonances and causes a shift in vowel formant frequencies, among other effects. If nasalization is nondistinctive, as it is in English, its presence or absence may have no effect on listener judgments. A matching process which compares the whole of the frequency range in a nasalized and a nonnasalized vowel will result in a large error measurement. In a feature-extraction process it should be possible to allow for the effects of such nondistinctive properties in the feature-detection operation.

12. *The mechanical recognizer must be able to cope with distortions due to the talker's acoustic environment.* The human listener is able to perform well in conditions of intense background noise, reverberation, and the addition of other sounds, such as speech due to other talkers.

Speech transmission can also lead to severe waveform distortion without greatly affecting the intelligibility of the signal to human ears. A mechanical recognizer must have the same ability if it is to match the performance of the human listener. This requires knowledge of how the human listener can perform in such conditions; this knowledge is very limited at present.

13. *Recognition of speech sounds at the acoustic level requires talker normalization.* A child learns to speak by imitation of more fluent talkers. The degree to which one person can imitate the speech sounds of another is limited by physical characteristics, in particular by the length of the vocal tract. The various vowel sounds are produced by controlling the shape of the vocal tract by means of the articulatory organs (tongue, lips, jaw, and velum). The range over which these vary in speech is a large proportion of the maximum possible variation; that is, the permissible "generation space" is almost completely occupied. This implies that when listening to the speech of different talkers, the human listener either detects meaningful features of the speech that do not depend on talker characteristics (invariant features) or else is able to judge the speech sounds of a particular talker in relation to that talker's own characteristics. Many of the recognition systems reported to date imply an acceptance of the first (feature invariance) condition, and this imposes severe limitations where more than one talker is involved. There is some evidence that talker normalization is invoked in the human listener, and Fant has discussed certain aspects of such a process, including the probability of nonlinear scaling in the normalizing process [67]. In an experiment by Gerstman [68] use was made of the Peterson and Barney [18] data discussed earlier. The original data showed considerable overlap in the F1/F2 plots of judged vowel quality when the talkers included men, women, and children, whereas the vowel sounds by a single talker led to little or no overlap. Gerstman normalized each talker's vowel formant measurements by determining the highest and lowest frequencies of F1 and F2 for the set of vowels by each, setting these measurements to 999 and 0, respectively, and then determining intermediate values by interpolation. This is approximately equivalent to expanding or compressing the frequency scales to give coincidence for the formants in /i/, /a/ and /u/. Replotting this talker-normalized data resulted in unique vowel-cluster boundaries for all but 34 of the 1,368 vowels tested. Each of those which were misclassified also resulted in nonunanimous classification by the panel of judges in the original experiment.

Such talker normalization cannot correct for vowel patterns which differ because of dialect or accent differences, as these are often due to the substitution of one vowel phoneme for another or to a consistent shift in vowel quality. Differences due to these causes must be recognized as a characteristic of the individual talker.

Since certain vowel formants are related to (often continuous with) characteristic resonances in the consonants, talker normalization should aid the identification of consonants as with vowels.

14. *The single-talker approach is of limited value in the development of a general speech-recognition device.* Some workers have developed recognition procedures based on the analysis of the speech of a single talker with a view to expanding the procedures, when proved successful, to cope with a larger range of talkers.

A recognition strategy which is based on features observed in a particular set of utterances by a single talker is open to criticism on several counts. One is that the chosen features may not be invariant when considering a wider range of utterances even by the same talker. Another is that the features may be appropriate to that talker alone and their use in the recognition operations may actually reduce the ability of the machine to recognize speech by other talkers. A third point is that modifying a sophisticated recognition strategy which makes use of such talker-specific data may be more difficult than developing the strategy from the start.

However, the possibility should not be overlooked that such limited-value data may be learned and utilized by the human listener.

15. *The use of language by a talker and the precision with which he articulates his speech depend on his assessment of the listener's ability to comprehend.* In an informal conversational environment, e.g., when chatting with a friend, the talker will generally be less careful about the way his speech is articulated, will be less formal or precise in his use of the language, and may even use a special vocabulary. This latter consideration also particularly applies where talker and listener have a specialized interest, say in a technical subject.

16. *The identification of sounds at the acoustic level requires knowledge of prosodic features.* The prosodic features are features of the speech sound which convey information other than phonemic information. They tell the listener something about the talker (sex, age, etc.), his emotional state, his attitude towards the listener and towards the subject of conversation, and so on. They also perform certain linguistic functions; thus in English the pitch pattern of a sentence may distinguish between a question and a statement, and in Chinese the "tone" of a word distinguishes it from other words in the vocabulary with otherwise similar pronunciation. The prosodic features are related to the range and the use of pitch variation, intensity, and rhythm, knowledge of which is essential in determining the stress pattern. The precision with

which a sound is articulated depends very much on its relation to the stressed syllables. It is possible that some very familiar utterances can be recognized almost entirely by analysis of the stressed sounds and knowledge of the context in which the utterances are spoken.

17. *The general-purpose recognizer must be able to take account of linguistic information.* The range of words which can appear at a particular point in a sentence is greatly restricted by the operation of the linguistic rules (grammatical, semantic, lexical, etc.) under which sentences are generated. This allows for error correction or the removal of ambiguity at the word or phrase level. Human listeners certainly make use of such constraints, and for similar performance the mechanical recognizer must do the same.

18. *Probabilistic information must be used with caution.* By probabilistic information we mean the probability that, for instance, one speech sound or word may follow another speech sound or word. The rejection of an unlikely candidate in a recognition process in favor of a similar, more likely one may improve the overall recognition scores but at the expense of message "quality." In one sense at least, an unlikely word conveys more information than one which is more likely. This danger has been pointed out by Flanagan [1, p. 162].

19. *The set of features to be detected in the recognition of a phoneme pattern may be very large.* Analysis of the acoustic correlates of phonemic quality has shown that data on a large number of features is necessary to distinguish between similar phoneme patterns. For instance, to distinguish /s/ from other patterns it may be necessary to observe the intensity and duration of the sound, the spectral transitions introduced by its juxtaposition with other sounds, its initial rate of rise of intensity, its position in relation to other sounds in a given utterance, the absence of features known to be characteristic of other classes of sound (e.g., a stop gap or voicing), etc. If less than the complete set of these features is utilized, the overlap with the feature sets of other sounds may cause ambiguity. The complete set may include features which it is difficult or undesirable to include on an automated basis, such as the meaning of the whole utterance in relation to some personal knowledge held by the listener; the point here is that distortions, such as phonemic substitution, leading to ambiguity which the listener can easily overcome by use of context, will often not be suppressed by the talker.

20. *Learning systems have a place in automatic speech recognition but cannot be valuably exploited until the basic principles of recognition have been determined.* Although in theory a learning system taking account of every possible measurable quantity can be trained to recognize human speech, it is at present much more efficient to employ human

ingenuity to isolate the factors on which human recognition is based. When these factors have been established and demonstrated, learning techniques will be of value in adapting the recognizer to suit different talkers, accents, vocabularies, etc., but simply connecting a spectrum analyzer to a learning net and training it to cope with speech patterns is unlikely to aid the development of a general speech recognizer in the foreseeable future.

21. *It should be possible to limit the size of the storage requirements by choosing the vocabulary to suit the topic of conversation.* The use of simple phoneme recognition in reported recognition systems has often been dictated by the available data storage capacity. Extending the unit of recognition to the word or phrase level will greatly increase the quick-access storage requirements. It should be possible to relate the choice of less frequently used (and therefore more numerous) vocabulary items to the assumed topic of conversation, based on human judgment or partial recognition of earlier parts of the conversation.

22. *General theories on speech perception are not sufficiently developed or proven to make their use in studies of mechanical recognition an obvious choice at this time.* Although the distinctive-features theory has been partially implemented for recognition purposes, the acoustic correlates of the full set of features have not yet been isolated, and there is little evidence that the features employed in recognition attempts to date provide a high degree of talker invariance or can be applied to a very wide range of utterances; the analysis-by-synthesis methods reported are somewhat slow and cumbersome and, except for some general considerations, the motor theory does not yet lend itself to a practical realization.

General Conclusion

The main finding which these conclusions illustrate is that significant advances in speech recognition are likely to come not from researches into signal analysis, adaptive pattern matching, or computer implementation (although these fields have valuable techniques to offer the speech researcher), but from studies of speech perception and generation, phonetics, linguistics, and psychology. We need a much greater understanding of the whole speech process before an automatic recognizer can be built whose performance will approach human ability. Much of this work must follow where others have led and a great deal of valuable information is available in the literature on general speech research. A study of writings on automatic recognition alone is not sufficient. An extensive list of publications dealing with automatic speech recognition is given in the bibliography following the references.

REFERENCES

1. J. L. Flanagan, "Speech Analysis Synthesis and Perception," Springer-Verlag, Berlin, 1965.
2. N. Lindgren, Machine Recognition of Human Language, *IEEE Spectrum,* **2:**(3 and 4) (1965).
3. T. Marill, Automatic Recognition of Speech, *IRE Trans. Human Factors Electron.,* **HFE-2**(1):34–38 (1961).
4. M. A. Saposhkov, The Speech Signal in Cybernetics and Communications, translation by *Joint Publications Res. Serv.,* 28117 (1965).
5. D. Jones, "An Outline of English Phonetics," 9th ed., Heffer and Sons, London, 1960; first published in 1918.
6. J. W. Strutt (Lord Rayleigh), "The Theory of Sound," vol. II, Dover Publications, New York, 1945 (first published in 1878).
7. G. O. Russell, "The Vowel," Ohio State University Press, 1928; summary in *J. Acoust. Soc. Am.,* **I**(1) (1929).
8. H. K. Dunn, Calculation of Vowel Resonances and an Electrical Vocal Tract, *J. Acoust. Soc. Am.,* **22:**740–753 (1950).
9. G. Fant, "Acoustic Theory of Speech Production, Mouton and Co., The Hague, 1960.
10. J. van den Berg, Myoelastic-Aerodynamic Theory of Voice Production, *J. Speech Hearing Res.,* **1:**227–244 (1958).
11. J. van den Berg, "Voice Production: The Vibrating Larynx," instructional film, University of Gronigan, 1960.
12. P. Lieberman, Intonation, Perception and Language, *Res. Monograph* No. 38, MIT Press, Cambridge, Mass., 1967.
13. P. F. MacNeilage and G. N. Sholes, An Electromyographic Study of the Tongue During Vowel Production, *J. Speech Hearing Res.,* **7**(3):209–232 (1964).
14. J. C. R. Licklider and I. Pollack, Effects of Differentiation, Integration and Infinite Peak Clipping upon the Intelligibility of Speech, *J. Acoust. Soc. Am.,* **20:**42–51 (1948).
15. R. K. Potter, G. A. Kopp, and H. C. Green, "Visible Speech," Van Nostrand, New York, 1947.
16. I. Lehiste and G. E. Peterson, Studies of Syllable Nuclei 2, Rept. No. 4, University of Michigan, 1960.
17. I. Lehiste, Acoustical Characteristics of Selected English Consonants, Rept. No. 9, University of Michigan, 1962.
18. G. E. Peterson and H. L. Barney, Control Methods Used in a Study of the Vowels, *J. Acoust. Soc. Am.,* **24**(2):175–184 (1952).
19. P. Ladefoged and D. E. Broadbent, Information Conveyed by Vowels, *J. Acoust. Soc. Am.,* **29:**98–104 (1957).
20. P. Delattre, Acoustic Cues in Speech, First Report, Haskins Lab., N.Y.: first appeared in French in *Phonetica,* **2:**108–118, 226–251 (1958).
21. M. Halle and K. N. Stevens, Analysis by Synthesis, in W. Wathen-Dunn and L. E. Woods (eds.), *Proc. Seminar Speech Compression Processing,* vol. 2, Paper D7, December 1959.
22. M. Halle and K. N. Stevens, Speech Recognition: A Model and a Program for Research, *IRE Trans. Inform. Theory,* **IT-8**(2):155–159 (1962).
23. A. M. Liberman, F. S. Cooper, K. S. Harris, and P. F. MacNeilage, A Motor Theory of Speech Perception, *Proc. Speech Commun. Seminar,* Stockholm, 1962.
24. C. G. M. Fant, Auditory Patterns in Speech, in W. Wathen-Dunn (ed.),

Proc. Symp. Models Perception Speech Visual Form AFCRL, 1964, MIT Press, Cambridge, Mass., 1967.

25. R. Jakobson, C. G. M. Fant, and M. Halle, Preliminaries to Speech Analysis, *Tech. Rept.* No. 13, Acoustics Laboratory, MIT, 1952, reprinted 1963.
26. K. H. Davis, R. Biddulph, and S. Balashek, Automatic Recognition of Spoken Digits, *J. Acoust. Soc. Am.,* **24**(6):637–642 (1952).
27. H. Dudley and S. Balashek, Automatic Recognition of Phonetic Patterns in Speech, *J. Acoust. Soc. Am.,* **30**(8):721–733 (1958).
28. J. Wiren and H. L. Stubbs, Electronic Binary Selection System for Phoneme Classification, *J. Acoust. Soc. Am.,* **28:**1082–1091 (1956).
29. H. F. Olson and H. Belar, Phonetic Typewriter, *J. Acoust. Soc. Am.,* **28**(6):1072–1081 (1956).
30. H. F. Olson and H. Belar, Phonetic Typewriter III, *J. Acoust. Soc. Am.,* **33**(11):1610–1615 (1961).
31. D. B. Fry, Theoretical Aspects of Mechanical Speech Recognition; also P. Denes, The Design and Operation of the Mechanical Speech Recognizer at University College London; both in *J. Brit. Inst. Radio Engr.,* **19:**211–229 (1959).
32. J. W. Forgie and C. D. Forgie, Results Obtained from a Vowel Recognition Computer Program, *J. Acoust. Soc. Am.,* **31**(11):1480–1489 (1959).
33. J. W. Cooley and J. W. Tukey, An Algorithm for the Machine Calculation of Complex Fourier Series, *Math. Computers,* **19:**297–301 (1965).
34. J. Suzuki and K. Nakata, Recognition of Japanese Vowels—Preliminary to the Recognition of Speech, *J. Radio Res. Lab. Tokyo,* **8**(37):193–212 (1961).
35. T. Sakai and S. Doshita, The Phonetic Typewriter, Information Processing 1962, *Proc. IFIP Congr.,* Munich, August–September 1962.
36. K. Nagata, Y. Kato, and S. Chiba, Spoken Digit Recognizer for Japanese Language, *NEC Res. Develop.,* No. 6, 1963.
37. T. B. Martin, A. L. Nelson, and H. J. Zadell, Speech Recognition by Feature Abstraction Techniques, *Tech. Rept.* AL-TDR-64-176, Air Force Avionics Laboratory, 1964 (AD 604526).
38. J. W. Falter, Feature Abstraction: An Approach to Speech Recognition, *Proc. IEEE Nat. Aerospace Electron. Conf.,* pp. 192–198, 1965.
39. J. Gazdag, A Method of Decoding Speech, *Tech. Rept.* No. 9, AFOSR-66-2385, University of Illinois, June 1966 (AD 641132).
40. L. Gilli and A. R. Meo, Sequential System for Recognizing Spoken Digits in Real Time, *Acustica,* **19**(1):38–48 (1967/68).
41. W. Bezdel, Discriminators of Sound Classes for Speech Recognition Purposes, *AFCRL Conf. Reprints,* Section B8, pp. 104–108, Conf. on Speech Communication and Processing, 1967.
42. P. W. Ross, A Limited-vocabulary Adaptive Speech-recognition System, *J. Audio Eng. Soc.,* **15**(4):414–419 (1967).
43. P. Denes and M. V. Mathews, Spoken Digit Recognition Using Time-Frequency Pattern Matching, *J. Acoust. Soc. Am.,* **32**(11):1450–1455 (1960).
44. G. Sebestyn, Automatic Recognition of Spoken Numerals, *J. Acoust. Soc. Am.,* **32**(11):1516 (1960). (Abstract)
45. W. F. Meeker, A. L. Nelson, and P. B. Scott, Voice to Teletype Code Convertor Research Program, Part II: Experimental Verification of a Method to Recognize Phonetic Sounds, *Tech. Rept.* No. ASD-TR 61-666, Wright-Patterson A.F., Ohio, 1962 (AD 288099).
46. B. Gold, Word-recognition Computer Program, Rept. No. 452, Research Laboratory of Electronics, MIT, June 1966.

47. P. N. Sholtz and R. Bakis, Spoken Digit Recognition Using Vowel-Consonant Segmentation, *J. Acoust. Soc. Am.*, **34**(1):1–5 (1962).
48. J. N. Shearme and P. F. Leach, Some Experiments with a Simple Word Recognition System, *IEEE Trans. Audio Electroacoust.*, **AU-16:**256–261 (1968).
49. R. F. Purton, Speech Recognition Using Autocorrelation Analysis, *IEEE Trans. Audio Electroacoust.*, **AU-16**(2):235–239 (1968).
50. S. H. Lavington and L. E. Rosenthal, Some Facilities for Speech Processing by Computer, *Computer J. Brit. Computer Soc.*, **9**(4):330–339 (1967).
51. G. W. Hughes, The Recognition of Speech by Machine, *Tech. Rept.* No. 395, MIT Research Laboratory of Electronics, 1961.
52. G. W. Hughes and J. F. Hemdal, Speech Analysis, Report AFCRL-65-681, Purdue University, 1965 (P 137552).
53. L. R. Talbert, G. F. Groner, J. S. Koford, R. J. Brown, P. R. Low, and C. H. Mays, A Real-time Adaptive Speech Recognition System, *Tech. Rept.* No. 6760-1 (ASD-TDR-63-660) (P 133441), prepared by Stanford Electronics Laboratory.
54. N. J. Nilsson, "Learning Machines," McGraw-Hill, New York, 1965.
55. J. A. Dammann, Application of Adaptive Threshold Elements to the Recognition of Acoustic-phonetic States, *J. Acoust. Soc. Am.*, **38**(2):213–223 (1965).
56. J. H. King and C. J. Tunis, Some Experiments in Spoken Word Recognition, *IBM J. Res. Develop.*, **10**(1):65–79 (1966).
57. D. Fraipont, Voice Actuated Address Mechanism. Report No. 3, Electronics Associates, Inc., 1966 (AD 633711).
58. C. F. Teacher and C. F. Piotrowski, Voice Sound Recognition, *Tech. Rept.* No. RADC-TR-65-184, Rome Air Development Center, July 1965 (AD 619964).
59. C. F. Teacher, H. G. Kellett, and L. R. Focht, Experimental, Limited Vocabulary, Speech Recognizer, *IEEE Trans. Audio Electroacoust.*, **AU-15**(3):127–130 (September 1967).
60. M. Weiss, A Study of Critical Instant Sampling of Speech Parameters for Automatic Recognition of Spoken Words, Rept. No. RADC-TR-65-371, Rome Air Development Center, July 1966 (AD 638380).
61. M. W. Cannon, A Method of Analysis and Recognition for Voiced Vowels, *IEEE Trans. Audio Electroacoust.*, **AU-16**(2):154–158 (1968).
62. D. R. Reddy, An Approach to Computer Speech Recognition by Direct Analysis of the Speech Wave, *Tech. Rept.* No. CS49, Computer Science Dept., Stanford University, September 1966; paper based on this report presented in *J. Acoust. Soc. Am.*, **42**(2):329–347 (August 1967) Computer Recognition of Connected Speech.
63. V. A. Kozhevnikov and L. A. Chistovich, Speech: Articulation and Perception. Translation by *Joint Publications Res. Serv.*, 30543 (1965).
64. P. Denes, On the Statistics of Spoken English, *J. Acoust. Soc. Am.*, **35**(6):892–904 (1963).
65. E. Peterson, Frequency Detection and Speech Formants, *J. Acoust. Soc. Am.*, **23**(6):668–674 (1951).
66. B. E. F. Lindblom and M. Studdert-Kennedy, On the Role of Formant Transitions in Vowel Recognition, *J. Acoust. Soc. Am.*, **42**(4):830–843 (1967).
67. G. Fant, A Note on Vocal Tract Size Factors and Non-uniform F-pattern Scalings, *Speech Transmission Lab. Quart. Progr. Status Rept. Roy. Inst. Technol. Stockholm*, No. 4/1966, pp. 22–30, January 1967.
68. L. J. Gerstman, Classification of Self-normalized Vowels, *IEEE Trans. Audio Electroacoust.*, **AU-16**(1):78–80 (1968).

BIBLIOGRAPHY

Baumann, R. H., J. C. R. Licklider, and B. Howland, An Electronic Word Recognizer, *J. Acoust. Soc. Am.*, **26**(1):137–138 (January 1954).

Bezdel, W., and J. S. Bridle, Speech Recognition Using Zero-crossing Measurements and Sequence Information, *Proc. IEE*, **116**(4):617–623 (April 1969).

Bezdel, W., and H. J. Chandler, Results of an Analysis and Recognition of Vowels by Computer Using Zero-crossing Data, *Proc. IEE*, **112**(11):2060–2066 (November 1965).

Bobrow, D. G., and D. H. Klatt, A Limited Speech Recognition System, Rept. No. 1667, Bolt, Beranek and Newman, Inc., May 1968.

Bobrow, D. G., and D. H. Klatt, Studies in Word Recognition by Computer, *J. Acoust. Soc. Am.*, **44**(1):385 (July 1968). (Abstract)

Chiba, S., Spoken Word Recognition by Multiple Linear Separation, *Rept. 6th Intern. Congr. Acoustics*, Tokyo, August 1968, Paper B-4-4, pp. B123–B126.

Chiba, S., and H. Sakoe, Calculation of Classification Functions Using a Large Number of Spoken Word Samples, *J. Acoust. Soc. Am.*, **47**(1, pt. 1):83 (January 1970). (Abstract)

Clapper, G. L., Machine Looks, Listens, Learns, *Electronics*, **40**(22):91–102 (October 30, 1967).

Clapper, G. L., Word Recognition System, *IBM Tech. Disclosure Bull.*, **11**(6):603–605 (November 1968).

Comer, D. J., The Use of Waveform Asymmetry to Identify Voiced Sounds, *IEEE Trans. Audio Electroacoust.*, **AU-16**(4): 500–506 (December 1968).

Denes, P., The Design and Operation of the Mechanical Speech Recognizer at University College London, *J. Brit. IRE*, **19**(4):219–229 (April 1959).

Denes, P. B., and T. G. von Keller, Articulatory Segmentation for Automatic Recognition of Speech, *Rept. 6th Intern. Congr. Acoust.*, Tokyo, August 1968, Paper B-4-9, pp. B143–B146.

Derkach, M., Heuristic Models for Automatic Recognition of Spoken Words, *Speech Transmission Lab. Quart. Progr. Status Rept. Roy. Inst. Technol. Stockholm*, No. 1/1970, April 15, 1970.

Dersch, W. C., Shoe-box, A Voice Responsive Machine, *Datamation*, **8**(6):47–50 (June 1962).

Ewing, G. D., and J. F. Taylor, Computer Recognition of Speech Using Zero-crossing Information, *IEEE Trans. Audio Electroacoust.*, **AU-17**(1):37–40 (March 1969).

Falter, J. W., and K. W. Otten, Cybernetics and Speech Communications: A Survey of Russian Literature, *IEEE Trans. Audio Electroacoust.*, **AU-15**(1):27–36 (1967).

Fant, G., The Nature of Distinctive Features, *Speech Transmission Lab. Quart. Progr. Status Rept. Roy. Inst. Technol. Stockholm*, No. 4/1966, pp. 1–14, January 1967.

Forgie, J. W., C. D. Forgie, and E. P. Dickey, A Recognition Program for English Fricative Consonants, *J. Acoust. Soc. Am.*, **33**(11):1676–1677 (November 1961). (Abstract)

Foulkes, J. D., Computer Identification of Vowel Types, *J. Acoust. Soc. Am.*, **33**(1):7–11 (January 1961).

Fujisaki, H., and N. Nakamura, Normalization and Recognition of Vowels, Research on Information Processing, *Ann. Rept. Eng. Res. Inst. Univ. Tokyo*, **28:**61–66 (1969).

Fukumura, T., and K. Adachi, Phoneme Recognition of Japanese Vowels Based Upon the Order Relations of Their Frequency-band Components, *Electron. Commun. Japan*, **47**(10):67–79 (October 1964).

Hemdal, J. F., and G. W. Hughes, A Feature Based Computer Recognition Program for the Modeling of Vowel Perception, in W. Wathen-Dunn (ed.), "Models for the Perception of Speech and Visual Form," pp. 440–453, MIT Press, Cambridge, Mass., 1967.

Hill, D. R., Automatic Speech Recognition—A Problem for Machine Intelligence, *Machine Intelligence,* **I**:199–226, Oliver and Boyd (October 1966).

Hill, D. R., An Esoteric Approach to Some Problems in Automatic Speech Recognition, *Intern. J. Man-Machine Studies,* **1**(1):101–121 (January 1969).

Hillix, W. A., M. N. Fry, and R. L. Hershman, Computer Recognition of Spoken Digits Based on Six Nonacoustic Measures, *J. Acoust. Soc. Am.,* **38**(5):790–796 (November 1965).

Hiramatsu, K., and K. Kotoh, A Spoken Digit Recognition System Using Error Correcting Procedure, *Rept. 6th Intern. Congr. Acoust.,* Tokyo, August 1968, Paper B-4-3, pp. B119–B122.

Hogan, D. L., Automatic Recognition of a Limited Set of Syllables, MIT *Quart. Progr. Rept. Res. Lab. Electron.,* No. 62, pp. 202–203 July 1961.

Hollabaugh, J. D., Methods for Phonemic Recognition in Speech Processing, MSC thesis, US Naval Postgraduate School, 1963 (AD 481756).

Holmgren, G. L., Speaker Recognition, Speech Characteristics, Speech Evaluation, and Modification of Speech Signal—A Selected Bibliography, *IEEE Trans. Audio Electroacoust.,* **AU-14**(1):32–39 (1966).

Inoue, S., and A. Kurematsu, Speech Recognition with Time-normalized Frequency Pattern, *Rept. 6th Intern. Congr. Acoust.,* Tokyo, August 1968, Paper B-4-5.

Keller, T. G. von, Automatic Recognition of Spoken Words, *J. Acoust. Soc. Am.,* **44**(1):385 (July 1968). (Abstract)

Ye Kirillov, N., and L. V. Fatkin, Experiments in the Recognition of Speech Sounds by Automatic Machines, Foreign Developments in Machine Translation and Information Processing, No. 107, *Joint Publ. Res. Serv.,* 15754 (October 1962).

Lecours, M., and J. J. Sparkes, Adaptive Spectral Analysis for Speech-sound Recognition, *IEEE Trans. Audio Electroacoust.,* **AU-16**(4):523–525 (December 1968).

Makhoul, J. I., Speaker-Machine Interaction in a Limited Speech Recognition System, *J. Acoust. Soc. Am.,* **47**(1, pt. 1):84 (January 1970). (Abstract)

Mendress, M., An Approach to the Computer Recognition of Single-syllable English Words, *J. Acoust. Soc. Am.,* **47**(1, pt. 1):83–84 (January 1970). (Abstract)

Miller, J. C., P. W. Ross, and C. M. Wine, An Adaptive Speech Recognition System Operating in a Remote Time-shared Computer Environment, *IEEE Trans. Audio Electroacoust.,* **AU-18**(1):26–32 (March 1970).

Nelson, A. L., M. B. Herscher, T. B. Martin, H. J. Zadell, and J. W. Falter, Acoustic Recognition by Analog Feature Abstraction Techniques, in W. Wathen-Dunn (ed.), "Models for the Perception of Speech and Visual Form," pp. 428–440, MIT Press, 1964.

Newell, A. F., and C. D. Nabavi, VOTEM: The Voice Operated Typewriter Employing Morse Code, *J. Sci. Instr.,* Series 2, **2**:655–657 (1969).

Ohlendorf, R. C., and C. L. Coates, Recognition of Spoken Digits Utilizing Sequential Patterns, *Tech. Rept.* No. 57, Electronics Research Center, University of Texas, November 1968 (AD 685128).

Olson, H. F., H. Belar, and E. S. Rogers, Speech Processing Techniques and Applications, *IEEE Trans. Audio Electroacoust.,* **AU-15**(3):120–126 (September 1967).

Paul, J. E., Jr., A Limited-vocabulary, Multi-speaker Automatic Isolated Word Recognition System, North Carolina State University, September 1969 (AD 696206).

Petrick, S. R., and H. M. Willet, Digital Automatic Word Recognition Procedure, *J. Acoust. Soc. Am.,* **32**(11):1517 (November 1960). (Abstract)

Robinson, E. F. V., Voice Control of Computers, *Bull. Radio Elec. Eng. Div. Nat. Res. Council Canada,* **18**(4):13 (October–December 1968).

Rogers, E. S., and E. G. May, Performance of a 200-syllable Communication System, *J. Acoust. Soc. Am.,* **41**(6):1594–1595 (June 1967). (Abstract)

Rogers, E. S., W. H. Jamison, and P. W. Ross, Syllable Coder Communication System, *Final Rept.,* Defense Communication Agency, Washington, May 1967 (AD 658530).

Sakai, T., and S. Doshita, The Automatic Speech Recognition System for Conversational Sound, *IEEE Trans. Electron. Computers,* **EC-12**(5):835–846 (December 1963).

Scarr, R. W. A., Word Recognition Machine, *Proc. IEE,* **117**(1):203–212 (January 1970).

Smith, C. P., A Phoneme Detector, *J. Acoust. Soc. Am.,* **23**(4):446–451 (July 1951).

Smith, J. E. K., and L. Klem, Vowel Recognition Using a Multiple Discriminant Function, *J. Acoust. Soc. Am.,* **33**(3):358 (March 1961). (Letter)

Trunin-Donskii, V. N., A. S. Firer, and G. I. Tsemel, Recognition of Spoken Word Ensembles with the Aid of a Digital Computer, Foreign Technology Division, Wright-Patterson, AFB, Ohio, February 1969 (AD 687227); *Computer Abstr.,* **13**(11): Abstr. No. 3100 (November 1969).

Tsemel, G., and V. Trunin, Words of Command, *Computer Weekly,* February 20, 1969.

Velichko, V. M., and N. G. Zagoruyko, Automatic Recognition of 200 Words, *Intern. J. Man-Machine Studies,* **2**(3):222–234 (July 1970).

Vicens, P., Aspects of Speech Recognition by Computer, Dept. of Computer Science, Stanford University, Calif., April 1969 (AD 687720); *Computer Abstr.,* **13**(11):Abstr. No. 3098 (November 1969).

Washizawa, S., M. Okamoto, T. Shiga, and S. Inomata, A Spoken Digit Recognition Scheme and Its Computer Simulation, *Rept. 6th Intern. Congr. Acoust.,* Tokyo, August 1968, Paper B-4-7, pp. B135–B138.

Zaytsev, V. H., Information and Interpolation Systems Recognition of a Limited Set of Words, *Sov. Autom. Control (IEEE),* **13**(2):28–33 (March–April 1968).

Speech Recognition by Machine: A Review

D. RAJ REDDY

Abstract—This paper provides a review of recent developments in speech recognition research. The concept of sources of knowledge is introduced and the use of knowledge to generate and verify hypotheses is discussed. The difficulties that arise in the construction of different types of speech recognition systems are discussed and the structure and performance of several such systems is presented. Aspects of component subsystems at the acoustic, phonetic, syntactic, and semantic levels are presented. System organizations that are required for effective interaction and use of various component subsystems in the presence of error and ambiguity are discussed.

I. Introduction

THE OBJECT of this paper is to review recent developments in speech recognition. The Advanced Research Projects Agency's support of speech understanding research has led to a significantly increased level of activity in this area since 1971. Several connected speech recognition systems have been developed and demonstrated. The role and use of knowledge such as acoustic–phonetics, syntax, semantics, and context are more clearly understood. Computer programs for speech recognition seem to deal with ambiguity, error, and nongrammaticality of input in a graceful and effective manner that is uncommon to most other computer programs. Yet there is still a long way to go. We can handle relatively restricted task domains requiring simple grammatical structure and a few hundred words of vocabulary for single trained speakers in controlled environments, but we are very far from being able to handle relatively unrestricted dialogs from a large population of speakers in uncontrolled environments. Many more years of intensive research seem necessary to achieve such a goal.

Sources of Information: The primary sources of information in this area are the *IEEE Transactions on Acoustics, Speech, and Signal Processing* (pertinent special issues: vol. 21, June 1973; vol. 23, Feb. 1975) and the *Journal of the Acoustical Society of America* (in particular, Semiannual Conference Abstracts which appear with January and July issues each year; recently they have been appearing as spring and fall supplements). Other relevant journals are *IEEE Transactions* (Computer; Information Theory; and Systems, Man, and

Manuscript received September 1, 1975; revised November 19, 1975. This work was supported in part by the Advanced Research Projects Agency and in part by the John Simon Guggenheim Memorial Foundation.

The author is with the Computer Science Department, Carnegie-Mellon University, Pittsburgh, PA 15213.

Reprinted from *Proc. IEEE*, vol. 64, pp. 501–531, Apr. 1976.

Cybernetics), *Communications of ACM, International Journal of Man-Machine Studies, Artificial Intelligence,* and *Pattern Recognition.*

The books by Flanagan [44], Fant [40], and Lehiste [84] provide extensive coverage of speech, acoustics, and phonetics, and form the necessary background for speech recognition research. Collections of papers, in the books edited by David and Denes [25], Lehiste [83], Reddy [121], and Wathen-Dunn [158], and in conference proceedings edited by Erman [34] and Fant [41], provide a rich source of relevant material. The articles by Lindgren [88], Hyde [66], Fant [39], Zagoruiko [171], Derkach [27], Hill [63], and Otten [113] cover the research progress in speech recognition prior to 1970 and proposals for the future. The papers by Klatt [74] and Wolf [163] provide other points of view of recent advances.

Other useful sources of information are research reports published by various research groups active in this area (and can be obtained by writing to one of the principal researchers given in parentheses): Bell Telephone Laboratories (Denes, Flanagan, Fujimura, Rabiner); Bolt Beranek and Newman, Inc. (Makhoul, Wolf, Woods); Carnegie-Mellon University (Erman, Newell, Reddy); Department of Speech Communication, KTH, Stockholm (Fant); Haskins Laboratories (Cooper, Mermelstein); IBM Research Laboratories (Bahl, Dixon, Jelinek); M.I.T. Lincoln Laboratories (Forgie, Weinstein); Research Laboratory of Electronics, M.I.T. (Klatt); Stanford Research Institute (Walker); Speech Communication Research Laboratory (Broad, Markel, Shoup); System Development Corporation (Barnett, Ritea); Sperry Univac (Lea, Medress); University of California, Berkeley (O'Malley); Xerox Palo Alto Research Center (White); and Threshold Technology (Martin). In addition there are several groups in Japan and Europe who publish reports in national languages and English. Complete addresses for most of these groups can be obtained by referring to author addresses in the *IEEE Trans. Acoust., Speech, Signal Processing,* June 1973 and Feb. 1975. For background and introductory information on various aspects of speech recognition we recommend the tutorial-review papers on "Speech understanding systems" by Newell, "Parametric representations of Speech" by Schafer and Rabiner, "Linear prediction in automatic speech recognition" by Makhoul, "Concepts for Acoustic-Phonetic recognition" by Broad and Shoup, "Syntax, Semantics and Speech" by Woods, and "System organization for speech understanding" by Reddy and Erman, all appearing in *Speech Recognition: Invited Papers of the IEEE Symposium* [121].

Scope of the Paper: This paper is intended as a review and not as an exhaustive survey of all research in speech recognition. It is hoped that, upon reading this paper, the reader will know what a speech recognition system consists of, what makes speech recognition a difficult problem, and what aspects of the problem remain unsolved. To this end we will study the structure and performance of some typical systems, component subsystems that are needed, and system organization that permits effective interaction and use of the components. We do not attempt to give detailed descriptions of systems or mathematical formulations, as these are available in published literature. Rather, we will mainly present distinctive and novel features of selected systems and their relative advantages.

Many of the comments of an editorial nature that appear in this paper represent one point of view and are not necessarily shared by all the researchers in the field. Two other papers appearing in this issue, Jelinek's on statistical approaches and Martin's on applications, augment and complement this paper. Papers by Flanagan and others, also appearing in this issue, look at the total problem of man-machine communication by voice.

A. The Nature of the Speech Recognition Problem

The main goal of this area of research is to develop techniques and systems for speech input to machines. In earlier attempts, it was hoped that learning how to build simple recognition systems would lead in a natural way to more sophisticated systems. Systems were built in the 1950's for vowel recognition and digit recognition, producing creditable performance. But these techniques and results could not be extended and extrapolated toward larger and more sophisticated systems. This had led to the appreciation that linguistic and contextual cues must be brought to bear on the recognition strategy if we are to achieve significant progress. The many dimensions that affect the feasibility and performance of a speech recognition system are clearly stated in Newell [108].

Fig. 1 characterizes several different types of speech recognition systems ordered according to their intrinsic difficulty. There are already several commercially available isolated word recognition systems today. A few research systems have been developed for restricted connected speech recognition and speech understanding. There is hope among some researchers that, in the not too distant future, we may be able to develop interactive systems for taking dictation using a restricted vocabulary. Unlimited vocabulary speech understanding and connected speech recognition systems seem feasible to some, but are likely to require many years of directed research.

The main feature that is used to characterize the complexity of a speech recognition task is whether the speech is connected or is spoken one word at a time. In connected speech, it is difficult to determine where one word ends and another begins, and the characteristic acoustic patterns of words exhibit much greater variability depending on the context. *Isolated word recognition systems* do not have these problems since words are separated by pauses.

The second feature that affects the complexity of system is the vocabulary size. As the size or the confusability of a vocabulary increases, simple brute-force methods of representation and matching become too expensive and unacceptable. Techniques for compact representation of acoustic patterns of words, and techniques for reducing search by constraining the number of possible words that can occur at a given point, assume added importance.

Just as vocabulary is restricted to make a speech recognition problem more tractable, there are several other aspects of the problem which can be used to constrain the speech recognition task so that what might otherwise be an unsolvable problem becomes solvable. The rest of the features in Fig. 1, i.e., task-specific knowledge, language of communication, number and cooperativeness of speakers, and quietness of environment, represent some of the commonly used constraints in speech recognition systems.

One way to reduce the problems of error and ambiguity resulting from the use of connected speech and large vocabularies is to use all the available task-specific information to reduce search. The *restricted speech understanding systems* (Fig. 1, line 3) assume that the speech signal does not have all the necessary information to uniquely decode the message and

	Mode of Speech	Vocabulary Size	Task Specific Information	Language	Speaker	Environment
Word recognition-isolated (WR)	isolated words	10-300	limited use	—	cooperative	—
Connected speech recognition-restricted (CSR)	connected speech	30-500	limited use	restricted command language	cooperative	quiet room
Speech understanding-restricted (SU)	connected speech	100-2000	full use	English-like	not uncooperative	—
Dictation machine-restricted (DM)	connected speech	1000-10000	limited use	English-like	cooperative	quiet room
Unrestricted speech understanding (USU)	connected speech	unlimited	full use	English	not uncooperative	—
Unrestricted connected speech recognition (UCSR)	connected speech	unlimited	none	English	not uncooperative	quiet room

Fig. 1. Different types of speech recognition systems ordered according to their intrinsic difficulty, and the dimensions along which they are usually constrained. Vocabulary sizes given are for some typical systems and can vary from system to system. It is assumed that a cooperative speaker would speak clearly and would be willing to repeat or spell a word. A not uncooperative speaker does not try to confuse the system but does not want to go out of his way to help it either. In particular, the system would have to handle "uhms" and "ahs" and other speech-like noise. The "—" indicates an "unspecified" entry variable from system to system.

that, to be successful, one must use all the available sources of knowledge to infer (or deduce) the intent of the message [107]. The performance criterion is somewhat relaxed in that, as long as the message is understood, it is not important to recognize each and every phoneme and/or word correctly. The requirement of using all the sources of knowledge, and the representation of the *task*, *conversational context*, *understanding*, and *response generation*, all add to the difficulty and overall complexity of speech understanding systems.

The *restricted connected speech recognition systems* (Fig. 1, line 2) keep their program structure simple by using only some task-specific knowledge, such as restricted vocabulary and syntax, and by requiring that the speaker speak clearly and use a quiet room. The simpler program structure of these systems provides an economical solution in a restricted class of connected speech recognition tasks. Further, by not being task-specific, they can be used in a wider variety of applications without modification.

The restricted speech understanding systems have the advantage that by making effective use of all the available knowledge, including semantics, conversational context, and speaker preferences, they can provide a more flexible and hopefully higher performance system. For example, they usually permit an English-like grammatical structure, do not require the speaker to speak clearly, and permit some nongrammaticality (including babble, mumble, and cough). Further, by paying careful attention to the task, many aspects of error detection and correction can be handled naturally, thus providing a graceful interaction with the user.

The (*restricted*) *dictation machine* problem (Fig. 1, line 4) requires larger vocabularies (1000 to 10 000 words). It is assumed that the user would be willing to spell any word that is unknown to the system. The task requires an English-like syntax, but can assume a cooperative speaker speaking clearly in a quiet room.

The *unrestricted speech understanding* problem requires unlimited vocabulary connected speech recognition, but permits the use of all the available task-specific information. The most difficult of all recognition tasks is the *unrestricted connected speech recognition* problem which requires unlimited vocabulary, but does not assume the availability of any task-specific information.

We do not have anything interesting to say about the last three tasks, except perhaps speculatively. In Section II, we will study the structure and performance of several systems of the first three types (Fig. 1), i.e., isolated word recognition systems, restricted connected speech recognition systems, and restricted speech understanding systems.

In general, for a given system and task, performance depends on the size and speed of the computer and on the accuracy of the algorithm used. Accuracy is often task dependent. (We shall see in Section II that a system which gives 99-percent accuracy on a 200-word vocabulary might give only 89-percent accuracy on a 36-word vocabulary.) Accuracy versus response time tradeoff is also possible, i.e., it is often possible to tune a system and adjust thresholds so as to improve the response time while reducing accuracy and vice versa.

Sources of Knowledge: Many of us are aware that a native speaker uses, subconsciously, his knowledge of the language, the environment, and the context in understanding a sentence. These sources of knowledge (KS's) include the characteristics of speech sounds (*phonetics*), variability in pronunciations (*phonology*), the stress and intonation patterns of speech (*prosodics*), the sound patterns of words (*lexicon*), the grammatical structure of language (*syntax*), the meaning of words and sentences (*semantics*), and the context of conversation (*pragmatics*). Fig. 2 shows the many dimensions of variability of these KS's; it is but a slight reorganization (to correspond to the sections of this paper) of a similar figure appearing in [108].

1. Performance	Nature of input Response time Accuracy	Isolated words? connected speech? Real time? close to real-time? no hurry? Error-free (>99.9%)? almost error-free (>99%)? occasional error (>90%)?
2. Source characteristics (acoustic knowledge)	Acoustic analysis Noise sources Speaker characteristics	Airconditioning noise? computer room? reverberation? Dialect? sex? age? cooperative? High quality microphone? telephone? Spectrum? formants? zerocrossings? LPC?
3. Language characteristics (phonetic knowledge)	Features Phones Phonology Word realization	Voiced? energy? stress? intonation? Number? distinguishability? Phone realization rules? junction rules? Insertion, deletion and change rules? Word hypothesis? word verification?
4. Problem characteristics (task specific knowledge)	Size of vocabulary Confusability of vocabulary Syntactic support Semantic and contextual support	10? 100? 1,000? 10,000? High? what equivalent vocabulary? Artificial language? free English? Constrained task? open semantics?
5. System characteristics	Organization Interaction	Strategy? representation? Graceful interaction with user? graceful error recovery?

Fig. 2. Factors affecting feasibility and performance of speech recognition systems. (Adapted from Newell *et al.* [108].)

To illustrate the effect of some of these KS's, consider the following sentences.

1) Colorless paper packages crackle loudly.
2) Colorless yellow ideas sleep furiously.
3) Sleep roses dangerously young colorless.
4) Ben burada ne yaptigimi bilmiyorum.

The first sentence, though grammatical and meaningful, is pragmatically implausible. The second is syntactically correct but meaningless. The third is both syntactically and semantically unacceptable. The fourth (a sentence in Turkish) is completely unintelligible to most of us. One would expect a listener to have more difficulty in recognizing a sentence if it is inconsistent with one or more KS's. Miller and Isard [101] show that this is indeed the case.

If the knowledge is incomplete or inaccurate, people will tend to make erroneous hypotheses. This can be illustrated by a simple experiment. Subjects were asked to listen to two sentences and write down what they heard. The sentences were "In mud eels are, in clay none are" and "In pine tar is, in oak none is." The responses of four subjects are given below.

In mud eels are,	*In clay none are*
in muddies sar	in clay nanar
in my deals are	en clainanar
in my ders	en clain
in model sar	in claynanar

In pine tar is,	*In oak none is*
in pine tarrar	in oak ? es
in pyntar es	in oak nonnus
in pine tar is	in ocnonin
en pine tar is	in oak is

The responses show that the listener forces his own interpretation of what he hears, and not necessarily what may have been intended by the speaker. Because the subjects do not have the contextual framework to expect the words "mud eels" together, they write more likely sounding combinations such as "my deals" or "models." We find the same problem with words such as "oak none is." Notice that they failed to detect where one word ends and another begins. It is not uncommon for machine recognition systems to have similar problems with word segmentation. To approach human performance, a machine must also use all the available KS's effectively.

Reddy and Newell [124] show that knowledge at various levels can be further decomposed into sublevels (Fig. 3) based on whether it is task-dependent *a priori* knowledge, conversation-dependent knowledge, speaker-dependent knowledge, or analysis-dependent knowledge. One can further decompose each of these sublevels into sets of rules relating to specific topics. Many of the present systems have only a small subset of all the KS's shown in Fig. 3. This is because much of this knowledge is yet to be identified and codified in ways that can be conveniently used in a speech understanding system. Sections III through V review the recent progress in representation and use of various sources of knowledge.

In Section III, we consider aspects of signal processing for speech recognition. There is a great deal of research and many publications in this area, but very few of them are addressed to questions that arise in building speech recognition systems. It is not uncommon for a speech recognition system to show a catastrophic drop in performance when the microphone is changed or moved to a slightly noisy room. Many parametric representations of speech have been proposed but there are few comparative studies. In Section III, we shall review the techniques that are presently used in speech signal and analysis and noise normalization, and examine their limitations.

There are several KS's which are common to most connected speech recognition systems and independent of the task. These can be broadly grouped together as task-independent aspects of a speech recognition system. Topics such as feature extraction, phonetic labeling, phonological rules, (bottom-up) word hypothesis, and word verification fall into this category. In Section IV, we will review the techniques used and the present state of accomplishment in these areas.

Given a task that is to be performed using a speech recognition system, one is usually able to specify the vocabulary, the grammatical structure of sentences, and the semantic and contextual constraints provided by the task. In Section V, we will discuss the nature, representation, and use of these KS's in a recognition (or understanding) system.

Control Structure and System Organization: How is a given source of knowledge used in recognition? The Shannon [140] experiment gives a clue. In this experiment, human subjects demonstrate their ability to predict (and correct) what will appear next, given a portion of a sentence.

Just as in the above experiment, many recognition systems use the KS's to generate hypotheses about what word might

Type of knowledge	Task-dependent knowledge	Conversation-dependent knowledge	Speaker-dependent knowledge	Analysis-dependent knowledge
Pragmatic and Semantic	A priori semantic knowledge about the task domain	Concept subselection based on conversation	Psychological model of the user	Concept subselection based on partial sentence recognition
Syntactic	Grammar for the language	Grammar subselection based on topic	Grammar subselection based on speaker	Grammar subselection based on partial phrase recognition
Lexical	Size and confusability of the vocabulary	Vocabulary sub-selection based on topic	Vocabulary sub-selection and ordering based on speaker preference	Vocabulary subselection based on segmental features
Phonemic and phonetic	Characteristics of phones and phonemes of the language	Contextual variability in phonemic characteristics	Dialectal variations of the speaker	Phonemic subselection based on segmental features
Parametric and acoustic	A priori knowledge about the transducer characteristics	Adaptive noise normalization	Variations resulting from the size and shape of vocal tract	Parameter tracking based on previous parameters

Fig. 3. Sources of knowledge (KS). (From Reddy and Newell [124].)

(1) Speed of Communication	Speech is about 4 times faster than standard manual input for continuous text.
(2) Total System Response Time	Direct data entry from remote source, which avoids relayed entry via intermediate human transducers, speeds up communication substantially.
(3) Total System Reliability	Direct data entry from remote source with immediate feedback, avoiding relayed entry via intermediate human transducers, increases reliability substantially.
(4) Parallel Channel	Provides an independent communication channel in hands-busy operational situations.
(5) Freedom of Movement	Within small physical regions speech can be used while moving about freely doing a task.
(6) Untrained Users	No training in basic physical skill required for use (as opposed to acquisition of typing or keying skills); speech is natural for users at all general skill levels (clerical to executive).
(7) Unplanned Communication	Speech is to be used immediately by users to communicate unplanned information, in a way not true of manual input.
(8) Identification of Speaker	Speakers are recognizable by their voice characteristics.
(9) Long Term Reliability	Performance of speech reception and processing tasks which require monotonous vigilant operation can be done more reliably by computer than by humans.
(10) Low Cost Operation	Speech can provide cost savings where it eliminates substantial numbers of people.

Fig. 4. Task demands providing comparative advantages for speech. (From Newell *et al.* [109].)

appear in a given context, or to reject a guess. When one of these systems makes errors, it is usually because the present state of its knowledge is incomplete and possibly inaccurate. In Section VI, we shall review aspects of system organization such as control strategies, error handling, real-time system design, and knowledge acquisition.

B. The Uses of Speech Recognition

Until recently there has been little experience in the use of speech recognition systems in real applications. Most of the systems developed in the 1960's were laboratory systems, which were expensive and had an unacceptable error rate for real life situations. Recently, however, there have been commercially available systems for isolated word recognition, costing from $10 000 to $100 000, with less than 1-percent error rate in noisy environments. The paper by Martin in this issue illustrates a variety of applications where these systems have been found to be useful and cost-effective.

As long as speech recognition systems continue to cost around $10 000 to $100 000, the range of applications for which they will be used will be limited. As the research under way at present comes to fruition over the next few years, and as connected speech recognition systems costing under $10 000 begin to become available, one can expect a significant increase in the number of applications. Fig. 4, adapted from Newell *et al.* [109], summarizes and extends the views expressed by several authors earlier [63], [78], [87], and [89] on the desirability and usefulness of speech—it provides a list of task situation characteristics that are likely to benefit from speech input. Beek *et al.* [17] provide an assessment of the potential military applications of automatic speech recognition.

As computers get cheaper and more powerful, it is estimated that 60–80 percent of the cost of running a business computer installation will be spent on data collection, preparation, and entry (unpublished proprietary studies; should be considered speculative for the present). Given speech recognition systems that are flexible enough to change speakers or task definitions with a few days of effort, speech will begin to be used as an alternate medium of input to computers. Speech is likely to be used not so much for program entry, but rather primarily in data entry situations [33]. This increased usage should in turn lead to increased versatility and reduced cost in speech input systems.

There was some earlier skepticism as to whether speech input was necessary or even desirable as an input medium for computers [116]. The present attitude among the researchers in the field appears to be just the opposite, i.e., if speech input systems of reasonable cost and reliability were available, they would be the preferred mode of communication even though the relative cost is higher than other types of input [109]. Recent human factors studies in cooperative problem solving [23], [110] seem to support the view that speech is *the* preferred mode of communication. If it is indeed preferred, it seems safe to assume that the user would be willing to pay somewhat higher prices to be able to talk to computers. This prospect of being able to talk to computers is what drives the field, not just the development of a few systems for highly specialized applications.

II. Systems

This section provides an overview of the structure of different types of speech recognition systems. To accomplish this, one needs to answer questions such as: what are the important concepts and principles associated with each of these systems, what are their distinguishing features, how well do they perform, and so on. It is not always possible to answer these questions. Very few comparative results based on common test data are available. In many cases all the returns are not yet in. There are so many possible design choices that most systems are not strictly comparable with each other. Therefore, it will be necessary to restrict our discussion to somewhat superficial comparisons based on accuracy, response time, size of vocabulary, etc.

In this section, we will examine the structure and performance of the first three classes of systems shown in Fig. 1: *isolated word recognition systems, restricted connected speech recognition systems,* and *restricted speech understanding systems.* We will illustrate the principles of design and performance by picking a few systems which are representative of the state of the art in each category. For the sake of brevity, we will leave out the words "isolated" and "restricted" for the rest of this paper. Unless otherwise indicated, it is to be assumed that we are always talking about isolated word recognition systems, restricted connected speech recognition systems, and restricted speech understanding systems.

A. Word Recognition Systems (WRS)

Here we will look at the structure and performance of three systems by Itakura [70], Martin [96], and White [161]. Given a known vocabulary (of about 30 to 200 words) and a known speaker, these systems can recognize a word spoken in isolation with accuracies around 99 percent. The vocabulary and/or speaker can be changed but this usually requires a training session. These systems, though similar in some respects, have several interesting and distinguishing features. Fig. 5 summarizes some of the features of these systems that affect cost and performance. Researchers desirous of working in the field of word recognition would also benefit from studying the structure and features of several earlier (and somewhat lower performance) systems by Gold [51], Shearme and Leach [141], Bobrow and Klatt [18], Vicens [152], Medress [98], Valichiko and Zagoruiko [151], Vysotsky *et al.* [153], Pols [117], Von Keller [154], Itahashi, Makino, and Kido [67], and Sambur and Rabiner [135].

All three systems use the classical pattern recognition paradigm as their recognition strategy. The general paradigm involves comparing the parameter or feature representation of the incoming utterance with the prototype reference patterns of each of the words in the vocabulary. Fig. 6 presents the flow chart of a typical word recognition system. The main decisions to be made in the design of a word recognition system are: how to normalize for variations in speech; what is the parametric representation; how does the system adapt to a new speaker or new vocabulary; how does one measure the similarity of two utterances; and how to speed up the matching process.

Normalization: Even when the speaker and the microphone are not changed, variations in speech occur as a result of free variation from trial to trial, as well as the emotional state of the speaker and the ambient noise level of the environment. These result in changes in amplitude, duration, and signal-to-noise ratio for a given utterance. Before a match with stored templates can take place, some form of normalization is necessary to minimize the variability. Itakura [70] uses a second-order inverse filter based on the entire utterance to achieve noise and amplitude normalization. Martin [96] identifies several types of noise related problems: room noise, breath noise, intraword stop gaps, and operator-originated babble. Some of these result in incorrect detection of beginning and end of the utterance. Most of the noise problems can be overcome by careful attention to detail, such as close-speaking microphones, looking for spectra that are typical of breath noise, rejecting utterances that do not get a close match to any of the words, and so on. White, before measuring distances, normalizes all filter samples by dividing by the total energy.

Parametric Representations: Itakura uses linear predictive coding (LPC) coefficients, Martin uses hardware feature detectors based on bandpass filters, while White uses a 1/3-octave filter bank (see Section III). White [161] has studied the effect of using different parametric representations. Results of this experiment are given in Fig. 7. It shows that the 1/3-octave filter bank and LPC yield about similar results, and using a 6-channel-octave filter bank increases the error rate from 2 to 4 percent while doubling the speed of recognition. Transforming the parametric data into a pseudophonemic label prior to match can lead to significant reduction of storage but the error rate increases sharply to 9 percent. Reference pattern storage requirement is also affected by the choice of parametric representation. Assuming an average duration of 600 ms per word, White requires from 2160 to 7200 bits of storage (depending on parametric representation) per reference pattern and Itakura requires 4480 bits, while Martin requires only 512 bits per pattern.

Training: Change of speaker or vocabulary is accomplished in all three systems by training the system to produce a new set of reference patterns. Both Itakura and White use a single reference pattern per word. A single reference pattern cannot capture all variations in pronunciations for even a single speaker. Thus when a word exhibits higher than acceptable error rate it is desirable to store additional patterns. But this

	ITAKURA	MARTIN	WHITE
1. Transducer	Telephone	Close speaking microphone	Close speaking microphone
2. Noise level	68 dB (A)	90 dB (A)	65 dB (A)
3. Parametric representation	LPC	Hardware feature extractor	1/3 octave filter bank
4. No. of templates per word	Single template	Average of multiple templates	Single template
5. Space required per reference pattern	4480 bits	512 bits	7200 bits
6. Computer system	DDP-516	Nova, PDP/11 or Microcomputers	SIGMA-3

Fig. 5. Distinctive aspects of three word recognition systems. (Compiled from Itakura [70], Martin [95], [96], and White and Neely [161].)

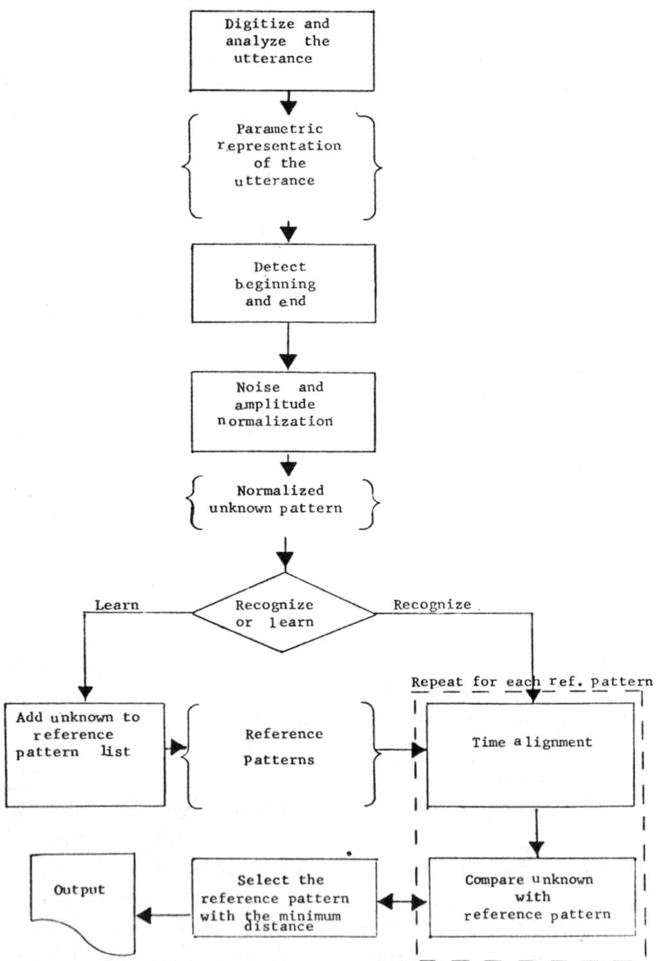

Fig. 6. Flow chart of a typical word recognition system.

requires additional storage and computation. Martin attempts abstraction of reference patterns by generating an average template from multiple samples.

Matching and Classification: Given an unknown input word, it is compared with every reference pattern to determine which pattern is most similar, i.e., has the minimum distance or maximum correlation to the unknown. This similarity measure is usually established by summing distances (or log probabilities as the case may be) between parameter vectors of the unknown and the reference. There are many design choices that affect the performance at this level, e.g., the choice of the basic time unit of sampling, the choice of the distance metric, differential weighting of parameters, and the choice of the time normalization function.

Preprocessing method	Alpha-Digit vocabulary % correct	Recognition time per utterance	Data Rate bits per sec approximate
20 channel (1/3 octave filters)	98%	30 sec	12,000
LPC	97%	20 sec	4,200
6 channel (octave filters)	96%	15 sec	3,600
Phone code	91%	2 sec	500

Fig. 7. Effect of parametric representation on accuracy and response time of a system. Preprocessing produces four different parametric representations arranged in order of increasing data compression (lower bit rate). Recognition accuracy goes down as compression goes up. Phone code attempts to give a single pseudophonetic label for each 10-ms unit of speech.

Itakura and White use dynamic programming for time normalization, while Martin divides the utterance into 16 equal time units. Itakura measures the distance between the unknown and the reference by summing the log probability based on residual prediction error every 15 ms. White measures the distance by summing the absolute values of the differences (Chebyshev norm) between the parameter vectors every 10 ms. Martin uses a weighted correlation metric to measure similarity every 40 ms or so (actually 1/16 of the duration of the utterance).

White shows that the nonlinear time warping based on dynamic programming is better than linear time scaling methods. He also shows Itakura's distance measure based on LPC linear prediction error yields about the same accuracy as other conventional methods. It is generally felt (based on speech bandwidth compression experiments) that significant loss of information results when speech is sampled at intervals exceeding 20 ms. However, note that Martin extracts averaged features based on longer time intervals and is not just sampling the signal parameters.

System	Vocabulary	Size	Noise	Microphone	Nunber of speakers	Accuracy (includes rejects if any)	Resp. time in times real time
Martin	Digits	10	—	Close speaking microphone (CSM)	10	99.79	Almost real-time
Martin	Aircraft ops.	11x12	—	CSM	10	99.32	Almost real-time
Martin	1 thru 34	34	90dB	CSM	12	98.5	Almost real-time
White	Alpha-digit	36	65	CSM	1	98.0	30
White	North Am. states	91	65	CSM	1	99.6	—
Itakura	Alpha-digit	36	68	Telephone	1	88.6	—
Itakura	Japanese geographical names	200	68	Telephone	1	98.95	22

Fig. 8. Performance characteristics of three word recognition systems. (Compiled from Itakura [70], Martin [95], [96], and White and Neely [161].)

Heuristics for Speedup: If a system compares the unknown with every one of the reference patterns in a brute-force manner, the response time increases linearly with the size of the vocabulary. Given the present speeds of minicomputers which can execute 0.2 to 0.5 million instructions per second (mips), the increase in response time is not noticeable for small vocabularies of 10 to 30. But when the size of vocabulary increases to a few hundred words it becomes essential to use techniques that reduce computation time. Itakura uses a sequential decision technique and rejects a reference pattern if its distance exceeds a variable threshold at any time during the match operation. This results in a speedup of the matching process by a factor of almost 10. White uses the duration, amplitude contour, and partial match distance of the first 200 ms as three independent measurements to eliminate the most unlikely candidates from the search list. Others have used gross segmental features [152] and pronouncing dictionary with phonological rules [67] in reducing search. But these require a more complex program organization.

Performance: Fig. 8 gives the published performance statistics for the three systems. It is important to remember that accuracy and response time are meaningful only when considered in the context of all the variables that affect the performance. Although recognition performance scores have been quoted only for systems ranging from 10 to 34 words, Martin's system has been used with vocabularies as high as 144 words. It is the only system that has been shown to work in very high noise (>90 dB) environments and with multiple speakers (using reference patterns which represent all the speakers). The accuracy of Itakura's system drops to 88.6 percent on the alpha-digit word list (aye, bee, cee, · · · , zero, one, · · · , nine). But note that it is the only system that uses a telephone as the transducer. In addition to restricting the frequency response to about 300 to 3000 Hz, the telephone introduces burst noise, distortion, echo, crosstalk, frequency translation, envelope delay, and clipping to list a few. In addition, the alpha-digit vocabulary is highly ambiguous. The fact that the system achieves about 1-percent error rate (and 1.65-percent rejection rate) on a less ambiguous 200-word vocabulary is indicative of its true power. White's system not only achieves high accuracies but also is notable for its system organization which permits it to use different parameters, different time normalization strategies, and different search reduction heuristics with ease. The important thing to remember is that each of these systems seems capable of working with less than 2-percent error rate in noisy environments given vocabularies in the range of 30 to 200. It seems reasonable to assume that accuracy will not degrade substantially with larger vocabularies. A useful indicator of this is the early system by Vicens [152] which achieved 91.4-percent with a 561-word vocabulary.

Future Directions: As long as the cost/performance requirements do not demand an order of magnitude improvement, the present systems approach will continue to be practical and viable. The improvements in computer technology have already brought the cost of such systems to around $10 000. However, if it becomes necessary to reduce the cost to the $1000 range, significant improvement to the basic algorithms will be necessary. The principal avenues for improvement are in the reference pattern representation and search strategies. Rather than storing a vector of parameters every 10 ms, it may be necessary to go to a segmentation and labeling scheme (see Section IV) as has been attempted by some earlier investigators [67], [152]. Rather than storing multiple reference patterns for multiple speakers, it will be necessary to find techniques for abstraction. It may also be necessary to use mixed search strategies in which a simpler parametric representation is used to eliminate unlikely candidates before using a more expensive matching technique. Since many of these techniques are essential for connected speech recognition, it is reasonable to assume that progress in that area will gradually lead to low-cost/high-performance word recognition systems.

B. Connected Speech Recognition (CSR)

In this section we will look at the structure and performance of four different connected speech recognition (CSR) systems: Hearsay-I and Dragon developed at Carnegie-Mellon University [7], [123]; the Lincoln system developed at M.I.T. Lincoln Laboratories [47], [48], [56], [97], [159], [162]; and the IBM system developed at IBM, T. J. Watson Research Center [10], [30], [31], [71], [72], [149], [150], [172], [173]. Hearsay-I was actually designed as a speech understanding system, but the semantic and task modules can be deactivated so as to permit it to run like a connected speech recognition system. Both the Dragon and Lincoln systems were designed to add task-specific constraints later, but in their present form can be looked upon as connected speech recognition systems. These systems have achieved from 55- to 97-percent word accuracies. Since a sentence is considered to be incorrect even if only one word in the utterance is incorrect, the sentence accuracies tend to be much lower (around 30 to 81 percent). With tuning and algorithm improvement currently in progress, some of these systems are expected to show significant improvement in accuracy. Researchers interested in CSR systems might also wish to look at the papers in [26], [28], [95], [120], [148], and [152].

Why Is Connected Speech Recognition Difficult? When isolated word recognition systems are getting over 99-percent accuracies, why is it that CSR systems are straining to get similar accuracy? The answers are not difficult to find. In connected speech it is difficult to determine where one word ends and another begins. In addition, acoustic characteristics of sounds and words exhibit much greater variability in connected speech, depending on the context, compared with words spoken in isolation.

Any attempt to extend the design philosophy of isolated word recognition systems and recognize the utterance as a whole becomes an exercise in futility. Note that even a 10-word vocabulary of digits requires the storage of 10-million reference patterns if one wanted to recognize all the possible 7-digit sequences. Some way must be found for the recognition of the whole by analysis of the parts. The technique needed becomes one of analysis and description rather than classification (moving away from pattern recognition paradigms toward hierarchical systems, i.e., systems in which component subparts are recognized and grouped together to form larger and larger units).

To analyze and describe a component part, i.e., a word within the sentence, one needs a description of what to expect when that word is spoken. Again, the reference pattern idea of word recognition systems becomes unsatisfactory. As the number of words in the vocabulary and the number of different contextual variations per word get large, the storage required to store all the reference pattern becomes enormous. For a 200-word vocabulary, such as the one used by Itakura [70], a CSR system might need 2000 reference patterns requiring about 8-million bits of memory, not to mention the time and labor associated with speaking them into the machine. What is needed is a more compact representation of the sound patterns of the words such as those used by linguists, i.e., representation of words as a sequence of phones, phonemes, or syllables. This change from signal space representation of the words to a symbol space representation requires segmenting the continuous speech signal into discrete acoustically invariant parts and labeling each segment with phonemic or feature labels. A phonemic dictionary of the words could then be used to match at a symbolic level and determine which word was spoken.

Since CSR systems do not have the advantage of word recognition systems, of knowing the beginning and ending of words, one usually proceeds left-to-right, thereby forcing at least the beginning to be specified prior to the match for a word. Given where the first (left-most) word of the utterance ends, one can begin matching for the second word from about that position. One must still find techniques for terminating the match when an optimal match is found.

However, the exact match cannot be quite determined until the ending context (the word that follows) is also known. For example, in the word sequence "some milk" all of the nasal /m/ might be matched with the end of "some" leaving only the "ilk" part for a subsequent match. This is a special case of the juncture problem (see Section IV). Techniques are needed which will back up somewhat when the word being matched indicates that it might be necessary in this context. (see also Section VIII of Jelinek [72].)

Finally, error and uncertainty in segmentation, labeling, and matching make it necessary that several alternative word matches be considered as alternative paths. If there were 5 words in an utterance and we considered 5 alternative paths after each word, we would have 3125 (5^5) word sequences, out of which we have to pick the one that is most plausible. Selection of the best word sequence requires a tree search algorithm and a carefully constructed similarity measure.

The preceding design choices are what make CSR systems substantially more complex than word recognition systems. We do not yet have good signal-to-symbol transformation techniques nor do we fully understand how to do word matching performance of CSR systems when compared with word recognition systems. However, researchers have been working seriously on CSR techniques only for the past few years, and significant improvements can be expected in the not too distant future. The following discussion reviews the design choices made by each of the four systems (Fig. 9).

Front End Processing: The purpose of the front end in a CSR system is to process the signal and transform it to a symbol string so that matching can take place. The first three design choices in Fig. 9 affect the nature of this signal-to-symbol transformation. The Dragon system uses the simplest front end of all the systems. It uses the 10-ms speech segment as a basic unit and attempts matching at that level. Given a vector of 12 amplitude and zero-crossing parameters every 10 ms, the system computes the probabilities for each of 33 possible phonemic symbols. To account for allophonic variations, it uses multiple reference patterns (vectors) to represent each phonemic symbol.

Hearsay-I uses amplitude and zero-crossing parameters to obtain a multilevel segmentation into syllable-size units and phoneme-size units. Every 10-ms unit is given a phonemic label based on a nearest neighbor classification using a predefined set of cluster centers. Contiguous 10-ms segments with the same label are grouped together to form a phoneme-size segment. A syllable-like segmentation is derived based on local maxima and minima in the overall amplitude function of the utterance. These larger segments are given gross feature labels such as silence, fricative, and voiced.

The Lincoln system is described in detail by Weinstein *et al.* [159]. The fast digital processor (FDP) computes LPC spectra, tracks formant frequencies [97], performs a preliminary segmentation, and labels the segments as one of vowel, dip (intervocalic voiced consonants characterized by a dip in amplitude), fricative, and stop categories. Formant frequencies, formant motions, formant amplitude, and other spectral measurements are used in further classifying the segments into phone-like acoustic–phonetic elements (APEL) labels.

The IBM system front end is based on the approach developed by Dixon and Silverman [31], [32], for pattern

	Hearsay-I	Dragon	Lincoln	IBM
Parametric representation	Amplitude + zero crossings in 5 octave bands	Amplitude and zero crossings in 5 octave bands	LPC Spectra formants	Spectrum
Segmentation	Heuristic multilevel (syllabic + phonetic)	None	Heuristic	Heuristic
Labeling	Two level prot. matching	Prototype matching	Feature based	Prototype matching
Word matching	Heuristic	Stochastic	Heuristic	Stochastic
Phonological rules	Ad Hoc	None (can be added)	Yes	Yes
Word representation	Phonemic base form	Network	Phonemic base form	Network
Syntax	Productions anti-productions	Finite state network	Productions anti-productions	Finite state network
Search	Left to right search best first	Left to right search all paths	Left to right search best first	Left to right search using sequential decoding (similar to best first)

Fig. 9. Design choices of the four connected speech recognition (CSR) systems. (Compiled from Reddy *et al.* [123], Baker [8], Forgie *et al.* [48], Baker and Bahl [10], and other related publications.)

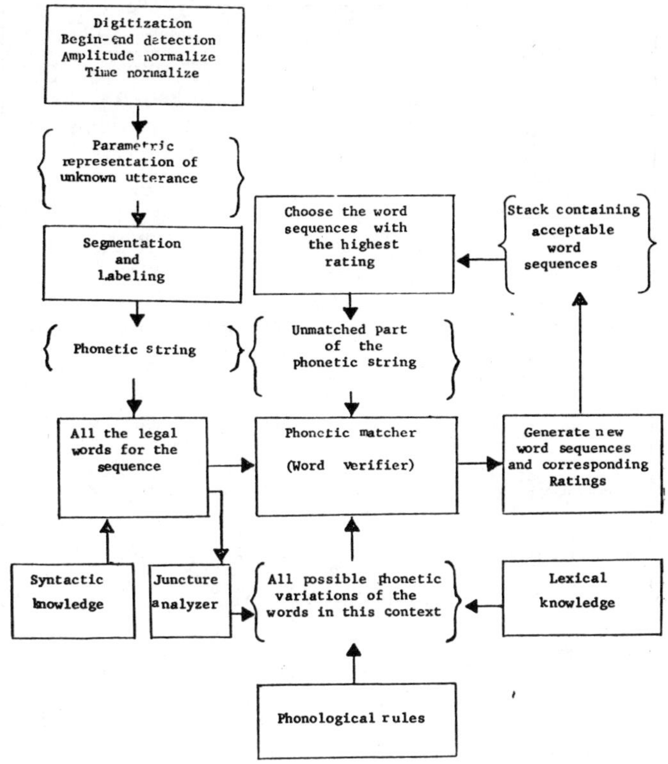

Fig. 10. Flow chart of a typical CSR system.

recognition using complex decision-making rules and dynamic segmentation [148]. The segmentation and labeling procedure uses energy, spectra, spectral change, an ordered list of five "most similar" classes, and their similarity values. The labeling is done by prototype matching as in the case of Hearsay-I and Dragon but using about 62 label classes.

Knowledge Representation: There are three types of knowledge that are usually required in a CSR system: phonological rules, lexicon, and syntax. The Dragon system has the most elegant representation of knowledge of the four systems [7]. All the knowledge is represented as a unified finite-state network representing a hierarchy of probabilistic functions of the Markov processes.

Hearsay-I organizes knowledge into independent and cooperating knowledge processes, which makes it easy to add or remove a knowledge source. The representation of knowledge within each process is somewhat arbitrary and depends on the needs of that process. Syntax is represented as a set of productions (generative rewriting rules) and antiproductions (analytic prediction rules). The lexicon contains only the phonemic base forms. Phonological information is embedded in various acoustic analysis procedures.

In the Lincoln system, syntactic constraints are represented by a set of production rules. Phonological and front-end-dependent rules are used to construct a lexicon from a base form dictionary [55], [56]. Other such rules are also applied during a heuristic word and matching process.

The IBM system uses a finite-state grammar and a directed graph representation of each lexical element [24]. Phonological rules are compiled into the lexicon. To account for the rules that do involve word boundaries, the graphs have multiple starting nodes labeled with conditions that must be met by preceding or following words. An important component of the IBM system is the extensive use of statistical information to provide transition probabilities within the finite-state networks representing task-dependent information. (See also Jelinek [72].)

Although both the Dragon and IBM systems use network representations and stochastic matching, they differ in several respects. Dragon uses an integrated representation of all the knowledge, whereas the IBM system has independent representations of the language, phonology, and acoustic components. Dragon evaluates the likelihood of all possible paths, while the IBM system uses sequential decoding to constrain the search to the most likely path.

Matching and Control: Fig. 10 is a flow chart of the recognition process of a typical CSR system. All the systems except Dragon use a stack (or a set) containing a list of alternative word sequences (or state sequences) arranged in descending order of their likelihoods (or scores) to represent the partial sentence analysis so far. Given the word sequence with the highest likelihood, the task-specific knowledge generates all the words that can follow that sequence. Each of these words is matched against the unmatched symbol (phonemic) string to estimate conditional likelihoods of occurrence. These are used to generate a new list of acceptable word sequences and their likelihoods. This process is repeated until the whole utterance is analyzed and an acceptable word sequence is determined. The Dragon system, rather than extending the best word sequence, extends all the sequences in parallel. The Markovian assumption permits it to collapse many alternative sequences into a single state, thus avoiding exponential growth.

The four systems differ significantly in the way in which insertion, deletion, and substitution errors are handled in the matching process, and the way in which likelihoods are estimated. Hearsay-I and Lincoln systems use heuristic techniques, while Dragon and IBM systems use the principles of stochastic modeling [72], [7] to estimate likelihoods. In Section IV, we will discuss techniques for word matching and verification in greater detail.

Performance: Fig. 11 gives some performance statistics for the four systems. The systems are not strictly comparable because of the number of variables involved. However, some

	Hearsay-I	Dragon	Lincoln	IBM
No. of Sentences	102	102	275	363
No. of Word tokens	578	578	-	-
No. of Speakers	4	1	6	1
No. of Tasks	5	5	1	2
Sentence Accuracy	31%	49%	49%	81%
Word Accuracy	55%	83%	-	97%
Response Time (x real-time)	9-44	48-174	15-25	25
Environment	Terminal room	Terminal room	Computer room	Sound booth
Transducer	CSM and telephone	CSM	CSM	HQM
Size of Vocabulary	24-194	24-194	237	250
Live Input	Yes	No	Yes	No
Date Operational	1972	1974	1974	1975
Computer	PDP-10	PDP-10	TX-2/FDP	360/91 and 370/168
Average No. of instructions executed per second of speech in million	3-15	15-60	45-75	30

Fig. 11. Performance statistics for four CSR systems. (From sources given for Fig. 9.)

general comparisons can be made. The IBM system has the best performance of the four, but one should bear in mind the fact that most of their results to date are based on relatively noise-free high-quality data for a single speaker. It is also the only system being improved actively at present. This tuning of the system should lead to even higher accuracies.

Hearsay-I and Dragon were run on the same data sets to permit strict comparison. Dragon yields significantly higher accuracy, though it is slower by a factor of 4 to 5. Hearsay-I yields much higher accuracies on tasks and speakers with which it is carefully trained (see Fig. 15). It was tested on several speakers and several tasks. As the vocabulary increases, its relatively weaker acoustic–phonetic module tends to make more errors in the absence of careful tuning. It was one of the first systems to be built and still is one of the very few that can be demonstrated live.

The Dragon system performance demonstrates that simple and mathematically tractable CSR systems can be built without sacrificing accuracy. Although searching all possible alternative paths becomes unfeasible for very large vocabularies, for restricted tasks with a few hundred word vocabulary, Dragon with its simpler program structure represents an attractive alternative.

The Lincoln system is the only one of the four that works for several speakers without significant tuning for the speaker. The 49-percent sentence accuracy represents the composite accuracy for all the speakers taken together. It was also tested with a 411-percent word vocabulary, yielding about 28-percent sentence accuracy over the same set of six speakers.

Future Directions: How can CSR systems achieve significantly higher performance and cost under $20 000? Better search, better matching, and better segmentation and labeling are all essential if the systems are to achieve higher accuracies. The best-first search strategy used by Hearsay-I and other systems leads to termination of search when it exceeds a given time limit. When this happens, it is usually because errors in evaluation have led to a wrong part of the search space, and the system is exploring a large number of incorrect paths. In most systems, this accounts for 20–30 percent of the sentence errors.

Dragon does not have the problem of thrashing since it searches all the possible extensions of a word (state) sequence. An intermediate strategy in which several promising alternative paths are considered in parallel (best few without backtracking), rather than all or the best-first strategies of the present systems, seems desirable. Lowerre [90] has implemented one such strategy in the Harpy system currently under development at Carnegie-Mellon University and has reduced the computation requirement by about a factor of 5 over Dragon without any loss of accuracy. The number of alternative paths to be considered is usually a function of the goodness of the parametric representation (and accuracy of the segmental labels). Continued research into this class of systems should lead to the development of low-cost CSR.

Accuracies in word matching and verification approaching those of word recognition systems, i.e., greater than 99 percent, are essential for the success of CSR. Since words exhibit greater variability in connected speech, this becomes a much more difficult task. Klatt [75] proposes the use of analysis-by-synthesis techniques as the principal solution to this problem. Near-term solutions include learning the transition probabilities of a word network using training data, as is being done by IBM, or learning the lexical descriptions themselves from examples, as is being attempted at Carnegie-Mellon University. There has been very little work on comparative evaluation of segmentation and labeling schemes. Further studies are needed to determine which techniques work well, especially in environments representative of real life situations.

C. Speech Understanding Systems (SUS)

In this section, we will study approaches to speech understanding systems (SUS's) design by discussing three systems, viz., Hearsay-II [36], [86], SPEECHLIS [166], and VDMS [127], [156], currently being developed, respectively, at Carnegie-Mellon University, Bolt Beranek and Newman, and jointly by System Development Corporation and Stanford Research Institute. We cannot give performance statistics for these systems as they are not working well enough yet. However, at least one earlier system, Hearsay-I, illustrates the potential importance and usefulness of semantic and conversation-dependent knowledge. Experiments on this system show that 25–30-percent improvement in sentence accuracies (e.g., from about 52 to 80 percent on one task) were achieved using chess-dependent semantic knowledge in the voice-chess task. Researchers interested in other attempts at speech understanding systems should look at [13], [20], [35], [47], [64], [123], [134], [152], [157], and [160].

What Makes Speech Understanding Difficult? In addition to the problems of having to recognize connected speech, SUS's tend to have the additional requirement that they must do so even when the utterance is not quite grammatical or well formed, and in the presence of speech-like noise (e.g., babble, mumble, and cough). The requirement is somewhat relaxed by the concession that what matters in the end is not the recognition of each and every word in the utterance but rather the intent of the message. The systems are also required to keep track of the context of the conversation so far and use it to resolve any ambiguities that might arise within the present sentence. Clearly, one can attempt to build CSR systems with all the preceding characteristics and yet not use any task-specific information. Here we will restrict ourselves to the apparent differences in approach between the CSR and the SU systems of the current generation.

How do the above requirements translate into specific problems to be solved? We still have the problem of determining when a word begins and ends in connected speech, and the problem of wide variability in the acoustic characteristics of the words. But the solutions adopted in CSR systems to solve these problems do not quite carry over to SUS. One can no longer proceed left-to-right in the analysis of an utterance because of the possibility of error or unknown babble in the middle of the utterance. Thus the useful technique of keeping an ordered list of word sequences which are extended to the right after each iteration has to be modified significantly.

Another design choice of CSR systems that leads to difficulties is the notion that there is a bottom-up acoustic analyzer (the *front end*) which generates a phonemic (or some such) symbol string, and a top-down language model (the *back end*) predicting possible word candidates at that choice point, which are then compared by a matching procedure. As the vocabularies get larger, often the roles have to be reversed. One cannot afford to match 1000 possible nouns just because the grammar predicts that the next word might be a noun. In such cases, the phonemic string may be used to generate plausible word hypotheses, while the language model is used to verify such hypotheses for compatibility and consistency. In general, one wants systems in which the role of knowledge sources is somewhat symmetric. They may be required to predict or verify depending on the context. The representations of knowledge required to perform these different roles will usually be different.

In CSR we have seen that at a given time one of several words might be possible given the acoustic evidence. This is what leads to the nondeterministic search, i.e., consideration and evaluation of an ordered list of alternate word sequences in the flow chart given in Fig. 10. This nondeterministic (and errorful) nature of decisions permeates all the levels of the speech decoding process, i.e., segmental, phonetic, phonemic, syllabic, word, phrase, and conceptual, and not just the word level. There is no such thing as error-free segmentation, error-free labels, and so on up the levels. This requires the representation of alternate sequences at all levels, not just the word level as in the case of CSR systems. Fig. 12 (from Reddy and Erman [122]) illustrates the consequences of this nondeterminism.

At the bottom of Fig. 12, we see the speech waveform for part of an utterance: '. . . all about . . .'. The "true" locations of phoneme and word boundaries are given below the waveform. In a recognition system, the choices of segment boundaries and labels to be associated with each of the segments are not as clear cut. (In fact, even getting trained phoneticians to agree on the "true" locations is often difficult.) A segmentation and labeling program might produce segment boundaries as indicated by the dotted lines connecting the waveform to the segment level. Given the segmental features, the phoneme represented by the first segment might be /aw/,

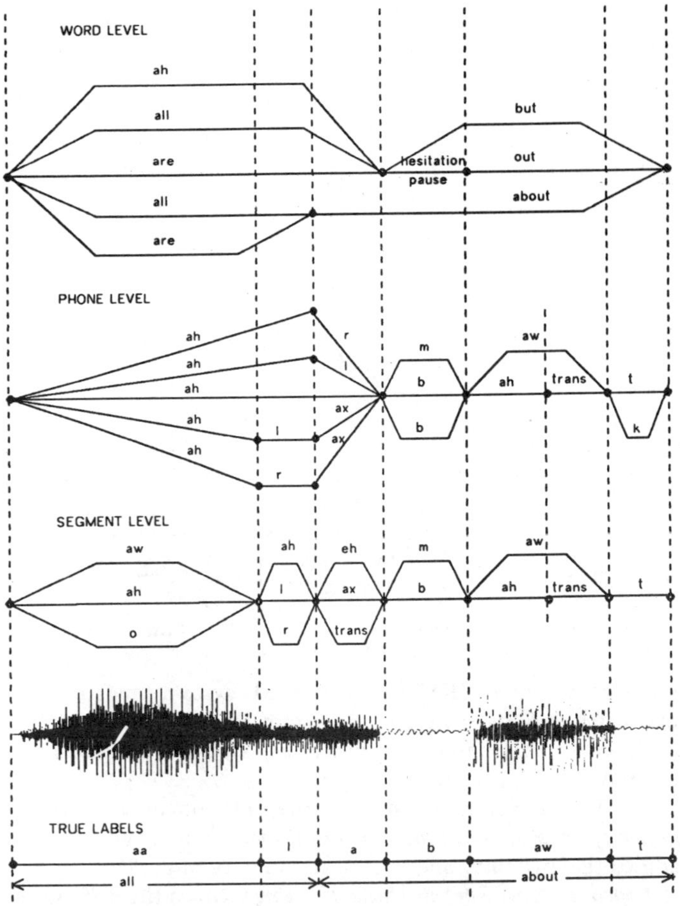

Fig. 12. Example of network representation of alternative choices at various levels. (From Reddy and Erman [122].)

/ah/, or /ow/. Similarly, several different labels can be given to each of the other segments. Given the necessary acoustic-phonetic rules, it is possible to combine, regroup, and delete segments, forming larger phoneme-size units, as shown in the figure. Note, for example, that /ah/ and /l/ are very similar, and it is not impossible that the minor parametric variability that caused the segment boundary at the lower level is just free variation. These phoneme hypotheses give rise to a multiplicity of word hypotheses such as 'ah but', 'all out', 'all about', 'all but', 'are about', and so on.

If, instead of selecting several alternate segmentations and following their consequences, we were to select a single segmentation and associate a single label with each segment, the resulting errors might make it impossible to verify and validate the correct word. Thus some form of network representation of alternate hypotheses at all levels is necessary in systems requiring high accuracy.

Even the lowest level decision about segmentation sometimes requires the active mediation of higher level knowledge such as the plausibility of a given word occurring in that position. Fig. 12 can be used to illustrate the point. The segment boundary at the word juncture of 'all' and 'about' is usually very difficult to find since the spectral characteristics of /l/ and the reduced vowel /ax/ tend to be very similar. In the event that a higher level process is fairly confident about this word sequence but there is no segment boundary, it could call upon the segmenter for a closer look, possibly using a different parametric representation. In general, SUS's require flexible means of cooperation and communication among different

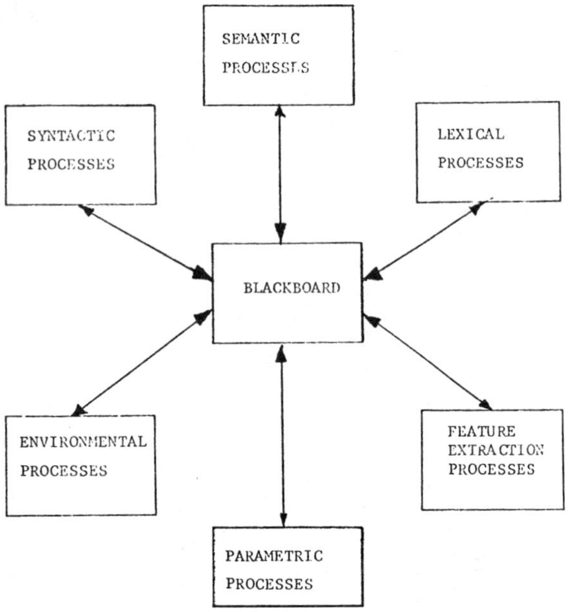

Fig. 13. Blackboard model used in Hearsay-II. (From Lesser *et al.* [86].)

knowledge sources (KS's). Since an SU system tends to have many more KS's than a CSR system, the system should be designed so that knowledge processes can easily be added and deleted.

Finally, the requirements of representation of *understanding, response generation, conversational context,* and *task* all add to the difficulty and overall complexity of an SUS.

Approaches to Speech Understanding: Given the difficulties that arise in SUS, it is clear that one needs significantly more sophisticated system design than those used in current CSR systems. At present, there is no clear agreement among researchers as to what an ideal system organization for an SUS might be.

In the VDMS system [127], the parser coordinates the operation of the system. In many respects the control flow resembles the one for CSR systems (Fig. 10) and is based on the best-first strategy. However, the simplistic notion of an ordered list of word sequences is replaced by a *parse net* mechanism which permits sharing of results and does not require strict left-to-right analysis of the utterance [115]. A language definition facility permits efficient internal representation of various KS's [128].

In the SPEECHLIS system [166], control strategies and system organization are derived through incremental simulation [168]. People located in different rooms simulate the various components and attempt to analyze an utterance by communicating via teletypewriter. Then one by one, people are replaced by computer algorithms having specified interface characteristics. A control strategy for SUS derived in this manner is described by Rovner *et al.* [131]. The final control structure is not available yet but is expected to be within the near future.

Perhaps the most ambitious of all the system organizations is the one used by the Hearsay-II system [86], [37]. Though it was designed with speech understanding systems in mind, it is viewed as one of the potential solutions to the problem of knowledge-based systems (KBS) architecture that is of general interest in artificial intelligence research. Other proposed solutions to the KBS architecture problem include Planner [62], production systems [106], and QA-4 [132].

Hearsay-II is based on a *blackboard* model (Fig. 13). The blackboard model conceives of each KS as an information gathering and dispensing process. When a KS generates a hypothesis about the utterance that might be useful for others, it broadcasts the hypothesis by writing it on the "blackboard"—a structurally uniform global data base. The hypothesis-and-test paradigm (see Section I-A) serves as the basic medium of communication among KS's. The way KS's communicate and cooperate with each other is to validate or reject each other's hypotheses. The KS's are treated uniformly by the system and are independent (i.e., anonymous to each other) and therefore relatively easy to modify and replace. The activation of a KS is data-driven, based on the occurrence of patterns on the blackboard which match the templates specified by the KS.

Most of the control difficulties associated with SUS appear to have a solution within the Hearsay framework. It is easy to delete, add, or replace KS's. The system can continue to function even in the absence of one or more of these KS's as long as there are some hypothesis generators and some verifiers in the aggregate. The blackboard consists of a uniform multilevel network (similar to the one in Fig. 12, but containing all the levels) and permits generation and linkage of alternate hypotheses at all the levels. A higher level KS can generate hypotheses at a lower level and vice versa. It is not necessary for the acoustic processing to be bottom-up and the language model to be top-down.

How does the recognition proceed in an asynchronously activated data-driven system such as Hearsay-II? Since there are not many systems of this type around, it is difficult for most people to visualize what happens. It is difficult to explain using flow charts which are primarily useful for explaining sequential flow of control. What we have here is an activity equivalent to a set of cooperating asynchronous parallel processors even when it runs on a uniprocessor. Generating and verifying hypotheses using several KS's is analogous to several persons attempting to solve a jigsaw puzzle with each person working on a different part of the puzzle but with each modifying his strategies based on the progress being made by the others.

What is important to realize is that within the Hearsay framework one can create the effects of a strictly bottom-up system, top-down system, or system which works one way at one time and the other way the next time, depending on cost and utility considerations. The ratings policy process, a global KS, combines and propagates ratings across levels facilitating focus of attention, goal-directed scheduling, and eventual recognition of the utterance. The focus-of-attention KS is used to determine an optimal set of alternative paths which should be explored further based on notions such as effort spent, desirability of further effort, important areas yet to be explored, and goal lists.

Knowledge Sources: Fig. 14 shows the design choices made by the three systems. Many of the low-level issues are common with CSR and do not require much discussion (see also Sections III, IV, and V). Here we will discuss the nature of the higher level knowledge sources used in each system.

The task for Hearsay-II is news retrieval, i.e., retrieval of daily wire-service news stories upon voice request by the user. The vocabulary size for the task is approximately 1200 words. The syntax for the task permits simple English-like sentences and uses the ACORN network representation developed by Hayes-Roth and Mostow [58]. The semantic and pragmatic model uses subselection mechanisms based on news items of

	Hearsay-II	Speechlis	VDMS
Microphone	Close speaking microphone	Close speaking microphone	Sony ECM-377 condenser microphone
Noise Level	Terminal room	Quiet office	Low (sound booth)
Parametric Rep.	LPC using Itakura metric	Formants and features	Formants and features
Segmentation	Parameter based	Feature based	Classification based
Labeling	Prototype matching	Heuristic	Heuristic
Word Hypothesis	Syllable based	Segment based	Syllable based
Word Verification	Markov Process	Analysis-by-Synthesis	Heuristic match with A-Matrix
Syntax	Restricted English	English-like	English-like
Semantics	Acorn net	Semantic net	Semantic net
Discourse Model	Topic based subselection	User model	Ellipsis and anaphora
Task	News retrieval	Travel Budget Manager	Submarine Data Base Management
Systems Control	Blackboard Model	Centralized Controller	Parser-Based

Fig. 14. Design choices of the three speech understanding systems. (Compiled from Lesser *et al.* [86], Woods [166], Ritea [127], and other related publications.)

1	2	3	4	5				6			
				Acoustic + Syntax				Acoustics + Syntax + Semantics			
Data set: Task/Speaker	Words in lexicon	No. of sentences	No. of words	%Sentences %Near miss	%Words	Average Time per sentence (sec)	Average Time per second of speech	%Sentences %Near miss	%Words	Average Time per sentence (sec)	Average Time per second of speech
1 Chess/Rn	31	14	82	43 100	87	11	6	100 100	100	9	5
2 Chess/Jb	31	19	86	74 95	93	12	9	100 100	100	8	6
3 Chess/Jb	31	21	105	15 50	69	15	8	48 90	88	13	7
4 Chess/(Tel) B1	31	25	99	52 84	78	7	6	80 88	88	7	6
Totals		79	352	46 80	81	11	7	79 93	93	9	6

Fig. 15. Performance of Hearsay-I speech understanding system. (From Erman [35].) Column 1 gives data set number, task, and speaker identification. Column 2 gives number of words in task lexicon. Column 3 shows number of sentences in data set. Column 4 gives total number of word tokens in data set. Column 5 gives results for HS-I system recognition with Acoustics module and Syntax module both operating. First subcolumn indicates percent of sentences recognized completely correctly. "Near miss" (indicated below that number in first subcolumn) indicates percent of times that recognized utterance differed from actual utterance by at most one word of approximate similar phonetic structure. Second subcolumn gives percent of words recognized correctly. Mean computation times on PDP-10 computer (in seconds per sentence and in seconds per second of speech) are shown in subcolumns three and four. Column 6 shows results for recognition using all three sources of knowledge (for Chess task only): Acoustics, Syntax, and Semantics modules. Subcolumns are similar to those of Column 5.

the data, analysis of the conversation, and the presence of certain content words in the blackboard.

The task for SPEECHLIS is to act as an assistant to a travel budget manager. It permits interactive query and manipulation of a travel budget of a company. It is meant to help a manager keep track of the trips taken or proposed, and to produce summary information such as the total money spent or allocated. The vocabulary is about 1000 words. The syntax permits a wide variety of English sentences and is based on the augmented transition network (ATN) formalism developed by Woods [164]. The parser is driven by a modified ATN grammar [15], [16] which permits parsing to start anywhere, not necessarily left-to-right. The semantic component is based on a *semantic net* and uses *case frame tokens* to check for the consistency of completed syntactic constituents and the current semantic hypotheses [103]. Semantics is also used to focus attention and to produce a representation of the meaning of the utterance. A discourse model is used to predict what the user might say next.

The task for VDMS is to provide interactive query and retrieval of information from a "submarine data base." The vocabulary for the task is about 1000 words. The language definition facility [128] permits the speaker to communicate in relatively natural English. A semantic net representation along with strategies for net partitioning help to organize and condense the semantics of the task [60]. The pragmatic component [29] permits processing of simple forms of conversation-dependent ellipses and anaphora (see Section V-D).

Status: None of the three systems discussed here is working well enough to report performance statistics. Many component parts of these systems are working, but there are still weak links in the total systems that make such measurements meaningless. In the absence of these, it is useful to look at the performance of Hearsay-I to understand the potential role of semantics and other task-dependent knowledge in speech understanding systems. Fig. 15 shows performance results of Hearsay-I on the voice-chess task, both with and without the use of semantics. In a set of experiments using 79 utterances containing 352 words from three speakers (one speaker using telephone input), the sentence accuracies of the system increased from 46 to 79 percent by the use of task-dependent semantics. Response time also improved by about 10–20 percent (11–9 s). This speedup illustrates the fact that more complexity need not always mean slower systems. It is difficult to extrapolate how well other systems might perform from this lone example which used a powerful semantic module, i.e., a chess program, to predict legal moves. However, most researchers agree that without semantic and/or pragmatic knowledge, the systems will be unable to recognize or interpret some of the nongrammatical and non-well-formed sentences that usually occur in conversations.

Future Directions: It is too soon to draw any conclusions, but a few general observations can be made. The main scientific question to be answered in the next few years will be: is *understanding* a necessary prerequisite for *recognition* or can the simpler CSR systems do the job? If SU systems can achieve higher accuracies or recognize utterances faster on a given task than a CSR system, then the answer can be affirmative. It will always be the case for simple tasks that CSR systems, with their simpler program organization, are more likely to be adequate and cost-effective. What is not known are the tradeoffs that occur with large vocabulary English-like languages in complex task situations.

The second question is how to simplify the structure of the present SU systems while continuing to make effective use of all the available knowledge. Will SU systems price themselves out of the market by being more complex than most computer programs we write? The present systems are large, unwieldy, slow, and contain too many *ad hoc* decisions without the benefit of careful comparative evaluation of potential design choices. This is to be expected given their pioneering status. Once these systems are working, the most important task will be to study design alternatives that will significantly reduce the cost and/or increase the performance.

III. Signal Processing for Speech Recognition

One of the first decisions to be made in the design of a speech recognition system is how to digitize and represent speech in the computer. The tutorial-review paper, "Parametric Representations of Speech" by Schafer and Rabiner [137], provides a comprehensive and in-depth treatment of the digital techniques of speech analysis. Usually the first steps in the recognition process are the division of the connected speech into a sequence of utterances separated by pauses and the normalization of the signal to reduce variability due to noise and speaker. In this section, we shall review the signal processing techniques that have found to be useful in performing these tasks. The books by Fant [39] and Flanagan [44] are recommended for those interested in a thorough understanding of the theory and practice of speech analysis.

A. Parametric Analyses of Speech

Analysis of the speech signal was perhaps the single most popular subject of the papers on speech research in the 1950's and 1960's. The book by Flanagan [44] summarizes much of this work and provides an excellent description of the most commonly used speech analysis techniques, such as the short-time spectrum, formants, zero-crossings, and so on. In recent years, advances in computer architecture, graphics, and interactive use of systems have significantly altered the way speech research is conducted [105], and have tilted the balance in favor of digital rather than analog techniques. Here we will briefly mention some of the techniques that are commonly used in speech recognition research today.

The simplest digital representation of speech is pulse-code modulation (PCM). The changes in air pressure caused by the speech are sampled and digitized by a computer using an analog-to-digital converter. The speech is sampled from six to twenty thousand times a second in speech recognition research, depending on the frequency response desired. The speech is usually quantized at 9 to 16 bits per sample. Schafer and Rabiner [137] report that 11 bits is adequate for most purposes. The higher sample accuracy used in some systems [77], [175] provides for the wide dynamic range of signal levels observed across speakers. Conventional automatic gain control techniques produce signal distortions and are not preferred by researchers. It is easier to throw away the unneeded resolution later than to train speakers to speak at a uniform level of loudness.

Given a linear PCM representation of speech, one can derive other representations commonly used in speech recognition. Most of these representations are based on the assumption that parameters of speech remain unchanged over a short-time period. The commonly used *short-time spectrum* can be obtained using an analog filter bank or calculated from the PCM speech using digital filtering techniques or the fast Fourier transform (FFT).

The most widely used technique in speech recognition systems today is the LPC technique pioneered by Atal [1]–[5] and Itakura [68], [69], and extended by Markel [94] and Makhoul [91]. The tutorial-review papers by Makhoul [92], [93] discuss in detail the use of this technique in speech analysis and recognition. The theoretical foundations of LPC are based on the fact that the model of an acoustic tube whose input is impulses or low-level noise is mathematically tractable, i.e., the important parameters of the tube can be determined from its output, and that the model is good enough in estimating the response of the vocal tract. The basic ideal behind LPC is that, given the acoustic tube model of the vocal tract, the present can be estimated from the immediate past, i.e., a speech sample can be expressed as a linear function of the preceding P speech samples. The coefficients of the linear function are determined by least square error fitting of the short-time speech signal. Given the coefficients, one can derive other parametric representations of speech, such as spectrum, formants, and vocal tract shape. Besides linear predictive coding (LPC), other commonly used parametric representations in speech recognition are the smoothed short-time spectrum based on DFT processing [175] and measurements based on amplitude and zerocrossings [11]. Silverman and Dixon [175] state that they have found DFT based processing of speech to be more desirable in their system than LPC based methods.

B. End-Point Detection

Division of connected discourse into utterances, i.e., detection of the beginning and ending of individual phrases is usually called end-point detection. Accurate determination of the end points is not very difficult if the signal-to-noise ratio is high, say greater than 60 dB. But most practical speech recognition systems must work with much lower S/N ratios, sometimes as low as 15 to 20 dB. Under these conditions, weak fricatives and low-amplitude voiced sounds occurring at the end points of the utterance become difficult to detect, leading to unacceptable error rates in high-accuracy systems. It is possible to detect end points accurately even in the presence of noise by careful attention to the algorithms. Gold [51], Vicens [152], and Martin [96] report on specific algorithms used by their systems.

The only careful study of this problem so far appears in a paper by Rabiner and Sambur [118]. They use the overall energy measure to locate an approximate end-point interval (N_1, N_2) such that although part of the utterance may be outside the interval, the actual end points are not within this interval. Precise end points are obtained by extending this interval in both directions to include any low-amplitude unvoiced fricatives at the beginning and end using a strict threshold on a zero-crossing measure.

Martin [96] reports on the use of a pattern matching technique to distinguish speech sounds from breath noise, which has its own spectral characteristics. Vicens [152] detects and rejects high-energy impulse noises, such as opening of the lips (when using a close-speaking microphone) and teletypewriter noise, by their very short duration followed by a long pause.

C. Noise Normalization

The single most important factor that affects the reliability and repeatability of speech recognition systems at present is the lack of proper attention to the sources of noise, i.e., background noise, microphone (or telephone) frequency response, reverberation noise, and noise from quantization and aliasing. Systems tend to be reliable as long as these sources of noise are kept invariant, but show a significant drop in performance as soon as the situation is altered. There have been a few studies on recognition in noisy environments [96], [104], and on the use of telephone as input device [38], [70]. But there are many questions that still remain unanswered.

Many system designs respond to the problems of noise by refusing to deal with this source of variability and requiring a new training session each time the environment, the microphone, or the speaker is changed. This seems acceptable in the short run but systematic studies into noise normalization techniques and the factors affecting the potential tradeoffs will be needed eventually.

Background Noise: This type of noise is usually produced by air-conditioning systems, fans, fluorescent lamps, typewriters, computer systems, background conversation, footsteps, traffic, opening and closing doors, and so on. The designers of a speech recognition system usually have little control over these in real-life environments. This type of noise is additive in nature and usually steady state except for impulse noise sources like typewriters. Depending on the environment, the noise levels will vary from about 60 dB (A) to 90 dB (A). Many of the noise sources have energies concentrated over certain portions of the spectrum and are generally not representable by white-noise experiments.

The most commonly used technique to minimize the effects of background noise is to use a head-mounted close-speaking microphone. When a speaker is producing speech at normal conversational levels, the average speech level increases by about 3 dB each time the microphone-to-speaker distance is reduced by an inch (when the distances are small). In absolute terms, the speech level is usually around 90 to 100 dB when the speaker-to-microphone distance is less than 1 in. Some systems use the so-called noise-canceling close-speaking microphones which are somewhat adaptive to the noise levels in the environment [126]. It is important that a close-speaking microphone be head mounted; otherwise even slight movement of the speaker relative to the microphone will cause large fluctuations in the speech level. Close-speaking microphones may also exhibit somewhat poorer frequency response characteristics. Careful experimental studies are needed to determine the microphone-related factors that affect the performance of a speech recognition system. Another method often used to reduce background noise derived from air conditioning, 60-Hz electrical hum, etc., is to high-pass filter the signal. (Cut-off frequency $\approx$80 to 120 Hz.)

Two signal processing techniques are generally used to normalize the spectra so as to reduce the effects of noise and distortion: inverse filtering and spectrum weighting. Silverman and Dixon [175] use quadratic spectral normalization to compensate for amplitude variations. Itakura [70] uses a second-order inverse filter based on the long-time spectrum of the entire utterance. This is intended to normalize the gross spectral distribution of the utterance. One could also use an inverse filter based on the noise characteristics alone rather than the whole utterance. Spectrum weighting techniques attempt to ignore those parts of the spectrum where the S/N ratio is low. This can be achieved by subtraction of the log noise spectrum from the log speech spectrum. This is equivalent to $[S_t + N_t]/N$, where S_t and N_t are the short-time spectra of speech and noise at time T, and N is the long-time average spectrum of the noise [170]. Another technique is to extract features only from those frequency bands where the signal spectrum exceeds the noise spectrum by at least 6 dB or more. The larger the difference, the less the impact due to noise.

Telephone Noise: Use of the telephone as the input device for a speech recognition system introduces several problems: the restriction of the bandwidth to 300 to 3000 Hz, the uneven frequency response of the carbon microphone, burst noise, distortion, echo, crosstalk, frequency translation, envelope delay, clipping, and so on. It is not known at this time how each of these problems affects the accuracy and performance of a system. In the case of isolated word recognition systems, we know [70] that there is little effect in the case of relatively unambiguous vocabularies, but the accuracy drops significantly for ambiguous words, like in the alpha-digit list. Further studies are needed to suggest noise normalization techniques which will improve the accuracy for telephone input systems. Use of a different microphone headset connected to the telephone systems and preemphasis and/or postemphasis to normalize for the frequency response characteristics have been suggested [38]. Techniques suggested for background noise normalization would also be applicable here.

Reverberation Noise: In rooms which have hard reflecting surfaces, there is a significant reverberant field. Unlike background noise, which is additive, reverberation is a multiplicative noise and cannot easily be suppressed. If the reverberation measurement of an environment indicates a significant reverberation component, acoustic treatment of the room may be necessary. One can reduce the effects of reverberation by using a close-speaking microphone and locating the input station away from hard reflecting surfaces if possible.

Sampling Effects: Speech input is filtered by passing through a low-pass filter prior to the sampling process to eliminate undesired high frequencies (aliasing) of speech and high frequencies of noise. The characteristics of the filter, especially its rolloff near the cutoff frequency, are superimposed on the spectrum of the speech signal. It is not known whether this has any significant effect on the performance of the system.

Future Directions: We do not yet have a clear idea of which of the many possible techniques of noise normalization work well and which do not, and what the accuracy and performance tradeoffs are. We need many careful experimental studies. However, some basic issues are clear, although very few systems seem to have paid any attention to them. In high-noise environments, it will be difficult to detect, recognize, and distinguish between silence, weak fricatives (voiced and unvoiced), voice bars, voiced and unvoiced /h/, and nasals in some contexts. In systems using telephone input it will be difficult to detect and distinguish between most stops, fricatives, and nasals. Systems must provide for some form of noise adaptation at the symbol (usually phonemic) matching level if they are to be noise-insensitive.

IV. Task-Independent Knowledge

There are many aspects of processing that are common to both connected speech recognition (CSR) systems and speech understanding (SU) systems. The associated knowledge and techniques are: the speech sounds and symbols (phones and phonemes), features associated with speech sounds (acoustic-phonetics), rules governing the insertions and deletions of speech sounds (phonological rules), stress and intonation patterns of speech (prosodics), and matching of speech sounds with higher level linguistic units (syllables and words). The knowledge associated with these techniques is primarily dependent on the language and is usually independent of the task to be performed. In this section we will present the knowledge, techniques, and present state of accomplishment associated with these task-independent aspects of speech recognition, i.e., phonemic labeling, phonology, word hypothesis, and word verification.

In the following discussion, the use of the terms *phone*, *phoneme*, and *syllable* are somewhat different from the conventional usage of these terms in linguistic literature. In linguistics, the use of these terms is motivated by either perceptual or articulatory (production) considerations. Our use of the terms is acoustically motivated. Thus the minimally distinctive character of a phoneme is based on acoustic considerations, i.e., two phonemes are distinct if they are acoustically separable. We choose to use the same terms rather than invent some new ones because the intent is the same even through the criteria for distinguishabilty are different.

A. Phonemic Labeling

We have already seen, while discussing the difficulties of CSR systems (Section II-B), that some form of signal-to-symbol transformation is necessary and that attempting to match using reference patterns (as in the case of word recognition) can lead to unwieldy and unextensible CSR systems. The common technique adopted by CSR and SU systems is to attempt to transform the speech into a phonemic (or some such) string, which is then matched to the expected phones in the word. This transformation of the speech signal into a sequence of phonemic symbols usually involves feature detection, segmentation, and labeling. The tutorial-review paper by Broad and Shoup [21] presents some of the basic concepts associated with the phonemic labeling problem. The book by Fant [40] provides a comprehensive discussion of the features of speech sounds and their relationship to phonemic labels. Here we will outline the techniques useful in machine labeling of speech.

Feature detection usually represents the detection of silence, voicing, stress, and so on. The purpose of segmentation is to divide the continuous speech signal into discrete units based on some measure of acoustic similarity. Labeling schemes associate a phonemic symbol with each segmental unit. Before this symbol sequence can be used in matching, it is necessary to apply phonological rules (Section IV-B) to combine segments, change labels based on context, delete segments such as transitions, and so on.

Different systems do these operations in different orders. Some systems segment the data first, use the averaged segmental parameters to detect features such as voicing and stress, and then attempt labeling. Other systems classify and label speech every 10 ms and use the resulting labels in segmentation. The former tends to be less sensitive to noise and segment boundary effects. The commonly used paradigm is to detect features, then segment, and then label.

Not all connected speech recognition systems use segmentation and labeling prior to matching. The Dragon system [9] matches the phonemic representation of the word directly at the 10-ms level. Bakis [12] reports significantly improved performance on the continuous digit recognition experiment using the segmentation-free word template matching technique. However, such techniques are likely to run into serious difficulties with large vocabularies involving a wide variety of juncture phenomena.

1) Feature Extraction: There are a large number of potential features one can extract from speech [40]. Many of these tend to be unreliable, and it is difficult to devise detection algorithms for them. Hughes and Hemdal [65] and Itahashi *et al.* [67] have attempted detecting various distinctive features with a limited success. However, certain basic features are extracted by almost all the systems: silence, voicing, and stress. These are usually based on two measurements: energy and fundamental frequency (pitch period) of the speech signal. Schafer and Rabiner [137] present the basic concepts and techniques useful in extracting energy and pitch measurements. One common measure of energy is to sum the absolute values of the speech samples over a 5-ms region. The papers by Sondhi [147], Gold and Rabiner [52], and Gillmann [50], provide several alternate techniques for extracting pitch periods.

Silence detection is usually based on a threshold applied to the energy function. Weinstein *et al.* [159] use a threshold of about 3 dB over the background noise level. When the energy falls below this threshold it is classified as a silence. The silence segment is then extended on both sides as long as the energy in the adjacent frames stays below a slightly higher threshold.

Voicing decision is usually based on the results of pitch extraction. If the period shows wide variability, it is treated as unvoiced [52]. In addition, concentration of energy in the high-frequency regions (3700–5000 Hz) when compared with low-frequency regions (100–900 Hz) is also an indication of unvoicing [159].

Stress decisions are usually based both on energy and on the pitch period. Much of the recent work on stressed syllable detection is based on the work by Lea *et al.* [79], [81]. Lea gives an algorithm for detecting stressed syllables from the rise–fall patterns of the pitch period (F_0) contours and the local maxima of energy. Although F_0 contours fall gradually in each breath group, it is possible to detect those maxima related to stress and they usually show rises over the gradually falling contour.

In addition to such primary features, several systems [136], [127] use other measures such as normalized linear prediction error, frequency of 2-pole linear prediction model, first autocorrelation coefficient, and energy in the 5–10-kHz region. Each of these features measures some quality of the signal such as lack of high-frequency energy or presence of voicing.

2) Segmentation: It is often said that "the problem with segmentation is that you can't segment." That is to say, there is no simple machine algorithm which will give phonemic boundaries. However, if one is satisfied with acoustic boundaries, i.e., boundaries associated with significant changes in the acoustic characteristics of speech, then it is possible to devise automatic algorithms to segment speech. The papers by Fant and Lindblom [42], Reddy [119], Reddy and Vicens [125], Tappert *et al.* [148], Dixon and Silverman [30], [31], Baker [11], and Goldberg [53] illustrate several attempts to segment connected speech into phonemic units with the understanding that some phonemic boundaries may be missed and some acoustic boundaries may be inserted where there are no phonemic boundaries.

Why is segmentation difficult? Figs. 16 and 17 (from Goldberg [53]) give examples where a boundary may be missing or added based on acoustic evidence. Fig. 16 gives the oscillogram of part of the word sequence 'been measured.' Note that it is impossible to say where /n/ ends and /m/ begins (vide the time period 121 to 132 centiseconds). The labels indicated at the bottom of the figure indicate an arbitrary choice on the part of the human segmenter. Fig. 17 contains part of the waveform of the word 'samples' and the corresponding spectrogram. Note that there is a significant variation in the parameters in the last 4 centiseconds (from 75 to 79) of the vowel resulting from coarticulation. Any attempt to ignore this variation can lead to errors in other contexts. A segmentation program based on acoustic measurements would normally insert an extra segment even though there is not a corresponding phoneme.

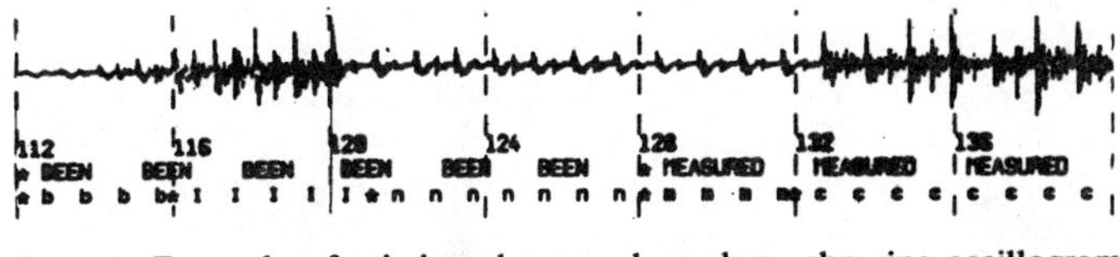

Fig. 16. Example of missing phoneme boundary, showing oscillogram (waveform) plot of part of the word sequence "been measured." Time scale is indicated on the first line below the plot in centisecond units. Second line shows a manually derived marker indicating which part of the waveform belongs to "been" and which part to "measured" (only parts of each word are visible in the plot). Third line shows manually derived markers indicating where various phonemes belonging to the words begin and end. The ending phoneme /n/ of the word "been" is assimilated with the beginning phoneme /m/ of the word "measured" as can be seen from the lack of any visible indication in the waveform. Boundary indicated at time 128 cs represents an arbitrary choice on the part of the human segmenter.

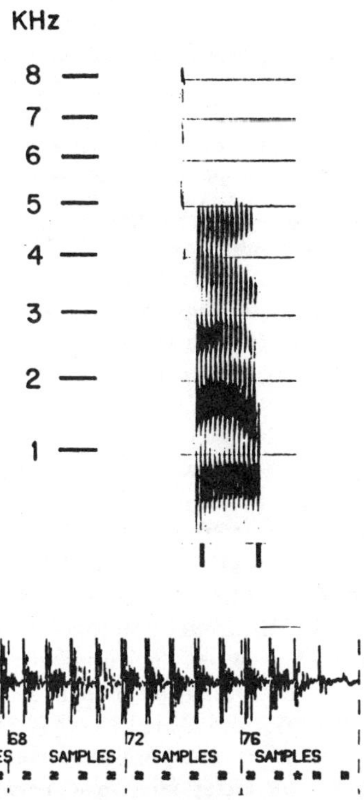

Fig. 17. Example indicating possibility of extra acoustic segments for a given phonetic segment. The waveform plot is similar to the one described in Fig. 16. The vowel /ae/ has significantly different parameters for the last 50 ms or so (from time unit 75 onwards) making it a candidate for an extra acoustic boundary.

There are many times when a boundary is expected but it is difficult to say exactly where it should be placed because of continuous variation. Fig. 18 illustrates an example of this. Looking at the waveform and the spectrogram for part of the word 'ratio,' it is difficult to say where /i/ ends and /o/ begins. Again the boundary indicated (* on line 3 between /i/ and /o/ at time 324) represents an arbitrary choice on the part of the human segmenter. If a machine segmentation program should place that boundary marker at a slightly different position (or time unit), it does not necessarily indicate an error of segmentation. In general, one will observe a few missing phonemic boundaries, some extra boundaries, and some cases in which the location of the boundary is shifted. These do not necessarily represent errors, but rather arise from the nature of the acoustic phenomena associated with phonemic symbols.

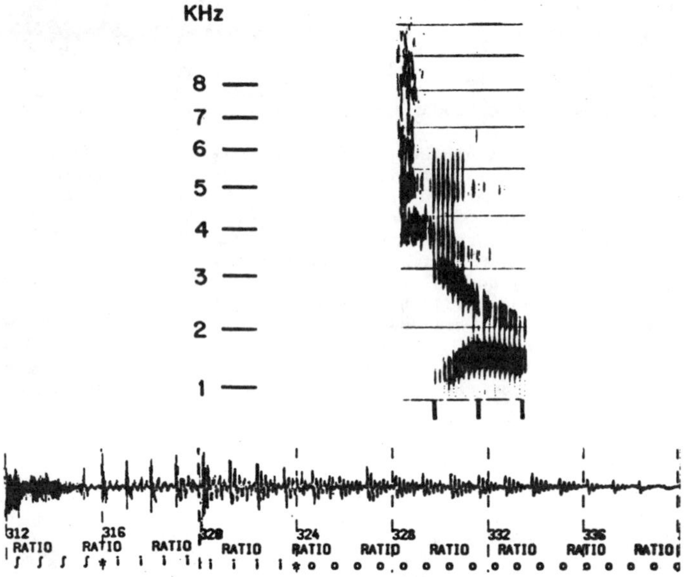

Fig. 18. Example of hard-to-place boundaries. The waveform plot is similar to the one described in Fig. 16. Note that it is difficult to say where /i/ ends and /o/ begins in the word "ratio"—boundary could be placed anywhere between time unit 324 and 330.

Another problem with segmentation is devising an appropriate acoustic similarity measure which indicates a boundary if and only if there is significant acoustic change. It is difficult to express in algorithm from intuitive notions of waveform similarity.

Segmentation techniques: Amplitude (or energy) is the single most important measure in segmentation [119]. It can be used to detect many of the boundaries. Sometimes it leads to extra segments in fricative sounds and missing segments in vowel/liquid sequences. Spectral characteristics of the sounds can be used to find additional boundaries that are missed by the gross segmentation based on amplitude. This additional segmentation may be based on heuristic techniques using speech specific information [31], [32], [136], [159], or algorithmic techniques based on a similarity metric on the parameter space [53]. The latter technique permits experimentation with and evaluation of different parametric representations of speech. The instantaneous frequency representation [11] yields the most accurate boundaries in nonsonorant speech (within 1 or 2 ms).

Fig. 19 shows typical segment boundaries placed by a machine segmenter [53]. The labels on the third and fourth rows under the waveforms in Fig. 19 show the human segmentation and labeling given for the utterance. The vertical lines indicate machine segmentation. Note that there are many more machine segments than there are phonemic boundaries. Examination of the waveform and spectrograms in the figure shows that many of the extra segments are in fact not errors in segmentation but a consequence of intraphone variability and transitions between phones.

Performance: There are many factors which must be considered in the evaluation of segmentation programs. Fig. 20 presents a list of some of the more important ones. Since reported performance evaluations of different programs may deal with only a few of these factors, direct comparisons are difficult to make.

Dixon and Silverman [31] report 6.9 percent missed segments with 10.5 percent extra segments over 6175 segments (8.5 min of speech). Recordings were made under sound booth conditions with high quality equipment. A single speaker was used and speaker specific training was employed. The segmenter also makes use of speech specific knowledge at the phonetic level. Dixon and Silverman report that recent work has further reduced these error rates to 5 percent missed and 6 percent extra.

Baker [11] reports 9.3 percent missed with 17.6 percent extra segments for 216 segments in 5 sentences spoken by 4 male and one female speaker. Recording conditions and equipment varied, and no speaker specific information at the phonetic level was used. The referent segmentation used in Baker's study included all segments indicated at the phonemic level. Hence, omissions of sounds by the speakers may have caused slightly higher missed segment rates than would be shown with a less conservative referent.

Goldberg [53] reports a 3.7 percent missed and 27.6 percent extra segments for 1085 segments in 40 sentences spoken under terminal room conditions (~65 dB (A)) using a close speaking microphone. Training was speaker specific and no speech specific knowledge was employed. The system was tested for several speakers with similar results. Goldberg introduces a model from signal detection theory to quantify the missed versus extra segment tradeoff. By adjusting a few thresholds, error rates (predicted by the model) of 11.7 percent missed and 11.7 percent extra can be achieved.

3) Labeling: Labeling is the process by which each segment is assigned a label. This can be done either heuristically [73], [120], [136], [159], based on speech specific information, or by using a nearest neighbor pattern classification technique [53], or both [31].

As in every other aspect of speech recognition, it is difficult to attempt comparative evaluation of different labeling schemes. There are three factors that affect accuracy and computation time of a labeling procedure: number of labels, number of alternate choices, and the correctness criteria. Weinstein *et al.* [159] report results of labeling accuracy for about 20 or the 35 APEL labels used in the Lincoln system. Dixon and Silverman [31] use 34 different phonemic class labels in their system. Goldberg [53] uses about 70 labels to account for various allophonic variations. The finer the desired phonemic transcription, the lower the accuracy.

The second factor that affects apparent accuracy of labeling is the *branching factor*, i.e., the number of alternate labels assigned to a segment, and is indicative of the degree of indecision of an algorithm. If you permit a large number of alternative choices, the correct label will appear sooner or later. Fig. 21 (from Goldberg [53]) illustrates the effects of the branching factor and the number of labels on accuracy. The figure shows that the labeling accuracy increases sharply when one considers several alternative choices. For example, the correct label appears as one of the choices 70–80 percent of the time if one considers 5 alternative choices (out of a possible 40) whereas it is the top choice only about 35 percent of the time.

The third and perhaps the most elusive factor is the label assigned to a segment by a human subject to be used for the evaluation of the machine labeler. Dixon *et al.* [174], [144] discuss the need for objective phonetic transcription and its importance in obtaining reliable performance statistics. Shockey and Reddy [142] show that subjective judgments of phoneticians seem to agree among themselves only about 51 percent of the time when labeling spontaneous connected speech in unfamiliar languages. Most of this variability is at-

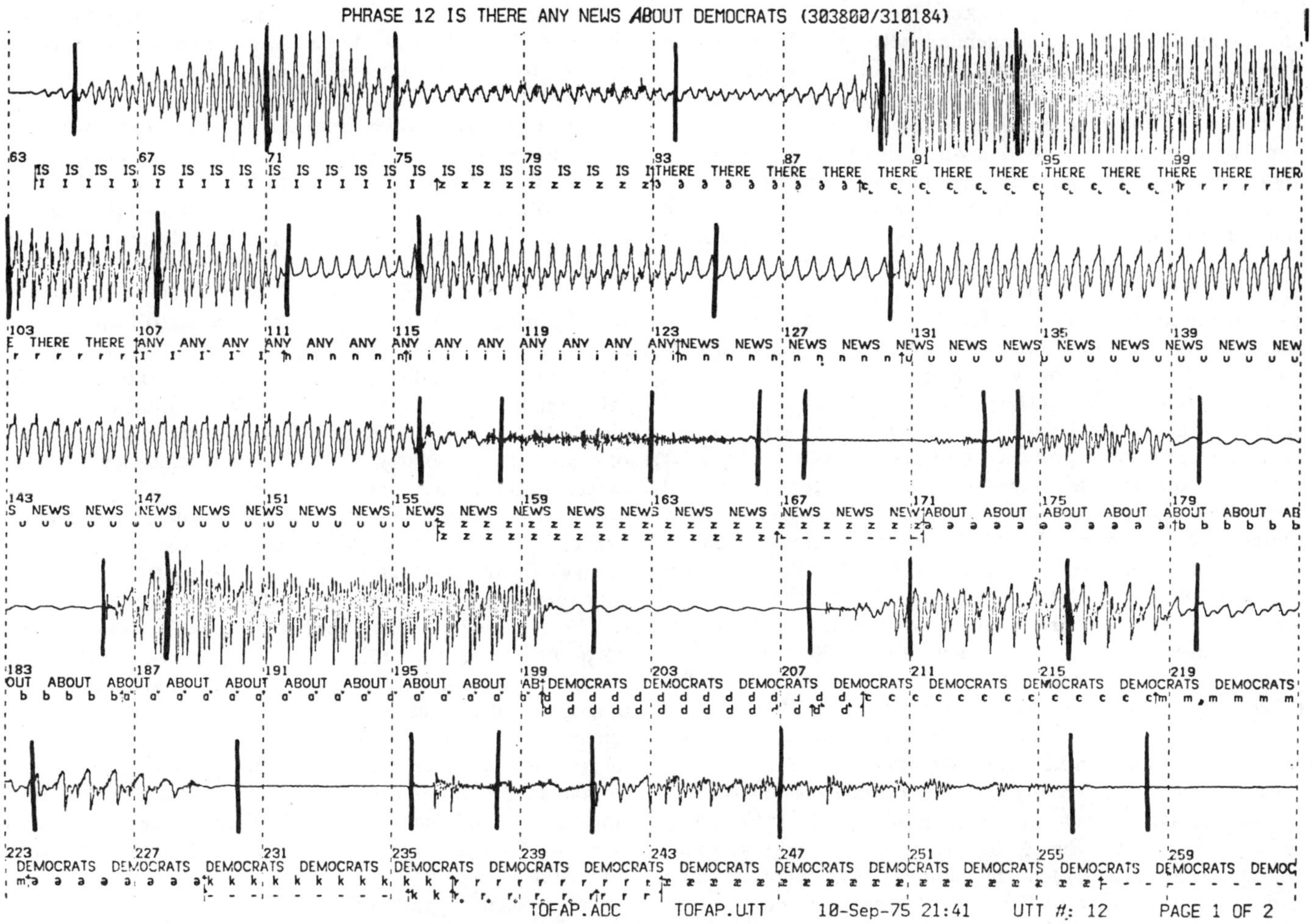

Fig. 19. Typical result of a machine segmentation "Is there any news about Democrats?" The waveform plot is similar to the one described in Fig. 16. Dark vertical lines indicate position of machine boundaries.

1. Recording conditions	Environmental noise Recording equipment (microphone!) Noise and amplitude pre-processing
2. Speaker variations	Number, sex, and age Speaker specific training
3. Use of speech specific knowledge	Phonetic and coarticulation rules
4. Performance measures	Missing vs. extra segment error rates Cost in speed and memory
5. Confidence of results	Quantity of data Nature and quality of "correct" segmentation (referent)

Fig. 20. Typical factors which may affect segmentation performance evaluations.

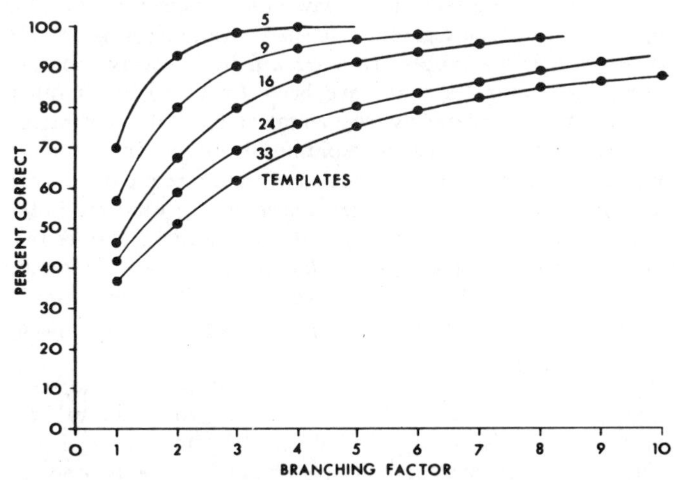

Fig. 21. Accuracy of labeling as a function of branching factor (number of choices per segment) and number of templates. The number below each curve indicates the number of template classes. The 5 classes consist of vowels, liquids, fricatives, nasals, and stops. Larger numbers of classes indicate finer subdivisions. The 33 classes are individual phonetic labels. (For further details, see Goldberg [53].)

tributable to the unfamiliarity with the language and the undistinctive character of many of the sounds in connected speech spoken by a native speaker. Carterette [22] says that phoneticians disagree on phonemic labels up to 20 percent of the time on a familiar language. Shoup [143] says that phoneticians with similar training and background disagree less than 10 percent of the time on phonetic labels while transcribing a familiar language. It is not known at this time how often the higher level linguistic cues are instrumental in determining the phone label and how often all the relevant information is available in the actual speech signal itself. Since we need some form of human segmentation and labeling to compare machine labeling with, it is clear that the accuracies reported are only as good as the manually derived labels we start with. Fig. 19 illustrates some of the problems with perceptual judgments associated with manually derived labels.

Some systems [159], [166] attempt *speaker normalization* based on vocal tract length estimates [155] or a vowel normalization procedure proposed by Gerstman [49]. The latter procedure observes the range of values for formant 1 and formant 2, and uses a linear scaling technique based on these values. Other systems [30], [53] achieve speaker normalization by using speaker-dependent prototype reference patterns associated with each label. Note that speaker normalization may be necessary and useful at many other levels besides the labeling level. Fig. 3 indicates many of the potential sources of improvement. In addition to vocal tract variations, one has to consider dialectal variations, vocabulary and grammatical preferences of the user, and a psychological model of the user predicting what action he might take next.

Performance: There are a few performance evaluations of labeling schemes given in the literature [31], [46], [53], [120], [159]. Of these, the performance results given by Dixon and Silverman [31] are the most comprehensive so far and are representative of the state of accomplishment to date in labeling connected speech. Dixon and Silverman report 61.7 percent accuracy at the phoneme level and 88.6 percent accuracy at the phoneme-class level.

B. Phonological Rules

In the preceding section, we saw how a speech utterance is segmented and each segment is labeled with one (or more) of a set of phonemic symbols. Here we will give some examples of knowledge and rules that have been found to be useful in combining and relabeling segmental units (with essentially phonemic labels). In natural continuous speech, the influence of surrounding vowels and consonants and stress patterns can lead to insertions and deletions of segments or variation in the expected acoustic characteristics of phonemes. The rules that govern this behavior are called *phonological rules.* Papers by Cohen and Mercer [24] and Oshika *et al.* [112] provide many examples of the nature and use of phonological rules in speech recognition systems.

Fig. 12 illustrates the need for rules that combine adjacent segments into larger sized units. In the word "about" the diphthong /aw/ is usually divided into two or more segments. Given the labels (or features) of individual segments, one can define diphthong detection rules which will combine the segments into larger units when an appropriate sequence of labels occurs. Often the onglide and offglide portion of a vowel are indicated as separate segments. In this case these segments are deleted using segment deletion rules. In Fig. 12, the initial part of /aa/ in "all" is an example of an onglide which has no phonemic significance of its own.

Fig. 22 gives some examples of insertion, deletion, and change rules that are used in CSR and SU systems. The comments associated with each rule explain the applicability of that rule. It is estimated that a few hundred such rules may be needed to explain the commonly occurring phonological variations.

Segment insertion rules are sometimes used to propose extra phonemic boundaries where no acoustic boundaries exist. Fig. 16 shows an example of word juncture where the ending sound of one word is the same as (or similar to) the beginning segment of the following word. This usually leads to a single longer duration acoustic segment. If the duration exceeds a threshold for that class of speech sounds, an extra boundary may be inserted (usually at the midpoint) to facilitate word matching.

Fig. 23 (from Oshika *et al.* [112]) illustrates the phonological variation that is pervasive in natural continuous speech. Notice the significant changes in the formant trajectories as one goes from isolated words to connected speech. It is especially noticeable in the realization of the words "you" and "the" in the connected utterance. In both these cases, the expected vowel characteristics have been significantly altered because of the context and stress. Any attempt to find a /u/-like sound in "you" during the word matching would lead to the rejection of that word as a possible choice for that portion of the utterance.

Fig. 23 also illustrates several other phonological phenomena. Note that a frication segment is inserted at the juncture of the words "did you" (pronounced as "did ja") where there was none in the isolated words. The fricative sounds at the juncture of "refresh screen" are merged into a single /sh/ sound, leading to the deletion of a segment. Oshika *et al.* [112] and Cohen and Mercer [24] provide a detailed discussion of the specification and use of phonological rules in speech recognition systems.

C. Prosodics

Prosodic features of speech, i.e., stress, intonation, rhythm, pauses, and tempo, augment the syntactic and semantic structure of language in helping to communicate the intended message. *Stress* patterns of speech help to distinguish between "light housekeeper" and "lighthouse keeper." *Intonation* helps to distinguish between "I will move, on Saturday" and "I will move on, Saturday." *Rhythm* in speech is illustrated by the example "John, who was the best boy in school, got the medal" where one usually observes an increase in the speech rate during the production of the parenthetical relative clause (almost as though each constituent of the sentence has to observe an equal-time rule). *Tempo* of speech and *pauses* provide additional distinctive patterns helpful in the interpretation of spoken language. These and other examples of prosodic knowledge, given in Lea *et al.* [81], illustrate the importance of prosodics in speech understanding research.

Stress and pause structure have been used to determine syntactic boundaries in utterances [81], [82], [111]. Although the boundaries cannot be placed exactly, they do indicate the general area within the utterance where a syntactic boundary may be expected. Rising and falling patterns of pitch contours have been used to determine whether an utterance is a question or an assertion. Research is presently under way [81] to determine other acoustic correlates of contrasting patterns of intonation, rhythm, and tempo in speech.

X → W/Y * Z means X can become W in the context of Y and Z

{ } means logical OR

( ) means enclosed segment is optional

;... indicates a comment

Insertion Rules

0 → (-) / n * s	; a silence segment may be inserted between /n/ and /s/
r → (s) (r) / t * i	; an /r/ occuring in the context of /t/ and /i/ may result in an optional fricative sound /s/
0 → (i) / t * u	; an /i/-like segment may appear in the context of /t/ and /u/

Deletion Rules

b → 0 / m *	; a /b/ might be missing when preceded by an /m/
{p, t, k} → 0 / * {p, t, k}	; an unvoiced stop may be missing in the context of another unvoiced stop

Substitution Rules

z → s / Unvoiced * Unvoiced	; a /z/ becomes devoiced in an unvoiced context
s → z / Voiced * Voiced	; an /s/ becomes voiced in a voiced context
{t, d} → Flap / Vowel $_1$ * Vowel $_3$	; an intervocalic /t/ or /d/ become flap-like

Fig. 22. Some typical phonological rules. (Compiled from Cohen and Mercer [24], Erman [35], and Hall [55].)

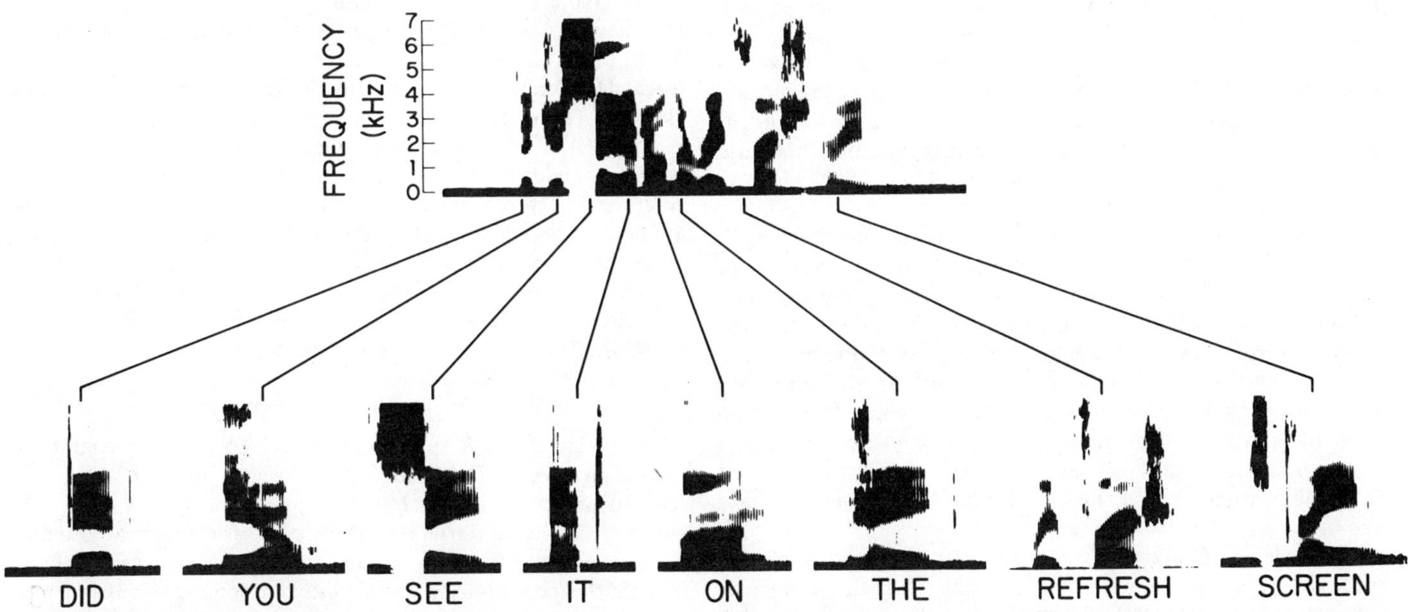

Fig. 23. Spectrograms of the words "did you see it on the refresh screen?" said in isolation, compared with spectrogram of the words in the continuous phrase. Note the significant differences in acoustic characteristics of the words "you" and "the" in the connected speech compared to the corresponding isolated words. (From Oshika *et al.* [112].)

Future Directions: It has been said that "prosodics play the role in spoken language that 'space' plays in written language." If this is so, we have been slow in making effective use of this source of knowledge. To be sure, amplitude (which is a measure of stress) has been used in segmentation and stress detection for a long time, but we are only just beginning to explore other uses of stress and intonation-related phenomena. Forgie [45] suggests that much of the nonlinguistic phenomena such as hesitation and stutter may be detectable from prosodic patterns of speech. This would make it easier to detect and ignore some of the speech-like noises and other nongrammaticality in spoken utterances. These considerations make prosodics an important area of study in speech recognition research.

D. Word Hypothesis

As the vocabularies get larger, it becomes expensive to match all the possible words that may appear in a given part of the utterance. In large vocabulary systems, the phonemic string is used to generate hypotheses for plausible words in a given location which are then verified by various higher level processes and/or more expensive low-level verifiers. There are two techniques presently being used in SU systems [100], [130], [146].

Rovner *et al.* [130] use partial sequences of phonemic descriptions and the expected phonemic patterns of the vocabulary to retrieve words from the lexicon that match the acoustic characteristics of the signal to some specified degree. The class of words scanned may be delimited by explicit enumeration, class membership, or phonemic length. Appropriate word boundary rules are used whenever an adjacent word is known.

Smith's word hypothesizer [146] detects syllables and uses them to retrieve and verify words that have matching syllable types. The syllable type is hypothesized using a Markov probability model to relate a sequence of phones to a sequence of states defining a syllable type. For each stressed syllable type, the program looks up all the words containing the same syllable type using an inverted lexicon, prunes away multisyllable words that do not match with adjacent syllable hypotheses, and rates and hypothesizes the remaining words. Smith reports that the program locates the correct word within the first two choices about 59 percent of the time given a 275-word vocabulary.

E. Word Verification

Matching and verification of hypothesized words, given the acoustic evidence from an unknown utterance, is basic to almost all speech recognition systems. In connected speech this usually implies matching the expected phonemic realizations of a given word with an unknown phonemic string possibly containing insertion, deletion, and substitution errors. Here we will illustrate the techniques employed by looking at the structure of three word verification techniques: heuristic matching [35], [55], stochastic matching [71], [150], [172], and analysis-by-synthesis [75], [12].

Heuristic Matching: Many of the connected speech recognition systems use this type of matching. Hall [55] of Lincoln Laboratories gives one of the clearest descriptions of the basic techniques involved. Matching process must account for three types of errors: some of the symbols in the phonemic string may be spurious (*insertion error*); some of the expected phonemes may be missing as a result of incorrect segmentation, or a result of being unsaid by the speaker (*deletion error*); or phonological context may have caused the segment to be identified as a different phoneme type (*substitution error*).

The basic matching techniques involves aligning the phonemic spelling of the word to be matched with the segmental (phone-like) labels while allowing for the possibility that some of the above types of error may have occurred. Alignment is usually based on the notion of "anchor points" in which stressed vowels and sibilants which are much less likely to be missed are aligned first, followed by the alignment of the remaining vowels and consonants. Once the alignment is completed, the degree of similarity between the word and the unknown phonemic string is defined as a weighted sum of the individual phoneme versus segment label similarity values. These similarity measures are usually available as a confusion matrix generated from a set of manually labeled training data.

Stochastic Matching: This type of matching is used in the IBM system [72], [150], [172] and in the Dragon system [7]. Given a finite-state representation of alternative pronunciations of a word with associated transition probabilities, a dynamic programming technique is used to perform matching left-to-right in a best-first manner. The best phonemic match and the corresponding likelihood are determined by matching all the possible phonemic variations of the word with the unknown segmental phoneme string. This technique, being more mathematically tractable, will probably become the standard technique in word matching. However, careful training procedures are needed to establish the transition probabilities in the graph representation of alternative pronunciations.

Analysis-by-Synthesis: Klatt [75] proposes the use of analysis-by-synthesis as the principal technique for word verification. He feels that phonological phenomena such as vowel reduction, flapping, palatalization, etc., are basically generative in nature and cannot be easily captured in terms of analytic rules. Klatt and Stevens' study of spectrogram reading [76] demonstrates the difficulty. In that study only 77 percent of the segments were correctly (or partially correctly) labeled during the analysis phase, while 97 percent of the words were correctly identified during verification.

Some form of analysis-by-synthesis procedure seems essential to transform an abstract representation of a word into an acoustic representation suitable for matching with the acoustic parametrization of the unknown utterance. Klatt gives the structure and description of an analysis-by-synthesis system which can be used as a word verification component. (see also Section IX of Jelinek [72].)

Future Directions: Whether matching must occur at the signal level, as in the case of analysis-by-synthesis, to achieve accurate recognition will depend on the success achieved by the heuristic and stochastic matching techniques. One would also have to investigate the store versus compute tradeoff in determining whether one can store a set of synthesized (or learned) reference patterns as in the case of word recognition systems (with the necessary juncture rules of course) or whether it is necessary to synthesize them each time. This would depend on the degree of variability and the number of reference patterns needed to cover the range of variability expected for each word. A mixed strategy in which those words that exhibit significant variability (such as function words) are verified by analysis-by-synthesis technique while all others are verified by one of the other techniques might be desirable.

V. Task-Dependent Knowledge

Specifying the task to be performed by a speech recognition system involves defining the *vocabulary* to be used, the grammatical structure of legal or acceptable sentences (*syntax*), the meaning and interrelationships of words within a sentence (*semantics*), and the representation and use of context depending on the conversation (*pragmatics*). Some recognition systems choose to ignore one or more of these KS's, partly because the notions of semantics and pragmatics are somewhat ill-defined and ill-understood at present, and partly because not all the KS's are necessary if the task is sufficiently restricted. The tutorial-review paper by Woods [167] presents a clear discussion of the role of syntax and semantics in speech. In this section, we will illustrate how these task-dependent KS's help to restrict and reduce the combinatorial explosion resulting from the error and uncertainty of the choices at the lower levels.

A major component of an SUS is to understand and respond to a message. There is a large body of literature on language understanding that is relevant. The books edited by Minsky [102], Simon [145], Rustin [133], Colby and Shank [138],

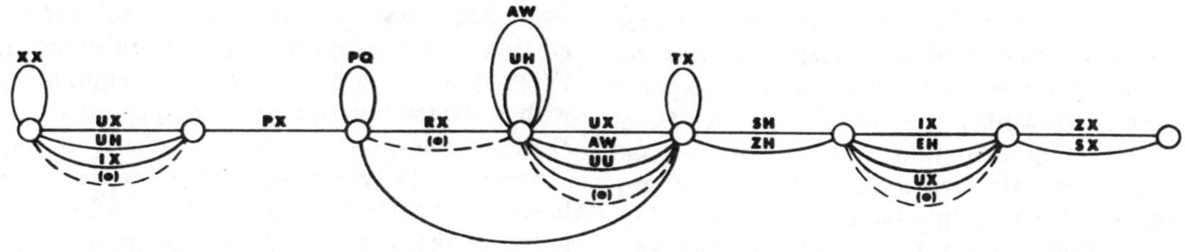

Fig. 24. Phonemic subgraph of the word "approaches" showing possible speaker variation. Branches corresponding to machine error phonemena and indications of second-order constraint have been omitted for clarity of representation. (From Paul *et al.* [114].)

Task	Size of Vocabulary	Language Entropy	Language EQV. Branching factor	Confusability Entropy	Confusability EQV. Branching factor
Digits	10	3.32	10	0.24	1.18
Alphabet	26	4.70	26	2.43	5.39
Alpha-digit	36	5.17	36	2.29	4.89
Chess	31	2.87	7.30	1.37	3.32
Lincoln	237	2.84	7.18		
Extended	411	3.36	12.61		
IBM	250	2.872	7.32		
Prog. language (no syntax)	37	5.21	37.00	1.92	3.78

Fig. 25. Confusability of some common vocabularies. (From Goodman [54].) The first two columns show the entropy per word (i.e., average number of bits it takes to represent a word in the language) and the equivalent branching factor. The last two columns show the confusability of the same vocabulary in terms of entropy (of a noisy channel) and branching factor. Note that the confusability of the digits vocabulary is low while the confusability of the alphabet ("aye," "bee," . . .) is much higher. Note that the average branching factors of the languages used by the systems shown in Figs. 9 and 11 are all less than 10 except for the extended Lincoln task.

Shank [139], and Bobrow and Collins [19] contain a number of the important papers in the natural language understanding area. In this section, we will restrict ourselves to those aspects of the task-dependent knowledge that are directly relevant to the problem of recognition of the utterance.

A. Vocabulary

The primary source of restriction in most speech recognition systems is the vocabulary. Performance of a system is not only affected by the size and dialectal variations of the vocabulary but also by the confusability among the words. The main design choice associated with this level is the representation of alternative pronunciations of the words. If the task permits, one might also wish to select words so as to minimize the confusability among them.

Representation of Phonemic Variation: Most of us know that words are pronounced differently in different contexts. The phrases "David and Robert" and "Fish'n chips" illustrate two different pronunciations of "and." The word "mostly" is sometimes pronounced without the /t/, as "mosly." What is not commonly realized is that much of this variability is rule governed and can be predicted by a set of phonological rules [24], [112]. Starting with a phonemic base form, one can create all possible alternative pronunciations. Early attempts represented each phonemic variation as a separate entry in the lexicon, but most present systems use a more compact network representation. Fig. 24 [114] illustrates the representation of many alternate pronunciations of "approaches" in the network form. Stress and syllable boundary information is also usually entered in the lexicon.

The lexical entries are sometimes preanalyzed to determine all the words that have the same syllable type and represented as an inverted dictionary where one can look up all the words that have the same syllable. This type of representation is useful in generating word hypotheses based on the phones and syllables observed in the symbolic representation of the unknown utterance.

Ambiguity: We saw in Section II how a system which gives 99 percent accuracy on a 200-word multisyllable vocabulary can drop to 89 percent accuracy on a 36-word alpha-digit list. This is because the letters of the alphabet (when pronounced as "aye," "bee," "cee," ···) are highly confusable. It is thus important to know not only the size of a vocabulary but also a measure of its confusability. Goodman [54] has studied the confusability of several vocabularies using both theoretical and experimental methods. Fig. 25 summarizes some of his results for several task domains. The first two columns show the entropy per word (i.e., average number of bits required to represent a word in the language) and equivalent branching factor. Thus for the digit sequence recognition task, where any of the 10 digits can follow at every choice point, the average branching factor is 10. However, the confusability of the digits vocabulary is not very high. Using the notion of entropy of a noisy channel, Goodman shows that, from a confusability point of view, the average branching factor for the digit task is only 1.18. For the spelling task (i.e., alphabet recognition task), the confusability is much higher, with a branching factor of 5.39.

Effect of Vocabulary Size on Accuracy: There have been no systematic studies in this area. The Lincoln system performance drops from 49 percent sentence accuracy to 28 percent when the vocabulary increases from 237 words to 411 words. (Note that the complexity of the language, as measured by the average branching factor, has also increased. Fig. 25 shows that the branching factor increased from 7.32 to 12.61—almost proportional to the increase in vocabulary in this case.) The Hearsay-I system shows a similar drop in performance in going from 30 to 194 words. What seems to be important is not so much the size but rather the confusability. In vocabularies that have not been carefully preselected, i.e., they might be assumed to have about the same percentage of words that are confusable, doubling the size of vocabulary seems to double the error rate. This linear increase is contrary to the earlier expectations that, as the vocabularies get larger, confusability among words (and hence the error rate) would only grow less than linearly. However, this linear increase should not be of concern if CSR systems can approach the accuracies being achieved by word recognition systems, i.e., greater than 99 percent accuracy at the word level.

Future Directions: Assuming that current trends in research and technology will continue, there is no reason, in principle at least, why we should not look toward *unlimited vocabulary recognition* systems. However, this will require significant advances in dictionary representation, word hypothesis, and word verification. There are several large phonemic dictionaries of English available in computer readable form [57]. Words that do not exist can be added using grapheme-to-phoneme translation techniques (see the paper by Jon Allen in this issue). Special techniques have to be devised to produce compact and easily retrievable representations of a dictionary containing on the order of a million entries.

Unstressed function words will always be a problem, whether we have a 1000-word system or an unlimited vocabulary system. To establish the feasibility of unlimited vocabulary recognition, we need to consider only the problems of locating and recognizing the rest of the words which can be expected to have at least one stressed syllable. Given the present and projected performances of word hypothesis procedures, fewer than one thousand of the million words are likely to be hypothesized around each stressed syllable. This candidate list can be further pruned to 10 or 20 words using stochastic word verification procedures discussed in Section IV. At this point the remaining words will have fine differences, such as between the words *sit* and *slit*. These will require analysis-by-synthesis, matching with prestored reference patterns for syllables, or some such technique. Any further ambiguities at this stage and prediction and detection of unstressed function words will require the active mediation of higher level processes, such as pragmatics.

B. Syntax

The grammatical structure of sentences can be viewed as principally a mechanism for reducing search by restricting the number of acceptable alternatives. Given a vocabulary of size N, if one permits any word to follow any other word such as "sleep roses dangerously young colorless," the number of possible sentences would be of the order N^L for utterances of less than L words in length. Syntactic structure imposes an ordering and mutually interdependent relationships among words such that only a subset of the N^L is in fact possible.

For example, the IBM New Raleigh task [10] containing 250 words permits only 1.4×10^7 sentences of the possible 250^8 ($\sim 10^{19}$), thereby reducing the search space by a factor of 10^{12}. A more meaningful measure for CSR systems is the average branching factor of the grammar, i.e., the average number of alternative word hypotheses possible at each point in the grammar. For the IBM New Raleigh task, this is about 8 out of the possible 250 words (with a maximum branching factor of about 24). Baker and Bahl [10] measure the complexity of a grammar in terms of the entropy of a word in the language. For the IBM task, the entropy was 2.87. (Note 2^{entropy} is also a measure of the average branching factor of the grammar.) One must also consider the confusability among the alternative words at each choice point. Fig. 25 (from [54]) shows the entropy and the average branching factor that can be expected as a result of the confusability of the vocabulary. Note that the average branching factors for several of the systems discussed in Section II are all less than 10.

Woods [165] proposes four categories to measure the constraint provided by a given grammar. The first two categories are finite-state grammars, the first one having a small branching factor (usually less than 30 at each choice point) and the second one having large branching factors (greater than 400 words at some choice points). Category III systems are artificial languages characterized by context-free grammars permitting recursion, and having large branching factors. Category IV systems are approximations to natural English grammars with considerably larger search space than even category III. Most systems built to data tend to be of the category I type.

Robinson [129] argues that the representation of grammar based on written language is likely to be of limited use. She proposes that the discovery of rules governing spoken language behavior and the development of performance grammars should be based on systematic study of conversational speech. She demonstrates some of the strategies and constraints operating in performance (and the rule-governed regularities they produce) by analysis of several task-oriented dialogs.

Representation: The most commonly used representation for grammars is some form of network representation. Woods [167] uses augmented transition network (ATN) grammars. An ATN consists of a finite-state transition diagram with embedded recursion added, and a set of registers which can hold arbitrary pieces of tree structure and can be modified depending on the actions (programs) associated with the arcs of the grammar. The ATN formalism is known to have the linguistic adequacy of a transformational grammar while providing more of the efficiency needed in parsing algorithms. The papers by Bates [15], [16], and Paxton [115] contain examples of the representation and use of transition network grammars.

Baker [7] and Jelinek, Bahl, and Mercer [71] view grammar as a probabilistic function of a Markov process and represents it as a finite-state network with transition probabilities including the self-transition probability (providing for recursion). Fig. 26 gives an illustration of Baker's representation of the chess grammar (transition probabilities not shown). This representation permits the Dragon system to determine the optimal match for the utterance using the dynamic programming algorithm.

C. Semantics

The term *semantics* means different things to different people. Here we use the term to denote the rules and relationships associated with the meaning of symbols. By this we mean the rules of language which tell us that the sequence of words "colorless yellow ideas" is not meaningful. It is not always possible to detect semantic inconsistency by looking at adjacent word pairs as in the previous example. The statements "Give me about a yard" and "Tell me about Tom" are acceptable, but "Give me about Tom" is not. Given a set of possibly disjoint words, semantic information must determine whether they are compatible and meaningful. The role of semantics in the recognition aspects of an SUS is analogous to that of syntax, i.e., it provides a mechanism for reducing search by restricting the number of acceptable alternatives. The papers by Woods [167], Nash-Webber [103], and Hendrix [60] illustrate the uses of semantic knowledge in speech understanding systems.

The principal technique used to represent this KS is a *semantic net*. Fig. 27 gives the structure of a semantic net fragment used by Hendrix [61]. A semantic net is used to represent objects, relationships among objects, events, rules, and situations. Such a net can be used to predict or verify possible word hypotheses in an unknown utterance. Given the concepts of *content* and *contains* and the meaning of the word "in," one may accept the statement "The bolts are in the box" and reject "The box is in the bolts" using such a semantic net.

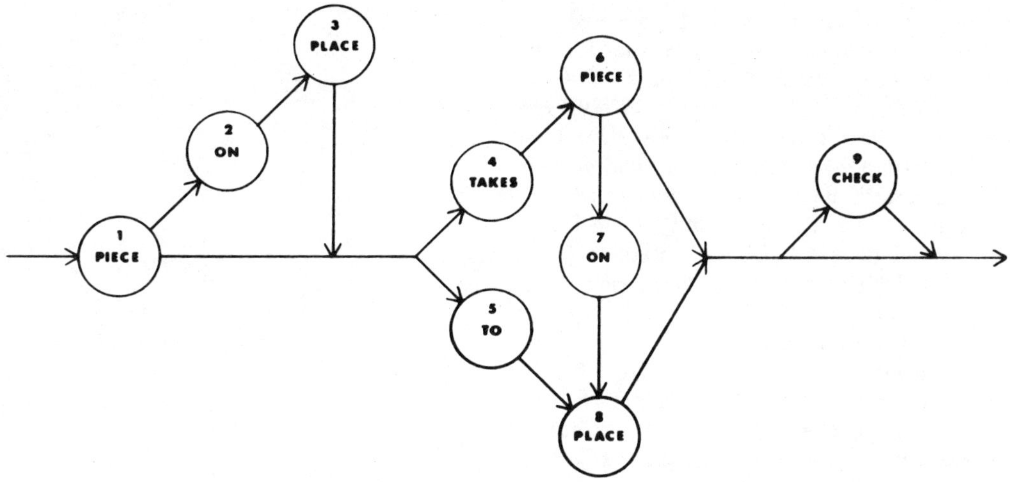

Fig. 26. Fragment of network grammar for Chess. (From Baker [7].)

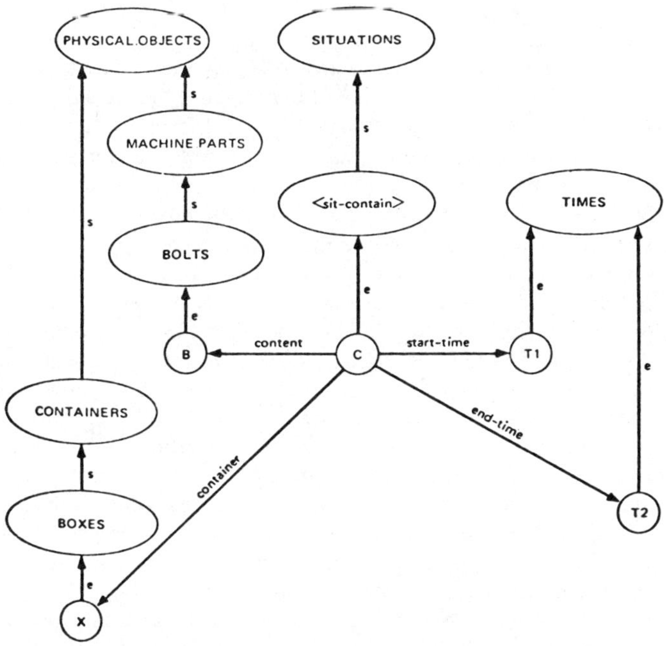

Fig. 27. Part of a typical semantic net. (From Hendrix [61].)

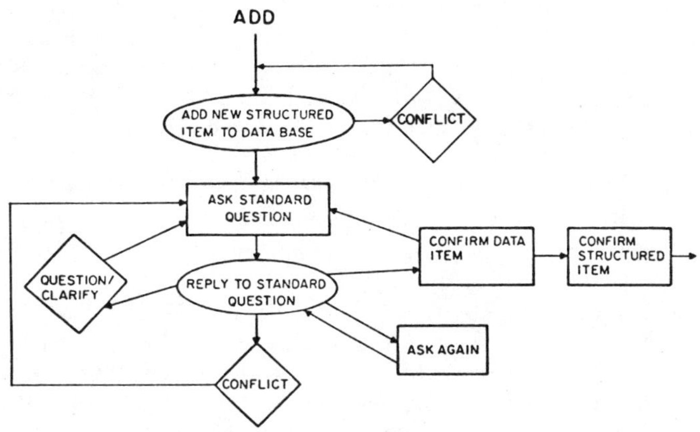

Fig. 28. User-oriented discourse model. (From Woods *et al.* [169].)

The chess task used by Hearsay-I [123] illustrates how knowledge about the partially recognized utterance can be used to constrain the hypotheses to a small set of words. For example, given that a word such as "captures" or "takes" appears in the partially recognized utterance, this information can be used to further restrict the search to the capture moves in a particular board position. This restricted set of moves is used to give high semantic preference to the key content words that may occur in the capture moves.

D. Pragmatics and Discourse Analysis

The term *pragmatics* usually leads to even more confusion and misunderstanding than *semantics*. Here we use it to mean conversation-dependent contextual information, i.e., task-related information accumulated so far through man–machine dialog. At a given point in the conversation, the user may use an elided (or non-well-formed) sentence or may use pronominal reference to a previous subject. For example, consider the sequence of questions, "How much does Tom weigh? How about John? What is his height?" It is obvious that in the second question one is asking for John's weight even though it does not appear explicitly. In the third question, does the term "his" refer to Tom or John? It is ambiguous, but the most plausible interpretation is that it refers to John, the subject of the immediately preceding utterance. Interpretation and validation of such questions based on pragmatics of the situation require the representation of dialog so that missing constituents can be inferred. Deutsch [29] uses a tree structure representation scheme for handling simple forms of ellipsis and anaphora.

The other main role of pragmatics is to predict the user behavior (user model) based on the dialog. Fig. 28 is a transition network diagram indicating the common modes of interaction found in travel budget management dialog [167]. It illustrates various possible modes of interaction of the user such as: user adds a new item to the data base, system points out contradiction, user asks a question, system answers, user makes a change, and so on. If the pragmatic knowledge can accurately ascertain the state of the user, it can be used to achieve syntactic subselection, i.e., only a small set of all the possible grammatical constructs would be likely in that situation. We do not yet have any system which has made effective use of user models, but several are attempting to do so.

VI. System Organization

System organization is a catch-all term that describes the art of transforming ideas into working programs. Given that many of the problems of connected speech recognition and understanding are not well defined, the issue of system organization assumes added importance. We know that all the available sources of knowledge must communicate and cooperate in the presence of error and uncertainty. We do not know how to do it effectively or efficiently. The system must work smoothly with high-data-rate real-time input and provide facilities for speaker- and task-dependent knowledge acquisition. The tutorial-review paper by Reddy and Erman [122] and the papers by Newell [107], Baker [9], Barnett [14], Erman [35], Fennell [43], Jelinek *et al.* [71], Jelinek [72], and Lesser [85] provide more detailed discussions of system organization issues. In this section, we will briefly review the problems of system organization.

Many of the principal issues of system organization were raised and discussed in Section II while studying the structure of various types of speech recognition systems and examining what makes such systems difficult to realize. In particular, we have seen how various systems were organized to permit several diverse sources of knowledge to communicate and cooperate, how search strategies were devised to deal with error and ambiguity, and how knowledge is represented and used. In this section, we will discuss some of the related issues of system organization which were not covered earlier.

A. Control Strategies in the Presence of Ambiguity and Error

There are several sources of error and ambiguity in speech recognition. In spontaneous (nonmaximally differentiated) connected speech many expected features (and phones) may be missing. Variability due to noise and speaker leads to errors. Incomplete and/or inaccurate KS's at each level introduce more errors. In simple hierarchical systems, these errors propagate through various levels, compounding the error rate. Thus every system organization must cater to the inevitability of errors and handle them in a graceful manner.

Given the errorful nature of speech processing, one has to consider several alternative hypotheses (or interpretations) since the hypothesis with the highest rating may not be the correct one. In Fig. 12, we see how the problem of error is transformed into a problem of uncertainty by considering several plausible alternative hypotheses. At that point the problem becomes one of search through this multilevel network to discover the best path that is consistent with all the KS's. There are several search techniques developed in the field of artificial intelligence that become potentially useful. We will consider two of these techniques that have been used in speech recognition.

The commonly used strategy is *best-first search*. This technique is used in Hearsay-I, Lincoln, and in a modified form in the IBM system (see Section II-B and Section V of Jelinek [72]). This technique is best explained by an example [122]. In Fig. 29, we see a tree of possible alternatives that had arisen in the analysis of the utterance "Are your headaches severe?" We find that there are nine alternatives for the first word: "have," "are," "where," and six others. The ratings indicating the likelihood, which can be derived either mathematically [71] or heuristically [55], are given under each word. Given that the word "have" has the highest rating (470), we begin to explore that path. "Have" is followed by a single alternative "you." The combined rating for the sequence "have you" is given under "you." The rating of 455 makes the sequence "have you" better than the other alternative paths. Proceeding along this path, we have three alternative words that can follow "have you." The sequence "have you had" receives the

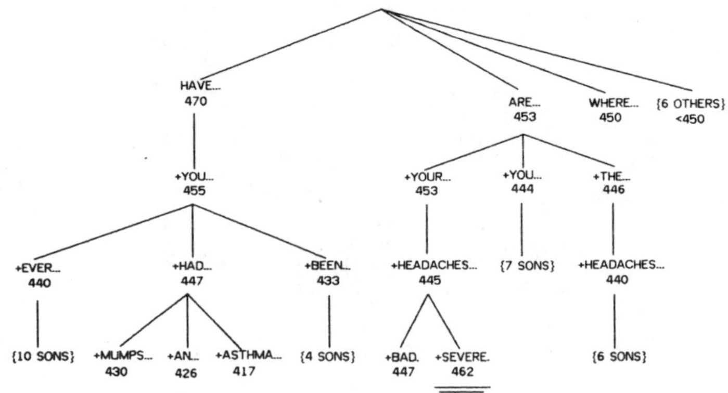

Fig. 29. Example of best-first search. (From Reddy and Erman [122].)

highest rating of 447 but is no longer the highest rated path. Search is suspended along this path and we begin exploring the alternatives that can follow "are." Of the three alternatives, the path "are your" has the highest rating of 453. Proceeding along this path, we get a rating of 445 for the sequence "are your headaches." Since this is lower than 447, we now suspend this search and resume search along the path "have you had." The highest rated sequence "have you had mumps" is lower than 445, so we resume the path of "are your headaches" again. Now we find that "are your headaches severe" has the highest rating of 462 and, being the end of a sentence, cannot proceed any further. We accept this as the most probable sentence and return it as the answer to the search.

Another technique that has been used in speech recognition is to *search all possible paths in parallel* but constrain the search only through those sequences which are valid paths in a specific network [7], [8]. This network is constructed to be an integrated representation of all the available KS's. Exponential growth is constrained through the use of a Markov assumption which limits the relevant context and collapses many alternative sequences to a single state. With this technique, search time is linear in the number of states in the network and in the length of the utterance.

There are several other search techniques, such as prosodically guided search [81], anchor points, focus of attention [86], a few alternative paths in parallel [90], and so on. The relative advantages and disadvantages of these techniques are not clearly understood.

B. Real-Time Input

Unlike most other forms of computer input, speech is critically *data directed*. That is, initiation and termination of the input depend on the incoming data rather than on program control. Thus a system must be prepared to continuously monitor the speech input device (analog-to-digital converter, filter bank, or what have you) to determine if the signal is speech or noise.

The *high data rates* associated with speech input (100 to 300 kbit/s) imply that a system cannot afford to have resident in primary memory more than a few seconds of speech data (usually no more than a single utterance). Thus the data must be immediately processed, placed in secondary storage, or played back. Keeping two high-data-rate devices serviced is not a major problem if the system is dedicated. However, if the system has a general-purpose operating system, special care must be taken to see that the device service overhead is low in order to avoid loss of data. This often becomes difficult to achieve with two active devices because of the costs associated with process synchronization, buffer service routines, and signal detection [35]. System primitives available within the system for performing these operations tend to be too slow and need to be reprogrammed.

C. Knowledge Acquisition

Every speech recognition system uses thresholds, templates, probabilities, and so on, based on measurements obtained on training data. In the case of word recognition systems, the problem is solved neatly since reference patterns capture noise, microphone, speaker, and phonological variability in a single step. In CSR systems, however, one has to deal with most of these sources of variability individually.

The first question that arises is what parameters will be seen when a sound is spoken. This depends not only on the parametric representation used but also on the speaker, the microphone used, and the noise in the environment. Systems using formant representation attempt to normalize speaker dependencies by estimating the shifts in formant trajectories, the length of the vocal tract of the speaker, etc. Systems that use prototype template matching require spectral templates (or some other parametric representation) for each sound to be recognized for each speaker. These in turn require a set of carefully manually segmented and labeled sentences for each speaker. Machine-aided segmentation and labeling has been attempted [6], but this requires a reasonable set of starting templates (the chicken and the egg problem).

The second question that arises is what phonemes are observed when a word (or a sequence of words) is spoken. Phonological rules predict some phenomena but they do not predict (at least not as yet) that a stop in some context can be three-quarters voiced and one-quarter unvoiced. Some systems attempt to accumulate such acoustic–phonetic phenomena from real data. Again, one needs manually labeled data or machine-labeled data for training of the system. Baker and Bahl [10] present the results of an interesting training method for automatically learning transition probabilities described in [71] and [72].

Many of the heuristic techniques used by various systems require substantial amounts of labeled data. This in turn necessitates the design of several interactive programs with graphical output for collection and validation of rules. Labeled data are also essential for systematic performance analysis of segmentation, labeling, syllable detection, word hypothesis, and word verification procedures.

VII. Conclusions

We have attempted to review the recent developments in speech recognition. The focus has been to review research progress, to indicate the areas of difficulty, why they are difficult, and how they are being solved. The paper is not intended as a survey of all known results in speech recognition and represents only one point of view of important issues, problems, and solutions.

The past few years have seen several conceptual and scientific advances in the field. We have already discussed many of these aspects earlier in the text. We will summarize them here.

1) For the first time we have available extensive analysis of connected speech. We know connected speech recognition is not impossible.
2) The role and use of knowledge are better understood. Almost all systems use knowledge to generate hypotheses and/or verify them.
3) Error and ambiguity can be handled within the framework of search.
4) Stochastic representations and dynamic programming provide a simple and effective solution to the matching problem.
5) Network representation of knowledge is a compact and computationally efficient way of generating and verifying hypotheses.
6) For the first time we have some techniques for the codification and use of phonological rules in speech recognition systems.
7) For the first time we have effective tools for the study of prosodics and the application of prosodic information to speech recognition.
8) There has been comparatively significant progress in the past five years in the areas of parameter extraction, formant tracking, feature detection, segmentation, and labeling.
9) Linear predictive coding and Itakura's distance metric represent effective digital techniques for analysis and matching at the signal level.

In spite of the significant progress, there are still several unsolved problem areas: signal processing associated with noise, telephone and speaker normalization, real-time live input providing graceful interaction with the user, careful and systematic performance analysis of the existing systems, and labeled data bases. In addition, continued progress is necessary in almost all the knowledge domains to establish optimal representation and use of different sources of knowledge.

We have indicated that it may be possible to build a $1000 isolated word recognition system, a $20 000 connected speech system, an unlimited vocabulary system, and so on. All of these seem feasible and can probably be realized within the next 10 years if the present momentum in speech recognition research can be continued. However, they may never be realized without significant and directed research effort. We are still far from being able to handle relatively unrestricted dialogs from a large population of speakers in uncontrolled environments. Many more years of intensive research seems necessary to achieve such a goal.

Acknowledgment

The author wishes to thank his colleagues L. Erman and A. Newell for their many valuable comments on various drafts of this paper, and also J. K. Baker, J. M. Baker, R. Dixon, J. Forgie, H. Goldberg, J. Shoup-Hummel, W. Lea, F. Jelinek, T. Martin, N. Neuburg, L. Rabiner, A. Rosenberg, H. Silverman, G. White, and J. Wolf for their comments on various parts of this paper.

References

[1] B. S. Atal and M. R. Schroeder, "Predictive coding of speech signals," in *Proc. 1967 Conf. Speech Communication and Processing*, pp. 360–361, Nov. 1967.
[2] ——, "Predictive coding of speech signals," in *Proc. Int. Congr. Acoustics*, C-5-4, Tokyo, Japan, Aug. 1968.
[3] ——, "Adaptive predicting coding of speech signals," *Bell Syst. Tech. J.*, vol. 49, no. 6, pp. 1973–1986, 1970.
[4] B. S. Atal and S. L. Hanauer, "Speech analysis and synthesis by linear prediction of the speech wave," *J. Acoust. Soc. Amer.*, vol. 50, no. 2, pp. 637–655, 1971.
[5] B. S. Atal, "Linear prediction of speech—Recent advances with applications to speech analysis," in [121, pp. 221–230].

[6] J. K. Baker, "Machine-aided labeling of connected speech," in *Working Papers in Speech Recognition II*, Tech. Rep., Comput. Sci. Dep., Carnegie-Mellon Univ., Pittsburgh, PA, 1973.
[7] —, "The DRAGON system—An overview," *IEEE Trans. Acoust., Speech, Signal Processing*, vol. ASSP-23, pp. 24-29, Feb. 1975.
[8] —, "Stochastic modeling as a means of automatic speech recognition," Ph.D. dissertation, Computer Sci. Dep., Carnegie-Mellon Univ., Pittsburgh, PA, 1975.
[9] —, "Stochastic modeling for automatic speech understanding," in [121, pp. 500-520].
[10] J. K. Baker and L. Bahl, "Some experiments in automatic recognition of continuous speech," in *Proc. 11th Annu. IEEE Computer Society Conf.*, pp. 326-329, 1975.
[11] J. M. Baker, "A new time-domain analysis of human speech and other complex waveforms," Ph.D. dissertations, Carnegie-Mellon Univ., Pittsburgh, PA, 1975.
[12] R. Bakis, "Continuous speech recognition via centisecond acoustic states," *J. Acoustic Society Amer.*, vol. 58 (to be presented at the 91st meeting of ASA).
[13] J. A. Barnett, "A vocal data management system," *IEEE Trans. Audio Electroacoust.*, vol. AU-21, pp. 185-188, June 1973.
[14] —, "Module linkage and communication in large systems," in [121, pp. 500-520].
[15] M. Bates, "The use of syntax in a speech understanding system," *IEEE Trans. Acoust., Speech, Signal Processing*, vol. ASSP-23, pp. 112-117, Feb. 1975.
[16] —, "Syntactic analysis in a speech understanding system," Ph.D. dissertation, Harvard Univ., Cambridge, MA, 1975. Also Rep. 3116, Bolt Beranek and Newman, Inc., Cambridge, MA, 1975.
[17] B. Beek, E. P. Neuburg, D. C. Hodge, R. S. Vonusa, and R. A. Curtis, "An assessment of the technology of automatic speech recognition for military application," NATO Rep. To be published by Rome Air Development Center, Rome, NY, 1976.
[18] D. G. Bobrow and D. H. Klatt, "A limited speech recognition system," in *Proc. AFIPS Fall Joint Computer Conf.*, vol. 33. Washington, DC: Thompson, 1968, pp. 305-318.
[19] D. G. Bobrow and A. Collins, *Representation and Understanding*. New York: Academic Press, 1975.
[20] R. Breaux and I. Goldstein, "Development of machine speech understanding for automated instructional systems," in *Proc. 8th NTECL/Industry Conf.*, Naval Training Equipment Center, Orlando, FL, Nov. 1975.
[21] D. J. Broad and J. E. Shoup, "Concepts for acoustic phonetic recognition," in [121, pp. 243-274].
[22] E. C. Carterette and M. H. Jones, *Informal Speech*. Berkeley, CA: Univ. of California Press, p. 16 ff, 1974.
[23] A. Chapanis, "Interactive human communication," *Sci. Amer.*, vol. 232, no. 3, pp. 36-42, 1975.
[24] P. S. Cohen and R. L. Mercer, "The phonological component of an automatic speech recognition system," in [121, pp. 275-320].
[25] E. E. David, Jr., and P. B. Denes, *Human Communication: A Unified View*. New York: McGraw-Hill, 1972.
[26] R. De Mori, S. Rivoira, and A. Serra, "A speech understanding system with learning capability," in *Proc. 4th Int. Joint Conf. Artificial Intelligence*, Tbilisi, USSR, 1975.
[27] M. Derkach, "Heuristic models for automatic recognition of spoken words," Quart. Progr. Status Rep., Speech Transmission Labs., KTH, Stockholm, Sweden, pp. 39-49, Jan-Mar. 1970.
[28] M. Derkach, R. Gumetsky, B. Gura, and L. Mishin, "Automatic recognition of simplified sentences constructed of the limited lexicon," in [41].
[29] B. G. Deutsch, "Discourse analysis and pragmatics," in [156, ch. VI].
[30] N. R. Dixon and H. F. Silverman, "A description of a parametrically controlled modular structure for speech processing," *IEEE Trans. Acoust., Speech, Signal Processing*, vol. ASSP-23, pp. 87-91, Feb. 1975.
[31] N. R. Dixon and H. F. Silverman, "A general language-operated decision implementation system (GLODIS): Its application to continuous speech segmentation," (to appear in *IEEE Trans. Acoust. Speech, Signal Processing*, vol. ASSP-24, 1976.
[32] —, "Some encouraging results for general purpose continuous speech recognition," in *Proc. 1975 Int. Conf. Cybernetics and Society*, San Francisco, CA, pp. 293-295, 1975.
[33] P. H. Dorn, "Whither data entry," *Datamation*, vol. 27, pp. 49-51, Mar. 1973.
[34] L. D. Erman, Ed., *Contributed Papers of IEEE Symp. Speech Recognition*, Carnegie-Mellon Univ., Pittsburgh, PA (IEEE Cat. 74CHO878-9 AE), 1974.
[35] —, "An environment and system for machine understanding of connected speech," Ph.D. dissertation, Comput. Sci. Dep., Stanford Univ., Tech. Rep., Comput. Sci. Dep., Carnegie-Mellon Univ., Pittsburgh, PA, 1974.
[36] —, "Overview of the Hearsay speech understanding research," *Comput. Sci. Res. Rev.*, Comput. Sci. Dep., Carnegie-Mellon Univ., Pittsburgh, PA, 1975.
[37] L. D. Erman and V. R. Lesser, "A multi-level organization for problem solving using many, diverse cooperating sources of knowledge," in *Proc. 4th Int. Joint Conf. Artificial Intelligence*, Tbilisi, USSR, 1975.
[38] L. D. Erman, and D. R. Reddy, "Implications of telephone input for automatic speech recognition," in *Proc. 7th Int. Congr. Acoustics*, vol. 3, Budapest, Hungary, 1971, pp. 85-88.
[39] C. G. M. Fant, "Automatic recognition and speech research," Quart. Progr. Status Rep., Speech Transmission Labs., KTH, Stockholm, Sweden, pp. 16-31, Jan-Mar. 1970.
[40] —, *Speech Sounds and Features*. Cambridge, MA: M.I.T. Press, 1973.
[41] —, Ed., *Proc. Speech Communications Seminar*, Stockholm, Sweden, 1974. To be published by Almquist and Wiksell Int. (Stockholm) and Wiley (New York), 1975.
[42] C. G. M. Fant and B. Lindblom, "Studies of minimal speech sound units," Quart. Progr. Status Rep., Speech Transmission Labs., KTH, Stockholm, Sweden, pp. 1-11, Apr.-June 1961.
[43] R. D. Fennell, "Multiprocess software architecture for AI problem solving," Ph.D. dissertation, Comput. Sci. Dep., Carnegie-Mellon Univ., Pittsburgh, PA, 1975.
[44] J. L. Flanagan, *Speech Analysis, Synthesis and Perception*. New York: Springer, 1972.
[45] J. W. Forgie, personal communication, 1975.
[46] J. W. Forgie and C. D. Forgie, "Results obtained from a vowel recognition computer program," *J. Acoust. Soc. Amer.*, vol. 31, pp. 1480-1489, 1959.
[47] J. W. Forgie *et al.*, "Speech understanding systems—semiannual Tech. Summary Rep.-May 1974," M.I.T. Lincoln Lab., Lexington, MA, 1974.
[48] J. W. Forgie, D. E. Hall, and R. W. Wiesen, "An overview of the Lincoln Laboratory speech recognition system," *J. Acoust. Soc. Amer.*, vol. 56, S27 (A), 1974.
[49] L. J. Gerstman, "Classification of self-normalized vowels, *IEEE Trans. Audio Electroacoust.*, vol. AU-16, pp. 78-80, Mar. 1968.
[50] R. A. Gillmann, "A fast frequency domain pitch algorithm," System Development Corp., Santa Monica, CA, unpublished rep., 1975.
[51] B. Gold, "Word recognition computer program," M.I.T. Lincoln Lab., Cambridge, MA, Tech. Rep. 456, 1966.
[52] B. Gold and L. Rabiner, "Parallel processing techniques for estimating pitch periods of speech in time domain," *J. Acoust. Soc. Amer.*, vol. 46, no. 2, pp. 422-449, 1969.
[53] H. G. Goldberg, "Segmentation and labeling of speech: A comparative performance evaluation," Ph.D. dissertation, Computer Science Department, Carnegie-Mellon University, Pittsburgh, PA, 1975.
[54] R. G. Goodman, "Language design for man-machine communication," Ph.D. dissertation (in preperation), Comput. Sci. Dep., Stanford Univ., Stanford, CA, 1976.
[55] D. E. Hall, "The linguistic module, Final report on speech understanding systems," M.I.T. Lincoln Lab., Lexington, MA, unpublished rep., 1974.
[56] D. E. Hall and J. W. Forgie, "Parsing and word matching in the Lincoln Laboratory speech recognition system," *J. Acoust. Soc. Amer.*, vol. 56, S27 (A), 1974.
[57] E. Hayden and J. Shoup, "SCRL computerized pronouncing dictionary," Speech Communication Res. Lab., Santa Barbara, CA, unpublished, 1975.
[58] F. Hayes-Roth and D. J. Mostow, "An automatically compilable recognition network for structured patterns," in *Proc. 4th Int. Joint Conf. Artificial Intelligence*, Tbilsi, USSR, 1975.
[59] F. Hayes-Roth and V. Lesser, "Focus of attention in a distributed logic speech understanding system," Comput. Sci. Dep., Carnegie-Mellon Univ., Pittsburgh, PA, Tech. Rep., 1976.
[60] G. G. Hendrix, "Expanding the utility of semantic networks through partitioning," in *Proc. 4th Int. Joint Conf. Artificial Intelligence*, Tbilisi, USSR, 1975.
[61] —, "Semantics," in [156, ch. V].
[62] C. Hewitt, "Description and theoretical analysis, (using schemata) of Planner: A language for proving theorems and manipulation models in a robot," M.I.T. Project MAC, Cambridge, MA, AI Memo. 251, 1972.
[63] D. R. Hill, "Man-machine interaction using speech," in *Advances in Computers*, F. L. Alt, M. Rubinoff, and M. C. Yovits, Eds., vol. II. New York: Academic Press, 1971, pp. 165-230.
[64] A. D. C. Holden, E. Strasbourger, and L. Price, "A computer programming system using continuous speech input," in [34].
[65] J. F. Hemdal and G. W. Hughes, "A feature based computer recognition program for the modeling of vowel perception," in [158, pp. 440-453].
[66] S. R. Hyde, "Automatic speech recognition: Literature, survey, and discussion," in [25].
[67] S. Itahashi, S. Makino, and K. Kido, "Discrete-word recognition utilizing a word dictionary and phonological rules," *IEEE Trans.*

Audio Electroacoust., vol. AU-21, pp. 239–249, June 1973.

[68] F. Itakura and S. Saito, "Analysis synthesis telephony based on the maximum likelihood method," in *Proc. 6th Int. Congr. Acoustics*, 1968, Paper C-5-5.

[69] —, "A statistical method for estimation of speech spectral density and formant frequencies," *Electron. Commun. Japan*, vol. 53-A, no. 1, pp. 36–43, 1970.

[70] F. Itakura, "Minimum prediction residual principle applied to speech recognition," *IEEE Trans. Acoust., Speech, Signal Processing*,vol. ASSP-23, pp. 67–72, Feb. 1975.

[71] F. Jelinek, L. R. Bahl, and R. L. Mercer, "Design of a linguistic statistical decoder for the recognition of continuous speech," *IEEE Trans. Inform. Theory*, vol. IT-21, pp. 250–256, May 1975.

[72] F. Jelinek, "Continuous speech recognition by statistical methods," this issue, pp. 532–556.

[73] I. Kameny, "Comparison of the formant spaces of retroflexed and nonretroflexed vowels," *IEEE Trans. Acoust., Speech, Signal Processing*, vol. ASSP-23, pp. 38–49, Feb. 1975.

[74] D. H. Klatt, "On the design of a speech understanding system," in [41].

[75] —, "Word verification in a speech understanding system," in [121, pp. 321–341].

[76] D. H. Klatt and K. N. Stevens, "On the automatic recognition of continuous speech: Implications from a spectrogram-reading experiment," *IEEE Trans. Audio Electroacoust.*, vol. AU-21, pp. 210–217, June 1973.

[77] J. S. Kriz, "A 16-bit A-D-A conversion system for high-fidelity audio research," *IEEE Trans. Acoust. Speech, Signal Processing*, vol. ASSP-23, pp. 146–149, 1975.

[78] W. A. Lea, "Establishing the value of voice communication with computers," *IEEE Trans. Audio Electroacoust.*, vol. AU-16, pp. 184–197, June 1968.

[79] —, "Intonational cues to the constituent structure and phonemics of spoken English," Ph.D. dissertation, School of Elec. Eng., Purdue Univ., Lafayette, IN, 1972.

[80] —, "Prosodic aids to speech recognition: IV—A general strategy for prosodically-guided speech understanding," Sperry Univac Rep. PX10791, 1974.

[81] W. A. Lea, M. F. Medress, and T. E. Skinner, "A prosodically guided speech understanding system," *IEEE Trans. Acoust. Speech, Signal Processing*, vol. ASSP-23, pp. 30–38, Feb. 1975.

[82] W. A. Lea and D. R. Kloker, "Prosodic aids to speech recognition: VI—Timing cues to linguistic structure and improved computer program," Univac Rep. Px11239, 1975.

[83] I. Lehiste, *Readings in Acoustic Phonetics.* Cambridge, MA: M.I.T. Press, 1967.

[84] —, *Suprasegmentals.* Cambridge, MA: M.I.T. Press, 1970.

[85] V. R. Lesser, "Parallel processing in speech understanding: A survey of design problems," in [121, pp. 481–499].

[86] V. R. Lesser, R. D. Fennell, L. D. Erman, and D. R. Reddy, "Organization of the Hearsay-II speech understanding system," *IEEE Trans. Acoust. Speech, Signal Processing*, vol. ASSP-23, pp. 11–23, 1975.

[87] J. C. R. Licklinder, "Man computer symbiosis," in *Perspectives on the Computer Revolution*, Z. W. Pylyshyn, Ed. Englewood Cliffs, NJ: Prentice-Hall, 1970, pp. 306–318. (First published in *IRE Trans. Hum. Factors Electron.*, vol. HFE-1, 1960).

[88] N. Lindgren, "Machine recognition of human language," *IEEE Spectrum*, vol. 2, Mar., Apr., May, 1965.

[89] —, "Speech—Man's natural communication," *IEEE Spectrum*, vol. 4, pp. 75–86, June 1967.

[90] B. Lowerre, "A comparative performance analysis of speech understanding systems," Ph.D. dissertation (in preparation), Comput. Sci. Dep., Carnegie-Mellon Univ., Pittsburgh, PA, 1976.

[91] J. Makhoul, "Spectral analysis of speech by linear prediction," *IEEE Trans. Audio Electroacoust.*, vol. AU-21, pp. 140–148, June 1973.

[92] —, "Linear prediction: A tutorial review," *Proc. IEEE* (*Special Issue on Digital Signal Processing*), vol. 63, pp. 561–580, Apr. 1975.

[93] —, "Linear prediction in automatic speech recognition," in [121, pp. 183–220].

[94] J. D. Markel, "Digital inverse filtering—A new tool for formant trajectory estimation," *IEEE Trans. Audio Electroacoust.*, vol. AU-20, pp. 129–137, June 1972.

[95] T. B. Martin, "Acoustic recognition of a limited vocabulary in continuous speech," Ph.D. dissertation, Univ. of Pennsylvania, Philadelphia, 1970.

[96] —, "Applications of limited vocabulary recognition systems," in [121, pp. 55–71].

[97] S. S. McCandless, "An algorithm for automatic formant extraction using linear prediction spectra," *IEEE Trans. Acoust., Speech, Signal Processing*, vol. ASSP-22, pp. 135–141, Apr. 1974.

[98] M. Medress, "Computer recognition of single-syllable English words," Ph.D. dissertation, M.I.T., Cambridge, MA, 1969.

[99] P. Mermelstein, "A phonetic-context controlled strategy for segmentation and phonetic labeling of speech," *IEEE Trans. Acoust., Speech, Signal Processing*, vol. ASSP-23, pp. 79–82, Feb. 1975.

[100] —, "Automatic segmentation of speech into syllable units," *J. Acoust. Soc. Amer.*, vol. 58, pp. 880–883, 1975.

[101] G. A. Miller and S. Isard, "Some perceptual consequences of linguistic rules," *J. Verbal Learning Behavior*, vol. 2, pp. 217–228, 1963.

[102] M. L. Minsky, Ed., *Semantic Information Processing.* Cambridge, MA: M.I.T. Press, 1970.

[103] B. Nash-Webber, "Semantic support for a speech understanding system," *IEEE Trans. Acoust., Speech, Signal Processing*, vol. ASSP-23, pp. 124–128, Feb. 1975.

[104] R. B. Neely and D. R. Reddy, "Speech recognition in the presence of noise," in *Proc. 7th Int. Congr. Acoustics*, vol. 3, Budapest, 1971, pp. 177–180.

[105] E. P. Neuburg, "Philosophies of speech recognition," in [121, pp. 83–95].

[106] A. Newell, "Production systems: Models of control structures," in *Visual Information Processing*, W. C. Chase, Ed. New York: Academic Press, 1973, pp. 463–526.

[107] —, "A tutorial on speech understanding systems," in [121, pp. 3–54].

[108] A. Newell, J. Barnett, J. Forgie, C. Green, D. Klatt, J. C. R. Licklinder, J. Munson, R. Reddy, and W. Woods, *Speech Understanding Systems: Final Report of a Study Group*, 1971. (Reprinted by North-Holland/American Elsevier, Amsterdam, Netherlands, 1973).

[109] A. Newell, F. S. Cooper, J. W. Forgie, C. C. Green, D. H. Klatt, M. F. Medress, E. P. Neuburg, M. H. O'Malley, D. R. Reddy, B. Ritea, J. E. Shoup, D. E. Walker, and W. A. Woods, "Considerations for a follow-on ARPA research program for speech understanding systems," available from Comput. Sci. Dep., Carnegie-Mellon Univ., Pittsburgh, PA, 1975.

[110] R. B. Ochsman and A. Chapanis, "The effects of 10 communication modes on the behavior of teams during co-operative problem-solving," *Int. J. Man-Machine Studies*, vol. 6, pp. 579–619, 1974.

[111] M. M. O'Malley, D. Kloker, and B. Dara-Abrams, "Recovering parentheses from spoken algebraic expressions," *IEEE Trans. Audio Electroacoust.*, vol. AU-21, pp. 217–220, June 1973.

[112] B. T. Oshika, V. W. Zue, R. V. Weeks, H. Nue, and J. Aurbach, "The role of phonological rules in speech understanding research," *IEEE Trans. Acoust., Speech, Signal Processing*, vol. ASSP-23, pp. 104–112, Feb. 1975.

[113] K. W. Otten, "Approaches to the machine recognition of conversational speech," in [63, pp. 127–163].

[114] J. E. Paul, A. S. Rabinowitz, J. P. Riganati, V. A. Vitols, and M. L. Griffith, "Automatic recognition of continuous speech: Further development of a hierarchical strategy," Rome Air Development Center, Rome, NY, RADC-TR-73-319, 1973.

[115] W. H. Paxton, "The parsing system," in [156, ch. III].

[116] J. R. Pierce, "Whither speech recognition?" *J. Acoust. Soc. Amer.*, vol. 46, pp. 1049–1051, 1969.

[117] L. C. Pols, "Real-time recognition of spoken words," *IEEE Trans. Comput.*, vol. C-20, pp. 972–978, Sept. 1971.

[118] L. R. Rabiner and M. R. Sambur, "An algorithm for determining the endpoints of isolated utterances," *Bell Syst. Tech. J.*, vol. 54, no. 2, pp. 297–315, 1975.

[119] D. R. Reddy, "Segmentation of speech sounds," *J. Acoust. Soc. Amer.*, vol. 40, pp. 307–312, 1966.

[120] —, "Computer recognition of connected speech," *J. Acoust. Soc. Amer.*, vol. 42, pp. 329–347, 1967.

[121] —, Ed., *Speech Recognition: Invited Papers of the IEEE Symp.* New York: Academic Press, 1975.

[122] D. R. Reddy and L. D. Erman, "Tutorial on system organization for speech understanding," in [121, pp. 457–479].

[123] D. R. Reddy, L. D. Erman, and R. B. Neely, "A model and a system for machine recognition of speech," *IEEE Trans. Audio Electroacoust.*, vol. AU-21, pp. 229–238, June 1973.

[124] D. R. Reddy and A. Newell, "Knowledge and its representation in a speech understanding system," in *Knowledge and Cognition*, L. W. Gregg, Ed. Washington, DC: L. Earlbaum Assoc., 1974, pp. 253–285.

[125] D. R. Reddy and P. J. Vicens, "A procedure for segmentation of connected speech," *J. Audio Eng. Soc.*, vol. 16, pp. 404–412, 1968.

[126] C. W. Reedyk, "Noise-cancelling electret microphone for light-weight head telephone sets," *J. Acoust. Soc. Amer.*, vol. 53, pp. 1609–1615, 1973.

[127] B. Ritea, "Automatic speech understanding systems," in *Proc. 11th Annu. IEEE Computer Society Conf.*, Washington, DC, Sept. 1975.

[128] J. J. Robinson, "The language definition," in [156, ch. IV].

[129] —, "Performance grammars," in [121, pp. 401–427].

[130] P. J. Rovner, J. Makhoul, J. Wolf, and J. Colarusso, "Where the

words are: Lexical retrieval in a speech understanding system," in [34, pp. 160-164].

[131] P. J. Rovner, B. Nash-Webber, and W. Woods, "Control concepts in a speech understanding system," *IEEE Trans. Acoust., Speech, Signal, Processing*, vol. ASSP-23, pp. 136-140, Feb. 1975.

[132] J. F. Rulifson *et al.*, "QA4: A procedural calculus for intuitive reasoning," AI Center, Stanford Res. Inst., Menlo Park, CA, Tech. Note 73, 1973.

[133] R. Rustin, Ed., *Natural Language Processing*. New York: Algorithmics Press, 1973.

[134] T. Sakai and S. Nakagawa, "Continuous speech understanding system LITHAN," Dept. Inform. Sci., Kyoto Univ., Kyoto, Japan, Tech. Rep., 1975.

[135] M. R. Sambur and L. R. Rabiner, "A speaker-independent digit-recognition system," *Bell Syst. Tech. J.*, vol. 54, pp. 81-102, 1975.

[136] R. Schwartz and J. Makhoul, "Where the phonemes are: Dealing with Ambiguity in acoustic-phonetic recognition," *IEEE Trans. Acoust., Speech, Signal, Processing*, vol. ASSP-23, pp. 50-53, Feb. 1975.

[137] R. N. Schafer and L. R. Rabiner, "Parametric representations of speech," in [121, pp. 99-150].

[138] R. C. Shank and K. M. Colby, *Computer Models of Thought and Language*. San Francisco, CA: Freeman, 1973.

[139] R. C. Shank, Ed., *Conceptual Information Processing*. Amsterdam, Netherlands: North-Holland, 1975.

[140] D. E. Shanon, "Prediction and entropy of printed English," *Bell Syst. Tech. J.*, vol. 30, pp. 50-64, 1951.

[141] J. N. Shearme and P. F. Leach, "Some experiments with a simple word recognition system," *IEEE Trans. Audio Electroacoust.*, vol. AU-16, pp. 256-261, June 1968.

[142] L. Shockey and R. Reddy, "Quantitative analysis of speech perception," in [41].

[143] J. Shoup, personal communication, 1975.

[144] H. F. Silverman and N. R. Dixon, "An objective parallel evaluator of segmentation/classification performance for multiple systems," *IEEE Trans. Acoust., Speech, Signal, Processing*, vol. ASSP-23, pp. 92-99, Feb. 1975.

[145] H. A. Simon and L. Siklossy, Eds., *Representation and Meaning*. Englewood Cliffs, NJ: Prentice-Hall, 1972.

[146] A. R. Smith, "A word hypothesizer for the Hearsay II speech system," in *Proc. IEEE Int. Conf. Acoustics, Speech, and Signal Processing*, Philadelphia, PA, Apr. 1976.

[147] M. M. Sondhi, "New methods of pitch extraction," *IEEE Trans. Audio Electroacoust.*, vol. AU-16, pp. 262-266, 1968.

[148] C. C. Tappert, M. R. Dixon, A. S. Rabinowitz, and W. D. Chapman, "Automatic recognition of continuous speech utilizing dynamic segmentation, dual classification, sequential decoding and error recovery," Rome Air Development Center, Griffiss AFB, Rome, NY, Tech. Rep. TR-71-146, 1971.

[149] C. C. Tappert, N. R. Dixon, and A. S. Rabinowitz, "Application of sequential decoding for converting phonetic to graphic representation in automatic recognition of continuous speech (ARCS)," *IEEE Trans. Audio Electroacoust.*, vol. AU-21, pp. 225-228, June 1973.

[150] C. C. Tappert, "Experiments with a tree-search method for converting noisy phonetic representation into standard orthography," *IEEE Trans. Acoust., Speech, Signal, Processing*, vol. ASSP-23, pp. 129-135, Feb. 1975.

[151] V. M. Velichiko and N. G. Zagoruiko, "Automatic recognition of 200 words," *Int. J. Man-Machine Studies*, vol. 2, pp. 223-234, 1970.

[152] P. Vicens, "Aspects of speech recognition by computer," Ph.D. dissertation, Comput. Sci. Dep., Stanford Univ., Stanford, CA, 1969.

[153] G. Ya Vysotsky, B. N. Rudnyy, V. N. Trunin-Donskoy, and G. I. Tsemel, "Experiment in voice control of computers," *Izv. Akad. Nauk SSSR, Tekn. Kibern.*, no. 2, pp. 134-143, 1970.

[154] T. G. Von Keller, "On-line recognition system for spoken digits," *J. Acoust. Soc. Amer.*, vol. 49, pp. 1288-1296, 1971.

[155] H. Wakita, "An approach to vowel normalization," Speech Communication Res. Labs., Santa Barbara, CA, Tech. Rep., 1975.

[156] D. E. Walker, W. H. Paxton, J. J. Robinson, G. G. Hendrix, B. G. Deutsch, and A. E. Robinson, "Speech understanding research annual report," Artificial Intelligence Center, Stanford Res. Inst., Menlo Park, CA, Project 3804, 1975.

[157] D. E. Walker, "The SRI speech understanding system," *IEEE Trans. Acoust., Speech, Signal Processing*, vol. ASSP-23, pp. 397-416, Oct. 1975.

[158] Walthen-Dunn, Ed., *Models for the Perception of Speech and Visual Form*. Cambridge, MA: M.I.T. Press, 1967.

[159] C. J. Weinstein, S. S. McCandless, L. F. Mondshein, and V. W. Zue, "A system for acoustic-phonetic analysis of continuous speech," *IEEE Trans. Acoust., Speech, Signal Processing*, vol. ASSP-23, pp. 54-67, Feb. 1975.

[160] C. Wherry, "VRAS: Voice recognition and synthesis," Naval Air Development Center, 1975.

[161] G. M. White and R. B. Neely, "Speech recognition experiments with linear prediction, bandpass filtering, and dynamic programming," in *Proc. 2nd USA-Japan Computer Conf.*, Tokyo Japan, Aug. 1975. Also to appear in *IEEE Trans. Acoust., Speech, Signal Processing*.

[162] R. A. Wiesen and J. W. Forgie, "An evaluation of the Lincoln Laboratory speech recognition system," *J. Acoust. Soc. Amer.*, vol. 56, S27 (A), 1974.

[163] J. J. Wolf, "Speech recognition and understanding," in *Pattern Recognition*, K. S. Fu, Ed. New York: Springer, 1975.

[164] W. A. Woods, "Transition network grammars for natural language analysis," *Commun. Ass. Comput. Mach.*, vol. 13, no. 10, pp. 591-602, 1970.

[165] —, "Proposal for research on English language and speech understanding," Bolt Beranek and Newman, Inc., 1975.

[166] —, "Motivation and overview of SPEECHLIS: An experimental prototype for speech understanding research," *IEEE Trans. Acoust., Speech, Signal Processing*, vol. ASSP-23, pp. 2-10, 1975.

[167] —, "Syntax, semantics and speech," in [121, pp. 345-400].

[168] W. A. Woods and J. Makhoul, "Mechanical inference problems in continuous speech understanding," *Artificial Intelligence*, vol. 5, pp. 73-91, 1974.

[169] W. A. Woods, M. A. Bates, B. C. Bruce, J. J. Colarusso, C. C. Cook, L. Gould, J. I. Makhoul, B. L. Nash-Webber, R. M. Schwartz, and J. J. Wolf, "Speech understanding research at BBN, Final report on natural communication with computers," vol. I, Bolt Beranek and Newman, Inc., Rep. 2976, 1974.

[170] B. Yegnanarayana, "Effect of noise and distortion in speech on parametric extraction," in *Proc. IEEE Int. Conf. Acoustics, Speech, and Signal Processing*, Philadelphia, PA, Apr. 1976.

[171] N. G. Zagoruiko, "Automatic recognition of speech," Quart. Progr. Status Rep., Speech Transmission Labs., KTH, Stockholm, Sweden, pp. 39-49, Jan-Mar. 1970.

[172] L. R. Bahl and F. Jelinek, "Decoding for channels with insertions, deletions, and substitutions with applications to speech recognition," *IEEE Trans. Inform. Theory*, vol. IT-21, pp. 404-411, 1975.

[173] L. R. Bahl, J. K. Baker, P. S. Cohen, N. R. Dixon, F. Jelinek, R. L. Mercer, and H. F. Silverman, "Experiments in continuous speech recognition," to appear in *Proc. IEEE Int. Conf. Acoustics, Speech, and Signal Processing*, Philadelphia, PA, Apr. 1976.

[174] N. R. Dixon and C. C. Tappert, "Toward objective phonetic transcription—An on-line interactive technique for machine-processed speech data," *IEEE Trans. Man-Mach. Syst.*, vol. MMS-11, pp. 202-210, 1970.

[175] H. F. Silverman and N. R. Dixon, "A parametrically-controlled spectral analysis system for speech," *IEEE Trans. Acoust., Speech, Signal Processing*, vol. ASSP-22, pp. 362-381, 1974.

Speech Recognition: A Tutorial Overview

George M. White
Xerox Palo Alto Research Center

Introduction

Research toward mechanical recognition of speech is laying the foundation for significant advances in pattern recognition and artificial intelligence. This paper explains the nature of some of these advances and provides an introduction to the state of the art of automatic speech recognition.

It is only a matter of time until automatic speech recognition (ASR) becomes a major force in man-machine communication because of the inherent advantages of speech communication and our increasing need to communicate with machines. The inherent advantages of speech arise from its universality, convenience, and speed. Even with the best communication aids of high technology, speech remains unrivaled as the fastest and most convenient way for human beings to communicate interactively. In experiments involving speech and other communication modalities (e.g., typing), information is exchanged almost twice as fast with speech as it is without speech.[1] Furthermore, the hands and eyes are free and the speaker has mobility, which other communication modes do not offer.

Progress toward economically viable automatic speech recognition systems has been slow but steady over the past 25 years, with a noticeable upturn in the rate of progress during the past five years. Isolated word recognition systems for small vocabularies with known speakers have become commercially successful during the past five years due largely to the lowered cost of adequate hardware. But while machines that recognize limited forms of *continuous* speech are beginning to appear as laboratory curiosities, it will probably be many years before machines recognize normal conversational speech. The reason is that the upgrading of existing recognition systems to encompass continuous speech requires more than reasonable advances in hardware technology. However it is only a question of time. Meanwhile this research is stimulating conceptual advances in pattern recognition and artificial intelligence, which in turn are drawing from the work in cognitive psychology, linguistics, psychobiology, and other fields far removed from acoustic analysis of speech.

In considering the varied aspects of speech recognition, whether by man or machine, we will begin with artificial intelligence and contextual information processing. We will move to a discussion of the sequence of events involved in recognizing an utterance beginning with the ear and ending with the brain. We will then move to recent advances in ASR, to theoretical problems, and finally to potential solutions.

There are several recent publications that complement the material covered here: Reddy[2] gives an excellent overview of the entire speech recognition field, covering isolated word recognition, continuous speech recognition, and speech understanding by computer. Martin[3] gives a good detailed description of isolated word recognition systems. Schroeder[4] describes human signal processing in "Models of Hearing." Makhoul[5] presents an excellent paper summarizing linear predictive coding (LPC), one of the most important innovations in speech research in recent years as explained in a later section.

Overview

The Power of Contextual Information. When we examine how people recognize normal speech, we discover that a high degree of intelligence is involved because of the need to use contextual information. It is a widely held view that speech contains many acoustically ambiguous sounds which make the use of contextual information absolutely essential. In attempting to implement contextual information processing algorithms for machine recognition of speech, we have come to the exciting realization that contextual information can do much more than resolve acoustic ambiguity: it can control the inner workings of pattern classifiers in such a way as to make them orders of magnitude more efficient. This can be achieved by dynamically allocating computational resources to the appropriate tasks. In other words, knowledge of global or historical events can provide dynamic control of local analysis in such a way that the amount of analysis required to recognize a pattern is dramatically reduced.

Reprinted from *Computer*, vol. 9, pp. 40–53, May 1976.

This notion is profoundly important to the development of pattern recognition and machine intelligence in general. The basic idea is to apply the "hypothesize and test" paradigm and use contextual information to supply the hypotheses. Techniques will be discussed in this paper for using contextual information to provide dynamic control of classifier operation for speech recognition and understanding. These techniques include use of nonacoustic sources of knowledge (e.g., semantic, syntactic, and pragmatic sources) and the use of speech sound subunits (features). Advancement of our ability to use contextual information is but one example of the fruitful merger of ideas from speech research and artificial intelligence. Let us look at some more examples.

Fundamental Problems of Machine Intelligence. Speech recognition research is concerned with at least four fundamental problems of machine intelligence. The first fundamental problem is how to "represent knowledge" to facilitate computational efficiencies. Knowledge can be represented as rules, procedures, templates, networks, etc., each of which has storage or computational advantages. The problem is how to combine storage and computation considerations to optimize system performance for a specific set of computational resource limitations. The second problem is how to represent and utilize contextual information, or in other words how to recognize patterns in a local analysis frame with the aid of properties found globally. The third problem is how to make a classification decision using advice from different knowledge sources (e.g., semantic, syntactic, pragmatic, prosodic, and acoustic sources). And the fourth problem is how to allow information from the execution of a procedure for one knowledge source to have an influence on the execution of procedures for other knowledge sources so that useless computation can be avoided. These are central problems in the field of artificial intelligence, and progress on them advances machine perception in general.[6] This increases the value of speech recognition research beyond the purely pragmatic goals of producing a usable tool in man-machine communication. These issues are explained in detail in a later section.

Intelligence and Speech Recognition Ability. Psychoacoustic experiments in which speech sounds are selectively masked with noise reveal that people have an amazing ability to restore missing phonemes, syllables, and words from continuous speech.[7,8] It is possible to arrange experiments so that various nonacoustic clues are present or absent in speech. The results show that listeners use semantic, syntactic, prosodic, pragmatic, as well as acoustic knowledge to restore acoustically ambiguous sounds and thereby to understand acoustically corrupted speech. (Semantic knowledge is general knowledge about the domain of discourse. Syntactic knowledge is a set of rules specifying legal sequences of words or similar units. Prosodic knowledge imputes meaning to the variation in pitch or stress in phrases. Pragmatic knowledge is a record of changes in the listener's world model occurring in the course of a conversation. For the purposes of this paper, we shall refer to all information arising from nonacoustic sources as "semiotic" information.) Normal speech has many naturally occurring corruptions that seem to require nonacoustic information. A puzzling question speech researchers have had to ask themselves is this: is it possible, and is it necessary, for machines to use these nonacoustic sources of knowledge to recognize speech?

Normal speech has many naturally occurring corruptions that seem to require nonacoustic information. A puzzling question speech researchers have had to ask themselves is this: is it possible, and is it necessary, for machines to use these nonacoustic sources of knowledge to recognize speech?

Some reputable scientists believe it is also impossible to provide all the necessary semiotic knowledge to machines in the foreseeable future. The most notable opinion of this sort came from Pierce[9] in 1969, who concluded that automatic speech recognition was a practical impossibility for this reason. (He made his judgment on the basis of the fact that more than 15 years of research in the field had failed to produce a significant speech recognition capability. The situation has changed since then.)

On the other extreme, there are those who believe that nonacoustic sources are not needed at all. They point to courtroom "shadowers" who are reputedly able to correctly transcribe entire dialogues while thinking about something else than the conversation they are transcribing. Most speech researchers take the view that nonacoustic knowledge is required. Just how much acoustic ambiguity is present in speech and just how much intelligence is required to deal with it are unsettled issues. If acoustic ambiguity is not inherent, it can be removed by speaking carefully. It is my opinion that speech is not inherently ambiguous (with minor exceptions); rather, it is filled with potential acoustic redundancy which speakers may choose (unconsciously) to reduce by omitting certain sounds and/or words. In other words, it is up to the speaker to determine how much acoustic ambiguity exists; it is not as if a speaker were powerless to remove acoustic ambiguity. Carefully pronounced isolated words are evidently not acoustically ambiguous, because they can be recognized out of context with no semiotic information to help identify them. On the other extreme, experiments show that one-fourth to one-half the words in normal conversational speech are, in fact, unintelligible when taken out of context and heard in isolation.[10] Certainly some of these ambiguities are uncontrollable. The exact amount of uncontrollable acoustic ambiguity for continuous speech is not known. And of course, there are many intermediate levels between the extremes of isolated utterances and continuous conversational speech. So the amount of intelligence (semiotic information-processing ability) required to recognize speech can vary from none to near-human levels of intelligence.

To draw attention to the fact that ASR strategies must be a function of the type of speech used, the speech community uses the terms "isolated word recognition," "continuous speech recognition," and "speech understanding" instead of simply "speech recognition." Systems that recognize a small number of words (less than 1000) and that require at least 0.1 second of silence between words are defined to be isolated word recognizers. Systems that deal with normal speech containing co-articulation and no word boundaries are defined to be continuous speech recognizers. Recognition systems that attempt to utilize semantic information (information arising from a model of the domain of discourse) are called *understanding* systems. Speech understanding systems presumably can recognize normal speech more accurately than speech recognizers with no understanding capability.

The Scope of Automatic Speech Recognition. What is possible and reasonable to expect of speech recognition, and who sponsors the work? The answers depend on the type of speech system. Isolated word recognition is relatively easy for small vocabularies (10-50 words) and for a small set of known speakers. Such recognition equipment is available today from at least four vendors (Threshold Technology, Inc., Perception Technology Corp., Scope Electronics, Inc., Dialog Systems, Inc.). On the other extreme we observe that real-time, continuous speech recognition systems accepting unrestricted vocabularies, unknown speakers, and many discourse topics are not conceivable with today's technology and knowledge. Intermediate in difficulty are continuous speech recognition/understanding systems limited in vocabulary size and number of speakers and requiring carefully pronounced speech on a particular topic. Such systems are just now becoming possible due largely to a $15 million five-year speech-understanding project sponsored by ARPA. The actual research has been performed at Bolt, Beranek and Newman; Carnegie-Mellon University; Lincoln Laboratory; Stanford Research Institute; System Development Corporation; Haskins Laboratories; Speech Communication Research Laboratory; Sperry-Rand, and the University of California at Berkeley. The goal of the ARPA Speech Understanding Project is to achieve continuous speech understanding for a 1000-word vocabulary for a specific task (e.g., making airline reservations) for a small number of speakers in near real time on a big computer (e.g., PDP-10). Such systems are certainly at the outer limits of today's technology. Details of the objectives of the ARPA projects are found in the work of Newell et al.[11]

The Army, Navy, Air Force, and National Security Agency all contribute directly or indirectly to the support of speech recognition research through their sponsorship of speech synthesis, speech compression, and speaker verification research, which all share the same technology as speech recognition. The biggest industrial sponsors for speech research are Bell Telephone Laboratories and IBM. Bell Laboratories supports general speech research topics and has a relatively small effort in speech recognition per se.

IBM has the largest industrial speech recognition effort with more than a dozen scientists at Yorktown Heights, N.Y. They hope to achieve continuous speech recognition to enter data into computers. It is generally acknowledged that within a decade more revenue will be generated by the data entry market than from the sale or lease of computer hardware. If only a small fraction of the data entry market involves speech, it could have significant economic impact.

Applications being served today by commercially available ASR equipment includes the following:

(1) data entry by quality control inspectors (Owens-Illinois Corp. uses it for inspection of t.v. faceplates; Ford Motor Company for assembly line inspection of cars; Continental Can for inspecting pull ring can lids; Tecumseh Products Co. for compressor inspection; Union Carbide for manipulating nuclear products at Oak Ridge, Tenn.; a semiconductor manufacturer uses it with microscopes, inspecting microscopic components);

(2) control of materials-handling equipment (United Airlines for baggage handling; Kresge for control of package routing system);

(3) special purpose computer programming (a manufacturer uses ASR to program automatic machine tools); and

(4) editing of financial information (EMI Ltd., England uses it to collect numerical data from a variety of sources to prepare monthly financial statistics).

Overview of the Act of Recognizing Speech

All speech recognizers, biological or mechanical, have transducers that convert sound waves to internal representations. All speech recognizers have internal models stored in memory of the acoustic patterns produced by speech acts that they match against internal representations of unknown speech Some models may be imagined as templates (e.g., word templates); other models as sets of rules (e.g., grammatical rules of English). Other models are implicit in the transfer functions of transducers (microphones, amplifiers, etc.) and data compressors.

We shall see how these models are related by following speech from the ear (or microphone) through the final act of being recognized. Figure 1 shows the flow of speech we will be discussing. Figure 2 is a flow diagram of an experimental recognition system that illustrates the similarity between mechanical and human speech recognition. As we follow the speech path, we will encounter the key ideas of data compression, directed search, and hierarchical data structures. Comparisons of mechanical and mental pattern recognition will be pointed out; and the uses of signal processing, pattern recognition techniques, and artificial intelligence will be mentioned. Most importantly, we shall see examples of the optimization of pattern classifiers through dynamic control by contextual information.

Modeling at the Ear. All speech sounds arriving at the ear may be modeled as a linear combination of sine waves with differing phases. Any device that can measure the relative intensities of component sine waves is called a power spectrum analyzer. It is generally believed that all acoustic information relevant to speech recognition is represented by the time evolution of the power spectrum, with the phase component being relatively unimportant. (Phase information is evidently used for localization of sound sources but not for speech information per se.[4] The human ear acts as a power spectrum analyzer, and most ASR systems perform some sort of spectral analysis early in the recognition process. It is not always necessary to perform spectral analysis; the initial encoding of speech may be in terms of autocorrelations of the amplitude variations of the speech waveform, or in terms of linear predictive codes,[12] or in terms of

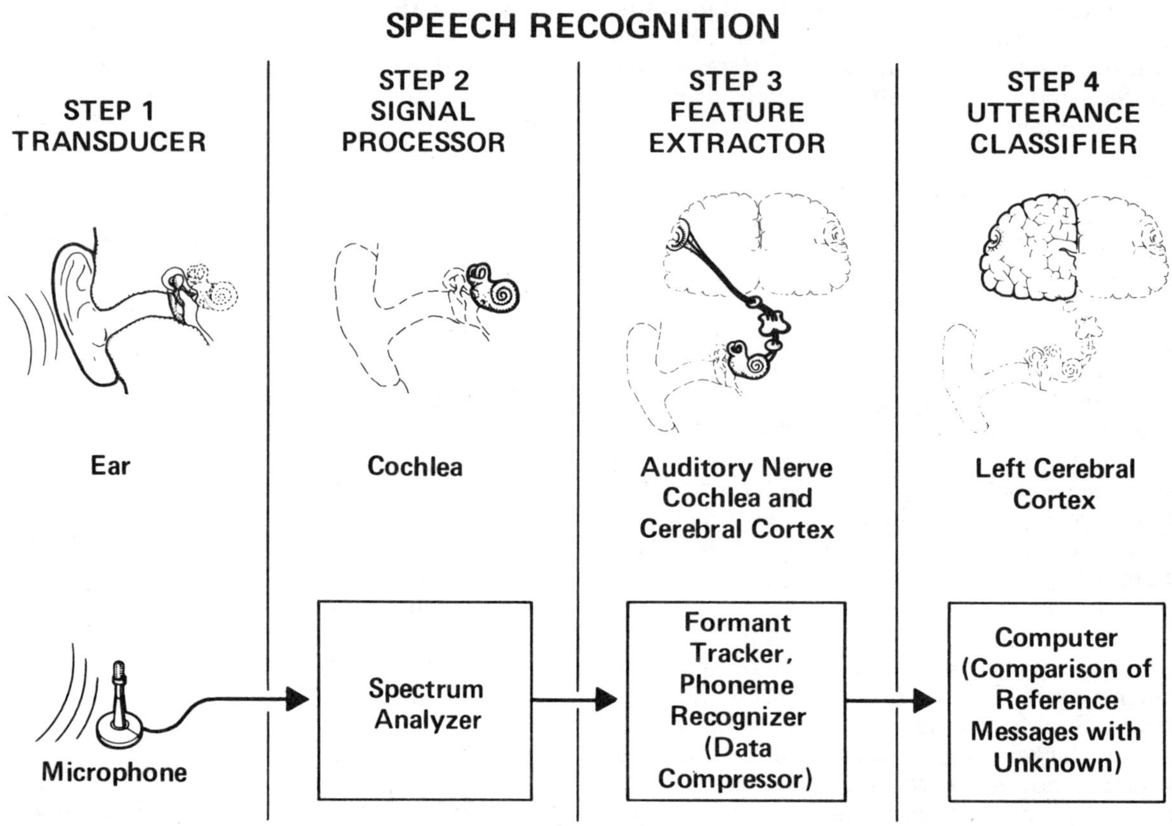

Figure 1. Overview of speech recognition showing parallels between human and machine recognition

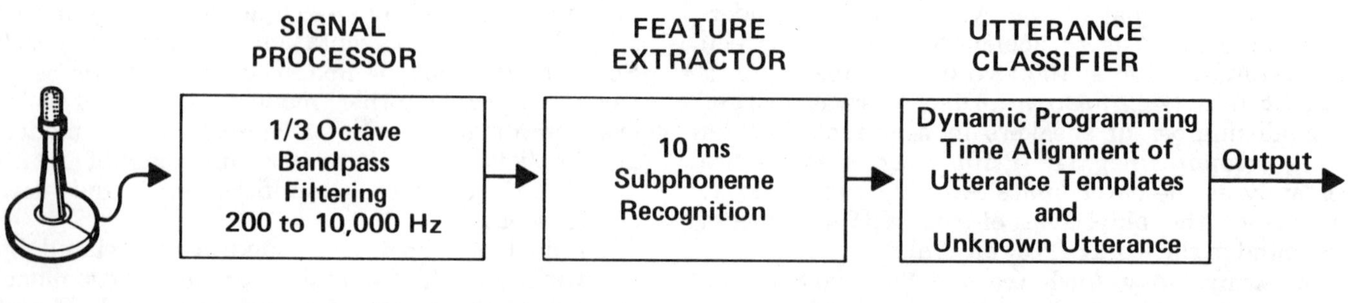

Figure 2. Flow diagram for an operational isolated utterance speech recognition, an example of the general structure shown in Figure 1

zero crossing statistics.[13] No matter how it is represented, spectral information must be explicitly or implicitly contained in all legitimate speech encodings. The initial analyses, whatever they are, produce *parametric representations* of speech, and take place in a part of the recognition system known in the literature as the "front end" or "bottom end" or "preprocessor" or "signal processor."

Data Compression and Formant Tracking. The initial parametric or "neuronal" representation of speech may contain redundant or irrelevant information that can be safely removed without requiring recognition of any speech sounds. The removal of extraneous information is called "data compression." After the act of data compression, all relevant information is represented with a smaller number of information theoretic bits; and this reduces the computational load for all subsequent processing be it neuronal or mechanical. There are a number of approaches to data compression but we shall focus on only one, formant tracking, which reveals a great deal about the nature of speech.

Formant tracking is the monitoring of time evolution of the major peaks of the power spectrum of speech. The formants are produced by the resonances of the vocal cavity. It is not clear that the ear-brain system tracks formants, nor is it clear that ASR systems need to. The reason it might be a good thing to do is that it has been demonstrated that *most* of the information content of speech is carried by the time evolution of the three principal formants (resonances). This was learned 25 years ago in experiments which employed transparent speech spectrograms to drive a speech synthesizer.[14] It was discovered that speech could be "painted" into a transparent strip of plastic by printing three or four thick black lines that corresponded to the time evolution of the formant frequencies. The transparent plastic with black strips was slid past an array of photoelectric cells that controlled oscillators with different frequencies. The output of the oscillators was combined and played through a loudspeaker. The result was intelligible speech. This showed that, indeed, all the necessary information was in the formants. This principle is the basis of formant vocoders[15]—devices that reduce speech to nothing more than formant frequencies, pitch, and amplitude information for the purpose of compressing and regenerating speech. The pattern of formants is the dominant feature of speech spectrograms, and speech spectrograms have taught us more about speech than any other tool.

From the point of view of ASR, the main advantage of tracking formants is that it provides a connection to the vast body of experimental data that have been collected over the years for speech in terms of spectrograms and formant frequencies. A secondary advantage is that it results in speech compression.

Automatic tracking of formants has always been difficult with available computational power, so its use in ASR has been limited until recently. But thanks to LPC (linear predictive coding), it is now much easier and has become a favorite technique of the ARPA Speech Understanding Project.[16]

There are other ways of compressing speech besides the use of formant tracking; one of the more promising is to recognize subpatterns in the speech. When subpatterns can be recognized, only the name of the subpattern need be saved and the detailed data representing the subpattern can be thrown away. This results in speech compression. Besides offering the advantage of speech compression, the recognition of subpatterns offers a means of dynamically controlling the operation of speech classifiers to achieve significant increases in efficiency. Let us now examine the operation of an actual recognition system to see how subpatterns might be used.

Intermediate Modeling. Once unknown speech sounds are transformed into neuronal or parametric representations, they can be grouped into word-sized chunks and matched against word prototypes. However, there are reasons to first recognize smaller units than words. To explain why, we will consider isolated word recognition without subword prototypes; that is to say, we will use only word prototypes. In particular, we will match every word prototype in the vocabulary against each unknown word. (With only minor variations, this is the scheme used in some very successful recognition systems.[12,17])

The first step in recognizing an unknown utterance is to divide it into short segments typically 10 milliseconds long. The second step is to compare the short segments with corresponding short segments in all the word prototypes. In other words, the unknown is time-aligned with each prototype, and the similarity between the short segments in the same time intervals is measured. The unknown utterance is classified by the word prototype that has the best overall similarity score for all its short segments.

Let us look more closely at the measurement of the similarity between unknown and prototype speech sounds in short time intervals. The similarity can be measured with a variety of similarity functions. These include correlation functions, filter functions, and geometric distance functions. Geometric distance functions are as good as any functions known, so we will not explain any similarity functions but geometric ones. Geometric functions operate in N-dimensional spaces defined by N parameters of parametric representations of speech[18,19] and are typified by Euclidean, Chebychev, and Hamming distance functions. For example, the similarity between two steady-state sounds can be defined to be inversely proportional to the Euclidean distance between the sounds, where the coordinates of each sound are defined to be its average passband energies in a bandpass filterbank.

This completes our description of word recognition techniques using word prototypes. The approach to word recognition of exhaustively matching all prototypes is inefficient and can be improved by using subword prototypes. Let us turn to phonemes as an example and see more explicitly what control and compression benefits are to be had from the recognition of subword prototypes.

The Value of Phoneme Recognition. Spoken words can be represented as strings of phonemes—the basic sound units of speech. In spoken English about 38 phonemes (16 vowels and 22 consonants) are typically used. There are two advantages of recognizing phonemes in a speech recognition system. Phonemes make possible (1) *selective recall of word prototypes* and (2) *reduction of memory requirements to store word prototypes*—i.e., data compression. Selective recall reduces the number of prototypes that need to be processed; and data compression reduces memory requirements. Let us examine both of these advantages, beginning with "selective recall of word prototypes."

Consider the word recognition scheme described above which processes templates serially until the correct template is found. When the correct template is matched against the unknown, the match is sufficiently good that it is clear the correct match has been found. At this point, the retrieval and matching of word templates can be stopped. Now, consider how much more efficient this process would be if there were some sort of *key* that could alter the order in which templates are processed so that the correct template would be more likely to be processed early. Phonemes provide such a key. The idea is to recognize phonemes first and use them to form words which then cause likely word templates to be processed. This is an example of the "hypothesize and test" paradigm. A rough classification decision is made on the basis of phonemic spelling, and this rough classification is verified by resorting to template matching. The computational expense of recognizing phonemes is small relative to that required for word recognition because there are many more words than phonemes, and phonemes are smaller than words. If phoneme recognition were perfect, then there would be no need to match word prototypes at all; properly spelled English words could be retrieved directly from memory using a dictionary indexed with phonemically spelled words. But phonemic strings may be full of errors, so it is necessary to be able to resort to template matching to verify tentative spellings. The important point here is that phonemes provide the means for improving the efficiency of the speech recognizer through enabling selective recall of prototypes.

Now let us consider briefly how phonemic encoding achieves data compression. The general principle is that data compression results from storing the names of phonemes rather than all the data that make up the phonemes themselves. The original data presumably could represent many more phonemes than need to be distinguished by having different names. To be more specific, if a given phoneme is a common element in a group of patterns, then data compression is achieved by storing the detailed information about the phoneme only once and then replacing the phoneme by its name wherever else it occurs. The name of the phoneme can then be used to find the detailed information about the phoneme whenever necessary. (For example, suppose it requires 100 bits to represent a phoneme in the representation produced by the signal processor. Suppose an average reference word is composed of 10 phonemes. Therefore it requires 10 × 100 bits to store the average word. But if the phonemes are replaced with their names, it requires only 6 × 10 bits since it requires only 6 bits to store the name of a phoneme. This represents a decrease from 1000 to 60 bits of memory to store the average word. Of course the reference representations of phonemes must be stored somewhere, and this requires 100 × 40 bits. It is clear that with less than four reference words, there is no advantage to using the names of the 38 phonemes (because it requires as much storage for the reference phonemes as it does to store four words without using phonemes). But by the time the number of words reaches 1000, the memory requirements are reduced by an order of magnitude through using *names* of phonemes instead of the phonemes themselves.)

In summary, the use of phonemes for encoding word prototypes is beneficial since it allows compression of the parametric representation of word prototypes and it allows dynamic control to search only a subset of the word prototype dictionary.

Phonemes Are Only One Type of Model Subunit. The use of subword prototypes other than phonemes is possible. The basic idea of subunits can be generalized to subunits of subunits, etc. The reasoning applied to justify the use of an initial type of subunit often can be applied to justify subunits of subunits. There is, of course, a limit to the number of levels of subunits that would increase the efficiency of a pattern classifier, but this limit will, for problems such as speech recognition, be greater than one. Thus a highly optimized system might have a large number of intermediate subunits (models) hierarchically organized between the signal processor and the higher centers that identify words or semantic units.

Does the Brain Model Complex Sounds in Terms of Simple Sounds? If highly optimized pattern classifiers organize patterns into hierarchies, then we might expect to find evidence of feature hierarchies in the brain. Indeed there is some neurological verification of the brain's use of hierarchical modeling. Specifically, this is what Hubel and Wiesel[20] seem to have found for the visual cortex. (They designated different levels in the hierarchy as "simple," "complex," and "hypercomplex" receptive fields.) In the auditory cortex, some nerves respond selectively to particular sounds, and the detection of simpler sounds seems to precede the detection of more complex ones. The possibility that more complex sounds are detected independently of simpler ones has not been ruled out.[21] Thus while

The ultimate purpose of speech communication is to communicate semantic information. We sometimes forget this and are inclined to view words as the final product.

preliminary indications are that neurological feature hierarchies exist, the evidence is inconclusive.

Pattern Recognition and Feature Extraction. We have been implicitly discussing "features" and "feature extraction" without explicitly defining the terms. The models (subunits) intermediate between the signal processor and the semantic interpreter are examples of "features," and the process of matching a model against unknown speech is an example of "feature extraction." Other sorts of models (features) are also possible. The field of pattern recognition has many mechanisms for generating features and transforming their representations. Whatever the strategy for generating intermediate features, the function of a feature must be to remove redundancy and irrelevant information from speech. This makes the ultimate classification decisions easier since the information that must be analyzed presumably has less "noise." An interesting description of about a dozen features useful in speech recognition appears in a dissertation by Martin.[22] Syntactic methods in pattern recognition appear to be a particularly promising approach for integrating traditional feature extraction ideas with modern digital computer technology. Fu[23] has written the first definitive text on the subject.

Human Auditory Feature Extraction. What is the biological counterpart of "intermediate models" and feature extractors? In man, experiments show that feature extraction begins in the auditory nerve, which passes through four or five synaptic junctions before arriving at the auditory cerebral cortex.[24] Figure 1 shows this schematically. Detection of more complicated sounds (e.g., entire words) is probably carried out with the aid of simple features and probably uses feedback from parts of the brain beyond the auditory cortex. But the way simple features relate to complex features in the auditory system is not understood.

Finally, from Features to Semantics. The ultimate purpose of speech communication is to communicate semantic information. We sometimes forget this and are inclined to view words as the final product. In fact, words may be more appropriately viewed as "features" of semantic patterns occupying a position in a feature hierarchy. Perhaps the principles of transforming phonemes into words can be applied to transforming words into meaning. Only during the past five years have such questions been seriously investigated, owing to the work of the ARPA Speech Understanding Project. Their main focus has been the transformation of phonemes (and sometimes syllables) into words with the aid of semiotic information. They attempt to use speech stress to spot semantic content words and phrase boundaries, to use the syntax of the spoken language to determine legal sequences of words, and to use a world model to determine if proposed sentences make sense. These various sources of knowledge are used to direct the "parsing" of spoken phrases and to achieve the benefits of dynamic control. It is particularly interesting that the Carnegie-Mellon University project actually employs a hierarchy of speech sounds. Systems of this sort should eventually result in a highly optimized system (based on the reasoning discussed on p. 45). The speech understanding systems that the ARPA contractors have built are major achievements for the field of artificial intelligence. However, these systems only scratch the surface. Many more years of work will be required before *practical* speech understanding systems are a reality. Many more years will be required before we fully understand how to increase the efficiency of pattern classifiers through the use of contextual information. Nevertheless, there is a great deal to be said about contextual information processing even now, as we shall see in our final sections.

Recent Progress

Significant progress on both theoretical and practical levels has been made since 1970, the time interval which concerns us here. In business applications, Threshold Technology, Inc. has become the first manufacturer of an economically significant recognition system. The Threshold system solved the problem of 90-dB background noise and breath noise of men lifting heavy loads in airport baggage sorting operations. The system is able to recognize about 20 numbers with almost 99% accuracy in this environment. Many other applications, such as automobile manufacture quality control, voice programming, and bookkeeping have successfully used TTI's automatic speech recognition system (see our "Overview" section).

Another outward sign of progress was the demonstration of operational continuous speech recognition systems by the ARPA contractors and IBM; this was the first demonstration of its kind in the 25-year history of ASR. IBM and Carnegie-Mellon University report recognition accuracies between 80 and 90% for a constrained vocabulary of 200-300 words for a specific task. Higher recognition scores are expected during this year, the final year of the ARPA speech understanding program.

Aside from outward signs of progress, there are significant underlying technical advances. These advances are characterized by replacement of complex heuristic computer programs by simple algorithms and mathematical descriptions. In essence, important subproblems have been identified, studied, and shown to admit simple solutions. (There are conceptual advances and advances in systems architecture which are not considered appropriate for the list below because of their complexity.)

Some of these technical advances are explained below. In summary, they are:

(1) *linear predictive coding* (LPC) for data compression and spectral smoothing (Atal,[25] Markel,[16] Makhoul,[5] Itakura[26]);
(2) *vocal tract area function* and *vocal tract length estimate* from LPC model of vocal track (Wakita[27,28]);
(3) *linear predictive residual* as a speech sound similarity measure for steady-state sounds (Itakura[12]);
(4) *dynamic programming* for time alignment of unknown and reference utterances (Sakoe et al.,[29] Itakura,[12] White and Neely[17]);
(5) *CEPSTRAL* and *COSH* distance functions for speech sound similarity measurement (Markel and Gray[19]);
(6) *Markov models* for representing the time evolution of a speech understander's state of knowledge (Baker[30]);
(7) *dimensionality reduction* of speech data by principal components analysis shows that parametric representations other than formant frequencies and bandwidths are just as adequate for the representation of speech data (Pols et al.[31]);
(8) *pitch tracking* by center clipping, infinite peak clipping, and autocorrelation analysis (Dubnowski et al.[32]);
(9) *convex hulls* in speech energy profiles for syllable segmentation (Mermelstein[33]); and
(10) *beginning and ending of utterance detection* by amplitude, zero crossings, and backtracking (Rabiner and Sambur[34]).

Other important developments include the generation of phonological rules (Oshika et al.,[35] Cohen and Mercer,[36] and Friedman[37]) and network data structures (especially semantic networks; see Hendricks[38]).

Linear predictive coding is the most important development in automatic speech recognition to occur in over a decade. It is a form of Wiener filtering (which has been known for more than a quarter century), but was evidently not applied to speech until the late sixties. The theory and practice of LPC are summarized in an excellent paper by Makhoul.[5] Its primary use is to represent speech in a highly compressed form and also to produce spectral smoothing that clearly reveals formants. The power of LPC does *not* lie in the accuracy of its representation of speech or speech spectra. Its power lies in the fact that it is a computationally efficient means of getting formant peaks and that it produces a compact representation of speech.

Linear predictive coding implicitly imposes a model of a nonbranching acoustic tube on speech. Wakita derives the important result that both the cross-sectional area and the length of the tube can be simply calculated along with the LPC coefficients. By normalizing a random speaker's vocal tract shape and length to some standard value, a major step forward is achieved toward independence of the need to retrain recognition systems for new speakers.

The linear predictive residual (LPR) is the error that remains when a linear predictive filter is applied to a time series representation of speech. This is also known as "matched filtering" in pattern recognition.[39] Itakura gives a computationally efficient formula for calculating the log ratio of two linear predictive residuals. He proceeds to show experimentally that such a ratio gives an excellent speech sound similarity measure when the unknown residual is used in the denominator and different template sounds are used in the numerator. It was later shown experimentally by White and Neely that this sound similarity measure is not superior in accuracy to traditional frequency domain similarity measures. However, the Itakura similarity function makes it possible to achieve significant computational economies in implementation by making it possible to perform all preprocessing and similarity measurements simply and in the *time* domain.

Dynamic programming is a well-known technique in operations research which, like LPC, has only recently made an impact on speech recognition. It is an extremely useful technique for achieving nonlinear time adjustment (warping) to align multisyllabic utterances. Although the technique had been used prior to 1970 in Japan, Russia, and France, the speech community in the U.S. did not start using it until 1974 when Itakura introduced it along with the linear predictive residual during his stay at Bell Labs. The power of dynamic programming revealed itself more forcefully when White and Neely showed that, on the one multisyllabic vocabulary they tested, a 20-fold reduction in error rate was obtained with dynamic programming compared to the best linear time alignment strategies known to them. They also pointed out that the excellent recognition scores obtained by the Itakura recognition system were due more to the use of dynamic programming and multisyllabic utterances than to the use of the Itakura similarity function, the log ratio of linear predictive residuals (LPR's).

The CEPSTRAL and COSH distance functions were recently proposed and tested as time domain similarity measures for speech sounds by Markel and Gray. They have properties that make them slightly preferable to the Itakura LPR measure.

Markov models made their debut in the speech community when Baker introduced the DRAGON speech-understanding system at Carnegie-Mellon University. Dynamic programming and Markov modeling result in the same algorithms for many speech problems, but Markov models have an advantage of more mathematical support. Baker's contribution was to point out that not only can time alignment be treated with Markov models, but syntactic, semantic, acoustic, and other knowledge domains can also be modeled as Markov processes.

Dimensionality reduction with principal components analysis is a standard technique in pattern recognition. It is essentially the same as the Karhunen Loeve technique (K. S. Fu),[40] analysis of variance, and factor analysis. Pols was able to use principal components analysis to identify Dutch vowel sounds as accurately as could be done by hand analysis of formant frequencies and bandwidths. This demonstrated that entirely automatic techniques are able, in fact, to perform as well at identifying vowels as laborious hand analyses. In my opinion there is no advantage to formant tracking as a technique for identifying vowels (and probably other sounds) over properly applied distance functions such as COSH, CEPSTRAL, Euclidean, and others in the properly defined spaces. The work of Pols is one of the only actual comparisons of formant tracking with another parametric representation on the same data base that substantiates this view. However, this view is apparently also held by IBM and CMU, since they both use this approach in their recognition systems. Dimensionality reduction can actually improve recognition accuracy as well as reduce data rates for representing speech. In an unpublished experiment in the author's laboratory, a two-dimensional subspace was found to be superior to a 20-dimensional bandpass filter space 1/3 octave bandwidth per channel, for discriminating between "B" and "D." (Note: there are many other methods besides principal components analysis for dimensionality reduction.)

Pitch tracking by center clipping, infinite peak clipping, and autocorrelation analysis is important for its accuracy and simplicity. The accuracy of this approach is reported to be as good as the CEPSTRAL approach—meaning that it is as good as the best known. Yet the algorithm is beautifully simple. Peak and center clipping produce a speech wave with only three states: -1, 0, 1. This reduces autocorrelation analysis to addition and subtraction, and it brings about a dramatic reduction in the computational burden associated with pitch tracking.

Syllable segmentation with convex hulls is a novel solution to an important problem. Almost every speech recognition researcher tries his hand on syllable or phoneme segmentation at one time or another. Paul Mermelstein has proposed a simple algorithm that will work on any continuous approximately convex function and will find the important dips and valleys. He applies his "convex hull" strategy to speech energy profiles and, indeed, does a good job of segmenting syllables in speech. But it would be misleading to suggest that the use of convex hulls solves the segmentation problem in general. The most reliable way to segment speech is to recognize its constituent sounds, and even this approach has errors. The value of convex hulls is their simplicity and the fact that good syllable segmentation is obtained most of the time.

Detecting the beginnings and endings of utterances is an age old problem that must be faced by every speech recognition system builder. The solution presented by Rabiner and Sambur is one of the simpler and more accurate ones in the literature, and as such it is noteworthy.

There are, of course, other important developments that are not included in the above list. The items on the list are there because their simplicity and importance will promote their widespread use. In a deeper sense, they are representative of the kinds of problems and solutions that, taken together, will ultimately solve the speech recognition problem.

The fundamental problems of speech recognition are exciting because they are general and their solutions will impact all aspects of machine perception.

Fundamental Problems: A Source of Inspiration

The fundamental problems of speech recognition are exciting because they are general and their solutions will impact all aspects of machine perception. The fundamental problems arise from the fact that the information needed to identify a speech sound is often not contained within the sound itself. The information is often spread over a larger time interval—i.e., it is often a function of contect. This phenomenon is extensive; it occurs frequently in all types of speech sounds: in phonemes, in syllables, in words, and even in sentences. This is an example of a fundamental problem in artificial intelligence in which local ambiguity is inherent in the data and can be removed only with information from global sources. Speech research is contributing to the solution of this general problem. We shall illustrate the nature of local ambiguity and methods for dealing with it through the example of phonemes.

If the approximately 38 phonemes of general American English could be recognized accurately, then it would be relatively easy to recognize an unlimited vocabulary of English words. Unknown speech would first be converted to strings of phonemes which would be converted to standard orthography by looking up words in a dictionary based on phonemic spelling. This approach has considerable appeal, and much ASR research has been expended on automatic phoneme recognizers.

Phoneme recognition has been attempted with and without feedback from the context surrounding phoneme. Those attempts which have used only local information have failed except for highly artificial speech. The information needed to identify a phoneme is often not present in the phoneme itself. For example, if vowels are preceded by consonants "l" or "r," the vowels are changed so much that they are quite often misclassified if taken out of context.[41] Phonemes are strongly affected by neighboring phonemes because of the physical inertia of the tongue and other articulators. Evidently speech is composed of a series of sound targets that speakers usually fail to reach but with no loss of intelligibility because listeners can properly interpret the "gestures" toward the sound targets by using contextual information.[42]

Attempts to circumvent the local phonemic ambiguity problem lead to the development of "phonological" rules governing the effects of phonemes on neighboring phonemes.[43] Phonological rules are a type of syntactic rule for phonemes (instead of words) telling what sequences of phonemes are legal. Phonological rules are usually intended to cope with commonly occurring coarticulation phenomena. It does not appear to be practical to design phonological rules to deal with erratic personal speaking idiosyncracies and mumblings. These are nonetheless very real sources of acoustic ambiguity that people have no trouble coping with. So we must look further than phonological rules in our search for a solution to the "local acoustic ambiguity" problem.

It is becoming increasingly clear that there is no single speech unit, nor is there any single set of rules, that satisfactorily avoids all commonly occurring acoustic aberrations in speech.

Attempts to avoid the local acoustic amgibuity inherent in phonemes also lead to the use of alternative units such as "transemes"[44] and to the use of larger units such as syllables or words.[45] The use of larger units is motivated by the fact that larger units tend to have smaller amounts of internal ambiguity. Syllables are more robust than phonemes; words are more robust than syllables. A significant source of experimental evidence demonstrating that larger models promote accuracy comes from the fact that the most accurate speech recognition systems known today use utterance prototypes rather than smaller units. For instance, White and Neely[17] were able to achieve 99.6% correct recognition for a 91-word vocabulary using utterance models (templates.) This is significantly better than any system attempting to work with a smaller unit. However, such high recognition scores apply only to isolated utterance recognition where all acoustic information necessary to identify a word is present in the word itself. Continuous speech often contains words that are acoustically ambiguous, which people recognize easily with contextual information but which machines using only word templates would fail to recognize. So the ultimate solution is not to be found even in the use of utterance-sized units.

It is becoming increasingly clear that there is no single speech unit, nor is there any single set of rules, that satisfactorily avoids all commonly occurring acoustic aberrations in speech. The solution to the problem seems to be approachable only asymptotically through the use of ever increasing numbers of larger units, models, rules, and other sources of knowledge. It is the need to combine large numbers of models and rules that is a significant challenge to artificial intelligence.

The following paragraphs explain more about various knowledge sources and the role of artificial intelligence in combining them.

For the purposes of this exposition, the word "model" means the same thing as "source of knowledge." The problem we face is how to use models differing in reliability and computational expense to optimize efficiency. Because larger models are typically more expensive to store and use, it is the author's opinion that larger units should be used in a "feedback" mode, being invoked only by the partial recognition of smaller units. This is based on the extremely important idea that the recognition of computationally cheap sound units can avoid the need to recognize some computationally expensive sound units.

A solution to the fundamental problem of local acoustic ambiguity is to have models of speech sounds at all levels (phoneme, syllable, word, phrase) and a strategy allowing lower models to call on higher models to resolve local ambiguities and a strategy allowing the higher models to call on lower models to request further analysis. The higher-level models are needed for accuracy; the intermediate level models are needed for conservation of computational resources (both memory and computation).

Note that higher-level models may be embodied in rules as well as templates. For instance, phonological rules and language syntax perform the function of removing local ambiguity by reference to a larger context. A particularly interesting set of rules are those that govern the application of "check morphemes"—suffixes, prefixes, or articles added to words or inserted in phrases which require agreement in person, gender, and temporal reference between words. Check morphemes may be separated by the entire duration of the sentence.[46]

Examples that illustrate the above ideas follow. To start, let us consider a detailed example of the problems that are encountered in attempting to use models for words only. In this example, no models are allowed for phonemes or syllables or other subword units. Word prototypes are encoded with representations derived from signal processing techniques.

The best signal-processing speech compression techniques known today require approximately 1000 bits per second to produce marginally intelligible speech. Given the typical computational requirements to match prototypes and unknowns, it is possible to show that general purpose computers are two orders of magnitude too slow to match an unknown utterance against several thousand utterance prototypes in real time. (The memory-to-processor bandwidth is too small and the processor speed itself is insufficient.) It is also true that there is not enough storage in most random access memories to store templates for several thousand words if the templates are stored in the original parametric representation of the signal processor.

So if word templates (prototypes) are to be encoded in terms of signal-processing representations at all, they must be stored on disk and used sparingly. In other words, the use of word prototypes may promote high accuracy, but encoding the prototypes in the representation produced by the signal processor requires so much storage and processor power that this approach must be limited to isolated word recognition for small vocabularies and to machines with significant computational power. The unavoidable conclusion is that the only reasonable alternative is to use intermediate sound units between the signal processor and the word classifier.

The three ARPA speech-understanding systems embody the major significant attempts to overcome acoustic ambiguity by the use of higher sources of knowledge. They do not share a unified approach to the problem of representing and using higher-level models. But they do share the assumption that semantic, grammatical, and phonological knowledge must be used to augment acoustic sources. They all use some sort of "hypothesize and test" paradigm from higher knowledge sources onto phoneme sequences. The phoneme strings predicted by (top down) analysis are compared to the string of phonemes produced by acoustic (bottom up) analysis. The use of higher-level models in this top down "predictive mapping" is one of the more important techniques of the ARPA speech understanding effort. It is particularly noteworthy that CMU's HEARSAY-II System actually uses a hierarchy of speech units to span the differences between higher-level and lower-level knowledge; they use subphonemes, phonemes, surface phonemes, syllables, words, and phrases to represent knowledge sources. (Recall that a hierarchy of sound units was suggested earlier as a mechanism for achieving significant computational economics.)

The CMU HEARSAY-II system seems to have the most clearly defined strategy for dealing with multiple knowledge sources. HEARSAY-II uses a "blackboard"—a structurally uniform data base—for communication between different sources of knowledge. Whenever any knowledge scource has something to say, it writes it on the blackboard for all other knowledge sources to see. The control of the computer processor is taken by the knowledge source that has the highest match between a pattern on the blackboard and one of its templates. The different knowledge sources may be implemented on asynchronous parallel processors.[54] The system can be bottom driven or top driven, or it can have a mixed bottom-top strategy.

The SRI-SDC system (VDMS) uses the recognition of phrases to tie its different knowledge sources together. It uses a parser to control which knowledge to use during the parsing of a phrase. It is noteworthy that reference prototypes are used for some phrases rather than for the words or phonemes that comprise them. In other words, the SRI-SDC approach is to admit that some phrases contain so much coarticulation and mumblings that it is unrealistic to try to decompose them into phonemes or even words. Such phrases are dealt with as basic units. This is certainly one of the more promising approaches to overcoming local acoustic ambiguity.

The development of the BBN SPEECHLIS system employed a clever incremental simulation to refine its strategy for coordination and control. People were placed in different rooms to perform functions such as acoustic analysis or semantic analysis but they were restricted to communicating through teletypes. The researchers derived protocols from studying the teletype record and then incrementally replaced the people by computer programs. The BBN system is known for its use of tree structures to index dictionaries and for its use of "islands of reliability" in parsing unknown speech. An island of reliability is a segment of a sentence that is identified with high confidence and serves as the starting point in left-to-right and right-to-left parsing. This idea was tried by Neely and White[55] for isolated utterances, but the BBN group is the first to promote its use in continuous speech.

In summary, the principal difficulty in ASR is not an inability to identify utterances for which there are adequate higher-level models (knowledge sources). The problem is an inability to use higher-level models in a reasonable amount of time and with a reasonable amount of memory. As Neuberg[47] wisely stated, our recent progress in ASR has been controlled more by advances in data processing technology than by advances in speech recognition techniques.[27] The problems are not so much due to our lack of understanding of speech as they are due to massive amounts of data that must be processed in real time.

There are two general ways to reduce the disparity between data processing needs and abilities. One way is to rely on faster hardware. The other way is to use artificial intelligence/pattern recognition techniques to optimize performance of existing hardware. More specifically, artificial intelligence/pattern recognition techniques can be used in conjunction with a number of "sources of knowledge" ("intermediate models" or "features") so that computationally inexpensive knowledge controls the application of more expensive knowledge. The next section elaborates on this point.

Improving System Performance

Frequently, the first thing that comes to mind when thinking about ways to improve a speech recognition device is the operation of comparing two elementary speech sounds: would not the accuracy of the system improve dramatically if the system could identify short speech sounds more accurately? It may come as a surprise that the answer is no. The gain from discovering more accurate speech sound similarity measures is relatively small. The major gains will come from being able to resolve local acoustic ambiguity with information arising from larger speech segments.

The important problems seem to be how to represent and use sources of knowledge arising from the global environments. It is only through the use of such knowledge that there can be hope of significantly increasing accuracy and reducing problems of insufficient computational power.

There are at least four categories of mechanisms for reducing the disparity between data rate processing needs and abilities: (1) special purpose hardware, (2) improved speech data compression techniques, (3) robust speech representations through normalization techniques, and (4) dictionary compression and directed search through the use of a hierarchy of speech subunits. Category (4) is the only approach concerned with contextual information. In (4), information from larger speech intervals is allowed to affect the resolution of local acoustic ambiguity in speech subunits. We will briefly examine each of these mechanisms. In giving estimates of performance improvement, we will use as a standard of comparison the performance of an isolated utterance system using utterance prototypes and an exhaustive search of the dictionary of prototypes. Assume the baseline system runs on a general purpose minicomputer.

Special-Purpose Hardware. An order of magnitude increase in data rate processing ability can be expected from new computer architecture. One way to achieve this is to alter conventional computer architecture by incorporating higher memory-to-processor bandwidths and special-purpose processors. Alternative approaches include the use of parallel processing[54] and/or acoustic surface waves[49] and/or custom LSI[48,50] and/or optical computers.[51] Some of these hardware developments could offer even greater performance improvements than an order of magnitude improvement, but this eventuality is difficult to predict. Of particular value, in conjunction with the hierarchical data structures to be described below, would be a large random access read only memory such as General Electric's BEAMOS memory, e.g., 32-million-bit capacity, 32-microsecond seek time, and 10-megabit bandwidth.[52]

Speech Encoding and Data Compression. Speech compression is not likely to reduce data rates by more than a factor of 4. The information theoretic minimum mean number of bits required to transmit speech information, including speaker's emotional state, identity, and semantic context, is probably between 100 and 200 bits per second. (For text-to-speech synthesis which has only semantic content, the data rate is approximately 75 bps.[15]) So speech compression is already within an order of magnitude of its theoretical limit. To hope that the theoretical limit will be achieved soon is unreasonable; a factor of 4 is more likely in the next decade than the theoretical maximum of 10.

Improved Representation through Normalization Techniques. Whatever prototypical speech units and subunits are used, the representation for them can be made more robust and less variable by normalization techniques. Using these normalization techniques means essentially that fewer templates or special rules are needed to represent a speech sound faithfully. This means that less processing needs to be done to match any unknown to a prototypical sound. This can speed up the overall recognition process. These techniques include normalization by (1) velocity, (2) amplitude, (3) time, (4) speaker spectra, (5) dynamic range, and (6) noise subtraction:

Velocity normalization is the shortening of steady-state speech segments to remove artificial variations in sound duration due to variations in speaking rate. ("Velocity refers to the time rate of change of the spectra.)

Amplitude normalization is the removal of speech amplitude as a parameter in speech sound similarity measurement. This ensures that a sound that varies in energy but not in its spectral composition is still interpreted as the same sound.

Time normalization is the stretching or shrinking of the length of time elapsed between given speech segments. The goal is to align the time of occurrence of unknown speech events relative to reference speech events to see how well they match. Dynamic programming is an excellent way of achieving this.

Speaker spectra normalization is the transformation of the power spectral density function in order to remove the effects of differing vocal tract lengths. This is required only for systems that attempt to recognize speech from different speakers without retraining. It can be achieved using the LPC model as shown by Wakita[27] or using bandpass filtered data as shown by Pols et al.[31]

Dynamic range normalization is the determination of the energy variations of speech in order to adjust thresholds to allow energy to be used in segmentation and segment labeling.

Noise subtraction normalization is the determination of the energy of ambient noise and the subtraction of that energy from the input signal so that only the speech signal is left.

To summarize, normalization techniques such as those listed above are useful in any approach, but will not deliver more than an order of magnitude improvement in recognition speed.

Improved Dictionary Compression and Search Strategies. Dramatic increases in data processing capabilities can be expected from using a hierarchy of speech sound subunits to promote dictionary compression and "directed search" dictionary retrieval strategies. Two orders of magnitude improvement can be expected for a vocabulary of 1000 words or more when the baseline system uses exhaustive search. The basic idea of directed search is that the identification of computationally cheap sound units makes the more expensive units easier to find in a dictionary. Computationally more expensive sound units are those that require more bits to store and more processing to match. Let us refer to such sound units as "larger units."

When the correct larger units are recalled from memory, the goodness match between the larger unit and the unknown speech will reveal which of the retrieved units are correct.

For instance, the partially correct spelling of a word unit in terms of phonemic subunits might make it possible to find the word in a dictionary without an exhaustive search. We might call this method "an imperfect match dictionary lookup strategy." An imperfect match dictionary retrieval method could be achieved by changing the spelling of the word until it hits an entry in the dictionary. Control of spelling changes could come from phonological rules, secondary spellings produced by acoustic analysis, or reference to more general sound classes—e.g., "nasal" in place of "M" or "N."

By using a hierarchy of sound units, the effective reduction in recognition time can be expected to be approximately a log function of vocabulary size rather than a linear function of vocabulary size. Thus the relative savings will be larger for larger vocabularies.

It is the author's opinion that a "hierarchical imperative" exists for the organization of pattern subunits and search strategies for more complicated pattern recognition problems. There is no other approach that offers so much potential for increasing the power of mechanical perception devices with existing hardware technology. Hierarchical organization provides contextual constraints by virtue of the fact that every subunit has the context provided by the larger units above it in the hierarchy. This contextual information can control the operation of pattern classifiers to achieve significant improvements in classifier efficiency. Properly applied contextual information is the most promising method to increase the apparent computational power of pattern recognizing machines. This is one of the more important points of this paper.

Finally, we have seen that hierarchically organized speech subunits and "directed search" are techniques that permit utilization of contextual information to control processing. These techniques are general and provide an example of techniques developed for speech recognition that apply to a great many problems in machine intelligence and pattern recognition. ■

Acknowledgments

I wish to thank Nilo Lindgren and Raj Reddy for constructive comments on this manuscript; K. S. Fu for inviting me to prepare it; and Jan Murphy for tireless assistance in transcribing my notes.

References

1. A. Chapanis, "Interactive Human Communication," *Scientific American*, Vol. 232 (3), pp. 36-42, 1975.

2. D. R. Reddy, "Speech Recognition by Machine: A Review," to be published in the *Proc. IEEE*, April 1976.

3. T. B. Martin, "Applications of Limited Vocabulary Recognition Systems," in *Speech Recognition: Invited Papers of the IEEE Symposium* (D. R. Reddy, ed.), Academic Press, New York, 1975.

4. M. R. Schroeder, "Models of Hearing," *Proc. IEEE*, Vol. 63 (9), pp. 1322-1352, September 1975.

5. J. Makhoul, "Spectral Analysis of Speech by Linear Prediction," *IEEE Trans. Audio Electroacoustics*, Vol. Au-21 (3), pp. 140-148, 1973.

6. E. Feigenbaum, Keynote Address, NATO Advanced Study Institute, Santa Cruz, California, July 1975.

7. A. M. Warren and R. P. Waren, "Auditory Illusions and Confusions," *Scientific American*, December 1970.

8. W. D. Marslen-Wilson, "Sentence Perception as an Interactive Parallel Process," *Science*, Vol. 189 (4198), July 18, 1975.

9. J. R. Pierce, "Whither Speech Recognition?" *J. Acoustical Society of America*, Vol. 46, pp. 1049-1051, 1969.

10. D. Klatt, MIT, personal communication.

11. A. Newell, J. Barnett, J. Forgie, C. Green, D. Klatt, J. C. R. Licklider, J. Munson, R. Reddy, and W. Woods, "Speech Understanding Systems: Final Report of a Study Group." Reprinted by North-Holland/American Elsevier, Amsterdam, 1973.

12. F. Itakura, "Minimum Prediction Residual Principle Applied to Speech Recognition," *IEEE Trans. Acoustics, Speech and Signal Processing*, Vol. ASSP-23 (1), pp. 67-72, February 1975.

13. R. J. Neiderjohn, "A Mathematical Formulation and Comparison of Zero-Crossing Analysis Techniques Which Have Been Applied to Automatic Speech Recognition," *IEEE Trans. Acoustics, Speech and Signal Processing*, Vol. ASSP-23 (4), pp. 373-379, August 1975.

14. P. B. Denes and E. N. Pinson, *The Speech Chain*, Doubleday, Garden City, New York, 1973.

15. J. L. Flanagan, C. H. Coker, L. R. Rabiner, R. W. Schafer, and N. Umeda, "Synthetic Voices for Computers," *IEEE Spectrum*, pp. 22-46, October 1970.

16. J. D. Markel, "Digital Inverse Filtering: A New Tool for Format Trajectory Estimation," *IEEE Trans. Audio Electroacoustics*, Vol. AU-20 (120), p. 137, 1972.

17. G. M. White and R. B. Neely, "Speech Recognition Experiments with Linear Prediction, Bandpass Filtering and Dynamic Programming," *IEEE Trans. Acoust., Speech and Signal Processing*, Vol. ASSP-24 (2), April 1976.

18. A. H. Gray, Jr., and J. D. Markel, "COSH Measure for Speech Processing," *90th Mtg., Acoustical Society of America*, Vol. 58 (1), p. S97, Fall 1975.

19. J. D. Markel and A. H. Gray, Jr., "Cepstral Distance and the Frequency Domain," *90th Mtg., Acoustical Society of America*, Vol. 58, p. 597, Fall 1975.

20. D. H. Hubel and T. N. Wiesel, "Receptive Fields and Functional Architecture of Monkey Striate Cortex," *Journal Of Physiology*, Vol. 195, pp. 215-243, 1968.

21. W. R. Webster and L. M. Aitkin, "Central Auditory Processing," *Handbook of Psychobiology*, Academic Press, New York, 1975.

22. T. B. Martin, "Acoustic Recognition of a Limited Vocabulary in Continuous Speech," Doctoral Thesis, University of Pennsylvania, 1970.

23. K. S. Fu, *Syntactic Methods in Pattern Recognition*, Academic Press, New York, 1974.

24. C. U. M. Smith, *The Brain: Towards an Understanding*, Capricorn Books, New York, 1972.

25. B. S. Atal and M. R. Schroeder, "Predictive Coding of Speech Signals," *Report 6th ICA, Tokyo*, Vol. II, C-5-4, 1968.

26. F. Itakura et al., "Analysis Synthesis Telephony Base on the Maximum Likelihood Method," *Report 6th ICA, Tokyo*, Vol. II, C-5-6, 1968.

27. H. Wakita, "An Approach to Vowel Normalization," Tech Report, Speech Communication Research Laboratories, Santa Barbara, 1975.

28. H. Wakita, "Direct Estimation of the Vocal Tract Shape by Inverse Filtering of Acoustic Speech Waveforms," *IEEE Trans. Audio Electroacoustics*, Vol. AU-21 (5), pp. 417-427, October 1973.

29. H. Sakoe et al., "A Dynamic Programming Approach to Continuous Speech Recognition," *Report 7th ICA, Budapest*, 20-C-13, 1971.

30. J. K. Baker, "Stochastic Modeling as a Means of Automatic Speech Recognition," Doctoral Thesis, Computer Science Department, Carnegie-Mellon University, 1975.

31. L. C. W. Pols, H. R. C. Tromp and R. Plomp, "Frequency Analysis of Dutch Vowels from 50 Male Speakers," *J. Acoustical Society of America*, Vol. 53 (4), pp. 1093-1101, 1973.

32. J. J. Dubnowski, R. W. Schafer and L. R. Rabiner, "Real Time Digital Hardware Pitch Detector Using Combined Peak and Center Clipping and a Simplified Autocorrelation Analysis," to be published in the *IEEE Trans. Audio, Speech and Signal Processing.*

33. P. Mermelstein, "Automatic Segmentation of Speech into Syllabic Units," *J. Acoustical Society of America*, Vol. 58 (4) pp. 880-883, October 1975.

34. L. R. Rabiner and M. R. Sambur, "An Algorithm for Determining the Endpoints of Isolated Utterances," *Bell Sys. Tech. J.*, Vol. 54 (2), pp. 297-315, February 1975.

35. B. T. Oshika, V. W. Zue, R. V. Weeks, H. Neu and J. Aurbach, "The Role of Phonological Rules in Speech Understanding Research," *IEEE Trans. Acoust., Speech and Signal Processing*, Vol. ASSP-23 (1), p. 104, February 1975.

36. P. S. Cohen and R. L. Mercer, "The Phonological Component of an Automatic Speech-Recognition System," in *Speech Recognition* (D. Raj Reddy, ed.), Academic Press, New York, 1975.

37. J. Friedman, "Computer Exploration of Fast-Speech Rules," *IEEE Trans. Acoust., Speech and Signal Processing*, Vol. ASSP-23 (1), p. 100, February 1975.

38. G. Hendricks, Doctoral Thesis, "Partitioned Networks for the Mathematical Modeling of Natural Language Semantics," Dept. of Computer Science, University of Texas, 1975.

39. K. Fukunaga, *Introduction to Statistical Pattern Recognition*, p. 91, Academic Press, New York, 1972.

40. K. S. Fu, *Sequential Methods in Pattern Recognition and Machine Learning*, Academic Press, New York, 1968.

41. I. Kameny, "Comparison of the Formant Spaces of Retroflexed and Nonretroflexed Vowels," *IEEE Trans. Acoust., Speech and Signal Processing*, Vol. ASSP-23 (1), p. 38, February 1975.

42. A. M. Liberman, F. S. Cooper, D. P. Shankweiler and M. Studdert-Kenney, "Perception of the Speech Code," in *Human Communication: A Unified View* (E. David, Jr., and P. Denes, eds.), McGraw-Hill, New York, 1971.

43. B. T. Oshika, V. W. Zue, R. V. Weeks, H. Neu and J. Aurbach, "The Role of Phonological Rules in Speech Understanding Research," *IEEE Trans. Acoust., Speech and Signal Processing*, Vol. ASSP-23 (1), p. 104, February 1975.

44. C. C. Tappert and N. R. Dixon, "A Procedure for Adaptive Control of the Interaction Between Acoustic Classification and Linguistic Decoding in Automatic Recognition of Continuous Speech," *Proc. 3rd Intern. Joint Conf. on Artificial Intelligence*, Stanford, California, August 1973.

45. O. Fujimura, "Syllable as a Unit of Speech Recognition," *Proc. IEEE Symp. Speech Recognition*, pp. 148-153, April 1974.

46. P. Beckmann, "Computerization of English," *IEEE Spectrum*, Vol. 8 (12), pp. 20-27, December 1971.

47. E. P. Neuburg, "Philosophies of Speech Recognition," in *Speech Recognition* (D. Raj Reddy, ed.), Academic Press, New York, 1975.

48. D. D. Buss, W. H. Bailey, R. W. Brodersen, C. R. Hewes, and A. F. Trash, Jr., "Applications of Charge-Coupled Device Transversal Filters to Communication," *Proc. Intern. Conf. Computer Communication*, June 16-18, 1975, San Francisco, California, IEEE Catalog No. 75 CH0971-2 CSCB, Vol. 1, pp. 2-4.

49. Gordon S. Kino and John Shaw, "Acoustic Surface Waves," *Scientific American*, Vol. 227 (4), p. 50, October 1972.

50. CE Chip (Computation Element chip) 1975 Winners I-R 100, *Industrial Research*, p. 42, October 1975.

51. *Proc. Intern. Optical Computing Conf.*, April 23-25, 1975, Washington, D.C., IEEE Catalog No. 75 CH0941-53.

52. BEAMOS (BEam Addressed Metal Oxide Semiconductor) 1975, Winners I-R 100, *Industrial Research*, p. 41, October 1972.

53. A. Schaff, *Language and Cognition*, McGraw-Hill, New York, 1973.

54. V. R. Lesser, "Parallel Processing in Speech Understanding Systems: A Survey of Design Problems," in *Speech Recognition* (D. Raj Reddy, ed.), Academic Press, New York, 1975.

55. R. B. Neely and G. M. White, "On the Use of Syntax in a Low-Cost Real-Time Speech Recognition System," *Proc. IFIP*, Stockholm, Sweden, pp. 748-752, August 1974.

An Assessment of the Technology of Automatic Speech Recognition for Military Applications

BRUNO BEEK, MEMBER, IEEE, EDWARD P. NEUBERG, AND DAVID C. HODGE

***Abstract*—The objective of this paper is to provide a summary of the state-of-the-art of automatic speech recognition (ASR) and its relevance to military applications. Until recently, speech recognition had its widest application in the development of vocoders for narrow-band speech communications. Presently, research in ASR has been accelerated for military tasks such as command and control, secure voice systems, surveillance of communication channels, and others. Research in voice control technology and digital narrow-band systems are of special interest. Much of the emphasis of today's military-supported research is to reduce to practice the current state of knowledge of ASR, as well as directing research in such a way as to have future military relevance.**

In coordination with the above-mentioned emphasis in military-supported research, this paper is divided into two major sections. The first section presents discussion of the state-of-the-art and problems in the various subareas of the ASR field. The second section presents a number of unsolved problems and techniques which need to be perfected before the solutions to a number of military applications of the ASR field are possible.

INTRODUCTION

THE OBJECTIVE of this paper is to provide a summary of the state-of-the-art of automatic speech recognition (ASR) and its relevance to military applications. Table I lists a number of military tasks for possible automation using speech recognition technology. Until recently, speech recognition has had its widest application in the development of vocoders for narrow-band speech communications. Presently, research in ASR has been accelerated in the following areas: speech understanding systems, voice control systems, automatic speaker verification (ASV), and narrow-band digital secure voice systems.

These areas, with the exception of speech understanding research, offer the potential for either immediate or near-term solution to a number of military problems. Research in voice control technology and digital narrow-band systems is of special interest. Much of the emphasis of today's military-supported research is to reduce to practice the current state of knowledge of ASR, as well as directing research in such a way as to have future military relevance.

Today, only a small number of applications exist for using ASR. However, as these systems prove to be reliable and cost-effective, their usage will increase in the near future. Already in use are voice data entry systems for inventory/supply record control [36]. These applications are limited to a small vocabulary, speaker-dependent, isolated word recognition system. These highly reliable systems allow for hands-free source data entry of the digits and a limited set of control words. As such, the voice data entry system eliminates manual transcription and keying operations.

TABLE I
MILITARY TASKS FOR POSSIBLE AUTOMATION

1) Security
- 1.1 Speaker Verification (Authentication)
- 1.2 Speaker Identification (Recognition)
- 1.3 Determining emotional state of speaker (e.g., stress effects)
- 1.4 Recognition of spoken codes
- 1.5 Secure access voice identification, whether or not in combination with fingerprints, facial information, identity card, signature, etc.
- 1.6 Surveillance of communication channels

2) Command and Control
- 2.1 System control (ships, aircraft, fire control, situation displays, etc.)
- 2.2 Voice-operated computer input/output (each telephone a terminal)
- 2.3 Data handling and record control
- 2.4 Material handling (mail, baggage, publications, industrial applications)
- 2.5 Remote control (dangerous material)
- 2.6 Administrative record control

3) Data Transmission and Communication
- 3.1 Speech synthesis
- 3.2 Vocoder systems
- 3.3 Bandwidth reduction or, more general, bit-rate reduction
- 3.4 Ciphering/coding/scrambling

4) Processing Distorted Speech
- 4.1 Diver speech
- 4.2 Astronaut communication
- 4.3 Underwater telephone
- 4.4 Oxygen mask speech
- 4.5 High "*G*" force speech

A large number of potential systems for military applications are now under study. These include:

1) Digital Narrow-band Communication Systems: A massive effort is underway to develop and implement an all-digital communication system [59].

2) Automatic Speaker Verification: An advanced development model has been fabricated for secure access control applications [14].

3) Training Systems: A limited speech understanding system is under study for use as a component in a military training system [20].

4) Distorted Speech Processing (Helium Speech): Helium speech unscramblers are being developed to allow for adequate diver-to-diver or diver-to-surface communications.

5) On-Line Cartographic Processing System: Studies are

Manuscript received April 20, 1976; revised March 21, 1977.

B. Beek is with the Rome Air Development Center, Griffiss Air Force Base, Rome, NY.
E. P. Neuberg is with the Department of Defense, Washington, DC.
D. C. Hodge is with the U.S. Army Human Engineering Laboratory, Aberdeen Proving Ground, MD.

Reprinted from *IEEE Trans. Acoust., Speech, and Signal Process.*, vol. ASSP-25, pp. 310–322, Aug. 1977.

underway to use speech recognition and voice response techniques with a cartographic point and trace processing systems [5]. Rome Air Development Center implemented an operational system for the Defense Mapping Agency (DMA) where bathymetric depth measurements are digitized using a real-time speaker-dependent, isolated word recognition system.

6) Word Recognition for Militarized Tactical Data Systems: Word recognition, speaker verification, and voice response will be used for message entry to a tactical data system [58].

7) Voice Recognition and Synthesis for Aircraft Cockpit: Existing word recognition systems are being tested and evaluated under simulated cockpit environments.

These studies and implementations are in various stages of investigation and/or development and represent a practical utilization of the emerging speech recognition technology.

This paper is divided into two major sections. The first section presents a discussion of the state-of-the-art and problems in the various subareas according to the outline of applications given in Table I.

The second section (summary) presents a number of unsolved problems and techniques required to be perfected before solutions to a number of military applications are possible.

I. Military Applications of ASR: State-of-the-Art

A. Security Applications

Automatic speech recognition may soon be extensively used in the area of security. Present and future military requirements shall place greater emphasis in this area as some of the critical technology is solved. First and foremost in terms of military applications is the problem of automatic speaker verification/identification [7], [22]. This security problem and others are in different stages of solution, some of which are discussed below.

1) ASV (Authentication): Speaker verification means the verification or rejection of an individual based on his speech patterns [11], [14], [53]. In general, each individual known to the ASV system has on file a number of samples of his speech. When he wishes to be verified by the system, he must first identify himself to the ASV system via a badge reader, keyboard, magnetic card, etc. Once he has identified himself, the ASV system requests that he speak a number of sentences, phrases, or words. After the individual complies, the ASV system analyzes the incoming data, compares them with its reference file, and makes a decision either to accept or reject the individual or requests additional data. ASV technology has a number of advantages that are not always available in other speech recognition problems. Namely, the speaker is cooperative; he is attempting to gain access to some function and hence will be on his best behavior. The speech data spoken by the individual are known to the ASV system; sentences and words are chosen to provide the greatest amount of discrimination. The acoustic environment can be either controlled (good signal-to-noise (S/N) ratio) or noise cancelling microphones can be used. Analysis of an individual's reference speech data may lead to extraction of customized features for that individual to maximize speaker discrimination. In the operational mode, where the individual tests the system, the ASV can, by analyzing the speech and finding it deficient (i.e., not loud enough, garbled, etc.), request individuals to repeat. Furthermore, the communication channel can easily be made identical for both reference and test.

A number of techniques are being investigated by Bell Laboratories, North American Rockwell, and others. Perhaps the most successful is that of Texas Instruments (supported by the United States Air Force/RADC) [14]. Their technique is as follows: each speaker, or potential user, prerecords a set of 16 words from which 32 sentences can be generated. Each word was selected to contain either a different vowel or diphthong. Only the vowel or diphthong region of the word is used for the speaker verification task. In each of these sentences, critical regions are chosen at which the overall amplitude is large (so that measurements are reliable) and some phonetic event seems to be occurring. These places are found by taking a Fourier spectrum every 10 ms, and looking for regions where spectra are changing rapidly with time (i.e., a transition). For each such transition, a matrix is formed which contains energies in some number of frequency bands from 300 to 2500 Hz, and at times for 100 ms surrounding the event. To score a reference against a test sentence, the incoming sentence is first Fourier transformed every 10 ms. Each template is scanned through the test sentence at 10 ms intervals and at each position is compared with the corresponding 100-ms-long matrix at that position; the distance measure is simply the sum of the squares of the differences between template elements and corresponding elements from the six minima is the score (against those six templates) for the sentence. If the score is below some threshold, the sentence is accepted (and thus the speaker is accepted).

This technique now produces results on the order of 1 percent rejection of true speaker, 2 percent acceptance of impostors, based on only one reference utterance for 120 speakers. Using two reference utterances reduces the false acceptance rate to less than 1 percent. Hence, ASV technology has proven highly successful for fixed context speaker verification when using cooperative speakers in a good S/N environment.

In addition, the technology has successfully coped with the problems of mimicry, day-to-day speaker variability, colds, sinus congestion, and respiratory ailments. In general, the technology can handle most operational requirements and achieve low Type I errors (true speaker rejections), as well as Type II errors (impostor acceptances) with certain tradeoffs depending on the specific application. For example, Type II errors can be lowered at the expense of increasing Type I errors and vice versa. Both types of errors can be reduced at the expense of having the user utter more speech data (i.e., utter two or three phrases instead of one).

The technology has been tested using a large data base and achieves low error rates with a high confidence level. The problem now is to optimize this technology so that it is compatible and acceptable to the user. The user must have complete confidence in the technology, and the problems involving human factors must be eliminated [21].

This is a research area of interest to the military (e.g., accepting or rejecting front-line tactical reports), in industry (e.g., controlling access to restricted areas), and in commerce (e.g., controlling access to money or information). There is a stated military requirement in the United States for a device to handle this problem under field conditions.

2) Speaker Identification (Recognition): This section describes several techniques for automatic speaker identification of an individual based on his voice characteristics [1], [7], [22], [32], [63]. Only those techniques will be discussed that have been evaluated in a set of experiments that encompasses a wide range of conditions. These techniques render recognition decisions automatically from continuous speech uncontrolled as to context [29], [67]. Hence, the techniques have the advantage of generating a speaker's reference library and testing unknown speech samples independent of spoken text. This advantage is important when one is collecting and analyzing speech data from an uncooperative speaker. At the present time, applications of greatest interest are the use of the voice signal for personnel identification in monitoring communication channels. Conditions that make this problem difficult in practice or real application are:

1) the communication system is of poor quality;
2) speakers are noncooperative;
3) recording and/or channel conditions are different for references and test samples;
4) deciding whether the speaker is a member of an original group of speakers.

This kind of problem arises in the military when, for example, one tries to keep track of a unit that is communicating by radio.

The techniques for the most part deal with analysis and classification of the speech signal in the frequency domain. Essentially, two different approaches have been extensively investigated:

1) extraction of voiced characteristics from long-term and short-term spectral characteristics [1], [22], [29], [67];

2) recognition of specific types of sounds, such as vowels, nasals, and/or fricatives as a prelude to the extraction of spectral characteristics.

Experiments have shown that long-term statistics of speech which include spectral and pitch distributions are pretty well determined by about 30 s of voiced speech [7], [32]. This technique, under laboratory conditions, has fairly low error rates ($\leqslant$5 percent) for up to 40 speakers. These statistics have not, so far, been upheld in an environment which includes channel noise and distortion.

At the present time, greater emphasis is being placed on analyzing an individual's speech signal when particular phonetic events occur. In this manner, the vocal-tract transfer function can be determined by a detailed spectrum analysis [64]. Peaks in the vocal-tract transfer function relate to the natural frequencies of the vocal tract and are called formants. It is postulated that measurements of these formants and other formant-related information may be speaker-specific. Combining a number of these measurements for a number of phonetic events can provide the data to identify a speaker.

A number of speech investigations have studied the use of a linear least-square, inverse filter formulation to estimate the formant trajectories of selected phonetic events [30], [34], [37], [56]. During this research it has been shown, both statistically and experimentally, which analysis conditions give the most stable or consistent parameters and how those same conditions give the best identification performance.

Much has been learned from past research in the field, but there still remain shortcomings which must be resolved in order to remove constraints on text, number of speakers, etc. There are continuing problems with speaker variability, context, and coarticulation effects (see Table II). Research is continuing in these areas, but only at a low level of effort.

3) Semi-Automatic Speaker Identification System: Perhaps the most controversial method of speaker identification is by the visual comparisons of speech spectrograms (also called "Voiceprints"). This method is not automatic, but subjective, and its reliability is disputed by many speech researchers [62].

A speech spectrogram is a three-dimensional plot representing time, frequency, and intensity of a sample of speech. Speaker recognition by visual comparison of spectrograms consists of subjectively matching loosely defined points of similarity (in spectrograms of identical utterances) found from the same person that are not found in pairs of spectrograms from different persons. This criterion prevents replication of the experimental results by independent investigations. As such, the "Voiceprints" have been the subject of controversy in the speech community. The advocates of "Voiceprint" are convinced that sound spectrograms are reliable enough to be admissible in a court of law. The opponent position is that the technique is good in a probabilistic sense, but not good enough to be used in convicting or freeing defendents. The situation at the moment is that the Voiceprint technique, administered only by this self-selected group of experts, is in fact being used in courts of law; however, several speech scientists are making strenuous efforts to bring the shortcomings of the technique to the attention of law enforcement officials.

The United States National Institute of Law Enforcement and Criminal Justice of the Law Enforcement Assistance Administration (LEAA) has undertaken the task of developing a computerized system to replace the subjective expert decision of "Voiceprints" by objective probabilistic decisions based on experiments performed on large speaker populations. A computerized hardware/software system has been developed to perform semi-automatic speaker identification [8]. This system will provide interactive displays to allow an operator to analyze quasi-steady-state portions of particular sounds of interest (phonemes). Analytical investigations have involved processing samples of speech of over 250 speakers from which 35 000 phonetic events were extracted. Algorithms were also developed to compute similarity measures based on various combinations of detected phonemes. It is the goal of this LEAA effort that when the semi-automatic speaker identification system is fully implemented and tested, it will overcome many of the current objections to the utilization of voice identification for courtroom evidence.

4) Surveillance of Communications Channels: This topic can include a number of items common to all major tasks listed in Table I. However, only two topics will be discussed due to military interest in these areas.

TABLE II
TECHNIQUES REQUIRING PERFECTION TO AUTOMATE MILITARY TASKS

1) Signal Conditioning

Some processing of speech signals may be necessary to compensate for different characteristics of input channels, such as overall signal level and differential delay. Also, it may be possible to preprocess to improve speech quality, or S/N ratio, or to remove long silences.

2) Digital Signal Transformation

The digitized speech signal is transformed in preparation for the extraction of parameters. Processes used include Fourier and Walsh transforms, correlation, LPC, and digital filtering.

3) Analog Signal Transformation and Feature Extraction

The signal can be transformed by hardware, such as filter banks and correlation devices. Transforms can be digitized for further processing, or parameters and features can be extracted in a continuous manner for presentation to decision networks or algorithms.

4) Digital Parameter and Feature Extraction

Calculations are done on the transformed signal to extract relevant parameters, such as formant tracking, pitch extraction and principle components analysis.

5a) Resynthesis

Speech parameters extracted, as mentioned above, in speech compression systems or stored in voice playback systems, must be transformed into acceptable acoustic speech signals.

5b) Orthographic Synthesis

In the translation of written materials to speech, a number of techniques must be developed. Some of these techniques are similar to those cited in the paragraphs above. One of the most important is the development of speech morphology.

6) Speaker Normalization, Speaker Adaptation, Situation Adaptation

The effectiveness of parameters in carrying relevant speech information depends on characteristics of individual speakers and on operational situations. This could mean that systems must be trained or must adapt to optimize parameters.

7) Time Normalization

In recognition of isolated utterances, normalization is imposed to compensate for local and global differences in speech rate. Both linear and nonlinear schemes can be used.

8) Segmentation and Labeling

Segment boundaries are set, e.g., at points of rapid change, formant positions, voicing, spectral shape or other parameters. Segments may be labeled probabalistically to acoustic-phonetic classes. Prestored knowledge of features and parameters for the various classes of segments are used in the decision.

9a) Language Statistics

Language statistics and partial recognition are used to predict and evaluate words at specific points in an utterance.

9b) Syntax

The grammar of the task is used to predict and evaluate word categories at specific points in an utterance.

9c) Semantics

Knowledge of the task domain is used to predict and evaluate subject matter at specific points in an utterance.

9d) Speaker and Situation Pragmatics

In determining the semantics of speech, certain aspects of the utterances are related to an underlying assumption about what the speaker would generally consider an appropriate response. The development of this type of knowledge is required for speech understanding systems. Knowledge of the situation that gave rise to the speaker's utterances is also required for reliable interpretation and execution of the task to be performed in response to the utterance.

10) Lexical Matching

Strings of linguistic-phonetic elements hypothesized by the linguistic part of the system are compared with strings of acoustic-phonetic elements derived from an utterance. A quantitative goodness of match is calculated.

11) Speech Understanding

All sources of knowledge (acoustic, phonetic, pragmatic, semantic, syntactic) are used in combination to reconstruct the utterance and/or determine its meaning.

12) Speaker Recognition

Speaker-specific parameters are extracted and compared with stored parameter sets from known speakers.

13) System Organization and Realization

Systems must be developed keeping in mind use by humans and cost-effective factors.

14) Performance Evaluation

Present development of all speech systems requires the determination of the quantitative value of each possible technique studied. Only by the use of stored speech samples is this performance evaluation possible.

a) Keyword Classification: The goal of this program is to recognize a keyword or a set of keywords embedded in narrow-bandwidth conversational speech as expected from a radio link. The reconnaissance of large amounts of speech information requires a need for economical data editing and scanning. An automatic method of detecting and classifying keywords would perform this function. The difficulties in providing this speech processing function are that the speaker is unknown, speech is continuous, and the speech signal is often degraded by noise and distortion. Problems also exist due to coarticulation and context, since the acoustic representation can be affected significantly by the acoustic environment of the keyword.

Two techniques have been investigated. The first is to recognize acoustic events simultaneously in free-running speech. A sequential logic made up of acoustic events can be designed for a keyword. This approach postulates that keyword detection will take place when the needed sequence of acoustic events occur. Another approach is to simply measure energy in selected frequency bands and match them against stored templates of the same measurement made on the keyword. Neither approach has yet proven successful, especially if the system has not been trained by the speaker. Considerable cost and effort have already been expended on research in this area; results have not been very promising. An experiment was performed using speech from a news-broadcast radio station as input; here the speech is carefully enunciated, the speakers are few, the communication channel is good, and there are frequently occurring words (such as the name of the radio station) [61]. In the best case, there was 80-90 percent recognition of the keyword, with nonnegligible false alarms. After a hiatus, military-sponsored research in this field is recommencing.

b) Language Identification: Numerous techniques have been applied to language identification due to a fluctuating military interest in this problem. The most general approach has been, as in speaker identification, to use pitch and spectral features. Most prominent features have been extracted from long-term speech spectra (usually voiced speech). The features are then used to generate statistics for the various languages of concern. Experimental tests using these statistics as representing the languages have proven that these approaches will not work, or they are too speaker-dependent to be useful. Recently, emphasis has been placed on the recognition of acoustic events within the speech signal which are reliable, stable, and speaker-independent. This work, and the work of the speech understanding group in devising methods of converting the acoustic signal into a chain of linguistic elements, offers considerable promise for a solution of this problem.

Experiments have been performed with perfect linguistic chains of this type, formed from a phonetician's hand transcription of speech in various languages [40]. These experiments show that the statistics of these chains, especially higher order statistics of digraphs and trigraphs, are a very powerful means of discriminating between languages given 1–2 min of speech.

Experiments were also performed on five languages involving over 100 different speakers using acoustic events extracted from continuous speech [28]. The data on each speaker were collected over a period of time to determine the effects of speaker variability on recognition performance. Fairly encouraging language recognition scores for three of the languages have already been attained. However, the other two languages were quite poorly recognized, indicating the need for further work. Experiments were also conducted on detecting a single language from many different languages. In one case, a language was detected successfully against several languages involving over 100 speakers with practically perfect detection and no false alarms [28].

B. Command and Control

Command and control, in the context of this paper, means voice communications with machines. These include:

1) limited word sets
2) connected word recognition (limited set of words)
3) continuous speech recognition/understanding.

1) Isolated Word Recognition: Speaker-dependent, limited vocabulary, isolated word recognition (10-50 words) has, for all intents and purposes, been solved under laboratory conditions [4], [6], [9], [25], [31], [33], [35], [42], [44], [46]-[49], [66]. A number of commercial companies in the United States and England are marketing isolated word recognizers. Voice data entry systems are already operating in a variety of industrial applications [36]. These include:

1) automated sorting systems, distribution of parcels, containers, and baggage
2) voice programming for machine tools
3) inspection system, i.e., measurement of TV face plates.

In general, automatic recognition processes can be viewed as a series of algorithms which reduce the relatively high-dimensional measurement space (time domain) to a single-dimensional recognition space. Each transformation, in turn, reduces the number of features that characterize the event. Ultimately, a minimum set of features is extracted and is used to generate a recognition pattern. The final transformation associates the pattern with one of a finite number of patterns of known events.

The most important problem to be solved in the isolated word situation, it seems, is locating the beginning and end of the word [36], [51]. According to many researchers in the field, if the word endpoints can be found, precisely, the exact process used in recognition becomes less critical. The beginning is usually easier to find on the basis of total energy in the signal. However, the end is often masked by breath noise after the word is over, and sophisticated speech/nonspeech separation techniques are needed. Once the endpoints are found, one extracts for the duration of the word, either continuously or at discrete times, some functions of the acoustic signal that are linguistically significant. In one system, for example, 32 functions are calculated continuously (by hardware), varying from something as simple as energy spectrum regions to a function indicating presence of a particular vowel (calculated by detecting voicing, and then looking at the energies in the frequency bands where the formants of that vowel should be found) [35]. These 32 features are sampled at 16 equally-spaced places throughout the word, and the resulting 16×32 matrix is used as a template to represent the word. In most systems, several tokens of each word are used to "train" the system; some use an average template to represent the word; others use templates for each word [35]. In the recognition mode, the matrix for an incoming word is calculated and matched against all the stored templates; the system decides that the incoming word is that word whose template is closest, according to some metric, to the new matrix. In most systems there is a distance threshold on the distance functions, and if the template fails to meet the distance criteria the word is rejected.

The difficult problem in isolated word recognition seems to be proper alignment of endpoints. Nonlinear time normalization does not seem to be necessary (especially if several training templates are stored), and although the particular functions used must obviously have linguistic significance, various systems using different sets of functions give satisfactory results. Some of the limitations of present systems are:

1) vocabulary is small—about 75 words
2) there is no speaker normalization procedure
3) there is no extrapolation of what the system learns on one training word [2) and 3) mean that every speaker must train the system on every word in the vocabulary]
4) the words must be spoken in a discrete manner.

2) Multispeaker, Isolated Words: Great emphasis is being placed today on the development of a speaker-dependent isolated word recognition system which operates over a good quality telephone network (bandwidth 300-3500 Hz) [50], [55], [58]. Experiments have shown that a relationship exists between word size, type of vocabulary, and speaker dependence as a function of recognition accuracy [52], [66]. Although most multispeaker recognition systems tend to be insensitive to variations in the rate of speech, problems still exist due to variations in a talker's speech characteristics and talker-dependent traits. Recent experiments have shown a multispeaker recognition system to be highly accurate in recognizing a small set of words (10–20) even in the context of connected speech [54], [68]. However, in these experiments, adjustments had to be made for an individual's characteristics by using a short learning phase. Also under experimental investigation is a speaker-independent connected digit recognition system to identify four digit code groups. These codes would be used in conjunction with an ASV system in lieu of a keyboard or badge reader. Being restricted to a finite length set of digits, error correcting codes, a few predetermined digits could be used to adapt the system [14].

3) Short Phrase Recognition: Item 2) above implies that isolated word recognition techniques are not sufficient for the short-phrase recognition task. There is, in fact, some military-sponsored research in the recognition of short strings of spoken digits and words. The total vocabulary of strings is too large to be handled by the isolated word algorithms, so two new problems must be faced. First, in place of the endpoint problem we have the segmentation problem: word boundaries must be found in connected text. Second, after words are located, the problem exists that words are altered according to context and according to position in the string. (For example, on the last word of a string the speaker usually allows both the amplitude and pitch to fall greatly.) The word-alteration problem might be solved by storage of more templates for each word, or by application of alteration rules; segmentation techniques are not as successful now as isolated word finders at determining word boundaries, even for a very small vocabulary such as the ten digits.

4) Continuous Speech Recognition (Speech Understanding): Speech understanding is interpreted to mean the capability to recognize any sentence that can be produced from a known vocabulary (lexicon), with known subject matter (semantics), using known grammatical rules (syntax) [13], [39], [41], [52], [68]. The conventional approach many are trying in order to get to this problem is to restrict lexicon, syntax, and semantics *drastically*, use high-quality speech (i.e., not limited to telephone bandwidth) and allow only one or a small number of speakers. A very restricted domain, for example, that is being investigated by one group is playing chess by voice [15]. (There are several computer programs that will play the user quite a good game of chess.) The lexicon consists of approximately 50 words. Syntax is very simple and semantics is trivial (few moves are even legal). A more complicated and more useful task domain is querying a data base by voice. An example of this is a query system pertaining to the Navy, of which one can ask questions such as "How many ships have length greater than 700 feet?," or "List all cruisers of the United States Navy."

All continuous speech recognition (CSR) systems so far constructed are large computer programs (100 000–200 000 instructions) on fairly large computers, typically a DEC PDP-10. The digitizing is done at 20 000 samples/s in most systems, allowing a bandwidth of about 10 kHz. Pitch extraction is performed in a variety of ways. With very few exceptions, spectral analysis is accomplished via linear predictive coding (LPC) and a Fourier transform, with formant tracking achieved by various ad hoc procedures [2], [3], [27], [50], [52], [68]. Vowel and fricative identification is implemented by matching LPC spectra taken every 10 ms against a stored template, or extracting formants and matching formant positions against formant templates. Stop identification is accomplished by recognizing short silences following bursts, and by observing formant transitions in adjacent vowels. Nasals, liquids, and glides are found by observing voicing with low overall energy, and then matching templates as if for vowels. In some systems, templates are formed by training the system on some specially constructed test sentences, producing a new set of templates for each speaker. In others, an attempt is made to normalize the speaker's parameters so that a single set of templates can be used for all speakers.

At the so-called "top end," the part that hypothesizes words to be matched against the incoming acoustic stream, fairly sophisticated new techniques are being used to decide what words are likely to appear at a given place in the sentence given a tentative partial recognition. Words are generally stored as a string of syllables or phonemes. Before that string is compared with the string of linguistic elements derived from the acoustic stream, it must be altered by application of phonological rules to take into account such things as context, amplitude, and duration changes induced by syntax and semantics, and local variations in the observed partial recognition. Matching algorithms for best recognition are still rather crude, and statistics of phones or phonemes are not used in the decision process. At a guess, the strings of linguistic elements that are being presented to the matching algorithms are something like 40 percent correct when compared to a phonetician's transcription, and probably the correct element is among the first five choices some 80 percent of the time. It is estimated by some that good recognition will require something like 90 percent first choices for the derived linguistic elements, and state-of-the-art is certainly two to three years from that goal [15].

There has never been a stated military requirement for CSR, but as with other processes, it would clearly be beneficial. The Defense Advanced Research Projects Agency (ARPA) has recently supported a very large research effort in CSR. Outside of the Department of Defense (DOD), the largest single effort is at IBM, which has a 15-man effort in progress [13]. The ARPA project culminated in late 1976. Limited progress has been achieved toward speech understanding goals, with the greatest success coming from the HARPY system, developed by Carnegie-Mellon University. The main targets of high accuracy on connected speech with a vocabulary of 1000 words were met by the HARPY system, with accuracy given in terms of total sentence accuracy, 91 percent, and semantic accuracy, 97 percent. Processing by the HARPY system takes about 20 times real time, and although HARPY is not a general task-free system, some constraints were not necessary such as the use of very high quality nonnoisy microphones; also, although HARPY makes substantial use of training, requiring the experimenter to adapt its word dictionaries, the amount of training required to add a new or additional speaker is not excessive [38].

C. Data Transmission and Communication

Extensive work in the area of speech transmission has been carried out. Generally, the programs tend to follow similar lines of attack, particularly with regard to the new innovation, LPC vocoders. Conventional vocoder systems have been widely used in military and government applications and are still under investigation. The following discussion outlines the United States programs for an all-digital communications system.

Because the United States DOD has decided to revamp its communications and go to an all-digital voice system, while keeping bandwidths low, massive compression techniques are being studied, developed, and realized in hardware and software [59]. Six defense agencies (see Appendix E) are carrying on and/or sponsoring research in the millions-of-dollars-per-year range. The following is a description of the techniques being pursued, and where in the study/research/development/implementation cycle they now stand.

1) Conventional Vocoders: Despite the tremendous popularity of the new LPC techniques, conventional vocoders are still being considered as candidates for the system [16]. One of the tests in the grand competition will be comparison with HY-2, which is a (by now) fairly old channel vocoder that has been used a great deal by the military. A new, all-digital, very reliable version of the HY-2 will be built and used in the tests. Besides this, new techniques are being examined to build better channel vocoders. (No other types of vocoders, such as Laguerre or harmonic vocoders, are being studied.) Some improvement seems to be possible in the coding of channel amplitudes; because of high correlation among amplitudes of the higher channels, coding of amplitude relative to the next lower channel is more economical than coding of amplitude itself. There is one development effort that is simply trying to build a classical channel vocoder, paying great attention to detail in order to improve quality. The implementation will in fact be digital, but all processes will be simulations of realizable analog processes, such as Lerner filters and the Gold pitch extractor.

Pitch extraction, which is of course a problem in all vocoders, not only channel vocoders, has improved since the last generation of vocoders, but is still very much an ad hoc process. Much of the activity in pitch detection seems to be an attempt to carry out known pitch detection schemes faster, and on computers with short words (16 bits). One new idea in pitch extraction is use of dynamic programming to track current pitch, based on estimates of past and future pitch.

2) LPC Vocoders: The main thrust of the consortium is toward a vocoder using LPC. The idea at its simplest, is to extract parameters through LPC and extract pitch, and reconstruct the input from these data at the other end. The LPC techniques that are being tried are those described by Atal, Markel, and Itakura [3], [27], [34]; these have all been set up in software, and are being realized in hardware. (Hardware here means very fast microprogrammable computers, hardwired to do the vocoder process. There are a number of these computers on the market, all with some degree of parallel processing and operating in the range of 100 ns/instruction.) Various LPC parameters have been analyzed, such as LPC coefficients themselves, reflection coefficients, and vocal-tract area functions; at present, reflection coefficients are in greatest favor, since they are fairly insensitive to noise. Many different rates of sending parameters have been tried; a good compromise between bit rate and quality seems to be to use 10- or 12- coefficient LPC and to send (update) the parameters every 16 or 20 ms. For smoothing purposes, the parameters are calculated more often and transmitted at the indicated rate.

Some LPC-related ideas that have been considered in the past but not tried are being experimented with, but have not been implemented into hardware or major software. One of these is pitch-synchronous LPC calculation. There seems to be a stability gain in doing this; however, since parameters are being transmitted at regular times, there is some uncertainty as to the best means of encoding. Another technique being examined is Kalman filtering. This is presently in the study stage, but certain problems have already emerged; it is more sensitive to noise than LPC and less stable. A possible use of Kalman filtering is to do short LPC's (on the order of 3 ms) and Kalman filter the coefficients. Both versions of Kalman filtering will have to be done pitch-synchronously.

3) Other Vocoders: Some novel hybrid vocoders are being considered, somewhat akin to voice-excited vocoders (VEV) [16], [45]. One such device will be a standard channel vocoder from 1-3 kHz, but the first 1000 Hz will be encoded by a fourth-order LPC calculation. Another will be a fairly standard VEV, in which the bottom 800 Hz are encoded by adaptive pulse-code modulation (ADPCM) or adaptive delta modulation (ADM). Still a third idea is to do the LPC calculation on the whole signal to obtain coefficients, then use the residual to convey the pitch; this will be done by filtering the residual by a low-pass filter and either sending it as is or compressing it via ADPCM or delta modulation, or even via a low-coefficient LPC.

The ARPA part of the consortium effort has some rather special aspects to it, since ARPA is concerned not only with speech compression, but also with the use of networks in communication. They have a network in which information is sent in 1000-bit packets, each containing the address of the recipient. These are switched at connection points in the network to whatever path toward the recipient is open at the time of arrival of the packet. Since different paths may cause different delays, the packets must be stored and reassembled at the receiving end. Clearly, this causes problems in real-time applications such as a voice communication system, and much of the ARPA work addresses these problems. Besides these special network problems, the ARPA effort is looking at another aspect of compression, which is removal of redundancy after a process like LPC or channel vocoding. There is some hope that by very careful editing of the redundant portion of the parameterized speech (especially silence), and accepting the resulting transmission delay, one can get high-quality vocoded speech at 1000 bits/s.

It is interesting to note that, except for this last notion of removal of redundancy, all compression efforts have a common underlying principle; they all try to separate the speech into a source function and a transfer function, encode these two separately, and reconstruct at the other end by convolution. No other model of speech compression is being considered.

D. Processing Distorted and Degraded Speech

1) Distorted Speech Process (Helium Speech): The use of a helium-rich mixture as a breathing gas solves physiological problems in the deep-sea or saturation diving situation, but gives rise to a problem of helium speech, the degradation of speech intelligibility [18], [54]. There is no question that effective speech communication must be provided for life support and for the effectiveness of divers in such situations. However, the present state-of-the-art for overcoming the problem is unsatisfactory.

Many attempts have been made to clarify the nature of helium distortions and then to build helium-speech unscramblers. Except for a few of them, almost all seem to have some shortcomings in understanding the underlying nature of helium distortions. It is due to: 1) the lack of insight into the basic mechanism of speech production and perception, 2) the focusing of attention only on narrow questions and on the small sets of data, and 3) the nonutilization of common knowledge and well-known techniques in the field of speech processing.

"Helium speech" occurs when divers perform saturation dives to depths of 200 ft and greater. An oxygen-helium mixture is breathed at pressures up to 450 lb/in^2. Marked changes in the resonant characteristics of the vocal tract result. The generalized effects of these conditions on speech are as follows.

1) There is a linear transformation of formant frequency above 500 Hz.

2) There is a nonlinear transformation of formant frequency below 500 Hz.

3) There is an apparent loss of energy in consonants compared to vowels.

4) Formant bandwidths do not increase with increasing pressure.

5) High-frequency energy decreases with increased pressure.

6) Low-frequency energy increases with increased pressure.

There has been little investigation of the effects of helium and pressure on vowel-consonant transitions. Behavioral characteristics of divers add to the problem. Some, for example, try to speak louder to overcome high ambient noise and this affects the consonant-vowel ratio further. The configuration of the mask and other life-support equipment also contributes to the problem.

The general approach taken in trying to unscramble helium speech involves linear shifting the vowel format frequencies down to the "normal" positions. This approach ignores the nonlinear low-frequency problem. The methods used fall into two categories: frequency domain processing and time domain processing. Frequency domain processing includes subtraction and vocoding. Time domain processing includes tape recorder manipulation, convolution processing, and digital coding schemes.

Typical examples of the two main methods used in unscrambling helium speech are given as follows:

a) Frequency Domain Processing

i) Frequency Subtraction: This involves subtracting a fixed frequency from the entire helium-speech spectrum [10]. It is generally accomplished by heterodyning a bandpassed version of the incoming signal by a carrier frequency, selecting one sideband, and then heterodyning it down in frequency. Another approach is to split the incoming signal into two subbands using bandpass filters. These bands are heterodyned up by a carrier frequency, then heterodyned downward by separately tuned oscillators. Frequency subtraction has been used in unscramblers developed by the Naval Applied Sciences Laboratory.

ii) Vocoder Techniques: Formant-restoring vocoders are used to compress the speech spectral envelope while preserving the harmonic structure of the speech signal [19]. Helium speech is introduced into a contiguous bank of bandpass filters whose outputs are full-wave rectified and smoothed by low-pass filters, yielding a slow time-varying signal that is proportional to the energy in the passband of a given analyzing filter. These signals are used to balance modulate an excitation signal derived from the original helium speech, and then are resynthesized through a bank of bandpass filters. This technique has been implemented in an off-line mode only.

b) Time Domain Processing

i) Tape Recorder Playback: This was one of the first techniques attempted to unscramble helium speech, and it involves recording the helium speech at one speed and then playing it back at one-half speed [24]. Off-line processing is required to restore the original time base. More recently, sophisticated recording and playback techniques, including revolving tape heads, etc., have been attempted.

ii) Digital Coding: Digital circuitry has been used in unscramblers built by Raytheon Company, Industrial Research Products, Inc., Westinghouse, and Singer. In general, the helium speech is sampled in real time, stored in a register, and then read out at a slower rate while bandpassing the signal. Some information is discarded in order to achieve proper frequency scaling. (Further details of these devices are proprietary, and hence not available.)

iii) Convolution Processing: This approach takes advantage of the fact that the shape of the vocal tract is the same under both helium and air speaking. The helium-speech waveform is first deconvoluted to obtain vocal-tract impulse response functions. Then an inverse can be constructed, and appropriate time scaling can be performed to compensate for the necessary changes in the velocity of sound.

On several of the existing scramblers, tests have been performed using rigorous and systematic procedures under a United States Navy contract by Hollien *et al.* [54] at the University of Florida. The results of these indicated that, in general, none of the unscramblers evaluated to date provides enough substantial improvement to allow for really adequate diver-to-diver or diver-to-surface communication. Mean unprocessed PB word intelligibility was reported to be about 16 percent, and mean unscrambled PB intelligibility was no better than about 40 percent. (Typical current military communication system criteria require 70 percent PB word intelligibility as mandatory and 80 percent as desirable.) Single digits can, of course, be received reliably with systems having PB intelligibility on the order of 50 percent, but good sentence intelligibility requires much higher values.

In general, it seems that helium-speech unscramblers do not work very well (although they may be in use because nothing better is available). Unsolved problems include the nonlinear shift at lower frequencies, formant transitions and consonants, and restoring consonant-vowel energy ratios. Hybrid systems involving both time and frequency domain processing are probably the next step in the development process.

In conclusion, a comprehensive study covering a wide range of speech phenomena is indispensable as it will lead to the following advantages: 1) providing useful data for designing a reasonable and practical unscrambler, 2) providing insight into the basic mechanism of speech production in media different from normal air, and 3) providing insight into the perceptual mechanism of speech in such media. Such studies are necessary for the improvement of helium speech.

2) Processing Degraded Speech: Programs are underway to enhance the intelligibility of speech signals transmitted over a low-quality communication channel. Techniques under investigation offer potential for the development of an automatic system for attenuating nonspeech signals which accompany speech and interfere with and occasionally obscure the information-bearing parameters of speech.

Two techniques were developed for enhancing the S/N ratio of speech received over a noisy channel. The first method is intended for use when the noise is wide-band and random. It is similar to homomorphic filtering, with the spectrum rooted (rather than logged) before being transformed. Test results showed the S/N ratio was somewhat improved without seriously distorting the character of the speech [65].

The second enhancement technique is useful when the interference consists of tones or can be decomposed into tones. It consists simply of transforming the speech-plus-noise to the spectrum domain, detecting and attenuating the tones, and retransforming the enhanced spectrum to the time domain. By use of this method, speech signals that were barely detectable at S/N ratios below -26 dB were made intelligible [65].

The enhancement process in its present configuration requires extensive hardware and software for real-time operation. The reason for this complex system is to transform the noisy speech signal in such a way as to easily remove the noise portion without appreciably affecting the voice signal.

A theoretical framework has been developed for the enhancement system, and meaningful experiments are underway [43]. While the enhancement process has been designed principally to enhance a voice signal immersed in wide-band noise, it is also providing insight into the enhancement of a voice signal subject to narrow-band noise.

3) Processing Stressed Speech: Other voice changes occur as a result of working in particular environments or being subjected to stressful (e.g., emergency) situations. For example, an aircraft pilot's voice characteristics may change as a result of *G*-forces. Threat, or other stress, may cause emotional changes in voice characteristics.

The state-of-the-art in this area appears to be that we are still investigating the extent of these changes in voice quality. Such research is being conducted largely by the DOD; civil projects seem to be largely ignoring these problems.

One project is being conducted by the United States Navy. Investigators are utilizing a dynamic flight simulator to study the effects of adverse flight conditions on voice quality. Typical variables include cockpit noise, high-*G* maneuvers, buffeting, mask breathing, cockpit temperature, and long-duration missions. Word sets being used include those expected to occur in communicating normal and emergency messages. The results will be used to determine: 1) conditions under which existing systems can be utilized, and 2) the extent of adaptability which must be designed into future speech recognition systems.

Stress-induced changes in voice quality may be studied in several ways. One way is to use task-induced stress. The subject is given a heavy workload and is required to make spoken responses. A paper by Hecker *et al.* suggests that knowledge of task-induced changes in voice quality is fairly complete [23].

Emotional stress-induced voice changes are more difficult to determine. An important aspect of this problem is how to induce emotional stress. Some study has been made of radio communications from pilots experiencing trouble. (In at least one case, the pilot crashed and was killed.) However, reference utterances are usually not available, and there is a lot of noise on the tapes. Simulated emergencies have been tried, but no one knows whether the extent of voice changes would be the same in a real emergency. A recent Army program [12] sought to attack this problem in the following way. Paid volunteer subjects were placed under hypnosis and lead via suggestion to relive traumatic experiences from their pasts. In one case, a man who had been a bomber crewman relived his experience of trying to release a live, 500-lb bomb that had become jammed in the bomb-bay. Speech was recorded before, during, and after such sessions. Data from this project are expected to provide evidence of stress-induced speech changes that must be taken into account in designing speech recognition systems.

II. Summary of Techniques to be Perfected and Unsolved Problems

Since its inception, research in ASR has progressed a long way. Man's most natural means of communication has undergone considerable analysis, resulting in a massive amount of equipment and documentation. Models of the speech mechanism have been developed and tested to demonstrate basic feasibilities. Earlier techniques have been considerably improved. Numerous independent and integrated efforts have been undertaken to further develop the speech genera-

TABLE III
STATE-OF-THE-ART AND UNSOLVED PROBLEMS

Processing Techniques	State-of-the-Art[1]	Unsolved Problems[2]
1) Signal Conditioning	A, except speech enhancement (C)	1, 15, 20, 23
2) Digital Signal Transformation	A	1, 15, 20
3) Analog Signal Transformation and Feature Extraction	A, except feature extraction (C)	1, 2, 6, 14–16, 20 24, 25
4) Digital Parameter and Feature Extraction	B	1, 2, 6, 14, 16, 20 24, 25
5a) Resynthesis	A	4, 7, 20, 25
5b) Orthographic Synthesis	C	4, 6–8, 19, 26–28, 29
6) Speaker Normalization Speaker Adaptation Situation Adaptation	C	15–17, 19, 20, 23–25, 29
7) Time Normalization	B	3, 16, 20, 25, 29
8) Segmentation and Labeling	B	1, 4, 5–9, 11, 13, 16, 18–20, 24, 25
9a) Language Statistics	C	5, 8, 9, 11, 12, 14, 20, 24, 25
9b) Syntax	B	6, 7, 9, 12, 14, 20, 25
9c) Semantics	C	6, 7, 9, 12, 14, 20, 25, 10
9d) Speaker and Situation Pragmatics	C	3, 6, 12, 14, 16, 18, 19, 23
10) Lexical Matching	C	7–9, 12–14, 20, 25
11) Speech Understanding	B–C	5, 9, 12, 14, 16, 18, 20, 23, 25
12) Speaker Recognition	A for speaker verification; C for all others	14, 16, 17, 19, 20, 24, 25
13) System Organization and Realization	A–C	21, 22
14) Performance Evaluation	C	1, 6–11, 18–20, 24–28

[1]Ratings: A = useful now; B = shows promise; C = a long way to go.
[2]See Glossary (Table IV) for problem definitions; list may not be exhaustive.

TABLE IV
GLOSSARY OF PROBLEMS AND DEFINITIONS

1) Detect speech in noise; speech/nonspeech.
2) Extract relevant acoustic parameters (poles, zeros, formant (transitions), slopes, dimensional representation, zero-crossing distributions).
3) Dynamic programming (nonlinear time normalization).
4) Detect smaller units in continuous speech (word/phoneme boundaries; acoustic segments).
5) Establish anchor point; scan utterance from left to right; start from stressed vowel, etc.
6) Stressed/unstressed.
7) Phonological rules.
8) Missing or extra added ("uh") speech sound.
9) Limited vocabulary and restricted language structure necessary; possibility of adding new words.
10) Semantics of (limited) tasks.
11) Limits of acoustic information only.
12) Recognition algorithm (shortest distance, (pairwise) discriminant, Bayes, probabilities).
13) Hypothesize-and-test, backtrack, feed forward.
14) Effect of nasalization, cold, emotion, loudness, pitch, whispering, distortions due to talker's acoustical environment, distortions by communication systems (telephone, transmitter-receiver, intercom, public address, face masks), nonstandard environments.
15) Adaptive and interactive quick learning.
16) Mimicking; uncooperative speaker(s).
17) Necessity of visual feedback, error control, level for rejections.
18) Consistency of references.
19) Real-time processing.
20) Human engineering problem of incorporating speech understanding system into actual situations.
21) Cost-effectiveness.
22) Detect speech in presence of competing speech.
23) Economical ways to adding new speakers to system.
24) Use of prosodic information.
25) Coarticulation rules.
26) Morphology rules.
27) Syntax rules.
28) Vocal-tract modeling.

tion, reception, and reproduction phenomena for specific military and civilian applications. This has increased the interaction among scientists of various disciplines. These include interchange and interaction in acoustic-phonetics, linguistics, signal processing, computer science, etc. In fact, international participation in the solution of the numerous ASR problems may also be at hand. European laboratories engaged in ASR are concentrating on statistical classification and theoretical models of detection, and are presently less involved in artificial intelligence techniques. Combining the various technologies could also lead to positive international cooperation.

A number of techniques must be perfected (and problems to be solved) before automation of the military tasks shown in Table I can be achieved. These techniques, together with their definitions and the state-of-the-art, are listed in Tables II and III. A glossary of problems and definitions is given in Table IV.

Although a great deal of emphasis is presently placed on the development of ASR systems for military applications, a much greater understanding of the speech process is required before ASR can approach human performance. Significant advances in ASR are not likely to come solely from research in pattern recognition (artificial intelligence) computer development and waveform/signal processing. Although these areas of investigation are important tools for ASR, the significant advances will come from studies in acoustic-phonetics, speech perception, linguistics, and psychoacoustic equipments.

APPENDIX A

FRENCH AGENCIES INTERESTED IN ASR

1) Government Laboratories

Ministry of Telecommunications
- Centre National d'Etudes des Telecommunications
- Ecole Nationale Superieure des Telecommunications

Ministry of Defense
- Laboratoire Central de l'Armement

Ministry of Education
- Faculte d'Orsay
- Faculte de Toulouse

Faculte de Nancy
Faculte de Grenoble, Institut de Phonetique
Commissariat a l'Energie Atomique

2) Firms

Thomson-CSF, Cagnes sur Mer
Thomson-CSF, Genevilliers
CGE-CIT
IBM-France

Appendix B

German Agencies Interested in ASR

Institut fur Kommunikationsforschung und Phonetic
Universitat Bonn
5300 Bonn
Adenauerallee 98a

Allgemeine Flektrizitats-Gesellschaft AEG-Telefunken
Bereich Forschung
7900 Ulm
Postfach 830

Lehrstuhl und Institut fur Allgemeine Nachrichtentechnik
Universitat Hannover
3000 Hanover
Callinstrabe 15

Fernmeldetechnisches Zentralmt
6100 Darmstadt
Postfach 800

Institut fur Nachrichtentechnik
Technische Universitat Braunschweig
3300 Branunschweig
Muhlenpfordstabe 23

Fachgebiet Ubertragungstechnik im Fachbereich Nachrichtentechnik
Technische Hochschule Darmstadt
6100 Darmstadt
Merckstrasse 25

Philips Forschungslaboratorium Hamburg Gmbll
Abt. Datentechnik
2000 Hamburg 54
Postfach 540840

Heinrich-Hertz Institut
1000 Berlin

Institut fur Datenverarbeitung
Technische Universitat Munchen
8000 Munchen 2
Arcisstrasse 21

Institut fur Phonetik und Sprachliche Kommunikation
Universitat Munchen
8000 Munchen 13
Schellingstrasse 7/11

Appendix C

Dutch Agencies Interested in ASR

Postal Research Laboratory (Dr. Neher-Laboratory)
St Paulusstraat 4,
Leidschendam
Speaker Verification (Drs. H. R. C. Tromp)

Institute for Perception TNO, Kampweg 5, Soesterberg
Analysis, Synthesis, Perception, and Automatic Recognition of Speech (Ir. L.C.W. Pols)

University of Nijmegen, Institute for Phonetics,
Erasmuslaan 40, Nijmegen
Speech Research (Prof. Dr. W. H. Vieregge)

Industrial Laboratory, Philips, Geldrop
Word Recognition (I. H. Slis)

Delft University of Technology, Department of Applied Physics, Subgroup on Pattern Recognition, Lorentzweg 1, Delft
All Aspects of Pattern Recognition (Prof. Dr. C. J. D. M. Verhagen)

Delft University of Technology, Department of Electrical Engineering, Laboratory for Information Theory, Mekelweg, 4, Delft
Speech Analysis and Recognition (Ir. C. Kamminga)

Appendix D

United Kingdom Agencies Interested in ASR

University of Keele
North Stafford Polytechnic
University of Essex, Department of Engineering
University of Essex, Language Centre
University College, London
Combridge University
Manchester University

Appendix E

United States Agencies Interested in ASR

1) DOD Research Laboratories

U.S. Army Electronics Command, Ft. Monmouth, NJ
Aerospace Medical Research Laboratory, Wright-Patterson AFB, Wright-Patterson, OH
AF Avionics Laboratory, Wright-Patterson AFB, Wright-Patterson, OH
Rome Air Development Center, Griffiss AFB, Rome, NY
Naval Electronics Laboratory Center, San Diego, CA
Naval Air Development Center, Warminster, PA
Naval Research Laboratory, Washington, DC
Naval Ship R&D Center, Bethesda, MD
Naval Training Equipment Center, Orlando, FL
Naval Undersea Center, San Diego, CA
Naval Underwater Systems Center, Newport, RI
National Security Agency, Ft. Meade, MD
Defense Communications Agency, Reston, VA

2) DOD Monitoring Agencies

U.S. Army Research Office, Durham, NC
AF Office of Scientific Research, Arlington, VA
AF Electronic Systems Division, Bedford, MA
Office of Naval Research, Arlington, VA
Defense Advanced Research Projects Agency, Arlington, VA

3) Consortium for All-Digital Communications System Research

National Security Agency, Ft. Meade, MD
Naval Research Laboratory, Washington, DC
Defense Communications Agency, Reston, VA
U.S. Army Electronics Command, Ft. Monmouth, NJ
Air Force Electronic Systems Division, Bedford, MA
Defense Advanced Research Projects Agency, Arlington, VA

4) Contractors for ARPA-Sponsored Research on Continuous Speech Understanding

Lincoln Laboratory, Lexington, MA
Bolt Beranek and Newman, Inc., Cambridge, MA
Carnegie-Mellon University, Pittsburg, PA
Stanford Research Institute, Menlo Park, CA
Systems Development Corporation, Santa Monica, CA
Sperry-Univac, Minneapolis, MN

References

[1] B. S. Atal, "Automatic recognition of speaker from their voices," *Proc. IEEE*, vol. 64, no. 4, pp. 460-475, 1976.

[2] ——"Linear prediction of speech—recent advances with applications to speech analysis," in *Speech Recognition: Invited Papers of IEEE Symposium*. New York: Academic, 1975.

[3] B. S. Atal and S. L. Hanauer, "Speech analysis and synthesis by linear prediction of the speech wave," *J. Acoust. Soc. Amer.* vol. 50, pp. 637-655, 1971.

[4] D. Becker, "Automatische Worterkennung mit Einem Linearen Quadratmittel-Klassifikator," in *Proc. NTG-G1Fachtagung*, "Cognitive Verhafen und System," Th. Einsele, W. Giloi, and H. Nagel, Eds. Berlin: Springer-Verlag, 1973, pp. 145-159.

[5] B. Beek, "Applications of speech processing for military applications," A. L. Gilbert, Ed., in *Proc. Workshop on Military Applications of Artificial Intelligence*, White Sands Missile Range, Juarez, Mexico, Oct. 1976, pp. 302-318.

[6] B. Beek and R. Vonusa, "An automatic isolated word recognition system—study and evaluation," Rome Air Dev. Cen. Tech. Rep. RADC-TR 70-129, Rome, NY, Oct. 1971.

[7] B. Beek *et al.*, "Automatic speaker recognition system," presented at the Agard Conf. on Artificial Intelligence, no. 94, London, England: Harford House, 1971.

[8] P. K. Broderick, J. E. Paul, and R. J. Renmick, "Semi-automatic speaker identification system," in *Proc. Carnahan Conf. Crime Countermeasures*, Univ. Kentucky, Lexington, 1975.

[9] R. Carre, "A summary of speech research activities in France," *IEEE Trans. Acoust., Speech, Signal Processing*, vol. ASSP-22, pp. 268-272, Aug. 1974.

[10] M. Copel, "Helium voice unscrambling," *IEEE Trans. Audio Electroacoust.*, vol. AU-14, pp. 122-126, Sept. 1966.

[11] S. K. Das and W. S. Mohn, "A scheme for speech processing in automatic speaker verification," *IEEE Trans. Audio Electroacoust.*, vol. AU-19, pp. 32-43, 1971.

[12] J. DeClerk, U.S. Army Electron. Command, Fort Monmouth, NJ, personal communication.

[13] N. R. Dixon and C. C. Tappert, "Toward objective phonetic transcription—an in-line interactive technique for machine-processed speech data," *IEEE Trans. Man-Machine Syst.*, vol. MMS-11, pp. 202-210, 1970.

[14] G. R. Doddington, "Speaker verification, vol. I-III," Rome Air Dev. Cen., Rome, NY, Tech. Reps. TR-74-179, TR-75-274, TR-76-262.

[15] L. D. Erman, Ed., "Contributed papers of IEEE Symposium on Speech Recognition," Carnegie Mellon Univ., Pittsburgh, PA, Apr. 1974, IEEE Catalog No. 74CH0878-9AE.

[16] J. L. Flanagan, *Speech Analysis, Synthesis and Perception*, 2nd ed. Berlin: Springer-Verlag, 1972.

[17] J. W. Forgie, D. E. Hall, and R. W. Wiesen, "An overview of the Lincoln Laboratory speech recognition system," *J. Acoust. Soc. Amer.*, vol. 56, p. S27 (A), 1974.

[18] T. A. Giordano, H. B. Rothman, and H. Hollien, "Helium speech unscramblers—A critical review of the state-of-the-art," *IEEE Trans. Audio Electroacoust.*, vol. AU-21, no. 5, pp. 436-444, Oct. 1973.

[19] R. M. Golden, "Improving naturalness and intelligibility of helium-oxygen speech, using vocoder techniques," *J. Acoust. Soc. Amer.*, vol. 40, pp. 621-624, 1966.

[20] M. W. Grady and M. B. Herscher, "Advanced speech technology applied to problems of air traffic control," in *NAECON 75 Record 541*.

[21] W. Haberman and A. Fejfar, "Automatic identification of personnel through speaker and signature verification-system description and testings," in *Proc. Carnahan and Int. Crime Countermeasures Conf.*, 1976, pp. 23-30.

[22] M. H. L. Hecker, "Speaker recognition—An interpretive survey of the literature," American Speech and Hearing Association, Mono. 16, Jan. 1971.

[23] M. H. L. Hecker, K. N. Stevens, G. von Bismarck, and C. F. Williams, "Manifestations of task-induced stress in the acoustic speech signal," *J. Acoust. Soc. Amer.*, 1968.

[24] K. Holywell and G. Harvey, "Helium speech," *J. Acoust. Soc. Amer.*, vol. 36, pp. 210-211, 1964.

[25] O. Hinrichs and J. Gonschorek, "Ein Spracherkennungsgerat mit Selbsttatiger Anpassung an Sprechgeschwindigkeit und Lautstarke," *Nachrichtentech. Z.*, vol. 24, pp. 177-182, 1971.

[26] F. Itakura, "Minimum prediction residual principle applied to speech recognition," *IEEE Trans. Acoust., Speech, Signal Processing*, vol. ASSP-23, Feb. 1975.

[27] F. Itakura and S. Saito, "On the optimum quantization of feature parameters in the Parcor speech synthesizer," Paper L4 in *Proc. 1972 Conf. on Speech Communications and Processing*, Air Force Cambridge Res. Lab., L. G. Hanscom Field, Bedford, MA, 1972, IEEE Cat. No. 72 CHO596-7AE.

[28] R. G. Leonard and G. R. Doddington, "Automatic classification of languages," Rome Air Dev. Cen., Rome, NY, Tech. Rep. TR-75-264, 1975.

[29] K. P. Li and G. W. Hughes, "Talker differences as they appear in correlation matrices of continuous speech spectra," *J. Acoust. Soc. Amer.*, vol. 55, pp. 833-837, 1974.

[30] J. Makhoul, "Linear prediction; A tutorial review," *Proc. IEEE*, pp. 561-580, Apr. 1975.

[31] H. Mangold, "Ein Spracherkennungssystem fur Isolierte Worte unter Schlechten Storbedingungen," presented at the 5th Conf. on Acoust., Budapest, Hungary, Apr. 1973.

[32] ——, "The individual differences with long time measurements of the speech signal," *Nachrichtentech. Z.*, vol. 22, no. 6, pp. 364-367, 1969.

[33] ——, "Investigation of a system for recognition of isolated words spoken in noisy surroundings," *Nachrichtentech. Z.*, vol. 27, no. 2, pp. 105-108, 1974.

[34] J. D. Markel, "Formant trajectory estimation from a linear least-square inverse filter formulation," Speech Commun. Res. Lab., Santa Barbara, CA, SCRL Mono. No. 7, Oct. 1971.

[35] T. B. Martin, "Applications of limited vocabulary recognition systems," in *Speech Recognition, Invited Papers of the IEEE Symp*. New York: Academic, 1975, pp. 55-71.

[36] ——, "Practical applications of voice input to machines," *Proc. IEEE*, vol. 64, pp. 487-501, Apr. 1976.

[37] S. S. McCandless, "An algorithm for automatic formant extraction using linear prediction spectra," *IEEE Trans. Acoust., Speech, Signal Processing*, vol. ASSP-22, pp. 135-141, 1974.

[38] M. F. Medress *et al.*, "Speech understanding: Report of a steering committee," Massachusetts Inst. Technol., Cambridge, to be published.

[39] E. P. Neuberg, "Philosophies of speech recognition," in *Speech Recognition, Invited Papers of the IEEE Symp.* New York: Academic, 1975, pp. 83-95.

[40] E. P. Neuberg, R. E. Wohlford, and A. S. House, "Preliminaries to the automatic recognition of speech," *J. Acoust. Soc. Amer.*, vol. 57, suppl. 1, p. S34, 1975.

[41] A. Newell *et al.*, "Speech understanding systems: Final report of a study group," 1971 (reprinted by North-Holland/American/Elsevier, Amsterdam, The Netherlands, 1973).

[42] D. J. P. J. Nierop, L. C. W. Pols, and R. Plomp, "Frequency analysis of Dutch vowels from 25 female speakers," *Acustica*, vol. 292, pp. 110-118, 1973.

[43] T. W. Parsons and M. Weiss, "Enhancing/intelligibility of speech in noisy or multi-talker environments," Rome Air Dev. Cen., Rome, NY, Rep. TR-75-155, AD-AO13767, 1975.

[44] E. Paulus, "The role of speech sounds in the perception and recognition of words," in *Zeichenerkennung durch Biologische*

und Technische Systeme, O. J. Grusser and R. Klinke, Eds. Berlin: Springer-Verlag, 1971, pp. 357-368.

[45] E. Paulus and D. Langle, "Die Anwendung der Karhumen-Loeve-Entwicklung fur die Digital Sprachanalyze und-Synthese," in *Proc. NTG-Fachtagung "Singalverarbeiting,"* W. Schubler, Ed. Berlin: Erlangen, 1973, pp. 362–369.

[46] L. C. W. Pols, "Real-time recognition of spoken words," *IEEE Trans. Comput.*, vol. C-20, pp. 972–978, 1971.

[47] —, "Dimensional representation of speech spectra," presented at the 7th Int. Congr. on Acoust., Budapest, Hungary, 1971.

[48] —, "Segmentation and recognition of monosyllabic words," in *1972 Proc. Conf. on Speech Communication and Processing*, Air Force Cambridge Res. Lab., L. G. Hanscom Field, Bedford, MA, 1972, IEEE Cat No. 72 CHO596-7AE.

[49] L. C. W. Pols, H. R. C. Tromp, and R. Plomp, "Frequency analysis of Dutch vowels from 50 male speakers," *J. Acoust. Soc. Amer.*, vol. 534, pp. 1093–1101, 1973.

[50] *Proc. Journees d'Etude sur la Parole (Annual Study Days on Speech) of Groupement des Acousticiens de Langue Francaise (GALF)*–lst in Grenobl 70, 2nd in Aix en Provence 71, 3rd in Lannion 72, 4th in Brussels 73, 5th in Orsay 74, 6th in Toulouse 75. (*Proceedings* can be obtained from Secretariat du GALF in CNET. Route de Tregastel, 22301 Lannion, France.)

[51] L. R. Rabiner and M. R. Sambur, "An algorithm for determining the endpoints of isolated utterances," *Bell Syst. Tech. J.*, vol. 54, no. 2, pp. 297–315, 1975.

[52] D. R. Reddy, "Speech recognition by machine: A review," *Proc. IEEE*, vol. 64, pp. 501-531, Apr. 1976.

[53] A. E. Rosenberg, "Automatic speaker verification systems: A review," *Proc. IEEE*, vol. 64, pp. 475–485, Apr. 1976.

[54] H. B. Rothman and H. Hollien, "Further evaluation of He02 unscramblers under controlled conditions," Rep. CSL/ONR-47 1, July 1972.

[55] M. R. Sambur and L. R. Rabiner, "A speaker independent digit recognition system," *Bell Syst. Tech. J.*, vol. 54, pp. 81–102, 1975.

[56] R. Schafer and E. L. Rabiner, "Digital representation of speech signals," *Proc. IEEE*, vol. 63, pp. 662–677, Apr. 1975.

[57] H. Schunk, "A transceiver from helium atmosphere," *Allg. Elek. Ges. Telefunken*, vol. 61, pp. 378–381, 1971.

[58] M. Simpson, "Word recognition for tactical data systems," A. L. Gilbert, Ed., in *Proc. Workshop on Military Applications of Artificial Intelligence*, White Sands Missile Range, Juarez, Mexico, Oct. 1976, pp. 302–318.

[59] T. Tremain, "Linear predictive coding systems," in *Conf. Rec. IEEE Int. Conf. on Acoust., Speech, and Signal Processing*, Philadelphia, PA, 1976, pp. 474–478, IEEE Cat. No. 76CH1067-8 ASSP.

[60] R. Turn, A. Hoffman, and T. Lippiatt, "Military applications of speech understanding systems," Defense Advanced Res. Proj. Agency, Arlington, VA, Rep. 1434, AD 787394, June 1974.

[61] V. A. Vitols and J. E. Paul, "An algorithm for detection of keywords in continuous speech," presented at Workshop of Sept. 1971, session III, paper I, Rome Air Dev. Cen., Rome, NY.

[62] "Voiceprint identification," *Georgetown Law J.*, vol. 61, issue 3, Feb. 1973.

[63] H. Wakita, "On the use of linear prediction error energy for speech and speaker recognition," *J. Acoust. Soc. Amer.*, vol. 57, suppl. 1, 1975.

[64] —, "Direct estimation of vocal tract shape by inverse filtering of acoustic speech waveforms," *IEEE Trans. Audio Electroacoust.*, vol. AU-21, no. 5, pp. 417–427, Oct. 1973.

[65] M. R. Weiss *et al.*, "Study and development of the intelligence technique for improving speech intelligibility," Rome Air Dev. Cen., Rome, NY, RADC-TR-75-108, 1975.

[66] G. White, "Automatic speech recognition: Linear predictive residual versus bandpass filtering," in *Proc. IEEE Int. Conf. on Cybernetics and Society*, Sept. 1975.

[67] J. J. Wolf, "Efficient acoustic parameters for speaker recognition," *J. Acoust. Soc. Amer.*, vol. 51, pp. 2044–2055, 1972.

[68] W. Woods, "Speech recognition–An overview," A. L. Gilbert, Ed., in *Proc. Workshop on Military Applications of Artificial Intelligence*, White Sands Missile Range, Juarez, Mexico, Oct. 1976, pp. 302–318.

[69] H. Yilmaz *et al.*, "Automatic speaker adaptation," Rome Air Dev. Cen., Rome, NY, Tech. Rep. RADC-TR-76-273, 1976.

Review of the ARPA Speech Understanding Project

Dennis H. Klatt

Massachusetts Institute of Technology, Cambridge, Massachusetts 02139

(Received 10 May 1977; revised 1 September 1977)

In September of 1976, four speech understanding systems were demonstrated, signifying the end of a five-year program of research and development sponsored by the Advanced Research Projects Agency (ARPA). The best performance was displayed by the Harpy system developed at Carnegie–Mellon University. Harpy satisfied a set of design goals that were specified at the beginning of the program, including the goal of understanding over 90% of a set of naturally spoken sentences composed from a 1000-word lexicon. After defining the nature of the speech understanding problem, the four systems are described and critically evaluated. Based on this review, a structure for a next-generation speech understanding system is proposed and parts of it are considered as a possible model of the early stages of speech perception. The perceptual model addresses the issue of lexical access and includes a decoding network composed of expected spectral sequences for all word strings of English.

PACS numbers: 43.10.Ln, 43.70.Sc, 43.70.Dn

INTRODUCTION

In November of 1971, the Information Processing Technology Office of the Advanced Research Projects Agency of the Department of Defense (ARPA) initiated a five-year research and development program with the objective of obtaining a breakthrough in speech understanding capability that could then be used toward the development of practical man—machine communication systems (Newell *et al.*, 1973). The specific goals set forth by an ARPA study group[1] are outlined in Table I. The objectives were to develop several speech understanding systems that accept continuous speech from many cooperative speakers of a General American dialect. Recordings were to be made in a quiet room using a good-quality microphone. Slight tuning of the system would be allowed to handle new speakers, but the users could be required to make only natural adaptations to the system. The language definition should include a slightly selected vocabulary of at least 1000 words and an artificial syntax appropriate to the limited task situation (e.g., a data management task). Less than 10% semantic error would be tolerated and the system would have to run in a few times real time using the next generation of computers [(i.e., machines capable of executing 100 million machine instructions per second (MIPS)]. These goals were to be achieved by November 1976.

Significantly (and deliberately) absent from the specifications were requirements that the demonstration tasks be relevant to real-world problems, that the languages be habitable, and that the systems be cost effective. These omissions helped to get the project focused on scientific and computational issues, but they have resulted in questions concerning the work remaining to develop future practical systems.

The study group emphasized the concept of speech understanding as opposed to speech recognition. They believed that the hope for the program lay in analyzing speech within the context of specific tasks that employed strong grammatical constraints, as well as strong semantic and dialogue constraints, so that many sources of knowledge could be brought to bear to attain successful understanding of what was said or intended by the speaker. Accuracy was to be measured by the correctness of the response and not by whether all of the words were correctly recognized.

There were two possible ways to meet the ARPA goals: (1) simplify the general speech recognition problem by finding ways to apply syntactic and semantic constraints and (2) improve upon previous speech recognition capabilities. As noted above, the steering committee emphasized the first alternative and recommended that funding be given to research groups that were composed mainly of computer scientists, not speech scientists. It turned out that the various research groups tried different combinations of the two strategies, but the only clearly successful speech understanding system, Harpy, relied heavily on the first technique. In fact, if the ARPA project were to be judged on its contributions to speech recognition and the speech sciences, rather than judging it against its stated goals, a more negative appraisal might have to be given.

The second column of Table I characterizes the performance of the Harpy speech understanding system, which was developed at Carnegie—Mellon University (Lowerre, 1976; Reddy *et al.*, 1977). Harpy essentially meets or exceeds each of the specifications. Given this set of criteria, Harpy performed the best of all the systems that were demonstrated at the end of the project.

A general overview of what has been accomplished during the past five years has been published by the

TABLE I. The ARPA five-year goals are compared with the performance of Harpy.

GOAL (Nov., 1971)	Harpy (Nov., 1976)
ACCEPT CONNECTED SPEECH	YES
FROM MANY	5 (3 MALE, 2 FEMALE)
COOPERATIVE SPEAKERS	YES
IN A QUIET ROOM	COMPUTER TERMINAL ROOM
USING A GOOD MICROPHONE	CLOSE-TALKING MICROPHONE
WITH SLIGHT TUNING/SPEAKER	20 TRAINING SENTENCES/TALKER
ACCEPTING 1000 WORDS	1011
USING AN ARTIFICIAL SYNTAX	AVG. BRANCHING FACTOR = 33
IN A CONSTRAINING TASK	DOCUMENT RETRIEVAL
YIELDING < 10% SEMANTIC ERROR	5%
IN A FEW TIMES REAL TIME	80 TIMES REAL TIME
ON A 100 MIPS MACHINE	ON A .4 MIPS PDP-KA10 USING 256K OF 36-BIT WORDS AND COSTING $5 PER SENTENCE PROCESSED

Reprinted with permission from *J. Acoust. Soc. Am.*, vol. 62, pp. 1345-1366, Dec. 1977.

ARPA steering committee (Medress *et al.*, 1977). The primary concern of this review is to compare and evaluate the structures and components of four speech understanding systems that were developed.[2] Only brief mention will be made of other activities that were carried out in support of the system development efforts. The remainder of the paper is divided into an initial section that sets forth the scientific problems to be solved, a section describing the four speech understanding systems, and a section concerned with an overall scientific evaluation of the program, a proposal for a second-generation speech understanding system, and a discussion of the implications of this research for models of the speech perception process.

The ARPA project, while large in funding terms, is only one of many past and present efforts to recognize spoken utterances. The reader is referred to other sources for a more complete picture. For example, there are reviews such as have been published by Lindgren (1965), Pierce (1969), Fant (1970), Hyde (1972), Wolf (1976), and especially Reddy (1976); conference proceedings such as have been edited by Erman (1974), Reddy (1975), Fant (1975), Teacher (1976), and Silverman (1977); and descriptions of other recent speech understanding systems such as have been published by Bahl *et al.* (1976), Jelenek (1976), De Mori *et al.* (1975), Sakai and Nakagawa (1975), Haton and Pierrel (1976), and Medress *et al.* (1977).

I. THE PROBLEM

At the beginning of the ARPA project, isolated word recognition by pattern matching techniques was enjoying some initial success. However, it was realized that many words appearing in sentence contexts varied dramatically in acoustic characteristics depending on the surrounding phonetic environment and depending on certain phonological processes of English (Stevens and Klatt, 1973; Oshika *et al.*, 1975), so a simple-minded pattern-matching word identification strategy could not be applied to the sentence understanding problem. Therefore it seemed necessary to follow a more traditional approach, the first step of which was to process the acoustic input to recover a phonetic transcription of what had been said. A phonetic transcription is a discrete representation of articulatory activity in terms of a sequence of configurational goals or states called phonetic segments.

The second step in the hypothetical understanding strategy would be to take the (probably errorful) phonetic transcription of an unknown utterance and try to find candidate words and word sequences that might be present. Consider the phonetic transcription:

[d ɪ ǰ ə h ɪ ɾ ɪ t ə t a m] (1)

No word boundaries are indicated in (1) because acoustic cues to word boundary locations are rarely present. The lexical search problem [to find the sequence of words corresponding to (1)] is extremely difficult because of the combinatorics of possible word boundary locations, because the phonetic transcription may contain substitution errors, omissions, and extra segments, and because the talker uses a system of phonological rules to modify and simplify the pronunciation of individual words in some sentence environments. For example, the normal way to say "Did you" is [d ɪ j ə], i.e., "Dija" but "you" is pronounced differently in "are you." The "t" in "hit" usually is realized as a very brief tongue flap [ɾ] in "hit it," but not in "hit some." The two adjacent "t"s of "it to" reduce to a single [t], resulting in (1) as the normal way to pronounce "Did you hit it to Tom?"

Each of the simplifications in (1) can be described by general phonological rules that presuppose an underlying basic representation for the word (called the phonemic representation). The phonemic string that would be stored in the lexicon for "you" might be /yu/. A phonological rule [d # y]→[ǰ] transforms the /y/ into [ǰ] if the previous word ends in a [d]. The application of inverse phonological rules for sentence decoding is complicated by the fact that there is no unique inverse rule in most cases. A [ǰ] that is observed could be the first or last sound of a word like "judge," or it could be the surface manifestation of /d/—/y/ in a word pair like "did you." Similarly an observed flap [ɾ] may indicate a word containing a /t/, a /d/, or possibly even an /n/. Almost any segment could be simultaneously the manifestation of the last phoneme of one word and the first phoneme of the next word.

All of these phonological phenomena result in lexical ambiguity so that even the best lexical hypothesis routines will propose many words that are not in the original sentence, simply due to fortuitous matches. The third step in the process would therefore be to use syntactic—semantic modules to weed out the false lexical hypotheses and put together a word string that represents what was spoken.

The block diagram shown in Fig. 1 summarizes what we have just said. Speech understanding systems may be thought to consist of two main components, a "bottom end" that converts acoustic data into lexical hypotheses and a "top end" that accepts lexical hypotheses and tries to find the most likely sentence that could have been spoken.

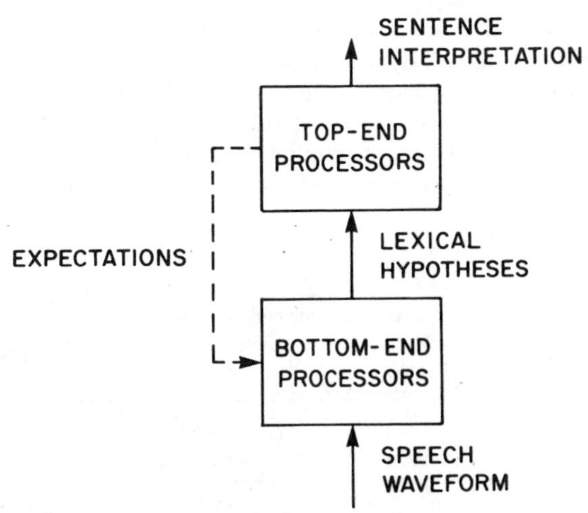

FIG. 1. Simplified overview of the speech understanding problem.

An important point to make concerning Fig. 1 is that the top end can provide the bottom end processor with constraints concerning what might be expected next. The relative success of the four speech understanding systems to be described is more highly correlated with the type of constraint provided by the top end than with any other variable. The most successful system, Harpy, exhaustively lists those and only those acoustic segment sequences that form acceptable input sentences, and the Harpy grammar severely constrains the acoustic alternatives much of the time. The advantage of applying strong constraints at the acoustic level is that one can avoid having to perform generalized phonetic recognition or generalized lexical hypothesization that would otherwise generate a large number of spurious hypotheses that have to be rejected later by the top end (a computationally costly and often difficult undertaking).

When the ARPA program began, it was believed that the scientific problems associated with top end design would be concerned with how to combine lexical hypotheses into larger and larger sentence fragments that are (1) syntactically acceptable, (2) semantically acceptable, (3) and plausible given what the user has said previously and some notion of what he/she wants to do. Syntactic analyzers used earlier in text processing applications would have to be modified to function in the face of errorful input, to consider and score multiple alternatives, and to include semantic knowledge before sufficient constraints could be applied effectively in the speech understanding context. The algorithms would have to be fast enough to permit evaluation of many word combinations and they would have to include sophisticated scoring algorithms to select among those alternatives that are grammatically acceptable. Progress in each of these areas is summarized in Sec. III.

The scientific problems associated with bottom end design when the ARPA program began included (1) selecting an acoustic representation, (2) improving segmentation and phonetic labeling strategies that had been developed previously, and (3) recognizing words that have undergone phonetic modifications at word boundaries and/or phonological recoding. Unanswered questions were: What kinds of improvements could be made to existing phonetic recognition strategies? How good does phonetic recognition have to be? Does one have to normalize for speaking rate? Can routines be made to work for any talker? How can one take advantage of prosodic cues (the pattern of voicing fundamental frequency, segmental durations, and intensity fluctuations), which indicate syllable stress and the syntactic structure of a spoken sentence? Progress in these areas and an interesting change in viewpoint are discussed in Sec. III.

TABLE II. Performance of the speech understanding systems as of November 1976. Statistics are based on more than 100 sentences spoken by several talkers, except for CMU Hearsay-II whose preliminary evaluation employed a smaller data set.

System	Sentences understood	Average branching factor
CMU Harpy	95%	33
CMU Hearsay-2	91, 74	33, 46
BBN Hwim	44	195
SDC	24	105

TABLE III. Task domains of the four systems and an example of an acceptable input sentence.

Group	Task	Sample sentence
SDC	FACTS ABOUT SHIPS	"How fast is the Theodore Roosevelt?"
BBN Hwim	TRAVEL BUDGET MANAGEMENT	"What is the plane fare to Ottawa?"
CMU Harpy	DOCUMENT RETRIEVAL	"How many articles on psychology are there?"
Hearsay-II	DOCUMENT RETRIEVAL	"How many articles on psychology are there?"

The block diagram of Fig. 1 describes a *system*. Some issues of speech understanding system design are obscured if one simply discusses component performance requirements. The system design problems extant at the onset of the ARPA program included (1) how to coordinate the effort to bring up and debug effectively a very large system, (2) how to define communication links between system components, (3) how to schedule activity among components, and (4) how to combine conflicting scores from different knowledge sources.

II. THE SPEECH UNDERSTANDING SYSTEMS

The performance of the final four speech understanding systems, when processing sentences composed from a 1000 word lexicon, is summarized in Table II. Also presented is one measure of the constraint provided by the syntactic and semantic knowledge. The average branching factor is defined here to be the average number of words that would have to be considered at each point along the correct left-to-right path through the syntactic production rules during the processing of a typical utterance. Branching factor has been shown to be a better measure of task difficulty than vocabulary size *per se*, although other aspects of the grammar and inherent confusibility of lexical items contribute to task complexity. Some systems do not process an utterance in a strictly left-to-right manner, but the estimated branching factors are roughly comparable.

Taking account of the range of task difficulties implied in part by the different branching factors, it is unclear whether there are large differences in ability among the top three systems. However, only Carnegie—Mellon University (CMU) was able to meet the ARPA goals. In judging the performance figures given in Table II, it should also be noted that System Development Corporation (SDC) was handicapped by the loss of one of their computers, which prevented them from making use of components being developed jointly with Stanford Research Institute.

The tasks employed by the three system builders are summarized in Table III. Also included is an example of a sentence accepted by each grammar. Each task involves data management of one sort or another. While only questions are given as examples in Table III, each

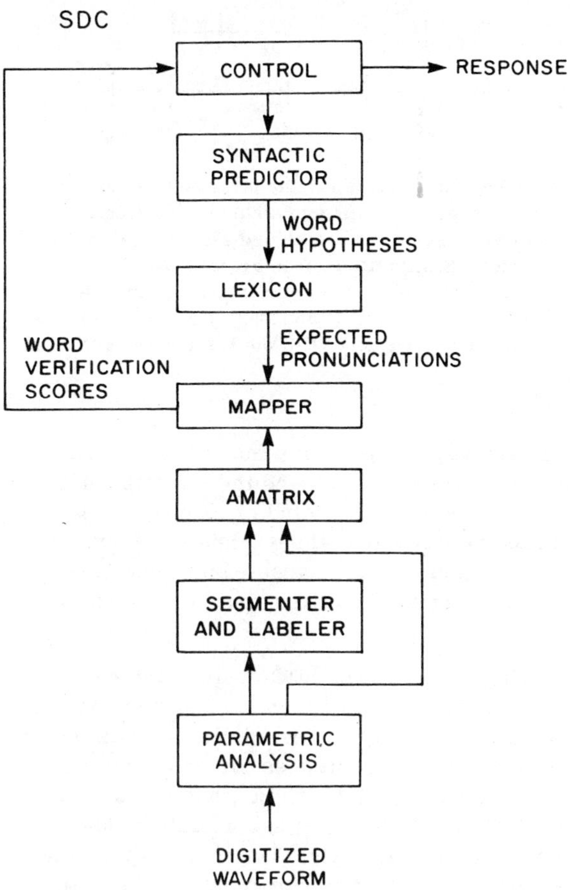

FIG. 2. Block diagram of the SDC system organization.

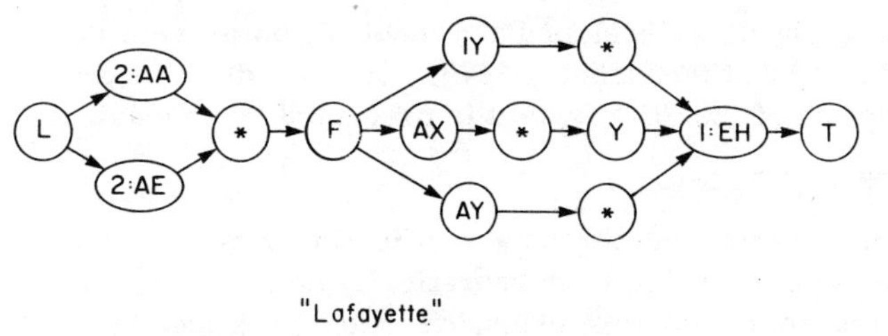

FIG. 3. Lexical representation in the SDC system for the word "Lafayette." Branches in the string indicate acceptable alternative pronunciations. The "*" is a syllable boundary symbol, and the "1" and "2" indicate relative lexical stress levels. Other phonemic symbols have the obvious interpretation. The advantages of a network representation for alternative phonetic pronunciations of words include compactness of form and efficiency of search compared with a simple list of alternatives.

of the systems was also capable of understanding commands and statements of various types.

A. Systems development corporation

The structure of the final SDC speech understanding system is shown in Fig. 2 (Ritea, 1975; Bernstein, 1976). Formant frequencies and other parameters are first extracted from the input waveform. A phonetic transcription is obtained, including several alternative labels for each phonetic segment, and all of this information is placed in a data array called the A-matrix for later examination by top-end routines.

The utterance is processed from left to right by first generating a list of all possible sentence-initial words. The control box then retrieves an abstract phonemic representation from the lexicon for each lexical hypothesis and computes expected phonetic variants, resulting in a phonetic graph representation such as is shown in Fig. 3. The phonetic graphs are sent, one at a time, to the mapper to see how good an acoustic match is obtained with the current position in the unknown utterance. The mapper is organized according to the syllable structure of a word and it examines the A-matrix in order to determine if the expected vowels and proper allophones of adjacent consonants are present. Since an exact match is unlikely, the mapper includes techniques for estimating the probability that the expected word is present given the phonetic and acoustic data. Performance of the mapper is indicated in Table IV.

On the basis of mapper scores, the control box decides which word or partial sentence hypothesis to pursue next, and generates a list of all words that can follow this sentence fragment. A similar "best-first" control strategy was used earlier in the Hearsay I speech understanding system (Reddy, Erman, and Neely, 1973)

TABLE IV. Performance statistics for three work verification components—the SDC mapper, the BBN verifier, and the CMU Hearsay-II verifier. The last row indicates that the SDC verifier is presented with lexical hypotheses from a syntactic module, whereas the BBN and CMU verifiers are preceded by lexical hypothesizers that screen out all but the best acoustic candidates.

	VERIFICATION DECISION					
	SDC		BBN		CMU	
LEXICAL PROPOSAL	ACCEPT	REJECT	ACCEPT	REJECT	ACCEPT	REJECT
CORRECT WORD	65	6	101	19	312	20
PERCENT	92%	8%	84%	16%	94%	6%
INCORRECT WORD	372	11,253	367	713	6462	6591
PERCENT	3%	97%	34%	66%	49%	51%
WORDS HYPOTH. CORRECT WORD	165		10		40	
ACOUST. SIMILARITY	RANDOM		BEST 5%		BEST 14%	

and in a system developed at Lincoln Laboratories (Klovstad and Mondshein, 1975). A more detailed description of the SDC system is presented in Appendix A.

Discussion of SDC

The mapper constitutes a verification strategy based on syllables, which is a theoretically attractive design for embedding context-dependent rules for expected manifestations of phonetic segments. The mapper is capable of rejecting a large fraction of the word hypotheses not in the sentence, but at a cost of rejecting about 10% of the words actually present. Fatal absolute rejections of correct words occurred either because the mapper lost track of which syllable was being processed or because a phonetic confusion occurred that had not been seen during a prior statistics-gathering run.

Unfortunately, the mapper performance is not good enough for a top-end system organization in which there is no mechanism for recovering from a single bad lexical matching score. It is unfortunate that SDC had so little time to design a more powerful top end after being prevented from using an SRI module, because a system can only perform as well as its weakest link.

The main criticism that can be made of the SDC effort is that their system failed its objectives in such a way that it is difficult to say what more restricted goals could be met by a modified system design. Is it simply a matter of shaking the bugs out of the system, or must one place further restrictions on the vocabulary and/or syntax? Or is it that the simple control strategy employed is essentially incapable of performing at an acceptable understanding rate in any moderate sized task because of the nature of speech and the inherent inaccuracies to be expected in any kind of mapper? Answers to these and other questions might have come from a year of system performance evaluation that was planned by the steering committee, but not funded by ARPA.

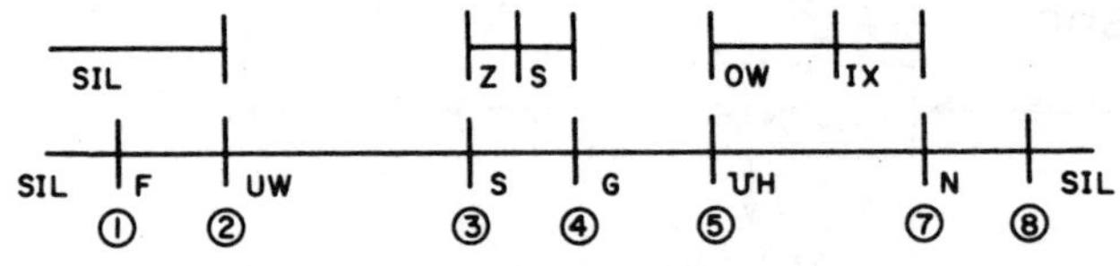

FIG. 5. A BBN segment lattice for the utterance "Who's going?" Alternative segmentations are displaced vertically, while each label represents the top choice among a set of 71 phonetic categories. Similarity scores are computed for all possible labels at each alternative segmentation point. For example, the segment starting at boundary (1) is labeled "F," but the correct phonetic segment "H" was the fourth best label choice.

An interesting aspect of the SDC system emerged in comparing its performance with an earlier version that did better on an easier task. The earlier system understood 65% of a set of test sentences formed from a 200-word lexicon and a more rigid syntax that was devoid of function words. Function words are usually acoustically reduced and difficult to identify. One might speculate that one reason for the poor performance of the more ambitious system was the dependence on function word recognition. Creation of a syntax that perhaps allowed some function words, but in no way depended on their identification to choose a path in the grammar, might be a better strategy for the realization of limited systems. (It is interesting to note that the Harpy grammar is essentially of this form.)

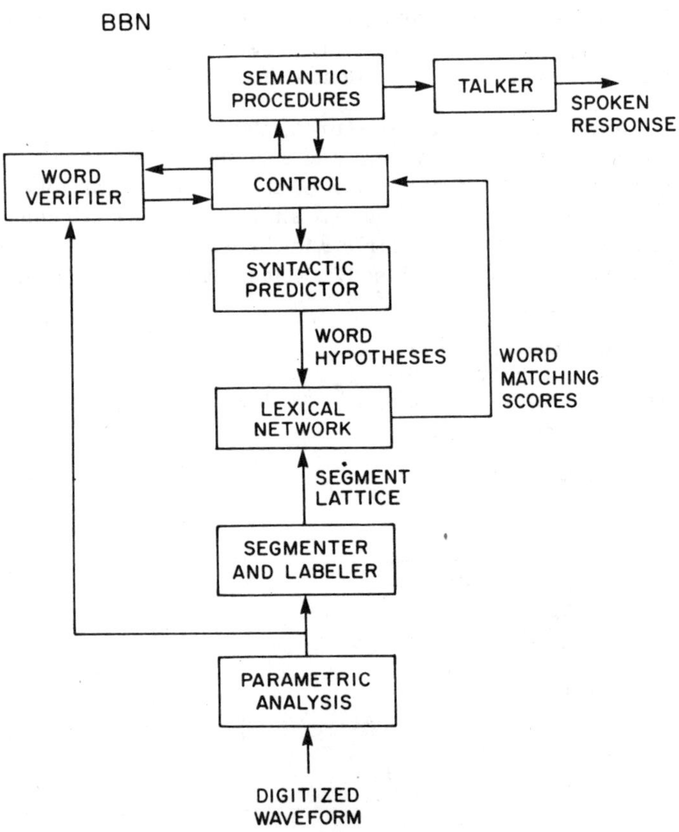

FIG. 4. Block diagram of the BBN Hwim system organization.

B. Bolt Beranek and Newman Inc. Hwim

The general organization of the BBN Hwim (Hear what I mean) system is shown in Fig. 4 (Woods *et al.*, 1976). As a first step in the processing of an unknown utterance, formant frequencies and other parameters are extracted from the digitized waveform. This information is used to derive a set of phonetic transcription alternatives that are arranged in a "segment lattice," as shown in Fig. 5. The advantage claimed for the lattice structure is that it can represent segmentation ambiguity in those cases where decisions are most difficult.

The identification process begins by searching through the segmental representation of the utterance for good matching words (anywhere in the utterance) that can be used as "seeds" for building up longer partial sentence hyptheses. The best-scoring initial word match is sent to a word verification component which returns to the parametric data to get a quasi-independent measure of the quality of the match. The method of verification is analysis by synthesis (Klatt, 1975).[3] The verification score is combined with the lexical matching score, and if the combined score is high, the word hypothesis is then sent to a syntactic predictor component which pro-

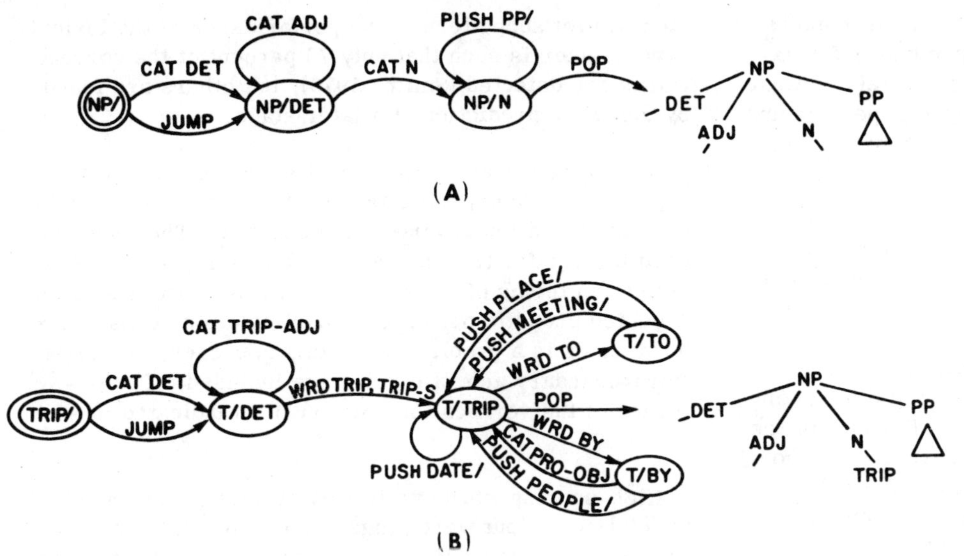

FIG. 6. A portion of the augmented transition network grammar. The network of part (a) defines acceptable noun phrases as consisting of the categories determiner, optional adjective string, noun, and optional prepositional phrases. A way to embed semantic constraints on the relations between words of an acceptable noun phrase is shown in part (b). Only one type of noun phrase concerning a trip is accepted by this fragment of the ATN grammar.

poses words that can appear to the left and to the right of the seed word, given the grammatical constraints. An augmented transition network grammar (Woods, 1970) is used to characterize syntactic and semantic constraints, in a manner that is illustrated in Fig. 6.

Matching scores are obtained for all of these word proposals, using a lexical decoding network (Klovstad, 1977). The lexical decoding network contains a representation of the expected phonetic realizations of each word in all possible phonetic contexts. To derive this network, a set of phonological rules (Woods and Zue, 1976) first transforms a phonemic lexicon into phonetic alternatives arranged in a tree structure, as shown in Fig. 7(a). Then a second set of word-boundary phonological rules attaches terminal nodes back to selected initial nodes of the tree, creating a network of permissible phonetic strings for all possible word sequences from the 1000-word lexicon. For example, the word "list" may be pronounced as [lis] in "list some" due to an optional word boundary phonological rule OPT {ST#S} → {S}, and this fact is captured in the network structure of Fig. 7(b). However, if "list" is to be recognized without the {t}, a word beginning with [s] must follow.

Each word receiving a good score from the lexical decoding network is combined with the seed word to produce a two-word hypothesis, a verification score is derived for the new two-word hypothesis and the hypothesis is then placed in an "event queue." The best scoring partial sentence hypothesis is always extended next. When a complete sentence is found, a deep structure representation of the word string can be sent to the semantic procedures component in order to compute an appropriate response. The response is spoken over a loudspeaker, using a speech synthesis by rule program. A more detailed description of the system is given in Appendix B.

Discussion of BBN

The BBN speech understanding system has a task domain with a more general syntax than the other systems, so it is difficult to judge how much better or worse the system design and individual components are. The same criticism applies to BBN that was leveled at SDC: The way in which the demonstration system failed to meet the ARPA goals makes it impossible to determine what more

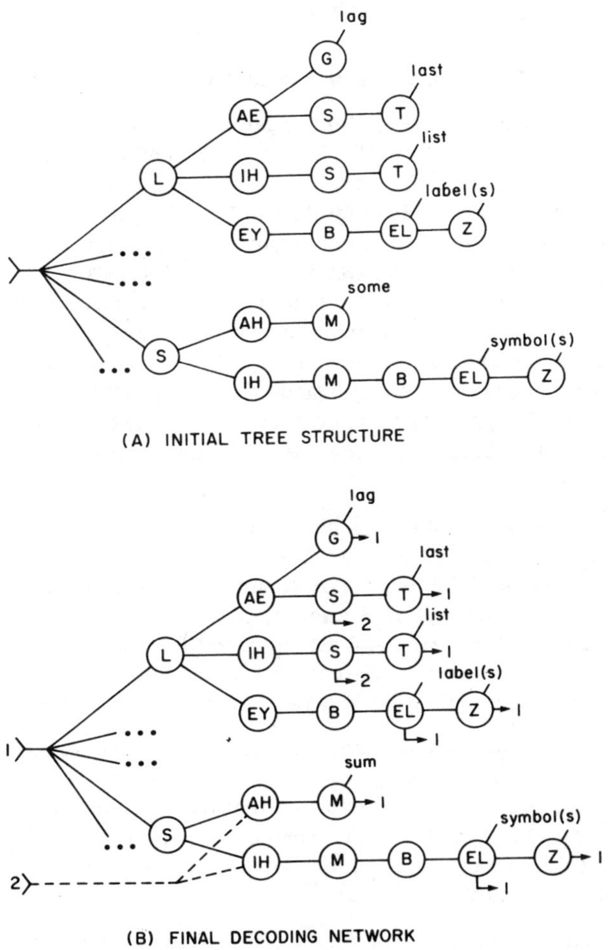

FIG. 7. The partial lexical tree for the phonetic representation of several English words shown in part (a) is transformed into a lexical decoding network for the recognition of sequences of words by application of a set of word-boundary phonological rules (Klovstad, 1977).

limited task domain might have resulted in acceptable performance. It would be interesting to know, for example, how much of an improvement in certain critical components is needed to achieve acceptable performance, or how much improvement would be gained by restricting the language definition in various ways.

The most interesting ideas to come out of the BBN project were a lexical decoding network incorporating sophisticated phonological rules, the technique of representing segmentation ambiguity by a lattice of alternatives, and the concept of word verification at the parametric level. However the performance of these components individually and as a total system did not seem to live up to their theoretical potential. Because of the slowness of the system, there was apparently not enough effort devoted to debugging and optimizing individual components in a system context. Specific problems that were never resolved were (1) how to ensure that the segment lattice was in fact providing more information than a linear string of best guesses, (2) how to normalize for talker differences, (3) whether sufficient data were analyzed to rely on the probability estimates of various phonetic confusions, extra segments, and missing segments, and (4) whether the system would perform significantly better if it were fast enough to evaluate many more partial sentence fragments.

C. Carnegie-Mellon University Hearsay-II

The CMU Hearsay-II system organization is shown in Fig. 8 (Lesser *et al.*, 1975; Lesser and Erman, 1977; Reddy *et al.*, 1977). The recognition process is similar in some respects to that employed in BBN Hwim, although the block diagrams and organizational philosophies are disparate. The CMU system configuration consists of a set of parallel asynchronous processes that simulate each of the component knowledge sources of a speech understanding system. Knowledge sources communicate via a global "blackboard" data base. When activated by the appearance of certain types of new information on the blackboard, a knowledge source tries to extend the analysis.

The information on the blackboard is divided into several major categories: sequences of segment labels, syllables, lexical items proposed, accepted words, and partial phrase theories. A knowledge source accepts information at one level and attempts to provide new information at a higher level (bottom-up analysis) or lower level (top-down prediction and verification).

Initially, amplitude and zero-crossing parameters are used to divide an utterance into segments that are categorized by manner-of-articulation features (Goldberg and Reddy, 1976). Good performance is obtained by avoiding the more difficult place-of-articulation decisions in the preliminary analysis.

A word hypothesizer lists all words having a syllable structure compatible with the partial phonetic representation. For example, there might be ten lexical items that are consistent with a fricative—stop—vowel—stop pattern, three items consistent with a fricative—stop—vowel subpattern, and five more items consistent with a stop—vowel subpattern. The performance of the lexical hypothesizer is such that only 70 percent of the correct words are detected (Smith, 1976), but others are found by top-down prediction at a later stage.

A word verification component scores each lexical hypothesis by comparing an expected sequence of spectra with observed linear-prediction spectra. The lexicon used for verification is adapted from Harpy and thus is defined in terms of expected spectral patterns instead of expected phonetic patterns. Coarticulation across word boundaries is a problem using this approach, but some word-boundary acoustic rules are included. Performance of the verification component is indicated in Table IV.

High-scoring words activate a syntactic component which tries to put words together into partial sentence theories. Grammatically acceptable adjacent words are also predicted since the word hypothesizer is not expected to get all of the words of the sentence. The control strategy is similar to that used by BBN in that best-scoring words or sentence-fragment pieces are sought anywhere in the utterance and extended to the left and/or to the right. CMU obtained significantly better performance with an island-driven strategy than BBN, but it is argued below that the Harpy left-to-right control strategy has advantages over any middle-out strategy. Once a complete sentence has been found, a response could be computed by accessing a data base. A more detailed description of the system is presented in Appendix C.

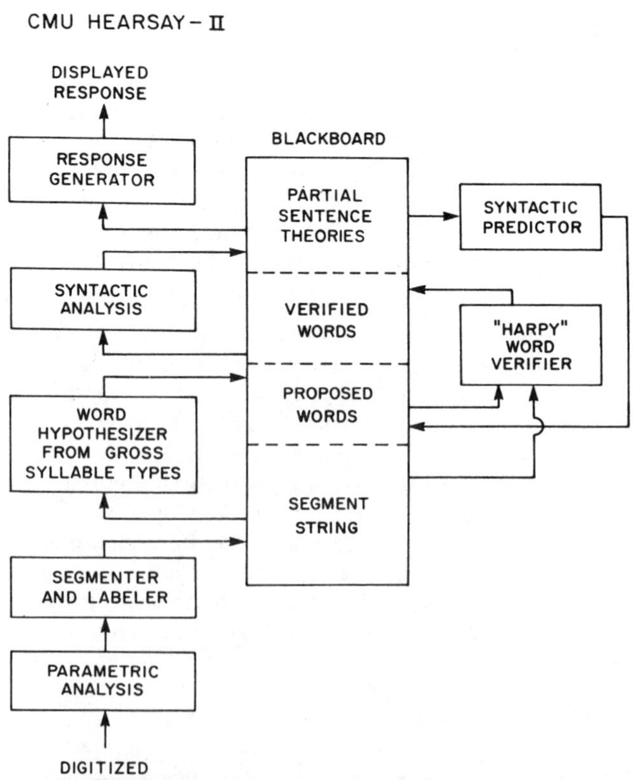

FIG. 8. A block diagram of the CMU Hearsay-II system organization.

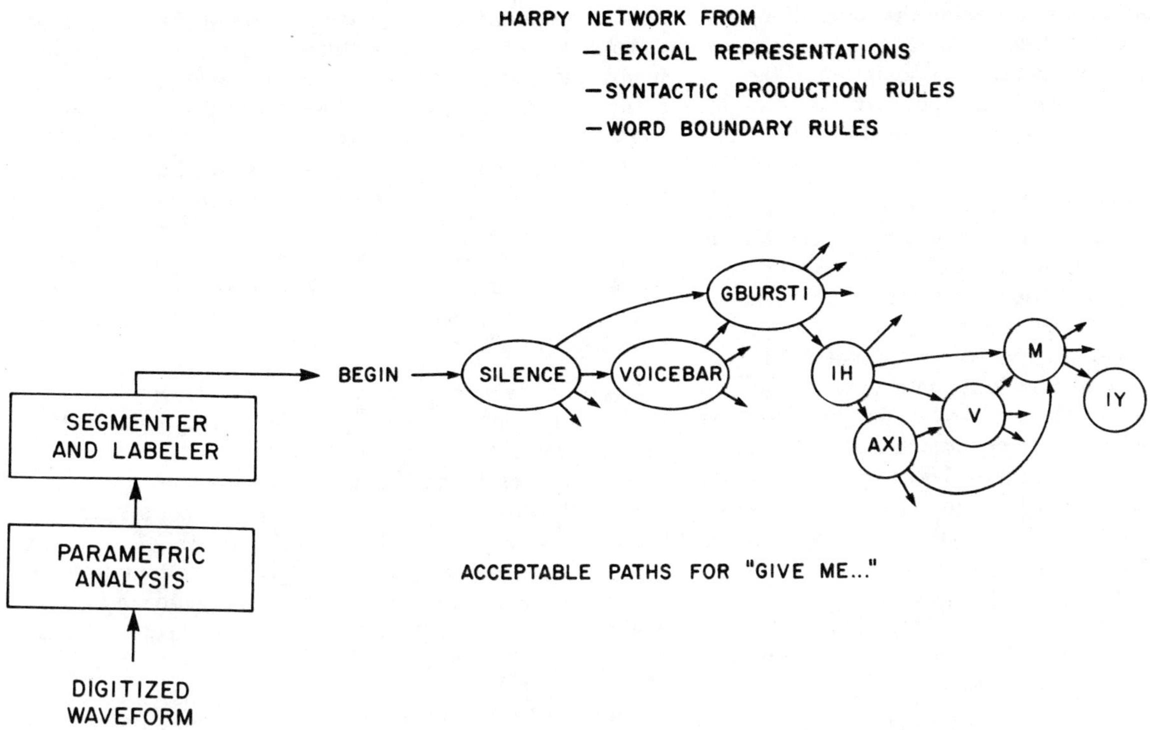

FIG. 9. A block diagram of the CMU Harpy system organization. Shown is a small (hypothetical) fragment of the Harpy state transition network, including paths accepted for sentences beginning with "Give me." Each node is named by the expected linear-prediction spectrum pattern. In general, many paths leave each node, corresponding to other possible sentence-initial words. A finite set of about 10**8 sentences (of length up to 8 words drawn from a 1011 word lexicon) can be recognized by the 15 000 state Harpy network.

Discussion of CMU Hearsay-II

Hearsay-II exhibited the best performance of the systems other than Harpy. Since it is not at all clear that Hearsay-II used components having better absolute performance, it is of interest to speculate on those aspects of the overall system design that account for its superior behavior. There are three essential reasons in my view: (1) as in the BBN system, absolute decisions (e.g., to reject a word hypothesis) were avoided by assigning graded scores so that component errors were not necessarily fatal, (2) computational efficiency issues were always of primary concern so that more alternatives could be considered, and (3) syntactic complexity (i.e., the average number of words to be considered to the right of any correct word) was directly controlled and reduced to a point where the system performance was acceptable. The use of strong syntactic and semantic constraints was encouraged by the ARPA goal structure, and should be utilized in future practical systems to improve performance.

D. Carnegie-Mellon University Harpy

The Harpy system, as implemented by Lowerre (1976), is shown in Fig. 9. The system includes a network of 15 000 states. Embedded in the state transition network are (1) all possible paths through the finite state grammar (i.e., a graph representation of all possible sentences), (2) alternate representations of all lexical items in terms of acoustic segments, and (3) a set of rules describing expected changes to acoustic segment sequences across word boundaries. The set of word-boundary rules, lexical representations, and grammar equations are automatically compiled into the efficient network representation shown in the figure.

The input utterance is divided into brief roughly stationary acoustic segments. Each segment is compared with 98 talker-specific linear-prediction spectral templates to obtain a set of 98 spectral distances, using the minimum residual error metric (Itakura, 1975). Template selection for a new talker is automatic, but requires that the user read about 20 selected sentences.

Each state in the network has an associated spectral template. The decoding strategy is to try to find the best scoring path through the state transition network by comparing the distance between the observed spectra and template sequences given in the network. Generally a state can accept a sequence of several sufficiently similar input segments, although some states are constrained so as to grab a specified minimum or maximum duration of the input.

Harpy is an extension of a Markov model of sentence decoding originally employed by Baker (1974) in a sentence recognition system called Dragon. In Dragon, a "breadth-first" dynamic programming strategy was used to find the optimal path through a network, but in the Harpy implementation a "beam-search" technique is used in which a restricted beam of near-miss alternatives around the best-scoring path are considered, thus reducing the search time significantly. Dragon also used *a priori* probabilities in choosing the most likely path through the network, while Harpy considers only spectral distance. A more detailed description of the CMU Harpy system is presented in Appendix D.

Discussion of CMU Harpy

Harpy and its predecessor Dragon represent a significant breakthrough in the application of simple structured models to speech recognition. It might seem to someone versed in the intricacies of phonology and the acoustic—phonetic characteristics of speech that a search of a graph of expected acoustic segments is a naive and foolish technique to use to decode a sentence. In fact such a graph and search strategy (and probably a number of other simple models) can be constructed and made to work very well indeed if the proper acoustic—phonetic details are embodied in the structure. The keys to success seem to me to be (1) the way that important structural aspects of language and speech can be folded into an initial network structure, (2) the possibility of optimizing of the network and the spectral templates using a very large body of training utterances, and (3) imposition of strong syntactic constraints.

Harpy is essentially a verification strategy. All alternative sentences are specified by the network, and the task is to verify which sequence of spectral states (path through the network) corresponds to the input sequence of spectra. It has been argued elsewhere (Klatt and Stevens, 1973) that verification of expected acoustic patterns for words is an easier task than phonetic analysis due to the inherent ambiguity of acoustic—phonetic decoding rules. To the extent that phonologists are better able to write generative than analytic rules to describe speech, the advantages of verification strategies will remain.

Due to syntactic constraints, the Harpy network is not particularly dense, so that minimal acoustic—phonetic distinctions are rarely required to distinguish between utterances. The present spectral sequence network may be capable of distinguishing minimal pairs of words quite well, but there is no direct evidence that it can, and some reason to doubt its detailed phonetic abilities given only 98 templates and limited word-boundary acoustic—phonetic rules. Even when syntactic constraints have been applied and the correct sentence has been identified, only 40% of the time does the top-scoring template match the expected template for each state in the best-scoring path through the network. If the templates were analogous to phonetic segments (which is roughly true for consonants in the current implementation, but not as true for vowels) this statistic would imply a less than 40% phonetic transcription performance in the absence of syntactic constraints, which is worse than in any of the other systems. However, there seems to me to be no fundamental limit to the ultimate transcription performance ability of Harpy-like networks if the lexical representations and word-boundary rules are sufficiently detailed.

The grammar on which Harpy and Hearsay-II were demonstrated was actually a member of a set of related grammars manifesting different branching factors and thus a range of task difficulties. One of the reasons for CMU's success was the ability to manipulate branching factor and observe changes to performance. This was a significant achievement given the ARPA objectives. Unfortunately, within the set of branching factors investigated, excellent performance was achieved only by using a rather low branching factor grammar, i.e., one that constrained acceptable sentences so that just two large syntactic classes were allowed: topics, and authors. Test sentences were always constrained so that at least one of these two classes appeared in each test sentence.

There clearly exist tasks for which a Harpy-like network would appear to be applicable [e.g., connected digit recognition or even perhaps air traffic control (Connolly, 1975)], but the languages for such applications will have to be fairly artificial and not a so-called "habitable subset of English" (Watt, 1968). Still the job of creating a Harpy system for a new task domain is not simple; it took careful analysis of 747 sentences to achieve the present level of Harpy performance on this particular 1000-word lexicon.

E. Other ARPA-funded speech understanding research

The ARPA project included a number of supporting efforts that were important to the task of creating the four large speech understanding systems just described. In this review, we have emphasized the systems, but a brief mention of the activities of the other contractors is provided in the paragraphs below.

1. Lincoln Laboratory

Researchers at MIT Lincoln Laboratory spent considerable effort on the development of phonetic recognition strategies (Weinstein *et al.*, 1975). Techniques included formant tracking and the use of formant transition information for stop place-of-articulation categorization. The performance and documentation of these strategies was probably the best of the initial system builders at the time when funds were re-allocated from five to the three research groups showing promise of putting together the best total systems. Lincoln staff also developed a lexical network representation (Klovstad and Mondshein, 1975) that later evolved into the BBN lexical decoding network.

2. Stanford Research Institute

When a planned joint SDC/SRI system development program was no longer possible, Stanford Research Institute staff were forced to carry out their development and testing of system components and strategies using a simple simulation of the behavior of a SDC mapper for word verification. Simulation proved to be a valuable technique for optimizing several system design choices concerning speed/accuracy tradeoffs, without the added run-time cost of using the actual mapper (Paxton, 1976; 1977). The results of the simulations were used, for example, to specify the performance required from the mapper for a given vocabulary size in order to obtain 90% sentence understanding, using a language definition that allows fairly general syntactic constructions, an independent semantic component, and capabilities for anaphoric references and ellipsis in processing sequential items in a dialogue (Walker, 1976).

3. *Special contractors*

As part of the overall research and development plan, funds were allocated to several research groups to provide support in the area of acoustic—phonetic analysis. The research contributions of the special smaller contractors[2] have not been discussed in this review. However, significant work was performed toward the development of phonological/phonetic rules for the description of spoken English sentences (Oshika *et al.*, 1975), prosodic decoding rules (Lea *et al.*, 1975), acoustic—phonetic recognition strategies (Mermelstein, 1975a; 1975b), and evaluation of the complexity of the grammars employed in the four systems (O'Malley, unpublished).

III. DISCUSSION AND CONCLUSIONS

Is there a need for speech understanding systems? Ochsman and Chapanis (1974) present evidence that man—man communication via speech is more natural and efficient than other modes of communication such as typing. This would presumably also be true of man—machine communication, especially for unskilled persons interacting with a system for either data input or information retrieval (Lea, 1968). It seems that the need for speech understanding systems is already present, and this need will grow as our dependence on computerized stores of information increases.

One answer to the demand for automated man—machine communication by voice might be a system that recognizes sentences formed by speaking a series of words separated by pauses (Herscher and Cox, 1976). It has been claimed that users can readily learn to insert short pauses between words, transforming the sentence recognition problem into an easier isolated word recognition problem. Coarticulation between words is minimized in this way and word identification by pattern matching is possible. Syntactic and semantic constraints can be applied to limit the set of acceptable words at each sentence location, and thus perform with a recognition rate significantly better than *P-to-the-N*th, where P is the probability of single word recognition, and N is the number of words in the pseudosentence.

Isolated word concatenation appears to have practical applications in many limited task domains (Martin, 1976). However, it is no more that a compromise solution to the attainment of fast natural communication with computers. The procedures have yet to be generalized to handle large vocabulary tasks, and it has not been shown that users are able to stay in the "pause-between-words" mode in a more complex task environment. There was and is a pressing practical need to study and develop procedures for simulating normal sentence understanding.

Given the demand for speech understanding by computers, was the ARPA project a good thing? The list of scientific achievements in the next section indicates that significant advances have been made in the speech understanding field. Yet if one spends three million dollars a year for five years and the best system turns out to be a one-man-year Ph.D. thesis, not all is well. The other projects sought to build more powerful general systems, but all failed to meet the ARPA goals.

It was potentially beneficial to shake-up the field with a large funding effort, and much good can still come from the ARPA project. On the other hand, it is disruptive to send funding oscillations through the basic research community and to subject science to fads and anti-fads. The danger now is that funds will be less available for the basic science that must be done in the speech analysis area before real further progress is made.

A. Scientific achievements of the ARPA program

The following paragraphs list a number of good ideas drawn from the four speech understanding systems and elsewhere.[4] In addition to identifying several scientific achievements of the ARPA program, this section is intended to summarize the state of the art and to suggest guidelines for the development of future speech understanding systems.

1. *System organization*

The structures of Harpy and Dragon represent a significant improvement in the realization of sentence verification procedures. System organization is immensely simplified by precompiling disparate knowledge into a uniform network representation at the spectrum level. A second new organizational concept comes from Hearsay-II and involves creation of a set of parallel asynchronous processes that communicate via a blackboard. As a conceptual model, the approach may be applicable in other problem solving domains.

2. *Grammar design*

The ability to manipulate grammatical complexity and observe changes to system performance as the task is simplified was an important factor in the success of CMU. The shift of attention from size of the lexicon to effective grammatical branching factor is an important advance in the quantification of task difficulty from the original ARPA goal of a 1000-word lexicon. It means that a difficult problem can be made easier by reducing the apparent size of the lexicon. What is needed now are techniques to reduce grammatical complexity while maintaining task objectives and retaining language habitability.

3. *Control strategy*

Control strategies that work from the middle out, starting with a good-matching content word utilize less syntactic constraint and have been found to cost a great deal more in complexity and computation time than strategies based on strict left-to-right processing through an utterance. If phonological rules handle function word variability well, then a strict left-to-right strategy with a breadth-of-search capability, as in Harpy, seems to be the best choice.

4. Semantics and context

Most semantic constraints employed by these systems are realized within the syntactic production rules. BBN Hwim contained a separate semantics module, but it was not used very much during sentence recognition. None of the four systems were able to use prior discourse information to reject a sentence such as "What is their registration fee?" because there was no assignable referent for "their." However, earlier, Hearsay-I (Reddy *et al.*, 1973) contained a chess-playing program that checked requested moves for plausibility.

5. Syntax

It is likely that almost any parser structure will do for simple speech understanding tasks in which all that is required is an enumeration of the possible lexical items following a given sentence fragment. In fact, the best solution for a finite grammar is very likely to precompile a list of the permissible word sequences into a network, as is done in Harpy.

The speech understanding project has benefitted from prior work on the automatic parsing (syntactic analysis) of written sentences. Powerful mechanisms such as an augmented transition network grammar and parser (Woods, 1970) have already been developed for processing word strings from left to right. While many grammar formulations could be considered, the augmented transition network grammar has the advantages of permitting semantic constraints to be written into the grammar and allowing many alternative parses to be computed efficiently in parallel (Woods, 1970). The grammar also includes simple methods of searching most-likely structures first and can produce structural representations that are ideal input for semantic processing routines involved in response generation.

6. Word identification/verification

Each word or morpheme of the lexicon has been specified at a fairly abstract phonemic level in several of the systems. This makes lexical development and augmentation much easier than if all possible detailed phonetic or acoustic forms must be listed. Phonological rules that operate within words and/or across word boundaries are used to expand the lexicon into multiple representations. Phonology seems to have come of age over the past few years in that formal rules of considerable predictive power have been developed. As a starting point the morphological expansions and phonological rules of Zue (Woods *et al.*, 1976, Vol. 3, pp. 57–72) might be used. Additional more general rules are to be found in the work of Cohen and Mercer (1975) and Oshika *et al.* (1975).

The potential role of the syllable in lexical verification was elaborated by SDC, who suggested that allophonic variations can be predicted in a relatively straightforward way if one begins verification at a syllable peak and then looks for acoustic evidence of adjacent consonants that are expected. The advantages of the syllable as a recognition unit are less clear. It might be argued that the dyad (Peterson, Wang, and Sivertsen, 1958), an interval from the middle of one phonetic segment to the middle of the next segment, is a unit having about the same theoretical advantages. There are far fewer dyad types than syllable types in English. Silverman and Dixon (1976) have employed the dyad as a recognition unit with good success for a single talker. The diad has been termed a "diphone" when used as a building block for speech synthesis (Dixon and Maxey, 1968).

Word identification in sentence contexts is possible only if the effects of phonetic/phonological recoding at word boundaries can be decoded. This requires that the phonological encoding rules be known, and that computational procedures be available for applying the inverse rules rapidly and selectively. To take the example of the rule [s t # s] → [s] as in "list some," it would be costly to test every [s] in an utterance for a possible underlying [s t # s], especially considering the number of word-boundary rules that would have to be treated in this way. The solution that comes from the BBN system is to incorporate word boundary phonology into the stored lexical representations by first constructing a lexical tree of expected phonetic sequences, and then transforming the tree into a phonetic-sequence network of the type shown in Fig. 7.

7. Acoustic-phonetic processing

An advance in the area of acoustic—phonetic processing has been the realization that *phonetic* segmentation and labeling is not necessary to word identification in connected speech. The Harpy philosophy of representing words by sequences of spectral templates in a network that takes into account word boundary phonology shows great promise.

The actual spectral representation (linear prediction spectral analysis) used in Harpy and the spectral distance measure (the minimum residual error) used are computationally very efficient, but probably not optimal and not related very closely to perceptual distance. For example, the metric does not incorporate overall spectral intensity and may therefore confuse a silence spectrum with some speech sound having a similar spectral shape. Also Harpy used only 98 templates to represent the entire inventory of spectral variations in speech. The excellent performance of Harpy may mean that the details of spectral representations and distance measures are not critical. On the other hand, perhaps even better performance in harder task domains is possible within the Harpy framework by using improved metrics.

Comparison of the general performance of the phonetic analysis components of the SDC, BBN, and CMU Hearsay-II systems in phonetic labeling with for example, Silverman and Dixon (1976), Weinstein *et al.*, 1975, and earlier work suggests that the contribution of the ARPA project to improved phonetic recognition strategies is not in proportion to the level of effort expended. Schwartz and Cook (1977) have recently attained 67%

correct phonetic transcription capabilities using 71 phonetic categories in a phonetic vocoder application, but their system is not well documented. There is a clear need for continued work in this area.

Shockey and Reddy (1975) discovered that linguists are actually not very consistent at phonetic transcription if the language is unfamiliar. From their data, they speculate that machines should not be expected to do better than 60%—70% correct phonetic transcription performance. We believe that their results may be a reasonable test of the current status of a universal phonetic theory, but they do not measure transcription abilities of listeners who are permitted to make use of the phonetic and phonological constraints of English. Recent experiments by Mark Liberman and Lloyd Nakatani (personal communication) suggest that listeners can transcribe English nonsense names embedded in sentences (and obeying the phonological constraints of English) with better than 90% phonemic accuracy. It is likely that machine performance must approach this figure before very powerful speech understanding systems are realized. Alternatively, perhaps the best bet is not to do phonetic labeling at all, as in Harpy.

Prosodic cues (fundamental frequency, segmental duration, and the intensity contour) suggest a stress pattern for the incoming syllable string, and thus could assist in lexical hypothesization. Prosodic cues also indicate clause boundaries, phrase boundaries, and, to a minor extent, word boundaries. While relatively little use was made of prosodic information in the four speech understanding systems, some ideas for prosodic analysis were proposed (Lea, Medress, and Skinner, 1975).

8. Use of statistics

Jelenek (1976) argues for the use of decision strategies that are based on the collection of an appropriate set of probabilities determined experimentally. Several of the speech understanding systems used estimates of the probability of a phonetic or lexical decision given the acoustic data in scoring the goodness of a theory, and each seems to have gotten into trouble by so doing. The problem is to analyze enough data to be sure of the probability of infrequent confusions. This is nearly impossible if one wants to take into consideration factors such as phonetic environment.

9. Acoustic analysis

It is now known that the important information-bearing elements of the speech code are contained in the magnitude spectrum of speech, i.e., in a sequence of well-chosen short-term spectra. Linear prediction spectra have proven to be a robust spectral representation having the additional advantages of being a pleasing visual idealization of speech, of having an existing simple metric for spectral comparisons, and of permitting the estimation of formant frequencies. On the other hand, it appears that filter banks designed carefully to take into account critical bands and other psychophysical constraints are equally useful as spectral representations (Klatt, 1976b).

10. Talker normalization

A surprisingly powerful method of talker normalization is incorporated in the Harpy system. About twenty known sentences are processed to derive talker-specific spectral templates automatically. These templates are capable of capturing a wide range of talker characteristics including important differences between men and women. Other talker differences such as differences in dialect are best overcome for the present by restricting system usage to talkers of a single fairly uniform dialect.

11. Response generation

The BBN Hwim system and CMU Hearsay-II included a data base and response generator (although these components were not usually connected during a recognition demonstration). In this sense, a distinction between speech understanding (is the response correct?) and speech recognition (are all of the words correct?) was realized. Cases where a correct response would be generated in spite of lexical identification errors were fairly frequent in Hearsay-II. To that extent, the systems described here represent the beginnings of true machine understanding of spoken language.

To generate a proper response, one must solve an information retrieval problem, choose an appropriate frame sentence for a response, and synthesize an audio output. Some progress in general solutions to these problems was achieved at BBN (Woods *et al.*, 1976; Klatt, 1976a).

12. Contributions to speech science

Many of the scientific achievements listed above impact on the speech sciences. One might have expected more in the way of detailed algorithms for the recognition of phonetic categories or descriptions of acoustic—phonetic details of sentences spoken by different talkers, but speech scientists should be made aware of advances such as the observations that (1) linear prediction spectra are a useful representation of speech for spectral analysis or formant frequency analysis (2) progress has been made in describing the steps involved in predicting the phonetic characteristics of words in sentences from a phonemic representation, (3) strategies exist for automatic phonetic transcription with performance of about 60%—70% correct, (4) talker normalization by acquisition of talker-specific spectral templates works surprisingly well, (5) lexical hypothesization need not include a step in which a phonetic transcription is derived, and (6) some of the computational structures suggested for a speech understanding system may in fact constitute a good model of sentence perception.

13. A proposed future system

A possible structure for a future speech understanding system that incorporates many of these ideas is shown in Fig. 10. An acoustic-segment lexical decoding network is generated off-line from a phonemically organized task-specific lexicon. A set of phonological rules, a diphone dictionary, and a set of word-boundary phono-

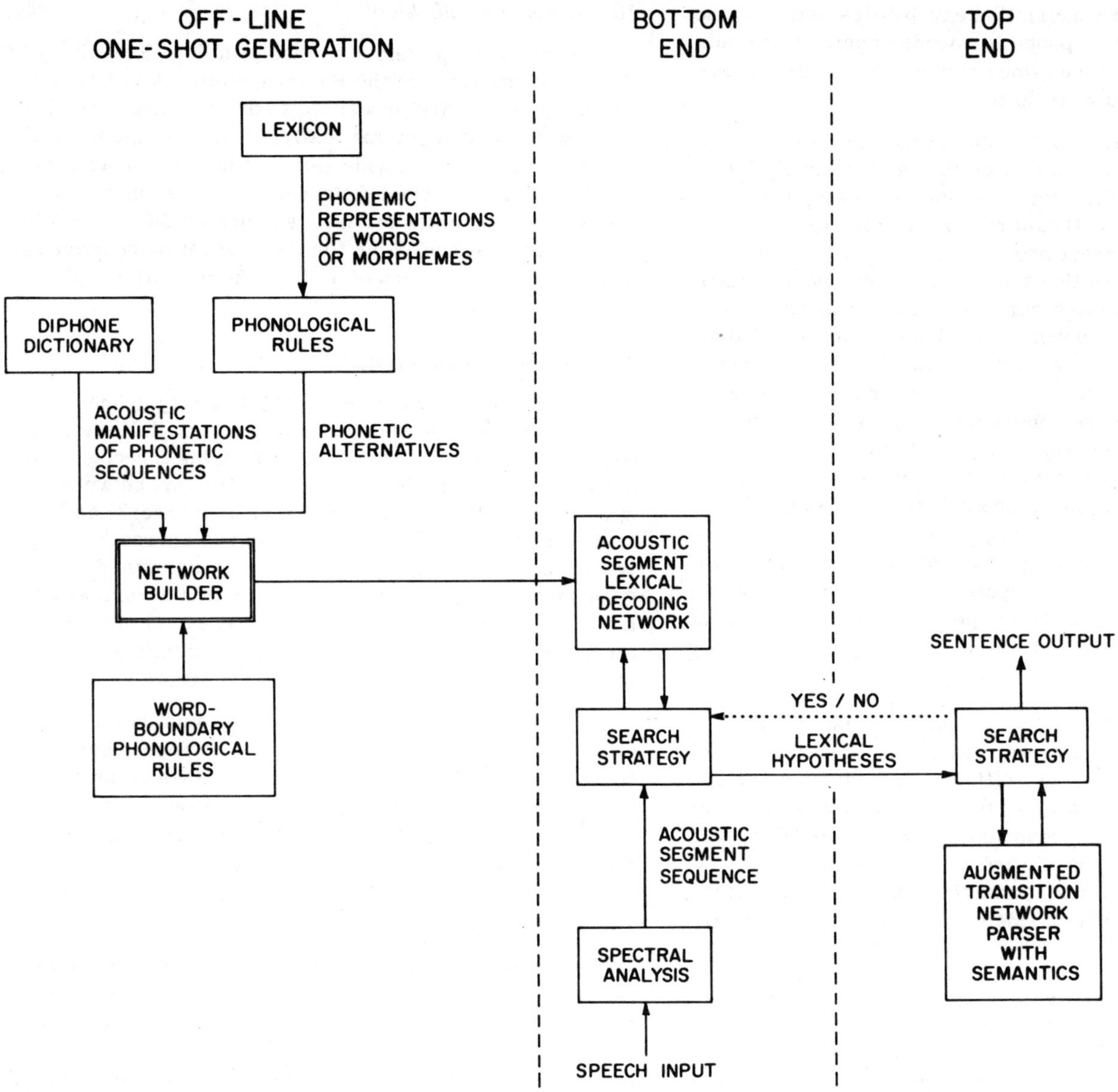

FIG. 10. Proposed structure for a future speech understanding or sentence recognition system.

logical rules convert the lexical representations into a network of expected acoustic segment sequences for all possible word sequences composed from the vocabulary. Each state of the network is represented by one of a moderate set of spectral templates.

A spectral template is envisioned to be something like a short-time spectrum, but the representation is refined to take into account critical bands, masking, loudness, and other limitations imposed by the peripheral auditory system. The comparison of spectral templates with input spectra is assumed to include sophisticated calculations depending on the types of spectra being compared. The decoding network includes a specification of duration limits for each template and an ability to normalize these durational constraints on the basis of estimates of local speaking rate or stress.

The bottom end is patterned after that of Harpy. An input sequence of acoustic segments is processed from left to right, always seeking the best path through the lexical decoding network. The resulting partial string of words is sent to the top end to see if the sequence is permitted by the grammar or if the next-best path through the network should be pursued instead. The Harpy talker normalization procedure of adaptive acquisition of talker-specific templates is assumed, although more than 98 spectral templates will probably be required to achieve optimum phonetic and lexical discrimination. There is no phonetic or phonemic level of representation at any stage in the bottom end recognition process, although important use is made of these linguistic concepts during network generation.

The top end uses an augmented transition network parser to monitor the word sequence proposed by the bottom end and to terminate immediately ungrammatical hypotheses. The first acceptable sentence that spans the input is sent to a semantics/response generation module (not shown) or is simply typed out if the system is being run in sentence recognition mode.

The keys to success of this proposed approach are the selection of a good set of spectral templates, development of a diphone dictionary that captures the acoustic characteristics of English phone sequences, and a set of phonological rules that can generate all possible phonetic manifestations of word sequences. Stated in this way, the task ahead is still formidable, but it is an interesting and well-defined challenge. The missing pieces must come from speech science: the computer sciences have done the job of providing a structure in which to embed speech knowledge for recognition purposes.

B. Relations to psychological models of speech perception

Previous psychological models of phonetic analysis include the motor theory of speech perception (Liberman *et al.*, 1962; 1967), analysis by synthesis (Halle and Stevens, 1962; Stevens, 1972b), multistage feature-based models (Pisoni, 1977), and quantal invariance models (Stevens, 1972a; Cole and Scott, 1974). An alternative psychological model of early stages in the speech perception process might be based on the organization shown in Fig. 10. This model makes four novel claims which, in terms of speech perception, must be looked upon as conjectures:

Conjecture 1: lexical decoding is usually direct, with no analysis-by-synthesis or other mechanism for rich information feedback from higher linguistic levels.

Conjecture 2: generative rules are used to precompile acoustic—phonetic and phonological knowledge into an appropriate decoding structure because analytic rules are too ambiguous and thus computationally inefficient.

Conjecture 3: there is no use made of a phonetic level of representation during sentence processing.

Conjecture 4: syntactic analysis is direct, using a precompiled network to characterize permitted sentence structures rather than a set of generative rules and an analysis-by-synthesis strategy.

These are independent claims. It is possible that any or all of them are true. The first claim has some support in the recent experimental work of Garrett (1977). The second claim is a theoretical argument that would be invalidated if, e.g., processing time for "list some" were greater than for "list one" due to the extra processing required to overcome [t] deletion in the one case. The third claim is superficially contradicted by numerous experiments concerned with the properties of phonetic feature detectors (see Studdert-Kennedy, 1975, for a review). However, if one looks carefully at these experiments, one can argue that none of them have invalidated the kind of template theory that we have in mind because the concept of phonetic similarity, as measured by the number of phonetic features that are shared, can be replaced directly by a concept of spectral similarity. The fourth claim already has its proponents (Wanner and Maratsos, 1978).

Research is needed to (1) investigate how pieces of the model might evolve during language acquisition, (2) determine how prosodic analysis is performed in such a model, (3) see how unfamiliar words are added to the lexicon, (4) determine how noise-corrupted speech is processed, and (5) make predictions that would distinguish the model from phonetic feature based models.

The model of Fig. 10 is probably too simple to be true. It is more likely that the central nervous system can make use of many strategies, including phonetic analysis and analysis-by-synthesis, in which case the conjecture made here is that, under normal circumstances, the primary way of initiating sentence analysis is indicated by the block diagram of Fig. 10.

C. Future research

The key to improved bottom-end performance (lexical hypothesization) in future speech understanding systems, it seems to me, is the transformation of a phonetic identification problem into a spectral state verification problem, as was done in Harpy. Phonetic representations for words of the lexicon are replaced by sequences of expected spectra and some durational constraints. This translation problem is nontrivial and required many trial-and-error iterations during Harpy development. The availability of a list of expected template sequences for all possible phonetic strings of English would considerably aid in bringing up new lexicons. The main objective of future research in this area should therefore be the accumulation of more detailed linguistic and acoustic—phonetic facts about English sentences.

Future research on top-end design might focus on the imposition of realistic semantic and task constraints and on computational efficiencies that will ultimately permit the use of more general grammars. Another worthwhile pursuit might be to interface a Harpy-like lexical recognition network to a top end with a nonfinite grammar, as in Fig. 10.

Additional research will be required to build a practical speech understanding system that has a complete human-engineered interactive capability. Problem areas in need of further work include the design of habitable languages, how to monitor the input to know when a signal is present (Rabiner and Sambur, 1975), including rejecting "umm's" and breath noise (Martin, 1975), how to know when an utterance is complete, whether it will be necessary for a user to see a display of the request and give a "yes"—"no" response, etc.

The steering committee prepared a follow-on research plan (Newell *et al.*, 1975) that took up a number of these issues and also proposed that the four speech understanding systems not be allowed to die. They argued that the systems required substantial additional debugging and tuning before reaching their full potential and that experiments were needed to better understand their capabilities and limitations. The committee proposed that the systems ought to be preserved as a resource for use by a wider community because considerable scientific insight might be gained from widespread experimentation with these systems. Based on the current funding picture, it appears that none of these recommendations will come to pass.

As a final note, we may ask "How hard is the sentence understanding problem in the limited contexts investigated during the ARPA project?" In 1970, when compared with isolated word recognition, the problems seemed immense. After the limited success of Harpy, one becomes more optimistic about the abilities of future systems. Still, the nature of the problem is elusive. Even the dimensions of task difficulty have yet to be adequately defined. Limited experience suggests that significant increases in difficulty are associated with increased grammar branching factor (caused by increased lexical size or increased syntactic freedom), the inherent acoustic ambiguity of words that must be distinguished, and the importance of unstressed function word recognition to sentence decoding. If these factors can be controlled in a particular task domain, speech understanding by machines is now a practical goal.

ACKNOWLEDGMENT

Preparation of this review was supported by the Advanced Research Projects Agency of the Department of Defense under Contract N00014-75-C-0533. I wish to thank everyone associated with the ARPA Speech Understanding Project who spent many hours helping me to understand these complex systems. Special thanks go to W. A. Lea, A. Newell, J. E. Shoup, D. R. Reddy, J. J. Wolf, and W. A. Woods for correcting some of my errors of judgment.

APPENDIX A. DETAILED DESCRIPTION OF THE SDC SYSTEM

A. Acoustic analysis

The speech waveform is digitized at 20 000 samples/sec with no prior frequency-domain preemphasis. The waveform is divided into 10-ms chunks, and the energy is computed for each chunk. Other parameters that are computed every 10 ms include zero crossing counts and the fundamental frequency contour. Fundamental frequency is extracted with a down-sampled center-clipped autocorrelation technique (Gillmann, 1975). A linear prediction spectral analysis is performed every 10 ms, using 24 coefficients and a 25.6-ms Hamming window. A formant tracker estimates which of the linear prediction poles are the four lowest formant frequencies over voiced intervals.

These parameters are used to apply gross phonetic labels to relatively stationary sequences of 10-ms spectra. Special routines then characterize vowel-like segments (Kameny, 1975; 1976) and frication spectra (Molho, 1976) in terms of phonetic labels with associated scores for the three best alternatives. A post-analysis pass smooths the label names through local continuity constraints. The resulting analysis is placed in an array called the A-matrix. Segmental identification is based on acoustic-phonetic recognition strategies having a good theoretical basis—formants for vowels, gross spectral shapes for fricatives and plosive burst onsets. However, the performance (first choice label correct about 50 percent of the time for 40 phonetic categories) suggests that there are not enough detailed facts about expected influences of coarticulation with adjacent phones in the algorithms.

B. Lexical representations

The format used to represent the word "Lafayette" in the lexicon was shown in Fig. 3. The pronunciation variants for this lexical item were generated automatically from a set of phonological rules (Barnett, 1974) and then stored in the form shown in Fig. 3 so as not to have to execute the rules each time a word is hypothesized by the top end. Similar lexical networks have been used in other speech understanding systems (Tappert, Dixon, and Rabinowitz, 1973; Tappert, 1975; Cohen and Mercer, 1975; Baker, 1975; Woods and Zue, 1976).

C. Word verification

The mapper forms the interface between the top end and the A-matrix. Each time a word is hypothesized, the mapper calls "phoneme sniffer" subroutines that give matching scores for each expected phoneme. The mapper is organized in terms of syllables, attempting to match a vowel nucleus first, then working outward to verify expected adjacent consonants. The best-scoring alternative of a lexical spelling lattice is found, and phoneme scores are combined by taking the geometric mean to get a total word score. Use of the geometric mean penalizes a single bad phonemic match. The control program converts this score into an estimate of the probability of correct verification (on the basis of a prior data collection experiment) and accepts the best word from a syntactic class if it exceeds a threshold. Other words from this syntactic class that exceed the threshold may be used later to form other sentence fragment hypotheses if the best word fails to generate an acceptable total sentence. Frequently there are unexplained temporal gaps and overlaps between the starting and ending times of adjacent words of a sentence hypothesis, so the control box also sends word pairs to the mapper for evaluation of word adjacency plausibility.

The phoneme sniffers first consult the list of phoneme labels in the A-matrix in their search for a match (Weeks, 1974). If there is not a direct match with the phoneme being sought, other parameters of the A-matrix may be examined. In other cases, a matching score is obtained by consulting a phoneme confusion probability matrix in which entries reflect the probability that phoneme x will be confused with phoneme y, as estimated from a limited data sample. Phonetic context, such as the fact that [t] and [k] are more likely to be confused before [i] than before other vowels, is not considered when using the confusion matrix.

One of the more difficult problems in structuring the mapper has been to keep track of the time position within the A matrix, and not to miss a syllable or detect extra syllables. Errors of this type are fatal if they reject a correct word, since the top end cannot overcome such a decision. Fatal errors (often of this type) occurred in 40% of the large set of utterances tested, indicating that the present mapper/A-matrix combination must be improved, or the exclusively top-down system strategy must be changed.

The mapper has been evaluated by making over 11 000 verification requests using the 1000-word lexicon in the course of attempting to recognize several sentences. Relevant performance statistics are given in Table IV. Of 71 correct words hypothesized, 65 were verified and 6 were (fatally) rejected. Of 11 000 decoy word proposals, all but 372 were correctly rejected. However, the 372 false "yes" answers mean that for each of the 65 correct responses by the mapper, there are on the average 6 false words accepted that must be rejected by syntactic constraints imposed by the top end as attempts are made to extend these false partial sentence theories.

APPENDIX B. DETAILED DESCRIPTION OF THE BBN HWIM SYSTEM

A. Acoustic analysis

The speech waveform is digitized at 20 000 samples/sec and the first difference is computed to remove the dc component and tilt the spectrum up somewhat. A 13-pole selective linear prediction analysis (Makhoul, 1975) is performed over the 0–5-kHz range every 10-ms using a 20-ms Hamming window. (Essentially no use was ever made of the 5–10-kHz information.) Formant frequencies are estimated as the lowest bandwidth poles in the linear prediction analysis during voiced intervals. Other parameters used for segmentation and labeling include the energy as a function of time in several different frequency passbands, a zero-crossing count, and fundamental frequency.

Segmentation and phonetic labeling is accomplished in several passes across the data, with each new pass refining the decisions made on an earlier pass. Segmentation ambiguity is represented by a lattice of alternatives, as shown in Fig. 5. For each segment of the lattice, all possible phonetic labels are given a rating score based on acoustic similarity and/or experimentally determined confusion probability. As in the SDC system, probability matrix entries were computed independent of phonetic context.

The performance of the segmenter has been evaluated for 124 sentences read by three talkers, using the dictionary spelling for the words of an utterance as the correct answer. For 2850 dictionary segments, the segmenter found 5127 segments arranged in a lattice such that, if one followed the most-correct path through the lattice, only 1.6% of the expected segmentation points were missed, and only 1.8% of the time did the best path contain an extra segment (Woods *et al.*, 1976, Vol. 2, pp. 9–39).

The labeling performance of the system was evaluated by considering the best path through the lattice, as defined above. With 71 possible phonetic labels, the rank-order distribution of the correct label ranges from 52% correct first choice to being within the top five label choices 83% of the time. This performance might appear to be somewhat better than that of the other systems, but it is not certain that the lexical matcher will find the best path through the lattice. Some high-scoring false word matches may be generated by using the alternative incorrect paths. A measure of information content would be needed to compare objectively the segment labelers used in the three systems.

The lexicon contains phonemic spellings for each word or morpheme. A set of phonological rules are applied to generate alternative pronunciations (Woods and Zue, 1976). On the average, a word begins with a single phonemic spelling and ends up with about two acceptable phonetic realizations after application of a modest set of phonological rules. Additional rules of the BBN phonological rule expansion system optionally delete or change some segment labels that are frequently missed by the acoustic–phonetic labeler. For example, a rule optionally deletes the /n/ in poststressed /nt/ clusters. If possible, it would have been better to make improvements to the labeler so that it could detect nasalization in these cases, but it is nevertheless very important for the lexicon to predict what is actually observed by the acoustic processing routines, and these special rules are one possible way of achieving this goal.

The entire lexicon of alternative pronunciations is folded into a single state transition network that incorporates word-boundary phonological rules and that can be searched very efficiently for lexical matches (Klovstad, 1977; Klovstad and Mondshein, 1975; Woods *et al.*, 1976, Vol. 3, pp. 12–27). The lexical decoding network is of sufficient theoretical interest for the design of future speech understanding systems that its general character will be described in some detail here. The first step in the creation of a lexical decoding network is to combine the expected phonetic spellings for all lexical items into a tree structure, as shown in Fig. 7a. Initial parts of words are combined with other words having the same beginning phonetic segments. The termination of each word is identified by one or more nodes in the tree, and these word-terminal nodes are unique insofar as the words of the lexicon have disjoint phonetic representations.

The tree shown in Fig. 7(a) is transformed into a network by application of a set of word-boundary pronunciation rules. Consider the word "list" in the tree. The pronunciation of "list" may be [l IH s] in the environment "list some," so the derived network representation of "list" shown in Fig. 7(b) has a path going from the [s] node of "list" directly to the second phone of all words starting with [s], and a path from the [t] node of "list" to the first phone of all words. This network structure captures a general word-boundary phonological rule stating that words ending in [s t] can be pronounced (optionally) without the [t], but that this can only happen if the following word begins with [s]. The rule is stated in a natural notation: OPT{S T # S}→{S} before being compiled into various modifications to the lexical tree. In this example, it is possible to accept the word "list" without seeing a [t], but only words starting with [s] can be matched thereafter.

It is possible to embed within this network structure any of the types of rules in the literature on word boundary phonology. The advantages of a lexical decoding network go beyond its being a concise statement of allowable phonetic strings corresponding to all word sequences of connected-word utterances. The network also allows computational (search) and storage efficiencies that can become significant as vocabulary size increases. Klovstad has developed scoring procedures for input phonetic strings having a missing segment or an extra segment by referring to experimentally determined probabilities of these phenomena. In my opinion, this is an attractive structure for representing lexical information in a generalized speech understanding system, although there are problems in accumulating sufficient statistics to score missing/extra segments properly.

B. Word verification by parametric synthesis

A word verification component is included in the BBN system to overcome the inherent inaccuracies in performance of the segmentation and labeling scheme by returning to the parametric level. One can be more certain about what acoustic data to expect if a word and, if possible, its phonetic context are given (Klatt and Stevens, 1973). The strategy is of some theoretical interest since it is a concrete example of an analysis-by-synthesis model of speech perception (Halle and Stevens, 1962).

Verification of a word begins by sending the phonemic representation, obtained from the lexicon, and adjacent phonemes, if known, to a speech synthesis-by-rule program (Klatt, 1976a), which was modified to predict spectra instead of generating waveforms (Woods *et al.*, 1976, Vol. 2, pp. 40–57). Verification scores are obtained by comparing 10-ms frames of synthesized spectra with selected spectral frames of the unknown utterance, using a dynamic programming algorithm to find the best possible alignment (Woods *et al.*, 1976, Vol. 2, pp. 58–68).

The performance of the verification component has been tested during operation of the speech understanding system. The distribution of verification scores for words that the lexical matcher thought were good word candidates during sentence recognition can be compared with an arbitrary threshold to obtain the performance figures shown in Table IV (Cook and Schwartz, 1977), although the system used graded scores rather than an absolute accept/reject threshold of the type implied by the contents of Table IV. The performance evaluation included three talkers, and a few changes were made (by hand) to the synthesis rules for each talker. Superficially, performance may seem poorer than for the SDC verifier, but the lexical matcher has removed nearly 95% of the worst matching words from consideration by the BBN verification component, while the SDC verifier processes all words permitted by the syntax.

Analysis by synthesis has been a popular model of the perceptual process. However, considering the computational cost of analysis-by-synthesis techniques and the problems of normalization for different talkers, it is the author's opinion that a more promising verification alternative for a computer system is the spectral-sequence verification strategy implicit in the Harpy speech understanding system.

C. Syntactic/semantic component

The syntactic component consists of an augmented transition network (ATN) parser; a portion of the ATN grammar is shown in Fig. 6 (Woods, 1970). The network indicates several possible paths that can be taken after a determiner has been found. The label PP is an abbreviation for a sub-network that recognizes prepositional phrases. The network is augmented with registers that are used to develop a quantified predicate calculus "deep-structure" representation for the sentence, i.e., the surface effects of certain grammatical transformations are undone to arrive at a standard syntactic representation appropriate for semantic interpretation. For example, there is a subject register, a "negative-particle-found" register, etc. The contents of the registers are modified as the parser discovers e.g., that the sentence is in the passive mode. This type of parser is considered by some psycholinguists to be the best current model of how a listener decodes the underlying structure of a spoken sentence (Wanner and Maratsos, 1977).

Semantic constraints are applied in the BBN system by adding them to the parsing grammar (although a separate semantic network was used for response generation). As an example of how semantic constraints are added, the general noun phrase subnetwork shown in Fig. 6(a) is expanded into a number of specialized noun phrase recognition networks, one of which is shown in Fig. 6(b).

Augmented transition net parsers were originally designed to process a sentence from left-to-right. However, the BBN parser has been modified to work in either direction or middle-out for the speech understanding application (Woods *et al.*, 1976, Vol. 4; Bates, 1975). Since the grammar is fairly general and complex, computational efficiencies are achieved by precomputing the answers to certain frequently asked questions concerning what can appear to the left and right of word hypotheses belonging to selected syntactic categories.

D. Control strategies

A speech understanding system can be divided into a set of quasi-independent components (this is especially true of the Hearsay-II system), each of which provides some information toward the ultimate decoding of the utterance. The problem of combining information from the segment lattice, the lexical decoding network, and the verifier is handled in the BBN system by a philosophy of transforming all scores into log likelihood ratios that can be added to form an overall score for a sentence fragment hypothesis. The idea is that scores can be more easily combined if each is based on the probability of being correct, as estimated from prior performance analysis for each component.

A number of control strategies were investigated at BBN as means to find the correct sentence without considering too many alternatives. Quick convergence is needed because, as currently implemented, the system is very slow. One strategy estimated the best possible matching score as a function of position within an utterance (using the lexical matcher to compare all lexical items with all possible segment starting positions). Partial sentence theories were then scored with respect to how far they fell short of reaching this maximum possible score. If a best-first search both to the left and right of a partial sentence theory were always pursued, BBN showed that the first sentence found had to be the best possible interpretation of the utterance. This optimal search theorem assumed that the initial scan gave an accurate estimate of the best possible score at any position in the utterance (not necessarily a good assumption since word boundary phonology was ignored in the initial scan).

Experience showed this strategy to be computationally costly whenever the segment lattice contained a phonetic error of a type not seen before in the probability-gathering stage. The system did not have time to recover from the resulting poor matching score for a correct word, so BBN modified the control strategy to work mostly from left to right, but to retain the theoretical advantage of initially jumping over the first few (less distinctly articulated) segments to find a seed word. The system then worked backward to find the word(s) to the left, and then worked strictly left-to-right. Strictly left-to-right sentence analysis is to be preferred in most speech understanding applications (and humans probably also process essentially left-to-right) because there are fewer local syntactic constraints that can be applied to a sentence fragment in the middle of an utterance.

The BBN system runs in about 1000 times real time on a PDP-KA10, which has a speed of about 0.4 MIPS (million instructions per second). This was a serious problem for system development and knowledge source debugging because it took a long time to accumulate performance data. BBN argued that a good deal can be learned about control issues by careful observation of system traces for only a few sentences. They claimed that it would be possible to implement the speech understanding system in real time on a large 100-MIPS machine by converting some of the code from INTERLISP to assembly language.

E. Response generation

The BBN system included a set of semantic procedures for accessing a data base to compute the response to an input utterance. An appropriate syntactic frame was selected to verbalize the response, and phonemic representations for the words of the response were sent to a speech synthesis by rule program (Klatt, 1976 a). The fully automatic generation of a spoken response to a correctly recognized sentence was demonstrated in February 1976.

APPENDIX C. DETAILED DESCRIPTION OF THE CMU HEARSAY-II SYSTEM

A. Acoustic analysis

The speech waveform is low-pass filtered to 5 kHz, digitized at 10 000 samples/sec, and filtered using a first difference to remove dc and tilt the spectrum up somewhat. The resulting waveform and a second waveform obtained from it using a low-pass smoothing filter are then divided into 10-ms chunks and characterized by a peak-to-peak amplitude and a zero-crossing measure. The two amplitude and zero-crossing functions are used to segment the utterance into intervals of relatively little acoustic change. Then each interval is assigned to one of several broad manner-of-articulation classes using a decision tree of logical threshold tests on the four parametric functions. The performance of the segmenter was compared with that of a hand segmentation. It was found that the segmenter missed 2% of the segments, hypothesized 20% extra segments, and gave a correct manner classification 90% of the time (Goldberg and Reddy, 1976).

A label was assigned to each quasi-phonetic segment (or several labels if they received about the same score) based on the distance between the linear prediction spectrum of the middle 10-ms frame of the segment and a set of 98 templates. The performance of the labeler was also evaluated. It was found that the correct label was the first choice 42% of the time and it was one of the five top choices 75% of the time, using 98 templates to represent 98 phonetic segment types and the minimum prediction residual distance measure to rank-order phonetic choices.

B. Word hypothesization

A word hypothesizer component takes as input the segment label string and tries to find word matches anywhere within the string, using the lexicon of stored representations for words. The hypothesizer is organized around the syllable structure of a word. All lexical items having the same syllable structure as a portion of the input (e.g., fricative—vowel followed by plosive—vowel) are proposed by the lexical hypothesizer. The technique is based on the assumption that manner-of-articulation decisions are more reliable than place-of-articulation decisions.

Performance evaluation of the word hypothesis component indicates that for a typical sentence, 50 words out of the 1000-word lexicon are hypothesized per word position, and the correct word is among the 50 about 70% of the time. Words can also be hypothesized top-down, using a syntactic predictor, so correct words missed by the word hypothesizer need not cause a fatal error in overall system performance.

C. Word verification

A word verification component is used to reduce the number of lexical hypotheses to be considered by the higher-level modules, and to rank order the merits of each accepted hypothesis. This component has the same structure as the Harpy system described below, i.e., a network consisting of sequences of expected spectral template alternatives for each word. Performance evaluation of the word verification component (Table IV) shows that, depending on the threshold employed, up to half the hypothesized words can be rejected while falsely rejecting only 6% of the correct words. The ratings of the verification component are such as to place the correct word in about fourth position, on the average, of the 50 or so words hypothesized to start at that position. This type of verification structure has great potential, but the Hearsay-II implementation does not presently account for very many phonetic and phonological interactions at word boundaries.

The observed scoring behavior of the verification component is not good enough to be used as an absolute ranking criterion when deciding, for example, whether to pursue one of two non-overlapping sentence fragments. Instead, scores at each position in a sentence are normalized with respect to the best matching word observed so far at that position (a strategy similar to that employed at BBN).

A second type of verification procedure is used to see if two words proposed to be adjacent are acoustically compatible with the segment label string. A special set of rules is employed to consider only the critical time interval, taking into account phonological processes occurring across word boundaries. During one run of sentence understanding, 7100 two-word hypotheses were processed by this component. One hundred and ninety five (i.e., 95% of the correct word pairs) were correctly accepted and 59% of the many decoy word pairs were correctly rejected.

D. Syntax, semantics, and control strategies

The syntax and semantics module uses the Cocke algorithm (Aho and Ullman, 1972) to list all possible words to the left or right of a high-scoring seed word. Verification scores are obtained for some or all of these word hypotheses, and the best-scoring word hypothesis is combined with the seed word to form a partial phrase. Many partial phrase theories are considered in parallel, and the parser is capable of saying whether adjacent partial phrases can be combined syntactically. All semantic knowledge contained in the system is presently embedded in the syntactic rules.

The control strategy is to expand larger sentence fragments first (depth first) because such fragments are not expected to occur randomly. However, since the correct word rarely has the best verification score, it is necessary to pursue many paths before a complete sentence is obtained. The first sentence found is not necessarily the best scoring possible sentence, so the recognition process continues until all remaining sentence fragments have a lower score.

The Hearsay-II system design with its blackboard concept permits a good deal of potential parallelism. For example, the components of the system might be implemented on a set of smaller computers connected in parallel (Bell *et al.*, 1973). Also, since each knowledge source is independent, taking its input from the blackboard and placing its output on the blackboard, knowledge sources can be changed fairly easily. The demonstrated advantage of this system design approach is that six months before the end of the project, the performance of Hearsay-II was such that an intensive effort was made to redesign nearly every component in the system, and even eliminate some of the components that provided little help. This resulted in a significant improvement in performance.

The Hearsay-II system ran in about 250 times real time on a PDP-KA10 (0.4 MIPS) computer. The final performance of Hearsay-II (Table II) is encouraging, although the evaluation was restricted to a small number of sentences from a single talker. Of interest is the fact that only 77% of the sentences were correctly *recognized* (all words correct) while 91% were *understood* correctly. It appears that the CMU grammar contains some desirable characteristics for the realization of computer understanding.

APPENDIX D. DETAILED DESCRIPTION OF THE CMU HARPY SYSTEM

A. Acoustic analysis

The preliminary acoustic analysis performed in Harpy is of interest because it obviates the need for sophisticated acoustic-phonetic decoding rules. A speech waveform is low-pass filtered at 5 kHz, digitized at 10 000 samples per second, and 14 linear prediction coefficients are computed every 10 msec. 10-ms frames are then grouped together into "acoustic segments" if sufficiently similar. Working from left to right, the control component takes the parametric representation for a frame and compares it with the first frame and the middle frame of the current segment. A new segment is proposed if either distance exceeds a threshold.

The linear prediction coefficients used to represent the combined segment are obtained from the sum of the autocorrelation coefficients of all the frames in the segment. On the average, segments consist of about three 10-ms frames, and there are thus two to three acoustic segments for every phonetic segment in a word. The process of grouping together 10-ms frames reduces the number of matches with the network, decreases the recognition time, and is intended to smooth out potential noise in the label sequences that are obtained from the linear prediction spectra. Each segment is characterized by a 14-pole spectrum, and the distances between this spectrum and a set of 98 spectral templates are computed using a minimum residual error measure (Itakura, 1975).

The system is sensitive to missing segments (being constrained not to skip a state in the network), but redundant sequences of labels are easily handled by including an implicit output path that returns to the same state for each state in the network. Therefore the segmenter is biased to produce extra segments rather than to miss an expected segment. The advantage of this simple strategy is that time normalization of the input stream is not required in the template matching process. Little phonetic constraint seems to be lost by allowing each state to grab as many acoustic segments as it can (subject to certain minimum and maximum times for remaining in particular states).

B. Template selection

The spectral template inventory was developed by starting with a single template for each phoneme (two for plosives, affricates, and diphthongs) and expanding the number of templates for cases where this simple approximation lead to recognition errors. Experimenter judgment was required to decide when to change a lexical representation using other available templates, when to add a word boundary rule, and when it was absolutely necessary to add to the template inventory. After processing over 700 sentences from a single talker, the number of templates reached 98, of which almost all of the additions helped describe voiced portions of consonant-vowel transitions.

C. Network generation

The Harpy grammar consists of a set of BNF statements that generate a finite list of acceptable sentences, where most sentences contain a word from a large class of "authors" and/or a large class of "topics." The lexical representation for each word consists of a state transition network of expected alternative sequences of spectral states, with duration limits given in parentheses for some of the states. A modest number of word-boundary rewrite rules are specified, but the coarticulatory phenomena covered are surprisingly few in number, and the restricted notation could not handle, for example, the {S T #S} phonological deletion example given earlier (unless the [s t] spectral sequence were replaced by a special dummy symbol). All this information is transformed into a 15 000 state network by a set of procedures that collapse common representations where possible, while assuring an ability to backtrack through the network once a terminal node is reached in order to determine what word sequence was spoken.

D. System tuning and talker normalization

The templates used in the segment labeler are tuned to each new talker, but the lexical representations stay the same for all talkers of a common dialect (it is acknowledged that a few phonetic alternatives may have to be added to improve performance for some individuals). Templates for a new talker are obtained by attempting to recognize a set of about 20 training sentences using someone else's template patterns. The system automatically generates a new set of template patterns from the label sequences used in a forced correct path through the network. For a 1000 word lexicon, it takes about a half hour to record and process the training sentences. This is perhaps more than intended by the ARPA steering committee specifications, but there is no doubt that the procedure contributes significantly to the very good performance of the system. Recent changes permit the system to adapt to a new talker dynamically by starting with a talker-independent set of templates and modifying their properties based on correctly understood input utterances (Lowerre, 1977) in a manner similar to that used in Hearsay I (Reddy, Erman, and Neely, 1973).

The Harpy system uses about 30 MIPSS (millions of instructions executed per second of speech). This is less than the computing time in the other systems, but it is far from real-time operation on the computer used (0.4 MIPS PDP-KA10). However, it is well within the target specifications of real-time response on a 100-MIPS future machine. Harpy also requires a large program space to store and manipulate its 15 000 state network representation of speech knowledge. The present program barely fits into 200K of 36-bit words, and it would probably not fit if the average branching factor of the grammar were increased.

[1]Members of the ARPA steering committee were F. S. Cooper, J. W. Forgie, C. C. Green, D. H. Klatt, J. C. R. Licklider (Ex-chairman), M. F. Medress (Acting Chairman), E. P. Newburg, A. Newell (ex-chairman), M. H. O'Malley, D. R. Reddy, B. Ritea, J. E. Shoup, D. E. Walker, and W. A. Woods.

[2]The original 5 system builders were a group at Bolt Beranek and Newman Inc. (BBN) headed by W. A. Woods, a group at Carnegie—Mellon University (CMU) headed by D. R. Reddy, a group at Lincoln Laboratories (LL) headed by J. Forgie, a group at Stanford Research Institute (SRI) headed by D. Walker, and a group at System Development Corporation (SDC) headed by B. Ritea. After two years, funding was concentrated on three main system builders. Smaller supporting research efforts were funded at Haskins Laboratories (F. S. Cooper), at Speech Communications Research Laboratory (J. E. Shoup), at Univac (M. F. Medress), and at Univ. California at Berkeley (M. H. O'Malley).

[3]In addition to serving on the ARPA advisory steering committee, the author also worked as a consultant during the development of the BBN system.

[4]No claim is made for the strict originality of these techniques. Even in the context of speech understanding systems, some of the ideas were preceded by or developed in parallel with research taking place elsewhere. For example, a major speech recognition effort was initiated at IBM about the same time as the ARPA project began (Bahl *et al.*, 1976; Jelenek, 1976). See Reddy (1976) for an excellent comparative review of progress in the field up to early 1976.

Aho, A. V., and Ullman, J. D. **(1972)**. *Theory of Parsing, Translation and Compiling* (Prentice-Hall, Englewood Cliffs, NJ).

Bahl, L., Baker, J., Cohen, P., Dixon, N., Jelenek, F., Mercer, R., and Silverman, H. **(1976)**. "Preliminary results on the Performance of a System for the Automatic Recognition of Continuous Speech," pp. 425–429 in Teacher (1976).

Baker, J. **(1975)**. "The Dragon System—An Overview," IEEE Trans. Acoust. Speech Signal Process. ASSP-23, 24–29.

Barnett, J. A. **(1974)**. "A Phonological Rule Compiler," pp. 188–192 in Erman (1974).

Bates, M. **(1975)**. "The Use of Syntax in a Speech Understanding System," IEEE Trans. Acoust. Speech Signal Process. **ASSP-23**, 112–117.

Bell, C., Chen, R., Fuller, S., Grason, J., Rege, S., and Siewiorek, D. **(1973)**. "The Architecture and Application of Computer Modules: A Set of Components for Digital Systems Design," Compcon 73, San Francisco, CA, pp. 177–180.

Bernstein, M. I. **(1976)**. "Interactive Systems Research: Final Report to the Director, Advanced Research Projects Agency," System Development Corporation, Santa Monica, CA, Report No. TM-5243/006/00.

Chomsky, N., and Halle, M. **(1968)**. *The Sound Pattern of English* (Harper and Row, New York).

Cohen, P. S., and Mercer, R. L. **(1975)**. "The Phonological Component of an Automatic Speech Recognition System," pp. 275–320 in Reddy (1975).

Cole, R. A., and Scott, B. **(1974)**. "Toward a Theory of Speech Perception," Psychol. Rev. **81**, 348–374.

Connolly, D. **(1975)**. "Minutes of the Speech Understanding Workshop," 81–82, Science Applications Inc., Arlington, VA.

Cook, C. C., and Schwartz, R. M. **(1977)**. "Advanced Acoustic Techniques in Automatic Speech Understanding," pp. 663–666 in Silverman (1977).

De Mori, R., Rivoira, S., and Serra, A. (1975). "A Speech Understanding System with Learning Capability," in *Proceedings of the 4th International Joint Conference on Artificial Intelligence* (Tbilisi, USSR).

Dixon, N. R., and Maxey, H. D. (1968). "Terminal Analog Speech Synthesis of Continuous Speech Using the Diphone Method of Segment Assembly," IEEE Trans. Aud. Electroacoust. **AU-16**, 40–50.

Erman, L. D., Ed. (1974). *Contributed Papers of the IEEE Symposium on Speech Recognition* (IEEE Catalog No. 74CH0878-9 AE).

Fant, G. (1970). "Automatic Recognition and Speech Research," Q. Prog. and Status Rep. **QPSR-1**, Speech Transmission Laboratories, KTH, Stockholm, Sweden, 16–31.

Fant, G., Ed. (1975). *Proceedings of the Stockholm Speech Communications Seminar* (Almqvist and Wiksell, Stockholm, and Wiley, New York).

Forgie, J. W., *et al.* (1974). *Speech Understanding Systems—Semiannual Technical Summary Report* (MIT Lincoln Laboratories, Lexington, MA).

Garrett, M. F. (1977). "Word and Sentence Processing," in *Handbook of Sensory Physiology, Volume* 8: *Perception*, edited by R. Held and X. Leibowitz (Springer-Verlag, Heidelberg).

Gillmann, R. A. (1975). "A Fast Frequency-Domain Pitch Algorithm," J. Acoust. Soc. Am. **58**, S63(A).

Goldberg, H. G., and Reddy, R. (1976). "Feature Extraction, Segmentation and Labeling in the Harpy and Hearsay-II Systems," J. Acoust. Soc. Am. **60**, S11(A).

Halle, M., and Stevens, K. N. (1962). "Speech Recognition: A Model and a Program for Research," IRE Trans. Inf. Theory **IT-8**, 155–159.

Haton, J.-P., and Pierrel, J.-M. (1976). "Organization and Operation of a Connected Speech Understanding System at Lexical, Syntactic and Semantic Levels," pp. 430–433 in Teacher (1976).

Hayes-Roth, F., and Lesser, V. R. (1976). "Focus of Attention in a Distributed-Logic Speech Understanding System," pp. 416–420 in Teacher (1976).

Herscher, M. B., and Cox, R. B. (1976). "Source Entry Using Voice Input," pp. 190–193 in Teacher (1976).

Hyde, S. R. (1972). "Automatic Speech Recognition: A Critical Survey and Discussion of the Literature," in *Human Communication: A Unified View*, edited by E. E. David and P. B. Denes (McGraw–Hill, New York).

Itakura, F. (1975). "Minimum Prediction Residual Principle Applied to Speech Recognition," IEEE Trans. Acoust. Speech Signal Process. **ASSP-23**, 67–72.

Jelenek, F. (1976). "Continuous Speech Recognition by Statistical Methods," Proc. IEEE **64**, 532–556.

Kameny, I. (1975). "Comparison of Formant Spaces of Retroflexed and Nonretroflexed Vowels," IEEE Trans. Acoust. Speech Signal Process. **ASSP-23**, 38–49.

Kameny, I. (1976). "Automatic Acoustic-Phonetic Analysis of Vowels and Sonorants," pp. 166–169 in Teacher (1976).

Klatt, D. H. (1975). "Word Verification in a Speech Understanding System," pp. 321–341 in Reddy (1975).

Klatt, D. H. (1976a). "Structure of a Phonological Rule Component for a Synthesis-by-Rule Program," IEEE Trans. Acoust. Speech Signal Process. **ASSP-24**, 391–398.

Klatt, D. H. (1976b). "A Digital Filter Bank for Spectral Matching," pp. 537–540 in Teacher (1976).

Klatt, D. H. (1978). "Speech Perception: A Spectral-Sequence Decoding Network as a Model of Lexical Access" (in preparation).

Klatt, D. H., and Stevens, K. N. (1973). "On the Automatic Recognition of Continuous Speech: Implications of a Spectrogram-Reading Experiment," IEEE Trans. Audio Electroacoust **AU-21**, 210–217.

Klovstad, J. W. (1977). "Computer-Automated Speech Perception System," Ph.D. thesis (MIT).

Klovstad, J. W., and Mondshein, L. F. (1975). "The CASPERS Linguistic Analysis System," IEEE Trans. Acoust. Speech Signal Process. **ASSP-23**, 18–123.

Lea, W. A. (1968). "Establishing the Value of Voice Communication with Computers," IEEE Trans. Audio Electroacoust. **AU-16**, 184–197.

Lea, W. A., Medress, M. F., and Skinner, T. E. (1975). "A Prosodically Guided Speech Understanding System," IEEE Trans. Acoust. Speech Signal Process. **ASSP-23**, 30–38.

Lesser, V. R., Fennell, R. D., Erman, L. D., and Reddy, D. R. (1975). "Organization of the Hearsay-II Speech Understanding System," IEEE Trans. Acoust. Speech Signal Process. **ASSP-23**, 11–23.

Lesser, V. R., and Erman, L. D. (1977). "A Retrospective View of the Hearsay-II Architecture," IJCAI-77 (in press).

Liberman, A. M., Cooper, F. S., Harris, K. S., and MacNeilage, P. F. (1962). "A Motor Theory of Speech Perception," *Proceedings of the Speech Communication Seminar*, (Royal Institute of Technology, Stockholm), Paper D3.

Liberman, A. M., Cooper, F. S., Shankweiler, D. S., and Studdert-Kennedy, M. (1967). "Perception of the Speech Code," Psychol. Rev. **74**, 431–461.

Lindgren, N. (1965). "Machine Recognition of Human Language," IEEE Spectrum **2**, March, April, May.

Lowerre, B. T. (1976). "The Harpy Speech Recognition System," Ph.D. thesis (Department of Computer Science, Carnegie–Mellon University, Pittsburgh, PA.)

Lowerre, B. T. (1977). "Dynamic Speaker Adaptation in the Harpy Speech Recognition System," pp. 788–790 in Silverman (1977).

Martin, T. B. (1975). "Applications of Limited Vocabulary Recognition Systems," pp. 55–71 in Reddy (1975).

Martin, T. B. (1976). "Practical Applications of Voice Input to Machines," Proc. IEEE **64**, 487–500.

Makhoul, J. (1975). "Linear Prediction: A Tutorial Review," Proc. IEEE **63**, 561–480.

Medress, M. F., Cooper, F. S., Forgie, J. W., Green, C. C., Klatt, D. H., O'Malley, M. H., Newburg, E. P., Newell, A., Reddy, D. R., Ritia, B., Shoup-Hummel, J. E., Walker, D. E., and Woods, W. A. (1977). "Speech Understanding Systems: Report of a Steering Committee," Sigart Newsletter **62**, 4–7 (April 1977); IEEE Trans. Prof. Commun. (1977) (in press).

Medress, M. F., Skinner, T. E., Kloker, D. R., Diller, T. C., and Lea, W. A. (1977). "A System for Recognition of Spoken Connected Word Sequences," pp. 468–473 in Silverman (1977).

Mermelstein, P. (1975a). "A Phonetic-Context Controlled Strategy for Segmentation and Phonetic Labeling of Speech," IEEE Trans. Acoust. Speech Signal Process. **ASSP-23**, 79–82.

Mermelstein, P. (1975b). "Automatic Segmentation of Speech into Syllable Units," J. Acoust. Soc. Am. **58**, 880–883.

Molho, L. M. (1976). "Automatic Acoustic-Phonetic Analysis of Fricatives and Plosives," pp. 182–185 in Teacher (1976).

Newell, A., Barnett, J., Forgie, J. W., Green, C. C., Klatt, D. H., Licklider, J. C. R., Munson, J., Reddy, D. R., and Woods, W. A. (1973). *Speech Understanding Systems: Final Report of a Study Group* (North-Holland/American Elsevier, Amsterdam).

Newell, A., Cooper, F. S., Forgie, J. W., Green, C. C., Klatt, D. H., Medress, M. F., Newburg, E. P., O'Malley, M. H., Reddy, D. R., Ritea, B., Shoup-Hummel, J. E., Walker, D. E., and Woods, W. A. (1975). *Considerations for a Follow-on ARPA Research Program for Speech Understanding Systems* (August 1975). Available from Computer Science Department, Carnegie–Mellon University, Pittsburgh, PA 15213.

O'Malley, M. H. (1975). "The Children of Lunar: An Exercise in Comparative Grammar" (unpublished).

Ochsman, R. B., and Chapanis, A. (1974). "The Effects of

10 Communication Modes in the Behavior of Teams during Cooperative Problem Solving," Int. J. Man–Machine Stud. **6**, 579–619.

Oshika, B., Zue, V. W., Weeks, R. V., Nue, H., and Aurbach. J. **(1975)**. "The Role of Phonological Rules in Speech Understanding Research," IEEE Trans. Acoust. Speech Signal Process. **ASSP-23**, 104–112.

Paxton, W. H. **(1977)**. *A Framework for Speech Understanding*, Ph.D. dissertation (Stanford University).

Paxton, W. H. **(1976)**. "Experiments in Speech Understanding System Control," Artificial Intelligence Center Technical Note 134, Stanford Research Institute Project 4762, Menlo Park, CA.

Peterson, G., Wang, W., and Silvertsen, E. **(1958)**. "Segmentation Techniques in Speech Synthesis," J. Acoust. Soc. Am. **30**, 739–742.

Pierce, J. R. **(1969)**. "Whither Speech Recognition," J. Acoust. Soc. Am. **46**, 1049–1051.

Pisoni, D. **(1977)**. "Speech Perception," *Handbook of Learning and Cognitive Processes, Vol.* 5, edited by W. K. Estes (Erlbaum, New Jersey).

Rabiner, L. R., and Sambur, M. R. **(1975)**. "An Algorithm for Determining the Endpoints of Isolated Utterances," Bell Syst. Tech. J. **54**, 297–315.

Reddy, D. R. **(1975)**. *Speech Recognition: Invited Papers Presented at the* 1974 *IEEE Symposium* (Academic, New York).

Reddy, D. R. **(1976)**. "Speech Recognition by Machine: A Review," Proc. IEEE **64**, 501–531.

Reddy, D. R., Erman, L. D., and Neely, R. B. **(1973)**. "A Model and a System for Machine Recognition of Speech," IEEE Trans. **AU-21**, 229–238.

Reddy, D. R., *et al.* **(1977)**. *Speech Understanding Systems Final Report* (Computer Science Department, Carnegie–Mellon University).

Ritea, B. **(1975)**. "Automatic Speech Understanding Systems," *Proceedings of the* 11*th IEEE Computer Society Conference*, Washington, DC, pp. 319–322.

Sakai, T., and Nakagawa, S. **(1975)**. "Continuous Speech Understanding System LITHAN," Technical Report, Department of Information Science, Kyoto University, Kyoto, Japan.

Schwartz, R. M., and Cook, C. C. **(1977)**. "Advanced Acoustic Techniques in Automatic Speech Understanding," (IEEE Catalog No. 663.666).

Shockey, L., and Reddy, D. R. **(1975)**. "Quantitative Analysis of Speech Perception," in Fant (1975).

Silverman, H. F. (Chairman) **(1977)**. "Conference Record of the 1977 IEEE International Conference on Acoustics, Speech and Signal Processing," Hartford, 9–11 May (IEEE Catalog No. 77CH1197-3 ASSP).

Silverman, H. F., and Dixon, N. R. **(1976)**. "The 1976 Modular Acoustic Processor (MAP): Diadic Segment Classification and Final Phoneme String Estimation," pp. 15–20 in Teacher (1976).

Smith, A. R. **(1976)**. "Word Hypothesization in the Hearsay-II Speech Understanding System," pp. 549–552 in Teacher (1976).

Stevens, K. N. **(1972a)**. "The Quantal Nature of Speech: Evidence from Articulatory-Acoustic Data," in *Human Communication: A Unified View*, edited by E. E. David and P. B. Denes.

Stevens, K. N. **(1972b)**. "Segments, Features, and Analysis by Synthesis," in *Language by Eye and by Ear*, edited by J. F. Kavenaugh and I. G. Mattingly (MIT, Cambridge, MA), pp. 47–52.

Studdert-Kennedy, M. (1975). "Speech Perception," in *Contempory Issues in Experimental Phonetics*, edited by N. J. Lass.

Tappert, C. C. **(1975)**. "Experiments with a Tree-Search Method for Converting Noisy Phonetic Representation into Standard Orthography," IEEE Trans. Acoust. Speech Signal Process. **ASSP-23**, 129–135.

Tappert, C. C., Dixon, N. R., and Rabinowitz, A. S. **(1973)**. "Application of Sequential Decoding for Converting Phonetic to Graphic Representation in Automatic Speech Recognition of Continuous Speech (ARCS)," IEEE Trans. Audio Electroacoust. **AU-21**, 225–228.

Teacher, C. (Chairman) **(1976)**. *Conference Record of the* 1976 *IEEE International Conference on Acoustics Speech and Signal Processing*, Philadelphia, PA, 12–14 April (IEEE Catalog No. 76CH1067-8 ASSP).

Walker, D. E. **(1975)**. "The SRI Speech Understanding System," IEEE Transl. Acoust. Speech Signal Process. **ASSP-23**, 397–416.

Walker, D. E. (Ed.) **(1976)**. "Speech Understanding Research: Final Technical Report," Stanford Research Institute, Menlo, Park, CA.

Wanner, E., and Maratsos, M. **(1977)**. "An ATN Approach to Comprehension," in *Linguistic Theory and Psychological Reality*, edited by J. Bresnan and M. Halle (MIT, Cambridge, MA).

Watt, W. C. **(1968)**. "Habitability," Am. Doc. **19**, 338–351.

Weeks, R. V. **(1974)**. "Predictive Syllable Mapping in a Continuous Speech Understanding System," pp. 154–158 in Erman (1974).

Weinstein, C. J., McCandless, S. S., Mondshein, L. F., and Zue, V. W. **(1975)**. "A System for Acoustic-Phonetic Analysis of Continuous Speech," IEEE Trans. Acoust. Speech Signal Process. **ASSP-23**, 54–67.

Weisen, R. A., and Forgie, J. W. **(1974)**. "An Evaluation of the Lincoln Laboratory Speech Recognition System," J. Acoust. Soc. Am. **56**, S27(A).

Wolf, J. J. **(1976)**. "Speech Recognition and Understanding," in *Digital Pattern Recognition*, edited by K. S. Fu (Springer-Verlag, Berlin).

Woods, W. A. **(1970)**. "Transition Network Grammars for Natural Language Analysis," Commun. Assoc. Comput. Mach. **13**, 591–602.

Woods, W. A., and Zue, V. **(1976)**. "Dictionary Expansion via Phonological Rules for a Speech Understanding System," 561–564 in Teacher (1976).

Woods, W., Bates, M., Brown, G., Bruce, B., Cook, C., Klovstad, J., Makhoul, J., Nash-Webber, B., Schwartz, R., Wolf, J., and Zue, V. **(1976)**. "Speech Understanding Systems: Final Technical Progress Report," Bolt Beranek and Newman, Inc. Report No. 3438, Cambridge, MA (in 5 volumes).

Part III
Discrete Utterance Recognition

Real-Time Recognition of Spoken Words

LOUIS C. W. POLS, MEMBER, IEEE

Abstract—First a survey is given of a number of published vowel and word recognition systems. Then a new real-time word recognition system is described that uses only a small computer (8K memory) and a few analog peripherals. The essentials of the procedure are as follows. During the pronunciation of a word, a spectral analysis is carried out by a bank of 17 ⅓-octave bandpass filters. The outputs of the filters are logarithmically amplified and the maximal amplitude of the envelope is determined and sampled every 15 ms. In this way a word is characterized by a sequence of sample points in a 17-dimensional space. Then a principal components analysis is performed, reducing the original 17 dimensions of the space to 3. After a linear time normalization, the 3-dimensional trace of the spoken word is compared with 20 reference traces, representing the 20 possible utterances (the digits, plus 10 computer commands). The machine responds by naming the best fitting trace. With the 20 speakers of the design set, the machine is correct 98.8 percent of the time.

Index Terms—Automatic speech recognition, pattern recognition, principal components analysis, real-time word recognition, spectral analysis, vowels.

Introduction

It is a generally accepted procedure to describe the properties of speech sounds in terms of their spectra as a function of time. A speech sound has a more or less constant frequency spectrum, and a sound transition can be described as a transition from one spectrum to another. This is displayed nicely in the spectrograms of words and sentences. Some 20 years ago investigators [42], [22] tried to develop rules for visual inspection of these spectrograms ("visible speech") in order to solve the problem of speech recognition. These first attempts at speech recognition in fact simply shifted the problem to another mode, since human interpretation (of the spectrograms) was still necessary. A discussion of the problems related with a human interpretation of spectrograms is given by Liberman *et al.* [33].

Probably the first attempt at automatic speech recognition was made by Kersta [28], who simplified the spectrograms to black and white mosaics, with the frequency scale divided in 200-Hz steps and the time scale in 67-ms steps. Master patterns were determined for each utterance and the incoming data were compared with those master patterns. The experiment was done by digital simulation using cards in which the patterns were punched; this was probably the first use of digital equipment in speech-processing research [10]. Real-time recognition is not possible with this approach, however, since the spectrographic data are not momentarily available. Two features of the early approaches, on-line data gathering and data reduction, have since received much attention. These will be described in more detail in the following section.

Manuscript received November 30, 1970; revised March 26, 1971. A preliminary version of this paper was presented at the IEEE Symposium on Feature Extraction and Selection in Pattern Recognition, Argonne, Ill., October 5–7, 1970.

The author is with the Institute for Perception RVO-TNO, Soesterberg, The Netherlands.

Survey of Vowel and Word Recognition Systems

A good survey of the literature up to 1965 is given by Lindgren [34]; see also a recent report by Hyde [27]. Considering the spectrograms, it is quite natural that the most important features of speech were thought to be the frequencies at which energy is greatest (formant frequencies). The positions of the formant frequencies were clearly visible as black bands in the spectrogram.

The classic work of Peterson and Barney [40] gives the formant frequencies and levels of 10 cardinal vowels spoken by 76 speakers (male, female, and children). Plotting the frequency of the second formant (F_2) against the frequency of the first formant (F_1) gives a representation of the vowels as points in a plane. This formant plane can be divided into areas that are specific for a certain vowel. The areas overlap, however, so a description of a vowel with only two parameters being F_1 and F_2 is perhaps not sufficient. Despite that, the data of Peterson and Barney are used repeatedly to improve the correct identification score [21], [53], [23], [4], using axis transformations and speaker-dependent corrections. Peterson and Barney extracted the positions of the formant frequencies by visual inspection of the spectrograms. For on-line speech recognition based upon formant frequencies, one needs, however, an automatic formant detector.

In 1959 Forgie and Forgie [20] developed a computer program to recognize vowels from their formant frequencies. The F_1–F_2 plane was divided into 11 rectangular regions. The position of a vowel sound in one of these 11 regions was determined by the maximal energy in 7 frequency bands. Each of these bands was composed out of 2 or 3 filter channels of a 35 bandpass filters system. A finer determination of the formant locations was made possible by using spectral derivative information. In certain cases F_0 and F_3 were determined as well. For 21 speakers the overall score was 88 percent. With the added use of vowel duration information, the score was raised to 93 percent.

Since then procedures for automatic formant detection have been improved [19] and the following new techniques have been invented: pitch synchronous analysis [35], analysis-by-synthesis [3], low-order spectral moments [48], fast Fourier transform [9], cepstrum [39], and chirp z transform [45]. Most of these new procedures are very useful for gathering data to use in the synthesis of speech, but are still not fast enough to detect the formant frequencies in real time. (Perhaps we must make an exception for a new technique proposed by Atal during the Symposium. Here

Reprinted from *IEEE Trans. Comput.*, vol. C-20, pp. 972–978, Sept. 1971.

speech signals are characterized by linear prediction of the speech wave. The predictor parameters then can be used to determine formant frequencies and bandwidths.) The automatic formant analysis procedure described recently by Schafer and Rabiner [45] still needs 120 times real time. In addition, we have seen that the formant frequencies are not entirely sufficient for vowel recognition. The problems in recognizing nasals, liquids, stops, and fricatives are probably even larger.

Another possibility is not to use the information about the formant frequencies directly, but rather to use it only to determine distinctive features [26]. But if the entire spectrum is available, then distinctive features need not be defined in terms of the formants only. For example, Bobrow, Hartley, and Klatt [5] defined their linguistic and nonlinguistic features directly, based upon the outputs of 19 bandpass filters. This was one of the most successful limited speech recognition systems. It could recognize about 100 words from different speakers. In order to make automatic recognition of continuous speech possible, Tappert *et al.* [49] even define 200 binary features in the frequency and in the time domain per subword segment. Each subword segment, a so-called "transeme," includes a transition from one steady state to the other.

Another approach is not to try to correlate the spectral information with any feature, but to hypothesize that if the complete spectral information is sufficient to discriminate different sounds, a straightforward algorithm must exist to separate these sounds. Fant [17] calls this the "engineering approach." Dudley and Balashek [15] built an analog digit recognizer based on this principle in 1958. The energy in 10 evenly spaced frequency bands was determined 24 times/s and these patterns were compared with 10 master patterns belonging to the phonemes i, I, ε, ɑ, o, u, n, r, f, and s. An incoming word was thus described as a sequence of phonemes (e.g., 9 = nnnnrɑɑɑrrεεnuunr). This sequence was then compared with the built-in reference sequences of all 10 possible words. In some cases different reference patterns for one word were stored in the memory matrices. The machine could recognize "his master's voice" almost perfectly and needed 330–500 ms for the recognition of one spoken digit.

Olson and Belar [38] also worked on the principle of comparing incoming data, syllable by syllable, with reference patterns (10 syllables: are, see, a, I, can, you, read, it, so, sir). The reference patterns were derived from the average of several pronunciations of the same syllable by one speaker. The energy in 8 frequency bands was sampled after 20, 60, 100, 140, and 180 ms and reduced to only 2 levels. For one speaker a 98 percent correct score could be achieved. In 1960 Denes and Mathews [12] simulated a spoken digit recognizer on a digital computer. The outputs of 17 evenly spaced bandpass filters were sampled every 14 ms with 10-bit accuracy and recorded on digital tape as a time-frequency pattern. This pattern was matched, using cross correlation, with the test patterns of each digit. A linear time normalization raised the correct score for 5 speakers from 88 to 94 percent. Gilli and Meo [24] worked with 17 $\frac{1}{3}$-octave bands (2 levels), sampled every 20 ms. The spoken digits were processed on-line by combinational networks that could recognize vowels, some consonants, or some typical transitions. For the 10 voices that were used to determine the reference patterns, the correct score was 100 percent; for the other voices the score was 70 percent.

Important questions for all speech recognition systems are: What filter system should one use (frequency range, number of filters, bandwidth)? In how many levels should one describe the filter output? What should the sampling time be? Successful systems differ markedly in these features. Becker's system [2], for example, used only four two-octave filters, described the energy per filter in only three levels, and looked to specific transitions in the words. For one speaker, an on-line recognition score of 94.7 percent could be achieved for 16 Danish words. Six band filters with increasing bandwidth were chosen by Washizawa *et al.* [51]. The outputs (in decibels) were sampled 20 times at moments proportional to the logarithm of time. The spectra derived in this way were compared with stored standard patterns, using a shortest distance concept. With this system the ten digits were recognized with 97 percent accuracy for both male and female talkers.

On the basis of psychophysical measurements [43], we prefer a particular type of filter system. This is also used by, for instance, a group of German workers [50], [55], [1]. They employ a set of 24 bandpass filters, with each filter one critical band wide. Every 100 ms, samples of the filter outputs are taken and these samples are reduced to zero or one values. Then, quite arbitrarily, the 24 channels are combined to give five. After time normalization (eight time samples per word) each word is described by a 5×8 binary matrix. This matrix is compared with all reference matrices derived from the average of 50 speakers. For the group of speakers, male and female, who were used also to derive the reference matrices, the correct recognition score was 82.5 percent. This reasonably high score for real-time recognition with a large group of speakers is even more promising if one considers that the information rate in the system is only 50 bits/s. Ohlendorf and Coates [37] used a similar system of 22 $\frac{1}{3}$-octave filters. The outputs of the filters were described in 12-bit accuracy and sampled at a 160/s rate. Per digit a system of more or less arbitrary rules was optimized. For example, if for eight succeeding samples, between the first and the fifteenth time sample, the energy in the 2000–3150 Hz region was larger than in the 6300–12500 Hz region, then a certain test label would be assigned the value one. For a given utterance to be recognized as a digit, certain conditions related to the test labels must be fulfilled. It may be possible that for more than one word all conditions are fulfilled. This explains that for this off-line system the correct score was 99.5 percent, whereas the incorrect score was 8.2 percent for a group of 14 male and 11 female speakers. Shearme and Leach [47] describe a more typical system consisting of 20 simulated bandpass filters and envelope detectors, sampled 100/s. A spectral profile is coded for each word and matched with a library of stored profiles (more than one per word). Thirty-two words, spoken by ten speakers, were recognized 90 percent correctly. Cannon [7] carried out an initial spectral analysis of 7 vowels using an electronic analog ear, which was a 24-section lumped parameter ladder network. Then 4 out of the 24 available outputs were arbitrarily selected to determine correlation functions. These functions were compared with seven averaged correlation sets. For ten speakers, and a linear adaptive procedure, a 97 percent correct score was achieved. Denes [11] used a set of 18 $\frac{1}{3}$-octave filters, and characterized each phoneme by the peak outputs of two filters. He also defined some additional features such as "duration of high-frequency energy" (this formed the basis of a $|t|$ detection circuit), and some linguistic information. A large set of words formed from nine consonants and four vowels and spoken by one voice, was recognized with a correct score of 72 percent.

If one accepts the usefulness of a set of $\frac{1}{3}$-octave filters because of its correspondence with certain psychophysical results, a disadvantage of all the above described approaches is still the quite arbitrary way of processing the outputs of the filters.

Dimensional Analysis of Speech

In general, any spectral analysis of speech can be described in terms of a multidimensional concept. The energy in each frequency band can be thought of as a coordinate value along a single dimension in a multidimensional space. There are as many dimensions as there are frequency bands. The number of possible values on each dimension is determined by the number of levels one uses to describe the energy in each band. Each speech sample then becomes a point in that multidimensional space [44]. To illustrate this technique we give the following example [30].

Using 18 $\frac{1}{3}$-octave filters the spectra of 12 Dutch vowels (100-ms segments) spoken by a group of 50 male speakers, were determined. This results in a cloud of 600 points in an 18-dimensional space. Being interested in vowel recognition one hopes of course that these 600 points will in fact fall into 12 clusters of 50 points. By simply looking to the data we can try to find the optimal rules for separating those 12 clusters. Since the samples from contiguous frequency bands are not independent, a data reduction is possible. Therefore, the data in different bands need not be combined arbitrarily; a well defined mathematical procedure can be applied. We used the so-called principal components analysis [25]. For this analysis, the variances along each dimension, and the covariances between the dimensions are calculated. Then a single new dimension in the space is determined which explains as much of the variance as is possible. This new dimension is a linear combination of the original 18 dimensions. The direction cosines of this dimension are defined by the first eigenvector of the covariance matrix. Then a second new dimension, orthogonal to the first new one, is determined to explain most of the remaining variance, and so on. For the above mentioned set of 600 Dutch vowels, four dimensions explained 75.4 percent of the total variance. In this 4-dimensional subspace one can determine the 12 average vowel positions and the maximum likelihood regions around these average positions. After combining three pairs of related vowels the nine remaining vowels were recognized, after a simple speaker dependent correction, with 98 percent accuracy for the 50 speakers. Using a modified discriminant analysis [36], the recognition results were not significantly better. Li *et al.* [32] as well as Boehm and Wright [6] used the same approach for a dimensional analysis of speech spectra. Kramer and Mathews [31] describe a similar procedure for transmitting a set of correlated signals. Watanebe [52] describes a comparable information compression procedure and gives as an example the positions of 12 vowels (spoken by 19 persons) in a plane derived from the 36-dimensional spectral data of the vowels. Favella *et al.* [18] analyzed seven Italian vowels, spoken by 35 speakers, with 12 $\frac{1}{3}$-octave filters. A principal components analysis was performed on these 245 points in 12 dimensions. One can extract from their data that three new dimensions, explain together 81 percent of the total variance. Chiba [8] describes a similar approach for digit recognition. The outputs of seven filters are sampled every 45 ms (9-bit resolution) giving maximally eight points per word. Each word is then described as a 56-dimensional vector. Linear discriminant functions are computed to isolate the patterns for each of the ten digits. Sebestyen [46] as well suggests describing the spectral properties of a digit with one multidimensional vector.

Another interesting feature of the above mentioned analysis of the 12 Dutch vowels [30] was the direct relationship between the 2-dimensional subspace (60.9 percent explained variance) and the F_1–F_2 plane. While in general the formant frequencies are very difficult to determine, the equivalent positions in the 2-dimensional subspace are very easy to find, even with a simple analog circuit [44]. If a perceptual confusion experiment is conducted with the same 600 vowel sounds the result is a confusion matrix from which a representation of the 12 vowels in a *perceptual* space can be derived. It appears that this perceptual space shows great correspondence with the physical subspace. This result has been substantiated by Pols, Van der Kamp, and Plomp [41] in a triadic comparison experiment. From this correspondence one might conclude that the subjects used, for their perceptual judgments, information comparable with that present in the physical representation of these signals.

The above mentioned results make it very promising to use this approach also for the development of an *on-line* speech recognition system. If a vowel can be described as a point in a space, then a whole word can be described as a set of points, or a trace in that space. An average trace can be determined for each word, by averaging over a number of speakers. The trace to be recognized must then be compared with the built-in reference traces and a score calculated which gives the probability that input trace represented a specific word. This approach has much in common with the word recognition systems described earlier, since it uses master patterns. The procedure needs no manual interpretations, however. It is straightforward and mathe-

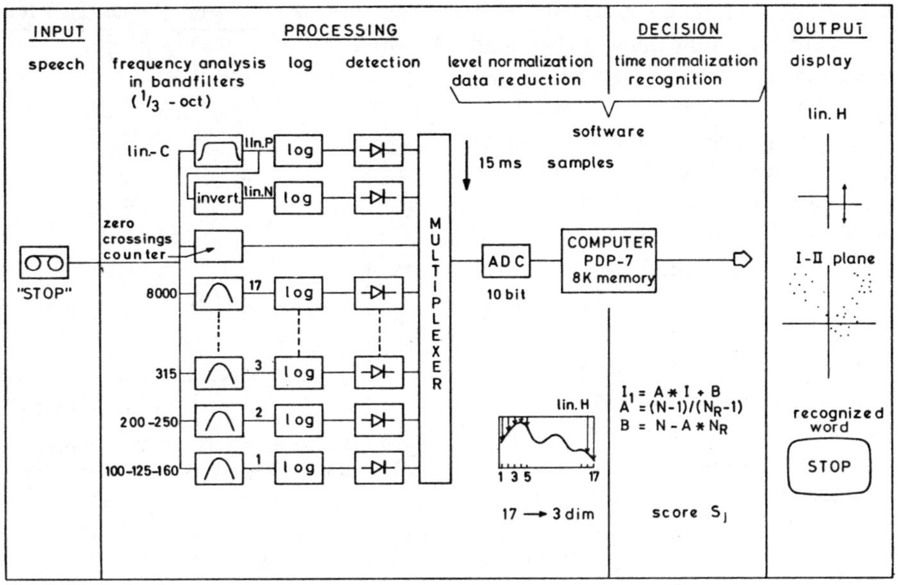

Fig. 1. Block scheme of the recognition system.

matically well defined. This means also that it is easy to transform the system, making it suitable for recognizing other groups of words, eventually in another language. In the following section the procedure will be described in detail.

Recognition of a Reduced Set of Words

Our system, shown schematically in Fig. 1, was developed both for the on-line analysis of running speech and for the recognition of a set of 20 Dutch words. The words were spoken once by a group of 20 male speakers in a silent room and recorded on magnetic tape. The word list consisted of the ten digits plus ten other words[1] which could be computer commands: PUNT (point), STOP, MIN (minus), FOUT (wrong), BEGIN, MAAL (times), DOE (do), MACHT (power), ALS (if), and GELIJK [equal(s)]. We had the idea that even with this reduced set of words already quite a lot of computer operations are possible. The word DO in combination with a number seems particularly powerful. For instance, DO ONE FOUR could mean: the following list of numbers must be interpreted as x_i, y_i values and the linear correlation coefficient must be computed. Each spoken word or number can be displayed on a screen after recognition, in order to have visual feedback and if necessary, to make correction possible.

The optimal subspace for the 20 words is of course different from the one described before for the 12 Dutch vowels. In order to make a principal components analysis possible, the covariance matrix for this speech material must first be derived. The words were analyzed by a set of 20 $\frac{1}{3}$-octave filters with center frequencies (f_c) from 100 to 8000 Hz. The three filters with $f_c = 100$, 125, and 160 Hz were combined, as were the two filters with $f_c = 200$ and 250 Hz, so in fact the system was reduced to a set of 17 filters. The filters in the low-frequency range were combined in order to have a filter system better corresponding to the critical bands in the auditory system. This combination also reduced the variance in the low-frequency filters, since now the fundamental frequency of voiced speech (male speakers) is always within the first filter band and the second harmonic is always within the second filter band. An 18th channel was added to give information about the overall level of the speech sample. This was simply a wide-band filter (*LIN-C*, −3 dB points at 32 and 8000 Hz). The output of this filter was used as a signal-no signal indicator. As long as the output is below a certain trigger value (*LI*) the other 17 filter outputs are not sampled. Once the level is above the *LI* value, and remains there for at least 2 ms, which means that the signal was no disturbing pulse, the frequency analysis starts. From that moment on every 15 ms (as long as the overall level is above the trigger level) the filter output, (after logarithmic amplification and envelope peak detection) are sampled. These 17 dB values are then fed to a computer (*DEC PDP*-7, 8K memory, 1.75-μs cycle time) via a 20-channel multiplexer. Because of the asymmetry of the speech waveform, both the largest positive (*LIN.P*) and negative (*LIN.N*) overall levels are transmitted, as well as the number of positive-going zero crossings in the precedings 15 ms. The 17 filter values are subtracted from the largest (positive or negative) overall level (*LIN.H*), producing 17 numbers, which are the SPLs in decibels below the overall level in each frequency band. The last operation is a level normalization, which in our opinion is very useful. The same level normalization is used by Zagoruiko [54] and Derkach [13]. It makes the analysis independent of the loudness level at which the words are spoken. A minor disadvantage is perhaps that one also misses the level distribution of the time samples within a word. If necessary, the *LIN-C* values can give that information.

One more remark about the used filter system may be worthwhile. It was a set of $\frac{1}{3}$-octave filters, which means that the bandwidth (Δf) of the filters increases with the

[1] /nœl/, /e:n/, /twe:/, /dri/, /vir/, /vɛif/, /zɛs/, /zϕv∂n/, /ɑχt/, /neγ∂n/, /pœnt/, /stɔp/, /mIn/, /fɑut/, /b∂γIn/, /ma:l/, /du/, /mɑχt/, /als/, /γ∂lɛik/.

center frequency (f_c). In fact, $\Delta f/f_c$ remains constant. This has as a consequence the fact that the time delay (τ) between maximum input and maximum output of the filters decreases with increasing center frequency. This time delay for the 8000 Hz filter is only 0.4 ms, but for the lowest filter combination 32 ms. While sampling the filter outputs this time delay is taken into account. However, this means that the sampling pattern crosses the 15 ms borders, and this makes the algorithm rather complicated. Out of neurophysiological experiments [29] it appears that this time delay also exists in the ear of the cat. It is measured as a latency of the first peak in the post-stimulus-time histogram for responses to clicks. This latency can be 4 to 5 ms for units with a center frequency around 300 Hz. The data are not exact enough to make it worthwhile to simulate the same latencies in our filter system, therefore, we completely corrected for the present time delays in the filter system. We can then be sure that the spectrum we measure for a given sound is the same, irrespective of the position of that speech sound within a word.

With an updating procedure, the 17-dB values for each 15-ms time sample are used to derive the 17×17 covariance matrix in real time. After analysis of the complete set of words the covariance matrix is at once available. A distribution of the variance along the 17 original dimensions is given in Fig. 2. The level-normalized spectra of vowels, nasals, and fricatives differ most in the high-frequency region. This explains why the variance in these frequency bands is highest. A principal components analysis of the covariance matrix produces three new dimensions which together explain 78.1 percent of the total variance (Dimension I—49.1 percent, Dimension II—18.8 percent, and Dimension III—10.2 percent). The fourth and higher dimensions each explain less than 5.6 percent, so we decided to work with a 3-dimensional subspace. The direction cosines of the three principal dimensions are given in Fig. 3.

Dimension I appears to discriminate between sonorants and nonsonorants since it separates the low- and high-frequency parts of the spectrum. The second and third dimensions have their highest weightings in the regions of the formant frequencies.

The next step in our recognition procedure is to determine the reference trace for each of the 20 words in the 3-dimensional subspace. Each word is analyzed again as previously described, but now the 17 numbers from each 15-ms sample are at once reduced to three coordinate values; these numbers are stored on magnetic tape. Special measures are taken to prevent that the analysis of a word stops when a silent period, for example, prior to a plosive, occurs. For that the multiplexer looks at the *LIN-C* filter for another 300 ms. If within this time, the level again exceeds the trigger level, the analysis is continued. When all the words are analyzed, a reference trace is computed for each word by averaging the 20 individual traces for that word. A problem with this technique is that the individual pronunciations of one word do not have the same duration and hence not the same number of samples, so a time normalization is necessary. One possible correct time normalization, apart from a nonlinear approach [14], is to treat the individual speech sounds within an utterance separately, taking into account the target positions (often not actually reached) of short sounds in a context. However, since this approach is not realizable for the moment, we used the much more simple procedure of linearly stretching or compressing the utterance as a whole. Since we judged it better not to make use of interpolated data, and considered the beginning, middle, and end of the word equally important, we simply omit a sample now and then or use one sample twice, depending upon the length of the individual word.

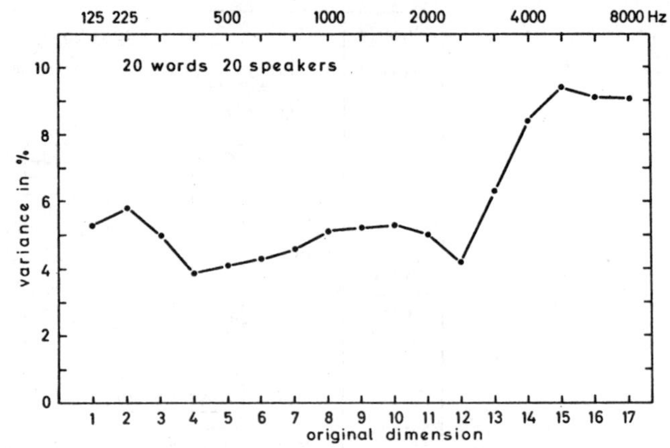

Fig. 2. Variance in each of the 17 original dimensions for all speech samples (20 speakers, 20 words). Total variance is 1862 dB^2.

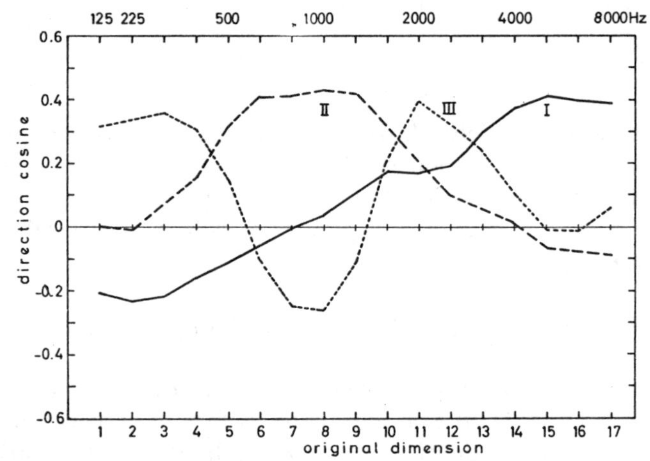

Fig. 3. Cosines of the angles between the computed Dimensions I, II, and III and the original 17 dimensions for the speech material of 20 times 20 words.

In order to compare the trace of the spoken word (N samples with coordinate values x_i, y_i, and z_i; $i=1, N$) with the 20 reference traces (N_j samples with coordinate values $\bar{x}_{ij}$, $\bar{y}_{ij}$, and $\bar{z}_{ij}$; $i=1, N_j$; $j=1, 20$) we defined a score which is a measure for the similarity between the two traces. This score is derived from the probability density (assumed to be normal) that a point will have a position between x and $x+\Delta x$

$$\frac{1}{\sigma\sqrt{2\pi}} \exp\left(-\tfrac{1}{2}(x-\bar{x})^2/\sigma^2\right) \cdot \Delta x. \tag{1}$$

Assuming independence of the dimensions and of the individual samples we can define

$$\frac{1}{\prod_{i=1}^{N_j} \{\sigma_{x_{ij}}\sigma_{y_{ij}}\sigma_{z_{ij}} \cdot (2\pi)^{3/2}\}} \exp\left[-\frac{1}{2}\sum_{i=1}^{N_j} \{(x_i - \bar{x}_{ij})^2/\sigma^2_{x_{ij}} + (y_i - \bar{y}_{ij})^2/\sigma^2_{y_{ij}} + (z_i - \bar{z}_{ij})^2/\sigma^2_{z_{ij}}\}\right]. \quad (2)$$

This is the probability that the trace of a spoken word belongs to the distribution of the jth reference trace. Since the number of samples (N_j) of the different reference traces is not the same, we normalize by taking the N_jth root of (2)

$$\frac{1}{(2\pi)^{3/2}\left(\prod_{i=1}^{N_j} \sigma_{x_{ij}}\sigma_{y_{ij}}\sigma_{z_{ij}}\right)^{1/N_j}} \exp\left[-\frac{1}{2N_j}\sum_{i=1}^{N} \{(x_i - \bar{x}_{ij})^2/\sigma^2_{x_{ij}} + (y_i - \bar{y}_{ij})^2/\sigma^2_{y_{ij}} + (z_i - \bar{z}_{ij})^2/\sigma^2_{z_{ij}}\}\right]. \quad (3)$$

Since we are mainly interested in the rank order of the values of (3) for the different reference traces, we neglect the constant factor and take the natural logarithm of (3) to reduce computation time. So we compute the following score

$$S_j = \frac{1}{N_j}\sum_{i=1}^{N_j} \{(x_i - \bar{x}_{ij})^2/\sigma^2_{x_{ij}} + (y_i - \bar{y}_{ij})^2/\sigma^2_{y_{ij}} + (z_i - \bar{z}_{ij})^2/\sigma^2_{z_{ij}}\} + P_j, \qquad j = 1, 20 \quad (4)$$

in which

$$P_j = 2 \ln\left(\prod_{i=1}^{N_j} \sigma_{x_{ij}}\sigma_{y_{ij}}\sigma_{z_{ij}}\right)^{1/N_j},$$

a constant for the jth reference trace. The word for which S_j is minimal is typed out as the word recognized.

The stored 3-dimensional traces of the 20 individual words of each of the 20 subjects were then, after linear time normalization, compared with the 20 reference traces. Using the score definition given in (4) 395 of the 400 words were correctly classified. If the word set had consisted only of the ten digits, those would have been recognized 100 percent correct. Furthermore, it appeared that making the number of samples in all the reference traces equal to 35 ($N_j = 35$ for $j = 1, 20$) did not influence the high accuracy. This procedure also reduced the computation time, since the samples of a spoken word were normalized once to 35 and then immediately were compared with *all* 20 reference traces. In the original procedure the number of samples of the incoming word had to be made equal to the number of samples of the reference trace with which it was being compared at that moment.

One must bear in mind that in this recognition procedure *only* spectral information was used. The recognition scores given above are the scores on the words which were also used to determine the reference traces. The recognition was programmed in Fortran, which is notoriously slow. A program in machine language has been written which makes it possible to execute the word recognition in real time. Recognition is completed 340 ms after the end of a word, and the most probable word is typed out or displayed on an oscilloscope screen. A real-time recognition of the 400 words from tape recording resulted in a misidentification of only seven words. For 16 out of the 20 talkers all words were correctly identified. New utterances from the same 20 speakers were correctly recognized 95.5 percent of the time. When the words were spoken by 20 new speakers the score was 93.8 percent correct, and even for 11 female talkers the score was 70 percent correct. In a preliminary test we transformed the system to a group of 17 English words. The 3-dimensional subspace was somewhat different, but the recognition scores were similar.

Discussion

We have seen above that with the dimensional approach, a very high correct score for a reduced set of words can be achieved. The word set makes it possible to speak to a computer in such a way that simple instructions and data input can be given. In fact for demonstration purposes we simulated a desk calculator which could add, subtract, multiply, and divide numbers which were spoken at a rate of about one word every second. Elder [16] also recently described a comparable on-line voice input computer processing system.

Despite the promising results, our approach of describing a complete word as a trace in a 3-dimensional space will never lead to a general word recognition system. For that we must abandon the idea of recognizing words as a whole and attempt to recognize phonemes, or phoneme-like parts in a word. This brings us directly to the problem of word segmentation.

Word segmentation and phoneme recognition can be based upon the same dimensional representation of speech spectra, especially if also such features as overall level and number of zero crossings are available and can be used. The sequence of transitional and stationary parts in a word can be determined on the basis of such properties as the overall level, the number of zero crossings, the position of and the distance between successive sample points in the subspace, the presence of silences within a word, etc.

We have just started research along this line. A first rough classification of speech sounds into sonorants and nonsonorants, and next into vowel-like, nasal-like, and voiced or unvoiced fricative-like sounds appears to be possible. Using optimal subspaces for each class will probably make a more detailed recognition possible.

Acknowledgment

The author wishes to express his thanks to L. W. M. Spiekman for developing the programs used for the on-line word recognition and to R. Plomp for many fruitful discussions.

References

[1] D. Anke and P. Hoeschele, "Einfache Erkennungsgeräte für die gesprochene Zahlen NULL bis NEUN," *Kybernetik*, vol. 4, June 1968, pp. 228–234.

[2] W. Becker, "Reduction of data flow using pattern recognition," in *1969 Colloque internationale sur la téléinformatique*, Paris, Mar. 26–28, pp. 259–268.

[3] C. G. Bell, H. Fujisaki, J. M. Heinz, K. N. Stevens, and A. S. House, "Reduction of speech spectra by analysis-by-synthesis techniques,"

J. Acoust. Soc. Am., vol. 33, Dec. 1961, pp. 1725–1736.

[4] W. J. Beninghof, Jr., and M. J. Ross, "Investigation of an efficient representation of speech spectra for segmentation and classification of speech sounds," *IEEE Trans. Audio Electroacoust*, vol. AU-18, Mar. 1970, pp. 33–42.

[5] D. G. Bobrow, A. K. Hartley, and D. H. Klatt, "A limited speech recognition system II," Bolt, Beranek, and Newman Rep. 1819, 1969.

[6] J. F. Boehm and R. D. Wright, "Dimensional analysis and display of speech spectra," *J. Acoust. Soc. Am.*, vol. 44, July 1968, p. 386.

[7] M. W. Cannon, Jr., "A method of analysis and recognition for voiced vowels," *IEEE Trans. Audio Electroacoust.*, vol. AU-16, June 1968, pp. 154–158.

[8] S. Chiba, "Spoken word recognition by multiple linear separation," in *1968 Proc. 6th Int. Congr. Acoust.*, Tokyo, Paper B-4-4, pp. B 123–126.

[9] J. W. Cooly and J. W. Tukey, "An algorithm for the machine calculation of complex Fourier series," *Math. Comput.*, vol. 19, Apr. 1965, pp. 297–301.

[10] E. E. David, "Artificial auditory recognition in the telephony," *IBM J. Res. Develop.*, vol. 2, Oct. 1958, pp. 294–309.

[11] P. Denes, "The design and operation of the mechanical speech recognizer at University College London," *J. British Inst. Radio Electron. Eng.*, vol. 19, Apr. 1959, pp. 219–229.

[12] P. Denes and M. V. Mathews, "Spoken digit recognition using time-frequency pattern matching," *J. Acoust. Soc. Am.*, vol. 32, Nov. 1960, pp. 1450–1455.

[13] M. Derkach, "Heuristic models for automatic recognition of spoken words," Speech Transmission Lab., Quarterly Prog. and Status Rep. STL-QPSR 1/1970, pp. 39–49.

[14] G. R. Doddington, "A method of speaker verification," *J. Acoust. Soc. Am.*, vol. 49, Jan. 1971, p. 139.

[15] H. Dudley and S. Balashek, "Automatic recognition of phonetic patterns in speech," *J. Acoust. Soc. Am.*, vol. 30, Aug. 1958, pp. 721–732.

[16] H. A. Elder, "On the feasability of voice input to an on-line computer processing system," *Commun. Ass. Comput. Mach.*, vol. 13, June 1970, pp. 339–346.

[17] G. Fant, "Automatic recognition and speech research," Speech Transmission Lab., Quarterly Prog. and Status Rep. STL-QPSR 1/1970, pp. 16–31.

[18] L. F. Favella, M. Reineri, and G. Righini, "On a mathematical procedure for detecting significant parameters in the classification of a statistical ensemble of phonema and its applications," *Kybernetik*, vol. 5, 1969, pp. 187–194.

[19] J. L. Flanagan, "Automatic extraction of formant frequencies from continuous speech," *J. Acoust. Soc. Am.*, vol. 28, Jan. 1956, pp. 110–118.

[20] J. W. Forgie and C. D. Forgie, "Results obtained from a vowel recognition computer program," *J. Acoust. Soc. Am.*, vol. 31, Nov. 1959, pp. 1480–1489.

[21] J. D. Foulkes, "Computer identification of vowel types," *J. Acoust. Soc. Am.*, vol. 33, Jan. 1961, pp. 7–11.

[22] R. H. Galt, unpublished notes, Oct. 2, 1951, referred to by David (1958).

[23] L. J. Gerstman, "Classification of self-normalized vowels," *IEEE Trans. Audio Electroacoust.*, vol. AU-16, Mar. 1968, pp. 78–80.

[24] L. Gilli and A. R. Meo, "Sequential system for recognizing spoken digits in real time," *Acustica*, vol. 19, 1967/1968, pp. 38–48.

[25] H. H. Harman, *Modern Factor Analysis*. Chicago: Univ. of Chicago Press, 1967.

[26] J. F. Hemdal and G. W. Hughes, "A feature-based computer recognition program for the modelling of vowel perception," in *Proc. Symp. Models for the Perception of Speech and Visual Form*. Cambridge, Mass.: M.I.T. Press, 1967, pp. 440–452.

[27] S. R. Hyde, "Automatic speech recognition. Literature survey and discussion," Res. Dep. Rep. 45, G.P.O., U.D.C. 534.78, 1968.

[28] L. G. Kersta, unpublished notes, July 1, 1947, referred to by David (1958).

[29] N. Y.-S. Kiang, *Discharge Patterns of Single Fibers in the Cat's Auditory Nerve*. Cambridge, Mass.: M.I.T. Press 1965.

[30] W. Klein, R. Plomp, and L. C. W. Pols, "Vowel spectra, vowel spaces and vowel identification," *J. Acoust. Soc. Am.*, vol. 48, Oct. 1970, pp. 999–1009.

[31] H. P. Kramer and M. V. Mathews, "A linear coding for transmitting a set of correlated signals," *IRE Trans. Inform. Theory*, vol. IT-2, Sept. 1956, pp. 41–46.

[32] K.-P. Li, G. W. Hughes, and A. S. House, "Correlation characteristics and dimensionality of speech spectra," *J. Acoust. Soc. Am.*, vol. 46, Oct. 1969, pp. 1019–1025.

[33] A. M. Liberman, F. S. Cooper, and M. Studdert-Kennedy, "Why are spectrograms hard to read," Haskins Lab., Status Rep. SR-10, Apr.-June 1967.

[34] N. Lindgren, "Machine recognition of human language, part I—Automatic speech recognition," *IEEE Spectrum*, vol. 2, Mar. 1965, pp. 114–136.

[35] M. V. Mathews, J. E. Miller, and E. E. David, "Pitch synchronous analysis of voiced sounds," *J. Acoust. Soc. Am.*, vol. 33, Feb. 1961, pp. 179–186.

[36] W. S. Mohn, "Statistical feature evaluation in speaker identification," Ph.D. dissertation, North Carolina State Univ., Raleigh, N. C., 1969.

[37] R. C. Ohlendorf and C. L. Coates, "Recognition of spoken digits utilizing sequential patterns," Information Syst. Res. Lab., University of Texas, Austin, Tex., Tech. Rep. 57, Nov. 1968.

[38] H. F. Olson and H. Belar, "Phonetic typewriter," *J. Acoust. Soc. Am.*, vol. 28, Nov. 1956, pp. 1072–1081.

[39] A. V. Oppenheim, "Speech analysis-synthesis system based on homomorphic filtering," *J. Acoust. Soc. Am.*, vol. 45, Feb. 1969, pp. 458–464.

[40] G. E. Peterson and H. L. Barney, "Control methods used in a study of vowels," *J. Acoust. Soc. Am.*, vol. 24, Mar. 1952, pp. 175–184.

[41] L. C. W. Pols, L. J. Th. v.d. Kamp, and R. Plomp, "Perceptual and physical space of vowel sounds," *J. Acoust. Soc. Am.*, vol. 46, Aug. 1969, pp. 458–467.

[42] R. K. Potter, G. A. Kopp, and H. G. Green, *Visible Speech*. Princeton, N. J.: Van Nostrand, 1947.

[43] R. Plomp and A. M. Mimpen, "The ear as a frequency analyzer II," *J. Acoust. Soc. Am.*, vol. 43, Apr. 1968, pp. 764–767.

[44] R. Plomp, L. C. W. Pols, and J. P. v. d. Geer, "Dimensional analysis of vowel spectra," *J. Acoust. Soc. Am.*, vol. 41, Mar. 1967, pp. 707–712.

[45] R. W. Schafer and L. R. Rabiner, "System for automatic formant analysis of voiced speech," *J. Acoust. Soc. Am.*, vol. 47, Feb. 1970, pp. 634–648.

[46] G. Sebestyen, "Automatic recognition of spoken numerals," *J. Acoust. Soc. Am.*, vol. 32, Nov. 1960, p. 1516.

[47] J. N. Shearme and P. F. Leach, "Some experiments with a simple word recognition system," *IEEE Trans. Audio Electroacoust.*, vol. AU-16, June 1968, pp. 256–261.

[48] J. Suzuki, Y. Kadokawa, and K. Nakata, "Formant-frequency extraction by the method of moment calculations," *J. Acoust. Soc. Am.*, vol. 35, Sept. 1963, pp. 1345–1353.

[49] C. C. Tappert, N. R. Dixon, D. H. Beettle, and W. D. Chapman, "A dynamic-segment approach to recognition of continuous speech," Rome Air Develop. Cen., Griffiss AFB, Rome, N. Y., Tech. Rep. RADC-TR-70-22, 1970.

[50] E. Terhardt, "Beitrag zur automatische Erkennung gesprochener Zahlen," *Kybernetik*, vol. 3, 1966, pp. 136–143.

[51] S. Washizawa, M. Okamoto, T. Shiga, and S. Inomata, "A spoken digit recognition scheme and its computer simulation," in *1968 Proc. 6th Int. Congr. Acoust.*, Tokyo, Paper B-4-7, pp. B 135–138.

[52] S. Watanabe, "A method of self-featuring information compression in pattern recognition," presented at the Bionics Symp., Dayton, Ohio, May 3–5, 1966.

[53] P. D. Welch and R. S. Wimpress, "Two multivariate statistical computer programs and their application to the vowel recognition problem," *J. Acoust. Soc. Am.*, vol. 33, Apr. 1961, pp. 426–434.

[54] N. G. Zagoruiko, "Automatic recognition of speech," Speech Transmission Lab., Quarterly Prog. and Status Rep. STL-QPRS 1/1970, pp. 32–38.

[55] E. Zwicker, W. Hess, and E. Terhardt, "Erkennung gesprochener Zahlworte mit Funktionsmodell und elektronischer Rechenanlage," *Kybernetik*, vol. 3, 1967, pp. 267–272.

Minimum Prediction Residual Principle Applied to Speech Recognition

FUMITADA ITAKURA, MEMBER, IEEE

Abstract—**A computer system is described in which isolated words, spoken by a designated talker, are recognized through calculation of a minimum prediction residual. A reference pattern for each word to be recognized is stored as a time pattern of linear prediction coefficients (LPC). The total log prediction residual of an input signal is minimized by optimally registering the reference LPC onto the input autocorrelation coefficients using the dynamic programming algorithm (DP). The input signal is recognized as the reference word which produces the minimum prediction residual. A sequential decision procedure is used to reduce the amount of computation in DP. A frequency normalization with respect to the long-time spectral distribution is used to reduce effects of variations in the frequency response of telephone connections.**

The system has been implemented on a DDP-516 computer for the 200-word recognition experiment. The recognition rate for a designated male talker is 97.3 percent for telephone input, and the recognition time is about 22 times real time.

I. INTRODUCTION

RECENTLY time-domain speech analysis based on linear predictability of signal waveform has been successfully adopted for efficient coding of a redundant speech signal [1], [2]. Motivated by these successes, several efforts have been made toward application of the linear predictor coefficients (LPC) for speech recognition [3], [4]. But the immediate use of LPC as feature parameters was not so successful as might be expected [5]. The lack of success may be partly due to the fact that the feature space spanned by LPC is too complicated to introduce a simple and effective measure of distance between elements in the space.

It may be natural to raise the question: what kind of distance measure should be used in the framework of the linear prediction technique? In order to discuss this question, let us consider a more simplified problem; given a short segment of signal, what is the optimal distance measure to test a hypothesis that the segment can be regarded as one generated by a model having specified LPC? The answer to this question might be extended to test a more complicated hypothesis; namely, that some input utterance can be regarded as a word having a specified pattern of LPC.

In this paper, an approach to this problem will be described from a statistical point of view, and it will be shown that the log likelihood ratio, which is the best criterion to test the hypothesis, is reduced to the logarithm of the ratio of prediction residuals, and can be used as a

Manuscript received March 29, 1974; revised October 2, 1974. This paper was presented at the IEEE Symposium on Speech Recognition, Carnegie-Mellon University, Pittsburgh, Pa., April 15–19, 1974.

The author is with the Acoustics Research Department, Bell Laboratories, Murray Hill, N. J. 07974 and the Electrical Communications Laboratories, Nippon Telephone and Telegraph Public Corporation, Musashino, Tokyo, Japan.

Reprinted from *IEEE Trans. Acoust., Speech, and Signal Process.*, vol. ASSP-23, pp. 67–72, Feb. 1975.

powerful distance measure. This result is applied to automatic recognition of isolated words, wherein a sequential likelihood ratio test is adopted to reduce the amount of computation.

II. DISTANCE MEASURE FOR AN ALL-POLE MODEL

An all-pole model of speech signal is as follows. The discrete-time signal $x(n)$ ($t = nT$, when T is the interval between samples) in a stationary segment of signal satisfies the system of difference equations

$$x(n) + a(1)x(n-1) + \cdots + a(p)x(n-p) = e(n) \tag{1}$$

where $\{a(i)\}$ are constants and $\{e(n)\}$ is a white noise or a quasi-periodic signal, with mean-squared value s. Because p is usually much less than the period of $\{e(n)\}$, $\{e(n)\}$ can be regarded as an uncorrelated signal as far as correlations between $q(<p)$ adjacent samples are concerned. In this paper, $\{-a(i)\}$ or simply $\{a(i)\}$ is called the LPC, and the mean-squared value s of $\{e(n)\}$, or power, is called the prediction residual.

The problem in this section is to derive a measure of distance, or dissimilarity, between a segment of signal $\mathbf{X} = (x(1),\cdots,x(N))$ and the model defined by (1). Here, for mathematical tractability, we assume that $\{e(n)\}$ is a Gaussian white noise. Then a set of parameters $\mathbf{P} = (s,a(1),\cdots,a(p))$ specifies the conditional joint probability density $p(\mathbf{X}/\mathbf{P})$, and if $N \gg p$, the logarithm of $p(\mathbf{X}/\mathbf{P})$ is approximately given by [6], [7]

$$L(\mathbf{X}/\mathbf{P}) = -(N/2)[\log 2\pi s + (1/s)\mathbf{aVa}'] \tag{2}$$

where $\mathbf{a}$ is a row vector $(1,a(1),\cdots, a(p))$, and

$$\mathbf{V} = [v(|i-j|)], \qquad (i, j = 0,1,\cdots p)$$

is a correlation matrix whose elements are defined by

$$v(i) = (1/N) \sum_{n=1}^{N-i} x(n)x(n+i). \tag{3}$$

Supposing that we have no knowledge about the absolute value of s and s is a free parameter (Case I), it is replaced by its estimate which maximizes $L(\mathbf{X}/\mathbf{P})$

$$\partial L(\mathbf{X}/\mathbf{P})/\partial s = 0, \qquad s = \mathbf{aVa}' \tag{4}$$

thus, from (2), we obtain

$$L'(\mathbf{X}/\mathbf{a}) = \max_s L(\mathbf{X}/\mathbf{P}) = -(N/2) \log \mathbf{aVa}' + C. \tag{5}$$

The vector $\hat{\mathbf{a}}$ which maximizes $L'(\mathbf{X}/\mathbf{a})$ is determined as a solution of the following system of equations:

$$\sum_{j=0}^{p} v(i-j)\hat{\mathbf{a}}(j) = 0, \qquad (i = 1,\cdots,p) \tag{6}$$

and the maximum value is as follows:

$$L''(X) = \max_{\mathbf{a}} L'(\mathbf{X}/\mathbf{a}) = -(N/2) \log \hat{\mathbf{a}}\mathbf{V}\hat{\mathbf{a}}' + C. \tag{7}$$

$L''(\mathbf{X})$ is the maximum value of the likelihood function when both s and $\mathbf{a}$ are assumed to be free parameters (Case II). From (5) and (7), the likelihood ratio for the Case I and II of free parameters is proportional to

$$d(\mathbf{X}/\mathbf{a}) = \log (\mathbf{aVa}'/\hat{\mathbf{a}}\mathbf{V}\hat{\mathbf{a}}'). \tag{8}$$

The quadratic forms $\mathbf{aVa}'$ and $\hat{\mathbf{a}}\mathbf{V}\hat{\mathbf{a}}'$ in (8) are prediction residuals, when the input signal $\mathbf{X}$ is operated by the model LPC $\mathbf{a}$ and the estimated LPC $\hat{\mathbf{a}}$, respectively.

If the model defined by $\mathbf{a}$ is close to the actual process which generates $\mathbf{X}$, then the $\hat{\mathbf{a}}$, which is the maximum likelihood estimate of $\mathbf{a}$, are close to the $\mathbf{a}$ and $d(\mathbf{X}/\mathbf{a})$ is close to zero; if not, $d(\mathbf{X}/\mathbf{a})$ is significantly large. More precisely, $d(\mathbf{X}/\mathbf{a})N$ will be asymptotically a χ^2 variate with p degrees of freedom, if $\mathbf{X}$ is a realization of a model having $\mathbf{a}$ as the parameter (null hypothesis) [12]. If the $d(\mathbf{X}/\mathbf{a})N$ is larger than the $\chi^2{}_{1-\alpha}(p)$, then the null hypothesis should be rejected at a given probability α of false rejection. In this sense, $d(\mathbf{X}/\mathbf{a})$ can be regarded as a distance measure between $\mathbf{X}$ and the hypothesized model (1) specified by LPC $\mathbf{a}$.

For small deviation of $\hat{\mathbf{a}}$ from $\mathbf{a}$, the distance of (8) can be approximated by

$$d'(\mathbf{X},\mathbf{a}) = [(\mathbf{a}-\hat{\mathbf{a}})\mathbf{V}(\mathbf{a}-\hat{\mathbf{a}})']/[\hat{\mathbf{a}}\mathbf{V}\hat{\mathbf{a}}']. \tag{8'}$$

This measure is apparently different from those which might be intuitively suggested in the space of $\{a(i)\}$ such as

$$d = (\mathbf{a}-\hat{\mathbf{a}})\mathbf{W}(\mathbf{a}-\hat{\mathbf{a}})'. \tag{9}$$

The main difference is in that, the weighting of the quadratic form in (9) is a constant matrix $\mathbf{W}$, while that of (8′) depends on the autocorrelation $\mathbf{V}$ of $\mathbf{X}$. This dependence of the weighting matrix on $\mathbf{V}$, or equivalently on $\hat{\mathbf{a}}$, is a natural consequence from the fact that the covariance characteristics of estimation error of $\mathbf{a}$ depends on the location of $\hat{\mathbf{a}}$ in the space of LPC. It is well known that the estimated covariance matrix of $(\mathbf{a}-\hat{\mathbf{a}})$ is proportional to the inverse of $\mathbf{V}/[\hat{\mathbf{a}}\mathbf{V}\hat{\mathbf{a}}']$ [12]. In the distance measure of (8′), the weighting for the difference $(\mathbf{a}-\hat{\mathbf{a}})$ is automatically adjusted in accordance with the probable error of the estimated parameter $\hat{\mathbf{a}}$.

Equation (8) can be rewritten in the form

$$d(\mathbf{X}/\mathbf{a}) = c + \log [(\mathbf{br})/(\hat{\mathbf{a}}\mathbf{r})] \tag{10}$$

where $(\mathbf{xy})$ means the inner product of two vectors, $\mathbf{r} = (v(i)/v(0))$, $(i = 0,\cdots,p)$, $c = \log (\mathbf{aa})$, and $\mathbf{b}$ is a vector $(1,b(1),\cdots,b(p))$ whose elements are defined by

$$b(i) = 2 \sum_{j=0}^{p-i} a(j)a(j+i)/(\mathbf{aa}). \tag{11}$$

The $\{b(i)/2\}$'s are the autocorrelation coefficients associated with the inverse filter of the all-pole model. The c is the log power of its impulse response. These modified parameters $\mathbf{b}$ and c are more convenient to compute $d(\mathbf{X}/\mathbf{a})$ than the $\mathbf{a}$ themselves.

III. ISOLATED WORD RECOGNITION

Each isolated word to be recognized can be expressed as a time pattern of LPC, which is called the reference pattern. The process in recognition is to find a reference pattern which produces the minimum distance to an input utterance.

Reference Pattern: The reference pattern $\mathbf{R}(k)$ for each word is stored as a matrix of the form

$$\mathbf{R}(k) = [c(m;k),\mathbf{b}(m;k)] \qquad (m = 1,\cdots,M(k),k = 1,\cdots,K) \qquad (12)$$

where $c(m;k)$ and $\mathbf{b}(m;k)$ are the modified parameters of LPC at the mth segment of the kth reference pattern, $M(k)$ is the number of segments in the reference pattern $\mathbf{R}(k)$, and K is the number of words to be recognized. Elements of the matrix $\mathbf{R}(k)$ are computed from a training utterance using (3), (6), and (11).

Recognition: An input utterrance is expressed as a time pattern of autocorrelation coefficients at the first p delays

$$\mathbf{r}(n), \qquad n = 1,\cdots,N \qquad (13)$$

where N is the number of segments in the input utterance. The distance between the nth segment of the input and the mth segment of a reference pattern $\mathbf{R}(k)$ is

$$d(n,m;k) = c(m;k) + \log [(\mathbf{b}(m;k)\mathbf{r}(n))/(\hat{\mathbf{a}}(n)\mathbf{r}(n))]. \qquad (14)$$

The value of $(\hat{\mathbf{a}}(n)\mathbf{r}(n))$ is obtained in the process of solving the linear equation (6).

If we assume statistical independence of $d(n,m;k)$ for $n = 1,\cdots,N$, it is reasonable to sum up $d(n,m;k)$ over the entire input utterance to give the total distance between the input and the reference pattern. Of course, m must be determined as a function of n

$$m = w(n). \qquad (15)$$

This function $w(n)$, which maps the input time axis onto the reference time axis, is called the time-warping function. This function should satisfy some boundary conditions as well as some continuity conditions. For brevity in the following discussion, it is assumed that $w(n)$ is subject to the following conditions.

Boundary Conditions:

$$w(1) = 1, \qquad w(N) = M(k). \qquad (16)$$

Continuity Conditions:

$$\begin{aligned} w(n+1) - w(n) &= 0, 1, 2 \qquad (w(n) \neq w(n-1)) \\ &= 1, 2 \qquad (w(n) = w(n-1)). \end{aligned} \qquad (17)$$

Fig. 1 shows the domain of possible (n,m) coordinates and an example of $w(n)$. The continuity conditions imply

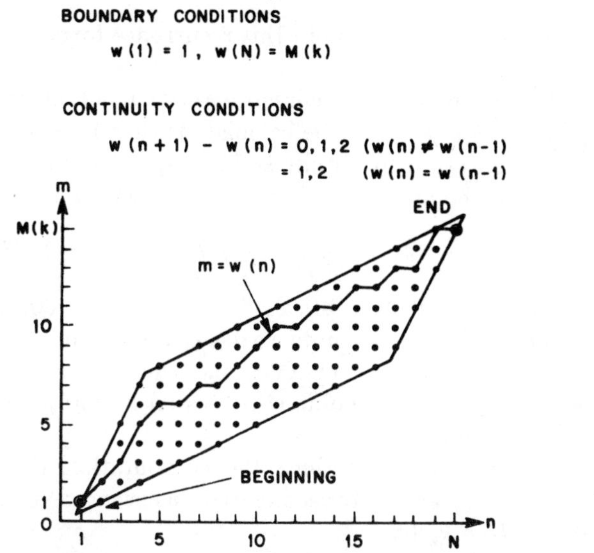

Fig. 1. An example of time-warping function. The parallelogram shows the possible domain of (n,m) coordinates.

that the ratio of instantaneous speed of the input utterance to that of the reference is bounded between 1/2 and 2 at every point. Let us denote the minimum value of the sum of $d(n,m;k)$ for all possible choices of the time-warping function by

$$D(k) = \min_{\{w(n)\}} \sum_{n=1}^{N} d(n,w(n);k). \qquad (18)$$

$D(k)$ is a distance between the input utterance and a hypothesized word k. A decision can be made on the basis of the minimum distance among $D(k), k = 1,2,\cdots,K$.

IV. DYNAMIC PROGRAMMING AND SEQUENTIAL DECISION

The distance $D(k)$ in (18) can be efficiently computed using the algorithm of dynamic programming (DP) [8]-[10]. Let us introduce the partial distance measure, in which the boundary conditions are $w(1) = 1$ and $w(n) = m$, and the continuity conditions are the same as the above, denoted by

$$D(n,m;k) = \min_{\{w(j)\}} \sum_{j=1}^{n} d(j,w(j);k). \qquad (19)$$

Then there follows the recurrence relation;

$$D(n+1,m;k) = d(n+1,m;k) + \min (D(n,m;k) \cdot g(n,m), D(n,m-1;k), D(n,m-2;k)) \qquad (20)$$

where

$$\begin{aligned} g(n,m) &= 1 (w(n) \neq w(n-1)), \\ &= \infty (w(n) = (n-1)). \end{aligned} \qquad (21)$$

In the recurrence relation (20), it is assumed that $d(n,m;k)$ outside the allowable domain in the (n,m) coordinates, shown in Fig. 1, is infinitely large. $D(k)$ is found at the last stage in this recurrence formula, that is, $D(k) = D(N,M(k);k)$.

As shown in the recurrence relation, at every lattice point, $d(n,m;k)$ must be calculated; therefore the amount of computation to obtain $D(k)$ is approximately proportional to the number of lattice points, which is nearly

$$L = (2N - M(k) + 1)(2M(k) - N + 1)/3. \quad (22)$$

For example, if $N = 40$, $M(k) = 40$, $K = 200$, the total number of lattice points to be examined in recognizing one word is nearly 112 000, and the processing time is 49 s, if one lattice point is processed in 420 μs, as is the case described later.

One method to reduce the computation time might be the procedure of sequential decisions. Now, let us define $D(n;k)$ by

$$D(n;k) = \min_m D(n,m;k). \quad (23)$$

$D(n;k)$ is the minimum distance between the first n segments of the input and a reference pattern $\mathbf{R}(k)$. If a reference pattern $\mathbf{R}(k^*)$ coincides with the input, it is expected that $D(n;k^*)$ takes lower values for all stages n. Therefore, if $D(n;k)$ is sufficiently large compared with probable excursion of $D(n;k^*)$, the reference pattern can be immediately rejected at an early stage without examining further segments. If not, the next stage is examined.

The threshold for rejection should be as low as possible under the constraint that the probability of false rejection is sufficiently small. Although it is desirable to get a threshold $T(n)$ which meets this requirement theoretically, it is difficult to find it in practice.[1] But, if we notice that the final decision is made on the basis of the relative values of $D(k)$, $T(n)$ might be determined depending on the actual realization of $D(n;k)$. The method used in the experiment is as follows.

The rejection threshold is assumed to be of the form

$$T(n) = S(n) + M \quad (24)$$

where M is a constant decision margin and $S(n)$ is the variable part of $T(n)$ and is updated at every stage in the DP. Initially $S(n)$ is so selected that it is not less than $D(n;k^*)$ for all cases when k^* coincides with the input word. Beginning with $n = 1$, $D(n;k)$ is sequentially computed. If $D(n;k)$ is less than $T(n)$ at the stage n, $S(n)$ is replaced by $D(n;k)$ to give a new threshold which will be used to compute $D(n;k+1)$. If a reference which is similar to the input is found, the threshold $T(n)$ is set to a lower value. Thereafter only references similar to the input are examined in detail and other references will be rejected at earlier stages. In the final decision only reference patterns which arrived at the last stage N are candidates for the recognized word. If no reference arrives at the last stage, the input is rejected as an inadequate input.

[1] If the reference pattern $R(k^*)$ is the true one and the assumptions of the model and the statistical independence of $d(n,m;k^*)$ for $n = 1,2,\cdots, N$ hold, the optimal $T(n)$ is given by $x_{1-\alpha}^2(pn)$, where α is the probability of false rejection.

V. EXPERIMENTAL PROCEDURE AND RESULTS

The recognition scheme described earlier has been implemented on a DDP-516 computer for a 200-word recognition experiment. The flow chart of the system is shown in Fig. 2. The 200 words are Japanese geographical names and were pronounced by a male speaker. The mean duration of the reference utterances is 600 ms, and the mean number of syllables is 3.5.

Speech Input: The experimental arrangement for the isolated word recognition is shown in Fig. 3. Each utterance is inputted to the computer using a conventional telephone set dialed through the Bell Laboratories PBX. The telephone set is placed beside the computer console and the noise level around it is about 68 dB(A). After passing through a lowpass filter whose 6 dB cutoff frequency is 3.0 kHz, the speech is sampled at 6.667 kHz and temporarily stored in disc memory. Each utterance is made within a fixed time interval of 1.2 s after listening to the start signal or manually pressing an initiating switch.

Autocorrelation Analysis: Hamming window of 200 samples (30 ms) is applied to the digitized signal. The window is advanced in steps of 100 samples (15 ms) to get the next segment. The instantaneous power within each window is computed, and if it exceeds the noise level, the first eight coefficients are computed. The speech signal duration is detected automatically by examining the power envelope from the forward and backward and neglecting low-level noise.

Normalization of Long-Time Spectrum: The gross spectral distribution of the input signal may be greatly affected by physical factors, such as transducer and line response, as well as by human factors, such as stress and physical condition. These factors may have serious effects on the stability of the system using LPC. Therefore, we have applied a normalization technique of input spectral distribution in the following way. The first two autocorrelation coefficients are averaged over the utterance interval after weighting by the instantaneous power level. For every utterance, a second-order inverse filter is designed by solving a two-variable linear equation. This filter is used to normalize the gross spectral distribution of the utterance. This is done by convolving the original autocorrelation coefficients and the autocorrelation coefficients of the impulse response of the second order inverse filter. The first six normalized autocorrelation coefficients are used to make both the reference patterns to recognize unknown inputs.

Making a Reference Pattern: The reference pattern for each word is generated by the method described in Section III. In this experiment p is 6, $\overline{M(k)}$, the average number of reference segments is about 40 (600 ms), and K, the number of words, is 200. The memory capacity for storing all the reference patterns is $(p + 1)\overline{M(k)}K = 56\,000$ words, and each computer word consists of 16 bits.

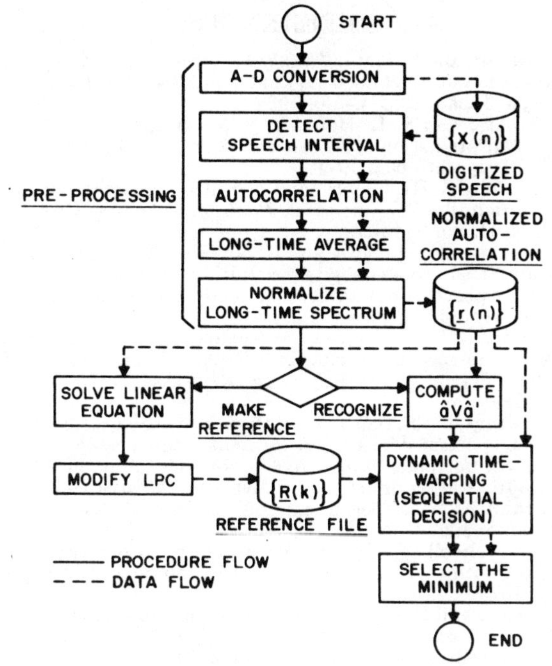

Fig. 2. Flow chart of isolated word recognition.

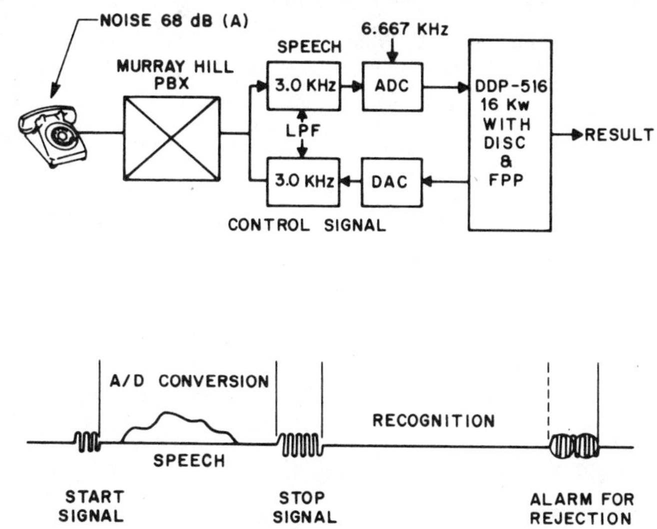

Fig. 3. Experimental arrangement of on-line isolated word recognition.

Recognition and Result: The recognition procedure has been described in Sections III and IV. The major processing in this phase is to compute the distance $d(n,m;k)$ defined by (14), and it is programmed using assembly language. The base of the logarithm is set to 2, and $\log x (1/2 \leq x < 1)$ is approximated by $2(x - 1)$. The computation time for the basic recurrence formula (20) at every lattice point is 420 μs including the computation of $d(n,m;k)$. The threshold margin is chosen as $M = 4$ on the basis of preliminary experiments. The average number of lattice points actually examined is 69 per reference pattern; that is, only 12 percent of L expressed by (22) in which the sequential decision scheme is not used. The total recognition time including the autocorrelation analysis and other preprocessing is about 12 s for one utterance, which is 22 times real time. The recognition rate is 97.3 percent and the rejection rate is 1.65 percent, when the designated talker inputs 2000 test utterances over an time span of three weeks.

VI. DISCUSSION

The main objective of this study is not to develop a particular isolated word recognition system, but is focused to assess experimentally the effectiveness of the proposed distance measure and the sequential decision scheme based on the distance. For this reason, the word recognition system is a straightforward realization of the proposed method without any ad hoc modification. Some parameters, such as intensity, voicing and pitch patterns, are intentionally not used, although they must be crucial in discriminating some words which have very similar patterns of LPC. Despite existence of some room for improvement, the experimental results may give a promising impression, considering the quality of the input signal and vocabulary size. But it must be admitted that the recognition rate is strongly influenced by a particular choice of vocabulary set. For example, if the vocabulary set is the English alphabet and digit

$$\{A,B,\cdots,Y,Z,1,2,\cdots,9,0\},$$

the recognition rate was 88.6 percent for 720 test utterances by the same speaker under the same conditions as in V. All digit input are correctly recognized, although "H" is incorrectly recognized as "8" twice out of 20 trials. Major misclassifications are listed in Table I. This result shows that the majority of confusions occur between pairs in which the vowel part is identical and the difference of the consonant part is relatively small and it is masked by the vowel part which is predominant in duration.

As compared with other word recognition methods of comparable vocabulary size [8], [11], the recognition rate of this method is nearly same or slightly better, despite, in this experiment, a conventional telephone set in a noisy environment is used as a speech input terminal. The complexity of recognition algorithm seems to be of the same order, judging from the processing time per word using computers of similar speed.

VII. CONCLUSION

A new measure of distance for an all-pole model of speech has been derived on the basis of the likelihood ratio criteria and is applied to automatic recognition of isolated words. An algorithm to find to the best match between the input pattern and a reference pattern is derived, in which the dynamic programming technique is used in conjunction with a sequential decision scheme. The system is implemented on a DDP-516 computer to recognize 200 isolated words. The validity of the scheme has been confirmed experimentally. Further work is in progress to

TABLE I
MAJOR MISRECOGNITIONS IN ALPHABET-DIGIT RECOGNITION

INPUT	RECOGNIZED	NO. of ERRORS
V	B or D	15
B	D	10
P	T or D	9
E	T	9
M	N	5
I	Y	5
	SUB TOTAL	53
	OTHER ERRORS	29
	TOTAL ERRORS / TOTAL TRIALS	82 / 720
	ERROR RATE	=11.4%

test the system for a greater number of talkers and for telephone connections switched over greater distances.

ACKNOWLEDGMENT

The author wishes to thank J. L. Flanagan for his guidance and stimulating discussions, and to acknowledge the help received from C. H. Coker and A. E. Rosenberg during implementation of the system.

REFERENCES

[1] F. Itakura and S. Saito, "Analysis synthesis telephony based on the maximum likelihood method," in *Proc. Int. Congr. Acoust.*, Tokyo, Japan, Rep. C-5-6, 1968.

[2] B. S. Atal and S. L. Hanauer, "Speech analysis and synthesis by linear prediction of speech waveform," *J. Acoust. Soc. Amer.*, vol. 50, pp. 637–655, 1971.

[3] M. Kohda, S. Hashimoto, and S. Saito, "Spoken digit mechanical recognition," *Trans. Inst. Electron. Commun. Eng.* (*Japan*), vol. 55-D, no. 3, 1972

[4] Y. Nakano, A. Ichikawa, and K. Nakata, "Evaluation of various parameters in spoken digits recognition," presented at the IEEE Conf. Speech Communication and Processing, Cambridge, Mass., Apr. 1972, Paper C4.

[5] H. Fujisaki and Y. Sato, "Evaluation and comparison of features in speech recognition," Faculty Eng., Univ. of Tokyo, Tokyo, Japan, Annu. Rep. Eng. Res. Inst., 1973, vol. 32, pp. 213–218.

[6] F. Itakura and S. Saito, "A statistical method for estimation of speech spectral density and formant frequencies," *Trans. Inst. Electron. Commun. Eng.* (*Japan*), vol. 53-A, pp. 36–43, 1970.

[7] S. Saito, T. Fukumura, and F. Itakura, "Statistically optimum discrimination of speech spectra," *J. Acoust. Soc. Japan*, vol. 23, no. 5, 1967.

[8] V. M. Velichiko and N. G. Zagoruiko, "Automatic recognition of 200-words," *Int. J. Man–Machine Studies*, vol. 2, pp. 223–234, 1970.

[9] H. Sakoe and S. Chiba, "A dynamic programming approach to continuous speech recognition," in *Proc. Int. Congr. Acoust.*, Budapest, Hungary, Rep. 20-C-13, 1971.

[10] ——, "Comparative study of DP-pattern matching techniques for speech recognition," Speech Res. Group, Acoust. Soc. Japan, Rep. S73-22, 1973.

[11] D. R. Reddy, "Segment synchronization problem in speech recognition," *J. Acoust. Soc. Amer.*, vol. 46, no. 1, p. 89, 1969.

[12] H. B. Mann and A. Wald, "On the statistical treatment of linear difference equations," *Econometrica*, vol. 11, pp. 173–217, 1943.

A Speaker-Independent Digit-Recognition System

By M. R. SAMBUR and L. R. RABINER

(Manuscript received July 9, 1974)

This paper describes an implementation of a speaker-independent digit-recognition system. The digit classification scheme is based on segmenting the unknown word into three regions and then making categorical judgments as to which of six broad acoustic classes each segment falls into. The measurements made on the speech waveform include energy, zero crossings, two-pole linear predictive coding analysis, and normalized error of the linear predictive coding analysis. A formal evaluation of the systems showed an error rate of 2.7 percent for a carefully controlled recording environment and a 5.6 percent error rate for on-line recordings in a noisy computer room.

I. INTRODUCTION

With the widespread growth in the use of digital computers, there has been an increasing need for man to be able to communicate with machines in a manner more naturally suited to humans. The realization of this need has motivated a great deal of research in automatic recognition of speech by computer.[1–3] Although only a moderate degree of success has been obtained in solving the problems associated with machine recognition of continuous speech,[4] a greater degree of success has been obtained in recognition of isolated words from a fixed vocabulary. The performance of these systems range from about 92 percent correct decisions for 561 isolated words by an individual for which the system has been carefully trained[5] to nearly error-free performance for the recognition of a limited vocabulary (e.g., the digits) also spoken by a speaker for which the system has been trained.[6] However, performance of many of these word-recognition algorithms is radically degraded when the system has not been tuned to the speech characteristics of the individual user. The subject of this paper is an isolated-word, digit-recognition system that achieves high accuracy without having to be trained every time a different speaker wishes to use the system.

The development of a speaker-independent limited-vocabulary word recognizer is inherently more difficult than a speaker-adaptive system that can use comparatively simple pattern-matching algorithms to recognize the input words. It has been argued that the extended effort needed to design a speaker-independent system is unnecessary in view of the relative ease of training an adaptive scheme to learn to recognize the speech of a new user. There are two major reasons why such arguments are invalid. For small vocabulary systems (e.g., digit recognizers) with a *large number* of potential users, it is not feasible to store training data for every possible user. Furthermore, most systems cannot train themselves on new speakers very rapidly. Thus, the turnaround time for new users is often a major factor limiting the use of speaker-dependent systems. For a large vocabulary (250 words), the time required for a new speaker to form reference patterns for all the words in the vocabulary can be prohibitive. In addition, the variation with time of a speaker's voice characteristics may necessitate frequent updating of his reference patterns. Finally, the design of a speaker-adaptive word-recognition algorithm is so dependent on the uniqueness of each talker that very little insight is gained in the actual problem of recognizing speech. On the other hand, it is hoped that the development of a speaker-independent scheme will contribute to an understanding of the acoustic attributes of speech that reliably distinguish the various sounds. Without such an understanding, it would be difficult to duplicate the human capacity of recognizing the speech of a wide variety of speakers.

This paper discusses a speaker-independent digit-recognition system that was implemented on the computer facility of the acoustics research department at Bell Laboratories. Section II discusses the basic speech parameters that are measured and shows how the digits can be classified from these features in a speaker-independent manner. This section includes a discussion of the various signal-processing techniques that are heavily relied on throughout the classification process. Section III discusses the digit-classification scheme. The classification procedure is a tree-like decision algorithm for which backwards tracing is allowed when one of the parallel-decision algorithms indicates a high probability of error. Section IV gives the results of a formal evaluation of the recognition system. Finally, the paper concludes with a discussion of the strong and weak points of the system and suggestions for how it can be improved.

II. FRAMEWORK OF THE RECOGNITION SYSTEM

Figure 1 is a block diagram of the overall digit recognition system that was implemented. Following endpoint alignment in which the

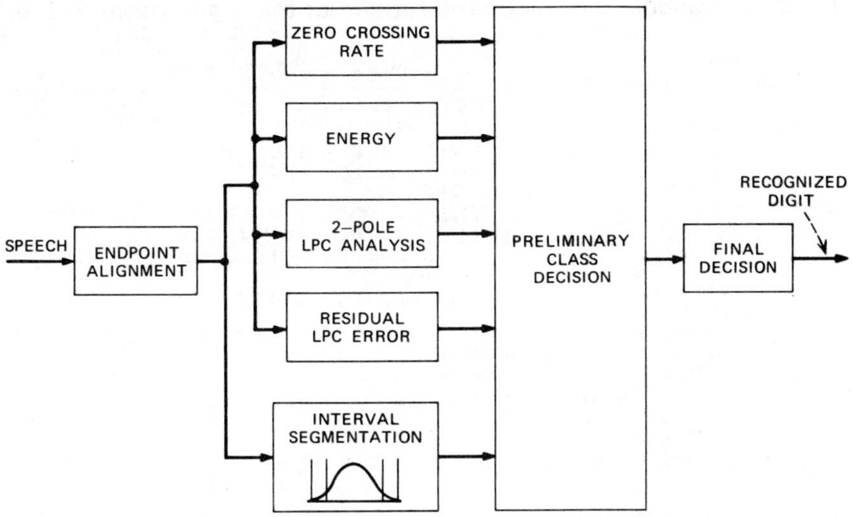

Fig. 1—Block diagram of the overall digit recognition system.

interval containing the word to be recognized is carefully determined, the speech is analyzed every 10 ms to obtain zero-crossing rate, energy, two-pole model linear-predictive-coding (LPC) coefficients, and the residual LPC estimation error. To aid in making preliminary classification decisions, the speech interval is segmented into three well-defined regions. All the speech information is fed in parallel into a preliminary decision-making algorithm that chooses one of several possible digit classes for the input utterance—e.g., one class contains the digits 1 and 9. A final decision is then made based on the presence or absence of certain key features in the input speech.

In this section, we show how the various digits can be characterized in terms of certain acoustic features. Then we discuss some key signal-processing functions that are heavily relied on in the decision algorithms and that contribute strongly to making the system speaker-independent.

2.1 Characterization of the digits

The elemental speech units (phonemes) that comprise English words can be classified into two broad categories, vowels and consonants. The vowels can be further classified into front (/i/, /I/, /e/, /ɛ/, and /ae/), middle (/ɝ/, /ʌ/), and back vowels (/u/, /U/, /ɔ/, and /o/). It is also convenient to subdivide the consonants into the categories noise-like (fricatives, plosives) and vowel-like (nasals, glides). Table I gives a list of the sequence of phoneme categories for each of the ten

Table I — Sound classes characteristic of the digits (from Ref. 6)

Digit	Sequence of Sound Classes
0	VNLC → FV → VLC → BV
1	VLC → MV → VLC
2	UVNLC → FV → BV
3	UVNLC → VLC → FV
4	UVNLC → BV → MV
5	UVNLC → MV → FV → VNLC
6	UVNLC → FV → UVNLC
7	UVNLC → FV → VNLC → FV → VLC
8	FV → UVNLC
9	VLC → MV → FV → VLC

VNLC = Voiced, noise-like consonant.
UVNLC = Unvoiced, noise-like consonant.
VLC = Vowel-like consonant.
FV = Front vowel.
MV = Middle vowel.
BV = Back vowel.

digits, 0 through 9.[6] Our approach toward speaker-independent recognition of the digits is to use a set of robust measurements to classify the phonemes into the six broad categories listed in Table I. By robust measurements, we mean acoustic parameters that give a general indication of the gross nature of each phoneme without being too dependent on the speaker's voice characteristics. Through a combination of parallel processing and self-normalization, the phoneme categories are determined and the spoken digit is recognized. We now discuss the criteria for the selection of the robust measurements that are used, the technique of self-normalization of measurements, and finally the method of parallel-processing of the data to give a speaker independent classification of the digits.

2.2 Robust measurements for digit recognition

The requirements for a recognition parameter to be selected as being a robust measurement are:

(*i*) The parameter can be simply and unambiguously measured.
(*ii*) The parameter can be used to grossly characterize a large proportion of speech sounds.
(*iii*) The parameter can be conveniently interpreted in a speaker-independent manner.

Based on the above requirements, the zero-crossing-rate and spectral-energy parameters are excellent candidates for robust measurements. These parameters can be used to effectively characterize the general acoustic properties of the sound categories listed in Table I. For example, noise-like sounds have a relatively high zero-crossing rate, relatively low energy, and a relatively high concentration of high-frequency energy. Thus, the noise-like sounds of any speaker can be characterized quite accurately based on these measurements. The term "relatively," in the above classification of noise-like sounds, can be conveniently interpreted for a given speaker by a simple self-normalization technique discussed later in this paper

To measure the distribution of spectral energy, a two-pole LPC analysis has been suggested by Makhoul and Wolf[7] as an excellent means of representing the gross features of the spectrum. Figure 2 (from Makhoul and Wolf[7]) shows the results of applying a two-pole model to a variety of speech sounds. This figure is a comparison of the spectra of several speech sounds obtained directly from FFT spectrum measurements compared with the spectra of the best two-pole LPC fit to the spectrum. For a two-pole LPC analysis, there is either one complex-conjugate pole or two real poles. In Fig. 2a, the spectra for the sound /sh/ as in the word "short" are plotted. For this example, the two-pole LPC analysis gives a complex conjugate pole at about 3000

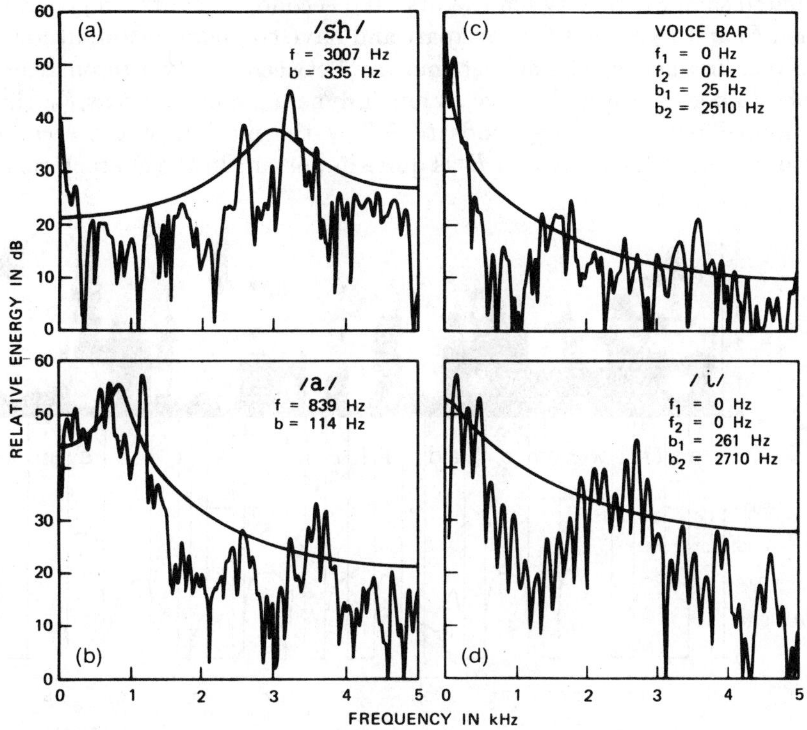

Fig. 2—Comparison of FFT spectra and two-pole LPC spectra for several speech sounds.

DIGIT-RECOGNITION SYSTEM

Hz—i.e., the region of maximum energy concentration in the spectrum. In Fig. 2b, similar results are shown for the vowel /a/ where the major concentration of energy in the spectrum is around 800 Hz. In the examples of Figs. 2c and 2d (a voice bar and the vowel /i/), the major concentration of spectral energy is around 0 Hz; thus, the two-pole LPC analysis gives two real poles in the right-half z-plane. From Fig. 2, it can be seen that the computed pole frequency gives a good indication of the location of the dominant portion of the spectral energy of the sound and can thus be effectively used to characterize sounds with relatively high-frequency or low-frequency concentrations of energy. For example, noise-like sounds are characterized by a relatively high-frequency spectral concentration of energy, while nasals and vowels generally have a much lower frequency for the energy concentration.

Figure 3 (also from Makhoul and Wolf[7]) illustrates the dynamic behavior of the computed pole frequency of the two-pole model and the corresponding spectrogram of the utterance, "Has anyone measured nickel concentrations · · · ." Examination of Figs. 2 and 3 shows that, for vowel-like sounds, the computed pole frequency is invariably situated somewhere between the first and second formants. In general, when F_1 and F_2 are not too far apart and have comparable amplitudes, the pole frequency falls almost midway between the two resonances. Since F_1 does not usually have as much dynamic movement as F_2, the computed pole frequency tends to follow the motion of the second formant. Since the motion of F_2 is quite important in the characteriza-

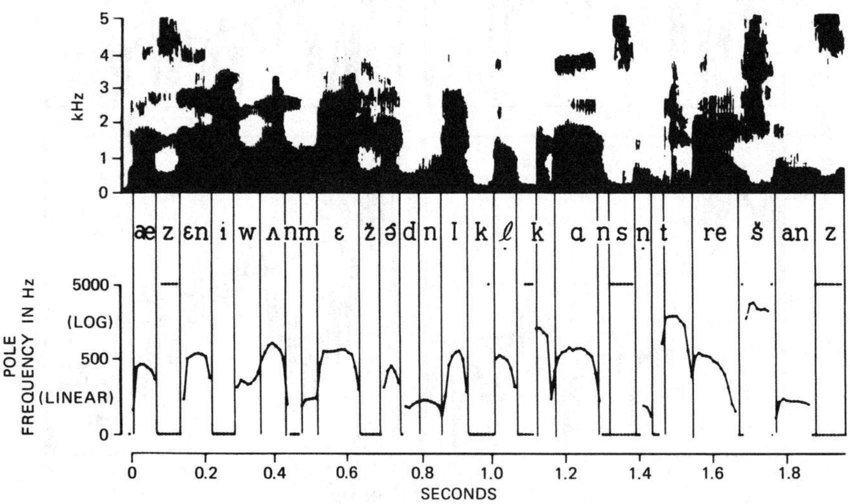

Fig. 3—Spectrogram and computed pole-frequency of two-pole LPC model for the utterance, "Has anyone measured nickel concentrations · · ·."

tion of the digits, the ability of the two-pole LPC analysis to track this motion has been used in the classification phase of the digit-recognition system.

It should be noted, however, that when either F_1 and F_2 are sufficiently far apart or the amplitude of F_1 is significantly greater than the amplitude of F_2, the pole frequency will either follow F_1 or result in two positive real poles. Figure 3 shows that, during the /i/ in the word "anyone," the pole frequency begins to dip sharply as the separation between F_1 and F_2 grows greater and finally results in positive real axis poles as the separation reaches some critical threshold. For nasal sounds, the energy is so highly concentrated near the first resonance that the two-pole model usually results in positive real axis poles, as seen in Fig. 3.

In addition to using the computed pole frequency as a measure of the location of dominant spectral energy and a characterization of the dynamic movement of F_2, the normalized error of the two-pole model contains important information about the spread of spectral energy. The normalized or residual error is defined as

$$V = 1 - a_1 r_1 - a_2 r_2,$$

where a_1 and a_2 are the two-pole LPC coefficients and r_1 and r_2 are the normalized autocorrelation coefficients. It can be shown that the more concentrated the energy spectrum, the lower the normalized error.[8] For speech sounds, the relative magnitude of the normalized error generally increases from sonorants to vowels and then to fricatives. Within the three vowel types, the back vowels have the lowest relative normalized error and the front vowels have the highest. By observing the relative changes in the pole frequency and normalized error, important information about the structure of the voiced region of the word can be obtained. An example of the usefulness of the pole parameter in specifying the speech sounds comprising the digits is given in the next section.

In summary, a reasonable set of robust measurements that have been implemented for this digit recognition algorithm is as follows:

(*i*) *Zero crossing rate*, which is defined as the number of zero crossings in a fixed frame length (on the order of 10 ms).
(*ii*) *Energy*, which is defined as the sum of the squared values of the speech waveform in a given frame.
(*ii*) *Normalized error* obtained from a two-pole LPC analysis of a given speech frame.
(*iv*) *Pole frequency* (or frequencies) obtained from a two-pole LPC analysis of a given speech frame.

DIGIT-RECOGNITION SYSTEM

2.3 Self-normalization of parameters

Almost all classification algorithms use some set of threshold levels in the decision process. Using a fixed set of thresholds leads to a large number of problems for speech recognition in that many of the thresholds are speaker- or time-dependent. To eliminate this difficulty, the technique of self-normalization of parameters was used in which many of the most significant thresholds were obtained from measurements made directly on the speech sample being recognized. Thus, for example, in the case of setting thresholds on zero-crossing rate to determine whether a sound is noise-like or nasal, a statistical description of the zero-crossing rate (ZCR) was made for the entire utterance. The statistical description consisted of measuring the mean of the ZCR and its standard deviation over the region of strong energy (i.e., the region where the energy exceeded 10 percent of the maximum energy of the utterance). Based on ZCR measurements, one criterion for classifying a segment as noise-like was if its ZCR exceeded a level one standard deviation *above* the mean during the segment. Figure 4 shows the ZCR measurements for the word "seven." Indicated in this figure are the average ZCR and a range of one standard deviation around this average. During the initial /s/, the ZCR is significantly above the threshold, as anticipated.

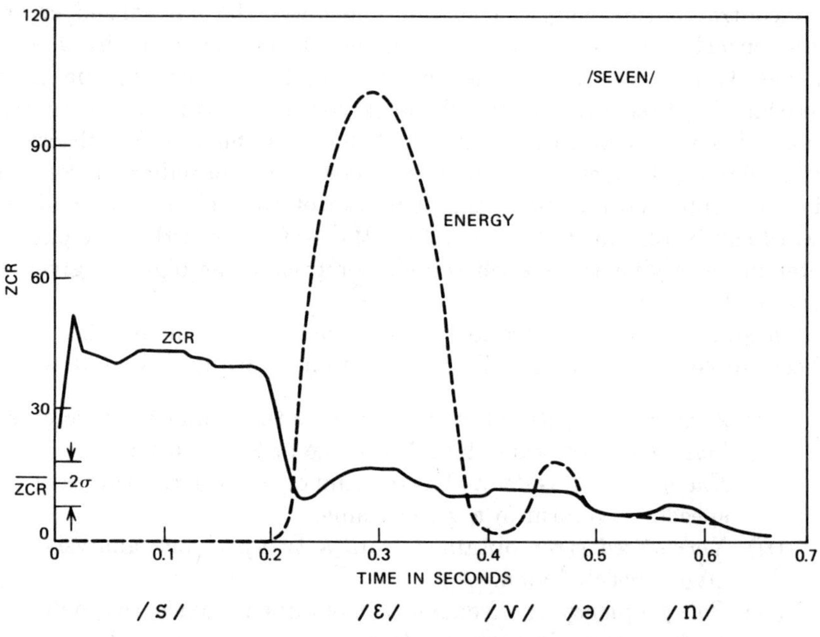

Fig. 4—Energy and ZCR for one example of the word "seven."

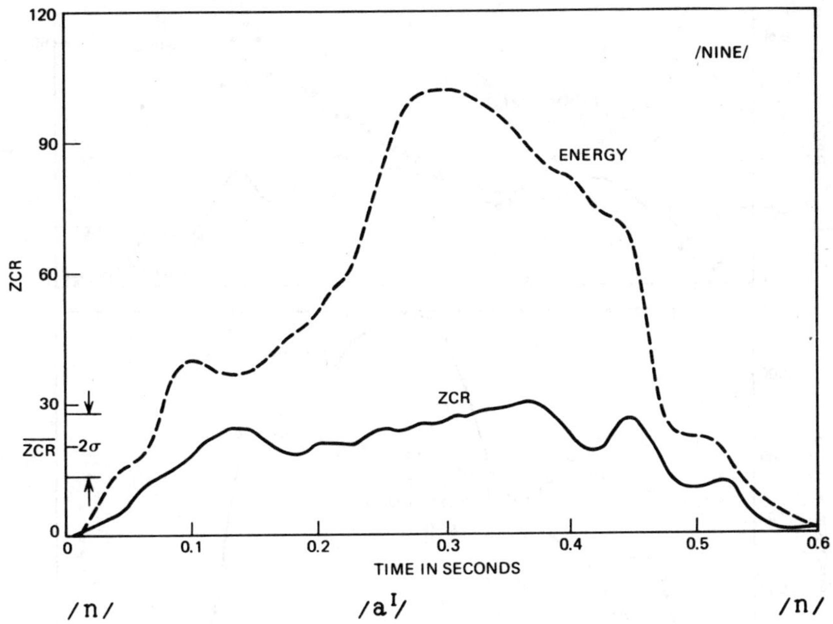

Fig. 5—Energy and ZCR for one example of the word "nine."

In much the same manner, a self-normalized ZCR threshold can be set for classifying a segment as a nasal-like sound. In such cases, the ZCR generally falls below a level one standard deviation *below* the average ZCR for the utterance. As an example, Fig. 5 shows the measured ZCR for the word "nine" and gives the spread of ZCR around the average value. For the initial and final nasals, the ZCR is much lower than the average and thus is a good indication of the nasals.

The idea of determining thresholds based on measurements made during the course of the utterance being recognized can be used for any or all measurements described in the preceding section. For example, Fig. 6 shows the two-pole model normalized error and the pole frequency for the word "nine." The nasal sections are clearly characterized by low normalized error and a zero-Hertz pole frequency. In contrast, Fig. 7 shows the same measurements for the word "six." Again, the noise-like sections are clearly depicted by the relatively high values of normalized error, pole frequency, and ZCR.

The transitional nature of the normalized error and pole frequency can be used to classify the vowels into types high, middle, and back. Figure 8 shows the normalized error and pole frequency throughout the word "two." After the frication region, which is marked by high normalized error and low energy, the normalized error uniformly

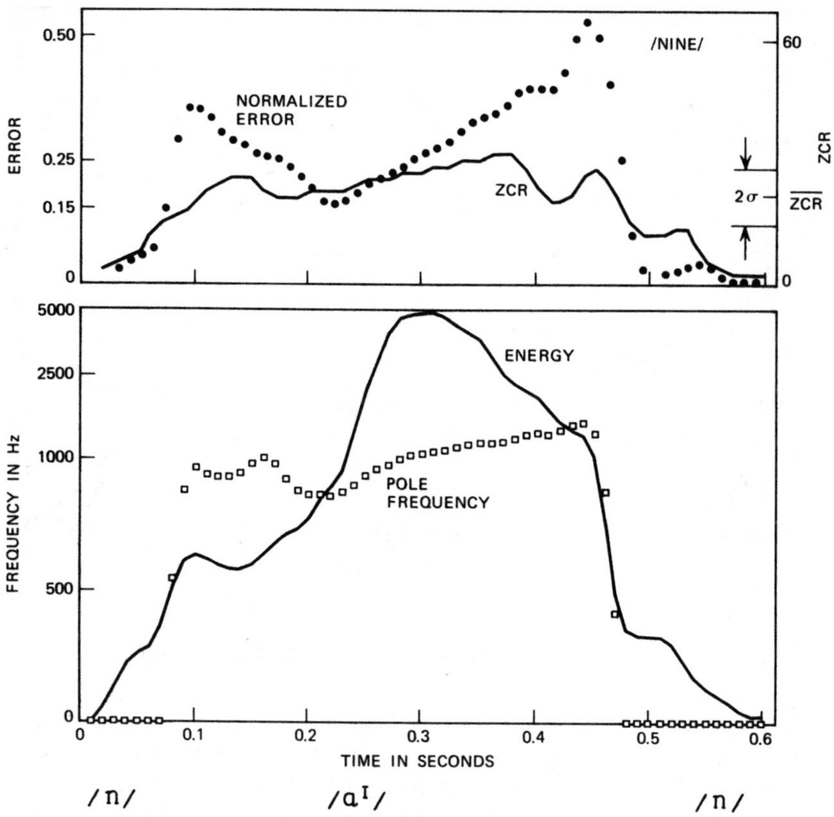

Fig. 6—Complete set of measurements for one example of the word "nine."

decreases. The decrease in the normalized error is due to the fact that the vowel nature changes from front (because of the /t/) to back. Thus, without specifying any absolute thresholds, the constituent structure of the voiced section of the word can be obtained by noting the relative changes in the normalized error. As described earlier, changes in the pole frequency can also be used to indicate the constituent vocalic structure. As seen in Fig. 8, the pole frequency is continually decreasing throughout the voiced region in the word "two," thereby indicating a continually decreasing second formant. As another example, Fig. 9 shows the parameters for the word "four." The gradually increasing normalized error and pole frequency are indicative of a progression from a back vowel to a middle vowel.

2.4 Parallel processing

Using the self-normalization technique, each robust measurement can, by itself, classify a speech sound into one of the six broad categories

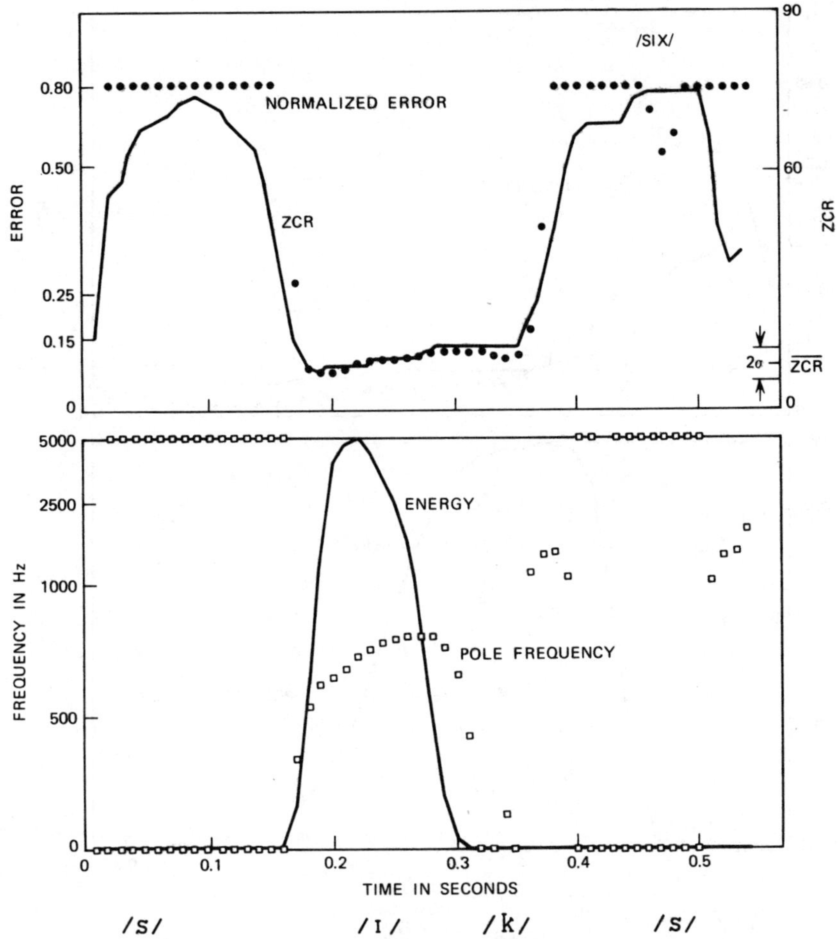

Fig. 7—Complete set of measurements for one example of the word "six."

of interest. Unfortunately, the classification will not be error-free; but if the results of all the measurements are "intelligently" pooled together, then the classification performance can be significantly enhanced. The operation of combining the measurements is termed parallel processing. Parallel-processing ideas have met with good success in other areas of speech processing.[9]

The idea of parallel processing as it is used here not only involves a suitable combination of the robust measurements but also the incorporation of certain structural constraints of the lexicon as additional input. For example, as seen in Fig. 9, the initial section of the word shows only a slight indication of the initial fricative /f/ (i.e., the high zero crossing and normalized error for the initial 10 to 20 ms of the

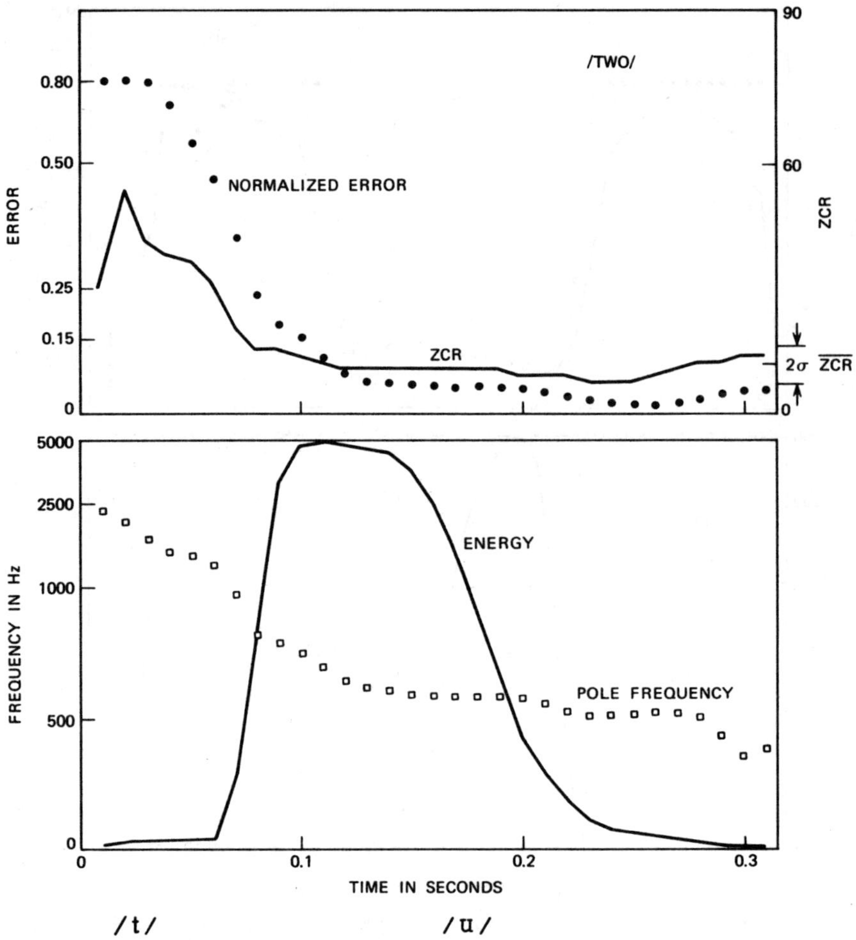

Fig. 8—Complete set of measurements for one example of the word "two."

word), and one might conclude that there is no frication. However, for the digits, it is known that only 1, 9, and 8 do not normally begin with frication. Since the ZCR, normalized error, and pole frequency are relatively too high for the digits 1 or 9, these digits can be safely omitted from consideration. In addition, a combination of the facts that the normalized error is low and increasing and that the pole frequency is increasing indicates that the voiced region in the word is more than likely composed of a back-type voiced sound followed by a middle-type voiced sound. Since the voiced section of the word "eight" is a front vowel sound, the odds are quite high that the word is not "eight." Additional evidence that the word is probably not "eight" can be

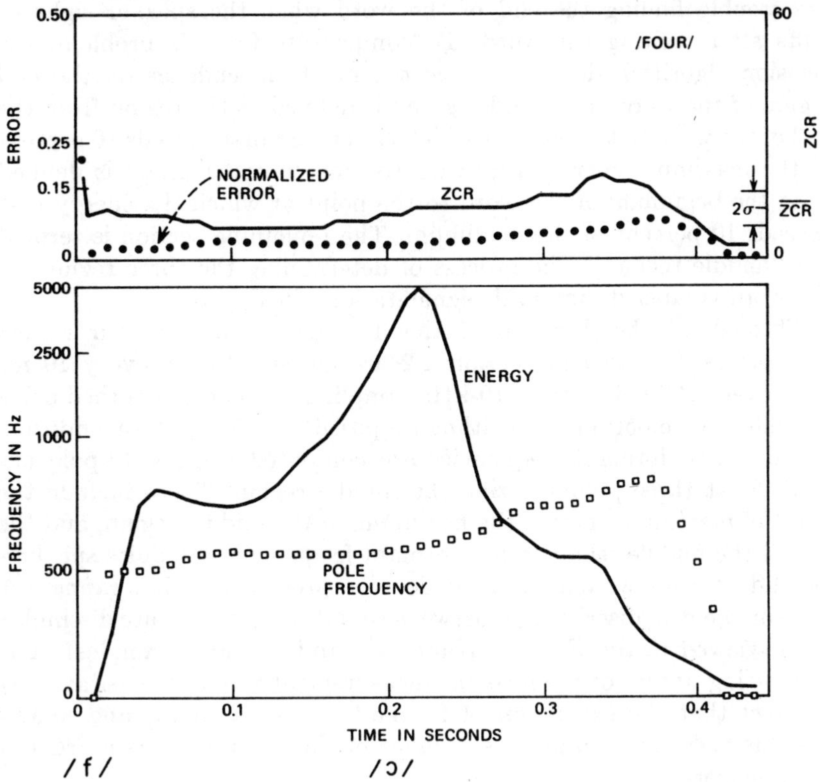

Fig. 9—Complete set of measurements for one example of the word "four."

obtained from the lack of a burst at the end of the spoken word. By pooling knowledge from the individual measurements with information about the structure of the words in the lexicon, the weak frication in the spoken "four" can be recognized. Thus, the major feature of parallel decisions is the ability to arrive at a correct decision even if one or more of the parallel inputs is in error. In the next section, we discuss the organization of the digit recognizer and the specific nature of the logic rules.

III. DIGIT RECOGNIZER

As seen from Fig. 1, the first step in the recognition scheme is the important problem of endpoint alignment (determining the location of the spoken word during the recording interval). The algorithm used in this scheme has been described by Rabiner and Sambur[10] and has been shown to give reasonably good results over a wide variety of speakers and background levels. However, the algorithm sometimes has trouble finding the end of the word when the speaker sighs or puffs after reciting the word. To compensate for this problem, the decision algorithm does not place too much dependence on the end region of the word. The "end region" is defined as the region from the end of the word to the point at which the energy first exceeds 10 percent of the maximum energy. Equivalently, an "initial region" is defined from the beginning of the word to the point at which the energy first exceeds 10 percent of the maximum. The remaining section is termed the "middle region." The process of determining the three regions of the word is labeled "interval segmentation" in Fig. 1.

Throughout the duration of the detected word, the four robust parameters discussed in Section 2.2 are measured once every 10 ms (i.e., every 100 points for a 10-kHz sampling rate) and smoothed using a nonlinear smoothing algorithm proposed by Tukey.[11] In addition, the first two formant frequencies are computed using a 12-pole LPC analysis at three points during the middle region. These include the point of maximum energy, the beginning of the middle region, and the end of the middle region. Since formant frequencies are quite speaker-dependent, they were used in the decision process only as a *supporting* measurement to discriminate between sounds that were quite dissimilar when viewed in the $F_1 - F_2$ plane (/i/ and /a/ are examples). The supporting nature of the formant measurement is also necessitated by the fact that the extraction of formants is not a simple and unambiguous task, and too great a reliance on these parameters is fraught with danger.

Following the measurement phase, a preliminary class decision is made for the utterance. An expanded view of the preliminary decision box is given in Fig. 10. The decision algorithm is in the form of a tree structure that traces down the most probable branch to arrive at the decided digit. However, it should be noted that there are provisions in the algorithm for back-tracking if some measurement strongly suggests that an error has been made.

The first branch in the tree is to decide whether or not the initial portion is nasal-like. As we discussed previously, this decision is based upon the fact that nasal-like sounds have relatively low ZCR, low normalized error, and low pole frequency. If a nasal-like beginning is detected, the preliminary choice is between 1 and 9. As a further check on this preliminary 1, 9 decision, the ending region is checked for nasal-like characteristics. If there is no evidence of initial nasal-like sounds, the digits 1 and 9 are removed from further consideration. When the initial region is deemed nasal-like, a relatively simple decision can be used to decide between 1 or 9. The digit 9 can be distin-

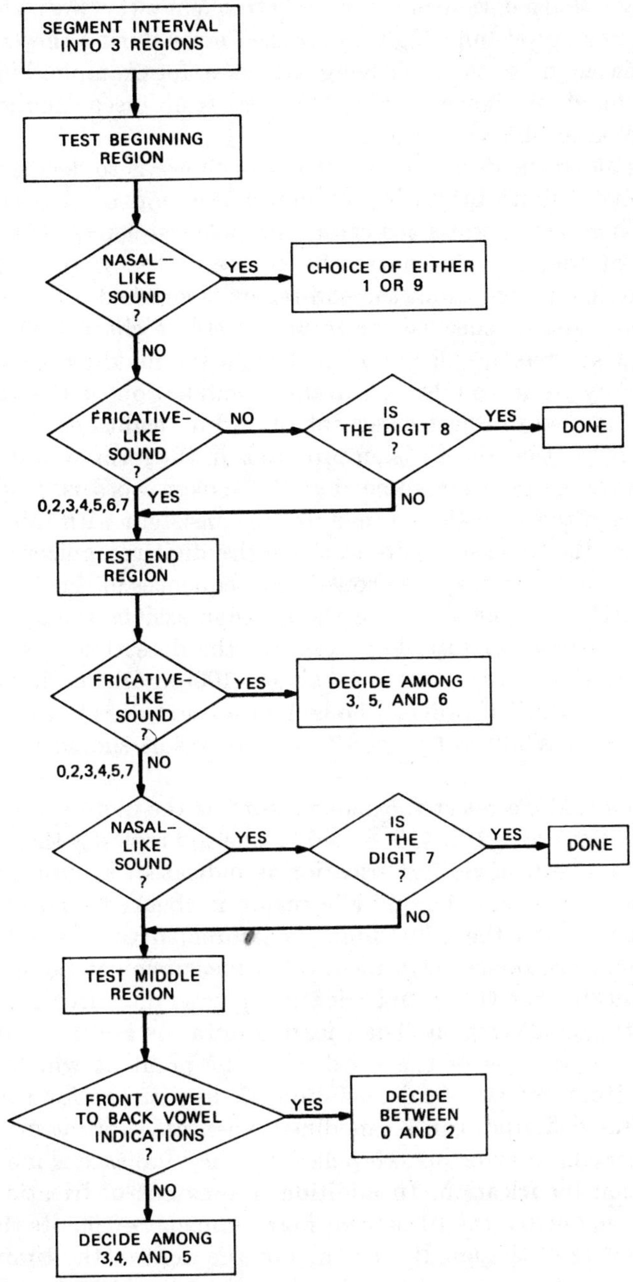

Fig. 10—Preliminary decision tree for digit classification algorithm.

DIGIT-RECOGNITION SYSTEM

guished by a sharp discontinuity in pole frequency (between the initial nasal and the vowel) and high normalized error during the transition from the nasal /n/ to the diphthong /aI/ (see, for example, Fig. 5). On the other hand, as shown in Fig. 11, there is no discontinuity at the end of the nasal-like section in 1.

Tracing along the decision tree, the next choice is to decide whether there is any definite indication of initial frication as shown by significantly high ZCR, normalized error, and pole frequency. The positive detection of frication eliminates the choice of the word "eight." If there is no definite frication, the end region is checked for a burst and the middle region is checked for front vowel-like characteristics. The formant parameters are also used to check if the middle region is composed of only front vowels. A suitable combination of the results of these tests is used to reject or accept the word "eight" as the digit. It should be noted that the decision process is in the form of a hypothesis test. In other words, we assume that the spoken word is "eight" and check to see if the acoustic parameters are consistent with this hypothesis. In fact, the basic structure of the entire digit recognizer is to first hypothesize and then test the acoustic consequences of this hypothesis. The parallel processing aspect of the decision assigns the appropriate weight to a particular test. For example, the detection of a burst at this point in the decision tree is an almost 100-percent indication that the word is "eight." However, the lack of a burst does not necessarily preclude the possibility of "eight," and this result should be weighed accordingly.

Assuming that we reject the spoken word as the digit 8, the remaining possibilities are 0, 2, 3, 4, 5, 6, and 7. The end region is then checked for fricative-like behavior. If frication is indicated, a hypothesis test on the digit 6 is made. The middle region is checked for front vowel characteristics, and the only timing measurement in the entire digit recognition program is performed. This measurement compares the relative duration of the initial frication plus ending frication to the length of the middle region. The frication duration is defined from the beginning (or ending) of the word until the point at which the ZCR remains within one standard deviation of the average for three time frames. This definition can be modified when any abrupt discontinuities in normalized error or two-pole frequency indicate a more probable location for frication. In addition, the extent of frication is not allowed to go beyond the 10-percent maximum energy points that form the boundaries of the middle region. For the digit 6, the timing ratio should be less than one and the middle region should be less than 250 ms. A combination of the results of the hypothesis test are used to verify that the spoken word was "six."

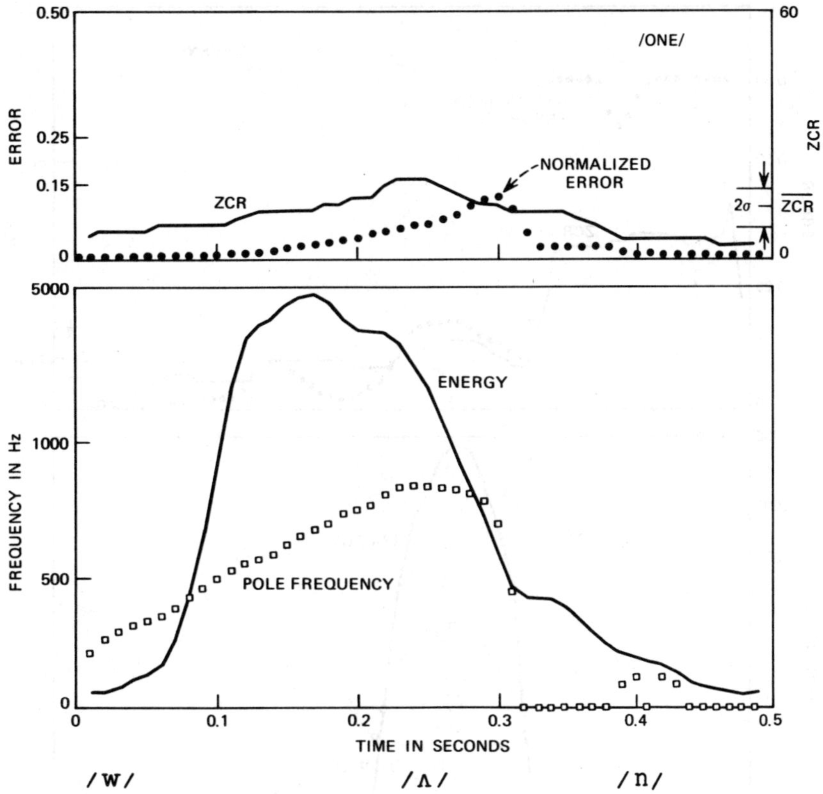

Fig. 11—Complete set of measurements for one example of the word "one."

If no frication is indicated during the ending region, a test for nasal-like behavior is made. If this test is positive, then a hypothesis test of the digit 7 is made. From Fig. 12, we can see that ZCR, two-pole frequency, and energy dip sharply during the consonant /v/. The hypothesis test consists of verifying these dips and checking the vowel characteristics on either side of the dip. Again, the combined output of the test determines whether to reject or accept 7.

If the digits 6 and 7 are eliminated from consideration, the middle region is analyzed to ascertain its structure. The preliminary analysis is achieved by noting the relative change in normalized error. If the normalized error increases, then the structure is characterized as an initial back vowel to a middle or front vowel. Thus, for increasing normalized error, the digits 3, 4, and 5 are considered the most likely. The relative change in the three-second formant measurements are used as supporting evidence to confirm the structure. For the digits

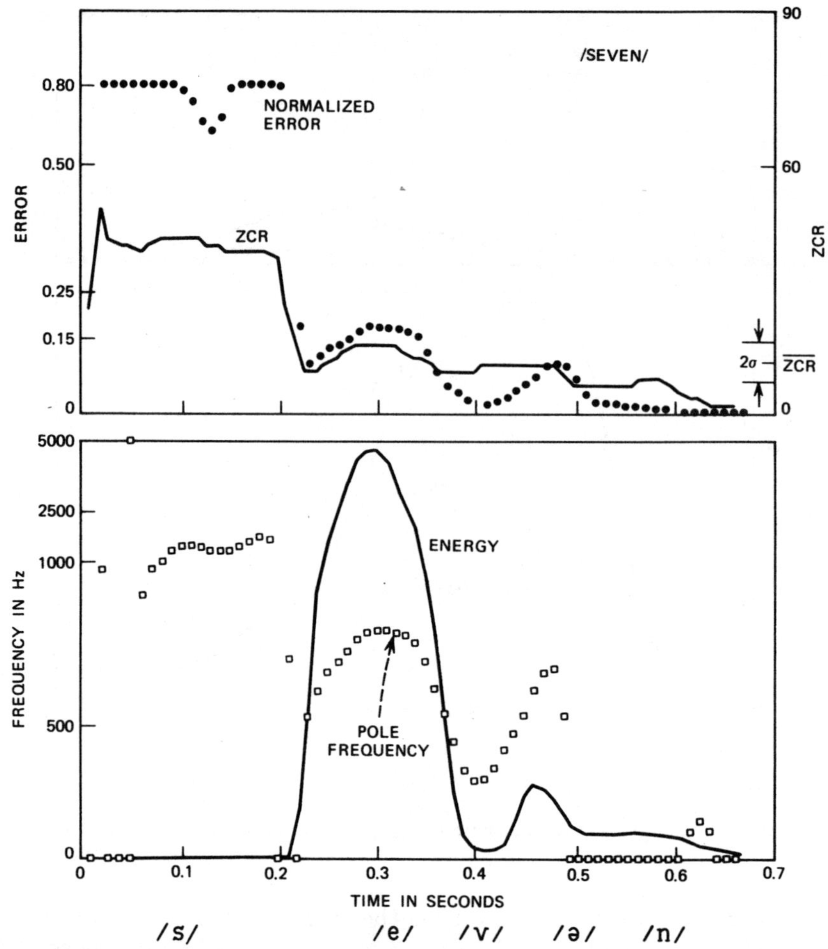

Fig. 12—Complete set of measurements for one example of the word "seven."

3, 4, and 5, F_2 should be increasing. The final decision among the possibilities 3, 4, and 5 is easily achieved on the basis of the robust parameters and formant measurements.

If the normalized error decreases during the middle region, the digits 0 and 2 are then the most probable choices. A decreasing F_2 helps support these choices. To decide between 0 and 2, a dip detector program is used to discover the presence of the sonorant /r/ as depicted by a slight dip in pole frequency, normalized error, and energy. Figure 13 shows the typical dip behavior for these parameters during the spoken 0. The presence (or absence) of a dip is checked with other measurements to verify the final decision.

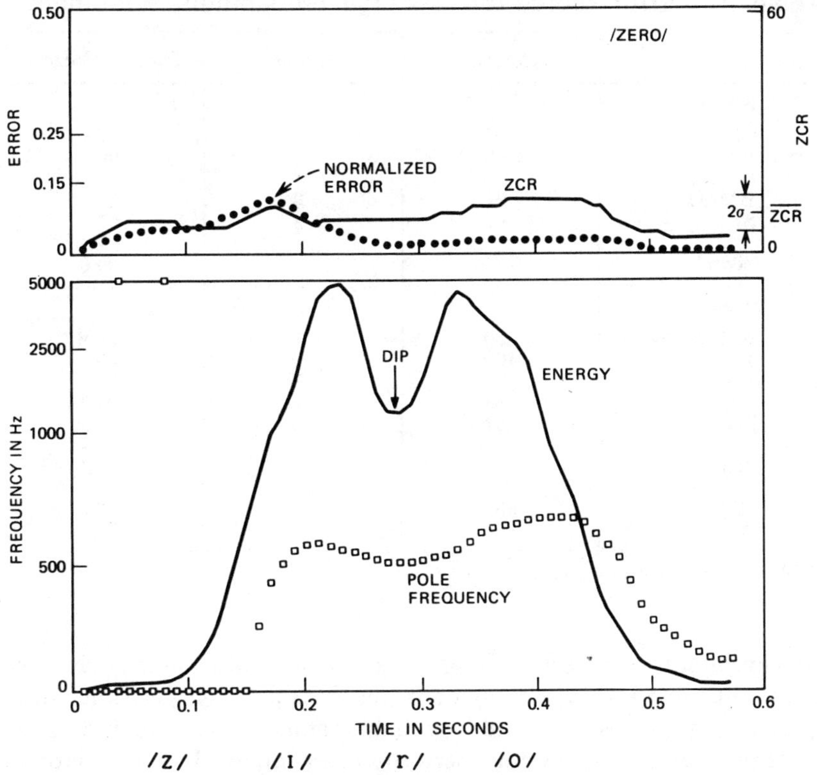

Fig. 13—Complete set of measurements for one example of the word "zero."

IV. EXPERIMENTAL RESULTS

The experimental test of the digit recognizer was conducted in two parts. The first part consisted of 10 speakers (five women and five men) who each made 10 complete recordings of the 10 digits. The recording sessions were spaced over a five-week period to include the effects of time variation in the testing. The recordings were made in a quiet room with a high-quality microphone. The decision algorithm was not designed for the characteristics of each particular speaker, so as to give a true test of the speaker-independent nature of the scheme. The results of this experiment are shown in Table II. The average error rate is 2.7 percent.

A confusion matrix for each of the 100 tests of each digit is presented in Table III. The confusion matrix indicates that all occurrences of initial frication were correctly detected by the decision algorithm. In only 6 out of 200 examples of the digits 1 and 9 was the initial nasal-

Table II — Error scores for first digit recognition experiment

	Correct	Wrong	Percent Correct
Women			
SK	97	3	97
KD	96	4	96
CMcG	96	4	96
BMcD	97	3	97
SP	97	3	97
Total			96.6
Men			
MS*	89	1	98.8
LR	100	0	100
RS	97	3	97
AR*	88	2	97.7
JH	97	3	97
Total			98.1
Sum	954	26	97.3

* Missed one recording session.

like consonant incorrectly determined. The confusion matrix also shows that most errors were made in the final detailed decision. More sophisticated processing would probably enhance the final decision and thereby make the system performance compatible with adaptive schemes.

Table III — Confusion matrix for first digit recognition experiment

		Word Spoken									
		0	1	2	3	4	5	6	7	8	9
Word Recognized	0	93	0	3	0	0	1	0	0	0	1
	1	0	96	0	0	0	0	0	0	0	0
	2	2	0	90	1	0	0	0	1	0	1
	3	2	0	2	97	0	0	1	0	0	2
	4	0	1	2	0	97	1	0	0	0	0
	5	0	0	0	0	0	96	0	0	0	1
	6	0	0	0	0	0	0	97	0	0	0
	7	1	0	0	0	1	0	0	97	0	0
	8	0	0	1	0	0	0	0	0	98	0
	9	0	1	0	0	0	0	0	0	0	93
Individual Errors		5	2	8	1	1	2	1	1	0	5
Total—26 errors out of 980 utterances											

Table IV — Distribution of errors for the second digit recognition experiment

	Number of Digits Incorrect			Total Percent Correct
	0	1	2	
Female (30)	11	15	4	92.3
Male (25)	17	8	0	96.8
Total (55)	28	23	4	94.4

To ensure the validity of these experimental results, another more challenging test was conducted. In this experiment, 55 speakers (30 women and 25 men) were selected at random and asked to give one rendition of the 10 digits. Instead of using a high-quality microphone in a quiet environment, the input speech was taken from a close-talking microphone alongside a chattering Teletypewriter. The decision was performed on-line, and the speaker was only instructed when to say each digit. The results for this experiment show an average error rate of 5.6 percent. In addition, no speaker tested did worse than 2 out of 10 wrong. The distribution of errors for this experiment is shown in Table IV. The distribution matrix indicates the generally good performance of the system.

It should be noted that there was no effort in our experimentation to select speakers with good diction. The speakers represent dialects from most of the regions in the U.S. In informal on-line demonstrations of the system, many non-American speakers (French, Japanese, Indian, German) tried having their English-pronounced digits recognized. The informal results were in good agreement with the other experiments. In addition, an informal attempt to "beat" the system by holding one's nose or using falsetto also proved generally unsuccessful.

V. DISCUSSION

The digit-recognition system that has been described in this paper can be considered as a first pass in the direction of speaker-independent speech recognition. Our approach has been to describe a variety of speech sounds in terms of a set of robust measurements. We then devised a tree-structured decision algorithm that used these measurements to characterize the acoustic features of the presented word. The sequence of branches in the tree was designed to resolve the most obvious sounds and then proceed to the more difficult decisions. Thus, the relatively easy problem of distinguishing between noise-like sounds and nasal-like sounds was attacked first, and the determination of the vowel-like constituents was then determined. The output of the preliminary decision tree was a small subset of the 10 possible digits that almost invariably included the spoken word. The major portion of the errors in the system were made in the box labeled "final decision" in Fig. 1.

The preliminary decision tree (Fig. 10) incorporated some original ideas about self-normalization that effectively eliminated the need for tuning the system to the characteristics of a given speaker. Such a decision tree can be extended to prune down a much larger lexicon and arrive at a small list of possible choices. Improvements in the method of selection within the list of possibilities could lead to speaker-independent systems that can truly compete with the performance of adaptive schemes. Such improvements could result by incorporating more sophisticated probabilistic methods into the framework of the "hypothesize-verify" technique proposed in this paper.

Our goal in the development of the digit-recognition system is to show that speaker-independent digit recognition is possible through an intelligent description of broad categories of speech sounds. This description uses what is known about the *necessary* characteristics of each category instead of blindly using pattern-matching algorithms to rigidly quantify the sounds. The later approach is doomed to failure for a large enough speaker population because it overlooks the fact that the information in the patterns contain as much personal information as linguistic information.

REFERENCES

1. Proceedings IEEE Symposium on Speech Recognition, Carnegie-Mellon University, April 1974.
2. Proceedings 1972 Conference on Speech Communication and Processing, April 1972.
3. A. Newell et al., *Speech Understanding Systems*, Springfield, Va.: National Technical Information Service, May 1971.
4. R. Reddy et al., "Working Papers in Speech Recognition," Carnegie-Mellon University, April 1972.
5. P. Vicens, "Aspects of Speech Recognition by Computer," Ph.D. thesis, Stanford University, April 1969.
6. T. B. Martin, "Acoustic Recognition of a Limited Vocabulary in Continuous Speech," Ph.D. thesis, University of Pennsylvania, 1970.
7. J. Makhoul and J. Wolf, "The Use of a Two-Pole Linear Prediction Model in Speech Recognition," Report 2537, Cambridge, Mass.: Bolt, Beranek and Newman, Inc., September 1973.
8. J. Makhoul and J. Wolf, "Linear Prediction and the Spectral Analysis of Speech," Report 2304, Cambridge, Mass.: Bolt, Beranek and Newman, Inc., August 1972.
9. B. Gold and L. R. Rabiner, "Parallel Processing Techniques for Estimating Pitch Periods of Speech in the Time Domain," J. Acoust. Soc. Am., *46*, No. 2 (August 1969), pp. 442–448.
10. L. R. Rabiner and M. R. Sambur, "An Algorithm for Determining the Endpoints of Isolated Utterances," to be published in B.S.T.J., *54*, No. 2 (February 1975).
11. J. W. Tukey, "Nonlinear (Nonsuperposable) Methods for Smoothing Data," 1974 EASCON Record, p. 673.

Practical Applications of Voice Input to Machines

THOMAS B. MARTIN, MEMBER, IEEE

Abstract—**Voice input to machine is the most natural form of man-machine communications. In this type of system the machine responds to the mode of communications preferred by the user, rather than vice versa. Many practical applications exist today for limited capability voice input systems. The first operational voice input systems have taken place with limited vocabulary, isolated word voice input systems. Most of these initial systems were for industrial applications in which the users' hands or eyes were already busy with their normal work requirements. Future developments in both new applications and increased capability voice input systems can be expected to considerably expand the usage of this form of man-machine communications.**

I. Introduction

SPEECH RECOGNITION is the ultimate step towards simplifying communications between man and machine. It is the process whereby a human operator can use ordinary spoken commands that can be recognized and interpreted by an automatic speech recognition (ASR) system. Historically, man's communications with machines or computers have been according to the operational requirements of the machine. To control machines or computers required learning the "language" of the machine or the manipulation of special dials or keys in the proper sequence and format. Any deviation from this unnatural machine language produced errors which were not easily detectable because of the complexities of the rules for man-machine communications.

The development of limited capability voice recognition systems has made it possible for the first time for humans to "talk" information directly into a computer, with no intermediate keying or handwritten steps involved, or to control mechanical systems with voice commands. Input to machines is simplified since the operator provides instructions in his natural language. The machine, therefore, adapts to the requirements of the human and greatly simplifies the task of man-machine communications.

The purpose of this paper is to describe practical limited vocabulary recognition systems. The discussion will be narrowed to a consideration of operational performance capabilities that can be achieved with limited-vocabulary ASR systems and of what practical value are such systems. It is hoped that this discussion will provide a base line of insight upon which future developments can be referenced.

Manuscript received August 1, 1975; revised September 19, 1975.
The author is with the Threshold Technology, Inc., Delran, NJ 08075.

II. Types of Voice Recognition Systems

All ASR systems can be considered as belonging to one of two categories: continuous (connected) speech systems or isolated (discrete) speech systems. The differences between these two types of systems can become obscure and overlapping when attempting to classify a particular approach as either isolated or continuous. Isolated speech systems can be defined as those systems that require a short pause before and after utterances that are to be recognized an entities.

The minimum duration of a pause that separates independent utterances is on the order of 100 ms. Anything shorter than 100 ms can be confused with the closure of stop consonants in the midst of continuous speech that can produce stop gaps approaching 100 ms in duration. In actuality, a stop gap can exceed a 100-ms duration. For example, the word "rapid" can be spoken with a relatively long silence interval after "ra-." For a cooperative speaker, however, a 100-ms minimum separation between words is a reasonable compromise value.

The speaking rate that can be achieved with isolated speech recognition systems is naturally much less than for connected

Reprinted from *Proc. IEEE*, vol. 64, pp. 487–501, Apr. 1976.

speech. Speaking rates over 300 words per minute can be achieved quite easily for short intervals of connected speech. The upper bound for an isolated word speaking rate has been measured informally for trained speakers reading digits in random order.[1] A rate of 120–125 digits/min was achieved with the best speakers. Each of the digits was classified correctly by a machine capable of recognizing isolated utterances. Measuring these rates is not possible without some objective measure that the words are not connected. The human ear is not a good judge of whether a brief pause actually exists between rapidly spoken words.

Average speaking rates between 30 and 70 isolated words (or phrases) have been achieved in factory environments by individuals using voice input systems during their entire 8-h working day, with the normal break for lunch. These average rates will include peak rates close to 120 words/min and lower than average rates during light workload requirements [24].

Another factor that should be mentioned concerns the duration of the utterances to be classified. A limited vocabulary system could be hypothesized in which each of the utterances in the limited vocabulary was of considerable duration. However, the limited vocabulary system described herein accepts isolated words and short phrases 2–4 s in duration [9].

III. Adaptation

One of the major obstacles to progress in the field of ASR is the variation in speech between individuals. Such differences have made the search for the "universal" speech recognizer a formidable task. A practical bypass of the problem can be achieved by adapting a recognition system to the characteristics of the user. Since interspeaker differences are far greater than intraspeaker differences, an order of magnitude of complexity can be eliminated by automatic speaker adaptation. It is for this reason that the first ASR systems to be used in practical applications have all employed speaker adaptation.

IV. Operational Considerations for Limited Vocabulary Applications

A. Noise Background

It is important to consider some of the practical aspects of a limited vocabulary speech recognition system intended for operational use. One of the first to be considered is interfering acoustical signals and noise background. If a system is to be used with a high-quality wide-ranging microphone, it will naturally pick up other sounds from within the immediate vicinity of the individual attempting to use the speech recognition system. There are two such solutions to this problem. The first solution is to remove the interfering sounds by placing the individual in an acoustically shielded environment. Should this be possible, noise backgrounds can be reduced generally to the point where they are noninterfering. However, the restrictions resulting from an acoustic enclosure are such that the mobility of the individual is reduced and can possibly eliminate any ability to perform any other functions. Many applications which are economically justifiable for a speech recognition system involve an individual who will do more than one function at a time. The purpose of the speech recognition system is to add to his capabilities or remove some of the overload on his manual or visual operations. Usually this type of an individual cannot be placed in a restrictive enclosure.

The second method of removing interfering sounds is to eliminate the noise at the microphone itself. Close-talking noise-cancelling microphones and contact microphones will both achieve a degree of noise cancellation. The contact microphone, however, does not pick up many of the attributes of the unvoiced frictional sounds. It is, therefore, a device which can be used only with a very limited capability speech recognizer. The contact microphone can also produce erroneous signals that are a result of body movement. Therefore, a close-talking noise-cancelling microphone worn on a lightweight headband or mounted in a handset is the optimum compromise between obtaining high-quality speech and reducing noise backgrounds.

B. Breath Noise

Once it is determined that a close-talking noise cancelling microphone is to be used for a speech recognizer, a very critical factor must be considered in the system. This factor relates to extraneous signals caused by breath noise. A highly trained speech researcher working in a laboratory will be able to pronounce distinct utterances to an automatic speech recognizer. Unconsciously he will control his breathing such that when he is producing the speech signal it is crisp and well pronounced. He can be lulled into a sense of false achievement until the first time an untrained speaker, having little or no interest in his work, speaks into the system with very poor results. A similar result will occur for an individual who is doing no physical movement whatsoever. This individual can achieve very high recognition accuracies on a particular system. However, once he begins to move around and perform other functions, recognition can deteriorate. The most likely cause for lower recognition accuracy in both cases is breathing noise. A strong tendency exists to exhale at the end of isolated words and to inhale at the beginning. Inhaling produces no significant direct air blast on the close-talking microphone, whereas exhaling can produce signal levels in a microphone comparable to speech levels. In a limited vocabulary, isolated word recognition system, the breath noise can be a serious problem.

Shown in Fig. 1 is a well-pronounced isolated utterance and a logically derived word boundary signal. Regardless of the method used for determining the word boundary it is very important that the actual beginning and ending of the word are determined. Accurate word boundary determination is the single most critical factor in an isolated word or phrase recognition system. Gross inaccuracies in word boundary detection can occur because of breath noise as shown in Fig. 2. The detrimental effects caused by the incorrect word boundary indication because of breath noise can be somewhat overcome by backing up a constant amount from a tentative initial word boundary indication. This is not a total solution, however, since many times the duration of the breath noise is longer than the speech signal and of comparable magnitude. Furthermore, the spectrum of the breath signal overlaps the spectrum where significant speech information occurs. In order to achieve recognition accuracies in a practical operational system equivalent to or superior to those rates obtainable with keying, it is necessary to separate speech from breath noise, regardless of the duration and magnitude of the breath noise. This can be achieved only by utilizing pattern recognition processing which discriminates between speech sounds (voice or unvoiced) and the frictional breath noises. The back-up duration will then be of a variable duration, depending on the duration of the breath noise.

[1] Tests conducted by author.

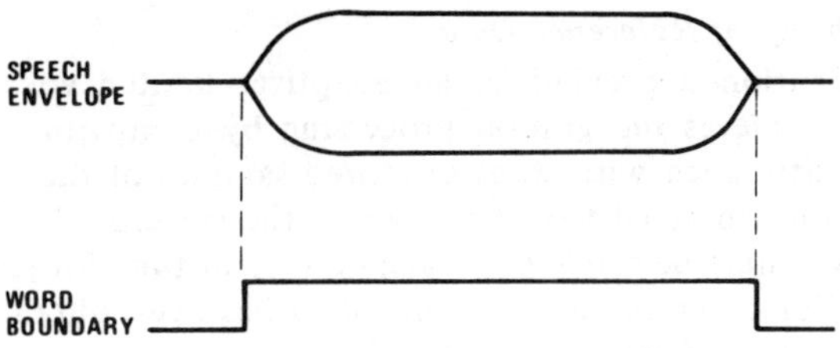

Fig. 1. High-quality speech.

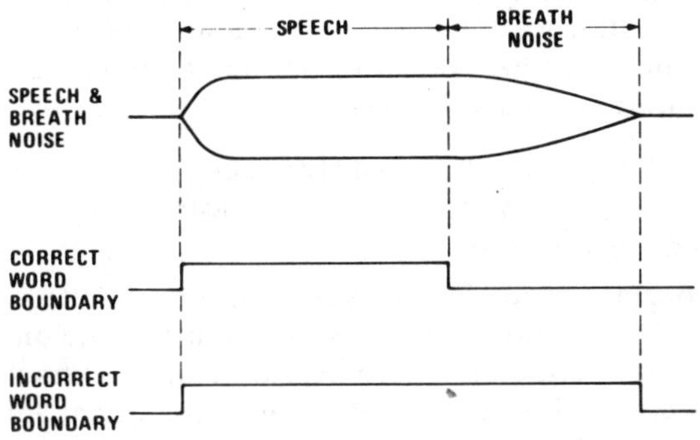

Fig. 2. Speech and breathing.

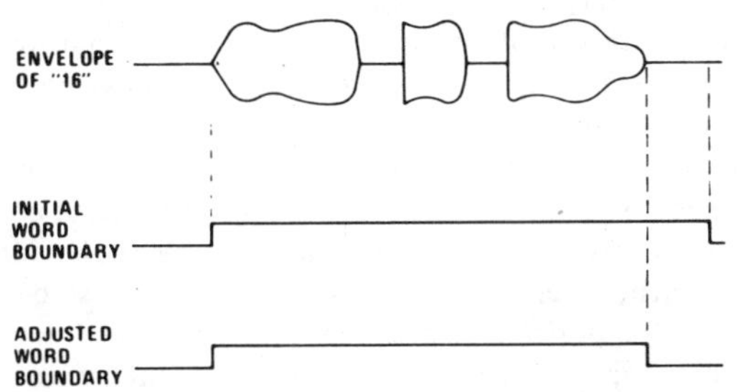

Fig. 3. Internal stop consonant pauses within a word.

C. Word Boundary Detection

It has already been mentioned in the discussion on breath noise that a variable back-up duration was desirable from an initially derived word boundary signal. If a variable back up is not used, a fixed duration back up can be of some value. An initial word boundary signal can be derived from a combination of amplitude of the speech signal overall or amplitude within predetermined spectral bands. This word boundary signal must not, however, be responsive to brief intervocalic pauses caused by the stop consonants and affricatives. Fig. 3 illustrates this point for the word "sixteen." The initial word boundary extends beyond the end of the word by an amount somewhat greater than the duration of the short pauses from the internal stop consonants. In this case an adjustment to the actual word boundary can be made by a fixed duration back up. The fixed duration back up will more accurately locate the end of the word, although the best results are obtained with variable back up.

D. Operator-Originated Babble

It is inevitable that an operator using an ASR system will wish to communicate with his supervisor or other individuals within his area. Regardless of the ease with which an ON/OFF switch can be utilized by an operator, he will occasionally forget to turn the microphone off and will begin to carry on a conversation with another individual. Since the operator will rarely use the words that are in the limited vocabulary the speech recognition system should generally reject the ordinary conversation. It is important in practical applications that a reject capability exists so that inadvertent conversations, sneezes, coughs, throat clearings, etc., do not produce spurious recognition decisions. Both audible and visual alerts can be supplied to the operator indicating that he is talking into a live microphone. This will minimize the number of inadvertent entries that are made into a speech recognition system. Another safeguard to prevent inadvertent message entry to the speech recognition system is to format the data entry sequence as much as possible so that after a block of data has been entered, a verification word is required before the entry is considered to be valid by the speech recognition system.

V. Human Factors of Voice Input

The reaction of a user to voice input is particularly important when the system is interactive. The voice input system must be programmed to avoid all unnecessary complexity and provide as natural a form of communications with the machine as is possible. Some of the factors which will influence the user and cause him to react to the "personality" of the voice input system are discussed below.

A. Multiple-Task Capability

ASR systems are unique in their ability to obtain data or commands from a user whose hands or eyes are already occupied in other functions. The only alternative in this situation is to have the data recorded by tape or by a listener, or to require the user to interrupt his other activities for the purpose of data input.

Since it is possible to achieve voice input simultaneous to other work activities, ASR systems can be employed for data entry by personnel not normally trained for such purposes. Data can be verbally entered at the source with no intermediate operations required. Factory data collection is a good example where voice input could be achieved directly at the source. Since data entry is not usually his primary function, the factory worker must feel that the ASR system provides job enrichment, improved productivity, or does not impede his normal activities.

Experience with multiple-task operations involving voice input as one of the functions has shown that an operator will achieve peak data entry rates after 3–4 months [12]. After this amount of experience, the operator knows the proper speaking rate, when to verify the data, and what words should be used at any particular instant of time.

B. Operator Mobility

By the use of a wireless transmitter an operator can have complete freedom of movement and still communicate with an ASR system. Small cigarette-pack size transmitters can provide a considerable range of operation. However, in such cases, feedback to the operator must be achieved by voice response or portable display since he would generally be outside the visual range of a fixed display.

C. Vocabulary Flexibility

An adaptive ASR system is trained for the speech characteristics of the user. Generally, this is achieved by providing samples of each word in the vocabulary as a set of reference data with which to compare future utterances. This reference data is usually stored for future use so that retraining need not be required each time an individual uses an ASR system. Because of the adaptive feature, a user is free to choose the most natural word to him for a particular function. For example, the word chosen to verify the accuracy of a block of data that has been spoken and displayed to a user could be either "GO" or "OK". The adaptive feature also makes it possible for limited vocabulary ASR systems to operate for any language.

D. Feedback, Editing, and Interaction

Immediate feedback must be given the user of a voice input system, either visually, aurally, or both. The feedback must be unambiguous and can greatly assist the user in accomplishing his voice input functions.

In an isolated speech recognition system, it is important to pace the user so that the minimum spacing is maintained and words are not run together. This can be achieved by an audible "ready" tone or visual indicator. An experienced user of an isolated word voice input system will quickly learn the fastest rate at which words can be spoken, after which the "ready" indicators are unnecessary. However, in the initial stages of using a voice input system the ready indicator is a valuable training aid to the operator.

A "reject" indicator similar to the "ready" indication can also be useful as discussed earlier in the section on operator-originated babble. The reject indication may also serve the purpose of subconciously training the operator to speak the vocabulary words used in a manner that can most easily be recognized by the ASR system.

Besides the elementary indications of "reject" and "ready," all spoken commands should be fed back to the operator for verification. This verification can take the form of a positive indication of correctness through a control word such as "OK" spoken after each command or each data field, or can simply be indicated by proceeding to the next command. Control words such as "erase" to delete the last command and "cancel" to delete an entire data block should also be provided.

It is in the area of conversational, interactive feedback that the greatest potential exists to assist the user of a voice input system. Feedback to the operator cannot only be used for verification, but also for prompting the user through an entry sequence, checking syntax, format and expected values and making special inquiries when the application requires such. In other words, voice input can be used for those applications requiring intelligent terminals.

E. Recognition Accuracy

Error rates in a practical ASR system must be sufficiently low to eliminate any loss of operator confidence or efficiency. Humans have a tendency to become oblivious to very low error rates in multitask operations. Corrections by voice must be sufficiently infrequent as to be no hindrance to the accomplishment of the intended task. If the error rate is high enough to interfere noticeably with the task, the operator will lose confidence and will not wish to use the voice input system. In a sense the operator makes a binary decision, i.e., the voice input system is either "good" or "bad." Interviews with users of operational voice input systems have shown that rarely is a voice input system accepted unless the error rate is very low. The acceptable error rate is critically dependent upon the particular application and the data entry rate. High voice data entry rates above 50 words or phrases per minute require lower error rates than those applications where the data rate is slow enough that the user has time to make corrections.

F. Stability of Reference Data

As mentioned previously, an adaptive, limited vocabulary system achieves recognition processing by comparing an unknown utterance with a set of stored samples of the vocabulary words obtained from the user of the system. This reference data must be stable over long periods of time for practical applications. Once the reference data has been obtained the operator should be able to use the voice input system with little or no "retraining." The ability to begin operations each day with no "warm up" or retrain will greatly enhance the operator's confidence. Similarly, he should not have to frequently interrupt his normal operations to retrain individual words during the course of operations.

VI. A General-Purpose Limited Vocabulary Voice Input System

A. Processing Functions

The four processing functions contained in a limited vocabulary voice recognition system, as shown in Fig. 4, consist of a microphone transducer, a preprocessor, feature extractor, and a final decision level classifier [9]. Early attempts at automatic speech recognition either deleted entirely the feature extraction process [1] or utilized a simplified form of template matching [2]. Experience with crude template matching soon led to the realization of its limitations. Slight variations of the individual speech samples of a particular word would result in gross misclassifications.

1. Preprocessor: It is possible to form many transformations of the speech signal to enhance certain properties and make them more easily detectable in an ASR system. However, speech is neither periodic nor aperiodic, but must be considered as a quasi-periodic signal so that analytical techniques that are developed must reflect temporal features of significance as well as spectral features. Maintaining this dual viewpoint throughout the analysis requires a modification of classical time-domain and frequency-domain analytical techniques. To retain both of these characteristics in a frequency analysis, a method which produces a short-duration spectrum is essential.

Frequency-domain representation of the speech signal is particularly advantageous since 1) it is known that the human auditory system performs a crude frequency analysis at the periphery of auditory sensation and 2) because it has been shown, by acoustical analysis of the vocalization system, that an exact description of the speech sounds can be obtained with a natural frequency concept model of speech production [3].

A periodic function of time possesses a power spectrum with finite amounts of power located at discrete points in the spectrum, commonly described as a line spectrum. An aperiodic function that contains finite energy and is Fourier transformable possesses an energy density spectrum that is a continuous function of frequency. For analyzing speech signals, it is desirable to obtain the spectral energy distribution and its variations as a function of time. Sufficient resolution must be maintained in both the frequency and time domains so that all of the information-bearing properties in both domains can be detected.

Speech analysis can be achieved either by direct analog spectrum analysis, through the use of the fast Fourier transform (FFT), or by linear predictive coding and cepstrum techniques. In all these methods, equivalent problems occur. The FFT produces a discrete spectrum which, with a sufficiently high

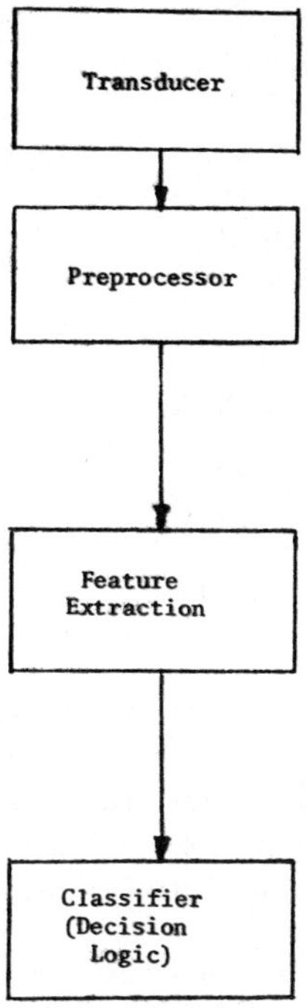

Fig. 4. Pattern-recognition process.

sampling rate, approaches that of the continuous Fourier transform. Many different types of data windows have been utilized in the FFT. The choice of the window is similar to the choice of the filter response in the analog spectrum analyzer. A "picket-fence" effect can occur both in the FFT and the analog spectrum analyzer representing the contributions of the individual filters in the analog analyzer or the separate coefficients of the various terms in the FFT calculation. The point to be made here is that spectrum analysis is only a possible first step in the processing of the speech signal. Considerable additional processing is required in order to achieve the detection and recognition of the information-bearing elements (significant features) of the speech signal which has been transformed to accentuate these elements in the preprocessor. However, an incorrect analysis procedure at the preprocessor can destroy the significant features prior to any processing to extract these features.

Recently, there has been an increased emphasis on time-domain speech analysis based on the linear predictability of speech waveforms. Linear predictive coding (LPC) has been successfully applied to efficient encoding for digital speech communications systems. These results have stimulated investigations of the usefulness of linear predictor coefficients as features for speech recognition. In a recent publication [4], White has concluded that bandpass filtering and linear predictive coding are approximately equivalent bases for measuring speech waveform similarity.

2. Feature Extraction: Considerable mathematical formalism has been developed for various automatic speech recognition processes. However, no general theory exists which can preselect the information-bearing portions of the speech signal. Therefore, the design of the feature extractor is heuristic and must use *ad hoc* or computer-assisted strategies. Only actual experimental data can prove the value of a particular feature set. It is this particular dilemma which has resulted in the recent increased emphasis given feature extraction research for pattern recognition systems.

The key processing function in a pattern recognition system is the feature extractor. Although there are many acceptable classification techniques which can operate on a set of features (measurements), no classification scheme can compensate for an inadequate feature set [5]. The more optimum the feature set, generally the less complex the classifier need be to achieve a given accuracy. The various acoustic features used in the speech recognition system to be described have been tested extensively with large speaker populations, in noisy as well as quiet backgrounds, and for many hours of on-line operations with untrained speakers [6], [7]. The features are useful for continuous speech applications [8] as well as isolated word recognition systems [9], [10]. The selected feature set used is sufficiently general to make it possible to add new arbitrary words at any time to the system. The judicious selection and reliable extraction of these critical speech features for virtually any operational environment is essential in a practical voice input system.

With reference to Fig. 5, the first two processing functions are accomplished principally by a hard wired preprocessor and feature extractor. This makes it possible to achieve real-time processing since only the classification function is performed in a general-purpose minicomputer.

Both the spectral shape and time derivative of the spectral envelope function are derived in the feature extraction process. The spectral shape and its changes with time are continuously measured over the frequency range of interest. Combinations and sequences of these measurements are processed to produce a set of 32 significant acoustic features, one of which is the initial estimate of word boundary. A more refined word boundary is obtained in the minicomputer using the variable-backup technique. The 32 acoustic features are functionally similar to those described in [7]. A hierarchy of features are measured together with a word boundary detection logic. This segmentation process is performed principally in hardware, although the final boundary detection is optimized through software processing in the minicomputer, as explained in Section IV-C.

3. Classifier: The classification (or decision) process is performed in software using a minicomputer. The minicomputer performs the multiplicity of functions shown in Fig. 5. For a spoken word, the 32 encoded features and their time of occurrence are stored in a short-term memory. When the end of the utterance is detected, the duration of the word is divided into 16 time segments and the features are reconstructed into a normalized time base. The pattern-matching logic subsequently compares these feature occurrence patterns to the stored reference patterns for the various vocabulary words and determines the "best fit" for a word decision. A total of 512 bits of information (32 features mapped into 16 time segments) are required to store the feature map of each utterance or reference pattern.

Since the voice input system is adaptive, it must be "trained" for individual talkers and/or words. The system can be automatically adapted or "tuned" to the voice characteristics of different users in a very short time period simply by speaking a small number of training samples into the device to provide a reference set of features. The system stores in memory an individual reference set of word features for each word in the vocabulary and for each talker in the system. Once having trained the system, new words spoken by a user into the device during normal operation are compared with the stored references and a "closest fit" is selected as the recognized word. It is also possible to obtain a "no-decision," or reject, when

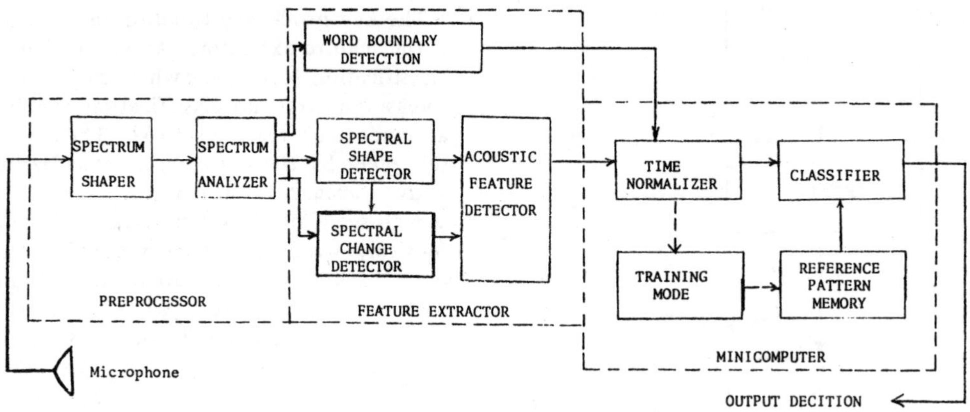

Fig. 5. Block diagram of voice input systems.

none of the characteristics of the words in the reference memory are close to the spoken word.

The decision technique employed can be described most simply by briefly reviewing the operation of the system training and recognition modes.

a. Training mode: During the training mode, the system automatically extracts a time-normalized feature matrix for each repetition of a given word. A consistent matrix of feature occurrences (between repetitions) is required before the features are stored in the reference pattern memory. A template threshold factor is chosen such that a feature occurrence (in a given time segment) is considered valid only when it occurs a minimum number of times relative to the number of training samples. Usually, this threshold factor is set to be between 30–50 percent of a feature's occurrences within the training samples. An example of a reference feature matrix for the word "erase" is shown in Fig. 6.

b. Recognition mode: In the operational mode, each new word spoken into the system is processed in a manner analogous to the training procedure—i.e., features extracted, digitized, and time normalized. The resultant test word matrix then is compared digitally to each stored reference matrix. Similarities and dissimilarities in each compared matrix are appropriately weighted and the net result provides a weighted correlation product. Correlation products also are generated after shifting the input word matrix ± 1 time segment. The stored reference word producing the highest overall correlation is selected as the test word, provided it exceeds a minimum correlation threshold value.

B. Special-Purpose Processing

1. Fixed Vocabulary Systems: For those applications in which both the vocabulary and the pronunciation of each word are fixed, it is possible to achieve enhanced performance by utilizing special-purpose processing. If it is known that two vocabulary words are minimal pairs or are phonetically quite similar, a final decision can be based upon a closer analysis of those portions of the words containing the dissimilarities. Consider, for example, the two possible words "fifteen" and "fifty." If initial processing indicates one of these two words is the most likely choice, a final choice can be made more accurate by heavily weighting the ending portions of the words in the correlation process with the reference samples.

An example of a vocabulary set with a high number of similar words is the English alphabet as it is normally pronounced. The letters "*a, b, c, d, e, g, p, t, v, z*" all end in the vowel /*i*/. The separation must be made on the characteristics of the beginning portions of each letter. Of course, it is possible to eliminate the problem entirely by using the phonetic alphabet pronunciation for each letter. However, if the normal pronunciation of the letters is employed, a close examination of the initial portions of each letter must be made in the ASR processing.

2. Universal Word Recognition: In some cases it is not always possible to obtain reference samples from each user of the ASR system. In such cases the exact vocabulary and preferred pronunciation (or minor variations thereof) must be known before any attempt can be made at automatic recognition of the vocabulary. A typical example falling in this category usually involves the digits and 2–3 control words [29].

3. Vocabulary Subgroupings: Another special-purpose function that can enhance a practical voice input system is a structured vocabulary resulting from the input format of a particular application. The user may have a large overall vocabulary size, but may only use subgroupings thereof as he goes through each step in the voice input sequence. This approach can only be used when the application is defined and all possible input alternatives are defined. Examples of this type of approach are described in [11]–[13].

VII. Recognition Accuracy

Isolated word recognition systems can be separated into those using high-quality speech and those using low-quality speech. Although no absolute distinction can be drawn between the two, high-quality speech systems are characterized as operational in a noise level typical of a laboratory or office environment. In addition, the user is performing only one task, namely pronouncing words for the purpose of a speech recognition test. Low-quality speech systems are operational in factory environments with operators performing a variety of functions including voice input.

Only recently have practical voice input systems been successfully applied to the latter category. A sparcity of performance data exists, therefore, for such systems.

A. Early Attempts at Digit Recognition

A summary of early attempts at spoken digit-recognition studies is presented in Fig. 7, together with some additional comments on some of the studies. The material presented in this table is only a partial survey of the work done and therefore is not all inclusive.

1. Davis, Biddulph, and Balashek [14]: One of the first attempts at digit recognition, this scheme separated the spectrum into two bands, above and below 900 Hz. The energy

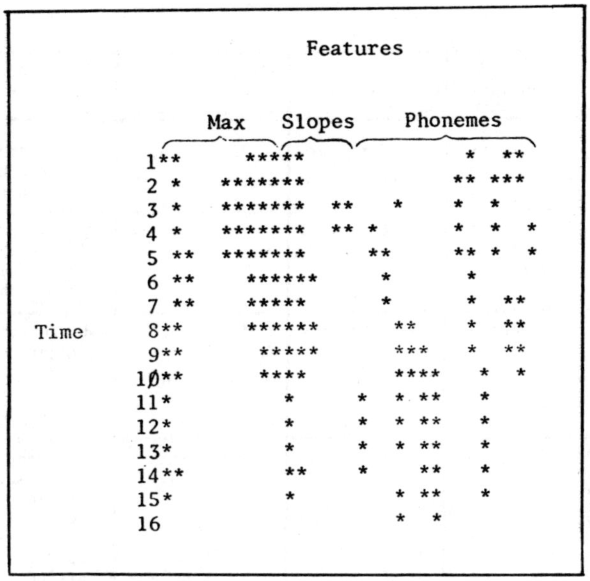

Fig. 6. Reference matrix for the word "erase."

Investigator	Vocabulary	No. of Talkers	Approx. Error Rate	Additional Facts and Comments
Davis, Biddulph & Balashek (Reference 14)	10 digits	1 talker	2 percent	Isolated speech, spectrum separated at 900 c/s, Formant 1 below, formant 2 above 900 c/s.
Dudley & Balashek (Reference 15)	10 digits	2 men	5 percent	Isolated speech.
Denes & Mathews (Reference 16)	10 digits	6 men	12 percent (without time normalization). 6 percent (with time normalization).	Non-realtime, computer simulation, isolated speech.
Sholtz & Bakis (Reference 17)	10 digits	25 men 25 women	2 percent error 2 percent reject	Non-realtime, computer simulation, vowel-consonant segmentation, isolated speech.
Dersch (Reference 18)	10 digits "plus","minus" "total",etc.	N/A	N/A	Real-time, each word is classified into three time segments with the detection of voicing as a registration point, isolated speech.
Nagata, Kato & Chiba (Reference 19)	10 digits (Japanese)	20 men	2.1 percent	Isolated speech
Musman & Steiner (Reference 20)	10 digits "plus","minus" etc. (German)	10 talkers	13 percent	Real-time
Shultz (Reference 21)	10 digits	25 men 25 women	3 percent	Isolated speech
King & Tunis (Reference 22)	10 digits "plus","minus" "times","over"	2 men 1 woman	approximately 1.0 percent	Isolated speech, used instantaneous peaks in spectrum and adaptive processing. Real-time input to computer. Used "forced decision" rules (no rejects allowed).

Fig. 7. Summary of early attempts at digit recognition.

Investigator	Vocabulary	No. of Talkers	Approx. Error Rate	Additional Facts and Comments
Hill (Reference 27)	16 digits	12 talkers	22 percent	Test data taken from 12 talkers not used to form reference data.
Medress (Reference 28)	100 digits polysyllable words	5 talkers	6 percent	One speaker of 5 used for reference data. Test data of 100 words, 20 from each speaker.
Bobrow & Klatt (Reference 33)	54 words	2 talkers	3 percent	Linguistic and non-linguistic features were used for recognition. Feature sequences used in classifier
Martin, Grunza (Reference 11)	10 digits	10 talkers	0.2 percent	Reference data 1 week old for 5 speakers and obtained immediately prior to test for other 5 speakers. Test data of 3,400 words. Real-time recognition.
	12 words	12 talkers	2.85 percent	Speaker wore operating M-100 microphone and MBU-5 oxygen mask. Real-time recognition. Test data of 1440 words
Martin (previously unpublished)	10 digits	1 talker	0 percent	Training data 6 months old. Experienced speaker - 1000 test words. Real-time recognition
Itakura (Reference 30)	200 words (Japanese)	1 talker	2.7 percent	Test data of 2000 words over 3 weeks. Twenty-two times real-time processing
	36 words Alphabet + digits	1 talker	11.4 percent	Normal pronunciation for all letters of alphabet. Test data of 720 words over 3 weeks. Twenty-two times real-time processing
White (Reference 4) (Tested system developed by Itakura)	91 polysyllabic words	1 talker	0.5 percent	Test data of 1820 words over 1 day. Ninety times real-time processing.
	36 words Alphabet + digits	1 talker	2 percent	Normal pronunciation for all letters of alphabet. Test data of 720 words over 2 days. Twenty-five times real-time processing
Martin (Reference 10)	34 words	12 talkers	1.5 percent	85 dB noise background, simultaneous handling of baggage. Vocabulary normal counting pronunciation for 1 through 34. Test data of 9149 words. Real-time processing.
Scott (Reference 29)	10 digits	30 talkers	2 percent	No training required. Live tests, untrained speakers. Test data of 9,300 words. Real-time recognition.
Sambur & Rabiner (Reference 32)	10 digits	10 talkers	2.7 percent	No training required. Test data of 980 words over 5 weeks.

Fig. 8. Performance of recently developed isolated word ASR systems.

rates in each band ("F_1" and "F_2") were then determined by axis-crossing counters. A "plot" of F_1 versus F_2 was made and compared with reference plots, and the recognition decision based on the best match. Good recognition scores (97–98 percent) were obtained when the equipment was adjusted for the particular talker, but needed to be readjusted for every change in talker.

2. *Dudley and Balashek [15]:* This attempt, again aimed toward recognizing spoken digits, combined a phonetic pattern recognizer in series with a word pattern recognizer. A bank of 10 filters was used, and the power output from the filters compared with reference patterns to recognize one of 10 "phonemes." The output of the phonetic recognizer was combined with sequence and duration information to obtain a "best match" with one of the stored reference patterns to recognize one of the 10 digits. Once again, the recognition accuracy was high only when the equipment was adjusted for the particular talker.

3. *Denes and Mathews [16]:* This approach utilized a computer simulation of a digit-recognition process. Time/frequency patterns of spectral energy were cross-correlated with reference patterns and a recognition decision was based on the highest correlation. An error rate of 12 percent was obtained, which was reduced to 6 percent by time-normalizing the word samples.

4. *Sholtz and Bakis [17]:* This approach generated power spectra, and the words were then segmented into consonants and vowels. These segments were classified into different categories and a recognition decision was based on a dictionary search. A recognition score of 97 percent was obtained with the internal dictionary adjusted for optimum results. This approach was more tolerant of interspeaker variations than previous attempts.

5. *Dersch [18] ("Shoebox"):* This word recognizer used "envelope asymmetry" to detect voicing, which was then used as a registration point for three time segments. Each time segment was then classified into one of several categories. This information plus sequence information was combined to give a recognition decision. The digits and "plus," "minus," "total," were recognized. No data were given on recognition scores or tolerance to interspeaker variations.

6. *King and Tunis [22]:* Their equipment consisted of a filter-bank voice-spectrum analyzer providing real-time input of measurement data to an IBM 1620-II digital computer. They sampled the spectrum and binary coded the instantaneous peaks of the speech-wave envelope as the input to the computer. Their system could handle a 30-dB dynamic range input signal and samples were taken at 30-ms intervals. Adaptive linear decision techniques were utilized to partition the decision space for recognition.

B. Recent Performance Results for Limited Vocabulary Systems

A partial listing of some of the recent performance results obtained with limited vocabulary isolated word recognition systems is shown in Fig. 8. Additional systems are described in [34]–[44].

1. *White [4] and Itakura [30]:* Both of these investigators tested recognition performance on a system originally developed by Itakura for the 36-word alphanumeric vocabulary with the normal pronunciation used for all letters of the alphabet. Itakura's system employs the linear predictive residual and dynamic programming. In comparing the two systems it must be pointed out that Itakura used a telephone to input speech which was low-pass filtered at 3kHz, sampled at 6.67 kHz and used 8 linear predictive coefficients. White used a high-quality microphone, 5-kHz low-pass filter, 10-kHz sample rate, and 14 linear predictive coefficients. White also used a slightly different dynamic programming strategy. These differences probably account for the lower error rates achieved by White.

White also compared the 14-coefficient linear predictive residual technique with a 20-channel bandpass filter bank and determined that the two methods have essentially the same power to measure the similarity of speech sounds.

2. *Medress [28]:* Medress attempted a limited experiment using an automatic speech recognition system which was independent of speaker. A total of 100 polysyllabic words were obtained as a reference set from one of the speakers. Five other speakers, one of whom was the reference speaker, then each pronounced 20 words on the list of 100. The 100 test words were recognized with an average error rate of 6 percent. The scores ranged from 100 percent for the speaker who produced the reference set down to 85 percent for one of the other four talkers.

3. *Martin and Grunza [11]*[2]*:* An indication of the performance of a recently developed isolated-word ASR system is contained in [11]. In June of 1974, 2400 repetitions of digits were used as test data from 10 speakers. Reference data for five of the speakers were obtained one week prior to the test and immediately before the test from the other five talkers. The error rate for these tests, with a real-time recognition system, was 0.2 percent. This same system was also tested by Martin (previously unpublished data) to determine the effects of time on the reference data. Training data that was six months old was used for one of the speakers, uttering 1000 test digits. The zero-percent error rate indicates there was no substantial fall off in accuracy over the six-month interval between when the original reference set was obtained and when the 1000 word test was conducted.

4. *Scott [29]*[3]*:* Scott has recently developed a digit recognition system which requires no adaptation for individual talkers. Tests were conducted with the 10-digit vocabulary using 30 speakers and a test data base of 9300 words. No adjustments were made for individual speakers, and a real-time recognition processor was utilized. An error rate of 2 percent was obtained for these tests. This is a significant accomplishment since most of the 30 speakers utilized for the tests had no prior experience with an ASR system. It is to be expected that universal digit recognition systems will be developed in the near future with error rates less than 1 percent.

5. *Sambur and Rabiner [32]:* Sambur and Rabiner have shown that a set of "robust features" can be measured and combined with a classifier to achieve universal digit recognition. A robust feature is defined as one which can be simply and unambiguously measured, grossly characterizes a large proportion of speech sounds, and can be conveniently interpreted independent of speaker. Only four robust features were used to categorize a region of a word into six broad acoustic classes. Evaluation tests were conducted over five weeks using five male and five female speakers. These tests resulted in an error rate of only 2.7 percent. The authors state that this is only a

[2] Work sponsored by AF Avionics Laboratory, Wright-Patterson AFB, OH.

[3] Work sponsored by Rome Air Development Center, Air Force Systems Command, Griffiss AFB, NY.

TEST CONDITIONS

Vocabulary:	34 Words (1 through 34) - pronounced normally as in counting 1 through 34.
No. of Speakers:	12 Total - 6 experienced 6 less than 1 hour experience
Noise Level:	85-90 dB of Machine Noise
Speaking Rate:	20-30 words/min.
Operator Task:	Loading sacks and bags on sorting conveyor while voice encoding each item.

TEST RESULTS

No. of Test Utterances	=	9,149
No. of Correct Responses	=	9,012
No. of Rejects & Incorrect Responses	=	137
% Recognition Accuracy	=	98.5%

Fig. 9. Performance results for 34-word vocabulary in high noise background.

first pass at universal digit recognition. It can be expected, therefore, that this technique could be developed further and compare favorably with adaptive systems.

C. Low-Quality Speech Systems

1. Automated Sortation: A series of tests were conducted in early 1974 with the limited vocabulary speech recognition system described in Section VI-A. The performance measurements were made for an operational system using employees who were voice encoding at the input to an automated conveyor sorter. The workers were subject to periods of relatively intense physical activity during periods of peak sorting rates. The noise background for the tests was 85–90 dB. The 34 word vocabulary utilized for the accuracy tests consisted of the digits 1 through 34. The normal pronunciations used in counting were utilized, e.g., 21 was pronounced as a single word "twentyone;" rather than the two separate words "two"–"one." The results from these tests are shown in Fig. 9. The overall recognition accuracy of 98.5 percent was obtained using 12 speakers, 6 of whom had less than 1 h of experience with the system.

Significant improvements have been made in recognition accuracy from that of early 1974. It is expected that general progress in speech recognition research will be reflected in exceptionally high recognition accuracies in future publications describing operational limited vocabulary systems.

2. Oxygen Mask Tests: A voice control system for evaluation in a high-performance aircraft cockpit simulator was tested with users wearing a pilot's normal oxygen mask [11].[4] The tests were conducted with each speaker breathing pressurized air or oxygen through a MBU-5 oxygen mask with a M-100 microphone. A standard CRU-69/A oxygen regulator was utilized in order to duplicate typical cockpit operations. Tests were conducted with 12 speakers, each using a different set of 12 words. An overall correct recognition rate of 97.15 percent was obtained with a standard system with no hardware or software changes made for the effects of the oxygen mask.

[4]Work sponsored by AF Avionics Laboratory, Wright-Patterson AFB, Ohio.

VIII. Typical Applications of Voice Input

Some of the applications in which voice input systems have already become operational are:

1. quality control and inspection
2. automated material handling
3. parts programming for numerically controlled machine tools
4. direct voice input to computers.

One of the characteristics common to most applications of voice input is that the operator's hands and/or eyes are already busy with other functions. The first voice input systems to be used by industry in these various applications were installed in late 1972 and early 1973 [23]. The results obtained from these initial operating systems indicated that a factory worker with minimal training can use a voice input system quite successfully. Recognition accuracies obtained were equal to or superior to keying accuracies obtained from the same personnel. Original training data for a speaker has been found to be stable over many months, thereby eliminating the need for frequent retraining and updating of the reference data.

A. Quality Control and Inspection

A normal procedure in industry for the inspection of products and the recording of defects is for an inspector or an inspection team to prepare a written report of any abnormal conditions. This manually prepared record of defects can be keyed into a computer from an on-line or off-line terminal. Several people, and much elapsed time, may be required to complete the procedure and prepare reports and there is abundant chance for error throughout. If it is required that the inspection data be captured at the source, it is necessary for the inspector to follow a rigid keyboard format in order to enter the defects as they are observed. This requirement usually substantially reduces the productivity of the operator and requires additional training in order to achieve the inspection function.

In most quality control and inspection processes the inspector's eyes and/or hands are occupied in the inspection task. By using a voice data entry system it is possible to combine the inspector's normal work requirements with a simultaneous entry of all the data that he measures and observes. With a voice data entry system, an inspector wearing a small microphone and having both hands free, follows a checklist appearing on an electronic display in front of him and simply describes each item's condition verbally. This inspection information, verbally entered into the system, provides status reports and can also be transmitted directly to a central computer. In addition to providing cost savings in entering the data, improvement in production quality results from both timely and accurate inspection reports.

1. Television Faceplate Inspection: Owens-Illinois Corporation has been using voice data entry equipment since early 1973 for the inspection of color television faceplates. In this application the inspector begins the operation by entering via a central teleprinter the type of television faceplate to be inspected, his employee number, shift, date, time, plunger number, survey number, and shop number. The information is retained by the system and printed as the heading on a final summary inspection report printed out at the conclusion of an inspection run.

The inspector is prompted through a complex measurement sequence by the visual display (Fig. 10) which indicates the name of the measurement to be taken, the nominal value, an "out-of-tolerance" condition, and the data being entered. The inspector verifies each measurement on the display with a control word such as "go" which inputs the data to the processor for computation and printout. As each entry is made it is compared by the computer to any applicable tolerance limits previously stored. If a measurement is out of tolerance, an indication of that is given to the operator so that he can make certain that measurement was correct. If the measurement is beyond all normal tolerance limits it is considered OUT OF MAX/MIN and the operator can proceed only by saying either the words "erase" or "override". In the case of saying "erase", the operator will repeat the measurement to be certain that it was out of MAX/MIN. In the case of "override" the operator indicates that he notices that the measurement was out of MAX/MIN but that it is also a correct measurement and the part should be rejected. The voice data entry system stores nominal values and tolerance limits for all measurements to be made. The operator need only call out those numbers that deviate from the nominal value. For example, if the nominal value is 20.000 and the tolerance is ±0.050, and if the inspector calls out "41," the display will indicate 20.041. If the inspector calls out "945" the display will flash OUT OF MAX/MIN since the measurements is 19.945 or 0.005 smaller than allowed.

Fig. 10. Visual display for TV faceplate inspection.

When the voice data entry system has accepted and stored all the data for an inspection run, mean and range measurements are computed. A summary inspection report is then printed out with all headings, data, and mean and range calculations. A separate listing of all out-of-tolerance measurements is included for immediate corrective action by the factory supervisory personnel.

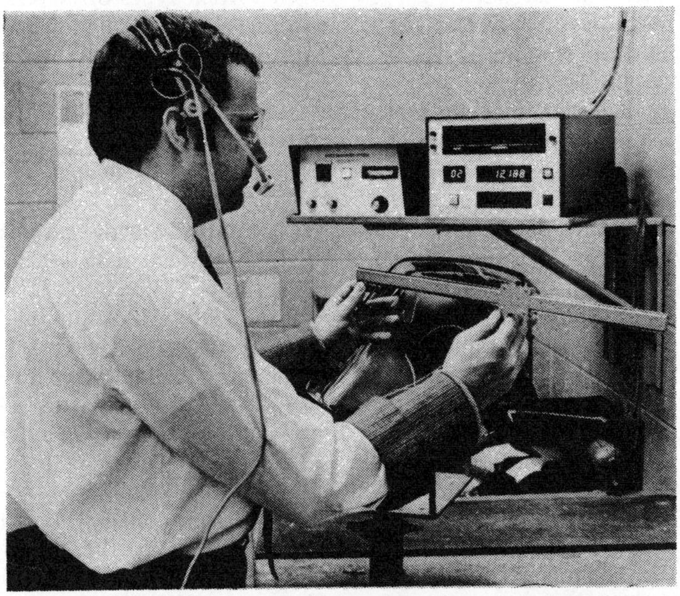

Fig. 11. Simultaneous inspection and voice data entry.

As shown in Fig. 11, the inspection of television faceplates is a particular example where an inspector must use both hands to manipulate, orient, and measure parameters using gauges and meters. There is also a simultaneous necessity to record the measurement data. In this case, the operator can achieve both tasks simultaneously and be guided through the measurement process by an interactive feedback display that verifies every step of the data entry, indicates the next measurement to be taken, and provides an alarm when out-of-tolerance values have occurred.

2. Inspection of Pull-Ring Can Lids: Voice data entry systems are also being used for the inspection of pull-ring can lids at major can manufacturing plants (Fig. 12). In this application, the operator is guided in a similar manner as in the Owens-Illinois television faceplate inspection application. The system has a two-line visual display which indicates the current state of the inspection process and prompts the inspector through his inspection sequence. The upper line of the display indicates to the operator the current inspection step. The lower line is used to display the data which the inspector enters by voice commands. Tolerances are stored in the computer such that the operator is alerted with both a REJECT light and an audio "beeper" indicating that an out-of-tolerance measurement has just been encountered.

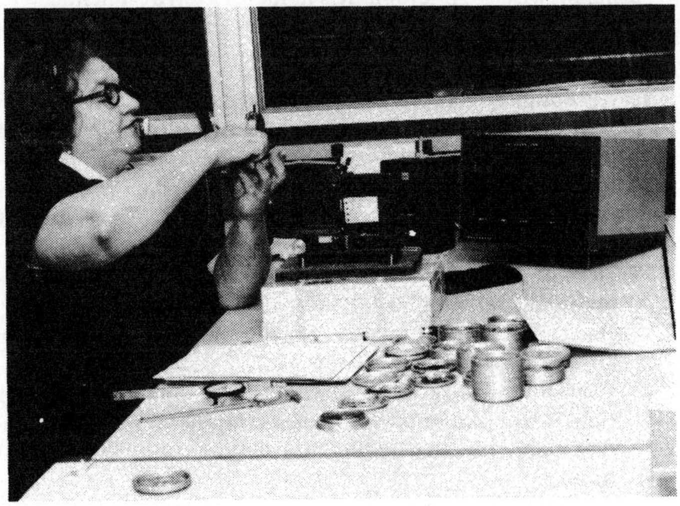

Fig. 12. Voice data entry of can lid inspection results.

The can lid inspection system contains an additional flexibility for an operator who wishes to utilize various meters and gauges in the order in which they become available from other inspectors performing similar functions. Under normal circumstances, the inspector would advance sequentially through each step and sample in a prescribed format. However, in those instances when an inspector wishes to deviate from the normal it is possible to advance to another data entry field while preserving the current inspection step. It is also possible for the inspector to skip over any measurements not currently required in the operation. This flexibility of operation is merely a result of the application software that resides in the central processor of the speech recognition system. Flexibility allows an operator the freedom to not enter all of the data in a major field at any one time. If he wishes to enter only partial data he may do so and later return to the original inspection point at the point of interruption. When all of the data has been entered for a shift, the system will print out a summary report showing all the defects in the proper categories in the proper sequence regardless of the sequence in which the operator entered the data.

The can inspection application is another example of an inspection function requiring the use of both hands during the inspection process. The pull-ring lid must be handled and placed in and out of gauges and, in certain types of meters, they must be rocked back and forth to find minimum and maximum points (Fig. 13). To capture these measurements would require the operator to break the inspection process at each inspection point and either manually record the data or key enter the data. With voice data entry it is possible to simultaneously enter the measurements while the manual manipulations are being carried out. Furthermore, the summary reports on the data that have been obtained from the various operators eliminate the need for all subsequent data keying operations.

3. Automobile Assembly Line Inspection: An automobile manufacturer installed an experimental voice data entry system for testing in assembly line inspection. The primary purpose of the experiment was to learn, first hand, the true impact of voice data entry on inspection applications in assembly operations. Specific objectives of the experiment were to determine 1) if such systems could operate accurately in an assembly plant environment; 2) if current plant personnel could utilize such systems without excessive training; 3) the impact this technology may have on the inspector's ability to perform his primary job responsibility; 4) the reactions of inspection personnel to voice data entry; 5) the desirability and feasibility of utilizing wireless microphones in factory environments.

After approximately two weeks of on-line multishift experimentation, the following conclusions were drawn.

1. Acceptable voice recognition accuracy was obtained on the assembly line. The voice data entry system performed accurately and reliably throughout the test.
2. Inspectors were able to successfully use the system with less than one day of experience. Usually a few hours of familiarization was sufficient.
3. Use of the system did not interfere with the inspector's ability to perform his job.
4. Inspector comments and behavior indicated a favorable attitude towards voice data entry.
5. Overall operation with a wireless microphone indicated that it has potential for in-plant use, thereby totally freeing an operator to enter information while having total mobility.

For the experiment, two on-line inspection stations were selected for use, one in the hard trim department and the other in the final inspection line. At the hard trim station, the inspector checked all items around the outside of the body of the vehicle and the interior dash area. In the actual inspection of each vehicle, the following steps were followed.

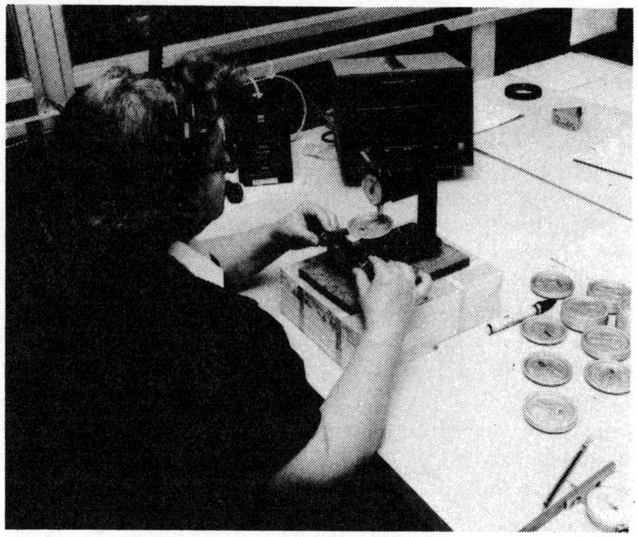

Fig. 13. Manual manipulations required during voice data entry.

1. The inspector would examine the vehicle in his normal manner. When he wished to record a defect, the inspector would:
   a) enter a two-digit item code by voice corresponding to the defective item. The speech recognition system would recognize the number and immediately flash on visual display the description of the item under consideration;
   b) the operator would then enter a single word description of the nature of the defect (e.g., loose, shy, inoperative, etc.);
   c) the inspector visually verified the displayed information and then entered the entire inspection item with the control word "go". The display was then cleared and a teleprinter would print the defect information on a defect label which would later be added to the inspection ticket attached to the car.
2. When the entire inspection of the vehicle was completed, the inspector would enter by voice the word "finished" followed by the control word "go." This action caused the printer to add the station number, the time, and date on the label which already contained the defects found on a particular vehicle.
3. This printed label would then be manually removed from the printer and subsequently placed on the inspection ticket.

Operation of the system on the final inspection line was basically the same as above. However, this inspector worked only on the left side of the vehicle mainly checking the electrical system.

4. Receiving Inspection: The receiving area of a corporation is typical of many such areas from which it is difficult to obtain timely and accurate information about the quantities arriving with each delivery. For example, compressors arriving at Tecumseh Products Company for service analysis required the writeup of a form for each compressor. The form required writing down such items as order no., item no., complete

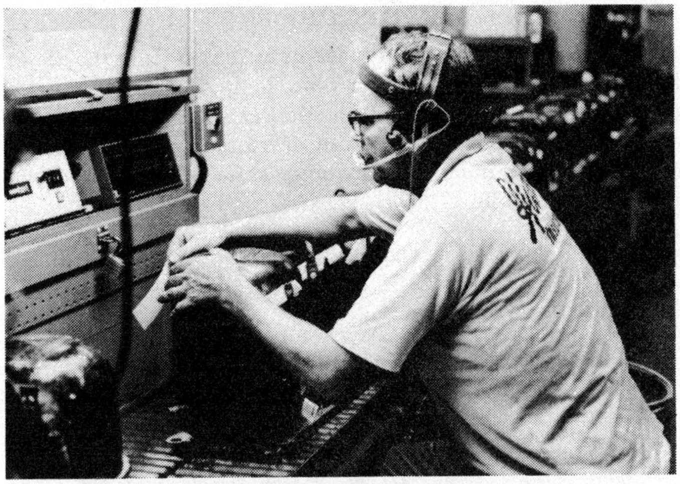

Fig. 14. Voice input for receiving inspection application.

serial plate data, customer tag no., etc. The combination of handling compressors and writing down the information was both time-consuming and error prone.

Once the receiving forms were filled out, they were sent to the data processing department for key-to-tape entry into computer. Here again was another possible source of delay and errors.

Tecumseh overcame all the problems at receiving by installing voice input equipment for direct data entry to a computer (Fig. 14). The operator speaks the data as he handles each compressor and is prompted through the entry sequence by the display. Illegal serial plate codes are checked as the operator enters the data. The operator is alerted so that correction is possible immediately rather than after the compressor has been sent to a repair area.

Since the data to be entered in the application is alphanumeric, the vocabulary consists of the digits, phonetic alphabet, and control words.

The system at Tecumseh has produced increased operator productivity and provided a considerably reduced response time to customers concerning the status of each compressor.

B. Automated Material Handling

Automated sorting equipment of various types has been developed in recent years for the rapid movement of materials from one point to another. Typically these materials consist of parcels, containers, baggage, sack mail, inventory, etc. Distribution and sorting centers use either belt or tray sorters and encoding at induction points to control the movements of the material. At each induction station a two-man team is usually employed (Fig. 15), one who orients the label face-up and another, seated at a keyboard, who keys in the destination code [31]. If one operator is used at the induction station, he must first handle each item, read the label, and then key the sorting code. A one-man operation is significantly slower than a two-man induction process.

Voice encoding for material handling applications can produce high sorting rates with a single operator at the induction station. Such systems have been in operation in a variety of applications starting in early 1973. All of these systems have resulted in increased operator productivity and reduced errors from the operators who formerly key-entered the sorting destination codes.

An example of an operational automated material handling system is the voice control package routing system installed by S. S. Kresge in November 1974 [24]. As shown in Fig. 16 parcels come to the operator's induction station where he simply states the destination code for each carton passing before him into his microphone headset. This code is recognized and a signal is produced at the conveyor belt as though it came from a keyboard entry. Individual cartons are then routed to the specific conveyor spurs according to the voice input codes for each carton. The system also provides a piece count for each individual operator at the induction station.

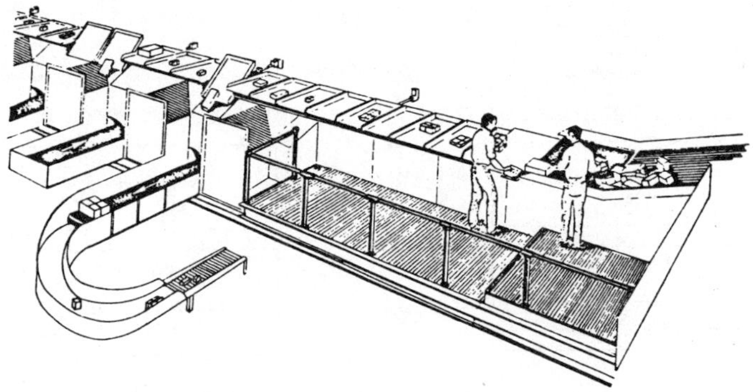

Fig. 15. Typical automated material handling system induction station (from [6]).

Fig. 16. Voice encoding for automated material handling system (from [24]).

Prior to the installation of the voice encoding system, the biggest single problem at the distribution center occurred at the induction location, where different size cartons tended to bunch and create difficulties for operators performing sortation. After testing various methods and types of encoding devices, S. S. Kresge installed voice activated sortation equipment which caused the bunching problem to be eliminated, productivity to be increased, and sorting errors to be reduced.

C. Parts Programming for NC Machine Tools

In the past, manufacturing control has centered around a company's central data processing facility. However, it is becoming increasingly apparent that decentralization of computer control—under direct supervision of those responsible for a particular manufacturing task—is the key to effective manufacturing control.

A traditional bottleneck in computer-based numerical control systems to date has been human interface problems associated with programming and software. An approach using voice programming has made it possible for factory supervisory personnel to control their own computer-based processes and programmable controllers. Voice programming appears to be the

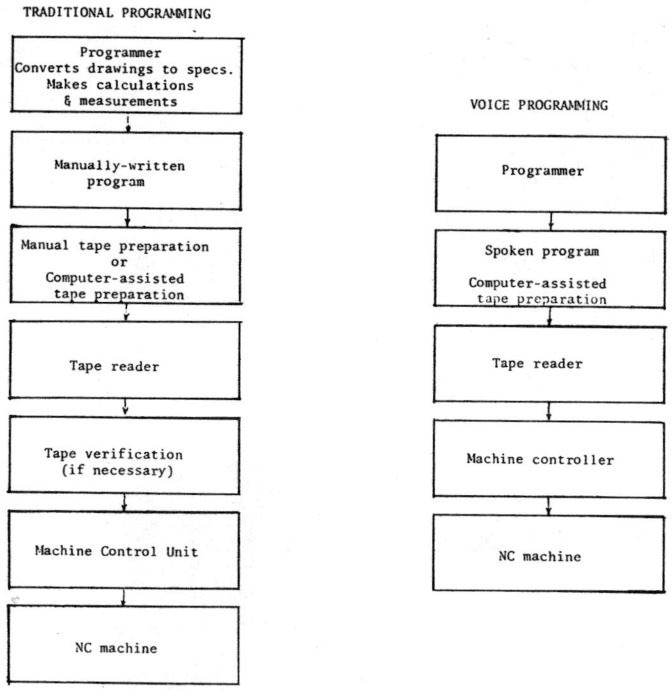

Fig. 17. Comparison of voice input and traditional parts programming.

ultimate step in simplifying communications between man and production machines.

Voice programming for numerical control (VNC) [13] allows factory personnel using normal English words to speak commands needed for parts programming, thereby eliminating the need to convert the information into a computer-compatible format. All the operator needs is a knowledge of blueprints and basic machine tool operations.

When using VNC, the individual simply calls out each basic operation. No special programming skills are needed. Instead of writing out programs or typing them according to a rigid programming format, the programmer simply speaks each machine command into a microphone. Each command is displayed sequentially for positive verification, after which the next entry required is displayed. Not only is the programmer led through each step by the visual display but the display provides a means for automatic error detection. The programmer's hands are free to handle prints or to perform required calculations. For a graphic comparison of traditional programming and voice programming, refer to Fig. 17, comparing standard methods of NC parts programming with VNC.

D. Government Applications

A report by Turn *et al.* [25] broadly summarized the military applications of automatic speech recognition systems. These applications fell into the general categories of equipment and process control, field data entry, cooperative man–computer tasks, and data management. Limited vocabulary voice input systems are under evaluation at various government agencies for applications such as:

1) controls for high performance aircraft cockpit simulators
2) air traffic control
3) entry of cartographic and bathometric data
4) aids for handicapped.

IX. Conclusions

The significant conclusion that can be drawn from the above discussion is that, for the first time, limited vocabulary voice input systems have moved from the laboratory to successful applications in industry. Future developments in both new applications and increased capability voice input systems can be expected to follow.

References

[1] G. S. Sebestyen, *Decision-Making Processes in Pattern Recognition.* New York: Macmillan, 1963.

[2] H. Dudley, and S. Balashek, "Automatic recognition of phonetic patterns in speech," *J. Acoust. Soc. Amer.*, vol. 30, pp. 721–739, Aug. 1958.

[3] J. L. Flanagan, *Speech Analysis, Synthesis & Perception.* New York: Academic Press, 1972.

[4] G. M. White and R. B. Neely, "Speech recognition experiments with linear prediction, bandpass filtering, and dynamic programming", *IEEE Trans. Acoust. Speech Signal Processing*, to be published.

[5] N. J. Nilsson, *Learning Machines.* New York: McGraw-Hill, 1965.

[6] T. B. Martin, H. Zadell, E. Grunza, and M. Herscher, "Numeric speech translating system," in *Automatic Pattern Recognition*, Washington, D.C.: National Security Industrial Association, pp. 113–141, May 1969.

[7] T. B. Martin, "Acoustic recognition of a limited vocabulary in continuous speech," Ph.D. dissertation, Univ. Pennsylvania, Philadelphia, May 1970. (Available from Univ. Microfilms, Ann Arbor, MI, Diss. 70-25,692.)

[8] T. B. Martin, H. J. Zadell, A. L. Nelson, and J. F. Schanne, "Continuous speech recognition and synthesis," *Tech. Rep.* AFAL-TR-67-210, Oct. 1967 (AD 821168).

[9] M. B. Herscher and R. B. Cox, "An adaptive isolated-word speech recognition system," in *Conf. Rec. 1972 Conf. Speech Communication and Processing*, pp. 89–92, (Newton, MA Apr. 1972, (AD-742236)).

[10] T. B. Martin, "Applications of limited vocabulary recognition systems," in *Speech Recognition: Invited Papers Presented at the 1974 IEEE Symposium.* New York: Academic Press, 1975, pp. 55–72.

[11] T. B. Martin and E. F. Grunza, "Voice control demonstration system," Tech. Rep. AFAL-TR-74-174, Wright-Patterson AFB, OH, June 1974.

[12] T. B. Martin and J. C. Collins, "Speech recognition applied to problems of quality control," in *1975 ASQC Tech. Conf. Trans.* (San Diego, CA) pp. 8–15, May 1975.

[13] M. F. Plute and R. B. Cox, "Voice programming—A new dimension to NC," in *NCS Proc. Tech. Conf. 1975—NC/CAM EXPO '75* (Washington, DC), pp. 89–97, May 1975.

[14] K. H. Davis, R. Biddulph, and S. Balashek, "Automatic recognition of spoken digits," *J. Acoust. Soc. Amer.*, vol. 24, p. 637, 1952.

[15] H. Dudley and S. Balashek, "Automatic recognition of phonetic patterns in speech," *J. Acoust. Soc. Amer.*, vol. 30, pp. 721–732, 1958.

[16] P. Denes and M. V. Mathews, "Spoken digit recognition using time-frequency pattern matching," *J. Acoust. Soc. Amer.*, vol. 32, pp. 1450–1455, 1960.

[17] P. N. Sholtz and R. Bakis, "Spoken digit recognition using vowel-consonant segmentation," *J. Acoust. Soc. Amer.*, vol. 34, pp. 1–5, 1962.

[18] W. C. Dersch, "Shoebox—A voice responsive machine," *Datamation*, vol. 8, pp. 47–50, 1962.

[19] K. Nagato, Y. Kato, and S. Chiba, "Spoken digit recognizer for the Japanese language," in *Preprint Audio Eng. Soc. Annu. Meet.*, Preprint 347, Oct. 1964.

[20] H. G. Musmann and K. H. Steiner, "Phonetische Addiermaschine," *Arch. Elek. Ubertragung*, vol. 19, pp. 502–510, 1965.

[21] G. L. Shultz, "Investigation procedures for speech recognition," in *Proc. Seminar on Speech Compression and Processing* (AF Cambridge Res. Center, Bedford, Mass., Sept. 28–30, 1959, Tech. Rep. 198).

[22] J. H. King, and C. J. Tunis, "Some experiments in spoken word recognition," *IBM J. Res. Dev.* vol. 10, no. 1, pp. 65–79, Jan. 1966.

[23] "Spoken words drive a computer," in *Business Week*, New York: McGraw-Hill, Dec. 2, 1972, pp. 36H-36L.

[24] "Tell your cartons where to get off!" in *Traffic Management*, Feb. 1975, Denver, CO: Cahners Publ., pp. 24–27.

[25] R. Turn, A. Hoffman, and T. Lippiatt, "Military applications of

speech understanding systems," Rep. R-1434-ARPA, June 1974 (available from ARPA under Order 189-1).

[26] M. W. Grady and M. B. Herscher, "Advanced speech technology applied to problems of air traffic control," in *NAECON 1975 Conf. Rec.*, Dayton, OH, pp. 541–546, June 1975.

[27] D. Hill and E. Wacker, "ESOTERIC-II—An approach to practical voice control: progress report," *Machine Intelligence*, Edinburgh, Scotland: Edinburgh Univ. Press, 1969, vol. 5, pp. 463–493.

[28] M. Medress, "A procedure for machine recognition of speech," in *Conf. Rec., 1972 Conf. Speech Communication and Processing*, pp. 113–116 (Newton, MA, Apr. 1972, (AD-742236)).

[29] P. B. Scott, "Voice input code identifier," Final Tech. Rep.–1975, Rome Air Development Center, Air Force Systems Command, Griffiss AFB, NY.

[30] F. Itakura, "Minimum prediction residual applied to speech recognition," *IEEE Trans. Acoust. Speech Signal Processing*, vol. ASSP-23, pp. 67–72, Feb. 1975.

[31] T. B. Martin, H. J. Zadell, E. F. Grunza, and M. B. Herscher, "Numeric speech translating system," in *Automatic Pattern Recognition*, pp. 113–141, May 1969, Washington, DC: Nat. Security Industiral Ass.

[32] M. R. Sambur and L. R. Rabiner, "A speaker independent digit recognition system," *Bell Syst. Tech. J.*, vol. 54, Jan. 1975.

[33] D. G. Bobrow and D. H. Klatt, "A limited speech recognition system," BBN Rep. 1667, Final Rep., Contract NAS 12-138, Bolt, Beranek and Newman, Inc., May 15, 1975.

[34] J. N. Shearme and P. F. Leach, "Some experiments with a simple word recognition system," *IEEE Trans. Audio Electroacoust.*, vol. AU-16, pp. 256–261, 1967.

[35] G. L. Clapper, "Automatic word recognition," *IEEE Spectrum*, vol. 16, pp. 57–69, 1971.

[36] V. M. Velichiko and N. G. Zagoruiko, "Automatic recognition of 200 words," *Int. J. Man-Machine Studies*, vol. 2, p. 223, 1970.

[37] K. Kido, H. Suzuki, S. Makino, and T. Matsouka, "Recognition of spoken words by use of spectral peaks and lexicon," paper presented at IEEE Symp. Speech Recognition, Carnegie-Mellon Univ., Pittsburgh, PA, Apr. 15–19, 1974.

[38] A. Ichikawa, Y. Nakano, and K. Nakata, "Evaluation of various parameter sets in spoken digits recognition," *IEEE Trans. Audio Electroacoust.*, vol. AU-21, pp. 202–209, June 1973.

[39] T. G. Von Keller, "An on-line recognition system for spoken digits," *J. Acoust. Soc. Amer.*, pp. 1288–1296, 1971.

[40] C. F. Teacher, H. G. Kellet, and L. R. Focht, "Experimental, limited-vocabulary speech recognizer," *IEEE Trans. Audio Electroacoust.*, vol. AU-15, pp. 127–130, 1967.

[41] L. C. W. Pols, "Real-time recognition of spoken words," *IEEE Trans. Computers*, vol. C-20, pp. 972–978, 1971.

[42] B. Gold, "Word-recognition computer program," MIT Res. Lab. *Electronics*, Cambridge, MA, Tech. Rep. 452, June 15, 1966.

[43] R. DeMori, L. Gilli, and A. R. Meo, "A flexible real-time recognizer of spoken words for man-machine communication," *Int. J. Man-Machine Studies*, vol. 2, pp. 317–326, 1970.

[44] J. W. Glenn, "Machines you can talk to," *Machine Design*, pp. 72–75, May 1, 1975.

Speech Recognition Experiments with Linear Predication, Bandpass Filtering, and Dynamic Programming

GEORGE M. WHITE, MEMBER, IEEE, AND RICHARD B. NEELY, MEMBER, IEEE

Abstract—Automatic speech recognition experiments are described in which several popular preprocessing and classification strategies are compared. Preprocessing is done either by linear predictive analysis or by bandpass filtering. The two approaches are shown to produce similar recognition scores. The classifier uses either linear time stretching or dynamic programming to achieve time alignment. It is shown that dynamic programming is of major importance for recognition of polysyllabic words. The speech is compressed into a quasi-phoneme character string or preserved uncompressed. Best results are obtained with uncompressed data, using nonlinear time registration for multisyllabic words.

I. INTRODUCTION

THIS paper discusses techniques used in automatic recognition of isolated utterances. The development of isolated word recognition systems is a challenging problem that can have a significant economical impact and can also provide acoustic analysis components for continuous speech recognition systems.

In this paper we select several of the more promising techniques described in the literature of isolated word recognition and combine and compare them in a set of controlled experiments. This is apparently the first published comparative study of its kind in recent years. One combination of techniques yields some of the highest recognition scores yet achieved for English vocabularies of 90 words or more. We combine or compare linear predictive coding [3] with bandpass filtering; dynamic programming [6] with linear time normalization; and "character-string encoding" (C.S. Code) [5] with a simple bandpass filter space representation of speech. The results of the comparisons are given in five tables in Section IV. The tables also report the effect on system performance of 1) vocabulary, 2) parametric representation, 3) time alignment, 4) C.S.Code and 5) a combination of time normalization and C.S.Code. Our results show that dynamic programming, which achieves nonlinear time scaling, is extremely useful for automatic speech recognition of multisyllabic utterances.

Nearly all successful isolated utterance recognition systems of today use utterance prototypes. An utterance "prototype" is a reference utterance against which unknown utterances are compared. Prototypes, or templates as they are sometimes called, are represented by a time sequence of acoustic "features." These features may be simply the output of a set of filters or they may be the output of complicated "feature extractors." We use linear predictive coding and bandpass filtering to provide features for representing utterance prototypes. In some cases, we then apply a data compression operation called C.S. Code which is a mapping of utterances into a string of quasi-phonemic labels. Comparison of an unknown utterance and a prototype takes place by aligning utterances and prototypes in time and then measuring the degree of similarity between sounds in the same time unit. We tested two different time alignment strategies and several "similarity measures." Time alignment and similarity measurements are grouped together and called utterance "classification" strategies. The measurement of features is called "preprocessing." Details of the preprocessing and classification techniques are given in the next section.

Manuscript received February 28, 1975; revised April 11, 1975 and September 19, 1975.

The authors are with the Palo Alto Research Center, Xerox Corporation, Palo Alto, CA 94304.

II. SPEECH RECOGNITION ALGORITHMS

The speech recognition systems compared in this paper had three stages: a *preprocessing* stage followed by a *data reduction* stage followed by a *classification* stage. The preprocessing stage used *linear predictive coding* (LPC) or *bandpass filtering*. The data reduction stage used *character-string encoding* or no *C.S.Code*. The classification stage used *linear time scaling* or *dynamic programming nonlinear time scaling* (Figs. 1-5).

Speech sound similarity is defined to be proportional to the distance separating two sounds in a vector space defined by bandpass filter parameters, linear predictive coefficients, or character strings. Vector spaces of 6 and 20 dimensions are defined by 6 and 20 channel filter banks. Linear predictive coding establishes a vector space of dimensionality equal to the number of predictive coefficients. Similarity measurement with *C.S.Code* takes place by measuring distances between reference points rather than the actual points.

To understand C.S.Code, consider the following. A succession of points in vector space is produced by successive time samples of speech. Each point is given a quasi-phonemic label. Each label is taken from a nearby reference point. (The reference points are established during a prerecognition "learning" stage during which about 20 steady-state speech sounds are encoded as reference points.) Establishing reference points for C.S.Code is the subject of previous publications [4], [5]. The succession of quasi-phonemic labels produced in this way are saved to represent speech and the original spectral information is discarded. Each reference point is taken to be an approximation to an original spectral point. In "matching" the spectra of two utterances that have been character-string encoded in this way, distances are measured between reference points. Encoding utterances as character strings introduces some class-

Reprinted from *IEEE Trans. Acoust., Speech, and Signal Process.*, vol. ASSP-24, pp. 183–188, April 1976.

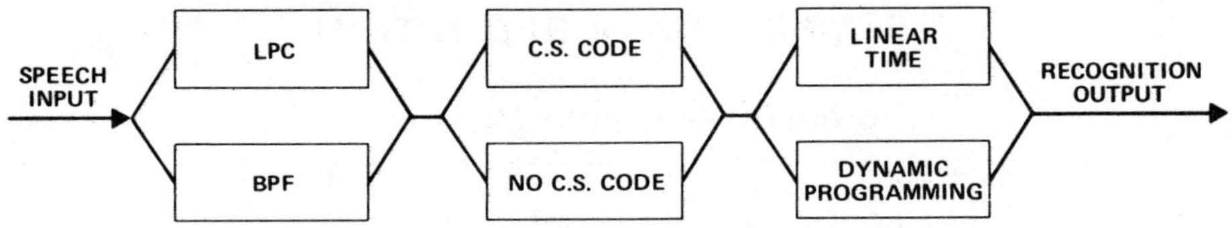

Fig. 1. Components of speech recognition system that were tested.

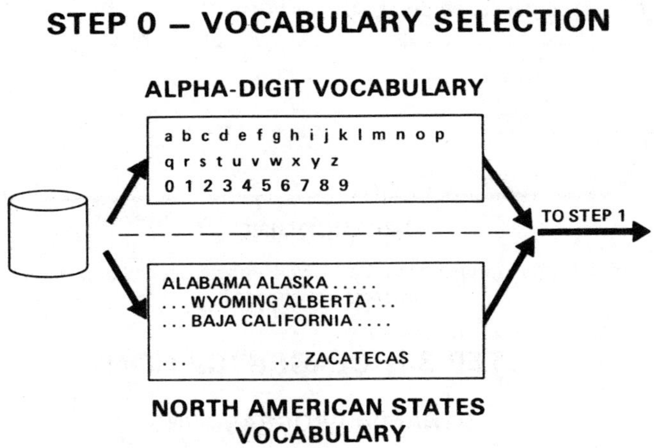

Fig. 2. Vocabulary selection. Two different vocabularies were selected from disc storage.

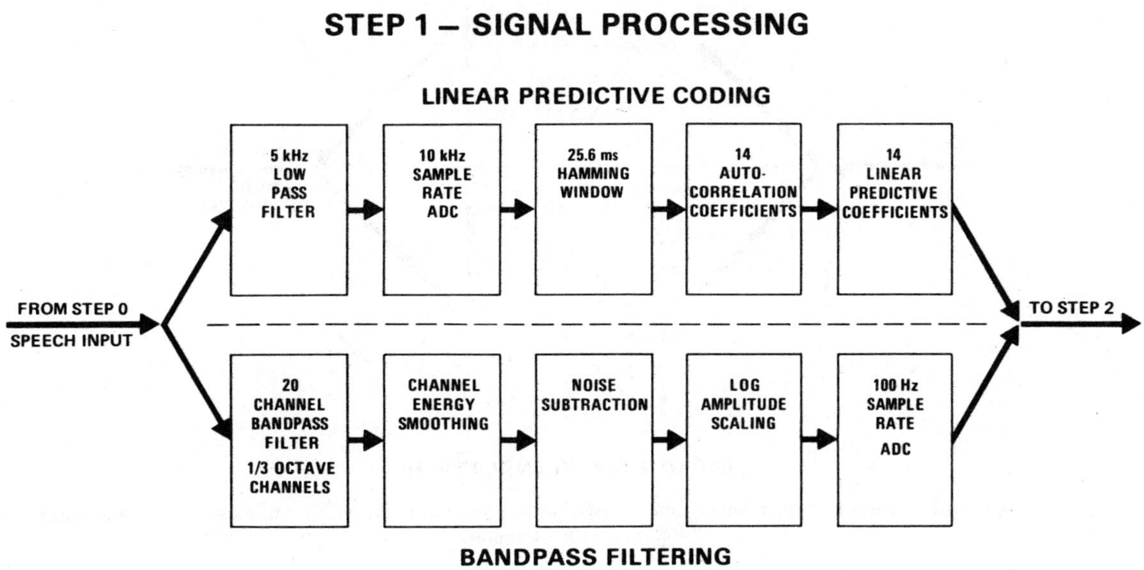

Fig. 3. Signal processing. Either LPC or bandpass filtering were used.

ification errors but it also greatly reduces the time and storage needed to process speech.

For the *bandpass filtering preprocessing* method, the *speech sound similarity measure* used was the Chebyshev norm (absolute value norm). This meant summing the absolute value of the differences of the coordinate values between the unknown and template every 10 ms. (We obtained slightly better results with the Euclidean norm, but it was not used because it was more expensive computationally. A similar result was obtained by Neroth [1] who compared the Chebyshev and Euclidean norms.) Before measuring distances, all filter samples were normalized by dividing by the total energy. (This normalization technique was previously used by Shearme and Leach [2].)

The *LPC preprocessing* method employed a *speech sound similarity measure* based on Itakura's linear predictive residual. A detailed description of the linear predictive residual is found in a paper by Itakura [3].

Of the two *time alignment methods*, linear time scaling is the simplest. *Linear time scaling* means that two utterance representations to be compared are stretched or compressed *linearly* so that they become the same length. Time normalized utterances are also shifted relative to one another in order to overcome misalignment due to poor detection of the beginnings and endings of utterances. However, nonlinear time translations within the interior of an utterance will still cause interior mismatch. *Dynamic programming*, however, does allow for nonlinear translation, and thus achieves better interior match-

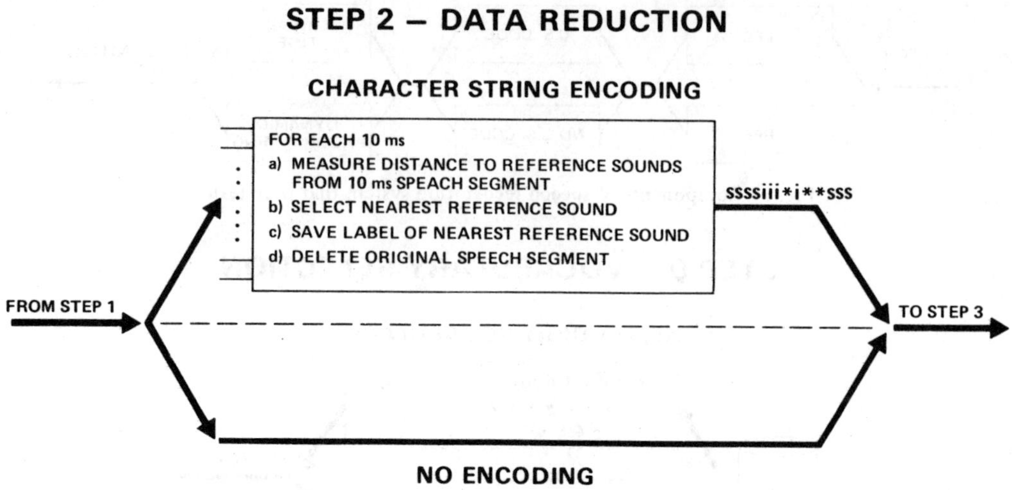

Fig. 4. Data reduction. The speech data sampled from Step 1 were either encoded as a character string of subphonemes *or* they were *not* encoded.

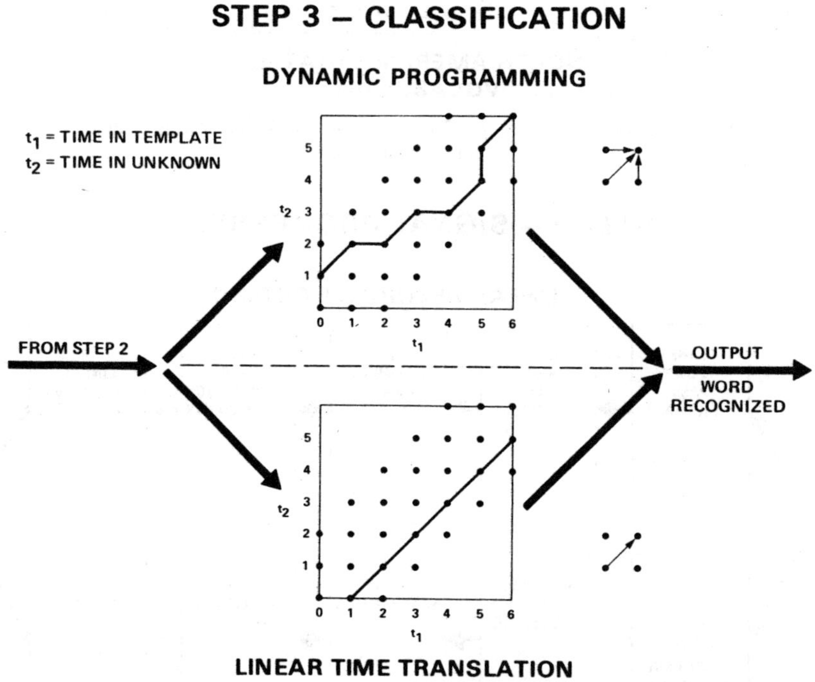

Fig. 5. Time alignment strategies. Either linear time translation or dynamic programming was used to align an unknown utterance with a template.

ing. Dynamic programming requires more computation, but significantly improves recognition results for multisyllabic utterances.

The dynamic programming equation used was

$$D_{ij} = d_{ij} + \min \{D_{ij-1}, D_{i-1j}, D_{i-1j-1}\}$$

where d_{ij} is defined to be the distance between the first utterance at time slice i and the second utterance at time slice j. D_{ij} is the total distance between the first and second utterances from their beginnings up to and including times i and j. The operation "min $\{a, b, c\}$" selects the smallest number from the set of numbers a, b, and c. For a more thorough discussion, see Itakura [3] or Sakoe and Chiba [6].

III. Experimental Conditions

All speech used in these experiments was recorded on analog tape. The tapes are available from the authors. A Telex noise canceling microphone model number CS-75 was used. The recordings were made in a laboratory room with a 65 dB(A) noise level from an air conditioner. Two different vocabularies were recorded. The Alpha-Digit vocabulary was spoken by G. White. It contains the names of the letters of the alphabet and the digits zero through nine for a total of 36 words. (The alphabet was spoken as "A, Bee, Cee, . . ." and not "Alpha, Bravo, Charlie, ...") This vocabulary was spoken five times over the period of two days. The other vocabulary, the North American States vocabulary, contains 91 names: the 50 states of the United States, plus 10 Canadian providences, plus 31 Mexican states. It was pronounced five times by R. Neely in one day in five different recording sessions.

A data base of digitized speech was prepared from analog tapes using either LPC or filter bank analysis. The parameters used to specify the LPC operation and the filter bank operation are as follows: LPC analysis used a 10-kHz sampling rate, 8-bit resolution, 4 dB per octave preemphasis, a 5-kHz low-pass filter, and linear amplitude scaling. Fourteen LPC coefficients were calculated every 12.8 ms and a 25.6-ms Hamming window was used. The filter bank analysis used a 100-Hz sampling rate with amplitude averaging between samples, a logarithmic amplitude scale, 4 dB per octave preemphasis, 8-bit log resolution, and either six one octave filters or 20 one-third octave filters. The filters covered the frequency spectrum from about 100 Hz to 10 kHz. The details of the hardware used to perform these LPC and bandpass filtering operations are given in the following paragraph.

Speech from an analog tape was passed through a Hewlett-Packard analog filter set model 8056A which is a set of 25 one-third octave Chebyshev filters. Spectral shaping (preemphasis) was obtained by adjusting the gain of each of the one-third octave filters to obtain an average gain of about 4 dB per octave about 1000 Hz. In the LPC experiment, speech was low-pass filtered to remove all frequencies above 5 kHz. The low-pass filter was obtained by adjusting the gains on the HP filter channels to -40 dB for the frequencies above 5 kHz. In LPC analysis, the output of the filter bank was passed directly to a 13-bit analog-to-digital converter (ADC). (Only 8 bits of resolution were actually used of the 13 bits possible.) In bandpass filter analysis, the output of the filter bank was passed to a bank of rectifier-integrator circuits and then to the ADC. (Each "rectifier-integrator" circuit rectifies the voltage from a filter channel, subtracts a constant voltage to remove effects of background acoustic noise, sums the resulting voltages for 10 ms, and finally converts the output voltages from linear to logarithmic scales.) The ADC then performed the analog-to-digital conversion and passed the resulting 8-bit numbers to a minicomputer. The digital data was stored on a disc to create a data base for our recognition experiments.

The five repetitions of the Alpha-Digit vocabulary and of the North American States vocabulary were used in recognition experiments to obtain 20 different vocabulary tests. A single repetition was used to "train" the recognizer. (Training consisted of simply storing one example of each word in the vocabulary as an utterance prototype.) The remaining four repetitions were then used to supply unknown utterances to test the accuracy of the recognizer. Next a different repetition from the original five was selected to generate prototypes and again the other four were used to test the recognizer. This process of selecting one repetition from five and testing on the remaining four was repeated five times thus creating 5 × 4 vocabulary tests. For the 36 word Alpha-Digit vocabulary, this resulted in 720 individual utterance tests. Similarly, 1820 utterance tests were obtained from the North American States vocabulary.

IV. Results

In the four tables below, each "percentage correct" was based on 1820 or 720 utterances depending on which vocabulary was used. The North American States vocabulary had 1820 utterance tests and the Alpha-Digit had 720 utterance tests.

For test 1 in Table I, preprocessing was done by a 20 channel filter bank, with $\frac{1}{3}$ octave bandwidth per channel; time alignment was done by dynamic programming; the percentage correct was 98 percent for the Alpha-Digit vocabulary and was 99.6 percent for the North American States vocabulary. In test 2, which differs from test 1 only in the time alignment strategy, the "linear time" normalization was achieved as follows. All utterances were stretched or compressed linearly to be the same length, namely 50 time units long. Reference utterances (prototypes) were compared to unknown utterances by summing up the 50 distances between unknown and reference sounds in the same time units. Then unknown utterances were shifted linearly right and left relative to the prototype and the total distance recalculated. The smallest "total distance" was assumed to be the result of the proper time alignment and was taken as the proper measure of utterance and prototype similarity.

An experiment using LPC recently reported by Itakura [3] shows an error rate of 11.4 percent on the Alpha-Digit vocabulary which is to be compared to our 3 percent error rate for the same vocabulary (Table II). Since the LPC technique we employed was essentially a replication of Itakura's system, the difference in scores requires an explanation. The differences between Itakura's system and ours arises primarily from the bandwidth difference for speech input. Itakura used essentially six LPC coefficients and a 6-kHz sampling rate for his recognition of speech input over a 3.0-kHz phone line. Our system used 14 LPC coefficients with speech input through an 8-kHz noise canceling microphone connection with a 10-kHz sampling rate. We also used a $\frac{1}{3}$ octave filter bank for spectral shaping to preemphasize high frequencies. We also used a slightly different (improved?) dynamic programming strategy (see Sakoe and Chiba [6]). We believe that the differences in scores arise essentially because our system has better access to high frequencies necessary to distinguish some of the words confused by the Itakura recognizer.

The most important result of the time alignment experiments (Table III) is an indication of the extraordinary recognition power of dynamic programming on multisyllabic utterances. A second result is that linear time normalization (with right and left shifting) is as good as dynamic programming on monosyllabic utterances.

The most interesting result shown in Table IV is that C.S.Code seems to reduce the advantage of using dynamic programming relative to linear time normalization.

V. Conclusions

The data base used in these experiments is relatively small. We ask the reader to bear in mind that these are preliminary conclusions.

One conclusion of our work is that *bandpass filtering* and *linear predictive coding* can provide approximately equivalent bases for measuring speech waveform similarity. In other words, a Chebyshev or Euclidean metric in a bandpass filter space is approximately equivalent to the log ratio linear predictive *residuals* in LPC space when typical LPC and filter bank parameters are used. The errors made by both LPC and filter bank recognition systems were nearly the same. Nearly all the errors arose from confusions between /b/ and /d/ and between /m/ and /n/. Our experiments have not concentrated on nasal sounds for which differences are most likely to be found be-

TABLE I
VOCABULARY EFFECTS

Test	Preprocessing Method	Time Alignment	Alpha-Digit Vocabulary (Percent Correct)	North American States Vocabulary
1	20 channel	Dynamic Programming	98 percent	99.6 percent
2	20 channel	Linear Shift	98 percent	90 percent

The Alpha-Digit vocabulary has 36 words, mostly monosyllabic. The North American States word list has 91 words, mostly polysyllabic. Test 1 uses 20 bandpass filter channels and dynamic programming, and gets recognition results of 98 percent correct for the Alpha-Digit vocabulary and 99.6 percent correct for the North American States. The larger vocabulary gets a significantly higher score. But in test 2 it gets a significantly lower score. Dynamic programming is not used in test 2. Linear time shifting (translation) is used in test 2. Thus the vocabulary used has a profound effect on the apparent advantage of different time alignment strategies.

TABLE II
PARAMETRIC REPRESENTATION EFFECTS
(PREPROCESSING EFFECTS)

Preprocessing Method	Time Alignment Method	Alpha-Digit Vocabulary (Percent Correct)	Recognition Time per Utterance	Data Rate Bits/s Approximate
20 channel	Dynamic Programming	98 percent	30 s	12 000
LPC	Dynamic Programming	97 percent	20 s	4200
6 channel	Dynamic Programming	96 percent	15 s	3600
C.S.Code	Dynamic	91 percent	2 s	500

Preprocessing produces four different parametric representations which are arranged in order of increasing data compression (lower bit rate). The recognition accuracy goes down as compression goes up. The similar results for LPC and bandpass filtering shows that they are essentially equivalent.

TABLE III
TIME ALIGNMENT EFFECTS

Preprocessing Method	Time Alignment Method	Vocabulary	Recognition Accuracy (Percent Correct)
20 channel	Dynamic Programming	North American	99.6 percent
20 channel	Linear Shift	North American	90 percent
20 channel	Dynamic Programming	Alpha-Digit	98 percent
20 channel	Linear Shift	Alpha-Digit	98 percent

Time alignment methods include linear time shifting and dynamic programming. Dynamic programming produces nonlinear time warping to achieve the best match between template and unknown utterances. Note that dynamic programming achieves 99.6 percent correct on the multisyllabic words of the North American states word list while linear time normalization achieves only 90 percent. Note, however, that there is no advantage for monosyllabic words of the alphabet plus digits.

tween the LPC and bandpass filtering approach. But with this exception, our work builds confidence in the similar power of the two approaches.

A second conclusion is that popular data reduction techniques may be damaging to the performance of recognition systems. Table II shows preprocessing techniques ranked according to degree of data compression. A strong correlation to recognition accuracy is evident. Although we do not claim to have proved it in this paper, these experiments suggest that standard data reduction techniques have significantly reduced accuracies in computer recognition of speech. We suggest that progress in speech recognition will be aided by special purpose data processors capable of dealing with significantly higher data rates than general purpose computers. This would be one way to avoid the crippling effects of present data compression "preprocessors." It would also promote the use of dynamic time alignment schemes such as offered by dynamic programming which require extra computation.

TABLE IV
C.S.CODE INTERACTION WITH TIME ALIGNMENT

Preprocessing Method	Time Alignment Method	Vocabulary	Recognition Accuracy (Percent Correct)
20 channel	Linear Time	Alpha-Digit	94 percent
20 channel	Dynamic Programming	Alpha-Digit	98 percent
C.S.Code	Linear Time	Alpha-Digit	89 percent
C.S.Code	Dynamic Programming	Alpha-Digit	91 percent

In going from linear time alignment to dynamic programming for 20 channel representation, there is an increase in accuracy from 94 percent to 98 percent. However, with C.S.Code, the accuracy only goes from 89 percent to 91 percent. It appears that C.S.Code reduces the advantage of dynamic programming over linear time normalization. Note that "linear shift" and "linear time" differ in that "linear shift" tries several "linear time" alignments and preserves the best one.

The importance of vocabulary in evaluating recognition systems was demonstrated in our experiments. Japanese recognition scores have been higher than American scores for the past several years. Our results lend support to the idea that the difference in scores may be due to language and vocabulary differences. In fact, we originally chose the North American States vocabulary in order to test this idea. Itakura [3] had reported a very good score, 97.3 percent correct on 200 Japanese geographical names. Each name had an average of 3.5 syllables. However, Itakura reported only 88.6 percent correct for the English alphabet plus digits (Alpha-Digit vocabulary). This led us to suppose that the differences in scores were largely due to vocabulary differences. In order to minimize the vocabulary differences, we looked for a similar multisyllabic word list and came up with the North American States vocabulary. Our results showed a large "vocabulary effect."

In closing, we offer a general opinion on speech recognition research. General purpose computers are unable to process uncompressed speech with adequate speed for real-time speech recognition using utterance template matching techniques and comparing all templates composing the recognizer's vocabulary. In most speech recognition systems an attempt is made to overcome this problem through a special "preprocessing" step designed to reduce the amount of data that reaches the computer. This data reduction is usually so severe that relevant information is thrown away. This is a major cause of low accuracy and lack of "robustness" of recognizers on most general purpose computers. Our research shows that relatively unsophisticated classification strategies perform very well if working with uncompressed speech data. The speech recognition research community would be well advised to pay more attention to those operations that it has come to call "preprocessing."

ACKNOWLEDGMENT

We thank D. R. Reddy for guidance and encouragement in our research. We also thank C. Hankins, P. Belew, and M. Wilmer for assistance in carrying out the experiments.

REFERENCES

[1] C. C. Neroth, "Audio graphic programming system," Ph.D. dissertation, Univ. California, Berkeley, pp. 41–45, 1972.

[2] J. N. Shearme and P. F. Leach, "Some experiments with a simple word recognition system," *IEEE Trans. Audio Electroacoust.* (*Special Issue on Speech Communication and Processing–Part II*), vol. AU-16, pp. 256–261, Mar. 1968.

[3] F. Itakura, "Minimum prediction residual principle applied to speech recognition," *IEEE Trans. Acoust., Speech, Signal Processing* (*Special Issue on IEEE Symposium on Speech Recognition*), vol. ASSP-23, pp. 67–72, Feb. 1975.

[4] G. M. White, "Speech recognition with character string encoding," in *Proc. 1972 IEEE Conf. Decision and Control*, New Orleans, LA, Dec. 13–15, 1972, TJ217,117.

[5] —, "Simple techniques for transforming speech to quasi-phoneme strings," in *Proc. Speech Communication Seminar*, Stockholm, Sweden, Aug. 1–3, 1974, pp. 225–231.

[6] H. Sakoe and S. Chiba, "A dynamic programming approach to continuous speech recognition," in *Proc. 7th Int. Congr. Acoustics*, 1971, Paper 20, p. C13.

[7] O. Fujimura, "Syllable as a unit of speech recognition," in *Proc. IEEE Symp. Speech Recognition*, Carnegie-Mellon Univ., Pittsburgh, PA, Apr. 1974, pp. 148–153; also in *IEEE Trans. Acoust., Speech, Signal Processing* (*Special Issue on IEEE Symposium on Speech Recognition*), vol. ASSP-23, pp. 82–87, Feb. 1975.

Dynamic Programming Algorithm Optimization for Spoken Word Recognition

HIROAKI SAKOE AND SEIBI CHIBA

Abstract—This paper reports on an optimum dynamic programming (DP) based time-normalization algorithm for spoken word recognition. First, a general principle of time-normalization is given using time-warping function. Then, two time-normalized distance definitions, called symmetric and asymmetric forms, are derived from the principle. These two forms are compared with each other through theoretical discussions and experimental studies. The symmetric form algorithm superiority is established. A new technique, called slope constraint, is successfully introduced, in which the warping function slope is restricted so as to improve discrimination between words in different categories. The effective slope constraint characteristic is qualitatively analyzed, and the optimum slope constraint condition is determined through experiments. The optimized algorithm is then extensively subjected to experimental comparison with various DP-algorithms, previously applied to spoken word recognition by different research groups. The experiment shows that the present algorithm gives no more than about two-thirds errors, even compared to the best conventional algorithm.

I. Introduction

It is well known that speaking rate variation causes nonlinear fluctuation in a speech pattern time axis. Elimination of this fluctuation, or time-normalization, has been one of the central problems in spoken word recognition research. At an early stage, some linear normalization techniques were examined, in which timing differences between speech patterns were eliminated by linear transformation of the time axis. Reports on these efforts indicated that any linear transformation is inherently insufficient for dealing with highly complicated fluctuation nonlinearity as well as that time-normalization significantly improves recognition accuracy.

DP-matching, discussed in this paper, is a pattern matching algorithm with a nonlinear time-normalization effect. In this algorithm, the time-axis fluctuation is approximately modeled with a nonlinear warping function of some carefully specified properties. Timing differences between two speech patterns are eliminated by warping the time axis of one so that the maximum coincidence is attained with the other. Then, the time-normalized distance is calculated as the minimized residual distance between them. This minimization process is very efficiently carried out by use of the dynamic programming (DP) technique. The basic idea of DP-matching has been reported in several publications [1]-[3], where it has been shown by preliminary experiment on Japanese digit words that a recognition accuracy as high as 99.8 percent has been achieved, indicating the DP-matching effectiveness.

This paper reports an optimum algorithm for DP-matching through theoretical discussions and experimental studies. Investigations were made, based on the assumption that speech patterns are time-sampled with a common and uniform sampling period, as in most general cases. One of the problems discussed in this paper involves the relative superiority of either a symmetric form of DP-matching or an asymmetric one. In the asymmetric form, time-normalization is achieved by transforming the time axis of a speech pattern onto that of the other. In the symmetric form, on the other hand, both time axes are transformed onto a temporarily defined common axis. Theoretical and experimental comparisons show that the symmetric form gives better recognition than the asymmetric one. Another problem discussed concerns slope constraint technique. Since too much of the warping function flexibility sometimes results in poor discrimination between words in different categories, a constraint is newly introduced on the warping function slope. Detailed slope constraint condition is optimized through experimental studies. As a further investigation, the optimized algorithm is experimentally compared with several varieties of the DP-algorithm, which have been applied to spoken word recognition by some research groups [3]-[6]. The optimized algorithm superiority is established, indicating the validity of this investigation.

Manuscript received February 17, 1977; revised September 7, 1977.

The authors are with Central Research Laboratories, Nippon Electric Company, Limited, Kawasaki, Japan.

II. DP-Matching Principle

A. General Time-Normalized Distance Definition

Speech can be expressed by appropriate feature extraction as a sequence of feature vectors.

$$A = a_1, a_2, ------, a_i, ------, a_I$$
$$B = b_1, b_2, ------, b_j, ------, b_J. \tag{1}$$

Consider the problem of eliminating timing differences between these two speech patterns. In order to clarify the nature of time-axis fluctuation or timing differences, let us consider an i - j plane, shown in Fig. 1, where patterns A and B are developed along the i-axis and j-axis, respectively. Where these speech patterns are of the same category, the timing differences between them can be depicted by a sequence of points $c = (i, j)$:

$$F = c(1), c(2), ------, c(k), ------, c(K), \tag{2}$$

where

$$c(k) = (i(k), j(k)).$$

This sequence can be considered to represent a function which approximately realizes a mapping from the time axis of pattern A onto that of pattern B. Hereafter, it is called a warping function. When there is no timing difference between these

Reprinted from *IEEE Trans. Acoust., Speech, and Signal Process.*, vol. ASSP-26, pp. 43-49, Feb. 1978.

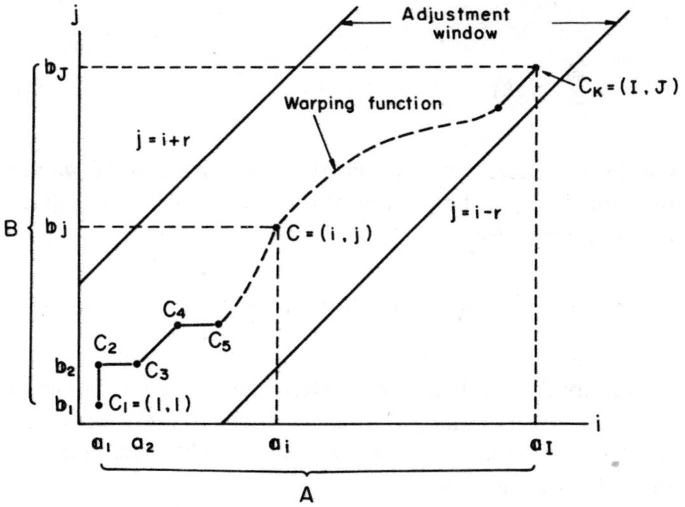

Fig. 1. Warping function and adjustment window definition.

patterns, the warping function coincides with the diagonal line $j = i$. It deviates further from the diagonal line as the timing difference grows.

As a measure of the difference between two feature vectors a_i and b_j, a distance

$$d(c) = d(i,j) = \| a_i - b_j \| \tag{3}$$

is employed between them. Then, the weighted summation of distances on warping function F becomes

$$E(F) = \sum_{k=1}^{K} d(c(k)) \cdot w(k) \tag{4}$$

(where $w(k)$ is a nonnegative weighting coefficient, which is intentionally introduced to allow the $E(F)$ measure flexible characteristic) and is a reasonable measure for the goodness of warping function F. It attains its minimum value when warping function F is determined so as to optimally adjust the timing difference. This minimum residual distance value can be considered to be a distance between patterns A and B, remaining still after eliminating the timing differences between them, and is naturally expected to be stable against time-axis fluctuation. Based on these considerations, the time-normalized distance between two speech patterns A and B is defined as follows:

$$D(A,B) = \operatorname*{Min}_{F} \left[\frac{\sum_{k=1}^{K} d(c(k)) \cdot w(k)}{\sum_{k=1}^{K} w(k)} \right] \tag{5}$$

where denominator $\Sigma\, w(k)$ is employed to compensate for the effect of K (number of points on the warping function F).

Equation (5) is no more than a fundamental definition of time-normalized distance. Effective characteristics of this measure greatly depend on the warping function specification and the weighting coefficient definition. Desirable characteristics of the time-normalized distance measure will vary, according to speech pattern properties (especially time axis expression of speech pattern) to be dealt with. Therefore, the present problem is restricted to the most general case where the following two conditions hold:

Condition 1: Speech patterns are time-sampled with a common and constant sampling period.

Condition 2: We have no *a priori* knowledge about which parts of speech pattern contain linguistically important information.

In this case, it is reasonable to consider each part of a speech pattern to contain an equal amount of linguistic information.

B. Restrictions on Warping Function

Warping function F, defined by (2), is a model of time-axis fluctuation in a speech pattern. Accordingly, it should approximate the properties of actual time-axis fluctuation. In other words, function F, when viewed as a mapping from the time axis of pattern A onto that of pattern B, must preserve linguistically essential structures in pattern A time axis and vice versa. Essential speech pattern time-axis structures are continuity, monotonicity (or restriction of relative timing in a speech), limitation on the acoustic parameter transition speed in a speech, and so on. These conditions can be realized as the following restrictions on warping function F (or points $c(k) = (i(k), j(k))$).

1) Monotonic conditions:

$$i(k-1) \leqq i(k) \text{ and } j(k-1) \leqq j(k).$$

2) Continuity conditions:

$$i(k) - i(k-1) \leqq 1 \text{ and } j(k) - j(k-1) \leqq 1.$$

As a result of these two restrictions, the following relation holds between two consecutive points.

$$c(k-1) = \begin{cases} (i(k), j(k) - 1), \\ (i(k) - 1, j(k) - 1), \\ \text{or } (i(k) - 1, j(k)). \end{cases} \tag{6}$$

3) Boundary conditions:

$$i(1) = 1, \ j(1) = 1, \text{ and}$$

$$i(K) = I, \ j(K) = J. \tag{7}$$

4) Adjustment window condition (see Fig. 1):

$$| i(k) - j(k) | \leqq r \tag{8}$$

where r is an appropriate positive integer called window length. This condition corresponds to the fact that time-axis fluctuation in usual cases never causes a too excessive timing difference.

5) Slope constraint condition:

Neither too steep nor too gentle a gradient should be allowed for warping function F because such deviations may cause undesirable time-axis warping. Too steep a gradient, for example, causes an unrealistic correspondence between a very short pattern A segment and a relatively long pattern B segment. Then, such a case occurs where a short segment in consonant or phoneme transition part happens to be in good coincidence with an entire steady vowel part. Therefore, a restriction called a slope constraint condition, was set upon the warping function F, so that its first derivative is of discrete form. The slope constraint condition is realized as a restriction on the possible relation among (or the possible configuration of) several consecutive points on the warping function, as is shown in Fig. 2(a) and (b). To put it concretely, if point $c(k)$ moves forward in the direction of i (or j)-axis consecutive m times, then point

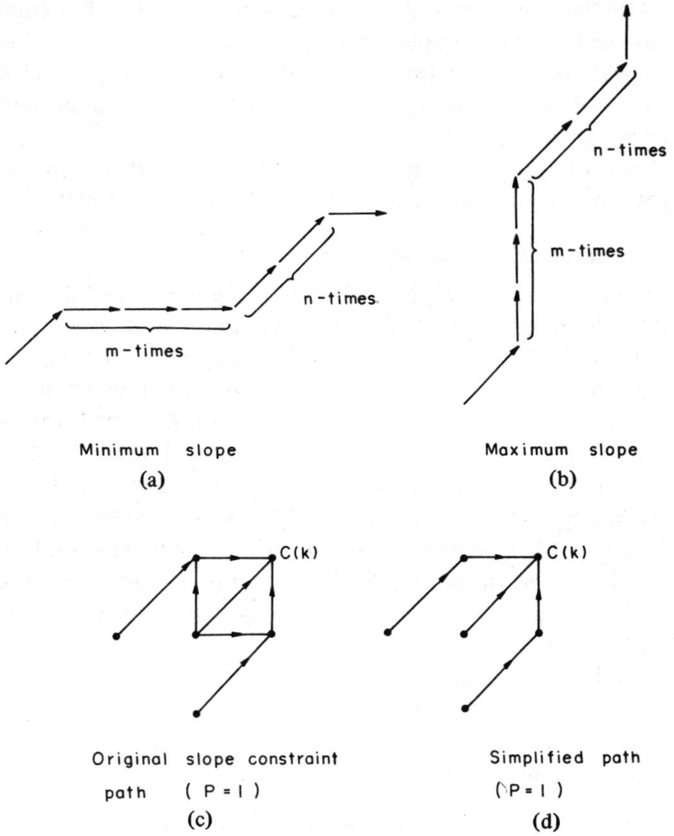

Fig. 2. Slope constraint on warping function.

$c(k)$ is not allowed to step further in the same direction before stepping at least n times in the diagonal direction. The effective intensity of the slope constraint can be evaluated by the following measure

$$P = n/m. \tag{9}$$

The larger the P measure, the more rigidly the warping function slope is restricted. When $p = 0$, there are no restrictions on the warping function slope. When $p = \infty$ (that is $m = 0$), the warping function is restricted to diagonal line $j = i$. Nothing more occurs than a conventional pattern matching no time-normalization. Generally speaking, if the slope constraint is too severe, then time-normalization would not work effectively. If the slope constraint is too lax, then discrimination between speech patterns in different categories is degraded. Thus, setting neither a too large nor a too small value for p is desirable. Section IV reports the results of an investigation on an optimum compromise on p value through several experiments.

In Fig. 2(c) and (d), two examples of permissible point $c(k)$ paths under slope constraint condition $p = 1$ are shown. The Fig. 2(c) type is directly derived from the above definition, while Fig. 2(d) is an approximated type, and there is another constraint. That is, the second derivative of warping function F is restricted, so that the point $c(k)$ path does not orthogonally change its direction. This new constraint reduces the number of paths to be searched. Therefore, the simple Fig. 2(d) type is adopted afterward, except for the $p = 0$ case.

C. Discussions on Weighting Coefficient

Since the criterion function in (5) is a rational expression, its maximization is an unwieldy problem. If the denominator in (5)

$$N = \sum_{k=1}^{K} w(k) \tag{10}$$

(called normalization coefficient) is independent of warping function F, it can be put out of the bracket, while simplifying the equation as follows:

$$D(A,B) = \frac{1}{N} \min_{F} \left[\sum_{k=1}^{K} d(c(k)) \cdot w(k) \right]. \tag{11}$$

This simplified problem can be effectively solved by use of the dynamic programming technique. There are two typical weighting coefficient definitions which enable this simplification. They are as follows.

1) Symmetric form:

$$w(k) = (i(k) - i(k-1)) + (j(k) - j(k-1)), \tag{12}$$

then

$$N = I + J, \tag{13}$$

where I and J are lengths of speech patterns A and B, respectively [see (1)].

2) Asymmetric form:

$$w(k) = (i(k) - i(k-1)), \tag{14}$$

then

$$N = I. \tag{15}$$

(Or equivalently, $w(k) = (j(k) - j(k-1))$, then $N = J$.)

The basic concepts of the symmetric and asymmetric forms were originally defined by Sakoe and Chiba [3]. The problem of their relative superiority has been left unsolved.

If it is assumed that time axes i and j are both continuous, then, in the symmetric form, the summation in (5) means an integration along the temporarily defined axis $l = i + j$. In the asymmetric form, on the other hand, the summation means an integration along time axis i. As a result of this difference, time-normalized distance is symmetric, or $D(A,B) = D(B,A)$, in the symmetric form, though not in the asymmetric form. Another more important result, caused by the difference in the integration axis, is that, as is shown in Fig. 3, weighting coefficient $w(k)$ reduces to zero in the asymmetric form, when the point in warping function steps in the direction of j-axis, or $c(k) = c(k-1) + (0, 1)$. This means that some feature vectors b_j are possibly excluded from the integration in the asymmetric form. On the contrary, in the case of symmetric form, minimum $w(k)$ value is equal to 1, and no exclusion occurs. Since discussions here are based on the assumption that each part in a speech pattern should be treated equally, an exclusion of any feature vectors from integration should be avoided as long as possible. It can be expected, therefore, that the symmetric form will give better recognition accuracy than the asymmetric form. However, it should be noted that the slope constraint reduces the situation where the point in warping function steps in the j-axis direction. The difference in performance between the symmetric one and asymmetric one will gradually vanish as the slope constraint is intensified.

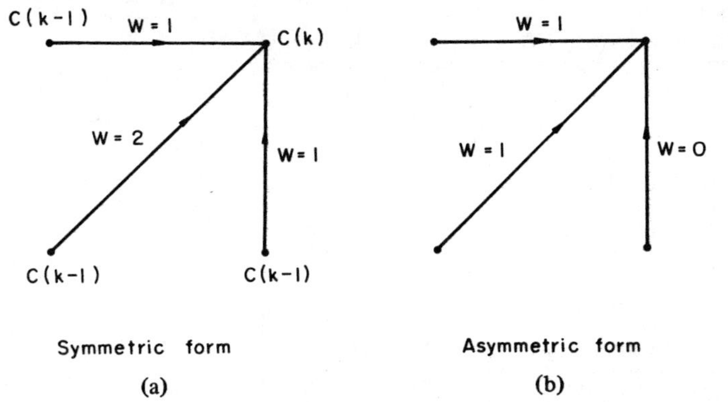

Fig. 3. Weighting coefficient $W(k)$ for both symmetric and asymmetric forms.

III. Practical DP-Matching Algorithm

A. DP-Equation

A simplified definition of time-normalized distance $D(A, B)$ given by (11) is one of the typical problems to which the well-known DP-principle [7] can be applied. The basic algorithm for calculating (11) is written as follows.

Initial condition:

$$g_1(c(1)) = d(c(1)) \cdot w(1). \tag{16}$$

DP-equation:

$$g_k(c(k)) = \min_{c(k-1)} [g_{k-1}(c(k-1)) + d(c(k)) \cdot w(k)]. \tag{17}$$

Time-normalized distance:

$$D(A, B) = \frac{1}{N} g_K(c(K)). \tag{18}$$

It is implicitly assumed here that $c(0) = (0, 0)$. Accordingly, $w(1) = 2$ in the symmetric form, and $w(1) = 1$ in the asymmetric form. By realizing the restriction on the warping function described in Section II-B and substituting (12) or (14) for weighting coefficient $w(k)$ in (17), several practical algorithms can be derived. As one of the simplest examples, the algorithm for symmetric form, in which no slope constraint is employed (that is $P = 0$), is shown here.

Initial condition:

$$g(1, 1) = 2d(1, 1). \tag{19}$$

DP-equation:

$$g(i, j) = \min \begin{bmatrix} g(i, j-1) + d(i, j) \\ g(i-1, j-1) + 2d(i, j) \\ g(i-1, j) + d(i, j) \end{bmatrix}. \tag{20}$$

Restricting condition (adjustment window):

$$j - r \leqq i \leqq j + r. \tag{21}$$

Time-normalized distance:

$$D(A, B) = \frac{1}{N} g(I, J), \qquad \text{where } N = I + J. \tag{22}$$

Calculation details are briefly depicted in Section III-B.

The algorithm, especially the DP-equation, should be modified when the asymmetric form is adopted or some slope constraint is employed. In Table I, algorithms are summarized for both symmetric and asymmetric forms, with various slope constraint conditions. In this table, DP-equations for asymmetric forms are shown in some improved form. The first expression in the bracket of the asymmetric form DP-equation for $P = 1$ (that is, $g(i-1, j-2) + (d(i, j-1) + d(i, j))/2)$ corresponds to the case where $c(k-1) = (i(k), j(k) - 1)$ and $c(k-2) = (i(k-1) - 1, j(k-1) - 1)$. Accordingly, if the definition in (14) is strictly obeyed, $w(k)$ is equal to zero while $w(k-1)$ is equal to 1, thus completely omitting the $d(c(k))$ from the summation. In order to avoid this situation to a certain extent, the weighting coefficient $w(k-1) = 1$ is divided between two weighting coefficients $w(k-1)$ and $w(k)$. Thus, $(d(i, j-1) + d(i, j))/2$ is substituted for $d(i, j-1) + 0 \cdot d(i, j)$ in this expression. Similar modifications are applied to other asymmetric form DP-equations. In fact, it has been established, by a preliminary experiment, that this modification significantly improves the asymmetric form performance.

B. Calculation Details

DP-equation or $g(i, j)$ must be recurrently calculated in ascending order with respect to coordinates i and j, starting from initial condition at $(1, 1)$ up to (I, J). The domain in which the DP-equation must be calculated is specified by

$$1 \leqq i \leqq I, \quad 1 \leqq j \leqq J,$$

and

$$j - r \leqq i \leqq j + r \text{ (adjustment window)}.$$

A practical procedure for calculating the time-normalized distance is shown in Fig. 4 as a flowchart.

IV. Experiments and Results

A. Experiment Outline

In order to quantitatively evaluate various types of DP-matching, several recognition experiments were conducted. The speech analyzer used through these experiments was a 10-channel bandpass filter bank which covered up to a 5.9-kHz frequency range. The output of each channel was time-sampled every 18 ms and was digitized in order that it could be fed into the digital computer (NEAC-3100). Automatic gain control effect was realized by dividing each filter output level by their sum total, at every sampling period. The so-called time-frequency amplitude pattern thus obtained was stored on a digital magnetic tape file. Recognition experiments were conducted for the speech pattern read out of this file. The recognition scheme used was the forced decision pattern matching method, where the input pattern (unknown) was decided to be of the same category as the reference pattern to which the maximum coincidence (that is the minimum time-normalized distance) was achieved. Distance $d(i, j)$ was measured by the Chebyshev norm, which was employed in the previous work [2]. Reference patterns were adapted to each speaker. That is, one repetition of the complete vocabulary, pronounced by each speaker, was used as the reference patterns for each speaker.

TABLE I
SYMMETRIC AND ASYMMETRIC DP-ALGORITHMS WITH SLOPE CONSTRAINT CONDITION $P = 0, \frac{1}{2}, 1$, AND 2

P	Schematic explanation	Symmetric / Asymmetric		DP-equation g(i, j) =
0		Symmetric	min	g(i,j-1)+d(i,j) g(i-1,j-1)+2d(i,j) g(i-1,j)+d(i,j)
		Asymmetric	min	g(i,j-1) g(i-1,j-1)+d(i,j) g(i-1,j)+d(i,j)
1/2	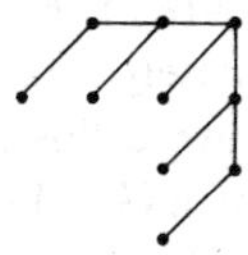	Symmetric	min	g(i-1,j-3)+2d(i,j-2)+d(i,j-1)+d(i,j) g(i-1,j-2)+2d(i,j-1)+d(i,j) g(i-1,j-1)+2d(i,j) g(i-2,j-1)+2d(i-1,j)+d(i,j) g(i-3,j-1)+2d(i-2,j)+d(i-1,j)+d(i,j)
		Asymmetric	min	g(i-1,j-3)+(d(i,j-2)+d(i,j-1)+d(i,j))/3 g(i-1,j-2)+(d(i,j-1)+d(i,j))/2 g(i-1,j-1)+d(i,j) g(i-2,j-1)+d(i-1,j)+d(i,j) g(i-3,j-1)+d(i-2,j)+d(i-1,j)+d(i,j)
1	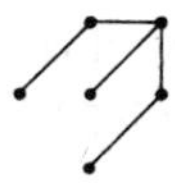	Symmetric	min	g(i-1,j-2)+2d(i,j-1)+d(i,j) g(i-1,j-1)+2d(i,j) g(i-2,j-1)+2d(i-1,j)+d(i,j)
		Asymmetric	min	g(i-1,j-2)+(d(i,j-1)+d(i,j))/2 g(i-1,j-1)+d(i,j) g(i-2,j-1)+d(i-1,j)+d(i,j)
2	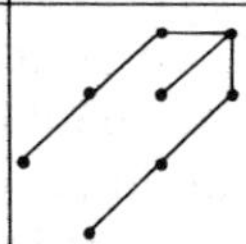	Symmetric	min	g(i-2,j-3)+2d(i-1,j-2)+2d(i,j-1)+d(i,j) g(i-1,j-1)+2d(i,j) g(i-3,j-2)+2d(i-2,j-1)+2d(i-1,j)+d(i,j)
		Asymmetric	min	g(i-2,j-3)+2(d(i-1,j-2)+d(i,j-1)+d(i,j))/3 g(i-1,j-1)+d(i,j) g(i-3,j-2)+d(i-2,j-1)+d(i-1,j)+d(i,j)

Experiments were conducted in three parts. The first part was carried out with the objectives of comparing the performances of symmetric form DP-matching and asymmetric form DP-matching, and optimizing the slope constraint condition. In the second part, further optimization of the slope constraint condition was investigated. In the final part of the experiments, the algorithm thus optimized was compared with several DP-algorithms proposed by different research groups.

B. Experiment (I)

The objective of this experiment was to compare symmetric form DP-matching and asymmetric form DP-matching performances, and to determine the best compromise for the slope constraint intensity (parameter P). Speech data used in this experiment were Japanese digit words (see Table II) isolatedly spoken by 10 male speakers. Six repetitions of the 10 digit words were made by each speaker. Then, for each speaker, each of the six repetitions was used as a reference pattern set. For each reference pattern set, the remaining five repetitions were supplied to recognition. Therefore, 10 (persons) $\times$ 6 (reference pattern sets) $\times$ 50 (input patterns) = 3000 (recognition tests) were conducted. The DP-matching subjected to this experiment covered both symmetric and asymmetric forms, with slope constraint condition of $P = 0, \frac{1}{2}, 1$, and 2. In each case, window length r was set equal to 6, which covered the utmost ±108 ms timing difference. A linear time-normalization method was also tested where the time axis of the input pattern was adjusted to that of the reference pattern with linear transformation.

Results are shown in Fig. 5 as two error rate curves. In this

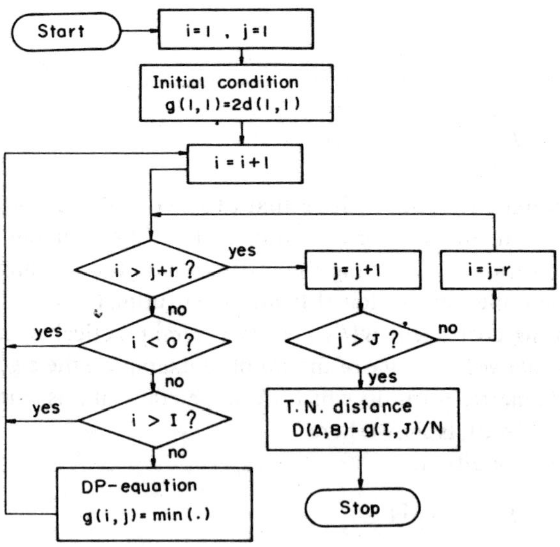

Fig. 4. DP-matching flowchart.

figure, it can be seen that the performance of the asymmetric form DP-matching is evidently inferior to that of the symmetric one, and that the difference in performance between them tends to vanish gradually as the slope constraint is intensified. It can also be seen that symmetric form DP-matching performance is utterly unaffected by a slope constraint of up to $P = 1$. On the other hand, the asymmetric form DP-matching performance is very effectively improved by slope constraint. The optimum condition is $P = 1$. When the slope constraint is intensified beyond $P = 1$, the performance of the asym-

TABLE II
TEN JAPANESE DIGITS AND THEIR PHONEMIC TRANSCRIPTIONS

0	1	2	3	4	5	6	7	8	9
rei	itʃi	ni	san	jon	go	roku	nana	hatʃi	kju

metric form, as well as that of the symmetric one tends to be degraded. Since extremely intensified slope constraint does not give any time-normalization, it is naturally understood that further growth in slope constraint will result in some worse performance than that of linear time-normalization method (0.8 percent error).

C. Experiment (II)

In order to further examine the effect of the slope constraint on the symmetric form DP-matching performance, another experiment was carried out for a 50-Japanese geographical name vocabulary. This vocabulary includes such confusing pairs of words as "Chiba"-"Shiga", "Okayama"-"Wakayama", "Fukushima"-"Tokushima", and "Hyogo"-"Kyoto". Each of two male speakers and two female speakers uttered six repetitions of the complete vocabulary. The first repetitions of each speaker were used as the reference patterns. The remaining five repetitions of each speaker were used as unknown input patterns, thus providing 4 (persons) × 50 (vocabulary size) × 5 (repetitions) = 1000 (recognition tests). The window length r here was set equal to 8, which covered utmost ±144 ms timing difference.

Results are shown in Fig. 6 for each of the slope constraint conditions. These results show that the slope constraint has a marked effect on the performance of the symmetric form DP matching, too. Optimum performance is also attained at $P = 1$.

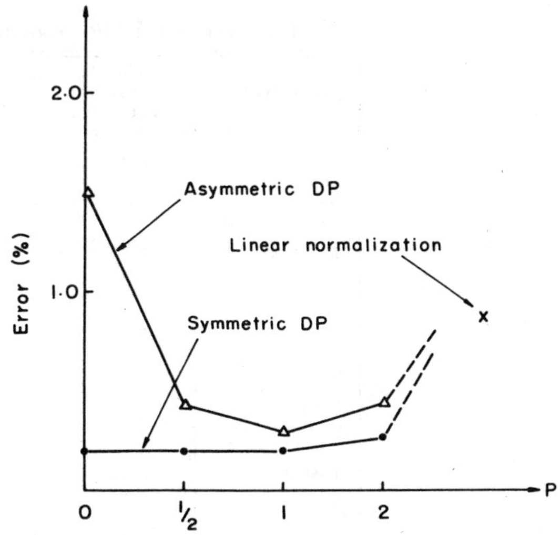

Fig. 5. Experiment (I) results (for Japanese digit words).

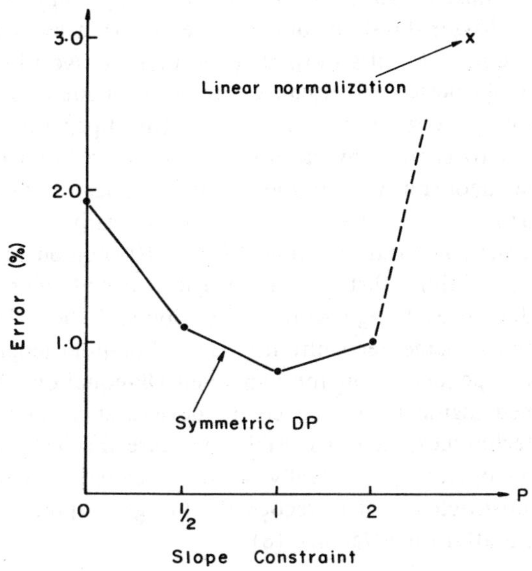

Fig. 6. Experiment (II) results (for 50 Japanese geographical names).

D. Experiment (III)

Various DP-algorithms have been applied to spoken word recognition, by different research groups. Four typical ones, including those proposed by Sakoe and Chiba [3], Velichko and Zagoruyko [4], White and Neely [5], and Itakura [6], were subjected to comparison with the algorithms described in this paper. Details of each algorithm are summarized in Table III. Some modifications were made to equalize the experimental condition, but these modifications are not harmful to time-normalizing abilities of algorithms. Both the Japanese digit data and Japanese geographical name data were again used as test data. Results are shown in Table IV. From these results, it can be observed that the symmetric form DP-matching with slope constraint $P = 1$, described in this paper, is the best of various DP-algorithms applied to spoken word recognition.

V. DISCUSSIONS

From the results shown in Fig. 5, it can be observed that the symmetric form DP-matching performance is significantly superior to that of the asymmetric one. It can also be seen that the difference in performance between them tends to decrease as the slope constraint grows. These observations completely agree with the theoretical discussions presented in Section II, indicating the validity of this investigation. From Figs. 5 and 6, it can be determined that the slope constraint condition with $P = 1$ is the optimum point for both symmetric and asymmetric forms. Moreover, as can be seen from Table I, the DP-equation for $P = 1$ is of the most simple form, next to that for $P = 0$. Thus, the slope constraint condition with $P = 1$ is favorable for computational economy, as well as for best performance. The slope constraint hardly affects the performance of the symmetric form DP-matching in case of Japanese digit vocabulary. This is perhaps due to the fact that, in case of Japanese digit words, the vocabulary size is so small and the separation between the words in the vocabulary is inherently so good that an optimally high recognition accuracy was achieved even without slope constraint. Nevertheless, the usefulness of the slope constraint for the symmetric form was established by the experiment on the Japanese geographical name data. Summing up these discussions, the symmetric form with slope constraint condition $P = 1$ is the optimum condition, when the speech patterns are time-sampled with a common and uniform sampling period.

TABLE III
FOUR VARITIES OF DP-ALGORITHMS SUBJECTED TO COMPARISON IN EXPERIMENT (III)

Algorithm	Initial Condition $g(1, 1) =$	Normalization Coefficient N	DP-equation $g(i, j) =$
Sakoe and Chiba [3]	$d(1, 1)$	I	$\min \begin{bmatrix} g(i-1, j) + d(i, j) \\ g(i-1, j-1) + d(i, j) \\ g(i-1, j-2) + d(i, j) \end{bmatrix}$
Velichko and Zagoruyko [4]	$a(1, 1)$	$\max\ [I, J]$	$\max \begin{bmatrix} g(i, j-1) \\ g(i-1, j-1) + a(i, j) \\ g(i-1, j) \end{bmatrix}$ where $a(i, j) = 1-d(i, j)$
White and Neely [5]	$d(1, 1)$	$(I + J)$	$\min \begin{bmatrix} g(i-1, j) + d(i, j) \\ g(i-1, j-1) + d(i, j) \\ g(i, j-1) + d(i, j) \end{bmatrix}$
Itakura [6]	$d(1, 1)$	I	$\min \begin{bmatrix} g(i-1, j) + \alpha \cdot d(i, j) \\ g(i-1, j-1) + d(i, j) \\ g(i-1, j-2) + d(i, j) \end{bmatrix}$ where $\alpha = \infty \quad (i(k-1) = i(k-2))$, $\alpha = 1 \quad (i(k-1) \neq i(k-2))$

The optimized algorithm was experimentally compared with several DP-algorithms, including those reported by other research groups. Results show that the present algorithm gives considerably better performance, for both Japanese digit data and Japanese geographical name data. This superiority can be attributed to careful investigations made to realize a pattern matching algorithm with rational characteristics of comparing each part of speech pattern evenly as far as possible.

As for the computational time, NEAC-3100 computer (index modified addition/substruction execution time is 8 μs) required about 3 s for each digit word recognition and about 30 s for geographical name recognition. These computational times scarcely depended upon the employed DP-equation. Recent high-speed digital integrated circuit devices and pipeline processor techniques made it feasible to realize the real time DP-matching operation. Actually, a DP-matching processor has been constructed which recognizes 60 geographical names in 300 ms after the utterance [8].

TABLE IV
EXPERIMENT (III) RESULTS

Algorithm \ Test data	Error rate (%): Japanese digit words	Error rate (%): 50 Japanese Geographical names
Sakoe and Chiba Symmetric P = 1 [in this paper]	0.2	0.8
Sakoe and Chiba Asymmetric P = 1 [in this paper]	0.3	1.3
Sakoe and Chiba [3]	0.3	1.5
Velichko and Zagoruyko [4]	2.0	2.7
White and Neely [5]	0.33	1.3
Itakura [6]	0.4	1.3
Linear method	0.87	5.9

VI. CONCLUSIONS

The optimum DP-algorithm, applied to speech recognition, was investigated. Two forms of pattern matching method, symmetric and asymmetric forms, were proposed along with a new technique called slope constraint. These varieties were then compared through theoretical and experimental investigations. Conclusions are as follows.

1) The symmetric form gives better recognition accuracy than the asymmetric form.

2) Slope constraint is actually effective. Optimum performance is attained when the slope constraint condition is $P = 1$.

The validity of these results was ensured by a good agreement between theoretical discussions and experimental results.

The optimized algorithm was then experimentally compared with several other DP-algorithms applied to spoken word recognition by different research groups, and the superiority of the algorithm described in this paper was established.

ACKNOWLEDGMENT

The authors wish to thank Y. Kato for his encouragement throughout this research.

REFERENCES

[1] H. Sakoe and S. Chiba, "A similarity evaluation of speech patterns by dynamic programming" (in Japanese), presented at the Dig. 1970 Nat. Meeting, Inst. Electron. Comm. Eng. Japan, p. 136, July 1970.

[2] —, "A dynamic programming approach to continuous speech recognition," in *1971 Proc. 7th ICA, Paper 20 C13*, Aug. 1971.

[3] —, "Comparative study of DP-pattern matching techniques for speech recognition" (in Japanese), in *1973 Tech. Group Meeting Speech, Acoust. Soc. Japan, Preprints (S73-22)*, Dec. 1973.

[4] V. M. Velichko and N. G. Zagoruyko, "Automatic recognition of 200 words," *Int. J. Man-Machine Stud.*, vol. 2, p. 223, June 1970.

[5] G. White and R. Neely, "Speech recognition experiments with linear prediction, bandpass filtering, and dynamic programming," *IEEE Trans. Acoust., Speech, Signal Processing*, vol. ASSP-24, pp. 183–188, Apr. 1976.

[6] F. Itakura, "Minimum prediction residual principle applied to speech recognition," *IEEE Trans. Acoust., Speech, Signal Processing*, vol. ASSP-23, pp. 67–72, Feb. 1975.

[7] R. Bellman and S. Dreyfus, *Applied Dynamic Programming*. New Jersey: Princeton Univ. Press, 1962.

[8] S. Tsuruta, H. Sakoe, and S. Chiba, "Real-time speech recognition system by minicomputer with DP processor" (in Japanese), in *1974 Tech. Group Meeting Speech, Acoust. Soc. Japan, Preprints (S74-30)*, Dec. 1974.

Part IV
Word Spotting

BRITISH ACOUSTICAL SOCIETY

"SPRING MEETING" at Chelsea College, London, S.W.3 on Wednesday 25th April / Friday 27th April, 1973.

SPEECH AND HEARING: Session 'C': Speech Properties and Recognition.

Paper No:

73SHC3

An Efficient Elastic-Template Method for Detecting Given Words in Running Speech

J S Bridle

Joint Speech Research Unit

1. Introduction In many applications of automatic speech recognition, such as voice input to computers, it will be necessary to decode a spoken command to produce a sequence of words which 'makes sense'.

In general, two utterances of the same word have different time-structures because of differences in pronunciation: some parts of the word become longer, others shorter, to varying extents. One approach to automatic speech recognition (the segmentation approach) attempts to identify phonemes as they occur, and thus reduce speech to a string of symbols similar to that which a phonetician might use to represent the utterance. Unfortunately there is no simple relationship between acoustic and phonetic descriptions of a speech signal.

An alternative approach is a template method in which we first use a measurement process to represent the speech signal as a small set of slowly varying functions of time. Words in the vocabulary are stored as 'templates' derived from actual spoken examples of the words. Typically, a template might be 50 regularly spaced samples of six measures. We assume that the same, or similar, words in the input speech will produce signals which are similar to the template, except that the time scales will be different. This assumption of similarity may of course turn out be as wrong as the acoustic-phonetic one above, but at this stage the possibilities for suitable measurement methods have not been fully explored.

In what follows we simplify the problem of recognising a sequence of words by considering the identification of a single word, represented by one template, but we retain the requirement that the word be picked out of a complete sentence, without prior segmentation into word units.

2. The non-linear time-distortion problem Before we can measure how similar to the template a portion of the input is, corresponding parts must be aligned in time. On a time-time diagram with time for the template drawn vertically and the input horizontally, any particular way of arranging the samples of the template against the samples of the input can be represented as a time-registration 'path', P, from the bottom to the top.

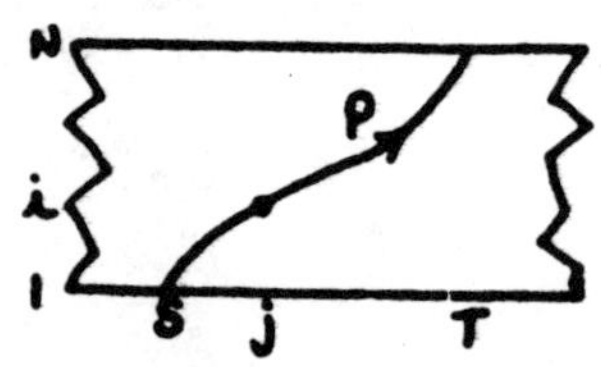

At any point (i, j) we can find the instantaneous similarity, A(i, j) between the ith time-sample of the template and the jth time-sample of the

Reprinted with permission from *British Acoust. Soc. Meeting,* April 1973, pp. 1–4.

input. The method of computing A should depend on the nature of the signals resulting from analysis of the speech.

A total fit function, TF(P), is a measure of the overall similarity between the template and the portion (S–T) of the input between the ends of such a path, evaluated along the path. TF should include the instantaneous similarities, the amount of time-scale distortion and the length of the path. We could say that an example of the template word occurs in the input if there is a complete path for which TF is greater than some threshold.

The problem is to find where such paths occur, without trying all possible paths. (Even on a 10 by 10 diagram, the number of paths from corner to corner of the type described in section 5 is more than one million).

3. Two methods One approach is to use a path-growing heuristic [1] which attempts to find good time-registration paths by examining the instantaneous similarity, A, in various directions from the growing tip of the path. Warren [2] and the author's unpublished work indicate that developments of such methods can give good results some of the time, but that wrong decisions can cause failure, even with two similar patterns.

A better approach is to use the principles of Dynamic Programming [3] to consider all optimum paths. It is only possible to do this properly if the fit function has a rather special property: that the best way, $\hat{P}(i, j)$, of getting to a point (i, j) should be independent of what happens beyond (i, j). In this case there exists a 'partial function', F(P(i, j)) which defines $\hat{P}(i, j)$ as the partial path to (i, j) which maximises F(P(i, j)).

$$\text{ie} \quad \hat{F}(i, j) = F(\hat{P}(i, j)) = \max_{P} \{F(P(i, j))\}$$

F can be defined incremently:

$$F(P(i-\alpha, j-\beta), (i, j)) = G(F(P(i-\alpha, j-\beta)), A(i, j), \alpha, \beta)$$

where $(i-\alpha, j-\beta)$ is the point on the path just before (i, j).

The crucial step is to recognise that $\hat{F}(i, j)$, (and therefore $\hat{P}(i, j)$) can also be defined (and computed) by a simple local operation:

$$\hat{F}(i, j) = \max_{\alpha, \beta} \{G(\hat{F}(i-\alpha, j-\beta), A(i, j), \alpha, \beta)\}$$

The sequence of values $TF(\hat{P}(N, T))$ can be thought of as the output of a time-flexible generalisation of a matched filter, and a detection threshold could be applied to decide where examples of the template word occur.

Now we must consider the all-important requirement on TF: the ability to recognise the first part of an optimum path without considering the rest of it. If the beginning and end of a candidate portion of input speech could be identified first, we could use a path-ength normalisation factor in TF which is independent of details of the path [4], but if we want to consider all paths on a strip, then at an intermediate point we cannot know how long the complete path will be. Therefore we cannot decide which of two paths up to this point is better if one has a high score so far but is long, and the other has a low score but is short.

It appears that it is too much to ask a method like this to detect the words as well as measure similarity. If we could detect, by other means, just one reliable acoustic event near the middle of the template word, then we could evaluate TF for the best path through this fixed point (always working towards the fixed point). The alternative, described below, is to concentrate on the detection aspect.

4. <u>The new method</u> F is defined for any partial path to (i, j), incremently, as

$$F(P(i-\alpha, j-\beta), (i, j)) = (1-\gamma). F(P(i-\alpha, j-\beta) + \gamma. H(A(i, j), \alpha, \beta)$$

with starting condition $F(1, j) = A(1, j)$

Thus F is a sum of recent values of instantaneous similarity along the path, with past values given exponentially decreasing weight, according to the value of γ. H applies an extra factor to A, according to the local time-distortion which is a function of the increments α and β.

F is a measure of the 'local similarity' at any point on a time registration path. We now say that a portion of the input pattern between points S and T is significantly similar to the template if there is a path from (1, S) to (N, T) for which F is above a threshold at every point on the path.

This criterion, which is superficially similar to the one for detection using total fit, in section 3, is very easy to implement. Paths are considered 'broken' as soon as F falls below the threshold, and $\hat{F}$ is defined in terms of unbroken paths. This results in a considerable saving of computation, because there will be large areas of the time-time diagram which cannot be reached by unbroken paths, and the instantaneous similarity, A, need not be evaluated in such regions.

When we find that a best unbroken path has reached the end of the template, then we have a section of the input which is locally similar to the template throughout its length, with due allowance for distortion of time scales.

5. <u>Details of present implementation</u> A(i, j), the instantaneous similarity between the ith time-sample of the template and jth sample of the input, is computed from the Euclidean distance, d, between the two points in measurement space.

$$A(d) = 1/(1 + d^2/\delta^2)$$

A is a bell-shaped function of d, with a maximum value of 1 when $d = 0$, and a value of 0.5 when $d = \delta$.

δ is made variable over the template, to allow for greater variation in some parts of the word, particularly at the beginning and the end.

Paths consist of horizontal, vertical and diagonal segments, as in [4]

$$\text{ie} \quad (\alpha, \beta) = \{(1, 0), (0, 1), (1, 1)\}$$

In the expression for F, A is attenuated by a factor k if a horizontal or vertical segment, corresponding to time distortion, is used.

When the point (i, j) is being considered, a one dimensional array of length N holds

$$\hat{F}(1, j), \hat{F}(2, j), \ldots \hat{F}(i-1, j), \hat{F}(i-1, j-1), \hat{F}(i, j-1), \ldots \hat{F}(N-1, j-1)$$

and the newly - calculated F(i, j) replaces F(i-1, j-1).

The figure illustrates the pattern of best unbroken paths produced in response to input sequences which are distorted in amplitude and time with respect to the template. The template and the input are artificial one-dimensional functions of time, chosen to illustrate the action of the process. δ is constant, and the resulting A(d) is illustrated on the same scale as the template. $k = 0$, so there is a high penalty for time-distortion. $\gamma = 0.3$

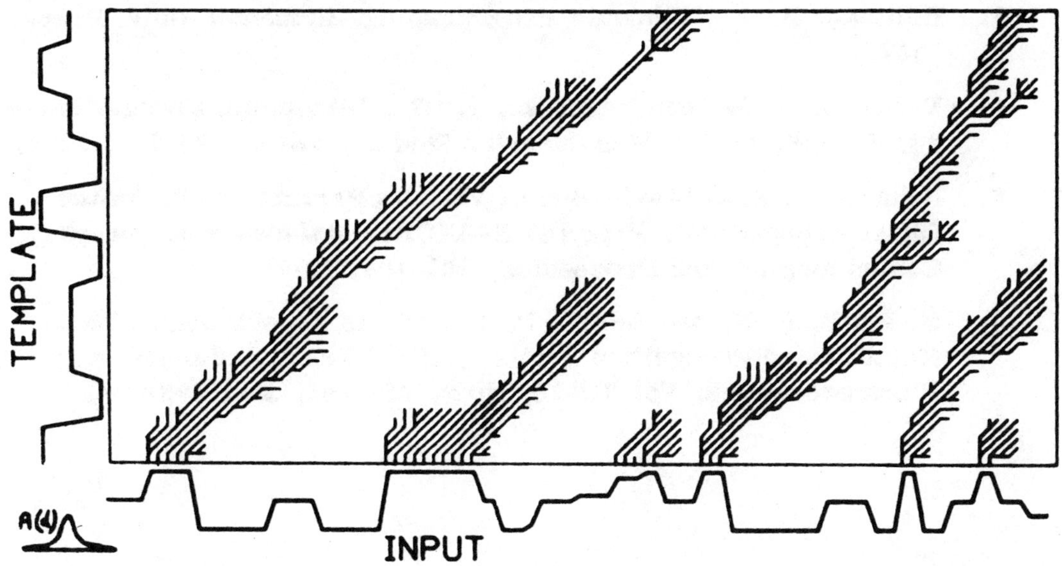

and threshold = 0.35. Note that the paths illustrated are optimum in terms of local fit only. They would not be best for an overall similarity measure.

6. Conclusions The method described will detect, in continuous functions of time, all portions which are locally similar to a template function throughout their length, with allowance for distortions of the time scale. The criterion for local similarity is a fairly simple one, and the smoothing time-constant and the sensitivity to distortions of amplitude and time can be adjusted separately.

Implementation is straightforward, and the amount of computation needed for each input sample is low, although the use of information from other sources (eg semantic information, or detection of particular acoustic events) may reduce this still further.

The method does not give a means of computing the overall similarity between the template and the isolated portion of the input. This could be an important disadvantage where a choice has to be made between two or more possible words.

It would seem difficult to incorporate into a method like this much of our detailed knowledge of the nature of the speech signal, or possible knowledge of the structure of the utterance which is being analysed.

Any application to automatic speech recognition depends on finding suitable methods of preliminary analysis of speech, and the associated instantaneous similarity function [5].

Since there is often more than one way of saying a word, it may be necessary to use more than one template per word [6], or to have a set of templates for each speaker.

7. References

1. Ellis, J. H., Electronics Letters, Vol 5, 335–6, July 1969.

2. Warren, J. H., 'A Dynamic Pattern Matching Algorithm with Applications to Automatic Speech Recognition', in Machine Perception of Patterns and Pictures, Institute of Physics, London, 1972.

3. Bellman, R. E., Dynamic Programming, Princeton Univ. Press, 1957

4. Velichko, V. M. and Zagoruko, N. G., 'Automatic Recognition of 200 Words', Int. J. Man-Machine Studies, Vol 2, 223-234, 1970.

5. Nakano, V. et al, 'Evaluation of Various Parameters in Spoken Digits Recognition', Proc IEEE-AFCRL Conference on Speech Communication and Processing, 101-104, 1972.

6. Shearme, J. N. and Leach, P. F., 'Some Experiments with a Simple Word Recognition System', IEEE Trans Audio and Electroacoustics, Vol AU-16, No 2, 256-261, June 1968.

WORD VERIFICATION IN A SPEECH UNDERSTANDING SYSTEM

Craig Cook

Bolt Beranek and Newman Inc.
Cambridge Mass. 02138

If, in a speech understanding system, word matching is performed at the phonetic level, then the accurate determination of the locations and identities of words present in an unknown utterance is necessarily limited by the phonetic segmentation and labeling. Verification offers an alternative strategy by doing a top-down parametric word match independent of segmentation and labeling. The result is a distance measure between the reference parameterization of a hypothesized word and the computed parameterization of the real speech. This distance is interpreted as the likelihood of that word having actually occurred over a given portion of the utterance.

1. Introduction

Given the results of the Klatt-Stevens spectrogram reading experiment [1], it seems clear that the ability to return to acoustic evidence for verifying word hypotheses is important to correct recognition. This is because one can verify the consistency of all acoustic clues with respect to the given word hypothesis. Assuming that phonological and coarticulation processes are described by rules which are generative in nature, we feel that an analysis-by-synthesis procedure is needed to overcome inaccuracies present in preliminary phonetic analysis and to decode the effects of the phonological rules. The synthesis phase of a word verification component must be able to transform a broad phonetic transcription into a parametric representation suitable for comparison with the acoustic parameterization of an unknown utterance.

To this end, we have written a high-level preprocessor to translate a set of phonological and acoustic-phonetic rules into a Fortran compilable synthesis-by-rule program [2]. The synthesis program takes into account phonological effects across word boundaries, altering the parameterization according to the context in which the hypothesized word may occur. This allows us to derive in near real-time a parametric representation of any word, given its phonetic transcription.

Speech recognition systems using templates extracted from real speech have achieved impressive results. White [3] has reported on an isolated word recognition application and Bridle [4] has described a technique for word spotting. For our particular application, we have chosen to use synthetic templates generated by a synthesis-by-rule program. This choice involved several considerations which are summarized below.

1) Using templates extracted from real speech requires storing a parameterization for each entry in the lexicon, which for large vocabularies may require a substantial amount of storage. On the other hand, the generation of synthetic templates requires only the storage of the synthesis program with a relatively small number of parameters.
2) In continuous speech, it is easier to deal with contextual effects of surrounding words by using synthetic templates. This is because we can deal with them at the phonetic level (see Section 4). These effects are particularly important for short function words.
3) In a multi-speaker environment, a system using real-speech templates will perform best if it is trained on each new speaker for the whole vocabulary. This technique is not practical for systems with very large vocabularies. However, in a synthesis program, it is possible to extract the speaker dependent parameters from a relatively small speech sample.

The chief limitation of using synthetic templates is their dependence on the ability of the synthesis program to generate accurate parameterizations. Inadequacies in the program may produce incorrect results in the verification component as a whole.

The verification component includes a time normalization routine and a parametric matching program. Time normalization is done using a dynamic programming algorithm based on a method first introduced by Itakura [5]. The algorithm involves a non-linear time warping based on the registration of the error metric, in this case the log ratio of the linear prediction residuals. We have modified Itakura's method to allow limited misalignment in time between the hypothesized word parameterization and its hypothesized position in the utterance. In actually computing the distance measure between these two, we sum the error metric between corresponding segments (frames), the correspondence having already been determined by the time normalization technique.

2. Synthesis-by-Rule

To synthesize the parametric representation of a hypothesized word, we use its phonetic spelling as given by the speech understanding system's phonetic dictionary. This transcription, plus any surface structure and available semantic information, serves as the input string to the phonological phase of a synthesis-by-rule program. This phase contains all of the program's phonetic rewrite rules plus a number of acoustic-phonetic rules dealing with phonological effects. After being processed by these rules, a more detailed phonetic transcription enters the phonetic phase of the program where a direct phonetic-to-parametric transformation is performed. The output parametric representation consists of a set of time

Reprinted from *1976 IEEE Internat. Conf. Record on Acoust., Speech, and Signal Process.*, April 12–14, 1976, pp. 553–556.

functions which would ordinarily control a terminal analog waveform synthesizer. The synthetic waveform is not needed in this application because matching is done at the spectral level between spectra extracted from the real speech and synthetic spectra computed from the parameters generated by the synthesis program. Parameters available for use in verification include:

1) three formant frequencies and bandwidths
2) a nasal pole-zero pair
3) amplitudes of voicing, aspiration, and frication sources
4) fundamental frequency.

The parameters currently used in word matching are a subset of those available from the synthesis program.

3. Spectral Matching

Our spectral distance measure is the log ratio of the linear prediction residuals. This metric was derived by Itakura [5] using maximum likelihood. Alternate expressions for this metric are given in Makhoul [6]. Briefly, the metric is defined as:

$$d = \log \frac{\sum_{i=-p}^{p} b_i' R_i}{\sum_{i=-q}^{q} b_i R_i},$$

where $\{R(i)\}$ are the autocorrelations of the matching signal and $\{b(i)\}$ and $\{b'(i)\}$ are the autocorrelations of the predictor coefficients for the matching and the reference signals respectively. "p" and "q" are the orders of the respective predictors. Here, the reference signal represents the real speech and the matching "signal" is represented by the synthetic spectrum. To compute the measured spectrum from the real speech, we divide the speech signal (sampled at 10 or 20 KHz) into 20 msec windows overlapped every 10 msecs. A preemphasized 14 pole LPC analysis (autocorrelation method) over 0-5 KHz is done for each window, and the roots of the polynomial are extracted by a pole solving routine [7]. Of the complex conjugate pairs, three pairs with frequency less than 3100 Hz are selected by a formant extraction routine. This procedure reduces the spectral model to a six-pole model defined from 0-3100 Hz. The actual predictor coefficients are then computed by multiplying the three complex conjugate pairs together and collecting terms assuming a sampling frequency of 6200 Hz. All of this preprocessing is computationally expensive but it need be done only once for the entire utterance and requires no extra computation beyond that already necessary for the initial acoustic analysis of our speech understanding system.

The synthesis-by-rule program computes a new set of synthesizer control parameters for every 10 msecs of speech. From these parameters, we derive an all-pole model defining the synthetic spectral shape for each frame of the synthesis. At present, we multiply together the pole pairs defined by the first three formant frequencies and bandwidths for a sampling frequency of 6200 Hz. We then shape the spectrum according to the source excitation generated for that frame.

Given both the measured spectra of an unknown utterance and the synthesized spectra of a hypothesized word, it remains to define a time registration between them. We use the same error metric to do both time normalization and computation of the spectral distance measure. Computing the time normalization means finding the frame-by-frame correspondence between the synthetic and real speech parameterizations. The sequence of these correspondences defines the optimal registration $W(n)$ as shown in Figure 1. The value of $W(n)$ is the frame number of the real speech which corresponds to frame number n of the synthetic parameterization. This means that for every frame of the synthetic parameterization, there is a frame in the utterance which corresponds to it. The reverse is not true, however. There are two sets of constraints which govern computation of the optimal path (Figure 1). These are the boundary conditions and the continuity constraints. In terms of $W(n)$, the boundary conditions are:

$$M-\Delta T_1 \le W(1) \le M+\Delta T_1 \qquad \Delta T_1=\Delta T_2=5$$

$$M'-\Delta T_2 \le W(N) \le M'+\Delta T_2$$

while the continuity constraints are defined as:

$$\begin{aligned} W(n+1)-W(n) &= 0,1,2 \quad (W(n)\ne W(n-1)) \\ &= 1,2 \quad (W(n)=W(n-1)) \end{aligned}$$

Note the continuity constraints imply that the relative durations of the synthetic and real-speech parameterizations must lie between 1/2 and 2. The parallelogram represents the space of all possible time registrations satisfying both sets of constraints.

Itakura [5] provides a detailed description of the computational procedure for finding the optimal registration. Our procedure is identical to his with one important exception. The endpoints of the registration are made variable to allow for uncertainty in the exact position of a given word. Within limits, the DP is allowed to find its own optimal alignment. Because of the configuration, all possible time normalizations as computed by the DP are of equal length in terms of the number of frames matched. The program must examine only those paths terminating at the top of the parallelogram to determine which one is optimal (i.e. has the smallest distance).

4. An Example

Within the scope of our speech understanding system, word matching is done at the phonetic level by the lexical retrieval component. An example of verifying a word which has been proposed by lexical retrieval is given below using the utterance "Give me a list of the remaining trips and their estimated costs" (Figure 2).

In this example, the phonetic transcription of the word "remain", including its lexical stress, is sent to the verification component. Also transmitted are the frame numbers delimiting the portion of the utterance over which the match is to occur. There may be contextual information in the form of an additional phone at one or both ends of the phonetic input string to be verified. This context is used in computing the synthetic parameterization but does not enter into the matching process. Here, no context was given so the program inserted silence ("SIL") at both ends automatically. The duration of the synthetic template is shown as the ordinate while the unknown utterance extends along the abscissa from the origin to the small vertical mark above the line. The two marks below the line locate the hypothesized alignment (frame numbers) as provided by lexical retrieval. The parallelogram is open slightly at both ends allowing the DP procedure limited freedom in selecting the end points of the optimal registration. For this case, the allowable variations are plus or minus 50 msecs although the one or both may be changed under program control.

The computed spectral distance is normalized by duration and subtracted from 1000. An ideal match having zero distance would have 1000 as its verified match score. In Figure 2, the match score is 724, which is a good score that indicates a likely match, where "remain" was matched against "remain"-ing. This score together with the frame numbers delimiting the optimal registration are transmitted back to the lexical retrieval component where they augment the score already computed for the phonetic word match.

5. Discussion

Although the synthesis-by-rule and matching programs are undergoing further development, we have made some general observations based on our experience with cases like the one above. Where the initial segmentation of an utterance is correct, a word's verification score is approximately the same as its phonetic match score. This agreement holds whether or not the word is correct. In some cases where segmentation or labeling errors have resulted in a prospective word receiving a low phonetic match score, verification was able to offset the effects of these errors by giving a good score to the correct word. The ability to verify a sequence of contiguous words has also been useful since a segmentation error can cause lexical retrieval to overlap the highest scoring occurrences of two words and thereby prevent their being matched sequentially. We are now studying how best to integrate these capabilities into control strategies being developed for the overall speech understanding system.

We are making an effort to improve the performance of the verification component in several respects. The current implementation requires 5-7 times real-time to perform the synthesis and matching procedures on a given word. This could be reduced by introducing a dynamic error bound which terminates execution of the matching algorithm if the distance measure exceeds a certain threshold. As the predictive capabilities of the synthesis-by-rule program improve, we are studying ways to integrate additional parameters into the framework of the existing error metric. One possibility is to use a separate distance measure to do time normalization. This would introduce another parameter into the overall matching process without increasing the dimensionality of the dynamic programming algorithm.

6. Conclusion

We have designed and implemented a verification component for a speech understanding system. The component generates synthetic parameterizations for hypothesized words and matches them onto an unknown utterance. Preliminary results indicate the usefulness of this technique in verifying word hypotheses in continuous speech.

Acknowledgement

The author wishes to thank J. Makhoul for discussions and comments on this paper. This research was supported by the Advanced Research Projects Agency of the Department of Defense and was monitored by ONR under Contract No. N00014-75-C-0533.

References

1. D.H. Klatt and K.N. Stevens, "Strategies for Recognition of Spoken Sentences from Visual Examination of Spectrograms," Bolt Beranek and Newman Report 2514, Cambridge Mass., June 1971.

2. D.H. Klatt, "Structure of a Phonological Rule Component for a Synthesis-by-Rule Program," presented at the 90th Meeting of the Acoustical Society of America, 3-7 November, 1975.

3. G. White, "Automatic Speech Recognition: Linear Predictive Residual versus Bandpass Filtering," Proceeding of the IEEE International Conference on Cybernetics and Society, September 1975

4. J. Bridle and M. Brown, "An Experimental Automatic Word-Recognition System," Joint Speech Research Unit Report No. 1003, Ruislip, Middlesex, U.K., December 1974

5. F. Itakura, "Minimum Prediction Residual Principle Applied to Speech Recognition," IEEE Trans. ASSP, 67-72, 1975.

6. J. Makhoul, "Linear Prediction in Automatic Speech Recognition," in <u>Speech Recognition</u> (D.R. Reddy, Ed.), New York: Academic Press, 1975.

7. J. Makhoul and J. Wolf, "Linear Prediction and the Spectral Analysis of Speech," Bolt Beranek and Newman Report 2304, Cambridge Mass., July 1973.

8. W.A. Woods et al., "Speech Understanding Systems, Annual Technical Progress Report" Bolt Beranek and Newman Report 3188, Cambridge Mass., December 1975.

9. R. Gillmann, "Automatic Verification of Hypothesized Phonemic Strings in Continuous Speech," Report TM-5-315, System Development Corporation, May 1974.

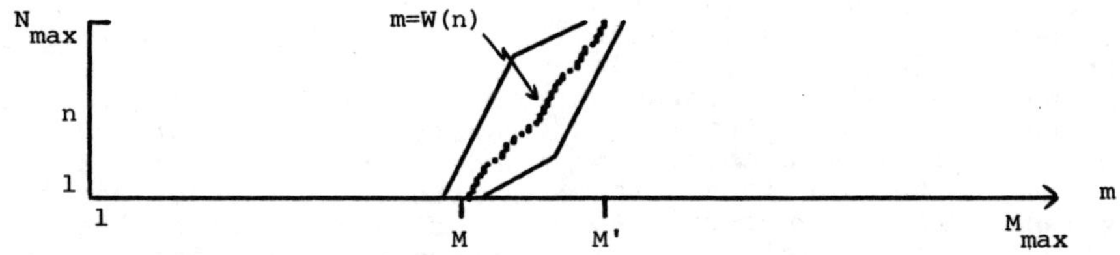

Figure 1

SIL * R IY M 1 EY N * SIL .
Matched : Left Boundary Time = 99 Right Boundary Time = 137
Verified : Left Boundary Time = 101 Right Boundary Time = 137
The Verified Score is 724

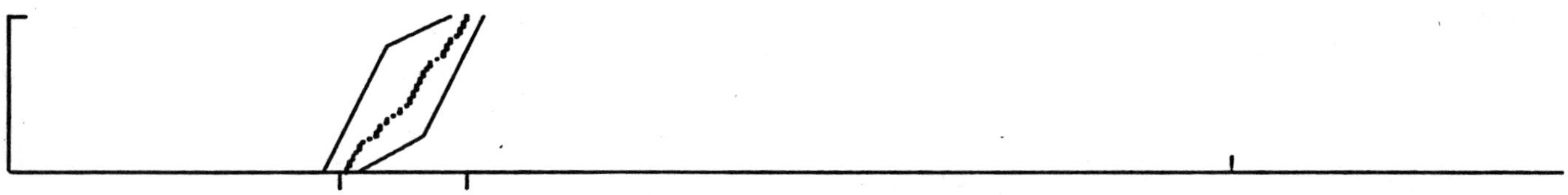

Figure 2

Detecting and Locating Key Words in Continuous Speech Using Linear Predictive Coding

RICHARD W. CHRISTIANSEN, MEMBER, IEEE, AND CRAIG K. RUSHFORTH, MEMBER, IEEE

***Abstract*–This paper considers the problem of automatically detecting and locating key words in a stream of continuous speech. The system described here is a template-matching procedure which uses as its basic waveform features a set of linear prediction coefficients. The similarity measure between a segment of the template and a segment of the incoming speech stream is taken to be a ratio of minimum prediction residuals. This similarity measure is used in conjunction with a dynamic-programming time-warp algorithm developed by Bridle and a novel method for using multiple templates. Using templates and incoming speech spoken by the same person in a quiet room, an accuracy in excess of 99 percent was obtained. Further experiments are described which explore cross-speaker word spotting and the effects of noise on system performance. The results of these experiments suggest that the technique described in this paper could well form the basis for a practical system.**

I. Introduction

AUTOMATIC speech recognition and understanding are currently receiving considerable attention [1], [2]. Most approaches to problems in these areas involve complicated procedures which rely on waveform segmentation, syntactic and semantic rules, and in some cases, elaborate statistical models. This complexity is probably necessary if the most general speech-recognition problems are to be solved.

In many cases of interest, however, the problem to be solved has special features which enable it to be solved using much simpler techniques. For example, the problem of recognizing isolated words from a finite vocabulary has typically been solved using simple features of the acoustic waveform, perhaps in conjunction with a time-registration procedure [3], [4].

In this paper we consider the problem of detecting and locating a specific word in a continuous speech stream. This problem, commonly referred to as the word-spotting problem, is clearly much simpler than the general problem of speech understanding, and we, therefore, might expect that a satisfactory solution could be obtained using a simpler system. On the other hand, the fact that the word to be detected is embedded in a continuous speech stream leads to some problems not present in the recognition of isolated words.

Considerable work has been done over the past several years on the problem of isolated word recognition, and several systems have been implemented. Most closely related to our work is the recent paper by Itakura [3], who considers the recognition of words spoken in isolation by a single speaker. His technique is a template-matching technique which uses linear prediction coefficients as the basic waveform features, the linear prediction residual as a measure of waveform similarity, and a nonlinear time-warping procedure based on dynamic programming to accommodate spoken words and reference templates of different lengths.

The problem of spotting words in continuous speech has received considerably less attention than has the isolated word-recognition problem. An early attempt to recognize connected digits using a dynamic-programming-based algorithm is reported by Sakoe and Chiba [5]. More recently, Bridle and Brown [6] have described a system for spotting words in continuous speech which uses as its basic waveform features the outputs of a channel vocoder together with a voiced-unvoiced decision. These features, appropriately weighted by empirical weighting coefficients, are then used to calculate a similarity measure between a frame of the reference template and a frame of the incoming speech. This frame similarity function is then used in conjunction with a time-warping algorithm based on dynamic programming to determine whether or not the key word is present in the incoming speech. The key to the success of this procedure is the time-warping algorithm which, unlike that of Itakura, is designed to work in a continuous speech stream rather than on isolated words.

The system which we describe below combines several features from the Itakura and Bridle systems with some additional modifications of our own. Our system, like that of Itakura, uses linear prediction coefficients as the basic waveform features and the minimum prediction residual as a measure of similarity between a portion of a stored reference template and a portion of the incoming speech stream. Our application of these ideas is somewhat different from that of Itakura, however. We combine our LPC-based similarity measure with the time-registration algorithm of Bridle and a novel way of using multiple reference templates to obtain the system described in detail in the next section. The main features of this system are the following:

1) The approach is based on template matching, and does not require waveform segmentation, syntactic information, or semantic information.

2) The basic waveform features used are linear prediction coefficients. Neither pitch information nor voicing information have been used.

3) The measure of similarity between a template frame and a frame of incoming speech is the minimum prediction residual.

4) Multiple templates are used in a novel way to improve performance and to provide for word spotting using templates and speech from different individuals.

We discuss the details of our approach in Section II. In

Manuscript received September 13, 1976; revised April 28, 1977.

R. W. Christiansen is with Eyring Research Institute, Provo, UT 84601.

C. K. Rushforth is with the Department of Electrical Engineering, University of Utah, Salt Lake City, UT 84112.

Reprinted from *IEEE Trans. Acoust., Speech, and Signal Process.*, vol. ASSP-25, pp. 361–367, Oct. 1977.

Section III we summarize the results of a number of experiments, and in Section IV we discuss these results and indicate some directions for future research.

II. System Description

In this section, we describe our approach to word spotting in somewhat more detail. Briefly, our system compares the incoming speech stream with one or more stored templates representing the word to be located. This is done by sliding the input speech past the template in a continuous fashion, with due regard for time registration. If the incoming speech and the template are sufficiently similar over some interval of time, the system indicates that the key word is present at that time. To show how this is accomplished, we first consider the construction of the template. We then discuss the processing of the incoming speech stream and the calculation of the similarity between a portion of the incoming speech stream and a portion of the stored template. We next describe the use of this local similarity measure in connection with the time-warping algorithm. Finally, we introduce a novel method of using multiple templates to improve the performance and increase the versatility of the system.

A reference template is created by having an individual speak the key word into a microphone. The resulting waveform is low-pass filtered at 4 kHz, and is then digitized using a 14-bit A/D converter running at 10 kHz. For further processing, the resulting digitized speech is partitioned into nonoverlapping segments (frames) of 256 samples each, corresponding to 25.6 ms in time. The samples in a given frame are then windowed using a Hamming window, and thirteen normalized autocorrelation coefficients are then calculated from this windowed speech frame. A version of Levinson's method is then used to calculate the predictor coefficients from these autocorrelation coefficients, and the linear prediction residual $a_T' R_T a_T$ is then calculated where a_T is the vector of prediction coefficients and R_T is the matrix of autocorrelation coefficients for that frame, and the prime denotes vector transpose. This process is repeated for each frame, and the quantities R_T and $a_T' R_T a_T$ are stored for each frame. These stored values provide all the information about the reference template that is needed for comparison with the incoming speech. For more details pertaining to these calculations, see [7].

The incoming continuous speech stream is initially processed in the same fashion as is the reference utterance, resulting in a vector a_s of prediction coefficients for a given frame. In order to calculate the frame similarity function between a given frame of input speech and a given template frame, we need the quantities R_T and $a_T' R_T a_T$ for the template frame, and the vector a_s of predictor coefficients for the input frame. We then define a frame similarity measure as

$$S = \frac{a_T' R_T a_T}{a_s' R_T a_s}. \tag{1}$$

This frame similarity measure is then used in conjunction with the dynamic-programming time-warp algorithm as described below. Note that we use S directly without taking its logarithm.

An obvious alternative to this procedure involves interchanging the roles of template and input speech. That is, we could calculate and store just the predictor-coefficient vector a_T for each template frame, and we could calculate R_s and $a_s' R_s a_s$ for each frame of incoming speech. We could then use as our similarity measure the quantity

$$\tilde{S} = \frac{a_s' R_s a_s}{a_T' R_s a_T}. \tag{1a}$$

We tried this alternative in a number of early experiments and observed no significant differences in performance from that achieved using (1). Hence, we used (1) throughout the remaining experiments.

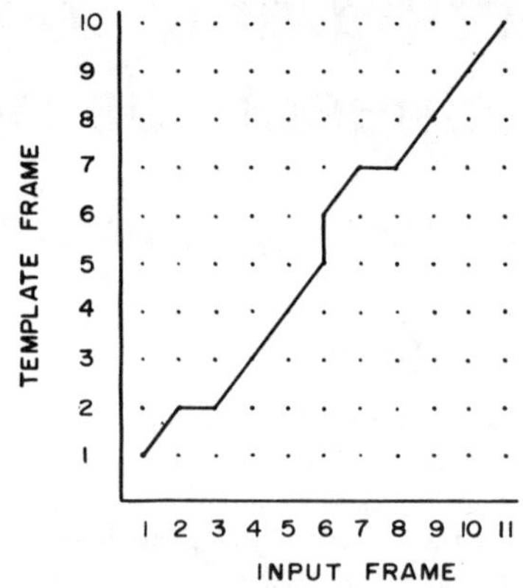

Fig. 1. Time-registration path.

Before turning to a discussion of the time-warp algorithm, let us consider the quantity S as defined by (1). The numerator $a_T' R_T a_T$ is the minimum prediction residual of a particular frame of the template. Assuming that we have used enough predictor coefficients, we expect this quantity to be rather small. The denominator $a_s' R_T a_s$ has the same form as the numerator, but involves the predictor coefficients from the incoming speech frame and the autocorrelation coefficients from the template frame with which comparison is being made. If these two frames are corresponding time segments of the same word, then the denominator should also be relatively small and S should be close to one. On the other hand, if there is no such correspondence between the input frame and the reference frame, we would expect the denominator to be larger and therefore S to be smaller. Thus, S appears to be a reasonable measure of similarity between different segments of speech. A more complete discussion of this measure may be found in [8].

In order to explain the time-warp algorithm, we first introduce the notion of a time-registration path. This concept is illustrated in Fig. 1. In this figure, the vertical scale corresponds to the stored reference word, and the horizontal scale corresponds to a segment of the incoming speech. The reference template is taken to be ten frames long; each template frame is represented by a row of dots. Similarly, each frame of the incoming speech corresponds to a column of dots. A time-registration path is represented on this diagram by connecting dots with a series of horizontal, vertical, and diagonal line segments. One particular path is shown in Fig. 1.

Since it is not computationally feasible to perform a direct search through all possible paths for each speech segment, a way must be found to make this search more systematic and efficient. Bridle and Brown [6] describe an efficient recursive search algorithm based on dynamic programming. We have incorporated this algorithm into our system without significant change, and we now describe its essential features. For additional discussion, see [6].

We first define a local similarity function evaluated at the ith frame of the reference template and the jth frame of the incoming speech stream on a given time-registration path by

$$L(i,j) = (1 - G)\,L(i - a, j - b) + KGS(i,j). \tag{2}$$

In this expression $(i - a, j - b)$ is the previous point on the path with (a, b) equal to $(0, 1), (1, 1)$, or $(1, 0)$, G is an empirical weighting constant, S is the frame similarity measure defined in (1), and K is a time-distortion penalty defined by

$$K = \begin{cases} 1 & \text{if } (a,b) = (1,1) \\ k & \text{if } (a,b) = (1,0) \text{ or } (0,1) \end{cases} \tag{3}$$

where $0 \leqslant k \leqslant 1$. When $i = 1$, we define

$$L(1,j) = S(1,j). \tag{4}$$

We say that the key word is present in a segment of speech if the local similarity function is above a previously chosen threshold Q at every point along the path. Because of the dependence on past frames, this does not imply that the similarity S between each pair of corresponding frames on the path must be large. The effect of an isolated pair of dissimilar frames can be overcome by nearby pairs which are similar.

The local similarity function is incorporated into a recursive search algorithm as follows. If there is no path to point (i,j) for which L is above the threshold Q for every point on the path, we set the detection function $A(i,j)$ to zero. Otherwise, $A(i,j)$ is assigned the maximum value of $L(i,j)$ over all paths to (i,j) for which $L > Q$ at every point. If the length of the template is N frames, then a nonzero value of $A(N,j)$ indicates the presence of the key word ending at frame j of the input speech stream. Since all acceptable paths are found, it is common for $A(N,j)$ to be nonzero for several successive input frames if the key word is present.

For computational purposes, $A(i,j)$ can be defined in terms of $A(i - 1, j - 1)$, $A(i, j - 1)$, $A(i - 1, j)$, and $S(i,j)$. To do this, we first define a new function

$$\text{STEP}(A,S,K) = \begin{cases} 0 & \text{if } A = 0 \\ 0 & \text{if } (1 - G)A + KGS < Q \\ (1 - G)A + KGS & \text{otherwise.} \end{cases} \tag{5}$$

We then have

$$A(i,j) = \max_{(a,b)} \{\text{STEP}\,[A(i - a, j - b), S(i,j), K(a,b)]\} \tag{6}$$

where $(a, b) = (1, 0), (1, 1)$, or $(0, 1)$. At the beginning of the template at point $(1,j)$, we have

$$A(1,j) = \max\,\{\tilde{S}(1,j), \text{STEP}\,[A(1, j - 1), S(1,j), k]\} \tag{7}$$

where

$$\tilde{S}(1,j) = \begin{cases} 0, & S(1,j) < Q \\ S(1,j), & S(1,j) > Q. \end{cases} \tag{8}$$

The processing of the input speech now proceeds one frame at a time. All the necessary information about previous input frames is contained in the quantities $A(1, j - 1), A(2, j - 1), \cdots, A(N, j - 1)$. Each j such that $A(N,j) > 0$ is identified as the last frame of an occurrence of the key word.

In the above discussion, we assumed that just one reference template had been stored. The restrictions on accuracy and flexibility that this would ordinarily impose are substantially eased by time warping to account for different word durations, and by amplitude normalization of the predictor coefficients to account for differing amplitudes and stress patterns. Even so, we might expect an improvement in performance if two or more templates are used to represent the key word, particularly if the templates and the incoming speech are from different speakers.

Multiple templates can be used in a variety of ways. For example, they might be combined in some way at the outset to form a composite template. Alternatively, they might be used separately in the procedure described above, with the final decision being based on the number of templates providing an acceptable match.

We use multiple templates in a somewhat different way. Although we form composite templates as suggested above, we do this dynamically as the speech arrives rather than statically at the beginning of the test. The composite template which is formed at any time is the one which provides the best match to the corresponding segment of incoming speech.

Our procedure is, in essence, a frame-by-frame adaptation of the nearest-neighbor decision rule used in pattern recognition [9]. The objective of that decision rule is to assign an observed vector X to one of N classes, $C_1, \cdots, C_N$. The only information available about the various classes is a set of representative samples from each class. The nearest-neighbor rule calculates the distance (suitably defined) from the input vector X to each of the available samples. If the sample closest to X is from class C_i, we assign X to C_i. The performance of the nearest-neighbor rule compares favorably with that of the optimum rule which uses complete statistical information about the classes (Bayes' rule).

In our adaptation of the nearest-neighbor rule, we construct M templates $T_1, \cdots, T_M$ using the procedure previously described. When the first speech frame arrives, we calculate the set of frame similarity functions $S_m(1, 1)$ between the first input speech frame and the first frame of the mth template for each $m = 1, \cdots, M$. We then select the largest of these frame similarity functions:

$$S_{\max}(1, 1) = \max_m S_m(1, 1). \tag{9}$$

If $S_{\max}(1, 1)$ exceeds the predetermined threshold, the first frame of the template which yielded $S_{\max}$ is chosen as the first frame of the composite template. If not, the second and succeeding frames of incoming speech are processed in the same way until the threshold is exceeded.

Once the composite template is started, we continue to compare incoming speech frames with frames from each template; in general defining

$$S_{\max}(i,j) = \max_m S_m(i,j) \tag{10}$$

TABLE I
WORD SPOTTING RESULTS FROM EXPERIMENT 1 (TEMPLATE AND SPEECH FROM SAME SPEAKER)

TEXT SPEAKER NO.	WORD	NUMBER OF OCCURRENCES	THRESHOLD Q	TIME WAVE PENALTY FACTOR RK	MISSES	FALSE ALARMS PER HOUR
1	Interrupt	18	.54	.55	0	0
	Processor	7	.47	.55	0	0
	Program	10	.47	.55	0	0
	Priority	6	.47	.55	0	0
2	Interrupt	18	.43	.70	0	0
	Processor	7	.43	.70	0	0
	Program	10	.43	.70	0	0
	Priority	6	.43	.70	0	0
3	Interrupt	18	.50	.63	0	0
	Processor	7	.54	.63	0	0
	Program	10	.50	.63	0	0
	Priority	6	.51	.63	0	0
4	Interrupt	18	.45	.60	0	0
	Processor	7	.45	.60	0	0
	Program	10	.46	.60	0	0
	Priority	6	.45	.60	0	0
5	Interrupt	18	.47	.65	0	0
	Processor	7	.47	.65	0	0
	Program	10	.47	.65	2	0
	Priority	6	.47	.65	0	0

where $S_m(i, j)$ is the similarity between the ith frame of the mth template and the jth frame of input speech. $S_{max}(i, j)$ is then used in the remainder of the algorithm just as $S(i, j)$ is in the single-template case. In the event that the match between input speech and templates remains good, this procedure results in the creation of a composite template, with each frame being chosen to produce the best local similarity. The resulting composite template may be constructed from frames from various templates in any order. Furthermore, different occurrences of the key word may yield different composite templates.

As we hoped, the use of multiple templates in the manner described above led to a significant improvement in system performance. Some results of performance evaluations are discussed in the next section.

III. EXPERIMENTAL RESULTS

In this section, we present the results of several experiments which we performed to evaluate the system described above. These results and their implications for future development of the system are discussed in Section IV.

In this initial phase of testing, we were primarily interested in determining the best performance achievable by the particular system configuration described above. Hence, we tuned the parameters Q, G, and k [see eq. (2)] to achieve the best possible performance for each speaker. A value of $G = 0.3$ worked well in all cases, but Q and k were varied from speaker to speaker and from word to word. Furthermore, the value of Q is sensitive to the number of templates used. Hence, there are important practical questions about the choice of these parameters in a realistic situation, which remain unanswered at this point. On the other hand, there are also many opportunities for system modification and optimization which remain unexplored. Thus, the results which we present here should be taken as suggestive of the power of the approach, but not as final and definitive performance figures.

Experiment 1: In this experiment, the passage of text reproduced in the Appendix was read by a speaker under quiet-room conditions. This same speaker then spoke the key words "interrupt", "program", "processor", and "priority" three times each in isolation to create three templates for each key word to be spotted. The multiple-template word-spotting procedure described in Section II was then applied separately for each key word. This basic experiment was repeated five times using five different speakers, four male and one female. In each case, the templates were taken from the same individual who spoke the continuous speech passage in which the words were to be located.

Counting repetitions of the same passage as different key words are sought, this experiment included a total of 205 occurrences of key words in approximately 40 min of continuous speech. The results of this first experiment are summarized in Table I. Overall detection accuracy was greater than 99 percent with no false alarms.

Experiment 2: The first experiment indicates that the system performs very well when recording conditions are good, and when the templates and the incoming speech are spoken by the same person. The second experiment was designed to give a preliminary indication of system performance when the templates and the incoming speech are spoken by different people.

For each of the four key words, three templates from Speaker 1 and three from Speaker 2 were used in combination to spot words in the text read by Speaker 5. This experiment was then repeated using the text read by Speaker 6. The results of this experiment are summarized in Tables II and III. In order to illustrate the tradeoff between misses and false alarms, the parameters Q and k were adjusted first to achieve no false alarms (Table II) and then to achieve no misses (Table III). In the first case, detection accuracy was 94 percent with no false alarms, while in the second case, there were 11 false alarms, but no misses. This amounts to about 40 false alarms per hour. In a realistic situation some compromise between these two extremes would probably be sought, although it is probably true that false alarms are less troublesome than misses unless their number becomes excessive.

Experiment 3: The previous two experiments were conducted in a quiet room to minimize the effects of outside disturbances and to provide an indication of the best achievable performance. Realistic environments are seldom this benign, and it is of some interest to consider the effects of various types of noise and degradation on system performance. Experiment 3 was a limited attempt to quantify the effects of additive white Gaussian noise on word-spotting accuracy.

In this experiment, the text and templates used were those of Speaker 1 from Experiment 1 described above. A collection of noise samples was obtained by passing the output of an analog white Gaussian noise generator through a 4 kHz low-pass filter and then through a 14-bit A/D converter operating

TABLE II
CROSS-SPEAKER WORD SPOTTING RESULTS FROM EXPERIMENT 2
(ADJUSTED FOR NO FALSE ALARMS)

TEMPLATE SPEAKER NO.	WORD	NUMBER OF OCCURRENCES	TEXT SPEAKER NO.	THRESHOLD Q	TIME WARP PENALTY FACTOR RK	MISSES	FALSE ALARMS
1 and 2	Processor	7	5	.46	.7	0	0
1 and 2	Processor	7	6	.50	.7	0	0
1 and 2	Priority	6	5	.53	.7	1	0
1 and 2	Priority	6	6	.45	.4	1	0
1 and 2	Program	10	5	.48	.6	0	0
1 and 2	Program	10	6	.46	.3	1	0
1 and 2	Interrupt	18	5	.55	.4	1	0
1 and 2	Interrupt	18	6	.50	.6	1	0

TABLE III
CROSS-SPEAKER WORD SPOTTING RESULTS FROM EXPERIMENT 2
(ADJUSTED FOR NO MISSES)

TEMPLATE SPEAKER NO.	WORD	NUMBER OF OCCURRENCES	TEXT SPEAKER NO.	THRESHOLD Q	TIME WARP PENALTY FACTOR RK	MISSES	FALSE ALARMS
1 and 2	Processor	7	5	.46	.7	0	0
1 and 2	Processor	7	6	.50	.7	0	0
1 and 2	Priority	6	5	.50	.7	0	1
1 and 2	Priority	6	6	.43	.2	0	1
1 and 2	Program	10	5	.48	.6	0	0
1 and 2	Program	10	6	.45	.3	0	2
1 and 2	Interrupt	18	5	.52	.6	0	2
1 and 2	Interrupt	18	6	.45	.3	0	5

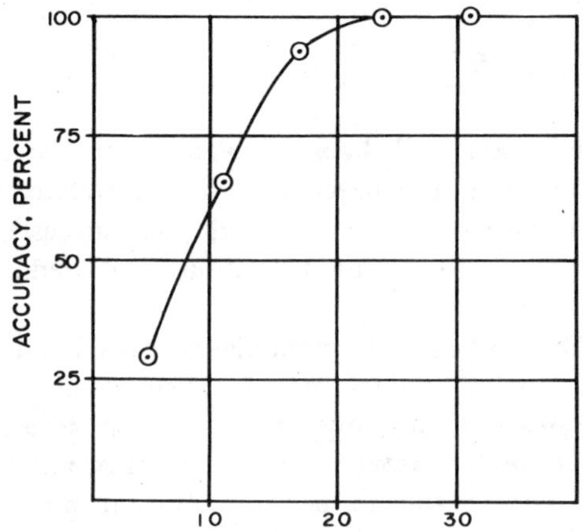

Fig. 2. Performance in presence of noise; no preprocessing.

at a 10 kHz sampling rate. This is the same digitizing procedure used for the speech waveforms. A noise sample N_n was added to each speech sample to yield the noisy speech sample $S_n + N_n$.

In order to quantify the results of this experiment, we must define a signal-to-noise ratio. For our purposes, the following definition suffices:

$$\mathrm{SNR} = \frac{\sum_{k=1}^{K} S_k^2}{\sum_{k=1}^{K} N_k^2} \tag{11}$$

where K is the total number of samples in the passage. This is just the ratio of the total signal energy to the total noise energy in the passage. It is an average measure which smooths out local variations, but since we are primarily interested in the relative performance with a given passage of speech and different amounts of noise, this measure is adequate for our purpose.

We first applied the word-spotting procedure of Section II directly to the noisy speech using noise-free templates and no preprocessing to reduce the effects of the noise. For purposes of comparison, we adjusted the system parameters in all cases to yield the same number of false alarms (about 1 every 4 min)

TABLE IV
SPOTTING ACCURACIES IN NOISY SPEECH

SNR (db)	NO PREPROCESSING	WIENER FILTERING
11.0	66%	95%
4.6	29%	68%

and then determined the number of key words correctly spotted. The results of this experiment are shown in Fig. 2.

We next applied standard Wiener filtering to the noisy speech samples. The improvement in performance achieved using Wiener filtering is shown in Table IV.

Experiment 4: Since there is considerable interest in the automatic recognition of spoken digits, we decided to make at least a preliminary application of our technique to this problem. Ten speakers, five males and five females, each spoke approximately 100 digits chosen from a table of random numbers. Speaker 2 spoke two sets of digits. One set was deliberately spoken to isolate the digits from one another, and the second was spoken with random speeds, emphasis, and groupings of numbers. The remaining speakers read the digits as they normally would over the telephone. This experiment was conducted in the quiet room, and in all cases, the templates and the stream of digits were taken from the same speaker.

The results of this experiment are summarized in Table V. The overall accuracy was 97 percent with only Speaker 7 dropping substantially below this figure.

In many cases, misses or false alarms were directly related to articulation. For example, the "t" was often missing from "eight". Speaker 7 yielded the poorest results, and she also exhibited the greatest apparent variability in speaking. For example, she sometimes rolled the "r" in "three" and sometimes not; sometimes the "t" was present in "eight" and sometimes not.

Experiment 5: The key words searched for in the first three experiments described above all had two or more syllables. To provide additional information on the performance of the system when the key word has just one syllable, we extracted a passage of text from a news magazine which contained the key word "Ford" twelve times and took approximately 1 min to read. In the absence of noise, perfect performance (no misses, no false alarms) was achieved using two templates

TABLE V
DIGIT RECOGNITION RESULTS

SPEAKER	NUMBER OF DIGITS	FALSE ALARMS	MISSES	PERCENT ACCURACY
1	100	0	0	100
2	98	0	4	96
2	119	0	2	98
3	96	1	0	99
4	100	0	0	100
5	100	0	2	98
6	100	1	1	98
7	100	6	14	80
8	100	0	0	100
9	100	0	2	98
10	100	2	2	96

from the speaker who read the text. As might be expected, however, performance in this case deteriorated more rapidly than in Experiment 3 as noise was added.

IV. SUMMARY AND CONCLUSIONS

In this paper, we have described the preliminary design and evaluation of a procedure for spotting key words in a continuous speech stream. This procedure uses linear predictive coding, the minimum prediction residual, and a time-registration algorithm based on dynamic programming. Preliminary evaluations have indicated that the basic technique holds considerable promise. We are confident that an improved system based on the techniques described here could be of considerable value in certain applications.

Much additional work remains to be done before the design of a practical system based on these techniques could be considered complete. We list here a number of avenues for further investigation.

1) We have made no serious attempt to optimize the LPC portion of the system (e.g., number of coefficients, bandwidth of low-pass filter, rate of updating, etc.); we simply chose values and parameters which seemed reasonable and stayed with our original choices.

2) We used the minimum prediction residual ratio directly. Perhaps taking the logarithm or some other function, with appropriate modification of the similarity calculation, would lead to improvements.

3) We did not use pitch or voicing information. Perhaps the addition of these or other parameters should be considered.

4) We typically tuned the parameters Q and k to achieve good performance. Since we were trying to determine the limits of performance for the given system configuration, this approach seemed justified. However, the sensitivity of system performance to these parameters and practical methods for choosing their values must certainly be looked at more carefully.

5) The entire issue of cross-speaker word spotting deserves a closer look. Certainly the imaginative use of multiple templates can be helpful, but it is not clear how the templates should be chosen. Perhaps templates could be artificially constructed from the speech stream under study (we have performed one such experiment with good success). Perhaps some sort of vocal-tract normalization would reduce speaker dependence.

6) We have given only preliminary consideration to the effects of noise. Certainly, more work should be done on this problem. Work is currently under way here in a somewhat different context to investigate the effects of noise on linear predictive coding and to develop efficient procedures for reducing these effects.

APPENDIX

PASSAGE READ BY SUBJECTS

A stack is a first-in last-out list. In a PDP-11, a stack is used automatically by program interrupts, subroutine calls, and trap instructions. When the processor is interrupted, the central processor status word and the program counter are saved (or "pushed") in the stack area, while the processor services the interrupting device. A return from interrupt instruction restores the interrupted program without software intervention. Interrupts are then automatically nested for fastest interrupt response and no program overhead.

The PDP-11 has an extremely flexible interrupt priority structure. The central processor recognizes interrupts on four separate lines. Many devices may be attached on each line with the device closest to the central processor given priority over the other devices on the same line. The hardware interrupt priority lines are interleaved by programmable central processor priority levels, thus allowing the running program to select the priority of allowable interrupts. Additional speed and power are added to the interrupt structure through the use of the PDP-11 fully vectored interrupt scheme.

When acknowledging an interrupt, the processor saves its program control and status word on the system push-down stack. Then, it establishes a new status and program counter from a set of interrupt locations unique to each device. Thus, no device polling is required. The program running in response to an interrupt may itself be interrupted by a device with a higher priority; these nested interrupts are allowed to any level. Subroutine call instructions also use the stack for storage of the return address. Hence, reentrant subroutines may be easily written. Reentrant subroutines make it possible to do real-time programming without using large amounts of core memory.

ACKNOWLEDGMENT

The authors are grateful to S. F. Boll for a number of helpful comments on linear predictive coding.

REFERENCES

[1] *IEEE Trans. Acoust., Speech, Signal Processing*, Feb. 1975.
[2] *Proc. IEEE Int. Conf., on Acoustics, Speech, and Signal Processing*, Philadelphia, PA, Apr. 12–14, 1976.
[3] F. Itakura, "Minimum prediction residual principle applied to speech recognition," *IEEE Trans. Acoust. Speech, Signal Processing*, vol. ASSP-23, pp. 67–72, Feb. 1975.
[4] G. L. Clapper, "Automatic word recognition," *IEEE Spectrum*, pp. 57–69, Aug. 1971.
[5] H. Sakoe and S. Chiba, "A dynamic programming approach to continuous speech recognition," in *1971 Proc. Int. Congr. on Acoustics*, Budapest, Hungary, 1971, pp. 65–68.
[6] J. S. Bridle and M. D. Brown, "An experimental automatic word-recognition system: Interim report," Joint Speech Research Unit, Middlesex, United Kingdom.
[7] J. Makhoul, "Linear prediction: A tutorial review," *Proc. IEEE*, pp. 561–580, Apr. 1975.
[8] S. F. Boll, "Waveform comparison using the linear prediction residual," Computer Science Dep., Univ. Utah, Salt Lake City, Rep. TM 7500.
[9] R. O. Duda and P. E. Hart, *Pattern Classification and Scene Analysis*. New York: Wiley, 1973, p. 98.

Part V
Continuous Speech: Automatic Speech Recognition

AN ACOUSTICALLY BASED CONTINUOUS SPEECH RECOGNITION SYSTEM

By James E. Paul, Jr. and Arthur S. Rabinowitz
Rockwell International
3370 Miraloma Avenue
Anaheim, California 92803

Summary

A continuous speech recognition system has been implemented as a research model. The system is partitioned into a digital acoustic frontend, an acoustic processor consisting of a phonetic segmenter and a dual (based on static and dynamic properties) classifier, and a linguistic processor. Based on initial training, performance across six male speakers and a total of 46 sentences includes an average word accuracy of 71 percent and a sentence accept rate of 52 percent.

Overview

A research model of a continuous speech recognition system has been implemented.[1,2,3] This system employs a 250-word vocabulary structured into a diverse syntax. Recognition is sentence-based, incorporating declarative, imperative, and interrogative structures.

A block diagram of the system is given in Figure 1.. The three modules that make up the software are:

- the digital acoustic analyzer for extracting spectral parameters,

- the acoustic processor for segmenting the speech signal into phonetic events and employing both static and dynamic properties of the acoustic signal to classify these events, and

- the linguistic processor for developing an orthographic representation of the machine-derived phonetic strings.

The acoustic analyzer consists of all processing between raw analog speech data and digital spectral characterization of that speech data. The sequence of processing includes analog-to-digital conversion of the raw speech signal at a 20 kHz sample rate, isolation of sentences in the raw speech data using an amplitude contour and a multithreshold detection algorithm, and digital spectral analysis of the isolated sentences. The spectral analysis procedure incorporates a dual spectral concept in which spectral estimates for a short-term (6.4 milliseconds) spectrum and a long-term (25.6 milliseconds) spectrum are produced every 6.4 milliseconds. These estimates are generated using data windowing, discrete finite Fourier transform (FFT), bandpass channelization, and channel spectral normalization.

The acoustic processor is composed of two primary stages: subword segmentation and dual classification. The subword segmenter establishes phonetic boundaries for a given sentence, based on spectral correlation with phonetic reference spectra. This correlation process employs multiple reference samples for each phonetic event (multimodal).

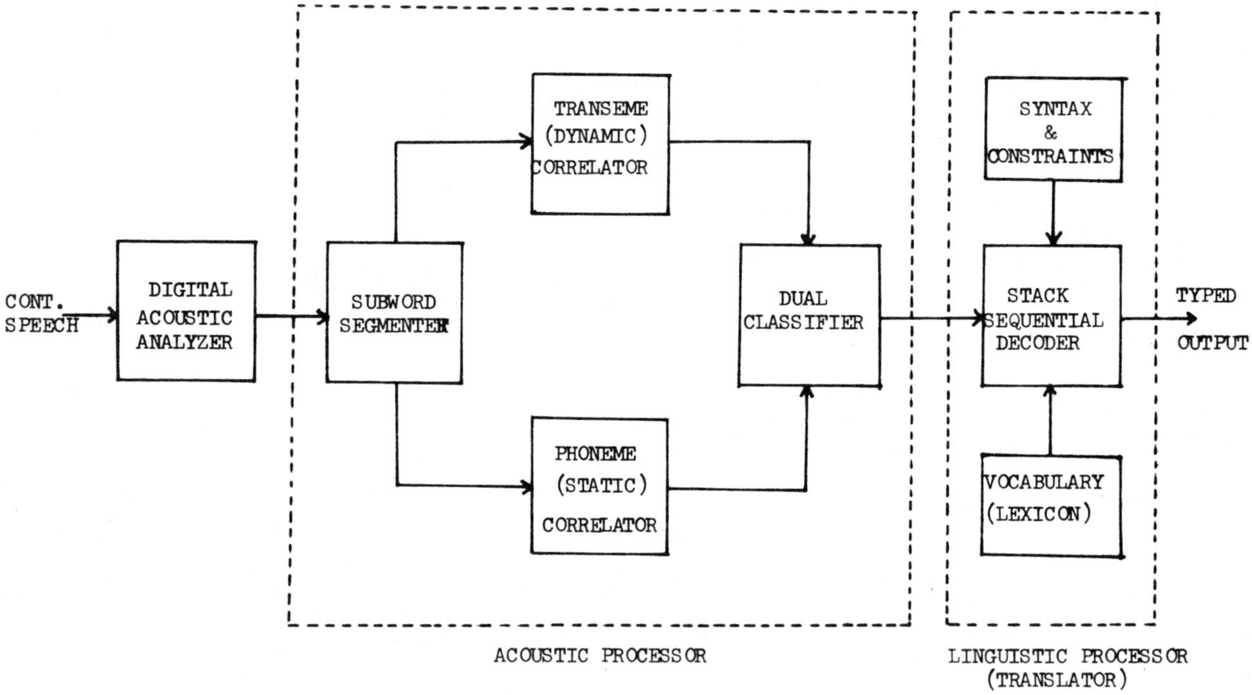

CONTINUOUS SPEECH RECOGNITION SYSTEM

FIGURE 1

The dual classifier utilizes phonetic correlations and phoneme pair (transeme) correlations to derive a preliminary phonetic string representing a given sentence. This preliminary phonetic string is then edited for the purpose of eliminating those events which are phonologically invalid.

Reprinted from *IEEE Symp. on Speech Recognition*, pp. 63–67, April 1974.

The function of the linguistic processor (translator) is the development of an orthographic (written) representation of the acoustic utterance. Translation is accomplished by the sequential decoding of the machine-derived phonetic string containing phonetic substitutions, omissions, and insertions. Information utilized includes multiple phonetic variations of each vocabulary member and error statistics associated with segmentation and dual classification processes. A stack[4] procedure is used.

System Description

Dual Digital Spectral Analysis

The requirements of parameterization of the speech signal for use in automatic recognition of continuous speech are: 1) pertinence to previously developed significant features; 2) long-time stability as measured by the mean square similarity of a parameterized input to a single input presented over a period of months (short-term stability is much more easily attained and hence is tacitly ignored); and 3) computational feasibility for ultimate real-time realization at a reasonable complexity to cost ratio.

The approach selected is based upon discrete finite Fourier transformation of the digitized speech signal. The input speech is lowpass filtered to 9.0 kHz and digitized to 15 bits at a 20 kHz sample rate.

The usual concern for tightly controlling the sharpness of cutoff and flatness of the in-band and out-of-band response of the bandpass filter (bpf) is not warranted for speech processing since the square flat window in the frequency domain is not the desired goal. Rather a flat bandpass with carefully controlled overlap to the next bpf is desired to aid in desensitizing the output to noninformation bearing variation in the fundamental frequency. The Hanning data window has been used. A 128 (6.4 msec) and a sliding 512 (25.6 msec) point transform are computed every 6.4 ms. For the Hanning window, this yields 64 primary filter spaced 156 Hz with 224 Hz one-half power points for the 128 point transform and 256 primary filters spaced 39 Hz with 56 Hz on-half power points for the 512 point transform. This permits subsequent stages of the system to call for finer time resolution for short-time events. The squared magnitude results are stored on tape in floating point form.

The primary filters are combined under program control to produce whatever width and shape filter is desired. Adjustment of bandpass filter parameters has yielded a configuration felt to be suitable for system start-up. Thirty-two filters have been implemented, crossing at 3 dB points (half-power) with less than 0.01 dB ripple. These are combined to yield the bandpass filter sections tabulated in Table for the 25.4 msec bpf set. The 6.4 msec bpf set consists of 12 contiguous bpfs, each 780 Hz wide (5 elementary filters) and center frequencies spaced from 409 Hz to 8989 Hz.

Segmentation

Segmentation of the acoustic signal into phonetic events is based on two sources of information: signal amplitude and correlations reference phonetic spectra.

The correlations are derived by computing the "distance" (using cosine measure) between each 25.6 msec spectral vector and members of a set of reference spectra. The events associated with the top five correlations are preserved. The reference spectra are represented in the correlation inventory in multimodal form, the intra phonetic modes being derived by a clustering process. The phonetic base and number of inventory modes given in Table 2.

TABLE 1

25.6 Millisecond ARCS Filter

Filter Number	Center Frequency	3 db Bandwidth	Number of Elementary Filters
1	155	195	5
2	370	234	6
3	604	"	6
4	838	"	6
5	1072	"	6
6	1306	"	6
7	1540	"	6
8	1774	"	6
9	2008	"	6
10	2242	"	6
11	2476	"	6
12	2710	"	6
13	2944	"	6
14	3197	273	7
15	3490	312	8
16	3841	351	9
17	4192	390	10
18	4601	429	11
19	5070	507	13
20	5616	585	15
21	6249	663	17
22	6943	741	19
23	7721	819	21
24	8579	897	23
25	9476	897	23

TABLE 2

Phonetic Base Giving Event Names, Examples, and Number of Referent Modes in Correlation Inventory

event	example	modes
GLIDES		
w	we	5
l	let	2
r	rob	5
NASALS		
n	not	5
m	me	5
VOWELS		
i	eve	3
I	it	3
ε	met	3
æ	at	3
ɝ	Bert	3
ʌ	Up	3
ɑ	father	3
ɔ	all	3
U	foot	3
u	boot	3

Derivation of a final phonetic string involves the following four stages of processing:

1. Determination of boundary events from steady-state phenomena. The procedure selects appropriate phonetic events, by rule, generally from correlation information on a segmentation indicator - specific basis.

2. Derivation of final transeme final - transeme initial events. From the five highest contiguous transeme pairs, the terminal (TF) and initial (TI) events of a boundary are developed on an indicator-specific basis.

3. Development of preliminary node and indicator strings. Initial event and indicator strings are derived from the correlation list at that boundary and from the information extracted in (2) above. Compatibility between phonetic events and indicators is maintained.

4. Development of final node and indicator strings. The sequences generated in (3) above are verified for consistency on a second-order basis. Correcting insertions, omissions, and substitutions are introduced by rule at those positions where contiguous events derived by the machine are invalid with respect to possible speaker production or in such cases where the preliminary event is incompatible with steady-state or dynamic classification information. Besides correcting errors generated by both the preceding segmentation and classification processing, non-phonemic speaker phenomena, e.g., aspirated releases, may be removed. Event indicator agreement is maintained.

The rules implemented for phonetic string derivation are similar to those used by Dixon and Tappert[3].

Linguistic Transformation

The function of the linguistic transformation stage is the conversion of a machine-derived phonetic transcription of the speaker's performance into an orthographic representation. A detailed description of the process in the continuous speech recognition system is reserved for Paper[5] W5 of this conference.

Preliminary Performance Analysis

Introduction

The speech base from which the following results were derived is quite limited and associated transeme and correlation inventories minimal with respect to those events expected in test material; therefore an overall assessment of this system cannot be drawn from these data alone. Additional gains in performance can eventually be achieved by the implementation of functions in domains which have not been explored within the context of the present system, e.g., closure of syntactic paths by the utilization of prosodic and semantic constraints, feedback of hypothesized phonetic strings to the acoustic level.

Source of Speech Material

Six male speakers were employed in the preliminary evaluation. Of these talkers, one expressed a Southern American dialect (speaker 006) and another displayed the effects of exposure to a language other than English (speaker 005). The speech of the remaining four can be considered General American English as broadly defined. All speech was recorded in a relatively noise-free chamber. Three of the speakers, 001, 002, and 003, were employed for training; i.e., their speech material was used for the generation of correlation and transeme inventories. The correlation inventory used spanned all phonetic types with, however, a limited number of tokens for each type. The transeme inventory was limited to approximately 200 events with the typical transeme reference resulting from the average of usually two or three tokens. This compares with the 550 to 600 transeme types desired in the inventory for spanning all possible phonetic input.

All sentences utilized in this evaluation were derived from a context-free (type 2) grammar. The number of words in the lexicon of this grammar is 250. The majority of the entries are high frequency types as given by the Dewey count. The number of possible sentences generated by this grammar is approximately 15.0×10^6; thus, the a priori probability of selecting the correct sentence is about $1/15 \times 10^6$. Only a fraction of the sentences of this sublanguage are semantically valid as no attempt was made to encompass any single problem domain. However, no semantic constraints are presently being imposed to restrict the search space of the phoneme-to-grapheme stage; therefore, performance with regard to this factor can be considered a worst-case. Certainly, the utilization of such constraints will effect substantial increments in recognition accuracy as paths inconsistent with the semantic domain are closed.

It should be mentioned that sentences of the sublanguage vary in length from three to eleven words and are of three general types: declarative, interrogative, and imperative. The use of differing sentence structures enables the eventual exploration of the effect of dissimilar suprasegmental contours on system performance.

Quantitative Performance Results

The total number of sentences processed in this preliminary evaluation was 46. The number of sentences n for each speaker varied somewhat. Recognition accuracies for each speaker are given in Table 3. The cumulative performance across all six speakers is also shown.

TABLE 3

Summary of System Performance Across Six Speakers

Speaker No.	001	002	003	004	005	006	All
Sentence accept rate	.83	.89	.44	.40	.33	.50	.52
Words out/words in (all sentences)	.98	.92	.74	.71	.71	.92	.82
Words correct/words out (all sentences)	.88	.74	.75	.67	.54	.58	.71
Words correct/words out (Correct Sent.)	.93	.76	.93	.76	.45	.69	.79
Words correct/words in (all sentences)	.88	.68	.55	.49	.39	.57	.58

TABLE 2 (CONTD)

event	example	modes
STOPS		
p	pot	1
b	be	1
t	to	1
d	do	1
k	key	1
g	go	1
x	(silence)	1
FRICATIVES		
low energy		
f	for	2
v	very	2
θ	thin	5
ð	then	5
high energy		
s	see	2
z	zoo	2
ʃ	she	2
ʒ	azure	2
ASPIRATES		
p'		1
t'		1
d'		1
k'		1
g'		1
h	he	3

The segmentation rules are similar to those developed by Dixon and Tappert[3]. The major difference in these rule sets are changes in time and amplitude thresholds for the new digital frontend, elimination of the rapid closure processor, and modification to the rule set to permit a more diverse syntax.

To summarize the segmentation rules, regions of low energy (closures and silences) are first detected; detection is based on a multi-threshold rule in which signal amplitude is utilized. These are removed from subsequent processing. Next, regions in which fricatives and aspirates display dominant positions in the correlation rankings are specified in the utterance.

The remaining unspecified regions of the utterance are categorized as stressed or unstressed. The stress level decision is based on a multi-threshold signal amplitude rule. The stressed and unstressed regions are processed separately. In each region, areas in which nasals, vowels, or glides play a dominant position in the correlation rankings are isolated and removed from the utterance.

For each specified region a segmentation indicator (nasal, fricative, unstressed vowel, etc.) is then derived and phonetic boundaries specified.

Transeme Classification

Transemes are defined as the dynamic interphonetic elements between the centers (steady-state region) of two adjacent phonetic events (as specified by the segmenter). Features are derived from these dynamic elements, and a correlation process is carried out. This correlation information is passed to the dual classifier for generating a hypothesized phonetic string.

A total of 395 binary-valued features are extracted from the initial, central, and terminal portions of each transeme. These features are derived from spectral measurements, slopes of transitional regions, spectral correlations, and segmentation indicators.

The transeme classifier assumes that a transeme inventory has been constructed from the feature vectors produced by the feature extraction process during a transeme phase. This inventory consists of references coded at two bits per position. The candidate input transeme, represented as a binary feature vector, is compared to each reference and a mismatch score

$$MM_j = \sum_{i=1}^{512} (D_i \oplus M1_{ij}) \cdot M2_{ij}, \quad j = 1, \ldots \text{ number reference transemes}$$

computed, where D_i is the ith bit of the candidate transeme, and $M1_{ij}$, $M2_{ij}$ are the two-bit coding of the ith position in the jth reference transeme. This mismatch score is normalized by the number of care positions in the jth reference to yield a correlation

$$\text{Normcor}_j = 100 - (MM_j \cdot 100)/\text{Number of care positions in reference } j$$

with values between 0 and 100. The highest five such correlations, together with the unnormalized mismatch scores, are retained.

The transeme inventory consists of approximately 200 different transeme events. These events are a subset of the larger 1000 + possible events and were chosen to span the sentence data used in developing this system. Admittedly, the transeme inventory is one of the weakest elements in this system as it is implemented. Dixon and Tappert[3] indicated that their inventory, consisting of approximately 600 transeme categories, is adequate to span a diverse vocabulary and syntax. The additional inventory entries for this system would require substantially more transeme labeling.

Dual Classification

a. Phonetic-String Derivation

The function of the dual classifier is the development of a phonologically consistent phonetic transcription to serve as input to the linguistic transformation stage. The information employed in this step of processing is of both a dynamic and steady-state nature. The utterance-specific inputs are: a) the five highest steady-state correlations, b) the correlation string event, c) the segmentation indicator, d) the amplitude value, e) the five highest transeme initial events, f) the five highest transeme final events, and g) temporal information.

References

(1) This program was sponsored by Rome Air Development Center (RADC) as a continuation of the IBM Automatic Recognition of Continuous Speech (ARCS) program. This system is architectually identical to the ARCS system and utilizes many of the elements developed by the IBM team.(3)

(2) J. E. Paul, A. S. Rabinowitz, J. P. Riganati V. A. Vitols and M. L, Griffith, "Automatic Recognition of Continuous Speech: Further Development of a Hierarchial Strategy," Rockwell International Corp., RADC-TR-73-319, 1973.

(3) N. R. Dixon and C. C. Tappert, "Intermediate Performance Evaluation of a Multi-Stage System for Automatic Recognition of Continuous Speech: An Exploratory Program," IBM Corp., RADC-TR-68-177, 1972.

(4) F. Jelinek, "Fast Sequential Decoding Algorithm Using a Stack IBM Journal of Research and Development," 13:675-685, 1972.

(5) A. S. Rabinowitz, "Phonetic to Graphemic Transformation by Use of a Stack Procedure," IEEE Symposium on Speech Recognition, Carnegie-Mellon University, 1974.

The DRAGON System—An Overview

JAMES K. BAKER

Abstract—**This paper briefly describes the major features of the DRAGON speech understanding system. DRAGON makes systematic use of a general abstract model to represent each of the knowledge sources necessary for automatic recognition of continuous speech. The model—that of a probabilistic function of a Markov process—is very flexible and leads to features which allow DRAGON to function despite high error rates from individual knowledge sources. Repeated use of a simple abstract model produces a system which is simple in structure, but powerful in capabilities.**

INTRODUCTION

TO ACHIEVE reliable speech recognition it is necessary to combine information from a variety of sources [4]. In addition to the direct acoustic information, valuable sources include the vocabulary, the grammar, and the semantics of the utterance. Extracting the information from each of these sources of knowledge is a difficult task, and the need to coordinate the various pieces of information makes the task even more difficult. For the DRAGON system a general theoretical model has been adapted to represent each of the important sources of knowledge. The sources of knowledge are organized into a hierarchical system such that the integrated system is again an instance of the same general model. The availability of this general theoretical framework has greatly simplified the DRAGON speech understanding system.

The general model which is used throughout the DRAGON system is that of a probabilistic function of a Markov process [2]. In this model there are two sequences of random variables $X(1),X(2),X(3),\cdots,X(T)$, and $Y(1),Y(2),Y(3),\cdots,Y(T)$. The X's correspond to internal states which are not observed and the Y's correspond to external observations whose distributions depend on the values of the X's. For example, the X's could represent the sequence of phones in an utterance and the Y's could represent the sequence of acoustic measurements. Alternatively, the X's could be the sequence of words in an utterance and the Y's could represent the sequence of phones and modifiers as the words are actually pronounced. Changing the frame of reference again, the Y's could represent the words of the utterance and the X's could represent the underlying sequence of syntactic-semantic states.

Manuscript received March 29, 1974. This research was supported in part by the Advanced Research Projects Agency of the Department of Defense under Contract F44620-73-C-0074 and is monitored by the Air Force Office of Scientific Research. This paper was presented at the IEEE Symposium on Speech Recognition, Carnegie-Mellon University, Pittsburgh, Pa., April 15–19, 1974.

The author is with the IBM Thomas J. Watson Research Center, Yorktown Heights, N. Y. 10598.

FEATURES OF THE DRAGON SYSTEM

The major features of the DRAGON system are

1) delayed decisions;
2) generative form of model;
3) hierachical system;
4) integrated representation;
5) general theoretical framework.

The various sources of knowledge are organized into a hierarchy of probabilistic functions of Markov processes. A network is constructed to provide an integrated representation of the hierarchy. Recognition of an utterance corresponds to finding an optimum path through the network. The optimum path if found by an algorithm which, in effect, explores all possible paths in parallel [1].

Delayed Decisions

In terms of the network representation, most speech recognition algorithms search for a suboptimum path through the network. A globally optimum path would clearly be superior, but with most models it is prohibitively expensive to compute. The Markov model of the

Reprinted from *IEEE Trans. Acoust., Speech, and Signal Process.*, vol. ASSP-23, pp. 24–29, Feb. 1975.

DRAGON system permits such a globally optimum path to be found by an algorithm such that the number of computations is linear in the length of the utterance.

The Markov assumption is a prescription to include "all relevant context" in formulating the state space of the process. By considering at each point in time all possible internal states, the algorithm searches all possible paths through the network. By combining paths when and only when they come to the same state at the same time, all decisions are delayed until the full effect of all context, past and future, has been considered.

Generative Form of Model

By having an external sequence (Y) depend probabilistically on an unobserved internal sequence (X), the system allows knowledge sources to be represented in a generative form [6]. Given the sequence of syntactic-semantic states one can generate the words. Given the words one can generate the phones. Given the sequence of phones one can generate the sequence of acoustic observations. But, computationally, this hierarchy of conditional probabilities can by reversed by applying Bayes' theorem. In analyzing a specific utterance one can proceed from the known observations to the internal states which must be inferred.

Hierarchical System

The sources of knowledge are organized into a hierarchy based on the following observation: the "top" levels of a speech recognition system change state less frequently than the "bottom" levels. Thus a single syntactic-semantic state corresponds to a sequence of several words; a single word corresponds to a sequence of several phones; and a phone corresponds to a sequence of several acoustic events. The hierarchy is not absolute—for example, syntax and semantics are mixed together into a single multilevel process—but it provides a convenient means for combining the Markov process which represent the individual sources of knowledge.

Integrated Representation

A network is constructed which represents the total hierarchy of Markov processes. The process as a whole fits the same general model as the pieces—it is a probabilistic function of a Markov process. All of the "knowledge" of the system is represented in a pair of simple data structures: the transition matrix of the network and the table of conditional probabilities connecting internal states to external observations. The main program of the system is based on the general model of a probabilistic function of a Markov process. All speech-specific knowledge is represented in the data structures, not in the program.

General Theoretical Framework

Having a general theoretical structure greatly simplifies the speech recognition system. It is both easier to implement and easier to understand. Its operations can be expressed explicitly by a simple set of mathematical equations. A powerful general system is constructed by repeated use of a flexible theoretical model.

Potential Problems and Disadvantages

Delayed decisions—searching all possible paths through the network—could lead to a combinatorial explosion in the number of computations. The Markov model completely prevents this combinatorial explosion. Alternate paths are recombined at exactly the same rate that new branches are formed. The total number of computations is linear in the length of the utterance.

The integrated representation of a hierarchical system could result in an excessively large state space. Care must be exercised as to what context must be included and what can be safely ignored. Experience indicates, however, that the network representation is a compact and powerful representation and speech recognition tasks with large vocabularies can be accommodated.

Representing all knowledge as conditional probabilities does not imply any loss of power, since the probabilities can be set to zero or to one whenever appropriate. However, it does require that estimates be computed for all the probabilities in the system. Fortunately, all these probabilities are easily estimated from the frequency of occurrence of corresponding events in a set of training utterances.

GENERAL MODEL

Let the sequence $X(1),X(2),X(3),\cdots,X(T)$ be the sequence of states of a Markov process [3] with transition matrix $A = (a_{i,j})$. Let $Y(1),Y(2),Y(3),\cdots,Y(T)$ be a sequence of random variables such that, for all t, $\Pr(Y(t) = k \mid X(t-1) = i,\ X(t) = j) = b_{i,j,k}$. Use a bracket and colon notation to abbreviate sequences. Thus $X[1:T] = X(1),X(2),X(3),\cdots,X(T)$ and $Y[1:T] = Y(1),Y(2),Y(3),\cdots,Y(T)$. The assumptions of the model are that

$$\begin{aligned}\Pr(Y(t) = y(t) \mid X[1:t] &= x[1:t],\ Y[1:t-1] = y[1:t-1]) \\ &= \Pr(Y(t) = y(t) \mid X(t-1) = x(t-1),\ X(t) = x(t)) \\ &= b_{x(t-1)x(t),y(t)} \qquad (1)\end{aligned}$$

and

$$\begin{aligned}\Pr(X(t) = x(t) \mid X[1:t-1] &= x[1:t-1]) \\ &= \Pr(X(t) = x(t) \mid X(t-1) = x(t-1)) \\ &= a_{x(t-1),x(t)}. \qquad (2)\end{aligned}$$

Under these assumptions,

$$\Pr(X[1:T] = x[1:T],\ Y[1:T] = y[1:T]) = \prod_{t=1,T} a_{x(t-1),x(t)} b_{x(t-1),x(t),y(t)} \qquad (3)$$

where a special extra state $x(0)$ is introduced and $a_{x(0),j}$ and $b_{x(0),j,k}$ are defined appropriately.

It is convenient to introduce a special notation for the total probability of all partial sequences resulting in a particular state at a particular time. Let

$$\alpha(s,j) = \Pr(X(s) = j, Y[1:s] = y[1:s])$$
$$= \sum_{x[1:s-1]} \prod_{t=1,s} a_{x(t-1),x(t)} b_{x(t-1),x(t),y(t)} \quad (4)$$

where the sum is over all possible sequences $x[1:s-1]$ and $x(s) = j$. The values of α for a given s can easily be computed from the values for $s - 1$. In fact,

$$\alpha(s,j) = \sum_i \alpha(s-1,i) a_{i,j} b_{i,j,y(s)}. \quad (5)$$

Conditional probabilities based on the known sequence $y[1:T]$ can be computed from the function α and a similar function computed backwards in time from the end of the sequence. For example,

$$\Pr(X(T) = j \mid Y[1:T] = y[1:T])$$
$$= \Pr(X(T) = j,$$
$$Y[1:T] = y[1:T]) / \Pr(Y[1:T] = y[1:T])$$
$$= \alpha(T,j) / \sum_i \alpha(T,i). \quad (6)$$

Each of the sources of knowledge needed for speech recognition can be represented with this general Markov framework.

REPRESENTATION OF KNOWLEDGE SOURCES

Representing Acoustic-Phonetic Knowledge

There are several choices in how to represent acoustic-phonetic knowledge. A decision must be made whether acoustic observations should be preprocessed by specialized procedures or whether the stochastic model should deal directly with the acoustic parameters. To simplify the exposition, consider just the case in which specialized preprocessing is done.

Assume that at each time t $(1 \leq t \leq T)$, an acoustic observation is made. Each such observation consists of a vector of values of a set of acoustic parameters, which in the stochastic model is represented by a vector-valued random variable $Y(t)$. There is a sequence of phones $P[1:J]$ which is produced during the time interval $1 \leq t \leq T$. Assume that the phones occupy disjoint segments of time, that is, assume there is a sequence $s_0 < s_1 < s_2 < s_3 < \cdots < s_J$ such that $P(j)$ lasts from observation $Y(s_{j-1})$ through observation $Y(s_j) - 1$. (Set $s_0 = 1$, $s_J = T$.)

Let $p[1:J]$ be the actual sequence of phones in an utterance and let $y[1:T]$ be the actual observed sequence of acoustic parameters. For convenience, also introduce a special initalization phone $p(0)$ which is assigned a special value to allow the initial probabilities to have the same form as the transition probabilities later in the sequence. Since the actual times $s_1,s_2,s_3,\cdots,s_{J-1}$ are not known, it is necessary to associate each arbitrary segment of time with some phone. For any pair of times t_1 and t_2 let $S(t_1,t_2)$ be that value of j for which the expression $(\min(s_j,t_2) - \max(s_{j-1},t_1))$ is maximized. If $t_2 \leq 1$ then set $S(t_1,t_2) = 0$.

The acoustic preprocessor tries to estimate a phonetic transcription from the acoustics alone. By looking for discontinuities or rapid changes in the acoustic parameters, the preprocessor divides the sequence $Y[1:T]$ up into K phone-like segments $Y[1:t_1-1], Y[t_1:t_2-1], Y[t_2:t_3-1], \cdots, Y[t_{K-1}:t_K]$. Then an attempt is made to classify each segment $Y[t_{j-1}:t_j-1]$ using some form of pattern recognition procedure. Let $t_0 < t_1 < t_2 < \cdots < t_K$ be the segment boundary times as decided by the preprocessor and introduce the random variable $D(t)$ which is 1 if there exists a k such that $t_k = t$ and is 0 otherwise. Let $F(k)$ be the label assigned by the preprocessor to the segment $Y[t_{k-1}:t_k-1]$. (For completeness, set $t_k = t_0 = 1$ for $k < 0$, and $t_k = t_K = T$ for $k > K$.)

For some pattern matching procedures it is possible to directly estimate conditional probabilities. When using such a procedure, let

$$B[p,k] = \Pr(Y[t_{k-1}:t_k-1] = y[t_{k-1}:t_k-1] \mid$$
$$P(S(t_{k-1},t_k)) = p). \quad (7)$$

The pattern matching procedure might yield only the label $F(k)$ representing a best guess as to the underlying phone. In such a case it is necessary to estimate the conditional probabilities from statistics of performance by the pattern matcher on training data. Let $f[1:K]$ represent the actual sequence of labels generated by the pattern recognizer for the utterance being considered. Then set

$$B[p,k] = \Pr(F(k) = f(k) \mid P(S(t_{k-1},t_k)) = p), \quad (8)$$

where the conditional probability is estimated by the frequency of such events in a set of training utterances.

In addition to estimating the probability of substitutions or confusions, it is necessary to estimate the probability of the preprocessor producing either too many or too few segments. The probability of such events may be estimated from their frequency of occurrence in a set of training utterances. Let

$$E[p_1,p_2,n] =$$
$$\Pr(D(t_{k-2}) = D(t_{k-1}) = D(t_k) = 1,$$
$$D[t_{k-2}+1:t_{k-1}-1] = 0,$$
$$D[t_{k-1}+1:t_k-1] = 0 \mid$$

$$P(S(t_{k-2},t_{k-1})) = p_1, P(S(t_{k-1},t_k)) = p_2,$$
$$S(t_{k-1},t_k) = S(t_{k-2},t_{k-1}) + n). \qquad (9)$$

If the acoustic preprocessor is reliable, then $E[p_1,p_2,n]$ should be small except for $n = 1$ and should be negligible for $n > 2$. In the DRAGON system, it has arbitrarily been assumed that $E[p_1,p_2,n] = 0$ for $n > 4$. Note that $E[p_1,p_2,0]$ is undefined and meaningless unless $p_1 = p_2$.

We can now estimate the conditional probability of the sequence $Y[1:T]$ given the sequence $P[1:J]$.

$$\Pr(Y[1:T] = y[1:T] \mid P[0:J] = p[0:J]) = \sum_{n[1:K]} \prod_{k=1,K} B[p(z(k)),k]E[p(z(k-1)),p(z(k)),n(k)], \qquad (10)$$

where $z(k) = \sum_{i=1,k} n(i)$ and the sum is taken over all sequences $n[1:K]$ such that $z(k) = J$. [By convention $z(0) = 0$.]

In order to apply the theory of a probabilistic function of a Markov process, it is necessary to specify the transition probabilities for the phone sequence $P[1:J]$. It is the task of the other sources of knowledge to specify these probabilities. Phonological rules may be represented either directly or indirectly in the estimates of $E[p_1,p_2,n]$ and $B[p,k]$, but all higher levels of the hierarchy deal only with the sequence $P[1:J]$ and are insolated from the acoustics $Y[1:T]$ or the labels $F[1:K]$.

Representation of Lexical Knowledge

This section discusses the computation of the conditional probability $\Pr(P[1:J] = p[1:J] \mid W[1:I] = w[1:I])$ where $W[1:I]$ is the sequence of words in the utterance and $P[1:J]$ is the sequence of phones. Knowledge of the sequence of words in an utterance is such a strong determiner of the sequence of phones that it is unusual to formulate the connection as a stochastic process. Nevertheless, the stochastic formulation can represent the same rules as other formulations and in a compact and computationally convenient form.

Let us first consider how alternate pronunciations of a particular word can be represented by a probability network. As an example, take the word "always" as used in the automatic recognition of continuous speech (ARCS), system (IBM Rockwell) [9], [5]. There are 432 pronunciations which are allowed. The ARCS system can have such a complete list of phonetic variants because it uses a network representation of the alternatives and constraints. Some speech understanding systems use an explicit list of alternate pronunciations, either generated automatically from a phonemic dictionary or preselected by hand. But an easy way to represent an exhaustive list of alternate pronunciations is by a network. The network representation for "always" is

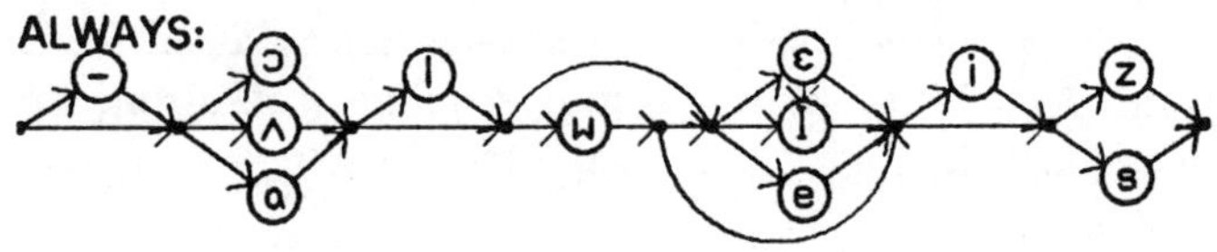

where the dots (.) are dummy nodes introduced so that the network can be shown in two dimensions. We have represented the phones as nodes rather than as arcs (which would be even more compact) because such a representation fits more easily into the integrated system. The node-based representation permits explicit representation of sequential constraints (such as the restriction that if /w/ is omitted, then the following vowel cannot also be omitted).

The network representing alternate pronunciations of a given word can either be derived by hand and stored in a dictionary of word networks, or can be derived by automatic procedures. The automatic procedures take a canonical pronunciation and apply phonological rules to produce a network representing all likely pronunciations of the word. Even if alternate pronunciations of words are not derived by rule, the phonological rules are still important because many of them can apply across word boundaries.

The process of applying phonological rules is one way in which the DRAGON system deviates from the conceptual hierarchy. The syntax and semantics of a particular task is represented by a network in which each node corresponds to a word. Using either a dictionary of canonical pronunciations or a word-network dictionary, a small network is substituted for each word node. The result is a network in which each node is an individual phone. The phonological rules are then repeatedly applied to the network. For each phonological rule the entire network is searched to find any nodes which satisfy the context conditions of the rule. Each rule provides an alternate pronunciation of some sequence of phones. If the alternate pronunciation is not already represented then an extra branch is created in the network representing the sequence of phones for the alternate pronunciation. This process applies across word boundaries as well as within words, depending on the phonological rule. Conditional probabilities for the different branches of the phonetic network are estimated from frequency of occurrence statistics for a set of hand transcribed sentences. Such probabilities could even be made dialect dependent or even talker dependent. Note that the training sentences only need to be phonetically transcribed, it is not necessary to know the time at which each phone occurs since at this level we are no longer dealing directly with acoustics.

The explicit representation of phonological rules in the network is easily achieved at an expense of doubling or tripling the number of nodes in the network. However, with this stochastic network model it is not essential that an exhaustive set of phonological rules be used. In fact, implementations of the DRAGON system have been made with no explicit phonological rules and only one canonical pronunciation for each word. The reason that this representation is possible is that any phonological phenomena which are not introduced explicitly will be treated at the acoustic-phonetic level. Thus phonological substitutions can be mimicked by adjusting the probabilities in the matrix $B[p,k]$ to include the probability that p is not the actual phone used by the talker but rather that some other phone q is spoken. Similarly, phonological insertions and deletions can be treated by adjusting the probabilities in the matrix $E[p_1,p_2,n]$. The disadvantage of this approach is that the matrices B and E represent less context than is available in the explicit representation of the phonological rules.

There is a serendipitous benefit in using the matrices B and E to represent acoustic-phonetic knowledge independently from the representation of the phonological rules. If the matrices B and E are estimated by running the acoustic preprocessor on a collection of test utterances, then any phonological rules which are left out in the prepared labeling of the test utterances are automatically absorbed into the estimates of B and E. Thus a perfect hand-labeled transcription of the test utterances is not only unnecessary, but undesirable. The best labeling for training purposes is an automatically generated labeling from a procedure knowing the sequence of words and having exactly the same lexical knowledge and phonological rules as the speech understanding system.

Representation of Syntactic and Semantic Knowledge

The syntax and semantics of a specific task domain can be represented by a multilevel network corresponding to a Markov process. Consider as a task a spoken chess move. Chess has a specialized grammar as well as a specialized vocabulary [6], [7]. Leaving aside a few special moves, a move can be represented by a path through the following network:

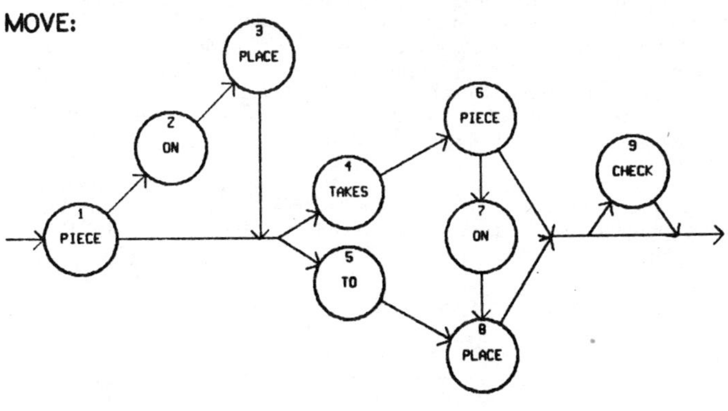

The nodes in the above network are not in general individual words, but are subgrammars which are themselves represented by networks. For example:

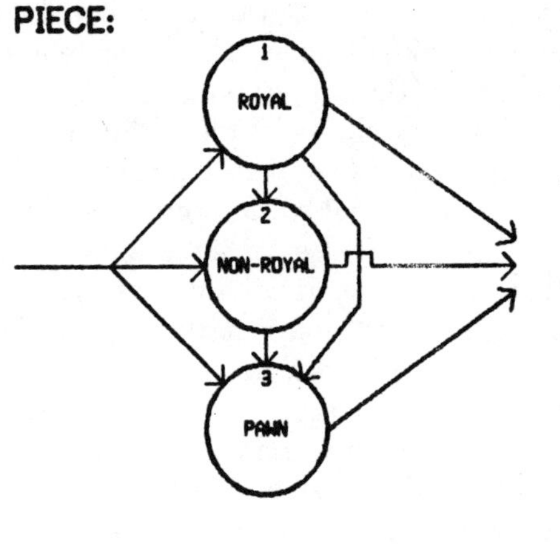

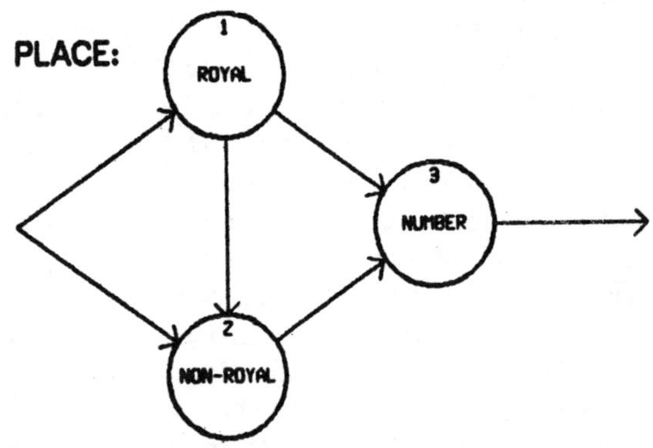

Again, the nodes can be expanded as networks:

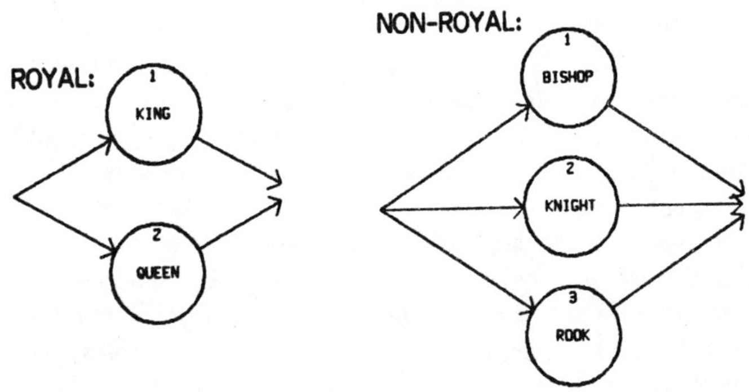

It is clear that any regular (finite state) grammar can be represented by a finite network. But in a speech understanding system the distinction between a regular grammar and an arbitrary context-dependent grammar is somewhat artificial. Consider the language of utterances generated by a particular grammar, not the sequence of words but the sequence of acoustic events. It is not unreasonable to assume, for example, that each entry in $B[p,k]$ is nonzero, although perhaps very small. Such a result would automatically be the case, for example, if the conditional probability distributions for the acoustic parameters are multivariate normal distributions.

But if each entry in $B[p,k]$ is nonzero, then at the acoustic level the language must include all possible sequences. Such a language can, of course, be represented by a finite network grammar. Thus, the issue becomes not one of generating the proper language, but rather one of modeling as accurately as possible the conditional probabilities, which can be context-dependent even for a context-free grammar. Context is represented in the network by having separate nodes for subgrammars which differ only with respect to context. For example, in the chess grammar there are two nodes marked "piece," one describing the piece which is moving and one describing a piece which is captured. There is clearly a tradeoff between the size of the state space and the amount of context which can be represented. For specialized tasks it is not difficult to achieve a reasonable representation of the grammar using most words at no more than two or three nodes. The transition probabilities for the grammar network can be estimated from statistics for a set of training sentences. A large set of training sentences should be used, but they only need to be transcribed orthographically, not phonetically, at this level of the hierarchy. If Bayesian statistics are used, the *a priori* probabilities could be set to achieve the same effect as a nonprobabilistic use of the grammar. The *a posteriori* probabilities would then be a strict improvement (as judged by the training sentences).

To the extent to which the statistics of the training sentences reflect the true probabilities for spontaneous utterances for the specific task, the probability network represents not only the syntax of the task but also all of the recognition information which can be obtained from the semantics of the available context. That is, assuming the probabilities are correct, the probability network is an optimal predictor for a given amount of context, and therefore predicts at least as well as a human who is given the same amount of context and who presumably understands the sentence (although the context in this case is not the whole sentence).

Inter-sentence semantics can also be introduced into the probability network. One way to use inter-sentence semantics is to employ a user model. Suppose there is a model for the user in a particular task which gives probabilities for the user transitioning among a finite number of states depending on the types of utterances which the user has made in the past. Conceptually this model fits in easily as an extra level in the Markov hierarchy. Computationally it requires that conditional probabilities be estimated separately for each user state. However, since the user transitions between states only between utterances, a given utterance is analyzed using only a single representation of the probability network. The probabilities in this single network are weighted averages of the probabilities for the various user states. A user model is especially valuable if certain key sentences trigger user state transitions with probability one and if for each user state a small subset of the general grammar is used. Then there is a savings in both computation and storage requirements.

PERFORMANCE RESULTS

The testing of the system is still at too preliminary a stage to make any definitive conclusions, but initial results are very promising. Simulation studies have shown that the system can perform well despite a high error rate in the acoustic preprocessor. In its first test with live speech input, the system correctly recognized every word in all nine sentences in the test.

ACKNOWLEDGMENT

The author wishes to thank L. Baum, who introduced him to the theory of a probabilistic function of a Markov process, and R. Reddy, whose encouragement, sponsorship, and personal examples have been his guiding light during this research.

REFERENCES

[1] R. E. Bellman, *Dynamic Programming.* Princeton, N. J.: Princeton University Press, 1957.
[2] L. E. Baum and J. A. Eagon, "An inequality with applications to statistical estimations for probabilistic functions of Markov processes and to a model of ecology," *Amer. Math. Soc. Bull.*, vol. 73, pp. 360–362, 1967.
[3] A. A. Markov, "Essai d'une recherche statistique sur le texte du roman 'Eugene Onegin' illustrant la liaison des epreuve en chaine," *Bull. de l'Academie Imperiale des Sciences de St. Petersbourg*, vol. VII, 1913.
[4] A. Newell *et al.*, "Speech understanding systems: final report of a study group," Comp. Sci. Dep., Carnegie-Mellon University, Pittsburgh, Pa., 1971.
[5] J. E. Paul *et al.*, "Automatic recognition of continuous speech: further development of a hierarchical strategy," Electron. Res. Div., Rockwell International, 1973.
[6] D. R. Reddy, "On the use of environmental, syntactic, and probabilistic constraints in vision and speech," Comp. Sci. Dep., Stanford University, Stanford, Calif., 1969.
[7] D. R. Reddy, L. Erman, and R. Neely, "A model and system for machine recognition of speech," Comp. Sci. Dep., Carnegie-Mellon University, Pittsburgh, Pa., 1972.
[8] D. R. Reddy *et al.*, "Working papers in speech recognition—I," Comp. Sci. Dep., Carnegie-Mellon University, Pittsburgh, Pa., 1972.
[9] C. C. Tappert *et al.*, "Automatic recognition of continuous speech utilizing dynamic segmentation, dual classification, sequential decoding, and error recovery," IBM Corp., 1971.

Design of a Linguistic Statistical Decoder for the Recognition of Continuous Speech

FREDERICK JELINEK, FELLOW, IEEE, LALIT R. BAHL, MEMBER, IEEE, AND ROBERT L. MERCER

Abstract—**Most current attempts at automatic speech recognition are formulated in an artificial intelligence framework. In this paper we approach the problem from an information-theoretic point of view. We describe the overall structure of a linguistic statistical decoder (LSD) for the recognition of continuous speech. The input to the decoder is a string of phonetic symbols estimated by an acoustic processor (AP). For each phonetic string, the decoder finds the most likely input sentence. The decoder consists of four major subparts: 1) a statistical model of the language being recognized; 2) a phonemic dictionary and statistical phonological rules characterizing the speaker; 3) a phonetic matching algorithm that computes the similarity between phonetic strings, using the performance characteristics of the AP; 4) a word level search control. The details of each of the subparts and their interaction during the decoding process are discussed.**

I. Introduction

MOST CURRENT attempts at automatic speech recognition are formulated in an artificial intelligence framework. A mini-universe of discourse is selected (e.g., repair of faucets [1], geophysical inquiry [2], or chess playing [3]) and described syntactically and semantically. This description deterministically limits the permissible set of utterances. A complex interaction of acoustic, syntactic, and semantic processors then directs the search for the spoken sentence. The search is often based on confidence, fit, and frequency metrics derived in an ad hoc intuitive manner.

In this paper we describe the structure of a linguistic statistical decoder (LSD) that will be implemented by the Speech Processing Group of the IBM Thomas J. Watson Research Center. It constitutes an attempt to model statistically various aspects of speech production and recognition and to use decision procedures familiar in the field of information transmission in order to recognize and transcribe speech. A statistics-based system was previously implemented by Dixon and Tappert [4], [5] at IBM, Raleigh, N.C.; this serves as the starting point for the efforts here.

Four problems of particular interest to information theorists will be introduced. None of these problems has received adequate analytic treatment in the literature. First, we must decode in a system in which the codewords are not under the control of the system designer. The information sequence is a sentence, and the corresponding transmitted codeword is the phonetic representation of the sentence, which is completely determined by the phonology of the language and the speaker. Second, there is a probabilistic relationship between the information sequence and the codeword that is transmitted. This is due to the fact that even a single speaker can pronounce the same sentence in many different ways. Third, the number of symbols in a codeword is a random variable, since word lengths and sentence lengths are variable. Finally, the recognition channel commits insertion and deletion errors in addition to the usual substitution errors. The insertion and deletion errors are due to imperfect segmentation, and the substitution errors are due to imperfect classification.

Fig. 1 is a block diagram of the speech recognition system. The acoustic processor (AP) uses signal processing and pattern recognition techniques to extract phonetic information from the acoustic signal. In the AP that we will consider here, this phonetic information is in the form of a phonetic string. In general, the AP may provide more detailed information and may even provide probabilistic information. The linguistic decoder then uses the structure of the language—its vocabulary, phonological rules, syntax, and semantics—to produce an orthographic transcription of the phonetic string.

The aim of this work is to recognize carefully spoken utterances that are produced in a relatively noiseless environment. The utterances are drawn from a corpus, which at present consists of two million words of patent applications in the field of laser technology. The vocabulary is roughly 10 000 words. We use this corpus to construct a statistical model of the language, and this is used by the LSD during the decoding process. The details of this model are discussed in Section IV. Sections II and III describe the speaker and AP models and the estimation of probabilities for them. In Sections V and VI we explain the principles and the implementation of the LSD. Section VII deals with some refinements of the model and decoder.

II. Front End Model

Fig. 2 is a diagram of the speaker-AP model, which will be referred to as the front end. It consists of three parts—an essentially phonemic dictionary, a set of phonological rules that models the speaker, and a noisy channel that models the AP. The front end accepts orthographic text as input and produces as output a string of symbols from a phonetic alphabet $A = (a_1,a_2,\cdots,a_K)$.

The phonemic dictionary and phonological rules are described in detail by Cohen and Mercer [6]. The phonemic dictionary contains a set of phonemic base forms for each word of the vocabulary. Each of these represents a basic pronunciation of the word from which a number of other

Manuscript received March 29, 1974.

F. Jelinek and R. L. Mercer are with the Computer Sciences Department, IBM Thomas J. Watson Research Center, Yorktown Heights, N.Y.

L. R. Bahl is with the Computer Sciences Department, IBM Thomas J. Watson Research Center, Yorktown Heights, N.Y., and also the Department of Electrical Engineering and Computer Science, Columbia University, New York, N.Y.

Reprinted from *IEEE Trans. Inform. Theory*, vol. IT-21, pp. 250–256, May 1975.

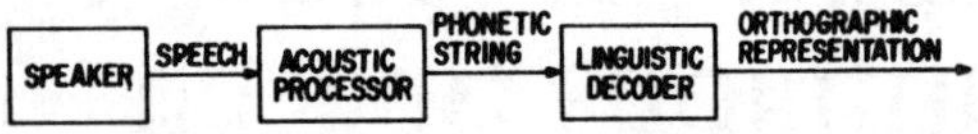

Fig. 1. Block diagram of speech recognition system.

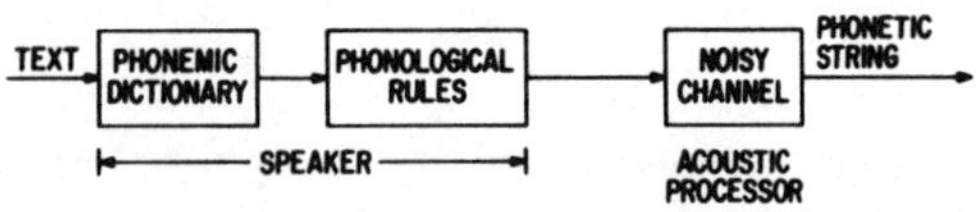

Fig. 2. Block diagram of front end model.

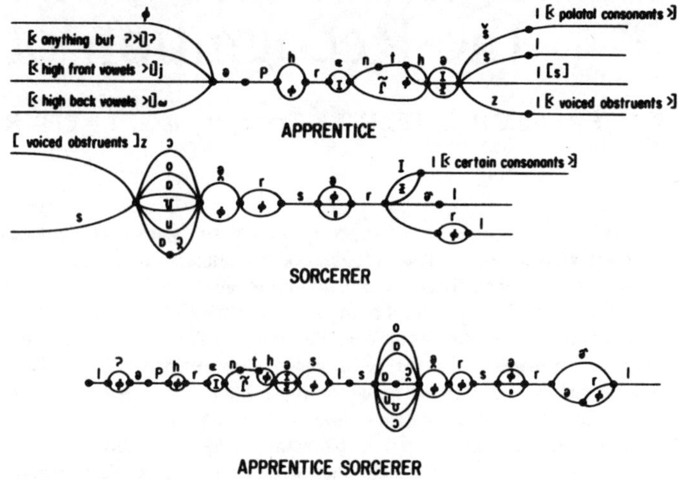

Fig. 3. Directed-graph lexical entries for *apprentice* and *sorcerer* and resultant graph for *apprentice sorcerer*.

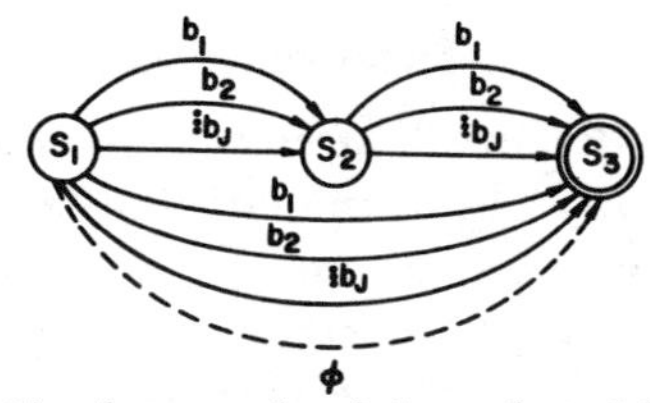

Fig. 4. Simple example of channel model for AP.

pronunciations are to be derived by the application of the phonological rules. For example, the word *library* has at least three phonemic base forms: /laˈbrɛri/, /laˈbrəri/, /laˈbɛri/.

The phonological rules account for variations in pronunciation due to surrounding words, differences in dialect and idiolect, rate of speech, etc. A typical phonological rule has the form $\alpha \rightarrow \beta/\gamma \_\_ \delta$, where α and β are strings over the phonetic alphabet A, and γ and δ are sets of such strings that define the context in which the rule can be applied. All rules are optional and apply on a single left-to-right pass through the base-form string.

The phonemic dictionary and the phonological rules comprise the speaker model in the following way. Given the string of words corresponding to a complete utterance, base forms for each of the words are selected with speaker-dependent probabilities. The phonological rules then apply to the base-form string with further speaker-dependent probabilities. Conceptually, this process generates all the possible pronunciations with associated probabilities. These are conveniently represented by a directed graph with a single starting node and a single ending node [7], such that any path through this graph traces out a possible pronunciation, with its associated probability obtained by forming the product of the probabilities on the branches. The actual application of the phonological rules to a base-form string is a very time-consuming process. Except for rules that operate across word boundaries, the rules are preapplied to the base forms to obtain a directed-graph representation of each word. To account for the rules that do involve word boundaries, the graphs have multiple starting and ending nodes that are labeled with the conditions that must be met by the preceding and following words, respectively. As an example, Fig. 3 shows the directed-graph lexical entries for *apprentice* and *sorcerer* and the resulting directed graph for *apprentice sorcerer* when preceded and followed by silence. Nodes that arise from application of the same set of phonological rules have the same probability distribution on their outgoing transitions. Those nodes in the graph through which all paths must pass are called confluent nodes. The phonology is such that, except for a few very short words, each directed-graph lexical entry has at least one confluent node.

The AP model is intended to account for the segmentation and classification errors that occur during the signal processing and pattern recognition process. The output alphabet of the AP is denoted by $B = (b_1, \cdots, b_J)$. Because of segmentation errors, the channel model must handle insertion and deletion errors as well as substitution errors. Models for such channels are discussed in detail by Bahl and Jelinek [8]. A simple example of such a model is one in which we associate with each input symbol $a_k \in A$ a probabilistic finite-state machine $F(a_k)$ that generates the possible outputs for the input a_k. Fig. 4 shows the state transition diagram of such a machine, which has initial state S_1 and final state S_3. Associated with states S_1 and S_2 are probability distributions on their outgoing transitions, and associated with each transition is an output produced by that transition. Some transitions, called null transitions, have no associated output. These are drawn in dotted lines and labeled with a ϕ in the state transition diagram. In the example of Fig. 4, the null transition from state S_1 to state S_3 represents a deletion, the remaining transitions from S_1 to S_3 represent substitutions, the paths from S_1 to S_3 via S_2 produce two outputs and, therefore, represent insertions. To accurately reflect the types of errors made by the AP, it may be necessary that the machines $F(\cdot)$ be associated not with single symbols from A but with strings of symbols from A. It may, of course, also be necessary to consider machines with more than three states.

Both the directed-graph lexical entries and the probabilistic finite-state machines $F(\cdot)$ are Markov chains. Given a word sequence $W_{1,m} = w_1, w_2, \cdots, w_m$, we can construct a composite Markov chain that generates all of the possible front end sequences for $W_{1,m}$ by first concatenating the directed-graph lexical entries for the words $w_1, w_2, \cdots, w_m$ and then embedding in each transition the finite-state machine $F(\cdot)$ associated with the label of that transition.

III. Estimation of Probabilities for Front End Model

To carry out the decoding process, we must know 1) the probabilities of the transitions in each directed-graph lexical entry, and 2) the probabilities of the transitions in each of the probabilistic finite-state machines $F(\cdot)$. One way of determining these probabilities is to transcribe by hand a large amount of speech data for each speaker. Regarding this transcription as the true input of the AP, one can in principle estimate the probabilities associated with the machines $F(\cdot)$ by comparison with the actual AP output for the same utterance. One could also estimate the probabilities associated with the directed-graph lexical entries by determining which path in the directed graph of the utterance is identical to the transcription. The amount of speech that must be transcribed to make reliable determinations in this manner is very large. Since hand transcription of speech is a very slow and expensive process, this makes the approach an unattractive one. Furthermore, different transcribers often produce different transcriptions for the same utterance, which leads us to question the consistency of this approach.

We now propose a method for estimating probabilities that does not involve hand transcription. Baum, Petrie, Soules, and Weiss [9] have described an iterative method for obtaining the maximum-likelihood estimate of the parameters of a Markov chain, given a sample of the output generated by the chain. Each iteration can be carried out by using the algorithm of Bahl, Cocke, Jelinek, and Raviv [10]. This method can be applied to the problem. We proceed as follows. Text is read by the speaker and processed by the AP, which produces a phonetic string. The composite Markov chain for this text is constructed by the method described in the previous section. The manner in which this chain is constructed places constraints on the probabilities associated with its transitions. For example, each subchain corresponding to a particular machine $F(a_k)$ must have the same probabilities. The method of Baum *et al.* may be applied to obtain maximum-likelihood estimates of the probabilities on the composite Markov chain. The probabilities associated with each subchain $F(a_k)$ can then be obtained by combining the probabilities associated with each occurrence of this subchain in the composite chain. This method requires some initial crude estimates of the probabilities, which can be obtained by examining a small amount of data.

Although the probabilities for the phonemic dictionary and phonological rule models will certainly be speaker dependent, those for the AP model will be much less so because the AP itself is trained to the individual speaker. Once probabilities have been estimated for many different speakers, it will be relatively easy to estimate probabilities for a new speaker by choosing as an initial estimate those of the known speaker who is dialectally most similar.

IV. Language Model

The aim of any speech recognition system is to determine for an acoustic signal A and a language L that sequence of words $W \in L$ which maximizes the *a posteriori* probability $\Pr\{W \mid A;L\}$. Now $\Pr\{W \mid A;L\} = \Pr\{W \mid L\} \cdot \Pr\{A \mid W;L\}/\Pr\{A \mid L\}$. The front end model provides us with $\Pr\{A \mid W;L\}$, and it is the function of the language model (LM) to provide us with $\Pr\{W \mid L\}$. The term $\Pr\{A \mid L\}$ in the denominator is independent of W and, therefore, need not be known.

We employ a probabilistic finite-state model to define the language L and provide us with the probabilities $\Pr\{W \mid L\}$. The probabilities associated with the model will be derived from the laser patent corpus. It should be noted that the decoding procedure is in no way dependent on the finite-state nature of the LM; it asks only for the probabilities $\Pr\{W \mid L\}$, caring nothing about how they are obtained.

We are well aware of the opinion held by linguists that finite-state models cannot account for the performance or competence of speakers of a natural language. The following arguments can be advanced in favor of finite-state models.

Current linguistic research and even many speech recognition efforts are primarily concerned with semantic interpretation, while the aim here is simply transcription. We know of no syntactic-semantic theory that is sufficiently developed to support a real corpus as large as ours. Furthermore, most of the arguments against finite-state models have been directed at word n-gram models in which the possible state transitions are determined by observing the $(n+1)$-grams that occur. For finite-state models in which the states are not word n-grams and in which the state transitions are determined by more sophisticated techniques, these criticisms are unfounded. No research into the adequacy of more general finite-state models has been done. With the availability of large computers, this appears to be an opportune moment to make such an investigation. Finally, one more advantage is that while there are many efficient computational techniques known for finite-state models, few techniques are available for models of any other type.

The states of the model are vectors of the form $S = (w_{-1},\cdots,w_{-k},s_{-1},\cdots,s_{-l},c_{-1},\cdots,c_{-m})$, where, $w_{-1},\cdots,w_{-k}$ are the k most recent words, $s_{-1},\cdots,s_{-l}$ are the parts of speech of the $l(\geq k)$ most recent words, and $c_{-1},\cdots,c_{-m}$ are the representatives of the m content classes (defined later) immediately preceding word w_{-k}. The purpose of including the most recent parts of speech in the states of the model is to make use of local grammaticality, while the purpose of the content classes is to use some information about long-range semantic content. As an example, consider the sentence: *The future of America depends on the availability of cheap energy*. Using D for determiner, N for noun, P for preposition, V for verb, and A for adjective, the corresponding part-of-speech sequence is *DNPNVPDNPAN*. If we assume that the only words that belong to content classes are *future* and *depend*, then for $k = 1$, $l = 2$, $m = 1$, the resulting state sequence would be (ϕ,ϕ,ϕ,ϕ), (The,D,ϕ,ϕ), (future,N,D,ϕ), (of,P,N,future(N)), (America,N,P,future(N)), (depends,V,N,future(N)), (on,P,V,depend(V)), $\cdots$, ($\cdot$,$\cdot$,N,depend(V)), where $S_0 = (\phi,\phi,\phi,\phi)$ is the initial state and ($\cdot$,$\cdot$,N,depend(V)) is a terminal state. Associated with a transition from state S_i to S_j is a word and its part of speech and the probability of that transition, which is denoted by $P(S_j \mid S_i)$.

We propose to obtain the transition probabilities by statistical analysis of the corpus. Thus it is necessary to label the corpus with parts of speech and to determine for it an appropriate set of content classes. Currently we are using a classification system of 29 parts of speech that have been obtained by conglomeration of the 133 parts of speech used by the Harvard Multiple-Path Syntactic Analyzer for English [12]. The part-of-speech labeling of the corpus is carried out by a probabilistic algorithm described elsewhere [13]. The algorithm agrees with human labeling roughly 98 percent of the time.

In the state description we have included the k most recent words explicitly. However, some words have significant statistical influence over a range of text; such words are called content words. Only adjectives, adverbs, nouns, and verbs are considered as possible content words. Since content words are of interest for their long-range effect, grammatical inflection due to number, tense, etc., is considered unimportant. Content words are, therefore, divided into equivalence classes called content classes, and one member of a class acts as a representative of that class.

For example, light (verb) represents the class {light (verb), lighted (verb), lighting (verb), lights (verb), lit (verb)}, while light (noun) represents the class {light (noun), lights (noun)}. Not all adjectives, adverbs, verbs, and nouns have long-range statistical influence. We have adopted the following procedure to determine those which do. After the text has been labeled with parts of speech, each of the potential content words is replaced by its representative. For each pair of representatives we determine the number of times they occur together within a specified span. If for any representative the co-occurrence statistics are significantly different from the average, then the class it represents is taken as a content class.

Once the text is labeled and the content classes determined, one may estimate the probabilities of transitions by determining the state sequence for the text and counting the transitions that actually occur. In estimating the probabilities, transitions that have never occurred should not necessarily be assigned zero probabilities. We are investigating several ways of estimating the probabilities of such transitions.

V. Decoding Principles

We now consider the decoding of the AP output on a sentence-by-sentence basis. Given the AP output $Y_{1,N} = y_1,y_2,\cdots,y_N$, we wish to find that sequence of LM state transitions $S_{0,M} = S_0,S_1,\cdots,S_M$ such that $\Pr\{S_{0,M}\} \cdot \Pr\{Y_{1,N} \mid S_{0,M}\}$ is maximized. State S_0 must be a sentence initial state and state S_M a sentence final state in the LM.

Corresponding to any state sequence $S_{0,m} = S_0,S_1,\cdots,S_m$, there is a unique word sequence $W_{1,m} = w_1,w_2,\cdots,w_m$ determined by the state transitions. The probability that the LM assigns to $S_{0,m}$ is denoted by $P(S_{0,m}) = P(S_1 \mid S_0) \cdot P(S_2 \mid S_1) \cdot \cdots \cdot P(S_m \mid S_{m-1})$.

Let $G(S_{0,m})$ be the graph embodying all possible phonetic realizations of the word sequence $W_{1,m-1}$ when followed by w_m, which provides the necessary phonological right context. Let g be a particular path through the graph (denoted by $g \in G(S_{0,m})$), and let $u(g)$ be the probability associated with g as determined by the speaker model. Now for a given front end output $Y_{1,n} = y_1,y_2,\cdots,y_n$ and a state sequence $S_{0,m}$, we define the conditional probability $Q(Y_{1,n} \mid S_{0,m})$ to be the probability that input $W_{1,m-1}$ (when followed by w_m) produces the output $Y_{1,n}$. Clearly,

$$Q(Y_{1,n} \mid S_{0,m}) = \sum_{g \in G(S_{0,m})} \Pr\{Y_{1,n} \mid g\} u(g). \tag{1}$$

Let $Q(Y_{1,N} \mid S_{0,m})$ denote the $(N + 1)$-vector

$$\{Q(\phi \mid S_{0,m}), Q(Y_{1,1} \mid S_{0,m}), Q(Y_{1,2} \mid S_{0,m}), \cdots, Q(Y_{1,N} \mid S_{0,m})\}.$$

An efficient method for computing $Q(\cdot \mid \cdot)$ is given in Bahl and Jelinek [8].

We assign to $S_{0,m}$ the likelihood $L(S_{0,m})$ given by

$$L(S_{0,m}) = P(S_{0,m}) \sum_{n=0}^{N} Q(Y_{1,n} \mid S_{0,m}) \cdot \Pr\{Y_{n+1,N} \mid Y_{1,n},w_{m-1},w_m,S_m\}. \tag{2}$$

The term $P(S_{0,m})$ is, of course, the *a priori* probability of the state sequence $S_{0,m}$. $\Pr\{Y_{n+1,N} \mid Y_{1,n},w_{m-1},w_m,S_m\}$ is the probability that the remainder of the output sequence $Y_{n+1,N}$ is produced by w_m (w_{m-1} merely provides the necessary left context) followed by some sequence of words ending in a period that can be produced from state S_m. Since we cannot know exactly how much of the output sequence $Y_{1,N}$ is accounted for by input $W_{1,m-1}$, it is necessary to sum over all possible values of n in (2). It should be noted that whereas $P(S_{0,m})$ involves the first m words, $Q(Y_{1,n} \mid S_{0,m})$ uses only the first $m - 1$ words, with w_m providing the right context for the directed-graph lexicon (DGL). Assuming that the pronunciation of the final word (which must be sentence terminal punctuation) is complete silence, the likelihood of (2) for a complete sentence $S_{0,M}$ becomes $P(S_{0,M}) \cdot \Pr\{Y_{1,N} \mid S_{0,M}\}$, which is exactly what we are trying to maximize. In fact,

$$\Pr\{Y_{n+1,N} \mid Y_{1,n},w_{m-1},w_m,S_m\} = \sum_i \Pr\{Y_{n+1,N}, I = i \mid Y_{1,n},w_{m-1},w_m,S_m\}$$

where I is a random variable whose value is the sentence length. When S_m is a terminal state, the only contribution to the sum is that for $I = m$, and thus $\Pr\{Y_{n+1,N} \mid Y_{1,n}, w_{m-1},w_m,s_m\}$ reduces to δ_{nN} (Kronecker delta).

In practice, the probabilities $\Pr\{Y_{n+1,N} \mid Y_{1,n},w_{m-1},w_m,S_m\}$ cannot be obtained exactly, but we can make a reasonable approximation by neglecting the dependence of $Y_{n+1,N}$ on w_{m-1}, w_m, S_m. It is possible to make a simple Markov model for the AP output and estimate its parameters by direct observation. Such a model will provide us with probabilities $\Pr\{Y_{n+1,N} \mid Y_{1,n}\}$, which we use instead of $\Pr\{Y_{n+1,N} \mid Y_{1,n},w_{m-1},w_m,S_m\}$ in (2). With this approximation, the likelihood function is, of course, no longer exact for incomplete sentences.

The LSD uses the stack algorithm of sequential decoding [14], [15] to find the most likely state sequence corresponding to a given front end output $Y_{1,N}$. Each partially decoded sequence $S_{0,m}$ is represented in the stack by an entry of the form $(S_{0,m};L(S_{0,m}))$. Entries in the stack are arranged in descending order of their likelihoods. We define the successors of an entry $(S_{0,m};L(S_{0,m}))$ to be the entries $(S_{0,m+1} = S_{0,m},S_{m+1};L(S_{0,m+1}))$ and $(S_{0,m}' = S_{0,m-1},S_m'; L(S_{0,m}'))$, where S_{m+1} is chosen such that $P(S_{m+1} \mid S_m) = \max_S \{P(S \mid S_m)\}$, and S_m' is chosen such that $P(S_m' \mid S_{m-1}) = \max_S \{P(S \mid S_{m-1}) \mid P(S \mid S_{m-1}) < P(S_m \mid S_{m-1})\}$. We assume that no two transitions out of S_{m-1} have identical probabilities. If they do, then the usual minor adjustment must be made in the definition of S_m'. Occasionally no S_m' exists, in which case there is only one successor.

Decoding proceeds as follows.

0) Initialize the stack to contain the single entry $(S_{0,1};P(S_{0,1}) \cdot \Pr\{Y_{1,N}\})$, where $S_{0,1} = S_0,S_1$ is chosen such that $P(S_1 \mid S_0) = \max_S P(S \mid S_0)$.

1) Let $(S_{0,m};L(S_{0,m}))$ denote the entry at the top of the stack, i.e., the one having maximum likelihood. If S_m is a final state, then we stop and accept $W_{1,m}$ corresponding to $S_{0,m}$ as the most likely input. Otherwise, we replace $(S_{0,m};L(S_{0,m}))$ by its successors, reorder the stack, and repeat step 1.

VI. Decoder Implementation

The decoding algorithm of the previous section is feasible only if an efficient technique can be devised for evaluating the likelihoods $L(S_{0,m})$. The probabilities $P(S_{0,m})$ are easily obtained from the LM using the recursion $P(S_{0,m}) = P(S_{0,m-1}) \cdot P(S_m \mid S_{m-1})$. The probabilities $\Pr\{Y_{n+1,N} \mid Y_{1,n}, w_{m-1},w_m,S_m\}$ have been approximated by $\Pr\{Y_{n+1,N} \mid Y_{1,n}\}$, which need to be computed only once for the output sequence $Y_{1,N}$. This leaves the evaluation of the probabilities $Q(Y_{1,N} \mid S_{0,m})$. An algorithm for computing these probabilities is discussed in [8]. The complexity of the calculation is roughly proportional to the product of the number of nodes in $G(S_{0,m})$ and N, the number of symbols in the output sequence. When computing $Q(Y_{1,N} \mid S_{0,m+1})$ and $Q(Y_{1,N} \mid S_{0,m}')$, it is not necessary to deal with the complete graphs for $G(S_{0,m+1})$ and $G(S_{0,m}')$ but only with the parts that differ from $G(S_{0,m})$. Let us denote by $G^*(S_{0,m})$ the subgraph of $G(S_{0,m})$ up to the rightmost confluent node and by $Q^*(Y_{1,n} \mid S_{0,m})$ the probabilities

$$Q^*(Y_{1,n} \mid S_{0,m}) = \sum_{g \in G^*(S_{0,m})} \Pr\{Y_{1,n} \mid g\} u(g), \qquad n = 0,1,\cdots,N.$$

The probabilities $Q^*(Y_{1,N} \mid S_{0,m})$ are obtained as a by-product of the computation of $Q(Y_{1,N} \mid S_{0,m})$. To compute the probabilities $Q(Y_{1,N} \mid S_{0,m+1})$ and $Q(Y_{1,N} \mid S_{0,m}')$, one need only know $Q^*(Y_{1,N} \mid S_{0,m})$ and those portions of the graphs $G(S_{0,m+1})$ and $G(S_{0,m}')$ that differ from $G^*(S_{0,m})$. Therefore, we store the vector $Q^*(Y_{1,N} \mid S_{0,m})$ with the stack entry for $S_{0,m}$.

Fig. 5 is a block diagram of the LSD. The decoding process is controlled by the word level search controller (WLSC), which maintains the likelihood stack. Each entry in the stack contains the path $S_{0,m}$, the likelihood $L(S_{0,m})$, the probability $P(S_{0,m})$, and the vector $Q^*(Y_{1,N} \mid S_{0,m})$.

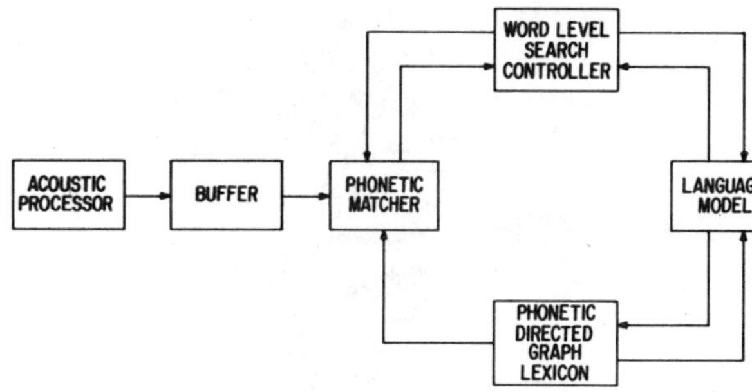

Fig. 5. Block diagram of LSD.

One iteration in the decoding process is as follows. The WLSC locates the path $S_{0,m}$ having the highest likelihood. The successors of $S_{0,m}$ must now be determined. To do so the WLSC sends the last three states of path $S_{0,m}$ to the LM. The LM determines S_{m+1} and the probability $P(S_{m+1} \mid S_m)$ and returns this information to the WLSC. Simultaneously the LM sends the word triplet w_{m-1},w_m,w_{m+1} corresponding to the state sequence $S_{0,m+1}$ to the DGL. The DGL uses these to determine the rightmost confluent node R of $G(S_{0,m})$ and $G^+(S_{0,m+1})$, which is that part of $G(S_{0,m+1})$ that lies to the right of R. The phonology is such that in virtually all cases R can be determined from w_{m-1} and w_m. At most, the DGL will need to know w_{m-2}, which could be provided by the WLSC through the LM if desired. The DGL sends $G^+(S_{0,m+1})$ to the matching algorithm. The matcher also receives $Q^*(Y_{1,N} \mid S_{0,m})$ from the WLSC and computes $Q(Y_{1,N} \mid S_{0,m+1})$ and $Q^*(Y_{1,N} \mid S_{0,m+1})$, both of which it returns to the WLSC. The WLSC can now complete the entry for $S_{0,m+1}$ and insert it in the stack. The procedure for computing the entry for the other successor $S_{0,m}'$ is similar. The WLSC terminates the decoding process when the top of the stack corresponds to a complete sentence.

The LM that we have described generates word and part of speech pairs, and consequently the decoder finds the most likely sequence of words and parts of speech for a given utterance. The likelihood of a word sequence can be obtained by summing up the likelihoods of all the state sequences that give rise to that word sequence. The decoder could then operate on these likelihoods to find the most likely word sequence. We believe, however, that the loss of performance caused by using state sequence likelihoods rather than word sequence likelihoods will be negligible.

VII. Refinements

One possible shortcoming of the LM is that it does not take advantage of any phonetic similarity between different words. The LM can be modified in the manner shown in Fig. 6. Fig. 6(a) shows a portion of the state transition diagram of the LM. All the transitions indicated have words whose phonetic representation starts with the phonetic sequence corresponding to *non*. The phonetic representations of *nonsense* and *nonsensical* agree even further as do those of *nonagenarian* (N) and *nonagenarian* (A). Fig. 6(b) shows a portion of a modified transition diagram that produces the same words with the same

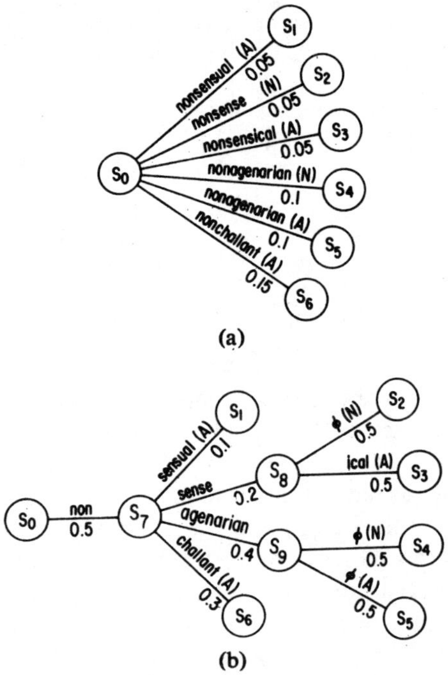

Fig. 6. Modification of LM state transition diagram to take advantage of phonetic similarity.

probabilities as Fig. 6(a), but takes advantage of the phonetic similarity of the words. The advantages of such a modification are twofold. First, the time used in computing $Q(Y_{1,N} \mid S_{0,m})$ is reduced because we need to compute these for *non* only once and use them for any word that starts with *non*. Second, the actual order of search may be altered beneficially, e.g., in Fig. 6(a), the transition S_0,S_6 will be investigated before either of the transitions S_0,S_4 or S_0,S_5, while in Fig. 6(b) S_7,S_9 (which is a combination of S_0,S_4 and S_0,S_5 in Fig. 6(a)) is investigated before S_7,S_6 (which corresponds to S_0,S_6 in Fig. 6(a)).

Although we have described the decoding algorithm as replacing the top stack entry with its successors, it may be better to consider replacing the top several entries with their successors simultaneously. Furthermore, it may be worthwhile to construct more than two successors for each stack entry.

Another possible modification to the decoding algorithm would be to allow a two-way search, i.e., a search in which we decode the received utterance simultaneously in the forward and the reverse directions. To construct a reverse decoder we must of course build a reverse LM which produces the sentences for the language in reverse order. This reverse model can be easily obtained for any finite-state machine by reversing the arrows in the state transition diagram and replacing the probability $P(S_j \mid S_i)$ by ${}^rP(S_i \mid S_j) = P(S_j \mid S_i) \cdot P(S_i)/P(S_j)$, where $P(S_i)$ is the probability that a path through the state transition diagram will include S_i. The initial states of the reverse machine are the final states of the original machine and *vice versa*. The forward machine defined by $P(S_j \mid S_i)$ and the reverse machine defined by ${}^rP(S_i \mid S_j)$ are then isomorphic under sequence reversal. We will use a left superscript r to indicate quantities related to the reverse model. A state sequence ${}^rS_{m_1,M}$ in the reverse machine corresponds to the transitions $S_{m_1} \leftarrow S_{m_1+1} \leftarrow \cdots \leftarrow S_M$, where S_M is a final state. The speaker and channel models are similarly reversible, since they too are finite state. Once the reverse models have been obtained, a reverse decoder that decodes from the end of the received sequence $Y_{1,N}$ can be implemented in exactly the same manner as the forward decoder of Sections V and VI. We can combine the forward and reverse decoders to give us a two-way decoder. This decoder would have two stacks, one for the forward paths and one for the reverse, and we would extend the top stack entry that has the greater likelihood. When extending a forward path, we would not only construct the two successors discussed in Section V, but also those successors that connect this forward path to a reverse path. Let S_{0,m_1} be a forward path and ${}^rS_{m_2,M}$ be a reverse path and let us assume that the transition $S_{m_1} \rightarrow S_{m_2}$ is possible in the LM. Then we would construct the successor $S_{0,m_2} = S_{0,m_1}S_{m_2}$ and determine the likelihood for the complete path $S_{0,M} = S_{0,m_1}S_{m_2}{}^rS_{m_2,M}$ from the entries for S_{0,m_2} and ${}^rS_{m_2,M}$. The *a priori* probability of the complete path is given by

$$P(S_{0,M}) = \frac{P(S_{0,m_2}) \cdot P({}^rS_{m_2,M})}{P(S_{m_2})}. \tag{3}$$

The probability $\Pr\{Y_{1,N} \mid S_{0,M}\}$ is obtained as

$$\Pr\{Y_{1,N} \mid S_{0,M}\} = \sum_{n=0,N} \Pr\{Y_{1,n} \mid W_{1,m_2}\} \cdot \Pr\{Y_{n+1,N} \mid {}^rW_{m_2+1,M}\} \tag{4}$$

where W_{1,m_2} and ${}^rW_{m_2+1,M}$ are the word sequences corresponding to S_{0,m_2} and ${}^rS_{m_2,M}$. The probabilities on the right side of (4) are, of course, easily obtained by extending $Q^*(Y_{1,N} \mid S_{0,m_2})$ and ${}^rQ^*(Y_{1,N} \mid {}^rS_{m_2,M})$, respectively. The likelihood of the complete path $S_{0,M}$ is obtained by multiplying $P(S_{0,M})$ and $\Pr\{Y_{1,N} \mid S_{0,M}\}$, which have been obtained from (3) and (4). Similarly when extending a reverse path, we would try to connect to partial forward paths.

It would, of course, require considerable computation to check which partial reverse paths are connectable to a forward path being extended. A simple heuristic technique for limiting the search is as follows. For any $S_{0,m}$, let $n_{\max}(S_{0,m})$ be that value of n (presumed unique) which maximizes $\Pr\{Y_{1,n} \mid S_{0,m}\}$. Then $n_{\max}(S_{0,m})$ is the most likely right boundary for $S_{0,m}$. Similarly, we can define $n_{\max}({}^rS_{m,M})$ to be the most likely left boundary for ${}^rS_{m,M}$. When trying to connect S_{0,m_1} to ${}^rS_{m_2,M}$, we check if $n_{\max}({}^rS_{m_2,M}) - n_{\max}(S_{0,m_1}) \le e$, where e is a small integer. If this condition is not met, we do not try to connect the two paths. To facilitate in checking this condition, we can keep for each $n = 0,1,\cdots,N$, a list of all forward paths $S_{0,m}$ such that $n_{\max}(S_{0,m}) = n$. Similar lists can be kept for reverse paths. To decide if $S_{0,m}$ should be connected to any reverse path, we consider only those reverse entries that are in the reverse path lists for $n_{\max}(S_{0,m}) + n'$, $n' \le e$. The basic idea here is that $n_{\max}(S_{0,m})$ gives us the most likely right boundary for $S_{0,m}$, and we should try to connect $S_{0,m}$ only to those reverse paths that have a likely left boundary close to

$n_{\max}(S_{0,m})$. At any time we need only save one complete path—i.e., the one with the highest likelihood—and if its likelihood is higher than the partial paths in both stacks, decoding is terminated.

Acknowledgment

The authors are grateful for the many suggestions they have received from the members of the Speech Processing Group, especially P. Cohen. They also wish to express their thanks to Dr. John Cocke for many stimulating discussions.

References

[1] D. E. Walker, "Speech understanding through syntactic and semantic analysis," in *Proc. 3rd Int. Joint Conf. Artificial Intelligence*, 1973, pp. 208–215.

[2] W. A. Woods, J. Makhoul, J. Wolf, and P. Rovner, "Organizing a system for continuous speech understanding," presented at the 85th Meeting of the Acoustical Society of America, Boston, Mass., Apr. 1973.

[3] D. R. Reddy, L. D. Erman, R. D. Fennell, and R. B. Neely, "The hearsay speech understanding system," in *Proc. 3rd Int. Joint Conf. Artificial Intelligence*, 1973, pp. 185–193.

[4] N. R. Dixon and C. C. Tappert, "Intermediate performance evaluation of a multi-stage system for automatic recognition of continuous speech," Tech. Rep. RADC-TR-73-16, 1973.

[5] C. C. Tappert, N. R. Dixon, and A. S. Rabinowitz, "Application of sequential decoding for converting phonetic to graphemic representation in automatic recognition of continuous speech (ARCS)," *IEEE Trans. Audio Electroacoust.*, vol. AU-21, pp. 225–228, June 1973.

[6] P. S. Cohen and R. L. Mercer, "The phonological component of an automatic speech-recognition system," in *Proc. IEEE Symp. Speech Recognition*, 1974, pp. 177–188.

[7] R. Alter, "Utilization of contextual constraints in automatic speech recognition," *IEEE Trans. Audio Electroacoust.*, vol. AU-16, pp. 6–11, Jan. 1968.

[8] L. R. Bahl and F. Jelinek, "Decoding for channels with insertions, deletions, and substitutions, with applications to speech recognition," to appear in *IEEE Trans. Inform. Theory*.

[9] L. E. Baum, T. Petrie, G. Soules, and N. Weiss, "A maximization technique occurring in the statistical analysis of probabilistic functions of Markov chains," *Ann. Math. Statist.*, vol. 41, no. 1, pp. 164–171.

[10] L. R. Bahl, J. Cocke, F. Jelinek, and J. Raviv, "Optimal decoding of linear codes for minimizing symbol error rate," *IEEE Trans. Inform. Theory*, vol. IT-20, pp. 284–287, Mar. 1974.

[11] N. Chomsky, *Syntactic Structures*. New York: Humanities, 1957.

[12] S. Kuno, "The multiple-path syntactic analyzer for English," Mathematical Linguistics and Automatic Translation, Computation Lab. Harvard Univ., Rep. NSF-8, 1963.

[13] L. R. Bahl and R. L. Mercer, "Part-of-speech assignment by a statistical decision algorithm," IBM Res. Rep., to appear.

[14] F. Jelinek, "A stack algorithm for faster sequential decoding of transmitted information," IBM Res. Rep., RC-2441, Apr. 1969.

[15] ——, "A fast sequential decoding algorithm using a stack," *IBM J. Res. Develop.*, vol. 13, pp. 675–685, Nov. 1969.

A SYSTEM FOR THE RECOGNITION OF SPOKEN CONNECTED WORD SEQUENCES

Mark F. Medress, Toby E. Skinner, Dean R. Kloker, Timothy C. Diller, and Wayne A. Lea

Sperry Univac Speech Communications Department, Univac Park, P.O. Box 3525, St. Paul, Minnesota 55165

ABSTRACT

Sperry Univac is developing a linguistically oriented computer system which recognizes natural spoken phrases and sentences without requiring extensive adjustments for individual users and without the need for each user to repeat every vocabulary word for system training. The recognition system produces a linguistic description of the unknown utterance by determining its component sound segments. Words from a dictionary, or lexicon, (represented in terms of the same linguistic segments) are then strung together and compared to the analysis segments to determine which syntactically allowed sequence of vocabulary words best matches the unknown utterance. Two data bases have been used recently for development and testing, including alphanumeric sequences constructed from a vocabulary of 36 words, and data management commands from a vocabulary of 64 words. For both data bases, average correct recognition scores were 95% for individual words, and 88% for complete sentences. Current plans for enhancing the recognition system include enlarging the vocabulary and number of recognizable sentence types, making additional use of prosodic information, and introducing phonetic verification rules and a word verification component. The ultimate goal of this development is to provide an effective sentence recognition system for natural and practical speech input to computers.

1. INTRODUCTION

During the past eight years, the Speech Communications Department at Sperry Univac Defense Systems has been developing effective procedures for verbal communication with computers.[1-5] The versatile system we are developing for the computer recognition of natural phrases and sentences does not require users to either pause artificially between words, or to repeat every vocabulary word several times for system training. It is also able to recognize speech from a number of similar talkers without adjustments for individual voice characteristics. With suitable vocabulary and syntactic restrictions, a wide variety of connected word sequences for practical speech input applications will be possible in the near future. Because of the linguistic framework used for recognition, the system can gracefully evolve to understand more natural sentences with the enhancement of syntactic and semantic analysis capabilities.

2. SPERRY UNIVAC SPEECH RECOGNITION SYSTEM

The principle components of the speech recognition system being developed at Sperry Univac are shown in Figure 1. In the first step of the recognition process, an acoustic analysis produces a representation of the incoming speech signal in terms of time-varying source, resonance, and energy functions. Next, the prosodic and phonetic analysis components derive a linguistic feature description of the phonetic segments in the unknown utterance. The segmental structuring component then performs a phonological transformation of the linguistic features to produce a linear sequence of analysis segments suitable for lexical matching. Finally, the word sequence hypothesizer uses syntactic constraints to direct the word matching component, which attempts alignment and scoring of analysis and lexical segments. The lexicon itself is produced by a generative phonological rules component, which automatically transforms standard dictionary pronunciations into likely alternative sequences of analysis segments. The word matcher aligns and scores the analysis and lexical segments with the aid of a scoring matrix, which is generated by a statistical analysis processor that correlates analysis segments with time-locked phonetic transcriptions for a data base of development utterances. The word sequence hypothesizer then strings together single word matches, and the highest scoring sequence that meets the syntactic constraints becomes the recognized utterance.

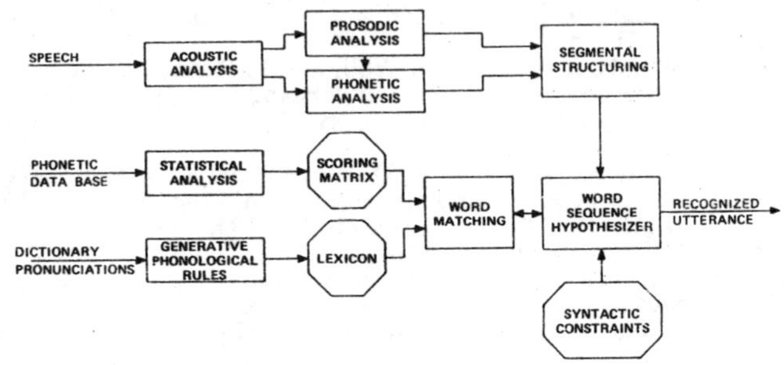

Figure 1. The Sperry Univac Speech Recognition System

2.1 Acoustic Analysis

To produce an acoustic analysis of the unknown utterance,[6,7] the analog speech waveform is low-pass filtered at 5 kHz and sampled at 10 kHz with a 12-bit A/D converter. An estimate of the rate of vocal cord vibration, or fundamental frequency, is determined from a 51.2 ms, center-clipped and autocorrelated window of time waveform samples, which is advanced at 10 ms increments. Spectral analysis is performed with a 25.6 ms Hanning window of software-preemphasized time samples, which is also advanced at 10 ms increments. A 256-point Fast Fourier Transform (FFT) of each window produces spectra used to compute time functions of spectral change, spectral prominance, and bandlimited energies. Smoothed spectra are also computed for each window to determine the first three formants, or vocal tract resonances. The smoothed spectra are produced by a 14-coefficient linear prediction analysis, and a 256-point FFT of the predictor coefficients biased 75 Hz off the $j\omega$-axis for peak enhancement.[8] The frequency and bandwidth of the lowest frequency complex pole are also derived from the linear prediction coefficients.

Reprinted from *1976 IEEE Internat. Conf. Record on Acoust., Speech, and Signal Process.*, April 12–14, 1976, pp. 434–437.

Thus, the acoustic analysis component provides the following fourteen time functions, with values derived every 10 milliseconds, for subsequent prosodic and phonetic processing:

From the time waveform –

1. Fundamental Frequency

From the Fourier Transform Spectra –

2. Total Energy (60 – 5000 Hz)
3. Sonorant Energy (60 – 3000 Hz)
4. High Frequency Sonorant Energy (650 – 3000 Hz)
5. Very Low Energy (60 – 400 Hz)
6. High Energy (3000 – 5000 Hz)
7. Low Energy (60 – 900 Hz)
8. Spectral Derivative
9. Frequency of Maximum Spectrum Amplitude

From the Linear Prediction Coefficients –

10. Lowest Frequency Complex Pole Frequency
11. Lowest Frequency Complex Pole Bandwidth

From the Off-Axis Linear Prediction Spectra –

12. First Formant Frequency
13. Second Formant Frequency
14. Third Formant Frequency

2.2 Prosodic Analysis

The prosodic analysis component provides information about the syllabic structure of the utterance from the Sonorant Energy function, which is high during sonorant syllabic nuclei and substantially lower during obstruents. Syllabic nuclei are located in regions of high energy bounded by substantial dips. Other procedures determine which syllables are stressed, based on first detecting fall-rise valleys in Fundamental Frequency (Fo) contours to segment the speech into intonational phrases, and then associating stresses with high-energy syllabic nuclei near the initial Fo rise in a phrase, and near to substantial Fo inflections at later points in each phrase.[9]

Vowels are later associated with, and identified at, the centers of the syllabic nuclei, after stripping away those portions of the nuclei that are automatically categorized as non-vowel sonorants. Long syllabic nuclei are used in detecting diphthongs, and syllable stress is used in assigning a reliability to each vowel.

2.3 Phonetic Analysis

The phonetic analysis process hypothesizes the locations and identifications of various sound classes throughout the utterance.[10-12] The parameter values derived during the acoustic analysis and the preliminary vowel nuclei locations provided by the prosodic analysis are used in this process. The basic phonetic classes are characterized by different manners of articulation, and include stops, sibilants, nasals, vowels, liquids, glides, and fricatives. Additional classification with regard to place of articulation is performed for stops, sibilants, vowels, and nasals; stops and sibilants are further distinguished with respect to their voicing feature.

The manner-of-articulation decisions are primarily based on formant characteristics of vocalic sounds and on energy distributions for the unvoiced sounds. Releases of stops (/P/,/T/, /K/,/B/,/D/,/G/,/Q/) are evidenced by an abrupt increase in Total Energy and a large Spectral Derivative. Sibilants (/S/, /SH/,/Z/,/ZH/) are indicated by their predominance of High Energy over Low Energy. Nasals (/M/,/N/,/NX/) are characterized by their dominance of Low Energy over High Energy, as well as their low First Formant Frequency and Lowest Frequency Complex Pole Bandwidth. Retroflex liquids (/R/) are indicated by their low Third Formant Frequency and their close Second and Third Formant Frequencies. Lateral Liquids (/L/) are indicated by a low First and Second Formant Frequency, a high Third Formant Frequency, and a discontinuity of their First Formant Frequency at its junctures to adjoining sounds. Labial glides (/W/) are characterized by their initially low First and Second Formant Frequencies, and a significantly rising Second Formant Frequency. Palatal glides (/Y/) are indicated by their initially very low First Formant Frequency and very high Second and Third Formant Frequencies; the First Formant Frequency proceeds to rise while the Second and Third Formant Frequencies are falling; the Lowest Frequency Complex Pole Bandwidth is extremely low; and the Second and Third Formant Frequencies closely approach one another during the glide. Voiced (/V/,/DH/,/DX/) and unvoiced (/F/,/TH/, /H/) fricatives are determined from previously unidentified regions of significant Total Energy, with the added requirement that the voiced fricatives are also accompanied by vocal cord vibration. All sound classes must persist for a minimum duration of at least 40 contiguous milliseconds, and all sonorants must be at least partially voiced.

The further place-of-articulation decisions are based on the Frequency of Maximum Spectrum Amplitude for stops and sibilants, and the Second Formant Frequency for nasals. Monothong vowels are identified as their nearest neighbor in the space of the first three formant frequencies, and diphthong vowels are identified by their initial vowel identities and the dynamics of their formant motion.[13] The voicing decision for sibilants and stops is made by examining the amount of concurrent voicing during sibilants, and the extent of post-release delay in voicing onset for stops.

Optimal threshold values used in some of the phonetic discrimination decisions are determined from a statistical analysis of development utterances. For example, in Figure 2, the data on Frequency of Maximum Spectrum Amplitude (FMSA)

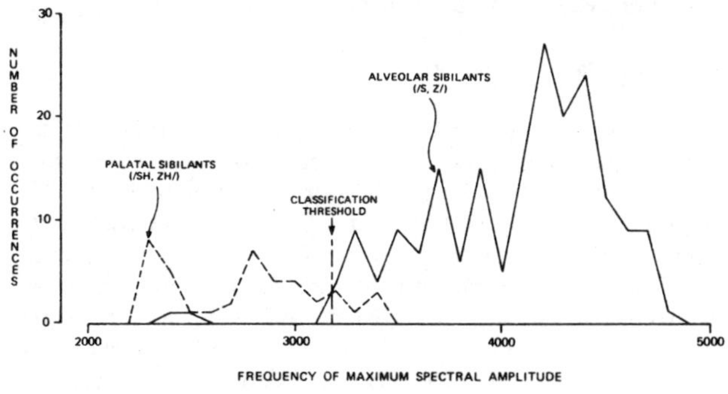

Figure 2. Sibilant Distribution for Frequency of Maximum Spectral Amplitude

from 233 sibilants was used to determine the value of the threshold for distinguishing sibilants with regard to place of articulation. Plotted are the number of occurrences of transcribed palatal (/SH,ZH/) and alveolar (/S,Z/) sibilants at 100 Hz quantitizations of the FMSA reported during the phonetic analysis process. From this plot, it was determined that a threshold value of about 3200 Hz provides for the best place distinction results. Optimal values for several other thresholds used in discriminatory decisions (e.g. stop and nasal place of articulation) were determined in a similar fashion.

The results of the phonetic analysis process are represented in the form of a two-dimensional lattice of features or sound classes versus time. An example phonetic analysis lattice for the utterance "six seven nine" is shown in Figure 3. Across the top

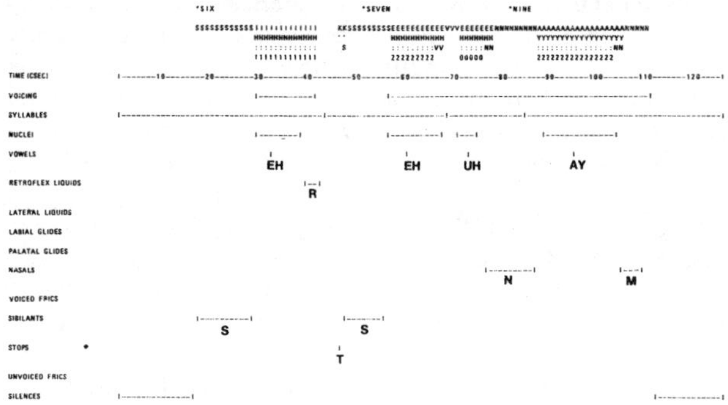

Figure 3. Phonetic Analysis Lattice for "Six Seven Nine"

of the lattice is a time-synchronous, manually-specified orthographic and phonetic transcription. The remainder of the chart is analytically derived. Voicing was found during the vowel of "six" and continuously throughout "seven nine", beginning with the first vowel in "seven". Four vowel nuclei were appropriately located, and the identities of the second and fourth vowels exactly coincide with the transcription. A false /R/ was located at the /IH/--/K/ juncture in "six". As expected, no /L/'s, /W/'s or /Y/'s were determined to be present during the utterance. Two nasals were found, the second of which was incorrectly identified as /M/. The voiced fricative /V/ was not found in the word "seven". Two sibilants were correctly located and subclassified as /S/'s during the analysis. The stop in "six" was also correctly located and subclassified with regard to voicing, but was incorrectly subclassified with respect to place of articulation and thus was partially misidentified as a /T/. No unvoiced fricatives were found, and segments of silence were located preceeding and following the utterance.

2.4 Segmental Structuring

In the next step of the recognition procedure, the lattice of phonetic information is organized into a non-overlapping sequence of segments to prepare for lexical matching.[14] The midpoint of each sound type on the lattice is used to define the order of segments. During this transformation, various phonological or segmental adjustments are made: some previously undetected vowels are recovered by relabeling certain isolated voiced fricatives; all /R–ER/ sequences are reordered to be /ER–R/ for consistency; all silences occurring before stops are deleted; and whenever two consecutive segments have the same manner of articulation, the least reliable is deleted. Features associated with each segment define the sound type, and stress and confidence measures are used to mark the analysis segment as highly reliable (HRS), optional (OPT), or intermediate in reliability. The analysis segments on the top of Figure 4 are the result of transforming the phonetic information in the lattice of Figure 3. The rest of Figure 4 is explained in the next section.

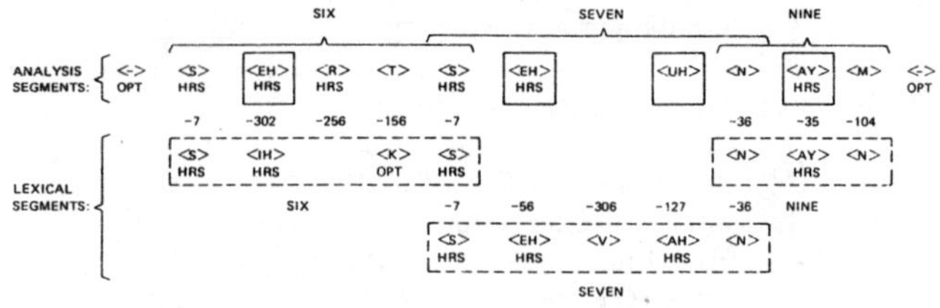

Figure 4. Analysis Segments and Lexical Matches for "Six Seven Nine"

2.5 Word Sequence Hypothesizer

The connected word sequence hypothesizer directs the word matching component in building, left-to-right, partial word sequences comprised of appropriate lexical entries that match throughout the string of analysis segments.[14,15] The matching procedure aligns analysis segments with lexical segments using vowels as anchor points, allowing extraneous and missing segments. The scoring procedure assigns a number taken from the scoring matrix (Figure 1) to every matched segment pair or mismatched segment. A pair score is the logarithm of the estimated conditional probability that the particular lexical segment was said given that the corresponding analysis segment was found. Scores for missed lexical segments and extraneous analysis segments are the logs of the conditional probabilities that the particular segment is a miss or false alarm. The scoring matrix is automatically computed from the incidence confusion matrix generated by the statistical analysis programs operating on the phonetic data base. If the segment is marked optional and cannot be aligned, it is ignored in the scoring. In Figure 4, the results are shown for aligning the lexical entries for "six", "seven", and "nine" with the analysis of "six seven nine". The numbers between the aligned segments are the log probability segment scores. They are all negative, since they are logarithms of numbers between zero and one. The word and phrase scores are simply the averages of the segment scores. Thus the word score for "six" is -145 -- the average of -7, -302, -256, -156, and -7; the phrase score for "six seven nine" is -110.

The strategy for building word sequences centers upon finding all good single word matches anchored around all appropriate analysis vowels. Figure 4 illustrates the end-product in word matching. The first word "six" was aligned by anchoring around the first vowel /EH/. (The analysis vowels are enclosed in solid boxes.) The next vowel after this match is the second /EH/, which is used for anchoring possible second words after "six". When the sequence "six seven" is found, the next vowel is the fourth one, /AY/, around which possible third words are aligned.

Figure 5 illustrates the process of arriving at the result given in Figure 4. Phrase scores are listed for the partial word sequences that are created in recognizing the utterance. First, the best one word matches are chosen from the many matches of lexical entries around the first vowel. Then, partial word sequences are created from the best one word matches using matches at succeeding vowels in the utterance. The partial sequences are extended this way until all the analysis vowels are used. At each step, the list of partial word sequences is pruned by keeping only the best scoring ones. The task syntax is used to select the lexical subset appropriate to the current position in the partial word sequence. In this example, each position in the three word sequence is limited to the numbers zero through nine.

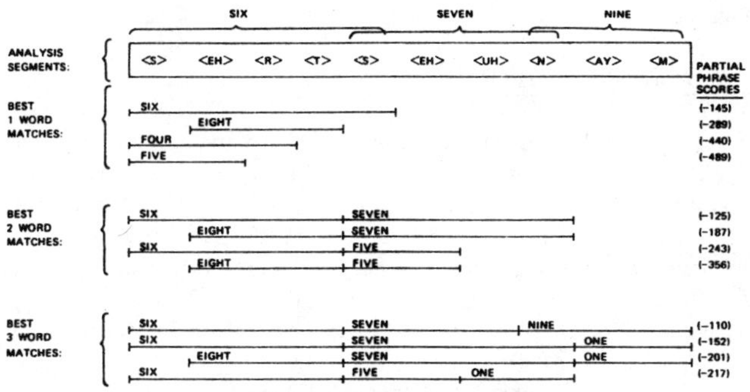

Figure 5. Partial Word Sequences in the Recognition of "Six Seven Nine"

2.6 Lexical Generation

Since word matching is performed on quasi-phonemic analysis segments, it is essential to produce a phonemic lexical representation for each word or phrase to be recognized. This lexical generation process has been automated so that initial representations of new entries can be added with ease, and without "training" the system. The procedure utilizes standard dictionary pronunciations as baseforms, and produces lexical variants incorporating both phonological generalizations and systematic characteristics of the Sperry Univac recognition system.

Automatic lexical generation[16] is accomplished by converting the dictionary pronunciation guides to system-compatible symbols, and then modifying the symbols by rules which insert, delete, and replace segments. More than 100 rules are currently in use. They are context sensitive, obligatory, and conjunctively ordered. The lexical strings produced contain segment labels, segment reliability, and stress information. The rules generate on the average about four lexical variants for each input baseform. The lexical variants reflect coarticulation effects both within and between words. Evaluation routines provide statistics on the use of the rules within a given lexicon.

Following the automatic generation, hand modifications were made to lexical entries which deviated significantly from the analytic results for the development data. Differences in performance between the automatic and hand modified lexicons are discussed in Reference 16.

2.7 Statistical Analysis

A number of statistical programs have been created which produce a wide variety of outputs.[17] These programs accept as input an algorithmically-produced correlation of analysis segments and listener-perceived transcription segments for each utterance. The correlation allows the creation of a segment confusion matrix, from which the scoring matrix is automatically derived for the word matching component. Other products of these programs include: charts permitting optimal settings of some threshold values (cf. Figure 2); printouts collecting all transcriptions and analysis strings for each lexical entry; charts indicating performance success in stress assignment and phone recognition (cf. Figure 7); and listings collecting acoustic parameter values for phones in particular contexts. By partially automating data analysis, performance evaluation, and system enhancement, our objectivity and accuracy have been increased, and our ability to evaluate and utilize much larger speech data bases has been extended.

3. SPEECH DATA BASES

During the past year three data bases were designed, recorded, digitized, and transcribed phonemically for use in developing and testing the capabilities of the recognition system.[18] The first two sets of data represent potential interactive tasks, while the third set is a collection of phonetically interesting sentences useful in developing phonetic level recognition procedures and in the formation of the scoring matrix.

The first of the task domains consists of two, three, and four word sequences of digits and "phonetic alphabet" words. This syntax is characteristic of many data entry tasks. The 36 word vocabulary is divided into four subsets of 8-10 words, and nine varieties of sequences are defined. Examples of these "alphanumeric" sequences are listed in Figure 6. The average branching factor (average number of word alternatives to the right of each word of the sentence[19]) for this task is 9.4. The syntax defines 25,842 potential sequences.

ALPHANUMERIC SEQUENCES

- Vocabulary size = 36
- Average branching factor = 9.4

e.g. Hotel niner
Sierra Alfa Zulu
Quebec Papa four three

DATA MANAGEMENT COMMANDS

- Vocabulary size = 64
- Average branching factor = 6.3

1. (Shift line) twelve (to) (position number) ten
2. (Transmit line) eighteen (to) (station) two
3. (Cursor) down seven
4. (Erase) field
5. (Flight index for) American forty nine
6. (Weather forecast for) Minneapolis
7. (Current weather for) Boston

Figure 6. Sample Connected Word Sequences for Speech Recognition Development and Testing

The second task addresses the recognition of utterances typical of data management or information retrieval languages, and is based upon a potential speech input application in air traffic control. The seven "command" types listed in Figure 6 define the permissable syntactic structures. The items in parentheses are fixed one-word subsets for that utterance type, while the underlined words are variable subsets consisting of the numbers 3-10, 10-19, or 20-90 by tens; the positions "up", "down", "left", or "right"; the objects "field", "line", or "page"; ten airline names; and ten city names. The total vocabulary size is 64, and the average branching factor is 6.3. The syntax defines a potential of 919 different utterances.

For each of the two task domains, 111 utterances were selected for recording and processing. The selection process was nearly random within the constraint that approximately equal exposure be provided for each lexical subset. About two-thirds of the utterances were used for development, and the remaining third was reserved as test material. For the third data base of phonetically interesting sentences, 20 phonetically balanced sentences[20] and 15 phonetically weighted sentences[21] were chosen, with a total of 229 different words. Three male talkers each recorded about one-third of the three data bases.

4. PERFORMANCE ANALYSIS

In evaluating the performance of the Sperry Univac speech recognition system, results were obtained on the segment, word, and phrase level. Since the segmental analyses are designed to be fairly insensitive to talker differences (and no adjustments were made for the three males in our data bases), and because no significant talker variations were found on the word and phrase level, all results have been pooled for the three talkers. First, segment performance is presented for the development portions of the alphanumeric sequences and data management commands. Then word and phrase recognition results are given for the development and test portions of each of these two data bases.

4.1 Segment Recognition

The performance of the phonetic analysis procedures are summarized in Figure 7. This data indicates the correspondence

SOUND CLASS (MANNER)	NUMBER PERCEIVED	NUMBER DETECTED	% MANNER OK	% PLACE OK IF MANNER OK	% VOICING OK IF MANNER OK	% FALSE ALARMS
RELEASED STOP (P,T,K,B,D,G,Q)	426	249	51%	70%	86%	13%
SIBILANT (S,Z,SH,ZH)	251	241	93%	97%	97%	3%
NASAL (M,N,NX)	284	224	68%	78%		14%
MONOTHONG VOWEL (IY,IH,EY,EH,AE,AA, AO,OW,UH,UW,AH,IX,ER)	891	840	93%	51%		3%
DIPHTHONG VOWEL (AY,OY,AW)	90	100		84%		
RETROFLEX LIQUID (R)	245	219	82%			8%
LATERAL LIQUID (L)	110	91	65%			22%
LABIAL GLIDE (W)	57	47	61%			26%
PALATAL GLIDE (Y)	28	15	29%			47%
UNVOICED FRICATIVE (F,TH,HH)	198	220	83%			25%
VOICED FRICATIVE (V,DH,DX)	80	195	61%			75%

Figure 7. Phonetic Analysis Performance for the 149 Development Sentences

between a listener's transcription of phonetic segments and the automatically produced analysis segments, totaled over the development data base of 149 alphanumeric sequences and data management commands. For each sound class, the listener decisions are indicated as number of segments perceived. The system's performance is summarized in the dimensions of: number of segments detected, percentage of perceived segments for which correct manner decisions were made, percentage of correct place and voicing decisions for those sounds having correct manner decisions (where appropriate), and percentage of false manner decisions.

For example, Figure 7 shows that 426 stops were transcribed by a listener, and 249 stops were hypothesized during the phonetic analysis process. Of the 426 transcribed stops, only 51%, or 217, were found as stops during the analysis. Of these 217 stops, 70% (or 152) received correct place of articulation classifications, and 86% (or 187) were correctly identified with regard to voicing. Of the 249 stops detected during the analysis, 13% (or 32) did not correspond with stops in the utterance transcription.

From an examination of Figure 7, it can be seen that best phonetic analysis performance occurred for vowels, sibilants, and retroflexives. Nasals, lateral liquids, labial glides, and unvoiced fricatives were classified with moderate success. Lowest phonetic analysis performance was obtained for stops, palatal glides, and voiced fricatives. In addition, results from the prosodic analysis show that 91% of the syllables were correctly located.

4.2 Word and Phrase Recognition

After adjusting all components of the recognition system for the development portions of our data bases, the system was stabilized and the test data base portions were processed to obtain test results. For both the alphanumeric sequences and the data management commands, the results are shown in Figure 8 for the correct recognition of the individual words in the phrase, as well as for the correct recognition of the complete phrases.

ALPHANUMERIC SEQUENCES

Speech Data	% Correct Individual Word Recognition	% Correct Phrase Recognition
Development	97% (225)	91% (75)
Test	93% (108)	83% (36)
Average	95% (333)	88% (111)

DATA MANAGEMENT COMMANDS

Speech Data	% Correct Individual Word Recognition	% Correct Phrase Recognition
Development	98% (256)	95% (74)
Test	91% (128)	78% (37)
Average	96% (384)	89% (111)

Figure 8. Word and Phrase Recognition Performance for the Development and Test Sentences

The number of words and phrases in each category are given in parentheses beside the percentage results. For the alphanumeric sequences, the correct phrase recognition was 91% for the 75 development phrases and 83% for the 36 test phrases. For the data management commands, the correct phrase recognition was 95% for the 74 development phrases and 78% for the 37 test phrases. The overall results are 88% correct for the alphanumeric sequences and 89% correct for the data management commands.

Analysis of the errors reveals that about half of the 30 words not found correctly had either an extraneous or a missing vowel, which is often fatal in a syllable based matching strategy. The other half of the errors did not cluster on particular words, but were instead distributed primarily on words of only one or two syllables.

5. SUMMARY

The speech recognition system being developed at Sperry Univac uses a linguistically oriented approach to recognize spoken natural phrases and sentences, without extensive adjustments for individual talkers, and without the need for each talker to repeat every vocabulary word for system training. An acoustic analysis is performed with autocorrelation, Fast Fourier Transform analysis, and linear prediction analysis to produce 14 time functions that describe voice fundamental frequency, bandlimited energies, and vocal tract resonances, or formants. A prosodic analysis component provides information about the syllabic structure of the utterance, including the preliminary locations of syllabic nuclei, as well as estimates of which syllables are stressed. A phonetic analysis component then determines the sound segments, or phonetic sequences, throughout the unknown utterance, including the locations and subclassifications of stops, sibilants, nasals, vowels, liquids, glides, and fricatives. This phonetic feature information is represented in a two-dimensional lattice of sound classes versus time. In preparation for lexical matching, a segmental structuring component next transforms the lattice of phonetic information into a non-overlapping sequence of analysis segments, making various phonological or segmental adjustments during the transformation.

To complete the recognition process, a word sequence hypothesizer determines which sequence of vocabulary words best matches the analysis segments of the unknown utterance. It uses syntactic constraints to direct a word matching component, which aligns and scores analysis segments with lexical segments. Vowels serve as alignment anchor points, and the word matching strategy allows both missed and extraneous segments. The word sequence hypothesizer works from left to right to build syntactically allowed word sequences from good single word matches. The best scoring sequence of words that spans all the analysis segments and satisfies the task constraints, is chosen as the recognized utterance.

The initial lexical representations of vocabulary words are produced automatically from standard dictionary pronunciations by a set of generative phonological rules. For some words, lexical entries are later hand-modified after observing analysis results. A number of statistical analysis programs, using algorithmically produced correlations of analysis and listener-perceived transcription segments, provide partial automation of data analysis, performance evaluation, and system enhancement.

During the past year, the Sperry Univac speech recognition system has been developed and tested on 222 alphanumeric sequences and data management commands from three male talkers. The two to four-word sequences of digits and "phonetic alphabet" words have a 36 word vocabulary and an average branching factor of 9.4, with over 25,000 syntactically allowed alphanumeric sequences. For the 111 sequences used for development and test, average correct recognition scores were 95% for individual words, and 88% for complete phrases. In the second task, seven types of data management commands are produced from a 64 word vocabulary. The syntax for this task allows 919 different sentences, and has an average branching factor of 6.3. Average correct recognition scores for 111 recorded sentences were 96% for individual words, and 89% for complete sentences.

In the near future, we plan to expand the recognition vocabulary to several hundred words, and to also increase the syntactic variety of sentences that can be recognized. Several possible system enhancements are expected to improve recognition performance, including additional use of prosodic information, and the incorporation of phonetic verification rules and a word verification component. Studies under way of noisy, bandlimited speech should eventually lead to successful speech recognition over typical communication channels. All of these planned improvements are designed to provide an effective sentence recognition system for natural speech input to computers in practical applications.

ACKNOWLEDGEMENT

The development of this speech recognition system has been funded by the Sperry Univac Independent Research and Development program. The authors are indebted to their colleagues in the Speech Communications Department, who have made important contributions to this development effort.

REFERENCES

1. Medress, M. F. (1972). "A Procedure for the Machine Recognition of Speech," Conference Record of the 1972 Conference on Speech Communication and Processing, IEEE Cat. No. 72 CHO 596-7 AE, pp. 113-116.
2. Lea, W. A., Medress, M. F., and Skinner, T. E. (1975). "A Prosodically-Guided Speech Understanding Strategy," IEEE Transactions on Acoustics, Speech, and Signal Processing, Vol. ASSP-23, pp. 30-38.
3. Beck, A. F., and Anderson, D. E. (1975). "Computer-Generated Voice in Air Traffic Control Applications," Proceedings of the IEEE 1975 National Aerospace and Electronics Conference NAECON '75, IEEE Cat. No. 75 CHO 956-3 NAECON 75, pp. 547-551.
4. Medress, M. F., and Skinner, T. E. (1976). "FY 1976 Final Report on Speech Processing Research," Sperry Univac Report No. PX 11650.
5. Skinner, T. E., Kloker, D. R., and Medress, M. F. (1976). "A Speech Recognition System for Connected Word Sequences," Conference Record of the 1976 IEEE International Conference on Acoustics, Speech, and Signal Processing, IEEE Cat. No. 76 CH1067-8 ASSP, pp. 434-437.
6. Skinner, T. E. (1973). "Speech Parameter Extraction: Fundamental Frequency, Spectral and Formant Frequency Processing," Sperry Univac Report No. PX 10376.
7. Skinner, T. E. (1974). "Speech Research Facility Parameter Processing System," Sperry Univac Report No. PX 10901.
8. Makhoul, J., and Wolf, J. (1972). "Linear Prediction and the Spectral Analysis of Speech," Bolt Beranek and Newman Report No. 2304.
9. Lea, W. A. (1976). "Prosodic Aids to Speech Recognition: IX. Acoustic-Prosodic Patterns in Selected English Phrase Structures," Sperry Univac Report No. PX 11963.
10. Skinner, T. E. (1975). "Acoustic-Phonetic Processing of Speech," Sperry Univac Report No. PX 11222.
11. Skinner, T. E. (1976). "Procedures for Identifying /ℓ/ and /w/ Sounds," Sperry Univac Report No. PX 11601.
12. Skinner, T. E. (1976). "Acoustic-Phonetic Processing of Speech: A Summary of FY76 Enhancements and Future Plans," Sperry Univac Report No. PX 11719.
13. McCandless, S. S. (1974). "Use of Formant Motion in Speech Recognition," Conference Record of the 1974 IEEE Symposium on Speech Recognition, IEEE Cat. No. 74 CHO 878-9 AE, p. 211.
14. Kloker, D. R. (1976). "A Connected Word Sequence Matching Strategy for Speech Recognition," Sperry Univac Report No. PX 11649.
15. Hall, D. E. (1974). Draft of a chapter on the Linquistic Module for the Lincoln Laboratory Speech Recognition System, M.I.T. Lincoln Laboratory, Sept. 17.
16. Diller, T. C. (1977). "Automatic Lexical Generation for Speech Recognition," Conference Record of the 1977 IEEE International Conference on Acoustics, Speech, and Signal Processing.
17. Diller, T. C., Kloker, D. R., Oredson, H. N., and Siebenand, J. F. (1977). "Steps Toward Automating Speech Data Analysis, Performance Evaluation, and System Enhancement," Sperry Univac Report No. PX 11825.
18. Diller, T. C., Kloker, D. R., and Skinner, T. E. (1976). "FY 1977 Development Data for the Automatic Recognition of Spoken Connected Word Sequences," Sperry Univac Report No. PX 11776.
19. Goodman, R. G. (1976). "Analysis of Languages for Man-Machine Voice Communication," Carnegie-Mellon University Ph.D. Thesis, Dept. of Computer Science.
20. Lea, W. A. (1974). "Sentences for Controlled Testing of Acoustic Phonetic Components of Speech Understanding Systems," Sperry Univac Report No. PX 10952.
21. "IEEE Recommended Practice for Speech Quality Measurements," IEEE Transactions on Audio and Electroacoustics, Vol. AU-17, Sept. 1969, pp. 225-246.

Some Preliminary Experiments in the Recognition of Connected Digits

LAWRENCE R. RABINER, FELLOW, IEEE, AND MARVIN R. SAMBUR

Abstract—This paper describes an implementation of a speaker independent system which can recognize connected digits. The overall recognition system consists of two separate but interrelated parts. The function of the first part of the system is to segment the digit string into the individual digits which comprise the string; the second part of the system then recognizes the individual digits based on the results of the segmentation. The segmentation of the digits is based on a voiced-unvoiced analysis of the digit string, as well as information about the location and amplitude of minima in the energy contour of the utterance. The digit recognition strategy is similar to the algorithm used by Sambur and Rabiner [1] for isolated digits, but with several important modifications due to the impreciseness with which the exact digit boundaries can be located. To evaluate the accuracy of the system in segmenting and recognizing digit strings a series of experiments was conducted. Using high-quality recordings from a soundproof booth the segmentation accuracy was found to be about 99 percent, and the recognition accuracy was about 91 percent across ten speakers (five male, five female). With recordings made in a noisy computer room the segmentation accuracy remained close to 99 percent, and the recognition accuracy was about 87 percent across another group of ten speakers (five male, five female).

I. INTRODUCTION

ONE of the most interesting areas of speech recognition is the problem of digit recognition. Although the applications to telephony alone would justify serious consideration of digit recognition methods, there are a wide variety of additional applications where voice input to a machine is extremely useful [2]. Among these applications are banking by voice, data input to a computer, and inventory and stock record keeping by machine.

Traditionally the approach to research in digit recognition has been to study the issues involved in recognizing isolated digits, spoken by a designated or one of a set of designated speakers [1], [3]-[7]. Although Martin has amply demonstrated the wide range of applications for such systems it is clear that for many applications of digit recognition (e.g., in telephony), these restrictions are highly undesirable.

Earlier work by Sambur and Rabiner [1] showed that a digit recognition accuracy on the order of 97 percent could be achieved with isolated digits across a broad range of male and female speakers. It was felt that these high scores justified experimentation with speaker independent systems for recognizing continuous digits.[1] It is the purpose of this paper to discuss such a system and to present results of experiments in recognizing strings of connected digits.

Fig. 1 shows a block diagram of the digit recognition scheme. The recorded digit string is first subjected to an endpoint analysis to determine where in the given recording interval the speech data occurs. The endpoint analysis is based on self-normalized measures of the energy and zero crossings of the

Manuscript received September 22, 1975; revised December 3, 1975. This work represents an equal contribution of the two authors.

The authors are with Bell Laboratories, Murray Hill, NJ 07974.

[1] The authors have recently become aware of similar work in the area of digit recognition at Perception Technology, Inc., Winchester, MA, Dialog Systems, Inc., Cambridge, MA, and Texas Instruments, Inc., Dallas, TX.

Reprinted from *IEEE Trans. Acoust., Speech, and Signal Process.*, vol. ASSP-24, pp. 170–182, Apr. 1976.

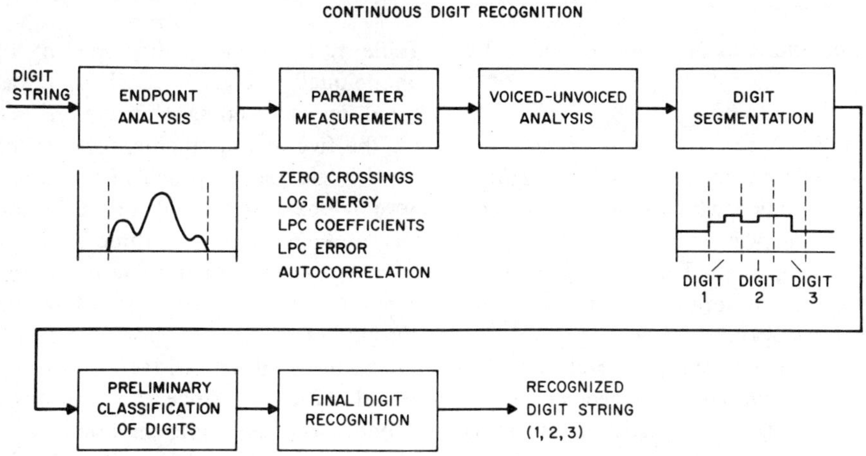

Fig. 1. Block diagram of the overall digit recognition system.

speech waveform, as described by Rabiner and Sambur [8]. Following endpoint alignment, the speech signal is analyzed 100 times/s, giving the following parameters:

1) Zero crossings
2) Log energy
3) Linear predictive coding (LPC) coefficients
4) LPC error
5) Autocorrelation coefficients

The measured parameters are then used in a statistical pattern recognition approach to give a voiced-unvoiced-silence contour of the utterance [9]. The voiced-unvoiced-silence contour is used along with some statistical information about the contour, and the speech energy measurements to segment the connected digit string into the individual digits. For the work to be described here it was assumed that all inputs were strings of three connected digits. This restriction on the number of digits could easily be removed with affecting any of the results to be presented. However, it is required that the number of digits in the string be specified.

Once the digits have been segmented, preliminary tests are made to check if the boundaries chosen by the segmentation algorithm might be grossly incorrect. In particular, classification tests on possibilities for any of the digits being 6, or 1, or 9 are made. Depending on the results of these tests the boundary locations of the individual digits are adjusted accordingly.

The final stage in the method is the digit recognition algorithm. This algorithm is similar in philosophy, but greatly different in details of implementation from the digit recognition algorithm described in [1]. The differences are due primarily to the coarticulation effects which are present with connected digits, but which are absent for isolated digits. In addition, there is a great deal less accuracy in the location of the digit boundaries for connected digits than there was for isolated digits. Thus a fairly large amount of processing is often required to make the final digit recognition.

The digit recognition system of Fig. 1 has been tested across a variety of speakers and transmission conditions. Experimental results have yielded about a 91 percent correct recognition score for ten subjects with recordings made in a soundproof booth using a high-quality microphone. For recordings made in a noisy computer room, an accuracy of 87 percent correct digit recognition was achieved across another group of ten speakers. Informal experiments showed the system to be capable of working on telephone line data if some modifications were made in the detailed recognition rules, and in the training data for the voiced-unvoiced-silence decision algorithm.

The organization for this paper is as follows. In Section II we discuss the method used to segment the connected digit string into the individual digits. Included in the section is a discussion of the various parameters which were used in the voiced-unvoiced-silence analysis, and for segmentation. In Section III the algorithm used to recognize the individual digits is described. Also described in this section is the method by which the digits are preliminarily classified to eliminate gross boundary errors, and the method of adjusting the boundaries based on the classification results. In Section IV an experimental evaluation of the overall recognition algorithm is described. Confusion matrices are included to show the types and distribution of recognition errors across the digits, and across different speakers. Finally, in Section V a general discussion of the problems of connected digit recognition is given.

II. Connected Digit Segmentation

In order to recognize the digits in the input string, it is necessary to accurately segment the input into the individual digits. Segmentation of speech is inherently an extremely difficult problem. However, for connected digit strings this problem is much more readily solved than for continuous speech in general. This is because by restricting the speech to be a string of digits known properties of the 10 possible digits can be used to accurately locate the digit boundaries. For example, it is easily shown that an interval of unvoiced speech or silence within the digit string denotes the beginning or end of a digit, i.e., there are no internal unvoiced or silence regions within the 10 digits (0-9).[2] Another observation about the digits is that, with a couple of exceptions, the energy contours of the digits have no internal local minima. Thus, excluding the noted exceptions, local minima of the energy

[2]Digits 6 and 8 can have internal silence or unvoiced regions. Such cases are treated directly using preliminary digit classification rules as discussed in Section III-B.

contour also are strong indications of digit boundaries within the digit string.

A. Voiced-Unvoiced Analysis

Based on the observations given above about the digits, a segmentation algorithm was studied which relied on an accurate voiced-unvoiced-silence analysis of the digit string, and the energy contour of the utterance. The voiced-unvoiced-silence analysis was made using a pattern recognition approach described by Atal and Rabiner [9]. The way in which this algorithm works is as follows. Each 10 ms interval of the utterance is classified as voiced speech, unvoiced speech, or silence, based entirely on measurements made on the signal during the prescribed interval. The classification of the interval into one of the three possibilities (voiced-unvoiced-silence) is based on a classical hypothesis-testing procedure in which a non-Euclidean distance is computed from the given set of measurements, for each of the hypotheses, and the minimum distance determines which class is selected. The classification algorithm had to be trained, a priori, to obtain the necessary statistics of the measurements for each of the three classifications.

The measurements which were used in the digit recognition experiment were the zero crossing count (number of zero crossings per 10 ms interval), the log energy of the interval, the first autocorrelation coefficient, the first LPC coefficient in a two-pole LPC analysis, and the LPC error of the two-pole analysis. These measurements differ from the ones described in [9] in that a two-pole LPC analysis was used rather than a 12-pole LPC analysis. The two-pole analysis was used because it was required in the final digit recognition phase of the system, and rather than perform two distinct LPC analyses, the method was trained on the two-pole analysis data. Additionally, the two-pole LPC analysis reduced the computation time considerably over an equivalent twelve-pole LPC analysis.

As mentioned above, the voiced-unvoiced classification algorithm requires a priori training to obtain the statistics for the measurements used in the analysis. Although the training is speaker independent (as long as a reasonable sampling of different speakers is used in the training set), the training is not independent of the transmission medium. Since three different transmission mediums were used in formal and informal evaluations of the recognition system, three sets of training data were used. The three conditions were the following.

1) Recordings made in a double-walled, soundproof booth using a high-quality microphone. This condition is called the high-quality speech.

2) Recordings made in a noisy computer room using a high-quality microphone. This condition is called the room-quality speech.

3) Recordings made over a dialed up telephone line using a telephone handset. These recordings went through the local Bell Laboratories PBX. This condition is called the telephone-quality speech.

Tables I-III show the training statistics for each of the five measurements, for each of the three classes, and for each of the three speech conditions. Table I is for high-quality speech; Table II for room-quality speech; and Table III is for telephone-quality speech. Each of these tables shows the measured means, standard deviations, and covariance matrices for the five measurements, for each of the classes, i.e., silence ($L = 1$), unvoiced speech ($L = 2$), and voiced speech ($L = 3$). Several observations can be made about the behavior of the measurements for these three conditions. It can be seen that the distributions of the five measurements for the room- and high-quality conditions are essentially the same for voiced and unvoiced speech; however significant changes have occurred in the distributions for silence. This result is what one would anticipate since the transmission system (the microphone) was the same in both cases; only the background silence characteristics have varied. This result is most readily seen in comparing the difference in means of the log energy between voiced speech and silence for high- and room-quality speech. For high-quality speech this difference is about 39.6 dB whereas for room-quality speech this difference is about 33.4 dB. Also the silence correlation coefficient mean is about 0.73 for high-quality speech, whereas it is about 0.91 for room-quality speech—a quite significant difference.

In comparing the distributions of the measurements for telephone-quality speech (Table III) with high-quality speech (Table I), many more differences are apparent. Although the statistical distributions of the measurements for voiced speech are quite similar, the strong band-limiting effects of a telephone line and a telephone handset are quite apparent for unvoiced speech and silence. For example, the average number of zero crossings for unvoiced speech is 49.5 for high-quality speech, whereas for telephone speech it is about 20.0. Thus the effectiveness of the zero crossing measurement in differentiating between voiced and unvoiced speech is greatly reduced for telephone speech. The reason this measurement is retained rather than replaced by a more effective measurement is for uniformity in the use of the digit recognition system. Since the same measurements are used for all three recording conditions, the only change required in the recognition system is the substitution of one training set of data for another set.

For purposes of illustration, Figs. 2 and 3 show plots of the distribution of two of the measurements for silence, unvoiced, and voiced speech for the room-quality speech. Also included in these plots are Gaussian curves that have the same mean and standard deviation as the measured data. Fig. 2 shows plots of the distributions of zero crossings; whereas Fig. 3 shows plots of the distributions of the first LPC coefficient in the two-pole LPC analysis. The differences in mean and standard deviations of the measurements, for the different classes, are readily obvious from these plots.

B. Digit Segmentation Rules

The digit segmentation algorithm is based on the results of the voiced-unvoiced-silence analysis discussed in the previous section, and also uses the energy measurements to aid in locating the digit boundaries. Fig. 4 shows a flow diagram of the digit segmentation algorithm. Based on N_D, the number of digits in the input string ($N_D = 3$ throughout this paper), the algorithm searches for two external boundaries

TABLE I
MEANS, STANDARD DEVIATIONS, AND COVARIANCE MATRICES FOR HIGH-QUALITY SPEECH

	Zero Crossings	Log Energy (Decibels)	First Auto-correlation	First LPC	LPC Log Error (Decibels)
1) Silence					
Mean	23.270	9.448	0.728	-0.955	6.672
Standard Deviation	7.672	3.424	0.120	0.205	3.403
	1.000	-0.557	-0.900	0.669	-0.749
Covariance Matrix	-0.557	1.000	0.529	-0.805	0.946
	-0.900	0.529	1.000	-0.671	0.741
	0.669	-0.805	-0.671	1.000	-0.859
	-0.749	0.946	0.741	-0.859	1.000
2) Unvoiced					
Mean	49.532	25.365	0.024	-0.046	11.436
Standard Deviation	8.891	5.747	0.260	0.400	2.892
	1.000	0.068	-0.921	0.895	-0.092
Covariance Matrix	0.068	1.000	-0.032	-0.007	0.943
	-0.921	-0.032	1.000	-0.978	0.143
	0.895	-0.007	-0.978	1.000	-0.200
	-0.092	0.943	0.143	-0.200	1.000
3) Voiced					
Mean	12.589	49.679	0.880	-1.469	26.793
Standard Deviation	5.367	6.095	0.085	0.289	4.241
	1.000	0.371	-0.821	0.450	-0.271
Covariance Matrix	0.371	1.000	-0.309	-0.041	0.525
	-0.821	-0.309	1.000	-0.711	0.447
	0.450	-0.041	-0.711	1.000	-0.780
	-0.271	0.525	0.447	-0.780	1.000

TABLE II
MEANS, STANDARD DEVIATIONS, AND COVARIANCE MATRICES FOR ROOM-QUALITY SPEECH

	Zero Crossings	Log Energy (Decibels)	First Auto-correlation	First LPC	LPC Log Error (Decibels)
1) Silence					
Mean	12.167	18.138	0.911	-1.388	13.061
Standard Deviation	3.739	3.928	0.053	0.180	2.372
	1.000	-0.239	-0.591	0.524	-0.499
Covariance Matrix	-0.239	1.000	0.124	-0.281	0.863
	-0.591	0.124	1.000	-0.802	0.515
	0.524	-0.281	-0.802	1.000	-0.682
	-0.499	0.863	0.515	-0.682	1.000
2) Unvoiced					
Mean	49.860	30.568	0.007	-0.041	13.086
Standard Deviation	16.093	4.860	0.441	0.482	2.161
	1.000	0.361	-0.971	0.948	0.331
Covariance Matrix	0.361	1.000	-0.370	0.366	0.954
	-0.971	-0.370	1.000	-0.977	-0.341
	0.948	0.366	-0.977	1.000	0.319
	0.331	0.954	-0.341	0.319	1.000
3) Voiced					
Mean	12.858	51.522	0.878	-1.490	28.373
Standard Deviation	5.491	5.745	0.109	0.379	4.715
	1.000	0.208	-0.778	0.635	-0.471
Covariance Matrix	0.208	1.000	-0.055	-0.158	0.487
	-0.778	-0.055	1.000	-0.838	0.627
	0.635	-0.158	-0.838	1.000	-0.847
	-0.471	0.487	0.627	-0.847	1.000

TABLE III
MEANS, STANDARD DEVIATIONS, AND COVARIANCE MATRICES FOR TELEPHONE-QUALITY SPEECH

	Zero Crossings	Log Energy (Decibels)	First Auto-correlation	First LPC	LPC Log Error (Decibels)
1) Silence					
Mean	13.804	14.711	0.891	-1.374	11.495
Standard Deviation	4.554	4.991	0.068	0.189	3.463
	1.000	-0.242	-0.771	0.499	-0.437
Covariance Matrix	-0.242	1.000	0.158	-0.665	0.939
	-0.771	0.158	1.000	-0.597	0.417
	0.499	-0.665	-0.597	1.000	-0.830
	-0.437	0.939	0.417	-0.830	1.000
2) Unvoiced					
Mean	19.987	29.819	0.788	-1.305	16.332
Standard Deviation	5.707	8.224	0.096	0.173	3.702
	1.000	0.095	-0.857	0.746	-0.159
Covariance Matrix	0.095	1.000	-0.054	-0.236	0.942
	-0.857	-0.054	1.000	-0.883	0.231
	0.746	-0.236	-0.883	1.000	-0.531
	-0.159	0.942	0.231	-0.531	1.000
3) Voiced					
Mean	12.858	51.319	0.896	-1.651	29.289
Standard Deviation	5.213	6.171	0.069	0.173	3.726
	1.000	0.361	-0.886	0.676	-0.256
Covariance Matrix	0.361	1.000	-0.316	0.094	0.598
	-0.886	-0.316	1.000	-0.837	0.372
	0.676	0.094	-0.837	1.000	-0.670
	-0.256	0.598	0.372	-0.670	1.000

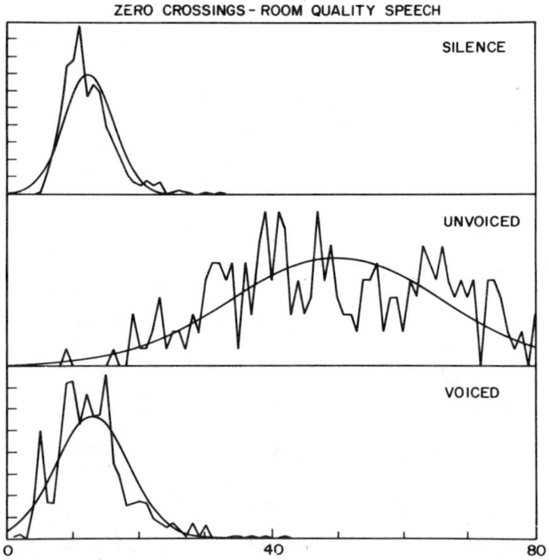

Fig. 2. Theoretical and measured probability density functions for the zero crossing measurement for room-quality speech.

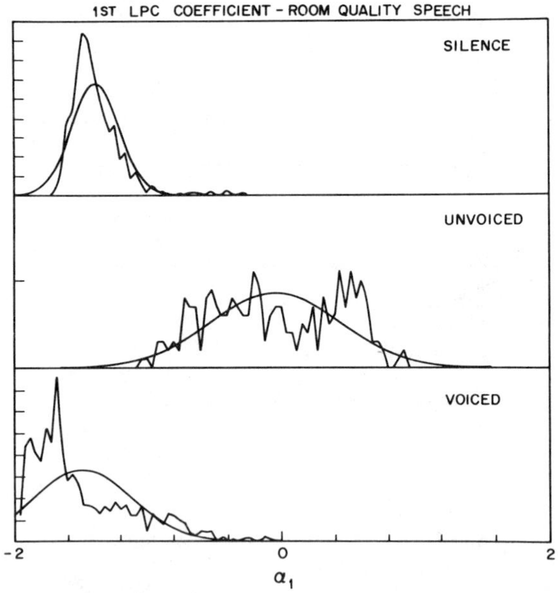

Fig. 3. Theoretical and measured probability density functions for the first LPC coefficient in a two-pole analysis for room-quality speech.

and (N_D - 1) internal boundaries. The external boundaries are generally the endpoints of the digit string as determined in the endpoint analysis. However the speech interval used for analysis is 100 ms longer both at the beginning and at the end of the utterance to account for possible endpoint location errors which can be corrected by the more sophisticated voiced-unvoiced-silence analysis. Thus the external boundaries are almost always located within 100 ms of the beginning and end of the analysis interval—as depicted in Fig. 1.

The internal boundaries are located using the procedure outlined in Fig. 4. First, all strong local minima of the energy contour of the utterance which occur in voiced regions are located and tagged. These minima are only possible candidates because the energy of the utterance can exhibit a strong dip both because of a word boundary, and because of a voiced fricative, e.g., /v/ in seven.

The next step in the algorithm is to locate one boundary in each nonvoiced region within the utterance, e.g., one digit

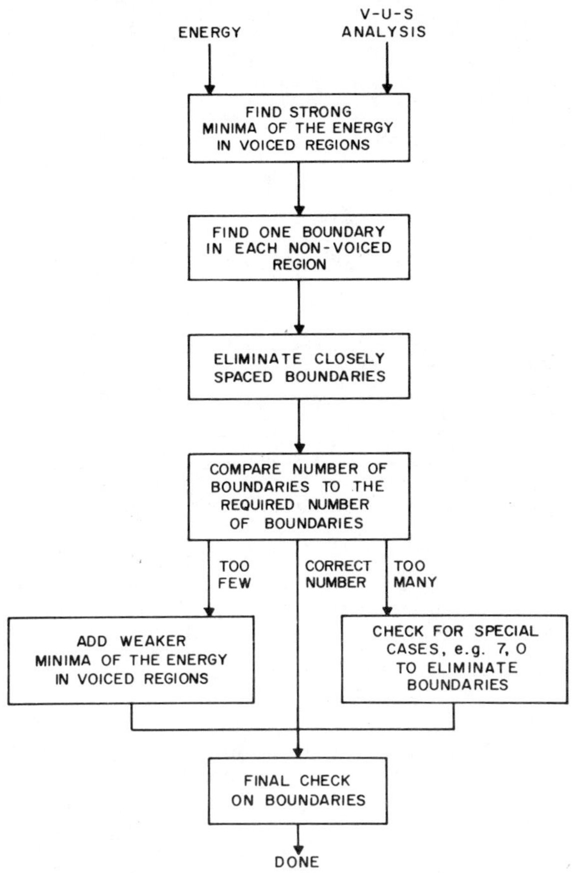

Fig. 4. Flow diagram for the digit segmentation algorithm.

boundary must occur with a silence, or unvoiced interval. The boundary locations are placed at the first nonvoiced interval within the region. The only exceptions to this rule (i.e., that the digit boundary occurs at the beginning of the nonvoiced region) are six, which ends in an unvoiced region, and eight, which ends in an interval of silence, and is sometimes followed by a stop burst at the release of the /t/. Methods of correcting the boundary locations for these cases are described in Section III where preliminary classification rules are used to adjust the boundaries within nonvoiced regions.

The first two steps in the flowchart of Fig. 4 showed ways of choosing candidates for the digit boundaries. The next step is to eliminate one boundary whenever two boundary candidates are too closely spaced (i.e., less than 150 ms apart). Appropriate logic decides which boundary candidate to eliminate in such cases.

The next step in the segmentation strategy is to compare the number of boundary candidates to the required number of internal boundaries. If there are too few choices, weaker minima of the energy contour are located and added as boundary candidates. If there are too many boundary candidates, checks are made for digits like seven, etc., for which spurious boundary candidates often occur and such boundary candidates are eliminated.

When the correct number of boundary candidates has been obtained, a final check is made on the boundaries for internal consistency, e.g., checks are made to insure each digit consists of only a single voiced region, etc.

To illustrate the operation of the segmentation rules, Figs. 5-9 show several examples of digit strings which were segmented using the rules discussed above. In each of these figures parts (a), (b), (c), and (d) show plots of the zero crossing contour, the log energy contour, a statistical measure of the certainty of the voiced-unvoiced-silence analysis, and the voiced-unvoiced-silence contour of the utterance, respectively. The statistical parameter shown in (c) is a measure of the probability that the decision made by the voiced-unvoiced-silence analysis is correct, and it varies from 0 to 1.0. The voiced-unvoiced-silence contour of (d) is a 3-level contour where level 1 is silence, level 2 is unvoiced speech, and level 3 is voiced speech.

Fig. 5 shows the segmentation boundaries for the digit string /721/. The initial boundary was placed at the beginning of the first unvoiced region, i.e., the /s/ is seven. The second boundary was placed at the initial interval of the second unvoiced region—corresponding to the /t/ in two. The third boundary was placed in the region of a local minimum of the log energy contour within the second voiced region. The exact boundary location is not at the absolute minimum of the log energy, but instead occurs somewhere within the region of the minimum. The exact location is determined by a series of complex decisions which will not be discussed. Although the correct location of the third boundary is not readily determined, it has been found that precise location of the boundaries within voiced regions is not required for reliable digit recognition. The final digit boundary is located at the beginning of the last silence region.

It should be pointed out that another possible candidate for a boundary location in Fig. 5 is at the strong local minimum in the log energy contour at the /v/ in seven. However, the segmentation rules were able to eliminate this case quite readily and instead choose the minimum in the second voiced region.

Fig. 6 shows a somewhat more complicated digit string—the string /191/. This input is all voiced—thus there are no convenient boundaries in unvoiced regions. In addition the local minima in the log energy plot are not very strong ones (e.g., the energy dips are not large ones), and the widths of these minima are quite large. Thus the choice of boundary locations was made at the next to last step in the segmentation algorithm. Listening tests showed that the location of these boundaries within the all-voiced regions was not critical due to the high degree of coarticulation in the speaking of such all-voiced digit strings.

Fig. 7 shows results for the segmentation of the digit string /650/. For this case there were three unvoiced regions and one boundary occurred at the beginning of each region. However the second boundary should actually be within the unvoiced region—not at the beginning of it. The dashed line in the figure shows where the boundary was moved by the preliminary classification algorithm which classified the initial digit as a six, and classified the following digit as one which might begin with an unvoiced region.

Finally, Figs. 8 and 9 show the three-digit sequence with which the segmentation rules had the most difficulty. It was the digit string /387/. Fig. 8 shows the segmentation

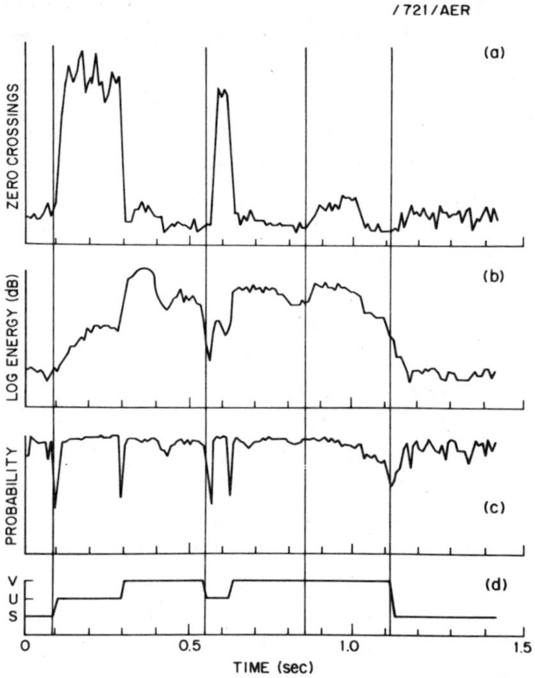

Fig. 5. Typical measurement contours and the resulting boundary locations for the utterance /721/.

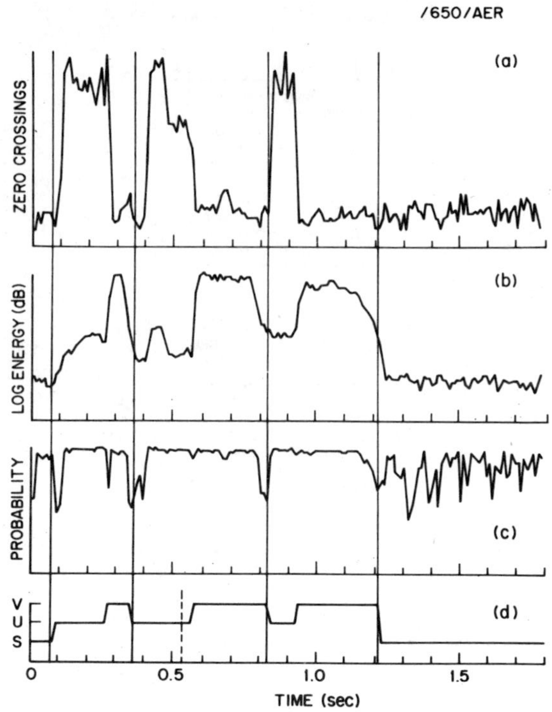

Fig. 7. Typical measurement contours and the resulting boundary locations for the utterance /650/.

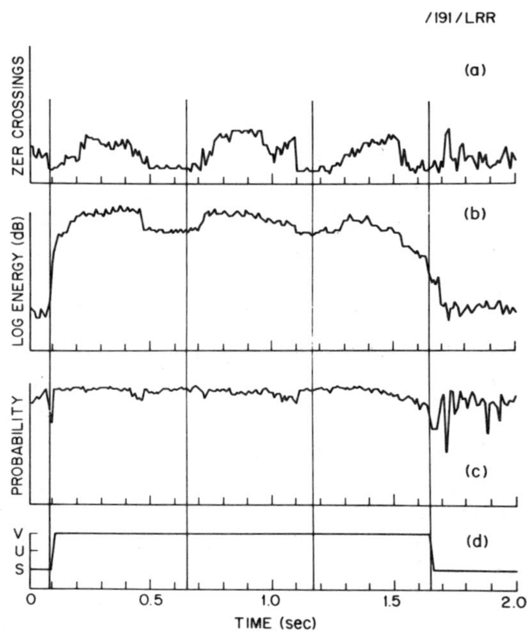

Fig. 6. Typical measurement contours and the resulting boundary locations for the utterance /191/.

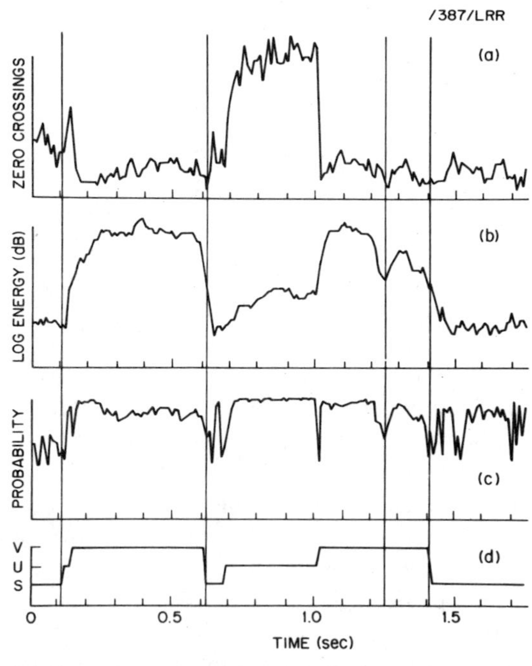

Fig. 8. Improper segmentation of the utterance /387/.

when the digit string was spoken fast, and Fig. 9 shows the segmentation when the digit string was spoken slowly and with emphasis on the /38/ rather than on the /7/.

The difference in emphasis is reflected in the relative durations of the frication in the initial /3/, and in the duration of the voiced regions of the /38/. The segmentation rules were not correct in placing a boundary at the /v/ in seven for the data of Fig. 8, whereas there was little difficulty segmenting the data of Fig. 9. It is also seen that the log energy during the voiced region of the /38/ of both Fig. 8 and Fig. 9 show no strong (or even weak) minima, indicating the presence of a boundary. However, for the data of Fig. 9, the relative durations strongly implied the presence of a boundary in the initial voiced region; even though no good location for the boundary could be found. For the data of Fig. 8, the relative durations implied the presence of a boundary in the second voiced region; hence the segmentation error.

An evaluation of the segmentation accuracy was made using 200 sequences of three digits recorded by ten different speakers in the computer room. Out of the 600 digits, only four were improperly segmented. An improper segmentation

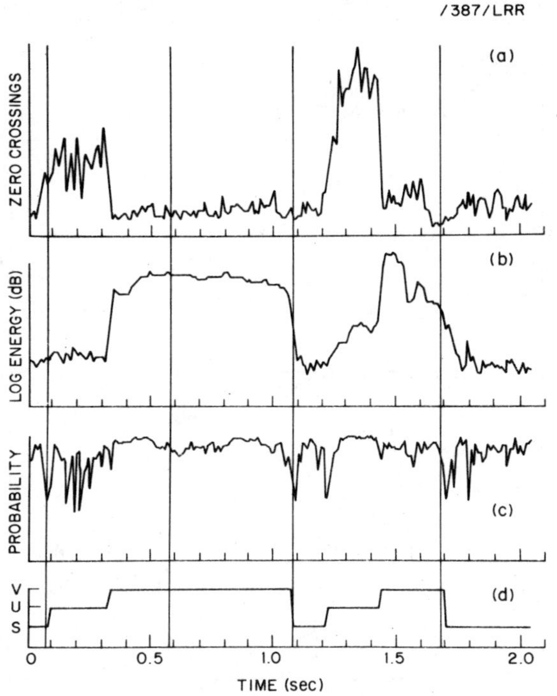

Fig. 9. Proper segmentation of the utterance /387/.

was defined as one in which a distinctly audible part of the preceding digit was included within the boundaries of the current digit being segmented. All of the errors occurred in cases similar to the one illustrated in Figs. 8 and 9. Thus a segmentation accuracy of about 99 percent was obtained on these three-digit strings.

III. Digit Recognition Algorithm

The next stage in the implementation of the recognition system is the identification of the digits within the boundaries determined by the segmentation algorithm. The digit recognition strategy that was used is similar to the one discussed by Sambur and Rabiner [1] for recognizing isolated digits but with several important modifications. The modifications are necessary to account for certain limitations in the segmentation algorithm. These limitations include:

1) impreciseness of the exact digit boundaries,
2) ambiguities in the assignment of boundaries for digits ending in unvoiced sounds, and
3) incorrect unvoiced-voiced decisions.

In addition, the effects of coarticulation must be incorporated in the recognition of connected digits. Before discussing the new aspects of the digit recognition algorithm, we shall briefly review the structure of the isolated digit scheme since this forms the framework of the present system.

A. Philosophy of Recognition

In the system for recognizing isolated digits, the approach was to describe the digits in terms of the six broad speech categories listed in Table IV. A set of robust measurements were then used to classify the sounds into the above categories. By robust measurements, we mean acoustic parameters that give a general indication of the gross nature of each phoneme without being overly dependent on the individual

TABLE IV [a]
Sound Classes Characteristic of the Digits

Digit	Sequence of Sound Classes
0	VNLC → FV → VLC → BV
1	VLC → MV → VLC
2	UVNLC → FV → BV
3	UVNLC → VLC → FV
4	UVNLC → BV → MV
5	UVNLC → MV → FV → VNLC
6	UVNLC → FV → UVNLC
7	UVNLC → FV → VNLC → FV → VLC
8	FV → UVNLC
9	VLC → MV → FV → VLC

VNLC Voiced, noise-like consonant.
UVNLC Unvoiced, noise-like consonant.
VLC Vowel-like consonant.
FV Front vowel.
MV Middle vowel.
BV Back vowel.

[a]After Martin [3].

speaker's voice characteristics. The robust measurements selected were:

1) Zero-crossing rate (ZCR), which is defined as the number of zero crossings in a fixed-frame length (on the order of 10 ms).
2) Energy, which is defined as the sum of the squared values of the speech waveform in a given frame.
3) Normalized error obtained from a two-pole LPC analysis of a given speech frame.
4) Pole frequency (or frequencies) obtained from a two-pole LPC analysis of a given speech frame.

To enable the system to perform without having to be trained every time a different speaker wishes to use the system, the technique of self-normalization was introduced. Self-normalization implies that the system does not use fixed threshold levels in the decision process, but instead calculates the appropriate decision thresholds from the speech input itself. Thus, for example, in the case of setting thresholds on ZCR to determine whether a sound is noise-like or nasal, a statistical description of the ZCR was made for each isolated digit. The statistical description consisted of measuring the mean of the ZCR and its standard deviation over the region of strong energy (i.e., the region where the energy exceeded 10 percent of the maximum energy of the utterance). Based on ZCR measurements, one criterion for classifying a segment as noise-like was if its ZCR exceeded a level one standard deviation above the mean during the segment. Fig. 10 shows the ZCR measurements for the word "seven." Indicated in this figure are the average ZCR and a range of one standard deviation around this average. During the initial /s/, the ZCR is significantly above the threshold, as anticipated.

The technique of "self-normalization" also implies that the decision process should avoid the use of absolute decisions and instead classify sounds according to the transitional nature of the various measurements. It was shown that for speech sounds, the relative magnitude of the normalized error generally increases from sonorants to vowels and then to frica-

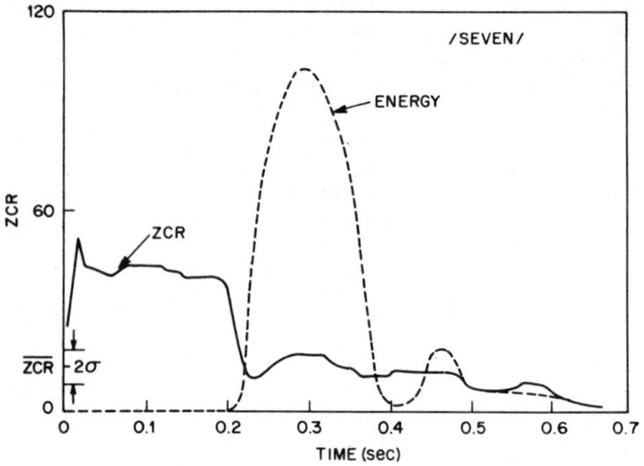

Fig. 10. Energy and ZCR for the digit 7.

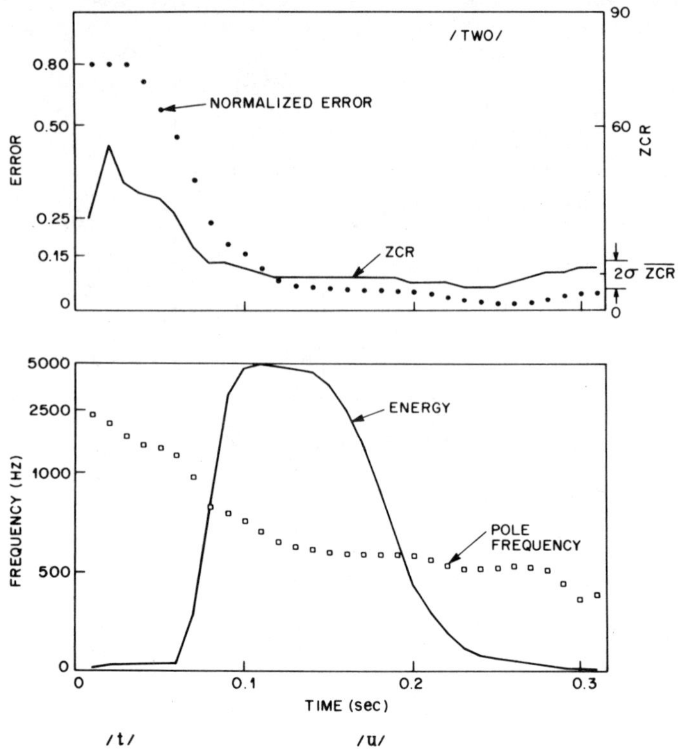

Fig. 11. Complete set of measurements for the digit 2.

tives. Within the three vowel types, the back vowels have the lowest relative normalized error and the front vowels have the highest. By observing the relative changes in the pole frequency and normalized error, important information about the structure of the voiced region of the word can be obtained. As an example, Fig. 11 shows the normalized error and pole frequency throughout the word "two." After the frication region, which is marked by high normalized error and low energy, the normalized error uniformly decreases. Thus the constituent structure of the voiced section is changing from a front vowel to a back vowel.

The final classification of the isolated digits was achieved by a "hypothesize-verification" scheme. In this method, the identity of the digit is first proposed and then the acoustic parameters are checked to see if they are consistent with this hypothesis. The sequence of consistency check was designed to verify the most obvious characteristic and then to proceed to the more difficult decisions. The essential strategy of the connected digit recognition is the same as the isolated scheme, but as noted above certain modifications were necessary. These modifications are described in the following subsections.

B. Preliminary Decisions

In Section II-B it was noted that the segmentation algorithm assigns a boundary location at the first nonvoiced interval within an unvoiced region. This rule is clearly not adequate for both the digit 6, which ends in an unvoiced region, and for cases when the final /t/ in 8 is released.

To partially overcome the limitation of this rule, a preliminary decision scheme was incorporated in the recognition system. One function of the preliminary digit classifier was to check for occurrences of the digit 6. The decision process first selects possible candidates for the digit 6. A "6 candidate" is defined as a digit with a voiced interval of less than 210 ms in duration that is surrounded by nonvoiced intervals and does not contain an internal boundary. Whenever a digit is preliminarily identified as a 6 using the above tests, it is automatically checked for the existence of a stop gap following the voiced interval. The determination of the presence of a stop gap is made by making measurements of the energy and zero crossings during the following unvoiced interval. A significant local minimum in the energy and zero crossing contours at the initial portion of the unvoiced interval is a strong indication of a stop gap. If the decision is that a stop gap exists, the voiced region is checked for front vowel like characteristics [1] and a positive indication confirms the digit as 6.

Assuming that a digit is classified as 6, there is still some ambiguity in locating the proper initial boundary for the following digit (of course if 6 is the final word, no problem exists). If the digit 6 is followed by 1, 9, or 8, then the boundary location should be placed at the first voiced interval following the 6; otherwise the location is within the preceding unvoiced interval. To resolve this ambiguity, a preliminary decision box has been incorporated to detect the digits 1 or 9.

Basically the 1, 9 decision involves checking the voiced interval following the digit classified as 6 to determine the existence of nasal like segments. A self-normalized ZCR threshold procedure was used as one indication of a nasal-like sound. The statistics of the ZCR were calculated in the voiced interval under investigation over those segments in which the energy exceeded 10 percent of the maximum energy in the interval and for which the two-pole frequency exceeded 375 Hz. The first criterion for a nasal-like sound to meet is that the ZCR rate should fall below a level one standard deviation below the average ZCR for three consecutive intervals. In addition, the nasal-like segment should exhibit a "relatively" low normalized error and the two-pole frequency should exhibit abrupt changes at the nasal-like boundaries. Fig. 12 shows the measured parameters for a typical pronounciation of the word "nine." The nasal segments of the word are clearly consistent with the characteristics verified by the decision rule.

To arrive at the final decision for the existence of the digits

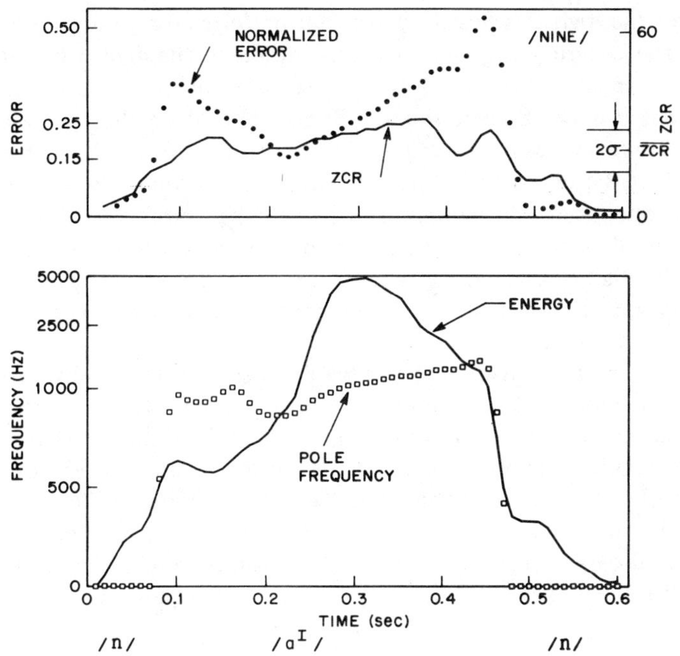

Fig. 12. Complete set of measurements for the digit 9.

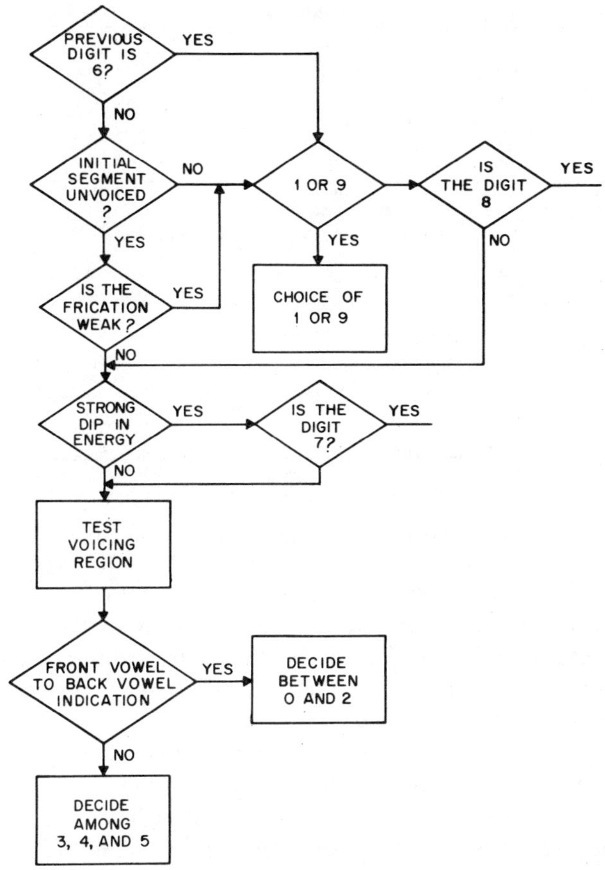

Fig. 13. Decision tree for the digit recognition algorithm.

1 or 9, the initial and final regions of the voiced interval must exhibit nasal-like characteristics. To avoid any possible confusion with the digit 7, an additional check is made any significant dips in the energy contour. These dips are strongly characteristic of the sound /v/ in 7. If the voiced interval contains a boundary location, this boundary location is allowed to float or wobble to account for a certain impreciseness in assigning internal boundaries in voiced regions. The wobbling of the boundaries is restricted to a range of ±30 ms and each possible boundary is checked for adjacent nasal like segments.

The preliminary recognition scheme does not check for the existence of the digit 8, but it is implicitly recognized in the final decision algorithm that the digit 8 is possible after the detection of the digit 6. In addition, if the digit 8 is recognized in the final decision algorithm and an unvoiced interval follows the recognized digit, it is implicitly assumed that the unvoiced interval is due to the release of the /t/ and a 1 or 9 check is undertaken. We now discuss the final digit recognition algorithm.

C. Digit Recognition

Fig. 13 illustrates the decision process used in the digit recognition algorithm. As can be noted from this figure, the results of the unvoiced-voiced analysis are *not* assumed to be error free. Thus if the initial segment of the bounded interval is classified as voiced, the decision is not automatically restricted to the digits 1, 9, and 8. Instead these digits are postulated as the most likely candidates and the acoustic parameters are then checked to verify these possibilities. The likelihood that the digit is either 1, 9, or 8 is quantified in terms of the probability (as measured in the voiced-unvoiced analysis) that the initial section of the word is voiced and the position of the word in the digit string. If the word is the first digit then there is a good chance that the weak fricatives /f/ and /th/ may not be classified as unvoiced.

The decision boxes shown in Fig. 13 are, for the most part, similar to the corresponding boxes used in the isolated digit recognition algorithm [1]. However, to account for the effects of coarticulation, the use of transitional changes in the second formant contour has been incorporated as a measurement feature. Used in parallel with the measured transitional changes in two-pole frequency and normalized error, an accurate decision can be obtained. The transitional nature of the second formant was derived by measuring F_2 at 3 locations in the segmented digit. The locations used in the measurement are the first point at which the probability of voicing exceeds 80 percent for three consecutive intervals, the point of maximum energy, and the first point after the maximum at which the energy dips below 15 percent of the maximum value. The formants were measured over a 20 ms interval by computing a linear prediction spectrum [10]. A peak-picking algorithm determined the second formant frequency. Fig. 14 illustrates the three LPC spectrums obtained for the digit 2. For this digit a fairly large drop in the second formant can be seen in comparing Fig. 14(a) and (c). Also, the third formant falls somewhat during the voiced region.

Since the complete details of the recognition algorithm are quite involved, we will only discuss the most prominent aspects of the decision rules for each box in Fig. 13. After a digit has been classified as beginning with a frication region, the energy contour is checked to determine if the energy dipped below 15 percent of the maximum value and then rose to a value at least 18 percent of the maximum. This

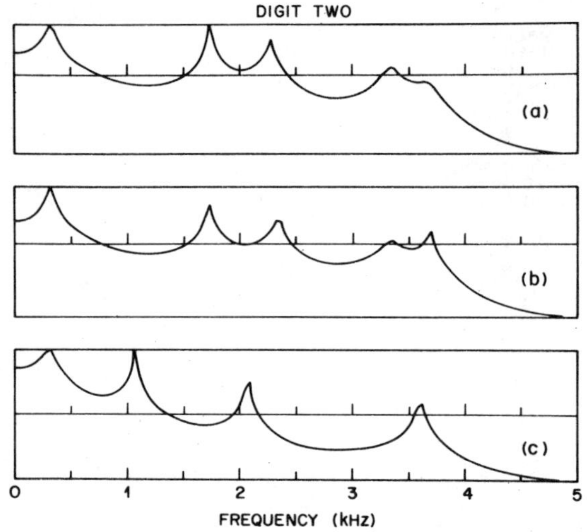

Fig. 14. Application of formants in the final recognition decision.

dip is an almost unfailing characteristic of the /v/ in the digit 7. Should such a dip occur, the ZCR of the digit is checked to see if it falls below the average during the end portion of the digit (after the second local maxima). If this condition is fulfilled, the digit is classified as 7.

If there is no strong dip in energy, the variations in the normalized error, the second formant and the two-pole frequency are calculated during the voicing region. A decrease in any two of these three measurements establishes the voiced region as having a front vowel to back vowel indication. The digits 0 and 2 are then the only candidates for recognition. The digit 0 differs from the digit 2 in the character of the energy contour and two-pole frequency. The digit 0 usually has a small but significant dip in energy during the consonant /r/ and a corresponding dip in two-pole frequency.

If the transitions in the parameters mentioned above are increasing rather than decreasing, the candidates for recognition are 3, 4, and 5. The digit 3 is characterized by it relatively high value of F_2 in the last measured formant location ($F_2 > 1700$ Hz). In addition, the two-pole frequency of the digit 3 is frequently zero at some point in the interval after the maximum energy, but before the energy dips below 20 percent of the maximum. This zero in the location of the two-pole frequency is attributed to the high second formant of the vowel /i/ in 3 [1], and is almost never observed for the other possible candidates (e.g., 4 and 5). The digit 5 can be separated from the digit 4 by its higher F_2 value in the end region and its higher values of two-pole frequency and normalized error. In addition, the two-pole frequency contour of the digit 4 is more uniformly increasing than the contour of 5.

When the candidates for recognition are 1, 9, and 8, the first decision made is whether the digit is 1 or 9. This decision has been discussed in the previous subsection. The digit 9 is separated from the digit 1 by the impulsive nature of the two-pole frequency and normalized error after the initial nasal-like section. The digit is identified as 9 if a total jump in two-pole frequency exceeding 200 Hz is obtained within 20 ms of the initial nasal-like section and the two-pole frequency in the interval also exceeds 600 Hz. The identification of the digit 8 is heavily dependent on formant measurements. The criterion employed for recognition of the digit 8 is that F_2 must exceed 1650 Hz in the three measured intervals. Based upon the Peterson and Barney [11] data, this criterion should be easily realized for this particular vowel. Since the digit 8 frequently begins with an unvoiced sound (8 is often pronounced with an initial /h/), the condition $F_2 > 2000$ Hz for all three intervals is applied for the recognition of 8 when the digit begins with an unvoiced sound. To aid in the recognition of 8, a burst detection algorithm, based on energy considerations, is also used.

It can be seen from the above discussion that the individual recognition rules are not simply written down. The sequential nature of the recognition algorithm implies vastly different recognition criteria for the digits depending on the results of earlier tests along the decision tree. The purpose of the above discussion was to provide a rough idea of the major features used to recognize the digits, without getting too involved with the individual tests which are made in the parallel decision mode.

IV. Experimental Evaluation

The entire digit recognition scheme of Fig. 1 was experimentally evaluated in two separate experiments. In one experiment ten speakers recorded a sequence of 100 7-digit telephone numbers read from a randomly generated list of telephone numbers. These recordings were included in the high-quality speech condition discussed in Section II-A. From these data 20 telephone numbers were chosen at random as test data for each of the speakers. (The processing time per utterance was several minutes. This limitation precluded using a much larger data base for evaluating the system.) The results of this experiment are described in Section IV-A.

The second experiment consisted of an evaluation of the system using room-quality recordings. For this experiment ten speakers (four of them were not in the first experiment) recorded ten randomly selected groups of three digits each. (Again the size of the data base was severely limited by the processing time per utterance.) The results of this experiment are discussed in Section IV-B.

Finally, an informal evaluation of the system was made using telephone-quality speech Section IV-C provides a discussion of the additional problems created using telephone-quality speech.

A. Experiment 1

The results of the first experiment are shown in Tables V and VI. Table V gives the error scores for each of the ten speakers (five female, five male). The range of the individual results is from 81.7 percent correct digit recognition, to 93.3 percent. The accumulated recognition scores for female and male speakers were 91.3 percent and 90.7 percent correct digit recognition, respectively. Thus the overall recognition accuracy for the ten speakers was 91 percent.

Table VI shows an analysis of where the digit errors occurred. This table shows the overall confusion matrix for the experiment. The entries which are circled are the cases which

TABLE V
ERROR SCORES FOR EXPERIMENT 1

Women	Correct	Errors	Percent Correct
SAW	56	4	93.3
CAM	53	7	88.3
SP	55	5	91.7
KD	56	4	93.3
BJM	54	6	90.0
Total	274	26	91.3
Men	**Correct**	**Errors**	**Percent Correct**
JLH	56	4	93.3
RWS	55	5	91.7
MRS	56	4	93.3
AER	49	11	81.7
LRR	56	4	93.3
Total	272	28	90.7
Overall	546	54	91.0

TABLE VI
CONFUSION MATRIX FOR EXPERIMENT 1

Experiment 1

		Digit Recognized											
		0	1	2	3	4	5	6	7	8	9	Number of Tries	Number of Errors
	0	36	1							2	2	41	5
	1		31	1							(7)	39	(8)
	2	(5)		59	1	1						66	(7)
	3				68					1		69	1
Digit	4					81	2					83	2
Spoken	5		1				49					50	1
	6							60				60	0
	7					1		1	63		1	66	3
	8		1	1	(11)				1	57	1	72	(15)
	9	1	2	2	2		2			3	42	54	(12)
												600	54

had the highest number of confusions. It is seen from Table VI that the following confusions occurred most frequently.

1) The digit 8 was recognized as the digit 3 eleven times out of 72 tries.
2) The digit 1 was recognized as the digit 9 seven times out of 39 tries.
3) The digit 2 was recognized as the digit 0 five times out of 66 tries.
4) The digit 9 was recognized as either 0, 1, 2, 3, 5, or 8 twelve times out of 54 tries.

These results show that the greatest number of recognition errors occurred when the digits 8, 9, 1, and 2 were spoken. This result is anticipated by the discussion in Sections II and III since these digits (especially in combinations) were the most difficult to segment reliably. The uncertainty as to the exact digit boundary led to higher reliance on the decisions within the digit for accurate recognition results, thereby leading to the results shown in Table VI.

Another source of error in this experiment was due to a low-level type of breath noise that several speakers used preceding initial eights. Because of the high-quality recording method, the analysis classified this initial breath noise as a short interval of unvoiced speech preceding the digit string. When the digit string began with an initial 8 (as occurred a large number of times) the combination of breath noise and eight caused the incorrect recognition of the eight as a three. This accounted for more than 20 percent of the errors in this experiment, as seen in Table VI.

B. Experiment 2

The results of the second experiment in which room-quality recordings were used are shown in Tables VII and VIII. Table VII gives the error scores for each of the ten speakers (five female, five male) in this experiment. The individual recognition accuracy varied from 73.3 percent to 96.7 percent in this experiment. The overall recognition accuracy was 86.7 percent across the ten speakers. For the female speakers the accuracy was 85 percent, whereas for the male speakers it was 88.4 percent.

Table VIII shows the confusion matrix for this experiment. Although the amount of data is quite small, the following confusions seem to occur most frequently.

1) The digit 1 was recognized as the digit 9 five times in 34 tries.
2) The digit 1 was recognized as the digit 4 four times in 34 tries.
3) The digit 2 was recognized as the digit 3 four times in 25 tries.
4) The digit 9 was recognized as either 0, 1, 3, 4, or 5 eight times in 33 tries.

The confusions occurring with the digits 1 and 9 were similar in nature to those which occurred in Experiment 1. The eight confusions for initial 8's were essentially eliminated in this experiment since the background noise level was sufficiently high to classify any breath noise as silence. Thus initial 8's were correctly recognized in most cases.

Although the room noise had some beneficial masking effects (e.g., the 8-3 confusion mentioned above), it can be seen that the higher noise level lowered the recognition accuracy by about 4 percent.

C. Telephone Recognition of Digits

An informal test of the recognition system was made using 3-digit sequences recorded over switched telephone lines. The purpose of the experiment was to see how much the band-limiting effects of the telephone line degraded the system performance using the same system as was used for high-quality and room-quality conditions.

For this informal experiment the voiced-unvoiced analysis used the training data of Table III. Two speakers (JLH and SAW) were used in this test. In spite of the fact that the five analysis parameters were not equally effective (and in some cases not at all effective) in separating silence from unvoiced speech from voiced speech, the analysis gave accurate results for 19 of 20 digit strings. For these 19 digit strings the segmentation program accurately (to within the stated limitations) segmented all 19 strings. The recognition accuracy, however, fell to about 64 percent for these 19 strings. An analysis of the types of errors showed that the effects of the

TABLE VII
ERROR SCORES FOR EXPERIMENT 2

Women	Correct	Errors	Percent Correct
CES	22	8	73.3
CAM	27	3	90.0
IE	27	3	90.0
SAW	27	3	90.0
GH	22	5	81.5
Total	125	22	85.0
Men	**Correct**	**Errors**	**Percent Correct**
REC	21	6	77.8
LRR	28	2	93.3
MRS	27	3	90.0
AER	29	1	96.7
JLH	25	5	83.3
Total	130	17	88.4
Overall	255	39	86.7

TABLE VIII
CONFUSION MATRIX FOR EXPERIMENT 2

Experiment 2

		0	1	2	3	4	5	6	7	8	9	Number of Tries	Number of Errors
	0	25			1	1						27	2
	1		22			(4)	1			2	(5)	34	(12)
	2			21	(4)							25	4
	3		1		34					2		37	3
Digit	4	1	1		1	29						32	3
Spoken	5				1	1	18				1	21	3
	6				1			36				37	1
	7					1			24			25	1
	8		1					1		21		23	2
	9	1	2		2	2	1				25	33	(8)
												294	39

band-limiting were particularly severe in the recognition stages which relied heavily on zero crossings and the two-pole analysis to classify the digits.

Although the general structure of the recognition stage could still be used on the telephone speech, the individual tests and decisions had to be greatly modified to account for the loss of information in the recognition parameters. Work on this aspect of the system is still in progress.

V. SUMMARY AND CONCLUSIONS

A system has been described for recognizing connected digits. The system is speaker independent and therefore can be used on speakers who have had no prior training in the use of the system. An evaluation of the recognition accuracy using strings of three connected digits showed scores of 91 percent correct recognition for high-quality speech, and 87 percent correct recognition for room-quality speech.

These recognition accuracies can be compared against similar scores obtained in other digit recognition schemes. Using isolated digits in a speaker independent scheme, Sambur and Rabiner [1] obtained digit recognition accuracies of 97 percent and 94 percent for high-quality and room-quality speech, respectively. The 6 percent degradation in the recognition accuracy scores is due primarily to the coarticulation effects which are present in connected digit strings which both makes it difficult to accurately locate the digit boundary, and makes the digit cues in the region of the digit boundaries somewhat unreliable for accurate recognition.

Another comparison which can be made is with the results reported by Martin [3]. Using 10 500 digits, Martin reported recognition accuracies of from 86.8 percent to 92.4 percent on strings of three digits. Although Martin used an order of magnitude more data than in the present study and, therefore, his recognition accuracies are statistically more reliable than those reported on here the results appear to be quite comparable. Additionally, the types of errors made in both studies are of a similar nature.

In summary, the digit recognition system discussed in this paper shows considerable promise for applications where recognition of connected digits is required. More sophistication in the digit recognition rules should help to raise the recognition accuracy. Additional flexibility is required to apply the system to telephone-quality speech due to the degradations caused by the band-limiting nature of the telephone line.

REFERENCES

[1] M. R. Sambur and L. R. Rabiner, "A speaker-independent digit-recognition system," *Bell Syst. Tech. J.*, vol. 54, pp. 81–102, Jan. 1975.

[2] T. B. Martin, "Practical applications of voice input to machines," *Proc. IEEE*, vol. 64, pp. 481–501, Apr. 1976.

[3] —, "Acoustic recognition of a limited vocabulary in continuous speech," Ph.D. dissertation, Univ. Pennsylvania, Philadelphia, 1970.

[4] T. G. Von Keller, "On-line recognition system for spoken digits," *J. Acoust. Soc. Amer.*, vol. 49, pp. 1288–1296, Apr. 1971.

[5] K. H. Davis, R. Biddulph, and S. Balashek, "Automatic recognition of spoken digits," *J. Acoust. Soc. Amer.*, vol. 24, pp. 637–642, Nov. 1952.

[6] P. B. Denes and M. V. Mathews, "Spoken digit recognition using time-frequency pattern matching," *J. Acoust. Soc. Amer.*, vol. 32, pp. 1450–1455, Nov. 1960.

[7] J. Suzuki and K. Nakata, "Recognition of spoken digits," *J. Inst. Elec. Comm. Eng.* (Japan), vol. 45, pp. 303–309, Mar. 1962.

[8] L. R. Rabiner and M. R. Sambur, "An algorithm for determining the endpoints of isolated utterances," *Bell Syst. Tech. J.*, vol. 54, pp. 297–315, Feb. 1975.

[9] B. S. Atal and L. R. Rabiner, "A pattern-recognition approach to voiced-unvoiced-silence classification with applications to speech recognition," *IEEE Trans. Acoust., Speech, Signal Processing*, to be published, June 1976.

[10] B. S. Atal and S. L. Hanauer, "Speech analysis and synthesis by linear prediction of the speech wave," *J. Acoust. Soc. Amer.*, vol. 50, pp. 637–655, Aug. 1971.

[11] G. E. Peterson and H. L. Barney, "Control methods used in a study of the vowels," *J. Acoust. Soc. Amer.*, vol. 24, pp. 175–184, Mar. 1952.

The 1976 Modular Acoustic Processor (MAP)

N. REX DIXON, MEMBER, IEEE, AND HARVEY F. SILVERMAN, MEMBER, IEEE

Abstract—**The modular acoustic processor (MAP), a complex experimental system for automatic derivation of phonemic string output for continuous speech, has stages dedicated to signal analysis, spectral classification, phonemic segmentation, phonemic (steady state) classification, phoneme boundary placement, dyadic (transitional) classification, and final phoneme string consolidation.**

This paper presents the concepts of and some details concerning these five stages. Results on a large body of continuous speech data, prepared by an automatic evaluation system, will also be presented.

I. Introduction

THE modular acoustic processor (MAP) is a large system, currently implemented in PL/I software, which has been developed for automatic derivation of phonetic-string description of continuous speech. The history of this development goes back to early 1967 when the automatic recognition of continuous speech (ARCS) project was begun under contract with the United States Air Force [1]. Four continuous, one-year studies were conducted at a low level at IBM in Research Triangle Park, NC. While the basic structure of the MAP approach was established during this period [2]-[4], a number of important aspects for a general system were treated only lightly, due to contractual requirements. In 1972, this project was transferred to IBM Research in Yorktown Heights, NY, where it was expanded. The goal of the current effort is automatic translation of high-quality continuous speech signals into standard orthography. In addition, the current effort is split equally into two parts, one dealing with acoustic-to-phonetic translation and the other with phonetic to standard orthographic translation.

Manuscript received April 28, 1976; revised December 15, 1976.

The authors are with the Department of Computer Sciences, IBM Thomas J. Watson Research Center, Yorktown Heights, NY 10598.

Since 1973, two versions of MAP have been completed as part of a continuing evolutionary process. It has become clear that even though constraints are imposed which are intended to simplify the problem—that is, limiting to a single, well-known talker in a high-fidelity environment—the level of difficulty is still very high. It is in cognizance of this fact that the authors have selected an evolutionary, rather than revolutionary approach to the solution of the problem. This implies whole-system consideration in the solution to the various subproblems and the conceptualization of any one stage. It is to be stressed that this effort has been directed toward the realization of a full-English (unrestricted vocabulary, etc.) acoustic-to-phonetic translation system. Hence, the performance data presented herein are based upon large, unconstrained texts, whereas MAP's use as a data source for linguistic processing has been exclusively on constrained text [5].

It will be the purpose of the present paper to describe the overall system structure of MAP-1976, and, more specifically, to relate some of the concepts involved in the several stages of the system.

II. Overall System Structure

Fig. 1 shows the major processing stages of MAP-1976. This basic structure is the same as that reported in [3], [4], and [6]. Virtually every block, however, has been extensively modified a number of times since [6] was written. While the current implementation will be described, experimentation is in progress which not only will alter many of the algorithms within the blocks, but if successful, will modify the system structure itself; the current idea is shown in Fig. 2.

Reprinted from *IEEE Trans. Acoust., Speech, and Signal Process.*, vol. ASSP-25, pp. 367–379, Oct. 1977.

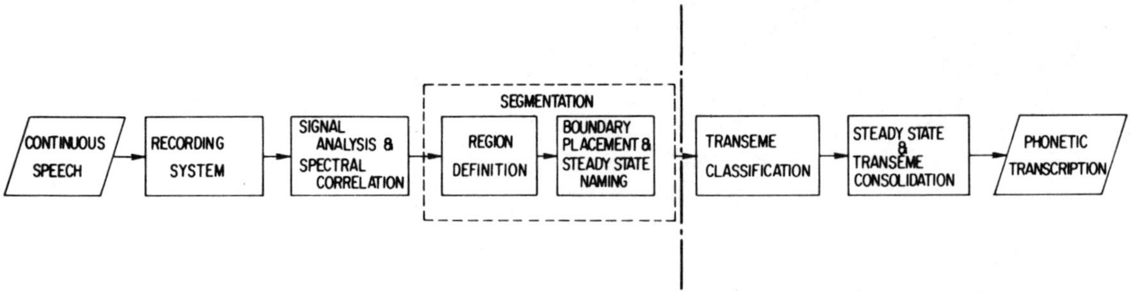

Fig. 1. Block diagram of MAP-1976.

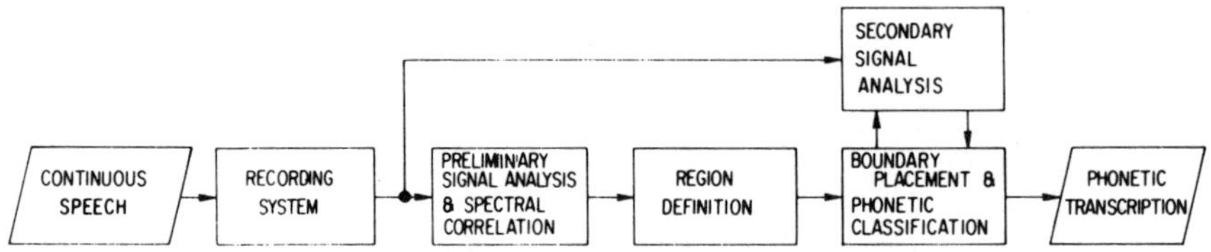

Fig. 2. Future version of MAP.

The acoustic signal for MAP-1976 is recorded directly onto digital tape using a sophisticated, high-fidelity system in which an IBM 1800 process-control computer simultaneously sends the digitized signal to a channel and prompts the speaker with text via a CRT. The signal is sampled at 20 kHz and quantized to 15 bits [6]. The tape is used as input to the rest of the MAP. Work is in progress which will provide for direct speech input to MAP and, therefore, interactive processing.

MAP-1976 uses a recognition-then-segmentation strategy in order to locate phonemic states. This is accomplished by first performing a spectral classification operation. These preliminary classifications are used, along with temporal, spectral change, and overall-energy information to identify candidate phoneme regions. These regions are then evaluated by the boundary placement and steady-state naming operation. Accepted regions are, where possible, phonetically labeled and an exact boundary is placed at the least transitional point in the region.

Unfortunately, not all states in speech can be labeled on the basis of steady-state information alone; some form of dynamic-event classification must be performed. In MAP-1976, the dynamic segment to be classified corresponds to the transition from one relative steady state to the next in time, and is called a *transeme.* It is also necessary to consolidate all classification information into a single phonemic estimate.

III. Signal Analysis and Spectral Correlation

In the analysis of speech signals for purposes of recognition, a number of decisions have been made. First, a frequency domain representation was selected because it offers a familiar form for interactive interpretation and affords the possibility of considerable data reduction, i.e., all phase information and much of the high-resolution magnitude information is not generally required for recognition. Also, it is convenient to compensate for deleterious low-frequency ambient effects in a frequency-domain representation. Second, nonpitch-synchronous (asynchronous) processing was selected because, at the outset, adequate synchronous processing was not in hand, and the need for such processing for recognition had not been demonstrated. Third, discrete Fourier transform (DFT) processing was selected after it was learned that analog hardware filterbank analysis, incorporating ALC, demonstrated inaccuracies when tracking rapidly changing events, and that an LPC analysis, because it was based upon an all-pole model, also had fundamental inaccuracies and was expensive [6].

The signal processor used is essentially that described in [7]. The parameter settings for this processor are selected for a best tradeoff between event representation and inaccuracies due to asynchronous processing. (The default settings in [7] are used.)

Recent experience with MAP-1976 has shown that, in fact, there are occasions in which a synchronous analysis is required. While this would improve nearly all spectral representations due to the fact that cepstral smoothing is no longer required, probably less than five percent of the phonemic events of interest would be substantially affected. Some preliminary work has been conducted into the development of an event-synchronous signal processing approach [8]. It is anticipated that event-synchronous processing will be incorporated into MAP at such time as this form of error represents a real block to further progress.

Using a fast Fourier transform (FFT) process on a fast, general purpose computer (IBM 360/91), a ratio of CPU time to speech time of 5:1 has been achieved. Recently, the new DFT algorithm due to Winograd [9] has been applied. This is the first system to incorporate the new technique. It reduces processing time to 3:1.

Following spectral analysis, each spectrum is compared against each of a carefully selected set of 33 steady-state spectral prototypes. There are several critical requirements for the spectral classification method. First, it must be *accurate*, i.e., during events which are definable as "steady state" relative to the set of classes being employed (the phonemes), the output must agree with the "correct" class. Second, the method must be *stable*, i.e., during these "steady states" the output must be unchanging. Third, the method must be *efficient*, both in its trainability and in its use. Finally, the method should be relatively *insensitive* to the expected within-event variation, e.g., overall-amplitude changes.

In our experience, methods which involve complex pattern

representation and classification fail to strike an acceptable tradeoff between efficiency and accuracy. In particular, the difficulty of the training problem grows rapidly as a function of pattern complexity. In fact, the amount of training data required for adding second-order statistics to a spherical pattern description rises dramatically in that all expected variations of each phoneme must be *appropriately* sampled. Since it is well known that for many phonemic events this variation is very large, the sampling problem is considerable.

Given a set of prototype classes, the experiments used to select the current spectral similarity algorithm are described in [10]. This algorithm has the following properties:

1) Power spectra data are piecewise-linearly reduced to a 40-point representation; 100 Hz per point from 0 to 3000 Hz and 500 Hz per point to 8000 Hz.

2) A minimum distance algorithm utilizing a linear mean (over the power spectrum) correction factor is used. A prototype and candidate whose means are close have essentially full mean compensation, while those with greater mean differences are compensated less.

The results from [10] show that the selected algorithm correctly classifies spectra (at the steady-state level) 64.7 percent of the time, and 95 percent of the time the correct prototype is among the top five.

A major factor in our recognition-then-segmentation approach is the selection of an "appropriate" set of states to be used as prototypes. A substantial amount of informal experimentation has indicated the following:

1) *Stops*—The voiced stops have formant information which allows them to be identified as a class and individually one from the others. Spectrally, voiceless stops appear as silence. Thus, a single prototype characterizes the three voiceless stops and silence.

2) *Aspirations*—Sufficient variation exists for each of the several stop aspirations to disallow discrimination among them as steady states. However, as a group, they are separable from other events.

3) *Aspirants*—A single prototype is included to characterize the essentially voiceless aspirant. The inclusion of a voiced cognate, however, causes much confusion with various vocalics, and, therefore, no voiced aspirant is in the set.

4) *Fricatives*—All of the major fricatives are included.

5) *Nasals*—The three major general American nasals are included. The addition of variants of these three leads to increased error.

6) *Flaps*—Flaps effectively have no steady state and are therefore not included.

7) *Glides*—The bilabial, palatal, lateral, and retroflex glides are included. However, the so-called "dark-l", "nonretroflexed r", etc., have been tried, but were unsuccessful.

8) *Vowels*—Ten major classes are discriminated. A more complete set tends to increase instability and hence has been rejected.

9) *Diphthongs*—Only two "diphthongs" are included for steady-state treatment. These are the so-called vocalic diphthongs [e, o].

In all cases, the final criterion by which the acceptability of some prototype set is evaluated is the degree to which the component classes contribute to consequent segmentation accuracy.

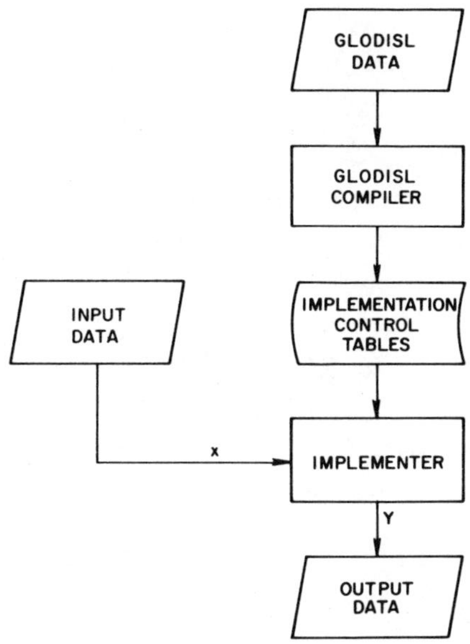

Fig. 3. Block diagram of GLODIS.

IV. Segmentation

In MAP-1976, segmentation consists of two major processes. First, regions corresponding to phonemic "states" are identified. Second, these regions are evaluated for validity, and, if accepted, boundaries are placed within them and a steady-state name assigned; if rejected, they are eliminated; in some cases, more boundaries are placed in a single region if evaluation indicates that a boundary has been missed.

A. Region Definition

A system has been developed for assembly and application of essentially heuristic rules for parsing the speech continuum into segmental regions. This sytem, called the General Language Operated Decision Implementation System (GLODIS), has been described in sufficient detail for replication in [11]. Fig. 3 shows the overall flow of GLODIS. Rules are defined in a special-purpose language called GLODISL. These are in turn compiled into machine readable tables which control the implementer. A block of speech data from previous stages, of about five seconds in length, serves as input to the implementer. The rules are applied sequentially to the whole block of data until the rule-set is exhausted.

In contrast to most systems, GLODIS is designed to allow great flexibility and convenience in rule generation and application. In no case is a rule "hard-wired," even in a programming sense. As a result, several different complex sets of rules have been investigated without modification to the GLODIS system itself.

Experience has shown that region identification by rule should be an hierarchical process. First in this hierarchy is the identification of stable, uncomplicated regions such as silence and the closures of voiceless stops on the basis of rules having to do with overall energy. Then, stop context is used to locate their associated aspirations. Spectral similarity evidence of aspiration is required for acceptance of these regions as aspirates. A similar set of rules is applied for voiced-stop/aspiration identification, using spectral similarity information rather than amplitude for the identification of the closure region. Similarly, other "easily" identifiable regions are found using spec-

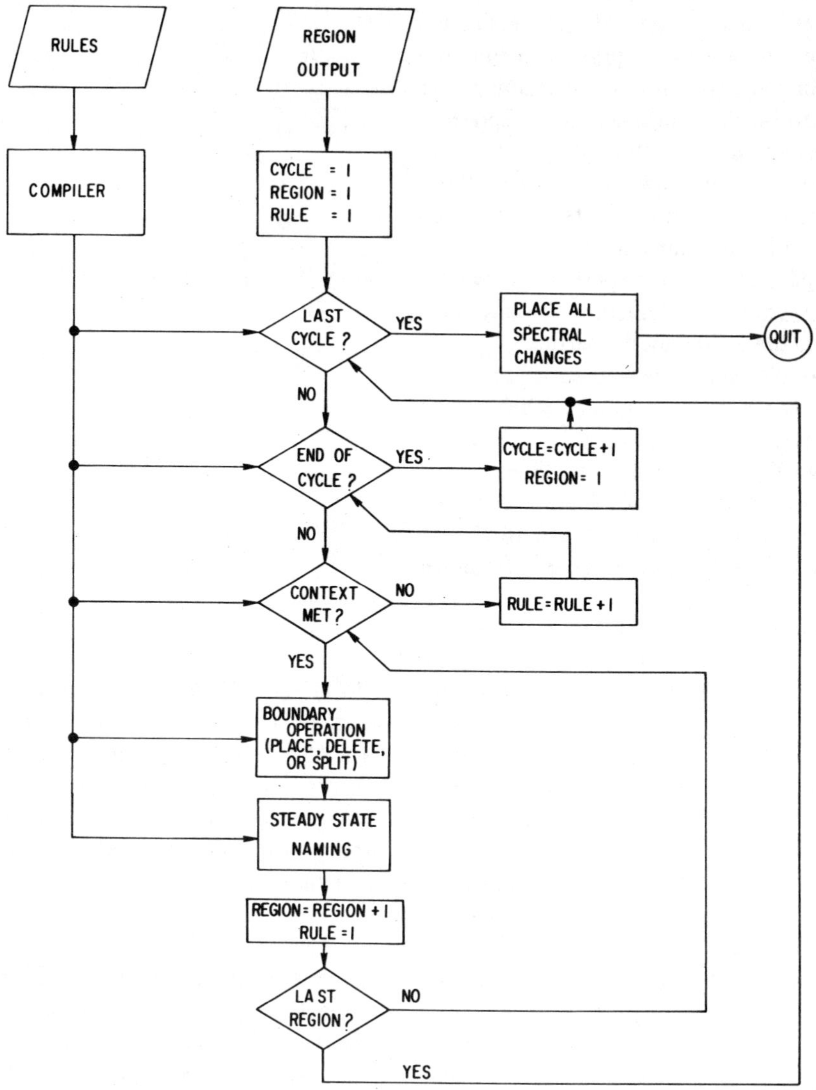

Fig. 4. Flow diagram of boundary placement and naming processor.

tral similarity and amplitude; these include fricatives, nasals, some vowels, some glides, and some flap-like events.

The basic principle of hierarchical segmentation is that the difficult events are basically context dependent, and are thus deferred until the context is provided by the earlier identification of events which are less dependent upon context. For example, one current rule in MAP-1976 tests an unidentified region, following a stop and preceding a vowel, for the presence of glide-related spectral similarity information. This relatively simple contextual rule serves, in many cases, to identify the second member of a stop-glide consonantal complex. There are also even more complicated, multistep, context dependent rules for the identification of diphthongs, vocalic on-glides and off-glides, assimilated aspirates, affricates, and heavily nasalized vowels.

MAP-1976 incorporates 72 rules consisting of 169 separate decision steps. These were developed interactively, as is indicated in Section VIII. It should be noted that evaluation, as it currently exists [11], [12], can be carried out only after the boundary insertion process, and thus, the development of the above rules included the parallel development of boundary placement operations.

B. Boundary Placement and Steady-State Classification

The final part of the segmentation process evaluates defined regions and accepts, rejects, or splits them. Accepted boundaries are placed within their respective regions and given a steady-state name. The last operation of this processor is the determination of points of maximal spectral change between steady states.

This processor also uses an operating system approach; it reads a special-purpose language and applies a compiler to develop control tables for the implementation stages as is shown in Fig. 4. The implementer has many features which are similar to those of the previous stage. However, the philosophy of rule application is somewhat different. Rather than the sequential application of all rules to all input data, here, the satisfaction of a particular rule terminates rule application for any "cycle" (or defined group of rules).

Under normal conditions, the task of this stage of processing is to place a boundary at the "most steady-state" point within a region and assign a steady-state name, usually on the basis of spectral similarity information. However, since region definition can be errorful, use is made of a deeper level of context to evaluate the validity of certain regions. To this end, a multicycle approach has been developed. Each cycle consists of a set of rules to be applied to the whole block of data. The first cycle simply evaluates, places, and names on the basis of input information. Subsequent cycles, however, may also use the results from previous cycles in addition to the input information. The context depth is also increased relative to the region definition stage. In that stage, environmental checking is limited to the immediate neighbors of a candidate region, while, here, environmental checking can be conducted over the four nearest neighbors to the candidate.

During the first cycle, silences are discriminated from unvoiced stops by applying a length criterion. Also, long steady-state regions may be split on the basis of identity and length. Nearly all other regions are accepted and named via spectral similarity. They are placed in a fashion appropriate to the class involved by using amplitude and/or spectral change functions. There are presently 29 rules involved in the first cycle.

The second cycle evaluates the acceptance, placement, and naming decisions using the context of the results from cycle one. Thus, zero-stress vowels are renamed, if they are of a given length and have an interconsonantal environment. Also, certain rapid closures are forced to a stop-flap if they are followed by stop-aspiration; palatal fricatives are changed to affricates; diphthong naming is made consistent; retroflexed vocalics are changed to glides; and on- and off-glide doublings are eliminated. These and several similar rules comprise the 35 rules of cycle two.

The third and final cycle in MAP-1976 is concerned with a final standardization of the parsed string. If, after two cycles of evaluation, two adjacent, short, same-name vowels have been accepted, then one is eliminated. Also, certain tentative regions which have not been confirmed, are rejected. Only four rules comprise cycle three.

V. History of the Transeme

It is well known that many phonemic events in speech are not uniquely describable in terms of their "steady-state" properties alone. For example, the voiceless stops are, in terms of their closures only, identical. This makes it necessary to inspect some type of transitional information for discrimination among these kinds of events.

The transeme, a recognition concept, had its origin in the early work on ARCS in 1967 [1].[1] This type of segment was based on work with the dyad [13] and subsequent work with the diphone [14]. Both of the latter were addressing the speech synthesis problem. It was thought that even though the quality of synthetic speech generated by dyad and/or diphone assembly was clearly synthetic, the intelligibility achieved indicated that a dyadic segment might be usable for speech recognition.

The transeme has been used as the dynamic-event unit during the entire evolution of MAP. However, a number of different system configurations, each using the transeme, have been implemented and investigated. For purposes of exposition, any transemic system can be described in terms of four major components. First, since various same-name transemes can, in their production, vary in duration, it is convenient to time-normalize all the tokens into a standard duration. Second, it is necessary to establish a method of encoding for purposes of event representation. Third, a classification method must be selected in order to determine the transemic class to which some unknown segment belongs. Finally, a method by which a set of prototypes will be developed must be established. These four components are illustrated in their relationships to an overall system in Fig. 5.

Table I is a concise presentation of the various methods which have been employed with regard to the four major components mentioned above. It can be seen that a number of significant changes were made between ARCS and the first complete version of MAP. These were motivated by the following:

1) It was desirable to make transeme classification as independent as possible from steady-state classification. For example, many of the binary encoding features of ARCS were based upon steady-state classification.

2) A more data-based time normalization seemed appropriate.

3) While ARCS performance seemed promising, it was felt that significant improvement would necessitate basic changes in the transeme operation.

4) Since the system had to be reimplemented as a result of a computer change, it was a convenient time to incorporate new concepts.

As was the case for ARCS, the first version of MAP proved to serve as a useful acoustic-to-phonetic transcriber in the context of a full recognition system utilizing a 250-word, finite-state grammar [5]. However, careful analysis of MAP performance indicated that considerable improvement would be required for more complex, less constrained input. Thus, MAP-1976 was developed, and it included a substantially different transeme system.

VI. MAP-1976 Transeme System

A. Training

The training procedures (prototype derivation) for transemes in MAP-1976 were considerably more complex than in preceding systems. As is shown by Table I, in previous systems, prototypes were derived by simply averaging (features in ARCS and spectral energies in MAP-1974) over all same-name tokens in a body of experimenter-transcribed text. Thus, *any* transcriber error was reflected in the final prototype representation, particularly where the number of tokens was small. The prototype set in ARCS was limited to those which could

[1] A *transeme* is defined as the dynamic, transitional region existing between successive, phonemic relative steady states with representation of the preceding steady state at its onset, and of the steady state following it at its coda.

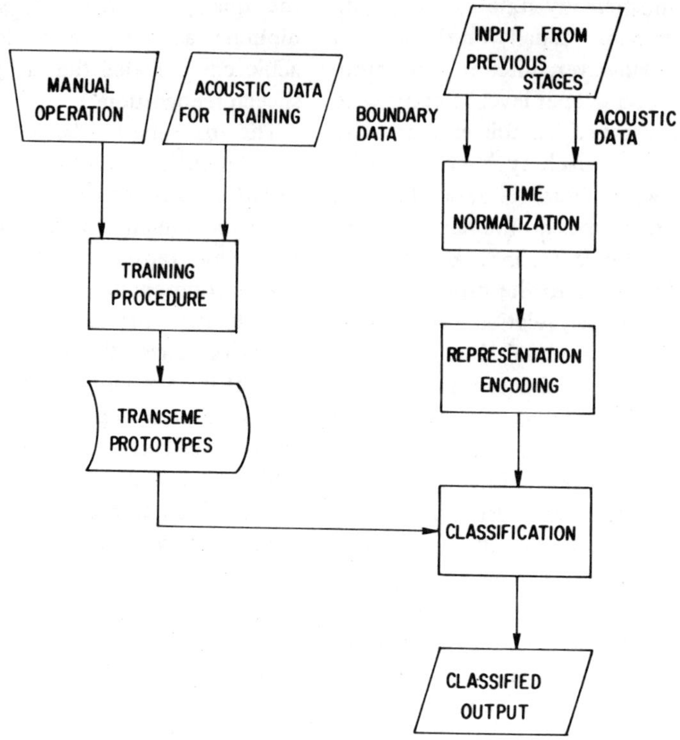

Fig. 5. Transeme classification system.

TABLE I
FEATURES OF TRANSEMIC CLASSIFICATION SYSTEMS

	Time Normalization	Representation Encoding	Classification	Training
ARCS	Heuristic, 11-Element Direct Mapping	200 Binary Features based on spectral energy & previous processing	Non-parametric perceptron method [8] / parametric minimum distance from mean	Token Averaging
MAP-1974	Functional 11-Element Mapping via Spectral Change Function	400 point normalized spectral image (16 bits/point)	15 point primary test: Direction Cosine / Sequential Similarity Detection [15]	Token Averaging
MAP-1976	Heuristic 7-Element Direct Mapping	210 point Normalized Spectral Image (8 bits/point / 210 point peak Valley image (4 bits/point)	Steady-State Limited Minimum distance from mean / Steady-State Limited Minimum absolute value distance	**Canonical Prototype Selection**

occur in the 250-word, finite-state language being used—approximately 600 classes. In MAP, however, there were no restrictions placed on the training set, the aim being representation for unconstrained English. MAP-1974 was trained on 10 min of unconstrained speech [11], which resulted in 1198 prototype classes. Table II shows the distribution of token representation in this set of prototypes. It is apparent that the effect of transcriber error could be profound in a substantial portion of these classes. Also, there was no post-transcription editing performed.

In an attempt to preclude this potential error, it was decided that single-token, canonical representations would be employed in MAP-1976. Since the distributional properties of within-class variation were not used, the use of a single, carefully selected token as a prototype seemed more appropriate than an edited "average" representation.

The training procedure for MAP-1976 is shown in Fig. 6. Here, some 18 min of unconstrained, rapid (16–20 phonemes per second in most parts), continuous speech was used for training. The training yields 1117 prototype classes. Fig. 7 shows the rate of acceptable prototype accumulation as a function of training-speech duration. It can be seen that the rate of accumulation beyond 9 min hardly justifies the use of manually transcribed, unconstrained text for additional train-

TABLE II
MAP-1974 PER-CLASS TOKEN DISTRIBUTION

No. Tokens	No. Classes
1	324
2	167
3	122
4	84
5	62
> 5	439

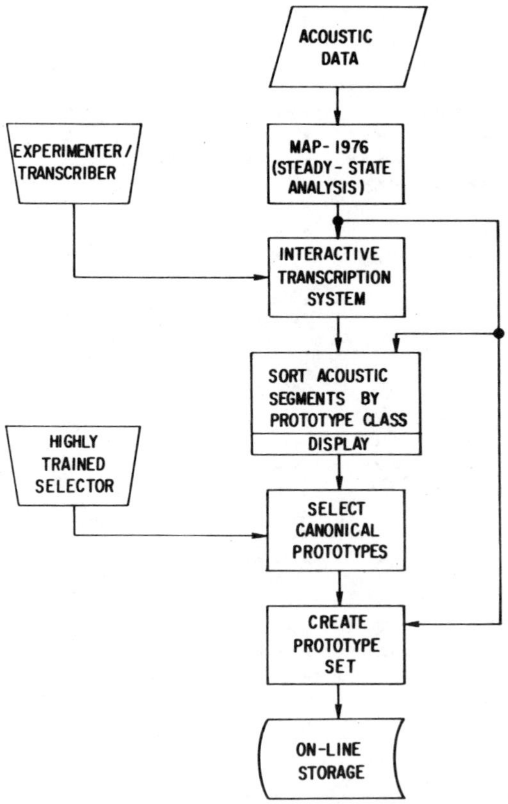

Fig. 6. MAP-1976 transeme training paradigm.

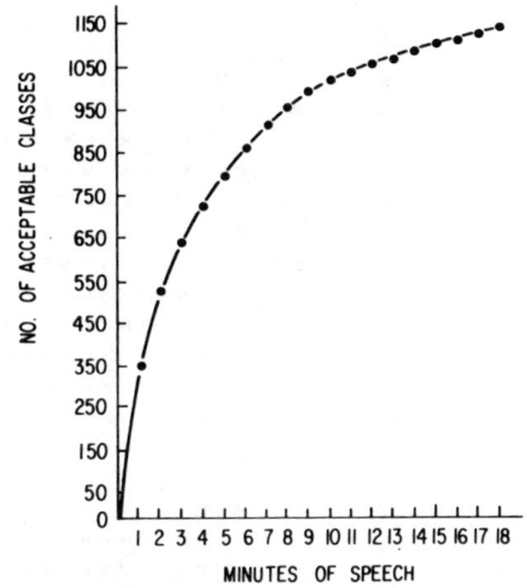

Fig. 7. Rate of acceptable-prototype accumulation as a function of training-speech duration.

ing. This would suggest that "holes" be filled by specially designed text.

An incidence matrix, showing the transemes included in MAP-1976, is given in Fig. 8. The first phonemic member of the transeme appears on the ordinate and the second on the abscissa. The alphabet is alphaphonetic, and, where possible, suggests the sound being described. In general, the second character of the alphaphonetic name is defined as follows:

X—null
Q—release or aspiration
F—flapped.

It is worthwhile stating that the transeme training process is a *very* arduous, long-term task and represents one of the unattractive aspects of this work. A primary concern in future work will be with automatic alternatives.

B. Time Normalization

As was shown in Table I, earlier systems utilized an 11-spectrum normalization. This number was based on the observation that the transemes averaged about 8/s for the 250-word vocabulary. However, for less structured text, it has been observed that the average intersteady-state duration was between 70 and 80 ms, and thus, a 7-spectrum normalized representation was selected for MAP-1976. The data are presented in Fig. 9.

Some detailed investigation of the functional time normalization of MAP-1974 indicated that, in many cases, spectral-change functions, of which several were tried, become unreliable for time normalization. For example, noise which is impossible to extract can effect large spectral-change magnitudes.

The heuristic algorithm used is quite straightforward; the first and seventh spectra are fixed to the preceding and following boundaries as determined by the previous boundary insertions. The fourth is fixed at the maximal change point; the remaining four are mapped directly or interpolated.

C. Representation Encoding

Earlier studies concerned with spectral correlation have indicated that a piecewise-linear, quantized, 30- to 40-point spectral representation is appropriate for phonemic classification [10]. A 30-point representation is used here to save on storage. A feature representation, such as the one used in ARCS, was not attempted in keeping with the desirability for independence from previous stages in the transemic representation itself. Two energy quantizations have been investigated. The first is straight 8-bit pulse-code modulation (PCM). The second is more complex and involves conversion from 8-bit PCM into a 4-bit peak/valley representation, where relative peak/valley height/depth is scaled. Each of these is currently available in MAP-1976.

D. Classification

If a transemic classification procedure is allowed to calculate full distance measures for each of the 1117 prototypes against every incoming candidate, the following problems arise:

1) The computation time consumed is prohibitive, even on a very fast computer.
2) Error can distribute itself wildly.
3) Unreasonable comparisons are made.

These facts led to the use of algorithmic, template-matching techniques for limiting the number of operations in MAP-1974

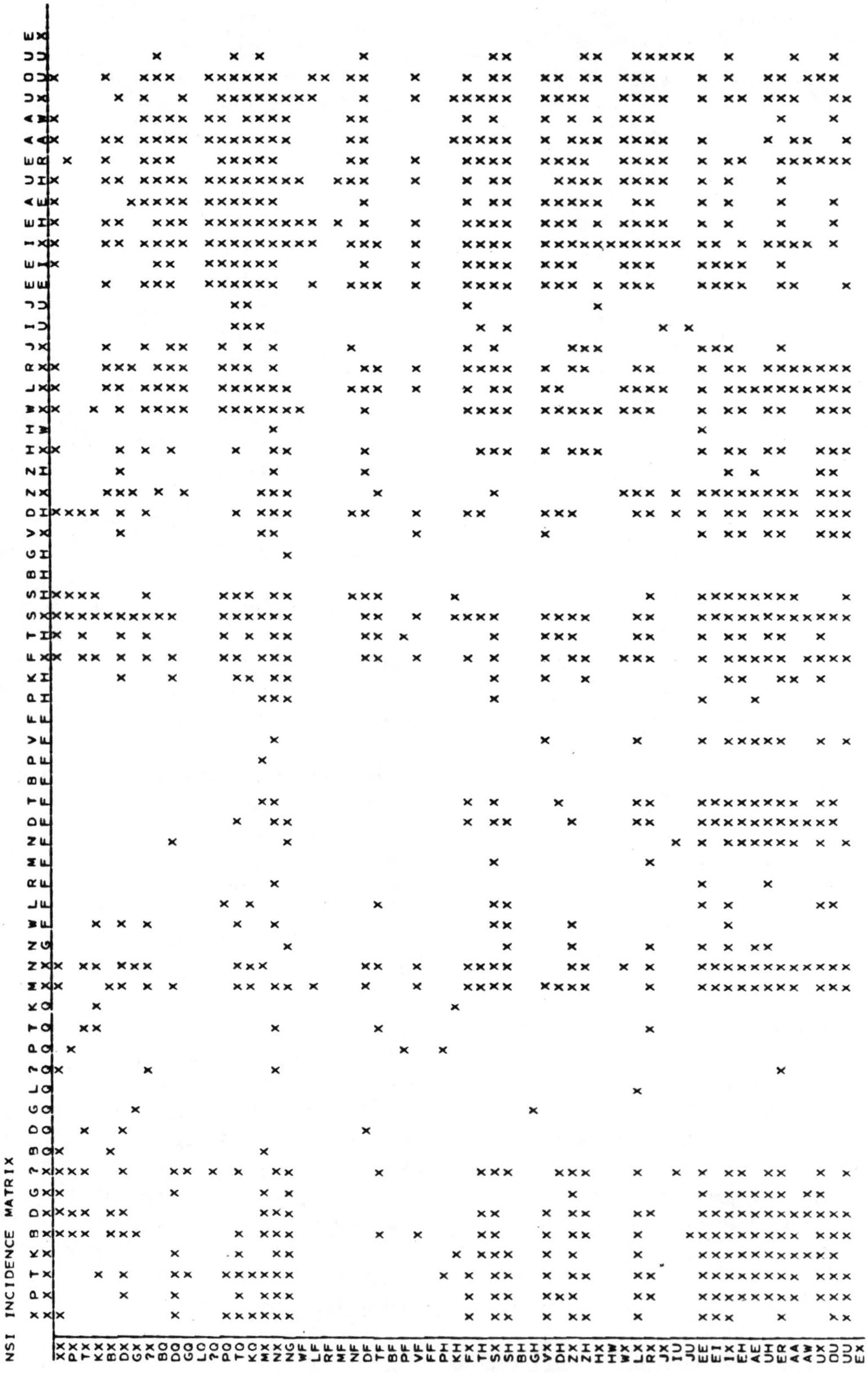

Fig. 8. Transeme incidence matrix.

[15]. While these tended to do their job, some errors, due to abnormal signal conditions, persisted.

A different approach to limiting is used in MAP-1976 which is based on the empirically derived confusion statistics at the steady-state level. Thus, not only is processing time saved, but error is limited so as to be not worse than that of steady-state classification. Fig. 10 shows the confusion-incidence matrix used for the limiting operation. The ordinate contains the steady-state names which may be outputted from the previous stage. The abscissa contains the desired output alphabet confusions. This matrix was derived using an automatic evaluator [12] on 4 min of carefully hand-transcribed text. Thus, a prospective list of prototypes to compare against a candidate is created as follows:

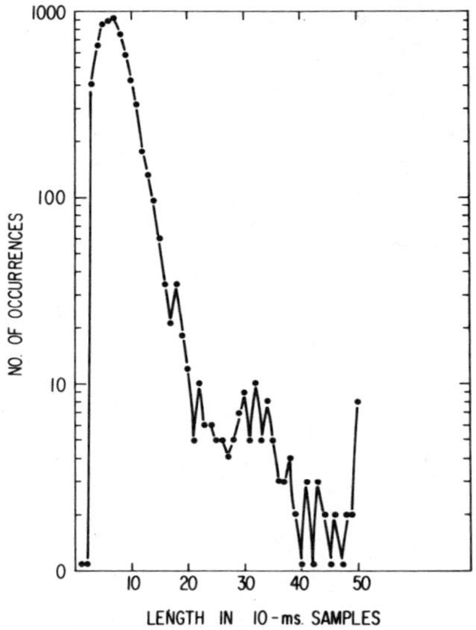

Fig. 9. Unnormalized-transeme duration distribution.

1) Lists of length N and M are created by obtaining from Fig. 10 the confusions of the two respective steady-state names put out by the segmenter.

2) A transemic list of length NM is obtained by a concatenation of each member of the N long list with each member of the M long list.

3) The final list is obtained by trimming the NM length list by the incidence of prototypes as given in Fig. 8.

4) An *a priori* probability is associated with each member of the final transeme list by multiplying the confusion probabilities from the steady-state confusion matrix of Fig. 10 corresponding to the two names making up the transeme.

This procedure reduces the average search to about 36 prototypes per candidate, an average reduction of 31 :1!

The actual measures of similarity used are the usual absolute value or Euclidean distance with or without mean compensation. Due to possible error in spectral-change placement, this similarity may be computed for several normalizations, each having a differently located spectral-change point. Only the maximum similarity is retained.

Finally, a weighted sum is derived from the transemic similarity and the *a priori* probability mentioned above. The ten best transemes are retained for processing by the consolidator.

VII. Consolidator

Perhaps the least amount of *a priori* "speech" knowledge exists relative to the consolidation of steady-state and transemic classification results. Both ARCS and MAP-1974 used completely heuristic, though, to some degree, data-based procedures. In MAP-1976, it was decided to make use of the confusion statistics available from the dynamic-segment classification output via the automatic evaluator.

At the consolidator, each phonemic state has three lists of candidates associated with it; a list of *steady-state* (*SS*) names, a list of *segment final* (*SF*) names derived from the last-half names of the best transemes preceding the state, and a list of *segment initial* (*SI*) names derived from the first-half names of the best transemes following it. The task of the consolidator is to select a final name from these lists.

In the current version, the "best" *SS* name is provided by the boundary selection and naming module. The following heuristic algorithm is used to determine a four-member list of quasi-probabilities for each of *SI* or *SF*, from their respective ten-deep transemic classification data:

1) The ten-deep lists are inspected to determine the first four unique names (in the list of ten, due to the dual nature of the transeme, repetitions of the same state may occur on each side) ($i = 1, 2, 3, 4$), their highest rank (r_i), and their frequency of occurrence in the list (f_i).

2) The scores are computed by

$$S_i = (f_i^{1/2}/r_i) \Big/ \sum_{i=1}^{4} (f_i^{1/2}/r_i). \tag{1}$$

3) The resulting four-member list is rank-ordered by S_i, implying $j(i)$, the new order.

4) A final score is computed using

$$\overline{S}_i = (S_i/j(i)) \Big/ \sum_{i=1}^{4} (S_i/j(i)). \tag{2}$$

These scores $\overline{S}_i$ are taken as probability measures $P(SI_i|SI \text{ data})$ and $P(SF_i|SF \text{ data})$. The output of this heuristic, the highest valued member in each case, is used as input to the automatic evaluator. Confusion matrices are thus derived from which the conditional probabilities $P(a_j|SI_i)$ and $P(a_j|SF_i)$ may be determined (where $a_j\, j \in [1, \text{alphabet length}]$ are the alphabet members). The final estimate is calculated using (3).

$$E(a_j|SI, SF \text{ data}) = \left[\sum_{l=1}^{4} P(a_j|SI_l)P(SI_l|SI \text{ data})\right] \cdot \left[\sum_{l=1}^{4} P(a_j|SF_l)P(SF_l|SF \text{ data})\right] \cdot P^{-1}(a_j). \tag{3}$$

The phonemic estimate is the alphabet member indexed by j where

$$\hat{j} = j \ni \max_{i \leqslant j \leqslant \text{alphabet length}} E(a_j|SI, SF \text{ data}). \tag{4}$$

Several assumptions have been made here. First, since the steady-state name was used to limit the inspection set for dynamic classification, the influence of the steady-state name on the transemic results is already very heavy. Thus, the steady-state name does not enter explicitly into (3). Also, it is clear that an assumption of *SI*, *SF* independence has been made.

VIII. Performance

A. Segmentation and Steady-State Classification

The stages described in this paper are all fully operational and have been used extensively as part of a full continuous speech recognition system. Results on the full system performance (for the immediate predecessor to MAP-1976) are given in [11] and [5]. The stages described herein have been evaluated against a careful phonetic transcription using an automatic system [12]. In light of their complexity, these stages perform rather efficiently. On an IBM 360/91, the ratio of CPU time to speech time for the various modules is as follows:

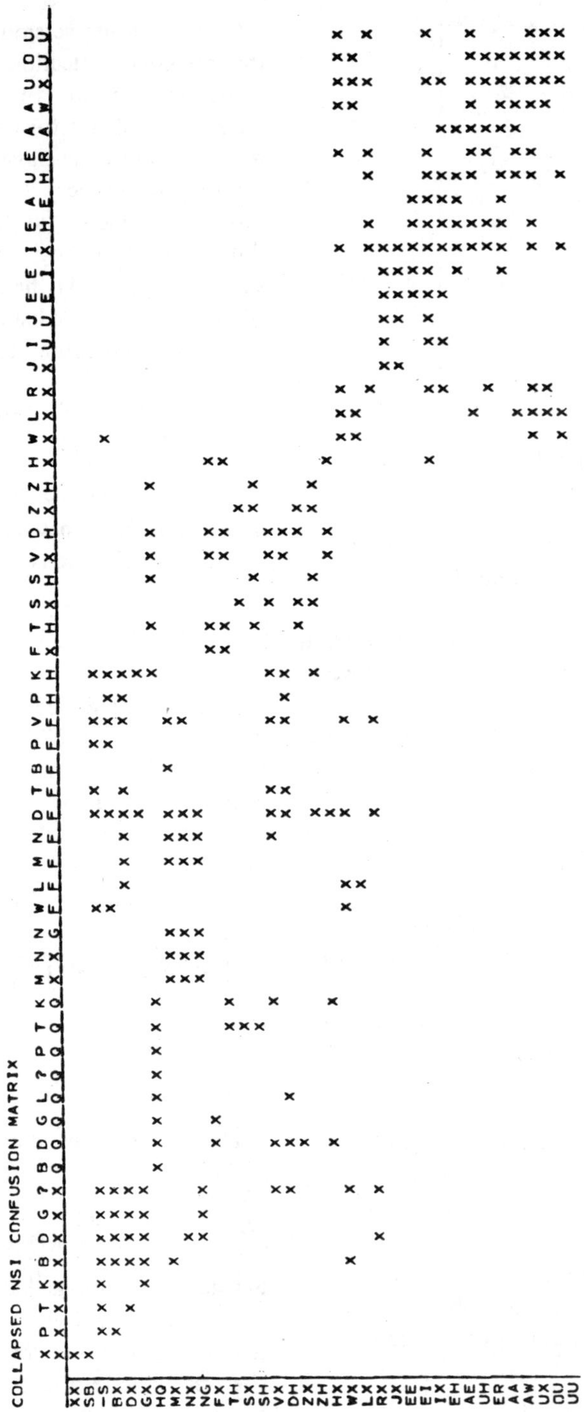

Fig. 10. Confusion–incidence matrix for limitation transeme classification.

Signal analysis	3:1
Spectral similarity	2:1
Region definition	2:1
Boundary placement	1:1.

The performance of the system described here is listed in Table III. It should be noted that the rules for the last two stages were first designed by observing the performance over the first minute. Then, after performance on the first minute was "acceptable," the first 2 min were used to check and augment the rules. The second 2 min of the 4 were not used for rule design. After each optimization stage, an automatic evaluation was conducted. Table II shows these results as well as a derived result from the 2 and 4 min evaluations, to show performance on the last 2 min (test data). These derived results are meant only to be indicative of a formal performance test.

The authors feel that a large portion of the remaining error is due to the inappropriateness of the data description given by the asynchronous signal analysis. The text of the test material is completely unconstrained and purposefully difficult, al-

TABLE III
SEGMENTATION PERFORMANCE

	First Minute	First 2 Minutes	First 4 Minutes	Last 2 Minutes
# of Boundaries	763	1504	3006	1507
% Missed	4.81	4.31	5.25	6.19
% Extra	2.75	3.69	4.88	6.07
Steady-State (Naming Accuracy %)	67.9	63.2	62.4	61.6
Within-Class (Naming Accuracy %)	88.6	87.5	86.3	85.1

TABLE IV
MAP-1976 OVERALL PERFORMANCE

	% Correct			
	# Tokens	Name	# Tokens	Class
SS	1998	57.9	2514	90.3
SI	2628	60.1	2628	80.2
SF	2644	60.3	2644	80.5
Final	2641	63.3	2641	83.2

TABLE V
MAP-1976 PERFORMANCE, BY PHONEME CLASS AND BY PHONEME

Class	Number of Tokens	% Correct	
		Name	Class
Silence	71	91.5	91.5
Unvoiced Stops	178	50.6	91.0
Voiced Stops	192	66.7	79.7
Voiced Aspirations	123	39.0	47.2
Unvoiced Aspirations	163	62.0	87.7
Nasals	215	83.7	98.6
Flaps	128	14.1	18.0
Voiced Fricatives	158	58.0	63.3
Unvoiced Fricatives	251	83.7	89.6
Aspirants	16	63.0	63.0
Glides	194	67.5	72.7
Vowels	952	81.2	95.3

though tightly controlled recording conditions are imposed. It is anticipated that any change in the experimental conditions would lead to increased error. The imposition of textual constraints would tend to reduce it.

B. Final Classification

The first set of performance results are based upon 4 min of unconstrained continuous speech as produced by a single, adult male speaker. These 4 min are among the 18 min of training data from which the canonical transemic prototypes were obtained. Also, the first 2 min of this segment were used extensively to train the segmenter. In addition, consolidator statistics were derived using this referent transcription. Thus, these results are considered only indicative of the expected performance. More extensive experiments using totally unrelated speech data are given later in this section.

It is to be noted in Table IV that the classification alphabet for *SS* is different from that for *SI*, *SF*, and the final output. Since it is not reasonable to expect individual classification of stop aspirations, voiceless stops, and flapped events on a steady-state basis, these were not included in the evaluation of steady-state naming performance. However, in the class performance, the voiced and unvoiced stop aspirations were merged into a single class and voiced versus voiceless stop discrimination was retained. On the other hand, all transemic and final evaluation maintained the individual identities of all names and classes.

Table V shows MAP-1976 performance at the level of specific-phoneme and phoneme-class accuracy. These and previous [1]-[4], [11] results indicate that for some classes of events, particularly those involving very rapid articulatory phenomena, such as some stops and stop aspirations, flaps and some voiced fricatives, a transemic-segment classification may not include enough phonetic context, especially under the constraints of asynchronous signal processing [8] and the non-feature-extracting, essentially straightforward, pattern classification procedures being utilized in MAP-1976. Therefore, work is in progress with the aim of incorporating other, more appropriate techniques involving synchronous signal processing, an adaptive level of segmentation, and more sophisticated data representation and classification methods.

Map performance was also measured on a second set of data (Tables VI and VII). These were based on a "New Raleigh" sentence model described in [5]. Table VI shows final segmentation and classification performance. Table VII presents final classification confusion and segmentation error at a fine-class level. It is to be stressed that these data are not training data, in any sense other than that the same talker was involved. In addition, more than one year separated the recording of these data and that of the training data.

IX. SUMMARY

In this paper, work begun in 1967 which has involved the evolution of a system for automatic phonemic transcription of continuous speech has been described. An attempt has been made to concentrate on those aspects which are conceptual, rather than those specific to implementation. Some results from the current working system have been presented.

Performance results have indicated the need for event-synchronous signal analysis, more automatic methods for event-prototype training, an event-dependent, supraphonemic level of classification, and better data representation and classification methods. Work is continuing which is aimed toward satisfying these needs.

TABLE VI
OVERALL PERFORMANCE FOR 36 "NEW RALEIGH" SENTENCES
(TOTAL PHONEMES = T = 1516)

Type	Error Ratio	%	Definition
SUBSTITUTION	440/1406	31.0	[S/(T-I]
. In Class	277/1406	19.0	
. Out of Class	163/1406	12.0	
TOTAL SEG ERROR	177/1516	11.7	[(I+D)/T]
. Insertion (I)	110/1516	7.2	[I/T]
. Deletion (D)	67/1473	4.6	[D/(T+(D-I))]

TABLE VII
OVERALL FINE CLASS CONFUSION BASED UPON 36 "NEW RALEIGH" SENTENCES

Input (Truth)	CLASS CONFUSION (%) Output (Actual)												Seg. Err.	
	SIL	UVS	VS	FL	UVA	VA	UVF	VF	A	N	G	V	INS	DEL
Silence	100												00	00
Unvoiced Stop		87	12				01						01	05
Voiced Stop		05	86	05	03						01		23	02
Flap		03	29	44			06	01		11	06		13	10
Unvoiced Aspirate			01		82	03	02	12					03	01
Voiced Aspirate					06	67	04	22					02	00
Unvoiced Aspirate							97	03					02	01
Voiced Fricative			01		05	04	05	85					10	06
Aspirant									100				00	00
Nasal			007	007						97		02	04	05
Glide											63	37	15	26
Vowel			004					006	002	004	04	94	08	03

REFERENCES

[1] C. C. Tappert, N. R. Dixon, D. H. Beetle, and W. D. Chapman, "A dynamic segment approach to the recognition of continuous speech: An exploratory program," Rome Air Dev. Cen., Rome, NY, Tech. Rep. TR-68-177, 1968.

[2] —, "The use of dynamic segments in the automatic recognition of continuous speech," Rome Air Dev. Cen., Rome, NY, Tech. Rep. TR-70-22, 1970.

[3] C. C. Tappert, N. R. Dixon, A. S. Rabinowitz, and W. D. Chapman, "Automatic recognition of continuous speech utilizing dynamic segmentation, dual classification, sequential decoding and error recovery," Rome Air Dev. Cen., Rome, NY, Tech. Rep. TR-71-146, 1971.

[4] N. R. Dixon and C. C. Tappert, "Intermediate performance evaluation of a multi-stage system for automatic recognition of continuous speech," Rome Air Dev. Cen., Rome, NY, Tech. Rep. TR-73-16, 1973.

[5] L. R. Bahl *et al.*, "Preliminary results on the performance of a system for the automatic recognition of continuous speech," in *1976 Int. Conf. Acoustics, Speech, and Signal Processing*, 1976, pp. 425-429.

[6] H. F. Silverman and N. R. Dixon, "A parametrically-controlled spectral analysis system for speech," *IEEE Trans. Acoust., Speech, Signal Processing*, vol. ASSP-22, pp. 362-381, Oct. 1974.

[7] N. R. Dixon and H. F. Silverman, "A description of a parametrically controlled modular structure for speech processing," *IEEE Trans. Acoust., Speech, Signal Processing*, vol. ASSP-23, pp. 87-91, Feb. 1975.

[8] H. F. Silverman and N. R. Dixon, "Transfer-characteristic estimation for speech via multirate evaluation," in *1976 Proc. IEEE EASCON Conf.*, Arlington, VA, Oct. 1975.

[9] S. Winograd, "On computing the discrete Fourier transform," in *Proc. Nat. Acad. Sci.*, Apr. 1976.

[10] H. F. Silverman and N. R. Dixon, "A comparison of several speech-spectra classification methods," *IEEE Trans. Acoust., Speech, Signal Processing*, vol. ASSP-24, pp. 289-295, Aug. 1976.

[11] N. R. Dixon and H. F. Silverman, "A general language-operated decision implementation system (GLODIS): Its application to continuous-speech segmentation," *IEEE Trans. Acoust., Speech, Signal Processing*, vol. ASSP-24, pp. 137-162, Apr. 1976.

[12] H. F. Silverman and N. R. Dixon, "An objective parallel evaluator of segmentation/classification performance for multiple systems," *IEEE Trans. Acoust., Speech, Signal Processing*, vol. ASSP-23, pp. 92-99, Feb. 1975.

[13] E. G. Peterson, W. S. Y. Wang, and E. Sivertsen, "Segmentation techniques in speech synthesis," *J. Acoust. Soc. Amer.*, vol. 30, pp. 739-742, 1953.

[14] N. R. Dixon and H. D. Maxey, "Terminal analog synthesis of continuous speech using the diphone method of segment assem-

bly," *IEEE Trans. Audio Electroacoust.*, vol. AU-16, pp. 40–50, Mar. 1968.

[15] D. I. Barnea and H. F. Silverman, "A class of algorithms for fast digital image registration," *IEEE Trans. Comput.*, vol. C-21, pp. 179–186, Feb. 1972.

[16] N. J. Nilsson, *Learning Machines.* New York: McGraw-Hill, 1965.

Part VI
Continuous Speech: Speech Understanding Systems

A Model and a System for Machine Recognition of Speech

D. RAJ REDDY, LEE D. ERMAN, and RICHARD B. NEELY

Abstract—This paper presents a model for machine recognition of connected speech and the details of a specific implementation of the model, the HEARSAY system. The model consists of a small set of cooperating independent parallel processes that are capable of helping in the decoding of a spoken utterance either individually or collectively. The processes use the "hypothesize-and-test" paradigm. The structure of HEARSAY is illustrated by considering its operation in a particular task situation: voice-chess. The task is to recognize a spoken move in a given board position. Procedures for determination of parameters, segmentation, and phonetic descriptions are outlined. The use of semantic, syntactic, lexical, and phonological sources of knowledge in the generation and verification of hypotheses is described. Preliminary results of recognition of some utterances are given.

Introduction

Most papers on speech recognition conclude by saying that it is necessary to use higher level linguistic cues to obtain acceptable recognition. The terms context, syntax, semantics, and phonological rules are used but attempts to utilize these sources of knowledge have not been successful because of the ill structuredness of these concepts. This paper represents a summary of several years of investigation to formulate an information processing model that would lead to efficient recognition of speech and in which the role of various sources of knowledge would be well defined.

At the 1969 spring meeting of the Acoustical Society, we presented several papers on the structure of a speech recognition system that was used to recognize a list of 500 isolated words and a syntax-directed connected speech-recognition system using a finite state grammar and a 16-word vocabulary (Vicens [37], Reddy [31], Neely [22]). Six amplitude and zero-crossing parameters of the incoming utterance were sampled every 10 ms and segmented. The segments were labeled to specify the phonetic class; the syntax was used for sentence analysis and word boundary determination, and prelearned acoustic and phonetic segmental descriptions of lexical items were used for word recognition.

Manuscript received April 30, 1972. This research was supported in part by the Advanced Research Projects Agency of the Department of Defense under Contract F44620-70-C-0107 and monitored by the Air Force Office of Scientific Research.

D. R. Reddy and L. D. Erman are with the Department of Computer Science, Carnegie-Mellon University, Pittsburgh, Pa. 15213.

R. B. Neely was with the Department of Computer Science, Carnegie-Mellon University, Pittsburgh, Pa. 15213. He is now with the Xerox Palo Alto Research Center, Palo Alto, Calif. 94505.

Several inherent limitations were apparent even as we developed the system. First, the vocabulary had to be reduced to 16 words because of word boundary ambiguity problems. For example, the word "large" had to be changed to "big" because of assimilation of the reduced vowel of "the" into the semivowel /l/ of "large" in the utterance: "Pick up the large block."

Second, we had to overcome the limitations of the syntax-directed methods. One could not blindly parse from left to right; rather, we had to locate anchor points from which parsing could proceed both backwards and forwards. This was necessary to compensate for machine errors in earlier stages and to compensate for the idiosyncrasies in speaker performance such as introduction of spurious words, repetition of words, and inclusion of hmm- and ha-like sounds.

Third, the simple hierarchical structure in which output from one process forms the input to the next was not adequate for the task. Errors introduced in each process tend to have multiplicative effect, i.e., if each of four processes introduced 10 percent errors, the cumulative error would be 34 percent. Further, the lack of feedback and feedforward of the simple hierarchical model meant any errors that got through were uncorrectable. The main virtue of the system was that it was the first demonstrable system to use syntactic and lexical constraints to recognize connected speech sentences (such as: "Pick up the big block at the bottom right corner").

For the past four years the authors have been attempting to develop a model and a system for connected speech recognition that did not suffer from the limitations mentioned previously, and that would serve as a research tool for speech-recognition research over a wide range of tasks. The following sections present the resulting model and an outline of the system implemented on a PDP-10 computer.

The Model

We were interested in developing a system capable of recognition of connected speech from several speakers with graceful error recovery, in close to real time, and easily generalizable to operate in several different task domains. We started with several requirements for the model.

1) Contributions of syntax, semantics, context, and other sources of knowledge towards recognition should be clearly evaluatable. Exactly what and how much does each contribute towards improving the performance of the system?

2) The absence of one or more sources of knowl-

Reprinted from *IEEE Trans. Audio Electroacoust.*, vol. AU-21, pp. 229–238, June 1973.

edge should not have a crippling effect on the performance of the model. That semantic context should not be essential for perception is illustrated by overheard conversations among strangers. That syntactic or phonological context should not be essential is illustrated by conversations among children. That lexical representation is not essential is illustrated by our recognition of new words and nonsense syllables.

3) When more than one source of knowledge is available, interactions between them should lead to a greater improvement in performance than is possible to attain by the use of any subset of sources of knowledge.

4) Since the decoding process is errorful at every stage, the model must permit graceful error recovery.

5) Increases in performance requirements, such as the real time requirement, increase in vocabulary, modifications to the syntax, or changes in semantic interpretation, should not require major reformulation of the model.

The model we have arrived at to satisfy these requirements consists of a small set of cooperating independent processes capable of helping in the decoding process either individually or collectively and using the "hypothesize-and-test" paradigm.

Each of the processes in our model is based on a particular source of knowledge, e.g., syntactic, semantic, or acoustic-phonetic rules. Each process uses its own source of knowledge in conjunction with the present context (i.e., the presently recognized subparts of the utterance) in generating hypotheses about the unrecognized portions of the utterance. This mechanism provides a way for using (much talked about but rarely used) context, syntax, and semantics in the recognition process.

The notion of a set of independent parallel processes, each of which is capable of generation and verification of hypotheses, is needed to satisfy the requirements 1) and 2) mentioned previously. In our model, the absence of a source of knowledge implies deactivating that process, and recognition proceeds (albeit more slowly and with lower accuracy) using the hypotheses generated by the remaining processes. The independence of the processes permits us to deactivate a source of knowledge and measure how and by how much that source of knowledge improves the system.

The need for parallel processes can be derived from the real-time performance requirement. If the system is to ever approach human performance, it must be able to answer trivial questions as soon as they are uttered (some times even before they are completed). This implies that various processes of the system should be able to operate on the incoming data as soon as they are able to do so without waiting for the completion of the whole utterance (as in a simple hierarchic model). The "coroutine" model, in which each process passes control to the next level when a "chunk" is perceived and regains control when a new chunk is needed, would be satisfactory. But this organization can lead to irrevocable loss of data if a higher level process does not return control in time to process new chunks of incoming speech. Thus, there must be at least two parallel processes, one of which is continuously monitoring the input speech and the other proceeding with recognition. This, in addition to requirements 1) and 2), suggests a model with parallel processes.

An important aspect of the model is the nature of cooperation between processes. The implication is that, while each of the processes is independently capable of decoding the incoming utterance, they are also able to cooperate with each other to help recognize the utterance faster and with greater accuracy. Process "A" can guide and/or reduce the hypothesis generation phase of process "B" by temporarily restricting the parts of the lexicon that can be accessed by B, or by restricting the syntax available to process B, and so on. This assumes that process A has additional information that it can effectively use to provide such a restriction. For example, in a given syntactic or semantic situation only a small subset of all the words of a language may appear.

The need for a hypothesize-and-test paradigm arises from 4). The "errorful" nature of speech processing at every stage implies that every source of knowledge has to be brought to bear to resolve ambiguities and errors at every stage of processing. This implies rich connectivity among various processes and involves both feedforward and feedback. The hypothesize-and-test paradigm represents an elegant way of obtaining this cooperation in a uniform manner.

The notion of hypothesize-and-test is not new. It has been used in several artificial intelligence programs (Newell [25]). It is equivalent to analysis-by-synthesis (Halle and Stevens [10]) if the "test" consists of matching the incoming utterance with a synthesized version of the hypothesis generated. In most cases, however, the test is of a much simpler form; for example, it is not necessary to generate the whole formant trajectory when a simpler test of the slope can provide the desired verification. This not only has the effect of reducing the computational effort but also increases the differentiability between phonemically ambiguous words.

Extendability and generalizability of the model is mainly an issue of implementation. It requires that representation of sources of knowledge be separate from and independent of mechanisms that operate on them. One way of achieving this is to represent the knowledge in a form most suitable for modification by the user and have a set of preprocessors that then transform the knowledge into the representation required by the system.

HEARSAY System

HEARSAY is a speech-recognition system that incorporates many of the ideas presented in the previous section and is presently under development at Carnegie-Mellon University. It is not restricted to any particular recognition task. Given the syntax and the vocabulary of a language and the semantics of a task, HEARSAY will attempt recognition of utterances in that language.

Fig. 1 gives an overview of the HEARSAY system. The EAR module accepts speech input, extracts parameters, and performs some preliminary segmentation, feature extraction, and labeling, generating a "partial symbolic utterance description." The recognition overlord (ROVER) controls the recognition process and coordinates the hypothesis generation and verification phases of various cooperating parallel processes. The TASK provides the interface between the task being performed and the speech recognition and generation (SPEAK-EASY) parts of the system. The system overload (SOL) provides the overall control for the system. A more detailed, but earlier, description of the goals and various components of this system are given in Reddy *et al.* [33] and Reddy [32].

Here we will describe the operation of the HEARSAY system by considering a specific task: voice-chess. The task is to recognize a spoken move in a given board position. In any given situation there are generally 20–30 legal moves and several thousand different ways of expressing these moves. The syntax, semantics, and vocabulary of the task are restricted, but the system is designed to be easily generalizable to larger tasks, which was not the case for our earlier systems. Larger syntax (e.g., a subset of English) and vocabularies (1000–5000 words) for a more complex semantic task will make HEARSAY slower and less accurate but are not likely to be crippling.

Fig. 2 shows the recognition process in greater detail. At present, it contains three independent processes: acoustic, syntactic, and semantic. We will give a short description of how these processes cooperate in recognizing "king bishop pawn moves to bishop four." Let us assume that this is a legal move (otherwise, at some stage of processing, the system will reject it as semantically inconsistent).

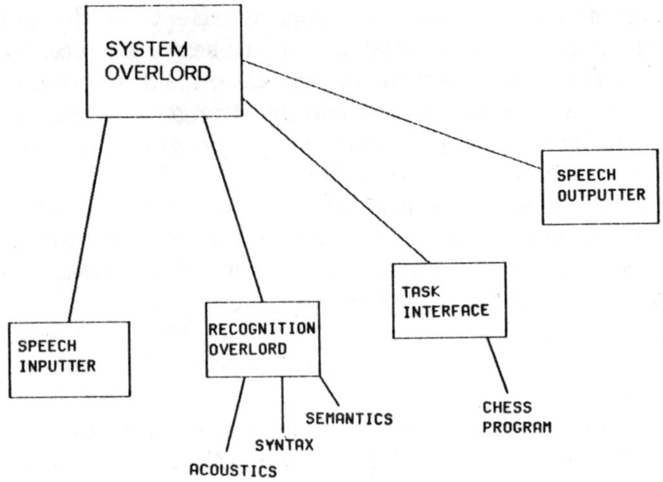

Fig. 1. Overview of the HEARSAY system.

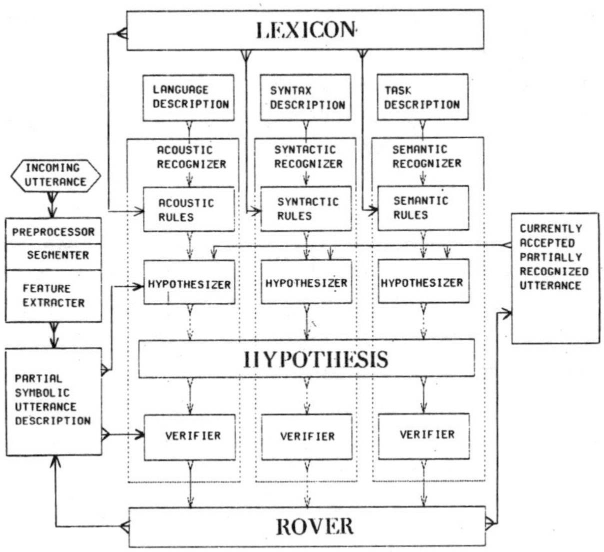

Fig. 2. Detail of the recognition process.

Parametric Level Analysis

The speech from the input device (microphone, telephone, or tape recorder) is passed through five octave bandpass filters (spanning the range 200–6400 Hz) and an unfiltered band. Within each band the maximum intensity and the number of zero crossings are measured for every 10-ms interval.

This results in a vector of 12 parameters every 10 ms. These parameters are smoothed and log transformed and a subset of the parameters is chosen for further processing. Fig. 3 gives the parameters used, at present, for part of the utterance "king bishop pawn . . . ." Each column represents a 10-ms time unit. Rows *P*1, *P*2, *P*3, and *AU* represent the log-amplitude parameters in the frequency bands 200–400, 400–800, 800–1600 Hz, and the unfiltered band, respectively. The amplitudes are quantized to 32 levels and represented as a single character (blank, 0–9, *A*-*U*, and *, which represents a value greater than 31). Rows *P*4 and *P*5 represent values that are functions of both amplitude and zero crossing in bands 1600–3200 and 3200–6400. Details of various operations on these parameters are given in Erman [6].

This vector of parameters (*P*1–*P*5 and *AU*) are compared with a standard set of parameter vectors to obtain a minimum distance classification for each time unit using a highly modified version of a procedure proposed by Astrahan [1]. The row labeled *PP* gives the classification for each 10-ms unit. The standard

```
          k       I         ŋ     b      I        ʃ          ə       p             ɔ            n
         .    :    .    :    .    :    .    :    .    :    .    :    .    :    .    :    .    :
P1          BMLJJKKKJJJJJJJJKKKKJCBEPSSTTTRPMDDA73200 LNOMG96311       8GGHIJJLLLMNNNNMMLKKKKKKF62
P2          6FHHFEEEDDDDDDDCB97622  DLLLLLJIEC72220   2DJHD51     00 BKOSRRRSRRQQRRRQQPPNHHFDC9731
P3               122232223200       13331             1650           AFJKLMNOQQQPQRRRRQMHA6631
P4     8HFHNT******RKLLMMNMKIHC     J******PMLNPPOMMJ7DPOL20           9CKLMMQSUUUUUTPPOONMMLD22
P5     9IJJC 2 2    0                     269FGEGGFE6                                 21
AU     20025LNONPPPMLLMMLLLKJIHGF61BLQSSSSQLIEDEDCB9 2BLNID600          CNQQRRRSSSSTTUTSSQOMLLLKJF84
PP    -FCC$$eIIIeeeINNNNNINNNNYMMDdVNIeeeeeIIIII$$$$SF+INIUD+++++--++-daaaaaa@@@@@@@@@AA@@&NN&UWdd+
SP    -CCC$$IIIIIIIINNNNNNNNNNNMMdddIIeeeeeIIIII$$$$+++NNN+++++++--++--aaaaaa@@@@@@@@@@@@NNNNWWdd+
VF    .fffffvvvvvvvvvvvvvvvvvvvvvvvv-vvvvvvvvvvvvvffff...vvv............vvvvvvvvvvvvvvvvvvvvvvvvvvv.
```

Fig. 3. Parameters and segmentation for "king bishop pawn · · · ." $P1$–$P5$ and AU (amplitude) are the input parameters. PP is the phone-like name given to the segment. SP is the locally smoothed PP. VF is a segmentation based on the SP's: · unvoiced, nonfricated; f unvoiced, fricated; v voiced, nonfricated; and z voiced, fricated.

set of parameters is obtained by selecting cluster centers from a training set of utterances containing various phonemes in neutral contexts. When a phoneme is represented by several articulatory gestures, more than one cluster center may be added to the standard set. Speaker characteristics and the noise characteristics of the environment or the transducer may be reflected in the standard set of clusters by recording the training set in that environment. Fig. 4 gives cluster centers for several representative sounds. A complete list of clusters used and the details of the speaker normalization program are given in Erman [6].

Remark 1: The labels in row *PP* of Fig. 3 are not to be confused with phonetic transcription. Accurate phonetic transcription, where possible, would require modifying the labels taking into account segment and sentence level context.

Remark 2: If one wanted to use formant frequencies and amplitudes (assuming they can be determined without mislabeling) one would reanalyze the training set for this parametric representation to determine the new cluster centers. Representing the parameters as a vector with a weighted distance metric defined on the vector space is all that is needed to use a new parametric representation in the HEARSAY system. There are several disadvantages to this approach, e.g., errors in labels, inability to take advantage of special features of a parametric representation, etc. However, this approach provides a convenient way of obtaining the best first approximation to the phonetic representation.

Remark 3: The tendency is to blame every error on inadequate parametric representations. We have gone from one set of amplitude and zero crossing parameters to three sets and now to five. Others divide the frequency range into 12, 17, 24, 32, and 48 regions or the full resolution given by FFT. The increase in noisiness of the parameters with increasing resolution makes it imperative that one transform the high resolution data to a smaller number of robust parameters such as the efforts by Li *et al.* [16] and Pols [28] in dimensionality reduction of spectra.

Remark 4: The parameters we use represent a crude spectrum. A mixed strategy in which finer analysis is performed only when necessary (Reddy [30]) seems more appropriate for an efficient realization of the system than obtaining every possible parameter at the start.

PP	P1	P2	P3	P4	P5	AU
d	22	14	5	8	0	18
s	0	0	0	47	39	9
m	30	10	2	2	0	33
u	43	30	11	7	0	39
a	37	62	44	38	0	59

Fig. 4. Several typical *PP*-cluster centers.

Remark 5: Spectral representation appears to be more robust than formant representation because of the likelihood of mislabeling a formant.

Remark 6: Parcor parameter representation (Itakura and Saito [14]) has also been used successfully (Nakano *et al.* [21]) and may have efficient machine realizations within the framework of the HEARSAY system.

Remark 7: Zero-crossing measurements and formant frequency measurements are more prone to error than energy measurements in a noisy environment. It appears more difficult to devise noise subtraction algorithms for frequency than for amplitude (Neely and Reddy [24]).

Segmentation

The purpose of segmentation is to divide the continuous parameter sequence into discrete phone-size chunks. This is usually based on an acoustic similarity measure (Reddy and Vicens [34]). Labeling every 10-ms unit by a phone-like cluster name permits the segmentation to be divided in terms of these labels. Fig. 3 shows two levels of segmentation for "king bishop pawn . . . ." The first level is derived by doing a local "smoothing" of the *PP* names assigned to each of the 10-ms segments; this is displayed on the row labeled *SP*. A segment is defined to be a contiguous run of a single *PP*, flanked by *PP*'s not the same as those in the run. This segmentation is approximately at the phoneme level but is, by itself, very unreliable.

A second level of segmentation is derived by associating a voiced/unvoiced decision and a fricated/nonfricated decision with each *PP*. These binary decisions, when applied to the *SP*'s (and modified with a few simple rules for smoothing and breaking of long segments according to significant local amplitude peaks), segment the signal very reliably. The row in Fig. 3 labeled *VF* indicates this segmentation for the sample.

Remark 1: It is now commonly agreed among all researchers that some form of segmentation of acoustic signals is necessary for connected speech recognition (see Fant and Lindblom [8], Reddy [29], Denes and von Keller [4], Broad [2], Medress [19], Dixon and Tappert [5], Klatt and Stevens [15], Stalhammar and Karlsson [35], Hemami and Lehiste [11]). No systematic evaluation has been made of these and other methods of segmentation that have been proposed or implemented. Our present view is that almost any of the schemes, given enough careful tuning, will work in a large majority of the cases; the more important question is then not how to segment, but rather how to use the segmentation without being crippled by the inevitable errors.

Remark 2: This use of segmentation represents a trend away from segmentation-free recognition schemes (Halle and Stevens [10]). However, segmentation-free recognition still seems to be a useful concept if one is mainly interested in isolated word recognition (Hill [12], White [39]).

Acoustic Recognizer

The role of the acoustic recognizer is to predict and verify syllables and words based on the features present in the incoming utterance, the present context, and the lexicon. The structure and phonetic description of syllables and words in the lexicon is prespecified. An entry for a word in the lexicon contains the phonemic spelling(s) of the word and annotations that are used to describe expected anomalies that cannot be predicted by rule from the phonemic spelling. A more detailed description of the lexicon and the preprocessing is given in Erman [6].

The acoustic recognizer has three sources of knowledge available for the generation and verification of hypotheses: acoustic, phonological, and vocabulary restrictions. The acoustic knowledge appears in the form of expected parameters (or features) for a phoneme in a neutral context. The phonological knowledge appears in the form of a coarticulation model that modifies the expected features based on context. The between-word coarticulation effects have to be determined wherever applicable through the use of the "currently accepted partially recognized utterance" (Fig. 2), which provides the boundary phonemes. The vocabulary restriction appears in the form of a valid subset of words in the lexicon that contain a given sequence of features.

The acoustic recognizer uses these sources of knowledge in two stages: the hypothesis and the verification. The acoustic hypothesizer does not have any knowledge of the syntax or semantics of the situation, but can use the gross features (such as /ʃ/ of "bishop") in the "partial symbolic utterance description" (Fig. 2) to retrieve those words of the lexicon that are consistent within the features present.

The task of a verifier is to determine whether a given hypothesis is consistent with the context presently available to it. For example, let us assume that alternative hypotheses of the words "king's," "pawn," "bishop," "queen's," and "knight" have been made in the context "king --- pawn · · ·" (where "---" represents the hypothesized words) and that the word actually spoken was "bishop." Detailed verification, by the acoustic verifier, of every phoneme of every option word is not necessary. All that is needed, in this example, are some simple tests that notice that there is a strong fricative indicated near the middle of the area of interest, which causes "pawn" and "knight" to be rejected, and some other simple tests on the vowel portion, e.g., duration, high/low, and front/back, which would indicate that both "queen's" and "king's" are unlikely, whereas "bishop" is highly likely.

A more detailed matching of features and the use of coarticulation rules at the word boundaries may, of course, be needed for other cases. Detailed matching often implies generation of a test. For example, if the verification to be made is among "sit," "spit," and "split," the presence of /s/, /I/, /t/ and the transitions between /I/ and /t/ are irrelevant. What is needed is the test for the presence or absence of a stopgap and for the presence of /l/-like formant structure following the stopgap.

Remark: That some form of hypothesization and verification is needed seems to be recognized by many researchers at this point. Halle and Stevens [10] proposed synthesis and match as a means of verification in their analysis-by-synthesis model. Hypothesis and verification for isolated word recognition was used in the Vicens–Reddy system (Vicens [38]). More recently, similar techniques have also been used by Klatt and Stevens [15], Lindblom and Svensson [18], Tappert *et al.* [36], and Itahashi *et al.* [13].

Syntactic Recognizer

The role of the syntactic recognizer is to predict phrases based on the syntactic structure of the language to be recognized and the context. The predicted phrases induce (specify) words that might appear in that context. The grammar for the voice-chess language is context free. The voice-chess grammar, specified as a set of BNF productions, is given in Fig. 5. For example, in this grammar, "<move>" is defined to be either "<move1>" followed by "<checkword>" or "<move1>." The total number of different utterances permitted by this grammar is about five million.

The role of the syntax hypothesizer is to use the syntactic source of knowledge to predict words. In

```
1.  <move>         ::= <movel> <check-word> | <movel>

2.  <movel>        ::= <regular-move> | <capture> | <castle>

3.  <castle>       ::= <castle-word> ON <uniroyal> SIDE
                       | <castle-word> <uniroyal> SIDE
                       | <castle-word>

4.  <regular-move> ::= <man-loc> <move-word> <square>

5.  <capture>      ::= <man-loc> <capture-word> PAWN EN-PASSENT
                       | <man-loc> <capture-word> <man-loc>

6.  <castle-word>  ::= CASTLE | CASTLES

7.  <move-word>    ::= TO | MOVES-TO | GOES-TO

8.  <capture-word> ::= TAKES | CAPTURES

9.  <check-word>   ::= CHECK MATE | CHECK

10. <man-loc>      ::= <man-spec> ON <square> | <man-spec>

11. <man-spec>     ::= <uniroyal> <unipiece> PAWN
                       | <uniroyal> <piece> | <uniroyal> pawn
                       | <unipiece> pawn | <man>

12. <square>       ::= <uniroyal> <piece> <rank> | <nopawn> <rank>

13. <man>          ::= KING | QUEEN | BISHOP | KNIGHT | ROOK | PAWN

14. <uniroyal>     ::= KING | QUEEN | KING'S | QUEEN'S

15. <unipiece>     ::= BISHOP | KNIGHT | ROOK
                       | BISHOP'S | KNIGHT'S | ROOK'S

16. <nopawn>       ::= KING | QUEEN | BISHOP | KNIGHT | ROOK

17. <piece>        ::= BISHOP | KNIGHT | ROOK

18. <rank>         ::= ONE | TWO | THREE | FOUR
                       | FIVE | SIX | SEVEN | EIGHT
```

Fig. 5. Voice-chess syntax.

CENTER	LEFT	RIGHT	HEAD
CASTLE	↑	↑	<castle-word>
CASTLES	↑	↑	<castle-word>
EN-PASSENT	PAWN	↑	<capture>
ON	<castle-word>	<uniroyal>	<castle>
PAWN	<capture-word>	EN-PASSENT	<capture>
SIDE	<uniroyal>	↑	<castle>
SIDE	<uniroyal>	↑	<castle>
<movel>	↑	<check-word>	<move>
<movel>	↑	↑	<move>
<check-word>	<movel>	↑	<move>
<regular-move>	↑	↑	<movel>
<capture>	↑	↑	<movel>
<castle>	↑	↑	<movel>
<castle-word>	↑	ON	<castle>
<castle-word>	↑	<uniroyal>	<castle>
<castle-word>	↑	↑	<castle>
<uniroyal>	ON	SIDE	<castle>
<uniroyal>	<castle-word>	SIDE	<castle>
<man-loc>	↑	<move-word>	<regular-move>
<man-loc>	↑	<capture-word>	<capture>
<man-loc>	↑	<capture-word>	<capture>
<man-loc>	<capture-word>	↑	<capture>
<move-word>	<man-loc>	<square>	<regular-move>
<square>	<move-word>	↑	<regular-move>
<capture-word>	<man-loc>	PAWN	<capture>
<capture-word>	<man-loc>	<man-loc>	<capture>

Fig. 6. Antiproductions for a subset of the syntax of Fig. 5. (The subset consists of productions 1-6.)

hypothesization the syntax recognizer uses only very local context to predict words. Predictions may be made either to the right or the left of already existing words. For example, if "--- moves-to ---" is given, then words may be hypothesized to the left of "moves-to" or to the right of "moves-to." Hypothesization uses only inexpensive methods, and often generates words that would not fit in the complete context of the sentence.

Traditional parsing schemes are not very useful in generating hypotheses. Further, the syntax recognizer must be capable of processing errorful strings containing spurious words and repetition of words. This implies that it must be capable of working both forwards and backwards. This is achieved in HEARSAY by the use of antiproductions.

Antiproductions act as a concordance for the grammar giving all the contexts for every symbol appearing in the grammar. They are used to predict words that are likely to occur following or preceding a word using only limited context. Fig. 6 gives antiproductions for productions 1-6 of the grammar of Fig. 5. These are produced automatically by a preprocessing program. In this figure, the symbols in the column labeled CENTER are the entries in the concordance. Each symbol in the subset of the grammar appears in this column once for each occurrence of it in the subset. The entries in the LEFT and RIGHT columns denote symbols that can appear to the left and right of the entry in the center column. When an ↑ appears in the LEFT or RIGHT column, it indicates that the original production did not have an entry to the left or right of that symbol.

When the LEFT (or RIGHT) context given in an antiproduction is satisfied, then the RIGHT (or LEFT) context is hypothesized for recognition. If the hypothesized symbol happens to be a nonterminal, then all the possible terminal symbols that can appear at the left of this nonterminal are hypothesized. Detailed descriptions of the structure and use of antiproductions will be given in Neely [23].

The role of the syntactic verifier is to accept or discard hypotheses using syntactic consistency checks. This is usually a more expensive process than hypothesization because it involves complete parsing of the partially recognized sentences. The verifier may work both on hypotheses that the syntactic hypothesizer has generated, as well as those generated by other hypothesizers.

Semantic Recognizer

The role of the semantic recognizer is to predict concepts based on the semantics of the task and semantics of the preceding utterance. A predicted concept (a legal move for voice-chess) is used in conjunction with the present context to predict a word that might appear in the utterance. The semantics of the task and the preceding utterances are captured for chess by the current board position. The board position for the utterance in discussion, "king bishop pawn moves to bishop four," is shown in Fig. 7.

HEARSAY has, as a subpart, a chess program (Gillogly [9]) that generates an ordered list of moves that are possible in that situation. A partial list of legal moves with numbers representing the likelihood of occurrence is given in Fig. 8.

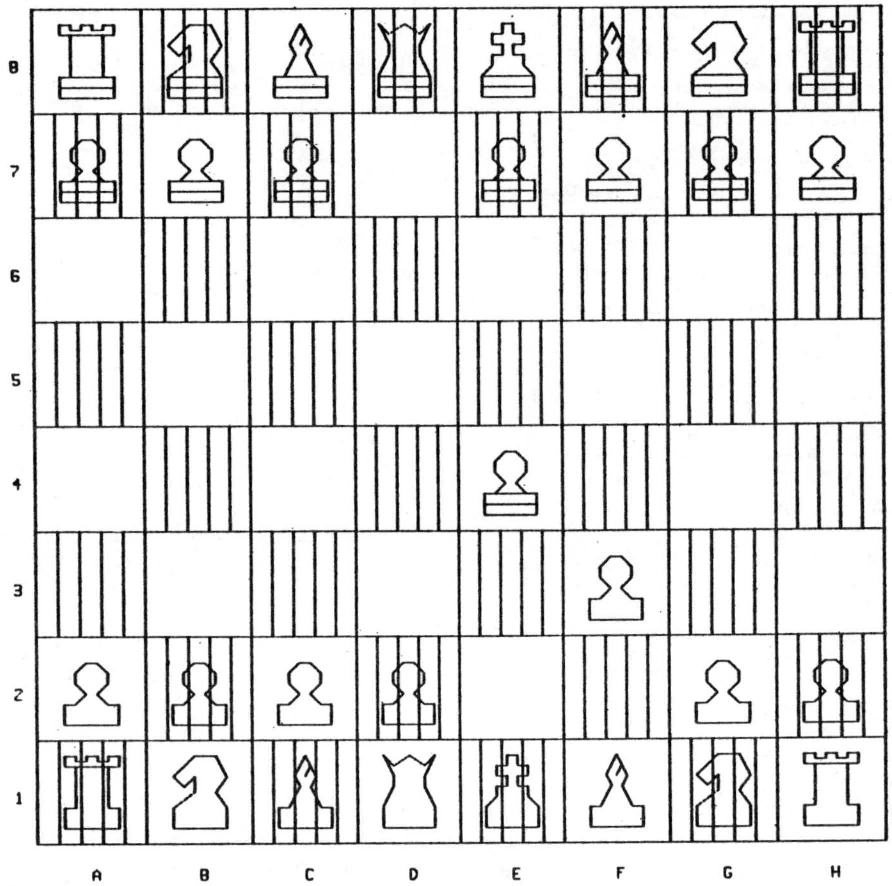

Fig. 7. Board position for utterance in discussion.

KBP/KB3XKP/K4	100
QP/Q2-Q4	50
QN/QN1-QB3	49
KB/KB1-QB4	48
KN/KN1-K2	47
QP/Q2-Q3	46
KB/KB1-K2	45
Q/Q1-K2	44
QBP/QB2-QB4	43
QBP/QB2-QB3	42
K/K1-KB2	41
K/K1-K2	40
KRP/KR2-KR4	39
KNP/KN2-KN4	38
QNP/QN2-QN4	37
QRP/QR2-QR4	36
KN/KN1-KR3	35
KNP/KN2-KN3	34
QNP/QN2-QN3	33
KRP/KR2-KR3	32
QRP/QR2-QR3	31
QN/QN1-QR3	30
KB/KB1-QN5CH	25
KBP/KB3-KB4	24
KB/KB1-QR6	12
KB/KB1-Q3	6

Fig. 8. Ordered list of legal moves supplied by the chess-playing program for the board position of Fig. 7.

The semantic hypothesizer uses the ordered list of moves for hypothesis generation. In our example the hypothesizer would concentrate only on the "non-capture" moves that start with the word "king." If there are none, then there is an inconsistency in the currently accepted partially recognized utterance. This may be due to an illegal statement or incorrect recognition. In the latter case, the partially recognized utterance is modified by replacing the weakest link by the second best choice for that position.

bishop	62
knight	62
bishop's	44
rook	41
on	41
knight's	38

ds hypothesized by semantic hy

Fig. 9. Words hypothesized by semantic hypothesizer.

Fig. 9 gives the words hypothesized by the semantic hypothesizer in the context of "king ---." Associated with each hypothesis is a rating (ranging from 1 to 100) indicating the semantic likelihood of the hypothesis. This likelihood is derived from the likelihoods of the projected legal moves from which the hypotheses are taken, and from intrasentence semantic clues. The semantic hypothesizer uses word- and phrase-level semantic consistency checks to restrict hypothesization. The structure and the mechanism used by the semantic hypothesizer are described in Neely [23].

Control of the Processes

Since the different recognizers are independent, the recognition overlord needs to synchronize the hypothesis generation and verification phases of various processes. Synchronization ensures that hypotheses generated by one process will be verified by all the other processes in the subsequent time slice. Several strategies are available for deciding which subset of the processes generates the hypotheses and which verify. At present this is done by polling the processes to decide which process is most confident about generating the correct hypothesis. In voice-chess, where the semantic source of knowledge is dominant, that module usually generates the hypotheses. These are then verified by the syntactic and acoustic recognizers. However, when robust acoustic cues are present in the incoming utterance, the roles are reversed with the acoustic recognizer generating the hypotheses.

The verification process continues until a hypothesis is found that is acceptable to all the verifiers with a high enough level of confidence. All the unverified hypotheses are stored on a stack for the purpose of backtracking at a later stage. Given an acceptable hypothesis, ROVER updates the currently accepted partially recognized utterance and updates the partial symbolic utterance description with additional features that were discovered during the process of hypothesis generation and verification. If the utterance still has unrecognized portions of speech and if the interpretation of the utterance is still unclear, then all the active processes are reactivated to generate hypotheses in the new context. If there are no unrecognized portions of speech in the utterance and the sentence is uninterpretable, the knowledge acquisition part of the system (unimplemented in the present system and not shown in Fig. 2) is activated to update the lexicon and the acoustic, syntactic, and/or semantic rules.

Preliminary Results

The system described in the preceeding sections has been operational since June 1972. We view HEARSAY as a continually evolving system that is expected to serve as a research tool for explorations in speech-recognition research at Carnegie-Mellon University. Fig. 10 gives some preliminary results of recognition by the system. More comprehensive results containing time, accuracy, and error analyses will be given in Erman [6] and Neely [23].

```
S: Actually spoken
R: Recognized by HEARSAY

1. S: PAWN TO KING FOUR
   R: PAWN TO QUEEN FOUR

2. S: KNIGHT TO KING'S BISHOP THREE
   R: PAWN   TO QUEEN'S BISHOP THREE

3. S: BISHOP TO KNIGHT FIVE
   R: PAWN TO QUEEN THREE

4. S: KNIGHT TO QUEEN BISHOP THREE
   R: KNIGHT TO QUEEN BISHOP THREE

5. S: PAWN TO QUEEN FOUR
   R: PAWN TO QUEEN FOUR

6. S: KNIGHT TAKES PAWN
   R: KNIGHT TAKES PAWN
```

Fig. 10. Some preliminary results from one run. (Approximately 4-7 times real-time processing on a PDP-10 computer.)

Discussion

Models of Speech Perception

This paper presents a model of speech perception that has been arrived at not so much by conducting experiments on how humans perceive speech but in the process of constructing several speech-recognition systems using computers. The emphasis has been on developing efficient recognition algorithms, with little attention to modeling of known human perceptual behavior. The general framework (for a model) that evolved is different from some previously proposed models by Liberman *et al.*, [17] and Halle and Stevens [10], which imply that perception takes place through the active mediation of motor centers associated with speech production. Our results tend to support "sensory" theories advanced by Fant [7], and others, in which speech decoding proceeds without the active mediation of speech motor centers.

If one eliminates the synthesis part of analysis-by-synthesis, then our model is most similar to that of Halle and Stevens [10]. The important distinction to remember is that once a hypothesis is generated, say of the words "sit," "slit," and "split," one should never want to verify the hypotheses by generating formant trajectories for the word or phrase. That phonemes /s/, /I/, /t/ occur in the hypothesized words is no longer relevant. All that is needed is a verification of the presence of stopgap and the /l/-like formant transition preceding the vowel. Another limitation of synthesis and match is that the noise might swamp the finer distinction required, i.e., the variability in speaker performance of /s/, /I/, /t/ might overshadow the positive contributions of a /p/ or an /l/.

Information-Processing Models

The model proposed in this paper raises several issues that may be of interest to speech scientists and cognitive psychologists interested in human speech perception. We would like to propose that, in addition to stimulus-response studies and neuro-physiological models, speech scientists should also make extensive use of information-processing models in the study of speech perception. The notion of an information-processing model reflects a current trend in cognitive psychology to view man as an information processor, i.e., that his behavior can be seen as the result of a system consisting of memories containing discrete symbols and symbolic expressions and processes that manipulate these symbols (Newell [26]). The main advantage of this approach to speech perception studies is that it permits a researcher to look at the total problem of speech perception at a higher functional and conceptual level than is possible with the other two approaches. (To attempt to study the total problem of speech perception by formulating a neurophysiological model would be like attempting to understand the workings of a TV set by looking at the flow of electrons through a transistor.)

One question that arises in this context is the nature of serial and parallel processing mechanisms used by humans. It is known that, at a higher problem-solving level, a human being behaves essentially as a serial information processor (Newell and Simon [27]). It is also known that parallel processing occurs at the preprocessing levels of vision and speech. What is not known is whether there are several independent processes or a single sophisticated process at the perceptual level that can use effectively all the available sources of knowledge.

The second question is how various sources of knowledge cooperate with each other. There are experiments (Miller and Isard [20], Collins and Quillian [3]) that can be interpreted to show that perception is faster or more intelligible depending on the number of available sources of knowledge. Any model of speech perception must deal with the nature and structure of the interaction between various sources of knowledge. Earlier models tend to ignore this question.

Summary and Conclusions

A casual reader of this paper would probably only notice the superficial aspects of the system: that it accepts voice commands to play chess, uses crude parameters, and is not very smart at using the acoustic-phonetic and other sources of knowledge. That is beside the point. The main contribution of this research is to provide a model and a framework in which the role of phonology, syntax, semantics, and other sources of knowledge can be systematically studied and evaluated. It is no longer necessary for us to be content with vacuous statements about the importance of syntax or semantics.

We chose voice-chess as a task not because it is important to play chess with a computer over telephone, but because chess provides a good area to evaluate our ideas about the role of various sources of knowledge in speech perception. Chess plays the role in our system that the fruit fly plays in genetics. Just as the genetics of *drosophila* are studied not to breed better flies, but to learn the laws of heredity, so we choose chess as a task because the syntax, semantics, and vocabulary of discourse are well defined and are amenable to systematic study.

Similarly, the acoustic parameters and phonological, syntactic, and semantic rules currently used by the HEARSAY system are not particularly important or interesting. What is important to note is that while each module is "stupid," the system still works and does do a creditable job in spite of its weaknesses. The interesting features are the interaction and cooperation among various modules and the correction of errors by various sources of knowledge.

The system described in this paper was demonstrated in June 1972, at a workshop on speech recognition. It represents the first system to demonstrate live, connected speech recognition using nontrivial syntax and semantics. We expect to actively modify the system to greatly increase its performance, as well as use it as an experimental tool for studying speech understanding, recognition, and perception.

Acknowledgment

The authors wish to thank A. Newell whose intellectual and moral support has been essential to sustain a long-term research effort of this kind in the midst of pessimistic predictions. We wish to acknowledge the important contributions of R. Fennell in the design and programming of ROVER and the global data structure. P. Karlton and B. Lowerre also helped in programming parts of the system. B. Broadley, P. Newbury, and J. Teter interfaced the speech devices to the PDP-10. G. Robertson and H. Wactlar made the necessary modifications to the PDP-10 monitor.

References

[1] M. Astrahan, "Speech analysis by clustering or the hyperphoneme method," Dep. Comput. Sci., Stanford Univ., Stanford, Calif., AI Memo 124, 1970.

[2] D. J. Broad, "Formants in automatic speech recognition," in *Proc. Int. Conf. Speech Commun. Processing*, 1972, pp. 295–298.

[3] A. M. Collins and M. R. Quillan, "Retrieval time from semantic memory," *J. Verbal Learn. Behav.*, vol. 8, 1969, pp. 204–267.

[4] P. B. Denes and T. G. von Keller, "Articulatory segmentation for automatic recognition of speech," in *Proc. 6th Int. Congr. Acoust.*, vol. B, 1968, pp. 143–146.

[5] N. R. Dixon and C. C. Tappert, "Derivation of phonetic representation by combining steady-state and transemic classification in automatic recognition of continuous speech," in *Proc. Int. Conf. Speech Commun. Processing*, 1972, pp. 319–321.

[6] L. D. Erman, Ph.D. dissertation, in preparation.

[7] G. Fant, "Auditory patterns of speech," in *Models for the Perception of Speech and Visual Form*, W. Wathen-Dunn, Ed. Cambridge, Mass.: M.I.T. Press, 1964.

[8] C. G. M. Fant and B. Lindblom, "Studies of minimal speech sound units," Speech Transmission Lab., Quarterly Prog. Stat. Rep., vol. 2, pp. 1–11, 1961.

[9] J. J. Gillogly, "The TECHNOLOGY chess program," *Artif. Intel.*, vol. 3, pp. 145–163, 1972.

[10] M. Halle and K. Stevens, "Speech recognition: A model and a program for research," *IRE Trans. Inform. Theory*, vol. IT-8, pp. 155–159, Feb. 1962.

[11] H. Hemani and I. Lehiste, "Interactive automatic speech segmentation," in *Proc. Int. Conf. Speech Commun. Processing*, 1972, pp. 291–294.

[12] D. R. Hill, "Man-machine interaction using speech," in *Advances in Computers*, vol. 11, F. L. Ait *et al.*, Ed. New York: Academic, 1971, pp. 165–230.

[13] S. Itahashi, S. Makino, and K. Kido, "Automatic recognition of spoken words utilizing dictionary and phonological rule," in *Proc. Int. Conf. Speech Commun. Processing*, 1972, pp. 327–330.

[14] F. Itakura and S. Saito, "Speech analysis-synthesis system based on the partial autocorrelation coefficient," presented at the 1969 Acoust. Soc. Jap. Meeting (see also "On the optimum quantization of feature parameters in the parcor speech synthesizer," in *Proc. Int. Conf. Speech Commun. Processing*, 1972, pp. 434–437).

[15] D. H. Klatt and K. N. Stevens, "Sentence recognition form visual examination of spectrograms and machine-aided lexical searching," in *Proc. Int. Conf. Speech Commun. Processing*, 1972, pp. 315–318.

[16] K.-P. Li, G. W. Hughes, and A. S. House, "Correlation characteristics and dimensionality of speech spectra," *J. Acoust. Soc. Amer.*, vol. 46, pp. 1019–1025, 1969.

[17] A. M. Liberman, F. S. Cooper, K. S. Harris, and P. F. MacNeilage, "A motor theory of speech perception," in *Proc. Speech Commun. Seminar*, vol. 2, 1962.

[18] B. Lindblom and S.-G. Svensson, "Interaction between segmental and non-segmental factors in speech recognition," in *Proc. Int. Conf. Speech Commun. Processing*, 1972, pp. 331–333.

[19] M. Medress, "A procedure for the machine recognition of speech," in *Proc. Int. Conf. Speech Commun. Processing*, 1972, pp. 113–116.

[20] G. A. Miller and S. Isard, "Some perceptual consequences of linguistic rules," *J. Verbal Learn. Behav.*, vol. 2, pp. 217–228, 1963.

[21] Y. Nakano, A. Ichikawa, and K. Nakata, "Evaluation of various parameters in spoken digits recognition," in *Proc. Int. Conf. Speech Commun. Processing*, 1972, pp. 101–104.

[22] R. B. Neely, "Experimental conversational computer system," *J. Acoust. Soc. Amer.*, vol. 46, p. 89(A), 1969.

[23] —, Ph.D. dissertation, in preparation.

[24] R. B. Neely and R. D. Reddy, "Speech recognition in the presence of noise," in *Proc. 7th Int. Congr. Acoust.* (Budapest, Hungary), vol. 3, 1971, pp. 177–180.

[25] A. Newell, "Heuristic programming: Ill-structured problems," in *Progress in Operations Research*, vol. 3, J. S. Aronofsky, Ed. New York: Wiley, 1971.

[26] —, "Remarks on the relationship between artificial intelligence and cognitive psychology," in *Non-Numerical Problem Solving*, R. Banerji and M. D. Mesarovic, Ed. Berlin, W. Germany: Springer-Verlag, 1970, pp. 363–400.

[27] A. Newell and H. A. Simon, *Human Problem Solving*. Englewood Cliffs, N.J.: Prentice-Hall, 1972.

[28] L. C. W. Pols, "Dimensional representation of speech spectra," in *Proc. 7th Int. Congr. Acoust.* (Budapest, Hungary), vol. 3, 1971, pp. 281–284.

[29] D. R. Reddy, "Segmentation of speech sounds," *J. Acoust. Soc. Amer.*, vol. 40, pp. 307–312, 1966.

[30] —, "Computer recognition of connected speech," *J. Acoust. Soc. Amer.*, vol. 42, pp. 329–347, 1966.

[31] —, "Segment-synchronization problem in speech recognition," *J. Acoust. Soc. Amer.*, vol. 46, p. 89(A), 1969.

[32] —, "Speech recognition: Prospects for the seventies," in *Proc. IFIP*, vol. 71, 1971, pp. I-5–I-3.

[33] D. R. Reddy, L. D. Erman, and R. B. Neely, "The C-MU speech recognition project," in *Proc. IEEE Syst. Sci. Cybern. Conf.*, 1970.

[34] D. R. Reddy and P. J. Vicens, "A procedure for segmentation of connected speech," *J. Audio Eng. Soc.*, vol. 16, pp. 404–412, 1968.

[35] U. Stalhammar and I. Karlsson, "A phonetic approach to ASR," in *Proc. Int. Conf. Speech Commun. Processing*, 1972, pp. 125–128.

[36] C. C. Tappert, N. R. Dixon, and A. S. Rabinowitz, "Application of sequential decoding for converting phonetic to graphemic representation in automatic recognition of continuous speech," in *Proc. Int. Conf. Speech Commun. Processing*, 1972, pp. 322–326.

[37] P. J. Vicens, "Use of syntax in the analysis of connected speech," *J. Acoust. Soc. Amer.*, vol. 46, p. 89(A), 1969.

[38] —, "Aspects of speech recognition by computer," Dep. Comput. Sci., Stanford Univ., Stanford, Calif., AI Memo 85, Ph.D. dissertation, 1969.

[39] G. White, private communication, Xerox Palo Alto Res. Cen., Palo Alto, Calif., 1972.

Motivation and Overview of SPEECHLIS: An Experimental Prototype for Speech Understanding Research

WILLIAM A. WOODS

Abstract—**SPEECHLIS is a research prototype of an intelligent speech understanding system which makes use of advanced techniques of artificial intelligence, natural language processing, and acoustical and phonological analysis in an integrated way to determine the interpretation of continuous speech utterances. This paper describes a number of the characteristics of the speech understanding task which influence the ways in which syntactic, semantic, pragmatic and lexical knowledge interact with acoustical and phonological information in the process of understanding speech utterances. The focus is on what the different knowledge sources have to contribute at different points in the analysis and the organization of a computer system to combine these different sources of information into an integrated system.**

INTRODUCTION

THIS PAPER describes a computer system under development at Bolt Beranek and Newman (BBN) for carrying out research in continuous speech understanding. The system is a research prototype of an intelligent speech understanding system which makes use of advanced techniques of artificial intelligence, natural language processing, acoustical and phonological analysis, and signal processing in an integrated way to determine an interpretation of a continuous speech utterance which is both syntactically and semantically plausible and consistent with the acoustic–phonetic analysis of the input signal.

We take as a point of departure that the information required to produce the correct interpretation of an utterance is not completely and unambiguously encoded into the speech signal, but rather that knowledge of the vocabulary and of syntactic, semantic, and pragmatic constraints of the language are used to compensate for uncertainties and errors in the acoustic realization of the utterance. This fact seems appropriately substantiated by human perceptual performance [10] and by Klatt and Stevens' spectrogram reading experiments [2]. In the latter, human experts attempting to decipher spectrograms achieved error rates of approximately 25 percent in "partial" phonetic transcription based on spectrographic evidence alone, but were 96 percent successful in identifying the words of the utterances when permitted to make use of knowledge of the vocabulary and of syntactic and semantic constraints. It is the matching of human performance in these experiments towards which the BBN speech understanding system (dubbed SPEECHLIS) aspires.

Manuscript received March 29, 1974. This paper was presented at the IEEE Symposium on Speech Recognition, Carnegie-Mellon University, Pittsburgh, Pa., April 15–19, 1974.

The author is with Bolt Beranek and Newman, Inc., Cambridge, Mass. 02138.

In a previous paper [12] we have described a method of "incremental simulation" which we have used to get a feeling for the types of interaction among the different sources of knowledge used during the understanding of a speech signal. In that paper, we postulated the decomposition of a speech understanding system into separate components and presented an illustrative example of their interaction in the analysis of an utterance. We also discussed the types of inference capabilities which would be required from the different components in a mechanical speech understanding system. In this paper we will describe how we have attempted to embody those capabilities in SPEECHLIS.

Whereas this paper gives an overview of the system and its motivations, separate papers [1], [6]–[9] give more detailed descriptions of the operations of individual components.

DOMAIN OF DISCOURSE

If one is to use knowledge of vocabulary, syntax, and semantics in a speech understanding system, it is necessary to select what vocabulary, syntax, and semantics to deal with. For our initial domain, because of its ready availability and its sophisticated syntax and semantics, we selected the domain of the LUNAR system [11], [13], a natural English question-answering system dealing with chemical analyses of the Apollo 11 moon rocks. The LUNAR system understands and answers such questions as:

"What is the average concentration of rubidium in high-alkali rocks?"
"List potassium/rubidium ratios for samples not containing silicon."
"How many rocks contain greater than 15 percent plagioclase?"

It contains a vocabulary of approximately 3500 words and a grammar for an extensive subset of general English. For our initial speech system, we have selected a subset of

Reprinted from *IEEE Trans. Acoust., Speech, and Signal Process.*, vol. ASSP-23, pp. 2–10, Feb. 1975.

approximately 250 words from LUNAR's vocabulary and a subgrammar of more restricted English from its grammar. In the future we intend to increase our vocabulary to over 1000 words, extend our grammar to include the entire LUNAR grammar, and include several additional domains of discourse unrelated to lunar geology.

KNOWLEDGE GATHERING

In order to gain a concrete understanding of the types of interaction required in using higher level linguistic knowledge to augment the front end (acoustic) analysis of the speech signal, we used "incremental simulations" to begin experimenting with the speech understanding system before completing its construction by "implementing" its components as combinations of computer program and human simulators. From these simulations, the following general conclusions were reached.

1) Small function words such as "a," "of," "the," etc., which are generally unstressed and short, have a high probability of matching accidentally in the signal. They are therefore unreliable cues by themselves on which to make a decision about an utterance and are unprofitable to look for on a "bottom up" or analytical scan of the utterance. However, when the hypothesized "content words" of the utterance are being parsed according to a grammar of English, syntactic knowledge is able to predict those places where such function words might occur, and in many cases, further semantic information is capable of predicting which function words are likely.

2) It is not generally possible with the current estimated level of performance of the acoustic analyzer to distinguish correct from incorrect word matches by acoustic word match scores alone. When a threshold of acoustic match quality is set sufficiently low to accept a high proportion of the correct word matches, a large number of accidental matches of other words are also accepted. The ratio of extraneous matches to correct ones depends on the setting of the threshold (as the threshold is relaxed the ratio gets higher), but for reasonable settings it may be on the order of 20 to 1. Moreover, it appears to be impossible to set the threshold sufficiently low to guarantee acceptance of all correct word matches without swamping the system with extraneous accidental matches. However in human simulations, although it required considerable thrashing around in difficult cases, it was generally possible to go back to selected regions of the utterance after partial lexical, semantic, and syntactic analysis and perform additional phonological and phonetic analysis and/or word matching to obtain the correct words. Although we are attempting to provide such processes in our system, they are likely to be more combinatoric in their searching for possibilities than the human simulation. It is far too early to predict the success of their performance.

3) The process of inferring an interpretation from a speech signal is inherently nondeterministic in the sense that it is frequently not possible to make a particular decision (such as which of several matching words is the correct one at a given position) without making an assumption and following out its consequences for the rest of the interpretation. Mechanisms must be provided for following out all of the alternative choices in order to find the correct interpretation.

4) No *a priori* order of scanning the utterance (such as left-to-right) for word matches and syntactic and semantic processing will be adequate in general since any given word may be garbled in its pronunciation or phonetic analysis and we may require a successful analysis of the rest of the utterance to recover the garbled word. Hence, classical left-to-right parsers will not suffice, nor will semantic interpretation rules such as those in LUNAR which are indexed solely under the head of the construction being interpreted (the head of the construction may be the word that is garbled and we may need to find the successful match of the rest of the rule in order to infer the garbled word).

5) The space of possible alternative computation paths which could lead to an interpretation of a signal is too vast to be searched in its entirety. In fact the set of possibilities which could be tried to get an interpretation when one has not found one yet is open-ended. Examples include relaxing the threshold of acceptability for word matches in the utterance (or in portions of it), trying the next best acoustical analysis of a given segment or combination of them, looking for possible alternative ways to segment the utterance into phoneme sequences, deciding to accept an interpretation of the utterance even though it is not syntactically well formed, or deciding to accept an interpretation which is not semantically meaningful. (I heard what you said but it doesn't make sense.) Because of the open-endedness of this search space, it is essential to devise strategies for searching it which devote their effort to the regions of the space most likely to yield the best interpretation and work out from there toward less and less likely interpretations. This requires the use of decision criteria to evaluate the goodness of a word match, and to weigh the alternatives of a more grammatical interpretation with poorer word matches against a sequence of better word matches which doesn't parse or doesn't make sense. It is critical to know the difference between reliable and unreliable clues and to juggle competing alternative partial interpretations so as to continually devote effort to the best ones.

6) Even with strategies for selectively pursuing alternatives according to their likelihood of success, the combinatorics of the situation are such that the system will be swamped with alternative possibilities unless special techniques are used to keep potentially different alternatives merged for processing operations for which they behave identically, splitting them up only when an operation being executed has a different effect for the different alternatives. One must avoid prematurely

multiplying combinations of cases. For example, one cannot afford to multiply out all of the possible sequences of phonemes which could cover the utterance.

The system which we have been developing has been designed to meet these requirements.

COMPONENTS OF THE SYSTEM

Principal Knowledge Components

As a consequence of examining the protocols and results of the Klatt and Stevens experiments, it was apparent that their performance was based on the capabilities of at least six conceptually distinguishable components.

1) An acoustic feature extraction component which performs the equivalent of a first-pass segmentation and labeling of the acoustic signal into partial phonetic descriptions, probably taking into account knowledge of phonological rules.

2) A lexical retrieval program which, on the basis of knowledge of the vocabulary and partial phonetic descriptions, retrieves words from the lexicon to be matched against the input signal.

3) A word verification component which, given a particular word and a particular location in the input signal, determines the degree to which the word matches the signal.

4) A syntactic component which is capable of judging grammaticality of an hypothesized interpretation of the signal and of proposing words or syntactic categories to extend a partial interpretation.

5) A semantic component which is capable of noticing coincidences between semantically related words which have been found at different places in the signal, judging the meaningfulness of an hypothesized interpretation, and predicting particular words or specific classes of words for extending a partial interpretation.

6) A pragmatic component, which is capable of making judgments and predictions as to the pragmatic likelihood of a given sentence being uttered by the speaker, taking into account whatever is known about the speaker and the situation.

In addition to these six components which correspond, to some extent, to different sources of knowledge that go into the determination of the preferred interpretation, there is clearly an additional component of a different sort—namely the decision process itself. In this component, which we have called the control component, reside the strategies for inferring an interpretation of the utterance, dealing with questions such as the following:

Where should one look for word matches first?
How much partial phonetic information is given as input to the lexical retrieval routine?
How good a word match score is required for the word to be given further consideration?
How and at what points does one use syntactic and semantic information to influence the interpretation?
How are alternative possible interpretations formed, managed, and resolved?
When should one temporarily abandon a given region of the utterance to concentrate on another region?
What information might be found elsewhere that might help, and how can it be used?

These and myriad other questions have answers (not necessarily optimal) embedded in the procedures used by the human experts to interpret the spectrograms in the Klatt and Stevens experiments. We need to capture similar strategies in the control component of our speech understanding system.

The Control Component

Clearly the strategies embedded in the control component, critical to the success of the system, are far from obvious. We have attempted to arrive at a reasonable set of such strategies by drawing on intuitions developed in incremental simulations. These strategies are being continually refined and extended as we gain more experience with the evolving SPEECHLIS.

The function of the control component centers around the creation, refinement, and evaluation of formal data objects called "theories," which represent alternative hypotheses about the utterance being interpreted. A theory contains the words hypothesized to be in the utterance and where they match, semantic hypotheses about how those words relate to each other, hypotheses about syntactic structure, and various scores reflecting the "likelihood" of the theory from different points of view (lexical match quality, semantic completeness, syntactic correctness, etc.). These theories generally represent only partial hypotheses, beginning with single word theories with little or no syntactic or semantic detail, constructing larger theories by refinement, and eventually building up to complete theories representing hypotheses for a sequence of words covering the entire utterance with complete syntactic structure and semantic interpretation. The task of the control component is to manage the creation and refinement of these theories, devoting its resources to expanding those theories which look best according to their various scores until one or more complete theories with acceptable scores are found. Control passes partial theories at various times to the syntactic and semantic components, which return them with evaluation scores or suspend them, after creating monitors for events (which could cause the refinement of a theory) and making proposals for word matches (which Control should recall the word matcher to look for). Monitors behave as active "demons" to give notices to control whenever events of the type which they are looking for occur. Each monitor remembers the theory which set it and a procedure which is to be executed to assimilate the event that triggers the monitor. The result of executing this procedure will be a new refined theory which may itself set additional monitors and make proposals.

In the next few sections, we will describe in a little

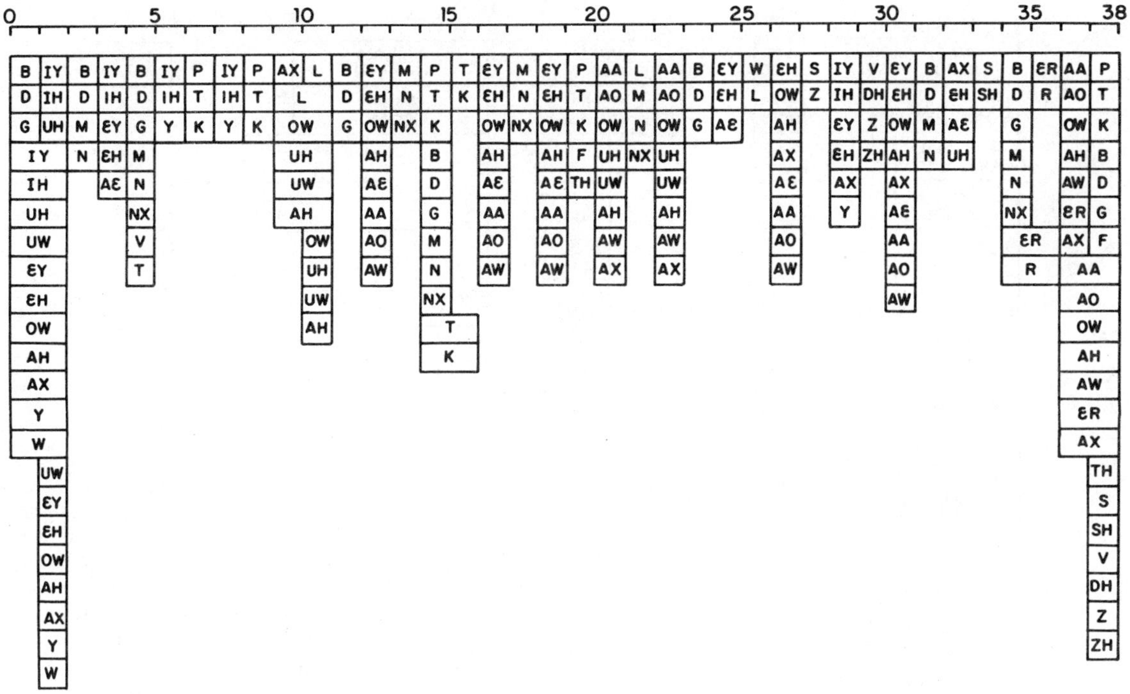

Fig. 1. Segment lattice.

more detail the various components of the current system. The scope of the current paper, however, will necessarily require these descriptions to be brief. For more detailed descriptions of the individual components the reader is again referred to [1], [6]–[9].

Acoustic–Phonetic and Phonological Analysis

In the acoustic end of our system, the speech signal is sampled at 20 kHz and stored on a disc file. All subsequent analysis is performed on the digitized signal. Using our recently developed method of "selective linear prediction" [3], [4] we perform a linear predictive (LP) analysis on the 0–5 kHz region of the spectrum. Presently, almost all our parameters are based on that portion of the spectrum, the exception being a parameter giving the spectral energy between 5–10 kHz, which is used for detection of frication. The parameters used in our segmentation and feature extraction are based on: energy of the signal, energy of the differenced signal, low-frequency energy, the first autocorrelation coefficient, the normalized LP error, energy-sensitive and energy-insensitive spectral derivatives, fundamental frequency, frequencies of a two-pole LP model [5], and poles of a 14-pole LP model. We have developed an initial set of algorithms for the nondeterministic segmentation of the utterance into a feature or segment lattice. Associated with each segment boundary are confidence measures that reflect the likelihoods of that point in the utterance being a segment boundary and of it being a word boundary. Another set of algorithms performs a feature analysis on each of the segments. We have concentrated thus far on the recognition of manner of articulation, e.g., vowel, nasal, lateral, retroflexed, plosive, fricative, and voiced–unvoiced. The only place of articulation recognition that we do is performed on the vowels and strident fricatives. Confidence estimates for each of the features and for the entire segment are also given.

The output of the acoustic–phonetic analysis is in the form of a segment lattice, an example of which is illustrated in Fig. 1. It compactly represents all of the possible alternative segmentations of the utterance and the alternative identities of the individual segments. This lattice is processed by a phonological rule component which augments the lattice with segments for possible underlying sequences of phonemes which could have resulted in the observed acoustic sequences. We associate with each added branch a predicate function which is later used by the word matcher to check for the applicability of the given phonological rule based on the specific word spelling and the necessary context. In this manner, the phonological rules are both analytic and partially generative. Other generative rules can be applied ahead of time to the dictionary phonemic spellings of words—such rules have been done manually in our current system.

Higher Level Linguistic Constraints

The current lexical retrieval and word matching component makes use of a phonetic similarity matrix for evaluating nonexact phoneme matches, phonologically motivated deletion likelihoods for each of the phonemes in a word, and rudimentary duration cues based on stress marks in the phonemic spelling of the word. Words with three or more phonemes which score above a threshold of match quality are placed in a "word lattice," an example of which is illustrated in Fig. 2. They are given individually to the semantic component which constructs

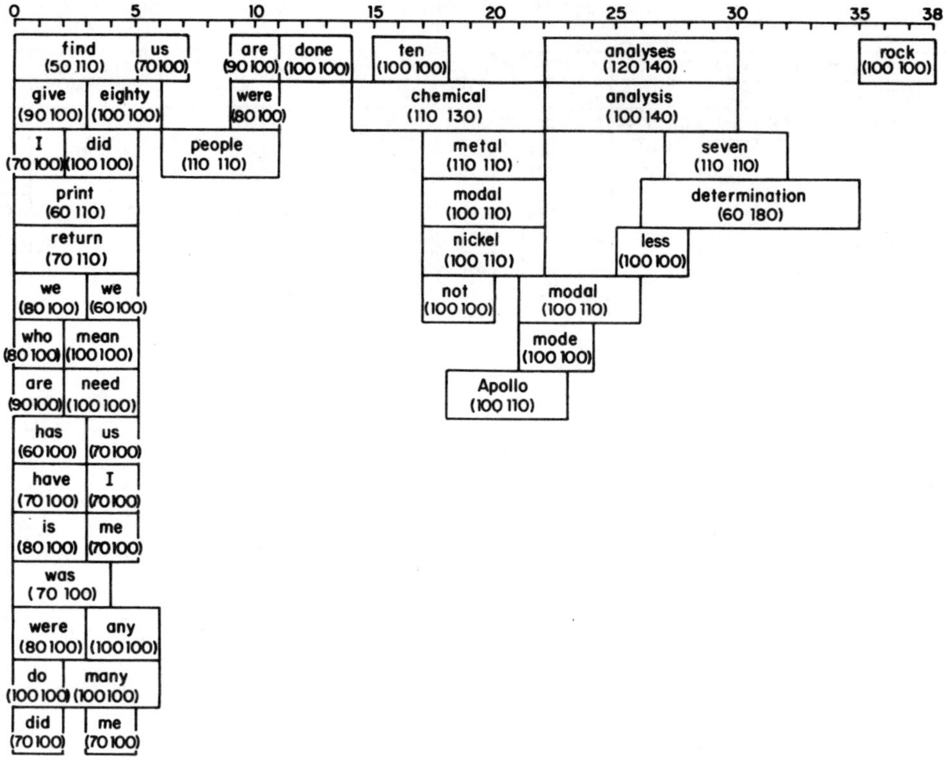

Fig. 2. Word lattice. Original utterance: "Have any people done chemical analyses on this rock?"

a one-word theory for each content word, monitors for words that could be semantically related to the given one, and generates events for each detected coincidence between two or more semantically related words or concepts. Each word is also checked for matching inflectional endings, and verbs are checked for possible auxiliaries to their left and at the beginning of the utterance.

The semantic coincidence events are sorted by the control component in order of their likelihood scores and at appropriate times are returned to Semantics for the construction of larger theories. In this way, multiple word theories are constructed which consist of semantically related content words which match well acoustically. When a theory becomes maximal (i.e., Semantics has no further words to add to it), it is passed to Syntax for syntactic evaluation. In addition to evaluation, Syntax picks up further words from the word lattice and proposes words (especially function words) to fill the gaps between the words originally provided in the theory. Syntax also monitors for syntactic categories of words which it could use to fill gaps. When Syntax completes a constituent (such as a noun phrase) it calls Semantics directly to verify the consistency between the syntactic structure of the constituent and the semantic hypotheses for its words.

The control strategy maintains a list of active theories, pending events, and proposed words and classes—all ordered by estimates of likelihood—and determines which theory/event/proposal to work on next at each point.

Some pragmatic inferences have been identified and embedded in the control strategy, but no systematic pragmatics component has been incorporated. The construction of semantic procedures for answering questions using the data base has not yet been implemented since we have previously done this once with the LUNAR system and have been devoting our effort instead to the new aspects of the system.

PRELIMINARY RESULTS OBTAINED

Since the current phase of the BBN speech project is more concerned with finding the problem areas and developing possible solution techniques, it is premature to expect statistical results such as percentage of utterances successfully understood. Rather, the principal product of the research at this point consists of experiences that suggest experiments yet to be done and techniques whose effectiveness has yet to be fully measured. The following are some examples.

The inclusion in the word matching function of simple duration checks for stressed phonemes and of deletion probabilities for each phoneme decreased the scores of many of the accidental word matches without effectively lowering the scores of the correct word matches. This suggests a host of experiments—how much improvement can you obtain?— With what cost?

The ambiguities of segmentation and labeling of the acoustic signal can result in the same word matching the input signal in approximately the same place in several different ways with slightly different end points and slightly different scores. From the point of view of the semantic associations invoked, these word matches are all the same and should not be dealt with by separate theories, one for each such match. This has resulted in the creation of a "fuzzy word match" which lumps together equivalent word matches into a single entity which is dealt with by Semantics as a single word match with ambiguous end points. This greatly reduces the number of theories processed.

A similar phenomenon occurs when several words from a single semantic class all match the signal at the same point (for example the pronouns "I," "we," and "us"). Again, since Semantics will initially do the same thing for each such word, these are grouped together into a "clump" which is treated as a single word until such time as later processing splits it up.

Certain acoustic–phonetic facts which are not currently dealt with by the segmenting and labeling component can cause recognizable pathologies at later stages of processing. For example, the fact that voicing frequently drops out before the end of frication in a voiced fricative followed by an unvoiced plosive may cause the segmenter to recognize a segment sequence /z, k/ as a sequence /z, s, k/ causing word matches for "samples" and "contain" which should be adjacent to have a spurious /s/ segment between them. This problem could be dealt with either by improving the initial segmentation and labeling algorithm, or by an analytic phonological rule to combine the voiced and unvoiced fricative in this context into a single voiced fricative, or by a higher level word adjacency test which considers two words to be adjacent if a spurious segment between them can be accounted for as an expected transition segment. This suggests experiments to be performed when the system is more fully developed to determine the most effective place to deal with this and similar problems.

It is possible to get alternative interpretations with almost equally good lexical, syntactic, and semantic evaluations—even two interpretations with exactly the opposite meaning. In all such situations which we have witnessed, there has been other information (such as prosodic or pragmatic information) available to make a choice, but it seems clear that the information which could be so used is open ended, and it is not clear how much is required in order to get acceptable performance even for our 250 word vocabulary, much less a 1000 word vocabulary.

The list of such questions which are being raised could go on and on, and would not be worth enumerating. However, the above list should be suggestive of the types of results which we hope to obtain.

A SAMPLE OF CURRENT PERFORMANCE

Issues of Evaluation

We have outlined the methodology and the current state of a project to develop advanced speech understanding capabilities by a process of continual incremental improvement of a system with initially crude capabilities in each of its individual components. An important consideration for such a program is a method for evaluating the progress of this evolutionary development in terms of the performance of the system or of its parts. How does one measure the improvement (or degradation) in system performance caused by a particular change to a strategy in one of the components? Although our current system has not yet reached the stage where we are prepared to run many utterances through it to compute statistics of performance, we have given some thought to what statistics of performance one would like to see and have made some initial measurements of them on test sentences.

Evaluation parameters fall into two classes, measures of precision and measures of accuracy. For example, in evaluating the performance of the segment labeler, precision measures the degree to which the label assigned uniquely specifies the phonemic identity of the segment, while accuracy measures the frequency with which the description is correct. There is clearly a tradeoff between these two measurements since one can achieve perfect accuracy by relaxing precision to the point where the description assigned is sufficiently vague to include all of the phonemes. On the other hand, one could only achieve perfect precision by choosing at every point the single most likely phoneme with a subsequent loss of accuracy. There are similar measures of precision and accuracy for the process of segmentation itself (as opposed to labeling) and the process of lexical retrieval and matching.

As a measure of precision in segmentation, we may take the branching ratio of the segment lattice, i.e., the number of segments per boundary. Accuracy in segmentation falls into two categories—the number of missing boundaries (i.e., segment boundaries which were not identified as potential boundaries in the lattice) and the number of extra boundaries (i.e., points in the utterance identified as boundaries in the lattice which were not segment boundaries and for which there is no "bridging" segment crossing that region of the utterance).

Specific precision and accuracy measures for segment labeling are the average number of phonemes per label (i.e., the number of phonemes subsumed under the description assigned to a segment) and the average percentage of errors in labeling (when the correct phoneme is not subsumed in the assigned description).

At the lexical level, we can measure the success of the initial lexical retrieval pass in terms of the number of correct words found (out of the total number of correct words to be found—an accuracy measure) and the "stray word ratio" (the ratio of the total number of words found to the number of correct words found—a precision measure).

Clearly there are precision–accuracy tradeoffs throughout the system. By merely adjusting the threshold of acceptable word match quality, the number of correct words found and the stray word ratio can be altered without any change at all in the algorithm being used for word matching.

	DWD-18				DWD-29			
	IDEAL	MANUAL	AUTO1	AUTO2	IDEAL	MANUAL	AUTO1	AUTO2
# segs in ideal segmentation	34				27			
# missing bdries	0	0	0	0	0	0	4	4
# extra bdries	0	0	0	0	0	0	0	0
# segs/bdry	1	1.2	1.3	1.3	1	2.0	1.5	1.5
% errors	0	12%	22%	10%	0	4%	43%	30%
# phonemes/label	1	6	4	3	1	4	4	3
# words ideal	9				8			
# words ≥ 3	8				5			
# correct words found		6	5	5		5	0	
# words found total		127	130	92		238	48	
# words missed		2	3	3		0	5	
stray word ratio (# words matched/ # correct)		21	26	18		48	-	

	have any people done chemical analyses on this rock	give me all lunar samples with magnetite
MANUAL	100 110 100 110 120 100	90 100 120 100 140
AUTO1	90 90 110 120 100	
AUTO2	100 90 120 140 100	

Fig. 3. Example of performance of acoustic-phonetic processing and lexical retrieval scan for "good" "big" words.

While we have not performed the necessary experiments to be able to give any conclusions about the behavior of these parameters as a function of differences in strategies, threshold levels, etc., and while the current components give only crude approximations to the performance which we expect, we have conducted a few tests which may serve as benchmarks. Fig. 3 gives the results of some tests (made in October 1973) on two utterances using three different acoustic analysis methods to produce the segment lattices. The first case (manual) is the result of a human spectrogram reading as in the first phase of the Klatt and Stevens experiments. The second case (auto 1) is the result of our first crude segmenting and labeling program which estimates only the manner of articulation of the segments and does not measure place of articulation. The third case (auto 2) makes use of a slightly improved version (but still crude) of the segmenting and labeling program, which tracks formants and estimates place of articulation for vowels. At the bottom of Fig. 3 is shown the word match score assigned by the lexical retrieval component to each of the correct words that it found. We did not run it on the auto 2 lattice for DWD-29.

Our current front-end analysis component tends to be better at some kinds of phonetic events than at others. This is a result of the almost encyclopedic amount of acoustic-phonetic and phonological knowledge which is required to deal with the different phenomena which can occur and the relatively short amount of time which we have had to embody this knowledge in computer algorithms. This difference is illustrated by the differences in performance between the two utterances DWD-18 ("Have any people done chemical analyses on this rock?") and DWD-29 ("Give me all lunar samples with magnetite.") The former seems to contain only phenomena with which the current programs deal reasonably well, while the latter contains such troublesome configurations as the "all lunar" sequence. In DWD-18, the performance of the auto 2 acoustic analyzer is superior to that of the manual analysis in terms of the precision and accuracy measures, but its errors are slightly different from those of the manual analysis, and in particular, its resulting transcription is such that the "people" word match which was found on the manual analysis was missed for auto 1 and auto 2. This is due to the effect of a phonological rule which the human apparently took into account in his analysis but which the mechanical analysis component did not know about. The phonological rule component which has been implemented since these experiments were run is capable of recovering this match.

Performance of Syntax and Semantics

For the higher level components of Syntax and Semantics the same types of precision and accuracy measurements no longer seem appropriate until one has processed large numbers of utterances and recorded the success rate; and even then, there is no natural notion of a precision measure. Questions of interest in the syntactic and semantic areas of the system include the following. How much effort is devoted to searching blind alleys before a correct interpretation of the utterance is found? How many false interpretations are accepted in addition to (or before) the correct one? Is the correct one found at all?, etc.

While we do not begin to have answers to these questions, we have run test cases which can serve as benchmarks. We will illustrate with a brief summary of the syntactic and semantic processing of a sentence DWD 24 ("How many samples contain silicon?") from a segment lattice obtained by mechanical segmentation and labeling. (Two editing changes were made to the lattice to manually simulate the effects of phonological rules.)

In the initial lexical retrieval scan of the segment lattice for this sentence, word matches for "sample," "contain," and "silicon" were found with acceptable acoustic scores, together with a number of other accidental word matches such as "contain" (in another place in the input), "occur," "occuring," "with," "content," "contents," and many others. In the formation of one-word theories, four different matches of "contain" were combined into a single fuzzy word match, four matches for "samples" and two for "sample" were combined into another single fuzzy match, and a number of other fuzzy word matches and semantic "clumps" occurred. Monitors placed by Semantics during processing of one-word theories detected coincidences between "samples" and "occur(ing)," between "contain" and "silicon," between "sample(s)" and "contain," and others. These events were ordered by their scores as assigned by the control component and the first two-word theory created was for "samples occur(ing)" (Theory 21). The second two-word theory was for "sample(s) contain" (Theory 22) and the third for "contain silicon" (Theory 23). There was also a theory for "sample(s)" and the other word match for "contain" (Theory 25). Theory 22 ("sample(s) contain") detected the match for "silicon" and produced Theory 26 ("sample(s) contain silicon"). Also Theory 23 ("contain silicon") detected the word match for "sample(s)," but it refrained from creating a duplicate of Theory 26 after detecting its presence. Theory 26 was then passed to Syntax for verification and further prediction.

The word matches for Theory 26 form a contiguous sequence of words from position six in the signal (60 ms from the beginning of the utterance) to the end, and Syntax was able to parse this sequence without knowing the word matches which occurred at the beginning of the sentence. After parsing the words that it was given, Syntax noticed word matches already in the word lattice for "many" and "any" ending at position six, proposed "much" and "there" and syntactic classes DET (determiner) and PREP (preposition), all ending at position six. It also set monitors at position six looking for the classes ADJ, ORD, DET, N, V, NEG, and PREP.

The notice for "any" from Syntax for Theory 26 resulted in a new theory for "any samples contain silicon" (Theory 30), which detected the word "give" to its left. However, Syntax rejected "give any samples contain silicon" as being ungrammatical. The notice for "many" combined with Theory 26 to give Theory 31 ("many samples contain silicon"), which in turn noticed several words ending at the left end of "many" including the word "how." The scores of the words and the strategies applied by Control are such that the 38th theory formed was the complete analysis, "how many samples contain silicone?"

In the process of this computation, Semantics had placed 48 monitors of various types on specific words and concepts in the semantic network. There were 48 events (resulting from notices from monitors) left unprocessed on the event queue and an unknown number of potential events which could have been noticed if processing were continued. Syntax had created 104 configurations and 142 transitions in its internal syntax tables, and set 51 monitors on positions in the word lattice.

Notice that although the potential search space is vast, and the control mechanism is set up to systematically cover the entire space (if necessary) looking for an interpretation of the utterance, the order of processing theories is such that we have found the correct analysis at a very early stage of the search, leaving the vast majority of the computations on other paths undone.

FUTURE DEVELOPMENTS

As a consequence of further experience with the gradually evolving SPEECHLIS and further thought on the matter, it is clear that we could benefit greatly from a component presumably not used by Klatt and Stevens in their experiment. This is a prosodic component which knows the required relationships between syntactic structure and meaning, on the one hand, and the intonation contour and stress patterns of a speech utterance, on the other. When one considers the inherent ambiguity of the speech utterance which is entailed by the loss of word and phoneme boundaries and the relative uncertainty of identification of the elementary units of phonetic "spelling," and when one contrasts this with the fact that sentences read aloud are capable of resolving syntactic ambiguities which are not resolvable in written form, it is clear that some additional information must be present in the spoken utterance beyond a mere sequence of vaguely blurred sounds. It appears that this additional information is provided in the subtle variations in pitch, energy, and segment duration which are present in the spoken utterance and which seemingly relate the speech signal directly to the syntactic structure of the utterance. Although not presently a part of SPEECHLIS, we plan to include such a component in the system in the near future. It is anticipated that such information will greatly reduce the number of possible syntactic analysis paths which must be considered in the current system.

Another development planned for the future, and on which we are now working, is a much more sophisticated word verification component. This component will take a word match proposed by lexical retrieval or other sources, which has passed the tests of the current word matching component, and will perform a type of analysis-by-synthesis derivation of the detailed behavior of formants, transitions, etc. This will then be compared against the acoustic analysis parameters of the speech signal to obtain a more reliable word match score than that currently obtained. We expect this component to greatly reduce the number of accidental word matches accepted for consideration by the higher level components.

CONCLUSIONS

We have presented a brief overview of the various components of the BBN speech understanding system together with a motivation for the structure of the system, the required capabilities of the individual components, and a brief description of how they work. More detailed descriptions of the individual components are contained in separate papers [1], [6]–[9]. The components of the current system are but crude approximations of the components which we plan to evolve, but they have been assembled into a total system in their current state in order to study their interactions. We believe that the development of the individual components will be more effective and the results more realistic if their development is done in the context of a total system rather than in isolation, and our experience so far bears this out. The project is now in a state where the interaction between the people working on acoustic analysis and those working on lexical retrieval and word matching as they try to make their components fit together has resulted in improvements to both sides, and this appears to be a continuing process.

A central issue of the BBN speech project is to gain insight into the ways in which the higher level linguistic components interact with the acoustic–phonetic and phonological components in the overall speech understanding process and to develop techniques for making this happen efficiently in mechanical speech understanding systems. We are especially concerned with discovering techniques which will be capable of dealing with a large vocabulary, a fluent English syntax, and a diversified range of semantic concepts, rather than attempting to optimize performance for small vocabularies and restricted syntax and semantics. We are concerned with finding the limits where increased vocabulary size, increased fluency of language, and increased range of semantic diversity cannot be handled by increased reliability in acoustic–phonetic and phonological analysis and word verification. Although the current capabilities of our system are but suggestive promises of what is to come, we think that the behavior of this minimal system on test sentences amply illustrates the potential power of the techniques which we have described. The full assessment of their capabilities must however await further development and testing.

ACKNOWLEDGMENT

The work described in this paper was done by members of the speech understanding project at Bolt Beranek and Newman, Inc. At the time of writing these included M. Bates, J. Colarusso, C. Cook, L. Gould, D. Klatt, J. Makhoul, B. Nash-Webber, P. Rovner, T. Scandora, R. Schwartz, and J. Wolf.

REFERENCES

[1] M. Bates, "The use of syntax in a speech understanding system," in *Proc. IEEE Symp. Speech Recognition*, Carnegie-Mellon Univ., Pittsburgh, Pa., Apr. 1974.

[2] D. H. Klatt and K. N. Stevens, "Strategies for recognition of spoken sentences from visual examination of spectrograms," Bolt Beranek and Newman, Inc., Cambridge, Mass., Rep. 2154, 1971.

[3] J. Makhoul, "Selective linear predictive spectral matching," presented at the 86th meeting of the Acoustical Society of America, Los Angeles, Calif.; also in Speech Understanding Res. Note 111, NIC 19951, 1973.

[4] J. Makhoul and J. Wolf, "Linear prediction and the spectral analysis of speech," Bolt Beranek and Newman, Inc., Cambridge, Mass., Rep. 2304, 1972.

[5] ——, "The use of a two-pole linear prediction model in speech recognition," Bolt Beranek and Newman, Inc., Cambridge, Mass., Rep. 2537, 1973.

[6] B. Nash-Webber, "Semantic support for a speech understanding system," in *Proc. IEEE Symp. Speech Recognition*, Carnegie-Mellon Univ., Pittsburgh, Pa., Apr. 1974; also this issue, pp. 124–129.

[7] P. Rovner *et al.*, "Where the words are: lexical retrieval in a speech understanding system," in *Proc. IEEE Symp. Speech Recognition*, Carnegie-Mellon Univ., Pittsburgh, Pa., Apr. 1974.

[8] ——, "Control concepts in a speech understanding system," Bolt Beranek and Newman, Inc., Cambridge, Mass., Rep. 2703, 1974; also in *Proc. IEEE Symp. Speech Recognition*, Carnegie-Mellon Univ., Pittsburgh, Pa., Apr. 1974; also this issue, pp. 136–140.

[9] R. Schwartz and J. Makhoul, "Where the phonemes are: dealing with ambiguity in acoustic-phonetic recognition," in *Proc. IEEE Symp. Speech Recognition*, Carnegie-Mellon Univ., Pittsburgh, Pa., Apr. 1974; also this issue, pp. 50–53.

[10] E. Wanner, "Do we understand sentences from the outside-in or from the inside-out?," *Daedalus*, pp. 163–183, Summer 1973.

[11] W. A. Woods, R. M. Kaplan, and B. Nash-Webber, "The lunar sciences natural language information system: final report," Bolt Beranek and Newman Inc., Cambridge, Mass., Rep. 2378, 1972.

[12] W. A. Woods and J. Makhoul, "Mechanical inference problems in continuous speech understanding," Bolt Beranek and Newman, Inc., Cambridge, Mass., Rep. 2565, Aug. 1973; also, *Artificial Intelligence*, pp. 73–91, Spring 1974.

[13] W. A. Woods, "Progress in natural language understanding—an application to lunar geology," in *1973 Nat. Computer Conf. and Exposition, AFIPS Conf. Proc.*

Organization of the Hearsay II Speech Understanding System

VICTOR R. LESSER, RICHARD D. FENNELL, LEE D. ERMAN, AND D. RAJ REDDY, MEMBER, IEEE

Abstract—**Hearsay II (HSII) is a system currently under development at Carnegie-Mellon University to study the connected speech understanding problem. It is similar to Hearsay I (HSI) in that it is based on the hypothesize-and-test paradigm, using cooperating independent knowledge sources communicating with each other through a global data structure (blackboard). It differs in the sense that many of the limitations and shortcomings of HSI are resolved in HSII.**

The main new features of the Hearsay II system structure are: 1) the representation of knowledge as self-activating, asynchronous, parallel processes, 2) the representation of the partial analysis in a generalized three-dimensional network (the dimensions being level of representation (e.g., acoustic, phonetic, phonemic, lexical, syntactic), time, and alternatives) with contextual and structural support connections explicitly specified, 3) a convenient modular structure for incorporating new knowledge into the system at any level, and 4) a system structure suitable for execution on a parallel processing system.

The main task domain under study is the retrieval of daily wire-service news stories upon voice request by the user. The main parametric representations used for this study are 1/3-octave filter-bank and linear-predictive coding (LPC)-derived vocal tract parameters [10], [11]. The acoustic segmentation and labeling procedures are parameter-independent [7]. The acoustic, phonetic, and phonological components [23] are feature-based rewriting rules which transform the segmental units into higher level phonetic units. The vocabulary size for the task is approximately 1200 words. This vocabulary information is used to generate word-level hypotheses from phonetic and surface-phonemic levels based on prosodic (stress) information. The syntax for the task permits simple English-like sentences and is used to generate hypotheses based on the probability of occurrence of that grammatical construct [19]. The semantic model is based on the news items of the day, analysis of the conversation, and the presence of certain content words in the partial analysis. This knowledge is to be represented as a production system. The system is expected to be operational on a 16-processor minicomputer system [3] being built at Carnegie-Mellon University.

This paper deals primarily with the issues of the system organization of the HSII system.

INTRODUCTION

THE HEARSAY II (HSII) speech understanding system is a successor to the Hearsay I (HSI) system [16], [17]. HSII represents, in terms of both its system organization and its speech knowledge, a significant increase in sophistication and generality over HSI. The development of HSII has been based on two years of experience with a running version of HSI, a desire to exploit multiprocessor and network computer architecture for efficient implementation [3], [4], [6], and a desire to handle more complex speech task domains (e.g., larger vocabularies, less restricted grammars, and a more complete set of knowledge sources including prosodics, user models, etc.). While from a conceptual point of view HSII is a natural extension of the framework that HSI posited for a speech understanding system, it differs significantly in its design and in its details of implementation.[1]

THE HEARSAY SYSTEM MODEL

HSI was based on the view that the inherently errorful nature of connected speech processing could be handled only through the efficient use of multiple, diverse sources of knowledge [13], [15]. The major focus of the design of HSI was the development of a framework for representing these diverse sources of knowledge and their cooperation [18]. This framework is the conceptual legacy which forms the basis for the HSII design.

There are four dimensions along which knowledge representation in HSI can be described: 1) function, 2) structure, 3) cooperation, and 4) attention focusing.

The *function* of a knowledge source (KS) in HSI has three aspects. The first is for the KS to know when it has something useful to contribute, the second is to contribute its knowledge through the mechanism of making a *hypothesis* (guess) about some aspect of the speech utterance, and the third is to evaluate the contribution of other knowledge sources, i.e., to verify and reorder (or reject) the hypotheses made by other knowledge sources. Each of these aspects of a KS is carried out with respect to a particular context, the context being some subset of the previously generated hypotheses. Thus, new knowledge is built upon the educated guesses made at some previous time by other knowledge sources.

The *structure* of each knowledge source in HSI is specified so that it is independent and separable from all other KS's in the system. This permits the easy addition of new

Manuscript received March 29, 1974; revised August 15, 1974. This research was supported in part by the Defense Advanced Research Projects Agency under Contract F44620-73-C-0074 and monitored by the Air Force Office of Scientific Research. This paper was presented at the IEEE Symposium on Speech Recognition, Carnegie-Mellon University, Pittsburgh, Pa., April 15–19, 1974.

The authors are with the Department of Computer Science, Carnegie-Mellon University, Pittsburgh, Pa. 15213.

[1] Several other organizations for speech understanding systems have been implemented over the past few years. Included among the more interesting ones are the SDC system [2], [20], the Bolt Beranek and Newman (BBN) SPEECHLIS system [21], [24], the DRAGON system [1], and the IBM system [9].

Reprinted from *IEEE Trans. Acoust., Speech, and Signal Process.*, vol. ASSP-23, pp. 11–24, Feb. 1975.

types of KS's and replacement of KS's with alternative versions of those KS's. Thus, the system structure can be easily adapted to new speech task domains which have KS's specific to that domain, and the contribution of a particular KS to the total recognition effort can be more easily evaluated.

The choice of a framework for *cooperation* among KS's is intimately interwoven with the function and structure of knowledge in HSI. The mechanism for KS cooperation involves *hypothesizing* and *testing* (creating and evaluating) hypotheses in a *global data base* (blackboard). The generation and modification of globally accessible hypotheses thus becomes the primary means of communication between diverse KS's. This mechanism of cooperation allows a KS to contribute knowledge without being aware of which other KS's will use its knowledge or which KS contributed the knowledge that it used. Thus, each KS can be made independent and separable.

The global data base that KS's use for cooperation contains many possible interpretations of the speech data. Each of these interpretations represents a "limited" context in which a KS can possibly contribute information by proposing or validating hypotheses. *Attention focusing* of a KS involves choosing which of these limited contexts it will operate in and for how much processing time. The attention focusing strategy is decoupled from the functions of individual KS's. Thus, the decision of whether a KS can contribute in a particular context is local to the KS, while the assignment of that KS to one of the many contexts on which it can possibly operate is made more globally. This decoupling of focusing strategy from knowledge acquisition, together with the decoupling of the data environment (global data base) from control flow (KS invocation) and the limited context in which a KS operates, permits a quick refocusing of attention of KS's. The ability to refocus quickly is very important in a speech understanding system, because the errorful nature of the speech data and its processing leads to many potential interpretations of the speech. Thus, as soon as possible after an interpretation no longer seems the most promising, the activity of the system should be refocused to the new most promising interpretation.

OVERVIEW OF HSI

The following is a brief description of the HSI implementation for this model of knowledge source representation and cooperation. This description will then be used to contrast the differences of implementation philosophy between HSI and HSII. (More complete descriptions of HSI are contained in [5], [12], [16], [17].)

HSI Implementation Overview

The global data base of HSI consists of partial sentence hypotheses, each being a sequence of words with non-overlapping time locations in the utterance. It is a *partial* sentence hypothesis because not all of the utterance need be described by the given sequence of words. In particular, gaps in the knowledge of the utterance are designated by "filler" words. The partial sentence hypotheses also contain confidence ratings for each word hypothesis and a composite rating for the overall sequence of words. A sentence hypothesis is the focal point that is used to invoke a knowledge source. The sentence hypothesis also contains the accumulation of all information that any KS has contributed to that hypothesis.

KS's are invoked in a lockstep sequence consisting of three phases: *poll*, *hypothesize*, and *test*. At each phase, all KS's are invoked for that phase, and the next phase does not commence until all KS's have completed the current one. The poll phase involves determining which KS's have something to contribute to the sentence hypothesis which is currently being focused upon; polling also determines how confident each KS is about its proposed contributions. The hypothesize phase consists of invoking the KS showing the most confidence about its proposed contribution of knowledge. This KS then hypothesizes a set of possible words (option words) for some (one) "filler" word in the speech utterance. The testing phase consists of each KS evaluating (verifying) the possible option words with respect to the given context. After all KS's have completed their verifications, the option words which seem most likely, based on the combined ratings of all the KS's, are then used to construct new partial sentence hypotheses. The global data base is then re-evaluated to find the most promising sentence hypothesis; this hypothesis then becomes the focal point for the next hypothesize-and-test cycle.

HSI Performance

The HSI system first demonstrated live, connected-speech recognition publicly in June 1972. Since that time, about three man-years have been spent in improving its performance. The system has been tested on a set of 144 connected speech utterances, containing 676 word tokens, spoken by five speakers, and consisting of four tasks, with vocabularies ranging from 28 to 76 words. On the average, the system locates and correctly identifies about 93 percent of the words, using all of its KS's. Without the use of the Semantics KS, the accuracy decreases to 70 percent. It decreases further to about 39 percent when neither Syntax nor Semantics are used. A more complete performance summary may be found in the Appendix.

HSI Design Limitations

There are four major design decisions in the HSI implementation of knowledge representation and cooperation which make it difficult to apply HSI to more complex speech tasks or multiprocessor environments.

The *first*, and most important, of these limiting decisions concerns the use of the hypothesize-and-test paradigm. As implemented in HSI, the paradigm is exploited only at the word level. The implication of hypothesizing and testing at only the word level is that the knowledge representation is uniform only with respect to cooperation at that level. That is, the information content of any element in the global data base is limited to a description at the word level. The addition of nonword level KS's (i.e., KS's cooperating via either subword levels, such as syllables or phones, or via supraword levels, such as phrases or concepts) thus becomes cumbersome because this knowledge must somehow be related to hypothesizing and testing at the word level. This approach to nonword level KS's makes it difficult to add nonword knowledge and to evaluate the contribution of this knowledge. In addition, the inability to share nonword level information among KS's causes such information to be recomputed by each KS that needs it.

Second, HSI constrains the hypothesize-and-test paradigm to operate in a lockstep control sequence. The effect of this decision is to limit parallelism, because the time required to complete a hypothesize-and-test cycle is the maximum time required by any single hypothesizer KS plus the maximum time required by any single verifier (testing) KS. Another disadvantage of this control scheme is that it increases the time it takes the system to refocus attention, because there is no provision for any communication of partial results among KS's. Thus, for example, a rejection of a particular option word by a KS will not be noticed until all the KS's have tested all the option words.

The *third* weakness in the HSI implementation concerns the structure of the global data base: there is no provision for specifying relationships among alternative sentence hypotheses. The absence of relational structures among hypotheses has the effect of increasing the overall computation time and increasing the time to refocus attention, because the information gained by working on one hypothesis cannot be shared by propagating it to other relevant hypotheses.

The *fourth* limiting design decision relates to how a global problem-solving strategy (policy) is implemented in HSI: policy decisions, such as those involving attention focusing, are centralized (in a "Recognition Overlord"), and there is no coherent structure for the policy algorithms. The effect of having no explicit system structure for implementing policy decisions makes it very awkward to add or delete new policy algorithms and difficult to analyze the effectiveness of a policy and its interaction with other policies.

OVERVIEW OF HSII

Experience with HSI (as described above) has led to several important observations about a more general, uniform, and natural structure for representing and operating on the (dynamic) state of the utterance recognition.[2]

1) The information contained in hypotheses at different levels of knowledge representation may be encoded in essentially identical internal structures, except for the primitive unit of information held in an hypothesis. This structural homogeneity in the global data base allows the actions of hypothesizing and testing at these various levels to be treated in a uniform manner.

2) The different types of knowledge (and their relationships) present in speech may be naturally represented in a single, uniform data structure. This data structure is three-dimensional: one dimension represents information levels (e.g., phrasal, lexical, phonetic), the second represents speech time, and the third dimension contains alternative (competing) hypotheses at a particular level and time. These three dimensions form a convenient addressing structure for locating hypotheses.

3) There is a conceptually simple and uniform way of dynamically relating hypotheses at one level of knowledge to alternative hypotheses at that level and to hypotheses at other knowledge levels in the structure. The resulting structure is an AND/OR graph with modifications which provide for temporal relationships and selective dependency relationships.[3]

System Structure

The main goal of the HSII design is to extend the concepts developed in HSI for the representation and cooperation of knowledge at the word level to *all levels of knowledge* needed in a speech understanding system, based on the preceding observations.

The generalization of the hypothesize-and-test paradigm to all levels of speech knowledge implies the need for a mechanism for transferring information among levels. This mechanism is already embodied in the hypothesize-and-test paradigm; that is, one can characterize two types of hypothesization a knowledge source might be called upon to perform: horizontal and vertical hypothesization. A hypothesization is *horizontal* when a KS uses contextual information at a given knowledge level to predict new hypotheses at the same level (e.g., the hypothesization that the word "night" might follow the sequence of words "day"–"and"), whereas a hypothesization is *vertical* when a KS uses information at one level in the data base to predict new hypotheses at a different level (e.g., the generation of a hypothesis that a [T] occurred when a segment of silence is followed by a segment of aspiration).

The HSII implementation of the hypothesize-and-test paradigm has also resulted in a generalization of the lockstep control scheme for KS sequencing employed by HSI. HSII relaxes the constraints on the hypothesize-and-test paradigm and allows the KS processes to run in an asynchronous, data-directed manner. A KS is instantiated as a *KS process* whenever the data base exhibits characteristics which satisfy a "precondition" of the KS. A *precondition* of a KS is a description of some partial state of the data base which defines when and where the KS can contribute its knowledge by modifying the data base. Such a modification might be adding new hypotheses proposed by the KS (at the information level appropriate for that KS) or verifying (criticizing) hypotheses which already exist.

[2] The meaning of these observations will be made more clear by the further descriptions that follow.

[3] This latter feature refers to "connection matrices" and is described below in more detail.

The modifications made by any given KS process are expected to trigger further KS's by creating new conditions in the data base to which those KS's respond. The structure of a hypothesis has been so designed as to allow the preconditions of most KS's to be sensitive to a single, simple change in some hypothesis (such as the changing of a rating or the creation of a structural link). Through this data-directed interpretation of the hypothesize-and-test paradigm, HSII KS's exhibit a high degree of asynchrony and potential parallelism. A side-effect of this more general control scheme for HSII is that the overall problem-solving strategy need not be centralized and implemented as a monolithic overlord, but rather can be implemented as *policy modules* which operate in precisely the same manner as KS's.

The three-dimensional data base, augmented by the AND/OR structural relationships specified over that data base, permits information generated by one KS to be: 1) retained for use by other KS's, and 2) quickly propagated to other relevant parts of the data base. This retention and propagation provide two important features for solving a complex problem in which errors are highly likely. First, quick refocusing can occur when a particular path no longer appears promising. Second, "selective" backtracking may be used; i.e., when a KS finds that it has made an incorrect decision, it does not have to eliminate all information generated subsequent to that decision, but rather only that subset which depends on the incorrect decision. In this way, information generated by one knowledge source is retained and is usable by itself and other KS's in other relevant contexts.

Summarizing, HSII is based on the views: 1) that the state of the recognition can be represented in a uniform, multilevel data base, and 2) that speech knowledge can be characterized in a natural manner by describing many small KS's. These KS's react to certain states of the data base (via their preconditions) and, once instantiated as KS processes, provide their own changes to the data base which contribute to the progress of the recognition. The hypothesize-and-test paradigm, when stated in sufficiently nonrestrictive (parallel) terms, serves to describe the general interactions among these KS's. In particular, changes made by one or more KS processes may trigger other KS's to react to these changes by validating (testing) them or hypothesizing further changes. The intent of HSII is to provide a framework within which to explore various configurations of information levels, KS's, and global strategies.[4]

From a more general point of view, the goal of HSII is to provide a multiprocess-oriented software architecture to serve as a basis for systems of cooperating (but independent and asynchronous) data-directed KS processes. The purpose of such a structure is to achieve effective parallel search over a general artificial intelligence problem-solving graph, employing the hypothesize-and-test paradigm to generate the search graph and using a uniform, interconnected, multilevel global data base as the primary means of interprocess communication.

[4] It is interesting to note that this generalized form of hypothesize-and-test leads to a system organization with some characteristics similar to QA4 [22] and PLANNER [8]. In particular, there are strong similarities in the data-directed sequencing of processes.

HSII SYSTEM DESIGN AND IMPLEMENTATION

One can derive from the description of the desired HSII recognition process given above several basic components of the required system structure. First, a sufficiently general *structured global data base* is needed, through which the KS's may communicate by inserting hypotheses and by inspecting and modifying the hypotheses placed there by other KS's. Second, some means for describing the various KS's and their internal processing capabilities is required. Third, in order to have knowledge sources activated in a data-directed manner, a method is required by which a set of *preconditions* may be specified and associated with each KS. Fourth, in order to detect the satisfaction of these preconditions and in order to allow KS's to locate parts of the data base in which they are interested, two mechanisms are needed: 1) a *monitoring mechanism* to record where in the data base changes have occurred and the nature of those changes, and 2) an *associative retrieval mechanism* for accessing parts of the data base which conform to particular patterns specified by *matching prototypes*.

Elements of the System Structure

The following sections outline the HSII implementation of the various basic system components.

Global Data Base: The design of HSII is centered around a global data base (blackboard) which is accessible to all KS processes. The global data base is structured as a uniform, multilevel, interconnected data structure.

Each level in the data base contains a (potentially complete) representation of the utterance; the levels are differentiated by the units that make up the representation, e.g., phrases, words, phonemes. The system structure of HSII does not prespecify what the levels in the global data structure are to be. A particular configuration, called HSII-C0 (Configuration Zero), is being implemented as the first test of the HSII structure. Fig. 1 shows a schematic of the levels of HSII-C0. A more detailed description and justification for parts of this particular configuration can be found in [23]. This configuration will be used as the basis for examples to illustrate various aspects of the HSII system.

Parametric Level: The parametric level holds the most basic representation of the utterance that the system has; it is the only direct input to the machine about the acoustic signal. Several different sets of parameters are being used in HSII-C0 interchangeably: 1/3-octave filter-band energies measured every 10 ms, LPC-derived vocal-tract parameters [10], and wide-band energies and zero-crossing counts.

Segmental Level: This level represents the utterance as labeled acoustic segments. Although the set of labels may

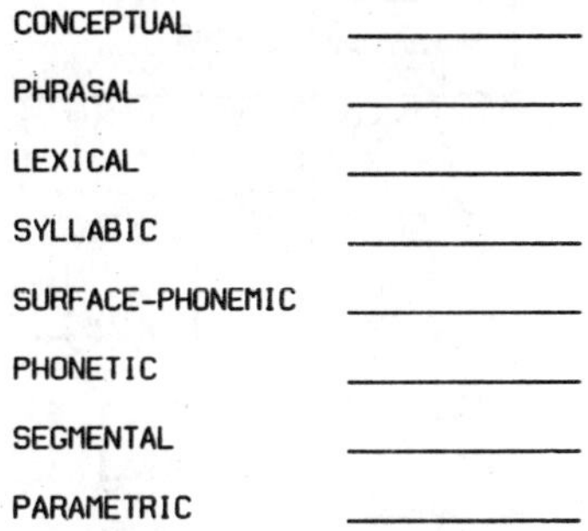

Fig. 1. Levels in HSII-C0.

be phonetic-like, the level is not intended to be phonetic—the segmentation and labeling reflect acoustic manifestation and do not, for example, attempt to compensate for the context of the segments or attempt to combine acoustically dissimilar segments into (phonetic) units.

As with all levels, any particular portion of the utterance may be represented by more than one competing hypothesis (i.e., multiple segmentations and labelings may co-exist).

Phonetic Level: At this level, the utterance is represented by a phonetic description. This is a *broad* phonetic description in that the size (duration) of the units is on the order of the "size" of phonemes; it is a *fine* phonetic description to the extent that each element is labeled with a fairly detailed allophonic classification (e.g., "stressed, nasalized [I]").

Surface-Phonemic Level: This level, named by seemingly contradicting terms, represents the utterance by phoneme-like units, with the addition of modifiers such as stress and boundary (word, morpheme, syllable) markings.

Syllabic Level: The unit of representation here is the syllable.

Lexical Level: The unit of information at this level is the word. (Note again that at any level competing representations can be accommodated.)

Phrasal Level: Syntactic elements appear at this level. In fact, since a level may contain arbitrarily many "sublevels" of elements structured as a modified AND/OR graph, traditional kinds of syntactic trees can be directly represented here.

Conceptual Level: The units at this level are "concepts." As with the phrasal level, it may be appropriate to use the graph structure of the data base to indicate relationships among different concepts.

The basic unit in the data structure is a *node*; a node represents the *hypothesis* that a particular element exists in the utterance. For example, a hypothesis at the phonetic level may be labeled as "T." Besides containing the hypothesis element name, a node holds several other kinds of information, including: 1) a correlation with a particular *time period* in the speech utterance,[5] 2) *scheduling parameters* (validity ratings, attention-focusing factors, measures of computing effort expended, etc.), and 3) *connection information* which relates the node to other nodes in the data base.

Structural relationships between nodes (hypotheses) are represented through the use of *links*; links provide a means for specifying contextual abstractions about the relationships of hypotheses. A link is an element in the data structure which associates two nodes as an ordered pair; one of the nodes is termed the *upper hypothesis*, and the other is called the *lower hypothesis*. The lower hypothesis is said to *support* the upper hypothesis; the upper hypothesis is called a *use* of the lower one. There are several types of links; in general, if a node serves as the upper hypothesis for more than one link, all of those links must be of the same type. Thus, one can talk of the "type of the hypothesis," which is the same as the type of all of its lower links. The two most important structural relationship types are SEQUENCE and OPTION.

A SEQUENCE node is a hypothesis that is supported by a (timewise) sequential set of hypotheses at a lower level (or sublevel—see below). For example, Fig. 2(a) shows a hypothesis of "will" at the lexical level supported by the (time-)ordered contiguous sequence of "W," "IH," and "L" at the surface-phonemic level. The interpretation of a SEQUENCE node is that all of the lower hypotheses must be valid in order to support the upper hypothesis.

An OPTION node is a hypothesis that has alternative supports from two or more hypotheses, each of which covers essentially the same time period. For example, Fig. 2(b) shows the hypothesis of "noun" at the phrasal level as being supported by any of "boy," "toy," or "tie," all of which are competing word hypotheses covering (approximately) the same time area.[6]

Fig. 3 is a example of a larger fragment of the global data structure. The level of a hypothesis is indicated by its vertical position, the names of the levels are given on the left. Time location is approximately indicated by horizontal placement, but duration is only very roughly indicated (e.g., the boxes surrounding the two hypotheses at the phrasal level should be much wider). Alternatives are indicated by proximity; for example, "will" and "would" are word hypotheses covering the same time span. Likewise, "question" and "modal-question," "you1" and "you2," and "J" and "Y" all represent pairs of alternatives.

This example illustrates several features of the data structure.

The hypothesis "you," at the lexical level, has two alternative phonemic "spellings" indicated; the hypothe-

[5] This time period is specified with an explicit estimation of fuzziness, even to the extent of spanning the entire utterance. As an extreme example, if a sequence of "phonemes" is being hypothesized from a "word" at the lexical level, the time boundaries of the phonemes are specified as "fuzzy" if information regarding their actual locations is not yet available.

[6] In addition to SEQUENCE and OPTION, there are two kinds of structural relationships which are generalizations of them: An AND node is similar to a SEQUENCE node except that there is no implication of any time sequentiality among the supports—they may overlap or be disjoint. An OR node is similar to an OPTION node in that the supports represent alternatives, but (as with the AND node) there is no time requirement.

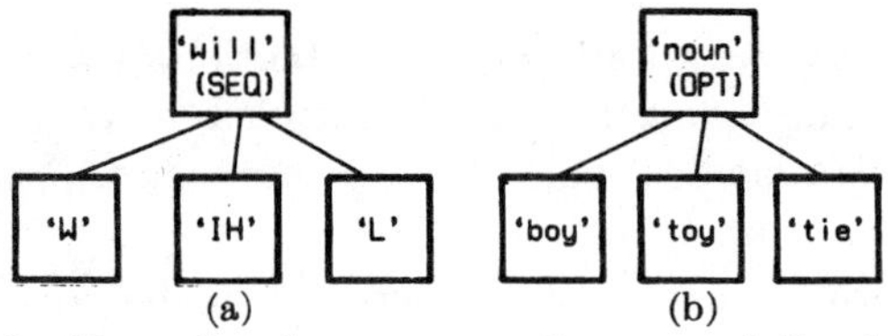

Fig. 2. Examples of SEQUENCE and OPTION relationships.

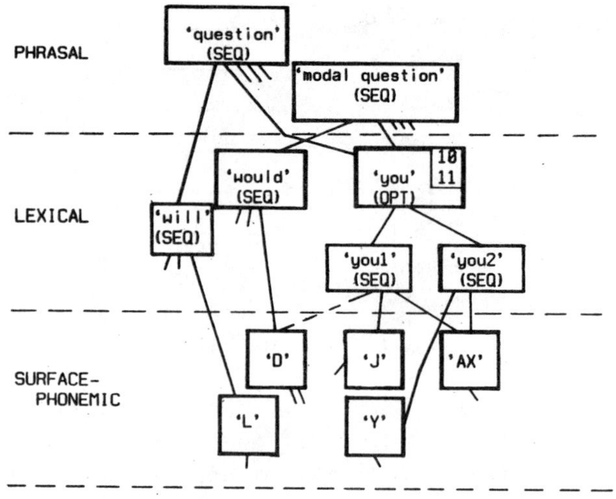

Fig. 3. Example of the data structure.

ses labeled "you1" and "you2" are nodes created, also at the lexical level, to hold those alternatives. In general, such *sublevels* may be created arbitrarily.

The link between "you1" and "D" is a special kind of SEQUENCE link (indicated here by a dashed line) called a CONTEXT link; a CONTEXT link indicates that the lower hypothesis supports the upper one and is contiguous to its brother links, but it is not "part of" the upper hypothesis in the sense that it is not within the time interval of the upper hypothesis—rather, it supplies a context for its brother(s). In this case, one may "read" the structure as stating " "you1" is composed of "J" followed by "AX" (schwa) in the context of the preceding "D." " (This reflects the phonological rule that "would you" is often spoken as "would-ja.") Thus, a CONTEXT link allows important contextual relationships to be represented without violating the implicit time assumptions about SEQUENCE nodes.

Whereas the phonemic spelling of the word "you" held by "you1" includes a contextual constraint, the "you2" option does not have this constraint. However, "you1" and "you2" are such similar hypotheses that there is strong reason for wanting to retain them as alternative options under "you" (as indicated in Fig. 3), rather than representing them unconnectedly. In general, the problem is that the use of a hypothesis implies certain contextual assumptions about its environment, while the support of a hypothesis may itself be predicated on a particular set of contextual assumptions. A mechanism, called a *connection matrix*, exists in the data structure to represent this kind of relationship by specifying, for an OPTION hypothesis, which of its alternative supports are applicable ("connected") to which of its uses. In this example, the connection matrix of "you" (symbolized in Fig. 3 by the two-dimensional binary matrix in the node) specifies that support "you1" is relevant to use "question" (but not to "modal-question") and that support "you2" is relevant to both uses. The use of a connection matrix allows the efforts of preceding KS decisions to be accumulated for future use and modification without necessitating contextual duplication of parts of the data base. Thus, much of the duplication of effort due to the backtracking mode of HSI is avoided in HSII.

Besides showing structural relationships (i.e., that one unit is composed of several other units), a link is a statement about the degree to which one hypothesis implies (i.e., gives evidence for the existence of) another hypothesis. The strength of the implication is held as information on the link. The sense of the implication may be negative; that is, a link may indicate that one hypothesis is evidence for the invalidity of another. Finally, this statement of implication is bidirectional; the existence of the upper hypothesis may give credence to the existence of the lower hypothesis and vice versa.

The nature of the implications represented by the links provides a uniform basis for propagating changes made in one part of the data structure to other relevant parts without necessarily requiring the intervention of particular KS's at each step. Considering the example of Fig. 3, assume that the validity of the hypothesis labeled "J" is modified by some KS (presumably operating at the phonetic level) and becomes very low. One possible scenario for rippling this change through the data base is the following.

First, the estimated validity of "you1" is reduced, because "J" is a lower hypothesis of "you1."

This, in turn, may cause the rating of "you" to be reduced.

The connection matrix at "you" specifies that "you1" is not relevant to "modal-question," so the latter hypothesis is not affected by the change in rating of the former. Notice that the existence of the connection matrix allows this decision to be made locally in the data structure, without having to search back down to the "D" and "J."

"Question," however, is supported by "you1" (through the connection matrix at "you"), so its rating is affected.

Further propagations can continue to occur, perhaps down the other SEQUENCE links under "question" and "you1."

KS Specification: A knowledge source is specified in three parts: 1) the conditions under which it is to be activated (in terms of the data base conditions in which it is interested, as described in the section on "preconditions" below), 2) the kinds of changes it makes to the global data base, and 3) a procedural statement (program) of the algorithm which accomplishes those changes. A KS is thus defined as possessing some processing capability which is able to solve some subproblem, given appropriate circumstances for its activation.

The decomposition of the overall recognition task into

various knowledge sources is regarded as being a natural decomposition. That is, the units of the decomposition represent those pieces of knowledge which can be distinguished and recognized as being somehow naturally independent.[7] Given a sufficient set of such KS's (that is, a set that provides enough overall connectivity among the various levels of the data base that a final recognition can be attained), the collection is called the "overall recognition system." Such a scheme of "inverse decomposition" (or, composition) seems very natural for many problem-solving tasks, and it fits well into the hypothesize-and-test approach to problem-solving. As long as a sufficient "covering set" for the data base connections is maintained, one can freely add new KS's, or replace or delete old ones. Each KS is in some sense self-contained, but each is expected to cooperate with the other KS's that happen to be present in the system at that time.

As examples of KS's, Fig. 4 shows the first set of processes implemented for HSII-C0. The levels are indicated as horizontal lines in the figure and are labeled at the left. The KS's are indicated by arcs connecting levels; the starting point(s) of an arc indicates the level(s) of major "input" for the KS, and the end point indicates the "output" level where the KS's major actions occur. In general, the action of most of these particular KS's is to create links between hypotheses on its input level(s) and: 1) existing hypotheses on its output level, if appropriate ones are already there, or 2) hypotheses that it creates on its output level.

The *Segmenter-Classifier* KS uses the description of the speech signal to produce a labeled acoustic segmentation. (See [7] for a description of the algorithm being used.) For any portion of the utterance, several possible alternative segmentations and labels may be produced.

The *Phone Synthesizer* uses labeled acoustic segments to generate elements at the phonetic level. This procedure is sometimes a fairly direct renaming of an hypothesis at the segmental level, perhaps using the context of adjacent segments. In other cases, phone synthesis requires the combining of several segments (e.g., the generation of [t] from a segment of silence followed by a segment of aspiration) or the insertion of phones not indicated directly by the segmentation (e.g., hypothesizing the existence of an [l] if a vowel seems velarized and there is no [l] in the neighborhood). This KS is triggered whenever a new hypothesis is created at the segmental level.

The *Word Candidate Generator* uses phonetic information (primarily just at stressed locations and other areas of high phonetic reliability) to generate word hypotheses. This is accomplished in a two-stage process, with a stop at the syllabic level, from which lexical retrieval is more effective.

[7] The approach taken in knowledge source decomposition is not an attempt to characterize somehow the overall recognition process and then apply some sort of traffic flow analysis to its internal workings in order to decompose the total process into minimally interacting KS's. Rather, KS's are defined by starting with some intuitive notion about the various pieces of knowledge which could be incorporated in a useful way to help achieve a solution.

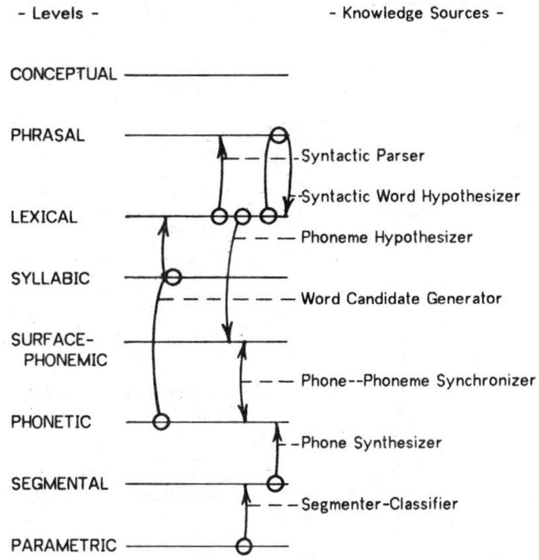

Fig. 4. First KS's for HSII-C0.

The *Syntactic Word Hypothesizer* uses knowledge at the phrasal level to predict possible new words at the lexical level which are adjacent (left or right) to words previously generated at the lexical level. ([19] contains a description of the probabilistic syntax method being used here.) This KS is activated at the beginning of an utterance recognition attempt and, subsequently, whenever a new word is created at the lexical level.

The *Phoneme Hypothesizer* KS is activated whenever a word hypothesis is created (at the lexical level) which is not yet supported by hypotheses at the surface-phonemic level. Its action is to create one or more sequences at the surface-phonemic level which represent alternative pronunciations of the word. (These pronunciations are currently prespecified as entries in a dictionary.)

The *Phone–Phoneme Synchronizer* is triggered whenever a hypothesis is created at either the phonetic or the surface-phonemic level. This KS attempts to link up the new hypothesis with hypotheses at the other level. This linking may be many-to-one in either direction.

The *Syntactic Parser* uses a syntactic definition of the input language to determine if a complete sentence may be assembled from words at the lexical level.

Fig. 5 shows the initial HSII-C0 KS's of Fig. 4 augmented with four additional ones which are being implemented or are planned.

The *Semantic Word Hypothesizer* uses semantic and pragmatic information about the task (news retrieval, in this case) to predict words at the lexical level.

The *Phonological Rule Applier* rewrites sequences at the surface-phonemic level. This KS is used: 1) to augment the dictionary lookup of the Phoneme Hypothesizer, and 2) to handle word boundary conditions that can be predicted by rule.

The primary duties of the *Segment-Phone Synchronizer* and the *Parameter-Segment Synchronizer* are similar: to recover from mistakes make by the (bottom-up) actions of the Phone Synthesizer and Segmenter–Classifier, re-

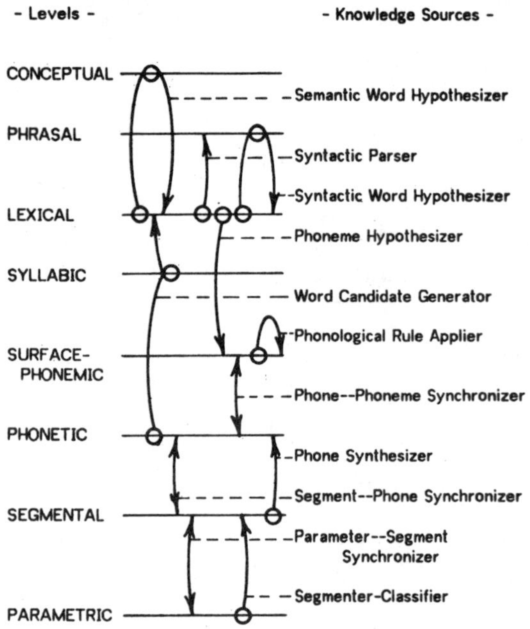

Fig. 5. Augmented KS set for HSII-C0.

spectively, by allowing feedback from the higher to the lower level.

The introduction of these knowledge sources indicates the modularity and extendability of the system in terms of both KS's and levels. In particular, notice that even though the purpose of some KS is stated as "correcting errors produced by other KS's," each KS is independent of the others. Yet additional KS's will be added to the configuration as the need for them is seen and as ideas for their implementation are developed.

In addition to the KS modules described above, all of which embody speech knowledge, several policy modules exist. These modules, which interface to the system in a manner identical to the speech modules, execute policy decisions, e.g., propagation of ratings, focusing of attention, and scheduling of other modules.

Matching-Prototypes and Associative Retrieval: The synchronous processing activity in HSII is primarily data-directed; this implies the need for some mechanism whereby one can retrieve parts of the global data base in an associative manner. HSII provides primitives for associatively searching the data base for hypotheses satisfying specified conditions (e.g., finding all hypotheses at the phonetic level which contain a vowel within a certain time range). The search condition is specified by a *matching prototype,* which is a partial specification of the components of a hypothesis. This partial specification permits a component to be characterized by: 1) a set of desired values, or 2) a DON'T-CARE condition, or 3) values of components of a hypothesis previously derived by matching another prototype. A matching prototype can be compared against a set of hypotheses. Those hypotheses whose component values match those specified by the matching prototype are returned as the result of the search. Associative retrieval of structural relationships among hypotheses is also provided by several primitives. More complex retrievals can be accomplished by combining the retrieval primitives in appropriate ways.

Preconditions and Change Sets: Associated with every KS is a specification of the data base conditions required for the instantiation of that KS. Such specifications, called *preconditions,* conceptually form an AND/OR tree composed of matching prototypes and structural relationships which, when applied to the data base in an associative manner, detect the regions of the data base in which the KS is interested (if the precondition is capable of being satisfied at that time). Alternatively, one might think of the precondition specification as a procedure, involving matching prototypes and structural relationships, which effectively evaluates a conceptual AND/OR tree. This procedure may contain arbitrarily complex decisions (based on current and past modifications to the data base) resulting in the activation of desired KS's within the chosen contexts. The context corresponding to the discovered data base region which satisfies some KS's precondition is used as an initial context in which to instantiate that KS as a new process. If there are multiple regions in the data base that satisfy the specified conditions, the KS can be separately instantiated for each context, or once with a list of all such contexts.

Whenever any KS performs a modification to the global data base, the essence of the modification is preserved in a *change set* appropriate to the change made (e.g., one change set records rating changes, while another records time range changes). Change sets serve to categorize data base modifications (events) and are thus useful in precondition evaluation since they limit the areas in the data base that need to be examined in detail. As currently implemented, precondition evaluators exist as a set of procedures which monitor changes in the data base (i.e., they monitor additions to those change sets in which they are interested). These precondition procedures are themselves data-directed in that they are applied whenever sufficient changes have been made in the global data base. In effect, the precondition procedures themselves have preconditions, albeit of a much simpler form than those possible for KS's. For example, a precondition procedure may specify that it should be invoked (by a system precondition invoker) whenever changes occur to two adjacent hypotheses at the word level or whenever support is added to the phrasal level. By using the (coarse) classifications afforded by change sets, the system avoids most unnecessary data base examinations by the precondition procedures. The major point to be made is that the scheme of precondition evaluation is *event driven,* being based on the occurrence of changes in the global data base. In particular, precondition evaluators are not involved in a form of busy waiting in which they are constantly looking for something that is not yet there.

Once invoked, a precondition procedure uses sequences of associative retrievals and structural matches on the data base in an attempt to establish a context satisfying the preconditions of one or more of "its" KS's; any given precondition procedure may be responsible for instantiating several (usually related) KS's. Notice that the data-directed nature of precondition evaluation and KS instantiation is linked closely to the primitive functions that are able to modify the data base, for it is only at points of modification that a precondition that was unsatisfied before may become satisfied. Hence, data base modification routines have the responsibility (although perhaps indirectly) of activating the precondition evaluation mechanism.[8]

Multiprocessing Considerations: Some Problems and Their Solutions

A primary goal in the design of HSII is to exploit the potential parallelism of the Hearsay system model as fully as possible. Several issues associated with the introduction of parallel KS processes into HSII will be described and their current solutions outlined.

Local Contexts: A precondition evaluator (process) is invoked based on the occurrence of certain changes which have taken place in the global data base since the last time the evaluator was invoked; these changes, together with the state of the relevant parts of the global data base at the instant at which the precondition evaluator is invoked, form a *local context* within which the evaluator operates. Conceptually, at the instant of its invocation, the precondition evaluator takes a snapshot of the global data base and saves the substance of the changes that have occurred to that moment, thereby preserving its local context.

The necessity of preserving this local context exists for several reasons: 1) HSII consists of asynchronous processes sharing a common global data base which contains only the most current data (that is, no history of data modification is preserved in the global data base), 2) since the precondition evaluators are also executed asynchronously, each evaluator is interested only in changes in the data base which have occurred since the last time that particular evaluator was executed (that is, the relevant set of changes for a particular precondition evaluator is time-dependent on the last execution of that evaluator), and 3) further modifications to the global data base which are of interest to a given KS process may occur between the time of that KS process's instantiation and the time of its completion (in particular, such modifications and their relationship to data base values which existed at the time of the instantiation of the KS process may influence the computation of that KS process). Hence, the problem of creation of local contexts exists, as do the associated problems of signaling a KS process when its local context is no longer valid and of updating these contexts as further changes occur in the global data base.

T1: start precondition evaluator PRE
(triggered by data base changes)
T2: PRE instantiates a knowledge-source process KS
T3: end PRE

T4: start KS
T5: after KS revalidation of precondition
<computation>
T6: KS modifies global data base
<computation>
T7: KS modifies global data base again
T8: end KS

Fig. 6. Timing sequence of a precondition evaluator and KS.

Consider the time sequence of events shown in Fig. 6. The precondition evaluator PRE is activated to respond to changes occurring in the global data base. PRE should execute in the context of changes existing at time T1 (since that context contains the changes which caused PRE to be activated). KS is instantiated (readied for running) at T2 due to further conditions PRE discovered about the change context of T1. Hence, PRE should pass the context of T1 as the initial environment in which to run KS.

By time T4, when KS actually starts to execute, other changes could have occurred in the global data base due to the actions of other KS processes. So KS should examine these new updating changes (those occurring between T1 and T4) and revalidate its precondition, if necessary. After revalidation, KS assumes the updated context of T5, and it proceeds to base its computation on the context of changes as of T5.

When KS wishes to perform an actual update of elements of the global data base at T6, it must examine the changes to the global data base that have occurred between T5 and T6 to see if any other KS processes may have violated KS's preconditions, thereby invalidating its computations. Having performed this revalidation and any data base updating, KS should update its context to reflect changes up to T6 for use in its further computation. At T7, KS must look for further possible invalidations to its most recent computations, due to possible changes in the global data base by other KS processes during the time period T6 to T7. When KS (which is an instantiation of some KS) completes its actions at T8, its local context may be deleted.

Changes occurring between instantiations of a KS are accumulated in the local contexts of the precondition evaluators and may become part of the local context of a future instantiation of a KS. Thus, the precondition evaluators are always collecting data base changes (since these evaluators are permanently instantiated), while individual KS instantiations accumulate data base changes only during their transient existence.

In practice, to create local contexts one need only save the contents of *changes* which occur in the global data base (thereby allowing the global data base to contain only the very latest values). In particular, no massive copy operations involving the global data base are required.

[8] One might think of HSII as a production system [14] which is executed asynchronously. The preconditions correspond to the left-hand sides (conditions) of productions, and the knowledge sources correspond to the right-hand sides (actions) of the productions. Conceptually, these left-hand sides are evaluated continuously. When a precondition is satisfied, an instantiation of the corresponding right-hand side of its production is created; this instantiation is executed at some arbitrary subsequent time (perhaps subject to instantiation scheduling constraints).

Thus, for each data base event caused by a modification primitive, the associated change[9] is distributed (copied) into the local contexts (which can now be characterized as *local change sets*,[10] referring to the previous discussion on change sets) of all KS processes and precondition evaluators who care. Notice that not every KS process and precondition evaluator cares about every change that takes place. For example, a fricative detector will not care about a data base change associated with the grouping of several words to form a syntactic phrase, but it is interested in the hypothesization of a word whose phonemic spelling contains a fricative.

In order for a KS (or precondition evaluator) process to be notified of changes which occur to particular fields of particular nodes which are in its local context, those fields need to be *tagged* with an alias (called a *tagid*) belonging to that KS instantiation. Then, whenever a modification is made to the global data base, a *message* signaling the change is sent to all who have tagged the field being changed. In addition, the contents of the change are also distributed to the local contexts of those KS's receiving the message. This data field tagging may be requested by either a precondition evaluator which is about to instantiate a KS based on the values of particular fields (which represent the context satisfying the precondition), or by a KS process, once instantiated, which may request additional fields to be tagged.

For example, in its search through the global data base for conditions satisying the preconditions of some KS, a precondition evaluator may accumulate references to the data fields which it has examined; and when the entire precondition has been found to be satisfied, the precondition evaluator tags those fields (for which it has accumulated references) with the name of the KS process it is about to instantiate. Similarly, having been invoked, a KS process might wish to do certain computations, but only if certain data fields are not altered; the KS process itself can tag these fields and thereby be informed of subsequent tampering with the tagged fields. Subsets of these tagged fields (the subsets being formed according to the tagid's chosen) form *critical sets* (specifying the fields of the local context for the KS process) which are *locked* (see below) every time the KS process wishes to modify the global data base. Thus, after having locked the critical set and prior to performing any update operations, the KS process can check to see whether any other KS process has made any changes which might invalidate the current KS's assumed context (and hence, perhaps, invalidate its proposed update).[11] For example, if a KS process is verifying a hypothesis in the data base because its rating exceeds 50 (i.e., the rating value represents part of the local context for the KS process), then before performing any modifications on the data base which depend on the assumption, the KS process should check to be sure that no other KS process has invalidated the rating assumption in the meantime.

In addition to maintaining local copies of the various relevant changes that have occurred since the instantiation of a KS process, a KS process may also include in its context various *supersets* of these changes. For example, if a knowledge source is interested in the values of changes in a node's begin-time or end-time, it might be worthwhile to include a superset which accumulates indicators pointing to changes in either begin-time or end-time (since checking such a superset for new elements would be quicker than checking each constituent subset individually). Note that supersets do not themselves contain any data values, but rather are pointers to changes contained in some one of its subsets. Further note that a KS need not contain in its local context all (or any) of the constituent subsets of a superset in order to have that superset in its local context.

Data Base Deadlock Prevention: Any KS process may request exclusive access to some collection of fields at any time. Thus, unless some care is taken in ordering the requests for such exclusive access, the possibility of getting into a deadlock situation exists (where, for example, one KS process is waiting for exclusive access to a field already held exclusively by a second KS process, and vice versa, resulting in neither process being able to proceed). Applying a linear ordering to the set of lockable fields and requesting exclusive access according to that ordering is a commonly used means of deadlock avoidance in resource allocation. However, this technique works only if all the resources (fields) to be locked are known ahead of time. The ability to tag a data field allows a KS process to locate and examine in arbitrary order the set of hypotheses that will form the context for a data base modification and then, only after the entire set of desired hypotheses (and links) has been determined, to lock the desired set and perform the modification.

Regarding the global data base as having orthogonal dimensions of information level versus utterance time further allows a convenient means of locking entire regions of the data base without explicitly naming the nodes or fields to be affected. This "blanket-locking" is called *region locking*. For example, a KS process might request the locking of a region consisting of the time interval from 50 to 80 centiseconds at the phonetic level. To assist in de-

[9] The information which defines the change consists of the locus of the change (i.e., a node name and a field name) and the old value of the field.

[10] An alternative to replicating the change information for the various KS processes is to maintain a single central copy of those data, passing only references to the centralized items to the various local contexts. The individual change items may then be deleted from their central change sets whenever there are no further outstanding references to that change.

[11] The characterization of local contexts according to specific data fields (which is made possible in part by the choice of levels in the global data base) helps to minimize the overhead associated with context maintenance. Also, the smaller the context, the more flexible the scheduling strategy may be (since it needs to be less concerned with the time required for a context swap on a processor).

termining such regions, each node in the global data base contains a bit vector whose high-order bits describe the time regions covered by the node and whose low-order bits contain the integer level number of that node. These region fields may be manipulated to allow locking of various regions in the data base. Note that a region-lock may be used to obtain exclusive access to a time region which need not contain any nodes yet (i.e., one may region-lock a "vacuum").

To eliminate the possibilities of deadlock, the actual locking operation is relegated to a system primitive, and a KS process is required to present to the locking primitive the entire set of fields to which it wants exclusive access. This set is then extended to include all fields in the critical set of the calling KS process, for the reasons relating to context revalidation given above. The system locking primitive can then request exclusive access for this union of data fields, on behalf of the KS process, according to a universal ordering scheme (such an ordering being possible since every node in the global data base essentially has a unique serial number) which assures that no deadlocks occur. Having been granted exclusive access to all desired fields at once, the KS process may then check to see whether there have been any changes to the tagged data fields. If there have been none, it can proceed to perform its modifications (which modifications are sent to the local contexts of others who care about such things). However, if there were changes, the KS process can, after examining the changed data fields, decide whether it still wants to perform the modifications. When the KS process is finished updating the data base, it releases all its locked fields by executing a system primitive unlocking operator. In particular, the system ensures that a KS process will not request two lock operations without issuing an intervening unlock operation. In this manner, any possibility of a data base deadlock is eliminated.

Goal-Directed Scheduling: The computational sequence of a typical HSII run may be characterized by considering the chronological sequence of states of the utterance recognition at any particular data base level. For example, if one considers the efforts in producing the word level and traces the development of the "best" partial sentences, the processing that will have been done is analogous to a general tree-search, where each node of the tree represents some partially completed sentence (with the eventual resultant sentence being one of the leaves of the tree). The problem now is to guide this tree searching so as to find the answer leaf in an optimal way (according to some measure of optimality). To achieve this end, *ratings* are associated with every hypothesis and link in the global data base (and thus with every partial sentence node of the analogous search tree). Using these ratings (which are effectively evaluation functions indicating the goodness of the work done so far with respect to a given partial sentence), one may employ tree-searching strategies to advance the search in some optimal manner.

To complicate matters further, however, HSII is intended to be a multiprocess-oriented system. Therefore, schemes must be devised for effectively searching a problem-solving graph using parallel processes, since one can conceive of pursuing several branches of the search graph in parallel by asynchronously instantiating various KS processes to evaluate various alternative paths. One must also take into consideration the underlying hardware architecture. The physical placement of the global data base and the KS processes will have a very definite influence on the scheduling philosophy chosen and the resultant system efficiency.

To aid in making scheduling decisions, one may associate with every node in the global data base some *attention-focusing factors*, which are indicators telling how much effort has been devoted to processing in this area of the search tree and how desirable it is to devote further effort to this section of the tree. Such attention-focusing factors may also be associated with various speech time regions to indicate interest in doing further processing on certain regions of the utterance, regardless of any particular information level. Furthermore, attention-focusing factors are associated with every data base modification, thereby distributing attention-focusing factors to the various change sets which constitute the local contexts of the processes in the system. The scheduler is one such process which might be especially interested in such focusing factors, as will be described below. The use of the various ratings and attention-focusing factors allows HSII to perform *goal-directed scheduling*, which is process scheduling so as to achieve "optimal" recognition efficiency. The thrust of goal-directed scheduling is that, while there may be many processes ready to run and work on various parts of the search tree, one should first schedule those processes which can best help to achieve the goal of utterance recognition. Notice that such search-tree pruning techniques as the alpha–beta procedure (which is essentially a sequential algorithm anyway) do not apply to HSII's nongame search trees, which do not have the constraint that alternating levels of the tree represent the moves of an opponent.

Goal-directed scheduling may be viewed as having two separate functions: 1) using the ratings and attention-focusing factors associated with the global data base components to schedule *KS processes* which have been invoked (readied for execution) in response to events previously detected in the global data base, and 2) using these same attention-focusing factors to detect important areas in the global data base which require further work, and invoking *precondition evaluators* as soon as possible to instantiate new KS processes to work in those important areas. Thus, the attention-focusing factors within the global data base serve to schedule both KS processes and precondition evaluators.

A KS process might be scheduled for execution because it possesses the only processing capability available to be applied to an important unexplored area of the data base. However, if there are many such processes ready to execute, the scheduler can perform a type of *means-ends* analysis in which those KS processes are scheduled which are likely to produce data base changes in which the system is currently interested (such interest being noted by high attention-focusing factors in a given change set). For example, if the data base contains focusing factors which highlight activity in a time region in which there are no structural connections between two adjoining levels, the scheduler would probably give a higher priority to a KS process which will attempt (as indicated in its external specifications) to make such a connection than to a KS process which is likely merely to perform a minor refinement on the ratings in one of the levels.

Another means of effecting goal-directed scheduling relates to the attention-focusing factors associated with various time regions of the utterance (such focusing factors reaching across all the information levels of the global data base). Using these time-region focusing factors, one can schedule KS processes which can contribute in a particular time region, or invoke precondition evaluators to instantiate some new KS processes to work within the desired time region.

SUMMARY, CURRENT STATUS, AND PLANS

In summary, HSII is a system organization for speech understanding that permits the representation of speech knowledge in terms of a large number of diverse KS's which cooperate via a generalized (in terms of both data and control) form of the hypothesize-and-test paradigm. KS's are independent and separable; they are activated in a data-directed manner and execute asynchronously, communicating information among themselves through a global data base. This global data base, which is a representation of the partial analysis of the utterance, is a three-dimensional data structure (in which the dimensions are level of representation, time, and alternatives) augmented by AND/OR structural relationships which interconnect elements of the data structure. This global data base structure permits information generated by one KS to be: 1) retained for use by other KS's, and 2) quickly propagated to other relevant parts of the data base. In addition to being a new representational framework for specifying speech knowledge, HSII is a system organization suitable for efficient implementation on a multiprocessor computer system. In particular, the system organization employs techniques which, while not violating the independence and modularity of KS's, permit: 1) avoidance of deadlock in the data base, 2) efficient implementation of data-directed sequencing of knowledge sources, and 3) goal-directed scheduling of asynchronously executable KS processes.

A preliminary, synchronous version of HSII has been operating on Carnegie-Mellon University's PDP-10 since January 1974. The fully asynchronous, multiprocess version of HSII is now in the final stages of being implemented, also on the PDP-10, and is expected to be running by August 1974. This multiprocess version of HSII will also contain the capability of simulating the effects of operating HSII in a multiprocessor environment. Experience with this multiprocess version of HSII, together with simulation data on the effects of operating in a multiprocessor environment, will form the basis for a multiprocessor version of HSII on a multi-miniprocessor computer (C.mmp). An initial implementation of HSII on C.mmp is expected to be completed in the first quarter of 1975.

A Carnegie-Mellon University technical report providing detailed examples of HSII's recognition process is planned for Autumn 1974.

APPENDIX I

HSI PERFORMANCE SUMMARY

Fig. 7 summarizes the performance of the HSI system as of Autumn 1973. The results are based on tests of 144 sentences containing 676 words, spoken by five speakers and using four different tasks (Chess, News Retrieval, Medical Questionnaire, and Desk Calculator) whose vocabularies range from 28 to 76 words. (More complete descriptions of the tasks are given in [5] and [12].)

Column 1 gives the data set number, task, and speaker identification. All of the speakers are male adults. Data set 4 was recorded over a long-distance telephone connection; the others were recorded in a fairly quiet environment using one of several medium to high-quality microphones. All of the utterances represent speech read from a script (as opposed to being spontaneous).

Column 2 gives the number of words in the task lexicon.

Column 3 shows the number of sentences in the data set; column 4 gives the total number of word tokens in the set.

Column 5 contains the results of recognition with just the Acoustics module (the acoustic-phonetic source of knowledge). The task lexicon is the sole restriction—the Syntax and Semantics modules are not used. The first subcolumn indicates the percent of times the correct word appears as the first choice of the Acoustics module in the hypothesis list. The second subcolumn indicates the percent of times the correct word is in the top two choices; the third shows the top three. In this mode each incorrect word recognition is overridden by specifying the correct word boundary positions (using carefully hand-segmented data) so that errors do not propagate.

Column 6 gives the results for the HSI system recognition with the Acoustics module and the Syntax module both operating. The first subcolumn indicates the percent of sentences recognized completely correctly. The "near-miss" (indicated below that number in the first subcolumn) indicates the percent of times the recognized utterance differed from the actual utterance by at most one word of

1	2	3	4	5 ACOUSTIC MODE			6 ACOUSTIC AND SYNTAX MODE				7 ACOUSTIC, SYNTAX, AND SEMANTIC MODE			
DATA SET: TASK/ SPEAKER	WORDS IN LEX	#SEN	#WORD	%IN #1	%IN #1 +#2	%IN #1 +#2 +#3	%SEN %NEAR MISS	%WOR	AVE T/SEN (Sec)	AVE T/S INP	%SEN %NEAR MISS	%WOR	AVE T/SEN	AVE T/S INP
1 CHESS/RN	31	14	62	61	79	85	43 100	87	11	6	100 100	100	9	5
2 CHESS/JB	31	19	86	44	69	78	74 95	93	12	9	100 100	100	8	6
3 CHESS/JB	31	21	105	39	68	73	15 50	69	15	8	48 90	88	13	7
4 CHESS/(TEL) BL	31	25	99	43	64	76	52 84	78	7	6	80 88	88	7	6
SUB-TOTALS		79	352	45	69	77	46 80	81	11	7	79 93	93	9	6
5 NEWS-RETREV/VL	28	19	104	30	53	67	21 42	63	13	7	XXX XXX	XXX	XXX	XXX
6 MED-QUES/JA	76	21	92	20	38	49	24 33	40	13	11	XXX XXX	XXX	XXX	XXX
7 DESK-CALC/JB	38	25	128	42	63	72	35 55	68	28	14	XXX XXX	XXX	XXX	XXX
TOTALS		144	676	39	61	71	38 64	70	15	9	79 93	93	9	6

Fig. 7. Performance results of the HSI system—Autumn 1973.

approximately similar phonetic structure. The second subcolumn gives the percent of words recognized correctly. The mean computation times on the PDP-10 computer (in seconds per sentence and in seconds per second of speech) are shown in subcolumns three and four.

Column 7 shows results for recognition using all three sources of knowledge (for the Chess task only): the Acoustics, Syntax, and Semantics modules. The subcolumns are similar to those of Column 6.

As one might expect, accuracy increases with the introduction of more KS's. It is also true that computation time decreases with more KS's; i.e., the additional KS's serve to reduce the size of the space that must be searched.

Performance differences across the different data sets are attributable to the following several sources:

1) Task lexicon size.

2) Phonetic content of the lexicons: many rules in the Acoustics module handle particular kinds of phonetic juxtaposition. Vocabularies as small as the ones used here do not exhaust all of these cases; each such vocabulary exhibits some cases not found in each of the others. Because a larger amount of effort has gone into the rules based on the Chess lexicon, that task also performs best.

3) Speaker differences.

It is encouraging that the performance using the telephone input (data set 4) does not appear to differ significantly from the other data sets, which use higher quality input. The labeling of acoustic segments is defined by a table of values derived from training syllables uttered by the speaker over the same channel used to input the test data; thus it is somewhat self-normalizing. Also, the system detects that there is very little higher frequency energy (in the case of the telephone input); this automatically triggers programmed readjustment of some thresholds and heuristics dealing with high frequency information.

ACKNOWLEDGMENT

We wish to acknowledge the contributions of the following people: A. Newell for his insights into the task of problem-solving, D. Parnas and L. Cooprider for their discussions on system design and decomposition, G. Gill for his untiring efforts in system implementation, and D. McCracken for his valuable criticism of the ideas as presented in this paper.

REFERENCES

[1] J. Baker, "The DRAGON system—an overview," in *Proc. IEEE Symp. Speech Recognition*, Carnegie-Mellon Univ., Pittsburgh, Pa., Apr. 1974, pp. 22–26; also, this issue, pp. 24–29.

[2] J. Barnett, "A vocal data management system," *IEEE Trans. Audio Electroacoust.* (*Special Issue on 1972 Conference on Speech Communication and Processing*), vol. AU-21, pp. 185–188, June 1973.

[3] C. G. Bell *et al.*, "C.mmp: the CMU multi-miniprocessor computer," Dep. Comput. Sci., Carnegie-Mellon Univ., Pittsburgh, Pa., Tech. Rep., 1971.

[4] C. G. Bell, R. C. Chen, S. H. Fuller, J. Grason, S. Rege, and D. P. Siewiorek, "The architecture and application of computer modules: a set of components for digital systems design," presented at COMPCON 73, San Francisco, Calif., pp. 177–180, 1973.

[5] L. D. Erman, "An environment and system for machine understanding of connected speech," Ph.D. dissertation, Dep. Comput. Sci., Stanford Univ., Stanford, Calif., 1974.

[6] L. D. Erman, R. D. Fennell, V. R. Lesser, and D. R. Reddy, "System organizations for speech understanding: implications of network and multiprocessor computer architectures for AI," in *Proc. 3rd Int. Joint Conf. Artificial Intelligence*, Stanford, Calif., Aug. 1973, pp. 194–199.

[7] H. G. Goldberg, D. R. Reddy, and R. L. Suslick, "Parameter-independent machine segmentation and labeling," in *Proc. IEEE Symp. Speech Recognition*, Carnegie-Mellon Univ., Pittsburgh, Pa., Apr. 1974, pp. 106–111.

[8] C. Hewitt, "Description and theoretical analyis (using schemata) of PLANNER: a language for proving theorems and manipulating models in a robot," Massachusetts Inst. Technol., Cambridge, project MAC, AI Memo. 251, 1972.

[9] F. Jelinek, L. R. Bahl, and R. L. Mercer, "Design of a linguistic statistical decoder for the recognition of continuous speech," in *Proc. IEEE Symp. Speech Recognition*, Carnegie-Mellon Univ., Pittsburgh, Pa., Apr. 1974, pp. 255–260.

[10] M. J. Knudsen, "Real-time linear-predictive coding of speech on the SPS-41 microprogrammed triple-processor system," in *Proc. IEEE Symp. Speech Recognition*, Carnegie-Mellon Univ., Pittsburgh, Pa., Apr. 1974, pp. 274–277; also this issue, pp. 140–145.

[11] S. Kriz, "A 16-bit A-D-A conversion system for high-fidelity audio research," in *Proc. IEEE Symp. Speech Recognition* Carnegie-Mellon Univ., Pittsburgh, Pa., Apr. 1974, pp. 278–282; also, this issue, pp. 146–149.

[12] R. B. Neely, "On the use of syntax and semantics in a speech understanding system," Ph.D. dissertation, Stanford Univ., Stanford, Calif., 1973.

[13] A. Newell *et al.*, *Speech Understanding Systems: Final Report of a Study Group*, 1971. Amsterdam, The Netherlands: North-Holland, 1973.

[14] A. Newell, "Production systems: models of control structures," in *Visual Information Processing*, W. C. Chase, Ed. New York: Academic, 1973, pp. 463–526.

[15] D. R. Reddy, L. D. Erman, and R. B. Neely, "The C-MU speech recognition project," in *Proc. IEEE Conf. System Sciences and Cybernetics*, Pittsburgh, Pa., 1970.

[16] ——, "A model and a system for machine recognition of speech," *IEEE Trans. Audio Electroacoust.* (*Special Issue on 1972 Conference on Speech Communication and Processing*), vol. AU-21, pp. 229–238, June 1973.

[17] D. R. Reddy, L. D. Erman, R. D. Fennell, and R. B. Neely, "The HEARSAY speech understanding system: an example of

the recognition processes," in *Proc. 3rd Int. Joint Conf. Artificial Intelligence,* Stanford, Calif., Aug. 1973, pp. 185–183.

[18] R. Reddy and A. Newell, "Knowledge and its representation in a speech understanding system," in *Knowledge and Cognition,* L. W. Gregg, Ed. Washington, D. C.: Erlbaum, ch. 10, to be published.

[19] E. Rich, "Inference and use of simple predictive grammars," in *Proc. IEEE Symp. Speech Recognition,* Carnegie-Mellon Univ., Pittsburgh, Pa., Apr. 1974, p. 242.

[20] H. B. Ritea, "A voice-controlled data management system," in *Proc. IEEE Symp. Speech Recognition,* Carnegie-Mellon Univ., Pittsburgh, Pa., Apr. 1974, pp. 28–31.

[21] P. Rovner, B. Nash-Webber, and W. Woods, "Control concepts in a speech understanding system," in *Proc. IEEE Symp. Speech Recognition,* Carnegie-Mellon Univ., Pittsburgh, Pa., Apr. 1974, pp. 267–272; also this issue, pp. 136–140.

[22] J. F. Rulifson *et al.*, "QA4: a procedural calculus for intuitive reasoning," AI Center, Stanford Res. Inst., Menlo Park, Calif., Tech. Note 73, 1973.

[23] L. Shockey and L. D. Erman, "Sub-lexical levels in the Hearsay II speech understanding system," in *Proc. IEEE Symp. Speech Recognition,* Carnegie-Mellon Univ., Pittsburgh, Pa., Apr. 1974, pp. 208–210.

[24] W. A. Woods, "Motivation and overview of BBN SPEECHLIS: an experimental prototype for speech understanding research," in *Proc. IEEE Symp. Speech Recognition,* Carnegie-Mellon Univ., Pittsburgh, Pa., Apr. 1974, p. 1–10; also this issue, pp. 2–10.

A Prosodically Guided Speech Understanding Strategy

WAYNE A. LEA, MARK F. MEDRESS, MEMBER, IEEE, AND TOBY E. SKINNER

Abstract—**Our strategy for computer understanding of speech uses prosodic features to break up continuous speech into sentences and phrases and locate stressed syllables in those phrases. The most reliable phonetic data are obtained by performing a distinguishing features analysis within the stressed syllables and by locating sibilants and other robust information in unstressed syllables. The numbers and locations of syntactic boundaries and stressed syllables are used to select likely syntactic and semantic structures, within which words are hypothesized to correspond to the partial distinguishing features matrices obtained from the segmental analyses.**

Portions of this strategy have been implemented and tested with hundreds of seconds of speech, involving fifteen talkers. A program for detecting syntactic boundaries from fall-rise patterns in fundamental frequency contours correctly detected over 90 percent of all predicted boundaries. An algorithm for locating stressed syllables (from fundamental frequency contours and high-energy syllabic nuclei) correctly located the nuclei of over 85 percent of all those syllables perceived as stressed by a panel of listeners. A study of segmental analysis results obtained by several other research groups showed that phonetic recognition clearly is most successful in the stressed syllables. Procedures for classification of stressed vowels, location and classification of sibilants, and location of stops, nasals, and [r]-like sounds have been implemented. Prosodic aids to parsing and semantic analysis are being investigated.

I. INTRODUCTION

THIS is a report on work currently in progress, which is directed toward the development of a system for computer understanding of spoken English sentences. The strategy for recognition, and several details of the acoustic and linguistic analysis procedures, are distinctive in that prosodic features (fundamental frequency contours, energy functions, and certain timing information) are used to break sentences up into grammatical phrases, locate the stressed syllables within those phrases, and guide procedures for both phone classification and higher level linguistic analysis (parsers and semantic analyzers).

The motivations for using prosodic patterns in speech understanding procedures are reviewed briefly in Section II, and an overall analysis-by-synthesis strategy is outlined. Section III describes the present implementation of the acoustic analysis procedures (including acoustic parameterization, location of reliably encoded phone classes, analysis of the sound structure of stressed syllables, and preliminary lexical matching procedures). A procedure for dividing continuous speech into phrases, by use of fall-rise patterns in fundamental frequency contours, has been described in detail in the literature [11], [12] and its successful performance on about 1000 s of continuous speech is reviewed in Section IV. In Section V, an algorithm for locating stressed syllables in continuous speech is described, and shown to successfully locate over 85 percent of the stressed syllables in connected speech.

To test the phone classification techniques, the prosodic feature extractors, the lexical analysis procedures, and the subsequent linguistic analyses, a set of test sentences has been designed which will isolate effects due to phonetic sequences, sentence intonation contours, constituent structure, positions of stressed syllables in constituents, and other linguistic and acoustic phonetic patterns. These test sentences are discussed in Section VI, along with the ways in which they will be used to: test alternative hypotheses about relationships between prosodic parameters and higher level linguistic structure; test performance of phone-recognition schemes (such as sibilant locators or stop locators, etc.); and determine the feasibility of prosodic aids to syntactic parsing and semantic analysis. Some implications about how a prosodically guided strategy impacts the selection of syntactic parsers and semantic analysis schemes are also discussed in Section VI.

A summary, and proposals for further work, are given in Section VII, and Section VIII lists pertinent references.

II. OUTLINE OF A PROSODICALLY GUIDED STRATEGY FOR SPEECH UNDERSTANDING

A traditional model of speech recognition has assumed that, by tracking the right "information-carrying" parameters, and using any of several pattern-matching phonemic-segment classification techniques, one could determine phonemic strings corresponding to these intended by the talker. Then, the phonemic strings may be applied to higher level linguistic analyses to determine words, phrases, and utterance meanings. We have argued elsewhere [10], [12], [22], [16], that successful understanding of spoken sentences involves *early* use of linguistic structure in combination with the *most reliable* acoustic information. Because of the structural redundancy provided by the listener's linguistic knowledge, a speaker does not have to encode into the acoustic waveform all of the features describing an utterance, and the features that he does choose to encode can vary from one repetition of a given sentence to the next. Indeed, in some utterances, whole phonemes or syllables may be "missing"

Manuscript received March 29, 1974; revised September 30, 1974. This paper is based on research supported by the Advanced Research Projects Agency of the Department of Defense under Contract DAHC 15-73-C-0310, ARPA Order 2010. This paper was presented at the IEEE Symposium on Speech Recognition, Carnegie-Mellon University, Pittsburgh, Pa., April 15–19, 1974. The views and conclusions contained in this document are those of the authors and should not be interpreted as necessarily representing the official policies, either expressed or implied, of the Advanced Research Projects Agency or the U. S. Government.

The authors are with the Defense Systems Division, Sperry Univac, St. Paul, Minn. 55165

Reprinted from *IEEE Trans. Acoust., Speech, and Signal Process.*, vol. ASSP-23, pp. 30–38, Feb. 1975.

from the pronunciation. A speech recognition system based on the acoustic manifestation of all phonemes or all distinctive features would thus frequently fail. In addition to this incompleteness and variability, the encoding of phonemic information is a complex one involving overlapping acoustic features and environmental dependency. Phonological rules and acoustic phonetic rules must be incorporated in systems to adequately characterize the complex process of encoding phonemic information into acoustic features. Some linguists have gone so far as to argue that syntactic cues must be used even before an adequate phonemic representation can be determined [7], [12]. Perception theorists also have argued that decisions about large linguistic units must be made before one fills in the phonemic details about an utterance (cf. review in [12]).

Speech understanding (by man or machine) then appears to involve making use of certain expectations and received cues to determine the syntactic structure (and semantic content) of an utterance. Given an hypothesis as to the surface syntactic structure, the perceiver uses phonological principles to determine a phonetic shape. The hypothesis will be accepted if its associated acoustic phonetic shape is not too radically different from the acoustic input [6, p. 24].

To make the preliminary syntactic hypotheses called for in the early stage of recognition schemes, without depending upon a complete segmental (phonemic) analysis, we have proposed the use of *prosodic features* to segment continuous speech into sentences and phrases and locate the prominent (or stressed) syllables in those phrases. The total framework within which such prosodic information is to be coupled with acoustic phonetic and structural information is illustrated in Fig. 1. This may be recognized to be an analysis-by-synthesis system, with what is usually called the "preliminary analysis" block here broken down into: a component for extracting prosodic features (energy, fundamental frequency, and voicing functions); a component for extracting phonetic parameters (spectral features and formants); a prosodic structure analysis which obtains phrase boundaries, rhythms, and stress patterns; a component for obtaining a partial representation of the phonetic segment structure (or "distinguishing features matrix") within stressed syllables and wherever other reliable phone categorizations can be accomplished; and a preliminary syntactic hypothesizer which uses phrase boundaries, rhythms, and stress patterns, together with allowable syntactic structures specified by the grammar, to predict the likely syntactic structure of the sentence. Following such preliminary analyses, the lexical hypothesizer proposes possible lexical entries for insertion in the sentence structure, based on the closest match between the partial distinguishing features representation of the input and the lexical entries in the lexicon. Contextual constraints, such as lexical categories that could occur at certain positions in the sentence structure, and likely words in certain semantic and task contexts, are used to guide the lexical hypothesizing.

The acceptable grammatical structures dictated by the grammar, and the constraints about what can be said based on the semantic structures and task domain, combine together with the lexical and syntactic hypotheses resulting from the preliminary analysis of the input speech, to yield a total hypothesis about the identity of the sentence spoken. The preliminary analysis should exclude from the parser's consideration all but a small subset of possible structures to hypothesize. The sentence hypothesizer then controls the order in which acoustic-phonetic patterns are generated, via the phonological rules (including acoustic-phonetic rules), for comparison with the input acoustic-phonetic patterns. It is anticipated that the comparisons between input and internally generated patterns will be done at the level of distinguishing features patterns and such prosodic patterns as phrase boundaries and stress patterns, but it is possible that some comparisons can best be done at the parameter level of formants and the like. Consequently, each of these three types of extracted patterns have been shown feeding to the comparator of Fig. 1, to be compared with the internally generated patterns.

The grammer, lexicon, semantic model, task model, and the basic analysis-by-synthesis blocks of sentence hypothesizer, phonological rules, and comparator are vital components in this strategy, but work has not progressed to the stage where they can be implemented, and they will not be discussed further in this paper. The preliminary analysis routines, however, have been implemented in at least an initial form, and will be discussed further below (Sections III to V). The overall strategy in general, and the preliminary analysis routines in particular, will ultimately have substantial effects on the form of parser, semantic analysis routines, and phonological rules implemented in the system, as will be illustrated in Section VII.

III. PRELIMINARY PHONETIC AND PROSODIC ANALYSES

The preliminary analysis components shown within the dotted lines in Fig. 1 provide all the information derived from the acoustic signal, which is to be compared with the stored and generated information in the other components. In Fig. 2 is shown the version of these preliminary analysis components that is currently implemented on the Sperry Univac speech research facility. Here we will briefly survey the various processes and resulting parameters and decisions that result from the "acoustic front end" shown in Fig. 2.

Hardware energy filters provide functions of *total energy* (TE) between 60 and 5000 Hz, *sonorant energy* (SE) between 60 and 3000 Hz, *high frequency energy* (HE) between 3000 and 5000 Hz, *low frequency energy* (LE) between 60 and 900 Hz, and *very low frequency energy* (VLE) between 60 and 400 Hz. The utterance beginning and end are determined from the TE function, and the beginnings and ends of all voiced portions in the utterance are determined from the VLE function. Only

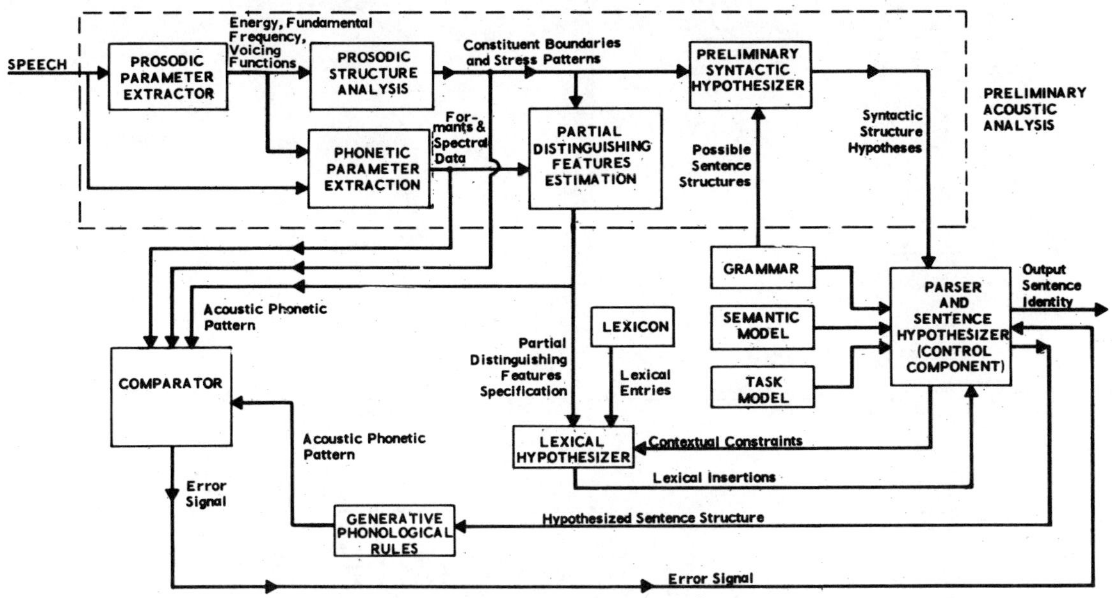

Fig. 1. Prosodically guided analysis-by-synthesis system.

within those regions recognized as voiced are spectral analyses, formant tracking and fundamental frequency tracking done each 10 ms. Thus, prosodic features are thereby used to limit the parametric computations to only those areas where the parameters are meaningful and useful.

Fundamental frequency (F_0) contours are used to detect boundaries between major grammatical units ("constituents"). Voicing boundaries and the SE function are used to locate all syllables (voiced portions bounded by substantial dips in energy) in the utterance. Then fundamental frequency contours, the syllabication results, and the constituent boundaries are used to locate the stressed syllables in the utterance. The formants F_1 and F_2 are used for categorizing each stressed vowel as either high-front, low-front, low-back, or high-back.

Within the region of the stressed vowel (bounded so as to include preceding or following consonants, but not to include surrounding syllables), analysis is done to locate all segments that might be an [r], an unvoiced stop, a nasal, a sibilant, or one of the "leftover" categories of silence, unvoiced consonant, or voiced consonant.

Throughout the utterance, a search is made for sibilants [s, ʃ, tʃ, z, ʒ, dʒ], indicated by a low value of the ratio LE to HE. The sibilants are further classified as anterior or palatal on the basis of the frequency region wherein the highest energy concentration occurs. Also throughout the utterance, a search is made for releases of unvoiced stops, indicated by silence followed by a rapid spectral change (high value of a spectral derivative), with accompanying proper voice onset time to rule out glottal stops and voiced stops. The formants are used to locate any r-like sounds ([r] or [ɝ], with a low F_3) and to locate nasals (with a very low F_1 of wide bandwidth).

The number and positions of constituent boundaries, stressed syllables, and syllable boundaries are total-sentence structure indications that may be used to rule out candidate sentences and direct the search for the most likely sentences to compare with. The sound structure in the region of the stressed syllable, and the locations of sibilants, [r]'s, unvoiced stop releases, and nasals provide some of the more reliable phonetic information needed for identifying a sentence. In the very simplified version of a sentence lexicon and lexical matching process as shown in Fig. 2, all the phonetic segments found are first ordered in time, and a comparison is made with lexical entries that specify only those structural and phonetic aspects that the analysis procedures can provide. More than one lexical entry is permitted for each sentence, to allow for expected cases of missing segments, or lack of certain constituent and syllable boundaries. These alternative lexical entries will eventually be generated by rules. Obviously, the lexical specification of sentences as total units is a temporary expediency which will be removed as techniques for constituent-by-constituent analysis, parsing, semantic analysis, and analysis-by-synthesis are developed.

The thrust of these preliminary analysis routines is to use prosodic features to guide one to the areas where the most reliable phonetic information is, and to use the incomplete phonetic information thus obtained, in combination with prosodic cues to sentence structure, to determine what sentence was said. Prosodic features limit the places where the most complex computations of parameters must be done, then break sentences up into grammatical constituents and then syllabicate and locate stressed syllables. Formants and other spectral features are used to categorize the stressed vowel and its surrounding consonants, and to locate any other speech sounds throughout the utterance whose detection is fairly reliable, regardless of stress level.

This approach to recognition is motivated by several factors. There is enough redundancy in speech, and enough evidence that listeners do large-unit recognition without

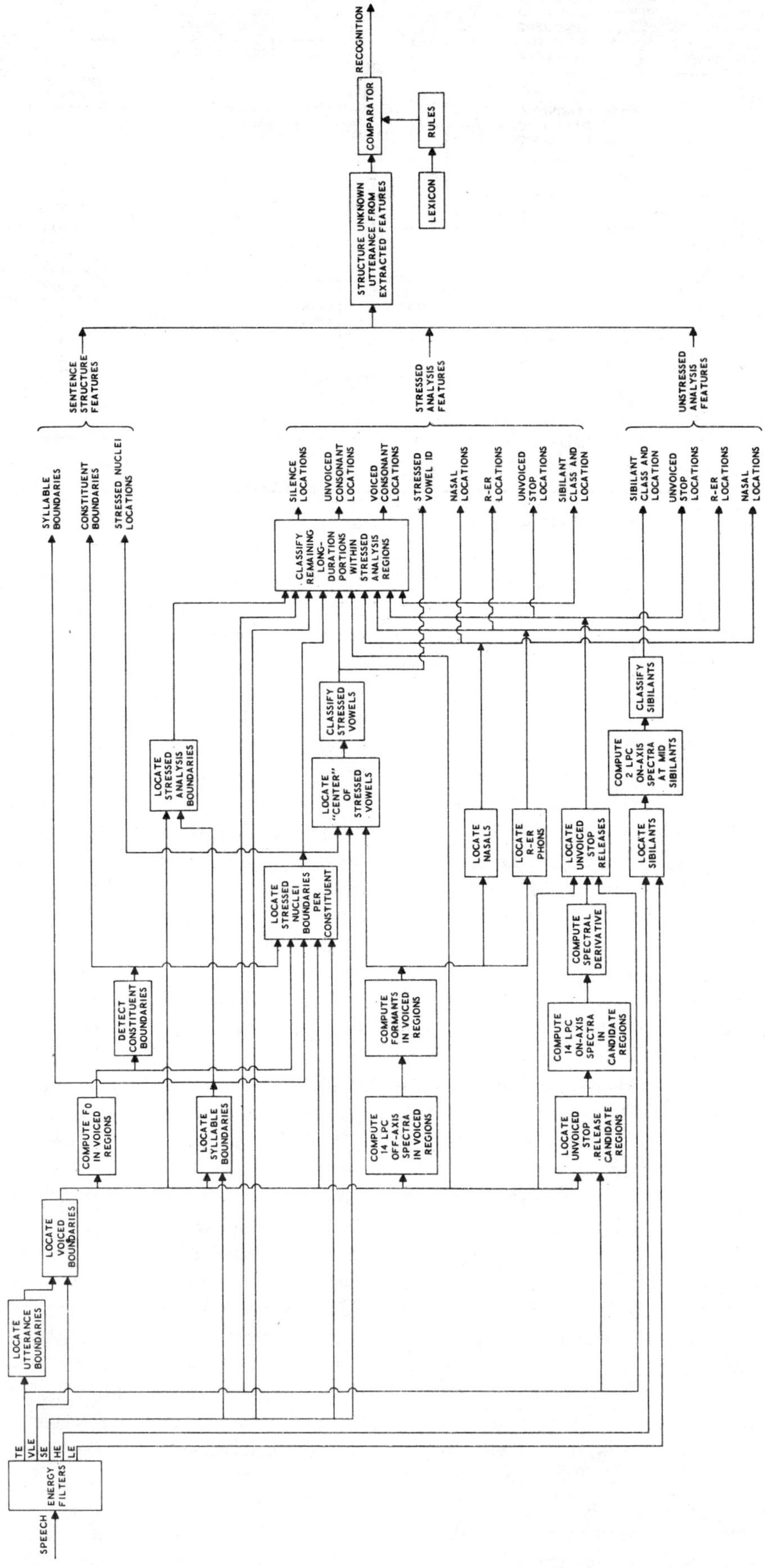

Fig. 2. Preliminary acoustic analysis components.

prior attention to all phonetic details of the speech, to suggest that all the phonetic structure need not be given equal attention in recognition schemes (cf. [12]). It has often been assumed that consonants and vowels should be more clearly articulated and easier to distinguish in stressed syllables than in unstressed or reduced syllables, so that a partial distinctive features analysis in the region of the stressed syllable should provide some of the most reliable phonetic information. Klatt and Stevens' (1973) work with sentence recognition from spectrograms did show best partial transcriptions of vowels occurring in stressed syllables. A recent analysis of the results in automatic segmentation and classification by five different speech recognition systems showed that in all cases vowels and obstruents are most reliably and accurately categorized in stressed syllables [13]. Error rates were as much as 2 to 8 times as large in unstressed and reduced syllables as they were in stressed syllables. In a similar study [18], with Univac's own initial methods for sibilant and unvoiced stop location, correct location scores were 20 percent higher in stressed syllables than in reduced syllables. Thus, the stressed syllable provides an "island of reliability" for best phonetic information. This explains the emphasis on the stressed syllable analysis in Fig. 2.

On the other hand, some phone categories can be detected with fairly high and somewhat uniform reliability, regardless of where they occur in an utterance. Sibilants were found to be correctly located in 66 percent of their occurrences in reduced syllables and 86 percent of their occurrences in unstressed syllables [18] and have proven repeatedly to be among the phone types most reliably located in stress-independent phonetic recognition [9], [21]. The characteristic low third formant of r-like sounds makes them among the easier sounds to recognize. The silences and sudden releases of unvoiced stops are also expected to be fairly easily detected. While sonorant consonants are among the most difficult phones to detect, and certainly difficult to distinguish among (cf. [27], [13]), their recognition scores were found to be almost unaffected by stress levels [13]. In fact, the syllabic nonvowel sonorants ([l̩, m, n]) which occur in reduced syllables are among the easiest nonvowel sonorants to detect [13]. Nasals are expected to be easier to locate than [l]'s or glides [y, w].

As segmental analysis tools are refined and augmented, the few broad categories of speech sounds obtained in Fig. 2 will be expanded.

To illustrate the use of the partial phonetic and prosodic specification obtained from the above analysis procedures, and to illustrate the lexical matching procedures, let us consider a specific case of the sentence "Who is the owner of utterance eight?" The primary lexical entry for this sentence would assert that it consists of 3 constituents, with the sequence S00S00S00S of stressed (S) syllables and other (0) syllables. The lexical specification of the phonetic sequence would be: — [UC][HBV] × [SIBA] × [LBV][NAS][r] × [LBV][VC][r] × [NAS][SIBA] [LFV][STOP] —. Here the stressed vowels are identified as high front (HFV), low front (LFV), and low back (LBV), and the nasals (NAS), anterior [SIBA] and palatal [SIBP] sibilants, r-like elements, unvoiced stops, unvoiced and voiced consonants (UC and VC), and silences (—) are indicated, while segments that are not categorizable are indicated by ×'s. Any structure which met these conditions on specified segments should be acceptable. Also, additional lexical entries for the same sentence can be introduced, to allow for distortions like failures to detect a nasal, or vowel categorization errors. Such additional lexical entries might later be generated by rules.

In the next two sections we shall consider how the algorithms actually work for detecting constituent boundaries and locating stressed syllables.

IV. USE OF PROSODIC FEATURES TO SEGMENT SENTENCES INTO PHRASES

An algorithm [11]–[15] has been implemented for segmenting speech into grammatical phrases, by marking phrase boundaries at the bottoms of fall-rise valleys in fundamental frequency (F_0) contours. Each 10 ms, a value of fundamental frequency was obtained by autocorrelating portions of the center-clipped speech waveform [18], and was converted from hertz to a logarithmic frequency (eighth tone) scale. In tests on over 500 s of speech, Lea had found that F_0 will usually decrease (about 7 percent or more, which is equivalent to five eighth tones) at the end of each major syntactic constituent, and then increase (about 7 percent or more) either at the beginning of the following constituent or after any unstressed syllables at the beginning of that following constituent. The Univac implementation of this algorithm was found to correctly detect about 90 percent of all predicted syntactic boundaries in another 500 s of speech, including spoken scripts, and questions, commands, and declarations intended for man-computer interaction. A refinement was introduced to eliminate some erroneous boundaries that were caused by consonantal influences on F_0 contours, yielding less than 5 percent false alarms in boundary detection.

The exact *location* of the constituent boundary is not accomplished by this algorithm, but success in stressed syllable location (see Section V) permits one to say that the boundary is located somewhere between the immediately preceding stressed syllable and the immediately following stressed syllable. More exact boundary location may be possible if the typical lengthening of phrase-final syllables and/or the detection of word boundaries can be accomplished. In any case, successful *detection* of boundaries permits one to tell how many constituents are in a sentence, and to give general indications about the lengths of phrases. The boundaries also permit stressed syllable location within constituents, to be discussed next.

V. STRESSED SYLLABLE LOCATION

Many studies have shown that peak F_0, local increases in F_0 [3], [10, ch. 5] and energy integrals [23] are among the best acoustic correlates of stress, at least in isolated words. Intonation studies have shown that, in connected texts, F_0 will peak near the first stressed syllable ("HEAD") of each breath group, and fall gradually until the last stressed syllable, after which may occur the rapid fall of an utterance-final "Tune I" contour or the rise in F_0 at the end of a "Tune II" contour (which marks "incompletion"). Fig. 3 illustrates how the acoustic correlates of rising F_0 and large energy integral are used in an algorithm for locating the stressed syllables within constituents of sentences (cf. [11], [14]). Constituent boundaries are marked by SYNTB in the plot of F_0 versus time. The increasing F_0 near the beginning of each constituent detected by the boundary detector is assumed to be attributable to the first stressed syllable in the constituent [11, Sect. 5]. A stressed "HEAD" to the constituent is thus associated with a portion of the speech which is high in energy with rising F_0, and bounded by substantial (5 dB or more) dips in energy. Other stressed syllables in the constituent are expected to be accompanied by local increases in F_0. Since the usual ("archetype") shape of the F_0 contour in a constituent is a rapid rise followed by a gradual fall in F_0, we expect that local "increases" in F_0 due to later stressed syllables will show local *rises above the gradually falling F_0 contour*, even if F_0 does not rise absolutely near the stressed syllable. The stressed syllable is located within a high-energy integral region near this local rise above the archetype F_0 contour.

Lea [11, Sect. 5] presented a detailed description of this algorithm for locating stressed syllables, based on the strategy just outlined, and reported an average of over 85 percent of all stressed syllables being correctly located, for over 400 s of speech, including spoken scripts and questions, commands, and declarations for man-machine interaction (involving fourteen talkers). To evaluate the algorithm, perception tests were performed to determine which syllables were actually perceived as stressed [13]. Besides showing considerable consistency in listeners' perceptions of stressed, unstressed, and reduced syllables, these tests provided the "standard" with which acoustic locations could be compared.

When other (simpler) algorithms for stressed syllable location (from energy integrals alone or from regions of increasing F_0 alone) were compared to this "archetype contour" algorithm, they were found to give lower scores of correct location, plus higher percentages of "false alarms" (perceptually unstressed syllables being found as stressed by the algorithm [14]).

The "archetype contour" algorithm has recently been implemented on the Univac speech research facility, and provides fairly accurate procedures for locating stressed syllables. The beginning and ending of each stressed nucleus are provided, as are the energy minima (syllable "boundaries") between syllables and the positions of peak energy in all nuclei. The stressed vowel is to be categorized on the basis of the formant structure at or near the time of peak energy in the stressed nucleus. The "stressed analysis region," wherein partial distinguishing features analysis is done, extends beyond the intersyllabic energy minima to the "5 dB down" border of immediately preceding or following syllabic nuclei. If unvoiced consonants immediately precede or follow the stressed nucleus, they are included in the stressed analysis region.

VI. PROSODIC AIDS TO STRUCTURAL ANALYSIS

Besides indicating the stressed analysis regions within which reliable phone categorizations may be done, prosodic features are also expected to indicate some aspects of the syntactic and semantic structures of a sentence. For example, intonation is the minimal differentiator between some declarations and questions, such as "All programs have been loaded" versus "All programs have been loaded?" Intonation contours have been asserted to provide data for "the recognition of immediate constituents and parts of speech syntax" [26, p. 77], such as distinguishing between "I'll move, on Saturday" and "I'll move on, Saturday", or the classic "They [are] [flying planes]" versus "They [are flying] [planes]" [20], [5]. Stress patterns or disjunctures are said to distinguish between "light housekeeper" and "lighthouse keeper," or between "large [tea cup rack]" and "[large tea cup] rack" [20], [6]. When two simple statements like "I saw a gray *house*" and "Joe saw a black *house*" are conjoined, to yield "*I* saw a *gray* house and *Joe* saw a *black* house," the indicated shift of highest stress or emphasis occurs, showing a regular effect of *coordination* on stress patterns [8].

Other syntactic and semantic structures have accompanying distinctive prosodic patterns, such as the pauses, distinct "comma intonation" contours, and rhythmic effects produced by parantheticals or appositive (nonrestrictive) relative clauses, such as in the sentence, "May, who knew the man in Rome, ran Maine" (to be contrasted to "Men who knew the man in Rome ran Maine", which is without such interruptive markers). In some sequences of noun phrase-prepositional phrase-prepositional phrase, intonation and other prosodic features may distinguish between such sentences as "Put [the block] [on the table [by the door]]!" versus "Put [the block [on the table]] by the door!" Stress patterns are also affected by placements of special emphasis and negation; for example, negation in an auxiliary verb will change its intonation contour, and the usual enclitic tie to preceding noun phrases can be lost [10], [1]. Cantrell [4] has suggested that there exists a form of "pitch concord" between noun phrases with coreference, so that in a sentence like "John told Bill that Harry had broken his bike", the pitch on "his" will be at different levels depending upon whether John, Bill, or Harry is the antecedent of "his." Some specially emphasized syllables are said to have accompanying *dips* in F_0 rather than the usually F_0 rises accompanying stress [25].

With all these interacting aspects of syntactic, semantic, and prosodic structure, and with the known effects of consonants and vowels on prosodic patterns [10], [19], it is difficult to determine just what can be learned about sentence structures from prosodic features in arbitrary

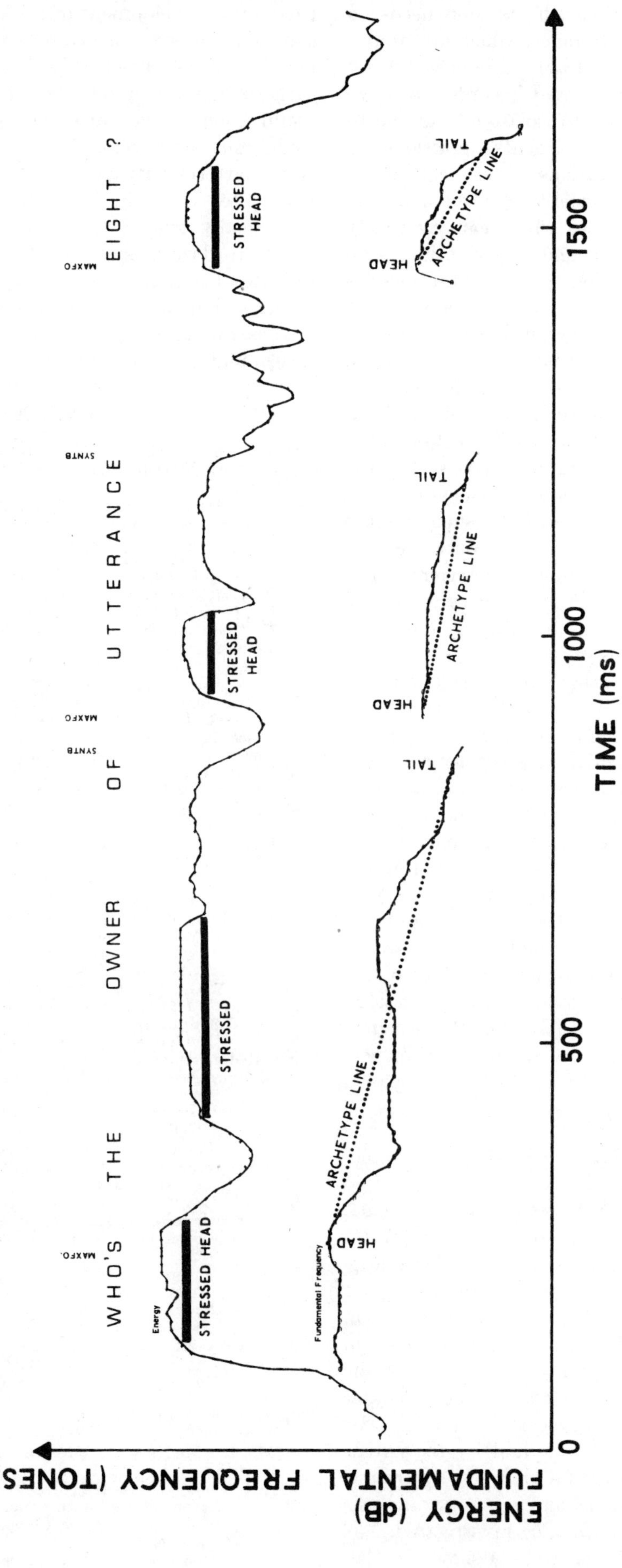

Fig. 3. Extraction of boundaries and stressed syllables from F_0 and energy contours.

sentences. To isolate the various effects, one needs to compare prosodic patterns in utterances which are similar except for only one or a few separable differences. A set of sentences has been designed (and recorded by five speakers, with three repetitions) to isolate effects due to sentence type, number of constituents, positions of stresses within constituents, various phrase categories, coordination, subordination, coreference, pronouns, etc. These sentences also include ones which can rigorously test success in sibilant location and classification, stop location, nasal location, and other segmental or distinguishing features classification. Such phonetic-test sentences include cases of the consonant under study combined with all vowels in word-initial CV sequences, all word-final VC sequences, and samplings of medial VCV sequences. Consonant clusters are also specifically included, as are word boundary effects, such as vowel hiatus and allophonic variations at word boundaries. Finally, these sentences include examples of several possible task domains for man-computer communication, such as voice compiling, information retrieval, air traffic control, etc.

From study of such sentences, one may determine what aspects of syntactic (and semantic) structure can be determined even with little or no information about the phonetic structure of the words or "leaves" of a syntactic tree. Syntactic parsers, on the other hand, usually address the problem of determining the labeled bracketing of a sentence, *given* the terminal string of words as input information. How then can prosodically determined syntactic structure be used to aid syntactic parsers? This problem is currently being investigated. One possibility is that prosodic patterns may be used to rule out (or decrease the priority of testing) candidate parses that do not agree with known constituent boundaries, stress patterns, or sentence intonations. Also, the "islands of reliability" provided by stressed syllable analysis would appear to encourage the use of a locally organized parser [24]. What can be done in "prosodic aids to parsing" will be more apparent after the analysis of the designed sentences and these preliminary investigations of parsers are completed.

VII. FURTHER WORK

Most of the system shown in Fig. 1 has not been implemented, and those portions that have been implemented (as illustrated in Fig. 2) are open to various refinements. The detection of constituent boundaries can be improved by use of sizes of F_0 falls and rises, plus contour shapes and timings between boundaries, to assign confidence levels to each detection. Stressed syllable location in nonneutral semantic contexts such as produce F_0 *dips* in emphasized syllables may be attempted. Other prosodic features (rhythm, pauses, word boundaries) need further study. Further phonetic subcategorization may be achieved within the stressed syllable and by the extension of stress-independent segmental analyses. The whole area of prosodic aids to parsing and semantic analysis is open for study, and is just now being investigated.

The total analysis-by-synthesis strategy shown in Fig. 1 demands development of a lexicon, selection of a grammar and parser (probably locally organized, such as Perry Miller's parser), development of a sentence hypothesizer and compilation of a comprehensive set of useful phonological rules. The semantic model and task model must be developed and the methods for comparing input patterns with generated patterns must be selected.

Despite the early stage of development of the total prosodically guided speech understanding strategy, the results to date in syntactic boundary detection, stressed syllable location, prosodically guided distinguishing-features analysis, and test-sentence design are important and encouraging steps toward the total design of the speech understanding system.

REFERENCES

[1] J. Allen, "Prosodic contours for auxiliary phrases," presented at the 86th Meeting Acoust. Soc. of Amer., Los Angeles, Calif., 1973.

[2] L. E. Armstrong and I. C. Ward, *Handbook of English Intonation*, 2nd ed. Cambridge, England: Heffer, 1926.

[3] D. A. Bolinger, "A theory of pitch accent in English," *Word*, vol. 14, p. 109, 1958.

[4] W. R. Cantrell, "Pitch, stress, and grammatical relations," in *Proc. 5th Regional Meeting, Chicago Linguist Soc.* Chicago, Ill.: Univ. of Chicago Press, pp. 1969, pp. 12–24.

[5] N. Chomsky, *Syntactic Structures*. The Hague, The Netherlands: Mouton, 1957.

[6] N. Chomsky and M. Halle, *The Sound Pattern of English*. New York: Harper and Row, 1968.

[7] N. Chomsky and G. A. Miller, "Introduction to the formal analysis of natural languages," in *Handbook of Mathematical Psychology*, R. D. Luce, R. R. Bush, and E. Glanter, Ed. New York: Wiley, 1963, pp. 269–321.

[8] L. R. Gleitman, "Coordinating conjunctions in English," *Language*, vol. 41, pp. 260–293, 1965.

[9] G. W. Hughes and J. F. Hemdal, "Speech analysis," Purdue Univ., Lafayette, Ind., for Air Force Cambridge Res. Lab., Bedford, Mass., Final Rep. AF 19 (628)-305, Proj. 5628, Task 562802, 1965.

[10] W. A. Lea, "Intonational cues to the constituent structure and phonemics of spoken English," Ph.D. dissertation, School of Elec. Eng., Purdue Univ., Lafayette, Ind., 1972.

[11] ——, "Syntactic boundaries and stress patterns in spoken English texts," Defense Syst. Div., Sperry Univac, St. Paul, Minn., DSD, PX 10146.

[12] ——, "An approach to syntactic recognition without phonemics," *IEEE Trans. Audio Electroacoust.*, vol. AU-21, pp. 249–258, June 1973.

[13] ——, "Evidence that stressed syllables are the most readily decoded portions of continuous speech," presented at the 86th Meeting Acoust. Soc. Amer., Los Angeles, Calif., 1973.

[14] ——, "An algorithm for locating stressed syllables in continuous speech," presented at the 86th Meeting Acoust. Soc. Amer., Los Angeles, Calif., 1973.

[15] ——, "Perceived stress as the 'standard' for judging acoustical correlates of stress," presented at the 86th Meeting Acoust. Soc. Amer., Los Angeles, Calif., 1973.

[16] W. A. Lea, M. F. Medress, and T. E. Skinner, "Prosodic aids to speech recognition: I. Basic algorithms and stress studies," Defense Syst. Div., Sperry Univac, St. Paul, Minn., DSD, PX 7940, 1972.

[17] ——, "Prosodic aids to speech recognition: II. Syntactic segmentation and stressed syllable location," Defense Syst. Div., Sperry Univac, St. Paul, Minn., DSD, PX 10232, 1973.

[18] ——, "Prosodic aids to speech recognition: III. Relationships between stress and phonemic recognition results," Defense Syst. Div., Sperry Univac, St. Paul, Minn., DSD, PX 10430.

[19] I. Lehiste, *Suprasegmentals*. Cambridge, Mass.: M.I.T. Press, 1970.

[20] P. Lieberman, *Intonation, Perception, and Language*. Cambridge, Mass.: M.I.T. Press, 1967.

[21] M. F. Medress, "Computer recognition of single-syllable English words," Ph.D. dissertation, Dep. Elec. Eng., Mass. Inst. Tech., Cambridge, Mass. 1969.

[22] ——, "A procedure for the machine recognition of speech," in *Proc. 1972 Conf. Speech Commun. and Processing*, Newton, Mass., 1972, pp. 113–116.

[23] M. F. Medress. T. E. Skinner, and D. E. Anderson, "Acoustic

correlates of word stress: A preliminary report," Defense Syst. Div., Sperry Univac, St. Paul, Minn., DSD, PX 6623.

[24] P. L. Miller, "A locally organized parser for spoken input," M.I.T. Lincoln Lab., Lexington, Mass., Tech. Rep. 503, 1973.

[25] K. L. Pike, *The Intonation of American English.* Ann Arbor, Mich.: Univ. Michigan, 1945.

[26] G. L. Trager and H. L. Smith, Jr., "An outline of English structure," *Studies in Linguistics: Occasional Papers 3.* Norman, Okla.: Battenburg, 1951.

[27] R. Newman, K. S. Fu, and K. P. Li, "A syntactic approach to the recognition of liquids and glides," in *Proc. 1972 Conf. Speech Commun. and Processing,* Newton, Mass., 1972, pp. 121–123.

A System for Acoustic-Phonetic Analysis of Continuous Speech

CLIFFORD J. WEINSTEIN, MEMBER, IEEE, STEPHANIE S. McCANDLESS, LEE F. MONDSHEIN, AND VICTOR W. ZUE

Abstract—**A system for acoustic-phonetic analysis of continuous speech is being developed to serve as part of an automatic speech understanding system. The acoustic system accepts the speech waveform as an input and produces as output a string of phoneme-like units referred to as acoustic phonetic elements (APEL's). This paper should be considered as a progress report, since the system is still under active development.**

The initial phase of the acoustic analysis consists of signal processing and parameter extraction, and includes spectrum analysis via linear prediction, computation of a number of parameters of the spectrum, and fundamental frequency extraction. This is followed by a preliminary segmentation of the speech into a few broad acoustic categories and formant tracking during vowel-like segments. The next phase consists of more detailed segmentation and classification intended to meet the needs of subsequent linguistic analysis.

The preliminary segmentation and segment classification yield the following categories: vowel-like sound; volume dip within vowel-like sound; fricative-like sound; stop consonants, including silence or voice bar, and associated burst. These categories are produced by a decision tree based upon energy measurements in selected frequency bands, derivatives and ratios of these measurements, a voicing detector, and a few editing rules.

The more detailed classification algorithms include: 1) detection and identification of some diphthongs, semivowels, and nasals, through analysis of formant motions, positions, and amplitudes; 2) a vowel identifier, which determines three ranked choices for each vowel based on a comparison of the formant positions in the detected vowel segment to stored formant positions in a speaker-normalized vowel table; 3) a fricative identifier, which employs measurement of relative spectral energies in several bands to group the fricative segments into phoneme-like categories; 4) stop consonant classification based on the properties of the plosive burst.

The above algorithms have been tested on a substantial corpus of continuous speech data. Performance results, as well as detailed descriptions of the algorithms are given.

INTRODUCTION

A SYSTEM for acoustic-phonetic analysis of continuous speech is being developed to serve as part of an automatic speech understanding system. The acoustic system accepts the speech waveform as input and produces as output a string of phoneme-like units which we refer to as acoustic-phonetic elements (APEL's).

Manuscript received March 29, 1974. This work was sponsored by the Advanced Research Projects Agency of the Department of Defense. This paper was presented at the IEEE Symposium on Speech Recognition, Carnegie-Mellon University, Pittsburgh, Pa., April 15–19, 1974.

C. J. Weinstein, S. S. McCandless, and L. F. Mondshein are with the Massachusetts Institute of Technology Lincoln Laboratory, Lexington, Mass. 02173.

V. W. Zue is with the Department of Electrical Engineering, Massachusetts Institute of Technology, Cambridge, Mass.

More specifically, the speech wave is broken into segments, each of which is tagged as one, or a choice of several, of these units called APEL's. This paper should be considered as a progress report, since the system is still under active development. Future work is expected to include not only improvements in APEL identification, but also development of different types of characterization of the speech signal in cases where the interaction of adjacent phonemes makes segment identification very difficult.

In this work we have been influenced by many previous and present workers in the field. We have listed some basic references [1]–[8] but refer the reader to previously compiled bibliographies [6]–[8], and to the collection of papers produced in the *Proceedings of the 1974 IEEE Symposium on Speech Recognition*. The additional references we have cited in the text certainly do not represent an exhaustive list.

System Overview

Before beginning the description of the current effort, let us list some of its aspects that we consider most important. These include: 1) careful initial segmentation of the waveform into broad acoustic categories; 2) sophisticated formant tracking based on linear prediction [9], [10] spectrum analysis; 3) heavy reliance on analysis of formant trajectories for detection, segmentation, and identification of glides, nasals, and diphthongs; 4) some detection of stress information, particularly in the location of weak or reduced vowels; 5) speaker-dependent tables and thresholds for most identification algorithms; 6) specialized types of classification algorithms directed toward specific phoneme classes; 7) a modular organization which allows for graceful modification of existing algorithms or addition of new ones; and 8) extensive testing and evaluation on a large corpus of continuous speech data.

An overview block diagram of the current acoustic-phonetic analyzer is shown in Fig. 1. The operations indicated in the top part of the diagram, including formant tracking and initial segmentation, generally require much computation of a signal processing nature and are implemented on the FDP [11]-UNIVAC 1219 computer facility at Lincoln Laboratory. Here the speed of the FDP is used to advantage, as both the linear prediction spectrum and the pitch tracking can be accomplished at a real-time rate. The classification and identification al-

Reprinted from *IEEE Trans. Acoust., Speech, and Signal Process.*, vol. ASSP-23, pp. 54-67, Feb. 1975.

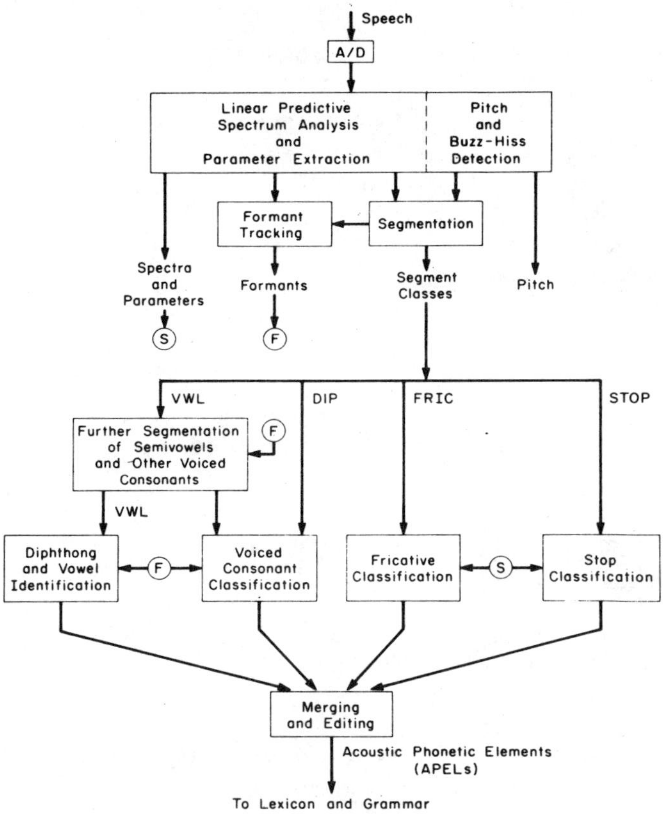

Fig. 1. Block diagram of acoustic-phonetic analysis system.

gorithms indicated in the bottom part of the diagram are implemented on the TX-2 computer facility, where advantage can be taken of compiler languages and the storage-retrieval facilities of the Lincoln Speech Data Base [12].

The initial segmentation algorithm (implemented on FDP-1219) breaks up the waveform into a series of segments, each of which is classified into one of four broad acoustic categories: VWL = vowel-like sound; DIP = volume dip within vowel-like sound; FRIC = fricative-like sound: and STOP = silence or voice bar, plus associated burst. Formant tracking [13] is carried out during voiced sounds (VWL and DIP segments). The formant tracker uses the peaks of the linear prediction spectrum as the initial formant estimates, but applies special techniques to deal with situations where these estimates are inadequate. For example, when a discontinuity in $F2$ or $F3$ indicates that these two formants may have merged into a single peak (as in /r/), the linear prediction spectrum is evaluated on a contour (in the complex z plane) closer to the poles to attempt to resolve the two formants.

The spectra, formant frequencies and amplitudes, and segmentation results are all passed to TX-2. Formant frequencies, formant frequency motions, and formant amplitudes are utilized (on TX-2) in identifying the vowels, diphthongs, and voiced consonants which make up VWL and DIP segments. Other spectral measurements are employed in the classification of stops and fricatives. The final output is the string of labeled segments called APEL's.

ACOUSTIC – PHONETIC ELEMENTS (APELs)

Vowels and Diphthongs	
i	beat
I	bit
ɛ	bet
æ	bat
a	Bob
u	boot
ɔ	bought
ʌ	but
ʊ	book
ɝ	bird
ə	about (weak vowel)
ay	buy
ɔy	boy
yu	compute
V	nonidentified vowel
ḷ	label (syllabic l)

Semivowels and Other Voiced Consonants	
N	met, net, sing
η	deletable N
w	wet, let
ω	deletable W
r	rent
ɾ	better (flapped t)
Δ	unclassified DIP

Fricatives	
f	fat, thing
s	sat, zoo
S	shut, azure
F	nonidentified fricative

Stops		Unvoiced	Voiced
unaspirated		–	+
aspirated	flat	p	b
	low	k	g
	mid	c	C
	high	t	d

κ indicates formant motion characteristic of post-vocalic /k/, /g/, or /η/

Fig 2. List of APEL symbols with their approximate phonemic significance.

An inventory of the APEL's now produced, with examples to indicate their approximate phonemic significance, is shown in Fig. 2. Some APEL's represent less specific phoneme classes than others. For example, the APEL N represents the three nasals as a class, while the APEL f represents either of two weak fricatives. The stops, although labeled as APEL's for convenience, are actually characterized by subphonemic features: voiced-unvoiced, aspirated-unaspirated, and features of the stop burst which will be described later. Some APEL's are designated deletable; for example, a segment labeled as η represents a nasal which was detected with relatively low confidence. The significance of the various APEL's will become more clear in the discussions below of particular algorithms.

Sample System Outputs

In Figs. 3 and 4, we show acoustic-phonetic analyses for two sample sentences. In each case, a linear prediction spectrogram is shown, with the automatically tracked formants superimposed on the spectrogram, and a time-aligned volume function displayed above the spectrogram. Directly below the spectrogram is phonemic transcription which has been entered by hand, and below that the machine-generated APEL's. Note that one to three choices are given for each APEL. In the first sentence, the initial phoneme /ɛ/ is correctly identified as the APEL ɛ on the third choice. (When possible confusion in notation exists, we will distinguish phonemes from APEL's by enclosing phonemes between slashes, as in /ɛ/.) The flapped-t in "edit" is identified properly as ɾ, but the /t/-/ð/ combination in the "edit the" is seen as the single APEL p. The two nasals in "phonemic" and the initial /l/ in "labels" are classified correctly, but

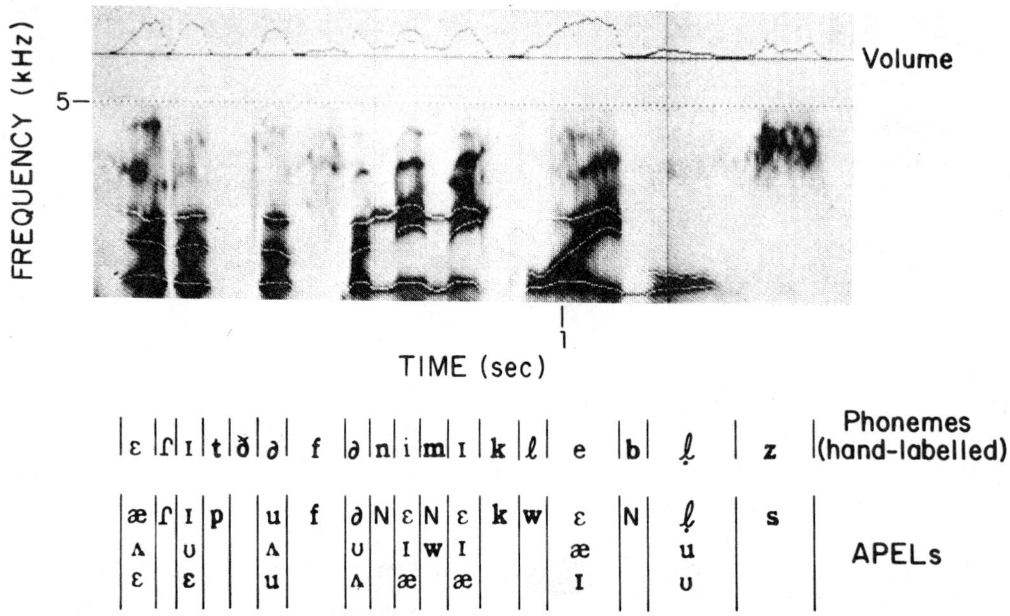

Fig. 3. Acoustic-phonetic analysis for the sentence, "Edit the phonemic labels." Hand-entered phonemic labels and machine-derived APEL's are aligned below the spectrogram.

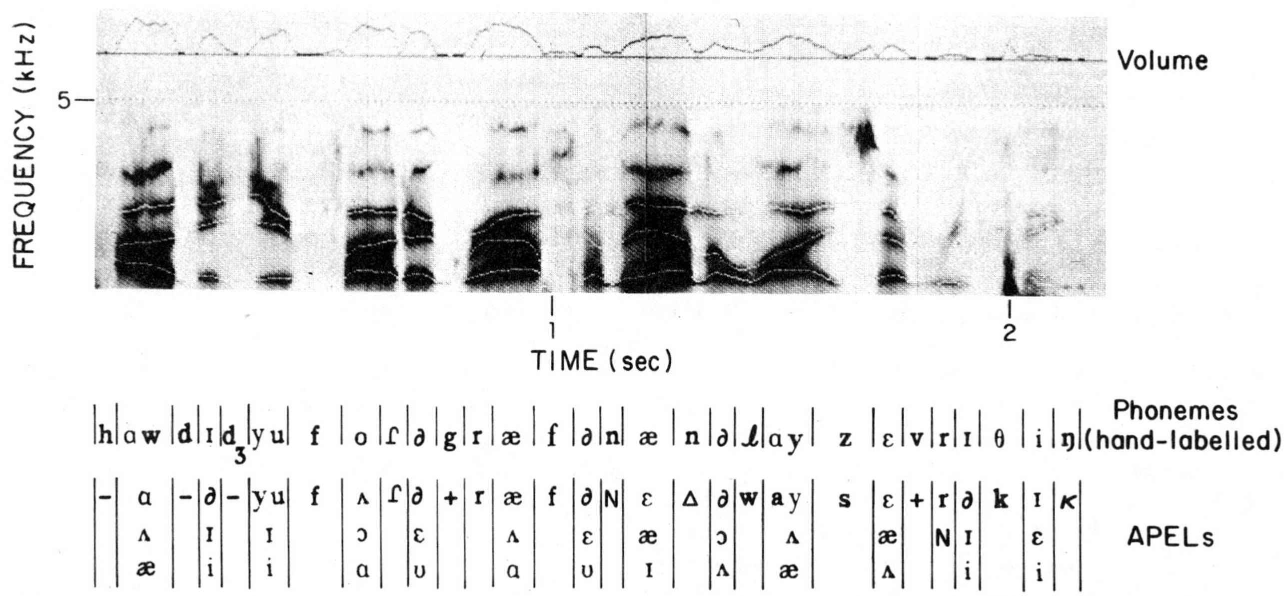

Fig. 4. Acoustic-phonetic analysis for the sentence, "How did you photograph and analyze everything?"

the voiced stop /b/ in "labels" is classified as a nasal. The final syllable in "labels" is detected as a syllabic ℓ. In the second sentence, the diphthongs /yu/ in "you" and /ɑy/ in "analyze" were correctly identified on the basis of their characteristic formant patterns. The $F2$–$F3$ merger due to the final /ŋ/ was detected, as indicated by the APEL κ. A typical type of error is illustrated where the weak fricative /θ/ in "everything" is misclassified as a stop. Several vowels, including those in second syllables of "photograph" and "analyze" are detected as weak vowels (designated by the APEL symbol) on the basis of energy comparison with adjacent syllables.

Labeling and Evaluation

We present a large amount of performance data in this paper. These data are based on a corpus of 111 sentences, averaging about 2.5 s in length and distributed among 7 speakers, including 6 males and one female (SM). The number of sentences spoken by the different speakers was as follows: RW 43, CW 24, SM 22, MH 8, IL 6, DK 4, and SC 4. A few sample sentences are given in the Appendix. The subject matter is generally command of a speech data base, and the sentences were not chosen to achieve any sort of phonetic balance.

The sentences were all phonemically hand-labeled. The level of our hand-labeling was chosen to be consistent with the desire to evaluate our identification programs; for example, the flapped-t, while not strictly speaking a phoneme, was specifically marked in our hand-labeling because we had developed a program to identify flapped-t. Our labels were selected by listening to the sentences and viewing spectrograms. In aligning the labels in time with the speech, we used the spectrogram and the results of our initial segmentation as guides. Use of the initial segmentation boundaries as tentative time markers greatly speeded up the labeling process; we felt that this procedure was justified because we were not trying to evaluate exact location of boundaries but rather their presence or absence, and the identity of the segments. Our labels, APEL's, and all other data are accessible in the Lincoln Speech Data Base [12]. Statistics were collected automatically or semiautomatically, depending on the nature of the algorithm tested. Although there are surely some minor errors in our labels, we feel certain that these have not disturbed the general trends of our performance statistics.

SPEECH INPUT AND SIGNAL PROCESSING

All the speech samples analyzed for this paper were recorded in the TX-2 computer room, using a small, directional, head set microphone (Roanwell Corporation, New York, P/N 116830-690). The microphone pickup was positioned to the right of the mouth opening, about $2\frac{1}{2}$ inches from the right edge of the lips. The computer was on during the recording session, but conditions were controlled so that extraneous noises such as teletypes were not present. The desire in using this recording environment was to simulate the type of conditions to be encountered in actual conditions of speech input to computers, but we found in general that our results compared well with similar results on speech recorded in much less noisy environments. The speech was passed through a 6-dB/octave analog preemphasis filter and a 5-kHz cutoff low-pass filter, sampled at 10 kHz, and sent to the TX-2 (and then into the Speech Data Base) through a 12-bit A-D converter. At the same time, another version of the same waveform, but unpreemphasized and sampled at 20 kHz, was also inputted into the Data Base. A digital tape of the 10-kHz waveform was made for processing on the FDP facility. (A hardware link between FDP and TX-2 is under development, but when this work was done, data transfer was achieved via digital tape.)

The basic signal processing operations are carried out on the FDP-1219 facility. A 14th order linear prediction analysis is carried out every 5 ms through a sliding 25.6-ms Hanning window, via an inverse filter method similar to that described by Markel [10]. From each set of predictor coefficients, a 256-point (40-Hz resolution) spectrum is computed; this is accomplished by evaluating the magnitude of the idealized vocal tract transfer function corresponding to the predictor coefficients, at equally spaced points on the unit circle in the z plane. The speed of the FDP is such that the coefficients and spectra can be calculated in about 0.7 times real time. All our spectral measurements are carried out on these linear prediction spectra. The spectral measurements (e.g., energy in a specified spectral band) which are used will be discussed below in the context of the algorithms to which they are applied.

A fundamental frequency estimate is computed every 5 ms via an algorithm developed by Gold and Rabiner [14]. This algorithm also produces a voiced-unvoiced decision every 5 ms, which is used in segmentation.

Formants are tracked during voiced sounds via an algorithm developed by McCandless [13]. This algorithm utilizes peaks of the linear prediction spectra as initial guesses at formant frequencies. In order to resolve difficulties as to which peak represents which formant, the algorithm anchors on strong vowel spectral frames where the situation is clear, and works out toward more ambiguous regions, applying careful editing based on formant continuity criteria. A key feature of the algorithm is formant enhancement, where a peak which is missing in the original spectrum is often recovered by computing a spectrum on a contour in the z plane inside the unit circle and, therefore, closer to the poles.

The information sent to TX-2 via digital tape includes the linear prediction coefficients, error, and spectra, the fundamental frequency, the formant frequencies and amplitudes, and the results of initial segmentation.

FIRST STAGE SEGMENTATION [15]–[17]

The purpose of first stage segmentation is to subdivide the problem of acoustic-phonetic analysis by segmenting the speech waveform into a few broad acoustic categories. The decisions of the initial segmentation algorithm are not taken as final; later algorithms not only classify segments, but frequently add new segments and (less frequently) delete segment boundaries produced by initial segmentation. As indicated in Fig. 1, there are four main categories produced by first stage segmentation: VWL = vowel-like sound; DIP = volume dip within vowel-like sound (typically an intervocalic voiced consonant); FRIC = fricative-like sound; and STOP = a sequence of one to three subsegments, including a silence or voice bar plus plosive burst (if present) and aspiration (if present). No attempt is made, in this initial segmentation phase, to detect nonintervocalic sonorants (nasals and glides) or to split up fricative clusters; these tasks were deferred because of the need for more sophisticated techniques, and will be discussed below. First stage segmentation basically consists of four major steps: 1) silence detection, 2) sonorant versus nonsonorant decision, 3) burst and aspiration versus fricative decision, and 4) dip detection. We will now describe these four steps, and then give some summary performance results on the segmentation algorithm.

Silence Detection

Initial silence detection (stop consonants, pauses) is made when a specified volume function falls below a threshold. In this case, the volume function used is rms (300–5000) (where rms (A − B) = root mean square of the sum of the squares of the spectral components in the range from A Hz to B Hz), measured for every spectral frame (every 5 ms). We will frequently use the term "volume" to refer to measurements of this type, making more specific definitions of the exact measurements when confusion might occur. The threshold was chosen to be about 3 dB higher than the background noise level on the input analog tape. Frames adjacent to those which passed the initial silence test are also called silence if their volume falls below a slightly higher threshold. A string of adjacent silence frames is called a silence segment, and any silence segment of less than two frames duration is eliminated. The reason for employing only the energy above 300 Hz in detecting silence was to allow voiced stops, which might have a low frequency voice bar, to be detected as silence. If the pitch detector indicates the presence of voicing throughout the duration of a silence segment, that segment is tagged as a voiced silence, or voice bar.

Sonorant Versus Nonsonorant Decision

With silence segments removed from consideration, the remainder of the utterance is segmented into "sonorant" and "nonsonorant" portions. This two-level grouping generally places vowels, nasals, and glides into the "sonorant" category; and the unvoiced fricatives, strong voiced fricatives (/z/, /ʒ/), and aspirations into the "nonsonorant" category. Flapped-t's generally are grouped with sonorant class. The phonemes /v/, /ð/, and /h/ are somewhat less consistent but tend to appear in the sonorant group when they occur in intervocalic context. Two criteria, a positive voicing indication from the pitch detector, and a predominance of low frequency energy over high frequency energy, are utilized to tag a frame as sonorant. If the pitch detector indicates no voicing, but the ratio r_1 = rms (100–900)/rms (3700–5000) is very high, the frame will be called sonorant. If the pitch detector indicates voicing, then the frame will be called sonorant unless r_1 is very low. Considerable editing is done to eliminate most sonorant and nonsonorant segments of less than five frames duration. A segment which is tagged as fricative-like due to strong high frequency energy, but has the pitch detector on throughout its duration, is called nonsonorant and passed to the fricative analysis algorithm, but retains a tag as a possible strong voiced fricative.

Burst and Aspiration Detection

The next step is to analyze the region immediately following each silence segment to determine the presence and location of a burst, and to make an initial decision, based on duration, as to whether an unvoiced segment following the silence is a fricative, or simply the aspiration following the stop. Burst detection is accomplished by analyzing a short-time high frequency energy function E_b near the end of the silence. Values of E_b are determined every 5 ms by passing the waveform through a simple first-differencing filter, rectifying the output and summing over the 5 ms or 50 sample frame. If the peak derivative of E_b near the end of the silence exceeds a threshold, the location of this peak is selected as the burst pointer. If the unvoiced segment following the silence exceeds 25 ms, then the stop is considered to be aspirated; in this case a burst pointer is created at the point of maximum E_b within 2 frames of the end of the silence segment. If an unvoiced segment following the silence exceeds 70 ms (14 looks), it is tagged as a fricative. Otherwise, the entire sequence of silence, burst, aspiration is tagged as a STOP, although the subsegmentation information is retained.

Generalized DIP Detector [18]

The sonorant segments are then analyzed by a generalized dip detector to locate intervocalic voiced consonants. In the first pass of the dip detector, the volume function used is rms (0–5000), computed every 5 ms but then lightly smoothed in time via a zero-phase digital filter whose impulse response $h(n)$ has only three nonzero values, $h(-1) = \frac{1}{4}$, $h(0) = \frac{1}{2}$, $h(1) = \frac{1}{4}$. Local maxima and minima of this volume function are then determined. As indicated in the bottom of Fig. 5, each minimum is tested against the surrounding maxima to determine if it meets the requirements to be called a DIP. If so, a segment is created with the boundaries set at the points of maximum slope in the volume function between the minimum and the two maxima. This first pass detects about 60 percent of the DIP's, but other valid DIP's are detected by similar processing of the remaining vowel-like regions on the basis of other volume functions. The sequence of events is indicated in Fig. 5. The rms (640–2800) is particularly useful for detecting nasals, where the major energy drop is in the second formant region. The heavily smoothed (6 passes through the simple smoothing filter) volume functions are useful for detecting long DIP's which were missed on the first pass due to extraneous maxima and minima of the volume function in the midst of a major valley. In Fig. 5, we distinguish four types of DIP's according to the volume functions which produced them. In later analysis of DIP segments, this distinction is ignored and all DIP's are treated equally. After all DIP's have been detected, the remaining sonorant segments are labeled VWL.

Some post-editing is carried out to correct some of the errors made by the DIP detector. If either of the VWL segments surrounding a given DIP is less than 25 ms in duration, then the DIP is considered spurious and is removed. Also, if the average volume near the center of the DIP is higher than the corresponding measurement for either of the two neighboring VWL segments, the DIP is removed.

Results of First Stage Segmentation

We now summarize the results of first stage segmentation on our 111 sentences corpus. There were 1002 VWL segments detected, of which 14 or 1.4 percent were considered to be false detections. Of the false detections, 7 were due to the insertion of a false DIP, which broke a single vowel into three segments; 2 were caused by false FRIC insertions due to voicing errors in the middle of a vowel. The remaining were actually unexpected weak vowels introduced by the speaker and should not be considered segmentation errors. For example, one speaker pronounced the word "second" as /sɛkəndə/. There were 16 hand-labeled vowels missed by the segmentation programs. Of these, 10 of the undetected syllables were short function words like "the" with a very short voicing duration and very low volume, and 6 were due to failure of the DIP detector to detect an intervocalic /r/ or /l/. For example, the underlined part of the word millisecond was marked as a single VWL segment.

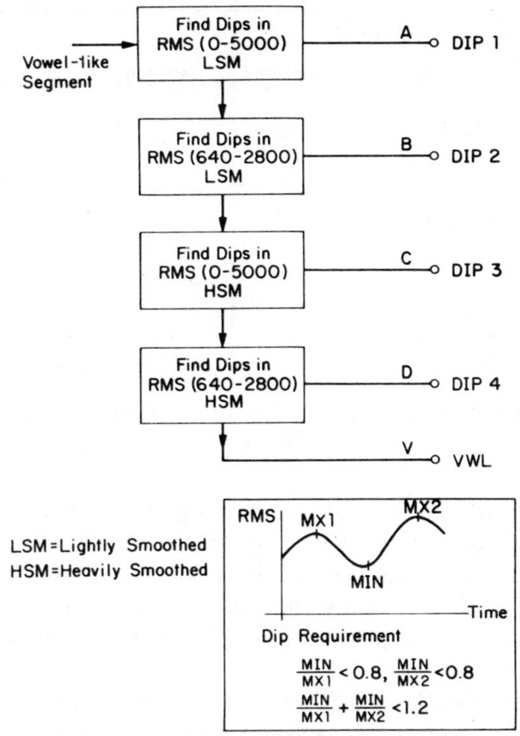

Fig. 5. Generalized DIP detector algorithm.

The phonemes detected as DIP's included 201 nasals and glides, 30 flapped-t's, 37 /v/'s and /ð/'s, 13 /h/'s, 14 stop consonants, and 4 glottal stops. No attempt was made in the initial segmentation to separate two consecutive voiced consonants; for example, in the word "only," the /nl/ would be marked as a single DIP. As mentioned above, there were 7 false DIP's during vowels and 6 failures to detect intervocalic glides. In general, the DIP detector did an excellent job of separating syllables, but detected a variety of phonemes. Later we will describe the algorithms used to subdivide the DIP's into narrower phonemic classes.

There were 246 strong fricatives (/s/, /z/, /ʃ/, /ʒ/) and 76 weak fricatives (mostly /f/, /θ/ but a few /v/, /ð/, /h/) detected as FRIC segments. There were 34 stop aspirations whose duration exceeded 700 ms, and which were therefore tagged as FRIC. Clearly a more sophisticated procedure is needed for separating aspiration from frication. Voicing detection errors caused 9 false FRIC's during vowel-like portions of speech. Less than 1 percent of the strong fricatives were not detected as FRIC, but there were 36 /f/ and /θ/ whose energy was so low that they were labeled STOP instead of FRIC. Of these missed weak fricatives, 25 were from two of the speakers (SM and CW); our suspicion is that better microphone placement might have increased the energy in the weak fricatives of these speakers.

About 94 percent of 320 stops present in the data corpus were correctly detected as STOP. Most of the missed stops were classified as DIP, with a few classified as FRIC. The extra STOP's were mostly composed of the missed weak fricatives mentioned above, but included a few intervocalic nasals which were labeled as voice bars.

Our general evaluation is that this segmentation program works well in carrying out its intended purpose—a rather accurate breakdown of the waveform into broad categories. The algorithm works well for a variety of speakers, and our experience (not documented here) is that it works well for a variety of recording environments. We have restricted the initial segmentation to making only the clearest decisions, and have left more detailed segmentation, finer classification, and error correction to the more sophisticated algorithms to follow.

ANALYSIS OF VOWEL-LIKE SOUNDS

We will discuss in this section the analysis of VWL and DIP segments. As shown above, these segments include primarily vowels, diphthongs, nasals, glides, but also include some other phonemes such as /v/, /ð/ and /ɾ/ (flapped t). The primary parameters used for further segmentation and classification of these sounds are the frequencies $F1$, $F2$, and $F3$ of the first three formants and the corresponding formant amplitudes. A dual approach, employing both steady-state and dynamic analysis of these parameters, is employed. Steady-state vowel identification is accomplished by comparing the formant positions at the center of a vowel to a speaker-normalized formant table containing target formant positions for each vowel. DIP's are classified both by a "steady-state" analysis of the spectral characteristics within the DIP and by a "half-syllable" analysis of formant trajectories from the minimum energy point in the DIP to a maximum energy point in each vowel adjacent to the DIP. Segmentation and identification on nonintervocalic voiced consonants, and identification of diphthongs, is also accomplished primarily via analysis for formant motions. We will now discuss some details of these algorithms and their performance.

Segmentation and Identification of Nonintervocalic Sonorants [19]

Nonintervocalic sonorants are detected by analysis of formant trajectories. Three algorithms are applied to test for sonorant segments: /r/ detection, detection of nasals as a single segment class, and detection of /l/'s and /w/'s as a single segment class. The algorithms are not exclusive: the same segment can be detected as a potential nasal and as a potential /l/ or /w/.

Prevocalic /r/ Detection: The algorithm for detection of prevocalic /r/'s is illustrated in Fig. 6. The slope of $F3$ is first examined on the left side of the VWL segment under consideration. If this slope is positive ($F3$ pulled down toward the left) for a time $T1$ which exceeds a threshold θ_T, and the composite measurement denoted as SCORE is less than a threshold θ_s, a prevocalic /r/ is considered to be detected. The boundary for the /r/ segment is placed, more or less arbitrarily, so as to chop off the leftmost $\frac{1}{3}$ of the VWL segment. The measurements entering into SCORE are taken over the time $T1$, and include the minimum of $F3$, the minimum and average differences between $F3$ and $F2$, and the total frequency change in $F3$. The requirements are such that $F3$ must be pulled low and close to $F2$ over a sufficiently long

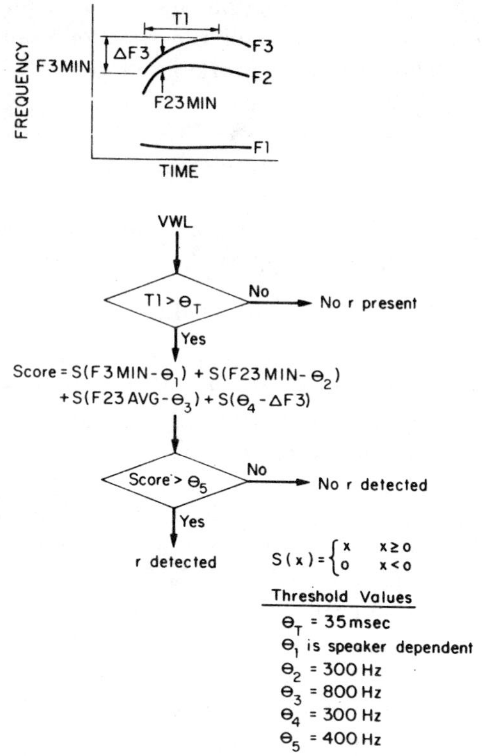

Fig. 6. Algorithm for detection of prevocalic /r/.

duration. Note that individual thresholds are used on each measurement and the SCORE function is designed such that a measurement only adds to SCORE if it fails to meet its threshold condition. This technique was found to be quite successful in dealing with the variety of vowels which might follow the /r/. If an /i/ followed the /r/, then often we would have $F3$ MIN $> \theta_1$ and $\theta_4 > \Delta F3$, but $F23$ MIN and $F23$ AVG would be below their thresholds. With an /a/ following the /r/, $F23$ AVG might exceed its threshold, but usually we would have $F3$ MIN $< \theta_1$ and $\theta_4 < \Delta F3$. We found that the measurements $F23$ MIN, $F23$ AVG, and $\Delta F3$, concerning difference between $F3$ and $F2$ and change in $F3$, were relatively speaker independent. Fixed thresholds were chosen for these measurements, but a speaker-dependent threshold was used for $F3$ MIN; a typical value for a male speaker is $\theta_1 = 1700$ Hz.

A performance summary on the prevocalic /r/ detector is given in Fig. 7. We have combined results on /r/ with results on identification of the vowel /ɜ/ (see below), because both cause similar formant behavior. As will be our general practice in this paper, we show actual counts, rather than percentages, in the confusion matrix. The data sample size is evident, and pertinent percentages can be calculated, based on either the input phonemes (by forcing the rows to sum to 100 percent) or the output APEL's (columns sum to 100 percent). The /r/-/ɝ/ confusions occur mostly in unstressed syllables, as in "spectrogram." Only 7 false /r/'s are detected in about 1000 syllables, with 15 of 88 (about 18 percent) prevocalic /r/'s undetected as either r or ɝ. We should note that excellent formant tracking is essential to this level of performance, since the formant tracker must resolve the difficult situation

Hand-Labelled Phonemes \ APELs	r Detected	ɝ Detected	No r or ɝ
Syllable Contains Prevocalic /r/	56	17	15
Syllable Contains /ɝ/	9	47	11
Syllable Contains No /r/ or /ɝ/	5	9	811

Fig. 7. Confusion statistics on detection of prevocalic /r/ and the vowel.

of two formants coming very close together. We have found that detection of post-vocalic /r/ is considerably more difficult than prevocalic /r/ detection and is complicated by the fact that many speakers tend to slur or omit post-vocalic /r/. A post-vocalic /r/ detector is not included in the current system.

Nonintervocalic Nasal Detection: The initial requirement for detection of a nasal segment is that a sequence of frames on the left or right side of a vowel have sufficiently low $F1$ frequency and low ratio of $F2$ amplitude to $F1$ amplitude. If this requirement is met, then a more stringent nasal test, similar to that for DIP's (see description below) is applied to determine whether a nasal segment should be created. This technique detects 80 percent of prevocalic nasals, but only about 60 percent of post-vocalic nasals. Part of the difficulty with post-vocalic nasals is that they are frequently shortened or evident only through nasalization of the preceding vowel. About 15 percent of the detected pre- or post-vocalic nasals were not actually nasals, but some other phoneme such as /w/, /l/, or /ə/. About 20 percent were false alarms in the sense that no phoneme was present. Most of the false alarms were post-vocalic, and occurred at the end of vowels with low $F1$ such as /i/, /e/, and /u/. This false alarm rate was sufficiently high that we chose to denote nonintervocalic nasals by the APEL η to distinguish them from the intervocalic nasals (the APEL N) which are detected with higher confidence.

Nonintervocalic /ℓ/ and /w/ Detection

We will describe the algorithm for prevocalic /ℓ/ and /w/; the post-vocalic case is treated similarly. The slope of $F2$ is examined on the left side of the VWL segment under consideration. If this slope is positive ($F2$ pulled down toward the left) for a sufficiently long time; and if $F2$ reaches a sufficiently low frequency near the left edge of the VWL; and if the average of $F3$-$F2$, over the time while $F2$ slope is positive, is sufficiently high, then a new segment is cut off the left part of the VWL segment and designated as the APEL ω. About 70 percent of pre- and post-vocalic /w/'s and /ℓ/'s are detected in this manner. However, presence of phonemes which are articulated with lip closure /f/, /p/, /b/, /m/, and /v/ also often cause an ω-segment to be created.

The presence of the APEL ω can be taken to indicate detection of either /w/ or /l/, or lip closure, since 97 percent of the detected ω's fall into these categories. The APEL ω is therefore a less reliable indication of the presence of /w/ or /ℓ/ than the corresponding intervocalic APEL, w.

Diphthong Identification [20]

After the voiced consonant segmentation just described has been carried out, each remaining VWL segment is subjected to special tests to detect the presence of the diphthongs /ay/ (buy) and /ɔy/, (boy) and the diphthong-like sound /yu/ (compute). Detection of a particular diphthong occurs when the formant trajectories in the VWL meet a set of criteria peculiar to that diphthong. The overall performance of these algorithms is quite good, with over 80 percent correct identification and false alarms in less than 1 percent of the remaining syllables.

The /*a*y/ detection algorithm is illustrated in Fig. 8. We require that the total duration T_v of the VWL exceed a threshold, that there be a region greater than $T_v/3$ in length where the slope of $F2$ is positive, and that the formant positions at a point $T_v/4$ from the left edge of the VWL be characteristic of a steady-state /*a*/. The test for this third requirement is carried out by comparing measured $F1$ and $F2$ with tabulated values for /*a*/ in a speaker-normalized vowel table, in a manner similar to that described below for steady-state vowel identifications. Then we require either that the rise in $F2$ exceed 300 Hz or that the duration of the vowel exceed 250 ms. This last duration test was helpful in detecting /*a*y/'s in words like file, time, or five where the influence of the following consonant caused the rise in $F2$ to be less than in other situations, but where it was found that the durations T_v and T_{pos} were longer than average. As seen in Fig. 9, this algorithm correctly detected 80 percent of the /*a*y/'s, with half the misses detected as /ɔy/. There were a few false detections, mostly with vowel and glide combinations like /le/ which have somewhat similar formant trajectories.

The /ɔy/ detector employs a strategy very similar to the /*a*y/ detector. $F1$ and $F2$ near the beginning of the VWL are required to reach positions close to those of a steady-state /ɔ/, and a sufficiently long region of increasing $F2$ is required, with a change in $F2$ of at least 750 Hz. There were only 9 /ɔy/'s in the 111 sentences, and all were correctly detected. In 3 cases, the diphthong /*a*y/, preceded by /w/ or /ℓ/, was detected as ɔy; and there were 3 additional false alarms.

The /yu/ detection algorithm applied a technique similar to the one previously described for /r/ detection. A set of measurements are thresholded and any that exceeds a threshold contributes a penalty to a score, proportional to how much it exceeds the threshold. The requirements are that $F1$ be low throughout the segment; that $F2$ be high on the left and have negative slope over at least $\frac{1}{3}$ of the segment; that $F3$-$F2$ become small near the middle of the segment; and that $F3$ decrease sharply from the beginning to the middle of the segment. The results are indicated in Fig. 9; 16 of 21 /yu/'s were detected, with 5 false alarms.

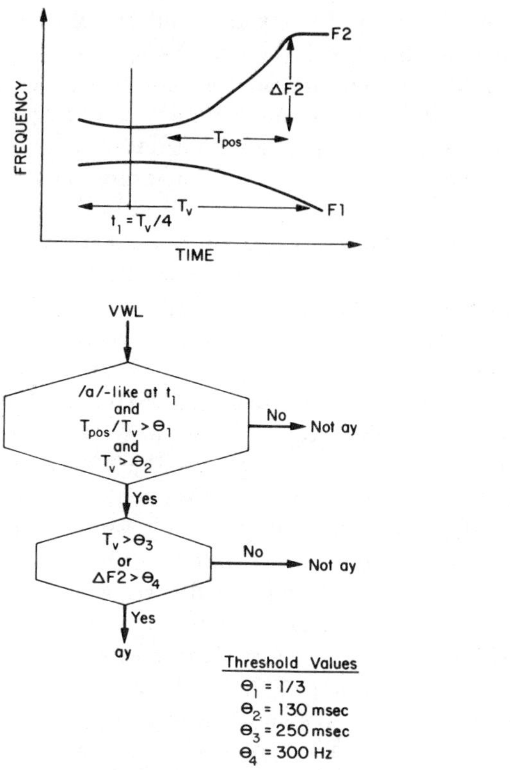

Fig 8. Algorithm for identification of the diphthong /*a*y/.

Hand-Labelled Phonemes \ APELs	ɔy	ay	yu	Other
/ɔy/	9			
/ay/	3	24		3
/yu/			16	5
Other Vowels	3	5	3	931

Fig. 9. Confusion statistics on diphthong identification.

Steady-State Vowel Identification [21]

Steady-state vowels are identified by comparing the measured formant positions at the temporal center of a VWL segment to the corresponding formant values in a speaker-normalized vowel table. The three top-ranked choices are produced, on the basis of distance from the vowels in the table. The fact that this simple classification scheme works reasonably well is, we feel, in large part due to the preprocessing which is done to restrict the set of "steady-state" vowels on which classification is attempted. By the methods discussed above, glides and nasals are detected and separated off from the VWL segment, and diphthongs are identified through their characteristic formant motions. Then weak (unstressed or reduced) vowels whose formant positions are quite dependent on their environment are tagged on the basis of energy comparisons with adjacent syllables. For the remaining VWL segments, a measurement is made of the average (over the segment duration) magnitude of the difference between $F2$ and the mean (over the segment duration) of $F2$. If this measurement is below a threshold (300 Hz was used in these experiments) the VWL segment is considered steady and identification is carried out. In the sentence corpus under investigation, 6 percent of the approximately 1000 detected VWL segments were identified as diphthongs, and 4 percent were labeled "unsteady." An additional 23 percent of the VWL segments were labeled as "weak" in the sense that the integrated energy in the weak VWL segment was less than that of either of its neighboring VWL segments. This simple weak vowel test worked quite well in detecting a majority of the reduced and unstressed vowels; refinements in detection of various levels of stress are now being implemented.

The remaining 67 percent of the VWL segments were considered to be steady state and were classified as indicated above. The procedure for generating a speaker-normalization vowel table is indicated in Fig. 10. Following Gerstman [22], formant normalization factors are obtained through a linear scaling of Peterson–Barney [23] data. Note that different factors are used for males and females. The speaker normalized table is obtained by the linear scaling procedure indicated in the figure. Note that only four measurements are needed for each speaker. For a male, $F1$ MIN and $F2$ MAX would be obtained from the vowel /i/, $F2$ MIN from /ɔ/ or /u/, and $F1$ MAX from /a/. The metric used in determining the distance of a particular vowel from one in the table is $d = |F1_m - F1_t| + \frac{1}{3}|F2_m - F2_t|$ where m and t denote measured and tabulated values, respectively. The top three vowel choices are obtained by measuring $F1$ and $F2$ at the VWL segment center, and determining d for all entries in the table. The vowel /ɝ/ is treated as a special case in that $F3$ is considered; if $F1$ and $F2$ are reasonably close to the tabulated /ɝ/ values, then ɜ will be lifted to first choice if $F3$-$F2$ is low near the segment center. We also have a detector for syllabic /ℓ/ (label) which requires $F3$-$F2$ to be high near the segment center. This steady-state classification procedure is actually applied to all VWL segments; however, if the VWL was detected as diphthong, weak, or unsteady, the "steady-state" identifications are relegated to second and third choices.

Of the vowels which were classed as steady state and assigned a first choice APEL from the set of 10 labels (i, I, ɛ, æ, *a*, ɔ, ʌ, ʊ, u, ɝ), 41 percent were identified correctly on the first choice, and 69 percent were identified correctly on one of the first three choices. There was no specific APEL for the phoneme /e/ (as in "bait"), but this phoneme was classified as ɛ about 45 percent of the time and as I about 35 percent of the time; in the summary data just given, classification of /e/ as ɛ was considered

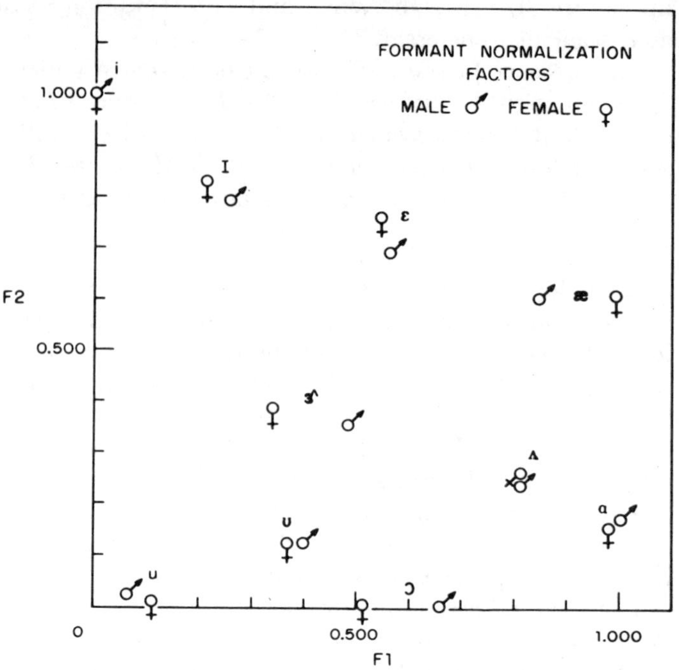

To determine formant table entry for any Speaker S, Sex X, and Vowel V:

$F1(V,S) = F1MIN(S) + F1X(V)\,F1Range(S)$
$F2(V,S) = F2MIN(S) + F2X(V)\,F2Range(S)$

F1MIN, F1Range, F2MIN, F2Range are determined empirically for each speaker from a calibration utterance

Fig. 10. Speaker-normalization procedure for vowels.

"correct." For similar reasons, classification of /o/ (boat) as ɔ was considered correct. A tabulation of some identification results on steady-state vowels is given in Fig. 11. The data presented include all cases where one of the 10 APEL labels listed above was produced as first choice, and where the hand-labeled input was one of the 10 corresponding phonemes, or the phonemes /e/ or /o/. Only the first choice output is tabulated in the matrix. Rather than present a 12 × 10 matrix, we have chosen to combine some of the rows and columns for easier reading. For example, the meaning of the entry in the top left hand corner is that 107 segments were hand-labeled as either /i/ or /I/ and identified as either i or I. The prominence of the diagonal is clear in the figure. A disturbing point is the number of (/i/, /I/) and (/e/, /ɛ/) inputs which were identified as (ʌ, ʊ). Further breakdown of the data shows that all of these entries were actually short vowel (/I/ or /ɛ/) inputs. The apparent misclassification was due either to reduction of the short vowel, or a coarticulation effect (as in the word "list") which resulted in lowered $F2$.

DIP Classification

A two-pronged attack is employed in classification of DIP segments. An analysis of formants and amplitudes within the DIP is combined with a "half-syllable" analysis of formant trajectories from the DIP into each of the neighboring VWL segments. This approach is similar in philos-

Hand-Labelled Phonemes \ APELs	i,I	ɛ	æ	a, ɔ	ʌ, ʊ	ɯ	ɝ
/i/, /I/	107	19			14	1	7
/e/, /ɛ/	40	86	18	5	22		1
/æ/		11	19	7	7		
/a/, /ɔ/, /o/				24	52		
/ʌ/, /ʊ/	2	2		1	22		4
/u/	5				3	11	1
/ɝ/	2	1			5	1	47

Fig. 11. Confusion statistics on steady-state vowel identification.

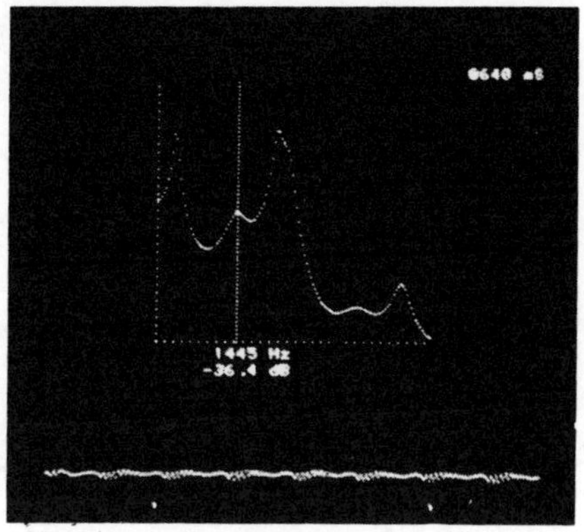

ophy to a previously reported dual classification technique [15], [24].

The trajectory analyses work from a maximum energy point in either a left or right VWL to the minimum energy point in the DIP, and consist of essentially the same algorithms as those described above for detection of nonintervocalic voiced consonants. In this section, we will describe only the "within DIP" or "steady-state" DIP classification algorithms. The combined algorithms produce 4 specific classes of DIP's: N for nasal, w for /w/ or /ℓ/, ɾ for flapped-t, r for /r/; and a default class Δ if none of these 4 classes are detected. Tests for all 4 classes are performed on all DIP's; if more than one test is passed, alternate APEL labels are produced.

The within DIP test for nasal [25] is illustrated in Fig. 12. The indicated formant frequency measurement and formant amplitude ratio measurements are averaged over 5 looks at the center of the DIP. $F1$ frequency must be low, $F1$ amplitude must be significantly higher than $F2$ amplitude (the effect of the nasal zero), but $F3$ amplitude must not be too low relative to $F1$ amplitude. The condition on $F3$ amplitude helps distinguish nasals from voice bars. Finally, the DIP duration must exceed 25 ms. The speaker dependent thresholds are based on measurements of $F1$ and the two amplitude ratios for several intervocalic nasals in a calibration sentence. The detector for /w/ and /ℓ/ requires the minimum (over the DIP) of $F2$-$F1$ to be small, the minimum of $F1$ to be small, and the minimum of $F3$ to be sufficiently large (to distinguish from /r/). The /r/-test requires the minimum of $F3$-$F2$ and the minimum of $F3$ to be below specified threshold values. The thresholds used in "within-DIP" testing for /w/, /ℓ/ and /r/ were the same for all male speakers, but different for the female speakers. The test for flapped-t simply requires that the DIP duration be less than 25 ms.

Composite results for DIP identification are given in Fig. 13. Focusing on the upper 4 rows of the matrix, it is clear that the DIP classifier worked quite well. A few calculations show that 82 percent of the nasals, /ℓ/'s, and /w/'s, /ɾ/'s, and /r/'s were correctly classified, 12 percent were left unclassified as Δ, and only 6 percent were misclassified. In the tabulation of these statistics, we would often face the situation where a DIP corresponded to more than one phoneme. Our convention was to make an entry in the matrix for each phoneme. For example, if the /nð/ in "on the" was detected as a single DIP and labeled as N, one entry would be added to the matrix for nasal labeled as N, and one for /ð/ labeled as N. Most of the 26 occurrences of /v/ or /ð/ labeled as N came about in this manner. We have been working on algorithms for subsegmentation of adjacent phonemes in DIP's, but have not yet achieved satisfactory results. Our dual approach in classification of DIP's worked to considerable advantage, increasing the percentage correct classification by more than 15 percent over either of the approaches separately. The "half-syllable" approach paid particular

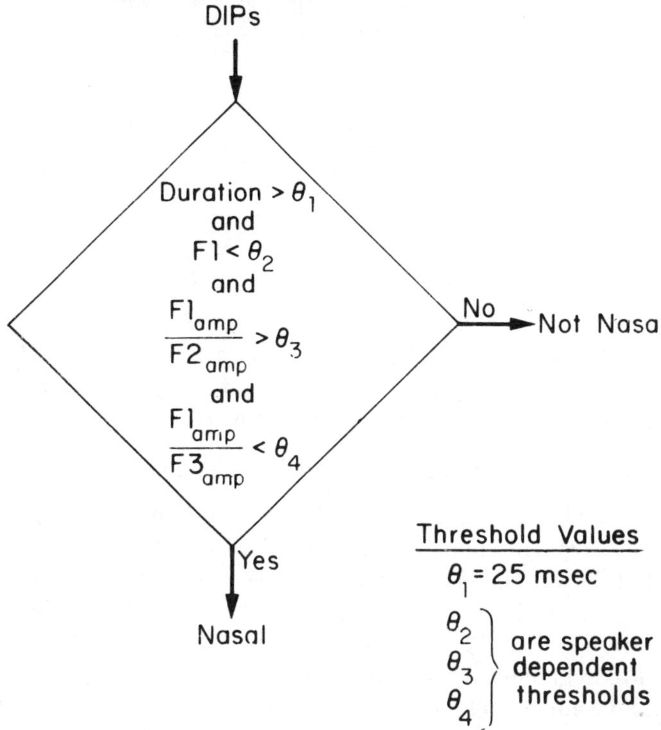

Fig. 12. Algorithm for identification of DIP's as nasals.

Hand-Labelled Phonemes \ APELs	N	W	ɾ	r	Δ
Nasals	97	2	2		16
/w/,/ℓ/	7	49			3
Flapped-t	2		20		8
/r/	1			20	1
/v/,/ð/	26	1			11
Vowels	2	2	3		
Other	11	2	4		10

Fig. 13. Confusion statistics on DIP classification.

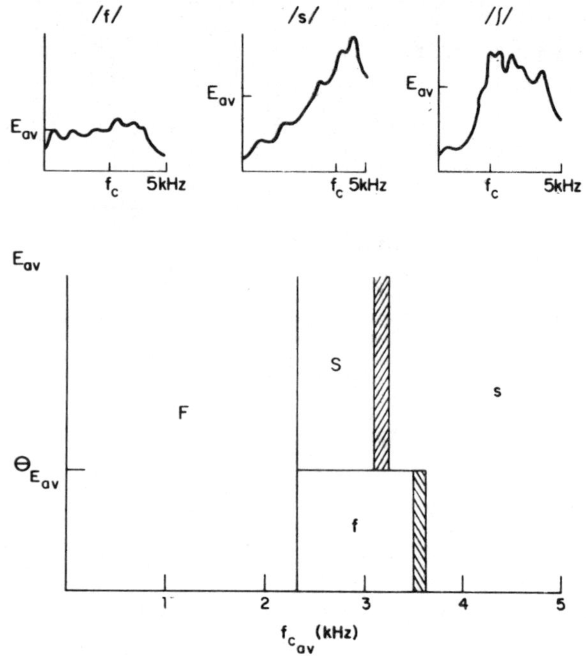

Fig. 14. Algorithm for fricative classification.

dividends in the detection of /r/'s, /w/'s, and /ℓ/'s where formant motions extend well into the vowel and segment boundaries are not clearly defined.

FRICATIVE CLASSIFICATION [26]

The basic fricative classification algorithm takes all FRIC segments and categorizes them into phoneme classes as follows: the APEL *f* designates the phonemes /f/ or /θ/, the APEL *s* designates /s/ or /z/, the APEL *S* designates /ʃ/ or /ʒ/, and the APEL *F* indicates that the FRIC segment did not meet the criteria for any of the above phenomes. The primary parameters used are segment duration, a measurement E_{av} of the volume (rms (0–5000)) averaged over 5 frames at the segment center, and a critical frequency f_{cav}. With $S(f)$ representing the spectral amplitude in a particular frame, and $\Delta f = 10\,000/256$, we define f_c for that frame as $f_c = k_c \Delta f$ where k_c is the largest integer for which

$$\sum_{k=k_c}^{k=127} S(k\Delta f) / \sum_{k=0}^{k=k_c-1} S(k\Delta f) \geq \theta_c.$$

In these experiments, θ_c was chosen as $\frac{1}{2}$, so that f_c corresponded to the center of mass of the spectrum. To determine f_{cav}, we average f_c over 5 frames at the center of the segment. The fricative classification algorithm has the option of segmenting the FRIC segment into two APEL segments, if distinct contiguous fricatives are detected (e.g., "voiceless fricative").

If the FRIC segment is less than 100 ms in duration, no additional segmentation is attempted. The FRIC is classified according to E_{av} and f_{cav} as indicated in the bottom half of Fig. 14. (In the overlap regions, two APEL choices are given.) The frequency regions defined on the figure were used for all speakers; a different set of regions was used for the female speaker. The volume threshold $\theta_{E_{av}}$ was empirically determined. The basic properties being exploited are illustrated by the spectra sketched in the top half of Fig. 14. The fricatives /f/ and /θ/ are weak and have relatively flat spectra; the spectral energy for /s/ and /z/ is skewed toward higher frequencies than for /ʃ/ and /ʒ/. A spectrum skewed too much towards lower frequencies leads to a suspicion that a segmentation error may have been made and that the segment may be vowel-like. If the FRIC segment is greater than 100 ms in duration, then separate classifications are made of the left and right halves of the segment. If these classifications are different, the FRIC segment is split into two APEL's.

Results of fricative classification are summarized in Fig. 15. The statistics indicate 91 percent correct classification, as determined by summing the diagonal elements in the first three rows and dividing by the sum of all elements in the first three rows. A few /v/'s which were called *f* and /tʃ/ and /dʒ/ called *S*, were included as correct classifications. As discussed under first stage segmentation, a number of stop aspirations were segmented as FRIC; they were further classified by the fricative algorithm as indicated. Of the few FRIC's produced due to voicing errors in vowels, about half were assigned the APEL *F* because of low f_{cav}. The double fricative detector performed successful segmentation and identification of 83 percent of adjacent but distinct fricatives. We are working on the problem of distinguishing /z/ from /s/ and /ʒ/ from /ʃ/ on the basis of the pitch detector voicing indicator. Some promising results have been obtained, but difficulties are caused by the fact that many /z/'s are devoiced in continuous speech, at least over part of their duration.

Hand-Labelled Phonemes \ APELs	s	f	S	F
/s/, /z/	202	7	4	1
/f/, /v/, /θ/	8	64	3	1
/ʃ/, /ʒ/, /tʃ/, /d_3/	4	2	26	
/h/	1	4	1	1
Aspiration after voiceless stops /p/, /t/, /k/	9	18	7	
Vowels		2	3	4

Fig. 15. Confusion statistics on fricative classification.

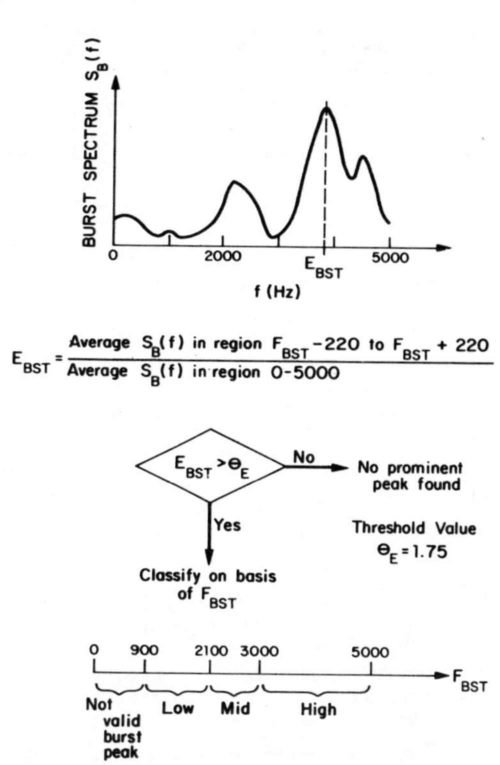

Fig. 16. Algorithm for stop burst classification.

CHARACTERIZATION OF STOP CONSONANTS [27]

The available cues for identifying the manner and place of articulation of stop consonants are 1) the presence or absence of voicing during the closure, 2) the spectral characteristics of the burst, and 3) the formant transitions out of and into adjacent vowels. The problem is complicated by the fact that often some of these cues are missing; for example, the burst may not be present, or the stop may be preceded by a fricative so that information on formant motion into the stop is not available. Our work includes some initial efforts in analyzing all three types of cues, with the major focus to date being analysis of the stop burst.

We classify stops as voiced or unvoiced depending on whether the pitch detector indicates voicing during the "silence" period. Our experience is that only a small percentage of the /b/'s and /d/'s and /g/'s are actually tagged as voiced by this method. However, when the voice bar is present, the stop is almost always a /b/, /d/, or /g/ rather than a /p/, /t/, or /k/.

As discussed above, bursts are detected and located by the primary segmentation program, which yields a decision as to whether a burst is present and a pointer to a single spectral frame representing the burst. This spectrum is analyzed to characterize the burst. The burst is classified according to the frequency location of the major concentration of energy in the burst spectrum, as indicated in Fig. 16. In the figure, F_{BST} is simply the location of the highest peak in the (linear predictive) burst spectrum; E_{BST} is a measure of the relative strength of this peak. If E_{BST} is sufficiently high, then a classification on the basis of F_{BST} is made as indicated. For aspirated /p/'s, E_{BST} will usually be below θ_E. A very low F_{BST} (<900) may arise when the burst location is incorrect (e.g., in the vowel), and is classified as not a valid burst peak. F_{BST} in the "LOW" region (900–2100) should generally represent /k/'s and /g/'s before back vowels, while /t/'s and /d/'s should have F_{BST} in the "HIGH" region. Some results on burst classification are given in Fig. 17. We have included in these statistics only those sounds for which an F_{BST} classification of LOW, MID, or HIGH was made, since these represent our only relatively specific classifications. Note the rather successful separation between (/t/, /d/) and those /k/ and /g/ which do not precede front vowels. As should be expected, /k/ and /g/ before front vowels have higher F_{BST} than /k/ and /g/ in other contexts. When directly followed by the glide /r/, /t/ and /d/ were generally found to have lower F_{BST}; in fact, 4 of the 5 /t/ and /d/ which had LOW F_{BST} were followed by /r/. For convenience, we label each STOP with 1 of 10 APEL's depending on the results of segmentation and burst analysis. The APEL assignments are indicated in Fig. 2; for example, the APEL *p* represents a STOP for which voicing was not detected, and a burst was detected with a spectrum whose major peak did not meet the criterion E_{BST}.

An algorithm has recently been developed to detect the characteristic formant motions into a post-vocalic /k/ or /g/. The requirement for detection of this motion is that $F2$ and $F3$ approach each other near the end of the vowel. In the current sentence corpus, 75 such motions were detected, of which 50 were considered to be correct (/k/, /g/, or /ŋ/ following the vowel). About $\frac{1}{3}$

Hand-Labelled Phoneme \ Burst Class	Low	Mid	High
k_1	32	2	2
k_2		22	13
/t/, /d/	5	31	104
/p/, /b/	1	9	3
Other	3	7	19

Notes:
k_2 includes /k/ and /g/ preceding the front vowels /i/, /I/, /e/, /ε/
k_1 includes all other /k/ and /g/
The affricates /tʃ/, /dz/ are included with /t/, /d/
"Other" includes primarily weak fricatives misidentified as stops

Fig. 17. Confusion statistics on stop burst classification.

of the "incorrect" detections were caused by post-vocalic /r/'s.

Our current efforts on stop consonants are primarily concerned with further analysis of formant transitions. We also feel that it would be worthwhile to study dynamic properties of the bursts, rather than restricting attention to a single frame. In our stop analysis so far, we have used a single set of thresholds for all speakers, but as our analysis becomes more complex, speaker-dependent classifications will have to be introduced.

DISCUSSION AND DIRECTIONS FOR FUTURE WORK

Initial experiments have begun on application of linguistic (lexical, syntactic, and semantic) programs to translate the current APEL's into sentences. Description of these experiments would be premature at this time and in any case is not the subject of this paper. We can say that the quality of APEL output seems high enough to support meaningful experiments in acoustic-linguistic linking. Some sentence recognition has been achieved with a 250 word vocabulary and a finite grammar capable of producing 4.8 million possible sentences (of which 10 examples are given in the Appendix). Meaningful error analysis, leading to suggested improvements in both acoustic and linguistic algorithms, has been possible.

The current acoustic-phonetic analyzer represents an integrated effort in which some attention has been paid to almost all the phonemes of English. The level of performance is best for strong steady-state vowels, diphthongs, strong fricatives, and intervocalic sonorants. More work needs to be done in all areas. In particular, we are just beginning to exploit formant transition cues in vowels to aid in identifying place of articulation for adjacent consonants, particularly stops and nasals. Alternate descriptions of the speech signals, in some cases more feature-like than phoneme-like, should be investigated. For example, detection of falling $F2$ at the edge of a vowel indicates the articulatory feature, lip closure, in the adjacent consonant. More investigation of the speaker normalization problem needs to be carried out. Additional information, such as stress and confidence measures, needs to be provided in order to aid acoustical-lexical matching programs in aligning and scoring dictionary entries against the acoustic stream. We intend to direct our future efforts both toward improvements in acoustic identification and toward the very closely related problem of acoustical-lexical matching.

APPENDIX

Sample Sentences from Data Corpus:

1) List the unvoiced fricatives from sentence one.
2) Delete the waveform from the data base.
3) Select all the nasals with tertiary stress.
4) Get all hand labels from the computer.
5) Skip over the second file on tape unit two.
6) Recalculate the minimum amplitude in the first vowel.
7) Give me the range of the third formant.
8) Move to the next file on tape unit one.
9) Erase the refresh screen.
10) Compute the effect of setting the threshold to eighty-five.

REFERENCES

[1] N. Chomsky and M. Halle, *The Sound Pattern of English* New York: Harper and Row, 1968.
[2] G. Fant, *Acoustic Theory of Speech Production.* The Hague, The Netherlands: Mouton, 1970.
[3] J. L. Flanagan, *Speech Analysis, Synthesis, and Perception,* 2nd ed. New York: Springer-Verlag, 1972.
[4] I. Lehiste, Ed., *Readings in Acoustic Phonetics.* Cambridge, Mass.: Mass. Inst. Tech Press, 1967.
[5] R. K. Potter, G. A. Kopp, and H. G. Kopp, *Visible Speech.* New York: Dover, 1965.
[6] A. Newell, Ed., "Speech understanding systems, final report of a study group," Nat. Tech. Inform. Serv., Springfield, Va., 1971.
[7] S. R. Hyde, "Automatic speech recognition, literature, survey, and discussion," Res. Dep., Dollis Hill, London, Rep. 35.
[8] N. Lindgren, "Machine recognition of human language—Part I," *IEEE Spectrum,* vol. 2, pp. 114–136, Mar. 1965; ——, "Machine recognition of human language—Part II," vol. 2, pp. 44–59, Apr. 1965.
[9] B. S. Atal and S. L. Hanauer, "Speech analysis and synthesis by linear prediction of the speech wave," *J. Acoust. Soc. Amer.,* vol. 50, pp. 637–655, 1971.
[10] J. D. Markel, "Digital inverse filtering—A new tool for formant trajectory estimation," *IEEE Trans. Audio Electroacoust.,* vol. AU-20, pp. 129–137, June 1972.
[11] B. Gold, I. L. Lebow, P. G. McHugh, and C. M. Rader, "The FDP, A fast programmable signal processor," *IEEE Trans. Comput.,* vol. C-20, pp. 33–39, Jan. 1971.
[12] *Speech Understanding Systems Semiannual Technical Summaries,* Lincoln Lab., Mass. Inst. Tech., Lexington, Mass., May 1972–Nov. 1973.
[13] S. S. McCandless, "An algorithm for automatic formant extraction using linear prediction spectra," *IEEE Trans. Acoust., Speech, and Signal Processing,* vol. ASSP-22, pp. 135–141, Apr. 1974.
[14] B. Gold and L. R. Rabiner, "Parallel processing techniques for estimating pitch periods of speech in the time domain," *J. Acoust. Soc. Amer.,* vol. 46, no. 2, part 2, pp. 442–448, Aug. 1969.
[15] C. C. Tappert, N. R. Dixon, D. H. Beetle, and W. D. Chapman,

"The use of dynamic segments in the automatic recognition of continuous speech," Rome Air Development Center, Griffiss Air Force Base, Rome, N. Y., Tech. Rep. RADC TR-70-22, 1970.

[16] B. Gold, "Word recognition computer program," Res. Lab. Electron., Mass. Inst. Tech., Cambridge, Mass., Tech. Rep. 452, June 1966.

[17] G. W. Hughes, "The recognition of speech by machine," Res. Lab. Electron., Mass. Inst. Tech., Cambridge, Mass., Tech. Rep. 395, 1961.

[18] A. N. Stowe, "Syllable segmentation in voiced environments," *J. Acoust. Soc. Amer.*, vol. 36, p. 1048, 1964.

[19] I. Lehiste and G. E. Peterson, "Transitions, glides, and diphthongs," *J. Acoust. Soc. Amer.*, vol. 33, pp. 268–277, 1961; also, I. Lehiste, Ed., *Readings in Acoustic Phonetics*. Cambridge, Mass.: Mass. Inst. Tech. Press, 1967.

[20] A. Holbrook and G. Fairbanks, "Diphthong formants and their movements," *J. Speech Hear. Res.*, vol. 5, pp. 38–58, 1962; also, I. Lehiste, Ed., *Readings in Acoustic Phonetics*. Cambridge, Mass.: Mass. Inst. Tech. Press, 1967.

[21] J. W. Forgie and C. D. Forgie, "Results obtained from a vowel recognition computer program," *J. Acoust. Soc. Amer.*, vol. 31, pp. 1480–1489, 1959.

[22] L. J. Gerstman, "Classification of self-normalized vowels," *IEEE Trans. Audio Electroacoust.*, vol. AU-16, pp. 78–80, Mar. 1968.

[23] G. E Peterson and H. L. Barney, "Control methods used in a study of the vowels," *J Acoust. Soc. Amer.*, vol. 24, pp. 175–184, 1952; also, I. Lehiste, Ed., *Readings in Acoustic Phonetics*. Cambridge, Mass.: Mass. Inst. Tech. Press, 1967.

[24] C. C. Tappert, W. D. Chapman, N. R. Dixon, and A. S. Rabinowitz, "Automatic recognition of continuous speech utilizing dynamic segmentation, dual classification, sequential decoding, and error recovery," Rome Air Development Center, Griffiss Air Force Base, Rome, N. Y., Tech. Rep. RADC-TR-71-146, 1971.

[25] O. Fujimura, "Analysis of nasal consonants," *J. Acoust. Soc. Amer.*, vol. 33, pp. 1865–1875, 1961; also, I. Lehiste, Ed., *Readings in Acoustic Phonetics*. Cambridge, Mass.: Mass. Inst. Tech. Press, 1967.

[26] J. M. Heinz and K. N. Stevens, "On the properties of voiceless fricative consonants," *J. Acoust. Soc. Amer.*, vol. 33, pp. 589–596, 1961; also, I. Lehiste, Ed., *Readings in Acoustic Phonetics*. Cambridge, Mass.: Mass. Inst. Tech. Press, 1967.

[27] M. Halle, G. W. Hughes, and J.-P. A. Radley, "Acoustic properties of stop consonants," *J. Acoust. Soc. Amer.*, vol. 29, pp. 107–116, 1957; also, I. Lehiste, Ed., *Readings in Acoustic Phonetics*. Cambridge, Mass.: Mass. Inst. Tech. Press, 1967.

THE HWIM SPEECH UNDERSTANDING SYSTEM

Jared J. Wolf and William A. Woods

Bolt Beranek and Newman Inc.
50 Moulton Street
Cambridge, Mass. 02138

Abstract

HWIM, the speech understanding system developed at BBN as part of the recent five-year ARPA Speech Understanding Research Project, is designed to "understand" naturally spoken utterances relevant to a task domain of travel budget management. Its vocabulary is over 1000 words, and its grammar permits a relatively habitable subset of natural English. HWIM contains sources of knowledge at the levels of acoustic-phonetics, phonology, vocabulary, syntax, semantics, factual knowledge, and discourse. This paper describes the system as a whole and presents its performance results at the end of the project.

Introduction

The HWIM (for Hear What I Mean) speech understanding system was developed as part of the recent five year program of automatic speech understanding research sponsored by ARPA at BBN and at several other sites [3]. This paper briefly describes HWIM's structure, components, and strategy and gives final performance results. More detailed accounts of some aspects of HWIM's components have been given in [1,2,4,6], and the complete system is described in [5].

HWIM's speech understanding is set in the context of a travel budget manager's automated assistant. It keeps track of trips taken and planned and the budgets to which costs are charged. This particular task is a simple example of the general resource management problem. Utterances processed by HWIM are assumed to be appropriate to this domain, and more specifically, of the type that the manager (as opposed to his assistant) would utter, such as "How much is left in the speech understanding budget?".

The Structure of HWIM

The structure of the HWIM system is shown in Figure 1. In this figure, components of the system are shown as boxes, and data structures are shown as ovals. Arrows illustrate flow of control, except in the lower right and lower center, where they illustrate flow of data. (Not shown are the control linkages between the Speech Control and the APR, PSA, and RTIME components.)

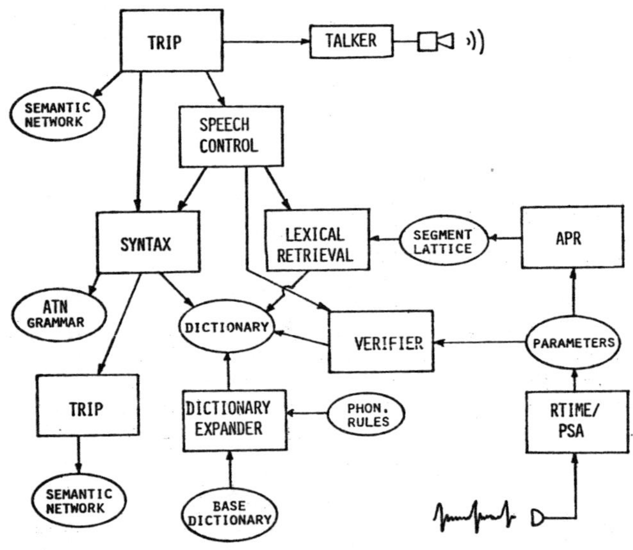

Figure 1. Structure of the HWIM system.

The HWIM system is implemented on TENEX, a virtual memory time-sharing operating system for the PDP-10 computer. HWIM is made up of a number of individual TENEX processes in a single multiple-process job structure. Each box shown in Figure 1 is implemented as a separate TENEX process (RTIME and PSA are actually separate processes).

The Components of HWIM

The TRIP component serves as the overall system controller, the data base manager and retriever, and the embodiment of HWIM's factual and discourse level knowledge sources. TRIP uses a semantic network to represent the travelers, destinations, meetings, trips, budgets, etc.

Reprinted from *1977 IEEE Internat. Conf. Record on Acoust., Speech, and Signal Process*, May 9–11, 1977, pp. 784–787.

that it must model. If it is presented with a typed request, it calls Syntax directly to parse and semantically interpret the request. If the request is spoken, then TRIP invokes the Speech Control component, passing to it discourse level expectations and receiving from it the semantic interpretation of the utterance. This interpretation, which is in a language akin to predicate calculus, is then manipulated by TRIP in its information retrieval role to carry out the user's request. TRIP's response to the user can be either typed or spoken, as appropriate. For the latter, TALKER, a speech synthesis program, is invoked.

The Dictionary Expander, although not a part of the running speech understanding system, is employed at system loadup time to expand the dictionary of baseform pronunciations by means of within-word and across-word phonological rules to encompass all predictable pronunciation variants. The current dictionary starts with 1138 base words, which are expanded to 1363 words by means of regular inflections, of which 1097 words are currently known to the grammar. These 1363 words are expanded into a total of 8642 pronunciations by the application of the phonological rules.

RTIME is the component used to acquire (digitize and store) the speech signal, and PSA is the signal processing component, which converts the speech signal into a parametric representation. This parametric form, used by the APR and Verification components, consists primarily of overall energy, energies in low-, mid-, and high-frequency bands, fundamental frequency, the first 3 formant frequencies, zero crossing rate, a spectral shape measure, and a 13-pole LPC spectral model.

The Acoustic-Phonetic Recognizer (APR) operates on the parametric representation of the utterance with acoustic-phonetic rules to produce a bottom-up phonetic hypothesis called the segment lattice, illustrated in Figure 2 below. The segment lattice allows for the representation of alternate segmentation paths where the acoustic evidence is not sufficiently unambiguous to permit unique segmentation decisions at this level. Each segment label, although shown as a single mnemonic label for the convenience of the experimenter, is in fact a vector of likelihood ratios L_j, one for each phoneme, giving an estimate of the likelihood of each phoneme P_j in light of the acoustic evidence. That is,

$$L_j = \frac{\Pr(\text{acoustic evidence} \mid P_j \text{ is correct})}{\Pr(\text{acoustic evidence})}$$

```
12      14      15        17
+------+        +---------+
|B     |        |J        |
|V     |        |H        |
|      |        |         |
12 13 14        15   16    17    18    19
--+--+--+-------+-----+-----+-----+-----+-
  |V |B |A      |N    |D    |I    |P    |
   D  V  O       V     H     X     K
   H             O
                 B
                 S
```

Figure 2. Segment lattice fragment for the word "budget". Time runs horizontally from left to right. The numbers denote segment boundaries, and the characters denote segment labels.

These likelihood ratios are derived from performance statistics of the APR program operating on a data base of utterances by five male speakers.

The Lexical Retrieval component, which embodies the lexical and phonological knowledge sources, is used to match dictionary word pronunciations against the segment lattice in two ways: (1) without regard to context, or (2) "anchored" off a previously found word match or set of word matches, with the effects of the adjacent words taken into account. In either case, it can seek either all words or only those in a specified set. It uses a tree-structured dictionary in order to do the matching and across-word phonological rule application most efficiently. It combines the segment lattice scores using Bayes' Rule to estimate the probability of the word match given the observed signal.

The Verification component takes a word pronunciation plus context (if any), generates an idealized time-varying spectral representation using a speech synthesis-by-rule program, and compares that against a region of the parametric representation of the utterance by means of a spectral distance metric and a dynamic programming algorithm. Because it uses generative rather than analytic acoustic-phonetic knowledge and matches a pronunciation against the parameters rather than the segment lattice, it provides a word matching capability largely independent of the Lexical Retriever, but at a higher computational cost.

The Syntax component embodies the syntactic, semantic, and pragmatic knowledge sources, and by invoking a second instantiation of the TRIP component, accesses the factual knowledge source as well. Its parser is built around a "pragmatic grammar", which accepts only those utterances that are grammatical in the usual sense, meaningful in the travel budget management domain, and appropriate to the pragmatic circumstance of a single speaker talking to a computer data management system and given the previous conversation. In this grammar, the usual NP, VP, and PP constituents are replaced by structures such as "meetings", "trips", and "budget items". This specialization considerably increases the predictive power of the grammar, since it does not permit phrases like "her next workshop", which, although formed from words in the HWIM vocabulary and acceptable in normal English grammar, is not appropriate to this task domain. The functions of the Parser are (1) to judge the grammaticality of a given word sequence, (2) to predict the possible extensions of a hypothesized word sequence, and (3) to build up a formal representation of the utterance, the semantic representation described earlier. It can parse utterances starting at any point in the utterance and working in both directions thereafter.

Control Strategy

The Control component uses the other components much like subroutines, making all decisions concerning resource allocation. The Control component contains about 25 flag variables that control different strategy options. Space does not permit more than the briefest description of one control strategy (a "left-hybrid, shortfall density" strategy [5]).

After an utterance has been acquired and the front-end processing has been done to produce a segment lattice, Lexical Retrieval is called to scan the lattice to determine the words that match best at the left end. Each of these words is scored and put on an event queue in order of a priority score derived from its likelihood. The Verification component is then used to further evaluate how well these words match the signal, and the queue gets reordered as the verification scores are factored in.

The top (best scoring) event on the queue is presented to Syntax as a theory (or hypothesis) for evaluation. Syntax makes proposals for all words and semantic categories that are possible at each end of this theory. These proposals are then given to Lexical Retrieval for anchored scans at both ends of the theory. For each word found, a word event, a one-word extension of the previous theory, is created, scored, and inserted in the queue at a position determined by the overall event score. The new events are given to Verification to have their new words verified.

This cycle of syntactic proposals by the top event, scans for the words proposed, and formation and verification of new events continues until an event is processed that spans the utterance and is acceptable to the grammar. Obviously, the number of such cycles (or new theories) required must be at least the number of words in the sentence, but such an optimum is rarely achieved. In some cases, the number of cycles required is on the order of 2 times the number of words; in others the number is much larger.

Among the possible strategy variations are policies for constraining the direction in which theories are allowed to grow, different methods of scoring the events to determine their positions in the queue, different ways of using the Verification component, and various other control heuristics.

Explaining the way that HWIM uses its various sources of knowledge to understand an utterance is a little bit like explaining how to high jump; the principles are few, but there are many practical details that are difficult to describe! For more details, see [5].

Performance

For the final performance test, a new set of 124 utterances spoken by three male speakers from whom previous utterances had been solicited were recorded. These utterances were processed with the final version (12 October) of HWIM. The test set comprised two tokens each of 62 sentences. Thirty-one of these sentences had been used in test utterances processed by earlier versions of HWIM, and the others were entirely new sentence types. The sentences were chosen so that we could use them to test the system on vocabularies of two sizes, 409 words and 1097 words. The utterances range in length from 3 to 13 words; the average length is 6 words or 1.8 seconds. The results are shown in Table 1.

In Table 1, the term "Semantically correct" refers to utterances whose word list was not entirely correct, but whose semantic interpretation, as generated by the Parser, was identical to that of the correct sentence. This is regarded as "correctly understood" in the sense of [3]. For example, the utterance "How much is left?" was understood as "What is left?", which is equivalent in this domain.

Of the incorrectly understood utterances, most were quite close to the correct sentence. For example, "Show me Bill's trip to Washington" was understood as "Show only Bell's trip to Washington" (i.e., Alan Bell, rather than Bill Woods.); "The registration fee is twenty dollars" was understood as "Their regis-

	BIGDICT 1097 words	MIDDICT 409 words
Correctly understood	54 = 44%	65 = 52%
All words correct	51 = 41%	59 = 48%
Semantically correct	3 = 2%	6 = 4%
Incorrect	45 = 36%	40 = 32%
Close to correct	29 = 23%	25 = 20%
Less correct	13 = 10%	10 = 8%
Very wrong	3 = 2%	5 = 4%
No response	25 = 20%	19 = 15%
Gave up	24 = 19%	18 = 14%
System broke	1 = 1%	1 = 1%
Estimated average branching (words)	196	67
Speed (times real time)	1350	1050

Table 1. Summary of final performance results, 124 utterances by three speakers.

tration fee is twenty dollars". Others were farther away from the correct sentence. For example, "Give me a list of the untaken trips" was understood as "Give Bill's fifty untaken trips". For some utterances, the system gave up without responding, after exceeding a preset limit of 150 theory evaluations without finding a complete interpretation. In all but a few such cases, at that point there was no hope that HWIM would correctly understand the utterance.

Whenever the Lexical Retrieval component is called to scan the segment lattice for a set of proposed words and classes, the number of words possible at that point is noted. This number ranges from over 900, at the left end of the sentence, to cases where the context allows only a single word to follow. The "Estimated average branching (words)" in Table 1 is the arithmetic mean of these branching factors.

The time required to understand an utterance is divided among the various components of the system in the following rough proportions:

RTIME/PSA	5%
APR	0
Lexical Retrieval	40
Verification	15
Parser	20
Control	20

The results for the smaller, 409 word vocabulary show an increase in the correctly understood utterances and a corresponding decrease in the incorrect and "no response" cases, but the improvement is far from dramatic. This suggests that the factor of 2.7 in vocabulary size (or the corresponding factor of 3 in average word branching) represents a much smaller change in the "difficulty".

We feel that the 44% "correctly understood" performance is a low estimate of HWIM's capabilities. Development of the system continued right up to three weeks from the end of the contract, and although this final version of the system was tested on a variety of utterances, time prevented the more thorough testing that we would have preferred. The final test runs uncovered many bugs, most of which did not bring the system to a halt, but definitely interfered with the process of finding the correct interpretation. Naturally, no changes could be made to the system during the test without invalidating the results already obtained and compromising the "new" status of the 124 utterance test set.

Acknowledgement

This research was supported by the Advanced Research Projects Agency of the Department of Defense and was monitored by ONR under Contract No. N00014-75-C-0053.

References

[1] Cook, Craig, "Word Verification in a Speech Understanding System," Conference Record, ICASSP-76, 553-556 (1976).

[2] Cook, Craig C., and Richard M. Schwartz, "Advanced Acoustic Techniques in Automatic Speech Understanding," elsewhere in these proceedings.

[3] Newell, A., J. Barnett, J. Forgie, C. Green, D. Klatt, J. C. R. Licklider, J. Munson, R. Reddy, and W. Woods, Speech Understanding Systems: Final Report of a Study Group (Amsterdam: North-Holland/American Elsevier, 1973).

[4] Schwartz, Richard M., and Victor W. Zue, "Acoustic-Phonetic Recognition in BBN SPEECHLIS," Conference Record, ICASSP-1976, 21-24 (1976).

[5] Woods, W., M. Bates, G. Brown, B. Bruce, C. Cook, J. Klovstad, J. Makhoul, B. Nash-Webber, R. Schwartz, J. Wolf, V. Zue, "Speech Understanding Systems, Final Technical Progress Report, Volumes I-V," Report No. 3438, Bolt Beranek and Newman Inc., Cambridge, Mass. (1976).

[6] Woods, William A., and Victor W. Zue, "Dictionary Expansion via Phonological Rules for a Speech Understanding System," Conference Record, ICASSP-1976, 561-564 (1976).

Dynamic Speaker Adaptation in the Harpy Speech Recognition System

Bruce T. Lowerre

Department of Computer Science
Carnegie-Mellon University, Pittsburgh, Pa. 15213

ABSTRACT

The Harpy speech recognition system works optimally when it "knows" the speaker, i.e. when it has learned the speaker dependent characteristics (speaker dependent parameters) of the speaker. There are three methods of learning these parameters. One way is to generate them from a set of training data which covers all the allophones that occur in the task language. A second method is to use "speaker independent" parameters with a resulting reduction in accuracy performance. Since it is inconvenient for a "new" speaker to say a set of training data before using the system and the low accuracy with speaker independent parameters is unacceptable, a third method has been devised to allow the system to dynamically learn the speaker dependent parameters while using the system. The new speaker starts with a set of speaker independent parameters. These parameters are then altered after correct recognition (which can be forced if necessary) to match the spoken utterance.

INTRODUCTION

This paper presents a method by which the Harpy is able to adapt to non-familiar speakers. The first section gives a short description of the Harpy system, its data structures, and its current performance. The following sections discuss the speaker variability issue and several approaches that have been taken towards its solution. These approaches include speaker specific tuning, speaker independent tuning, and dynamic speaker adaptation. The last section discusses how these averaging techniques can also be used in isolated word recognition systems.

THE HARPY SYSTEM

The Harpy system is the first system to be demonstrated with a vocabulary of over 1000 words. The system was demonstrated at the completion of the five year Advanced Research Projects Agency (ARPA) speech research project in September, 1976. It had a sentence accuracy, across five speakers (both male and female), of 91% and ran in about 30 MIPSS (a MIPSS is millions of machine instructions executed per second of speech). Since that time, improvements have been made in the speed of the system. The current system runs in less than 7 MIPSS. The system is a recognition system rather than an understanding system since it uses no semantic knowledge about the task in decoding the utterance. However, there are several other sources of knowledge in the system such as syntactic, lexical, word juncture phenomena, speaker characteristics, and intrinsic phoneme durations (see Lowerre, 1976 for complete details).

In the Harpy system, the syntactic, lexical, and word juncture knowledge are combined together into one integral network representation similar to that of the Dragon system (Baker, 1975). The syntactic knowledge is specified by a context free set of production rules for the task language. A dictionary is used to represent the lexical knowledge. The dictionary contains symbolic phone spellings and specifies alternate pronunciations of the words in the task language. Word juncture rules are also included in the network to account for inter-word phonetic phenomena. The network consists of a set of states and inter-state pointers. Each state has associated with it phonetic, lexical, and duration information. The pointers indicate what states may follow any given state. Two special states in the network, the initial state and the final state, indicate the starting point and ending point for all utterances respectively. The network is, therefore, a complete (and pre-compiled) representation of all possible pronunciations of all possible utterances in the task language. This network is used to guide the recognition process.

The recognition process of the Harpy system is based on the Locus model of search. The Locus model rejects all but a narrow beam of paths around the most likely path through the network. These "best" paths are searched in parallel with one pass through the speech data and therefore does not require backtracking.

The following is a short description of the recognition process: The utterance is digitized at 10 KHz. This continuous signal is segmented into consecutive acoustically similar sound units (based on distance measures of the data) and autocorrelation values and linear predictor coding (LPC) coefficients are extracted for each segment. The segments are then mapped to the network states based on the probability of match (distance match) of the LPC data and the expected phones of each state. The matching of the LPC's and the network states is accomplished by use of phone templates. The templates contain the idealized parameters for each phone that occurs in the network states and they may be either speaker specific or speaker independent. The metric used for this matching is Itakura's minimum prediction residual error (see Itakura, 1975).

Reprinted from *1977 IEEE Internat. Conf. on Acoust., Speech, and Signal Process.*, May 9–11, 1977, pp. 788–790.

The mapping scheme used is a modified graph search in which heuristics are used to reduce the number of paths that are checked. The result is that only a few "best" paths are searched in parallel during the recognition processes thus greatly reducing the computational overhead.

Results The current system achieves a sentence accuracy of 90.0% and a word accuracy of 94.3% on a 1011 word task and runs in 6.8 MIPSS.

SPEAKER ADAPTATION IN THE HARPY SYSTEM

Speaker variability Speaker variability generally occurs in three forms, dialectic, contextual, and acoustic. Dialectic variability involves changes in the pronunciation of words among speakers. Contextual variability involves changes in word pronunciation do to the context of the words. Acoustic variability results from vocal tract changes among speakers. Either or all types of variability can occur when changing speakers. The Harpy system attempts to recognize these different variabilities and to separate the effects made by each. Dialectic variability is an effect across a broad group of speakers and the variability is encoded into the lexicon. Many dialects can be encoded into the lexicon or different lexicons can be used for different dialects. The current Harpy system uses the "mid-western American" dialect of English. The contextual variability is handled in the word juncture phenomena rules and, to a lesser extent, in the lexicon itself. The acoustic variability is a speaker dependent phenomenon and can be separated from the other types of variability.

Approach to speaker variability Many proposals and attempts have been made, from such groups as SDC, BBN, Lincoln Labs, etc., as to how to handle the speaker variability problem. These proposals include such ideas as vowel formant normalizations as an attempt to determine speaker independent characteristics of the speech signal. The Harpy system handles speaker variability by the use of phone templates to capture the vocal tract characteristics. We achieve this by identifying all the unique sounds that occur in the task language (called phones). It is important to realize that these phones may or may not bear a resemblance to what may be usually thought of as a phonetic sound in the English language. For example, there are usually several occurrences of one vowel (allophones) in our set of phones each of which has a unique name. Also, there could be a single phone which represents what is usually thought of as a combination of phones (e.g. the phone "WH" represents the characteristics of the aspiration sound when pair "K W" that occures together as in the word "queen"). Each of the phones used in the Harpy system represents one unique phonetic sound.

Phonetic knowledge in the Harpy system The Harpy system uses a phonetic dictionary (along with word juncture rules) to represent the lexicon of the task language. The spellings in the dictionary are strings of phones (along with a special syntax) which are used to represent primary and alternate pronunciations of the words in the lexicon. The phonetic dictionary is a representation of the actual realizations of the task language words rather than a pronunciation dictionary. A set of speaker dependent phone templates (one per phone) is used to match the symbolic lexicon to the actual acoustic signal. The phones of the lexicon represent all the unique phonetic sounds that occur in the task language. Since the lexicon contains symbolic spellings which are speaker independent and there is a one to one mapping of the templates to the phones, the acoustic speaker variability can be handled effectively by using a unique set of templates for each speaker. The templates model speaker dependent vocal characteristics. For example, the dictionary spelling for "CONCERN" is "(← (-,0),-) (K,0) (IH7,IH3) N S ER (N,DX)". Optional paths are enclosed within parenthesis and are separated by commas (the "0" represents the null option). The spelling is interpreted as either a voice bar ("←") followed by an optional silence ("-") or just a silence, followed by an optional "k", followed by either a "IH7" or "IH3", followed by an "N", followed by a "S", followed by an "ER", followed by either an "N" or "DX". See McKeown, 1977, for an example network.

Averaging of template exemplars The success of the speaker dependent phonetic templates depends of the ability to average many exemplars of each phone together to generate each template. This averaging enables the automatic cancelation of errors (provided they are small). Since the template is an average, there is no need to find the single "ideal" exemplar that best fits all occurrences of the phone. The averaged template will usually match all exemplars of the phone in the training data to a high degree of accuracy. If a match of an exemplar in the training data is too far from the average template, then this indicates a missing phone.

The metric used by the Harpy system is Itakura's minimum prediction residual error of the LPC data. A method was needed to average samples together that could be used for generating the templates for this metric. The method we use is to sum the autocorrelation data of the samples that are used in generating the template. The justification of this is that the LPC's are independent of the number of autocorrelation samples that are used to generate them. The obvious danger is that non-similar sounds may be averaged resulting is a poor spectrum. This is a real problem and is handled by a semi-automatic procedure for generation of the phones, templates, lexicon, and word juncture rules described below.

Speaker specific tuning The phones, templates, lexicon, and word juncture rules are generated from a set of training data that contains occurrences (and hopefully all contexts) of all the words in the lexicon. A semi-automatic iterative procedure is used to generate (or more precisely, update) these knowledge sources. There is a "chicken-egg" problem with this iterative procedure in that the data sources must already exist in order to update them. The generation of the initial knowledge sources is a tedious manual boot-strapping procedure. The training data must be carefully hand labeled (both at the word level and the phone level) and initial guesses are made about what phones, word spellings, juncture rules, etc. are needed. This manual effort is the main bottle-neck for developing larger vocabulary systems. Automatic methods must be developed before larger systems can be attempted.

The following is the semi-automatic procedure used to update the data sources: The Harpy system is run in a forced recognition mode with a previously generated set of templates (which can be from some other speaker) to produce a parsing of the phones to the acoustic data. This forced recognition can be done either by using a unique network for each utterance (which represents only the one utterance) or by considering only paths in a large network that represent each single utterance. The parsings generated from the forced recognition runs are used to locate the autocorrelation data for the averaging of the templates. After the averaging is completed, a new set of templates is generated and used to again run the training cycle. This cycle is run several times until the templates converge. If the templates do not converge, then this indicates an error in either the lexicon or word juncture rules or a missing phone which must be manually analyzed and corrected.

Speaker independent tuning The speaker dependent templates are an averaging of many phone exemplars for each template. Since there is a unique set of templates for each speaker, they capture the individual vocal tract characteristics. This idea of capturing vocal tract characteristics by the use of templates can be extended to multiple speakers. When a number of these speaker dependent sets of templates are generated, another set of templates can be generated from all of them by a similar averaging technique. This set of templates, since they are an averaging of several speakers, will be speaker independent. The performance with speaker independent templates will of course be lower than with the speaker dependent templates. For example, one experiment done with connected digits gave the following result: Ten speakers (including males and females) were used to produce ten speaker dependent sets of templates. The average word accuracy for all ten speakers (when tested on the speaker dependent templates with a total of 1000 three word utterances) was 98%. These ten template sets were then used to generate a set of speaker independent templates. These same ten speakers plus ten new speakers were then tested with the system. The word accuracy for all 20 speakers (on 1200 utterances) was 93%. An interesting observation is that there was no significant difference between the accuracies of the ten speakers whose templates were used to generate the speaker independent set and the ten new speakers.

Dynamic speaker adaptation The high error rate (7%) with the speaker independent templates makes this alternative to the handling of acoustic variability unacceptable. Further, the training cycle mentioned earlier to generate the speaker dependent templates is inconvenient do to the large amount of training data needed and is computationally expensive. A third scheme was devised which allows a new user the immediate use of the system but also allows for the speaker dependent vocal characteristics. This is the dynamic tuning of the speaker templates. A new speaker to the system starts with the set of speaker independent templates. The system will, upon all correct recognitions, automatically average the autocorrelation data with the corresponding templates and update the template parameters. The first occurrence of a phone spoken by the speaker will replace the speaker independent template. Further occurrences of the same phone will add to the average of the template. This will result in the phone template being altered quickly for the first occurrences of a phone and a gradual fine tuning of the template by additional occurrences of the phone. In this method, the system quickly adapts itself to the speaker's acoustic characteristics. If the system makes an error in recognition, one can either speak the same utterance again with the hope that it will be recognized correctly the second time or the system can be rerun on the same utterance and forced to recognize the utterance. To force a recognition, the appropriate switch is set and the correct utterance is typed to the system. The system will then only consider paths in its network which represent the spoken utterance.

The error rate when first starting is, of course, 7% but quickly drops off towards the 2% error rate of the speaker dependent templates. The time needed for the updating of the templates is zero during the actual recognition but requires up to one times real time after recognition depending on the number of templates that are updated. Therefore, the overhead of doing the dynamic speaker adaptation is minimal.

DISCUSSION

Summary In this paper we have considered several sources of variability in the connected speech signal, i.e. dialectic, contextual, and speaker dependent variability, and described how the Harpy system attempts to cope with all these sources of variability. The dialectic and contextual variability are encoded into the lexicon and word juncture rules. The speaker dependent sources of variability are handled by averaging phone parameters (i.e., the autocorrelation coefficients, not the LPC's) from among several exemplars of a given phone by the same speaker (for speaker specific templates) or from many speakers (for speaker independent templates). In the case of dynamic adaptation, a set of speaker independent templates are used initially and the system automatically alters the templates during use to adapt to the specific speaker.

It appears straight forward to adopt the above techniques for isolated word recognition systems also. Given several training samples of the same word, one can align the speech signal by dynamic programming techniques and average the autocorrelation coefficients as in the connected speech case. Since this averaging would be independent of word representation used, i.e. whether one uses segmentation and phone templates to represent words or the conventional brute force word templates, one can still use the above averaging technique to generate better templates.

REFERENCES

Baker, J. K. (1975), "Stochastic Modeling as a Means of Automatic Speech Recognition", (Ph.D. Thesis, Carnegie-Mellon Univ.), Tech. Rep., Comp. Sci. Dept., Carnegie-Mellon University, Pgh, Pa.

Itakura, I. (1975), "Minimum Prediction Residual Principle Applied to Speech Recognition", IEEE Trans., ASSP, 23 67-72.

Lowerre, B. T. (1976), "The Harpy Speech Recognition System", (Ph.D. Dissertation, Dept. of Comp. Sci.), Carnegie-Mellon University, Pittsburgh, Pa.

McKeown, D. (1977), "Word Verification in the Hearsay II Speech Understanding System", 1977 IEEE International Conference on Acoustics, Speech and Signal Processing, Hartford Ct.

Part VII
Reviews of Speaker Recognition

Automatic Speaker Verification: A Review

AARON E. ROSENBERG, MEMBER, IEEE

Abstract—The relation of speaker verification to other pattern-recognition problems in speech is discussed, especially the distinction between speaker verification and speaker identification.

The prospects for automatic speaker verification, its settings and applications are outlined. The techniques, evaluations, and implementations of various proposed speaker recognition systems are reviewed with special emphasis on issues peculiar to speaker verification. Two large-scale operating systems using different analysis techniques and applied to different settings are described.

I. Introduction

PATTERN-RECOGNITION problems are among the most challenging and fascinating areas in speech research. The speech pattern recognition facility of human beings is remarkable. It is easily taken for granted and is only appreciated when one attempts to make machines perform similar tasks. Some of the speech-pattern-recognition problems of current interest are speech recognition, speaker recognition, language identification, diagnosis of speech pathologies, and even characterizing emotional state and attitude by voice analysis. Of these, by far the most attention has been given to speech recognition. This problem has had as much fascination and potential payoff for the speech researcher as the conversion of lead to gold had for the alchemist. (With intelligent circumscription of the problem, the chances of success for the speech researcher seem much better than those of the alchemist (cf. papers by Martin, Reddy, and Jelinek in this issue).)

Speaker recognition has also received a great deal of attention among speech researchers. It seems to be a problem which is an order of magnitude less difficult than speech

Manuscript received September 15, 1975; revised October 31, 1975.
The author is with Bell Laboratories, Murray Hill, NJ 07974.

Reprinted from *Proc. IEEE*, vol. 64, pp. 475–487, Apr. 1976.

recognition because it is not necessary to extract the message-bearing information from the speech waveform to be able to characterize the speaker of the message. It is nevertheless a difficult and challenging problem and like speech recognition has more chance of success when it is intelligently circumscribed. The speaker-recognition[1] problem in general is treated in the paper by Atal in this issue. The particular circumscription of the speaker-recognition problem which has already achieved a modicum of success and which has a considerable potential practical payoff is speaker verification.

The more general problem, speaker identification, may be stated as follows. Out of a total population of N speakers, find that speaker whose reference pattern is most similar to the sample pattern of an unknown speaker. Since the sample pattern is compared to each of the N reference patterns and since there is a finite probability of an incorrect decision for each comparison, it is apparent that the overall probability of an incorrect decision must be a monotonically increasing function of N.

The speaker-verification problem may be stated as follows. The sample pattern of an unknown speaker together with a claimed identity is given. Determine whether the sample pattern is sufficiently similar to the reference pattern associated with the claimed identity to accept that claim. In this case just one comparison of patterns is required regardless of the size of the population. Thus the probability of an incorrect decision is generally independent of the population size.

It is possible to treat the distinction between speaker verification and speaker identification more formally and arrive at this same conclusion. However, the assumptions generally made are that the impostor is drawn from the same population as the true speaker and that all speakers are equally likely to be an impostor. In fact, it may be that a speaker with a high probability of acceptance is more likely to be an impostor, i.e., a determined mimic, and that the *a priori* probability of such a speaker grows as the population of speakers is allowed to increase.

With the exception of the above *caveat*, it is seen that the speaker verification is a more tractable problem than the more general speaker identification problem in that the error rate is independent of the population size. Also, only a single comparison of unknown pattern to reference pattern and a simple accept or reject decision is required. This allows faster computation and less complexity than the compound comparisons and decisions required for speaker identification.

Doddington [13] has provided a formal treatment of the distinction between speaker identification and speaker verification including a simulation for normally distributed speaker measurements. Expected error rate is computed as a function of population size. An example of these computations is shown in Fig. 1.

Thus speaker-verification systems are theoretically capable of handling large as well as small speaker populations, with limitations only with regard to storage capacity and speed of access to reference patterns. For this reason there has been a good deal of impetus recently towards developing commercially practical speaker-verification systems. Some of the possible applications include banking and credit authorizations, access to secure information or premises, and carrying out transactions from remote locations by telephone or other voice communication links.

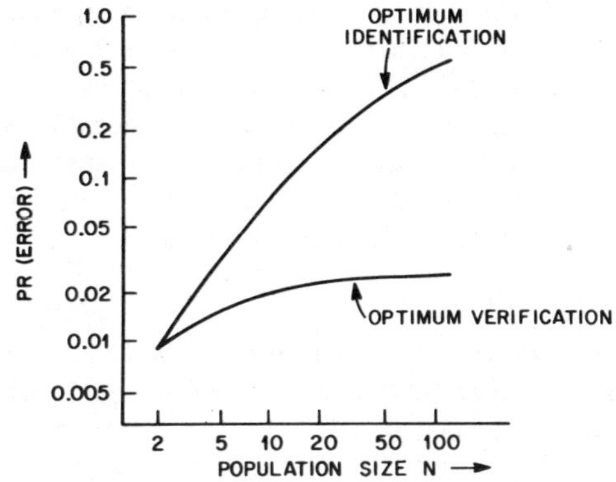

Fig. 1. Expected error rate for speaker verification and speaker identification as a function of population size; results from a computer simulation by Doddington [13].

This paper deals almost exclusively with automatic techniques for speaker verification. There are two other techniques for speaker verification which are dependent on subjective abilities. These are auditory comparison of speakers and visual comparison of spectrograms or other speech features which can be displayed. Visual comparison of spectrograms (voiceprint analysis), is especially controversial because of the wide claims of applicability put forth by its advocates and the large variation in performance found in various evaluations of the technique. References to both auditory and visual techniques will be found in the bibliography.

A basic assumption for most automatic speaker verification systems is that the speakers in the customer set are cooperative. That is to say, they make no overt attempts to alter their speaking behavior from trial to trial. With this restriction, present automatic speaker verification methods have little forensic application.

II. Approaches to Speaker Verification

Much of the theory and techniques of speaker verification is common to speaker identification. These are adequately covered in the paper by Atal in this issue. However, we will review them again here with emphasis on techniques and issues peculiar to speaker verification.

One dichotomy for speaker-recognition systems is whether there is a text prescribed for speakers to utter or not. In most investigations of automatic speaker-recognition systems there is a prescribed text. In those systems which are stated to be text independent there are still some restrictions on the nature of the material, usually the length [3], [16], [23], [30]. Another class of systems, although strictly speaking not text independent, are often stated to be potentially text independent if the speech material used as input is general enough to contain certain specified speech events which can be extracted for analysis [11], [19], [46], [50], [52]. In this class of systems a certain amount of recognition and segmentation of speech events is required prior to analysis for purposes of speaker recognition.

Text independent speaker recognition, with restrictions on the length and context of the speech material, is the operating mode for speaker recognition by audition or by visual analysis of spectrograms. In such cases the speakers are not required to be cooperative and in many forensic applications, in fact, are not expected to cooperate.

[1] The term speaker recognition in this paper refers to the general category of problems which includes speaker identification, speaker verification, speaker classification, etc.

As indicated in the introduction, for many applications the speakers are expected to be cooperative so that a prescribed text is perfectly feasible. Text-dependent systems are the subject of most investigations in speaker recognition and are the ones which are the closest to practical implementation in a speaker verification mode. The prescribed texts are usually sentence-long utterances or isolated words.

A. Speech Signal Processing

The most frequently used preprocessor for speaker recognition systems is the filter bank. The filter bank, widely used in other areas of speech analysis, is a series of contiguous bandpass filters spanning the useful frequency range of speech. The output of each filter is rectified, smoothed, and sampled say every 10 ms to obtain the energy of the signal over the specified passband. The summed output of the filter bank can be considered as the short-time power spectrum of the input speech signal. Filter banks can provide a highly efficient and comprehensive analysis of speech signals. Although digital representations of filter banks are potentially computationally superior and provide reproducible measurements, analog configurations provide an on-line analysis of speech which can be input to a digital computer for further processing. The tandem combination of analog filter bank and digital computer is capable of providing a fast responding speaker recognition system. A disadvantage of filter bank analysis is an inherent inflexibility since all subsequent processing is tied to combining measurements of the individual filter outputs. Pitch and formant analysis, for example, is difficult to achieve from filter bank processing alone. Very often filter bank processing is used in combination with other analyses such as pitch, formant, and overall energy [11], [52]. The few systems that do not rely on filter-bank techniques generally make use of pitch, intensity, formant, and LPC analysis [2], [32], [44], [46].

B. Analysis Techniques

Analysis and possibly feature selection follow the basic processing. Analysis in this paper is considered to be the process in which the raw measurements, from a filter bank for example, are combined or restricted to certain speech segments in such a way as to reduce the dimensionality of the original measurement space while at the same time preserving or enhancing speaker discriminability according to a prescribed system design. It is the central process in a system, the process which makes the most of the designer's intuitive ideas or theoretical knowledge. It can be considered a feature selection process. But in this paper feature selection is considered to be a statistical process in which a subset of the entire set of analyzed features which is most useful in discriminating speakers is selected by a statistical technique.

In many filter bank systems, analysis does not proceed beyond the processing of raw spectral data. In these systems spectral energy matrices are operated on directly by statistical decision techniques to carry out the speaker-recognition tasks [5], [29], [38], [39]. The simplest treatment of the raw spectral data by prescribed design is the formation of long-term spectral averages by summing and averaging the spectral energies over the utterance time interval [5], [16], [30], [41]. Other transformations of filter bank data include conversion to cepstral measurements [31] and extraction of formants [12], [32], [52].

Perhaps the most sophisticated and potentially powerful reductions of raw analysis data are those in which some segmentation of the input speech is required. There are two goals for speech segmentation. The first goal, where prescribed texts are used as speech input, is to precisely align corresponding speech events in reference and test utterances. This alignment allows the comparison of equivalent events and is required to compensate for expected variations in the occurrence of speech events in the repetition of a given utterance by a given speaker. This type of segmentation is best described as time registration. Some successful automatic time registration techniques have been investigated [12], [13], [26], [32], [43].

The second goal for segmentation is to locate and isolate acoustic features or events which insight and investigation have shown to be powerful discriminants for speakers. Ideally, as Wolf [52] remarks, such cues should occur naturally and frequently in normal speech, be easily measurable, not change over time or be affected by the speaker's health, background noise or transmission characteristics, and not be consciously modifiable by the speaker. Two studies [46], [52], investigated a large set of extracted acoustic features and tested their relative effectiveness. Feature extraction also played a central role in the investigations of Das and Mohn [11] and Hair and Rekieta [21], [22]. Although the extraction of specific speech events for speaker recognition purposes is potentially very powerful, segmentation is an extremely difficult problem. Most of the investigations have used manual segmentation schemes. An automatic segmentation scheme was reported by Das and Mohn [11], but it is quite complex. In addition it was not entirely reliable since 10 percent of the test utterances were rejected because of segmentation failure.

As a specific example, the segmentation and analysis of nasal consonants has attracted considered attention due to the conjecture that the acoustical properties of nasal consonants are strongly speaker dependent and that there is little movement of the articulators during phonation [19], [46], [50], [52]. Most of these investigations measured spectral characteristics of individual nasal consonants. However, one investigation carried this type of analysis one step further (Su *et al.* [50]). It was hypothesized in this study that differences in the spectra of a particular nasal consonant due to coarticulation with following vowels is also strongly speaker dependent and even less likely to be subject to conscious modification.

Another distinct mode of analysis is the transformation of raw data into functions of time or contours. Most often the speech input is prescribed sentence-long utterances. The hypothesis is that the time functions of many acoustic features have strong speaker dependent characteristics. Some of the features that have been investigated as time functions are pitch, intensity, formants, and predictor coefficients [2], [12], [32], [42], [44].

C. Statistical Feature Selection and Decision Techniques

Statistical feature selection and decision techniques are important elements of any speaker recognition scheme. The most common statistical feature selection technique is that of the F-ratio or analysis of variance [2], [5]. For this purpose several statistics are computed over the set of training of reference utterances provided by each speaker. These include the mean feature vector and covariance matrix of the elements of the feature vector. To compute the F-ratio a between-talkers covariance matrix B, which is a measure of the dispersion of the feature vector means, and a within-talkers covariance matrix W, which is the average of the individual talker covariance matrices, are computed. The F-ratio given by

$$F = a^t Ba / a^t Wa$$

is maximized to find a set of eigenvectors $a_1, a_2, \cdots$, which linearly transform the original feature vector into a space in which the speaker feature vector means are maximally separated relative to the within-talkers covariance. As a special case, if the correlations between the components of the feature vector are ignored, i.e., if the off diagonal elements in B and W are set equal to zero, the F-ratio provides an ordering of the separability between speaker means in terms of the original individual coordinates [11], [21], [22], [39], [52]. A subset of these coordinates with the largest F-ratio is selected as the new feature vector. Mohn [34] describes the distinction between the general technique and the special case.

A different approach to statistical feature selection is to select those features which from processing a set of training or reference utterances through the designated speaker recognition system provide the lowest error rate [44], [46]. If the original feature vector has a relatively high dimensionality, it is important to adopt a systematic and efficient procedure for investigating as many possible lower order subsets of this vector. One such approach is that of the "knockout" tournament [44], [46].

Decision techniques are all based on the computation of a distance which quantifies the degree of dissimilarity between the feature vectors associated with pairs of utterances. There are many distance metrics that have been investigated. Let r_i be the ith reference vector and x an unknown test vector. The most common distance metric is the simple Euclidean distance.

$$\|x - r_i\| = ((x - r_i)^t (x - r_i))^{1/2} = \left(\sum_j (x_j - r_{ij})^2\right)^{1/2}$$

where x_j and r_{ij} are the jth components of x and r_i, respectively. Other possibilities are $\Sigma_j |x_j - r_{ij}|$, and $x \cdot r_i / \|x\| \, \|r_i\|$ which is the cosine of the angle between x and r_i. There have been several investigations in which the various distance metrics have been compared [8], [16], [30].

The simplest decision rule is that of the "nearest neighbor." For speaker identification this means that distances are calculated from the unknown vector to each reference vector and the speaker corresponding to the minimum distance is designated the identified speaker. That is if $D(x, r_{jn})$ represents the distance between an unknown test vector and the vector corresponding to the nth utterance of the jth speaker we select J if

$$\min_{j,n} D(x, r_{jn}) = D(x, r_{JU})$$

where r_{JU} is the vector corresponding to a particular utterance U of speaker J. The nearest neighbor principle has been used by several investigators [16], [31], [38]. For speaker verification, the minimum distance for the claimed identity J, $D(x, r_{JU})$, is compared against a threshold to decide whether to accept or reject.

At the next level of sophistication explicit account is taken of the distribution of the feature vectors for each class. For example, prototype vectors can be calculated by computing the mean feature vector for each speaker

$$m_j = \frac{1}{N} \sum_n r_{jn}.$$

The nearest neighbor procedure is then the determination of

$$\min_j D(x, m_j).$$

This decision is obviously more efficient than the more general search over both speakers and utterances, but it assumes that the set of m_j are good prototypes, i.e., that the r_{jn} form well-behaved clusters by speakers. This nearest neighbor prototype approach has been used by Bunge [8], Furui *et al.* [16], Glenn and Kleiner [19], and Hair and Rekieta, [21], [22]. Still another level of sophistication is added to this approach by weighting the components of the feature vector inversely by the calculated variances of these components over each individual speaker's utterances. This weighting has the effect of giving more influence in the distance calculation to those components of the feature vector which are more strongly clustered. This approach has been used in [8], [16], [21], [22], [32], [39], [42]–[44], [52].

Since this latter technique provides a weighting of the components of the feature vector it is, in effect, providing statistical feature selection. In fact, the feature vector can be weighted by the inverse of the entire covariance matrix of the feature vector over each individual speaker's utterances provided the number of utterances available is sufficiently larger than the number of components (Furui *et al.* [16]). Another possible weighting is the inverse of the pooled covariance matrix over all speakers W, if the individual covariance matrices are not too disparate [3], [16], [46]. Finally, consideration can be given to the between-speakers covariance matrix B as well as W using the weighting provided by the F-ratio procedure described earlier.

The techniques discussed above all provide a linear weighting of the feature vector using moments of the distribution of reference or training vectors. Another class of procedures establishes linear weightings of the feature vectors by so-called nonparametric techniques, such as ADALINE or linear threshold elements (Nilsson). The weights are calculated by operating iteratively on the set of training feature vectors so that the vectors associated with each speaker are optimally separated by hyperplanes which are specified by the weights. Nonparametric decision procedures have been investigated by Das and Mohn [11], Hargreaves and Starkweather [23], and Li *et al.* [29].

An important extension of decision techniques is the use of sequential strategies. In a sequential strategy, each identification or verification trial is transformed into a series of trials. At each trial there is an option to defer decision to the next trial if the distance associated with the trial is too close to a predetermined decision threshold. The procedure terminates on the trial in which a decision is made. In practice, a limit is placed on the number of trials, with a special decision category if the limit is exceeded. A sequential procedure is useful if trial-to-trial measurements are not strongly correlated. Sequential strategies are especially useful in on-line speaker verification implementations. Doddington has demonstrated the effectiveness of such strategies in reducing error rate [13]. Some of these results are described later in this paper.

III. Evaluations and Implementations

In this section, we will briefly describe the evaluation and results of some of the systems whose techniques are sketched in the previous section. We will also discuss some of the factors which affect the evaluation and implementation of systems.

A. Large Populations

There are not many systems in which a significantly large sample of speakers and utterances has been used for an evaluation, or in which the collection and recording of the sample has been accomplished under "real world" conditions. Most studies, in fact, can be considered preliminary investigations of particular speaker-recognition techniques with no special claims to be "real-world" systems operating outside the laboratory. Since a goal of this paper is to emphasize practical systems, particular attention is paid in the next section to two systems which come closest to operating in the "real world". These are the Texas Instruments entry control system which at this date has made over 150 000 verifications over a period of a year on a population of 180 users and the Bell Labs telephone system which made over 4500 verifications over a five-month period on a population of approximately 100 users.

Other large test populations have been reported by Bricker *et al.* [5], Das and Mohn [11], and Hair and Rekieta [21], [22]. The population tested by Bricker *et al.* consisted of 172 talkers each of whom recorded five replications of digit names in a single session. The recordings were made with high quality equipment but in a somewhat uncontrolled environment. In the speaker identification experiment which was carried out accuracies as great as 94 percent could be achieved if information from more than one word per speaker is included in the analysis.

Das and Mohn made use of a population of 118 male talkers including 50 "customers" who provided 20 replications of a test phrase in five sessions held once per week and 68 impostors who provided 20 replications in a single session. These were high-quality recordings made in a sound booth. In the speaker verification experiment carried out by these experimenters an equal-error rate of 1 percent was obtained although decisions could not be made on 10 percent of the utterances submitted.

Hair and Rekieta utilized single-word recordings from approximately 40 speakers, male and female, collected in eight or nine sessions held once per week. These were also high-quality recordings obtained in a sound booth. Equal error rates of less than 1 percent were reported. An unreported number of utterances were excluded due to "bad colds."

B. Intersession Variability and Reference File Maintenance

In addition to the desirability of testing a large population of speakers there are other considerations to be examined with regard to the experimental data base. One of the most important considerations is the time period over which utterances are collected and the methods used to establish and maintain reference patterns over this period. Intersession variability for a given speaker was recognized as a significant effect in some of the earliest investigations reported [11], [23], [31]. In the speaker verification experiment reported by Luck [31], it was found necessary to include speech samples taken over a 5-week period in the reference data for an adequate representation of the speaker's voice. The problem of long-term variation has been examined in some detail in the investigations of Furui *et al.* [16]-[18]. With their data base they were able to examine the effects of intervals of up to 18 months between samples. In [16], the best identification and verification rates were obtained when the reference data was calculated from 4 samples taken at intervals of 3 months. The data base used by Sambur also extended over a long period—up to 3.5 years. The only feature reported by Sambur to be strongly affected by this interval was average pitch.

In any practical speaker verification system the problem of maintaining reference files over extended periods of time is an immediate concern. It is quite clear that a verification system which requires several reference or training samples collected over an extended period of time before the system can be accessed for actual use has little practical value for most applications. This problem and methods to deal with it are discussed again in the descriptions of the Texas Instruments an Bell Labs systems.

C. Speaker Characteristics

The composition and characteristics of the speaker population are other important considerations. Many evaluations have included only male talkers. (Two investigations, Atal [2] and Hargreaves and Starkweather [23], employed only female talkers.) The difficulties associated with analysis of female speech are well known. The fundamental problem is the loss of spectral resolution compared with analysis of male speech.

Temporary and chronic speech irregularities are important characteristics of a speaker population and must be considered in the light of each type of analysis. For example, nasal congestion associated with upper respiratory disorders is likely to modify the spectral characteristics of many sounds especially nasal consonants. Laryngeal inflammation can have a profound effect on pitch measurements. Diplophonia, a condition associated with a husky or raspy voice quality, will also disturb pitch measurements. Any overt speech pathology is likely to have a serious effect on almost every type of analysis. Especially severe effects can be expected from one of the most common types of pathology, that of stuttering.

There is also a subtle change in speaking behavior to be expected when speakers are removed from the formal experimental environment of a sound booth. In their normal home or work environment speakers are likely to lose their experimental "set" or attitude. They may become less attentive, impatient, easily distracted or, generally speaking, less "cooperative."

D. Recording Environment and Transmission Conditions

Factors which can loom large over the implementation of a speaker-recognition system are the recording environment and the conditions governing the transmission of the speech signal to the processor. Until recently these factors have received little attention. Most evaluations have been carried out in the hothouse atmosphere of the sound booth and high-quality recordings. Eventually, however, one must consider whether these conditions represent a fair approximation to conditions that are expected in a practical application. For an application such as entry control as in the Texas Instruments system, this may be the case. Even here, however, one might find it difficult to control such conditions as angle of incidence and distance from the microphone and certain kinds of background noise.

The most severe effects can be expected when a recognition transaction is carried out over remote communication links where it is possible that either or both the recording environment and the transmission conditions will vary from transaction to transaction. The most obvious situation of this type is recognition transactions over dialed-up telephone lines. This is the principal setting proposed for the Bell Labs speaker-verification system, and its evaluation over dialed-up telephone lines is described in a later section. Dialed-up telephone lines have been used in the evaluation of one other speaker verification system, that of Li *et al.* [29]. In the design of such systems, careful allowance should be given to the effects of background noise and room reverberation at the source and the reduced bandwidth, distortion, and line disturbances over a dialed-up line. In addition, the possibility of variation of these conditions from one transaction to another must be considered. Spectral amplitude measurements of a critical nature are especially susceptible under such conditions and for that reason are avoided in the Bell Labs system. Some spectral normalization techniques have been suggested to compensate for some of these conditions. Doddington [13] and Glenn and Kleiner [19] normalize the spectral data vector obtained from their filter bank output by the sum of the filter outputs for each measurement. This normalization has the effect of stabilizing the measurements with respect to overall changes in signal level. Furui [18] has employed an inverse filtering technique. Long-time spectral measurements calculated over a given speaker's speech sample are used to construct a second-order inverse filter which characterizes the gross spectral distribution of the input signal. This filter is applied to the instantaneous input signal of the speaker. This approach has also been used successfully by Itakura [26] in a speech-recognition system. This type of normalization will tend to cancel out the broad characteristics of the source and radiation spectrum as well as that of the transmission system.

E. Mimic Resistance

An important question which must be answered for a speaker recognition system is how well can the system resist the effects of determined mimics. A related question is, can the system discriminate among closely related members of a family such as siblings, especially indentical twins. These questions are especially important for speaker-verification systems since the intended applications of these systems are usually ones in which there could be a large payoff if the system is successfully defrauded.

Four mimic investigations have been reported. The most extensive investigation was undertaken at Bell Labs by Lummis and Rosenberg [33]. Four professional mimics were employed to mimic eight customer voices. The initial acceptance rate for these mimics was high but a considerable degree of mimic protection was achieved in later versions of the system. The Bell Labs mimic experiment is described in more detail in a later section. Doddington [13] employed two of these mimics to test the Texas Instruments system. They provided imitations of 6 speakers. Doddington, too, found that mimic acceptance was significantly greater than acceptance of casual impostors.

A mimic experiment was reported by Hair and Rekieta [22]. A professional performer specializing in impersonations provided imitations of 6 speakers. Although some increase in similarity was observed for individual features in their verification scheme, the attempt at acceptance when all features were combined was unsuccessful. Luck [31] also performed a mimic experiment. The mimics were not professionals but were selected from the population of casual impostors used in the evaluation. Three mimics were afforded the opportunity to imitate a single speaker out of the customer set. Only the mimic who was the worst casual impostor significantly improved his performance (but not enough to be accepted).

The evaluation of a system's resistance to mimics depends on the definition of a skilled mimic. Since the skills required of a mimic vary from system to system and since subjective impressions can be quite faulty, the most reliable definition of a skilled mimic is not based on a priori appraisal. It is simply one who can significantly increase his acceptance as an impostor by deliberate imitation. This makes mimic evaluation difficult since one cannot be certain in advance who is a skilled mimic. One generalization seems clear however. This is that mimics who depend on caricature for their imitations are poor candidates since most effective systems will not tolerate exaggeration of speaker characteristics.

The systems that are more likely to be mimic resistant are those which make strongly physiologically correlated measurements rather than measurements correlated with behavior or learned characteristics. This is discussed in the description of the Bell Labs systems since many of its measurements are correlated with behavior. On the other hand, systems whose measurements are physiologically oriented may not be able to discriminate among close family members. An experiment with an identical twin impostor in the Bell Labs systems showed that even though the voices were physiologically identical, the twin impostor was not able to imitate his brother's speaking behavior well enough to be accepted by the system even when he was given every opportunity to do so. More study of identical twins is merited.

IV. Detailed Large-Scale Systems Descriptions

A. Texas Instruments Entry Control System

A practical method of automatic speaker verification has been under development at Texas Instruments under the direction of Doddington. The speech input is sentence-long utterances and the analysis provides spectral amplitude information on precisely located sections of the utterance. A block diagram of the analog processing is shown in Fig. 2. Each bandpass filter is composed of two-pole-pair sections with an approximate 220-Hz bandwidth. The center frequencies are spaced uniformly between 300 and 3000 Hz. The low-pass filters cutoff at 20 Hz. The filter outputs are sampled 100 times per second and digitized. (The most recent version uses a digital filter bank with 14 instead of 16 channels.) Each filter output is quantized to 3 bits with the levels chosen so that each is approximately equiprobable. For reference data storage in the most recent versions an additional 4 bits per filter output is required for adaptation purposes so that each time sample requires $14 \times 7 = 98$ bits. Succeeding stages of processing take place in a digital computer.

Within each test utterance several key points are specified to provide time registration and for data comparison. In the most recent implementation the test material consists of 4-word phrases each word being a CVC monosyllable. The key points are chosen at regions of maximum energy in the vowel portion of each word. A reference pattern consists of 6 spectral amplitude samples taken every 20 ms through a 100-ms interval around the key point. Thus each phrase is associated

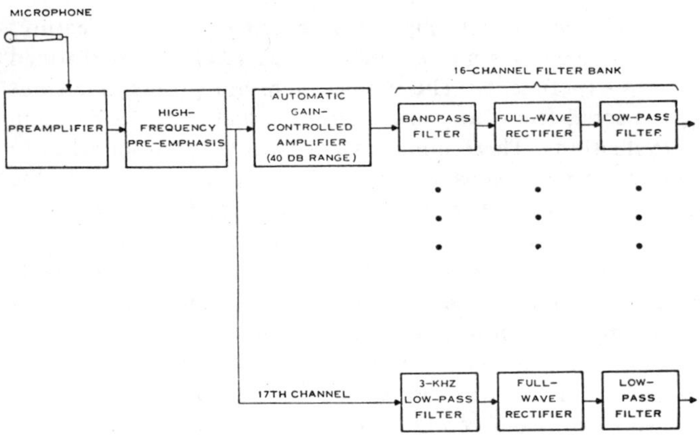

Fig. 2. Functional block diagram of the analog processing of the Texas Instruments system [13].

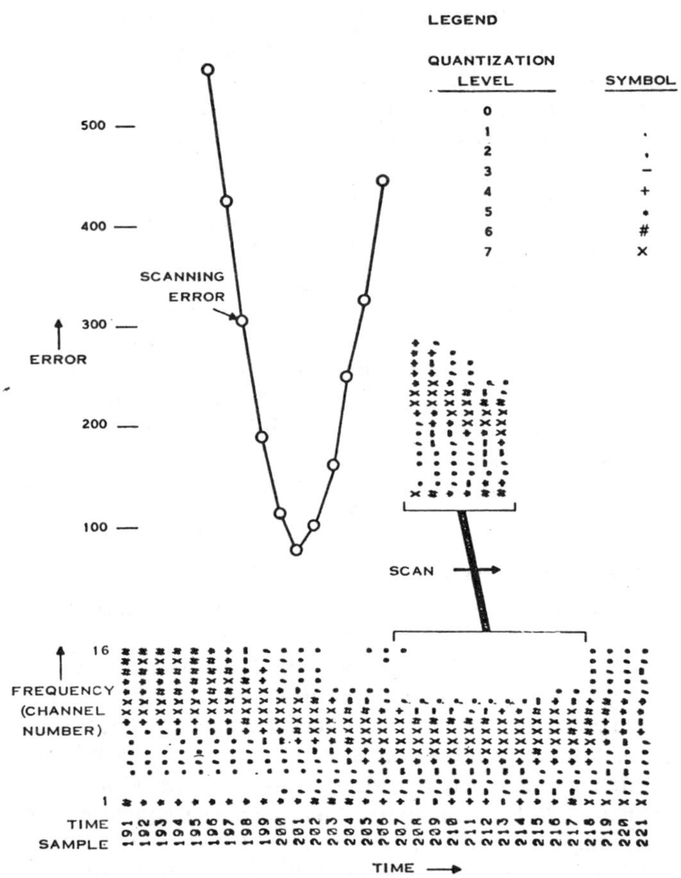

Fig. 3. Key point location by error function scanning [13].

with four reference patterns, each represented by $6 \times 98 =$ 588 bits of information.

In the verification process each reference pattern is scanned across the spectral amplitude sample vectors of an incoming test phrase to locate the corresponding key points in the test phrase. In the scanning process a squared error difference is computed every 10 ms between the incoming spectral data pattern and each corresponding reference pattern. An error function is obtained for each reference pattern and the minimum of each error function determines the location of each key point in the incoming utterance. This scanning process is illustrated in Fig. 3. Once all the key points are located in the input sample utterance no further measurements are necessary. The decision function is simply the average scanning error at these points normalized by an estimate of the expected scanning error for the speaker under consideration. If all the key points cannot be located in an input phrase the strategy is to request an additional phrase. The estimate of the expected scanning error is computed during a series of initial training sessions. (In the most recent implementation a single enrollment session is required.)

Doddington has reported two evaluations. In both evaluations the data was collected in a sound booth using a dynamic microphone. In the first evaluation 10 females and 40 male "customers" provided 100 recording sessions of five phrases over a span of 2 months. Approximately 70 impostors, with approximately the same female–male ratio, provided 20 sessions each. Although a verification response was provided during data collection the results reported by Doddington represent an evaluation from digital recordings after the recording sessions were completed. In this evaluation the first 50 sessions were designated training sessions.

Using the recordings from the 70 member impostor population and customer recordings from the 50 test sessions a verification equal-error rate of approximately 1.6 percent was obtained for a single phrase with one phrase held in reserve. In this strategy, in the event that the key points in the primary phrase cannot be registered a second phrase is scanned to locate key points. If registration fails for both phrases the speaker is unconditionally rejected. The number of unregistered customer utterances is very small, less than 1 percent, but the number of unregistered impostor utterances is quite high, approximately 50 percent.

The error rate decreases dramatically with the use of 2 or more phrases. The decision function is simply the average of the decision function for each phrase used. For 2 phrases the equal error rate falls to 0.42 percent, for three phrases the error rate falls to 0.23 percent.

A sequential decision strategy using only as many phrases as are necessary to achieve a given level of confidence is a more efficient multiple-phrase strategy. In the sequential decision strategy examined by Doddington the speaker is accepted after the first phrase if the decision function is less than some threshold. Otherwise additional phrases are requested combining the decision functions at each stage. For this strategy the customer reject rate was established at 1 percent and the concurrent accept impostor rate was measured as 0.01 percent. The average number of phrases required of customers was less than 1.5.

Doddington tracked the average customer decision function (or reject rate) over the 6-week period of the test and observed a distinct increasing trend over the entire period as seen in Fig. 4. It is obvious then that some sort of periodic reference file adaptation is required as the customer accesses the system.

The influence of upper respiratory infections was also investigated. In 5.5 percent of the true speaker trials, the speakers reported that their voices were "not normal." At the decision level for which normal voice speakers were rejected at a 1-percent rate, "not normal" speakers were rejected at a 2-percent rate. The increase in rejection rate is significant but not alarming since the probability of acceptance is still quite high.

Also, two of the professional mimics used in the Bell Labs study were engaged to attempt to defeat the system. Each mimic chose 5 male speakers to mimic after listening to recordings from a selection of 35. The mimics were then pro-

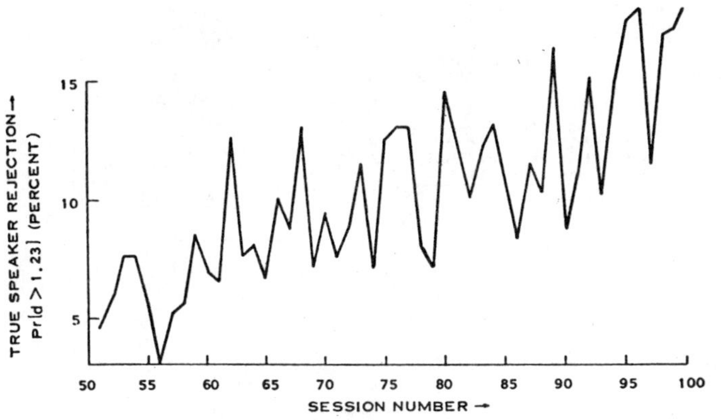

Fig. 4. True speaker rejection rate as a function of session number (adjusted to a nominal 10-percent reject rate).

TABLE I
MONOSYLLABIC WORDS USED TO COMPOSE 4-WORD NONSENSE PHRASES (DODDINGTON [13])

Cool	birds	stopped	west
Small	bugs	sing	down
Huge	twigs	sang	deep
Strange	toads	stood	wild

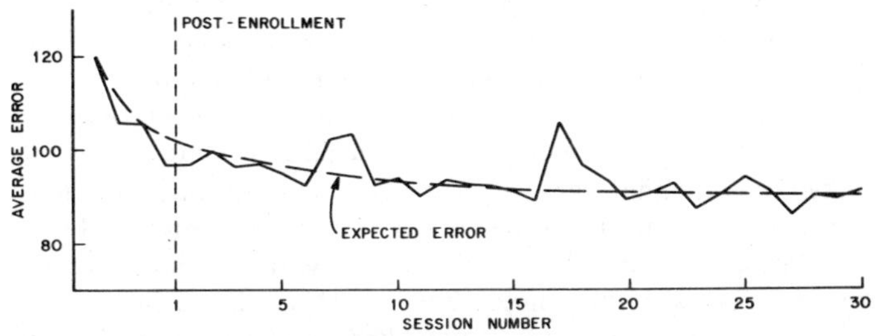

Fig. 5. Average scanning error a function of session number when reference patterns are adapted session by session.

vided with repetitive recordings of each of his 5 chosen speakers and were also allowed to listen to each voice in person. The mimic trials were performed on-line with immediate feedback for degree of success. For a one-phrase decision function it was found that the probability of mimic acceptance was approximately twice that of casual impostors.

In the second evaluation reported by Doddington the speaker set consisted of 63 male speakers who over the span of one month provided an average of 25 verification sessions. The impostor set consisted of 2 sessions each from 60 male speakers. The sample utterances consisted of 16 monosyllabic words organized in a set of 4-word sentence-like nonsense phrases. There were 32 allowable phrases in the set. At each trial the speaker was instructed by means of voice prompting to utter a phrase selected at random. A list of the words used to compose the phrases is given in Table I.

The initial training for this evaluation consisted of an enrollment session in which enough phrases were collected so that each of the 16 words was presented 5 times. A reference pattern was constructed for each word based on the location of key points from at least five repetitions of each word. Initial training was extended by 4 post-enrollment sessions to establish an adapted set of reference patterns and to estimate speaker variability.

Each verification session consisted of the utterance of 4 test phrases. Adaptation was allowed if the decision function averaged over all 4 phrases was less then some threshold. Adaptation consisted of refreshing the reference pattern by averaging it with a small fraction of the corresponding input sample pattern. The estimated scanning error and the timing between key points in the phrase were also adaptively updated.

For this evaluation the equal error rate obtained for a single phrase was approximately 4 percent. Again there is marked improvement with the use of more than one phrase. With two phrases the error rate decreased to 1.5 percent and with the use of all 4 phrases the error rate is 0.5 percent. With the use of a sequential strategy in which an average of 1.3 phrases is required for verification the true speaker reject rate is 0.3 percent with an accompanying 1 percent accept impostor rate.

It was found that scanning error when plotted as a function of session number decreases more or less uniformly to an asymptote after an initial elevation. This finding is similar to the trend for the threshold function and error rate for the Bell Labs system. This is shown in Fig. 5 for a subset of 17 speakers who completed at least 30 sessions. Doddington attributes this trend to the use of session-by-session adaptation of reference patterns. This behavior is in contrast to the trend shown in Fig. 4 where no adaptation was employed.

At this writing, Doddington has installed an operational entry control system for use at a Texas Instruments computer facility. The verification data from this installation are available for evaluation. Approximately 180 users, 13 percent female, make an average of more than 400 entries per day. Using a 4-phrase sequential decision strategy, an impressive customer reject rate of 0.3 percent is achieved with a 1-percent impostor accept rate. (The impostor accept rate is calculated from off-line cross-comparisons.) The average number of utterances required per transaction is 1.3. The average verification time is 5.8 s.

In summary, the Texas Instrument automatic speaker verification system achieves a high level of performance making efficient use of computer processing with respect to both execution time and storage. The fast execution time allows the comfortable use of a multiphrase sequential decision strategy which provides impressive error rates.

The use of a filter bank preprocessor to provide the basic measurements on the speech signal is largely responsible for the fast processing times and high level of accuracy. It seems likely, however, that to maintain the effectiveness of such measurements a relatively large signal-to-noise ratio (Doddington suggests 30 dB) and uniform transmission conditions are required. The system in its present configuration is particularly well suited to the principal application for which it was designed—access control. In this type of application the speaking environment and transmission conditions are the same from trial to trial. A sound booth is used to provide a uniform low-noise speaking environment.

B. Bell Labs Systems

The Bell Labs automatic speaker verification system has been under development since 1970 under the aegis of several investigators. The original implementation was carried out by Doddington, presently at Texas Instruments, for his doctoral dissertation based on a suggestion by J. L. Flanagan [12]. It has since been studied and improved by Lummis [32], Sambur, and Rosenberg [42]–[44].

From the outset it was hoped to provide a system which would tolerate variable and degraded environmental and transmission conditions as might be experienced by use of the system over dialed-up telephone lines. Perhaps the most important distinguishing characteristics of the Bell Labs system are the choice and method of measurements which were deemed most likely to meet these goals. Measurements are chosen which are largely insensitive to the phase and/or spectral amplitude distortions likely to be encountered in the telephone plant. Examples of measurements that have been studied are pitch, overall intensity, formant frequencies and linear predictor coefficients. The measurements are calculated as a function of time over prescribed sentence-long utterances so that the emphasis is on the variations of these features rather than on absolute measurements at fixed instants of time or averages taken over long intervals of time. To a large extent, then, measurements obtained in this manner are strongly correlated with the inflectional or prosodic behavior of the speaker. To the extent that absolute measurements of pitch, formants, and predictor coefficients are obtained the analysis is partially correlated with physiological characteristics. There is no question, however, that there is a strong dependence in this system on the analysis of speaking behavior simply because this information is relatively slowly time varying, phase insensitive, and broad band.

A simplified block diagram of the Bell Labs system is shown in Fig. 6. A marked interval is provided for input of a sentence-long sample utterance. The input signal is digitized at a 10-kHz sampling rate. For pitch and intensity analysis the input is low-pass filtered typically at 900 Hz. For predictor coefficient or formant analysis the input is subject to 3000-or 4000-Hz low-pass filtering. For each feature analyzed a measurement is made every 10 ms (or 20 ms for predictor coefficients). Calculations on the intensity function are used to delimit the end points of the actual utterance within the recording interval. The time functions for each analyzed feature, subjected to 16-Hz low-pass smoothing, between the delimited end points are designated contours and are the basic patterns for the verification process. A typical set of contours is shown in Fig. 7. The intensity or gain contour is normalized to the peak intensity measurement resulting in a contour of relative intensity values. The pitch contour in the more recent implementations is extracted by means of the time-domain parallel processing technique of Gold and Rabiner [20]. Predictor coefficient measurements are obtained by the covariance method (Atal and Hanauer [1]). Following analysis, the set of sample contours are compared with a set of reference contours associated with the claimed identity. The reference contours are obtained by averaging and combining sets of contours previously obtained from sample utterances of the person whose identity is claimed. Before comparing the sample and reference contours an additional operation, time registration, is carried out. In this operation, the events of the sample contours are brought into the best possible time registration with the corresponding events of the reference contours. This operation attempts to compensate for normal expected variations in speaking behavior which may displace corresponding events from repetition to repetition of a given utterance. The intensity contour is used as the guide contour for this operation. In the latest implementation a dynamic programming algorithm is utilized. First, the sample intensity contour is linearly stretched or compressed to the standardized length of the reference intensity contour. Then a distance is calculated between the ith point of the sample contour and the jth point of the reference contour for each i and j. The dynamic programming algorithm is used to find the path of least accumulated distances through the matrix of distances (d_{ij}). The optimal path establishes the warping function required to replot the sample contour registered to the reference contour. The warping function obtained for the guide intensity contour is applied to all other contours analyzed for the sample utterance. Time registration of the intensity contour is illustrated in Fig. 8.

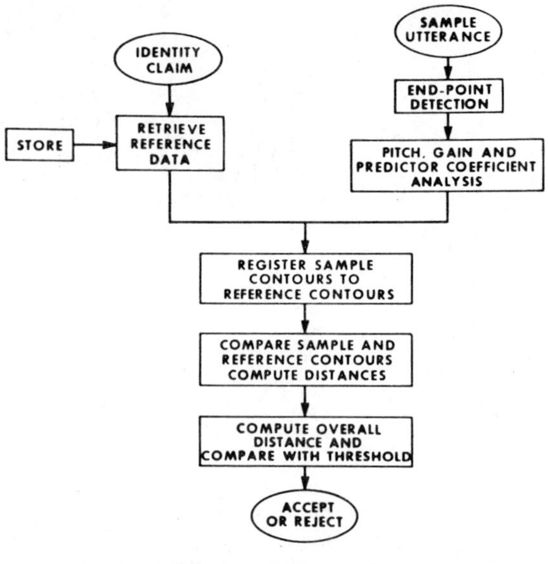

Fig. 6. Functional block diagram of the Bell Labs system.

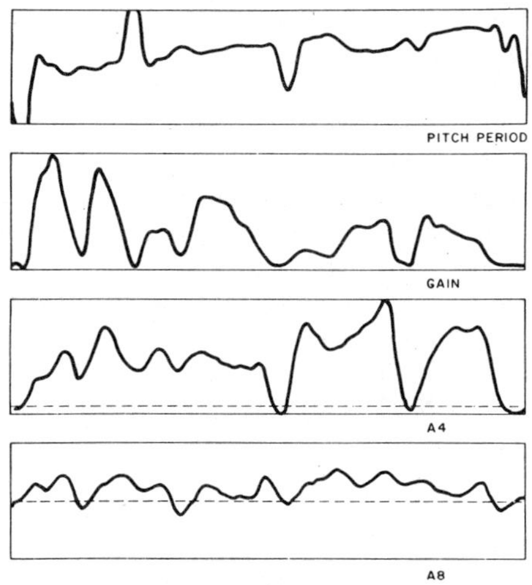

Fig. 7. A typical set of sample contours plotted as a function of time through a sample utterance. Included are pitch period, gain, and A4 and A8, the fourth and eighth coefficients of an eighth-order linear predictor.

Following registration, the contours are divided into 20 equal length segments as shown for intensity in the bottom panel of Fig. 8. In each segment, a set of measurements is applied to both the sample and reference contours and a squared difference is calculated specifying the dissimilarity between the contours for a particular measurement. The squared difference for each measurement and segment is weighted inversely by a variance which is calculated from the set of sample contours used to construct the reference. The effect of the variances is to weight those segments in which a particular measurement is

TIME REGISTRATION

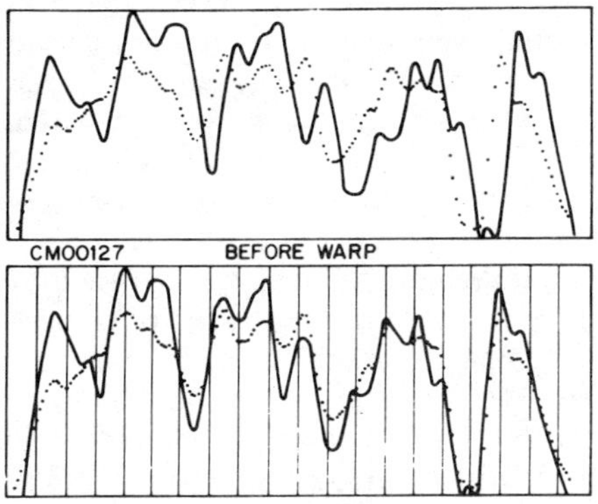

Fig. 8. Contour time registration. The dotted curve in each panel is a reference gain contour; the solid curve is a sample gain contour. The top panel shows the contours with end-points aligned, but before internal registration. The bottom panel shows the results of registering the sample contour to the reference contour.

more consistent over the set of sample contours. The various segment-by-segment measurements characterize the shape of the contours. In addition, there are distances based on the overall cross correlation of sample and reference contours and distances based on the amount of warping required to register the sample contours to the reference contours. Detailed descriptions of the measurements and distances can be found in [32], [42]-[44].

An overall distance is obtained by a simple average over the entire set of individual distances or over a subset of these distances. In recent implementations, speaker-dependent subsets have been calculated which select those measurements which are most effective in separating the overall distance distributions of customer and impostor sample utterances for each customer. The overall distance is compared with a speaker-dependent threshold distance to determine whether to accept or reject the identity claim. The threshold distance is estimated from the overall distance distributions of a set of customer sample utterances and a set of impostor sample utterances. For the purposes of evaluation an equal-error threshold is estimated.

Four distinct evaluations of the system have been carried out, the original evaluation and succeeding ones associated with major modifications. In addition, a study was carried out to determine the sensitivity of the system to the effects of professional mimics and a parallel study was undertaken to examine the ability of human listeners in a speaker verification task using the same speech samples used to evaluate the original system.

The first evaluation was carried out by Doddington [12] using recordings collected from a population of 40 male speakers. High-quality recordings were obtained from the speakers seated in a sound booth. At least two days elapsed between consecutive utterances. Eight of the speakers were designated customers and provided 15 utterances each. The remaining 32 speakers were designated impostors, providing just one utterance each.

The feature analysis employed by Doddington was a complete formant analysis (Schafer and Rabiner [47]) resulting in 3 formant contours plus a pitch and intensity contour. For each customer 3 reference files were constructed from 3 different subsets of 10 of the 15 sample utterances. The remaining 5 utterances for each customer were reserved for test utterances together with the 32 impostor utterances. An overall average equal error rate of approximately 1.5 percent was obtained. The importance of time normalization was underscored by the result that the error rate increased by a factor of 4 if only end-point alignment of sample and reference utterances were performed. Lummis provided some modifications of the system including time registration based on the intensity contour instead of the second formant contour. Using the same data base of utterances essentially the same average error rate of the order of 1 or 1.5 percent was obtained. Lummis also demonstrated that the distances extracted from the formant contours seemed to provide a negligible contribution to the performance of the system.

Two parallel studies were undertaken using the same 40-speaker data base. In the first study [33], professional mimics were subjected to intensive listening and training sessions prior to providing sample recordings. Mimic utterances provided by the four best mimics were processed by the system in the same manner as the original set of utterances. With threshold distance set for a customer reject rate of approximately 1.5 percent, it was found that mimic utterances were accepted at a 27-percent rate, compared to the 1.5-percent rate for casual impostors. In this study, in contrast to the earlier observations, it was found that formant information was a significant factor in the performance of the system. It is worth noting that the mimicking required a great deal of skill. The group of four chosen for evaluation were culled from an initial group of some 25. None of the mimics in the final group was primarily an entertainer. In fact, any mimic utterance that smacked of caricature was readily rejected by the system. In addition, one of the original eight customers had an identical twin. Even when this twin was afforded the same opportunity which the mimics had, to listen and rehearse his brother's utterances, his sample utterances were rejected by the system.

The second study undertaken in parallel with the original evaluation investigated the ability of human listeners to perform a speaker verification task [42]. The subjective tests were of the paired-comparison type in which each test presentation consisted of a challenge and comparison utterance. Listeners were required to respond whether the challenge and comparison utterances were from the same or different speakers. The comparison utterances were all drawn from either the set of impostor utterances or from a distinct set of utterances provided by the same speaker of the challenge utterance. Human listeners performed the speaker verification task with an average error rate of approximately 4 percent, with the false-alarm rate (customer rejection) about equal to the miss rate (impostor acceptance), a significantly higher rate than the automatic system. When the professional mimic utterances were included in the test presentations the miss rate increased to 22 percent, about the same level of performance as the automatic system.

A third modification and evaluation was undertaken by Rosenberg and Sambur to investigate the possibility of replacing the rather difficult and time consuming analysis of formants and improving the effectiveness of the system with respect to the efforts of professional mimics. In addition, a new and larger data base was obtained to provide a more statistically reliable evaluation of performance. The new data base was extracted from 50 recording sessions for each of 22 male speakers designed customers and one recording session for each of 55 male speakers designed impostors. The recording sessions were held over a period of two months with no more

TABLE II
ERROR RATES (ROSENBERG AND SAMBUR [44])

	Pitch + Intensity	Pitch + Intensity + 2 Pred. Coeff.
All measurements (equal-error)	6%	4%
Selected (speaker dependent) Measurements (equal-error)	3%	1.5%
Mimic acceptance rate (selected measurements, old data base)	16%	4%

than two sessions per customer per day. Two sentences were processed from each recording session, the all-voiced sentence "We were away a year ago" used in the previous evaluation and another all-voiced sentence, "I know when my lawyer is due."

Linear predictor coefficient analysis was chosen to replace the formant-analysis because of its relative simplicity of computation. In a sense, formant analysis can be considered as an extension of linear predictor analysis, but for the purpose of obtaining speaker characterizing features there is no essential reason to extend the analysis to the computation of formants. An eight-order predictor analysis was employed with the fourth and eighth coefficients plotted as a function of time to provide contours. (Contours provided by two widely spread predictor coefficients were found to provide effective speaker discrimination.) In addition, a speaker-dependent measurement selection procedure was investigated which selected those measurements which best discriminated each customer from imposters. The results of this evaluation are summarized in Table II.

"All measurements" refers to the speaker-independent measurement technique of earlier evaluations. Distances calculated from these measurements provide an error rate of the order of 4 percent, somewhat greater than what was obtained in the earlier evaluations. The speaker-dependent selected-measurement technique provides error rates of the order of 1.5 percent. In both cases the inclusion of predictor coefficients in the analysis results in a significant reduction in error over the use of just pitch and intensity. The mimic data base was reprocessed using these techniques and in this case there was a striking reduction in error with the inclusion of predictor coefficients. Mimic acceptance was reduced to the tolerable level of 4 percent.

The fourth evaluation of the system has brought access of the system and recording of utterances into the "real world" [42]. Over 100 "customers" accessed the system and recorded their test utterances from their own telephones via ordinary dialed-up lines to a data set interfaced with a computer. Identity claims were made by keying in an identification number on a Touchtone® dial. Instructions and responses to the customer were made by means of a programmed voice-response system (Rosenthal *et al.* [45]). To provide a more tractable system for this evaluation, only pitch and intensity were included in the analysis. Initial reference files were established for each customer by processing a set of 5 sample utterances collected in a single session. Following this initial session, the customers were instructed to call the system nominally once each work day for a verification trial. The data for each verification trial in which the customer's identity was accepted was used to periodically refresh the customer's reference file and adaptively update the accept/reject thresholds.

Over the five-month period of evaluation an average of approximately 50 trials per customer were collected. Tabulation of errors over all the customer trials was used to calculate the customer reject rate. The accept impostor rate was calculated by tabulation of errors in periodic off-line cross comparison of customer sample files with the reference files of other customers of the same sex. Overall average error rates of 9 or 10 percent were obtained for both reject customer and accept imposter. (Estimated equal-error thresholds were used.) It was found that both the reject customer and accept impostor error rates were high for the customer's initial calls to the system, of the order of 15 percent, and declined to stable values of the order of 4 percent after a settling-in period of some 20 trials.

Thus when the customer's speaking behavior is stabilized and when the reference file has been sufficiently adapted by periodic refreshing, the error rate is of the order of 4 percent, which is approximately the benchmark achieved in the previous laboratory evaluation for pitch and intensity analysis. Although an extensive survey of the telephone plant environment was not possible in this evaluation it was encouraging to find no special adverse effects on performance due to either telephone transmission or customer speaking environment.

In agreement with Doddington, the results indicated that a considerable reduction in error rate can be obtained with a deferred decision strategy.

The current activity for this system includes reintroduction of LPC analysis for telephone evaluation and the integration of the system into generalized man–machine communication by speech systems.

V. CONCLUSION

An immediate conclusion of this paper is that speaker verification is emerging as a practical technology. That the future will bring new and improved systems is certain. There is a ready market for practical systems in many areas where it is desired to extend and automate valuable informational and transactional services to larger and larger groups of customers, while at the same time ensuring that these services are provided only to those who are authorized to receive them.

However, one should not lose sight of the fact that there are still large gaps in our knowledge with respect to speaker recognition techniques. The most important issue, and likely to be a long-standing one, is the specification of the most effective measurements to apply to the speech signal for the purposes of speaker discrimination. This really is a two-part issue since an intrinsically effective feature may prove to be impractical if it cannot be reliably extracted from the speech signal, especially when confronted with variable or degraded recording environments and/or transmission links. For example, measurement of nasal coarticulation as proposed by Su *et al.* [50], is a very sophisticated approach to speaker discrimination but the measurement may be difficult to carry out reliably in a practical system. Thus there are two needs. The first need is for more insight and more theoretical study on intrinsically effective speaker discrimination measurements. The second need is for more thorough investigations of the effect of recording environment and transmission characteristics on proposed speaker discrimination measurements to ensure a good match between the type of analysis and the type of application for the system.

Another issue remaining is the choice of statistical feature selection and decision techniques. Pattern-recognition theory is well advanced so that there is a good selection of these techniques from which to choose. The question is how sophisticated must these techniques be to be effective. A good bet is that if the basic analysis provides measurements which are sufficiently reduced in dimension and suitably normalized, then the statistical operations can be quite simple and computationally effective.

An issue which has not been discussed at all in this paper is that of the economic feasibility of speaker verification. A central concern here is the cost of customer reference data storage. Reference file storage for the Texas Instruments system has been considerably optimized and requires approximately 1200 bytes per customer [14]. There exists a 90-Mbyte disk pack drive with a price tag of approximately $30 000. Such a pack could serve some 75 000 customers at a cost of 40¢ per customer. Processing costs are harder to estimate since it depends on how many transactions are required per unit time, the time required for each transaction, multiplexing capabilities, the cost of special purpose hardware, and transmission costs.

In another paper in this issue, Flanagan has described the integration of automatic speaker verification into a 3-mode man-machine voice communication system. The other modes in this system are computer voice response and automatic recognition of words spoken in isolation by designated speakers. Although the system is primitive in comparison with the sophistication of the HAL-3000 of "2001" fame, it is an augury of things to come. The goal of communication with machines by means of man's most natural mode of communication—speech—is enormously significant. Automatic speaker verification will play an important role in this new technology. We can imagine that if automatic voice dialing becomes a reality, the same voice-dialing utterances might be used for authorization for billing!

References

[1] B. S. Atal and S. L. Hanauer, "Speech analysis and synthesis by linear prediction of the speech wave," *J. Acoust. Soc. Amer.*, vol. 50, pp. 637–655, 1971.

[2] B. S. Atal, "Automatic speaker recognition based on pitch contours," *J. Acoust. Soc. Amer.*, vol. 52, pp. 1687–1697, 1972.

[3] —, "Effectiveness of linear prediction characteristics of the speech waves for automatic speaker identification and verification," *J. Acoust. Soc. Amer.*, vol. 55, pp. 1304–1312, 1974.

[4] R. H. Bolt, F. S. Cooper, E. E. David, P. B. Denes, J. M. Pickett, and K. N. Stevens, "Speaker identification by speech spectrograms: some further observations," *J. Acoust. Soc. Amer.*, vol. 54, pp. 531–534, 1973.

[5] P. D. Bricker, R. Gnanadesikan, M. V. Mathews, S. Pruzansky, P. A. Tukey, K. W. Wachter, and J. L. Warner, "Statistical techniques for talker identification," *Bell Syst. Tech. J.*, vol. 50, pp. 1427–1454, 1971.

[6] P. D. Bricker and S. Pruzansky, "Effects of stimulus content and duration on talker identification," *J. Acoust. Soc. Amer.*, vol. 40, pp. 1441–1449, 1966.

[7] —, "Speaker recognition," in *Contemporary Issues in Experimental Phonetics*, N. J. Lass, Ed. Springfield, IL: Charles C. Thomas, 1975.

[8] E. Bunge, "Automatic speaker recognition by computers," in *Proc. Carnahan Conf. Crime Countermeasures*, 1975.

[9] R. Carré, "A summary of speech research activities in France," *IEEE Trans. Acoust. Speech Signal Processing*, vol. ASSP-22, pp. 268–272, 1974.

[10] R. O. Coleman, "Speaker identification in the absence of intersubject differences in glottal source characteristics," *J. Acoust. Soc. Amer.*, vol. 53, pp. 1741–1743, 1975.

[11] S. K. Das and W. S. Mohn, "A scheme for speech processing in automatic speaker verification," *IEEE Trans. Audio Electroacoust.*, vol. AU-19, pp. 32–43, 1971.

[12] G. R. Doddington, "A method of speaker verification," Ph.D. dissertation, Univ. Wisconsin, Madison, 1970.

[13] —, "Speaker verification—Final report," Rome Air Development Center, Griffiss AFB, NY, Tech. Rep. RADC 74-179, Apr. 1974.

[14] —, "Speaker verification for entry control," presented at WESCON, 1975.

[15] J. L. Flanagan, *Speech Analysis Synthesis and Perception*, 2nd ed. New York: Springer-Verlag, 1972.

[16] S. Furui, F. Itakura, and S. Saito, "Talker recognition by long-time averaged speech spectrum," *Electron Commun. Jap.*, vol. 55-A, pp. 54–61, 1972.

[17] S. Furui and F. Itakura, "Talker recognition by statistical features of speech sounds," *Electron. Commun. Jap.*, vol. 56-A, pp. 62–71, 1973.

[18] S. Furui, "An analysis of long-term variation of feature parameters of speech and its application to talker recognition," *Electron. Commun. Jap.*, vol. 57-A, 1974.

[19] J. W. Glenn and N. Kleiner, "Speaker identification based on nasal phonation," *J. Acoust. Soc. Amer.*, vol. 43, pp. 368–372, 1968.

[20] B. Gold and L. R. Rabiner, "Parallel processing techniques for estimating pitch periods of speech in the time domain," *J. Acoust. Soc. Amer.*, vol. 46, pp. 442–448, 1969.

[21] G. D. Hair and T. W. Rekieta, "Automatic speaker verification using phoneme spectra," *J. Acoust. Soc. Amer.*, vol. 51, p. 131(A), 1972.

[22] —, "Mimic resistance of speaker verification using phoneme spectra," *J. Acoust. Soc. Amer.*, vol. 51, p. 131(A), 1972.

[23] W. A. Hargreaves and J. A. Starkweather, "Recognition of speaker identity," *Language and Speech*, vol. 6, pp. 63–67, 1963.

[24] M. Hecker, "Speaker recognition: An interpretive survey of the literature," *ASHA Monogr.* 16 (Amer. Speech and Hearing Assoc., Washington, DC, 1971.

[25] Information Center for Hearing, Speech, and Disorders of Human Communication, *Bibliography: Speech identification by eye, ear, and machine*, Johns Hopkins Medical Inst., Baltimore, MD, 1975.

[26] F. Itakura, "Minimum prediction residual principle applied to speech recognition," *IEEE Trans. Acoustics, Speech, Signal Processing*, vol. ASSP-23, pp. 67–72, 1975.

[27] L. P. C. Jansen, "Speech identification by means of some relations between the parameters of vowel sounds," National Physical Research Laboratory, CSIR, Pretoria, South Africa, Rep., 1973.

[28] L. G. Kersta, "Voiceprint identification," *Nature*, vol. 196, pp. 1253–1257, 1962.

[29] K. P. Li, J. E. Dammann, and W. D. Chapman, "Experimental studies in speaker verification using an adaptive system," *J. Acoust. Soc. Amer.*, vol. 40, pp. 966–978, 1966.

[30] K. P. Li and G. W. Hughes, "Talker differences as they appear in correlation matrices of continuous speech spectra," *J. Acoust. Soc. Amer.*, vol. 55, pp. 833–837, 1974.

[31] J. E. Luck, "Automatic speaker verification using cepstral measurements," *J. Acoust. Amer.*, vol. 46, pp. 1026–1031, 1969.

[32] R. C. Lummis, "Speaker verification by computer using speech intensity for temporal registration," *IEEE Trans. Audio Electroacoust.* vol. AU-21, pp. 80–89, 1973.

[33] R. C. Lummis and A. E. Rosenberg, "Test of an automatic speaker verification method with intensively trained mimics," *J. Acoust. Soc. Amer.*, vol. 51, p. 131(A), 1972.

[34] W. S. Mohn, "Two statistical feature evaluation techniques applied to speaker identification," *IEEE Trans. Computers*, vol. C-20, pp. 979–987, 1971.

[35] K. O. Mead, "Identification of speakers from fundamental frequency contours in conversational speech," Joint Speech Research Unit, Rep. 1002, 1974.

[36] National Academy of Sciences–National Research Council, Committee on Hearing, Bioacoustics, and Biomechanics, Research on speaker verification, Report of working Group 53, 1971.

[37] N. J. Nilsson, *Learning Machines.* New York: McGraw-Hill, 1965.

[38] S. Pruzansky, "Pattern-matching procedure for automatic talker recognition," *J. Acoust. Soc. Amer.*, vol. 35, pp. 354–358, 1963.

[39] S. Pruzansky and M. V. Mathews, "Talker-recognition procedure based on analysis of variance," *J. Acoust. Soc. Amer.*, vol. 36, pp. 2041–2047, 1964.

[40] S. Pruzansky and B. A. Stevens, "Speaker recognition, 1937–1973," Bibliography 266, Bell Lab., 1974.

[41] G. S. Ramishvili, "Experiments on automatic verification of speakers," in *Proc. 2nd Int. Joint Conf. Pattern Recognition* (Copenhagen, Denmark), pp. 389, 393, 1974.

[42] A. E. Rosenberg, "Listener performance in speaker verification tasks," *IEEE Trans. Audio Electroacoust.*, vol. AU-21, pp. 221–225, 1973.

[43] —, "Evaluation of an automatic speaker verification system over telephone lines," to be published in *Bell Syst. Tech. J.*, 1976.

[44] A. E. Rosenberg and M. R. Sambur, "New techniques for automatic speaker verification," *IEEE Trans. Acoustics, Speech Signal Processing*, vol. ASSP-23, pp. 169–176, 1975.

[45] L. H. Rosenthal, L. R. Rabiner, R. W. Schafer, P. Cummiskey,

and J. L. Flanagan, "A multiline computer voice response system utilizing ADPCM coded speech," *IEEE Trans. Acoustics, Speech, Signal Processing*, vol. ASSP-22, 339-356, 1974.

[46] M. R. Sambur, "Selection of acoustic features for speaker identification," *IEEE Trans. Acoustics, Speech, Signal Processing*, vol. ASSP-23, pp. 176-182, 1975.

[47] R. W. Schafer and L. R. Rabiner, "System for automatic formant analysis of voiced speech," *J. Acoust. Soc. Amer.*, vol. 47, pp. 634-648, 1970.

[48] J. N. Shearme and J. N. Holmes, "An experiment concerning the recognition of voices," *Language and Speech*, vol. 2, p. 123, 1959.

[49] K. N. Stevens, C. E. Williams, J. R. Carbonell, and B. Woods, "Speaker authentication and identification: A comparison of spectrographic and auditory presentations of speech material," *J. Acoust. Soc. Amer.*, vol. 44, pp. 596-1607, 1968.

[50] L-S Su, K-P Li, and K. S. Fu, "Identification of speakers by use of nasal coarticulation," *J. Acoust. Soc. Amer.*, vol. 56, pp. 1876-1882, 1974.

[51] O. Tosi *et al.*, "Experiment on voice identification," *J. Acoust. Soc. Amer.*, vol. 53, p. 2030, 1972.

[52] J. J. Wolf, "Efficient acoustic parameters for speaker recognition," *J. Acoust. Soc. Amer.*, vol. 51, pp. 2044-2055, 1972.

[53] M. A. Young and R. A. Campbell, "Effects of context on talker identification," *J. Acoust. Soc. Amer.*, vol. 42, pp. 1250-1254, 1967.

Automatic Recognition of Speakers from Their Voices

BISHNU S. ATAL

Abstract—This paper presents a survey of automatic speaker recognition techniques. The paper includes a discussion of the speaker-dependent properties of the speech signal, methods for selecting an efficient set of speech measurements, results of experimental studies illustrating the performance of various methods of speaker recognition, and a comparison of the performance of automatic methods with that of human listeners. Both text-dependent as well as text-independent speaker-recognition techniques are discussed.

I. Introduction

MOST OF US ARE aware of the fact that voices of different individuals do not sound alike. This important property of speech—of being speaker-dependent—is what enables us to recognize a friend over a telephone. The ability of recognizing a person solely from his voice is known as speaker recognition. Speaker recognition by human listeners is a common experience and has been known for a long time [1], [2]. More recently, with the availability of digital computers, speech scientists have wondered if automatic and objective methods can be devised to recognize a speaker uniquely from his voice [3]-[10]. In many speech applications, it is often difficult to duplicate human performance by machines. In the case of speaker recognition, fortunately, this is not true. Not only successful speaker recognition by machines is possible, presently available experimental evidence suggests that the performance of machines in many instances exceeds that of human listeners [11].

The early work on speaker recognition was almost completely limited to human listening. A considerable part of this research was motivated by the desire to produce natural sounding speech from vocoders and similar speech processing devices. Although vocoder-generated synthetic speech was quite intelligible, it was often deficient with respect to the recognizability of the speakers. This particular problem led to a search for the factors which convey the speaker-dependent information in speech. The principal aim of these studies was not just to determine the accuracy with which listeners could identify speakers but to answer the fundamental question: how do listeners differentiate among speakers? Unfortunately, it is not easy to find a satisfactory answer to this question. The question about perceptual bases of speaker recognition and their acoustical correlates remains largely unresolved.

The availability of digital computers for processing of speech signals probably provided the greatest impetus to research on automatic speaker recognition. The motivation for such research stemmed from both a curiosity to see if human performance could be duplicated by machines and a promise of providing new and indeed revolutionary services in many diverse fields. Efficient banking and business transactions, controlled access of a facility or information to selected individuals, and a new tool for the law-enforcement agencies are among the many possible applications of automatic speaker recognition.

This paper presents a survey of the progress achieved towards automatic speaker recognition.[1] We will review in the remainder of this introductory section some of the fundamental aspects of the problem. Why is speaker recognition possible? What are the sources of interspeaker variability and how are

Manuscript received August 15, 1975; revised October 8, 1975.
The author is with Bell Laboratories, Murray Hill, NJ 07974.

[1] The term speaker recognition as used in this paper refers to any decision-making process that uses some features of the speech signal to determine if a particular person is the speaker of a given utterance which will include tasks such as identification, verification, discrimination, and authentication of speakers.

Reprinted from *Proc. IEEE*, vol. 64, pp. 460–475, Apr. 1976.

they manifested at the acoustic level? We will also discuss the differences among the various tasks in speaker recognition: speaker identification versus speaker verification and text-dependent versus text-independent speaker recognition. In Section II, we describe different acoustic parameters of speech and present techniques for selecting an efficient set of parameters for speaker recognition. Speaker-recognition procedures employed in various experimental studies on speaker recognition are presented in Section III. The performance of different speech parameters for speaker recognition is discussed in Section IV. In Section V, some results concerning the performance of human listeners are presented and compared with machine performance. Finally, in Section VI, we present some thoughts on "what have we achieved so far?" and "where do we go from here?"

Speech is produced as a result of a complex sequence of transformations occurring at several different levels: semantic, linguistic, articulatory, and acoustic. In general, differences in these transformations are likely to show up as differences in the acoustic properties of the speech signal. Speaker-related variations in speech are caused in part by the anatomical differences in the vocal tract and in part by the differences in the speaking habits of different individuals [12]. The anatomical differences relate to the fixed structural differences in the shape or size of the vocal tract which can vary considerably from one person to another. The differences in the speaking habits, on the other hand, result from the manner in which persons have learned to use their speech mechanism. Such differences show up in the temporal variations of speech characteristics of different individuals. Intonation patterns of individuals represent a good example of such variations. In speaker recognition, one attempts to exploit both anatomical as well as learned differences to distinguish speech of one speaker from that of another.

So far, we spoke primarily of interspeaker variations in speech. We must also consider intraspeaker variations—those occurring within different speech utterances of a single speaker [13]. Intraspeaker variations occur even though the texts of two utterances are identical. Such variations are caused by many factors such as the differences in the speaking rates, the emotional state of the speaker, his health, etc. The differences in the speaking rates can often be minimized by nonlinear deformation of the relative time scales of two utterances. It is desirable to select for speaker recognition those acoustic parameters of speech which show low intraspeaker but high interspeaker variability.

Often, in many speaker-recognition applications, it is possible to reduce the intraspeaker variability by requiring that the text of the unknown and reference utterances of a speaker be the same. It is still interesting to know if such a restriction is really necessary for successful speaker recognition. After all, human listeners do not need this restriction in order to recognize a person. Indeed, in most practical situations, the spoken text is different from one occasion to another. Although a large number of experimental studies in speaker recognition have dealt with a text-dependent format, a few recent studies have described methods suitable for both the text-independent and the text-dependent situations [14]–[16]. Generally speaking, text-independent speaker recognition is the more difficult of the two, since one must now cope with the additional variability due to the differences in the texts of the unknown and the reference utterances. We will be discussing the results of both kinds of studies in this paper.

One can think of two different applications of speaker recognition. In the first one, speaker identification, the task is to assign an unknown utterance to one person in a group of several known speakers. In the second application, speaker verification, the task is to verify if the unknown utterance was spoken by the claimed speaker. Although these two problems have quite a lot in common, the recognition procedures employed in each problem can be very different. In some sense, the verification procedure is much simpler than that of identification. Verification requires a binary decision, namely, that of accepting or rejecting the claimed identity of an utterance. In practice, it means comparing the unknown utterance with a reference utterance of the claimed speaker and deciding if the two are similar enough. Superficially, the task of identification requires comparisons with reference utterances of all speakers, which is likely to be impractical with a very large number of speakers. For applications involving a large number of speakers, which is of great practical interest, some method which limits the comparisons to only a few reference utterances must be used [7], [17]. For example, by using proper tree-structures algorithms, the number of comparisons involved in the search can be made independent of the number of speakers. Unfortunately, not much work has been done in this respect. Nevertheless, successful development of such techniques is essential for satisfactory speaker identification in large populations.

The main emphasis of this paper is on automatic methods of speaker recognition. We will present some results with respect to the performance of human listeners in situations comparable to those encountered by the machine, thus allowing us to compare the performance of the automatic methods with that of human listeners. This is not to suggest that the human performance should serve as a benchmark of achievement for the automatic methods. On the contrary, we wish to show that automatic methods are, in many cases, more accurate than human listening.

II. Selection of Speech Parameters for Speaker Recognition

A. Desirable Properties for Speaker-Recognition Parameters

The problem of speaker recognition may be divided into two parts: measurement and classification. In the first part, a number of measurements are made on the speech utterance to provide a set of parameters representing the speaker-dependent information of speech. In the second part, appropriate decision rules are used either to assign the measurements to one of the speakers or to verify if the measurements have originated from the speech of the claimed speaker. We will discuss the measurement problem in this section.

A large variety of parameters can be extracted from the speech signal either directly from the waveform or after spectral transformation to the frequency domain [18]. One of the most important steps towards achieving successful speaker recognition is the selection of speech parameters capable of efficiently representing the speaker-dependent information in speech. Procedures for selecting an efficient set of acoustic parameters have been discussed extensively in the literature [19]–[22]. Wolf, in a recent paper [19] on this subject, has outlined a set of desirable characteristics for suitable speaker-recognition parameters. Ideally, the chosen speech parameters should be as follows:

1) efficient in representing the speaker-dependent information;

2) easy to measure;
3) stable over time;
4) occur naturally and frequently in speech;
5) change little from one speaking environment to another; and
6) not be susceptible to mimicry.

B. Parameter Evaluation

Let us consider the problem of selecting a set of suitable speech parameters. Obviously, we must define first a reasonable criterion of effectiveness. We can then rank the different parameters in order of their measured effectiveness. The ideal measure of effectiveness is the probability of error in recognizing a speaker. This choice does, however, create some practical problems. The error probability depends not only on the parameters but also on the nature of classification rules. Thus the error probability cannot be determined without specifying the classification rules. The computing of error probability is generally quite time-consuming, particularly with a large number of speakers. It is, therefore, desirable to choose a measure of effectiveness which reflects the basic properties of the parameters alone in discriminating one speaker from another and is not dependent on the choice of the classification rules. Theoretically, one could avoid this problem by using optimal classification rules. However, it is not a practically sound idea since one would then be required to rank order not only the different speech parameters but also the different classification rules. Of course, the error probability is an ideal measure of effectiveness if the parameters are to be evaluated for a specific classification rule and indeed experimentally determined error probabilities have been used extensively for evaluating the performance of practical speaker-recognition systems.

A set of measurements made on an utterance may be thought of as mapping the utterance into a point in a multidimensional parameter space. Different utterances of the same speaker will generate a set of points in the parameter space whose distribution can be described by a multivariate probability density function. Roughly speaking, a set of measurements would be effective in discriminating between speakers if the distributions of different speakers are concentrated at widely different locations in the parameter space. For a single measurement parameter, this amounts to saying that a good measure of effectiveness would be the ratio of interspeaker to intraspeaker variance, often referred to as the F ratio [19], [21]–[22]. The F ratio is defined as

$$F = \frac{\text{variance of speaker means}}{\text{average intraspeaker variance}} = \langle[\mu_i - \bar{\mu}]^2\rangle_i / \langle[x_\alpha^{(i)} - \mu_i]^2\rangle_{\alpha,\, i} \tag{1}$$

where $x^{(i)}$ is the parameter value from the αth repetition of an utterance spoken by the ith speaker, $\langle\,\rangle_i$ indicates averaging over the speakers, $\langle\,\rangle_\alpha$ indicates averaging over the different utterances of a speaker,

$$\mu_i = \langle x_\alpha^{(i)}\rangle_\alpha \tag{2}$$

is the estimated mean value of the parameter for the ith speaker, and

$$\bar{\mu} = \langle \mu_i \rangle_i \tag{3}$$

is the estimated overall mean value of the parameter averaged over all speakers.

For normal variables (having Gaussian probability density function), the F ratio has the nice property that the probability of misclassifying a speaker i to speaker j is a monotonically decreasing function of F. In general, however, the F ratio has no simple relationship to the probability of error. Still, it has been found very useful in evaluating the effectiveness of parameters. Pruzansky and Mathews [21] used this technique to select a small subset of features from a much larger set consisting of the quantized spectrographic data. They compared the performance of a number of parameters with large F ratios with the performance of the same number of parameters with small F ratios. As an example, with a subset consisting of 10 percent of the total number of parameters, the probability of error increased from approximately 18 percent for the largest F ratios to approximately 50 percent for the smallest F ratios, thus demonstrating the utility of the F ratio for selecting efficient speaker-recognition parameters.

The major disadvantage of evaluating parameters individually is that interparameter correlations are not taken into account. For example, if the parameter is highly correlated with another parameter, the performance of the two together would not be much better than either of the parameters alone. The individual evaluation of parameters can thus result in the selection of redundant parameters. It is advantageous to consider the parameters together as a vector. The concept of F ratio can be extended to the multidimensional case. We define two covariance matrices: an interspeaker covariance matrix B and an intraspeaker covariance matrix W. These matrices are defined as

$$B = \langle[\mu_i - \bar{\mu}]\,[\mu_i - \bar{\mu}]^t\rangle_i \tag{4}$$

$$W = \langle[x_\alpha^{(i)} - \mu_i]\,[x_\alpha^{(i)} - \mu_i]^t\rangle_{\alpha,\, i} \tag{5}$$

where $x_\alpha^{(i)}$ is a vector representing the measurements from the αth repetition of an utterance spoken by the ith speaker,

$$\mu_i = \langle x_\alpha^{(i)}\rangle_\alpha \tag{6}$$

is the estimated mean vector for the ith speaker, and

$$\bar{\mu} = \langle \mu_i \rangle_i \tag{7}$$

is the estimated overall mean vector averaged over all speakers. A suitable measure of effectiveness of a set of parameters for discriminating between different categories is "divergence," originally defined by Kullback [24] as a measure of uncertainty in the data. The divergence is given by [24], [25]

$$D = \langle[\mu_i - \mu_j]\,W^{-1}\,[\mu_i - \mu_j]^t\rangle_{i,\, j} \tag{8}$$

where W^{-1} is the inverse of the matrix W and the superscript t indicates the transpose of a vector. Equation (8) can also be written as

$$D = \mathrm{Tr}\, W^{-1}\, \langle[\mu_i - \mu_j]\,[\mu_i - \mu_j]^t\rangle_{i,\, j} \tag{9}$$

$$= \mathrm{Tr}\, W^{-1} B \tag{10}$$

which is an obvious generalization of the concept of the F ratio to the multidimensional case [6], [25]. For a one-dimensional case, (10) reduces to $D = F$.

The divergence was used by the author to find an efficient representation of pitch contours of different speakers [6], [25]. Originally, the pitch contours were specified by 40 equally-spaced samples along the time scale. These 40 pitch values were converted to 40 Karhunen–Loève components [26] and partitioned into 4 groups of 10 each in order of decreasing variance. Each group of parameters was used to

TABLE I
THE DIVERGENCE AND THE PERCENTAGE OF CORRECT IDENTIFICATIONS FOR THE FOUR GROUPS OF KARHUNEN–LOÈVE COMPONENTS

Group	Divergence	Percentage of Correct Identifications
1	44.9	93
2	3.5	57
3	1.2	20
4	0.8	11

identify a speaker from an ensemble of 10 speakers. The percentage of correct identifications and the divergence for each of the four groups is shown in Table I. In each case, a decrease in divergence is accompanied by a decrease in the identification accuracy.

The divergence D takes account of the interparameter correlations and thus is a more appropriate measure of the effectiveness of a set of parameters than the F ratio. Of course, correlation is a measure of linear dependence between two parameters. A small correlation between two parameters does not imply lack of any relationship between them. Wolf [19] describes a technique for estimating pair-wise interparameter dependence (not necessarily linear) between a set of parameters. His method is based on estimating the degree of overlap between the parameter distributions of the individual speakers. Such a measure of interparameter dependence could prove to be useful for isolating cases of strong nonlinear dependence between the parameters.

C. Types of Acoustic Parameters

Acoustic parameters of speech can be broadly classified into two groups: steady-state (time-invariant) and time-varying. Ideally, one would like to think that the speaker-defining parameters should reflect fixed characteristics of the speech signal and therefore be time-invariant. Time-invariant parameters can be obtained either by averaging the time-varying behavior of the parameter or by performing measurements which reflect fixed anatomical properties of the vocal tract. The main advantage of the time-invariant parameters is that they are essentially independent of the spoken message and are therefore suitable for text-independent speaker recognition. However, they may suffer from important disadvantages. A large class of speaker-dependent properties of speech result from the idiosyncrasies in the speaking habits of individuals and these by nature vary from one sound to the other. Such useful speech characteristics cannot be represented by time-invariant parameters. Furthermore, time-averaged voice characteristics, such as average pitch or average spectrum, may be subject to easy mimicry since it would appear difficult that an impostor could easily mimic the entire time variation of a parameter.

Among the time-varying parameters, one should distinguish between parameters which are defined continuously as a function of time versus the parameters which are defined selectively for certain speech events. Both of these types have their merits. Continuously defined parameters are easier to measure but could result in a large set of data having a high degree of redundancy. Such redundancies can be identified by using the techniques based on the F ratio or the divergence as discussed earlier. Selective measurement of parameters at appropriately chosen locations in the utterance avoids this problem but requires the identification of the proper locations in the speech utterance—a task difficult to perform automatically. Most of the speaker-recognition work has been done with parameters measured at regularly spaced intervals in an utterance, and consequently, a large part of the results presented in this paper are related to such measurements. Both Wolf and Sambur [19], [20] have discussed selectively defined parameters exclusively and their published work is an important source of information for evaluating such measurements for speaker recognition.

D. Model of Speech Production

Speech sounds are produced as a result of acoustical excitation of the vocal tract which consists of the cavities in the pharynx and the mouth. The entire vocal tract can be thought of as an acoustic tube terminated by the lips at one end and by the vocal cords at the other end. The shape of the vocal tract is changed continually during speech production by the movement of different articulators such as the tongue, the jaw, and the lips. For most sounds, the sound is radiated at the lips. In the case of nasal consonants, the front part of the vocal tract is closed and the vocal tract is coupled through the velar opening to the nasal cavities, thereby producing sound radiation from the nostrils. During the production of nonnasal sounds, the velar opening is closed and no sound is radiated from the nostrils.

There are three important modes of exciting the vocal tract. It is customary to classify sounds according to their mode of excitation. Voiced sounds are produced as a result of excitation by a series of nearly periodic pulses generated by the vocal cords. Examples of voiced sounds are vowels, semivowels, voiced stops, and nasals. The fundamental frequency of the vocal-cord vibrations is determined by the mass and tension of the vocal cords, and by the subglottal air pressure. Both the tension of the vocal cords and the subglottal air pressure change during speech production. The range of fundamental frequency in speech from a normal adult is about 60 to 400 Hz. Unvoiced sounds are produced when the vocal tract is excited by a noise-like turbulent flow of air at a point of constriction. The resulting excitation has a relatively uniform spectrum. Examples of unvoiced sounds are various fricatives, such as *f*, *s*, *sh*, etc. and voiceless stop consonants like *p*, *t*, and *k*. Finally, the plosive sounds are produced by making a complete closure, building up pressure behind the closure, and abruptly releasing it. Examples of plosives are stop consonants like *b*, *d*, *g*, *p*, *t*, and *k*. In continuous speech, combinations of different types of excitation mentioned above are also used.

A simplified model of speech production can be made by representing the vocal tract as a linear time-varying filter excited either by a periodic pulse source or by a white-noise source as shown in Fig. 1. The output of the vocal tract is then expressed as a convolution between the excitation function and the impulse response of the time-varying linear filter representing the vocal tract. Thus, the speech signal $s(t)$ is given by

$$s(t) = \int_{-\infty}^{t} e(\tau)\, v(t, \tau)\, d\tau \tag{11}$$

where $e(t)$ is the excitation function, and $v(t, \tau)$ is the response

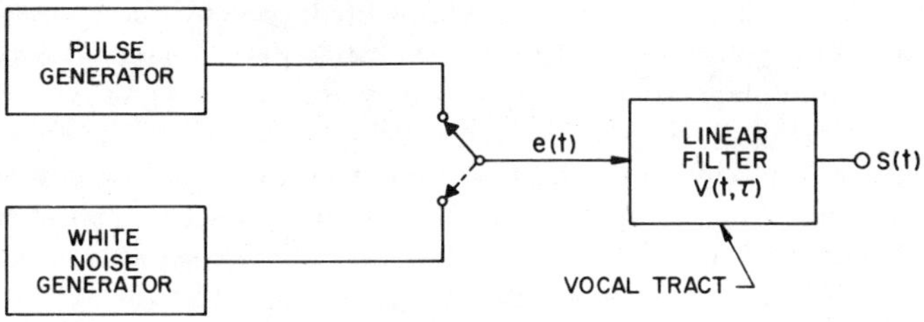

Fig. 1. Block diagram of a functional model of speech production.

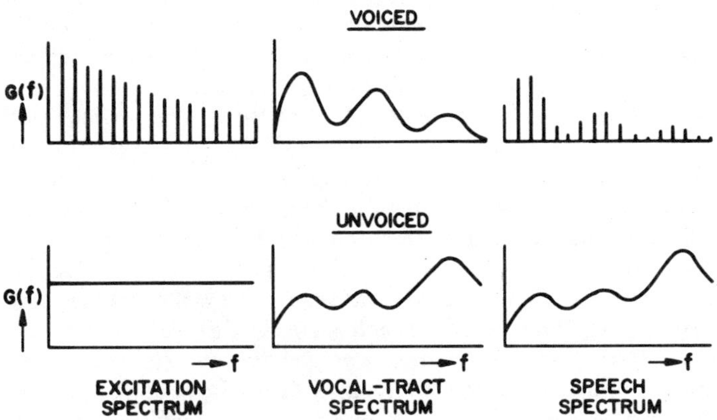

Fig. 2. Spectra of voiced and unvoiced sounds.

of the vocal tract at time t to a delta function input applied at time τ. For most sounds, the shape of the vocal tract changes slowly compared to the variations in the excitation waveform. Thus the speech production can be considered to be a quasi-stationary process. The quasi-stationarity of the model permits us to look at the speech characteristics in the frequency domain. For voiced speech, the vocal excitation function is nearly periodic with slowly varying periods. Its spectrum consists of a series of harmonics whose amplitude falls off at approximately 12 dB per octave. The spacing between adjacent harmonics is determined by the period of the vocal-cord vibrations. The spectrum of the vocal-tract response consists of a number of resonances whose locations depend upon the vocal-tract shape. The voiced-speech spectrum is thus composed of harmonically related frequencies whose amplitudes are determined by the vocal-tract response at these frequencies. For unvoiced speech, the excitation spectrum is uniformly distributed over a wide frequency range; the speech spectrum for these sounds reflects entirely the vocal-tract response. Such idealized representations of spectra for voiced and unvoiced speech are given in Fig. 2.

E. Short-Time Spectral Representation of Speech

A useful concept for describing properties of nonstationary signals such as speech is the time-varying or "short-time" spectrum [18], [27], [28]. In such a "short-time" representation, only a portion of the signal in the neighborhood of the present time is included in computing the spectrum. Mathematically speaking, for a signal $s(t)$, the short-time power spectrum is defined as a function of frequency f and time t as

$$G(f, t) = \left| \int_{-\infty}^{+\infty} s(\tau)\, w(t - \tau)\, e^{-j2\pi f\tau}\, d\tau \right|^2 \tag{12}$$

where $w(t)$ is a suitable window function. For most practical cases, the effective duration of $w(t)$ is in the vicinity of 20 to 30 ms. The frequency range of interest in speech usually extends from 0 to 10 kHz. The short-time spectrum of speech contains nearly all of the important information in speech and has formed the basis for most of the present methods of characterizing speech in a parametric form.

In the earlier days before the availability of fast digital computers, the short-time power spectrum was obtained by passing speech through a bank of band-pass filters. The energy at the output of each band-pass filter provided a good estimate of the short-time spectrum at the center frequency of the filter. The number of band-pass filters is governed by the bandwidth of each filter and the range of frequencies to be covered. An example of such a system is described in [19]. It consists of a 36-channel filter bank with center frequencies spaced linearly between 150 and 1650 Hz and logarithmically thereafter to 7025 Hz.

On a digital computer, the short-time power spectrum is obtained directly by using (12). A suitable window function $w(t)$ is the "Hamming" window [29] defined as

$$w(t) = \begin{cases} 0.54 + 0.46 \cos 2\pi t/T, & -T/2 \leq t \leq T/2 \\ 0, & |t| > T/2 \end{cases} \tag{13}$$

where the duration T is typically 25 ms. An example of the short-time power spectrum of speech for a voiced speech sound is shown in Fig. 3. The fine structure corresponding to the regularly spaced peaks in the spectrum is due to the periodicity of the voiced speech; the frequency spacing between the peaks is the pitch frequency. The amplitude of the peaks—often described as the spectral envelope—is a function of both the glottal-pulse shape and the vocal-tract response. Since the fine structure is determined completely by a single parameter, the pitch frequency, it is usually desirable to separate the fine structure of the spectrum from the envelope. Such a decomposition leads to a compact description of the spectrum.

F. Description of Acoustic Parameters

In the early work on speaker recognition, spectrographic data (time-frequency-energy pattern of speech) was almost exclusively used in speaker-recognition studies. Since then, a wide variety of additional measurements, based on both frequency and time-domain analyses, have been investigated for application to automatic speaker recognition. Many of these parameters are related to some property of the short-time power spectrum. We present here a brief description of the acoustic parameters which have been found useful for speaker recognition. The intention here is not to give an exhaustive list of parameters but to provide a fair sampling of different speech characteristics capable of distinguishing one speaker from another. The description of speech analysis methods for obtaining speech parameters is omitted here. An excellent survey on different speech analysis techniques and various parametric representations of speech appears in [18].

1) Intensity: One of the simplest characteristics of any signal is its intensity. For nonstationary signals such as speech, the intensity must be defined as a function of time. A suitable definition would be

$$E(t) = \int_{t-T/2}^{t+T/2} s^2(\tau)\, d\tau \tag{14}$$

where T is the averaging interval. The choice of T is somewhat

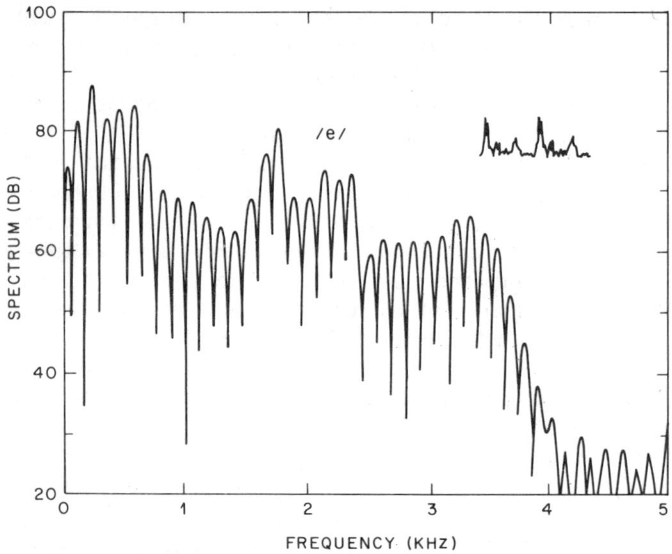

Fig. 3. **An example of the short-time spectrum of voiced speech.**

arbitrary; a value in the range 10 to 30 ms is adequate in most cases. The variations in intensity of speech are caused by the variations of both the subglottal pressure as well as the vocal-tract shape as a function of time and represent an important source of speaker-dependent information in speech [30]–[31].

2) Pitch: Pitch is the fundamental frequency of the vocal-cord vibrations. Accurate measurement of pitch has received considerable attention in speech research. Voice pitch can be determined either in the time domain by direct measurement of the period of the speech waveform or in the frequency domain by computing the frequency spacing of the spectral peaks [6], [32]–[35]. The temporal variation of pitch represents an important speech characteristic and has been found to be effective for automatic speaker recognition [6], [25].

3) Short-Time Spectrum: The definition of short-time spectrum given in (12) provides a three-dimensional representation of the speech signal, the coordinates being time, frequency, and energy. The short-time spectrum provides a complete (although not a very compact) description of the acoustical characteristics of speech. Both the exact representation of the short-time spectrum, defined in (12), and its approximation by filter-bank outputs have been found to be effective for automatic speaker recognition. [3], [4], [7], [8], [21].

4) Predictor Coefficients: Linear prediction analysis is an important method of characterizing the spectral properties of speech in the time domain [18], [36]–[39]. In this analysis method, each sample of the speech waveform is predicted as a linear weighted sum of the past p samples. The weights which minimize the mean-squared prediction error are called the predictor coefficients. Typically, 12 predictor coefficients are adequate for speech band-limited to 5 kHz. The predictor coefficients vary as a function of time and it is usually sufficient to compute them once every 20 ms.

5) Formant Frequencies and Bandwidths: Formant frequencies are defined as the resonance frequencies of the vocal tract. These too are speaker dependent. The chief difficulty with the formants lies in their measurement. Several methods have been described in the literature which provide a partial solution to the problem of determining formant frequencies [40]–[43]. Still, accurate and reliable determination of formants for both male and female speakers poses very difficult problems.

6) Nasal Coarticulation: In connected speech, due to slow movement of the articulators, the vocal-tract shape at any given time depends not only on the phoneme being spoken at that time but also on the neighboring phonemes. This phenomenon is known as coarticulation and it has been suggested that the nature of coarticulation in a given context is speaker dependent. One difficulty in using such information for speaker recognition is in obtaining a quantitative measure of such differences from speech. Coarticulation during the production of nasal consonants has been found useful for speaker recognition [45]. In this study, an acoustic measure of nasal coarticulation in a consonant–vowel context was obtained by measuring the spectral difference between the mean spectrum of a nasal consonant followed by a front vowel (such as /i/) and that of the same consonant followed by a back vowel (such as /a/).

7) Spectral Correlations: Significant degree of correlation exists between the short-time spectrum at different frequencies. These correlations have been found to vary consistently from one speaker to another [45]. Stable evaluation of such correlations, however, requires averaging over long utterances; about 30 s of speech is considered a minimum.

8) Timing and Speaking Rate: Relative timing of different speech events in spoken utterances differ from one speaker to another. Doddington has described a novel way of measuring such differences by determining the nonlinear deformation of the time axis of one utterance relative to that of another [10], [46].

III. Speaker-Recognition Procedures in Experimental Studies

Several computer-based studies have been conducted to test the feasibility of automatic speaker recognition. The objectives of these studies have been twofold: one to provide data about the comparative performance of different speech parameters in representing interspeaker differences and the other to determine the performance in terms of the error rates achieved in a complete speaker-recognition system using a selected set of parameters. A word of caution is in order here about interpreting the results of different speaker-recognition studies. These results depend on the task involved in the experiment—such as speaker identification or verification, text-dependent or text-independent speaker recognition. A meaningful comparison of results between these different cases cannot be made. Even in the absence of such differences, the comparisons may still not be straightforward. Every speaker-recognition study needs a data base consisting of several utterances spoken by many speakers. Unfortunately, there are no standard set of rules to be followed in collecting such a data base of speech utterances. The differences in data base can originate from several sources: number of speakers, type of speaker population, speech material, recording conditions, the time span over which the speech data is collected, and the elapsed time between the collection of test and training data. The decision rule employed for classification could also have a significant influence on the performance achieved in different studies. However, the results, in most cases, provide a rough measure of performance.

A. Collection of Speech Data

Ideally, the data base for speaker-recognition studies should include a large number of speakers. Collection of speech data from a large number of speakers poses many practical problems. Consequently, most studies use a relatively small population of speakers. Very few studies have tested speech data from one hundred or more speakers [7], [8], [47], [48]. In many cases, only male or female speakers have been used exclusively. With a small number of speakers, it is preferable not to include speakers with widely different speech characteristics. For example, male and female voices can often be distinguished from each other on the basis of average pitch alone. A small population study using speakers with widely different voice characteristics is not likely to provide a critical test of the suitability of a set of speech parameters for automatic speaker recognition. In some of the early work on speaker recognition, both the test and reference utterances were recorded in a single session. Later on, it became obvious that the results from such studies can be misleading. A speaker can often maintain a high degree of stability in his speaking habits over a short interval of time. However, the intraspeaker variability can often increase significantly with an increase in the time interval between recordings of test and reference utterances. As an example, Furui *et al.* have reported that percentage-recognition rate decreased from 96 percent to 52 percent when the interval between recordings of test and reference samples was increased from 3 days to 3 months [16]. Thus one must be careful about using the results from those speaker-recognition studies in which all the utterances from a speaker were collected over a short interval of time.

B. Formation of Training and Test Sets

In most speaker-recognition systems, a training set of speech utterances is used to obtain a statistical characterization of the acoustical parameters of the various speakers. In testing the performance of these systems, it is essential that the speech utterances used in the training process be kept separate from the utterances used to test the performance. In fact, clever pattern-recognition procedures can often be devised to work very well on the utterances in the training set. But there is no assurance that these procedures would work equally well on another set of utterances not used in the training process. The use of an independent test set would show if indeed the training procedure has learned the true characteristics of a speaker which are common to all of his utterances and not just to those represented in the training set.

C. Temporal Alignment of Utterances

Speech events in two utterances—even though they have the same text and are spoken by the same speaker—are seldom synchronized in time. This effect is attributable to the differences in the speaking rates. In comparing time-varying parameters, it is necessary that these be derived from similar speech events in the reference and the test utterances. Approximate time synchronization can be achieved by aligning the beginning and the end of the two utterances. More accurate synchronization can be obtained by pattern-matching techniques using nonlinear time deformation [30], [46], [49]. An alternative procedure would be to identify a number of "landmarks" in the utterances and to align the utterances by linear stretching or compression of the time scales between the landmarks [8].

D. Speaker-Classification Procedure

A speaker-recognition system involves two basic functions: measurement and classification. The measurement and selection of speaker-dependent parameters were discussed earlier in Section II. The classification is concerned with the decision-making process of determining if a particular person is the speaker of a given utterance.

The speaker-classification problem can be viewed as an exercise in statistical decision theory. A set of parameters derived from an utterance can be thought of as representing the utterance by a point in a multidimensional parameter space. In principle, the distribution of points corresponding to different utterances of a speaker can be characterized by a multivariate probability-density function. For speaker identification, the decision rule to assign a given point in the parameter space to a particular speaker would call for the selection of a speaker who has the highest probability of generating the given set of parameters. Similarly, the task of speaker verification (or authentication) would call for deciding if the probability of the parameters being generated by the claimed speaker is large enough for the particular application at hand. However, a straightforward application of this simple idea is not practically feasible. Even with relatively few parameters, the estimation of the multivariate probability-density function requires a very large number of utterances from a speaker. It is more practical to choose a parametric form of the probability density with some unknown parameters whose values could be estimated from the utterances in the training set. A convenient choice for this purpose is the well-known multivariate Gaussian density function. The Gaussian density function has an important property that is completely determined by its mean vector and a covariance matrix. The assumption of Gaussian density for the parameters is not as arbitrary as it might seem to be. For the decision rule to be correct, it is sufficient that the density be essentially unimodal and approximately Gaussian in the center of its range—a property often found to be true for physical measurements. Needless to say that such a decision rule would also be optimum for arbitrary monotonic functions of the Gaussian probability-density function.

As mentioned earlier, the Gaussian density is completely specified by its mean vector and a covariance matrix. An appropriate choice of the mean vector is the sample mean vector $\mu^{(i)}$ defined in (6), with the averaging being done over the various utterances of a speaker in the training set. The covariance matrix, strictly speaking, is also speaker dependent. However, in most practical situations, it is not possible to determine an accurate estimate of the matrix for each speaker. A more tractable choice for the covariance matrix is the pooled intraspeaker covariance matrix W defined in (5) representing an average matrix for all of the speakers. The N-dimensional Gaussian density function for the ith speaker is then written as

$$g_i(x) = (2\pi)^{-N/2}\, |W|^{-1/2} \exp\,[-1/2(x - \mu_i)^t W^{-1}\, (x - \mu_i)] \tag{15}$$

where $|W|$ is the determinant of the matrix W. Let us consider speaker identification first. If we assume that the unknown utterance could have originated from any speaker in the population with equal apriori probability and that the cost of making an error is the same for all speakers, the optimum decision rule would assign the unknown utterance to the speaker j if [50]

$$g_j(x) > g_i(x), \qquad \text{for all } i \neq j. \tag{16}$$

Since logarithm is a monotonic function, the decision rule of

(16) can be rewritten as

$$d_j(\boldsymbol{x}) < d_i(\boldsymbol{x}), \qquad \text{for all } i \neq j \tag{17}$$

where

$$d_j(\boldsymbol{x}) = [(\boldsymbol{x} - \boldsymbol{\mu}_j)^t W^{-1} (\boldsymbol{x} - \boldsymbol{\mu}_j)]^{1/2}. \tag{18}$$

The above rule simply assigns the unknown utterance to a speaker on the basis of a minimum-distance classification rule. The quantity $d_j(\boldsymbol{x})$ of (18) would be called the distance between a vector representing the unknown utterance and the mean (reference) vector for the jth speaker. The commonly used Euclidean distance is a special case of this general definition and is obtained by equating the covariance matrix W by an Identity matrix in (18), thereby replacing the quantity under the square-root sign by the sum of the squared differences along each coordinate. However, the Euclidean distance does not provide the correct decision rule if the speech parameters show significant interparameter correlations or have widely different intraspeaker variances.

The distance metric $d_j(\boldsymbol{x})$ defined in (18) has several important properties: the distance $d_j(\boldsymbol{x})$ is invariant with respect to any arbitrary nonsingular transformation of the parameters. To prove this result, consider a representation of the utterances in the N-dimensional parameter space. Let T be a $N \times N$ matrix representing the linear transformation. The unknown utterance is represented in the transformed space by a vector $\hat{\boldsymbol{x}}$ given by

$$\hat{\boldsymbol{x}} = T\boldsymbol{x}. \tag{19}$$

The reference utterance of the jth speaker in the transformed space is given by

$$\hat{\boldsymbol{\mu}}_j = T\boldsymbol{\mu}_j. \tag{20}$$

The distance $\hat{d}_j$ between $\hat{\boldsymbol{x}}$ and $\hat{\boldsymbol{\mu}}_j$ is then given by

$$\begin{aligned} \hat{d}_j &= [(\hat{\boldsymbol{x}} - \hat{\boldsymbol{\mu}}_j)^t \hat{W}^{-1} (\hat{\boldsymbol{x}} - \hat{\boldsymbol{\mu}}_j)]^{1/2} \\ &= [(\boldsymbol{x} - \boldsymbol{\mu}_j)^t T^t \hat{W}^{-1} T(\boldsymbol{x} - \boldsymbol{\mu}_j)]^{1/2}. \end{aligned} \tag{21}$$

Since $W^{-1} = T^t \hat{W}^{-1} T$, it follows that $\hat{d}_j = d_j$. This property of the distance metric of being invariant with respect to arbitrary linear transformations of the parameters is very useful. The distance metric of (18) would provide identical results with two parameter sets if they are linearly related to each other. For example, the Fourier transform is a linear transformation. Thus several frequency and time-domain representations of speech would be expected to provide similar results with this particular metric.

Consider the distribution of utterances in an N-dimensional parameter space. The non-Euclidean distance metric $d_j(\boldsymbol{x})$ is equivalent to the measurement of Euclidean distance after a suitable linear transformation of the parameters. This can be seen as follows: the covariance matrix W is a positive-definite and symmetric matrix and can thus be written as a product $W = CLC^t$, where C is a unitary matrix ($CC^t = I$), and L is a diagonal matrix with its ith element given by λ_i. The non-Euclidean distance measure of (18) is equivalent to the Euclidean distance if all the vectors are multiplied by a matrix $L^{-1/2} C^t$. This matrix transformation has the interesting property that the intraspeaker covariance matrix in the transformed space is the Identity matrix. Thus the transformed parameters have no interparameter correlations and have equal intraspeaker variances; the Euclidean distance is the proper distance measure under such conditions.

A distance metric can be regarded as a means of combining the contributions of a large number of measurements into a single measure of dissimilarity between two utterances. A good measure of distance must weight the contributions of different measurements in order of their importance in producing small intraspeaker variations. The distance metric of (18) does indeed possess this property while the Euclidean distance does not.

Both the Euclidean distance and the non-Euclidean distance metric obtained under the assumption of a Gaussian probability-density function of the parameters have been used in speaker-recognition studies with success. Some studies have used the degree of crosscorrelation between the two utterances—the unknown and the reference—as a measure of similarity between the two. In vector notations, the crosscorrelation is defined as

$$\rho_i = (\boldsymbol{x}^t \boldsymbol{\mu}_j)/[(\boldsymbol{x}^t \boldsymbol{x})(\boldsymbol{\mu}_j^t \boldsymbol{\mu}_j)]^{1/2} \tag{22}$$

The crosscorrelation measure has an important property that it is unchanged even if either $\boldsymbol{x}$ or $\boldsymbol{\mu}_j$ or both are multiplied by a constant. This property need not always be a desirable one but can be used with considerable advantage in some situations where parameter variations introduced by some random scale factor are to be ignored.

The distance metric of (18) and the crosscorrelation measure of (22) are also applicable to the speaker-verification problem. Here, the claimed identity of a speaker would be verified if the distance was less than a preselected threshold value or if the crosscorrelation exceeded the threshold value.

IV. Results of Experimental Studies

A fairly large number of speaker-recognition studies have been conducted during the past decade or so. It would not be possible to present in this paper an exhaustive survey covering all of them. Rather, we would attempt to use the results obtained in such studies to illustrate the effectiveness of various speech characteristics discussed earlier for automatic speaker recognition. Particular attention will be given to those results which enable one to compare the recognition performance of different sets of parameters.

Both speaker-recognition tasks, identification and verification, have been investigated in past experimental studies. Of the two, the identification task is more suited for comparing the performance of different parameters. In speaker identification, a single error rate can provide a measure of the performance, while in speaker verification, two kinds of errors, namely, the probabilities of false verification and false rejection as functions of a threshold parameter, determine the performance. Also, the identification accuracy is a more sensitive indicator of the ability of a parameter for discriminating speakers. Consequently, a large portion of the results in this section will relate to studies in speaker identification. Practical aspects of the speaker-verification problem are discussed in a companion paper by Rosenberg [48]. This paper also provides valuable details about the performance of a speaker-verification system being tested at Bell Laboratories under realistic practical environments [49]. To avoid duplication, this particular study will not be included in this paper.

A. Short-Time Power Spectrum

We will discuss here the results from two studies which have used the short-time power spectrum of speech for speaker identification. The first of these [3] is probably one of the earliest investigations on automatic speaker recognition. In this study, the spectrum analysis was accomplished by passing speech through a 17-channel filter bank covering the frequency range 100–7000 Hz. The first 16 channels were approximately equally spaced along a Koenig scale from 200–4000 Hz. The speech data consisted of 4 repetitions of 10 words excerpted from sentence-length utterances spoken by 10 speakers (7 male and 3 female). Each word was represented by a three-dimensional array describing spectrum as a function of frequency and time. The temporal alignment of the words was achieved by lining up the maximum of the energy-versus-time function of each word. For each speaker, three utterances of each of the ten words were used to form the reference pattern for that individual. The procedure used for recognition of speakers consisted of crosscorrelating the spectrographic pattern of the test utterance of each word with each of the ten reference patterns for that word using the product-moment definition of the correlation. The speaker corresponding to the reference pattern with the highest correlation was recognized as the speaker of the test utterance. Speakers were correctly recognized for 89 percent of the 393 cases tested. Results for individual speakers ranged from 77 percent to 98 percent. The recognition rate was not uniformly good for all of the words and ranged from 74 percent to 97 percent approximately.

In the same study, the three-dimensional time-frequency-intensity patterns were reduced to two dimensions by averaging over time for each of the 17 frequency bands. The averaging produced an intensity-versus-frequency array for each word. With the time dimension eliminated, speakers were still recognized correctly for 89 percent of the utterances—no change from the previous case. However, when the three-dimensional patterns were reduced to two dimensions by eliminating the frequency dimension, the recognition rate dropped to 47 percent thus implying that spectral information is more important than the energy-time information for speaker recognition. The low recognition rate may partly be due to the poor temporal alignment of speech events in the test and reference patterns. Such misalignment is not detrimental to the time-averaged spectral data but is highly critical in obtaining proper results from the energy-time data. Later studies by Doddington, using nonlinear time warping, show that intensity-versus-time variation in speech is very effective for speaker recognition [30], [31].

The same speech data was employed in another study by Bricker *et al.* [7]. Using the non-Euclidean distance metric of (18), they found a recognition rate of 97 percent for the two-dimensional spectral data. The non-Euclidean distance measure reduced the error rate by a factor of approximately 4 as compared to the simple crosscorrelation measure. The study was also extended to a much larger data base consisting of 172 speakers. The speech data in this study consisted of five digits spoken in isolation. The spectral data was obtained by using a 20-channel filter bank over the frequency range 20–2900 Hz. The speech data was recorded in an unattended booth in a relatively noisy concourse. The results of their study indicated that a fairly high recognition rate can be maintained even with such a large number of speakers. Based on the speech data from a single digit, the recognition rate was 84 percent; it increased to 94 percent by combining the information from two digits.

Both of the above studies succeeded in demonstrating the importance of spectral information in speech for speaker recognition. However, there is some difficulty in using time-averaged spectra for practical speaker-recognition systems. The spectral data as used in the above studies is strongly affected by the frequency characteristics of the recording and the transmission apparatus. Any variations in the frequency characteristics—not an uncommon occurrence—would be an additional source of randomness in the spectral data which could cause an adverse influence on the performance.

B. Parameters Derived by Linear Prediction of Speech Waveform

Speech analysis based on linear predictability of its waveform is carried out efficiently on digital computers. The predictor coefficients thus offer a convenient choice of parameters for speaker recognition. Recently, a number of studies have been carried out to determine the suitability of these parameters for speaker recognition [14], [51], [52].

The use of linear prediction parameters for automatic speaker recognition is desirable for several reasons. Most important of these is that it eliminates the necessity of deciding as to which of the speech characteristics—such as a particular formant frequency or its bandwidth or some property of the glottal wave—would be suitable for speaker recognition. The predictor coefficients represent the combined information about the formant frequencies, their bandwidth, and the glottal wave. Moreover, being independent of the pitch and intensity information, the predictor coefficients could be used to improve the reliability of another method of speaker recognition based on pitch and intensity information. The linear prediction analysis is also conveniently implemented by digital hardware.

In the linear prediction model [18], [36]–[39], one represents the combined filter transfer function of the vocal tract, the radiation, and the glottal-wave shape by a discrete all-pole linear filter with p poles as shown in Fig. 4. This filter is described completely by a set of p coefficients $a_1, a_2, \cdots, a_p$, defining the linear prediction characteristics of the speech waveform. The predictor coefficients are determined by minimizing the mean-squared prediction error between a speech sample and its linearly predicted value from the past p samples and are given as solutions of a set of linear simultaneous equations [18], [36]

$$\sum_{k=1}^{p} \phi_{jk} a_k = \phi_{jo}, \qquad j = 1, 2, \cdots, p \tag{23}$$

where

$$\phi_{jk} = \sum_{n} s_{n-j} s_{n-k} \tag{24}$$

$$s_n = n\text{th speech sample}$$

and

$$a_k = k\text{th predictor coefficient.}$$

The value of p is approximately determined by the number of poles of the vocal tract and the glottal wave within the frequency range of the speech signal. For speech band-limited to 5 kHz, a typical value of p is 12.

We present here a summary of the results reported in detail in [14]. In this study, the speech data base consisted of 60 utterances spoken by 10 speakers. All of the speakers were female and they spoke the sentence "May we all learn a yellow lion roar" with six repetitions. The speech recordings were made in an anechoic chamber using a high-quality microphone

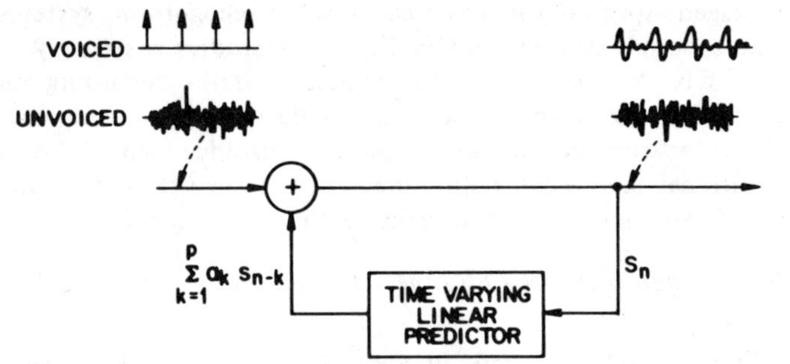

Fig. 4. All-pole model of speech production used in linear prediction analysis.

on two different days 27 days apart. On each day, the recordings were made in three separate sessions. The speech signal was band-limited to 5 kHz prior to analysis in the computer. In the analysis, each utterance was divided into 40 segments of equal duration. Approximate temporal alignment of the segments was achieved by making the segment durations in an utterance proportional to the duration of the utterance which ranged between 1.8 and 2.8 s. The silent portions and pauses in an utterance were eliminated automatically from the segments.

The basic parameter data used in this study consisted of 12 predictor coefficients obtained at 40 uniformly spaced time frames for each of the 60 utterances (6 repetitions × 10 speakers). Five utterances for each speaker were used to compute the reference vectors while the remaining sixth one was used as a test vector. Each of the six repetitions was used in turn as the test vector for each of the 10 speakers. The identification decision was based on the non-Euclidean distance measure defined in (18). The pooled intra-speaker covariance matrix was obtained by averaging over 50 utterances of the 10 speakers in the training set.

A number of different parametric representations of speech derived from the all-pole representation were examined to determine if any one of them is more effective than the other for speaker recognition. Amongst the parameters examined were the predictor coefficients, impulse response of the all-pole filter, autocorrelation function, area function, and cepstrum function of the impulse response—all of which have the interesting property that they can be derived from each other. The mathematical relationships between these different representations are discussed in detail in [14] and are omitted here except for the cepstrum function which proved to be the most effective of all for speaker recognition. The cepstrum by definition is the inverse Fourier transform of the logarithm of the transfer function [18], [53]. For the all-pole filter of Fig. 4, the logarithm of the transfer function is written as

$$\ln H(z) = C(z) = \sum_{n=1}^{\infty} c_n z^{-n} \tag{25}$$

where z is the usual z-transform variable [55]. The desired relationship between c_n's and a_n's is given by [14], [53]

$$\begin{aligned} c_1 &= a_1 \\ c_n &= \sum_{k=1}^{n-1} (1 - k/n)\, a_k c_{n-k} + a_n, \qquad 1 < n \leqslant p \\ c_n &= \sum_{k=1}^{n-1} (1 - k/n)\, a_k c_{n-k}, \qquad n > p. \end{aligned} \tag{26}$$

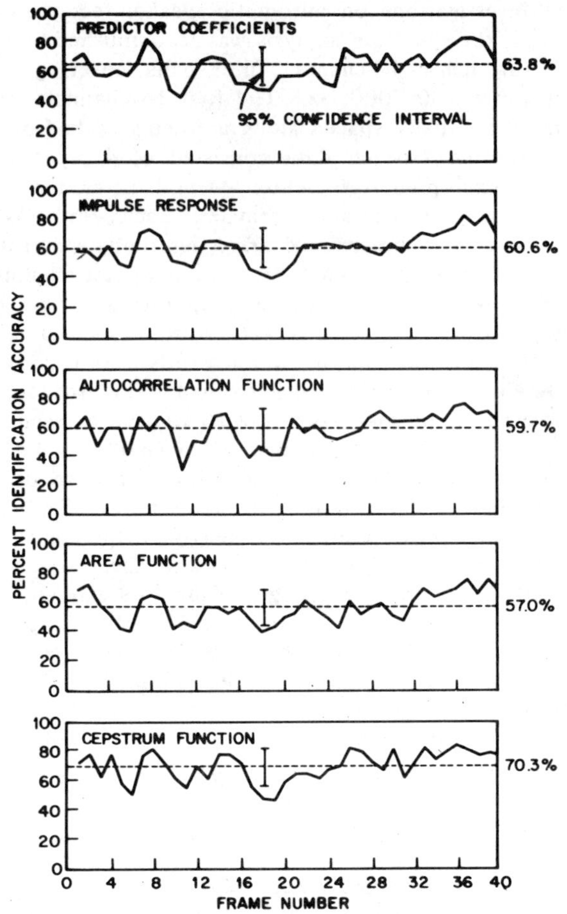

Fig. 5. Percent identification accuracy for different parametric representations of speech derived by linear prediction. Each result is based on a single frame of speech approximately 50 ms in duration.

The recognition accuracy for each of the 40 segments for the five sets of parameters is shown in Fig. 5. The number of parameters p in each case is 12 and each result is based on a total of 60 judgments. The recognition accuracy varied from one segment to another—the average standard deviation is approximately 6.0 percent. However, most of the time the variation is within the 95 percent confidence interval. The identification accuracy averaged over the 40 segments was found to be 63.8 percent for the predictor coefficients, 60.6 percent for the impulse response, 59.7 percent for the autocorrelation function, 57.0 percent for the area function, and 70.3 percent for the cepstrum function. These identification scores are quite high considering the fact that each segment has a duration of approximately 50 ms. The cepstrum function provided the highest score while the area function provided the lowest. The 95 percent confidence interval for the mean is approximately 2 percent. The mean identification score of cepstrum is thus significantly higher than the other parameters.

The identification accuracy was also determined as a function of the duration of speech included in computing the distances. An average distance was computed by averaging the distances from the individual frames. The results are shown in Fig. 6 for the 12-parameter cepstrum function. The solid curve was obtained when the duration was increased from zero onwards starting at frame 1 at the beginning of an utterance while the dashed curve was obtained when starting at the middle of the utterance. The differences between the two curves are obviously due to different texts of the two portions of the

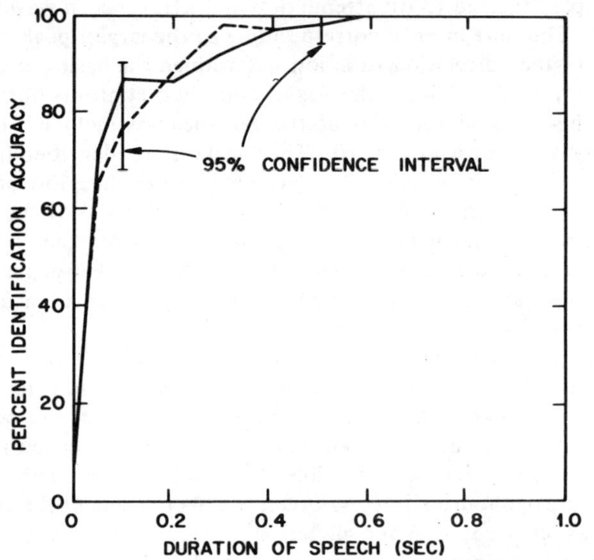

Fig. 6. Percent identification accuracy as a function of the duration of the speech sample based on 12 cepstrum parameters. The solid curve is for speech starting at the beginning of the utterance, while the dashed curve is for speech starting at the middle of the utterance.

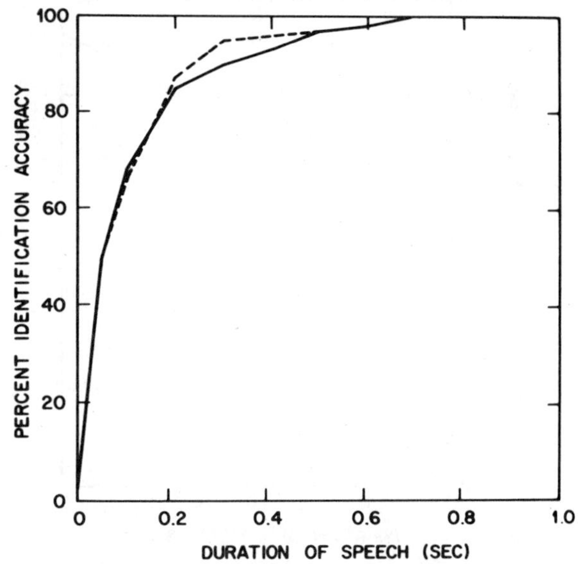

Fig. 7. Percent identification accuracy as a function of speech duration when the time average of the cepstrum parameters is eliminated from the data. The solid curve is for speech starting at the beginning of the utterance, while the dashed curve is for speech starting at the middle of the utterance.

utterance. The 95 percent confidence intervals are also marked at two places suggesting that the differences between the two curves are probably not significant. The recognition accuracy is approximately 80 percent for a duration of 0.1 s and is greater than 98 percent for durations of 0.5 s and higher. These results are very similar to those reported by Pruzansky for the spectral data [3].

All of the linear prediction parameters discussed so far are also affected by the frequency response of the recording apparatus as well as the transmission system. The cepstrum parameters, however, have the additional advantage that one can derive from them a set of parameters which are invariant to any fixed frequency-response distortions introduced by the recording apparatus or the transmission system. The new parameters are obtained simply by subtracting from the cepstrum parameters their time averages performed over the entire utterance. This result follows directly from the property of the cepstrum; namely, it is the logarithm of the overall transfer function. Since, the transfer function of the transmission system introduces a frequency-dependent multiplicative factor in the overall transfer function, the net result in the cepstrum is an additive frequency-dependent factor. If this factor does not vary in a short interval of a few seconds—a typical duration of an utterance—it is eliminated by subtracting the time-averaged cepstrum. The identification accuracy as a function of the duration of the spoken material based on the cepstrum parameters with their time averages removed is shown in Fig. 7. The significance of the solid and dashed curves is the same as in Fig. 6. There are no major differences between the two curves. The results show an identification accuracy of 68 percent for a duration of 0.1 s and an accuracy of greater than 98 percent for a duration of 0.6 s and higher. On comparing these results with the ones in Fig. 6—where the temporal averages were not removed—one finds the identification accuracy to be slightly lower (68 percent as compared to 80 percent for a duration of 0.1 s) but not significantly so. In fact, for durations larger than about 0.3 s, the differences are very minor. This result is not surprising. An increase in duration brings in more phonemes in the recognition process causing a decrease in the error rate. This decrease is slower in the case of Fig. 6 owing to higher correlation between the parameters of different phonemes. The higher correlations are introduced by the average frequency response of the utterance which is common to all phonemes in the utterance.

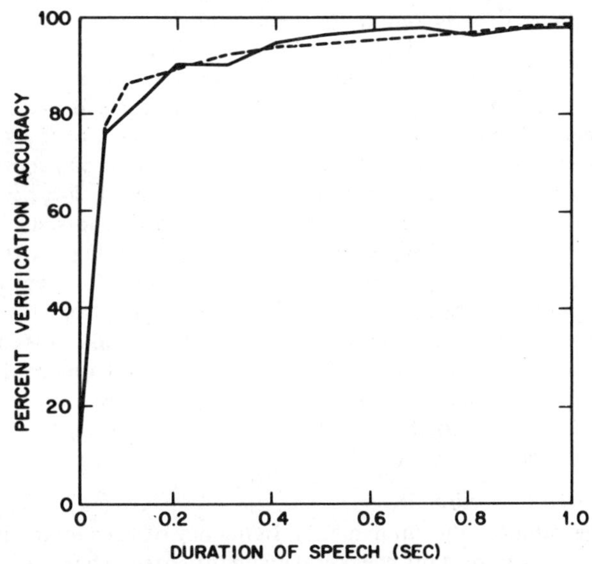

Fig. 8. Percent verification accuracy as a function of speech duration based on 12 cepstrum parameters with their time averages subtracted out. The solid and the dashed curves refer to the same conditions as in Fig. 7.

Tests were also conducted to determine the effectiveness of cepstrum parameters for automatic speaker verification. The speaker was verified if the distance between his utterance vector and the reference vector of the claimed speaker was smaller than a preselected threshold value. The results are shown in Fig. 8. A verification accuracy of 90 percent was achieved for a duration of 0.2 s and of 98 percent for a duration of 1.0 s.

The possibility of text-independent speaker recognition was also investigated in this study. Twelve cepstrum parameters

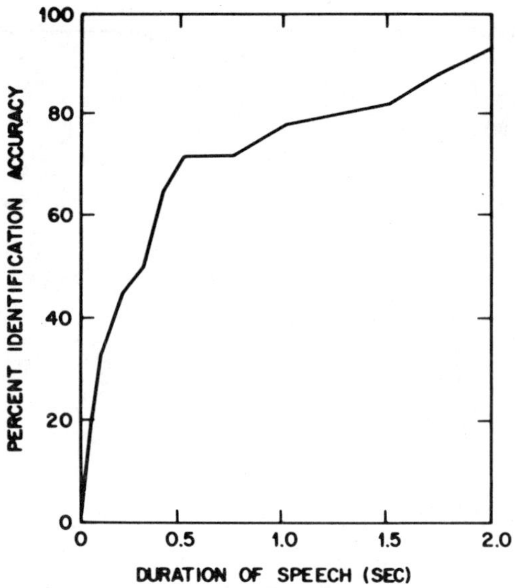

Fig. 9. Percent identification accuracy as a function of speech duration when the texts of the test and reference speech samples are different.

were again used with the distance measure of (18). The time synchronization between the reference and the test utterances was destroyed by cutting each utterance into 40 equal segments and later recombining them in random order to form a new utterance. The identification accuracy as a function of the duration of the spoken material is shown in Fig. 9. The identification accuracy is only 17 percent for a duration of 50 ms but increases to 72 percent for a duration of 0.5 s and to 93 percent for a duration of 2 s. The recognition accuracy, although lower than in the text-dependent case, is surprisingly high considering the difficult nature of the task involved.

A recent study by Furui and Itakura [55] using PARCOR coefficients [37, 39] reports similar results both for identification and verification tasks. The speech data base for the speaker identification study consisted of 4 words spoken by 9 speakers over a period of 3 months and yielded a recognition rate of 99.1 percent. The number of speakers were increased to 37 for the verification task and resulted in an accuracy of 99.2 percent.

C. Pitch Contours

The pitch or the fundamental frequency of vocal-cord vibrations is an important speaker-dependent speech characteristic. Several studies [6], [10], [19], [25], [30] have found pitch to be an effective parameter for automatic speaker recognition. The average pitch for a speaker varies considerably from one individual to another but by itself is not sufficient to distinguish between many speakers. A more interesting source of speaker-dependent information is the entire pitch contour describing the variation of pitch as a function of time in a sentence-length utterance. Pitch has an important advantage over the spectral information since it is not affected by frequency characteristics of the recording or the transmission system. A speaker-identification study based exclusively on the pitch information is described in [25]. The speech data base employed in the study is identical to the one used for the linear prediction characteristics [14] and thus it allows us to compare the relative performance of pitch and linear prediction information for speaker identification.

The pitch analysis in this study [6, 25] was carried out by performing a short-time correlation analysis on the cubed and low-pass filtered (3-dB attenuation at 1 kHz) speech waveform [6]. The time interval corresponding to the largest peak in the short-time correlation function determined the basic period of the waveform. Two examples of the pitch contours obtained by this method for each of the ten speakers included in the study are shown in Fig. 10. The speakers are identified in the figure by their initials. The ordinate is the duration of the pitch period in ms (pitch period is the reciprocal of the fundamental frequency) and the abcissa represents the time in seconds. The pitch contours are strongly speaker-dependent and yet are quite stable within the utterances of a single speaker.

For speaker identification, each pitch contour was represented by 40 samples spaced uniformly along the utterance. The pitch data was further compressed to a smaller set of parameters by the Karhunen–Loève (KL) transformation [26]. This compression was possible due to high correlations between neighbouring pitch samples. A 20-component KL representation accounted for all but 0.5 percent of the total variance. As before, five utterances of each speaker were used to form his reference pattern while the sixth one served as the test pattern. The identification decision was based on a non-Euclidean distance metric essentially similar to one described in (18). The overall percentage of correct identifications based on a total of 60 judgments was found to be 97 percent. A number of different recognition procedures were also tested on the same data to compare them with the non-Euclidean distance metric. The minimum-distance classification rule based on the Euclidean distance yielded only 68 percent correct identifications leading to the conclusion that the non-Euclidean distance metric reduced the misidentification rate from 32 percent to 3 percent—a reduction by a factor of over 10. The decision rule based on the crosscorrelation measure of (22) yielded a recognition rate of 70 percent—same as obtained by the Euclidean distance measure.

A somewhat different description of the pitch contours is obtained by describing each contour by the first-order probability distribution of the pitch samples in the contour. The first four central moments of the distribution yielded a recognition rate of 78 percent. Such a description retains information only about the variability of pitch in an utterance but not about the exact sequence of pitch variations as a function of time. For example, a particular sequence of pitch samples can be arranged in any arbitrary order without affecting the moments. These results suggest that the temporal information in the pitch contours is essential for reliable speaker recognition.

The results from the above study demonstrate the importance of pitch for automatic speaker recognition. These results can be directly compared with the results described earlier for the 12 cepstral coefficients [14]. The pitch-contour data provided a recognition accuracy of 97 percent for a speech utterance about 2 s in duration. On the other hand, a recognition accuracy of 98 percent was achieved for the 12 cepstral coefficients with a duration of only 0.5 s which is four times shorter than needed for pitch contours. Since the cepstral coefficients represent information about the spectral envelope of the speech signal, these results suggest that the spectral envelope is much more effective than the fine structure of the spectrum for automatic speaker recognition. Interestingly, a similar result was obtained by Miller in a study [56] involving human listeners to determine the relative importance of articulatory and source characteristics for speaker identifiability.

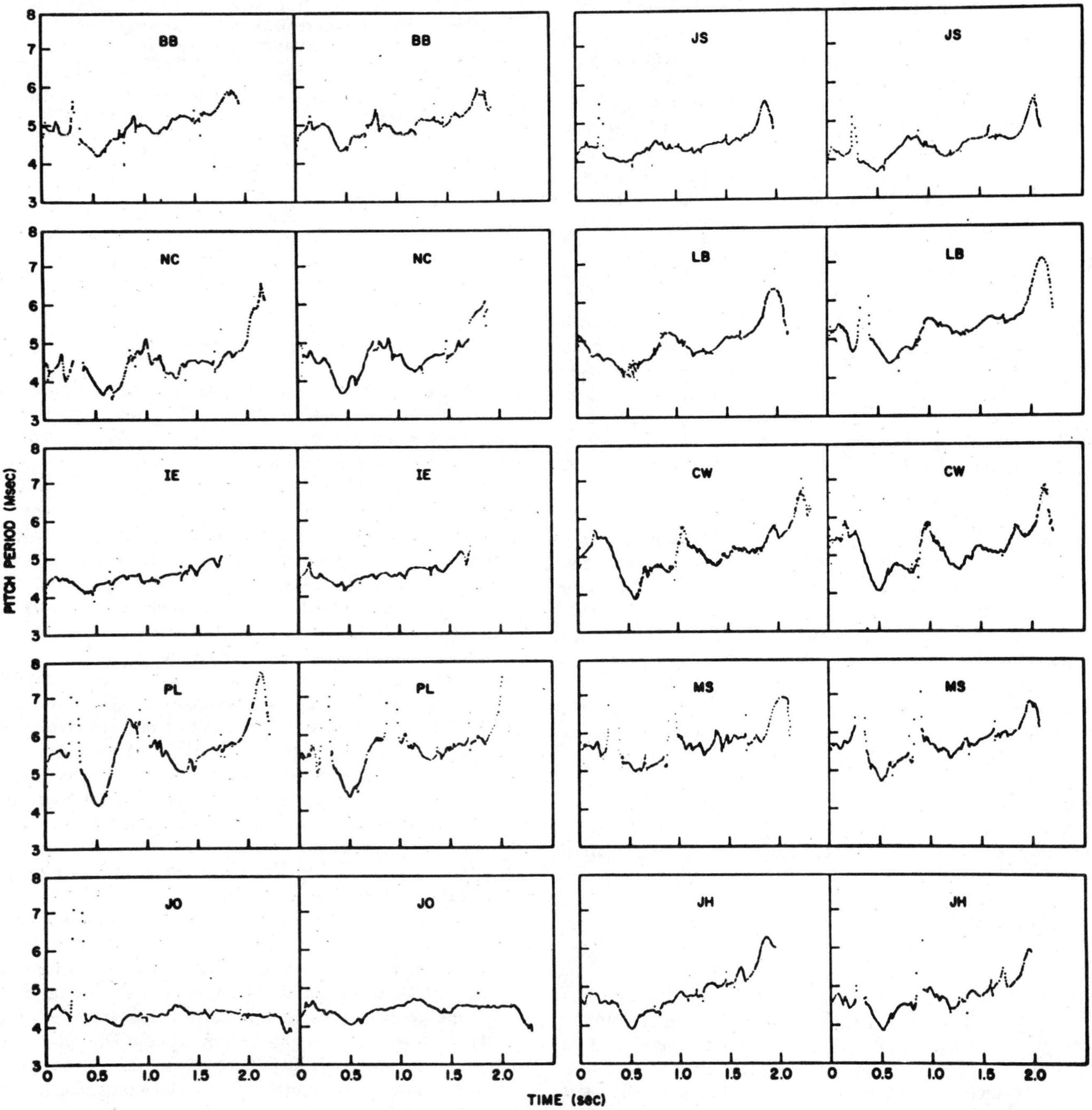

Fig. 10. Some examples of the pitch contours for the ten speakers. The sentence spoken was "May we all learn a yellow lion roar".

D. Spectral Correlations

The samples of short-time power spectrum of speech at different frequencies show significant correlations. Since these correlations are caused by the vocal-tract resonances, they are expected to be speaker dependent. These correlations are also a function of the text of the speech utterance used in computing the correlations. Such text dependence can be avoided by including a sufficiently long utterance containing a variety of speech events. Li *et al.* [45] have examined the correlational properties of speech spectra in considerable detail. Their main conclusions are: 1) the estimates of the correlation coefficients converge to a set of stable values after about 30 s of speech material is included; 2) the correlations exhibit strong speaker dependent behavior. Spectral correlations are usually characterized by a matrix of spectral correlations. In another study, Li and Hughes [15] measured the quantitative differences between the spectral correlation matrices of different speakers and of different utterances of the same speaker. The intraspeaker differences were found to be consistently less than the interspeaker differences. For a population of 30 speakers, the distribution of the two differences—interspeaker and intraspeaker—had about 1 percent overlap. These results suggest that the spectral correlations could be very useful for text-independent speaker recognition.

V. Speaker Recognition By Human Listeners

The results presented in the last section demonstrate clearly the feasibility of automatic speaker recognition—at least within the laboratory environment. The performance of automatic speaker recognition systems under "real world" conditions is discussed by Rosenberg in a companion paper [48]. In this section, we will present some results concerning the performance of human listeners in speaker recognition.

The question "How accurate are the automatic methods compared to the human listeners?" comes up quite often in any discussion on speaker recognition. It is also a question which is rather difficult to answer owing to the differences in the tasks performed by the automatic methods and the human listeners. For example, in order to perform satisfactorily, the present automatic methods require that the texts of the test and the reference utterances be identical. On the other hand, such a restriction is seldom necessary for human speaker recognition; the human listeners can recognize familiar voices with high accuracy irrespective of the text being spoken. A comparison between automatic methods and human listeners usually ends up in the selection of a speaker-recognition task that can be performed reasonably well by automatic methods, which is obviously unfair to human listeners. The results presented in this section should thus be interpreted with considerable caution.

A number of experimental studies have been conducted to investigate different aspects of human speaker recognition [57]-[63]. Several of these have been aimed at finding the perceptual factors which are important in human speaker recognition [59], [60]. The results of such studies however cannot be directly used for comparing the performance with automatic methods. At least two studies [61]-[62] have been reported in which the task before the human listeners was comparable to the one faced by the automatic methods—that is of identifying the speaker of an unknown utterance by direct listening to speech samples corresponding to the reference and the test utterances.

One of the earliest studies on speaker recognition by human listeners was conducted by McGehee [58]. The study included 5 speakers who read a paragraph of text to a group of listeners *unfamiliar* with the talkers. The identification accuracy was found to depend upon the elapsed time interval between the test and training sessions. For example, the identification accuracy decreased from 83 percent for a time interval of 1 day to 69 percent for a time interval of 2 weeks.

A more comprehensive study involving human listeners was carried out by Bricker and Pruzansky [61] in an attempt to determine the influence of the duration and phonetic content of the spoken utterance on the identifiability of speakers. Their study included 10 speakers and 16 listeners who were familiar with all of the speakers. The listeners were however not able to access the reference samples of different speakers for comparison during the test session. Each speaker recorded all of his material in a single session. The average identification score together with the durations of the spoken material are shown in Table II. The identification scores ranged from 56 percent for vowel excerpts to 98 percent for sentence-length utterances. The identification score was found to increase with the number of phonemes in the utterance. The scores presented in Table II are the average values for the 16 listeners. The individual scores varied considerably. As an example, for the vowel excerpts, the range of variation was between 39 and 75 percent.

Another study which allowed the listeners to hear the reference samples of the speakers is reported in [62]. This study included eight known speakers whose samples were available to the listeners for comparison in the tests. The speech material consisted of five repetitions of 11 words. A total of 10 listeners participated in the tests. The identification scores varied between different words, between different speakers, and between different listeners. The approximate identification score averaged over all the speakers and listeners was 89 percent for monosyllabic words and 91 percent for two-syllable words, phrases, and sentences. The identification score was not found to improve significantly once the number of syllables exceeded two. The average length of the two-syllable words was slightly under 1 s. The error rates for different words differed by a factor of 2.5 to 1. The error rates for different listeners differed by a factor of 3 to 1.

TABLE II
IDENTIFICATION SCORES OF HUMAN LISTENERS FOR FIVE TYPES OF SPEECH MATERIAL

Speech Material	Duration msec	Percent Correct
Vowel excerpts	117	56
CV excerpts	117	63
Monosyllables	498	81
Disyllables	446	87
Sentences	2400	98

A recent study by Rosenberg [11] reports the performance of human listeners in a speaker-verification task. The listeners were asked to respond whether a pair of test and reference utterances were spoken by the same or different speakers. The speech utterance was a 2-s long all-voiced sentence "We were away a year ago". The human listeners achieved an accuracy of 96 percent correct within a population of 40 speakers. An automatic method using formant, pitch, and intensity data from the same set of utterances provided a verification accuracy of 98 percent.

These studies provide a rough estimate of the performance of human listeners in identifying speakers. A strict comparison between the identification scores of automatic methods and human listeners cannot be made due to the differences in the speech data base as well as the differences in the test formats. However, it is interesting to compare these results with those presented in Fig. 6 based on the 12 cepstral parameters. The performance of the automatic method is at least comparable if not better. In this particular case, the results are quite intriguing if one considers the fact that human listeners could use the pitch, the intensity, and the timing information, as well as the spectral information, while the automatic method was constrained to use only the spectral envelope information contained in the 12 cepstral parameters.

VI. Concluding Remarks

The research on automatic methods for speaker recognition has reached a turning point. It is a proper time to look back and ask some basic questions. What have we learned so far? What are the remaining unresolved problems? Where do we proceed from here?

One of the original objectives of research on automatic speaker recognition was to find out if computers could be programmed to recognize speakers from their voices. It is obvious that automatic speaker recognition within small speaker populations is possible—at least, under laboratory environments—and, in this sense, the objective has been fulfilled.

A somewhat different motivation for speaker-recognition research came from a desire to isolate speaker-dependent parameters of speech from message-dependent ones. So far, little progress has been made in this respect. Most of the present evidence suggests that speaker-related and message-related information in speech are mixed in a fairly complicated fashion at the acoustic level. Almost every acoustic parameter derived from speech is speaker-dependent to some extent. Fortunately, the ability to define a set of simple and physically meaningful parameters for speech conveying information solely about the speaker is not crucial for the success of automatic methods. Modern statistical techniques enable us to combine the contributions of a large number of parameters—each of them individually might carry only a limited amount of information about the speaker—into a single measure which is highly selective in representing speaker-related information in speech. Our present knowledge of many of the transformations occurring during speech production at different levels—semantic, linguistic, articulatory, and acoustic—is very limited. Perhaps satisfactory answers to a number of basic questions relating to the manner in which speaker-related information is embedded in speech must wait till we gain a better understanding of the various physical processes involved in human speech production.

The motivation for future speaker-recognition research would come in part from a desire to find practical and economical applications of automatic speaker recognition. Past studies have left unanswered many questions of practical importance. For example, can the results based on small speaker populations be generalized to include large ones? Most practical applications are likely to involve considerably more speakers than have been used in experimental studies so far. The accuracy with which a particular speech parameter can be determined often depends upon the speaking environment. Results based on speech recorded under conditions which are free from noise and reverberation cannot be expected to provide a realistic estimate of the performance under practical conditions. One cannot always assume that the parameter-extraction method found to work well with a few speakers would continue to work satisfactorily for a large number of speakers. Very often, the speaker-recognition performance is found to depend upon the elapsed time between the recordings of the reference and the test utterances. It is inconvenient in practical systems to update the reference utterance of various speakers at frequent intervals. More research is needed to identify speech characteristics which show a high degree of stability over time. Finally, most speaker-recognition studies so far have used cooperative speakers who are not interested in fooling the machine, not a realistic situation for practical systems. Studies are needed to test the performance under the conditions where the impostors have some motivation to mimic.

References

[1] F. McGehee, "The reliability of the identification of human voice," *J. Gen. Psychol.*, vol. 17, pp. 249–271, 1937.

[2] I. Pollack, J. M. Pickett, and W. H. Sumby, "On the identification of speakers by voice," *J. Acoust. Soc. Amer.*, vol. 26, pp. 403–406, May 1954.

[3] S. Pruzansky, "Pattern-matching procedure for automatic talker recognition," *J. Acoust. Soc. Amer.*, vol. 35, pp. 354–358, Mar. 1963.

[4] W. Hargreaves and J. A. Starkweather, "Recognition of speaker identity," *Lang. Speech*, vol. 6, pp. 63–67, 1963.

[5] K. P. Li, J. E. Dammann, and W. D. Chapman, "Experimental studies in speaker verification using an adaptive system," *J. Acoust. Soc. Amer.*, vol. 40, pp. 966–978, Nov. 1966.

[6] B. S. Atal, "Automatic speaker recognition based on pitch contours," Ph.D. dissertation, Polytech. Inst. Brooklyn, Brooklyn, NY, June 1968.

[7] P. D. Bricker *et al.*, "Statistical techniques for talker identification," *Bell Syst. Tech. J.*, vol. 50, pp. 1427–1454, Apr. 1971.

[8] S. K. Das and W. S. Mohn, "A scheme for speech processing in automatic speaker verification," *IEEE Trans. Audio Electroacoust.*, vol. AU-19, pp. 32–43, Mar. 1971.

[9] J. E. Luck, "Automatic speaker verification using cepstral measurements," *J. Acoust. Soc. Amer.*, vol. 46, pp. 1026–1032, Oct. 1969.

[10] G. R. Doddington, "A method of speaker verification," Ph.D. dissertation, Univ. Wisconsin, 1970.

[11] A. E. Rosenberg, "Listener performance in speaker verification tasks," *IEEE Trans. Audio Electroacoust.*, vol. AU-21, pp. 221–225, 1973.

[12] P. Garvin and P. Ladefoged, "Speaker identification and message identification in speech recognition," *Phonetica*, vol. 9, no. 4, pp. 193–199, 1963.

[13] M. H. L. Hecker, *Speaker Recognition: An Interpretive Survey of the Literature, ASHA Monogr.* 16 (American Speech and Hearing Association, Washington, DC), Jan. 1971.

[14] B. S. Atal, "Effectiveness of linear prediction characteristics of the speech wave for automatic speaker identification and verification," *J. Acoust. Soc. Amer.*, vol. 55, pp. 1304–1312, June 1974.

[15] K. -P. Li and G. W. Hughes, "Talker differences as they appear in correlation matrices of continuous speech spectra," *J. Acoust. Soc. Amer.*, vol. 55, pp. 833–837, Apr. 1974.

[16] S. Furui, F. Itakura, and S. Saito, "Talker recognition by long-time averaged speech spectrum," *Electron. Commun. Jap.*, vol. 55A, pp. 54–61, Oct. 1972.

[17] J. H. Friedman, J. L. Bentley, and R. A. Finkel, "An algorithm for finding best matches in logarithmic time," Stanford Linear Accelerator Center Rep. SLAC-PUB-1549, Feb. 1975. This paper has been submitted for publication in the Communications of the ACM.

[18] R. W. Schafer and L. R. Rabiner, "Digital representations of speech signals," *Proc. IEEE*, vol. 63, pp. 662–677, Apr. 1975.

[19] J. J. Wolf, "Efficient acoustic parameters for speaker recognition," *J. Acoust. Soc. Amer.*, vol. 51, pt. 2, pp. 2044–2055, June 1972.

[20] M. R. Sambur, "Selection of acoustic features for speaker identification," *IEEE Trans. Acoust., Speech, Signal Processing*, vol. ASSP-23, pp. 176–182, Apr. 1975.

[21] S. Pruzansky and M. V. Mathews, "Talker-recognition procedure based on analysis of variance," *J. Acoust. Soc. Amer.*, vol. 36, pp. 2041–2047, Nov. 1964.

[22] W. S. Mohn Jr., "Two statistical feature evaluation techniques applied to speaker identification," *IEEE Trans. Comput.*, vol. C-20, pp. 979–987, Sept. 1971.

[23] S. Kullback, *Information Theory and Statistics.* New York: Wiley, 1959, p. 6.

[24] T. Marill and D. M. Green, "On the effectiveness of receptors in recognition systems," *IEEE Trans. Inform. Theory*, vol. IT-9, pp. 11–17, Jan. 1963.

[25] B. S. Atal, "Automatic speaker recognition based on pitch contours," *J. Acoust. Soc. Amer.*, vol. 52, pp. 1687–1697, Dec. 1972.

[26] S. Watanabe, "Karhunen-Loève expansion and factor analysis," in *Trans. IV Prague Conf. Information Theory, Statistical Decision, Functions, Random Processes.* Prague: Academia Publishing House, Czechoslovak Academy of Science, 1967, pp. 635–660.

[27] M. R. Schroeder and B. S. Atal, "Generalised short-time power spectra and autocorrelation functions." *J. Acoust. Soc. Amer.*, vol. 34, pp. 1679–1683, Nov. 1962.

[28] J. L. Flanagan, *Speech Analysis Synthesis and Perception*, 2nd ed. New York: Springer-Verlag, 1972, pp. 141–161.

[29] R. B. Blackman and J. W. Tukey, *The Measurement of Power Spectra.* New York: Dover, 1959.

[30] G. R. Doddington, "A method of speaker verification," *J. Acoust. Soc. Amer.*, vol. 49, pt. 1, p. 139(A), Jan. 1971.

[31] R. C. Lummis, "Speaker verification by computer using speech intensity for temporal registration," *IEEE Trans. Audio Electroacoust.*, vol. AU-21, pp. 80–89, 1973.

[32] A. M. Noll, "Cepstrum pitch determination," *J. Acoust. Soc. Amer.*, vol. 41, pp. 293–309, Feb. 1967.

[33] M. M. Sondhi, "New methods of pitch detection," *IEEE Trans. Audio Electroacoust.*, vol. AU-16, pp. 262–266, June 1968.

[34] B. Gold and L. R. Rabi. Parallel processing techniques for estimating pitch periods of speech in the time domain," *J.*

Acoust. Soc. Amer., vol. 46, pp. 442–449, Aug. 1969.

[35] J. D. Markel, "The SIFT algorithm for fundamental frequency estimation," *IEEE Trans. Audio Electroacoust.*, vol. AU-20, pp. 367–377, Dec. 1972.

[36] B. S. Atal and S. L. Hanauer, "Speech analysis and synthesis by linear prediction of the speech wave," *J. Acoust. Soc. Amer.*, vol. 50, pt. 2, pp. 637–655, Aug. 1971.

[37] F. Itakura and S. Saito, "An analysis-synthesis telephony system based on maximum likelihood method," *Electron. Commun. Japan*, vol. 53A, pp. 36–43, 1970.

[38] J. Makhoul, "Linear prediction: A tutorial review," *Proc. IEEE*, vol. 63, pp. 561–580, Apr. 1975.

[39] J. D. Markel, A. H. Gray, Jr., and H. Wakita, "Linear prediction of speech: Theory and practice," Speech Communications Res. Lab., Santa Barbara, CA, SCRL Monogr. 10, Sept. 1973.

[40] R. W. Schaefer and L. R. Rabiner, "System for automatic formant analysis of voiced speech," *J. Acoust. Soc. Amer.*, vol. 47, pp. 634–648, Feb. 1970.

[41] J. Olive, "Automatic formant tracking by a Newton-Raphson technique," *J. Acoust. Soc. Amer.*, vol. 50, pt. 2, pp. 661–670, Aug. 1971.

[42] J. D. Markel, "Digital inverse filtering—a new tool for formant trajectory estimation," *IEEE Trans. Audio Electroacoust.*, vol. AU-20, pp. 129–137, June 1972.

[43] S. S. McCandless, "An algorithm for automatic formant extraction using linear prediction spectra," *IEEE Trans. Acoust., Speech, Signal Processing*, vol. ASSP-22, pp. 135–141, Apr. 1974.

[44] Lo-Soun Su, K. -P. Li, and K. S. Fu, "Identification of speakers by use of nasal coarticulation," *J. Acoust. Amer.*, vol. 56, pp. 1876–1882, Dec. 1974.

[45] K. P. Li, G. W. Hughes, and A. S. House, "Correlation characteristics and dimensionality of speech spectra," *J. Acoust. Soc. Amer.*, vol. 46, pt. 2, pp. 1019–1025, Oct. 1969.

[46] G. R. Doddington, J. L. Flanagan, and R. C. Lummis, "Automatic speaker verification by nonlinear time alignment of acoustic parameters," U. S. Patent 3, 700, 815, issued Oct. 24, 1972.

[47] A. E. Rosenberg, "Evaluation of an automatic speaker verification system over telephone lines," *Bell Syst. Tech. J.*, to be published in 1976.

[48] A. E. Rosenberg, "Automatic speaker verification systems: a review," this issue, pp. 475–487.

[49] F. Itakura, "Minimum prediction residual principle applied to speech recognition," *IEEE Trans. Acoust., Speech, Signal Processing*, vol. ASSP-23, pp. 67–72, Feb. 1975.

[50] T. Y. Young and T. W. Calvert, *Classification, Estimation, and Pattern Recognition.* New York: American Elsevier 1974, pp. 24–26.

[51] M. R. Sambur, "Speaker recognition and verification using linear prediction analysis," Ph.D. dissertation, Massachusetts Inst. Technol., Cambridge, Sept. 1972.

[52] A. E. Rosenberg and M. R. Sambur, "New techniques for automatic speaker verification," *IEEE Trans. Acoust., Speech, Signal Processing*, vol. ASSP-23, Apr. 1975.

[53] A. V. Oppenheim and R. W. Schafer, "Homomorphic analysis of speech," *IEEE Trans. Audio Electroacoust.*, vol. AU-16, pp. 221–226, June 1968.

[54] J. R. Ragazzini and G. F. Franklin, *Sampled-Data Control Systems.* New York: McGraw-Hill, 1958.

[55] S. Furui and F. Itakura, "Talker recognition by statistical features of speech," *Electron. Commun. Jap.*, vol. 56A, pp. 62–71, Nov. 1973.

[56] J. E. Miller, "Decapicitation and recapicitation, a study of voice quality," *J. Acoust. Soc. Amer.*, vol. 36, p. 1876 (A), Oct. 1964.

[57] Reference 13, pp. 24–49.

[58] F. McGehee, "An experimental study in voice recognition," *J. Gen. Psychol.*, vol. 31, pp. 53–65, 1944.

[59] G. L. Holmgren, "Physical and psychological correlates of speaker recognition," *J. Speech Hearing Res.*, vol. 10, pp. 57–66, 1967.

[60] W. D. Voiers, "Perceptual bases of speaker identity," *J. Acoust. Soc. Amer.*, vol. 36, pp. 1065–1073, June 1964.

[61] P. D. Bricker and S. Pruzansky, "Effects of stimulus content and duration on talker identification," *J. Acoust. Soc. Amer.*, vol. 40, pp. 1441–1449, June 1966.

[62] K. N. Stevens, C. E. Williams, J. R. Carbonell, and B. Woods, "Speaker authentication and identification: A comparison of spectrographic and auditory presentations of speech material," *J. Acoust. Soc. Amer.*, vol. 44, pp. 1596–1607, Dec. 1968.

[63] F. R. Clarke and R. W. Becker, "Comparison of techniques for discriminating among talkers," *J. Speech Hearing Res.*, vol. 12, pp. 747–761, 1969.

Part VIII
Speaker Recognition Systems

A Scheme for Speech Processing in Automatic Speaker Verification

S. K. DAS
W. S. MOHN
IBM Corporation
Research Triangle Park, N. C. 27709

Abstract

Experiments investigating adaptive pattern recognition in automatic speaker verification are reported. A binary decision confirming or rejecting a speaker's purported identity is required. The experiments involve 7000 phrase length utterances of 118 speakers. An average misclassification rate of one percent with a "no decision" rate of ten percent is obtained. Other experiments indicate that the utterances used for training purposes should preferably be collected over a relatively long period of time.

Manuscript received July 15, 1970.

I. Introduction

The problem of speaker verification continues to be a challenge to many investigators [1], [2], [4]. In this problem, the identity of a person who utters a certain phrase is confirmed from an analysis of the phrase and some knowledge of the speaker's speech characteristics obtained from earlier utterances of the same phrase. The person is referred to as a "real" speaker. At the same time, the system should be able to reject other speakers who might falsely claim to be the real speaker. Thus, they are referred to as "impostors." A real speaker and the impostors represent the two classes that the verification system is designed to separate.

Implementation of a speaker verification system involves a combination of speech processing techniques and pattern recognition methodology. This will be clear from Fig. 1, which depicts the proposed system. Utterances of a suitable phrase are first tape recorded by all of the speakers. These analog utterances are then digitized by using a vocoder type of speech analyzer (Section II). These are the preliminary steps of speech processing and are carried out in hardware. The digitized data are stored on digital tapes and form the input to a software system. The first stage of this software system serves to segment the utterances (Section III). This is essentially a pattern recognition scheme in which various events in the utterances are identified. The identified events are used to align the utterances properly so that appropriate features can be extracted from the segmented data (Section IV). This is a further stage of speech processing and is expected to yield feature sets suitable for speaker discrimination. These feature sets are used in a pattern recognition task for creating one reference profile for each real speaker or, in a different operational mode, for making a verification decision (Section V).

It is interesting to compare the tasks of the segmentation and the feature extraction process. The first one is designed to detect corresponding events from various utterances of all speakers. Thus, it places emphasis on phenomena that are similar among the speakers, but different among the events constituting the speech sample. On the other hand, the feature extraction procedure is designed to obtain features which distinguish speakers from one another. Thus, it places emphasis on phenomena that are different among the speakers, but are similar in terms of the speech events.

This paper describes principally the procedures followed in data collection, digitization, segmentation, and feature extraction. The techniques for creating a reference profile for a speaker and for eventual decision making are dealt with briefly since they have been described in detail elsewhere [1]. The structure of the verification system is such that it is fully automatic after its implementation. This feature is essential in order that the system can be feasible in practical applications and in order that a large-scale experiment such as the one reported here for performance validation may be under-

Reprinted from *IEEE Trans. Audio Electroacoust.*, vol. AU-19, pp. 32–43, Mar. 1971.

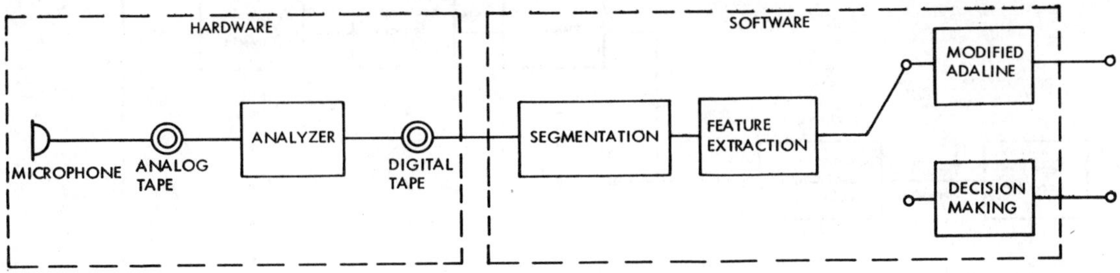

Fig. 1. Experimental setup.

taken. The last section of the paper includes some comments about the experiments and some observations regarding possible future work.

II. Data Collection

One of the significant factors that distinguishes this work from earlier reported experiments in the same field by other research workers is the size of the data base [2]–[4]. In speaker verification, large amounts of data are required for several reasons. In the case of each real speaker, sufficient data must be available to "train" the verification system, and an independent set of utterances must be available to later test the system. In the case of impostors, many speakers must be available to test the system's sensitivity to nonreals, and in some cases to "train" the system in the first place. Complications arise in the collection of sufficient data since each speaker must be sampled at a number of different times to gain a representative sample of his speech variability. In other words, all of the training utterances cannot be gathered at one time if accurate verification of later utterances is desired. It has been found that utterances should be collected over a period of several weeks, ideally being spread uniformly over that period. It is difficult to gather such data in a controlled manner so one is forced to schedule recording sessions in which several utterances are collected at one time.

An easy way to organize a recording session would be to have the speaker repeat the chosen verification phrase a number of times, one right after the other. This violates the requirement that the utterances must be representative of isolated examples from the speaker as would be encountered in practical use. Therefore, some task must be inserted between each utterance to "neutralize" the speaker. The data collection procedure about to be described followed these guidelines.

The five phrases listed in Table I were selected for the data collection phase. They were selected according to the following criteria: 1) each must be made up of words familiar to the speakers; 2) each should begin with a high-energy sound to cause reliable starting of the digitizing hardware; 3) each should contain points that allow reliable segmentation of key phonetic events; and 4) each should also contain a maximum number of independent phonological events carrying speaker-specific information. A randomized ordering containing each phrase exactly ten times was created. At a given recording session, a speaker was asked to enter an acoustically treated chamber which effectively isolated the speaker acoustically from the laboratory and reduced sound reflection within the chamber. In the chamber, the speaker seated himself at a small table upon which was located a phrase indicator, a digital indicator, and a ten-digit keyboard. The speaker placed a Koss KR2+2 headset and boom-mounted microphone combination on his head. The microphone was connected to the inputs of one track of each of five tape recorders [Ampex 351–2's) to separate phrases by type. The other track of each tape recorder was used to record tones resulting from key depressions of the ten-digit keyboard. The tape recorders were interlocked so that only one could be running at a time. The phrase indicator lights were lit to indicate which phrase should be spoken. The digital indicator was simply a counter to indicate how far through the list of 50 phrases the recording has progressed.

TABLE I

Five Experimental Phrases

1) Check Intermediate Allowance
2) Check Numeric Interrogation
3) Check Available Terminals
4) Check Allowable Clearance
5) Check Preliminary Correlation

Note: All phrases recorded; only 3) digitized.

During operation, a tone coded label was recorded on each tape recorder to identify each speaker. Next, the experimenter started the tape recorders in the sequence indicated by the randomization list. As a tape recorder was started, the digital counter was incremented, the speaker keyed in the counter reading and then uttered the phrase. Generally, the speaker could not anticipate which phrase was coming next, and there was a guaranteed pause between utterances caused by the phrase-labeling keyboard task and the time during which the experimenter outside the chamber switched from one tape recorder to another. This procedure resulted in the production of sets of tapes, each containing only a single phrase, thereby simplifying eventual experimental processing.

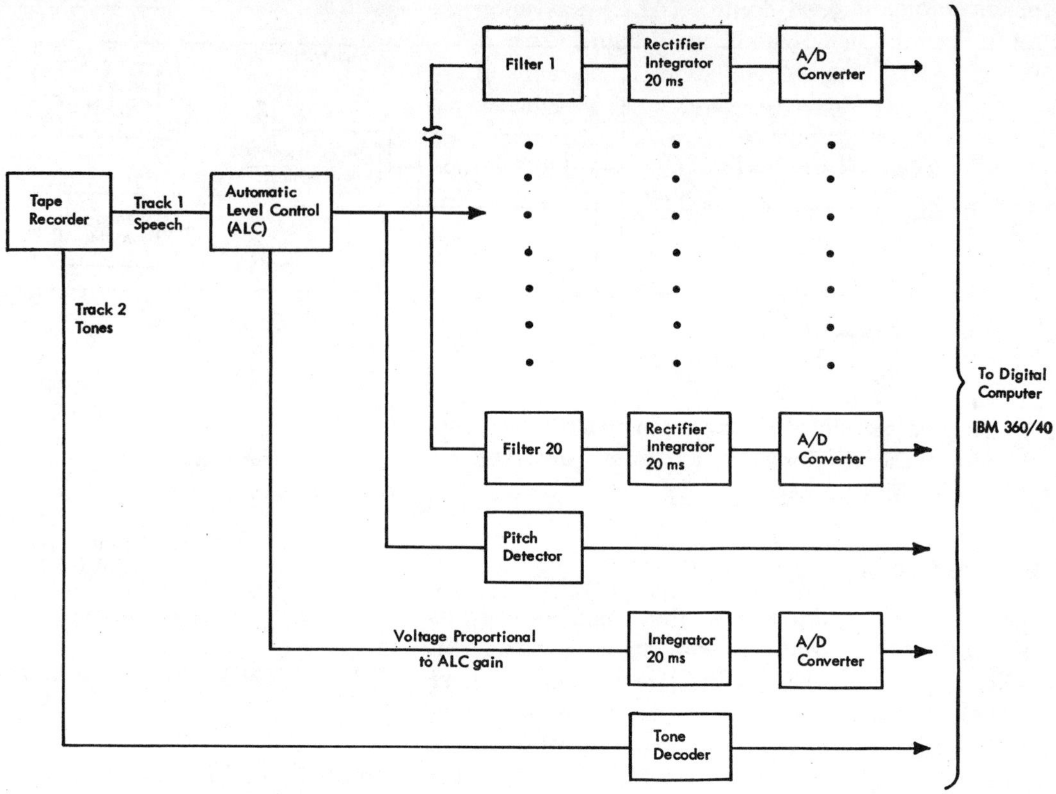

Fig. 2. Automatic digitizing system.

After the experimenter had obtained 50 utterances, the speaker was asked to leave the chamber and rest for five to ten minutes. Following this pause, the speaker reentered the chamber and the same list of phrases was recorded, in the same sequence as before. This full set of 100 utterances, 20 for each phrase, constituted a single recording session. This procedure allowed the collection of a great many utterances while maximizing utterance independence under the given time constraints and not occupying too much of each speaker's time.

The original plan called for a recording period covering five weeks using speakers who were male engineers and scientists in the laboratory. During this time, the speakers, who were arbitrarily designated as "reals," were expected to attend one recording session a week. Meanwhile, each of the speakers designated "impostor" was asked to make one recording session. Thus, each real was to produce 100 utterances of each phrase while each impostor produced only 20. Fewer were needed from each impostor since his utterances were eventually to be used for either training or testing but not both. Initially, 58 people were designated as reals and 69 as impostors. For several reasons the recording period exceeded five weeks and not all of the speakers produced a full set of utterances. This was the result of speakers being transferred, absent, or otherwise unable to attend their recording sessions on time. This resulted in only 50 usable reals and 68 usable impostors. A total of 7180 utterances of each phrase was collected by this procedure. However, the useful number was somewhat less than this for reasons about to be discussed.

TABLE II

Filter-Bank Specifications

Filter Number	Center Frequency (Hz)	±6.0 dB Bandwith (Hz)
1	188	250
2	459	250
3	715	250
4	969	250
5	1220	250
6	1472	250
7	1725	250
8	1975	250
9	2225	250
10	2475	250
11	2725	250
12	2991	290
13	3300	330
14	3659	390
15	4083	460
16	4586	550
17	5194	670
18	5954	860
19	6932	1110
20	8203	1450

The digitizing system is shown in Fig. 2. The speech analyzer consists of 20 bandpass filters covering the range of center frequencies from 188 to 8203 Hz. The center frequency and the bandwidth of each filter are listed in Table II. The output of each filter is full-wave rectified and passed to a resettable integrator with a 20-ms integration time. The value of each integral is logarithmically coded as a four-bit value spanning a 30-dB range. In addition, an automatic level control (ALC) acts upon the input to keep the signal within the dynamic range of the A/D converters. The average value of the gain of the ALC is also A/D converted every 20 ms. Finally, a separate fundamental frequency (F_0) measurement circuit quantizes and ditigizes the measured values of F_0 every 20 ms. The analyzer is described in more detail elsewhere [1], [5].

In addition to the speech analyzer, the digitizing system as a whole consisted of three parts: a tape recorder, a device for converting the tones on a second analog tape track to label information, and a digital computer system. The digitizing program performed the following functions. It first detected the speaker's identity from the initial tone sequence. Next, the phrase number was detected and the analyzer began digitizing the speech track following the receipt of the last tone. Digitizing continued until either 6 s had elapsed or the tone sequence for the following utterance began. The 6-s figure made the digitized record length reasonably short, yet while truncating very few utterances. Only one phrase, "check available terminals" has been digitized to date.

After the data were digitized, several steps were taken to insure that only valid examples of the phrase were kept for further analysis. This reduction process is summarized in Table III. (The set of analog utterances was 87 less than the planned number because speakers sometimes did not appear for recording sessions or did not provide the proper number of utterances at a recording session.) Occasional analog recordings were not digitized due to tone decoding error or digitizing program error. Some digitized utterances were removed if the person monitoring the digitizing detected either an incorrect or improperly spoken phrase, or if an utterance was digitized with the wrong label.

A program was written to eliminate silence before "check" and after "terminals." Utterances were eliminated if, after the removal of leading and trailing silence, less than 50 samples remained. It was found experimentally that no one said the full phrase in less than 1 s. This data base of almost 7000 utterances was placed on disk storage so that the next steps of segmentation and feature extraction could be performed efficiently. At this point, of the 7093 utterances of the phrase which had actually been uttered by our speakers, about 98 percent (6926) were still available and thought to be valid, properly labeled examples of "check available terminals."

TABLE III

Presegmentation Utterance Rejection

	Number of Utterances
Theoretical original analog tape	7180
Usable original analog tape	7093
Not digitized (tone sequence errors, program errors, etc.)	47
Initial digital tape	7046
Operator detected digitizing errors	59
Unrecoverable labeling errors	25
Phrase too short after silence removal	36
Resulting digitized set	6926

III. Segmentation

The previous section describes the process of collecting and digitizing the speech samples for the verification experiments. Since all the speech samples pertain to a single phrase, generally each digitized utterance may be assumed to be a collection of a known set of phonetic events in a fixed sequence. On the average, it takes about 1.5 s to pronounce the experimental phrase and considerable variations in speaking rate in different parts of different utterances are inevitable. These cause the time intervals elapsed between the various events to be inconsistent from one utterance to the next. Thus, some of these events must first be identified so that approximately identical parts of various utterances can be compared to each other. This process of identification of events is termed "segmentation."

For several reasons, the process of segmentation is one of the most critical steps. The importance of accurately performing this step cannot be overemphasized. Gross recognition errors are likely to occur if incorrectly segmented utterances are used for later processing. Previous investigators have often based their utterance alignment on the event with the maximum amplitude or energy [3], [4]. For some reported experiments, segmentation has been performed manually [6]. The former procedure is not suitable for our experiments due to the complexity of the uttered phrase; the points of maximum amplitude or energy will not be consistent with respect to the various events of interest in many utterances. The manual procedure is unacceptable due to the proposed large scale of our experiments and due to our intention to make the system fully automatic. Thus, it is necessary to adopt the laborious method of studying a number of spectrograms and devising a set of rules to detect the phonetic events of interest. The task is complicated by the broadness of the range of intraspeaker and intra-utterance variations that can be expected in the spectral representation of a given event. The crux of the segmentation scheme lies in taking into account such wide variations and yet not misidentifying any event. Due to such demands, the software programs which are designed to accomplish segmentation often become so involved with various conditional loops and branches that it is impossible to present a detailed account of their operation here. Thus, in this section, only the segmentation philosophy will be outlined; no attempt will be made to describe all of the rules.

Another matter of importance is to determine the generalization capability of the designed segmentation rules. It has been established that this is often an iterative procedure [1] in which alternate stages of designing and testing are conducted. Thus, the rules are first designed by using several utterances; next, the rules are tested for generalization on a comparable number of new utterances. If segmentation is not of desired accuracy, this test set is combined with the original design set to form the new design set. The rules derived from this design set are then tested on a comparable separate set of utterances. This process is repeated until the generalization is sufficiently accurate. At least the last generalization test should be on a considerable number of utterances from many new speakers whose utterances have never entered into the previous design stages. This should provide some confidence in the accuracy obtained. During each of the preceding design stages, the utterances in the design set must be hand-segmented by inspecting the digital spectrograms and the implicit rules followed in this process must be transformed into a set of software programs. During the generalization test, the utterances selected for this purpose are also hand-segmented in a similar manner and the segmentation points determined by the software programs are compared against the hand-segmented points for acceptability. The criteria for acceptance are entirely subjective. Thus, if an event is of short duration in an utterance, a difference of even one time sample between the hand-segmented and the program-generated points may be objectionable; but, for an event of relatively long duration, slight discrepancies of one or two time samples may be quite acceptable.

It should be clear from the previous discussion that a large amount of effort must be devoted to implementing the segmentation strategy. Some help may be obtained in the above implementation if an interactive display facility (such as an IBM 2250) is used on line. Possibilities of this approach are outlined in Section VI. In the present experiments, the phonetic event corresponding approximately to "v" in "available" is located first. (The events will be given various names for ease of description even though the names may not correspond to these phonetic events precisely in time. The important point to note is that as long as the events are determined satisfactorily in the utterances in their expected locations, the particular names attributed to these events are of little concern.) The only reason for this selection is the conviction arrived at after studying many spectrograms of the test phrase that this is the easiest event to detect with some certainty. After "v" is found, the knowledge of its location is used to determine the events of "available terminals" corresponding roughly to "l," "b," "t," "e," "s," and "m" in that sequence. Further description of the strategy of detecting these events is given in the following paragraphs. No segmentation point in "check" is determined since it is believed that little speaker-dependent information can be extracted from the pronunciation of this word as the first word of the phrase. It is pointed out here that this method of segmentation is subject to criticism. Some probable ways of improving on this approach are outlined in Section VI.

In order to locate "v," it is necessary to scan a digitized utterance from its beginning. Some simple preliminary rules are used first to find a probable location for "v"; then, a more stringent set of rules is applied to verify if it indeed is "v." If it is not "v," the scanning proceeds again.

In the preliminary set of rules, it is helpful to look for sufficient energy in filter 4 to filter 8 (844 to 2100 Hz). This is approximately the region of the second formant which appears relatively strongly at "v." Thus the filter values in this range are compared against an experimentally determined threshold. Among the more precise set of rules for detecting the presence of "v" are the following: 1) the closure before "-ble" must occur within a reasonable time period from the proposed location of "v." The criterion for what is reasonable was determined during hand-segmentation of the design data. 2) The shape of the second formant within the period from "v" to closure before "-ble" must conform to the characteristics normally encountered in the design utterances. Some variations may be expected in this shape. For example, even though the second formant often increases in frequency at the beginning of this interval, occasionally no conclusive rise is detected. The program should be able to handle these variations. 3) The first formant (filter 1 to filter 3) should be sufficiently prominent. This is determined by comparing with a second threshold.

Sometimes a "v" detected by the program is several samples earlier than what is judged to be the proper location of "v." To remedy this situation, an attempt is always made to find a second "v" location after the first one is located using the previously described plan. If a second "v" is found and if it is within a short interval from the first, the second one is taken to be the proper "v" location. As an additional confirmation, the ALC gain waveform is also checked for its typical shape around this point.

The location of "l" in "available" is determined next. The second formant which appeared strongly at "v" continues up to the this point. Thus, it is necessary to track the second formant starting from "v" and determine the location where this formant stops dropping in frequency. This point is called "l."

Next, the events called "b" and "t" are detected. "b" is evidenced by the rise of voiced energy following the b-closure. "t," similarly, is marked by the t-release aspiration following the t-closure. Two programmed functions of the digitized data were written to detect the presence of voicing and frication. The former considered the power in the lowest three filters and the latter considered the power in the upper 12 filters. The power in a set of contiguous filters was calculated by converting the log-encoded filter values produced by the hardware back to linear power scale, summing, and then reconverting to log scale. Thus, the frequency band (defined by the 6-dB points) of 63 to 840 Hz was used for voicing detection and 2100 to 8900 Hz for fricative detection. The latter range extends to somewhat lower frequencies than would normally be needed for pure fricatives but it was used to detect the T-release which was sometimes more D-like than T-like. The power in each of these bands was compared to an appropriate threshold to characterize each sample as V (primarily voicing), F (primarily frication), B (both), or none of these. To handle what unreliability remained in the F/V-finding program, the rules for "b" and "t" mentioned above were refined as follows.

The "-ble" section was determined to begin at the last continuous set of V samples before the first F samples following the previously determined segmentation point "l" (in "-vail"). The specific sample labeled "b" in this "-ble" section was that showing the sharpest increased in amplitude as evidenced by the sharpest drop in ALC gain. Thus, "b" reflects the b-release. The "t" in "term-" was found in an analogous way.

The sample labeled "e" in "term-" is the first sample of the V section immediately following the sample labeled "t."

Using these F and V functions, the first sample of the fricative ending "terminals" was called "s." The "ending" fricative was defined to be the first fricative following the last voiced sample in the utterance. Fig. 3 describes an example of the operation of these rules.

These rules have been stated in some detail to show how the apparently simple task of detecting closures in the phrase "check available terminals" can become involved when it is desired to find these closures accurately over an essentially unlimited set of talkers. Even these rules were designed only for male speech.

The last segmentation point detected is "m" in "terminals." This is done primarily by noting the behavior of the second formant region (filters 4, 5, and 6 or 844 to 1587 Hz) after "e." At "m," this formant is least prominent. The ALC waveform shape is also taken into consideration in selecting a final location.

As mentioned before, the segmentation design procedure utilizes a number of utterances in an iterative manner. For the present experiments, a total of about 300 utterances from 20 speakers was used at the final stage of the design process. The generalization capability of the segmentation strategy was checked by testing the rules on approximately 300 utterances of 20 new speakers not included in the design process. One or more of the desired events were undetected in approximately ten percent of the test utterances. Suitable techniques for dealing with these utterances may be devised at a later time. For the present experiments, however, these utterances were simply eliminated from further consideration. Thus, the phrase rejection rate was ten percent. Among the remaining utterances of the test set, "b" was detected incorrectly in one utterance and "m" appeared to be wrong in 24 utterances. When "b" was misidentified, it caused errors in the locations of "t," "e," "s," and "m" as well. One predominant source of error in "m" detection seemed to be the misrecognition of "n" in "terminals" as "m." Besides these, no other errors were apparent.

At this stage, the evaluation of the segmentation strategy was complete. Latter processing steps were carried out without any manual intervention. The total set of 6926 utterances was processed under the segmentation strategy outlined in the preceding paragraphs. Except for the utterances automatically flagged due to the phrase rejection procedure described above,

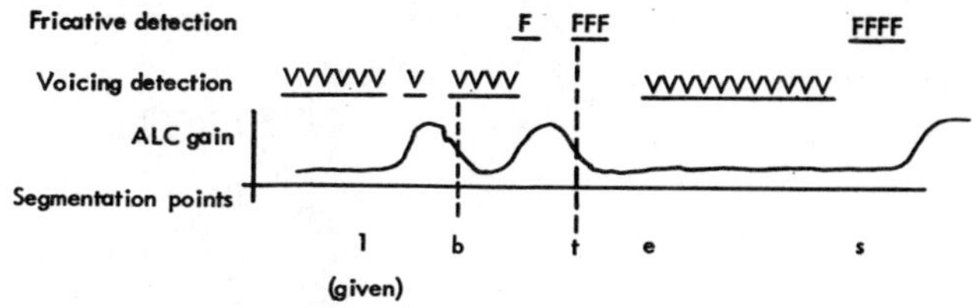

Fig. 3. Example of operation of *l*, *b*, *t*, and *s* finding rules.

all the other utterances segmented in this manner were used as inputs to the next software stage of feature extraction. No attempt was made to disregard the utterances that were segmented incorrectly since that would violate our principle of making the system fully automatic.

IV. Feature Extraction and Evaluation

Most investigators currently agree that the feature extraction step is one of the most crucial in the solution of practical pattern recognition problems. The segmentation effort described in the previous section would be viewed by some as simply a kind of feature extraction. We have chosen to look upon it as a preprocessing step allowing the extraction of more sophisticated features than would be otherwise available.

A total of 405 different features were calculated for each utterance based upon these segmentation points. The features were in general, multilevel discrete approximations to continuous features. Their discrete nature was dictated by the quantization performed by the analysis hardware. The set of features included essentially all that were considered potentially useful. Some features were suggested by various articles in literature [3], [6].

The forms of the various sorts of features will be given below. Reference should be made to Fig. 4(A)–(C) which diagramatically shows all of the features. Only those shaded were eventually used in decision making. (See subsequent paragraphs regarding evaluation procedure.)

Filter Averages

The most common type of feature was the so-called filter average. Each of these was the combination of values of one or more filters for one or more time samples. In each case, the filter values were first converted from a log to a linear scale averaged over the required number of filters and the average finally reconverted to log scale. The number of filters used for the different features ranged from one to all 20. Some features used filters in the regions of the first, second, third, or higher formants by utilizing filters 1 through 4, 5 through 12, 13 and 14, and finally 15 through 20. The choice of "all filters" was meant to give some measure of the total power in that time sample.

The number of time samples involved in a filter average was also one of three choices, short, medium, or long. A short interval was from one to three time samples (20 to

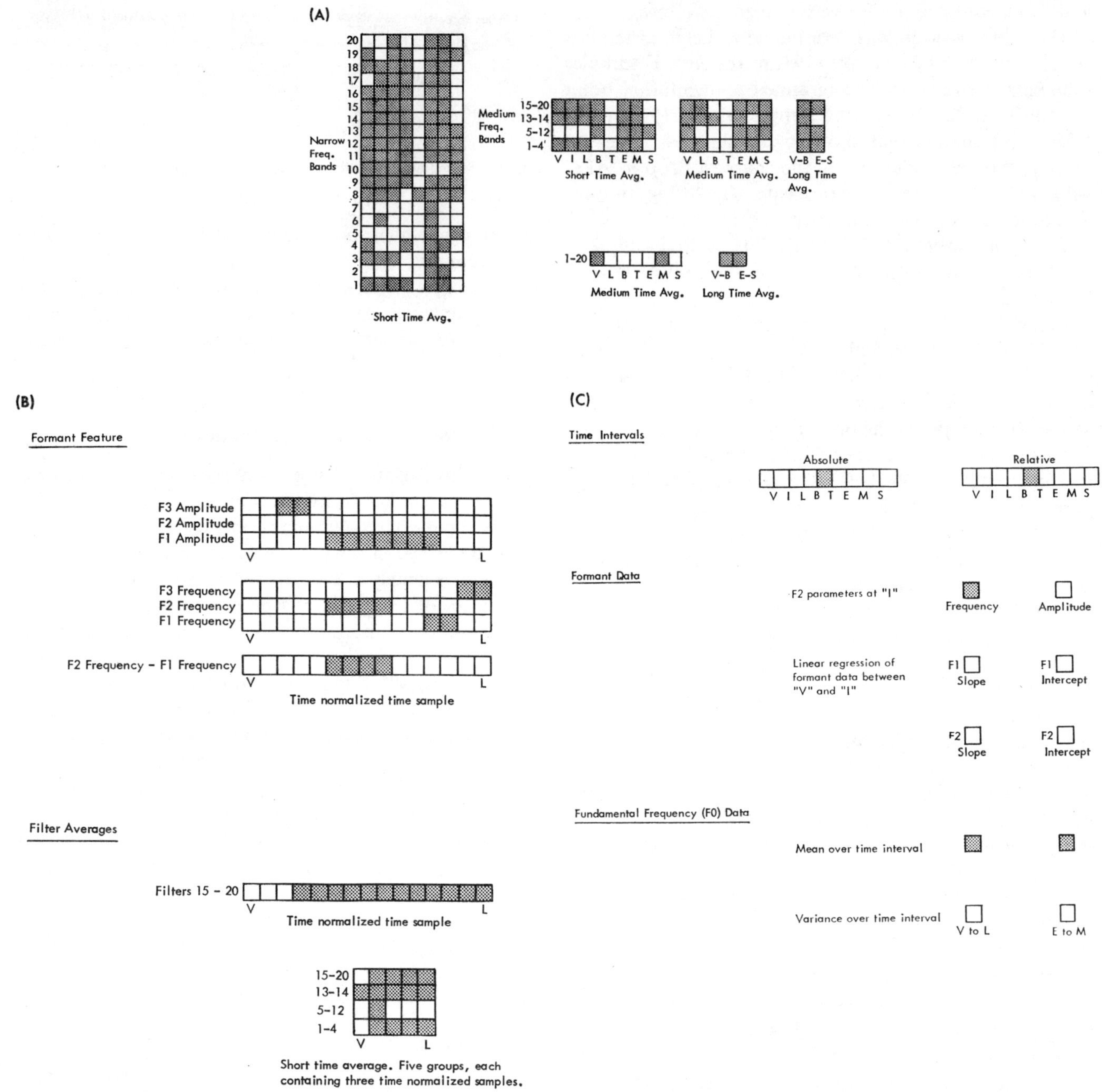

Fig. 4. (A) Features used for speaker verification (filter averages). (Note: Vertical labeling refers to the filters involved in the average. Horizontal labeling refers to the time samples involved in the average. Each block thus defined represents one feature. Only those shaded were retained for later decision making.) (B) Features used for speaker verification (from time-normalized data). (C) Features used for speaker verification (miscellaneous).

60 ms) at a segmentation point. The length varied based upon the particular segmentation point. A medium length interval extended from one segmentation point to the sample immediately preceding the following segmentation point. The long time intervals were between segmentation points "v" and "b," and "e" and "s." This covers all filter averages except those involving time normalized data described below.

Time Normalized Data

Utterances vary in length and simple use of time-frequency-power matrices may not result in sufficiently powerful features. Much of this dependence upon changes in time scale can be eliminated by simple linear time normalization defined as follows. One may take the sampled filter value function represented by a horizontal row in the time-frequency matrix and linearly interpolate between adjacent sample points. The piecewise linear function can now be resampled with a fixed number of time samples. This was done for the array of samples beginning with "v" and ending with "l." An arbitrary length of 15 samples was chosen for the resampling. Thus a new 20×15 array was formed.

Within the time normalized data two new sets of filter averages were calculated. For one set the array was divided into four frequency bands as before and five equal time intervals of three samples each. The other took only the top frequency band (filters 15 through 20) and considered each new sample independently.

Formant Data

Formant data was extracted in both normal and time normalized data. The following interpolation was performed in the frequency domain in both cases. A four point interpolation formula was used to estimate the power in a hypothetical filter placed between two real filters. The four points were the values produced by the two real filters immediately above and the two immediately below the hypothetical filter in frequency. Thus, the original 20 filters were augmented by 19 interpolated filters to produce a total of 39 upon which formant analysis was performed.

Formant detection operated in two stages. First, each time sample was treated independently, and local peaks were detected in the frequency-interpolated spectrum. These peaks were the input data to the second stage in which three were chosen and labeled the first, second, and third formants, taking into account the normal characteristic of formants not to change greatly in frequency from time sample to time sample. A particular formant at a particular time sample was specified by two parameters: its amplitude measured by the value of the filter output at the peak, and its frequency measured as that of filter numbers 1 through 39. These parameters were included for all 15 time normalized samples for all three formants. In addition, the difference in frequency between F1 and F2 was included in all 15 samples. Other formant features were extracted from the original non-time normalized data also. These were the frequency and amplitude of the second formant peak characterizing the sample labeled "i" in "-vail-" and the intercept and slope information for linear approximations to F1 and F2 between "v" and "i."

Time Difference

Both absolute and relative time differences were included among the features. Time was measured in number of time samples between each adjacent pair of segmentation points. These absolute measures were made relative by normalizing with respect to the number of time samples between "v" and "s." In each case, the time interval from the k-release to "v" and from "s" to the end of the phrase were included.

Pitch Frequency

The fundamental-frequency measurement circuit supplied an estimate of F_0 every sample period, but some of the estimates are meaningless due to a lack of voicing. A voiced–unvoiced decision was not made. To increase the likelihood of meaningful data, only the intervals "v" to "l" and "e" to "m" were chosen for F_0 feature extraction. Two features were calculated in each interval: the mean F_0 value and its variance over those several samples. This completes the list of 405 features extracted for every utterance.

Feature evaluation was performed to eliminate those features that were relatively uninformative for speaker separation. Analysis of variance was the evaluation method employed. This method was applied by Pruzansky in a speaker identification problem involving different features [3]. Analysis of variance essentially takes the ratio (called the F-ratio) between two variances. In the numerator is the variance of the means of a particular feature for different speakers. This quantity will be large if there is considerable variation from speaker to speaker, a desirable condition. In the denominator is the average of the variances of the same feature for different speakers. That is, a variance for the feature is calculated for each speaker and these variances averaged. If this quantity is small, it indicates that on the average, the values of the feature for utterances of each speaker stay close to the mean of the feature for each speaker, another desirable condition. By forming the ratio of these quantities, a single measure of each feature's usefulness is calculated. The larger the F, the better the feature. The equation defining F exactly is

$$F = \frac{\left(\sum_{i=1}^{k} r_i - k\right)\left[\sum_{i=1}^{k}\left\{\left(\sum_{j=1}^{r_i} x_{ij}\right)^2 \Big/ r_i\right\} - \left(\sum_{i=1}^{k}\sum_{j=1}^{r_i} x_{ij}\right) \Big/ \left(\sum_{i=1}^{k} r_i\right)\right]}{(k-1)\left[\sum_{i=1}^{k}\sum_{j=1}^{r_i} x_{ij}^2 - \sum_{i=1}^{k}\left\{\left(\sum_{j=1}^{r_i} x_{ij}\right)^2 \Big/ r_i\right\}\right]}$$

where

x_{ij} feature value for jth utterance of ith speaker
r_i number of utterances of ith speaker
k number of speakers.

The quantities r_i are not equal for two reasons. First, as mentioned before, not all speakers produced the same number of utterances and some others were eliminated because of missing segmentation points. In these cases, no features existed for that utterance. Second, it is possible for some, but not all, of the features to be missing in an

TABLE IV
Testing Rank Correlation Between Pairs of Analysis of Variance Rank Orders

	Kendall (t)					Spearman (r)			
	S1U1	S2U1	S1U2	S2U2		S1U1	S2U1	S1U2	S2U2
S1U1	1.00	0.54	0.69	0.54	S1U1	1.00	0.73	0.86	0.73
S2U1	0.54	1.00	0.49	0.71	S2U1	0.73	1.00	0.66	0.88
S1U2	0.69	0.49	1.00	0.52	S1U2	0.86	0.66	1.00	0.70
S2U2	0.54	0.71	0.52	1.00	S2U2	0.73	0.88	0.70	1.00

Note: 1.00 = perfect correlation. 0.00 = random and independent. S1, S2 = speaker groups 1 and 2. U1, U2 = utterance groups 1 and 2.

otherwise acceptable utterance. For example, the algorithm for finding formants sometimes finds no peak and must indicate that the formant feature does not exist. This condition is flagged in the feature by insertion of a unique value, such as a negative formant amplitude. The feature evaluation program must take this into account and not allow the negative value to enter into mean and variance calculation. Similarly, during later training and recognition, averages were substituted for missing features in order not to bias the dot product toward either real or impostor category.

In all, four different analyses of variance were carried out. The purpose of separate tests was to check the consistency of rank from one group of utterances to another, both within the same speakers and across different groups of speakers. A base of 50 speakers was first divided in half. The utterances from each of the resulting groups of 25 speakers were further halved so that each of two groups contained about ten utterances from each speaker. Therefore, the four analyses of variance were each based on about 250 different utterances. The result of each analysis of variance was an ordered list of the 405 features based on the F-ratio.

For computational convenience, a subset of 100 of the features was extracted and the four rank orders of these compared. The comparison tool used was the Kendall and the Spearman coefficients [7]. Both coefficients are designed to produce a value of zero if the lists being compared are randomly ordered with respect to each other, and a value of unity if they are in exactly the same order. Table IV shows these results for all pairs of rankings. To calculate significance, the least significant value (Kendall $(t) = 0.49$) was converted to a normal scale and it was found that the probability of attaining a value even that large by chance was the same as the probability that a normally distributed variable will be greater than 7.2 standard deviations from its mean, an infinitesimal probability. One must conclude that all of the rank orders produced by analysis of variance are significantly correlated and that ten utterances from each of 25 speakers are sufficient to evaluate features with confidence that the results will be applicable to other utterances and other speakers.

The four rank order lists were combined in the manner suggested by Kendall, namely by assigning a composite rank for each feature based upon the average of its rank in the four original lists. This composite list was used for all later feature value judgments. For example, the top 200 of the 405 were used in most of the experiments to be reported. These are the features indicated by shading in Fig. 4(A)–(C). The obvious weakness of this and most other simple ranking techniques of feature evaluation is the lack of consideration of feature dependence. It is true that each of the shaded features is individually better for speaker verification than any of the nonshaded features by an objective measure. It is probably not true that the set of 200 shaded features is better as a whole than all other sets of 200 features chosen from the 405. Consideration of this and other related problems is given elsewhere [5].

V. Decision Experiments

The preceding sections have indicated how the utterances are digitized and segmented and how suitable features are extracted and ranked. At this stage, the decision experiments can be carried out. The results of these experiments will show the validity of the whole procedure. If verification of speakers from their voices is at all feasible by this method, it should be apparent from these results.

Once again, to make the experiments somewhat significant, many utterances from a large number of speakers should be used. Then, some confidence can be placed in the results.

In the present case, there are 50 real speakers whose utterances are used to test the validity of the proposed approach. As described in Section II, a total of approximately 100 utterances spanning a period of five recording sessions is available from each of these speakers. These utterances are divided into two equal groups of 50 for the purposes of eventual training and recognition.

1) First group of real speakers' utterances. Those collected during first two sessions and first half of the third session.

2) Second group of real speakers' utterances. Those collected during the remaining part of the third session and during the last two sessions.

Beside these 50 speakers, some utterances from a separate set of 68 speakers are also available. These are the impostors. Two groups are again formed.

1) First group of impostor utterances. About nine utterances from each of 29 speakers assigned to the impostor category.

2) Second group of impostor utterances. All utterances (about 20 from each) from the remaining 39 speakers assigned to the impostor category.

A modified version [1] of the classical Adaline technique is utilized for the training and recognition procedure inherent in the decision process. During training, this technique employs several training utterances and creates a reference profile or weight vector W for each of the real speakers. The training utterance set consists of the first group of utterances from the real speaker for which the weight vector is desired and the first group of impostor utterances. The recognition set is comprised of the second group of utterances from the same real speaker and the second group of impostor utterances. After the weight vector is formed for a real speaker, recognition is performed by using this vector and the recognition set of utterances. Thus, the recognition data is completely separate from the training data.

The weight vector W is such that, for a convergent training procedure [1],

$$W \cdot R > K \mid W \mid$$

and

$$W \cdot I < -K \mid W \mid$$

where R is any utterance from the real training set, I is any one from the impostor training set, K is some finite constant, and the symbol $(\cdot)$ implies inner product operation. The value of K was set to 5 for the current experiments. This choice was a compromise and was made after some preliminary investigations on convergence time, generalization ability, and other such related factors [1].

During recognition, the inner products of the weight vector with the recognition utterances are determined. A threshold is then selected so that the percentage of misclassified real utterances is equal to the percentage of misclassified impostor utterances. This single percentage is plotted in Fig. 5 in histogram form. It is clear that except for a small number of speakers, the error rate of misclassification is generally low. Mean error rate is one percent. An investigation carried out on the speaker with the highest error rate has revealed that this high error rate can be attributed largely to segmentation inaccuracies. It is possible that an improved segmentation strategy will decrease the overall error rate on all speakers. In this connection, it may be mentioned that the effect of segmentation error is serious for the utterances from the real speaker only. Such utterances with wrong segmentation points lead to wrong feature sets and are likely to produce wrong decisions. On the other hand, erroneous feature sets for impostor utterances resulting from inaccurate segmentation are not likely to cause these utterances to be misclassified as utterances from the real speakers.

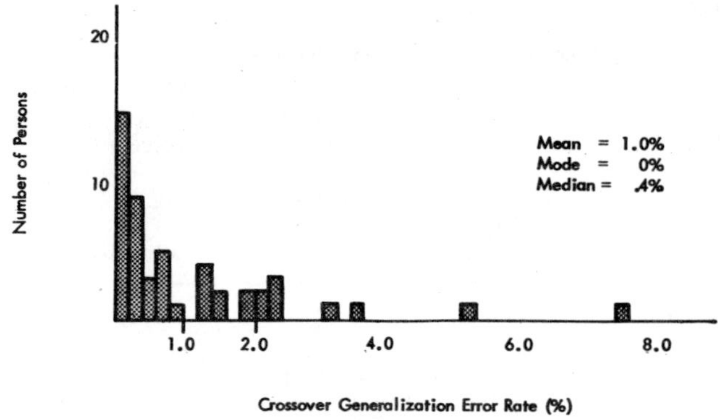

Fig. 5. Generalization error histogram.

Another experiment using six real speakers will now be reported. The objective is to test the hypothesis that utterances collected during one session only are less desirable for training purposes than the utterances obtained during a larger number of sessions. The following rationale was employed for forming such a hypothesis. One may argue that the utterances spoken during one session tend to be rather "similar" to one another and do not depict typical variations of speech patterns that may be expected at later instances of time. Thus, the weight vector derived from the utterances of one session is not likely to be representative. However, if utterances are collected in at least two sessions which are separated by a prudent time interval, many of the person's possible speech variations are encountered and the weight vector is likely to be more representative. No investigations about what constitutes a suitable time interval between two sessions have been made in the following experiment.

In the first part of the experiment, only the first 20 utterances produced by each real speaker in the first session are used for training. Training utterances of the impostors and recognition utterances of both the real and the impostors are unchanged from the earlier experiments. In previous terminology, only the first group of utterances from the real speaker is different; the second group of real utterances and the two groups of impostor utterances are the same as before. The error rates for the six real speakers are shown in the row marked "1–20" of Table V. The column marked "Average" gives the average errors rates across the six speakers.

TABLE V

Results with Various Number of Training Utterances

Real Utterances of Group I	Speaker 1 Percent	Speaker 2 Percent	Speaker 3 Percent	Speaker 4 Percent	Speaker 5 Percent	Speaker 6 Percent	Average Percent
1–20	9.1	2.0	1.7	1.6	5.9	0	3.4
1, 3, · · · , 39	3.6	1.4	0.5	0.5	3.5	0	1.6
1–50	3.1	1.2	2.1	0.8	3.4	0	1.8

In the second part of the experiment, only 20 utterances of the real speaker are again used for training, but, this time, they are the alternate 20 utterances from the first *two* sessions, numbered 1, 3, 5, · · · , 39. The total number of training utterances is kept constant so that it does not enter as a variable in the experiment. Other three groups of utterances are held fixed as before. The error rates are shown in the row labeled "1, 3, · · · , 39" of Table V. The number in the last row of this table marked "1–50" are the original error rates for these six speakers when the first 50 utterances from each of them are used for training. Comparing the three rows of results, it may be observed that the utterances of one session represented in the row "1–20" indeed lead to higher error rates than the utterances obtained during two sessions shown in the row "1, 3, · · · , 39." Utterances of *three* sessions which results in the error rates of the row "1–50" seem to have no added value over the utterances of two sessions. Occasional discrepancies in the general trend of results were noted, but no explanations for these occurrences were apparent.

Finally, it is pointed out that these conclusions about the number of sessions suitable for gathering training utterances may depend on the particular speakers employed, instructions given to them, and other such factors as mentioned in Section II.

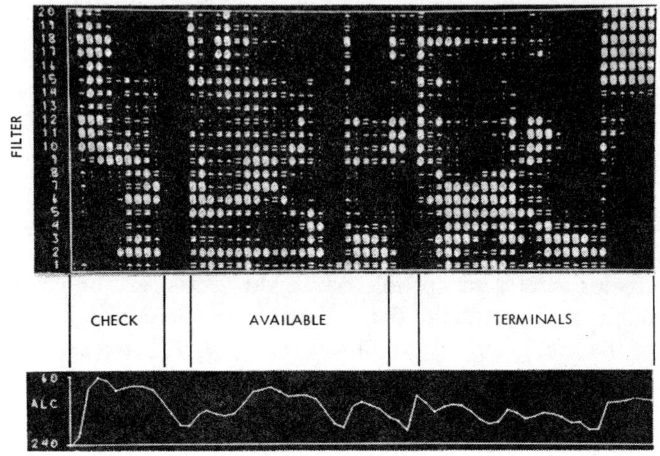

Fig. 6. Spectrogram display in IBM 2250.

VI. Comments and Further Work

The experiments reported in this paper and in [1] have used a realistic data base which is believed to be larger than any other data bases previously reported in the same area of work. This data base permits the experimenter to draw more meaningful conclusions and grants him considerable freedom in satisfactory implementations of various algorithms.

One problem pointed out in Section III is the relatively high (ten percent) phrase-rejection rate. This rate could possibly be lowered in at least two ways. First, it is necessary to invent more effective segmentation techniques. This means that events in more utterances will be successfully detected leading to a lower rejection rate. Next, a technique for dealing with utterances which has one or more missing events needs to be found. This will also yield reduced phrase-rejection rate.

A possible way of improving the segmentation procedure is by adopting a strategy of detecting individual events independently. Later, these events may be correlated to verify that they occur in their expected sequence.

Considerable facility in the design of a segmentation strategy may be gained by utilizing an interactive display system. The system should have the provision for displaying the results obtained from the experimenter's program in a convenient form as well as the digitized spectrogram of the speech. Then, the user could modify various parameters of his program on-line and observe the effect in a short time. A good understanding of the capabilities and limitations of his program may be obtained in this manner. Fig. 6 shows a digital spectrogram display in an IBM 2250.

One of the important aspects of speaker verification missing in this research is the utilization of the utterances of female speakers. It is quite likely that the segmentation and feature selection strategies developed in the present paper will be inadequate for the female speech. Thus, a study of female utterances should be undertaken. Other important areas of research in the verification problem may be mentioned. Investigations regarding the effect of colds or other symptoms that may affect speech quality can be carried out. Sensitivity of the verification system to impostors trying intentionally to mimic a real speaker needs to be studied. Such impostors should include speakers with formal training in speech since they are effectively able to control various characteristics of their voice. Siblings of real speakers should also be considered since their voice may be "similar" to the voice of the real speakers due to their possibly similar physical speech apparatus or environmental background.

In summary, effective automatic speaker verification has been demonstrated, the results of collecting training utterances over one or more number of sessions have been investigated, and some further areas of research have been pointed out.

Acknowledgment

The authors wish to thank their associates in the Speech Processing and other Advanced Technology Departments, for invaluable assistance in theory, hardware design and construction, data gathering and preprocessing, and programming. Special credit is due Dr. N. R. Dixon who composed the five phrases listed in Table I, designed the data-taking paradigm, advised the authors regarding many aspects of the feature extraction process, and helped check the acceptability of the segmentation results.

References

[1] S. K. Das and W. S. Mohn, "Pattern recognition in speaker verification," in *1969 Fall Joint Computer Conf., AFIPS Conf. Proc.*, vol. 35, pp. 721–732.

[2] K. P. Li, J. E. Dammann, and W. D. Chapman, "Experimental studies in speaker verification, using an adaptive system," *J. Acoust. Soc. Am.*, vol. 40, Nov. 1966, pp. 966–978.

[3] S. Pruzansky, "Talker-recognition procedure based on analysis of variance," *J. Acoust. Soc. Am.*, vol. 36, Nov. 1964, pp. 2041–2047.

[4] J. E. Luck, "Automatic speaker verification, using cepstral measurement," *J. Acoust. Soc. Am.*, vol. 46, Oct. 1969, pp. 1026–1032.

[5] W. S. Mohn, "Statistical feature evaluation in speaker identification," Ph.D. dissertation, Dept. Elec. Eng., North Carolina State Univ., Raleigh, July 1969.

[6] J. W. Glenn and N. Kleiner, "Speaker identification based on nasal phonation," *J. Acoust. Soc. Am.*, vol. 43, Feb. 1968, pp. 368–372.

[7] M. G. Kendall, *Rank Correlation Methods*. New York: Hafner, 1962.

Identification of speakers by use of nasal coarticulation*

Lo-Soun Su,[†] K.-P. Li,[‡] and K. S. Fu

School of Electrical Engineering, Purdue University, West Lafayette, Indiana 47907
(Received 25 May 1974; revised 12 September 1974)

A new approach, based on the statistical properties of the nasal spectra, has been used to quantitatively study the coarticulation of nasal consonants, with the vowels following them in isolated /hə'CVd/ utterances. The spectral differences between the mean spectra of nasals followed by front vowels and those of nasals followed by back vowels were used as the acoustic measure of the coarticulation of [m] and [n] with the following vowel [V]. The coarticulation between [n] and [V] was found to be only about one-third of that between [m] and [V]. The coarticulated nasal spectrum, particularly between [m] and [V], was found to have strongly idiosyncratic characteristics, which are not likely to be modified in natural speech. A method was therefore developed by which the coarticulation between [m] and [V] was taken as the acoustic clue and the speaker was identified by use of a correlation decision criterion. Coarticulation was found to give more reliable clues than the nasal spectrum alone, which had earlier been found to be one of the best acoustic clues for identifying speakers.

Subject Classification: 70.40, 70.62, 70.65, 70.30.

INTRODUCTION

In the belief that the automatic identification of speakers may soon be extensively used for security, and in the hope that work on this subject will lead to theories in the process of speech production as byproducts, more researchers are working in this area now than a decade ago. A good review of speaker identification by use of hearing, voice print, and machine was given by Hecker.[1] Several other studies have also been reported recently.[2–8]

Previous work makes it plain that speakers can be recognized provided that interspeaker variability is greater than intraspeaker variability. Techniques that reduce intraspeaker variability more than they reduce interspeaker variability would be expected to improve the reliability of speaker identification.

Most of the acoustic clues used in the past were based on voice differences due to structural differences in the articulatory organs, such as vocal and nasal cavities.[1–8] The acoustic clues in question, however, can be modified during the speech production process, and thus may not necessarily represent the speaker's normal speech characteristic. To circumvent this disadvantage, we have to turn to acoustic clues that cannot be controlled consciously. In this paper, these clues are analyzed and extracted from speech spectra with the intention of applying them to the automatic identification of speakers.

As is well known, almost all speech processes have speaker-dependent characteristics. An example is the prevoicing of a voiced stop following a voiceless phoneme.[5] This is only one of the coarticulation processes that are controlled by the neuromuscular system of the speaker. Other coarticulation processes too may be idiosyncratic.

Coarticulation is an important phenomenon that has not yet been fully accounted for by speech production theory. Phoneticians have long known that phoneme strings are sensitive to context, but the general rule underlying the context-dependent properties has not been sufficiently elaborated. In 1966, Ohman presented important acoustic evidence and a theory to account for coarticulation.[9] Since then, numerous others have studied this topic.[10–12] All of them were concerned with formulating the acoustic characteristics of natural-sounding speech signals. Their methods—high-speed cinematography,[10,11] sonographs,[9] and EMG studies[12]—however, are not only time consuming, but also difficult to quantify.

This paper reports experiments designed and conducted to extract the speaker-dependent characteristics of coarticulated sounds from the spectra in a form that can be quantified, and analyze them for clues to be used in identifying speakers.

I. THE COARTICULATION OF NASAL CONSONANTS AND THE FOLLOWING VOWEL CONTEXT

A. Basic analysis

Nasal consonants are produced with the vocal cavity closed and with energy radiated from the nasal cavity.[13,14] A complete closure is made toward the anterior orifice of the oral cavity either by the lips, by the tongue at the alveolar ridge, or by the tongue dorsum at the velum. The velopharyngeal port is fully open during the nasal phonation; thus, energy is transmitted chiefly through the nasal cavities.

Henke[15] has proposed an articulatory model in which a phonetic sequence is scanned a few units in advance, and some characteristics of impending sounds are anticipated if they do not conflict with the characteristics of sounds that immediately precede them. Thus, during the sequence C_1VC_2, a feature of C_2 might be anticipated during the production of C_1, provided it does not conflict with any characteristic of C_1 or V. This model has been verified by Moll and Daniloff,[11] who used it in successfully predicting the velar movement in CVVN and NVC sequences. It also gives a good explanation of data on lip protrusion and jaw opening.[16]

Reprinted with permission from *J. Acoust. Soc. Am.*, vol. 56, pp. 1876–1882, Dec. 1974.

As one would expect, the Henke model can also predict the tongue coarticulation between nasal consonants and the following vowel context. If the nasal consonant is followed by a vowel, the tongue anticipates the following vowel segments and moves to the vowel position during the nasal phonation.[15,16] The extent of this coarticulation depends on whether the tongue takes a specific position to produce the nasal consonant. In English, the tongue has no distinctive function for [m],[17] but has important functions for [n] and [ŋ]. For [m] before [V], therefore, we would expect more lingual coarticulation than for [n] and [ŋ] before [V].

If there were little or no coarticulation between a nasal consonant [C] and the following vowel [V], then, in a large number of samples, the mean spectrum of [C] followed by front vowels, designated as $\overline{X}_{Cf}$, and that followed by back vowels, designated as $\overline{X}_{Cb}$, would remain stable and would coincide. With coarticulation, these spectra would differ. Since the difference is caused primarily by coarticulation, it might serve as a measure of the coarticulation. If it is calculated for each individual speaker, then, from the results, one might be able to derive a gross estimate of the speaker's coarticulation process.

In this study, we should mention, we are concerned only with the acoustic characteristics caused by coarticulation. Although the difference between $\overline{X}_{Cf}$ and $\overline{X}_{Cb}$ is caused primarily by the underlying coarticulatory process, it may also be due in part to structural differences in the oral and nasal cavities of individual speakers. For speaker identification, however, the difference itself, not the cause of it, is what matters.

The formants (poles of the transfer function) of nasal consonants are formed chiefly by the main path, the pharyngeal and nasal cavities. Therefore, the basic formant structures of nasal consonants are essentially the same. The closed oral cavity, which functions as a side-branch resonator coupled to the main path, forms the antiformants (zeroes of the transfer function). Since the oral cavity takes on a different shape and size for each nasal consonant, nasal consonants have different antiformants, which fall within different and distinctively defined regions. As Fujimura[14] has shown, the antiformant of [m] is between 750 and 1250 Hz, that of [n] is between 1450 and 2200 Hz, and that of [ŋ] is above 3000 Hz. Taking into consideration both formants and antiformants, Fujimura found that the antiformant brings the formants into its vicinity; the result is a formant–antiformant cluster around the antiformant region. The coarticulation under study is attributable to the modification of the oral cavity as it affects the formant–antiformant cluster of the nasal spectra. Therefore, the frequency range used in this experiment, from about 250 to 3681 Hz, should be adequate to characterize the spectra of [m] and [n]. (Because /ŋ/ occurs only at postvocalic syllable final position, it was not considered in this study.)

B. Description of the data

Isolated /hə'CVd/ utterances were phonated by two adult males (ASH and GWH, both with phonetic training) and two adult females (MH and CH). Here, /C/ can be only /m/ or /n/. For /V/, three front vowels /i, e, æ/ and three back vowels /u, o, a/ were used. Thus, there were six [CV] utterances. Each speaker pronounced the corpus three times, for a total of 36 utterances. The utterances were ordered randomly for each repetition. The recordings were made in a sound-treated environment with a Brüel and Kjær half-inch condenser microphone and an Ampex recorder.[6]

In the processing, the speech signals were first passed through a spectral shaping circuit. The shaping had a flat frequency response above 2200 Hz, and a + 6-dB/oct asymptotic slope below that point. The speech signals were then fed into a filter bank that had a range from 250 Hz to 10 kHz. After being rectified and smoothed, the signals were sampled every 10 msec. The time samples thus obtained were digitized by use of a ten-bit analog-to-digital converter, and then logarithmically transformed into a 35-dimensional vector by use of a hybrid system.[19] Only the outputs of the first 25 filters, ranging from 250 to 3681 Hz, were used. A digital computer was first used to print out the digital outputs of the filter bank. The spectral samples of the nasal consonant for each utterance were then manually selected for the analysis.[6]

C. Qualitative study

Daniel Jones[20] noticed the coarticulation between /m/ and the following vowel context. According to Jones, "When a vowel follows, the position of the tongue during the production of /m/ approximates to the position required for that vowel. To that extent, therefore, it may be said that there are subsidiary members of the phonemes." He further remarked, "With most speakers, however, these differences of tongue position are slight and their effects on the acoustic quality of the sound are negligible." Fujimura[14] and Fujimura and Lindquist[21] also found the context-sensitive property of [m] with respect to the following vowels.

In this section, the nasal samples due to coarticulation are projected on a two-dimensional eigenvector space for visual analysis. Essentially, the procedure is to find the principal components (or the ordered eigenvectors of a covariance matrix) of the spectral data.[18,19] These components yield a convenient set of orthonormal coordinates, and their variances characterize the statistical properties of the spectral data. The new coordinate system maintains the original statistical characteristics, but in an ordered form. The first few eigenvectors are found to be closely related to major acoustic features of the linguistic units under study.[19] In the present experiment, the analysis of nasal spectra shows that the important acoustic information—total energy, and the first and second locations of formants and antiformants—is conveyed in the first few eigenvectors. For a qualitative study, then, the projection of samples on the first few eigenvectors generally should sufficiently reveal the clustering properties of the samples.

Eigenvectors of the covariance matrix of all the time samples of [m] and [n] for each speaker were calculated.

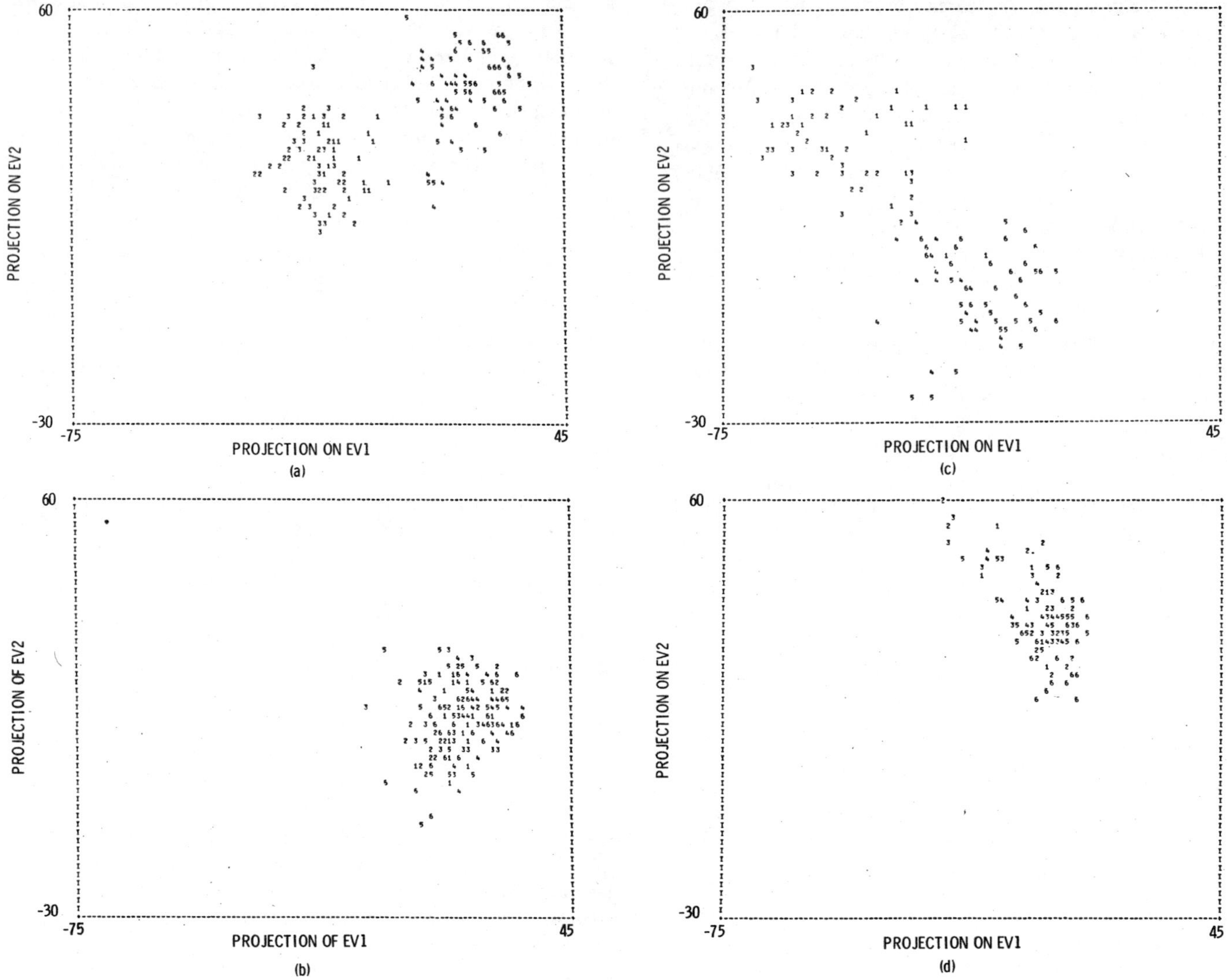

FIG. 1. Two-dimensional patterns on EV1–EV2 for male speakers. 1./hə′mid/; 2./hə′med/; 3./hə′mæd/; 4./hə′mad/; 5./hə′mod/; 6./hə′mud/. (a) [m] spectral samples for ASH; 77 time samples for $[m_f]$, 76 for $[m_b]$. (b) [n] spectral samples for ASH; 160 time samples. (c) [m] spectral samples for GWH; 55 time samples for $[m_f]$, 60 for $[m_b]$. (d) [n] spectral samples for GWH; 121 time samples.

The number of time samples for each speaker ranged from 236 to 313. Since only 25 dimensions were used in the analysis, all four covariance matrices should be considered stable.

After the eigenvectors for each speaker were obtained, time samples were projected on EV1 and EV2 to form a two-dimensional distribution pattern. Figures 1 and 2 are computer plots of the two-dimensional distribution patterns of time samples of [m] and [n] for the four speakers; the coordinate represents projection on EV1, the ordinate on EV2. Each numerical value (1–6) stands for one time sample followed by the corresponding six vowels, as shown in the figures. Because most of the samples are concentrated near the clustering centers, there are numerous overlapping time samples in these regions. If two time samples overlap, only the one that bears the larger numerical value is shown. However, the total number of time samples is given in the figures. From Figs. 1 and 2, one can see that time samples of $[m_f]$ and $[m_b]$ form two distinct clusters, whereas time samples of [n] form only one. This evidence is consistent for all four speakers. However, the detailed clustering properties (cluster distribution, the scattering of two clusters, etc.) for each speaker are quite different. These differences indicate qualitatively the characteristic of the coarticulation process is speaker dependent.

The next section reports an effort to apply these results to speaker identification.

D. Quantitative study

To perform the quantitative analysis, we first define

$\bar{Y}_{Cf}$ = 25-dimensional mean spectra of $[C_f]$ time samples

$$= [\bar{y}_{Cf}(1),\ \bar{y}_{Cf}(2), \ldots,\ \bar{y}_{Cf}(25)]\,, \qquad (1)$$

$\bar{Y}_{Cb}$ = 25-dimensional mean spectra of $[C_b]$ time samples

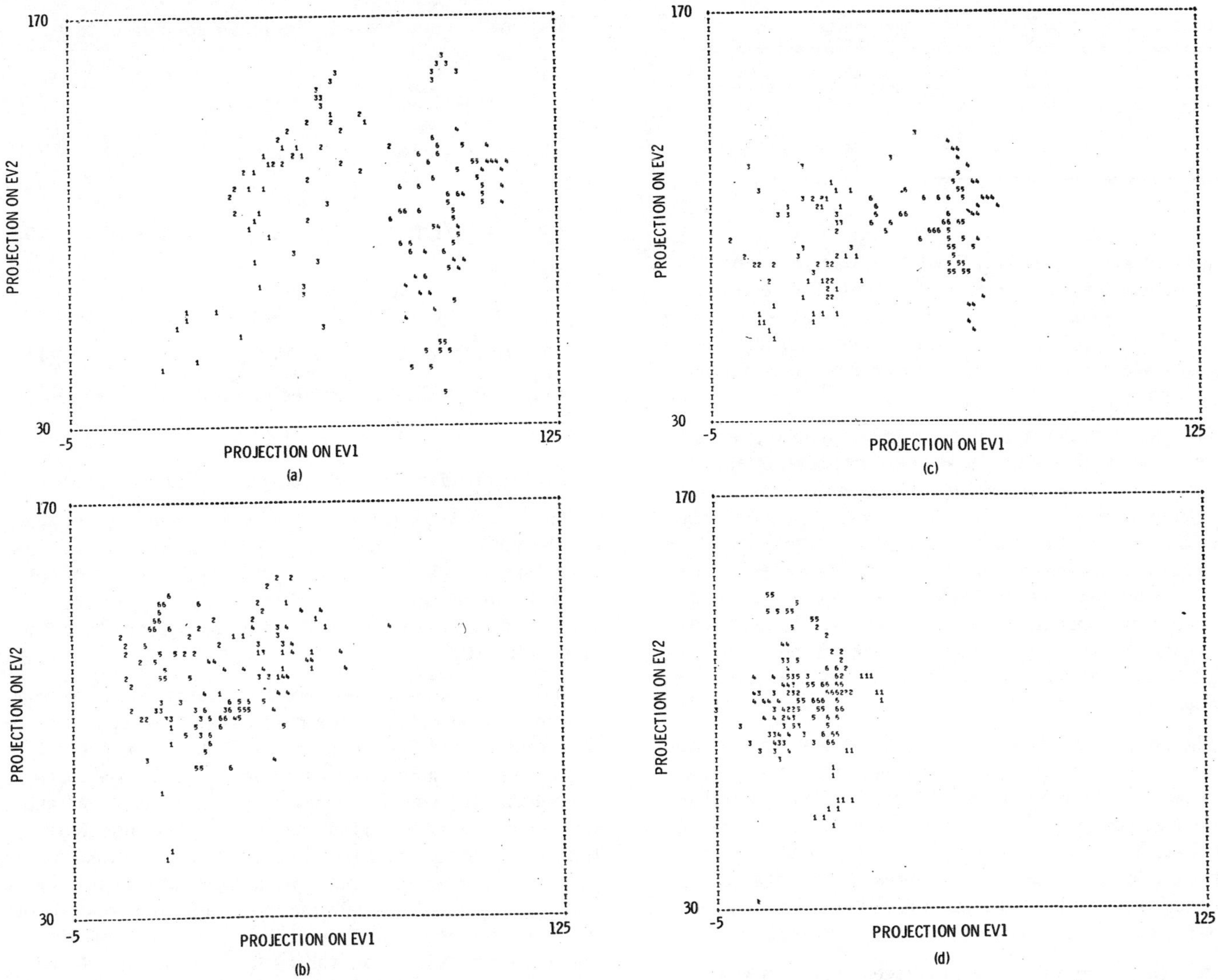

FIG. 2. Two-dimensional distribution patterns on EV1–EV2 for female speakers. (a) [m] spectral samples for MH; 64 time samples for [m_f], 70 for [m_b]. (b) [n] spectral samples for MH; 164 time samples. (c) [m] spectral samples for CH; 66 time samples for [m_f], 75 for [m_b]. (d) [n] spectral samples for CH; 151 time samples.

$$= [\bar{y}_{Cb}(1),\ \bar{y}_{Cb}(2),\ \ldots,\ \bar{y}_{Cb}(25)]\ , \tag{2}$$

where

$$\bar{y}_{Cf}(k) = \text{the } k\text{th component of vector } \overline{Y}_{Cf}\ , \tag{3}$$

$$\bar{y}_{Cb}(k) = \text{the } k\text{th component of vector } \overline{Y}_{Cb}\ , \tag{4}$$

and [C] represents either [m] or [n]. Then, the Euclidean distance between $\overline{Y}_{Cf}$ and $\overline{Y}_{Cb}$ can be expressed by

$$DIST\ (\overline{Y}_{Cf},\ \overline{Y}_{Cb}) = \left\{ \sum_{k=1}^{25} [\bar{y}_{Cf}(k) - \bar{y}_{Cb}(k)]^2 \right\}^{1/2} . \tag{5}$$

$DIST\ (\overline{Y}_{Cf},\ \overline{Y}_{Cb})$ is used for measuring the gross estimate of coarticulation. By calculating $DIST\ (\overline{Y}_{mf},\ \overline{Y}_{mb})$ and $DIST\ (\overline{Y}_{nf},\ \overline{Y}_{nb})$ for each speaker, we obtain an estimate of the difference in [m] and [n] spectra attributable mainly to the coarticulation of the nasal consonants with front and back vowels.

The Euclidean distance between the mean spectra of [m_f] and [m_b], designated by $DIST\ (\overline{Y}_{mf},\ \overline{Y}_{mb})$, and that between the mean spectra of [n_f] and [n_b], designated by $DIST\ (\overline{Y}_{nf},\ \overline{Y}_{nb})$, were calculated for four speakers. The results are listed in Table I. As Table I shows, the coarticulation measure for [nV] is about one-third of that for [mV]. The reason, as was mentioned earlier, is that the tongue blade is less free to move during part of the [n] phonation. Although structural differences in the oral and nasal cavities may cause some differences between the spectra of $\overline{Y}_{Cf}$ and $\overline{Y}_{Cb}$, the difference between these spectra should primarily reflect the change of coarticulation for [mV] and [nV]. Hence, we may conclude that the coarticulation between [m] and [V] is much greater than that between [n] and [V], as would be predicted by use of Henke's model.[15]

II. THE SPEAKER IDENTIFICATION EXPERIMENT

Wolf[5] remarked that for the identification of speakers the most reliable clue is the one that "concerns a rapid event which is not likely to be consciously modifiable." He attempted to identify speakers according to the pre-

TABLE I. $DIST(\bar{Y}_{Cf}, \bar{Y}_{Cb})$ of four speakers.

Speaker	ASH	GWH	MH	CH
$DIST(\bar{Y}_{mf}, \bar{Y}_{mb})$	39.90	46.38	50.93	43.08
$DIST(\bar{Y}_{nf}, \bar{Y}_{nb})$	8.27	11.62	16.06	17.43

voicing of a voiced stop following an unvoiced segment. This parameter, however, yielded only limited information. In addition, it required high-quality recording, because the voicing feature always occurs in the lower-frequency domain, where background noise is hard to suppress.

The phenomenon Wolf used is only one of numerous coarticulation processes that are controlled by the neuromuscular system of the speaker. In general, any coarticulation process that has strongly speaker-dependent characteristics can be used in identifying speakers. As was demonstrated qualitatively in the preceding section, the acoustic characteristics caused by the coarticulation of [m] and the following vowel are speaker dependent. To see how effectively they can be used in identifying speakers, an experiment was designed and conducted.

The characteristics of each individual's coarticulation were represented by a measurement of the separation between the samples of $[m_f]$ and $[m_b]$. Two separation measures are used. The first, the difference between the mean spectra $\bar{Y}_{mf}$ and $\bar{Y}_{mb}$, would presumably indicate how the two clustering centers are separated. The second, the standard deviation along each dimension, would indicate how the samples are scattered.

In order to compare the effectiveness of the coarticulation measure with that of other acoustic clues, we chose a decision criterion similar to one used in previous studies.[2,5,6] We define correlation coefficients for different separation measures as in Eqs. 6 and 10, where r stands for reference speaker and t for test speaker:

$$\rho_{ij} = (D_{ri} \cdot D_{tj})/(|D_{ri}| \cdot |D_{tj}|) , \quad i, j = 1\text{–}4 \text{ or } 1\text{–}10 , \tag{6}$$

where

$$D_{ri} = \text{difference between the mean spectra of reference speaker } i = (\bar{Y}_{mf} - \bar{Y}_{mb})_{ri} , \tag{7}$$

$$D_{tj} = \text{difference between the mean spectra of test speaker } j = (\bar{Y}_{mf} - \bar{Y}_{mb})_{tj} , \tag{8}$$

$$|D_{yz}| = DIST_{yz}(\bar{Y}_{mf}, \bar{Y}_{mb}) , \quad y = t \text{ or } r, \ z = i \text{ or } j . \tag{9}$$

Further,

$$r_{ij} = (V_{ri} \cdot V_{tj})/(|V_{ri}| \cdot |V_{tj}|), \quad i, j = 1\text{–}4 \text{ or } 1\text{–}10 , \tag{10}$$

where

$$V_{ri} = \text{standard deviation vector of reference speaker } i = [\sigma(1), \sigma(2), \ldots, \sigma(25)]_{rj} , \tag{11}$$

$$V_{tj} = \text{standard deviation vector of test speaker } j = [\sigma(1), \sigma(2), \ldots, \sigma(25)]_{tj} , \tag{12}$$

$\sigma(k)$ = standard deviation along the kth dimension.

The first two phonations of each utterance were used for the reference pattern, and the third for testing. The correlation coefficients for the four speakers were calculated and arranged in matrix form by use of differences and standard deviations of mean spectra (see Tables II and III).

Data were taken for ten more speakers, all male faculty members and graduate students in the Department of Audiology and Speech Sciences of Purdue University, in exactly the same way as for the first four speakers, except that the vowels used were /i, I, e, u, o, a/ and that each utterance, again /hə'mVd/, was phonated six times at intervals of about 2 sec. Two phonations were used for the reference pattern, and two others for the test pattern. The correlation matrices for two kinds of measure are shown in Tables IV and V. With either separation measure, as Tables II–V show, the identification score for both the group of four speakers and the group of ten male speakers was 100%.

Spectra of nasals have thus been demonstrated to be efficient acoustic clues for identifying speakers. Let us now compare the nasal coarticulation measure used in this study with the measure involving nasal spectra. In previous work,[5] acoustic clues have been evaluated and compared by the analysis-of-variance method. A more reliable method, we have found, is actually to perform the experiment (or, in our case, compute the correlation matrices) with different acoustic clues and compare the differences between the diagonal coefficients and the off-diagonal coefficients of the resulting correlation matrices. The difference $\Delta\rho$ or Δr ($\Delta\rho = \rho_{ii} - \rho_{ij}$ and $\Delta r = r_{ii} - r_{ij}$; $i \neq j$ and $i, j = 1\text{–}4$ or $1\text{–}10$)

TABLE II. ρ matrix for four speakers.

Test speaker	Reference speaker			
	ASH	GWH	MH	CH
ASH	<u>0.93</u>	0.74	0.64	0.51
GWH	0.77	<u>0.93</u>	0.49	0.32
MH	0.63	0.40	<u>0.90</u>	0.67
CH	0.47	0.20	0.74	<u>0.90</u>

TABLE III. r matrix for four speakers.

Test speaker	Reference speaker			
	ASH	GWH	MH	CH
ASH	<u>0.98</u>	0.95	0.92	0.93
GWH	0.95	<u>0.98</u>	0.94	0.94
MH	0.91	0.91	<u>0.98</u>	0.90
CH	0.92	0.93	0.94	<u>0.98</u>

TABLE IV. ρ matrix for ten male speakers.

Test speaker	Reference speaker									
	1	2	3	4	5	6	7	8	9	10
1	0.94	−0.15	0.62	0.77	0.71	0.79	0.47	0.80	0.37	0.67
22	−0.16	0.88	0.45	0.03	0.36	0.35	0.44	−0.20	0.68	0.18
3	0.64	0.17	0.91	0.59	0.63	0.76	0.49	0.53	0.39	0.70
4	0.65	0.02	0.57	0.94	0.50	0.83	0.60	0.74	0.57	0.74
5	0.69	0.37	0.42	0.29	0.74	0.50	0.18	0.40	0.39	0.30
6	0.61	0.20	0.85	0.81	0.70	0.96	0.74	0.68	0.63	0.81
7	0.20	0.28	0.68	0.59	0.47	0.67	0.91	0.24	0.66	0.59
8	0.79	−0.31	0.50	0.76	0.55	0.72	0.23	0.96	0.18	0.58
9	0.26	0.57	0.60	0.55	0.53	0.72	0.74	0.29	0.93	0.52
10	0.59	−0.07	0.50	0.78	0.34	0.66	0.48	0.61	0.31	0.87

between the diagonal coefficients and the off-diagonal coefficients is calculated for both the ρ matrix and the r matrix. In general, $\Delta\rho$ is several times as large as Δr. We may therefore conclude that the vector between two clustering centers $\overline{Y}_{mf}$ and $\overline{Y}_{mb}$ is a better separation measure than the standard deviation vector.

The percentage distributions of $\Delta\rho$ for nasal coarticulation, the [n] spectra of isolated words,[2] and nasal spectra in continuous speech[6] are plotted in Fig. 3. For nasal coarticulation, both the minimum and the average values of $\Delta\rho$ are several times as large as for [n] spectra. At the peaks of distribution, $\Delta\rho$ is 0.01 to 0.018 for the spectra of nasals in continuous speech, 0.1 to 0.18 for [n] spectra in isolated words, and 0.32 to 0.57 for nasal coarticulation. Thus, for an arbitrary threshold of $\Delta\rho = 0.1$, the identification error would be 100% for nasal spectra in continuous speech, 32% for [n] spectra in isolated words, and only 1.1% for nasal coarticulation. All of these indicate that nasal coarticulation is the best clue of the three for identifying speakers.

Chow performed a similar experiment with a group of 33 naive native speakers.[22] Of the subjects, 23 were undergraduate students at Purdue University and the rest were the ten male subjects used in this study. The distribution of $\Delta\rho$ was found to be similar to that plotted in Fig. 3, except that 15% of $\Delta\rho$ was negative because five of the 33 speakers were misidentified.

III. CONCLUSIONS AND DISCUSSION

The Euclidean distance between the two clustering centers $\overline{Y}_{Cf}$ and $\overline{Y}_{Cb}$ along each dimension can be used as a measure of the coarticulation of both [m] and [n] with the following vowel context. This measure may also include the effect of structural differences introduced by the oral and nasal cavities.

A speaker-dependent characteristic, the coarticulation between [m] and the following vowel context, can be used as an acoustic clue for identifying speakers. This clue is more reliable than nasal spectra. Also, since it concerns a rapid event, it is not likely to be consciously modified in natural speech.

In Chow's experiment,[22] when the population was increased from ten to 33, the speaker identification score dropped from 100% to 85%, as usually happens in such an experiment when the acoustic clues are tested in a larger population. The reason was thought to be that 23 of the speakers were untrained: an untrained speaker tends to display more intraspeaker variability than a trained one.[22] Without intensive tests of a large population, then, it would not be wise to state an absolute figure purporting to represent the performance of the coarticulation measure. However, we have demon-

TABLE V. r matrix for ten male speakers.

Test speaker	Reference speaker									
	1	2	3	4	5	6	7	8	9	10
1	0.99	0.97	0.96	0.96	0.96	0.96	0.95	0.97	0.95	0.96
2	0.98	1.00	0.96	0.94	0.95	0.97	0.96	0.98	0.97	0.98
3	0.94	0.95	0.98	0.93	0.91	0.95	0.92	0.94	0.92	0.95
4	0.95	0.95	0.97	0.99	0.94	0.96	0.94	0.94	0.96	0.96
5	0.94	0.93	0.90	0.92	0.98	0.92	0.90	0.92	0.94	0.91
6	0.95	0.97	0.96	0.92	0.93	0.99	0.95	0.95	0.96	0.98
7	0.93	0.95	0.94	0.95	0.94	0.95	0.99	0.92	0.98	0.97
8	0.96	0.97	0.95	0.93	0.91	0.96	0.93	0.99	0.93	0.95
9	0.95	0.97	0.96	0.93	0.94	0.98	0.96	0.94	0.99	0.97
10	0.97	0.98	0.96	0.97	0.94	0.97	0.96	0.97	0.96	0.99

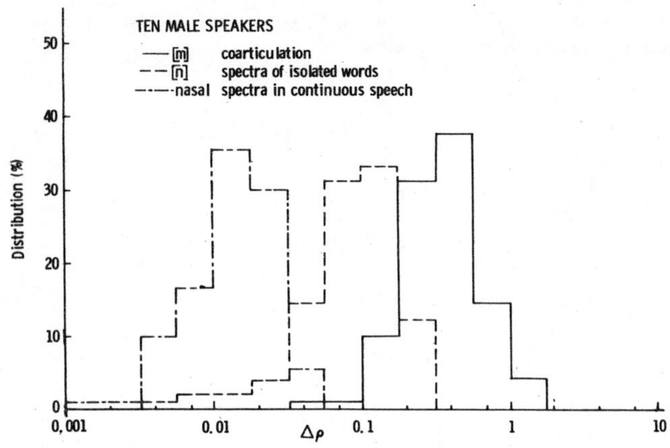

FIG. 3. Distribution of Δρ using nasal coarticulation, [n] spectra of isolated words, and nasal spectra in continuous speech as acoustic features for speaker identification.

strated that this measure is more reliable than the measures based on the known features of nasal spectra.

ACKNOWLEDGMENTS

We would like to thank Dr. Raymond G. Daniloff of the Department of Audiology and Speech Sciences of Purdue University for many helpful discussions. We would also like to thank Dr. Yoshiyuki Horii of the same department for helping us collect the digitized speech data. Thanks are also due to Mr. Thomas J. Way of IBM for editing the manuscript of this article.

*This research was supported by the Air Force Office of Scientific Research, Air Force Systems Command, USAF, under Grant No. AFOSR 69-1176.

†Present address: IBM System Products Division, Hopewell Junction, N. Y. 12533.

‡Present address: TRW Systems Group Inc., One Space Park, Redondo Beach, Calif. 90278.

[1]M. H. L. Hecker, *Speaker Recognition*, ASHA Mono. 16, (1971).

[2]J. W. Glenn and N. Kleiner, "Speaker Identification Based on Nasal Phonation," J. Acoust. Soc. Am. 43, 368–372 (1968).

[3]B. S. Atal, "Automatic Speaker Recognition Based on Pitch Contours," J. Acoust. Soc. Am. 52, 1687–1697 (1972).

[4]K. S. Das and W. S. Mohn, "A Scheme for Speech Processing in Automatic Speaker Verification," IEEE Trans. Audio Electroacoust. AU-19, 32-43 (1971).

[5]J. J. Wolf, "Efficient Acoustic Parameters for Speaker Recognition," J. Acoust. Soc. Am. 51, 2044–2056 (1972).

[6]L. S. Su and K. S. Fu, "Automatic Speaker Identification Using Nasal Spectra and Nasal Coarticulation as Acoustic Clues," Tech. Rep. TR-EE 73-33, Purdue U. (1973).

[7]K. N. Stevens, C. E. Williams, J. R. Carbonell, and Barbara Words, "Speaker Authentication and Identification: A Comparison of Spectrographic and Auditory Presentations of Speech Material," J. Acoust. Soc. Am. 44, 1496–1607 (1968).

[8]K.-P. Li and G. W. Hughes, "Talker Differences as They Appear in Correlation Matrices of Continuous Speech Spectra," J. Acoust. Soc. Am. 55, 833–837 (1974).

[9]S. E. G. Ohman, "Coarticulation in VCV Utterances: Spectrographic Measurements," J. Acoust. Soc. Am. 39, 151–168 (1966).

[10]R. G. Daniloff and K. L. Moll, "Coarticulation of Lip Rounding," J. Speech Hear. Res. 11, 707–721 (1968).

[11]K. L. Moll and R. G. Daniloff, "Investigation of the Timing of Velar Movements During Speech," J. Acoust. Soc. Am. 50, 678–684 (1971).

[12]V. A. Kozhevnikov and L. A. Chistovich, *Speech Articulation and Perception*, Joint Publ. Res. Serv., U. S. Dept. Commerce, TT:65-31233 (1966).

[13]J. L. Flanagan, *Speech Analysis, Synthesis and Perception* (Academic, New York, 1965), pp. 19–20.

[14]O. Fujimura, "Analysis of Nasal Consonants," J. Acoust. Soc. Am. 34, 1865–1875 (1962).

[15]W. L. Henke, "Dynamic Articulatory Model of Speech Production Using Computer Simulation," Ph.D. dissertation, M.I.T. (1966).

[16]R. Daniloff and R. Hammarberg, "On Defining Coarticulation," J. Phon. 3, 239–248 (1973).

[17]R.-M. S. Heffner, *General Phonetics* (Univ. Wisconsin P., Madison, Wisc., 1969), 5th Ed., p. 142.

[18]S. S. Wilks, *Mathematical Statistics* (Wiley, New York, 1962).

[19]K.-P. Li, G. W. Hughes, and A. S. House, "Correlation Characteristics and Dimensionality of Speech Spectra," J. Acoust. Soc. Am. 46, 1019–1025 (1969).

[20]D. Jones, *An Outline of English Phonetics* (Heffer, Cambridge, England, 1960), 9th Ed., pp. 168–172.

[21]O. Fujimura and J. Lindquist, "Sweep-Tone Measurements of Vocal Tract Characteristics," J. Acoust. Soc. Am. 40, 541–558 (1971).

[22]S. M. Chow, "A Brief Report on Speaker Identification Experiment," personal communication (1973).

DEVELOPMENT OF ANALYTICAL METHODS FOR A SEMI-AUTOMATIC SPEAKER IDENTIFICATION SYSTEM

by

Dr. J. E. Paul, Jr.
Dr. A. S. Rabinowitz
Dr. J. P. Riganati
Dr. J. M. Richardson
Rockwell International
Anaheim, Calif. 92803

Summary. The purpose of this paper is to describe the analytical studies leading to the development of the Semi-Automatic Speaker Identification System, the SASIS. In this system, segments of speech are extracted from two speech utterances and are computer-analyzed to yield a statistical measure indicating whether or not the utterances were said by the same or different speakers.

The analytical studies involved the collection and processing of speech data from over 250 speakers from which was extracted over 35,000 phonetic-event tokens. A study of the discriminating power of individual phonetic events, along with a study of coarticulation effects on these same events, was conducted. A unique set of 30 features was defined for each of the resultant 13 phonetic categories used by the SASIS in carrying out speaker identification. A weighted Euclidean distance measure was selected for measuring speaker similarity within a phonetic category, and a desensitized Fisher discriminant was incorporated to combine these individual distance measures into an overall measure of similarity between the speaker of two spoken utterances. A set of likelihood tables, indexed by similarity measure and the phonetic events used, was derived to determine the probability that the utterances were uttered by the same or different individuals.

Introduction

In recent years, speaker identification through the use of voiceprints has been an important and much publicized source of evidence in investigative activities and in criminal court proceedings. Speaker identification techniques currently in use are hampered by time-consuming, manual methods. The subjective nature of those methods has also led to controversy over their admissibility in courts of law.

In order to overcome these drawbacks, the Law Enforcement Assistance Administration, through the National Institute of Law Enforcement and Criminal Justice under Contract J-LEAA-025-73, has supported an effort to develop improved methods and equipment. The SASIS program, conducted by the Electronics Research Division (ERD) of Rockwell International under subcontract to The Aerospace Corporation, is a project to develop techniques for quantitative, reliable, computer-aided speaker identification. This effort consisted of an algorithm development, or analytical phase, and a prototype development phase, conducted concurrently.

The prototype system utilizes a minicomputer and associated peripherals to accept analog speech signals for processing and statistical comparison. In the criminal speech sample processing operation, specific phonetic events that have been found to have a high degree of discriminating power are identified and labeled by the operator using an interactive graphic display terminal. When a suspect sample is obtained, the same phonetic events are selected for processing. In the comparison phase, each selected event from the criminal sample is compared with the like event from a suspect sample. The points of comparison are well defined and yield quantitative results on a repeatable basis. The comparison results for all phonetic events are then combined into a statistically interpretable overall similarity measure. A more detailed treatment of the prototype system is given in these proceedings (1).

This paper treats the analytical studies carried out in developing the algorithms and procedures and the overall quantitative evaluations employed in the prototype system.

The problems that had to be solved and the tasks that had to be carried out in the SASIS analytical studies included:

1. Design of phonetically and statistically valid speech data bases and recording procedures;

2. Recruitment, screening, scheduling, and recording of over 250 speakers;

3. Processing of the data bases to examine, analyze, label, extract, and catalog over 35,000 phonetic tokens;

4. Research on the effects of coarticulation on speaker comparison;

5. Development of a large set (162) of candidate feature measurements and refining of that set down to the 30 best features for each phonetic type;

6. Research on the effects on speaker comparison of the channel over which the speech is transmitted and the acoustic surroundings at the speaker location;

Reprinted from *1975 Carnahan Conf. on Crime Countermeasures*, pp. 52-64, May 1975.

7. Development of optimum techniques for combining features into distance measures, and distance measures into similarity measures;

8. Development of statistically valid system performance testing techniques.

Background

Speech is usable for identification because it is a product of the speaker's individual anatomy and linguistic background. When air is expelled from the lungs, it passes through the glottis, which is the opening bounded on either side by the vocal folds. When the vocal folds are drawn together and air from the lungs is forced through them, they vibrate, making a buzzing sound. This sound is modified as it passes through the vocal tract, which is the tube formed principally by the pharyngeal cavity and the oral cavity. The shape of the vocal track serves to concentrate sound energy at certain frequencies and reduce it in others. During speech, the shape of the vocal track is continuously modified by movements of the tongue, lips, and other vocal organs. Thus, the quality of the speech sounds a speaker produces represents the sizes and shapes of his vocal organs and the way he uses them in speaking. Therefore, speech characteristics vary from speaker to speaker. The effect is termed inter-speaker (between speakers) variability. Speech analysis also reveals variability when the same speaker utters a given sound several times. This is called intraspeaker (within speaker) variability. Intraspeaker variability arises because the physiological activity necessary to make speech sounds need not be exactly controlled to effect adequate communication.

The speech signal produced by a given individual is affected by both the organic characteristics of the speaker (in terms of vocal tract geometry) and learned differences due to ethnic or social factors.

Research leading to the conception of the SASIS can be divided into two broad categories, one treating manual spectrographic comparison (voiceprint) techniques and the other treating automatic or semi-automatic computer-assisted speaker identification techniques.

It is generally acknowledged that voice spectrograms (voiceprints) contain significant information about speaker identity. The spectrographic comparison method has been used extensively in forensic applications but has been recently under increasing criticism from the linguistic community (2, 3, 4). The primary deficiencies in the voiceprint technique are subjectivity on the part of the voiceprint examiner and lack of continuous training of the examiner's discriminant ability.

The voiceprint research has contributed to the conception of the SASIS in establishing a definite need for the system's objectivity and introducing the concept of voice identification to the investigative and forensic application areas. The methodology of voiceprint comparison is poorly documented in the published literature, but basically attempts to match relevant areas of corresponding spectrograms for an identification decision. This method differs significantly from the SASIS in that it relies primarily upon the dynamic properties of the spectrum, whereas the SASIS approach analyzes steady-state segments of phonetic events.

The computer-assisted approach to speaker identification has also been investigated, and several systems have been proposed (5). Most techniques developed prior to SASIS have attempted to be completely automatic, based on digital spectrographic comparison of samples of speech from groups of speakers. Typically, such systems require the speakers to say a sequence of specified words, which are automatically segmented and compared using Fourier LPC or analog filter measurements. Such automatic segmentation techniques are not yet advanced to the state where these systems can deal with the kind of unconstrained speech found in criminal utterances. Therefore, the emphasis by the law enforcement community has been on techniques such as in the SASIS, which make use of the best and most dependable capabilities of both the human operator and the computer.

A prior study at Stanford Research Institute (SRI) was sponsored through the Law Enforcement Assistance Administration (LEAA) under Title I, Omnibus Crime Control and Safe Streets Act of 1963, and relates directly to applications of computer-assisted speaker recognition to law enforcement (6). This pilot study made use of interactive graphics to segment and label vowels in recorded sentences. The spectral analysis via linear predictive filtering was carried out on each vowel segment. Comparison between speakers was made, correlating the LPC spectral measurements for several vowels across different utterances of the same sentences. Based on highly restricted sentence material, the SRI study concluded that, if a decision could be avoided in 30 percent of the time, identification with error rates of less than 1 percent could be achieved.

The present study, by broadening the scope of the investigation and extending the techniques of the SRI work, has resulted in a significant reduction in the previously achieved identification error rates.

Analytical Procedures

Approach

The SASIS analytical studies project was divided into 20 tasks, each treating a particular aspect of algorithm development. The organization and sequential order of the individual task developments is shown in Figure 1. For clarity and ease of presentation, the analytical tasks are not presented in this paper in the chronological order of Figure 1, but are summarized in topic form.

Audio Data Acquisition

Two audio data bases were recorded during the course of the investigation. These data bases are defined as follows:

Data Base I - The pilot data base on which initial system design is based. This base consists of 25 General American English (GAE) dialect speakers saying 20 phonetically balanced sentences on two separate occasions, separated by approximately two weeks.

Data Base II - The system optimization and evaluation data base. This base consists of

193 GAE, 21 Chicano, and 18 Black Urban dialect speakers saying 10 phonetically balanced sentences on two separate occasions, separated by one to two weeks.

As shown in Figure 1, the sentence material used in Data Base II was based on detailed analysis of the material recorded in Data Base I. Each data base required two tasks: designing the sentences and recording the speakers.

The sentence design task was carried out in three phases: phoneme selection, vocabulary design, and sentence construction. A basic 14-phonetic-event set, Table 1, was selected for Data Base I and, following analysis, was reduced to 13 phonemes for Data Base II, dropping the schwa [ə]. This resulting candidate phoneme set constitutes the basis on which speaker identification is carried out.

A number of factors were taken into consideration in selecting the candidate phoneme set. Vowels were selected in nonnasalized, stressed positions since they have been shown to have good discriminating ability and are easily labeled. Fricatives and stop releases were not selected because they show less intraspeaker variability and are difficult

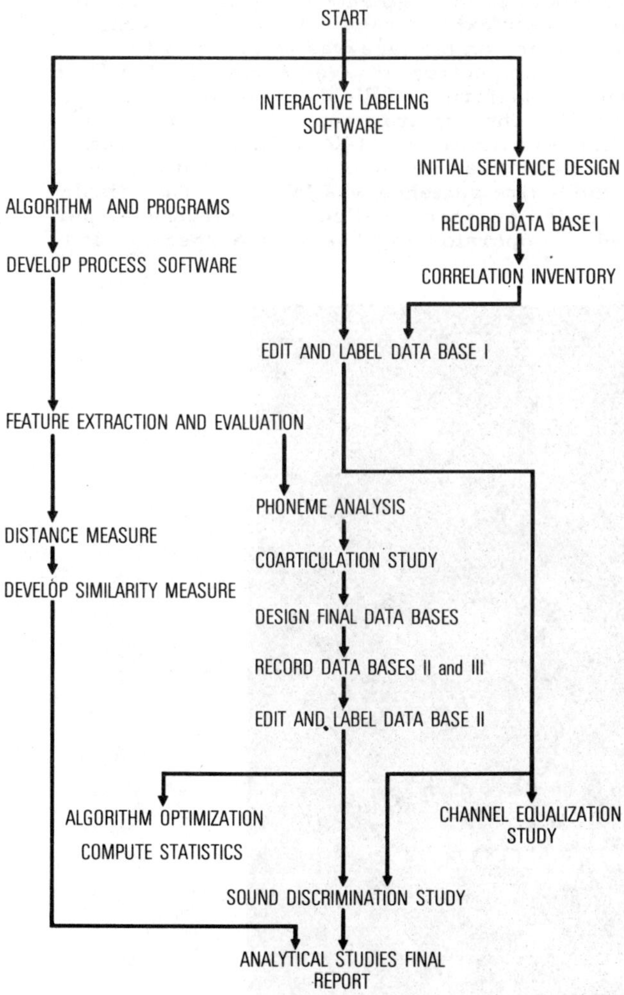

Figure 1. Task Organization of Analytical Studies Showing Sequence of Task Developments

Table 1. Candidate Phoneme Event Set for SASIS

The schwa was later dropped, leaving the first 13 phonetic events as the basis on which speaker identification is carried out. The events are numbered from 23-33.

Event No.	Event	Example
23	i	eve
24	I	it
25	ɛ	met
26	a	ask
27	ɑ	father
31	ʌ	up
32	ɝ	bird
28	ɔ	all
29	ʊ	put
30	u	boot
20	m	me
21	n	no
22	ŋ	sing
33	ə	the (schwa)

to analyze. Diphthongs and glides were not selected due to the lack of steady-state intervals for analysis.

In order to consider the effects of coarticulation on the candidate phonetic events, a set of phonetic contexts was specified to be included in the sentence material. Context here is defined as the two phonetic events in juxtaposition to the candidate event. These three events are referred to collectively as a triad. By specifying the context, a measurement of coarticulation effects was carried out. Coarticulation refers to the influence of one phonetic state, during articulation, on another and results principally from the dynamics of lip and tongue motion.

A diverse set of contexts was incorporated into Data Base I, which was analyzed to consolidate contexts having similar effects and to reduce the context requirements on Data Base II. The context of a phonetic event was specified for this study in terms of hub position, i.e., the position of the second major resonance, or formant (7). Hubs were quantified into low, middle, and high positions. For each vowel, tokens were represented with the same hub position on either side for low, middle, and high positions. Nasals were not considered in context since the effect of hub context on them is considered minimal.

The vocabulary was designed from the specified triads, and sentences were constructed from the vocabulary. Declarative, interrogative, and imperative sentence structures were used with emphasis on longer sentences to minimize end effects. A total of 20 sentences were designed for Data Base I, incorporating 167 labelable triads. Ten sentences with 61 labelable triads were composed for Data Base II.

Sentence recording was carried out in a semi-anechoic sound booth measuring 56 × 48 × 105 inches. The sound booth contained two dynamic microphones, positioned approximately 12 inches from the speaker's lips and 20 degrees either side, as well as a conventional telephone instrument. The two microphones were mixed on one channel of a tape recorder, and the telephone was recorded by the second channel. The sound booth also included two wall speakers, one as an intercom channel for the recording supervisor to communicate with the subject speaker and the other over which prerecorded instructions were played.

For Data Base I, 25 male General American English (GAE) speakers were recruited and recorded on two occasions, separated by approximately two weeks. Documentation of the speaker's linguistic characteristics was maintained. Recording was directed by the supervisor, who monitored the speaker during recording.

Each sentence was played to the speaker followed by a tone directing him to say that sentence. The speaker was recorded through the telephone handset and the dynamic microphones, though only the telephone data were employed during analysis.

Data Base II was recorded in a similar fashion. A total of 193 GAE, 21 Chicano, and 18 Black Urban dialect male speakers were recorded on two occasions using the 10-sentence set designed for this data base. A total of 119 audio tapes were required to record the two data bases.

Interactive Labeling and Segmenting Phonetic Data

A computer interactive graphics procedure was developed to permit analog-to-digital conversion (digitizing) of the recorded speech sentences, selecting and labeling candidate phonetic events within the sentences, and segmenting three pitch periods of the steady-state portion of each selected phonetic event. A total of over 35,000 events were labeled and segmented from Data Base I and Data Base II.

The first phase of this procedure involved digitizing the prerecorded spoken sentences. The audio from the telephone channel was passed through the combination of a C-2 telephone channel simulator and a 3.2-kHz, low-pass sampling filter. The resultant audio was sampled at 6.8 kHz by the analytical studies computer. The sentence digitizing was controlled by an operator at the interactive graphics console. He first instructed the computer to sample 10 seconds of speech after which a display of the smoothed energy in the digitized signal was displayed on the CRT (Figure 2). The operator next isolated the sentence with a set of electronic crosshairs, or cursors. He then verified the sentence using digital-to-analog playback between the cursors and judged whether to accept or reject the utterance. Upon acceptance, complete speaker and sentence identification information was entered, and the isolated sentence was automatically stored on a digital output tape by the computer.

The digital sentence tape was then processed by the labeling and segmentation program in order to identify and extract candidate phonetic events. Each sentence on the tape was transformed to a digital voice spectrogram (voiceprint) via the Fast Fourier Transform and displayed on the CRT (see Figure 3). The spectrographic display frame on the CRT was limited to 1100 milliseconds. The operator advanced the display a frame at a time until the entire sentence was labeled. This display phase of the program, called the macrophase, permitted the operator to observe the spectral and

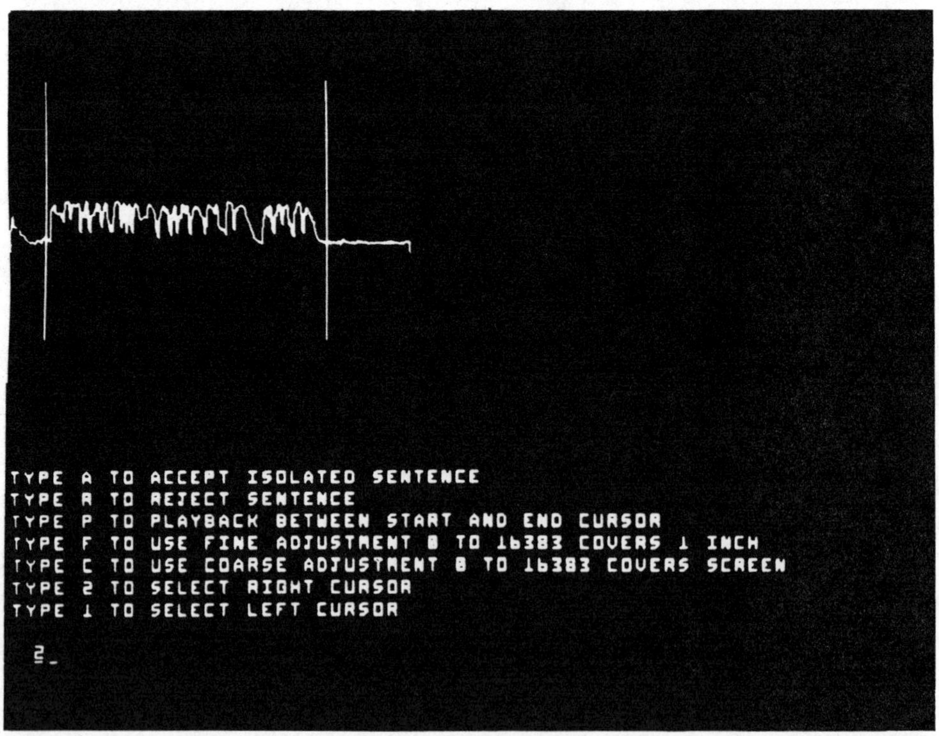

Figure 2. Interactive Graphics Display During Sentence Digitizing Showing Amplitude Contour and Cursor-Isolated Sentence

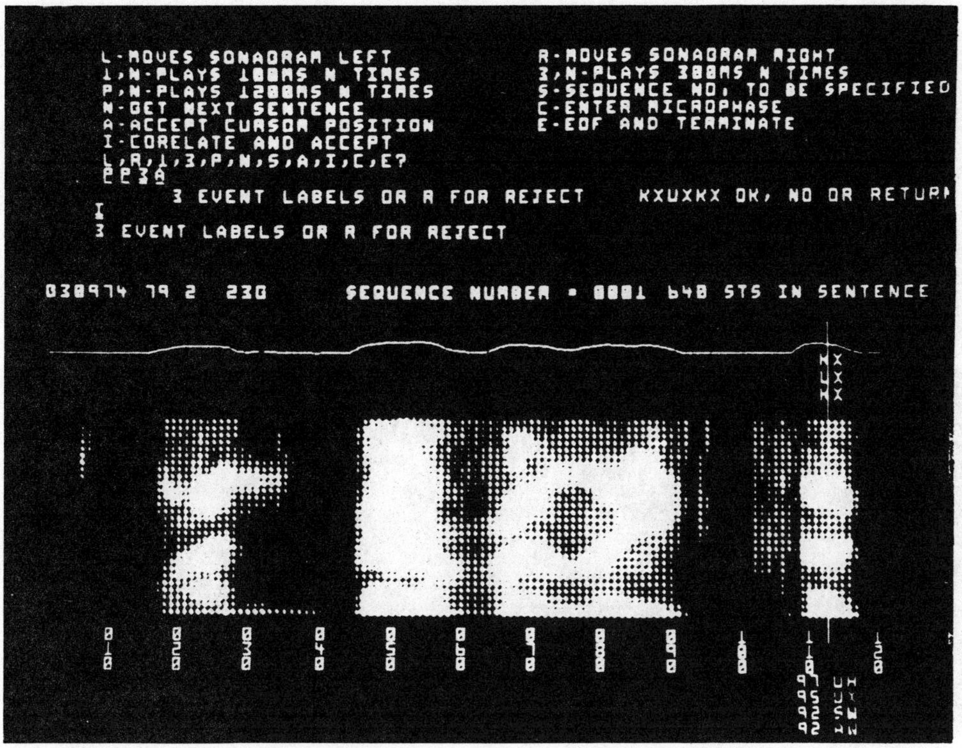

Figure 3. Interactive Graphics Display of Macrophase During Labeling Showing Spectrogram of "When Beverly Cooks..." with the /U/ in "Cooks" Labeled

amplitude characteristics of the utterance and to locate with a cursor the candidate phonetic events. The operator established the identity of the candidate phonetic event by making use of several aids including observing the spectrum, playing back via digital-to-analog converter the speech in the interval centered on the cursor, and requesting that the computer judge the identity by correlating the spectral sample designated by the cursor with a set of reference spectra stored in the computer.

Following the macrophase, a three-pitch period interval of the steady-state portion of each labeled phonetic event was segmented in the microphase. During this phase of the program, 75 milliseconds of the speech waveform from each labeled phonetic event in the macrophase was displayed on the CRT (Figure 4). The operator utilized two cursors to specify the beginning and end of a three-pitch period interval for that phonetic event. This interval was then played back (concatenated 10 times) to the operator for label verification. Upon acceptance by the operator, the three-pitch-period waveform, along with label data, was stored in an output file by the computer. In this fashion, over 35,000 phonetic-event tokens were labeled and segmented from the two data bases.

Phoneme Analyses and Coarticulation Study

Two studies were carried out, utilizing the phonetic tokens from Data Base I, to evaluate the speaker discriminating power of each phonetic event and to consolidate phonetic contexts that have similar coarticulative effects. The results of these two studies were incorporated into the criteria specifying Data Base II sentence design.

In carrying out the phoneme analysis study, it was first necessary to determine the mode in which two phonetic events from different recordings should be compared. Three modes were considered and included:

1. Context independent - any two phonetic events of the same type are suitable for comparison.

2. Context dependent - any two phonetic events of the same type are suitable for comparison if their hub contexts are the same.

3. Text dependent - two phonetic events of the same type are suitable for comparison if they occur in the same identical phonetic contexts.

Comparison was carried out by measuring the F-ratio of the correlations between pairs of candidate phonetic events. The F-ratio is a figure of merit, having larger values when the events have a greater discriminating value. The F-ratio increases monotonically from context independent to text dependent, by a factor of approximately 2:1 across all phonetic event categories. Text dependency was selected as the SASIS basis of comparison.

The purpose of phoneme analyses was to rank the discriminating power of individual phonetic categories. Several ranking procedures were carried out in the text-dependent mode. These include two F-ratio rankings and one ranking based on the SASIS operating characteristic (SOC) curves.

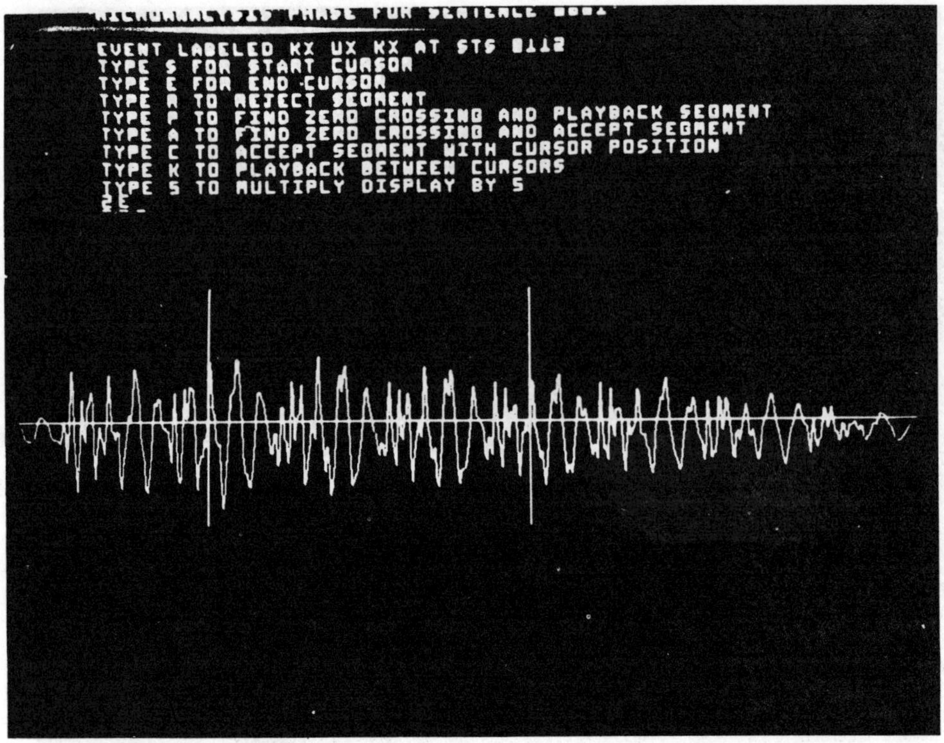

Figure 4. Interactive Graphics Display of Microphase Showing Cursor-Isolated Three-Pitch-Period Segment from /U/ of "Cooks"

Comparison based on the SOC curves was selected because these curves (to be discussed later) yield a better appraisal of performance in the region of intraspeaker/interspeaker overlap, the region of greatest speaker confusion. Table 2 gives the rankings from this comparison. From these experiments it was concluded that front vowels, high vowels, and nasals appear to possess greater speaker discrimination capability than other types.

The set of three defined contexts (low hub-vowel-low hub, middle hub-vowel-middle hub, and high hub-vowel-high hub) for each vowel were reduced to an average of two hubs for each vowel in the coarticulation study. Context was not considered in the case of nasals, since the effect on them is considered minimal. The analysis of hub contexts was carried out in a qualitative manner, plotting the spectrum for each hub context for each phonetic category and combining those contexts experiencing similar effects. It was concluded that the mean spectra for most vowel types embedded in high hub consonantal contexts differs little from those for mid hub consonantal contexts. The mean spectra for high and middle cases of a phonetic type were usually substantially different from that of the low hub consonantal context.

Feature Extraction

The next step in developing the speaker identification process was that of extracting useful features from the three-pitch-period speech segments isolated during the labeling process. The features extracted from these time waveforms were the parameters on which identification was based.

A feature is a digital parameter extracted from the speech time series carrying information about the speaker's identity. It is desirable that the

Table 2. Ranking of Event by SOC Curve Under Text-Dependent Constraint

The distance measure used was the weighted Euclidean operating on 30 features.

Highest Ranked
U
u
i
m
I
a
ɔ
n
ŋ
ʌ
ɝ
ɑ
ɛ
Lowest Ranked

feature measure some aspect of the signal which distinguishes one speaker from another, i.e., that the interspeaker variations are substantially greater than the intraspeaker variations of that feature. An additional desirable property of a feature is that it contributes information to the identification process not found in other features in the feature set, i.e., that it be reasonably uncorrelated with other features. If this latter property is not satisfied and the subsequent identification function is incapable of decorrelating the features, then identification performance is usually degraded.

A feature extraction task was undertaken as part of the analytical studies to define a unique set of 30 features for each phonetic event category. This feature selection process was carried out in three phases, as follows:

1. Define a large set of features using a heuristic procedure;

2. Evalute each feature on a first-order basis (without regard to interfeature dependencies) and derive weights for each feature;

3. Select a subset of features for each phonetic event category using a second-order (interfeature correlation) selection procedure.

The end product of this study was a set of features along with a corresponding set of weights defining the quantitative value of each feature in the identification process. The weights were used by the distance measure in computing inter-phonetic-event distances.

The first step in the feature selection process was definition of a candidate set of features. The set was designed to extract speaker information from the speech process. No consideration was given to interfeature dependencies in defining the candidate set, since the purpose of the feature selection phase was to decorrelate features.

The features selected were of a static nature; i.e., they were extracted from the isolated three-pitch-period interval of acoustic speech data. No information was derived from the acoustic signal external to this interval. This static constraint prohibited use of transitional information used in the subjective voice-spectrogram-comparison procedures. Two additional constraints were factored into the definition process and included observing the telephone channel bandwidth and requiring that feature rules be implementable on the prototype SASIS system without excessive complexity.

A set of 162 candidate features was defined as the basis from which 30 were eventually selected for each phonetic type. These features, which are summarized in Table 3, were based on Fourier, linear predictive filter, and time domain measurements.

The next step in the feature selection process is the evaluation of individual features based on a figure of merit. The evaluation process is carried out for each of the 162 features for each of the 13 phonetic types. The F-ratio was applied to each feature independently (8). It measured the relative usefulness of a feature for discriminating among speakers and computed from the data sample values in the following manner:

$$F = \frac{\text{variance of speaker means}}{\text{mean of individual speaker variances}}$$

The F-ratio computed applied the text-dependency constraint in determining means and variances.

The final phase of the feature selection task was that of selecting a 30-feature subset of the 162 candidate features for each phonetic event category. The subset selected was the set of features subsequently used in the distance measure computation for that phonetic event. The selection process employed was based on the F-ratio derived in the feature evaluation phase and on the 162-dimensional feature correlation matrix. The process involved a sequential procedure that made use of the F-ratio rank ordering of the features and the interfeature cross-correlation matrix. In the selection process, the next feature accepted had (1) the highest F-ratio and (2) a correlation coefficient no greater than 0.6 with features already selected.

Table 3. Summary of 162 Candidate Features from Which 30 Features Were Selected for Each Phonetic Category

Features	Description
1-13	Fourier spectral derivatives measuring slope of spectrum from 300 to 2900 Hz.
14-31	Special features measuring ratios of spectral energy in various segments of the spectrum.
32-35	Time domain features measuring autocorrelation and pitch period.
36-92	Fourier spectral measurements including (a) 25 200-Hz-wide measurements from 300 through 3200 Hz and (b) 32 assorted bandwidths across the same spectrum.
93-99	Linear-predictive-filter-derived special features including formant bandwidths and locations, and rms estimation error.
100-162	Linear predictive tenth-order filter spectral estimates every 53 Hz from 53 through 3346 Hz.

The two parameters, the subset of 30 features and the maximum interfeature correlation coefficient of 0.6, were derived empirically from Data Base I. The feature sets were derived from Data Base I and were optimized using 75 randomly selected speakers from Data Base II.

The feature sets selected in this process were usually found to include parameters measuring pitch period, spectral derivative, and estimates in the region of the second and third formants and spectral ratios sensitive to formant regions. Spectral derivatives and estimates for the first formant were not usually selected, except for the low vowels, where that formant rises above the lower frequency cutoff of the telephone channel.

Merging: Reduction of System Complexity Without Loss of Significant Phonetic Events

Fourteen phonetic events were labeled in the various data bases. Operationally, it is desirable to be able to use the system if any subset of these is present. Various notions for extracting and clustering the statistical information contained in the data bases were conceptually explored before the determination was made that the most reasonable match, to both the forensic application of SASIS and the schedule of data availability, was to tabulate the performance for all possible subsets. Consideration of disc storage and table computational time suggests a set of 10 events yielding 1023 subsets as a reasonable tabulation goal. An analysis was carried out to determine if this is indeed a reasonable goal and, if so, specifically how it was to be attained without discarding any useful phonetic events. The solution is to discard one phonetic event and to merge three pairs of events. This merging process enables the system to retain the information in these phonetic events but to suppress their effect on the combinatorial explosion. The pairs are chosen to minimize the degradation in performance. The degradation that does result is very small.

Event /ə/ was eliminated from consideration for the following reasons:

1. It is the single event with the least number of tokens available.

2. It is not well represented in the data base (labeled only in "the").

3. Although /ə/ occurs with a total relative frequency of over 90 percent, this is actually a lopsided average of over 16 percent unstressed and 0.04 percent stressed. Its unstressed, aperiodic structure makes it difficult to label and, as implied by (1) above, it frequently is unlabelable.

4. As a frequently occurring unstressed neutral, it is very likely to result in confusions with many other unstressed events, resulting in a large variation in performance.

Hence, for the purposes of SASIS, there are 13 phonetic events considered.

The relative frequency of occurrences of the SASIS phonetic events was tabulated. These data were extracted to prevent the possible merging of two phonetic events, each of which had a very high percentage of occurrence. If this were to occur, the resultant event class would be too large a fraction of the total and the results of SASIS would be excessively sensitive to the presence of this event class.

The criteria used for selecting three pairs of the 13 events to be merged relate to (1) the most likely phonetic confusion pairs chosen in terms of similarity on the vowel quadrangle, (2) similarity of event pairs as viewed by measures relating to the overlap of intraspeaker and interspeaker distributions, and (3) the correlation coefficients computed separately on intraspeaker and interspeaker data. Several sets of the form shown in Table 4 were considered. The final result is to merge set (1) in the table; i.e., (25-26) (ɛ-a), (27-28) (α-ɔ), and (29-30) (U-u).

Table 4. Candidate Sets of Phonetic Events for Merging

	(1)	(2)	(3)	(4)	(5)
Phonetic Confusion Pairs:	25-26 27-28 29-30	25-26 27-28 21-22	25-26 27-28 23-24	21-22 23-24 29-30	26-28 23-24 29-30
	(6)	**(7)**	**(8)**	**(9)**	**(10)**
High Intra and Inter Correlation:	31-26 25-24 28-27	26-25 31-28 29-24	31-28 25-24 29-26	25-24 28-26 27-31	28-26 31-25 29-24

Distance and Similarity Measures

Overview: A Two-Step Approach. Many structures are feasible to map features extracted from phonetic events into a similarity measure between two utterances. The following structure describes the architecture within which this investigation was conducted:

1. Any one of 10 phonetic event groups may be present in the base (or reference) sentence(s) (or utterance(s)).

2. For each event to be used in the base sentence (in the form of one or more triads), the query (or suspect) sentence(s) have one or more triads.

3. For each event present in the base sentence, a single distance measure is obtained by comparison of allowable triad pairs or tokens (those having the same sentence position).

4. Complete or partial sentence repetitions are explicitly handled by the distance measure.

5. The similarity measure explicitly allows any combination of the 10 events to be present and produces a likelihood ratio whose reliability is, of course, a function of the data upon which it is based (number of distances, which distances, number of tokens upon which the distances were based).

6. Guidelines for interpretation of the likelihood ratio are presented which may be used to make a same, different, or insufficient data decision (a "two choice open decision": TCOD).

Figure 5 shows the two-step distance and similarity structure.

Distance Measure Development. While the formal properties of a metric must be kept in mind, engineering applications in the pattern classification context have generalized the intuition behind this structure to include a wide variety of measures to compare pattern points (elements of a basic set). The two-step process described in Figure 5 was chosen for SASIS because it provides enough degrees of freedom to permit obtaining a reasonable solution given the time and schedule constraints and the *a priori* unknown nature of the data. The overall similarity measure certainly may be viewed as a metric. We chose to apply this terminology only to the first step of the development.

The distance being sought is to be a measure of the separation between the feature representation of the steady state portion of identical triads in identical sentence position. Since a phonetic event is expected to be found in several such triad pairs, for a given operational comparison of a base and query sentence, the distance measure must specifically take this into account. Since repetition of the query sentence has not been part of the data bases collected, the operational form remains to be defined and the distance measure results given below do not consider this aspect of the operation.

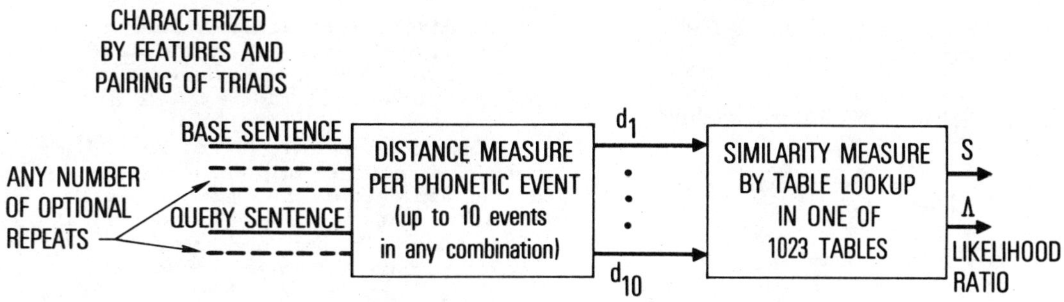

Figure 5. Two-Step Distance and Similarity Structure

A frequently used, geometrically based, measure of distance is the Euclidean form, which may be interpreted as motivated by an energy criterion and second order statistics. For classification purposes, a large distance between any pair of components (features) tends to dominate the result. This suggests that alternate forms, such as a weighted sum, a saturating "local" distance, or powers other than the square, may be less sensitive to individual features and may more suitably represent the separation of triads.

Distance measures were evaluated based on comparisons of SASIS operating characteristic curves (SOC curves). The curves represent the cumulative error distribution that would result if specific values of similarity measure were used in making decisions regarding whether two voice samples came from the same or different speakers. Figures 6(a) and 6(b) indicate how the SOC curves are derived. The SOC curves are used as an evaluation figure of merit that indicates sensitivity in the ϵ_1 and ϵ_2 overlap region.

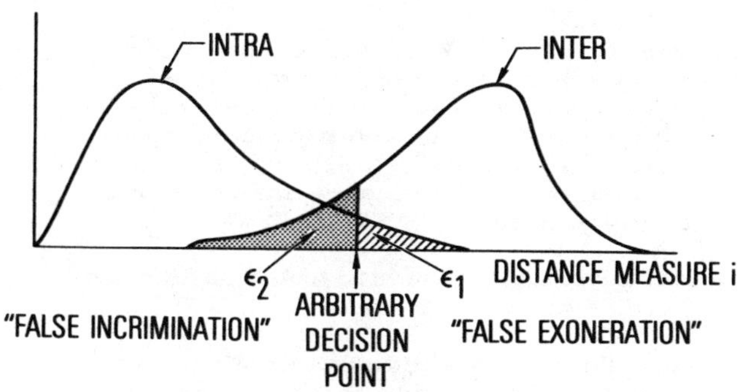

Figure 6(a). Intraspeaker and Interspeaker Normalized Histograms

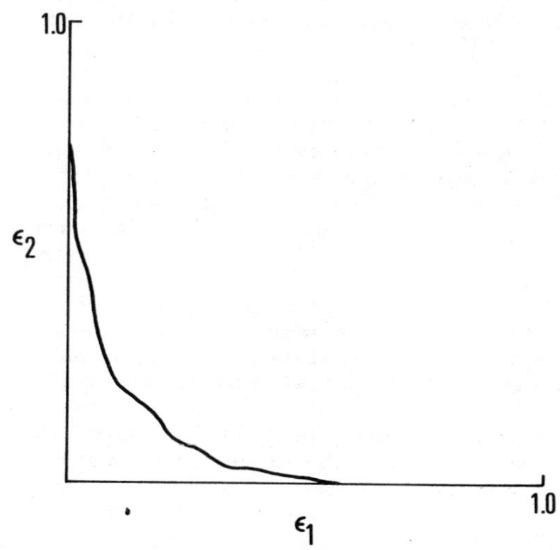

Figure 6(b). SOC (SASIS Operating Characteristic)

Figure 7 presents a summary of SOC comparisons made for all 14 phonetic events for the first seven distance measures listed in Table 5. The ideal no-overlap condition is represented by the two axes. If the curves cross, a subjective judgment must be made. Of course, this may be made

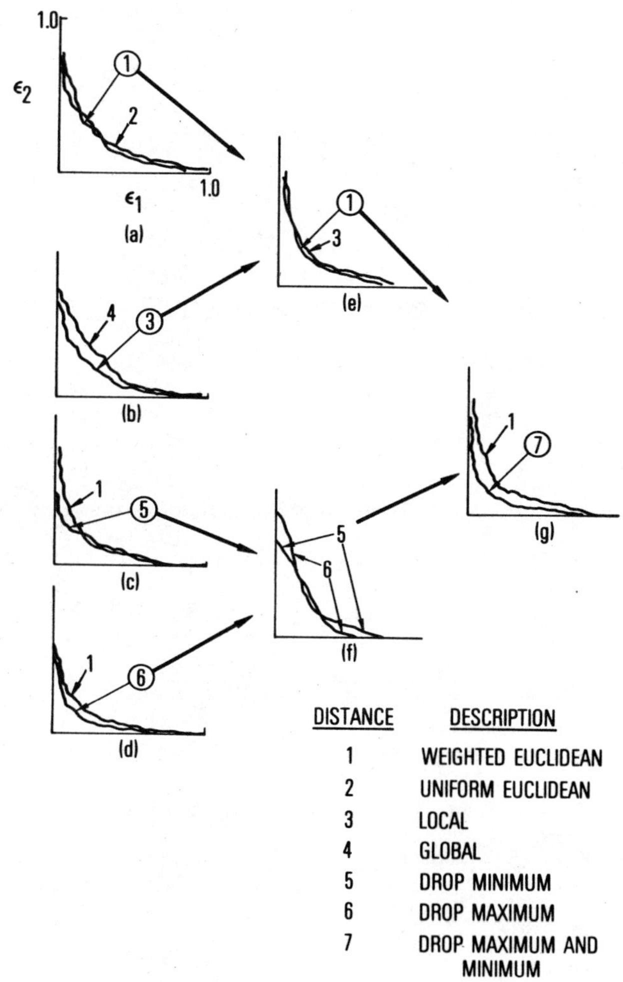

Figure 7. Summary of Comparison of Distance Measures $d_1, \ldots, d_7$

Table 5. Distance Forms Considered Per Triad Pair

$$d_1^2 = \sum_{i \epsilon I} W_i^2 (x_i - y_i)^2 \qquad \text{weighted Euclidean}$$

$$d_2^2 = \sum_{i \epsilon I} (x_i - y_i)^2 \qquad \text{uniform Euclidean}$$

$$d_3^2 = \sum_{i \epsilon I} g_i[(x_i - y_i)^2] \qquad \text{local}$$

$$\text{where } g_i[T] = \begin{cases} g_i(2.5\,\sigma_i), & T \geq 2.5\,\sigma_i \\ T, & T < 2.5\,\sigma_i \end{cases}$$

I = subset of total number of features available

x_i, y_i = values of feature i for two corresponding phonetic events from distinct utterances X and Y

W_i = an arbitrary weight associated with feature i

σ_i = standard deviation of feature i

$$d_4^2 = \sum_{i \epsilon I} g_i[(x_i - y_i)^2] \qquad \text{global}$$

$$\text{where } g_i[T] = \begin{cases} T, & T \geq 2.5\,\sigma_i \\ g_i(2.5\,\sigma_i), & T < 2.5\,\sigma_i \end{cases}$$

<u>data edited forms</u>

$d_5^2 \sim d_1^2$ except drop minimum per speaker comparison

$d_6^2 \sim d_1^2$ except drop maximum per speaker comparison

$d_7^2 \sim d_1^2$ except drop minimum and maximum per speaker comparison

<u>discriminant forms</u>

$$d_8 = \Sigma\, W_i\, \overline{d}_i$$

where $d_i = (x_i - y_i)^2$

$\overline{d}_i$ = average d_i over matching triad pairs

$W_i = [E(\overline{d}_i/\text{intra}) - E(\overline{d}_i/\text{inter})]\ \text{Var}(\overline{d}_i/\text{inter})^{-1}$

$$d_9 = \Sigma\, W_i\, Z_i$$

where $Z_i = (x_i - \mu_i)(y_i - \mu_i)$

$\mu_i = \frac{1}{2}$ average speaker triads $(x_i + y_i)$

$\overline{Z}_i$ = average Z_i over matching triad pairs

$W_i = [E(\overline{Z}_i/\text{intra}) - E(Z_i/\text{inter})]\ \text{Var}(\overline{Z}_i/\text{inter})^{-1}$

quantitatively, for example, defining the area under the SOC curve as an auxiliary figure of merit. This has not been done because the use of the SOC curve is already a qualitative comparison.

Distance form d_1, the weighted Euclidean metric, is not the optimum measure when the SOC curves are used as the figure of merit. However, the differences between this measure and the best of the above alternatives are slight. The data editing forms have the subjectively annoying characteristics of being inapplicable when the data are sparse. The discriminant function forms are apparently erratic over the data examined. The global/local thresholding conjectures actually made the SOC curves worse. Hence, the upshot of this investigation was to confirm the utility of the generally used properly weighted Euclidean sum. There is no doubt that superior measures are attainable, but none has been found which is significantly and consistently better from the viewpoint of the figures of merit employed.

<u>Similarity Measure Development</u>

For a given phonetic event class, e, the distance between two speakers (who may or may not be the same person) is denoted by d_e. For a particular operational speaker comparison, there are one or more phonetic event classes and their corresponding distances, yielding a vector

$$\overline{d} = \left\{ d_e \,|\, e \,\epsilon\, \mathcal{S}_e \right\}$$

whose components are the individual phonetic event distances that are present (this set is denoted by $\mathcal{S}_e$). The similarity measure must accept this vector $\overline{d}$, of dimension 1 to 10, and produce a quantitative measure of similarity between the two speakers that has (1) statistical significance and (2) an understandable interpretation.

An ideal similarity measure would satisfy the following criteria:

1. It must be insensitive to sampling fluctuations in the training set; i.e., it must have almost the same value when computed for two different random samplings of the same parent population.
2. It must converge to a definite limit as the size of the training set increases.
3. It must be a good measure in the case of low false incrimination probabilities. (If it is used as an investigative tool, this is less important.)
4. It must be as free of subjective elements as possible.
5. Whatever subjective elements exist must be of a kind that is widely accepted by workers in information sciences, in particular, mathematical statistics.
6. The measure must be of such a nature that it can be used by the law enforcement community.

7. It must be easy to compute for a multiplicity of sets $\mathcal{S}_e$ of phonetic events available for comparison purposes.

Given the distance vector $\bar{d}$ of dimension K between 1 and 10 (i.e., there are K particular events present for a particular speaker pair comparison), mappings or transformations of $\bar{d}$, into a scalar S, of the following form have been investigated:

$$S = \bar{a}^T \bar{d} + \bar{d}^T B \bar{d}$$

where $\bar{a}$ is a constant vector of dimension K and B is a constant K × K matrix. The motivations for consideration of this set of transformations come from several directions:

1. The form is readily amenable to analysis.
2. It is optional with respect to figures of merit and functional forms that are widely used in mathematical statistics.
3. It reasonably satisfies the criteria listed above.
4. It represents a logical extension of previous work.

A series of experiments was conducted for the purpose of comparing the levels of performance of various candidate similarity measures.

Three metric forms were empirically examined:

1. The Fisher linear discriminant

$$S = \bar{a}^T \bar{d}$$

where $\bar{a}$ = [E($\bar{d}^T$/same speaker class) - E($\bar{d}^T$)/different speaker class)] C^{-1}

2. The linear discriminant for the case of the separating plane perpendicular to the vector connecting the class means (C = I)

$$S = \bar{a}^T \bar{d}$$

where $\bar{a}$ = E($\bar{d}^T$/same speaker class) - E($\bar{d}^T$/different speaker class)

3. The uniform linear discriminant

$$S = \bar{a}^T \bar{d}$$

where $\bar{a}^T = [1\ 1 \ldots\ 1]$.

The primary criterion of performance used was total area of the SOC curve. For each of the three metrics above, 24 SOC curves were developed. Twelve plots were generated by repeatedly defining the metric to be a function of the N highest ranked types of the SOC ranking, based on the distances of single phonetic events. The parameter N, therefore, ranged from 2 to 13 and the weight vector $\bar{a}$ was recomputed for each value of N. In a similar manner, the remaining 12 curves resulted from the N lowest ranked types. The resulting three sets of SOC curves and plots of the error rate as a function of dimensionality at $\epsilon_1 = \epsilon_2$ were qualitatively compared.

Based on results, a decision was made to use the Fisher metric, but with a suitable desensitization of the covariance matrix to reduce the degradation experienced at higher dimensionality and dependency on the intrinsic characteristics of Data Base II.

Additional empirical results indicate that the inclusion of appropriate nonlinear terms can provide additional speaker separation beyond that attainable by a linear sum of distances. However, because of the highly subjective nature of performing a suitable nonlinear form through empirical study, this task was beyond the scope of this work. Although the linear form selected is certainly suboptimal, it is quite well matched to the problem structure, in view of the limited analytical exploration described above. The fact that the data became available largely at the end of this examination played a significant role in the posing of the hypotheses and the resulting procedure described above.

System Evaluation

A basic philosophy employed during the development of this system has been to avoid restrictive assumptions whenever possible and to explicitly state all assumptions that must be made, accompanied, where it is reasonable to do so, by demonstration or illustration of their validity. This must especially be true for the evaluation and the associated statistical interpretations.

Data Organization. The General American English (GAE) portion of Data Base II consists of 193 speakers in two sessions numbered nonconsecutively from 1 to 233. Since the method used to record and number speakers has some possibility of producing groups of similar speakers (because of similar backgrounds, jobs, etc.), the speaker numbers were randomized. The data from the first 75 speakers from this randomized list are selected for the training portion of the system evaluation procedure; the remaining 118 are selected for the testing portion.

The data organization is shown in Figure 8. Intraspeaker comparisons are found on the main diagonal. Only those interspeaker comparisons shown shaded are used. This data editing procedure allows manipulation of 25 × 25 matrix subportions within the core limitations of the computer at no significant sacrifice in statistical significance because (1) all the intraspeaker comparisons are fully utilized; (2) an order of magnitude more interspeaker comparison than intraspeaker comparison data is considered (considerably more are available--all the unshaded regions of Figure 8--but their use is costly and cumbersome and adds very little to the significance of the results); (3) the prerandomization of the speaker selection order assures that the data in the shaded regions are taken from throughout an original matrix that might have been constructed from the unrandomized list of speakers.

A tabulation of the number of distance tokens available shows that the number of tokens available per speaker comparison ranges from 0 to 9 and is

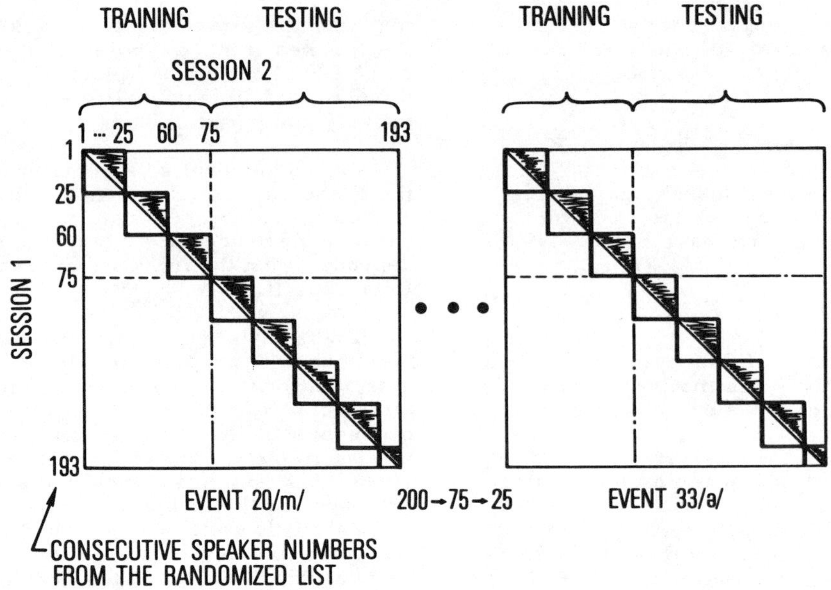

Figure 8. SASIS Data Base II Organization for System Evaluation

clustered between 4 and 6 for most events. It is desirable to so structure these data that the statistics obtained are representative of those which will be found operationally. To this end, the following assumption has been made:

> A realistic number of triad pairs from which a distance is calculated, per phonetic event available, is three.

Since the distance used for a phonetic event is an average over the number available, the available tokens have been grouped in three's for the calculations made on this base.

Given that there are 10 phonetic event classes defined, the data structuring described above is further described in Figure 9. The block of 100 numbers is available for any speaker comparison of the form: Speaker i Session 1 versus Speaker j Session 2, with i and j arbitrary and each in the range 1,..., 193.

From any one block such as that shown in Figure 9 a large number of "pseudo comparison sessions" may be generated. Based on the assumptions above, each of the 10 numbers on each of the 10 lines represents a realistic distance between the two speakers, i and j, for the particular phonetic class indicated by the line. A "pseudo comparison session" is defined as follows:

1. Select n of the 10 phonetic event classes, for any value of n = 1,..., 10 (this may be done, of course, ${}_{10}C_n$ ways).

2. Select any arbitrary one of the 10 numbers from the first phonetic event class; then select the corresponding value (e.g., the 5th) from each of the other phonetic event classes (this may be done 10 ways).

The total number of "psuedo comparison sessions" for a single comparison block is now

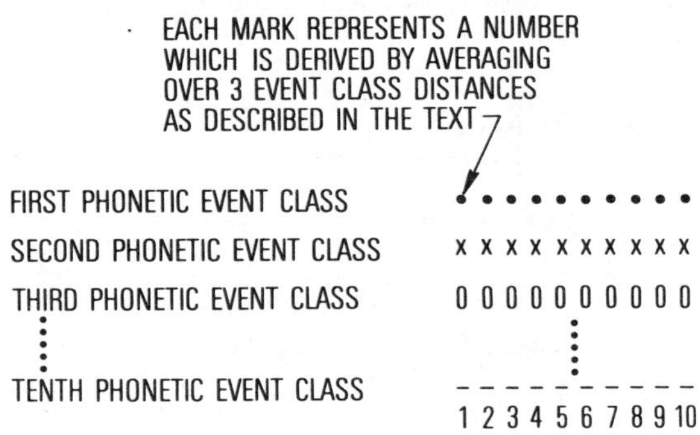

Figure 9. Data Structure for Any Speaker Pair Comparison of the Form: Speaker i Session 1 Speaker j Session 2

$$\sum_{n=1}^{10} {}_{10}C_n \cdot 10 = 10 \cdot (1023) = 10230 \approx 10^4$$

<u>Considerations for Presenting the Results.</u> The 118 GAE speakers in the testing portion of Data Base II are used to calculate the system performance. The results have been tabulated in the forms shown in Table 6.

Table 6 is the first sheet of a 1023-page detailed tabulation for all combinations of the 10 events. It lists the similarity measure, density values, distribution values, and the resulting likelihood ratio Λ and may be used to obtain the 95 percent confidence interval for the probabilities and Λ. Examination of the full set shows that the results generally improve as the number of events increases, as would be expected, but that certain event combinations are significantly superior to others. The improvement is much more marked in the low numbers of events region. This indicates that the number of events used is sufficient to extract substantially all the information that is available under the SASIS problem formulation. The

Table 6. First Sheet from 1023-Page Detailed Tabulation

09:19:32 SASISTAB REAL-TIME MONITOR 3.1 PAGE 1

SIM	LAMBDA	E1	E2	P1	P2	SIM	LAMBDA	E1	E2	P1	P2	SIM	LAMBDA	E1	E2	P1	P2	SIM	LAMBDA	E1	E2	P1	P2
0.00	100.00	100	0	34	31	1.72	9.13	56	6	37	2	3.40	0.13	5	39	1	7	5.09	0.01	0	84	0	6
0.07	31.23	96	3	0	0	1.75	8.27	52	6	23	4	3.44	0.13	5	40	2	8	5.12	0.01	0	85	0	5
0.10	31.23	96	3	0	0	1.79	7.44	50	6	25	2	3.47	0.12	4	40	2	10	5.16	0.01	0	85	1	6
0.13	31.23	96	3	0	0	1.82	6.87	48	7	19	3	3.50	0.11	4	41	2	11	5.19	0.01	0	86	0	5
0.17	31.23	96	3	0	0	1.85	6.33	46	7	25	3	3.54	0.10	4	42	2	13	5.22	0.01	0	86	0	6
0.20	30.97	96	3	0	0	1.89	5.75	43	7	16	4	3.57	0.10	4	44	4	10	5.26	0.01	0	87	0	4
0.24	30.97	96	3	0	0	1.92	5.26	42	8	22	4	3.61	0.08	3	45	1	11	5.29	0.01	0	87	0	5
0.27	30.97	96	3	0	0	1.95	4.75	39	8	19	5	3.64	0.08	3	46	2	10	5.32	0.01	0	88	0	4
0.30	30.97	96	3	0	0	1.99	4.27	38	8	13	3	3.67	0.07	3	47	12	9	5.36	0.01	0	88	0	5
0.34	30.97	96	3	0	0	2.02	3.99	36	9	18	6	3.71	0.05	2	48	1	8	5.39	0.01	0	89	0	4
0.37	30.97	96	3	1	0	2.06	3.56	34	9	8	5	3.74	0.04	2	49	0	10	5.43	0.01	0	89	0	4
0.40	30.94	95	3	0	0	2.09	3.31	34	10	17	4	3.77	0.04	2	50	1	12	5.46	0.01	0	90	0	5
0.44	30.94	95	3	0	0	2.12	3.03	32	10	9	4	3.81	0.04	2	51	1	9	5.49	0.01	0	90	0	5
0.47	30.94	95	3	0	0	2.16	2.84	31	11	15	7	3.84	0.04	2	52	1	12	5.53	0.01	0	91	0	5
0.51	30.94	95	3	10	0	2.19	2.54	30	11	8	5	3.88	0.04	1	53	1	10	5.56	0.01	0	91	0	3
0.54	30.61	94	3	0	0	2.22	2.37	29	12	8	4	3.91	0.03	1	54	1	10	5.59	0.01	0	91	0	4
0.57	30.61	94	3	1	0	2.26	2.24	28	12	20	5	3.94	0.03	1	55	2	9	5.63	0.01	0	92	0	3
0.61	30.58	94	3	2	0	2.29	2.00	26	13	22	6	3.98	0.03	1	56	1	11	5.66	0.01	0	92	0	3
0.64	30.52	94	3	3	0	2.33	1.75	24	13	7	5	4.01	0.02	1	57	1	12	5.69	0.01	0	92	0	3
0.67	30.42	94	3	11	0	2.36	1.64	23	14	9	7	4.04	0.02	1	58	3	15	5.73	0.01	0	93	0	3
0.71	30.06	93	3	1	0	2.39	1.51	22	15	8	6	4.08	0.02	1	60	3	10	5.76	0.01	0	93	0	3
0.74	30.03	93	3	3	0	2.43	1.40	21	15	5	6	4.11	0.01	0	61	3	9	5.80	0.01	0	93	0	2
0.78	29.94	92	3	10	0	2.46	1.31	21	16	8	5	4.14	0.01	0	61	1	9	5.83	0.01	0	94	0	1
0.81	29.61	91	3	13	0	2.49	1.23	20	16	7	7	4.18	0.01	0	62	0	9	5.86	0.01	0	94	0	3
0.84	29.19	90	3	3	1	2.53	1.14	19	17	11	7	4.21	0.01	0	63	0	8	5.90	0.01	0	94	0	2
0.88	28.19	90	3	1	0	2.56	1.03	18	18	3	6	4.25	0.01	0	64	0	10	5.93	0.01	0	94	0	3
0.91	28.16	90	3	14	2	2.59	0.98	18	18	6	6	4.28	0.01	0	65	0	10	5.96	0.01	0	94	0	3
0.94	26.09	88	3	4	0	2.63	0.92	17	19	9	7	4.31	0.01	0	66	0	9	6.00	0.01	0	95	0	3
0.98	25.97	88	3	5	0	2.66	0.84	16	20	11	6	4.35	0.01	0	67	0	8	6.03	0.01	0	95	0	3
1.01	25.82	87	3	6	0	2.70	0.77	15	20	7	5	4.38	0.01	0	68	0	9	6.07	0.01	0	95	0	2
1.04	25.65	87	3	9	0	2.73	0.71	15	21	6	10	4.41	0.01	0	69	0	7	6.10	0.01	0	96	0	2
1.08	25.38	86	3	7	1	2.76	0.65	14	22	13	8	4.45	0.01	0	69	0	10	6.13	0.01	0	96	0	2
1.11	24.46	85	3	13	1	2.80	0.57	13	23	4	7	4.48	0.01	0	70	0	8	6.17	0.01	0	96	0	3
1.15	23.42	84	3	16	1	2.83	0.54	12	23	4	9	4.52	0.01	0	71	0	9	6.20	0.01	0	96	0	2
1.18	22.35	82	3	14	2	2.86	0.50	12	24	4	8	4.55	0.01	0	72	0	10	6.23	0.01	0	96	0	1
1.21	20.85	81	3	12	0	2.90	0.47	12	25	6	7	4.58	0.01	0	73	0	9	6.27	0.01	0	97	0	2
1.25	20.54	80	3	14	0	2.93	0.44	11	26	5	9	4.62	0.01	0	74	0	7	6.30	0.01	0	97	0	1
1.28	20.18	78	3	11	1	2.97	0.40	10	27	3	8	4.65	0.01	0	75	0	7	6.33	0.01	0	97	0	2
1.31	19.40	77	4	8	1	3.00	0.38	10	27	11	9	4.68	0.01	0	75	0	8	6.37	0.01	0	97	0	1
1.35	18.73	76	4	8	1	3.03	0.33	9	28	4	7	4.72	0.01	0	76	0	9	6.40	0.01	0	97	0	1
1.38	18.10	76	4	22	3	3.07	0.31	9	29	5	9	4.75	0.01	0	77	1	9	6.44	0.01	0	97	0	2
1.42	16.40	73	4	31	2	3.10	0.28	8	30	3	9	4.78	0.01	0	78	0	8	6.47	0.01	0	97	0	1
1.45	15.04	70	4	19	3	3.13	0.27	8	31	7	8	4.82	0.01	0	79	0	10	6.50	0.01	0	98	0	1
1.48	13.76	68	5	18	1	3.17	0.24	7	32	4	10	4.85	0.01	0	80	0	7	6.54	0.01	0	98	0	1
1.52	13.14	67	5	19	1	3.20	0.22	7	33	3	10	4.89	0.01	0	80	1	6	6.57	0.01	0	98	0	1
1.55	12.52	65	5	19	2	3.23	0.20	6	34	3	11	4.92	0.01	0	81	0	8	6.60	0.01	0	98	0	1
1.58	11.70	63	5	8	2	3.27	0.19	6	35	3	10	4.95	0.01	0	82	0	7	6.64	0.01	0	98	0	1
1.62	11.14	62	5	10	2	3.30	0.17	6	36	2	9	4.99	0.01	0	82	0	6	6.67	0.01	0	98	0	1
1.65	10.50	61	5	25	2	3.34	0.16	6	37	4	12	5.02	0.01	0	83	0	7	6.71	0.01	0	98	0	1
1.69	9.02	58	6	23	2	3.37	0.15	5	38	6	11	5.05	0.01	0	84	0	4	6.74	0.01	0	98	0	0

20 MAX 21 NX

fact that the higher order curves do not asymptote to perfect separation may be interpreted as stating that the intrinsic dimensionality of the formulation is less than 10. It is especially important to note at this point that these results, of course, depend on the ability of the data organization and processing to represent realistic operational data. The perfect separation case may be approached more nearly, for example, by removing the requirement that the data be structured into triad-pair triplets and averaging over all the data in the base. This indicates that the results presented will be conservative, indicating more overlap than is actually present if more samples are available operationally.

References

1. Broderick, P. K., J. E. Paul, and R. J. Rennick, "Semi-Automatic Speaker Identification System," 1975 Carnahan Conference on Crime Countermeasures, University of Kentucky, Lexington, Ky.

2. "People vs E. D. Law," Opinion expressed in Appellate Report, August 13, 1974, Court of the State of California, 5 Crim. No. 1516 (Swp. Ct. No. 26331).

3. Papcun, G., and P. Cadeferged, Two "Voiceprint" Cases, 1973, Acoustical Society of America 86th Meeting, Los Angeles, Calif. LL15.

4. Poza, F., "Voiceprint Identification: Its Forensic Application," 1974, Proceedings of the 1974 Carnahan Crime Countermeasures Conference, University of Kentucky, Lexington, Ky.

5. Hecker, M. H. L., "Speaker Recognition - An Interpretive Survey of the Literature," 1971, ASHA Monographs No. 16.

6. Becker, R. W., F. R. Clarke, F. Poza, and J. R. Young, "A Semi-Automatic Speaker Recognition System," 1972, SRI Project 1363 - prepared for Michigan Dept. of State Police, East Lansing, Mich.

7. Potter, R. K., G. A. Kopp, and H. G. Kopp, "Visible Speech," 1966, Dover Publications, Inc., New York, N. Y.

8. Pruzansky, S., and M. V. Mathews, "Talker-Recognition Procedure Based on Analyses of Variance," 1964, JASA 36:11, pp. 2041-2047.

PERSONAL IDENTITY VERIFICATION USING VOICE[1]

Dr. George R. Doddington
Texas Instruments Incorporated, P.O. Box 6015, Dallas, Texas

SUMMARY

An entry control system using voice verification is now in use at Texas Instruments. This system, which has performed over 200,000 verifications during the past year and a half, is the first completely automatic system based upon a personal attribute to provide high operational security. Performance is ensured by randomized selection of the verification utterance, on-line adaptation of voice reference data, and impostor detention. User verification requires less than 6 seconds.

Verification is based upon a four-word utterance. The words are randomly selected from a set of sixteen monosyllabic words. A sequential decision strategy is used which requires from one to four utterances for verification. Voice prompting of the randomized utterance helps to stabilize the user's pronunciation.

The desired level of impostor rejection is 99.0%. At this rejection level, user acceptance is 99.9%. The average number of utterances required for this level of performance is 1.35, and the average verification time is 5.6 seconds. This verification time includes both voice prompting and user response.

The speech reference data storage requirement per user is 9,408 bits for all sixteen words. This reference storage requirement includes provision for on-line adaptation of the reference file. Frequent usage, say once per week or more frequently, is desirable in order to maintain the quoted level of performance.

Several interesting applications of speaker verification are not discussed in this paper. These include speaker verification over the telephone for business transactions, and speaker identification of non-cooperative speakers. These problems are difficult because of the uncontrolled speech signal environment. Research is being conducted in these application areas.

WHY USE VOICE?

Lock and key are the traditional means of identity verification for entry control. More recently, the use of badges, secret numbers and computer control has greatly improved the flexibility and usefulness of entry control systems. However, virtually all (automatic) entry control systems in use today share a serious shortcoming: verification of identity is based upon possession of an artifact and is thus vulnerable. The ultimate solution is to verify a person's identity based upon a personal attribute unique to him.

A person's speech is a useful personal attribute for identity verification and is well suited to computer processing. The use of speech also provides other advantages, including an inexpensive transducer (microphone), fast verification without special manual procecures, and a flexible medium for controlling verification performance. The primary limitation in using speech is that the speech signal is inherently dynamic. Speech characteristics change with time and cooperation of the user is required to minimize the variability of the speech measures.

PERFORMANCE PARAMETERS

Many factors must be considered in adequately describing or specifying the performance of an identity verification system. Verification errors, total verification transaction time, and operating protocol are important in user acceptance and overall system performance. The key parameter, however, is verification error rate.

Verification errors may be categorized as Type I or Type II. A Type I error is the rejection of the claimed identity when in fact the identity claimed was true. A Type II error is the acceptance of the claimed identity when in fact the identity claimed was false.

Sources of Errors

Verification errors may be attributed to three causes:

1. Variations in speech by the same speaker.
2. Similarities in speech between speakers, and
3. Problems in automatic measurement, comparison and time registration.

Variations by the same speaker are the source of Type I errors. Abnormal variations in the voice include laryngitis and the common cold. These variations often cause user rejection. Occasionally, normal variations in rate of speech, voice quality and articulation may also contribute to user rejection.

Similarities between speakers are the

Reprinted from *Proc. ELECTRO-76*, May 11-14, 1976, pp. 22-4, 1—5.

source of Type II errors. In addition to an occasional natural similarity, a potential for Type II errors exists through artful mimicry or through the use of a tape recording. Appropriate choice of speech measurements can minimize the probability of successful mimicry. The use of a tape recording can be defeated by randomized construction of speech data.

Problems in measurement include variations in the speech signal environment, errors in time alignment between input and reference speech, errors in feature extraction algorithms, and inadequate representation of speech characteristics. Variations in speech signal environment include differences between microphones and differences in mouth-to-microphone distance and azimuth.

Useful Speaker Discriminating Measures

A variety of speech signal measurements are available with useful speaker discrimination characteristics. The choice of measures involves a trade-off between speaker discrimination capability, ease of measurement, and ease of mimicry. The performance of some commonly used speaker discriminating measures is rated in Table 1.

Some degree of speaker verification is afforded by long-term averages of speech characteristics. However, the use of a point-by-point comparison of input and reference speech data as a function of time provides a superior verification capability. In this case, of course, an added requirement exists for reliable time registration.

Table 1. Performance Ranking of Some Speaker Discriminating Measures.

Measure	Level of Discrimination	Ease of Measurement	Difficulty of Mimicry
Waveform envelope	Good	Good	Fair
Voice pitch period	Good	Fair	Fair
Relative amplitude spectrum	Good	Good	Good
Vocal tract resonant frequencies	Good	Poor	Good

SPEAKER VERIFICATION TECHNOLOGY

Texas Instruments has developed a speaker verification technology which provides high-performance entry control. Technology development has been sponsored by the U.S. Air Force Systems Command (RADC and ESD). Verification is based upon the relative amplitude spectrum of the speech signal and is implemented in a mini-computer system. The verification is highly mimic resistant.

Speech Processing

The relative amplitude spectrum of the speech signal is provided by a 14-channel digital filter bank. Each channel comprises a 4-pole recursive bandpass filter, a full-wave rectifier, and a 4-pole lowpass Bessel filter with cutoff frequency 20 Hz. Each channel has a bandwidth of 220 Hz. The 14 channels are uniformly spaced in frequency and span the range of frequencies from 300 to 2700 Hz. Filter bank output is sampled every 10 milliseconds. Let $A_j = \{a_{ij}\}$ be the filter bank output vector. a_{ij} is the amplitude for channel i and time sample j.

A_j undergoes three preprocessing steps before verification processing. First, vocal tract resonances are enhanced by eliminating contributions to the spectrum which vary slowly with frequency:

$$(A_j)_R = A_j - c_{1j}P_1 - c_{2j}P_2 \tag{1}$$

c_{kj} is the inner product of A_j and P_k. P_k is the kth order orthonormal polynomial basis vector. Second, A_j is normalized by the average value of A_j:

$$(A_j)_N = \frac{1}{c_{0j}} (A_j)_R \tag{2}$$

Finally, the normalized amplitude vector is quantized to three bits in order to facilitate later data comparison operations:

$$(a_{ij})_Q = q \text{ iff } (a_{ij})_N \in (\phi_{iq}, \phi_{iq+1}) \tag{3}$$

The $\{\phi_{iq}\}$ are chosen so as to provide a uniform first-order distribution of quantized amplitudes.

Each speaker's reference data is a set of reference matrices. Each reference matrix is defined so as to represent the speech signal in the neighborhood of some reference time point j_o. Six quantized amplitude vectors comprise the reference matrix:

$$R_{j_o} = [A_{j_o-5}\ A_{j_o-3}\ A_{j_o-1}\ A_{j_o+1}\ A_{j_o+3}\ A_{j_o+5}] \tag{4}$$

Reliable and accurate time registration between the reference matrix and the input speech signal is essential for high-performance speaker verification. Time registration is established by a continuous comparison of each reference matrix with the corresponding matrix formatted from the input data. The Euclidean squared error norm is used as a means of comparison:

$$e_{kj} = ||X_j - R_k|| \tag{5}$$

That value of j which minimizes e_{kj} is taken to be the point of correct time registration. Because the time span of the reference matrix is small (0.1 second), only time translation is required to provide an accurate comparison between input and reference speech.

Verification Strategy

No additional data comparison is made in computing the verification decision function. The minimum error for each reference point, e_m, as computed during time registration, is used to form the decision function d:

$$d = (\Sigma_k e_k)/(\Sigma_k \hat{e}_k) \tag{6}$$

$\hat{e}_k$ is the expected minimum error which is estimated for each reference point and each speaker. The speaker's identity is accepted if d is less than or equal to d_T. d_T is a fixed speaker-independent threshold.

The speech utterances used for verification are nonsense sentences of four monosyllabic words. Each verification utterance is randomly constructed from a set of 16 monosyllabic words. An example set is shown in Table 2. Each vowel in the set is required to be distinct. Word function and phonetic environment are independent of the randomization. There are 32 possible randomizations.

Each verification system user must generate reference speech data and parameter estimates during an enrollment session. This enrollment session also serves to accustom the speaker to the verification procedures. Five sets of utterances (20 utterances total) are required in the enrollment session. The first set of utterances is used to define initial reference patterns for each of the 16 words. A reference pattern is chosen at the center of each word. The remaining four replications of each word are used to refine the speech reference data and to estimate speaker parameters.

Table 2. An Example Set of Words Used To Construct Randomized Verification Utterances.

Good	Ben	called	hard.
Proud	Bruce	swam	near.
Strong	Jean	came	north.
Young	Joyce	served	high.

Verification performance improves with the number of utterances used to form a decision, as shown in Table 3. The decision function for multiple-utterance verification is the simple average of the decision functions for each utterance. A trade-off will often be necessary between verification performance and verification time. In this case, a sequential decision strategy may be used to minimize the verification time with negligible degradation of verification performance. Verification performance for such a strategy is summarized in Table 4. In this strategy an automatic retry is performed if the user can not be verified after 4 phrases. The average number of phrases required of true speakers for this strategy is 1.35.

Table 3. Verification Performance Versus Number of Utterances at a 1% Impostor Acceptance Level.

Number of Utterances	% Type I Error
1	13.0
2	2.3
3	0.8
4	0.3

Table 4. Verification Performance for a Sequential Decision Strategy.

% of Speakers Accepted	True Speakers	Impostors
on 1st phrase	75.24	0.24
2nd phrase	18.60	0.08
3rd phrase	4.87	0.11
4th phrase	0.95	0.13
on retry	0.28	0.26
Total	99.94	0.82

In computing the verification performance shown in Tables 3 and 4, only male speakers were used and impostor attempts were casual. That is, the verification utterance was said in each speaker's normal speaking voice. Previous studies indicate that, for the verification measures used here, a talented professional mimic may be expected to double the probability of successful impersonation over that which a casual impostor can achieve. Tables 3 and 4 are thus at a professional mimic acceptance level of less than 2%.

Speech reference data and speaker parameters are adaptively updated each time the speaker successfully verifies his identity. The update procedure is a simple weighted average of input data and reference data.

$$R_{new} = (1-\alpha)R_{old} + \alpha X \quad (7)$$

$\alpha = 1/16$ is a compromise between rapid reference update and accurate reference estimation. Adaptation is necessary in order to provide high-performance speaker verification with changes in a speaker's voice and speech habits. The inclusion of the adaptation feature more than doubles the speech data memory requirement (from 3 bits per datum to 7 bits per datum).

The Verification System

Seven components comprise the speaker verification system.

1. An identification keyboard or badge reader serves to identify the user and select the correct speech reference file.

2. An 8-bit D/A converter is used for voice response. Instructions to the user such as "louder please" and "verified, thank you", and prompting of the selected verification utterance are made by voice response. The speaker then merely repeats the prompting utterance. It is believed that this procedure stabilizes the pronunciation of the utterance by the speaker and thus minimizes Type I error.

3. A microphone and digital filter bank are used to provide the frequency analysis of the speech signal.

4. A minicomputer provides all speaker verification and system control functions. Sufficient computer power is available to perform two verifications simultaneously or four verifications in a queued mode with no wait.

5. A moving-head disc provides speech reference data storage. With provision for adaptation, the storage of speech data for 16 reference patterns requires 9,408 bits.

6. A control teleprinter is used for operator interaction and control and for verification summary output.

7. A control line/sense line interface enforces the verification decision and fully automates the entry control.

AN EXAMPLE ENTRY CONTROL SYSTEM IN OPERATION

The Corporate Information Center (CIC) at Texas Instruments requires positive control of personnel entering and leaving the central computer room. A manned guard station at the facility entrance has traditionally met this requirement. The need for increased flexibility and higher security led to the installation of a fully automated entry control system based on speaker verification. This system has been in operation for over one and one half years.

System Description

Entry is controlled by a 4' x 5' control booth. The inside and outside doors of the control booth are computer monitored and controlled. At least one door is locked at all times. Both doors are locked during verification. The verification terminal in the control booth includes both a microphone and a badge reader. Entrant identification is made with the employee badge.

Upon entering the booth from the outside the user is greeted with "Good morning". After both booth doors are closed and locked and the user has identified himself, speaker verification of his identity is performed. Upon successful verification the user is notified with "Verified, thank you". If the user is not verified, he remains locked in the booth. Figure 1 illustrates normal booth usage during verification.

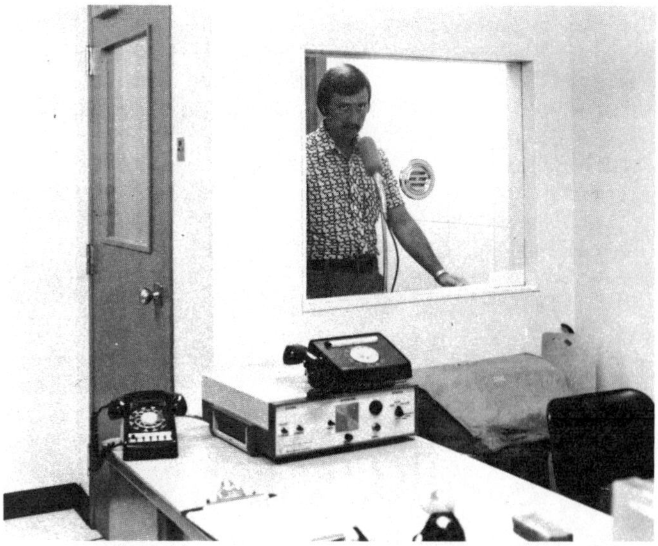

Figure 1. A View Of The Voice-Controlled Booth From Inside CIC During Verification.

No verification of identity is required upon exiting the computer room. After badge identification and door closure, the user is signaled with "Thank you, bye-bye".

More than one person is allowed in the control booth at one time. This increases entry/exit throughput significantly and is achieved by making the entire floor of the booth a weight scale. During enrollment the weight of each user is discreetly recorded along with his speech data.

Flexible control of entry authorization is achieved by assigning one of three authorization levels to each user. Entry is granted to a user only when the computer facility status is at his authorization level or lower.

System Performance

Over 200 users are authorized entry and are enrolled on the speaker verification system. Thirteen percent of the users are women. An average of more than 400 entries are made per day. Well over 200,000 verifications have been performed since the system was installed.

Verification performance has been in good agreement with that predicted from experimental data. The probability of rejecting a valid user is 0.1% and the average number of phrases required for verification is just under 1.3. This slightly better performance may be attributed to a complete adaptation of the user to the verification system.

[1]Technology development was sponsored by the Air Force Systems Command.

The residual Type I verification errors have proven acceptable to the users. Typically, when a user's identity is rejected a speech abnormality is obvious to the user. For example, it has been observed that more phrases are required for verification when the user has a cold.

An operational parameter of crucial importance to entry/exit throughput is the control booth occupancy time. This is the time required for door opening, control transaction, and door closure. Table 5 presents an analysis of booth occupancy time. Note that the entry time for additional users appears higher than what might be anticipated. This is caused by the requirement (during entry only) that all users be in the booth and that the door be closed before the first verification may begin.

Table 5. Average Entry Control Booth Occupancy Time (in seconds).

	First User	Each Additional User
Entry	16.3	12.3
Exit	11.5	3.5

Initial user acceptance of the verification system was gained gradually over a two to three month period. Dissatisfaction centered on the new non-negligible time required for entry. New users now being enrolled on the system accept the control and verification procedures and adapt to the system almost immediately.

Speaker Recognition Using Orthogonal Linear Prediction

MARVIN R. SAMBUR

Abstract—Recent experiments in speech synthesis have shown that, by an appropriate eigenvector analysis, a set of orthogonal parameters can be obtained that is essentially independent of all linguistic information across an analyzed utterance, but highly indicative of the identity of the speaker. The orthogonal parameters are formed by a linear transformation of the linear prediction parameters, and can achieve their recognition potential without the need of any time-normalization procedure. The speaker discrimination potential of the linear prediction orthogonal parameters was formally tested in both a speaker identification and a speaker verification experiment. The speech data for these experiments consisted of six repetitions of the same sentence spoken by 21 male speakers on six separate occasions. For both identification and verification, the recognition accuracy of the orthogonal parameters exceeded 99 percent for high-quality speech inputs. For telephone inputs, the accuracy exceeded 96 percent. In a separate text-independent speaker identification experiment, an accuracy of 94 percent was achieved for high-quality speech inputs.

I. Introduction

In the past few years, a great deal of research has been directed towards finding speech characteristics that are effective for automatic speaker recognition [1]-[3]. Ideally, an effective speaker recognition feature should measure some aspect of the acoustic signal that reflects the unique properties of the speaker's vocal apparatus, and contains little or no information about the linguistic content of the speech. If the selected recognition feature is indicative of both the speaker and what is being said, then the full speaker discrimination potential of the feature is only realized when the recognition process is confined to a comparison of speech samples with exactly the same linguistic component. The nontrivial and nonerror free operations of segmentation and time normalization are usually required to guarantee the success of systems that depend on such features [4].

The most effective features presently employed in automatic speaker identification systems are pitch [7], gain [7], and the linear prediction characteristics of the speech waveform [3], [7]. The first two parameters are related to the properties of the speaker's glottal source and the linear prediction parameters are indicative of the talker's vocal tract. Since these three features are by themselves sufficient to produce a high-quality synthesis of the speech utterance [6], they must necessarily contain a high degree of information about the speaker's identity. Unfortunately, these parameters are also quite obviously influenced by the exact linguistic content of the speech signal and can, therefore, not be regarded as "ideal" recognition measurements.

Manuscript received October 22, 1975; revised February 11, 1976.
The author is with Bell Laboratories, Murray Hill, NJ 07974.

In order to determine the speaker identifying properties of the speech signal, it is natural to look for guidance from the results of speech synthesis experiments. A recent experimental study has shown that by an appropriate eigenvector analysis of the linear prediction parameters, a set of orthogonal parameters are obtained that can be used to achieve a high-quality synthesis of the original utterance [5]. The interesting aspect of these orthogonal parameters is that only a small subset of the parameters demonstrate any significant variation across the analyzed utterance. The remaining orthogonal parameters are essentially constant and, for purposes of synthesis, are completely specified by their measured mean values across the utterance. Since one of the aspects of the speech that is remaining constant is the speaker, these orthogonal parameters may be indicative of the talker's identity. This hypothesis was reinforced when a subsequent experiment indicated that if the same eigenvector analysis is applied to the same utterance spoken by another speaker, the resulting mean values of the corresponding orthogonal parameters are different. The implications of these experimental results are that a set of orthogonal linear prediction parameters can be obtained for a given speaker that contain almost no linguistic information and a possible high degree of information about the speaker's identity. To verify these implications, the set of orthogonal linear prediction parameters were formally examined for their ability to differentiate speakers. The results of this examination are presented in this paper. Before presenting the details of the experimentation, we shall review the concept of orthogonal linear prediction.

II. Orthogonal Linear Prediction

In the field of speech research, the term linear prediction refers to a highly successful representation of the speech signal $\{s_n\}$ as the output of an all-pole filter $H(z)$ that is excited by a sequence of pulses separated by the pitch period for voiced sounds, or pseudorandom noise for unvoiced sounds [6]. This model implies that within a frame of speech the output speech sequence is given by

$$s_n = \sum_{k=1}^{p} a_k s_{n-k} + Gu_n \tag{1}$$

where p is the total number of real and complex poles attributed to the vocal tract and glottal wave, u_n is the appropriate input excitation, G is the gain of the filter, and the a_k's are the linear prediction coefficients (LPC's) that characterize the filter. Fig. 1 illustrates the frequency domain, as well as the equivalent time-domain representation of linear predic-

Reprinted from *IEEE Trans. Acoust., Speech, and Signal Process.*, vol. ASSP-24, pp. 283–289, Aug. 1976.

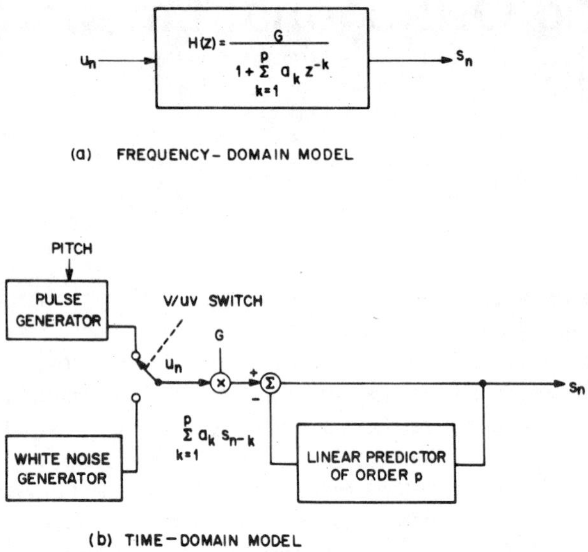

Fig. 1. Discrete model of speech production as employed in linear prediction.

tion speech production. To account for the nonstationary character of the speech waveform, the parameters a_k of the modeled filter are periodically updated during successive speech frames.[1]

It is sometimes convenient to characterize the filter $H(z)$ in terms of a nonuniform acoustic tube formed by cascading p uniform cylindrical sections of equal length [6]. The p area coefficients, A_i, are uniquely related to the linear prediction coefficients by

$$\frac{A_i}{A_{i+1}} = \frac{1+\alpha_i}{1-\alpha_i}, \quad A_{p+1} = 1 \quad 1 \leqslant i \leqslant p \tag{2}$$

where the α_i's are termed the parcor coefficients [6]. If we denote $a_i^{(k)}$ as the ith LPC for a kth pole linear prediction model, then

$$\alpha_i = a_i^{(i)}, \quad i = 1, \cdots, p. \tag{3}$$

The area coefficients and parcor coefficients provide an alternate representation of the linear prediction characteristics of the speech wave.

The technique of orthogonal linear prediction was introduced to exploit the experimental observation that the linear prediction parameters were considerably redundant. This redundancy implies that a conventional eigenvector analysis can be used to reduce the dimensionality of the linear prediction space [8]. The eigenvector analysis involves the generation of a set of statistically uncorrelated parameters that are formed by a linear combination of the given linear prediction parameters.[2] The redundancy in the linear prediction parameters is reflected in the fact that only a small subset of the orthogonal parameters will demonstrate any significant variation across an analyzed utterance. The remaining orthogonal parameters can be effectively considered constant and only a knowledge of their particular mean values are needed to achieve high-quality speech synthesis [5].

To determine the the orthogonal parameters, we first calculate the covariance matrix, R of the linear prediction parameters across the given utterance [10]. Denoting x_{ij} as the ith linear prediction parameter in the jth frame, the elements of R are

$$r_{ik} = \frac{1}{J-1} \sum_{j=1}^{J} (x_{ij} - \bar{x}_i)(x_{kj} - \bar{x}_k), \tag{4}$$

where

$$i, k = 1, 2, \cdots, p$$

and

$$\bar{x}_i = \frac{1}{J} \sum_{j=1}^{J} x_{ij}, \tag{5}$$

and J is the number of frames in the utterance. Given the covariance matrix, the statistical variance (eigenvalue) of each orthogonal parameter is first found by solving the set of simultaneous equations [8]

$$|R - \lambda I| = 0 \tag{6}$$

where I is the identity matrix, λ is the eigenvalue, and $|Q|$ denotes the determinant of any matrix Q.[3] Mutually orthogonal eigenvectors are then derived as solutions of the equation[4]

$$\lambda_i \boldsymbol{b}_i = R\boldsymbol{b}_i \quad i = 1, 2, \cdots, p \tag{7}$$

where $\boldsymbol{b}_i$ is a vector with p elements. In terms of the linear prediction parameters, the ith orthogonal parameter, φ_i, in the jth frame is given by

$$\varphi_{ij} = \sum_{k=1}^{p} b_{ik} x_{kj} = x_j' b_i. \tag{8}$$

To illustrate the behavior of the linear prediction parameters and their corresponding orthogonal parameters, Table I contains a listing of the determined eigenvalues (variances) of the calculated orthogonal parameters across the utterance "I was stunned by the beauty of the view" spoken by a typical talker. The table shows that the higher numbered orthogonal parameters have a relatively small variance and can, therefore, be considered essentially constant across the utterance for the analyzed speaker. We shall now discuss the result of our speaker recognition experiment that establish these orthogonal parameters as indicative of the speaker's identity.

III. Speaker Recognition Experimentation (Text Dependent)

A. Speech Data

The speaker recognition experiment involved 21 male speakers with no noticeable dialect. The speech data for the text-dependent study consisted of six repetitions of the same

[1] A frame is a segment of speech thought adequate to assume stationarity of the speech process. Typical frame lengths employed range from 10 to 30 ms.

[2] Statistically uncorrelated parameters are referred to as orthogonal parameters.

[3] Equation (6) is a pth-order polynomial in λ. There are p solutions of this equation; $\lambda_1, \lambda_2, \cdots, \lambda_p$.

[4] A convenient Fortran program for obtaining the eigenvectors from the covariance matrix is listed in the *IBM Scientific Subroutine Package Manual* on p. 164.

TABLE I
MEASURED EIGENVALUES FOR THE ORTHOGONAL PARAMETERS DERIVED FROM THE STATISTICS OF THE LOG AREA, PARCOR, AND LPC'S OBTAINED IN A TYPICAL ANALYZED UTTERANCE

	Log Area	Parcor	LPC's
1	3.27	0.25	14.1
2	1.23	0.17	1.73
3	0.42	0.07	0.34
4	0.35	0.06	0.24
5	0.24	0.05	0.14
6	0.18	0.03	0.08
7	0.12	0.02	0.06
8	0.10	0.02	0.03
9	0.09	0.02	0.02
10	0.07	0.01	0.01
11	0.07	0.01	0.004
12	0.02	0.007	0.003

sentence spoken by each speaker on six separate occasions. The sentence analyzed was "I was stunned by the beauty of the view." The recordings were made in a quiet environment on six different days spaced over a period of three weeks.

The speech signal was sampled at 10-kHz sampling rate after bandpass filtering from 100 Hz to 4 kHz. Each utterance was then subjected to a 12th-order linear prediction analysis using the autocorrelation method to obtain the various linear prediction parameters (parcor, area, and LPC's). The analysis was conducted over contiguous speech frames of 20-ms duration. Although no time normalization was applied to the utterances, an automatic procedure was used to eliminate the consideration of silent portions and pauses in the utterance. These intervals were determined by energy and zero-crossing rate measurements [9].

B. Recognition Procedure

In the experimental study, each set of six repetitions of an utterance for a speaker was partitioned into a design and test set. The utterances in the design set were used to evaluate each individual's reference orthogonal parameters, and the utterances in the test set were used to test the effectiveness of the orthogonal parameters. Each of the utterances rendered by a given speaker was used in turn as the test set, and the remaining five samples were used as the design set.

To evaluate the *unique* orthogonal parameters for the mth speaker, we first determine the reference covariance matrix for the mth talker. This matrix is defined as the weighted average of the calculated covariance matrices in the design set. Denoting R_{lm} as the calculated covariance matrix across the lth utterance in the mth speaker's design set, we define

$$R_{\text{ref}}^{(m)} = \frac{1}{\sum_{l=1}^{L} J_{lm}} \sum_{l=1}^{L} J_{lm} E_{lm} \tag{9}$$

where J_{lm} is the number of frames[5] in the lth utterance and L is the number of utterances in the design set ($L = 5$ in this experiment). The orthogonal parameters for the mth speaker are then derived using $R_{\text{ref}}^{(m)}$ and (4)–(7). The mth speaker's orthogonal parameters are then obtained from the linear prediction parameters using the derived conversion matrix $[b_i]_m$ and (8).

In the introductory section of this paper, we noted that the least significant orthogonal parameters of a given talker are, for purposes of speech synthesis, completely specified by their mean values. Thus we can characterize the orthogonal parameters of the mth speaker by the conversion matrix $[b_i]_m$ and the mean values of the orthogonal parameters as determined in the design set. Denoting ϕ_{ijm} as the value of the ith orthogonal parameter for the mth speaker in the jth frame, then the average value of the ith orthogonal parameter for the mth speaker is given by

$$\bar{\phi}_{im} = \frac{1}{\sum_{l=1}^{L} J_{lm}} \sum_{l=1}^{L} \sum_{j=1}^{J_{lm}} \phi_{ijm}. \tag{10}$$

Now let us assume that we are presented with an utterance spoken by some unknown speaker and we wish to measure the dissimilarity between the unknown speaker and the mth speaker. Since the orthogonal parameters are by definition statistically uncorrelated, one logical measure of dissimilarity is

$$d_m = \sum_{i=p'}^{p} \left(\frac{\bar{\phi}_{im} - Z_i}{\sqrt{\lambda_{im}}} \right)^2 \bar{J}_m \tag{11}$$

where Z_i is the mean value of the ith orthogonal parameter calculated across the utterance of the unknown talker via $[b_i]_m$ and (8), λ_{im} is the reference eigenvalue for the ith orthogonal parameter of the mth speaker, $(p' - 1)$ is the number of leading orthogonal parameters not included in the summation, and

$$\bar{J}_m = \frac{1}{L} \sum_{l=1}^{L} J_{lm} \tag{12}$$

is the average number of frames in the utterances of the mth speaker's design set. This metric measures the weighted distance between the mean values of the orthogonal parameters for the presented utterance and the mean values calculated for the orthogonal parameters in the design set. The weighting factor in the distance computation is the eigenvalue of each orthogonal parameter. It can be shown that $\lambda_{im}/\bar{J}_m$ is the uncertainty or variance in the estimation of the true mean values of the orthogonal parameter from the limited design set [8, p. 345], and thus d_m is just the standard distance measure for comparing uncorrelated recognition features (the features are the calculated mean values of the mth speaker's orthogonal parameters).

The orthogonal parameters of a given speaker can not only be specified in some sense by their mean values, but also by their variance (eigenvalue) across a given utterance.[6] It can

[5] To obtain a statistically stable estimate of the orthogonal parameters, it is advisable that the duration of the utterances be approximately 1.5 or more seconds ($J_l \geq 75$). However, for shorter durational utterances, this condition can be avoided by increasing the number of utterances in the design set ($L > 5$).

[6] Note that if we calculate the orthogonal parameters determined for speaker A across an utterance of speaker B, there is no guarantee that the least significant orthogonal parameters will still be relatively constant for speaker B.

be shown that under certain broad conditions, the estimates $\overline{\phi}_{im}$ and λ_{im} are statistically uncorrelated [8, p. 349] and thus the metric d_m can be expanded to include the variance information by

$$D_m = d_m + \frac{1}{2}\sum_{i=p'}^{p}\left(\frac{V_i - \lambda_{im}}{\lambda_{im}}\right)^2 \cdot \overline{J}_m \tag{13}$$

where V_i is the measured variance of the ith orthogonal parameter of the mth speaker calculated across the presented utterance and $(\sqrt{2}/\sqrt{\overline{J}_m})\,\lambda_{im}$ is the standard deviation in the estimation of each eigenvalue [8, p. 349]. D_m is again the standard distance measure for comparing uncorrelated recognition features (the features are the calculated mean values and variances of the mth speaker's parameters).

C. Experimental Results

1) Identification: For a speaker identification evaluation,[7] the distance d_m (or D_m) is computed for a presented utterance spoken by some unknown speaker. The unknown speaker is then identified as the mth speaker if d_m (or D_m) is the smallest distance among the entire set of d_m's (D_m's). An error results when the actual speaker is not the mth talker. Fig. 2 illustrates the basic structure of the speaker identification scheme.

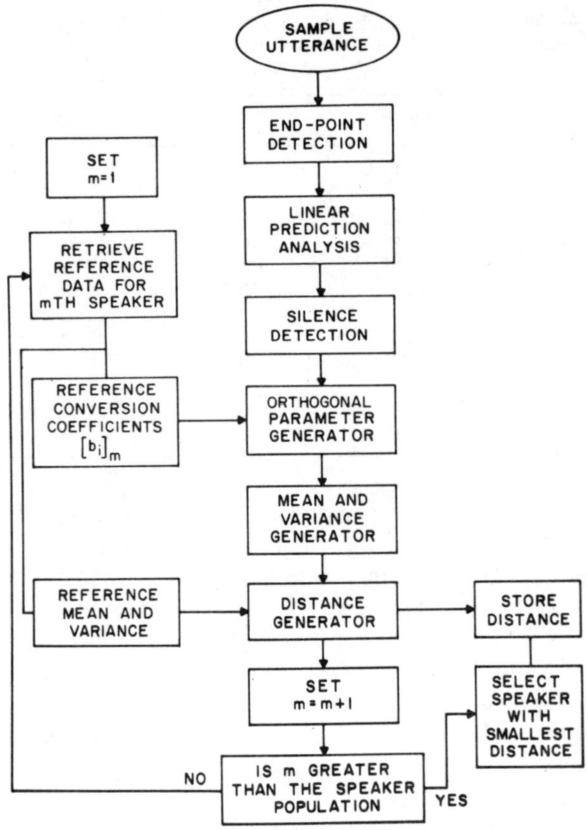

Fig. 2. Block diagram for speaker identification.

The identification accuracy of the orthogonal parameters was ascertained for the ensemble of 21 speakers. Since each of the six repetitions was used in turn as the test set for each of the speakers, a total of 126 judgments were made. The identification accuracy of these judgments is illustrated in Table II. The three results depicted in this table are, for the orthogonal parameters, calculated from the LPC's the log area ratio coefficients,[8] and the parcor coefficients in accordance with (4), (5), and (8). The percent identification accuracy is tabulated against the number of orthogonal parameters used to calculate the distance d_m and D_m [$(13 - p')$ in (11) and (12)]. Thus an accuracy of 30 percent was obtained for the orthogonal parameters of the LPC's when only the least significant orthogonal parameter was used in the distance calculation ($p' = 12$) and d_m was the distance metric. The identification results presented in Table II tend to saturate after the use of approximately the six or seven least significant orthogonal parameters ($p' = 7$ or $p' = 6$, respectively). This observation is consistent with the synthesis experimentation discussed in [5]. This experimentation showed that high-quality speech synthesis can be obtained with the use of only the first five or six most significant orthogonal parameters. The remaining orthogonal parameters are relatively constant and are apparently associated with the identity of the speaker as surmised by the results depicted in Table II. However, it should be noted that the last two significant orthogonal parameters did not afford a great deal of speaker identification potential. These parameters may reflect other aspects of the speech signal that are fixed. For example, they may be partially indicative of the constant frequency response of the recording apparatus and transmission system.

Overall, the distance metric D_m achieved a higher accuracy than the metric d_m. In addition, the orthogonal parameters obtained from the parcor coefficients and the log area ratio coefficients outperformed the orthogonal parameters obtained from the LPC parameters. The superiority of the log area ratio and parcor orthogonal parameters can probably be attributed to their direct relationship to the physical properties of the speaker's vocal tract (see Introduction).

2) Speaker Verification: For speaker verification,[9] the distance between the unknown sample and the reference parameters of the claimed speaker, m, is compared with a threshold value. If d_m (or D_m) is smaller than the threshold value, the speaker is verified; otherwise, he is rejected. Fig. 3 illustrates the basic structure of the verification scheme. In the speaker verification tests, one of the 21 speakers was designated as the speaker to be verified and the remaining talkers were considered impostors. Table III contains the average equal-error for the three types of parameters investigated. The equal-error rate is established by using a decision threshold that produces the same probability of incorrectly rejecting the true speaker as the probability of accepting an impostor. The performance of the orthogonal parameters for speaker verification purposes is quite similar to the results established for speaker recognition. The implication of the

[7] For a speaker identification test, the task is one of identifying the unknown speaker from among a host of possibilities.

[8] The log area ratio coefficients = $\log (A_i/A_{i+1})$.

[9] The task for a speaker verification test is to verify the identity claim of the unknown speaker.

TABLE II

		Number of Orthogonal Parameters											
		1	2	3	4	5	6	7	8	9	10	11	12
LPC Orthogonal Parameters	D_m	44.2	75.1	88.8	95.8	96.9	96.8	96.8	96.0	96.8	96.8	96.8	96.8
	d_m	30.1	47.2	50.0	66.7	83.3	94.4	95.2	95.2	96.0	96.0	96.0	96.0
Parcor Orthogonal Parameters	D_m	55.3	79.2	93.7	96.8	99.2	99.2	99.2	99.2	99.2	99.2	99.2	99.2
	d_m	38.1	48.2	53.0	65.7	84.9	95.2	96.0	97.6	97.6	97.6	97.6	97.6
Log Area Orthogonal Parameters	D_m	53.1	77.0	93.7	96.0	98.9	98.9	99.2	99.2	99.2	99.2	99.2	99.2
	d_m	37.1	49.2	53.0	65.7	83.3	95.2	96.0	97.6	97.6	97.6	97.6	97.6

Speaker identification accuracy for the three linear prediction orthogonal parameters as a function of the number of least significant orthogonal parameters used for computation of distance. The metrics D_m and d_m are given in (11) and (12).

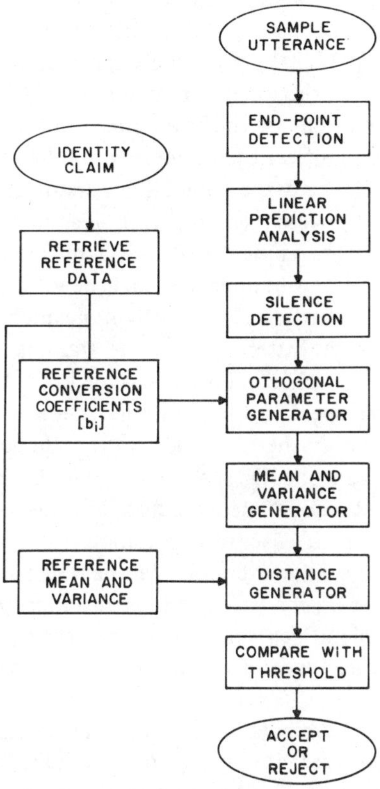

Fig. 3. Block diagram for speaker verification.

verification scores correspond to those discussed in the previous section.

IV. Text-Independent Speaker Recognition

In many practical applications, it is desired to recognize a speaker from an utterance that does not exactly correspond to the text of the reference samples. The differences in the text of the test and the reference utterances introduce an additional variability to the problem that many automatic speaker recognition systems can not handle. In the previous section, it was demonstrated that the orthogonal linear prediction parameters could achieve a high speaker recognition accuracy without the need for any elaborate time normalization or speech segmentation schemes. Thus it may be assumed that text-independent speaker recognition can be readily achieved using the system of orthogonal parameter recognition. However, it should be appreciated that the normalization of the linguistic content of the analyzed utterance was really achieved by statistical averaging. To guarantee the success of a text-independent application of the system, the reference data must be large enough to model the overall distribution of speech sounds that are likely to occur.

To examine the potential of the orthogonal parameters for text-independent recognition, the original 21 speakers were asked to record six additional sentences. The sentences were the following:

1) We were away a year ago.
2) Every salt breeze comes from the sea.
3) I know when my lawyer is due.
4) Our yacht slid around the point into the bay.
5) May we all learn a yellow lion roar.
6) I was stunned by the beauty of the view.

The new recordings were produced on six separate occasions and processed in the manner of Section III-A.

As a first examination, the data obtained for the original analysis of the sentence "I was stunned by the beauty of the view" were used as the reference and the new sentences were used as the test data. The peak identification results using the parcor orthogonal parameters ranged from 52 to 73 percent for first five above sentences and 99 percent for the last sentence in which the text of the test and reference samples were identical.

We next expanded the reference data to include all but one of the available sentences. The remaining sentence was used as the test utterance and a total of six separate tests were made. The identification scores in this experiment ranged from 100 percent (I know when my lawyer is due) to 87 percent (Every salt breeze comes from the sea). The total results are shown in Table IV and indicate an accuracy near 94 percent. These results are an encouraging indication that text-independent speaker recognition is quite possible using orthogonal linear prediction provided the distribution of speech sounds in the reference set is not too different from the relative occurrence of sounds comprising the test set.

V. Speaker Recognition for Telephone Inputs

With the increased use of telephone communications, it is desirable that any speaker recognition system maintain a high level of accuracy for speech inputs transmitted over telephone lines. Unfortunately, the telephone communication channel is band-limited from about 300 to 3000 Hz and much of the

TABLE III

		Number of Orthogonal Parameters											
		1	2	3	4	5	6	7	8	9	10	11	12
LPC Orthogonal Parameters	d_m	59.5	75.4	76.2	80.9	85.7	90.4	92.0	92.0	92.0	92.0	92.0	92.0
	D_m	61.1	75.2	79.3	84.9	90.4	94.4	95.2	94.4	95.2	95.2	95.2	95.2
Parcor Orthogonal Parameters	d_m	75.4	83.3	89.1	94.4	95.2	95.2	95.2	95.2	95.2	95.2	95.2	95.2
	D_m	76.2	84.9	89.7	96.0	97.6	98.4	99.2	99.2	99.2	99.2	99.2	99.2
Log Area Orthogonal Parameters	d_m	74.6	83.3	88.3	93.8	95.2	95.2	94.4	95.2	95.2	95.2	95.2	95.2
	D_m	76.2	84.9	89.7	96.0	97.6	98.4	99.2	99.2	99.2	99.2	99.2	99.2

Speaker verification accuracy for the three linear prediction orthogonal parameters as a function of the number of least significant orthogonal parameters used for computation of distance. The metrics D_m and d_m are given in (11) and (12).

TABLE IV
TEXT-INDEPENDENT IDENTIFICATION RESULTS USING THE PARCOR ORTHOGONAL PARAMETERS AND THE METRIC D_m

Number of Orthogonal Parameters	Identification Accuracy
1	28.1
2	38.1
3	50.5
4	76.2
5	84.0
6	89.7
7	92.9
8	92.9
9	93.7
10	93.7
11	93.7
12	93.7

low- and high-frequency speaker identifying properties of the speech are removed. In addition, a different pair of telephone lines is typically obtained each time a new telephone call is initiated, and thus the telephone channel is slightly, but randomly, changed for each new telephone call. These problems have made speaker recognition for telephone inputs quite difficult.

To ascertain the performance of the orthogonal linear prediction approach to speaker recognition for telephone inputs, the 21 speakers each recorded six additional utterances of the sentence "We were away a year ago."[10] The utterances were transmitted over local telephone lines after band-limiting from 300 to 3000 Hz. For the transmission of each utterance, a new local telephone line was initiated. The telephone-quality utterances of the speaker were then used for a speaker identification experiment using the system of Fig. 2. For this experiment the number of utterances in the design set was again 5 ($L = 5$) and a 12th-order LPC analysis was used ($p = 12$). Using the metric d_m, the identification accuracy was a disappointing 87.3 percent and the accuracy using D_m was an even more disappointing 83.3 percent.

After examining the data from the above experiment, it was observed that the distortions due to the telephone channel were most apparent in the distances associated with the four least significant orthogonal parameters. To understand this influence of the telephone channel, it should be noted that across a *given* utterance the characteristics of the telephone transmission media are essentially constant, and less variable than both the characteristics of the speaker and the linguistic content of the utterance. Thus, if the measured linear prediction parameters of a *given* telephone utterance are orthogonalized [from (4)-(8)], it can be expected that the first few most significant orthogonal parameters would be indicative of the linguistic content of the utterance (synthesis experiments [5]), the least significant parameter would be indicative of the telephone media, and the remaining parameters would be indicative of the speaker (recognition results for high-quality media). However, as noted above, a different pair of telephone lines may be obtained for each new telephone call and thus the characteristics of the telephone media may not be constant across the utterances in the training set. Since the orthogonalization scheme involves averaging over several utterances of a given speaker, the telephone media can no longer be represented by only the least significant orthogonal parameter. The transmission media variability spreads the representation of the telephone media across the last few significant parameters. These last few parameters are then partially indicative of the characteristics of the speaker *and* the telephone transmission media. The large distances associated with the four least significant parameters are due to the differences in the telephone media for an utterance outside the training set.

To avoid the problems of telephone media variability, it was decided to increase the order of the LPC analysis to 14 ($p = 14$). By using a 14th-order analysis, it was hoped that four poles would model the telephone media and ten poles would model the attributes of the speech. It was also hoped that an orthogonalization of the linear prediction parameters would then result in the four least significant orthogonal parameters being totally indicative of the characteristics of the telephone line. In effect, by over-specifying the number of poles needed to model the speech signal, we are leaving room for the variability of the media to be represented by the four least significant orthogonal parameters without spreading the variability across the parameters representing the speaker.

Consistent with these hopes, two modified metrics d_m' and D_m' were used for telephone inputs. These metrics are defined as

$$d_m' = \sum_{i=p'}^{p-4} \left(\frac{\bar{\phi}_{im} - Z_i}{\sqrt{\lambda_{im}}} \right) \bar{J}_m \tag{14}$$

and

$$D_m' = d_m + \sum_{i=p'}^{p-4} \left(\frac{V_i - \lambda_{im}}{\lambda_{im}} \right)^2 \bar{J}_m . \tag{15}$$

[10] The utterances were collected over a three-week period.

The new metrics are exactly the same as those defined in (11) and (13), but implicitly ignore the distances associated with the four least significant orthogonal parameters. For this modified system, the identification accuracy increased dramatically to 94.4 percent for the metric d'_m and 96.03 percent for the metric D'_m. These results confirm the fact that the four least significant orthogonal parameters are indicative of the telephone transmission media. Thus the effects of the telephone channel are partially avoided by ignoring these parameters. Of course, the band-limiting effects of the phone line can never be avoided and the accuracy for this transmission media is necessarily less than the previous results obtained for high-quality media.

VI. Conclusions

The effectiveness of the linear prediction orthogonal parameters for speaker recognition (identification and verification) was evaluated in this paper. The recognition accuracy for high-quality inputs exceeded 99 percent for the log area ratio and parcor orthogonal parameters and slightly lower for the LPC orthogonal parameters. For telephone input the accuracy exceeded 96 percent.

The important advantage of employing the linear prediction orthogonal parameters for speaker recognition is that a significant subset of these parameters are relatively constant across an analyzed utterance, and can thus be considered independent of the linguistic information and indicative of the speaker. Because of this linguistic independence, it is not necessary to time-normalize or segment the utterance to realize the full potential of the parameters. Another advantage is that the calculation of the linear prediction orthogonal parameters is an unambiguous, clearly defined operation that is easily determined from the speech signal. In addition, the linear prediction orthogonal parameters are independent of pitch and intensity information and can presumably be used to augment the recognition potential of these measurements. Finally, in view of the linear prediction orthogonal parameter's characterization of the speaker and not the linguistic content of the utterance, it may be possible to achieve text-independent speaker identification using these parameters.

References

[1] M. R. Sambur, "Selection of acoustic features for speaker identification," *IEEE Trans. Acoust., Speech, Signal Processing*, vol. ASSP-23, pp. 176-182, Apr. 1975.

[2] J. J. Wolf, "Efficient acoustic parameters for speaker recognition," *J. Acoust. Soc. Amer.*, vol. 51, pp. 2044-2056, 1972.

[3] B. S. Atal, "Effectiveness of linear prediction characteristics of the speech wave for automatic speaker identification and verification," *J. Acoust. Soc. Amer.*, vol. 55, pp. 1304-1312, 1974.

[4] G. R. Doddington, "A method of speaker verification," *J. Acoust. Soc. Amer.*, vol. 49, p. 139(A), 1971.

[5] M. R. Sambur, "An efficient linear prediction vocoder," *Bell Syst. Tech. J.*, Dec. 1975.

[6] B. S. Atal and S. L. Hanauer, "Speech analysis and synthesis by linear prediction of the speech wave," *J. Acoust. Soc. Amer.*, vol. 50, p. 637, 1971.

[7] A. E. Rosenberg and M. R. Sambur, "New techniques for automatic speaker verification," *IEEE Trans. Acoust., Speech, Signal Processing*, vol. ASSP-23, pp. 169-176, Apr. 1975.

[8] H. Cramér, *Mathematical Methods of Statistics*. Princeton, NJ: Princeton Univ. Press, 1951.

[9] L. R. Rabiner and M. R. Sambur, "Some preliminary experiments in connected digit recognition," presented at the 90th meeting of ASA, San Francisco, CA, Nov. 1975.

[10] H. L. Van Trees, *Detection, Estimation and Modulation Theory*. New York: Wiley, 1968.

AUTOMATIC SPEAKER RECOGNITION FOR USE OVER COMMUNICATION CHANNELS

Melvyn J. Hunt, John W. Yates and John S. Bridle

Joint Speech Research Unit
Eastcote Road
Ruislip, Middlesex, U.K.

SUMMARY

A system is described for the automatic comparison of speakers given short samples of their speech. The method does not depend on knowing what is being said, and is to a large extent independent of the degradations likely to be suffered by the speech during transmission. A small computer has been used to generate statistics on fundamental frequency and spectral shape information produced by a real-time cepstrum processor. Fundamental frequency is intrinsically resistant to most transmission degradations, and the spectral statistics taken are independent of linear spectral shaping. A useful level of recognition performance has been obtained using a total of 154 20s samples of read speech from thirteen typical speakers of British English.

1. INTRODUCTION

The work described in this paper is part of an attempt to develop a completely automatic means of speaker identification. Such a facility might be useful, for example, in the early stages of a police investigation where a telephoned message is to be compared with the recorded voices of a large number of suspects. The requirements, then, are that the system should be text independent and that as far as possible it should work on speech that has been degraded by transmission over communications channels such as the telephone. Satisfying these requirements entails some disadvantage in terms of accuracy of identification on high-quality speech and in terms of the length of speech sample needed. We are aiming for a system that would take as input a twenty second sample of telephone quality speech from an unknown speaker. The output would be a list of the five or ten percent of the speakers known to the system whose voices are most similar to that of the unknown speaker. Atal (1) has provided a clear and comprehensive account of the general principles and considerations involved in this sort of investigation.

Speaker recognition research requires the use of large quantities of speech, so for reasons of speed and storage limitations it is desirable to interpose a hardware speech processor between the analogue speech recording and the general purpose computer. At the outset of the work described in this paper we were aware that the fundamental frequency of the voice was likely to be useful for speaker recognition (2), and that the periodicity of the speech signal was not affected by the usual channel distortions. We considered that the 'cepstrum' method described by Noll (3) would be well suited to estimating fundamental frequency in telephone speech, so we processed the speech with a hardware implementation of Noll's method. With a 5 kHz sampling rate this 'cepstrum processor' produces an estimate of the fundamental period every 20 ms. It also provides the intermediate results of short-term log power spectrum and its cosine transform, the cepstrum.

2. THE SYSTEM

2.1 Overview

Because of the difficulty of selecting specific phonetic features automatically in telephone speech, we have confined ourselves to considering the overall statistical properties of the speech. We have written programs to reduce a twenty second speech sample to a set of about thirty numbers describing its statistical behaviour. We refer to these numbers as 'input parameters', and we hope that a suitably transformed set of them will characterise the speaker.

After the input parameters have been produced the rest of the system provides facilities for testing, displaying and transforming them, adding and deleting parameters, dividing data into sets containing selected speakers or selected groups of recordings and finally attempting recognition. By using small, modular programs all accessing files of a standard format, we have a flexible vehicle for carrying out pattern recognition experiments. Beyond the point where the input parameters are produced the system is quite independent of what features in the speech produced them, or indeed of the fact that they are concerned with recognising people from their voices at all.

In a speaker recognition experiment a group of speech samples is taken from each of a number of speakers. The speech samples are subsequently divided into two groups - a group to be used to train the system and a group representing unknown samples to be used to test recognition. The samples are reduced to parameter sets and recognition performance will depend on how tightly the sets from each speaker - or more generally, recognition class - cluster in the parameter space relative to the separation between speakers or classes. The training set is used to select useful input parameters and to find a transformation of them that will lead to

Reprinted from *1977 IEEE Internat. Conf. Record on Acoust., Speech and Signal Process.*, May 9-11, 1977, pp. 764-767.

tight clustering.

2.2 Parameter Selection and Transformation

An estimate of the usefulness of a parameter taken in isolation is provided by the ratio of its between-class to within-class variance, usually known as the F ratio. Low values of this ratio can be used to weed out unpromising input parameters.

Frequently, though, several apparently promising parameters will be highly correlated with one another, so that their contribution to overall recognition performance cannot be assessed individually. Insofar as the correlations are linear, the technique known as linear discriminant analysis (LDA) can be used. In the quantity known as 'divergence' (1) LDA provides an estimate of the likely recognition performance of a subset of the input parameters. At the same time it specifies the linear transformation of the input parameters which makes the within-class covariance for the training set isotropic and which condenses the discriminating power of the input parameters into as few transformed parameters as possible.

The transformation specified by LDA will be optimal for recognition if the training set is representative of the properties of the test material, and if the distributions within classes are multivariate normal and differ between classes only in their means. LDA cannot, for example, deal with non-linear correlations, and the transformation it specifies can be distorted by single uncharacteristic examples within a class. To check for these possibilities we can inspect scatter plots of selected pairs of input or transformed parameters on a display screen. We also carry out crude tests (skew and kurtosis) of normality for each parameter individually. Non-linear transformations of the parameters can be effected and tested using a BASIC program in which the transformation required is specified at run time.

2.3 Recognition Phase

The transformations determined from the training set are applied to both the test and training sets. The test set can then be used to measure recognition performance. The sets of parameters in the training set for each speaker are averaged to produce a centroid intended to characterise that speaker. A sample from the test set is then ascribed to the speaker whose centroid is closest to its parameter set. Since LDA makes the estimated within-speaker covariance isotropic, there is no need to weight the parameters in the recognition phase and a simple Euclidean distance metric can be used.

Instead of using the distances from the test sample to the centroids, one could look at the distances to all the individual samples in the training set and use a modified k-nearest-neighbour rule as the recognition criterion. We have a fairly large number of classes with a small number of approximately normally distributed samples within each class. In this situation the advantage of considering the training samples separately would probably be small and would not justify the increased computational effort involved.

3. CHOICE OF FEATURES

3.1 Fundamental Frequency

The repetition rate of glottal excitation in voiced speech, appearing as harmonic structure in the spectrum, is a feature which is resistant to moderate amounts of almost all the distortions encountered in communications channels. Statistics of the values of fundamental frequency estimated by the cepstrum processor during a speech sample should therefore be reasonably channel independent. This independence can be helped by a sensible choice of statistics. For example, high-order moments should be avoided since these will be heavily affected by outlying, probably spurious, points. In work carried out so far we have also avoided statistics concerned with longer-term features in the intonation pattern. This is because reliable estimation of such statistics requires long samples of speech; they are probably more dependent on the situation the talker is in than short-term statistics and it is difficult to devise measures of long-term features which are not liable to be disrupted by sudden bursts of noise.

3.2 Spectrum Envelope Measures

The spectrum envelope characteristics of speech are a function of the glottal pulse shape, the intrinsic dimensions of the vocal tract and the state of the articulators. Such characteristics are therefore promising sources of speaker identification information. The cepstrum processor provides a compact description of the spectrum envelope in the low-order cepstrum coefficients.

Spectrum shape measures are in general very susceptible to transmission distortions. It is, however, possible to devise measures derived from low-order cepstrum coefficients which are unaffected by moderate amounts of linear filtering. The principle on which these measures are based has already been described by Atal (1). Briefly, any spectrum shaping effect will appear as a multiplicative factor in the power spectrum, and so will be additive in the log power spectrum and in any linear transformation of this spectrum such as the cepstrum. If the spectrum shaping effects of the channel are constant over the speech sample, any measure of the variability in the cepstrum coefficients about their means will be unaffected by spectrum shaping. In choosing statistics of low-order cepstrum coefficients, then, one should only use measures which are unaffected by the addition of a constant value to all samples, for example, moments about the mean and differences between consecutive values of a coefficient.

In practice, even with high signal-to-noise ratios, the finite word lengths used in computing the cepstrum coefficients result in the invariance property holding only for moderate amounts of spectrum shaping. Moreover, such measures have no special resistance to the effects of non-linear distortions and additive noise, though some degree of immunity to short-term high-level noise bursts can be obtained by taking statistics only on sections of recordings judged to be voiced speech from their harmonic structure.

4. SPEECH MATERIAL

The material used in this study consisted of radio weather forecasts read by professional meteorologists and recorded from an FM broadcast receiver. Weather forecasts form a particularly convenient body of speech material: they consist of two or three minutes of read speech produced by typical speakers of British English who are not professional announcers or actors; they occur at regular times of day and the speaker's name is always announced; finally, individuals normally remain part of the team of weather forecasters for several years, so that long-term changes in voices can be studied. Although no special care was taken in making the recordings, they are certainly of higher quality than might be expected on communications channels such as telephones.

We collected recordings from thirteen speakers, eleven men and two women. For one of the male speakers it was unfortunately impossible to collect more than one recording. Consequently, this speaker had to be excluded from many of the experiments.

Two separate data sets were made from the recordings. The first consisted of just the fundamental frequency information for 330 thirty-second extracts from the forecasts. This corresponds to about 25 extracts per speaker taken from an average of six weather forecasts. The second contained both fundamental frequency information and the first eight cepstrum coefficients. In this set there were a total of 149 twenty-second extracts taken from exactly two forecasts for twelve speakers, plus five twenty-second extracts from the single forecast of the thirteenth speaker.

5. EXPERIMENTS

5.1 General Considerations

There can be two quite separate products of speaker identification experiments: one can use them to discover ways of obtaining improved recognition performance, and one can use them to test the performance of an existing system. Although they are superficially similar, the two kinds of experiments often have conflicting requirements. Performance testing demands strict separation of test and training sets. Not only must no speech extract occur in both sets, but also all extracts from the same recording session must be kept together in one set or the other. Moreover, the test set can only be used once if it is not to provide feedback which would help to train the system and thus give unrealistically optimistic results. By contrast, performance improvement often requires repeated use of the same test set; to do otherwise would be very expensive on data and would be an unnecessary source of variability in the results. A less rigorous separation of test and training sets may also provide a more convenient experimental procedure and a more effective use of a limited data set.

Our own experimental work so far has been primarily directed towards performance improvement and the data base was set up with this in mind. Although we have attempted some rigorous performance testing the unsuitable data base leads to results which probably understate the capabilities of the present system.

Visual inspection of scatter plots of values of pairs of the parameters we have tried has revealed no obvious non-linear correlations or bad values and our simple tests have not indicated peculiar distributions for any of our parameters. Consequently, we have so far confined ourselves to linear transformations of the input parameters.

5.2 Performance Improvement

The procedure adopted in the performance improvement work was to use the whole of the data set to determine the linear transformation to be applied. Each sample is then taken in turn and its effect removed from its own centroid before recognition of that sample is attempted.

The data set containing only fundamental frequency information was used exclusively for performance improvement. The first point we investigated was the form in which the fundamental frequency, or 'F_o', information should be used, ie whether one should take statistics on the distribution of linear frequency, linear period or log frequency. To do this we chose some simple input parameters and compared for the three cases the recognition performance and the values of divergence produced by the LDA. Log frequency turned out to be better than linear period, and, rather to our surprise, linear frequency was best of all. In seeking to explain this result it may be relevant that the mel scale of subjective frequency approximates to linear objective frequency in the range of human F_o.

We next investigated the most suitable F_o input parameters to use. Statistics were taken of the individual values of F_o and of first and second-order differences of adjacent values of F_o. First we tried some simple statistics: means, mean deviations and some low-order moments about the mean. At a slightly more complex level we investigated parameters based on possible correlations between F_o and its rate of change, and parameters indicating the proportions of time that F_o is rising or falling. Finally, we tried taking simple statistics of F_o with F_o first partitioned into periods when it was rising or falling or when its curvature was in a particular range.

In general, the simplest statistics were found to be the most useful: statistics of F_o were more useful than those involving differences in F_o, means were more useful than measures of variation about the mean, and partitioning the F_o track before taking statistics of it did not prove worthwhile.

The group of six input parameters which appeared to give the best recognition performance was determined. This consisted of the mean, the mean deviation, the second and third moments about the mean, the proportion of time F_o was falling, and the second moment about the mean with each value multiplied by the sign of the deviation from the mean. These parameters were then used in the validation experiments with the data set which included cepstrum coefficients. Obviously, the long-term mean could only be used for F_0 and not for the cepstrum data, but the other five parameters were computed for each of the eight cepstrum coefficients. There were therefore 46 input parameters in all.

Before carrying out the performance-testing experiments we undertook some preliminary investigations using the 'performance improvement' procedure on the new data set. To retain the validity of the performance tests, nothing discovered here was used to modify those tests.

The six F_0 parameters taken as a group were found to be much more effective for recognition than the five parameters of any one cepstrum coefficient. This result can be attributed to the fact that for both F_0 and cepstrum parameters the overall mean is the most useful single parameter, but in the cepstrum case it cannot be used if resistance to spectrum shaping effects is required. When, however, twenty or more of the better cepstrum parameters are taken together they are much more effective than the six F_0 parameters, and experience with the other data set showed that recognition based on F_0 statistics would not be much improved by adding more parameters. The cepstrum parameters appeared to be quite independent of the F_0 parameters in that the error rates for the two groups taken separately could be multiplied together to predict the error rate for the combined set.

By using the five parameters for each cepstrum coefficient in eight separate recognition experiments we compared the usefulness of each of the eight coefficients. While the usefulness did vary between coefficients there was certainly no tendency for the higher quefrency coefficients to be less useful. It appears, therefore, that performance might be substantially improved by including more coefficients.

In order to investigate correlations between the instantaneous values of the different cepstrum coefficients we computed covariance matrices for each speaker. Significant correlations were found, and the correlations were similar for all speakers. The correlations were therefore removed by carrying out a principal components analysis of the covariance matrix averaged over all speakers. The parameters of the principal components corresponding to low variability were neither better nor worse than those corresponding to high variability. Moreover, a subset consisting of the best parameters of the principal components gave no better recognition performance than a subset made up of the best parameters of the untransformed cepstrum coefficients.

5.3 Performance Testing

Using techniques developed on the F_0 - only set, peformance testing experiments were carried out on the data set containing cepstrum information. Since we had speech data from at most two weather forecasts per speaker the training set could contain information from only one forecast for the speaker being tested. The input parameters to be used were chosen by taking the 31 out of 46 whose F-ratios in the training set were highest. We tried two ways of organising the performance testing experiments.

The first way was to split the data into two sets each containing data from one weather forecast for each speaker, the thirteenth speaker with only one forecast being omitted. The two sets were then alternately used as test and training set. 133 samples out of 149 (89%) were correctly identified. If the system had produced a list of two possible names for the unknown speaker, it would have included the correct name 147 times out of 149.

The second way of organising the experiment was to make the test set consist of just one forecast with the rest of the data forming the training set. This has the advantage that an unknown sample can be identified as one of 13 speakers rather than one of 12, and it provides more information for the LDA, though in an unbalanced way because the speaker to be recognised contributes roughly half as much information to the LDA as the other speakers do. In fact, the results were very similar, with 132 (89%) correct identifications and 143 correct identifications when a list of two names was allowed.

There is good evidence that extracts taken from the same forecast are much more similar than extracts taken from different forecasts: if extracts from both forecasts were included in the training set (ie performance improvement mode) performance rose from 89% to 100%; and if the system was asked to identify the particular forecast that an extract was taken from, recognition performance was 75%. It seems likely, then, that the testing experiments would have given better and more realistic recognition scores if it had been possible to include data from several forecasts in the training set.

6. CONCLUSIONS

The set of statistical features used here gives a useful level of speaker recognition performance with some resistance to transmission distortions, and this performance can probably be improved by including more cepstrum coefficients. It remains to be seen whether the performance can be maintained when the system is tested on telephone quality conversational material.

ACKNOWLEDGEMENTS

We wish to thank the British Meteorological Office for letting us use the weather forecast material, and Miss P. S. Shillabeer for helping with the experiments.

REFERENCES

1. B. S. Atal, "Automatic Recognition of Speakers from their Voices", IEEE Proceedings, Vol 64, pp 460-475, April 1976.

2. K. O. Mead, "Identification of Speakers from Fundamental Frequency Contours in Conversational Speech", JSRU Research Report No 1002, March 1974.

3. A. M. Noll, "Cepstrum Pitch Determination", J. Acoust. Soc. Amer., Vol 41, pp 293-309, February 1967.

AUTOMATIC SPEAKER RECOGNITION SYSTEM AUROS FOR SECURITY SYSTEMS AND FORENSIC VOICE IDENTIFICATION

by

E. Bunge

Philips GmbH Forschungslaboratorium Hamburg,
2000 Hamburg 54, Germany

Abstract. AUROS is a versatile research tool for investigating the influence of different parameters to the speaker recognition security. The structure of this new modular system for automatic speaker identification and verification is described. Results obtained using AUROS are being discussed.

Introduction

In crime investigations (bomb threats, kidnapping, etc.) authorities are often facing the problem of identifying persons by comparing recorded voices. It is well known, that the human listener's capability of recognizing voices is considerably high. But due to the extreme large range of variations that is inherent to human speech production, the human performance in identifying persons by their voices is restricted to a value that is below a margin to be used for evidence at law courts.[1,2]

The same holds for visual comparison of optical data derived from the speech signal e.g. the frequency-energy-time plots "voice prints". Although a few skilled experts in this field obtained high recognition scores, the "reading" of these plots is highly subjective and not reproducible.[3] The need for reproducible, objective answers concerning a voice comparision, led to research in the field of automatic and semi-automatic speaker recognition by computers.[4,5,6,7,8]

In speaker recognition, forensic identification, being a multi-class problem, has to be distinguished from the two-class problem of speaker verification. In the latter case, an assumed or claimed identity will be stated or denied by comparing the actual recorded voice to the voice data of the real speaker, which had been evaluated by the system before.

In forensic speaker identification, an unknown voice is compared to a stored voice pattern library, and, according to a similarity criterion, the system will find out, to which person this actual voice belongs.

Both aspects, speaker identification and speaker verification are investigated in the AUROS project (AUtomatic Recognition Of Speakers by Computers) by the Philips GmbH, Research Laboratory, Hamburg, cooperating with Heinrich Hertz Institute of Communications Technology, Berlin GmbH.*)

Description of the AUROS System

The basic problems related to automatic speaker recognition are the variability of human speech and the large amount of data to be processed within short time intervals.[7] To overcome these difficulties, real time speech analysis techniques have to be combined with statistical techniques of pattern recognition. To take into account the different ways of disguising a voice, which is typical for non-cooperative speakers in the forensic application, a very flexible system, allowing many alternatives to optimize for given boundary conditions has been set up at Philips Research Labs. Fig. 1 shows the general structure of the AUROS system. Details of the algorithms incorporated in the system can be found elsewhere.[8]

The AUROS system consists of a general purpose computer for pattern recognition and a set of new real-time signal analysis processors, as well as a dedicated computer for simulation purposes. Most of the processors perform two-stage statistical analysis: in the time domain, as well as in the spectral domain, groups of events are detected segmentwise and are described by their moments and their distributions. A second set of analysis procedures based on linear transformations like FFT, Walsh Hadamard transformation and inverse filtering are used to evaluate off-line Cepstrum, formant frequencies, formant bandwidths and pitch. The analysis

*)The described work was supported by the German federal ministry for research and technology (BMFT) under no.081 2014. Only the author is responsible for the contents of this publications.

Reprinted from *Proc. 1977 Internat. Conf. on Crime Countermeasures—Sci. & Eng.*, July 25-29, 1977, pp. 1-7.

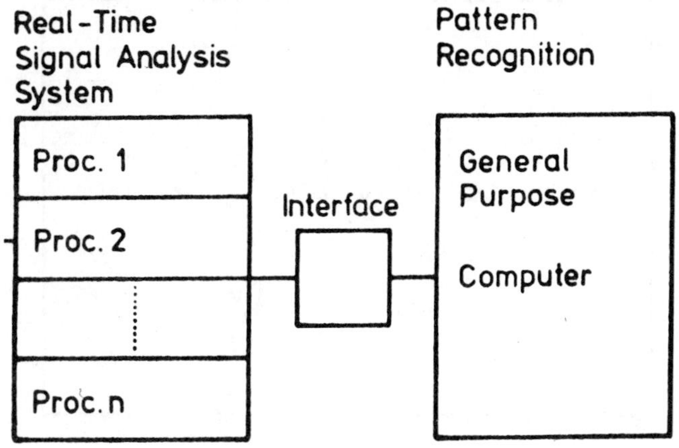

Figure 1. Principle structure of the speaker recognition system AUROS.

data are fed to the general purpose computer for statistical evaluation of voice reference patterns and automatic classification. For pattern recognition purposes, a large set of classification methods is available, e.g. minimum risk classificators, distribution-free tolerance region classificators, Mahalanobis classificator and nearest neighbour classificators. Different distance measures and different methods for probability density approximation can be chosen, thus providing a large variety of methods.

The different speech signal analysis processors and the various pattern recognition methods can be combined to a special task-adapted subsystem by a supervising program. An own programming language PATSY was developed to control the AUROS system. The system inputs are voices, either picked up by microphones for on-line recognition or recorded on magnetic tape for off-line tasks with large voice data bases. The output of the system are graphs of the different feature vectors, statistical data concerning the reliability of a decision, recognition rates for identification experiments and error rates for false acception and false rejection, describing verification experiments; the confusion matrices are evaluated as well.

The AUROS system is considered to be a powerful and universal research tool for investigation of security aspects in commercial and forensic speaker recognition.

Principle of Automatic Speaker Recognition

The general approach to the speaker recognition problem can be described by three phases:
1. Preprocessing the speech signal
2. Training the system
3. Testing the performance.

These three phases will be described in detail.

The Preprocessing Phase

The basic idea of the preprocessing phase is not to use the high dimensional redundant speech signal for the recognition procedure, but to describe it by a low dimensional set of features being typical mainly for the speaker's identity. In speaker recognition there are three general ways of feature extraction.

Short-time Analysis with Preceding Segmentation. The principle of this procedure is that the speaker specific information is already contained in a short segment of ca. 50 ms of the speech signal. So, using a segmentation algorithm, a special segment of this length, e.g. a few pitch periods of a nasal sound are cut out of the acoustical signal. To this segment, transformations like Fourier transformation or Walsh transformation or Ceptrum transformation are applied. The coefficients of these transformations can be used as feature vectors for the following pattern recognition procedures.

Fig. 2 shows three examples for short-time analysis of a 256 point segment of vowel "a": a) Fourier transformation, b) Walsh transformation, c) Cepstrum.

The problem of short-time feature extraction is the accuracy of the preceding segmentation algorithm: if the defined segment in the acoustical signal is not found exactly, the following steps are not meaningful since representations of physically different events are being compared.

Contour Analysis. Contour analysis describes the temporal structure of an utterance. The acoustical signal is segmented aequidistantly. For each segment, only one feature, e.g. the pitch period or the energy is evaluated. The sequence of these segment features forms the resulting contour curve. Fig. 3 shows as an example the pitch contour of a 2,5 s sentence, which was obtained by applying Cepstrum analysis and peak detection to approximately 100 segments of the speech signal.

Hereby the number of segments is identical with the dimensionality of the resulting feature vector. This means as a consequence, if a given sentence is spoken slowly, the dimensionality will be high (because many segments are produced), and if it is spoken fastly, a low dimensionality will be achieved. However, since the pattern recognition algorithms assume equal dimensionality for each speaker, complicated time normalization methods have to be applied to the contour vectors to stretch them for fast speakers and to compress them for slow speakers. These time normalization or time warping methods are complicated and very computation time-intensive.[5] Using contour analysis for feature extraction in speaker recognition means restriction to code-word

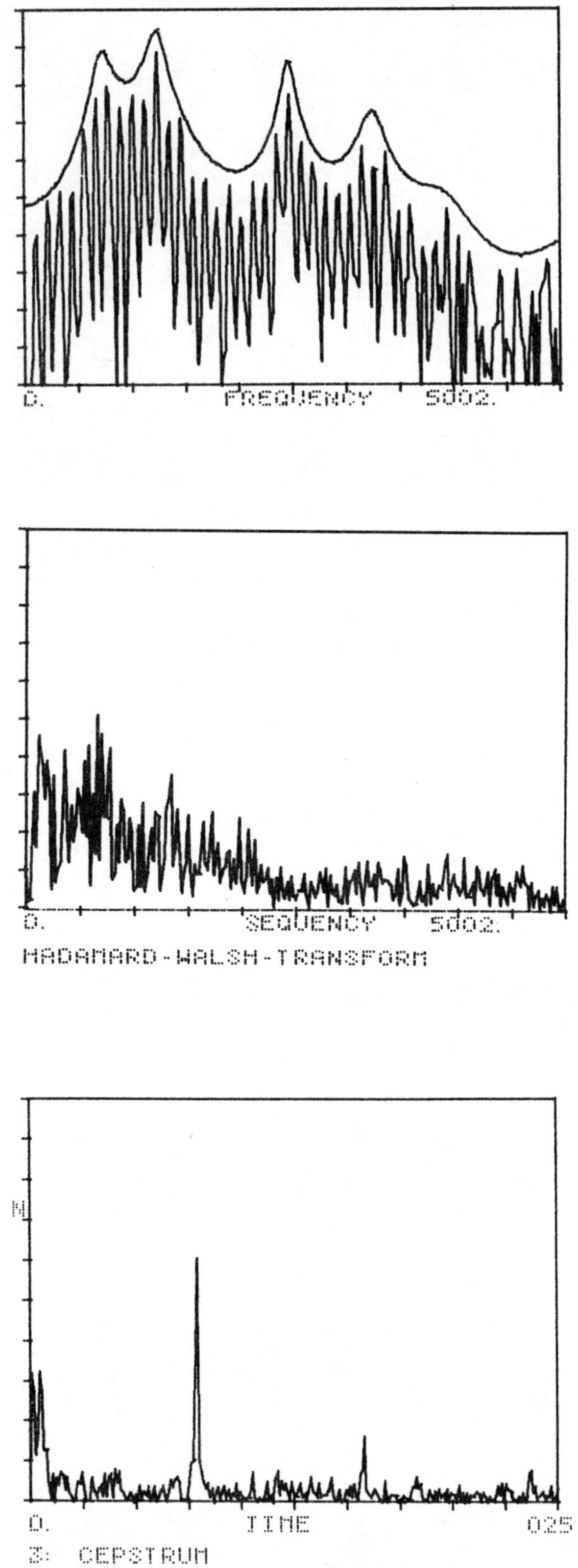

Figure 2. Examples for short-time analysis of the vowel "a"
a) Fourier transformation and inverse filtering
b) Walsh transformation
c) Cepstrum.

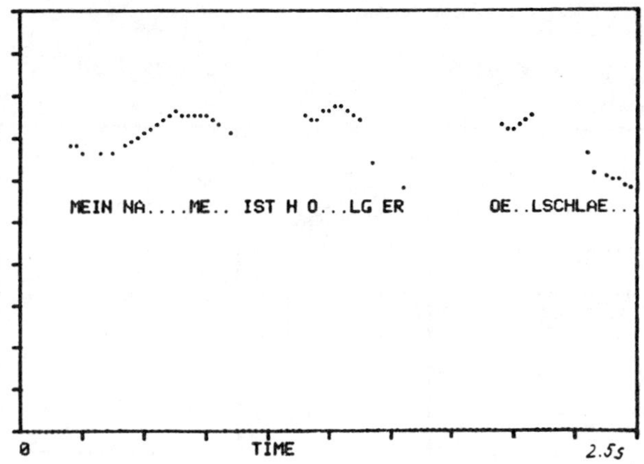

Figure 3. Pitch contour as example for contour analysis.

related recognition. Text-independent recognition is not possible since the time normalization methods are adapted to a special given code word.

Statistical Speech Signal Analysis. The speech signal is split in a sequence of 20 ms segments by aequidistant segmentation. For each segment, the coefficients of short-time analysis methods like FFT, autocorrelation, LPC, Cepstrum or any other transformation are evaluated. From the sequence of those sets of coefficients a feature vector is combined either by evaluating the mean value vector or by approximating probability densities of event groups. This kind of statistical feature extraction allows text-independent speaker recognition, assuming that the processed speech signal is at least 10 s long. There are no segmentation and no time normalization problems. For this reason these methods were preferably used within this research project.

Training Phase

To characterize the voice of a speaker it is necessary to combine the analysis results of a few utterances (at least 10) to a typical voice reference, since one utterance does not contain sufficient information, due to the non-reproducibility of human speech.[7] The evaluation of the voice reference is done by pattern recognition methods during the training phase. Details of the algorithms used in AUROS, can be found in [8,9].

The principle of some pattern recognition methods used for speaker recognition is as follows:

Each feature vector, generated by prepocessing the speech signal, can be mapped as a pattern point in the n-dimensional feature space. Each utterance of a speker produces a new point in this space. The entirety of all pattern points of the training phase forms a cloud in the n-dimensional space. The characteristics of a voice now can be described by the properties of this cloud.

Distance Classificators

For each speaker class separately, the centre of gravity of the cloud of pattern points is evaluated and stored as reference vector. An unknown pattern point is assigned to the speaker class to which the centre of gravity is the nearest. While class description by centres of gravity or meanvalue vectors is the principle of the "Minimum Distance" classificator, the "Nearest Neighbour" classificator preserves the cloud of points for each class and associates a pattern point to that class, to which the nearest neighbour point belongs. Within the AUROS system the distance classificators can be modified by a large number of different distance measures, including the Mahalanobis distance

$$d(\underline{X},\underline{M}) = (\underline{X}-\underline{M}) \sum^{-1} (\underline{X}-\underline{M})^T \qquad (1)$$

which was found to yield high recognition rates. (Σ^{-1} being the inverse pooled covariance matrix of all classes). The Mahalanobis classificator was realized by applying a decorrelating whitening transform to the data, thus producing a unity covariance matrix, and using "Minimum Distance" classificator with Euclidean distance measure in the rotated feature space.

Distribution-free Tolerance Region Classificators

In principle, the enveloping hypersphere of the cloud of pattern point is evaluated in a manner that avoids intersections between different classes. The equation of this hypersphere or tolerance region represents the voice characteristics for this type of classificator. For classifying an unknown pattern point, it is checked for each class whether this point lies within its hypersphere or not. If the point cannot be found in any tolerance region, it will be rejected.

Minimum Risk Classificators

The n-dimensional pattern space is divided into subspaces with equal volume. For each subspace the conditional probability density (CPD) is approximated by counting the number of pattern points in this area separately for each class. The CPD for a given class and a given subspace tells how probable it is, that a pattern point of this class lies within that subspace. For classification of an unknown pattern point, it is checked in which subspace it lies, and the values of the according CPD's for this subspace are compared. The unknown point then is classified into the class with the highest CPD.

The CPD evaluation can be performed by histogram techniques or by Parzen window approximation alternatively. Details of the algorithms used for minimum risk classificators can be found in [8,9].

Reliability Test Phase

During the reliability test phase, utterances, that have not been used for training, are offered to the system for automatic classification. The number of correct classifications and false rejects are counted in order to establish a confusion matrix and to evaluate the error rates being typical for the system performance.

Fig. 4 shows a simplified speaker verification experiment with real data. Speaker X repeated a text for 10 times. Each time a long-term spectrum was evaluated. Fig. 4a shows a plot of these 10 feature vectors. The non-reproducibility is easy to be seen. In a "model" training phase, a tolerance region is constructed in form of a mask by connecting all minimum and maximum values (Fig. 4b). For verification, the speaker X repeated the same text, and the analysis result was compared with the reference. It was accepted, as this long-time spectrum was within this tolerance region (Fig. 4c). When speaker Y claimed to be speaker X, he was rejected (Fig. 4d), as his curve did not fit the tolerance templet.

Results

For system performance evaluations, three large voice data bases have been used in the experiments.

Base 1: 2500 utterances of 41 male and 9 femal speakers, each utterance lasting 11 s. Equal texts each time.

Base 2: 2500 utterances of 41 male and 9 female speakers, each utterance lasting 11 s. 50 different texts

Base 3: 2500 utterances of 41 male and 9 femal speakers, each utterance lasting 2 s, equal texts each time.

In the experiments, the influence of different parameters on the obtained recognition rate has been investigated.

The Influence of the Length of the Spoken Message

In early experiments, utterances of 4 min were used to demonstrate, that speakers can be identified independent of the spoken text.[7] As this length, however, is unrealistic for practical use, the utterances were shortened.

Using data base 2, it could be proved, that text-independent identification is still possible with a textlength of approximately 11 s, as long, as different textes are used for the training phase. In this experiment, a recognition rate of 99.6% could be obtained, using long-time averaged spectra for signal analysis and

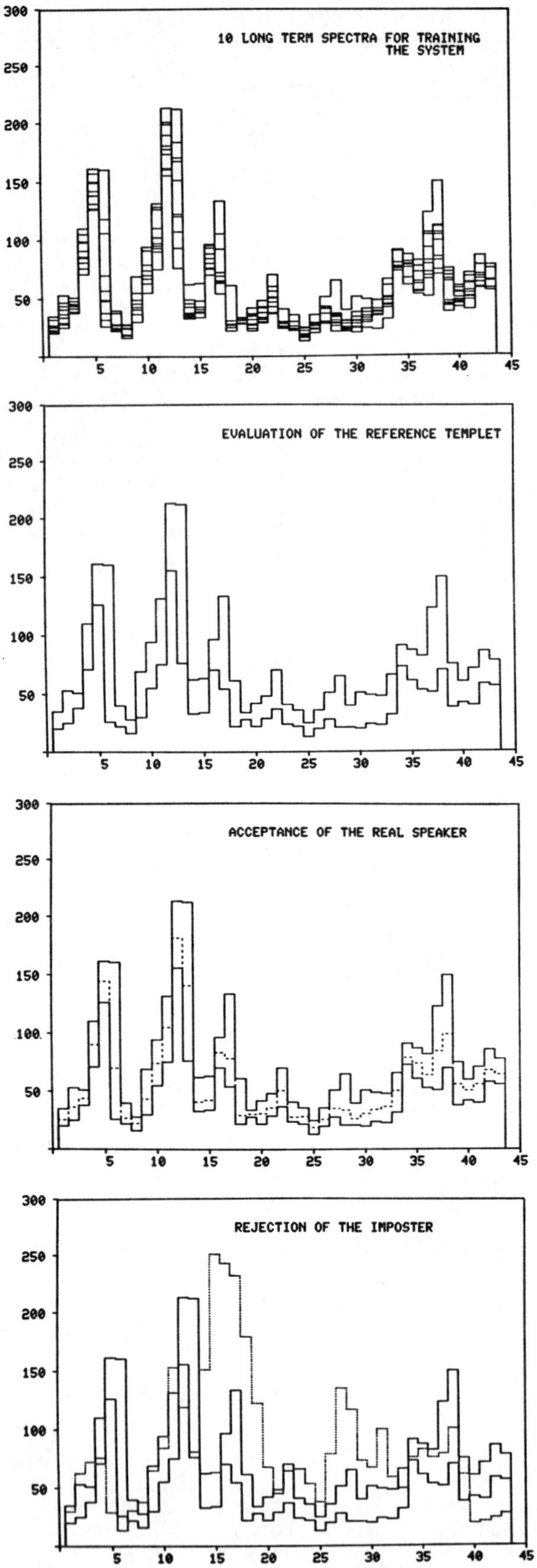

Figure 4. Example of a speaker verification experiment using 10 samples for training and averaged spectra as feature vectors.

minimum distance classificator with modified crosscorrelation coefficient as a distance function. The data were normalized to equal pattern energy and weighted according inverse parameter variances.[8] Twenty samples were used for training and thirty samples for testing for each of the 50 speakers. Training and testing data sets were non overlapping.

When decreasing the message length below 11 s, the influence of the text spoken became more and more obvious, and at last dominated, so that the variations of the analysis data were more due to the text than to the speaker's identity. A text length of 11 s seemed to be a limit for textindependent speaker recognition at high recognition rates.

In textdependent recognition, however, using data base 3, a recognition rate of 99.5% could be obtained for a textlength down to 2 s.

The Influence of Signal Analysis Methods and Pattern Recognition Algorithm to the Recognition Rates

All 2500 utterances of data base 3 were analysed by seven different statistical methods. For classification of these seven data sets, three different algorithms were used: Minimum distance classificator, nearest neighbour classificator and Bayes classificator, using histogram techniques for prohability density approximation.

The analysis methods used were: zero crossing interval analysis in two different frequency bands, distribution of energy levels, long time averaged spectrum and distribution of local features like relative minima, relative maxima and positive slopes in short time spectra. Fig. 5 shows as an example four of the statistical feature vectors. Without discussing the details, the results can be summarized as follows: analysis in the frequency domain is superior to analysis in the time domain (zero crossing statistics). The highest recognition rates of 99% and better, with 0% rejection rate were obtained by the distribution of relative maxima in short time spectra and by the averaged spectra. The best suited classificator in these experiments was the Bayes classificator. Normalization of the feature vectors to equal energy was important for the performance. Details of the algorithms used are described in [8].

The statistical methods for speech signal analysis, used here, seem to be very well suited for speaker recognition purposes. The analysis is performed in real time by specially designed hardware processors.

Sample Size For Training the System

In speaker verification, a distance measure between test sample and reference pattern is evaluated. If the distance

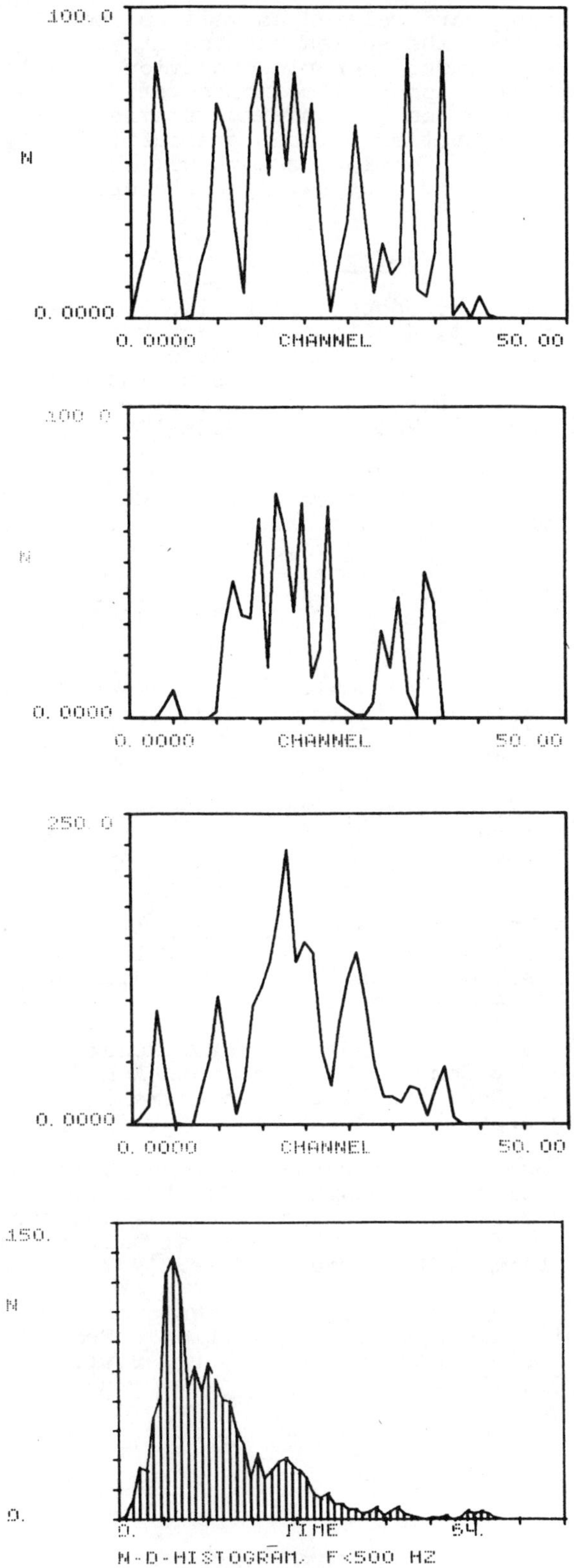

Figure 5. Statistical long-time speech analysis
a) distribution of relative maxima in short-time spectra
b) distribution of relative minima in short-time spectra
c) long-time averaged spectrum
d) zero crossing interval histogram

function exceeds a threshold, that had been established during the training phase, the test pattern will be rejected, otherwise it will be accepted and the identity claim will be stated.

Fig. 6 shows the threshold value as a function of the sample size of the training phase: the threshold was initially evaluated using two samples, and the third sample of the same class was verified. Then, this third sample was included for training, a new threshold was evaluated and the fourth sample was verified and so on, up to 49 samples for training. The function of the threshold value is drawn as a curve, while the actual distance for verification is plotted as a bar. As long as the bar is below the threshold, the sample is correctly accepted, otherwise it is falsely rejected as in the case of the third bar. By adding this sample to the training phase, the threshold, which was obviously too small, is increased, thus classifying the next samples correctly. After another correction at a sample size of 9, the threshold adapts nearly asymptotically to a value at which no false rejects occur. For this picture the false acception rate was 0%.

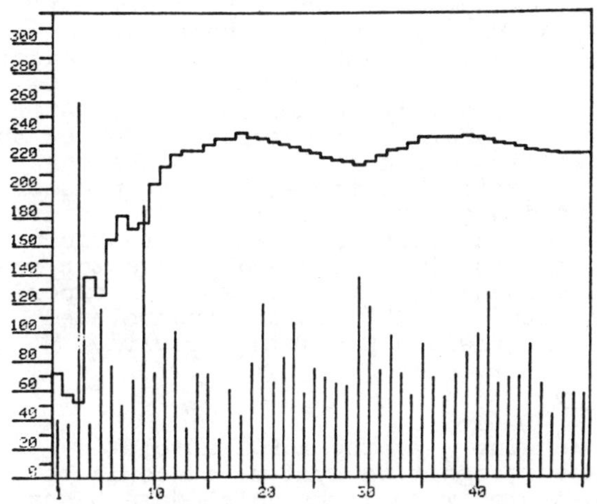

Figure 6. The decision threshold for speaker verification as a function of the sample size of the training phase

In general, the verification experiments showed that about 10 - 20 samples for the training phase seem to be necessary to obtain reliable results. The same sample size holds for identification experiments.

Applying the verification system to the two voice data bases with 2500 samples, each yielded error rates of about 1% for false accept and fals reject in both cases, codewordrelated as well as text-independent.

Elimination of Telephone Line Distortions

Any kind of spectral measurement will be affected by the superposition of telephone line transfer characteristics. To avoid, that the influence of varying transfer characteristics of dialled telephone line outweights the voice characteristics, a new analysis method for speaker recognition has been introduced.[8] The new feature vectors, the modified spectral standard deviation profiles (MSP vector) are a function only of the voice characteristics, and are not affected by the channel transfer functions.

The jth component S_{bj} of this novel feature vector is expressed in equation 2:

$$S_{bj} = \frac{\sum_{i=1}^{I} \left| a_j X_{ij} - \frac{1}{I} \sum_{i=1}^{I} a_j X_{ij} \right|}{\frac{1}{I} \sum_{i=1}^{I} a_j X_{ij}} \quad (2)$$

In the nominator, the modified standard deviation of the jth spectral component is evaluated, describing the short-time changes of the speech signal. This term still contains the frequency weighting factor a_j of the unknown transfer function. The averaged spectrum in the denominator, on the other hand, mainly describes the long-time properties of the voice superimposed by the unknown line characteristic. As the unknown weighting factor a_j occurs in numerator and denominator, it disappears, and by this, the influence of unknown transfer functions is eliminated and the vector remains unchanged, First recognition experiments with MSP vectors and related functions yielded promising results.

Summary

Working with the AUROS automatic speaker recognition system, it could be demonstrated with large voice data bases, that speaker identification and speaker verification can be performed automatically, codeword related as well as independent from the spoken message at error rates < 1% under economic conditions. While the system response time for a verification task is below one second, the statistical feature extraction methods are carried out in real-time. Continuous work will be done in the field of recognizing non-cooperative speakers.

References

1. R. Bolt, E. Cooper, E. David, P. Denes, J. Pickett, K. Stephans, "Speaker Identification by Speech Spectrograms: A Scientist's View of its Reliability for Legal Purposes", J. Acoust. Soc. of America, Vol. 47, 597-612, 1970.
2. A. Rosenberg, "Listener Performance in Speaker Verification Tasks", IEEE Trans. Audio Electroacoust., Vol. Au-21, 221-225, 1973.
3. L.G. Kersta, "Voiceprint Identification", Nature, Vol. 196, 1253-1257, 1962.
4. B.S. Atal, "Automatic Recognition of Speakers from their Voices", Proc. of the IEEE, Vol. 64, No. 4, 460-475, April 1976.
5. A.E. Rosenberg, "Automatic Speaker Verification: A Review", Proc. of the IEEE, Vol. 64, No. 4, 475-487, April 1976.
6. G.R. Doddington, "Speaker Verification - Final Report", Rome Air Development Center, Griffiss AFB, NY, Techn. Rep. RADC 74-179, April 1974.
7. E. Bunge, "Automatic Speaker Recognition by Computers", Proc. 9th Ann Carnahan Conf. on Electronic Crime Countermeasures, Lexington, Ken., May 1975.
8. E. Bunge, "Comparative Systematic Investigations on Automatic Identification and Verification of cooperative Speakers, Ph.D. Dissertation, Technical University of Darmstadt, Germany, Febr. 1977.
9. E. Bunge, "Statistical Techniques for Automatic Speaker Recognition", Proc. of the "DAGA 76", Heidelberg, Sept. 1976, VDI Verlag.

Long-Term Feature Averaging for Speaker Recognition

JOHN D. MARKEL, MEMBER, IEEE, BEATRICE T. OSHIKA, AND AUGUSTINE H. GRAY, JR., MEMBER, IEEE

Abstract—The potential benefits of long-term parameter averaging for speaker recognition were investigated. Parameters studied were pitch, gain, and reflection coefficients. Parameter variability was computed over various averaging lengths from one frame averaging (in effect, no averaging) to 1000 frame averaging (about 70 s of speech). It was demonstrated that the between-to-within speaker variance ratio, measured over several speakers, was significantly increased by performing long-term averaging of the parameter sets. The reflection coefficient averages for k_2 and k_6, respectively, were shown to produce the highest variance ratios.

I. INTRODUCTION

THERE have been several studies on the choice of acoustic features in speaker recognition tasks [14], [19], [22]. Average fundamental frequency has been found to be a useful discriminating feature [13], as have gain measurements [2], [10] and long-term speech spectra [4]-[6], [9]. Perceptual studies indicate that "there is at least weak evidence that a voice that is distinctive to listen to also has distinctive spectrographic patterns" [20], and that dimensions of "characteristic pitch" and "characteristic loudness" may be posited to differentiate among speakers [21]. These speaker characteristics can be distinguished from the acoustic cues which signal linguistic elements, e.g., phonemes or words. For example, the realization of the word "bit" by a female child is acoustically very different from the same word pronounced by an adult male, yet the words are generally understood to be equivalent while the speakers are clearly different. It appears, then, that listeners adapt to speakers' *voice* characteristics (as well as their *linguistic* characteristics).

Manuscript received May 13, 1976; revised December 13, 1976 and March 15, 1977. This research was supported by the Advanced Research Projects Agency of the Department of Defense and was monitored by the Office of Naval Research under Contract N00014-73-C-0221.

J. D. Markel and B. T. Oshika are with the Speech Communications Research Laboratory, Inc., Santa Barbara, CA 93109.

A. H. Gray, Jr., is with the Speech Communications Research Laboratory, Inc., Santa Barbara, CA 93109 and the Department of Electrical Engineering and Computer Science, University of California, Santa Barbara, CA 93109.

All this suggests that there are long-term characteristics which can be used in text-independent speaker recognition tasks. Such characteristics include long-term averages related to fundamental frequency, gain, and spectral averages.

The motivation for long-term averaging in text-independent speaker recognition is based upon a result from statistical sampling theory.

We assume that $\{p(i)\}$ defines statistically independent, identically distributed samples of the parameter p with true mean μ_p and variance σ_p^2. (For example, $\{k_1(i)\}$ corresponds to the reflection coefficient k_1 samples for each analysis frame.) If $x = \langle p(i) \rangle$ defines a *feature* based upon long-term averaging of p, where

$$\langle p(i) \rangle = \frac{1}{L_v} \sum_{i=0}^{L_v - 1} p(i), \tag{1}$$

and L_v is the number of voiced analysis frames used in the averaging, then the variance of x is given in terms of the original

Reprinted from *IEEE Trans. Acoust., Speech, and Signal Process.*, vol. ASSP-25, pp. 330–337, Aug. 1977.

parameter variance σ_p^2 by

$$\sigma^2 [\langle p(i) \rangle] = \sigma_p^2 / L_v. \tag{2}$$

The sample variance as a function of L_v is an important figure of merit for a particular feature. For example, if the features are more tightly clustered together about the sample mean as L_v increases from $L_v = 1$ (no averaging), then the intraspeaker variability is decreased, and the parameters would be expected to result in higher performance in text-independent speaker recognition tasks. Although no "true mean or true variance" exists for real speech because of physiological variations in human speech, it is reasonable to assume that at least some convergence or clustering of parameters will occur with long-term averaging.

The purpose of this paper is to define several sets of potentially useful long-term features and then to investigate their statistical properties as a function of the averaging length L_v. In addition, discrimination tests are presented over a small homogeneous set of speakers to illustrate the potential benefits of long-term averaging for unconstrained text-independent speaker recognition.

II. Features

To discuss the applicability of long-term feature averaging in a quantitative manner, we have chosen three different feature sets as the basis for analysis. Some of these features reflect physiological characteristics more closely than others.

A. Fundamental Frequency Features

Due to physiological considerations such as the length and thickness of the vocal folds, and respiratory muscle patterns, the phonation of a particular vowel with "normal effort" may result in differing rates of vocal fold vibration (corresponding to the acoustical correlate of fundamental frequency) for different speakers. For example, a child will have a high fundamental frequency compared to an adult because of the child's smaller vocal folds.

Although fundamental frequency, along with intensity and duration, is a controllable attribute of stress and intonation which may vary widely, each person appears to have a mean fundamental frequency value which, if averaged over a sufficiently long period of time, is relatively constant over a reasonable time span and is independent of linguistic content [8].

In addition, the standard deviation of the fundamental frequency over a long interval of time may carry important speaker-dependent information. For example, if the speaker is judged to be a monotone speaker, then the standard deviation would be expected to be relatively small. However, if the speaker is thought to be an "expressive" or "forceful" speaker, it would be expected to be relatively large.

B. A Gain Feature

It seems reasonable to assume that one of the characteristics that contributes to a speaker's identity is the amount of intensity or gain variation in his speech over time. Subjectively, the amount of gain variation is possibly correlated with the perception of "dynamic" versus "flat" voices. The actual gain variation is also a function of phonetic content, word and phrase stress, and discourse context. For example, for a constant subglottal pressure, the acoustical output energy for an /a/ is about 5 dB greater than for a /u/. Also, a larger gain variation would be expected with an exclamatory as opposed to a normal declarative sentence. Our assumption is that, over a sufficiently long interval of speech, gain variation can be considered part of the individual speaker's characteristics. That is, a speaker who is judged overall to be an "emphatic" speaker will have larger gain variation than one who is judged to have a usually monotonous voice.

In the measurement of gain variation, it is very important that results be only a function of speaker characteristics and not absolute system gain. Furthermore, because of the distinctly different production mechanism between voiced and unvoiced speech, it is desirable to measure the gain variations only during voiced speech. A normalized gain variation which satisfies desired physical properties is now defined. If $R(n)$ defines the energy of N speech samples $\{s(l)\}$ in frame n, then

$$R(n) = \sum_{l=0}^{N-1} s^2(l). \tag{3}$$

The sample mean and sample variance of $R(n)$ over L_v voiced frames is then defined by

$$\bar{R} = \langle R(n) \rangle \tag{4}$$

and

$$\sigma_R^2 = \langle (R(n) - \bar{R})^2 \rangle \tag{5}$$

where $\langle \cdot \rangle$ will be used throughout to denote averaging over L_v voiced frames. The normalized gain variation δ is then defined by

$$\delta = \sigma_R / \bar{R}. \tag{6}$$

If the overall system gain is changed by a constant value, δ is unaffected. Furthermore, δ is nonnegative with $\delta = 0$ only when $\sigma_R = 0$. Physically, $\delta = 0$ means that the speech envelope (more precisely, the frame energy) is unchanged over the complete range of voiced speech analyzed.

C. Spectral Features

It is well established in the literature that one of the acoustical features that tends to differentiate one particular speaker from another during voiced speech production is the glottal sound source shape [15].

Although the spectral slope of a single glottal pulse can vary over a wide range from nearly whispered speech to very intense vocal effort, for normal conversational speech it is expected that an average glottal source spectrum could be obtained over a relatively long interval of speech that would have relatively small intraspeaker variability.

Unfortunately, glottal volume velocity waveform estimation from speech is a nontrivial task [7], [12], [16]. A more direct method for automatic real-time analysis is to use a parameter set that is related to the smooth characteristics of the spectrum, which is independent of fundamental frequency or gain. With linear prediction analysis, obvious possibilities are filter coefficients, reflection coefficients, or log area functions. Sambur [17] compared these coefficients in a speech recognition experiment and decided to make use of the reflection coefficients. Although reflection coefficients are nonlinearly related to the more physically meaningful smooth-spectral and log-spectral model from linear prediction analysis, there is ample evidence that they do contain important speaker-dependent information that is not contained in fundamental frequency- or gain-related parameters. For example, in the case of a first-order filter, $M = 1$, a smooth spectral model can be physically and mathematically related to the first reflection coefficient. This model [11, p. 139] has a spectral flatness given by

$$\Xi(1/A) = 1 - k_1^2. \tag{7}$$

If the speech sample being analyzed has a nearly flat spectral trend, k_1 approaches zero and the spectral flatness approaches unity. As the spectral slope increases negatively, k_1 approaches -1 and the spectral flatness approaches zero.

Based upon the spectral matching properties of linear prediction [11, p. 134], we would assume that preemphasis of the data would be beneficial since the reflection coefficients would then carry more information about the spectral structure at higher frequencies.

It would also seem reasonable that if long-term, spectrally related features are desired which minimize intravariability, only voiced speech should be analyzed. Substantial differences exist in the physiological mechanisms which produce voiced and unvoiced sounds. Since the excitation for unvoiced speech is generally assumed to have a flat spectrum, the difference in spectral slope between voiced and unvoiced sounds may be on the order of 8-16 dB. With only voiced sounds, some variation will still occur since different articulator positions will cause variations on the acoustic loading at the glottis, affecting the glottal source shape. This variation, however, is expected to be substantially less than that due to glottal source variations in voiced-unvoiced speech production.

D. Summary of Feature Definitions

As *features* we study the following.

1) F_0 average

$$x_1 = \overline{F}_0 = \langle F_0(n) \rangle. \tag{8}$$

2) Standard deviation of F_0

$$x_2 = \sigma_{F_0} = \langle [F_0(n) - \overline{F}_0]^2 \rangle^{1/2}. \tag{9}$$

3) Sample gain variation

$$x_3 = \sigma_R / \overline{R} \tag{10}$$

where

$$\overline{R} = \langle R(n) \rangle \tag{11}$$

and

$$\sigma_R = \langle [R(n) - \overline{R}]^2 \rangle^{1/2}. \tag{12}$$

4) Spectrally related features (reflection coefficient averages)

$$x_{i+3} = \langle k_i(n) \rangle \quad \text{for } i = 1, 2, \cdots, M. \tag{13}$$

The *feature vector* x is defined by

$$x^T = [x_1 x_2 \cdots x_{3+M}] \tag{14}$$

where T denotes transpose.

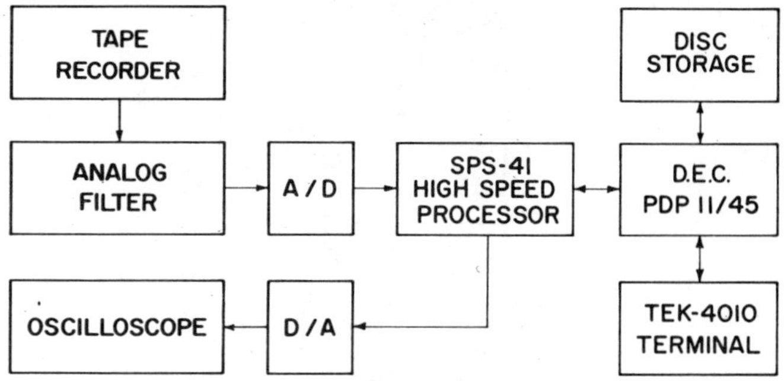

Fig. 1. Block diagram of system for processing speech.

III. Procedures

A. Data

The data used for the analysis were obtained during interviews of four speakers. Each interview was then edited so that only the interviewees' voices remained. The total duration of each edited interview (including pauses) was typically 15-18 min. The total data base used for this study was approximately one hour in duration. No special precautions or recording conditions were imposed on the experiment. Interviews were conducted in normal room environments with a dynamic microphone and an audio tape recorder. So that a small number of speakers could be used with some generality in extrapolating results, a homogeneous population of four male speakers was chosen, each having somewhat similar speech characteristics and relatively narrow fundamental frequency ranges. Histograms of the raw nonaveraged fundamental frequency values showed substantial overlap among the four speakers.

B. Digital Processing of Data

The audio tape was digitally processed using the system shown in Fig. 1. Each test segment was recorded onto a disk using conventional procedures. A novel part of the procedure is based upon the use of a high-speed signal processor and oscilloscope (for visual feedback during processing). Using an array-processing software system, it is possible to process the data in real time at a 50 Hz analysis frame rate from a Fortran environment. Processing includes modified cepstral pitch period and voicing detection, gain calculation, linear prediction analysis for reflection coefficients, and a running mean and mean-square computation of these parameters.

The procedure for generating output feature vectors to be used in the statistical analysis is shown in Fig. 2. A counter for frame n is incremented and one frame of speech is analyzed. The parameters used are: sampling frequency f_s = 6.5 kHz, number of analysis coefficients $M = 10$, number of samples for reflection coefficient computation = 128, and the number of samples for F_0, and gain parameter analysis = 256 (40 ms). The analysis frame rate is 50 Hz. Preemphasis of the speech data is applied using a differencer, $1 - z^{-1}$.

Fundamental frequency estimation is performed with a modified cepstral technique. After the spectrum has been computed, a symmetrical window function is applied that smoothly tapers from unity at 1000 Hz to zero from 1500 Hz to $f_s/2$. This simple modification resolves most of the voicing problems one obtains with the usual cepstral analysis method since only

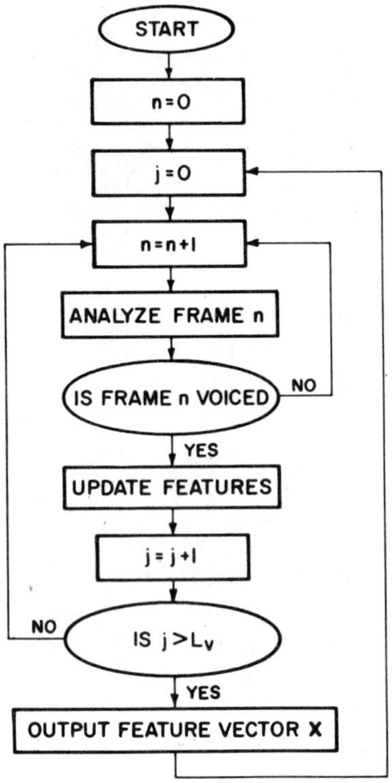

Fig. 2. Procedure for generating output feature vectors.

the most consistent region of harmonic structure is used [3]. Two frames of delay are included in the system so that some amount of error detection and correction can be applied in the pitch period estimation. One additional test has been found necessary for obtaining meaningful feature vectors. A max (F_0) and min (F_0) value are chosen for the speaker being analyzed to ensure against gross errors causing the fundamental frequency features from being dramatically affected. If min $(F_0) < F_0 <$ max (F_0), the frame is judged to be voiced and the long-term averages are updated. The frame counter is incremented and if $l > L_v$, the resultant features vector x is output to disk, l is reset to zero, and analysis then continues.

IV. Experiments

A. Experiment 1–Statistical Variation as a Function of L_v

The complete edited audio tape for speaker D (approximately 18 min in duration) was analyzed to extract long-term averaged feature vectors for several L_v conditions. As a time reference, $L_v = 1000$ corresponds to approximately 70 s. The total number of vector samples obtained is approximately inversely proportional to L_v.

The unbiased variance estimate of the feature $x = \langle p(i) \rangle$ based upon the speech parameter p is

$$\sigma^2(x) = \frac{1}{L_f - 1} \sum_{i=0}^{L_f - 1} [\langle p(i) \rangle - \bar{x}]^2 \tag{15}$$

where

$$\bar{x} = \frac{1}{L_f} \sum_{i=0}^{L_f - 1} \langle p(i) \rangle. \tag{16}$$

Each $p(i)$ explicitly denotes an individual feature, and L_f is the number of feature vectors obtained over the total speech duration. Note that L_f is actually a function of L_v since the total duration is fixed. The sample mean x is thus independent of L_v except for sampling variation in the real-time analysis because it is not possible to start analysis at precisely the same location on the audio tape when L_v is changed. The true variance σ_p^2 is estimated from $\sigma_p^2 = \sigma^2(x)$ with $L_v = 1$. Features which themselves are based on variances (such as $x_2 = \sigma_{F_0}$ and $x_3 = \sigma_R/\bar{R}$) do not allow for a true variance estimate. The sample standard deviations of the fundamental frequency-related features are shown in Fig. 3 as a function of L_v. The estimated standard deviation about the long-term fundamental frequency averages is reduced from about 18 Hz for $L_v = 10$ to about 6 Hz for $L_v = 1000$. These values are somewhat higher than the long-term F_0 averages reported by Horii [8]. However, this experiment is based upon unconstrained conversational speech, whereas Horii's experiment was based upon a reading of the "Rainbow Passage."

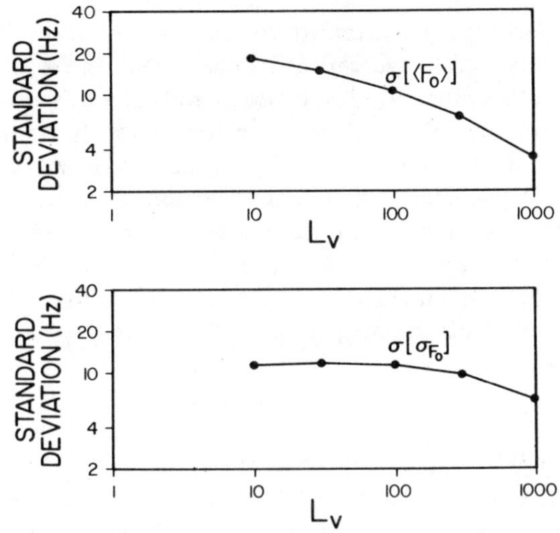

Fig. 3. Standard deviation of F_0 related features as a function of the number of voiced frames L_v.

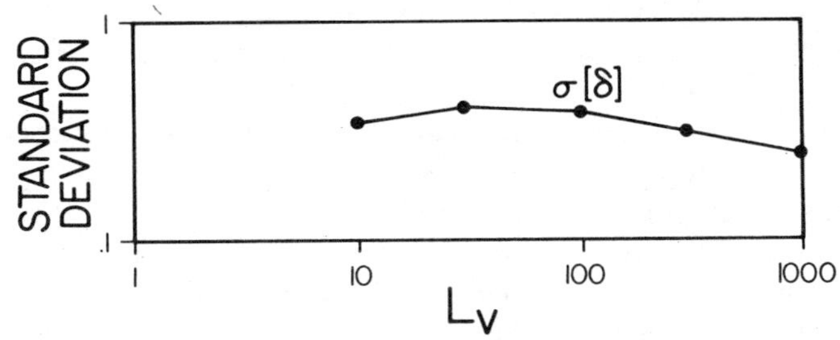

Fig. 4. Standard deviation of gain related features as a function of the number of voiced frames L_v.

The estimated standard deviation of the $x_2 = \sigma_{F_0}$ feature is surprisingly constant, until at least on the order of 7-10 s of speech ($L_v > 100$) have been analyzed. Increasing L_v from 100 to 1000 decreases $\sigma(x_2)$ from 12-6 Hz.

The variability of the gain variation feature, $\sigma(x_3)$, as shown in Fig. 4, follows a similar pattern. This particular feature appears to be a very weak function of L_v.

In Fig. 5(a), the estimated standard deviation of the $\langle k_1 \rangle$ and $\langle k_{10} \rangle$ features for speaker D are shown as being representative of the reflection coefficient feature set characteristics. Although the estimated standard deviation does not decrease as

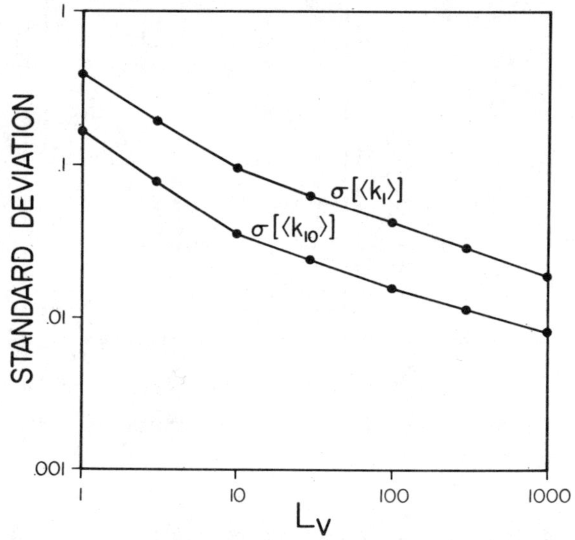

(a)

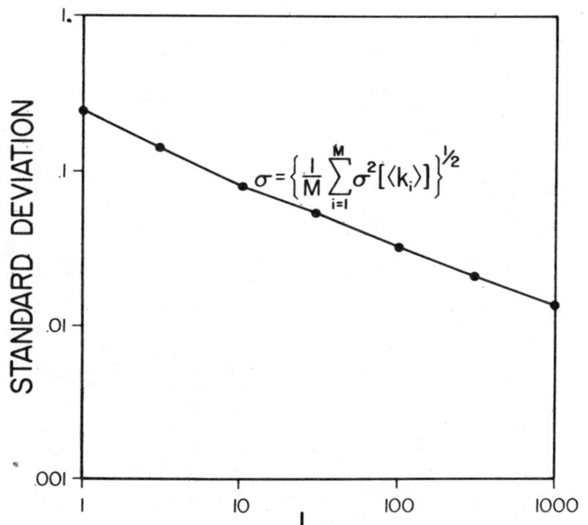

(b)

Fig. 5. (a) Standard deviation of reflection coefficient averages as a function of the number of voiced frames L_v. $\langle k_1 \rangle$, $\langle k_{10} \rangle$ deviations. (b) Standard deviation of reflection coefficient averages as a function of the number of voiced frames L_v. rms of all coefficient variances.

rapidly as predicted by sampling theory for the case of independent samples because of intraspeaker variability, the decrease is substantial and is surprisingly linear on a log-log scale. Instead of a $L_v^{-1/2}$ relation, the standard deviation of the reflection coefficient features appears to approximately decrease proportionally to a $L_v^{-1/3}$ model beyond $L_v = 10$.

The rms deviation over all $\langle k_i \rangle$ averages is shown in Fig. 5(b). Over a range of L_v from 10 to 1000, the $L_v^{-1/3}$ model is still seen to be very accurate for predicting the decrease in reflection coefficient feature parameter variation as L_v is increased. The measured exponent value is certainly dependent upon the particular speaker. However, it appears to vary only slightly from the model discussed for the several other speaker measurements.

The estimate of the true variance for the k_1, k_{10}, and overall parameter variance is also shown in Fig. 5(a) and (b) at $L_v = 1$.

A second way of qualitatively showing the effect of long-term averaging is to show two-dimensional scatter diagrams for various values of L_v. Fig. 6 shows a scatter plot of $\langle k_2 \rangle$ versus $\langle k_1 \rangle$ samples. Each point is based upon L_v samples from the edited audio tape for speaker *D*. Shown with the data are two-sigma ellipses with the principal axes. A dramatic decrease in the dispersion of the data is seen as L_v increases.

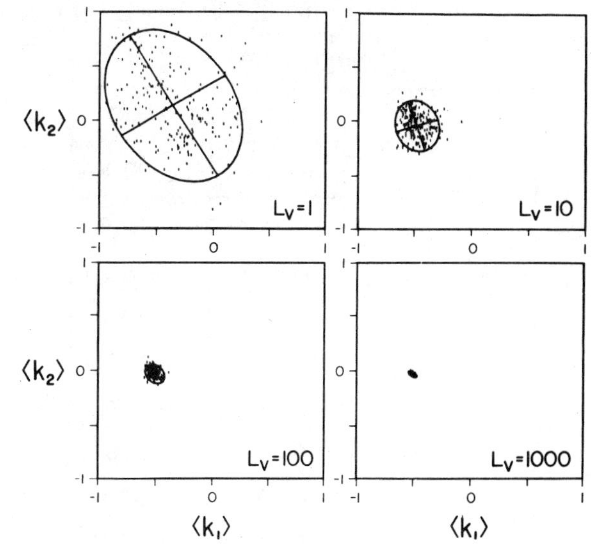

Fig. 6. Scatter plots of $\langle k_1 \rangle$, $\langle k_2 \rangle$ features for different L_v with two-sigma ellipses and principal axes.

B. Experiment 2–Discrimination as a Function of L_v

The approach taken here is to investigate the effectiveness of long-term averaging for speaker recognition using the ratio of the between-speaker variance and the within-speaker variance, without specifying particular speaker recognition experiments. Since the mathematics of this procedure (Fisher discriminant method) is discussed elsewhere [1], only the necessary details will be summarized below.

A within-speaker covariance matrix W is computed, and then a normalized between-speaker covariance matrix B' is found in terms of the matrix B of Bricker *et al.* [1] from

$$B' = B/L_f \tag{17}$$

where L_f is the number of feature vectors. The normalization is included so that B' will depend only upon the sample means, not upon the number of feature vectors. Eigenvalues and eigenvectors of the equation

$$B'\boldsymbol{\phi}_k = \lambda_k W \boldsymbol{\phi}_k \tag{18}$$

are then obtained. The eigenvalues are ordered from highest to lowest, and as the number of speakers, four, is less than the number of features, thirteen, all but the first three eigenvalues are zero [1]:

$$\lambda_1 \geq \lambda_2 \geq \lambda_3 \geq \lambda_4 = \lambda_5 = \cdots = \lambda_{13} = 0. \tag{19}$$

A new coordinate system is defined using the eigenvectors of (18) as base vectors, so that the new coordinate vector $\boldsymbol{y}$ is related to $\boldsymbol{x}$ through the linear transformation

$$\boldsymbol{y} = \boldsymbol{\phi}^T \boldsymbol{x} \tag{20}$$

where $\boldsymbol{\phi}$ is the matrix whose columns are the eigenvectors of (18). The eigenvalues of (18) represent the variance ratios in the directions of the eigenvectors with λ_1 being the maximum

TABLE I
VARIANCE RATIOS OF LONG-TERM AVERAGE FEATURE SET FOR $L_v = 100$ AND $L_v = 1000$

FEATURES	VARIANCE RATIO	
	$L_v = 100$	$L_v = 1000$
$x_1 = \langle \bar{F}_0 \rangle$	0.332	2.321
$x_2 = \langle \sigma_{F_0} \rangle$	0.004	0.043
$x_3 = \langle \delta \rangle$	0.119	0.329
$x_4 = \langle k_1 \rangle$	0.081	0.305
$x_5 = \langle k_2 \rangle$	2.721	16.118
$x_6 = \langle k_3 \rangle$	0.221	1.216
$x_7 = \langle k_4 \rangle$	0.367	2.023
$x_8 = \langle k_5 \rangle$	0.307	2.002
$x_9 = \langle k_6 \rangle$	2.315	11.452
$x_{10} = \langle k_7 \rangle$	0.155	0.650
$x_{11} = \langle k_8 \rangle$	0.511	2.591
$x_{12} = \langle k_9 \rangle$	0.185	0.977
$x_{13} = \langle k_{10} \rangle$	0.403	0.978

TABLE II
VARIANCE RATIOS OF TRANSFORMED LONG-TERM AVERAGE FEATURE SET FOR $L_v = 100$ AND $L_v = 1000$

TRANSFORMED FEATURES	VARIANCE RATIO	
	$L_v = 100$	$L_v = 1000$
y_1	10.959	115.368
y_2	0.972	7.956
y_3	0.393	1.730
y_4	0	0
⋮	⋮	⋮
y_{13}	0	0

variance ratio, λ_2 being the next largest (in a direction orthogonal to $\boldsymbol{\phi}_1$), etc. Variance ratios can also be computed in the original coordinate system as a method for measuring relative effectiveness of features.

Tables I and II show the variance ratios in the original and transformed coordinate systems, respectively, for $L_v = 100$ and $L_v = 1000$. Except for the fact that parameter correlation is not taken into account, the variance ratio values can be taken as quantitative measures of the original parameter's effectiveness in speech recognition. For example, we see that σ_{F_0} provides very little discrimination among speakers, whereas $\langle k_2 \rangle$ appears to provide the maximum discrimination among speakers over all parameters. It is seen that the first dimension in the new coordinate system results in a substantially increased variance ratio.

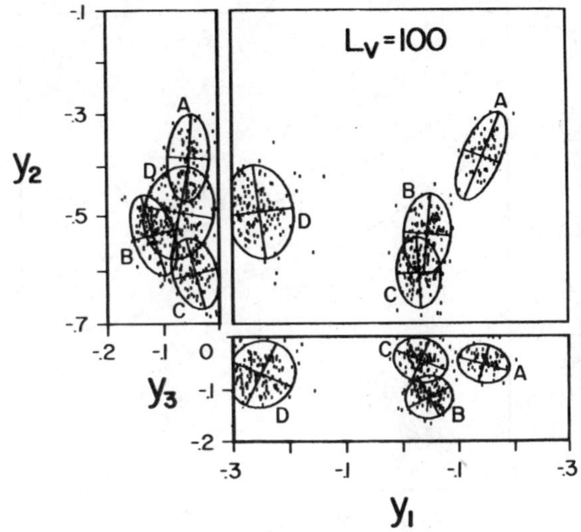

Fig. 7. Scatter plots for speakers *A-D* along first three Fisher discriminant dimensions ($L_v = 100$).

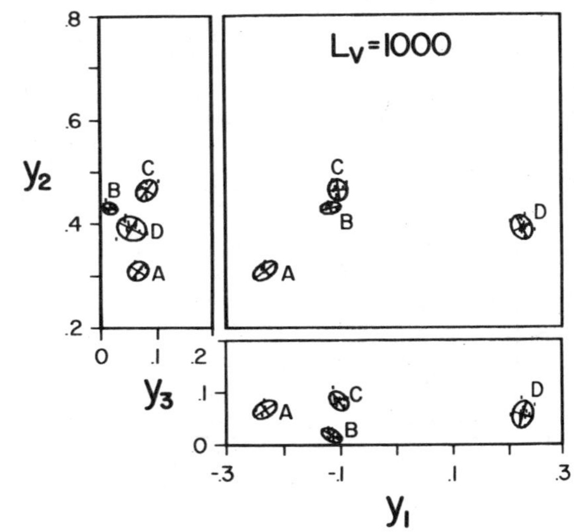

Fig. 8. Scatter plots for speakers *A-D* along first three Fisher discriminant dimensions ($L_v = 1000$).

Two-dimensional scatter plots of the first three transformed dimensions are shown in Fig. 7 for $L_v = 100$ and in Fig. 8 for $L_v = 1000$. The results are based upon the four speakers *A-D*. Also shown are two-sigma ellipses and the principal axes for each speaker distribution. In Fig. 7 it is seen that *A* and *D* are essentially uniquely separated from *B* and *C* in at least one plane ($y_1 - y_2$). A relatively large overlap does occur, however, for *B* and *C* in all planes. A cursory comparison of Fig. 7 and the relative sizes of clusters in Fig. 6 will illustrate that substantial benefits in discriminating against different speakers have been obtained over using no averaging ($L_v = 1$) or very limited amounts of averaging ($L_v = 10$).

In Fig. 8, it is seen that by performing long-term averaging with $L_v = 1000$, perfect discrimination is obtained, in this instance based upon only a two-dimensional transformed feature representation.

The variance ratios for the input feature variables are shown in Table I for $L_v = 100$ and $L_v = 1000$. If the variables were statistically independent, these ratios would differ by a multiplicative factor of 10 rather than the smaller factors indicated in the figure. The ordering of the features in terms of variance ratios is of some interest. The fifth feature, k_2, clearly shows the largest variance ratio, with the ninth feature, k_6, the next largest. These coefficients correspond to the coefficients for the highest power of z^{-1} in the models of order 2 and 6 found from linear prediction analysis. The two-pole model has been used in earlier recognition tasks [18].

The variance ratios for the first three features, fundamental frequency, its standard deviation, and sample gain variation, are smaller than what one might expect from intuition. Part of the reason may lie in the fact that the speakers were chosen to have similar fundamental frequency ranges.

The variance ratios for the new coordinate system, the eigenvalues of (18), are shown in Table II. From these ratios and the scatter diagrams of Fig. 8, it can be seen that very clear separation of the speakers is indicated for the long-term average case of $L_v = 1000$ by using only the first two coordinates, y_1 and y_2, in the direction of the eigenvectors $\boldsymbol{\phi}_1$ and $\boldsymbol{\phi}_2$.

V. Discussion

A. Parameter Variability Over Days, Weeks, Etc.

This initial study has been restricted to the study of long-term averages taken from one session. This is probably the reason why the standard deviation of the long-term averages tends to have a monotonically decreasing behavior. Although some amount of intraspeaker variability is reflected in the data, additional variability will occur when results are obtained from sessions separated by days, weeks, or months later. In several studies over linguistically constrained units, this effect has been shown to be severe beyond several months for short text-dependent segments [4]. A large data base extending over several months is now being generated for studying these effects in conversational speech.

B. Accuracy of Voicing Decisions

Since all long-term statistics are made only during voicing, it is very important to know that realistic voicing decisions are made. Spectral slope and normalized gain variation are direct computations requiring no decisions (except for voicing) and are, therefore, very robust.

If the threshold setting for voicing and pitch period detection is set too high or too low, the effect can be catastrophic. At one extreme, if the voicing threshold is too high, very few frames will be included in the statistics as being voiced (although they will be very reliable estimates) and, furthermore, transitions in which considerable fundamental frequency variations may occur are likely to be missed, causing the measured fundamental frequency standard deviation to be unrealistically small.

At the other extreme, if the threshold is too low, there will be a tendency to define fundamental frequencies near the maximum allowable frequency (minimum pitch period) (near 400 Hz) during actual voiced speech and at random values throughout the rest of the allowable range during unvoiced speech. Although a pitch period and voicing decision program with several frames of delay is used for error detection and correction, it is essentially impossible to separate accurate estimates from gross errors beyond some reasonable threshold.

C. Assumptions Versus Experimental Results

It was assumed that $\langle F_0 \rangle$ carries important speaker information. The $\sigma[\langle F_0 \rangle]$ versus L_v graph in Fig. 3 showed a significant monotonic decrease as L_v was increased. In addition, the variance ratio was relatively high (even though speakers were purposely chosen with similar fundamental frequency ranges). Therefore, this assumption appears valid. The assumption that $\sigma[\sigma_{F_0}]$ is meaningful does not appear to be true for conversational speech. The variance ratio for this feature is extremely small. This result contradicts that shown by Mead [13], where the use of the first through the fourth moments of F_0 and of the first four differences of F_0 (resulting in 20 features) was suggested. Our experience indicates that unless hand-marked or hand-corrected F_0 contours are used, very significant biases in results can occur because of very few gross errors in F_0 estimation. Higher order differences and moments only magnify these biases.

The standard deviation of the gain deviation feature as a function of L_v shows a weak relationship to expectations from statistical sampling theory. In addition, the variance ratios for the gain deviation feature are relatively small. Although some discrimination is obtained, what we have seen is that not only is there substantial intraspeaker variability for this parameter, but that, in addition, considerable overlap in the gain feature values occurs between speakers. Other measures of fundamental frequency and gain variations may prove to be more useful than the ones used here, which are essentially based upon root mean squares taken about the averages. One possibility is the use of the ratio of geometric and arithmetic means as used in evaluating spectral flatness [11].

The long-term averages of the reflection coefficients as a set appear to be the most significant features for speaker recognition. Not only does the standard deviation of the long-term averages show a substantial decrease as a function of L_v, but in addition, the variance ratios are seen to be relatively large for most of the parameters.

D. Observations on Reflection Coefficient Averaging

Although $\sigma(\langle k_{10} \rangle) < \sigma(\langle k_1 \rangle)$ for all L_v, in Fig. 5(a), one should not be misled into thinking that $\langle k_{10} \rangle$ is a better feature for speaker recognition. This result occurs because k_1 inherently has a larger standard deviation than k_{10} ($\langle k_1 \rangle = k_1$ for $L_v = 1$). The important fact to note is that whatever the parameter deviation is without averaging, due to either linguistic content or intraspeaker variability, it decreases as $L_v^{-\alpha}$ where $\frac{1}{3} \leqslant \alpha \leqslant \frac{1}{2}$ when long-term averaging is applied.

In a recent paper [17], the use of orthogonal linear prediction parameters for use in text-independent speaker recognition studies was suggested. Although very high recognition scores were shown using the orthogonal linear prediction parameters, we would suggest that substantial reduction in scores would occur if unconstrained data bases as described here were used. Whatever scores are obtained using, in effect, $L_v = 1$, our results qualitatively indicate that substantial improvements could occur by incorporating long-term averaging.

Each orthogonal parameter was obtained from a linear combination of all reflection coefficients as

$$\Phi_i = \sum_{j=1}^{M} c_{ij} k_j \tag{21}$$

where the c_{ij} terms were obtained from a principal component analysis. The averaged parameters would then be

$$\langle \Phi_i \rangle = \sum_{j=1}^{M} c_{ij} \langle k_i \rangle. \tag{22}$$

Although Fig. 6 shows only the dispersion characteristics for $\langle k_1 \rangle$ and $\langle k_2 \rangle$, similar characteristics are obtained for all the coefficients. The amount of data dispersion will be primarily due to the value of L_v, not the fact that a linear combination of the k_i terms (or the $\langle k_i \rangle$ terms) has been obtained.

E. Computational Considerations

Studies of this type place a premium on the available processing speed of the computer system. It became clear early in the study that small- or medium-scale computer capability was insufficient. For example, the analysis method described runs in approximately 100 times real time if all operations are implemented only on the PDP-11 system. The relatively small data base of speakers for this study would have required over 100 hours of processing time.

Except for the nontrivial costs in software development, we have found that attaching a high-speed processor to the main computer system provides a very economical solution to the requirements for real-time processing.

VI. Summary

The properties of long-term feature averaging for three sets of fundamental frequency related, gain related, and spectrally related parameters have been investigated. Based upon the Fisher discriminant method, the rank ordering of the parameter sets in importance was shown to be spectral, fundamental frequency, and then gain. It was also shown that over a long duration from $L_v = 10$ to $L_v = 1000$, the standard deviation of the sample means of the reflection coefficient vectors decreased proportionally to $L_v^{-1/3}$.

A small number of speakers with relatively homogeneous characteristics was used to illustrate the effects of long-term averaging. The data base was of nontrivial duration, somewhat greater than one hour in length. Furthermore, the text was unconstrained conversational speech, recorded under normal room noise conditions. Analysis was performed in real time with a high-speed signal processor.

Presently, other spectral representation methods are being investigated and a data base is being developed for performing text-independent speaker recognition tests without any linguistic or structural constraints.

References

[1] P. D. Bricker, R. Gnanadesikan, M. V. Mathews, S. Pruzansky, P. A. Tukey, K. W. Wachter, and J. L. Warner, "Statistical techniques for talker identification," *Bell Syst. Tech. J.*, vol. 50, pp. 1427-1454, 1971.

[2] G. R. Doddington, "A method of speaker verification," Ph.D. dissertation, Univ. of Wisconsin, Madison, 1970.

[3] O. Fujimura, "An approximation to voice aperiodicity," *IEEE Trans. Audio Electroacoust.*, vol. AU-16, pp. 68-72, 1968.

[4] S. Furui, "An analysis of long-term variation of feature parameters of speech and its application to talker recognition," *Electron. Commun. Jap.*, vol. 57-A, pp. 34-42, 1974.

[5] S. Furui and F. Itakura, "Talker recognition by statistical features of speech sounds," *Electron. Commun. Jap.*, vol. 56-A, pp. 62-71, 1973.

[6] S. Furui, F. Itakura, and S. Saito, "Talker recognition by long-time averaged speech spectrum," *Electron. Commun. Jap.*, vol. 55-A, pp. 54-61, 1972.

[7] J. N. Holmes, "Low-frequency phase distortion of speech recording," *J. Acoust. Soc. Amer.*, vol. 58, pp. 747-749, 1975.

[8] Y. Horii, "Some statistical characteristics of voice fundamental frequency," *J. Speech Hearing Res.*, vol. 18, pp. 192-201, 1975.

[9] U. Kosiel, "Statistical analysis of speaker-dependent differences in the long-term average spectrum of Polish speech," in *Speech Analysis and Perception*, vol. 3, W. Jassem, Ed., Polish Academy of Sciences. Warsaw, Poland: PWN-Polish Scientific Publishers, 1973, pp. 117-120.

[10] R. C. Lummis, "Speaker verification by computer using speech intensity for temporal registration," *IEEE Trans. Audio Electroacoust.*, vol. AU-21, pp. 80-89, 1973.

[11] J. D. Markel and A. H. Gray, Jr., *Linear Prediction of Speech*. Berlin, Heidelberg, New York: Springer-Verlag, 1976.

[12] J. D. Markel and D. Wong, "Considerations in the estimation of the glottal volume velocity waveforms," submitted to *IEEE Trans. Acoust., Speech, Signal Processing.*

[13] K. O. Mead, "Identification of speakers from fundamental frequency contours in conversational speech," Joint Speech Res. Unit, Rep. 1002, 1974.

[14] W. S. Mohns, "Statistical feature evaluation in speaker identification," Ph.D. dissertation, North Carolina State Univ., Raleigh, 1969.

[15] A. E. Rosenberg, "Effect of glottal pulse shape on the quality of natural vowels," *J. Acoust. Soc. Amer.*, vol. 49, pp. 583-590, 1970.

[16] M. Rothenberg, "A new inverse-filter technique for deriving the glottal air flow waveform during voicing," *J. Acoust. Soc. Amer.*, vol. 53, pp. 1632-1645, 1973.

[17] M. R. Sambur, "Speaker recognition using orthogonal linear prediction," *IEEE Trans. Acoust., Speech, Signal Processing*, vol. ASSP-24, pp. 283-289, Aug. 1976.

[18] M. R. Sambur and L. R. Rabiner, "A speaker independent digit recognition system," *Bell Syst. Tech. J.*, vol. 54, pp. 81-102, 1975.

[19] K. N. Stevens, "Sources of inter- and intra-speaker variability in acoustic properties of speech sounds," in *Proc. 7th Int. Congr. of Phonetic Sciences*, A. Rigault and R. Charbonneau, Ed. The Hague: Mouton, 1972.

[20] K. N. Stevens, C. E. Williams, J. R. Carbonell, and B. Woods, "Speaker authentication and identification: A comparison of spectrographic and auditory presentation of speech material," *J. Acoust. Soc. Amer.*, vol. 44, pp. 1596-1607, 1968.

[21] W. D. Voiers, "Perceptual bases of speaker identity," *J. Acoust. Soc. Amer.*, vol. 36, pp. 1965-1973, 1964.

[22] J. J. Wolf, "Efficient acoustic parameters for speaker recognition," *J. Acoust. Soc. Amer.*, vol. 51, pp. 2044-2056, 1972.

Author Index

Subject Index

A

B

C

D

E

F

G

T

U

V

W

EDITORS' BIOGRAPHIES

N. Rex Dixon (M'76) was born in Ecorse, Michigan, on February 24, 1932. He received the B.A. degree in psychology and speech pathology from Western Michigan University, Kalamazoo, the M.A. degree in speech pathology and audiology from Indiana University, Bloomington, and the Ph.D. degree in speech and hearing sciences and psychology from Stanford University, Palo Alto, California, in 1958, 1960, and 1966, respectively.

During the academic year 1960-61, he served on the faculty at Cornell University, Ithaca, New York. In 1963 he became a staff member in communication sciences at the IBM Research Laboratory, San Jose, California. During the academic year 1963-64, he served as a staff member in the Foreign Student Program at Stanford University. He also served on the faculty at San Jose State College during the academic year 1964-65. In 1967 he transferred to IBM Systems Development Division at Research Triangle Park, North Carolina, as an Advisory Scientist in speech processing technology. In 1972, he transferred back to the Research Division at the Thomas J. Watson Research Center, Yorktown Heights, NewYork, where he is presently a staff member in speech processing. Since joining IBM, he has been involved in the investigation of problems relating to automatic document indexing, speech synthesis, automatic speech recognition, speaker verification, and evaluation methods for speech processing. In North Carolina, he also served as an adjunct faculty member at North Carolina Central University, Durham, and at North Carolina State University, Raleigh.

Dr. Dixon serves as Chairman of the Technical Committee on Speech Processing and as Associate Editor for Speech Processing on the Editorial Board of the IEEE Acoustics, Speech, and Signal Processing Society (ASSPS). He is a member of the ASSP Administrative Committee.

Thomas B. Martin (S'58, M'60, SM'77) was born in Burlington, Iowa on June 23, 1935. He received the B.S. degree, with magna cum laude honors, in electrical engineering from the University of Notre Dame in 1957 and the M.S.E.E. and Ph.D. degrees from the University of Pennsylvania in 1960 and 1970, respectively.

Dr. Martin is the founder of Threshold Technology Inc. He is a Director of the Company and served as Engineering Vice President until January 1974 at which time he was promoted to Executive Vice President. In April 1974 he assumed his current position of President of Threshold. He has worked in the field of automatic speech recognition since 1960 and was one of the first to recognize the practical applications of this technology.

Prior to joining Threshold, Dr. Martin was employed for 13 years by RCA Corporation where he was the head of the Speech Processing Group in the advanced Technology Laboratories. During this time he was nominated as a team member for the 1969 and 1970 RCA David Sarnoff Outstanding Team Award in Engineering.

Dr. Martin is a member of IEEE, Acoustical Society of America and Tau Beta Pi. He has published more than 40 papers and has given many talks to professional societies, conventions and universities. He has been awarded 14 patents and has several pending. He has also taught at the graduate level and has held the honorary position of an Adjunct Associate Professor in the Physiology Department of Thomas Jefferson University.

He is part Chairman of the IEEE Committee on Speech Processing and the IEEE Subcommittee on Pattern Recognition Problems in Speech. He was Co-Chairman of the 1971 IEEE/RADC Workshop on Speech Processing and was Program Chairman for the 1976 IEEE International Conference on Acoustics, Speech & Signal Processing (ASSP). He has also served as an elected member of the Administration Committee for the IEEE ASSP Society and the IEEE Systems, Man & Cybernetics Society. He has acted as an associate editor for the IEEE Transactions on ASSP.